Advanced Biology

Michael Roberts
Former Head of Biology at Marlborough and Cheltenham Colleges

Michael Reiss
Reader in Education and Bioethics at Homerton College, Cambridge

Grace Monger
Former Head of Science at The Holt School, Wokingham

Delta Place
27 Bath Road
Cheltenham GL53 7TH
United Kingdom

First published by Nelson 2000

ISBN 978-0-17-438732-9
9 8 7 6
08

Printed and bound in China by Midas Printing International Ltd.

Acknowledgements

The authors and publisher wish to thank Geoffrey Harper for compiling the index, Zooid Pictures for the picture research and the following for permission to reproduce questions from past examination papers, which are copyright material:

The Associated Examining Board and Southern Examining Group, Edexcel Foundation, Northern Examinations and Assessment Board, Northern Ireland Council for the Curriculum Examinations and Assessment, Oxford, Cambridge and RSA Examinations Board and the Welsh Joint Education Committee.

Every effort has been made to trace all the copyright holders, but where this has not been possible the publisher will be pleased to make any necessary arrangements at the first opportunity.

Thank you

The authors and publisher would like to thank the following friends and colleagues who have helped us in the production of this book.

Mr David Alford
Dr Mark Avery
Dr Michael Berridge
Dr J.A. Bailey
Professor Barbara Banks
Mr John Barker
Professor Colin Blakemore
Dr Michael Brimicombe
Dr Peter Brandham
Dr Brian Bush
Professor Anthony Campbell
Mrs Barbara Case
Dr Jenny Chapman
Dr David Chisholm
Mr Joe Conaghan
Dr Jonathan Cooper
Dr Sally Corbett
Dr Jenny Croft
Dr Basiro Davey
Dr Kenneth Dickstein
Dr David Dover
Professor Gabriel Dover
Professor Dianne Edwards

Mr Glyn Evans
Dr Richard Firn
Dr Peter Forey
Dr T.J. Flowers
Dr C.S. Foster
Dr Peter Gasson
Dr Maurice Grindle
Dr B.L. Gupta
Professor J.L. Hall
Dr Jack Hannay
Dr Kate Hardy
Dr Geoffrey Harper
Dr D.A. Hartley
Mr Beverley Heath
Dr David Herries
Mr Tony Hilliar
Dr Peter Hogarth
Dr Harry Hudson
Dr Neil Ingram
Dr Geilan Ismail
Dr Tim King
Dr Patricia Kohn
Dr Peter Kohn

Dr John Land
Professor Rachel Leech
Professor Gordon Leedale
Professor Henry Leese
Dr Adrian Lister
Dr Bill Mackie
Dr Mike Majerus
Professor John Marshall
Professor James McInerney
Dr Ann Mullinger
Dr James Parkyn
Dr Jim Penny
Dr Bruce Reed
Professor Tom ap Rees
Dr Moira Sheehan
Dr Mark Tester
Dr Mike Tipton
Mr Stephen Tomkins
Professor A. Deri Tomos
Professor David Walker
Dr Joanna Walker
Dr Max Walters
Dr E.J. Wood

Contents

Part 1
Part 2
Part 3
Part 4
Part 5
Part 6
Part 7
Part 8
Index

Part 1
Part 2
Part 3
Part 4
Part 5
Part 6
Part 7
Part 8
Index

Introduction

How to get the most from this book

Biology has been described as the science of the twenty-first century. Recent years have seen tremendous advances in medicine, agriculture and other applied aspects of the subject while the ethical implications of biology – such as arise with cloning, genetic engineering, the extinction of species, etc. – seem never to be out of the news.

This book has been written to help you understand what biology is all about. It may be that you are studying Advanced Subsidiary (AS) or Advanced (A) GCE Biology or Human Biology, or another advanced course. It may be that you are about to go to college or it may be that you simply want a well-written and up-to-date account of modern biology, Whatever your needs, we have tried to ensure that this volume meets them.

This book, *Advanced Biology*, has its roots in two earlier books: *Biology: A Functional Approach* (by Michael Roberts) and *Biology: Principles and Processes* (by Michael Roberts, Michael Reiss and Grace Monger). In this way we hope to have preserved the best of those two books while adding many new features appropriate for today.

The organisation of this book

We have divided the 44 chapters in this book into eight parts:

- Part 1 *Molecules to Organisms*
- Part 2 *Respiration, Nutrition and Transport*
- Part 3 *Regulation and Defence*
- Part 4 *Response and Coordination*
- Part 5 *Reproduction, Growth and Development*
- Part 6 *Heredity and Genetics*
- Part 7 *Organisms and their Environment*
- Part 8 *Evolution of Life.*

To help those of you tackling AS and A GCE specifications, we have done our best to ensure that topics mainly covered in the second year of Advanced GCE, the A2 part of it, are mostly in the second half of the book. This doesn't mean that you can ignore the second half the book if you are simply taking an AS in Biology! But it does mean that you may find it sufficient to read parts of it only. To help you know exactly which bits of the book are needed for your own specifications, we have provided a detailed analysis of the AS, A GCE specifications and International Baccalaureate (IB) syllabus on the website. For more information about this, see the section 'Other help available' overleaf.

Chapter features

Each of the eight parts of the book is divided into a number of chapters and each chapter has the same sorts of features:

- **Introduction** explaining what the chapter is about.
- **Numbered headings** dividing the chapter into manageable chunks. For example, Chapter 2, *The chemicals of life*, has seven such headings:
  - 2.1 Water
  - 2.2 Minerals (inorganic ions)
  - 2.3 Organic compounds
  - 2.4 Carbohydrates
  - 2.5 Lipids
  - 2.6 Proteins
  - 2.7 Vitamins.
- **Readable text** in which we have made a particular effort to engage your interest and keep technical terminology to a minimum. Important terms are highlighted in **bold** and explained.
- **Photographs** to illustrate points made in the text.
- **Diagrams**, **graphs** and other **illustrations** to provide evidence for conclusions drawn in the text.
- **Support boxes** to build on GCSE Science or other courses at this level and summarise the basic essentials of a topic.
- **Extension boxes** to cover material found only in a small number of the specifications, or which we feel may be of particular interest to some of you. Some are written by invited experts to highlight a particular point or give some of the historical background to a piece of research.
- **Cross-references** to other parts of the book. Minor cross-references are simply indicated in the text. Major cross-references are indicated by the symbol ▶ which is usually placed in the margin.
- **Red flags** next to major headings to indicate that the section contains material about **Health & Disease**.
- **Blue flags** next to major headings to indicate that the section contains material about **Biotechnology**.
- **Summary** in which the key points of the chapter are provided in a numbered list.
- **Practice questions** to test your understanding of the chapter and enable you to develop certain **key skills**. Most of these questions are taken from Advanced GCE past papers; some have been written by us. We have not provided answers

to these questions so you may find your teacher or lecturer setting some of them for homework. Your teacher or lecturer will be able to help you appreciate which questions are most suitable for AS and which for A2 Advanced GCE.

NB: When answering essay-type examination questions, it is useful to note the following guidelines which normally appear at the beginning of the question and vary slightly according to the awarding body:

Marks will be awarded for scientific content, the coverage of the topic and for coherence. Diagrams should be included only if they are relevant to and complement the rest of the answer.

Answers should be illustrated by large, clearly labelled diagrams wherever suitable. Extra marks are awarded for quality of expression.

Marks are sometimes specifically allocated, e.g. 16 marks for scientific content and 4 marks for orderly presentation and quality of English.

Other features of the book

As well as features within each chapter, you should also note the following four sections:

- The **Contents** section on pp. iii to vi. This lists all the chapters with their major headings. In addition, both Biotechnology flags and Health & Disease flags are shown to indicate where these two areas of biology are covered.

- A short **Statistics Appendix** on pp. 778 to 780. This will be a useful reference when you are attempting questions where statistical analysis of data is required.

- The **Index** on pp. 781 to 793. If you can't find something in the contents section, try the index. It has been written so that you can quickly find any important biological topic.

Other help available

If you need additional information, we particularly recommend the website that accompanies this book which you can find at **www.advanced-biology.co.uk**. Here you can find other helpful information including the following material specially developed to accompany this book:

- Information on the **chemical and physical basis of biology**. If you aren't doing Advanced GCE Chemistry or Physics you may find this of value.

- Detailed analyses of the main **AS** and **A GCE** specifications and **International Baccalaureate Diploma Programme**, showing how this book can be used to cover the requirements of the various Awarding Bodies.

- A detailed contents list with links to **other sites of interest** related to topics in the chapters.

- Suggestions for ways in which **key skills can be developed** using the material provided in this book.

Finally, **practical work,** including project work, is presented in a companion volume to this book written by Roberts, M., King, T. & Reiss, M.

Michael Roberts
Michael Reiss
Grace Monger

Chapter 1

The nature of biology

T he word **biology** comes from Greek: *bios* – 'life', *logos* – 'knowledge'. It is the study of life and living things (organisms), and is an enormous, rapidly developing subject involving many allied disciplines such as chemistry, physics, mathematics, geology and psychology. You have only to glance through the current issues of the British scientific journal, *Nature*, or its American equivalent, *Science*, to appreciate the extent and ramifications of biology. Well over a million original papers are published in the biological (including medical) sciences every year, ranging from descriptions of new species to analyses of chemical reactions in organisms (*figure 1.1*).

With so much information flowing from research laboratories, it is difficult to gain that broad overview of the subject which is essential for understanding its principles. It is therefore the principles that we stress in our book.

There are many ways of approaching biology. For example, one might approach it through the structure of organisms, or perhaps through the environment. Ours is a *functional* approach, having as a pervading theme the way biological systems work.

1.1 The branches of biology

Traditionally biology has been divided into **zoology**, the study of animals, and **botany**, the study of plants. However, in recent years the distinction between these two areas of the subject has become increasingly blurred by the development of new disciplines which span both. Another major subdivision, **microbiology**, embraces a vast assortment of mainly microscopic organisms (**microorganisms**), most of which are neither animals nor plants. Within microbiology come such subjects as **bacteriology**, the study of bacteria, **mycology**, the study of fungi, and **virology**, the study of viruses.

In the 19th and early 20th centuries, biologists were mainly concerned with describing the structure (**anatomy**) of animals and plants, together with their classification (**taxonomy**). Anatomical studies included the microscopic structure of organs and tissues – **histology** as it is called. Similar descriptive studies were carried out on the stages through which animals developed – **embryology**. In more recent times there has been a shift of interest towards the way organisms work, resulting in the growth of animal and plant **physiology**. Embryological studies have become more functional too, as scientists have attempted to discover the mechanisms which direct development. This important area of biology is called **developmental biology**.

In the course of the last century these functional studies have become increasingly chemical, employing the talents of chemists as well as biologists. The first professorship of **biochemistry** in Britain was established at Liverpool University in 1902. London followed in 1912, and Cambridge in 1914. Now biochemistry is very much a subject in its own right with university departments all over the world.

Biochemical studies have shown us that in many respects the traditional division of biology into botany and zoology is an artificial one. Animals and plants – indeed all organisms – are made of cells. Research on cells, the study of **cell biology (cytology)**, has made it clear that in both their structure and functioning all cells have much in common. This similarity is also seen in the way an organism's characteristics are passed on to its offspring, the study of **heredity** or **genetics**.

The word genetics is derived from the word **gene**, the term used to describe the physical entities by which inherited characteristics are transmitted from parents to offspring. Research on the structure and properties of molecules in cells has helped us to

Figure 1.1 Over one million original papers are published in the biological and medical sciences every year. The picture shows the Scientific Periodicals Library at Cambridge University. In 1998 this library was taking 2597 scientific journals in 26 languages from 64 countries.

Support

Biology and biologists

Many attempts have been made to explain what biology is and what biologists do. One of the most elegant and succinct was suggested by E.J.W. Barrington, formerly Professor of Zoology at Nottingham University: *The business of organisms is to stay alive until they have reproduced themselves and the business of biologists is to understand how they do it.*

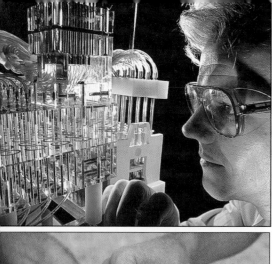

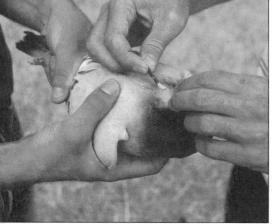

Figure 1.2 The settings are different, but these two biologists share the same basic purpose, to understand life and living organisms.
A A technician is examining a cell harvester. This device is essentially a filter which is used to separate cells from the medium in which they are suspended.
B A pigeon is being ringed. The ringing of birds enables their movements and habits to be studied.

understand what genes consist of and how they work. Spectacular advances have been made in this area in the last 60 or 70 years. It is known as **molecular biology** and, like biochemistry, is now an established subject in its own right.

So, looking back, there has been a gradual shift of interest from anatomical description of the whole organism to functional studies of cells and their constituent molecules. This does not mean that all modern biologists are engaged in cellular or molecular research. The older, more traditional studies still have an important part to play in building up a complete picture of life and living organisms (*figure 1.2*).

From the earliest times, people have been fascinated by the ways and habits of living things – **natural history** as one would call it. These pursuits, often carried out by enthusiastic amateurs, can provide very useful information. At the professional level, such studies fall into two main categories: **behaviour** and **ecology**.

At one time behaviour studies consisted of lengthy descriptions of the activities of animals, particularly birds. Today the approach is more analytical and experimental, increasingly using the techniques of nerve physiology.

Ecological studies are important, not least because they affect the future of the human race and other forms of life. Our hopes of reducing global pollution, protecting the environment and sustaining the world's biodiversity and natural resources will depend on advances in this field. Scientists have taken these matters seriously for years; now politicians are doing so. Ecological studies are demonstrating how humans can derive material benefits from the environment without destroying it: **conservation** as opposed to exploitation.

Levels of organisation

What emerges from this brief survey is that living organisms can be studied at different levels of organisation (*figure 1.3*). Thus a molecular biologist studies the organism at the level of its component molecules, a cell biologist at the level of its cells, and a physiologist at the level of its tissues and organs. In contrast, an ecologist studies organisms mainly at the level of populations and communities.

Recognition of these levels of organisation has led scientists and philosophers to look at organisms in two different ways. At one extreme the organism is regarded as a machine made up of a collection of parts – organs, molecules and so on. This **mechanistic approach** involves **reductionism**, the idea that an organism can be understood by *reducing* it to its component parts. At the other extreme the organism is regarded as having special qualities which make it more than the sum of its parts and which can only be understood by considering the whole organism. This is called the **holistic approach** from the Greek word *holos*, 'whole'.

1.2 Methods of investigation in biology

Biology is a science and, as such, it uses the methods of science. Most biological investigations start with an **observation**. What is observed may be a structure, a process, a disease, a behaviour pattern or the occurrence of an organism in a particular habitat. As a scientist, the biologist reacts to an observation by asking questions about it. What is this structure for? What causes this disease? And so on.

To answer such questions, the biologist gathers as many relevant facts (**data**) as possible and then puts forward an **hypothesis**. An hypothesis is a tentative theory – an intelligent guess. To take an example, virtually all cells have a nucleus. This observation enables us to hypothesise that the nucleus is essential for the life of a cell.

If an hypothesis is to lead anywhere it must be possible to make **predictions** from it. For example, if it is true that the nucleus is essential for the life of a cell, we can predict that a cell deprived of its nucleus will die. A prediction is therefore a logical deduction from the

Level of organisation	Definition	Who works at each level
 community	all the different species living in a particular locality	ecologists
 population	all the individual organisms of a species in a particular locality	
 organism	a self-reproducing system capable of growing and maintaining itself	geneticists ethologists
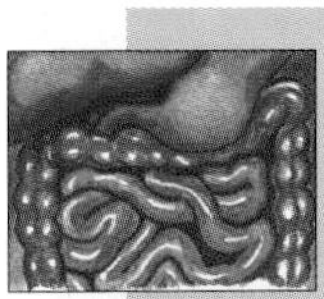 organ system	a group of organs which carries out a particular function	anatomists
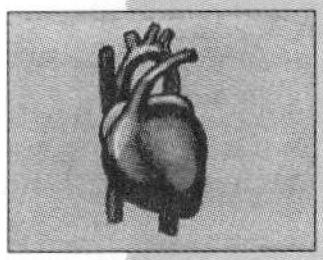 organ	a group of tissues which carries out a particular function	physiologists histologists developmental biologists
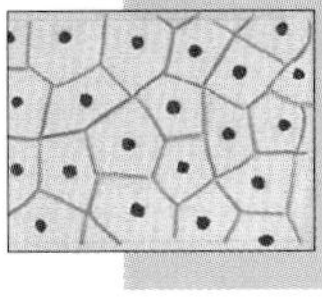 tissue	a group of cells which carries out a particular function	
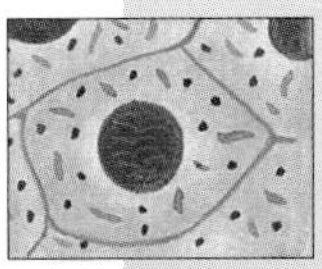 cell	the basic structural unit of an organism consisting of a group of organelles surrounded by a membrane	cell biologists
 organelle	a structure inside the cell which carries out a particular function	
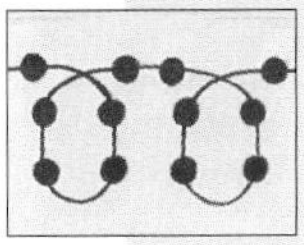 molecule	a group of atoms linked together in a particular arrangement	biochemists molecular biologists geneticists

Figure 1.3 The different levels of organisation in biology and who works at each level. The distinctions are not rigid. For example, a physiologist may work on individual cells as well as on tissues and organs, and a geneticist may work on populations as well as on individual organisms. Occasionally an ecologist may venture into cell biology or biochemistry if the problem being investigated takes a turn in that direction. Can you think of any circumstances in which that might happen?

hypothesis. Thinking up an hypothesis and making a prediction is a purely theoretical exercise and can be done in an armchair.

The next step is to test the prediction to find out if it is correct. Usually this entails performing an **experiment**. There are many different types of experiment but all involve setting up a *contrived* practical situation in which the experimenter manipulates the variables. In the case of our cell example, an obvious experimental test would be to remove the nucleus from a cell and see if the cell dies. So the testing of an hypothesis, unlike its formulation, is a practical activity – an *empirical* process.

Sometimes, testing a single prediction is enough to decide that an hypothesis is false, but often several different predictions are made from the same hypothesis and all of them tested. If all the predictions turn out to be correct, the hypothesis is supported. If any turn out to be wrong, the hypothesis must be reviewed and, if necessary, abandoned.

The procedure outlined above is summarised in figure 1.4. It is called, rather pompously, the **scientific method**. However, there is nothing particularly special about it. Essentially the same procedure is adopted by a doctor making a diagnosis, a mechanic trying to find what's wrong with a car, and a police detective investigating a crime.

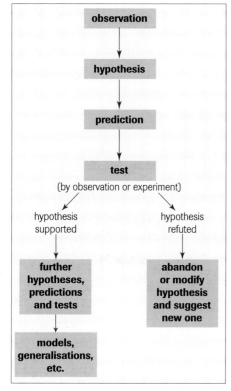

Figure 1.4 The main steps in the scientific method.

Support

Doing experiments

Hypotheses stand or fall on the experiments that are carried out to test them. It is therefore imperative that when testing an hypothesis the right experiment should be done in the right way.

To revert to our cell example, with the aid of micromanipulators and a sufficiently powerful binocular microscope, it is possible to remove the nucleus from a large cell like *Amoeba* by sucking it out with a very fine pipette. It is found, as predicted, that the cell dies. But can we be certain that death is caused by the absence of the nucleus and not by damage inflicted on the cell during the operation? To answer this we must set up a **control**: a second cell has its nucleus removed in exactly the same way and then put back again. The same amount of damage is done to the cell but it is not deprived of its nucleus. The control cell does in fact survive, confirming that it is the absence of the nucleus which causes death.

Not all biological experiments require a control, but many do. The control provides a standard with which the experimental situation may be compared. However, for the comparison to be fair, the control and experimental situations must be treated in exactly the same way except for the condition which you are studying. In general terms, *all variables must be identical except the one whose effect is being investigated*. In the cell example, the variables which should be kept the same are the amount of damage done to the cell, and environmental conditions such as the temperature and composition of the medium in which the cell is kept. The variable being investigated is the presence or absence of the nucleus. Manipulating variables is an integral part of most biological experiments.

One further point. It is not sufficient to do an experiment only once. It must be repeated many times, and consistent results obtained, before the hypothesis can be accepted. In the case of the cell investigation, one would set up a *group* of cells without nuclei, perhaps 50 in all – the **experimental group** – and another group of cells with nuclei – the **control group**. It might happen that all the cells in the experimental group die and all those in the control group survive, but in biological experiments it usually turns out that only a proportion of tests give the expected results. In such cases it may be necessary to analyse the results statistically to be certain that the differences are not due to chance.

The progress of science

Once an hypothesis is supported, further questions can be asked. For example, if we have obtained evidence that the nucleus is essential for the life of a cell, we can ask what the nucleus does which makes its presence necessary. Further hypotheses can then be suggested, for example that the nucleus controls certain processes that go on in the surrounding cytoplasm. From this hypothesis new predictions can be made and new experiments carried out. In this way science progresses, each discovery paving the way for the next.

What sets the pace of scientific progress? To some extent it is the rate at which new observations and hypotheses are made. However, limits are also imposed by the technology available. Cells were not discovered until the light microscope was invented in the 17th century, and their detailed internal structure (ultrastructure) remained unseen until the electron microscope came into use in the 1930s. There are many instances in biology, as in other sciences, of new technology leading to a burst of fresh discoveries.

Variations of the scientific method

The scientific method, as described here, characterises much biological research but not all of it. For example, a biologist may carry out observations or experiments with no particular hypothesis in mind. The results of such investigations further our knowledge and can prompt us to ask questions from which testable hypotheses may arise.

Modifications of the scientific method are also used in areas of biology where experiments are difficult or impossible to perform. For example, in palaeontology, the study of fossils, hypotheses are usually tested by amassing circumstantial evidence rather than by experiment; and in taxonomy, the classification of organisms, the methods are largely descriptive and mathematical.

Sometimes, when experimentation is not feasible, an attempt may be made to **correlate** different sets of data. For example, the hypothesis that smoking causes lung cancer has been tested by taking groups of people and correlating the incidence of lung cancer with the number of cigarettes smoked per day. In such investigations statistical analysis is used to assess the likelihood that the suspected connection is genuine and not caused by chance.

▶ Statistical tests, page 778

Theories

An hypothesis can never be proved, only supported. The validity of an hypothesis rests on the gradual accumulation of evidence. As more and more evidence comes to hand, the hypothesis gains increasing acceptance and may eventually become a **theory**.

A theory is similar to an hypothesis but more firmly established. An example is the theory of evolution. Though not proved, the theory of evolution is supported by an impressive body of evidence which even its most ardent critics find hard to deny.

Generalisations, laws and models

Enough cells have been looked at for us to say with reasonable certainty that most, if not all, cells have a nucleus. Such a statement is called a **generalisation**.

Generalisations play an important part in biology for they enable us to build up a system of principles and concepts which form the framework of the subject. They also permit us to make predictions about things that are not yet known. For example, the generalisation that organisms contain DNA allows us to predict that when a new species of organism is discovered, its cells will also contain DNA. Generalisations allow us to predict the characteristics of organisms we have never seen, the features of habitats we have never visited and the properties of materials we have never tested.

Although generalisations are useful, they can be misleading because sometimes there are exceptions. For example, the statement that all cells have a nucleus has some notable exceptions - human red blood cells for example. Generalisations should therefore be worded carefully. It is better to say 'most cells have a nucleus' rather than 'cells have a nucleus'.

Some generalisations appear to have no exceptions and are therefore held to be universally true. It is customary to call such generalisations **laws**. Examples are the laws of thermodynamics and Mendel's laws of inheritance. But even these seemingly inviolable laws are constantly being questioned and scrutinised for possible revision or replacement. Mendel's laws, for instance, have many exceptions as is made clear in Chapter 33.

A term much used these days by scientists is **model**. A model is a system of ideas, based on numerous observations and experiments, which help to explain a particular phenomenon. An example is the fluid mosaic model explaining the structure of the cell surface membrane (*page 57*). Models are useful in biology for, as the name suggests, they can be readily modified in the light of new discoveries.

It is important to bear in mind that all scientific investigations are carried out within the context of current models which may influence our observations and how we interpret them. There have been many cases in the history of biology of scientists being misled by preconceived ideas based on the models prevailing at the time. Can you think of any examples?

1.3 **What is life?**

The honest answer is that we cannot say categorically what life is. The best we can do is to list those attributes of living organisms that distinguish them from non-living matter. These are as follows:

■ Reproduction

Reproduction, the production of new individuals from pre-existing ones, is a basic feature of all living organisms. It takes place in different ways but always involves certain giant molecules (macromolecules) producing copies of themselves, in other words **replicating**. Molecular biologists have identified and characterised these molecules. They are **nucleic acids**, the main one being **deoxyribonucleic acid** (**DNA**). Encoded in this complex molecule are the instructions required for the development and activities of the cells and therefore ultimately of the whole organism. In certain viruses a similar nucleic acid called **ribonucleic acid** (**RNA**) is used instead of DNA.

■ Respiration

Respiration, the controlled transfer of **energy** in living organisms, is essential for life. Everything an organism does is dependent on chemical processes which are ultimately energy-consuming. Energy, the capacity to do work, is obtained by the organism from molecules such as glucose. This does not happen in a single reaction. Rather, the molecules are gradually dismantled, small amounts of energy being transferred at various stages of the process. The energy is used to synthesise molecules of a substance called **adenosine triphosphate** (**ATP**). The energy contained in ATP is then used to power a wide range of biochemical processes. ATP is of universal occurrence in living organisms and is itself a basic feature of life.

■ Nutrition

The molecules which living organisms use as their source of energy are obtained from food in the process of feeding (nutrition). Food also provides substances needed for other purposes such as growth, maintenance and repair.

There are two fundamentally different methods of nutrition. Animals and certain other organisms take in ready-made organic substances (**heterotrophic nutrition**). Other organisms, notably plants, take in simple inorganic substances which they then build up into complex organic substances (**autotrophic nutrition**). The main type of autotrophic nutrition is **photosynthesis** in which sunlight is the natural source of energy.

■ Excretion

The chemical reactions that occur in organisms result in the formation of **waste products**, often toxic, which must be disposed of in some way. These include nitrogenous compounds such as ammonia or substances derived from it. The disposing of these waste products is what is meant by excretion. Usually they are expelled from the organism. However, plants generally retain much of their excretory waste, storing it in a harmless form.

■ Growth

New individuals, produced by reproduction, grow. Of course some inanimate objects grow too – crystals, for example – but the mechanism is different. A crystal grows by new matter being added at the surface. An organism grows from within by taking in substances from outside and incorporating them into its internal structure. This is called **assimilation**. In organisms, growth is controlled so that it occurs in the right places and at the right time. Single-celled organisms grow by increasing their cell size, multicellular organisms by increasing their cell size and cell number.

■ Responsiveness

It is characteristic of living organisms that they react to changes in their surroundings. The changes are called **stimuli** (singular: **stimulus**) and the reactions are called **responses**. Responses evoked by stimuli range from rapid ones like the withdrawal of one's hand from a hot object, to much slower ones like the growth of a plant towards light.

Although plants tend to respond slowly to stimuli, there are some interesting exceptions: insectivorous plants such as the one in figure 11.9 on page 181 respond very quickly to touch, as do the leaves of the sensitive plant *Mimosa pudica*.

Even seemingly simple organisms respond to stimuli. For instance, single-celled organisms such as *Amoeba* and *Paramecium* move away from noxious substances in their environment.

■ Movement

Responding to stimuli usually means moving in some way, and this is another characteristic of living organisms. Even plants, which at first appear to be an exception, can move. For example, time-lapse films show the stem tips of bramble and honeysuckle waving around as if searching for a support to climb up, though of course these movements are too slow for us to see them with the naked eye.

Movement occurs inside plants too: for instance, chloroplasts can sometimes be seen circulating inside the cells of the Canadian pondweed *Elodea*. This kind of movement cannot be explained by purely physical forces such as diffusion. It is an active, energy-requiring process arising from within the cells.

Organisms do not necessarily display all of the above characteristics all the time, but they all show them at some stage in their lives.

We might sum up by saying that a living organism is a self-reproducing system capable of growing and maintaining its integrity by the expenditure of energy. Life is the sum total of all these things.

1.4 Some basic concepts

As we look at organisms, we cannot help being struck by the way their structure and physiology seem to suit them for living in their particular environments. We say the organism is **adapted** to its environment. Figure 1.5 shows some particularly striking examples of adaptation, but in fact every species is adapted to its environment to a degree: it must be to survive.

In what ways need an organism be adapted? It must be adapted in such a way that it can defend itself from attack by other organisms, compete successfully for food and other

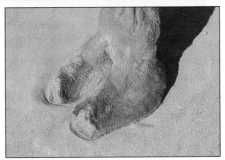

Figure 1.5 Three examples of adaptation in animals.
A The pattern of colours in the skin of this puff adder helps it to blend with its natural background, thus giving it admirable camouflage.
B The streamlined shape and flippers of the dolphin are adaptations for swimming.
C The splayed-out foot of the camel prevents the foot sinking into the soft sand. This is just one of a large number of adaptations which camels possess for living in the desert.

Size scale

Although all organisms have certain fundamental features in common, they vary enormously in all sorts of ways, not least in size. At one extreme is the blue whale *Balaenoptera musculus* which can exceed 30 metres in length. At the other extreme are bacteria with diameters of less than one millionth of a metre (10^{-6} m). Viruses are even smaller, though they are not normally regarded as organisms (*page 76*).

For convenience it is customary to express the dimensions of small organisms not in metres but in **millimetres** (mm), **micrometres** (µm) or **nanometres** (nm):

- a millimetre is a thousandth of a metre (10^{-3} m);

- a micrometre is a thousandth of a millimetre (10^{-6} m);

- a nanometre is a thousandth of a micrometre (10^{-9} m).

Cells are such that it is most convenient to express their dimensions in micrometres. The organelles inside them, being much smaller, normally have their sizes expressed in nanometres, as do viruses and other very small biological objects (*illustration*).

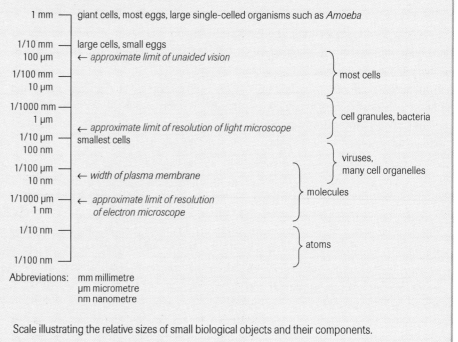

1 mm	— giant cells, most eggs, large single-celled organisms such as *Amoeba*
1/10 mm 100 µm	— large cells, small eggs ← *approximate limit of unaided vision*
1/100 mm 10 µm	— most cells
1/1000 mm 1 µm	— cell granules, bacteria ← *approximate limit of resolution of light microscope*
1/10 µm 100 nm	— smallest cells
1/100 µm 10 nm	— viruses, many cell organelles ← *width of plasma membrane*
1/1000 µm 1 nm	— molecules ← *approximate limit of resolution of electron microscope*
1/10 nm	— atoms
1/100 nm	—

Abbreviations: mm millimetre
µm micrometre
nm nanometre

Scale illustrating the relative sizes of small biological objects and their components.

essentials, respond appropriately to changes in its environment, and live long enough to reproduce its kind. In short, the organism must be able to maintain all those processes which we listed earlier as fundamental to living organisms.

One further aspect of adaptation should be mentioned. It must ensure that the organism's cells always experience those conditions which permit efficient functioning. This is achieved by a wide range of mechanisms which together keep the physical and chemical conditions inside the organism constant. This is called **homeostasis**, and it will come up repeatedly in this book.

From the principle of adaptation another principle arises, namely that the structure of an organism and its component parts are closely related to the functions they perform. Guts, kidneys, gills, lungs, stems and leaves all demonstrate this close relationship between structure and function (*see figure 1.6 for example*). This concept is not restricted to whole organisms and organs; it also applies to individual cells and molecules, as we shall see in later chapters.

Adaptation and the close relationship between structure and function can be explained by a further concept: **evolution**. It is generally believed that present-day species have arisen by a process of gradual evolution from pre-existing forms that lived in the past, this being achieved by **natural selection**.

Figure 1.6 The leaf of the giant water lily of the Amazon, *Victoria amazonica,* illustrates the close relationship between structure and function. The leaves have a diameter of up to 2 metres. The vertical margin round the edge of each large floating leaf, seen in the top picture, prevents the leaves overlapping which would reduce the area for photosynthesis. The thick fibrous ribs on the underside of the leaf, seen in the lower picture, prevent the leaf from collapsing and hold it out flat, exposing it to the Sun and maximising photosynthesis. Reminiscent of fan vaulting, this strong construction is said to have been the inspiration for the design of the roof of the Crystal Palace in London.

The theory of evolution by natural selection originated with Charles Darwin and Alfred Russel Wallace in the middle of the 19th century. Today it forms the backbone of biology: it makes sense of the discoveries that have been made, and it gives a direction to research. This is not to say that everyone believes in it unquestioningly. Indeed, it comes under attack quite often, sometimes by biologists themselves, and its detailed claims are constantly under review.

1.5 Applied biology

Applied biology is the application of the biological sciences to human affairs. Thus defined, applied biology includes **medicine**, **veterinary science**, **agriculture**, **horticulture**, **forestry** and **environmental management**.

For thousands of years microorganisms have been used for manufacturing bread and alcoholic drinks such as beer and wine. The use of microorganisms for the benefit of humans is part of **biotechnology**. Nowadays this term has taken on a wider meaning and embraces all aspects of applied biology that have a technological slant.

Today biotechnology is a rapidly growing branch of industry. Two developments in particular have made this possible. One is the use of **enzymes** – organic catalysts which speed up chemical reactions in living organisms. Enzymes can be extracted from microorganisms, purified and then used in a wide range of manufacturing processes. The second development is our ability to manipulate an organism's genes so that the organism produces something useful for us. This is called **genetic engineering** and it is bringing about a revolution in the way many biologically important substances are manufactured.

Advances in applied science give us power to control our environment and improve the quality of human life. But power can be misused, resulting in pollution, over-use of our natural resources, and destruction of the environment. At one time these were thought of as essentially local phenomena, but in recent years it has become apparent that they are happening on a global scale. The depletion of the ozone layer, global warming and acid rain are three pressing examples. One reason for studying biology is to understand how an ever-expanding human population can survive on this planet without irreparably harming the very environment that gives us life.

Summary

1. Biology, the study of life and living organisms, is divided into numerous subjects which include **zoology**, **botany**, **microbiology**, **taxonomy**, **anatomy**, **physiology**, **biochemistry**, **cell biology (cytology)**, **heredity (genetics)**, **molecular biology**, **behaviour** and **ecology**.

2. Living organisms can be studied at different levels of organisation, e.g. the **molecular**, **cellular**, **organ**, **organism**, **population** and **community levels**.

3. The **scientific method** starts with **observations** which lead to the formulation of **hypotheses** from which **predictions** are made. The predictions are usually tested by **experiment**.

4. An experiment may require an appropriate **control**, i.e. a standard with which the experimental results may be compared. All **variables** should as far as possible be kept constant except for the one being investigated.

5. The progress of science is limited by the rate at which new observations and hypotheses are made, and by the technology currently available.

6. Generalisations are helpful in biology, and models provide a flexible approach which can be useful.

7. Characteristics shared by all living organisms are: **reproduction**, **respiration**, **nutrition**, **excretion**, **growth** (by **assimilation**), **responsiveness**, and **movement**.

8. Basic biological concepts include **survival**, **adaptation**, **homeostasis** and **evolution** by natural selection.

9. Applied biology includes agriculture, medicine and environmental management. **Biotechnology**, particularly **genetic engineering**, is of growing importance in society.

For general advice on these questions and advice on answering essay-type questions, see pages vii and viii.

1. Sugar beet is a root crop often grown as a commercial source of sugar. It has been suggested that the yield of the crop can be affected if weeds are allowed to grow amongst the rows of sugar beet plants.

Plan an investigation which you personally could carry out to test the hypothesis that the growth of weeds will reduce the yield of sugar beet. You should give your answer under the following headings.

(a) Plan of the investigation to be carried out. (6)

(b) Recording of the raw data measurements, presentation of the results and methods of data analysis. (6)

(c) Possible limitations of your method and an indication of further work that could be undertaken. (4)

(Total 16 marks)

London 1997

2. It has been suggested that learning is affected by background noise.

Plan an investigation which you personally could carry out to test the hypothesis that background noise reduces the ability to learn. You should give your answer under the same headings as in question 1.

(Total 16 marks)

London 1997

3. A student investigated the relationship between the birth weight of babies born to mothers who had smoked during pregnancy compared with those who had not. She visited a large maternity hospital daily for 6 days and recorded the birth weight of each baby born during this period. She also recorded whether or not each mother had smoked during pregnancy.

An extract from her laboratory notebook is shown below.

NEWTOWN MATERNITY HOSPITAL

Weight of baby at birth / kg

Date	Smoking mothers	Non-smoking mothers
18.9.94	3.20 , 3.10 , 2.96	3.22 , 4.11 , 3.01 , 3.79
19.9.94	4.10 , 3.62 , 3.11, 3.40	3.16 , 3.57 , 3.92
20.9.94	2.71 , 3.52 , 3.20	3.62 , 3.59 , 3.36 , 3.82
21.9.94	3.30 , 3.17 , 2.82 3.69 , 3.35	3.47 , 2.99 , 3.32 , 3.18
22.9.94	3.53 , 3.27 , 3.81 3.09	3.52 , 3.89 , 3.76
23.9.94	3.16 , 2.39 , 2.59	3.59 , 3.49 , 2.98 , 3.67

(a) (i) Prepare a table and organise the data in a suitable way so that the birth weights of the babies from the two groups of mothers can be compared. (4)

(ii) Use the data in your table to present the information in a suitable graphical form. (4)

(b) Suggest *three* other variables which could have been taken into account in this investigation. (3)

(Total 11 marks)

London 1996

4. A group of students carried out an ecological investigation into the distribution of two species of trees in a wood. They found that one species (A) was more common on dry, well-drained soils whilst the other species (B) was more common where the soil was wet and poorly drained. They produced the hypothesis that one reason for this was that the leaves of species B lost water vapour more quickly than the leaves of species A.

To test this hypothesis they collected a sample of 100 g of leaves from species A and a sample of 100 g of leaves from species B. They then hung each sample on a line to dry in identical conditions in the laboratory. Both samples were then reweighed each hour for five hours.

An extract from the records of this investigation is shown below.

Species A Mass after	1h	2h	3h	4h	5h	
	92.5	81.0	64.0	57.2	51.6	in g
Species B Mass after	1h	2h	3h	4h	5h	
	72.5	45.9	31.0	24.1	20.8	in g

(a) (i) Calculate the loss in mass compared to the original mass, for each sample every hour. Then organise the data in a suitable table so that the loss in mass for each sample can be compared. (4)

(ii) Use the data in your table to present this information in a suitable graphical form. (4)

(b) What conclusions can you draw from the results of this investigation? (2)

(Total 10 marks)

London 1998

5. What are the basic properties of living things? What arguments would you present to show that (a) a crystal, and (b) a candle flame are not alive, and that (c) an oak tree is alive?

(Total 13 marks)

Chapter 2

The chemicals of life

Cells, tissues and organs are composed of chemicals, many of which are identical with those found in non-living matter. Others are unique to living organisms.

Chemical compounds are conventionally divided into two groups: **organic** and **inorganic**. Under the organic heading are included all the complex compounds of carbon. All other compounds are classified as inorganic. Both are found in living things.

In 1828, the German chemist Friedrich Wöhler synthesised the organic compound urea in the laboratory. Until then it was almost universally believed that organic compounds could only be formed in living organisms.

The main organic compounds found in organisms are **carbohydrates**, **fats**, **proteins**, **nucleic acids** and **vitamins**. Of the inorganic constituents, **minerals** and **water** are among the most important. Their proportions in the human body are summarised in table 2.1.

All these chemical substances, or the raw materials for making them, come from the environment. They must be obtained as **nutrients** in sufficient amounts if the organism is to function efficiently and lead a healthy life. As humans, we obtain these nutrients from our food and, together with dietary fibre, they form the constituents of a **balanced diet**, with the exception that we can make nucleic acids from other, smaller chemicals and therefore do not need nucleic acids in our diet. The lack of a necessary substance in our diet leads to a **deficiency disease** (*page 35*).

In this chapter we shall review the structure and function of these cell constituents, apart from nucleic acids. Because of their special role in transmitting genetic information, nucleic acids will be dealt with in a later chapter (*Chapter 34*).

Table 2.1 The approximate percentage composition by mass of the human body shown separately for women and men. There is considerable variation between individuals in the relative amounts of the different chemical constituents, particularly fat.

Substance	Percentage of body mass	
	Woman	Man
Water	57	64
Fat	23	15
Protein	16	17
Carbohydrate	2	2
Other organic (including vitamins)	1	1
Inorganic (apart from water)	1	1

▶ Nucleic acids, page 603

2.1 Water

Water is by far the most abundant component of organisms. Most human cells are approximately 80 per cent water, and 60 per cent of the whole body is made up of it. As J.B.S. Haldane used to say, even the Archbishop of Canterbury is 60 per cent water. Life probably originated in water, and today numerous organisms make their home in it. Water provides the medium in which all biochemical reactions take place, and it has played a major role in the evolution of biological systems.

The importance of water as a medium for life springs from its abundance on the surface of the Earth and from five of its properties: its **solvent properties**, **heat capacity**, **surface tension**, **freezing properties** and **transparency**. Let us look at each of these in turn.

Water as a solvent

At atmospheric pressure, water is a liquid between 0 and 100°C. The distance of the Earth from the Sun is such that, over much of the Earth's surface, water exists as a liquid. Were the Earth either a little nearer to the Sun, as Venus is, or a little further from it, as is Mars, life would almost certainly never have evolved here because water would exist either as a solid or as a gas, rather than mostly as a liquid.

Water's properties as a solvent depend on the fact that it is a **polar molecule** with positively charged hydrogen atoms and a negatively charged oxygen atom. For reasons which are explained in the box on the next page, other polar molecules – which include most small biological molecules – readily dissolve in water. This is of great significance because many of the chemical reactions in cells take place in aqueous solution.

Why water's polarity makes it a good solvent

A polar molecule is one which has an unevenly distributed electrical charge, so there is a positive region and a negative region. Water's polarity is caused by its shape. Instead of being in a straight line (180°), the angle between the two hydrogen atoms is only 105°:

$$\overset{2\delta^{-}}{\underset{\delta^{+}}{H}} \overset{O}{\underset{105°}{}} \overset{}{\underset{\delta^{+}}{H}}$$

Now consider what happens if a crystal of sodium chloride, NaCl, is placed in water. The positive sodium and the negative chlorine ions part company and go into solution. This is because the slight negative charge on the oxygen of the water attracts the sodium ion, while the slight positive charges on the hydrogen ions attract the chlorine ion. You can see this to the right where the chlorine ions are indicated by large circles with a − inside, the sodium ions are indicated by smaller circles with a + inside and each water molecule is represented by two dark circles (the hydrogens) and a single larger white circle (the oxygen):

Water is therefore a good solvent for many substances. Ionic solids like salt, and polar molecules such as sugars and amino acids, readily dissolve in it. The only small biological molecules that do not dissolve in water are lipids, whose lack of polarity renders them insoluble. However, even lipids can be made partially soluble by having polar groups added to them, and this has been important in the development of cell membranes (*page 56*).

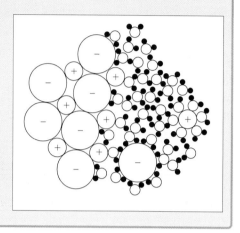

Water is unusual among small molecules in being a liquid at ordinary temperatures. The positively charged hydrogen atoms of one molecule are attracted to the negatively charged oxygen atoms of nearby water molecules, leading to the formation of small clusters of water molecules. The hydrogen–oxygen attraction that holds water molecules together is known as **hydrogen bonding**. We shall see later that, although it is not strong compared with some other types of bonding, the hydrogen bond plays an important part in holding certain organic molecules together.

Water's thermal properties

Water's thermal properties relate to its **specific heat capacity**. A substance's specific heat capacity is the amount of energy (in joules) required to raise the temperature of 1 gram of that substance by 1°C. Water has a very high specific heat capacity compared with other liquids. In other words, a large increase in energy results in a comparatively small rise in temperature of the water. This means that water is good at maintaining its temperature at a steady level, irrespective of fluctuations in the temperature of the surrounding environment.

The importance of this from the biological point of view is that the range of temperatures in which biochemical processes can proceed is quite narrow and most organisms cannot tolerate wide variations in temperature. The high specific heat capacity of water helps to keep the temperature of organisms from varying too much.

Water's high latent heat of vaporisation

As well as having a high specific heat capacity, water also has a high **latent heat of vaporisation**. The latent heat of vaporisation is the amount of energy required to turn one gram of a liquid into a vapour. If water had a lower latent heat of vaporisation, ponds and soils would dry up more quickly and air humidity would vary more greatly than it does.

Surface tension of water

Surface tension is the force that causes the surface of a liquid to contract so that it occupies the least possible area. It is caused by the attractive forces that hold the molecules of the liquid together. At everyday temperatures water has the highest surface tension of any known liquid except mercury.

The strong cohesive forces which exist between water molecules play an important part in the movement of water upwards through vessels and tracheids in the stems of plants (*page 250*). Were these forces much weaker, trees could not be so tall. Surface tension also allows the surface film of standing water to support and provide a habitat for certain aquatic organisms (*figure 2.1*).

Figure 2.1 Pond skater supported on water by the force of surface tension.

▶ The ascent of water up the stem, page 256

Water's freezing properties

Most liquids increase in density, and so decrease in volume, on solidifying as the molecules become more densely packed together. Water is most unusual in that the reverse is the case. As a result, ice floats on liquid water. Indeed, water has its greatest density at 4°C. This means that in winter the warmest water, namely water at around 4°C, is often at the bottom of a lake. As a result, lakes more than a metre or two in depth rarely freeze right through.

Even in the coldest winters organisms, including large fish, may survive at the bottom of lakes. It has been calculated that if it were not for ice floating on water, the oceans would all be frozen solid except for a thin layer of liquid water near the surface.

Water's transparency

This obvious feature of water is very important biologically. Were water opaque, very few organisms could live in it, for the absence of light would prevent plants and other primary producers from photosynthesising (*figure 2.2*). That water is transparent is also of great significance to animals living in water, for it allows them to see.

2.2 Minerals (inorganic ions)

In biology the terms **minerals** and **inorganic ions** are used interchangeably. A **mineral salt** is a substance such as sodium sulphate that is made up of oppositely charged inorganic ions.

Some minerals are needed in relatively large amounts. These include the cations calcium (Ca^{2+}), iron (Fe^{2+} or Fe^{3+}), magnesium (Mg^{2+}), potassium (K^+) and sodium (Na^+), and the anions chloride (Cl^-), nitrate (NO_3^-), phosphate (PO_4^{3-}) and sulphate (SO_4^{2-}). These ions are referred to as **major mineral elements** or **macronutrients**.

Minerals needed in smaller amounts are called **trace elements** or **micronutrients**. They include cobalt (Co^{2+}), copper (Cu^{2+}), manganese (Mn^{2+}), molybdenum (generally found as MoO_4^{2-}) and zinc (Zn^{2+}). There is no hard and fast dividing line between major mineral elements and trace elements. Furthermore, some trace elements needed by animals are not required by plants, and vice versa. For instance, iodide (I^-) is an essential trace element for many animals, including ourselves, but does not seem to be required by plants.

Evidence for the importance of minerals

Just because a mineral is found in an animal or a plant, it does not mean that it is necessarily essential. It is quite difficult to show which minerals really are essential for animals. In some cases farm animals or pets have been found to recover from mysterious ailments when given minute supplements of a mineral previously lacking from their diets. This provides evidence that the mineral is an essential one.

Recently it has been shown that some highly toxic elements, such as arsenic, are required by humans in the most minute amounts. The evidence for this comes from people unfortunate enough to be unconscious for several years and kept alive by intravenous drip

Figure 2.2 Giant kelp photosynthesising several metres under water in the Pacific Ocean.

feeds containing a balanced diet. Sometimes such people eventually develop strange skin disorders. It has been found that adding tiny quantities of arsenic or vanadium cures their skin complaint. You will be relieved to know that normally each of us gets enough, but not too much, arsenic in our diet for good health.

It is easier to find out which minerals are needed by plants. Plants can be grown in deionised water or purified sand to which are added in turn various minerals. In this way, a mineral that is needed can be identified, for its exclusion leads to the development of visible symptoms (*figure 2.3*). In extreme cases the plant may show stunted growth or even death.

Some soils have very low levels of certain minerals needed by plants. For instance, in parts of Eastern Australia, molybdenum is the limiting nutrient. The addition of just 50 g ha^{-1} has greatly increased the productivity of the land. The effectiveness of such small amounts suggests that the mineral has a catalytic role.

Figure 2.3 Manganese deficiency in a rose; an example of the consequences of a mineral deficiency in a plant. Manganese is required for photosynthesis. Deficiency symptoms include chlorosis (yellowing) between the leaf veins.

Functions of minerals

The more important minerals, with details of their functions, deficiency symptoms and main sources for humans are listed in table 2.2. Their functions are many and varied but can be summarised as follows:

- **As constituents of large organic molecules** Proteins contain nitrogen and often sulphur as well. Enzymes frequently contain metal ions such as copper, iron or zinc. Phospholipids, as their name suggests, contain phosphorus. Nucleic acids contain phosphorus and nitrogen.

- **As constituents of smaller molecules** Adenosine triphosphate (ATP) contains phosphorus. Phosphorus is also often required for the activation of small organic molecules. For instance, glucose is phosphorylated (has phosphorus added to it) before it is broken down in respiration. The hormone thyroxine contains iodine.

- **As constituents of certain pigments** The two best-known biological pigments are haemoglobin and chlorophyll, which contain iron and magnesium respectively. Iron is also found in the cytochromes, a group of pigments of great importance in energy transfer.

- **As constituents of structures** Calcium and phosphorus are found in bones. Calcium is found in plant cell walls.

- **As determinants of the anion–cation balance in cells** Sodium, potassium and chloride ions are particularly important in this regard, especially in nerves, muscles and sensory cells where they are involved in the transmission of impulses.

- **As determinants of water potential** Mineral salts, together with other solutes, determine the water potential of cells and body fluids. In most organisms the water potential is not allowed to fluctuate outside quite narrow limits.

Extension

Absorption of iron

A number of factors affect the absorption of minerals by organisms. For example, the absorption of iron is affected by the source of the iron (haem or non-haem), the presence of inhibitors or enhancers of absorption and the amount of iron already stored in the body.

Table 2.2 Summary of the principal mineral elements required by organisms.

Element	Obtained as	Functions	Deficiency symptoms in humans and flowering plants	Main sources for humans
Calcium	Ca^{2+}	Involved in selective permeability of plasma membranes and intracellular communication; activates certain enzymes; constituent of bones, teeth and plant cell walls	Poor growth of skeleton, soft bones (rickets), muscular spasms, delayed clotting; stunted growth in plants	Milk, cheese, fish, drinking water if hard
Chlorine	Cl^- by plants $NaCl$ by animals	With Na^+ and K^+ helps determine solute concentration and anion–cation balance in cells	Shortage of NaCl causes muscular cramp	See sodium
Cobalt	Co^{2+}	Constituent of vitamin B_{12}; involved in nitrogen fixation	Pernicious anaemia	Most foods
Copper	Cu^{2+}	Activates certain enzymes; required for formation of haemoglobin	Certain metabolilc disorders; young leaves permanently wilted	Most foods
Fluorine	F^-	Found in bones and teeth; prevents dental caries	Weak teeth, especially in children	Drinking water
Iodine	I^-	Constituent of thyroxine	Goitre	Sea fish, shellfish, drinking water and vegetables if soil contains iodine
Iron	Fe^{3+}	Constituent of haemoglobin and myoglobin, also ferredoxin and cytochromes involved in electron transfer; activates certain enzymes including catalase	Anaemia; young leaves chlorotic (yellow)	Liver, kidneys, beef, eggs, cocoa powder, apricots, drinking water if soil contains iron
Magnesium	Mg^{2+}	Activates many enzymes; constituent of chlorophyll and bones	Older leaves chlorotic	Nearly all foods
Manganese	Mn^{2+}	Activates certain enzymes; involved in photosynthesis	Malformation of skeleton; young leaves chlorotic with dead spots	Most foods
Molybdenum	MoO_4^{2-}	Activates certain enzymes in nitrogen metabolism	Slight retardation of growth in plants	Most foods
Nitrogen	NO_3^- or NH_4^+ by plants; protein, etc. by animals	Constituent of proteins, nucleic acids, porphyrins, ATP, cytochromes, auxin, etc.	Protein deficiency disease (kwashiorkor); chlorosis and stunted growth in plants	Protein foods e.g. milk, meat, eggs, soya beans
Phosphorus	$H_2PO_4^-$ by plants; protein, etc. by animals	Constituent of plasma membrane (as phospholipid), certain proteins, all nucleic acids and nucleotides; required for phosphorylation; also found in bones and teeth	Poor growth in plants; leaves dark green to red	Most foods
Potassium	K^+	Helps determine anion–cation balance in cells. Activates many enzymes; involved in stomatal opening.	Yellow edges and tips to plant leaves	Prunes, potatoes, brussels sprouts, mushrooms, cauliflower, beef, liver, fish
Sodium	Na^+	Helps determine solute concentration and anion–cation balance particularly in excitable tissues such as nerve and muscle	Muscular cramp	As NaCl in table and cooking salt, bacon, salty fish, cheese
Sulphur	SO_4^{2-} by plants; protein by animals	Constituent of certain proteins and vitamins	Chlorosis in young leaves	Sulphur-containing protein foods
Zinc	Zn^{2+}	Activates various enzymes	Thick malformed leaves with dead spots	Most foods

Covalent and ionic bonds

A covalent bond is one where two atoms *share* electrons. In carbon dioxide, CO_2, for example, each oxygen atom shares two electrons with the carbon atom.

In an ionic bond there is a complete *transfer* of electrons from one atom to another. In sodium chloride (NaCl) for example, the sodium donates one of its electrons to the chlorine.

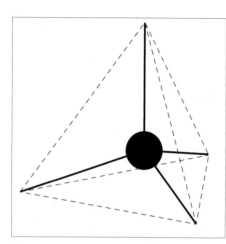

Figure 2.4 The carbon atom can make four bonds with other atoms. These bonds are arranged symmetrically so that if their ends were joined up (dotted lines) the resulting shape would be a regular tetrahedron.

Table 2.3 Naturally occurring single sugars (monosaccharides) have between three and seven carbon atoms.

Number of carbon atoms in a monosaccharide	Name
3	Triose sugar
4	Tetrose sugar
5	Pentose sugar
6	Hexose sugar
7	Heptose sugar

2.3 Organic compounds

Many of the molecules in organisms contain hundreds or even thousands of atoms. Such large molecules are characteristic of life. Surprising as it may seem, few molecules containing more than about six atoms exist naturally unless made by living organisms. Organic compounds are therefore immensely important in living things.

The construction of organic molecules

An organic compound contains at least two, and often many more, atoms of carbon. Organic compounds owe their complexity to the **carbon atom**. Carbon has a **valency** of four which means that in its compounds every carbon atom forms four **covalent bonds**. This accounts for the variety and complexity of organic molecules.

To make this clearer, think of the way an organic molecule is built up. Starting with a single carbon atom one can visualise adding on further carbon atoms (or other atoms for that matter) in any of four different directions. In this way elaborate three-dimensional molecules can be constructed, the carbon atoms forming a skeleton to which other atoms (hydrogen, oxygen, nitrogen and so on) are attached.

The carbon atom is shown in figure 2.4. The variety, complexity and sheer size of organic molecules are caused by the bonding behaviour of the carbon atom. It is doubtful whether life as we know it could ever have evolved without it.

The other principal elements found in organic molecules are **oxygen** and **hydrogen**. Oxygen has a valency of two which means that it may link carbon atoms together or form side chains. Hydrogen, with its valency of one, can only occupy terminal positions in a molecule. **Nitrogen** is found in many organic compounds – proteins, nucleic acids and porphyrins for instance. It usually has a valency of three.

Many important organic compounds are formed by relatively small organic molecules (**monomers**) linking together to form larger, more complex molecules (**polymers**). This process of **polymerisation** contributes to the structural versatility of biological substances.

2.4 Carbohydrates

Carbohydrates contain only the elements carbon, hydrogen and oxygen. The ratio of hydrogen to oxygen is, with a few exceptions, the same as in water: two hydrogen atoms for every oxygen atom. Carbohydrates are the most abundant class of biomolecules. In animals their main function is to act as an easily accessible source of energy. They carry out this role in plants too, but here they also have an important structural function.

Carbohydrates include **sugars**, **starch**, **cellulose** and **glycogen**. As a group, carbohydrates are most conveniently classified on the basis of their size, and this is the approach adopted here. We shall start with the smallest and simplest carbohydrates, the monosaccharides.

Monosaccharides

The word **monosaccharide** literally means 'single sugar'. Monosaccharides have the general formula $(CH_2O)_n$. The letter n equals the number of carbon atoms in the molecule and its value may lie between 3 and 7 (*table 2.3*). Six is the most common number, giving 6-carbon sugars or **hexoses**.

The hexose sugars

The best-known and most abundant hexose is **glucose**. Glucose, like all hexose sugars, has the formula $C_6H_{12}O_6$. This tells us that there are six carbon, twelve hydrogen and six oxygen atoms in each molecule, but it gives no information as to how these are arranged in three dimensions. This information is better shown by the *structural* formula given in figure 2.5.

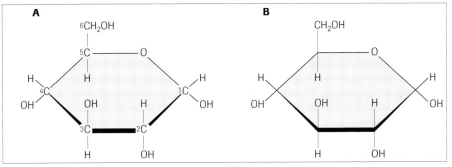

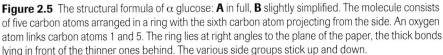

Figure 2.5 The structural formula of α glucose: **A** in full, **B** slightly simplified. The molecule consists of five carbon atoms arranged in a ring with the sixth carbon atom projecting from the side. An oxygen atom links carbon atoms 1 and 5. The ring lies at right angles to the plane of the paper, the thick bonds lying in front of the thinner ones behind. The various side groups stick up and down.

Understanding the three-dimensional structure of glucose is important for understanding the properties of carbohydrates in general. Look at figure 2.5. First, notice the shape of the molecule: it is a ring whose sides are formed by five carbon atoms and one oxygen atom. Secondly, notice the side branches. Some of these end in hydrogen atoms, others in OH (hydroxyl) groups and one of them in a CH_2OH (alcohol) group. Each group occupies a particular position with respect to the carbon atoms of the ring. This is made clear in the structural formula by numbering the carbon atoms 1 to 6 in a clockwise direction, starting with the one at the extreme right – the only carbon atom in glucose that is bonded to two oxygen atoms.

It is the positions of the side groups that determine the nature of the sugar and its properties. The type of glucose whose structural formula is shown in figure 2.5 is called **α glucose**. If, however, the H and OH groups attached to the first carbon atom are interchanged, another sugar with slightly different properties results: **β glucose** (*figure 2.6*). Another sugar is formed by swapping the CH_2OH group at position 6 with the H at position 1, and at the same time swapping the H and OH groups at positions 2 and 3: this is **fructose**.

All these sugars share the formula $C_6H_{12}O_6$ but they differ in their molecular structure: in the language of the chemists they are **isomers**. There is little point in multiplying examples; the important thing is that the type of sugar is determined by the positioning of the atoms in the molecule. The implications of this for the properties of more complex carbohydrates will become clear later.

Monosaccharides are soluble, taste sweet and form crystals. They share these properties with their slightly larger relatives, the disaccharides, which are built up from monosaccharides.

Disaccharides

Two monosaccharide molecules may combine to form a **disaccharide** or 'double sugar'. The process is one of **condensation** involving the loss of water. A single molecule of water is removed from a pair of monosaccharide molecules, as shown at the bottom of figure 2.7. As a result, a covalent bond (resulting in the formation of a **glycosidic link**) is established, joining the two monosaccharide molecules together. The general formula of a disaccharide formed from two hexose sugars is $C_{12}H_{22}O_{11}$. In appropriate conditions disaccharides can be broken down into monosaccharides by adding water (**hydrolysis**).

When a bond is formed between carbon atom 1 of one glucose and carbon atom 4 of another, the result is a 1–4 linked compound called **maltose**. Large concentrations of maltose are found in some germinating seeds – barley, for example.

Other disaccharides formed from hexose sugars include **sucrose** and **lactose**. Sucrose results from the union of glucose and fructose; it is the main form in which carbohydrate is transported in plants and is particularly abundant in the stems of sugar cane and the roots of sugar beet, which are the sources of commercial sugar (*figure 2.8*). Lactose results from the union of glucose and galactose, another hexose sugar. Lactose is the sugar found in milk.

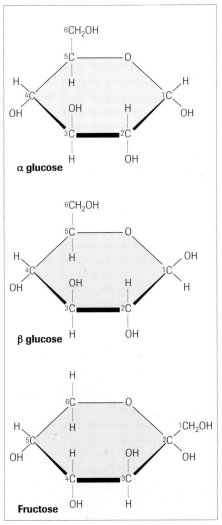

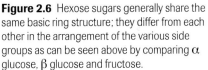

Figure 2.6 Hexose sugars generally share the same basic ring structure; they differ from each other in the arrangement of the various side groups as can be seen above by comparing α glucose, β glucose and fructose.

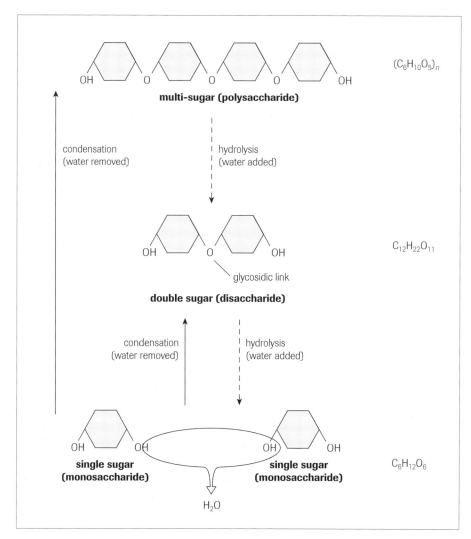

$(C_6H_{10}O_5)_n$

multi-sugar (polysaccharide)

condensation
(water removed)

hydrolysis
(water added)

$C_{12}H_{22}O_{11}$

glycosidic link

double sugar (disaccharide)

condensation
(water removed)

hydrolysis
(water added)

**single sugar
(monosaccharide)**

**single sugar
(monosaccharide)**

$C_6H_{12}O_6$

H_2O

Figure 2.7 Removal of water from monosaccharide molecules results in the formation of disaccharides and polysaccharides. Addition of water reverses this process.

Figure 2.8 *Left* Sugar beet being harvested. Sugar beet is a biennial plant of temperate regions. It stores sugar in swollen roots during the first year prior to producing flowers and seeds in the second year. *Right* Sugar cane being harvested. Sugar cane is a perennial grass of the tropics and subtropics. Sugar is stored in its long thick stems.

How sweet is sugar?

The sugar that people buy for use in cooking is almost pure sucrose. Other sugars taste either sweeter or less sweet than sucrose. If we call the sweetness of sucrose 1 (for reference), then the degrees of sweetness of other common sugars are as follows:

Lactose   0.2
Maltose   0.3
Galactose   0.3
Glucose   0.7
Sucrose   1
Fructose   1.7

Because fructose is sweeter than sucrose, it is often used in the manufacture of sweets and diet foods as the same sweetness can be obtained for fewer calories.

However, sugars are not the only compounds that are sweet. Saccharin is 500 times sweeter than sucrose, although chemically it is quite distinct from sugars:

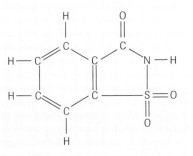

Certain proteins taste even sweeter than saccharin. One such protein is obtained from serendipity berries, the fruit of a West African plant. This protein is 2500 times as sweet as sucrose.

New low-calorie sweeteners are being developed by the food industry. One is a dipeptide called aspartame. This compound is about 200 times sweeter than sucrose and lacks the slightly bitter aftertaste often found with saccharin.

Polysaccharides

Under appropriate conditions, monosaccharides may link up through glycosidic bonds to form a **polysaccharide** or 'multi-sugar' as shown in figure 2.7. In its final form, a polysaccharide consists of a long chain which may be folded or branched and in which the total number of monosaccharide units is variable.

The general formula for polysaccharides formed from hexose sugars is $(C_6H_{10}O_5)_n$. Here n may vary from as little as 40 to over 1000. Polysaccharides are insoluble in water, do not taste sweet and cannot be crystallised.

The compact structure of a polysaccharide makes it ideal as a storage carbohydrate. By building up free monosaccharide molecules into an insoluble polysaccharide, sugars can be stored in a compact form in which they will not diffuse out of the cell nor exert an osmotic effect within the cell. When occasion demands, free sugars can be obtained from the polysaccharide by hydrolysis. These sugars may then be used for the release of energy or for the synthesis of new compounds.

The best-known polysaccharides are the polymers of glucose: **starch**, **glycogen** and **cellulose**. Starch and cellulose are found in plants, glycogen in animals. Starch consists of a mixture of two sorts of molecule: **amylose** and **amylopectin**. The chemical characteristics of amylose, amylopectin, glycogen and cellulose are listed in table 2.4.

Table 2.4 Biochemical characteristics of the four most abundant polysaccharides.

Polysaccharide	Basic monomer	Glycosidic bond	Branching	Relative molecular mass
Amylose	α glucose	1 — 4	None	$4 \times 10^3 - 1.5 \times 10^5$
Amylopectin	α glucose	1 — 4 and 1 — 6	≈ 4%	$5 \times 10^4 - 1 \times 10^6$
Glycogen	α glucose	1 — 4 and 1 — 6	≈ 9%	$≈ 5 \times 10^6$
Cellulose	β glucose	1 — 4	None	$≈ 2 \times 10^5 - 2 \times 10^6$

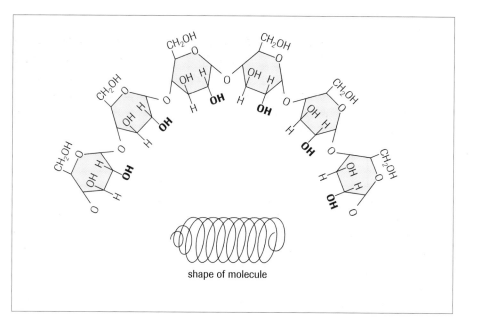

shape of molecule

Figure 2.9 Starch mainly consists of a long chain of 1–4 linked α glucose units of which six are shown here. The chain is coiled into a helix forming, in effect, a cylinder in which most of the OH groups potentially capable of forming cross-linkages project into the interior. These OH groups are shown in red. There are six glucose units for every complete turn of the helix.

Starch

Most starches consist of about 20–30 per cent **amylose** and 70–80 per cent **amylopectin**. Amylose only has bonds between the carbon 1 of one monomer and the carbon 4 of its neighbour, so it is an unbranched polysaccharide. However, although unbranched, it is not a long straight molecule. Instead it spirals, resulting in the formation of a helix (*figure 2.9*).

Amylopectin, like amylose, mainly consists of glucoses joined by 1–4 bonds. However, it has branches at roughly 4 per cent of its monomers. These branches occur between the carbon 6 of the glucose in the main chain and the carbon 1 of the first glucose in the branch chain. The two-dimensional shape of amylopectin is shown diagrammatically in figure 2.10. Its three-dimensional shape is difficult to represent on paper. Essentially it consists of a spiral with other spirals coming off it at irregular intervals.

In both amylose and amylopectin, the bonding between adjacent α glucoses means that in the resulting helix the OH groups capable of forming hydrogen bonds project into the interior. This means that adjacent helices are not linked.

Amylose and amylopectin are usually found together, packed into starch grains (*figure 2.11A*). Although starch grains are particularly abundant in storage organs such as potato tubers, they are found in most parts of a plant.

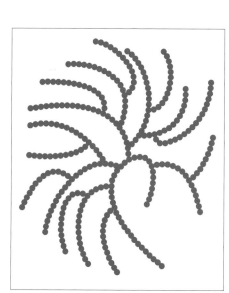

Figure 2.10 Amylopectin is a branched polysaccharide which is found in starch. This diagram shows its two-dimensional structure.

Figure 2.11 Starch and glycogen as they appear in cells. **A** Photomicrograph of potato cells showing starch grains, the pink oval bodies. Magnification ×200. **B** Electron micrograph of a section through part of a liver cell showing glycogen granules (small black dots) in the cytoplasm. Magnification ×15 000.

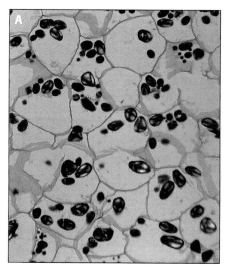

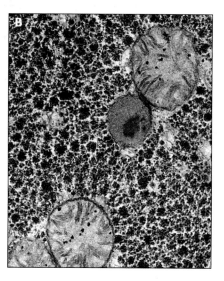

Glycogen

Glycogen is the storage carbohydrate of animals. As indicated in table 2.4 it consists of long, profusely branched chains of α glucose molecules linked by 1–4 or 1–6 glycosidic links. Glycogen is more soluble than starch and exists in the cytoplasm as tiny granules (*figure 2.11B*). It is particularly abundant in the liver and muscles. Each of us has approximately 500 g of glycogen in our bodies, only enough for about 90 minutes of flat-out exercise. If we use it all up, we have to rely on our fat reserves.

▶ Obesity, page 154

Cellulose

Cellulose is found in plant cell walls and is a polysaccharide consisting of long, straight chains of β glucose molecules linked by 1–4 glycosidic bonds. The way the sugar molecules are oriented means that OH groups stick outwards from the chain in opposite directions. These can form hydrogen bonds with neighbouring chains, thereby establishing a kind of lattice (*figure 2.12*). This is in marked contrast to the way starch molecules arrange themselves and explains why cellulose has structural properties lacking in starch.

A single cellulose chain may contain as many as 10 000 sugar units with a total length of 5 μm. The strength of the glycosidic bonds, together with the cross-links between adjacent chains, makes it tough, like rubber.

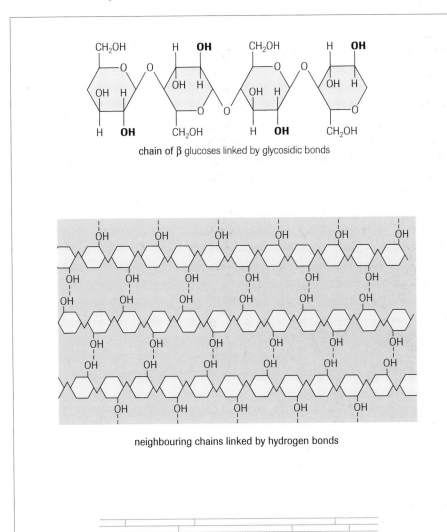

chain of β glucoses linked by glycosidic bonds

neighbouring chains linked by hydrogen bonds

resulting shape of cellulose molecule

Figure 2.12 Cellulose consists of a straight chain of β glucose units joined together in such a way that the OH groups capable of forming cross-linkages project from both sides of the chain. These OH groups are shown in red. They are capable of forming hydrogen bonds with neighbouring OH groups, resulting in the formation of bundles of cross-linked parallel chains as indicated. Compare with figure 2.9.

Cellulose in the cell wall

In the cell wall, groups of about 60 to 70 cellulose chains are massed together to form ribbon-like **microfibrils** each about 3.5 nm in diameter. Under the electron microscope it can be seen that these are laid down in layers, the microfibrils of each layer running roughly parallel with each other but at an angle to those in other layers. The microfibrils of successive layers are frequently laid down at right angles and are interwoven as can be seen in the illustration.

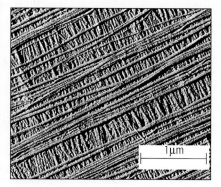

Electron micrograph of cellulose microfibrils (shadowed) showing how the microfibrils of successive layers in a cell wall are often laid down at right angles to one another.

In the cell wall, the cellulose microfibrils are embedded in a gel-like organic matrix containing **hemicelluloses** and **pectins**. Hemicelluloses are short polysaccharides that bind tightly but non-covalently to the surface of the cellulose microfibrils and to each other, thus holding the microfibrils in a complex three-dimensional network. There are many different sorts of hemicelluloses, each containing a variety of sugars such as glucose, xylose, galactose and fructose.

Pectins are another group of polysaccharides found in cell walls. They are characterised by the presence of many acidic, negatively charged residues. Because of their negative charge, pectins bind tightly to cations, and in the cell wall calcium ions (Ca^{2+}) are found associated with pectins, forming **calcium pectates**. Calcium pectates are particularly abundant in the **middle lamella**, the region that serves to cement together the cellulose walls of adjacent cells (*page 42*).

The result of the association between cellulose microfibrils, hemicelluloses and pectins is a material of great strength and structural complexity. The cell wall of a plant can be likened to reinforced concrete: the matrix of hemicelluloses, pectins and the occasional glycoprotein is equivalent to the concrete, the cellulose microfibrils to the metal framework within the concrete.

Despite its strength, the plant cell wall is fully permeable to water and solutes. This is because the matrix is riddled with minute, water-filled channels through which salts, sugars and other small polar molecules can readily diffuse. Moreover the molecules of the matrix are strongly hydrophilic ('water-loving') with the result that in normal circumstances the cell wall is saturated with water like a sponge.

Lignification

Certain plant cells, notably those concerned with providing strength and conducting water, become **lignified** during their development, and this is an important step in the formation of **wood**. In this process **lignin** is deposited in the spaces between the cellulose molecules, making the cell wall much more rigid, and rendering it less permeable. Lignin is not itself a carbohydrate but a complex polymer of various aromatic alcohols and amino acid-like substances.

Once lignification is complete the cell can no longer absorb materials and so dies. Hence, fully lignified tissue is always dead. Its function of providing mechanical strength is entirely due to its ligno–cellulose composition. Its ability to transport water and minerals is due to the fact that lignification involves loss of the cell contents, resulting in the formation of hollow, waterproof tubes (*page 252*).

Other sugar compounds

Simple sugars such as pentoses and hexoses can easily link up with other molecules to form more elaborate compounds. One of the most important associations is between phosphoric acid (H_3PO_4) and sugar.

Phosphorylation of hexose sugar is a necessary first step in the breakdown of sugar in respiration (*page 142*). Phosphorylation is also involved in the formation of **nucleotides**. In this case a pentose sugar links up with an organic base at position 1 and a phosphoric acid molecule at position 5. Nucleotides are the building blocks of nucleic acids such as deoxyribonucleic acid (DNA). Nucleotides also have other significant functions, for example in respiration (*page 141*).

Some sugars contain nitrogen: they are called **amino sugars**. An example is given in figure 2.13. A polysaccharide that contains amino sugars is called a **mucopolysaccharide**. Mucopolysaccharides are found in the basement membranes of epithelia, the matrix of connective tissue, the synovial fluid in vertebrate joints and in the cell walls of prokaryotes.

▶ Deoxyribonucleic acid, page 603

They also occur in **chitin**, a compound found in the walls of fungal hyphae and the exoskeletons of arthropods. Chitin is an important biological material. It is widespread in nature and combines strength with durability.

2.5 Lipids

Lipids are insoluble in water but soluble in organic solvents. Like carbohydrates, they contain carbon, hydrogen and oxygen. However, a lipid contains much less oxygen than a carbohydrate of the same size. Lipids, as we shall see, may also contain small amounts of other elements, such as phosphorus.

Lipids may be divided conveniently into two groups. The first consists of **fats** and **oils**. The second includes **steroids** and **terpenes** together with fat-soluble vitamins and some other compounds.

The structure of fats and oils

Natural fats and oils are compounds of **glycerol** (whose systematic name is propane-1,2,3-triol) and **fatty acids**. The only difference between a fat and an oil is that at room temperature fats are solids and oils are liquid. This is because the fatty acid molecules in oils are smaller than those in fats, or because of the presence of one or more double bonds in some oils.

Glycerol is a small molecule with the formula $C_3H_8O_3$. The arrangement of the carbon, hydrogen and oxygen atoms is shown in the following structural formula:

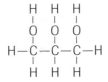

There is only one sort of glycerol, but fatty acids show considerable structural variation. Indeed, the physical and chemical properties of a particular lipid depend on the fatty acids which it contains.

The general formula of a saturated fatty acid is $C_nH_{2n}O_2$. A more informative way of writing this is $CH_3(CH_2)_nCOOH$ where n varies but is generally an even number between 14 and 22. To give an example: in **stearic acid**, a common constituent of body fat, there are 16 CH_2 groups. The formula of stearic acid is therefore $CH_3(CH_2)_{16}COOH$.

The full structure of stearic acid is shown in figure 2.14. You can see that for the most part it consists of a single chain of carbon atoms to which are joined hydrogen atoms, giving rise to a **hydrocarbon chain**. The molecule terminates in an acid carboxyl (COOH) group. This end of the molecule can therefore form hydrogen bonds with water, but overall the molecule is insoluble in water due to the presence of so many CH_2 groups.

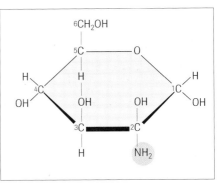

Figure 2.13 Glucosamine, one of the simplest amino sugars. The hydroxyl (OH) group at position 2 of α glucose is replaced by an amino group (NH_2). In other amino sugars the nitrogen-containing side group may be more complex. Amino sugars can form long chains just as ordinary sugars can. Chitin, for example, is a polymer of acetylglucosamine.

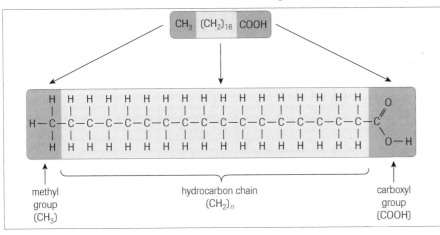

methyl group (CH_3)   hydrocarbon chain $(CH_2)_n$ carboxyl group (COOH)

Figure 2.14 The general formula of a saturated fatty acid is $CH_3(CH_2)_nCOOH$. The fatty acid depicted here is stearic acid with a total of 18 carbon atoms. The systematic name of stearic acid is octadecanoic acid.

A glance at figure 2.14 tells us that this particular hydrocarbon chain contains the maximum possible number of hydrogen atoms: all the bonds between neighbouring carbon atoms are single bonds, so no more hydrogen atoms could be added to the molecule. Such fatty acids are said to be **saturated**. Some fatty acids, however, have one or more double bonds connecting neighbouring carbon atoms. They therefore have fewer hydrogen atoms than they might, and are said to be **unsaturated**. For instance, oleic acid, found in both animal and plant fats, has a double bond between its two central carbons:

$$CH_3 \, (CH_2)_7 - \overset{\displaystyle \overset{H}{|}}{C} = \overset{\displaystyle \overset{H}{|}}{C} - (CH_2)_7 - COOH$$

Coronary heart disease and diet

Coronary heart disease arises when the blood supply to the heart muscle is reduced by obstruction in the coronary arteries. This obstruction is usually the result of a mass of connective tissue and fat deposits building up in the wall of the artery. This is called an **atherosclerotic plaque**. It slows the flow of blood along the artery and may eventually cause the blood to clot, blocking the artery. Such a blockage in one of the coronary arteries will prevent blood reaching part of the heart. If the plaque is fairly small, only a small portion of the heart will lose its blood supply. If, though, one of the larger coronary arteries is blocked, the result will be a heart attack, technically known as a **myocardial infarction**.

Careful medical research has shown that many factors increase a person's chance of suffering a heart attack. These **risk factors** include being male, getting old, having close relatives who have had heart attacks, smoking, being overweight, taking too little exercise, having high blood pressure and eating too much salt or saturated fat (*page 241*) or too little fibre. We cannot do much about our gender, age or relatives. However, the other risk factors are more under our control.

The relationship between fat intake and the risk of coronary heart disease is a complicated one which has still not been fully sorted out. It does seem clear though that a high level of **saturated fats** and **cholesterol** in the diet is associated with an increased risk of coronary heart disease (*page 241*). Fats which have just one double bond per fatty acid do not seem much better for us than saturated fats. Fats with two or more double bonds per fatty acid (**polyunsaturated fats**) seem to reduce the risks.

Foods that are high in saturated fats include animal fats such as butter, cream and lard. However, switching to a low-fat diet does not guarantee that you will not get a heart attack. Some people, such as the Masai people of East Africa, have a diet that is very high in animal fats, yet have a very low rate of heart disease. But then they do not smoke, are not overweight and take a lot of exercise.

The synthesis of fats and oils

Fatty acids and glycerol are the sub-units of fats and oils. In the synthesis of a fat or oil, three fatty acid molecules combine with one glycerol molecule to form a **triglyceride**.

As with the construction of disaccharides and polysaccharides from monosaccharides, this process involves a condensation reaction in which water is lost. As you can see in figure 2.15, each of the OH (hydroxyl) groups in the glycerol molecule reacts with the COOH (carboxyl) group of a fatty acid. In this reaction water is removed and an oxygen bond (known in this case as an **ester bond**) is established between the glycerol and the fatty acid. As glycerol possesses three hydroxyl groups, three fatty acids attach themselves to the glycerol and three molecules of water are removed.

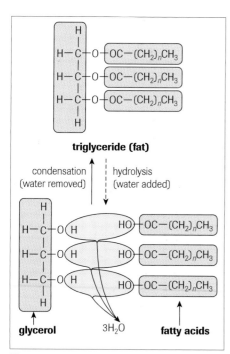

Figure 2.15 The removal of three molecules of water from a molecule of glycerol and three fatty acid molecules results in the formation of a triglyceride. The diagram shows the simplest sort of triglyceride in which three identical saturated fatty acids react with glycerol.

The functions of fats and oils

Although carbohydrates provide the most important direct source of energy in organisms, mass for mass fats yield approximately twice as much energy on combustion as do carbohydrates. This is because they contain relatively little oxygen. When a carbohydrate molecule is respired, some of the necessary oxygen comes from the carbohydrate itself. When, however, a fat is respired, more oxygen needs to be obtained from the atmosphere.

The fact that a given mass of fat stores considerably more energy than the same mass of carbohydrate (or protein) is one reason why animals usually carry around much more fat than carbohydrate. Fat deposits beneath the skin and elsewhere represent potential sources of energy which can be drawn upon when required (*page 149*). Fats and oils are also used as food stores in some plant seeds.

Another property of fat is that it conducts heat energy only very slowly, making it a good insulator. Animals which live in cold climates therefore have extensive fat stores. In polar bears and other Arctic and Antarctic animals, large deposits of **sub-cutaneous fat** occur beneath the skin (*figure 2.16*). In whales and seals this fat is known as **blubber**. Blubber, and lipids in general, can also provide **protection** for the organism and **buoyancy**.

Figure 2.16 Polar bear with cubs. Polar bears have large subcutaneous fat deposits. These serve both as fuel reserves and as insulation.

Fats play a major role in the structure of the **plasma membrane**. Here they are combined with phosphoric acid to form **phospholipids**. In the formation of a phospholipid the phosphoric acid reacts with one of the three hydroxyl groups of glycerol. The other two hydroxyl groups of glycerol react with fatty acid chains in the usual way (*figure 2.17*). The part played by phospholipids in the functioning of the plasma membrane is explained on page 57.

Lipids may also act as a source of **metabolic water**. When respired they yield water and carbon dioxide. Some desert animals are so efficient in their conservation of water that they never need to drink it. Instead they obtain their water either from fat metabolism or directly from the foods they eat.

The structure and functions of steroids

Apart from fats and oils, **steroids** are the most important lipids in animals and plants. Steroids consists of four interlinked rings of carbon atoms. Vitamin D is a steroid, but probably the best-known steroid, on account of the publicity it has received as a constituent of the diet, is **cholesterol**.

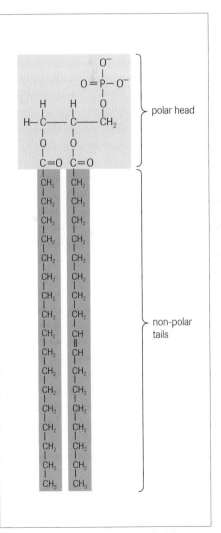

Figure 2.17 A typical phospholipid of the sort found in the plasma membrane. Notice the small polar head and the two non-polar tails. This molecule results from the reaction of one molecule of glycerol with two fatty acid molecules and a molecule of phosphoric acid.

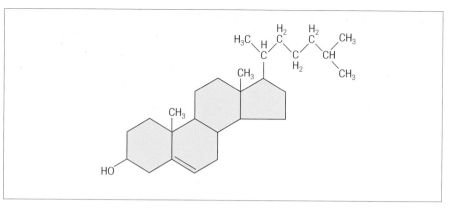

Figure 2.18 The structure of cholesterol, a steroid. All steroids have four rings of carbon atoms but differ in the side groups attached to the carbon atoms.

The structural formula of cholesterol is shown in figure 2.18. Despite its bad press, some cholesterol is essential. Cholesterol is found in the membranes of animal cells where it helps to keep the membranes fluid (*page 58*). Other important steroids are derived from cholesterol. They include the sex hormones **progesterone** and **testosterone**, and the hormone **aldosterone** secreted by the adrenal cortex. Bile salts, such as **glycocholate** and **taurocholate**, are polar metabolic products of cholesterol needed for the normal digestion of lipids.

Other lipids

A number of other important biological molecules are also lipids. Vitamins A, E and K are **terpenes**, compounds similar to steroids but somewhat smaller. Other terpenes include turpentine and rubber and the plant growth regulators gibberellic acid and abscisic acid.

Because they are insoluble in water, lipids often reduce the loss of water by evaporation from organisms. Plant cuticles contain various **waxes** and a mixture of compounds collectively called **cutins**. Cutins and waxes are synthesised by the epidermis and then secreted on to the surface of the plant. A related lipid, **suberin**, is found in tree bark, and in the Casparian strip in roots where its function depends on its impermeability to water.

In animals, waxes again serve in water conservation and are found in arthropod cuticles, vertebrate skin, bird feathers and mammalian fur.

2.6 **Proteins**

Proteins play a number of vital roles in all organisms. Unlike carbohydrates and lipids they always contain nitrogen as well as carbon, hydrogen and oxygen. In addition, sulphur is often present and sometimes phosphorus and other elements.

The structure of proteins

Proteins are built up from **amino acids**. There are over 100 naturally occurring amino acids and they all have an NH₂ (amino) and a COOH (carboxyl) group, as shown below:
Proteins differ in the nature of the R group. The simplest amino acid is **glycine**, in which R

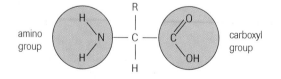

is a hydrogen atom. In **alanine** it is CH₃, in **cysteine** it is CH₂SH, and so on.

Although there are over 100 naturally occurring amino acids, only 20 are used in the biosynthesis of proteins. The names of these 20 amino acids are listed in table 2.5, together with the R groups of six representative examples.

Amino acids unite to form proteins in much the same manner that monosaccharides combine to form polysaccharides, and fatty acids and glycerol combine to form fats and oils. The first step in this process involves the union of two amino acids (*figure 2.19*). A reaction occurs between the amino group of one amino acid and the carboxyl group of another: a molecule of water is removed in a condensation reaction and the two amino acids become joined by a **peptide link** to form a **dipeptide**.

Names of the twenty amino acids

Non-essential	Essential
Alanine	Isoleucine
Arginine*	Leucine
Asparagine	Lysine
Aspartic acid	Methionine
Cysteine	Phenylalanine
Glutamic acid	Threonine
Glutamine	Tryptophan
Glycine	Valine
Histidine*	
Proline	
Serine	
Tyrosine	*essential in children

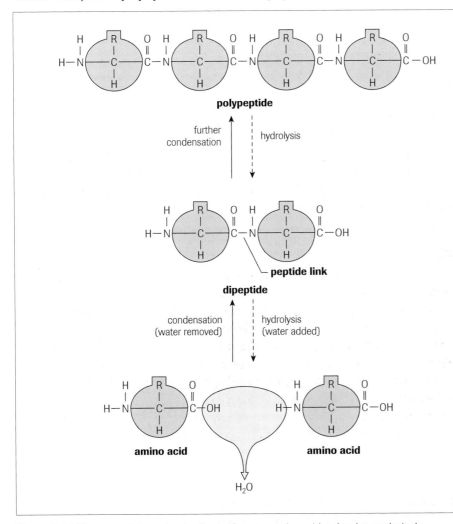

Figure 2.19 The removal of a molecule of water from two amino acid molecules results in the formation of a dipeptide. Further condensation leads to the formation of a polypeptide.

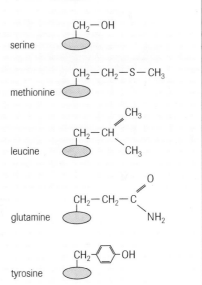

Table 2.5 *At the top* is a list of the naturally occurring amino acids involved in protein synthesis. Non-essential amino acids can be synthesised in the body and are therefore not needed in the human diet. Essential amino acids cannot be synthesised and are therefore needed in our diet. Arginine and histidine, both required for growth, are non-essential in adults but essential in children. *Below* are shown the R groups of six amino acids to illustrate the range of variation in their chemical structure. While the R group is variable, the remainder of the molecule, i.e. the part responsible for forming peptide linkages, is common to all the amino acids. In each case only the R group is shown in full; the rest of the molecule is represented by the shaded oval. Notice that nitrogen and sulphur are present in the R groups of some amino acids.

Continued condensation reactions lead to the addition of further amino acids, resulting in the formation of a long chain called a **polypeptide**. Polypeptides may be composed of up to around 400 amino acids.

Although only 20 amino acids are used in the natural synthesis of proteins, the number of possible ways in which they can be combined is almost infinite. The individuality of a particular protein is determined by the sequence of amino acids comprising its polypeptide chains, together with the pattern of folding and cross-linkages. Some proteins contain only a few of the 20 amino acids; others contain all of them. The total number of amino acids in a protein molecule may be as few as 40 or as many as several thousand.

The primary and secondary structure of proteins

The **primary structure** of a protein is the order of the amino acids of which its polypeptides are composed. The only bonds recognised at this level of protein structure are the covalent bonds between successive amino acids.

The **secondary structure** refers to the way the chain of amino acids folds or turns upon itself as a result of hydrogen bonding (*page 12*). The first elucidation of the secondary structure of a protein was achieved in 1951 by Linus Pauling of the California Institute of Technology.

The alpha-helix

Pauling worked on **keratin**, the structural protein found in hair. He was able to demonstrate that the keratin molecule consists of a greatly elongated polypeptide chain twisted into a helix, the so-called **alpha-helix**, rather like an extensible telephone cord (*figure 2.20*). Successive turns of the helix are linked together by weak hydrogen bonds situated between the amino groups of one turn and the carboxyl groups of the next. We now know that many other proteins besides keratin are built on a helical plan.

What is the function of the alpha-helix? Undoubtedly it helps to maintain the shape of the molecule. The alpha-helix, with its links between successive twists, is a much more stable and robust structure than a straight, untwisted polypeptide chain would be. Alpha-helices are found in proteins such as enzymes and antibodies, where the important feature of the molecule is its precise three-dimensional shape and surface contours.

The beta-pleated sheet

Subsequently Linus Pauling, in collaboration with Robert Corey, discovered another type of secondary structure, called the **beta-pleated sheet**. In this, hydrogen bonding between parallel chains results in a flat structure which becomes folded, as shown in figure 2.21.

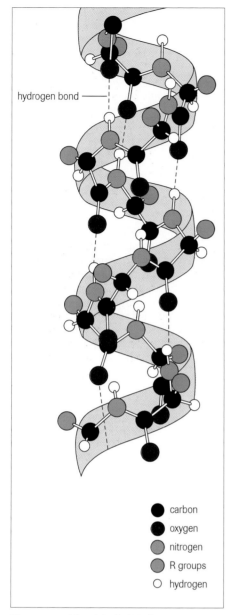

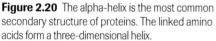

hydrogen bond

- ● carbon
- ● oxygen
- ● nitrogen
- ● R groups
- ○ hydrogen

Figure 2.20 The alpha-helix is the most common secondary structure of proteins. The linked amino acids form a three-dimensional helix.

Figure 2.21 The beta-pleated sheet is the other secondary structure found in proteins. Here the linked amino acids form flat sheets. The colours of the atoms are as in figure 2.20.

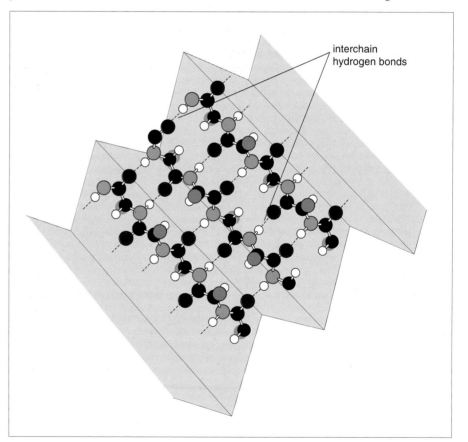

interchain hydrogen bonds

Beta-pleated sheets occur less often than alpha-helices. They are found in a number of structural proteins, for instance silk, and also in some portions of globular proteins, for instance the enzyme lysozyme. By and large beta-pleated sheets are found in proteins whose function requires strength. Silk, for example, is for its thickness, one of the strongest substances known.

The tertiary structure of proteins

The **tertiary structure** refers to the way a polypeptide folds and coils to form a complex molecular shape (*figure 2.22*). The polypeptide may be folded and cross-linked at intervals. The cross-links may be of several sorts including hydrogen bonds, ionic bonds and sulphur bridges. The sulphur bridges are the strongest and contribute to the great toughness of certain proteins.

Conjugated proteins

Many structures in organisms consist of a protein combined with another molecule to form a **conjugated protein**. The non-protein component to which the protein is attached is called the **prosthetic group**. Egg yolk, haemoglobin and other pigments are all examples of conjugated proteins. In egg yolk the prosthetic group is phosphoric acid; in haemoglobin it is an iron-containing pigment called haem (*page 218*).

If a protein is combined with a carbohydrate, the resulting compound is called a **glycoprotein**. Usually the protein forms the core of the molecule and the carbohydrate consists of a branched polysaccharide chain projecting from it. Mucus and synovial fluid contain glycoproteins with lubricative properties. Glycoproteins also occur in the matrix of connective tissue and in the eukaryotic plasma membrane (*page 57*).

Proteins may also combine with fat (triglyceride) to form **lipoproteins**. These too are components of the plasma membrane. They also occur in the blood, for it is mainly in the form of soluble lipoproteins that lipids (including cholesterol) are transported in the bloodstream, for example from the liver to the body's fat depots (*page 273*).

The quaternary structure of proteins

The **quaternary structure** is only present when a protein consists of two or more polypeptides. It refers to the way these polypeptides are arranged to form the biologically active protein. For instance, the pigment haemoglobin, found in red blood cells, contains four tightly packed polypeptide chains whose spatial arrangement is vital for the efficient functioning of the molecule (*page 219*).

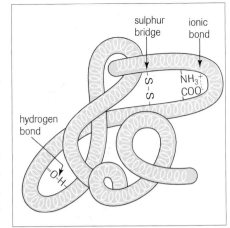

Figure 2.22 The tertiary structure of a hypothetical polypeptide showing some of the different sorts of bonds that can hold a polypeptide chain of a protein together and so help maintain the tertiary structure. The strongest of these bonds are those of the sulphur bridges, as these are covalent bonds. The bonds that link the amino acids together within each chain are also covalent bonds.

The functions of proteins

The function of a protein is directly related to its shape. In general proteins fall into two groups: **globular** and **fibrous**.

Globular proteins

In globular proteins, such as globulin itself and the hormone insulin (*page 269*), the polypeptide chains are tightly folded to form a more-or-less spherical shape such as that shown in figure 2.22 on the previous page. One of the most important classes of globular proteins is **enzymes**, organic catalysts whose function is to speed up chemical reactions in organisms. Enzymes are nearly always proteins and the functioning of an enzyme is directly related to its shape (*page 128*).

Globular proteins are also used in the construction of microfilaments and microtubules in cells (*page 52*). Microfilaments are polymers of the protein **actin**, and microtubules are polymers of the protein **tubulin** (*figure 2.23*).

Globular proteins are also important in buffering, as explained in the box on page 29. They are generally water soluble, though on account of their large size they do not go into true solution but form **colloidal suspensions**. Collectively such colloids have a very large surface area and, since they have a strong capacity to absorb water and other substances, they are important in holding molecules within the cell.

Among the many other classes of globular proteins, special mention should be made of **antibodies**. Each of us can make hundreds of thousands of different antibodies, which bind to particular disease-causing agents and toxins (*page 323*).

Other globular proteins are found in membranes where they are mainly involved in the transport of substances into and out of the cell and its membrane-bound organelles.

Fibrous proteins

Fibrous proteins are insoluble and consist of long, parallel polypeptide chains cross-linked at many points along their length. They are essential constituents of many structures in the body. The fibrous protein **keratin**, for instance, is found in skin and in hairs, feathers, nails, hooves and horns (*figure 2.24*).

Collagen is another fibrous protein. It is the most abundant protein in vertebrates, making up a third of their total protein mass. We are largely held together by collagen as it is found in bones, cartilage, tendons, ligaments, connective tissue and skin (*page 65*). Collagen is also found in the cornea of the eye. Collagen fibres have a tensile strength greater than that of steel. Under the electron microscope they show a characteristic banding pattern (*figure 2.25*). Careful analysis has shown that they consist of three polypeptide chains coiled round each other in a **triple helix**. The resulting structure is like a plaited rope and has great strength.

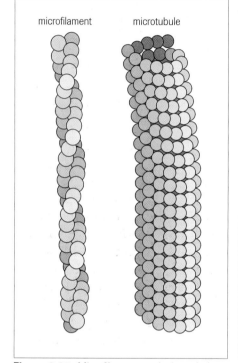

microfilament   microtubule

Figure 2.23 Microfilaments and microtubules are composed of globular proteins (represented by the spheres above). In the microfilament the globular protein molecules are in chains twisted round each other. In the microtubule they are arranged helically around a hollow space. Molecules can be added, or removed, at the ends, which explains the transitory nature of these structures (*page 52*).

Figure 2.24 Scimitar oryx. The hair, hooves and horns of this animal are almost pure keratin.

Figure 2.25 Shadowed collagen fibres from the neck tendon of a bird seen under the electron microscope. The banding pattern is characteristic of collagen.

Other fibrous proteins include myosin which is found in muscle, and elastin found associated with collagen in connective tissue (*page 65*).

Protein as an energy source

Like carbohydrate and fat, protein can be broken down with the transfer of energy. However, protein is normally only used as a substantial source of energy when eaten in excess or when an animal is starving. For humans, the possibility that tissue protein may be used as a source of energy is one of the dangers of going on so-called 'starvation diets'. Under such conditions, though, the body tends to utilise less essential tissues first, such as the skeletal muscles. Vital organs such as the heart and brain initially remain unaffected.

Proteins and the diet

In an animal's cells the various proteins are assembled from the necessary amino acids. As indicated in table 2.5 on page 27, adult humans can synthesise 12 amino acids in sufficient quantities for them not to be required in the diet. They are therefore called **non-essential amino acids**. The remaining eight amino acids cannot be synthesised by the body itself, at any rate not fast enough, so they have to be supplied in the diet. Consequently they are known as **essential amino acids**. A further two amino acids are essential for growth and cannot be made in sufficient amounts by children. Children therefore have ten essential amino acids.

Synthesis of the non-essential amino acids involves a process called **transamination**. In this, the amino acid group of one of the dietary amino acids changes places with the keto group of a carbohydrate derivative which is thereby converted into a new amino acid (*figure 2.26*).

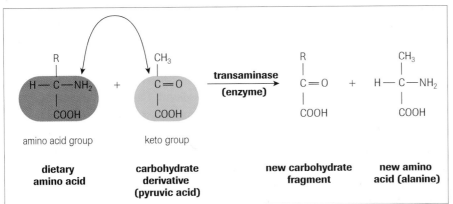

Dietary reference values

Dietary Reference Values (DRVs) are numbers which indicate how much energy and nutrients people need in their diets. Obviously such figures differ from person to person depending on such things as their mass, growth rates, activity, gender (whether male or female), pregnancy and lactation. In addition, there are slight individual differences even when all such factors are taken into account.

The way in which energy requirements depend on these various factors is described on pages 151 to 152. Dietary reference values are also produced for protein, fat, carbohydrate, vitamins and minerals. Nowadays, maximum safe upper levels as well as minimum needed levels are published.

Most of us, of course, manage pretty well without paying any attention to dietary reference values. However, they are of considerable value to caterers and dieticians planning meals for people in such cicumstances as famine relief, long-stay hospitals and prisons.

Figure 2.26 How the body makes non-essential amino acids by transamination. Under the influence of a transaminase enzyme, the amino acid group of the dietary amino acid changes place with the keto group of the carbohydrate derivative which in this example is pyruvic acid. This results in the formation of a new amino acid, in this case alanine.

Production of mycoprotein

A **mycoprotein** is a protein made by a fungus – 'myco' coming from the same root as 'mycelium' (*page 92*). Mycoproteins are an increasingly important example of biotechnology being used in the food industry.

For example, you have probably heard of or eaten **Quorn**™ (TM meaning that the name is 'trademarked'). Quorn is made by the fungus *Fusarium graminearum*. This fungus can be grown cheaply as it thrives on a substrate of grain and flour wastes. Its mycelium is high in protein and fibre, yet low in salt and cholesterol. It is also fairly tasteless! This is an advantage since the addition of suitable flavourings (*page 38*) can persuade eaters that they are eating chicken or beef – and the product is acceptable to vegetarians too.

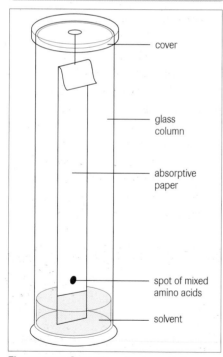

Figure 2.28 Separation of amino acids by paper chromatography. A small amount of solvent is put into a glass column. A strip of absorptive paper, containing a concentrated spot of the mixture of amino acids near its lower end, is hung in the glass column so that its end dips into the solvent. The solvent moves slowly up the strip carrying the amino acids with it. These travel at different speeds and so become separated. The strip is dried and treated so that the positions of the amino acids show up clearly.

Most plant proteins contain fewer essential amino acids than most animal proteins. Vegetarians therefore take care to eat a wide range of plant proteins so as to be sure they get all the necessary amino acids. Some plant products, such as soya beans, provide a particularly rich source of the various essential amino acids, at least compared with other plants.

Lack of one or more of the essential amino acids can result in retarded growth and various other symptoms depending on which particular amino acids are in short supply.

The analysis of proteins

Proteins are key compounds in the working of the body. Often it is an error in the body's synthesis of a particular protein that leads to genetic diseases such as sickle cell anaemia and cystic fibrosis. Understanding such diseases often involves identifying and characterising the proteins responsible. For this and other reasons, protein analysis is important in biology.

The first step in analysing a protein is to separate it from others that may be mixed up with it. A blood sample, for instance, contains many different proteins. A commonly used technique for separating proteins is **electrophoresis**. The technique relies on the fact that large, charged molecules such as proteins migrate in an electric field. The rate of migration varies from one protein to another, depending on the size, shape and charge of the molecule, so they become separated from one another (*figure 2.27*).

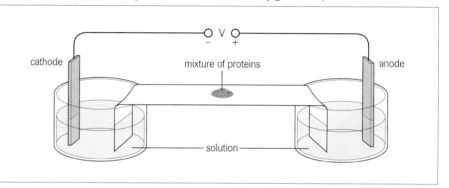

Figure 2.27 Separation of proteins by electrophoresis. A strip of absorptive paper, to which the mixture of proteins is applied, is placed between two dishes containing a suitable conducting solution. When a potential difference is applied, the proteins migrate towards one of the electrodes. If positively charged, they migrate towards the negative electrode (cathode); if negatively charged, they migrate towards the positive electrode (anode). The rate at which the proteins move depends on their size and charge.

The next step is to determine the sequence of amino acids in the protein, that is, its primary structure. The precise methods used to determine the primary sequence of a protein are complex and have changed in recent years as a result of automated approaches. Nevertheless, two techniques are central: **progressive hydrolysis** of the protein and **chromatography** of the resulting amino acids.

Progressive hydrolysis involves removing the amino acids from the polypeptide one at a time by the use of hydrolysing enzymes. The mixture of amino acids is then subjected to chromatography.

There are various sorts of chromatography, but the simplest is **paper chromatography** (*figure 2.28*). A concentrated spot of the mixture of amino acids is placed on a sheet of absorptive paper which is then dipped in a suitable solvent. The solvent rises up the paper and carries each amino acid at a speed which depends on its physical and chemical properties. By comparing how far the amino acids have travelled after a given length of time with a reference collection showing the distance travelled by the 20 different amino acids, the amino acids can be identified.

Analysing protein structure is easier said than done, and it was not until 1953 that the first naturally occurring protein had its primary sequence determined. In that year Frederick

Extension

Working out the shape of a protein molecule

As we have seen, there is more to a protein than its primary structure. How can the three-dimensional shape of the molecule be ascertained? Here again spectacular progress has been made. The approach makes use of a technique developed by the physicist Sir Lawrence Bragg. In 1913 Bragg determined the precise atomic structure of sodium chloride by a technique called **X-ray crystallography**. Since then this technique has been used in the analysis of many other molecules, including proteins.

The technical problems in X-ray analysis are formidable but the principle is simple enough. A beam of X-rays is fired at the protein crystal. The X-rays are deflected by the atoms in the protein molecules and the way in which they are scattered, the **X-ray diffraction pattern**, is recorded on a photographic plate located behind the crystal. Between each firing the crystal is rotated slightly so that the X-rays hit all sides of it, thus enabling a complete analysis to be made.

Proteins are large molecules composed of thousands of atoms. Their X-ray diffraction patterns are correspondingly complex, and this makes analysis of the data a difficult and laborious business. However, with the aid of computers, it is now possible to derive from X-ray diffraction patterns the precise positioning of the atoms and the shape of the whole molecule.

X-ray crystallography allowed the elucidation of the alpha-helix and beta-pleated sheet in the 1950s. By the 1960s the same techniques had been refined to the point where the Cambridge biologists John Kendrew and Max Perutz were able to announce the complete structures of, respectively, myoglobin and haemoglobin, both oxygen-carrying proteins. For this, Kendrew and Perutz shared a Nobel Prize in 1962. Once the structures of myoglobin and haemoglobin had been discovered it became easier to understand how they functioned.

Myoglobin is the simpler of the two. Even so, it has a relative molecular mass of 17 600 and contains over 2500 atoms which show up as groups of spots on X-ray photographs. On analysis it turns out that the molecule consists of a single polypeptide chain made up of 153 amino acids. The polypeptide chain is coiled to form an alpha-helix, and this in turn is folded on itself into a roughly spherical shape. Various kinds of chemical bond, together with electrostatic attraction, keep the folds of the chain together and help to maintain the shape of the molecule.

Myoglobin is an example of a conjugated protein: attached to the polypeptide chain is a flat group of atoms, the prosthetic group, consisting of a central iron atom surrounded by rings of carbon and nitrogen atoms. This prosthetic group is **haem** and it is to the iron atom in the middle that the oxygen molecule becomes attached. Haem belongs to a class of organic compounds known as **porphyrins**.

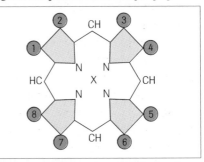

The general structure of a porphyrin. A variety of side groups can exist at positions 1 to 8, so that many different porphyrins occur. Various metal ions may be found at X. In chlorophyll the element is magnesium, in haemoglobin it is iron. Porphyrins are also found in cytochromes – coenzymes required in respiration.

Haemoglobin is a larger and more complex molecule than myoglobin. It contains 574 amino acids in all, almost four times as many as in myoglobin. The mole-cule is composed of four polypeptide chains arranged around four haem groups. Each polypeptide chain has stretches of the alpha-helix and this is folded and held together in much the same way as the single polypeptide chain is in myoglobin.

Sanger (*figure 2.29*) of Cambridge University worked out the structure of insulin, a hormone produced by the pancreas and involved in blood sugar regulation. Insulin is quite a small protein, containing only 51 amino acids. Since then many other proteins have had their primary structures determined.

Figure 2.29 Frederick Sanger, discoverer of the sequence of amino acids in the hormone insulin, an achievement for which he was awarded the Nobel Prize in 1958. When Sanger announced that he wanted to find out the structure of a naturally occurring protein, his professor told him he was mad! In 1980 he was awarded a second Nobel Prize, this time for his work on the chemical structure of genes. He is the first British scientist to have been awarded two Nobel Prizes.

2.7 Vitamins

Vitamins are a mixed assortment of organic compounds which are grouped together, not because of any chemical affinity between them, but because they are all needed in the diet in small amounts. The chemical structures of vitamins A (retinol), B_1 (thiamine) and C (ascorbic acid) are shown in figure 2.30. The importance of vitamins can be appreciated from the ill-effects which follow if an organism is deprived of one of them.

Figure 2.30 Vitamins vary greatly in their structure. This shows the chemical structures of retinol (vitamin A), vitamin B_1 (thiamine) and vitamin C (ascorbic acid).

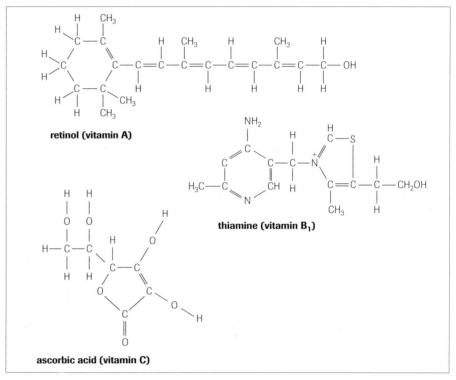

retinol (vitamin A)

thiamine (vitamin B_1)

ascorbic acid (vitamin C)

Scurvy and the discovery of vitamin C

Apart from famine, scurvy is probably the nutritional deficiency disease that has caused the most suffering in recorded history. Some of the earliest descriptions of what is now known as scurvy come from the diaries kept by Europeans, such as the great Portuguese explorer Vasco da Gama, while on board ship in the late 15th century. Before that time, scurvy occurred only rarely among sailors. However, as voyages became longer, the problem of scurvy became more serious. During the 18th century, the British navy lost more sailors through scurvy than through enemy action.

During the 17th and early 18th centuries, many cures for scurvy were suggested and there was some evidence that fresh fruit could help. Unfortunately, none of the experiments had what would

nowadays be considered adequate controls. Because of this, the results were generally inconclusive. In 1746, however, James Lind, a Scottish ship's surgeon, kept a group of 12 sailors all with scurvy 'as similar as I could have them' in the same quarters. He then divided the men into six pairs and fed them different diets. After six days the men whose diet included two oranges and a lemon a day were greatly improved, the men who drank just over a litre of cider a day were somewhat improved, and the others were no better. Lind concluded 'that oranges and lemons were the most effectual remedies for this distemper at sea'.

Unfortunately this trial seems to have made very little impression among the writers on scurvy over the next 50 years, and it is only quite recently that Lind's

work has been praised as an exemplary example of biological experimentation (*page 4*).

At the beginning of the 20th century some leading scientists still thought that unsanitary surroundings, overwork, mental depression, bad meat, sterilisation of milk and exposure to damp and cold could all contribute to the disease. However, in 1907 two Norwegians, Axel Holst and Theodor Frölich, showed that scurvy could be produced, and cured, by diet. They worked on guinea pigs and found that fresh cabbage, lemon juice and apples could all alleviate the symptoms of scurvy. It is because of their work that the term 'guinea pig' is used for an experimental subject.

Table 2.6 Vitamins required by humans.

Name	Function	Principal sources	Deficiency diseases
Fat soluble			
A (retinol)	Enters into photochemical reaction in rods in retina of eye	Meat, fish, carotenoid pigments in vegetables, particularly carrots	Xerophthalmia (drying and degeneration of cornea) leading to blindness
D (calciferol)	Absorption and utilisation of Ca^{2+} for bone formation	Fish liver oil and the action of sunlight	Rickets (softening of bones)
E (tocopherol)	Not known for certain	Most foods	Sterility in rats
K	Required for synthesis of certain blood-clotting factors	Synthesised by intestinal bacteria	Prolonged clotting time
Water soluble			
B_1 (thiamine)	Required as coenzyme in respiration	Many foods, especially husks of wheat grains and brown rice	Beri beri: wasting of muscles, circulatory failure and paralysis
B_2 (riboflavine)	Forms flavine coenzyme FAD required in respiration	Leafy vegetables, fish, eggs	Sore mouth, eyes and skin
Nicotinamide	Forms coenzymes NAD and NADP required in respiration and photosynthesis respectively	Meat, fish, milk, eggs	Pellagra: diarrhoea, dermatitis and mental disorder
B_5 (pantothenic acid)	Forms coenzyme A required in respiration	Most foods	Fatigue, poor motor coordination, sleep disturbance
B_6	Forms coenzyme required for synthesis of amino acids by transamination	Most foods	Convulsions, kidney stones
B_{12} (cobalamin)	Coenzyme in carbon transfer in nucleic acid metabolism.	Meat, eggs, dairy products	Pernicious anaemia, neurological disorders
Folic acid	Coenzyme in carbon transfer in nucleic acid metabolism	Green vegetables, legumes, whole wheat products	Anaemia, gastrointestinal disorders
Biotin	Required as coenzyme for fat synthesis, amino acid metabolism and glycogen formation	Legumes, vegetables, meat	Under experimental conditions: dermatitis, muscle pains and depression
C (ascorbic acid)	Required for hydroxylation of a precursor of collagen	Citrus fruits and green vegetables	Scurvy

Indeed this was how they were discovered. In 1912 the English biochemist Frederick Gowland Hopkins showed that rats fed on a diet containing only proteins, fats, carbohydrates, minerals and water eventually became unhealthy. However, the daily addition of a small amount of milk soon restored their health. The crucial ingredients in the milk came to be known as vitamins.

At first vitamins were simply given letters (vitamin A, B, etc.). Later some of them were given names and some were found to consist of more than one vitamin. We shall classify vitamins into fat-soluble and water-soluble. Both sorts come from a wide variety of sources, and their absence causes a wide range of **deficiency diseases**. The details are summarised in table 2.6.

Fat-soluble vitamins

Vitamin A (**retinol**) is required for the photochemical reactions involved in light perception by the rod cells in the eye (*page 387*). Although it occurs in many foods, it is particularly abundant in liver, especially polar bear liver. Indeed, Arctic explorers have been poisoned by excessive amounts of vitamin A as a result of eating too many polar bear livers.

Vitamin D is present in few natural foods except fish liver oil. However, one form in which it occurs, **cholecalciferol** (**vitamin D₃**) is synthesised by the action of sunlight on a natural precursor found in the skin. Because of this, vitamin D deficiency is rare except in climates where there is very little sunlight or in cultures where people spend very little time in natural sunlight. Under these circumstances, vitamin D deficiency may lead to **rickets**, a condition in which the bones fail to develop properly and remain soft (*figure 2.31*).

Figure 2.31 Young boy suffering from rickets which has resulted in severely bowed legs.

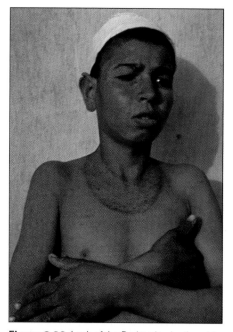

Figure 2.32 Lack of the B-vitamin nicotinamide results in the deficiency disease pellagra, one symptom of which is coarsening of skin exposed to sunlight. Other symptoms include abdominal pains and diarrhoea. Acute deficiency results in mental disorder and delirium.

Vitamin E (tocopherol) is known to prevent some forms of infertility in rats. However, no human has ever been found to be short of this vitamin and its biochemical function in humans is still uncertain.

Vitamin K is needed for normal blood clotting (*page 228*). Interestingly, intestinal bacteria synthesise the vitamin for us. Because of this, the only way deficiency can occur is if we lose most of our intestinal bacteria, for example by taking antibiotics for months on end.

Water-soluble vitamins

The **B-vitamins** form a group of eight water-soluble substances which for historical reasons are named: B_1 (thiamine), B_2 (riboflavine), nicotinamide, B_5 (pantothenic acid), B_6, B_{12} (cobalamin), folic acid, biotin.

These eight vitamins are examples of **coenzymes**, complex non-protein compounds needed for the action of enzymes (*page 123*). For example, **thiamine (vitamin B_1)** serves as the coenzyme in several important reactions in carbohydrate metabolism involving the removal or transfer of aldehyde groups. Another important B-vitamin is nicotinamide. Insufficient of this leads to **pellagra** (*figure 2.32*).

Vitamin C or **ascorbic acid** is perhaps the best-known vitamin. It is ironic therefore that its precise biochemical function is still unknown, despite the fact that lack of it has long been known to cause scurvy. If you are ever asked what humans share in common with guinea pigs, red-vented bulbuls, Indian fruit bats and certain species of fish and monkeys, the answer is that they are the only animals known to require vitamin C in their diet. Other organisms can synthesise it from glucose. As you would expect, therefore, the structure of vitamin C is similar to that of glucose (*figure 2.30 on page 34*).

Extension

Pellagra and the discovery of the vitamin that prevents it

Until the First World War it was generally thought that pellagra was caused by infectious microorganisms. However, Joseph Goldberger, an Austrian-American doctor, found that prisoners in a Mississippi prison developed the disease when given a diet lacking meat and milk.

Goldberger then attempted to contract the disease by exposing himself to the clothing, bedding and excreta of the prisoners. However, he did not get the disease. His failure to develop pellagra suggested that the disease was due, not to an infectious agent present in the prisoners, but to something absent from the prisoners' diet. Goldberger called the missing nutrient the P-P (pellagra-preventing) factor and after his death it was sometimes called vitamin G in his honour.

Extension

Dorothy Hodgkin

Dorothy Hodgkin was born in 1910 in Cairo and her early education was in the Middle East and Africa. As a teenager she was attracted by archaeology as well as chemistry, but decided to study the latter at Oxford. After taking her doctorate at Cambridge she returned to Oxford. In the 1930s she was one of the first people to use and develop the technique of X-ray crystallography. Her major research triumphs included the determination of the three-dimensional structures of penicillin, vitamin B_{12} and insulin. Her work has led to a better understanding of the functioning of these compounds, and has been of considerable medical importance.

In 1964 she received the Nobel Prize, the only woman from Britain to do so, and the year after became the first woman to receive the Order of Merit since Florence Nightingale. In 1970 she was made Chancellor of Bristol University. She achieved all this despite suffering from terrible rheumatoid arthritis all her life. She died in 1994.

One of the most notable contributors to our knowledge of biochemistry, including vitamins, was Dorothy Hodgkin.

Food additives

Various chemicals, natural or artificial, are added to our food by the manufacturers. Guest author Colin May discusses some of these food additives.

A **food additive** is a substance which is added to a food for a specific technical purpose but which is not normally consumed as a food in itself or as a characteristic ingredient of a food. Typically additives are used to improve the food's appearance, texture, flavour or keeping quality, or to make processing possible or easier. Their use is controlled under International Food Standards and European Law, and only approved substances may be used. In the European Union detailed directives set out lists of additives which have been approved for safety, their permitted concentrations and the foods in which they may be used. Once an additive has been declared to be safe, it is given an **E-number**. There are approximately 300 E-numbered additives altogether.

Some additives provide alternatives to traditional ingredients or processes, whilst others have unique functions in the wide range of ready-prepared convenience foods available today. The main types of additives are as follows:

Emulsifiers

There are two kinds of emulsion in foods: an **oil-in-water emulsion** where small droplets of oil are dispersed through water, e.g. milk; and a **water-in-oil emulsion** where small droplets of water are dispersed through oil, e.g. margarine. Oil and water, being immiscible, normally separate into two layers with the oil on top. In the presence of an emulsifier, however, the oil and water are prevented from separating with the result that each is evenly dispersed in the other.

The effect of the emulsifier is therefore to stabilise the food, i.e. to keep it in a particular state. Stabilisers are a category of food additives in themselves; in addition to emulsifiers, they include gelling agents, thickeners and substances that affect the texture of the food.

Emulsifiers illustrate an important general principle, namely that when selecting an additive care must be taken to ensure that the one chosen gives the best effect for the particular food or process in which it is going to be used. For example, an emulsifier used for a water-in-oil emulsion would have a quite different effect on the texture and stability of a food from that produced by an emulsifier for an oil-in-water emulsion.

Sweeteners

Sweetness is a desirable feature of many foods, including confectionery, soft drinks, cakes and desserts. Traditionally, sweet ingredients such as **honey**, **sugar** or **glucose syrups** have been used. As well as adding sweetness, these substances affect the bulk, texture and stability of the food, and at sufficient concentration they also contribute to preservation, as in jams and sweets.

Sugars vary in their sweetness (see extension box on page 19). Glucose syrups are made by hydrolysing starch with acid or enzymes, and their sweetness depends on how much of the starch is broken down into particular sugar fragments (glucose, maltose, etc.). Other sugars, such as lactose, which is found in milk, have very little sweet taste.

Sugars are simple carbohydrates and are a ready source of energy. Today many people want to control their energy intake while still enjoying sweet foods, so reduced-energy foods are very popular. Aspartame, saccharin and other **artificial sweeteners** can provide intense sweetness and each has a slightly different taste profile. Some are therefore more suited to particular foods, and often mixtures give the best taste. These sweeteners do not provide the bulk or texture of natural sugars, so other ingredients are often added to artificially sweetened products. In cases where sugar would provide nutrition for spoilage microorganisms, artificial sweeteners may be added to give a slight sweetness, as for example in prepared salads and dips.

Colours

It has been said that we eat with our eyes as well as our mouths, and coloured ingredients such as saffron, turmeric, spinach and tomato are traditionally used to give colour as well as flavour (green lasagne verde for instance). **Colour additives** are used to restore the colour of processed foods (e.g. canned peas), to maintain a consistent colour in foods and drinks whose ingredients are liable to seasonal changes in colour, or to make prepared foods more acceptable.

Colours may be extracted from natural sources (which may be food or non-food) or they may be purely artificial. The law requires that both should be demonstrably safe at the concentrations to be used. Examples of natural colours are β–carotene, extracted from carrots; annatto, a yellowish pigment extracted from the fruits of the tropical annatto tree; and cochineal, a bright red pigment extracted from the cochineal insect of South America and the Canary Islands. Tartrazine and Sunset Yellow are examples of synthetic azo colours ('azo' refers to the particular arrangement of atoms in the molecule). Natural colours have to be used in higher concentrations than synthetic ones to give similar effects, so ensuring their safety is just as important as for synthetic colourings.

A few synthetic colours have been shown to cause adverse reactions in some people. However, the number of people affected is far fewer than for common food allergies and intolerance to certain natural foods such as wheat, milk, nuts and shellfish. Nevertheless, this has encouraged manufacturers to make greater use of natural colours, despite the fact that they are often less stable and more expensive to use. Care is needed even with natural colourings: for example, there is some concern that wider use of annatto could result in people exceeding the acceptable daily intake (ADI).

Antioxidants

Oxidation of fats and oils in foods causes **rancidity**, making the food unpalatable. This happens much more rapidly with unsaturated fats and oils than with the saturated fats used more typically in the past. However, consumers still expect the foods they buy to have a longer shelf life.

In fats and oils themselves, **oil-soluble antioxidants** such as tocopherol (vitamin E) or synthetic antioxidants are used. In low-fat products it may be better to use **water-soluble antioxidants** such as ascorbic acid (vitamin C). However, it is also possible to convert ascorbic acid into a fat-soluble ester, such as ascorbityl palmitate, thereby making it effective in high-fat foods. Water-soluble antioxidants can also be used to control oxidative browning in cut fruits and vegetables.

Preservatives

The safety of some preservatives is controversial, but their correct use contributes to both the shelf life and safety of foods. They control the growth of microorganisms which can spoil food and even cause food poisoning.

Sorbic acid and sorbates are some of the most widely used preservatives and have been shown to be particularly safe. They occur naturally in some fruits and berries. They are particularly effective against moulds, which can spoil food and in some cases generate dangerous toxins.

Benzoic acid and benzoates also occur in nature and are used in some acidic drinks and fruit products because they are particularly effective against yeasts as well as moulds which thrive on these sorts of foods. However, at high levels they give the food a distinctive taste, which limits their use.

The Romans used **sulphur dioxide** to preserve wine, and this is still one of its biggest uses. Sulphites have advantages in certain foods because they can control bacteria as well as yeasts and moulds, and they also inhibit browning reactions which affect the taste and colour of, in particular, dried foods (try tasting dried apricots with and without sulphite). Sulphur dioxide is important in preserving the traditional British sausage.

Sulphur dioxide is also used to preserve food ingredients temporarily during processing or storage because it can be expelled subsequently from the food by boiling. It is used in this way during the production of glucose syrups and maltodextrins, and in the preservation of fruit pulps prior to processing.

Usually sulphur dioxide reacts with other food components, so that little of it is present in the free form. This is important because high levels of free sulphur dioxide have occasionally caused serious reactions in asthmatics who are sensitive to aspirin and related compounds. This has happened when sulphur dioxide has been used on salads in self-service restaurants and similar situations where most of it remains in the free form. As with nut allergies, it is vital to provide proper information so that susceptible individuals can avoid the risk.

Finally, **nitrates** and **nitrites** are useful preservatives in cured meats and canned meat products. In such foods anaerobic conditions may occur, and these additives prevent the growth of *Clostridium botulinum*, a particularly dangerous and often fatal pathogenic

bacterium. Only nitrates and nitrites are effective against it, so they have to be used. However, their use is carefully controlled because there is a possible association between nitrite and cancer.

Other substances

Enzymes are important processing aids which, because they are usually inactivated in the final food product, are not regarded as food additives and are not given E-numbers. Some of their uses in food production are given on page 134.

Most **flavourings** are not regulated as food additives because there are so many of them and they are used at very low concentrations in the final food. They include extracts from flavoursome foods and ingredients (e.g. orange oil, vanilla extract, herb and spice extracts), chemicals which are identical to those found in foods (e.g. vanillin, ethyl acetate and many others) and a few which are synthetic and not found in foods. Meaty flavours can be made by reacting sugars and amino acids, a process which also occurs in meat when it is cooked.

Some additives do not themselves provide flavour but increase the effect of natural flavours present in the food. These **flavour enhancers** include monosodium glutamate and ribonucleotides, both of which are normal constituents of foods. Monosodium glutamate gained a reputation for causing dizziness and nausea. However, the evidence for this is flimsy, and in any case at the levels used it does not cause any adverse effects except on certain individuals who are exceptionally sensitive to it.

Dr May is a past Chairman of the Food Additives and Ingredients Association.

1. The main organic constituents of organisms are **carbohydrates**, **lipids**, **proteins**, **nucleic acids** and **vitamins**. Inorganic constituents include **minerals** and **water**.

2. The importance of water as a medium for life derives from its **solvent properties**, **heat capacity**, **surface tension**, **freezing properties** and **transparency**.

3. Minerals (**inorganic ions**) perform a wide range of functions in organisms. **Major mineral elements** (**macronutrients**) are needed in relatively large amounts; **trace elements** (**micronutrients**) in smaller.

4. **Carbohydrates** contain only carbon, hydrogen and oxygen, with a ratio of approximately two hydrogen atoms to one oxygen atom in each molecule. They provide easily accessible stores of energy, and in plants they also play an important structural role (cellulose). They are classified into **monosaccharides**, **disaccharides** and **polysaccharides**.

5. Monosaccharides such as glucose can be built up into disaccharides and polysaccharides such as starch or glycogen by **condensation**. Polysaccharides and disaccharides can be broken down into monosaccharides by **hydrolysis**.

6. Polysaccharides include starch, which is a polymer of α glucose, and cellulose, which is a polymer of β glucose. Cellulose may become impregnated with lignin to form the basis of wood.

7. **Lipids** include fats, oils and related substances. They contain little oxygen and do not dissolve in water. Fats and oils are compounds of **glycerol** and **fatty acids** which can be united by condensation and split by hydrolysis. They are important sources of energy.

8. Cell membranes contain **phospholipids**, which contain phosphoric acid in addition to glycerol and fatty acids. Animal cell membranes also contain cholesterol, a steroid. A number of hormones are also steroids.

9. Proteins are composed of numerous **amino acids** which join by a condensation reaction to form **polypeptide chains**. The order of amino acids constitutes the **primary structure** of the protein.

10. The chain of amino acids may be coiled into an **alpha-helix** or arranged into a **beta-pleated sheet** to give the protein its **secondary structure**. Further coiling or folding gives the protein its **tertiary structure**. Finally, several polypeptide chains may combine with one another to give the protein its **quaternary structure**.

11. Proteins may be **globular** or **fibrous**. The former are usually soluble and perform many regulatory functions (e.g. as enzymes), while the latter fulfil structural roles (e.g. collagen).

12. An important function of globular proteins is **buffering**. They owe this function to the presence of both positively and negatively charged groups in amino acids.

13. Humans can synthesise about half of the 20 naturally occurring amino acids involved in protein synthesis. The remainder, known as **essential amino acids**, are required in the diet. Most animal and some plant proteins contain a high proportion of the essential amino acids. Non-essential amino acids can be made from essential amino acids by **transamination**.

14. A mixture of proteins can be separated by **electrophoresis**. Progressive hydrolysis followed by **chromatography** enables the amino acid sequence of a protein to be established. **X-ray crystallography** can be used to work out the three-dimensional shape of the protein.

15. **Vitamins**, a mixed collection of organic compounds, are required by organisms in small amounts for various metabolic purposes. Some of them function as **coenzymes**.

For general advice on these questions and advice on answering essay-type questions, see pages vii and viii.

1. The diagram shows two of the glucose molecules which are joined together in a molecule of starch.

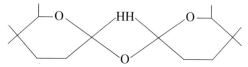

(a) Amylase digests starch by hydrolysing it.

   (i) Explain what is meant by hydrolysis. (1)

   (ii) By means of a similar diagram, show the products of hydrolysis of this molecule. (2)

(b) Much human food is cooked and eaten while it is hot. In an investigation it was found that the mean temperature of potato eaten during a meal was 68°C. Suggest where the starch in this potato is digested during its passage through the gut. Explain your answer. (4)

(Total 7 marks)

NEAB 1996

2. Write an essay on the structure and functions of lipids.

(Total 15 marks)

London 1998

3. (a) The diagram shows a molecule of glutamic acid. Glutamic acid is a non-essential amino acid.

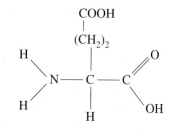

   (i) Copy the diagram and draw a ring round the part of the molecule which is found only in glutamic acid and not in other amino acids. (1)

   (ii) Briefly describe how a non-essential amino acid can be made in the body. (2)

(b) An 18 year-old girl requires a certain amount of protein. In a non-vegetarian, this requirement can be met by 37.1 g of protein in the diet. In a vegetarian whose diet contains a large proportion of unrefined cereal and vegetables, this requirement is met by 43.6 g of protein in the diet. Suggest an explanation for this difference. (2)

(Total 5 marks)

AEB 1998

4. It is thought that the amount of fat in the diet and the proportions of saturated and polyunsaturated fatty acids in the fat have an influence on the health of individuals.

The table below shows the composition of 100 g edible portions of meat and poultry.

Component	Beef Lean meat	Beef Fatty meat	Lamb Lean meat	Lamb Fatty meat	Pork Lean meat	Pork Fatty meat	Chicken
Energy/kJ	517	2625	679	2762	615	2757	508
Protein/g	20	9	21	6	21	7	21
Fat/g	5	67	9	72	7	71	4
Iron/mg	2	1	2	1	2	2	1

(a) Suggest why lean lamb and lean pork have a higher fat content than have lean beef or chicken. (2)

(b) Protein and fat form 25% by weight of lean beef but 76% of fat beef. Comment on this difference. (2)

(c) Lean meat contains very little Vitamin D. Suggest a reason for this. (1)

(d) Comment on the difference in energy content of 100 g of lean pork and 100 g of chicken. (2)

(e) Comment on the difference in the iron content of lean beef and lean pork. (2)

(f) Lamb fat contains 52% saturated fatty acid whereas chicken fat contains 35% saturated fatty acid. Explain why chicken is considered to be a more healthy food than lamb. (3)

(Total 12 marks)

London 1996

5. The diagram shows part of a protein molecule.

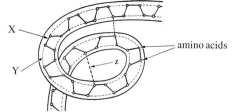

(a) Name the level of protein structure which is shown. (1)

(b) Suggest a function that such a structure might perform in the body. (1)

(c) Explain what structural feature allows the performance of this function. (2)

(d) Name the bonds labelled **X** and **Y**. (2)

(e) Name one other type of bond which might form the bond labelled as **Z**. (1)

(Total 7 marks)

WJEC 1997

Chapter 3

The cell as a basic unit

Cells carry out the essential processes that make the organism a living entity. There is really no such thing as a *typical* cell but, as we shall see, cells share certain features and they are of almost universal occurrence in living organisms.

The cell is the basic structural and functional unit of an organism, and so it is not surprising that biologists have devoted a great deal of attention to its structure and the processes which go on inside it. The study of cells continues to be an exciting area of research as more sophisticated techniques become available for studying them.

In this chapter we shall look mainly at the structure of cells and their component parts. We shall not say much about the functional aspects at this stage for they will be dealt with much more fully in later chapters.

3.1 Cells as revealed by the light microscope

You will probably examine your first cells with the light (or optical) microscope and it is therefore best to start by considering the structure of cells as seen with this instrument. It was with a simple light microscope that cells were first discovered (*extension box below*).

Extension

The cell theory

Cells were first described in 1665 by Robert Hooke, a scientist of great talent and versatility who was an accomplished technician as well as a biologist. He designed one of the earliest optical microscopes with which he examined, amongst other things, thin sections of cork. He discovered that cork is composed of numerous box-like structures which we now know to be dead cells. Though Hooke coined the word cell for these structures, he did not realise their significance.

As more and more material was examined under the microscope, it gradually became apparent that the great majority of organisms are composed of cells. This idea is embodied in the **cell theory**. First proposed by M.J. Schleiden and Theodore Schwann in 1839, the cell theory states that cells are of universal occurrence and are the basic units of an organism.

In 1849 cell division was described for the first time, and this led to a further facet being added to the cell theory. In 1859 Rudolf Virchow proposed that all cells come from pre-existing cells. This had not been appreciated before: Schwann thought that new cells arose from tiny particles in the fluid between cells.

During the 20th century, biologists have used increasingly powerful microscopes to study the structure of cells. At the same time various biochemical techniques have been used to unravel the chemical reactions and molecular structures that occur inside cells and are fundamental to the processes of life.

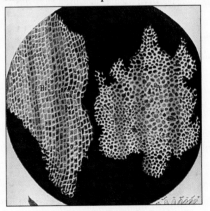

Robert Hooke's drawing of cork cells from his famous *Micrographia* published in 1665.

An animal cell as seen with a light microscope

The whole cell has a diameter of about one fiftieth of a millimetre (20 μm). It is bounded by a thin **plasma membrane** (also called the **cell surface membrane**). This encloses the **cytoplasm** which surrounds the **nucleus**.

On first examination the cytoplasm appears to be a homogeneous substance, but closer inspection of cells stained with special dyes shows it to contain numerous granules and inclusions. Food materials, for example **glycogen** (a polysaccharide), are stored in the cytoplasm and it is here that complex chemical reactions take place, building up materials and supplying energy for the cell's activities.

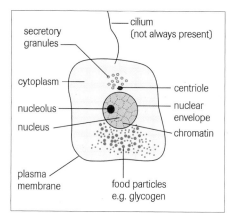

Figure 3.1 The structure of a generalised animal cell as seen under the light microscope. In suitable circumstances certain other structures can just be detected in the cytoplasm. These include mitochondria and the Golgi apparatus, both of which are described in detail later.

Figure 3.2 A typical plant cell with the nucleus near the side of the cell.

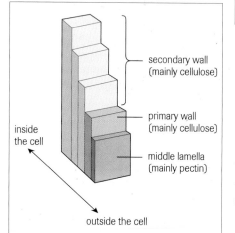

Figure 3.3 The various layers which make up the cell wall of a typical plant cell. Pectin is explained on page 22. The middle lamella and primary wall have considerable 'give' and are stretched as the cell grows and expands. The secondary wall consists of several layers of cellulose which are laid down in succession after growth has ceased. In some cells the secondary wall is hardened by impregnation with lignin to give wood, or with suberin to give cork.

The **centriole**, found just outside the nucleus, plays an important part in the formation of **cilia** and **flagella**, slender motile 'hairs' that project from the surface of certain cells. The behaviour of the centriole is also related to the way cells divide when they multiply.

The nucleus is bounded by a **nuclear envelope** and contains a dense body called the **nucleolus**, together with a material called **chromatin** which condenses into distinct bodies called **chromosomes** when the cell undergoes division. The chromosomes carry hereditary material in the form of **deoxyribonucleic acid** (**DNA**) which determines the organism's characteristics and transmits these to subsequent generations. The structure of a typical animal cell as seen with a light microscope is illustrated in figure 3.1.

Later we shall have much to say about the functions of the nucleus. For the moment you should appreciate that it is vital for the continued life of the cell (*page 620*). Although important chemical reactions take place in the cytoplasm, the nucleus is essential for directing these activities.

A plant cell as seen with a light microscope

As you can see in figure 3.2, most of the structures found in an animal cell also occur in plant cells. A typical plant cell, however, has certain additional features.

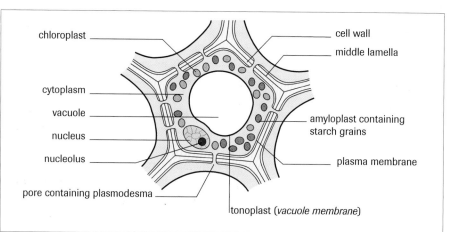

The centre of the cell is taken up by a large **vacuole** filled with a solution containing sugars and salts, the **cell sap**. The cell is bounded by a plasma membrane, beyond which is a comparatively thick **cell wall** made largely of the polysaccharide carbohydrate **cellulose**. This is tough but slightly elastic. The vacuole and cell wall play a major part in maintaining the shape and form of the cell, as we shall see in Chapter 7.

The central position of the vacuole means that the cytoplasm is confined to the sides of the cell. In most plant cells the nucleus is located somewhere in this peripheral cytoplasm, but not uncommonly it is suspended in the middle of the vacuole by slender strands of cytoplasm.

Another consequence of the vacuole is that the cell has two membranes bounding the cytoplasm. In addition to the plasma membrane lining the outer surface of the cytoplasm (in contact with the cellulose wall), there is a membrane lining the inner surface bordering the vacuole. This membrane is called the **vacuole membrane** or **tonoplast**.

The cell wall is laid down during the development of the cell, and starts as a thin layer of **pectin** on the inner side of which cellulose, secreted by the outer part of the cytoplasm, is laid down. This constitutes the **primary wall**. Further layers of cellulose make up the **secondary wall** (*figure 3.3*). The cellulose is strengthened by another polysaccharide called **hemicellulose** (*page 22*). The point of demarcation between one cell and the next, known as the **middle lamella**, represents the fused pectate walls of the two adjoining cells.

Two levels of cellular organisation

Biologists today recognise a major distinction between two types of cell. The type shown in figures 3.1 and 3.2 is called a **eukaryotic cell**. This means 'good or true nucleus' and reflects the fact that these cells have a clearly discernible nucleus. This is typical of the majority of organisms, including all animals and plants.

The other type of cell is called a **prokaryotic cell**, meaning 'before the nucleus'. Such cells do not have a nucleus, though they do have a long compacted strand of DNA in the middle of the cell. This type of cell is found in the Prokaryote kingdom which includes bacteria.

The distinction between eukaryotic and prokaryotic cells is one of the most fundamental dividing lines between living organisms. It is far more significant than the difference between animal and plant cells, both of which are eukaryotic.

The definitions above are based only on the presence or absence of a nucleus. However, there are many other differences between eukaryotic and prokaryotic cells. In particular, eukaryotic cells have a full complement of membrane-bound **organelles** in their cytoplasm, whereas prokaryotes lack such organelles.

Inside a prokaryotic cell

A bacterium can be taken to illustrate the main features of a prokaryotic cell (*illustration 1*). The cell is filled with **cytoplasm** but there is no membrane-bound nucleus. Instead there is a long strand of DNA with the ends joined to form a ring. This is sometimes referred to as the bacterial chromosome, though the term is misleading because it is much simpler than eukaryotic chromosomes. The ring of DNA is concentrated in certain areas of the cell and is called the **nucleoid**. In addition there may be smaller rings of DNA called **plasmids** which serve as additional chromosomes. In many disease-causing bacteria these

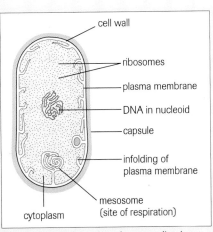

Illustration 1 Diagram of a generalised bacterium to illustrate the structure of a prokaryotic cell.

plasmids are associated with resistance to antibiotics.

The cytoplasm contains **food storage particles**, enzymes and tiny granules called **ribosomes** where proteins are synthesised. The **mesosome**, formed by an infolding of the plasma membrane, is the site of respiration. Other smaller infoldings of the plasma membrane perform a similar function and may also be involved in the formation of the cell wall.

Some bacteria are photosynthetic. They possess small membrane-lined **chromatophores** containing a pigment called **bacteriochlorophyll** which is similar to, but chemically simpler than, the chlorophyll of plants. The chromatophore is a simple spherical body and lacks the complex internal structure typical of plant chloroplasts.

Other bacteria feed on organic substances: they secrete digestive enzymes across the cell surface and absorb the soluble products of digestion back into the cell.

Bacterial cells are lined with a **plasma membrane** which is similar to that of eukaryotic cells except that there are fewer types of phospholipid present. Outside the plasma membrane is a **cell wall** of variable thickness which is made of a substance unique to bacteria, called

peptidoglycan. This consists of a mucopolysaccharide and a polypeptide combined together and is quite different from the cellulose cell wall of plants. The cell wall helps to support the cell and maintain its shape.

Some bacteria possess, in addition to the cell wall, a slimy **capsule** which gives them extra protection against ingestion by phagocytes and may prevent them from drying out.

Certain bacteria have **flagella** for movement. However, they lack the internal structure typical of the flagella of eukaryotes (*page 54*). The bacterial flagellum is a hollow cylindrical thread equivalent to one of the microtubules inside a eukaryotic flagellum. It is shaped like a corkscrew and propels the cell, not by waving as does a eukaryotic flagellum, but by rotating about its axis like a propeller. It is one of the few rotating devices found in living organisms.

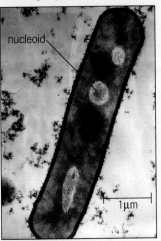

Illustration 2 Electron micrograph of the bacterium, *Bacillus subtilis*.

When a prokaryotic cell divides, the DNA replicates and the two strands move into the new cells without the aid of the elaborate spindle apparatus found in eukaryotes.

So, the prokaryotic cell is much simpler than the eukaryotic cell. However, both have DNA, ATP and much the same range of enzymes and coenzymes. At the chemical level they are fundamentally similar.

Although each cell appears to be enclosed in a box of cellulose it is by no means isolated from its neighbours. The cellulose cell wall is interrupted at intervals by narrow pores carrying fine strands of cytoplasm which join the living cells to one another. These are called **plasmodesmata** and they facilitate the movement of materials between cells. We shall return to them presently.

Granules and inclusions found in the cytoplasm include hollow ovoid or spherical bodies called **plastids**. There are two main kinds of plastids found widely in plant cells:

■ **Amyloplasts:** these contain the **starch grains** which represent the major form of storage carbohydrate, equivalent to glycogen in animal cells.

■ **Chloroplasts:** these contain the green pigment **chlorophyll** which plays a crucial role in photosynthesis, the process by which plants manufacture food materials.

3.2 Fine structure of eukaryotic cells

Eukaryotic cells are typical of most organisms including ourselves and are characterised by the possession of a nucleus and membrane-bound organelles (*support box on previous page*).

In a sense, organelles stand in relation to the cell as organs do to the whole organism. For example, some organelles have a digestive function, breaking down complex molecules inside the cell. They are analogous to the gut of an animal, although they have an entirely different structure.

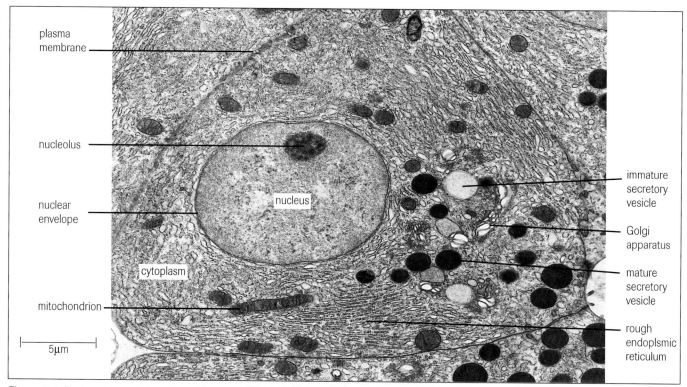

Figure 3.4 Electron micrograph of a very thin section of a pancreas cell.

Figure 3.4 is an electron micrograph of an animal cell and figure 3.5 is a diagram of an animal cell based on detailed examination of numerous electron micrographs. Figure 3.6 is a similar diagram of a plant cell.

Endoplasmic reticulum

You will see immediately that the cytoplasm, far from being a homogenous substance, is a highly organised material. It consists of a soluble ground substance or matrix called the **cytosol** containing a system of parallel flattened cavities lined with a thin membrane about 4 nm thick (nm is the symbol for nanometre, a thousandth of a micrometre).

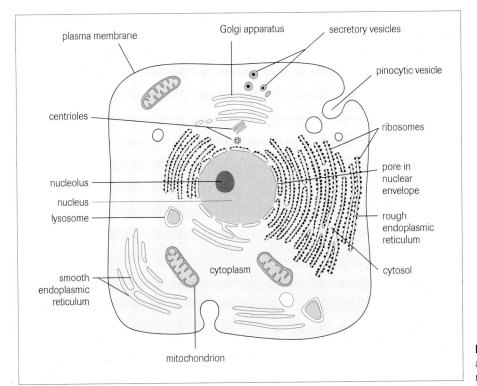

Figure 3.5 Fine structure of a generalised animal cell based on studies with the electron microscope.

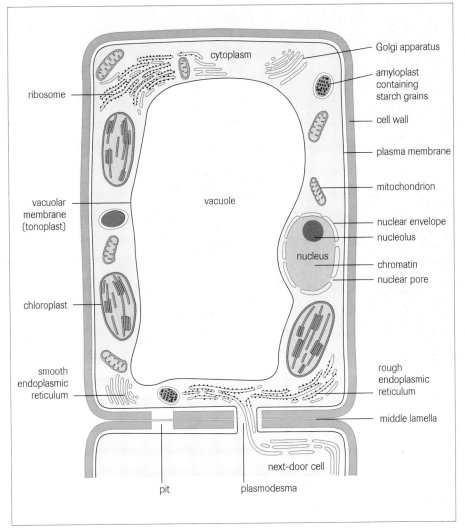

Figure 3.6 Fine structure of a generalised plant cell based on studies with the electron microscope.

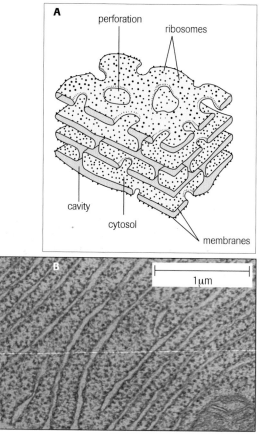

Figure 3.7 The endoplasmic reticulum consists of a series of parallel membranes, encrusted with ribosomes, enclosing a system of interconnected flattened cavities.
A Diagram of part of the endoplasmic reticulum.
B Electron micrograph of endoplasmic reticulum in a pancreas cell.

This membrane system is known as the **endoplasmic reticulum**, or **ER** for short. The cavities are interconnected as shown in figure 3.7 and the lining membranes are continuous with the nuclear envelope. Attached to the cytosol side of the membranes are numerous small bodies called **ribosomes**. Manufactured in the nucleolus, these are the sites where proteins are synthesised in the cell. In places the ribosomes are clustered together in small groups called **polyribosomes**.

The bulk of the endoplasmic reticulum in most cells is studded with ribosomes and is known as **rough endoplasmic reticulum**. Its general function is to isolate and transport the proteins which have been synthesised by the ribosomes. Many of these proteins are not required by the cell in which they are made but are for export, i.e. they are secreted by the cell. Such proteins include enzymes and hormones.

The endoplasmic reticulum is thus a kind of intracellular transport system helping to move materials from one part of the cell to another. The nuclear envelope is pierced by tiny **pores**, thus providing a route by which materials can move from the nucleus to the cytoplasm and vice versa (*figure 3.8*).

In certain parts of some cells the endoplasmic reticulum lacks ribosomes and is known as **smooth endoplasmic reticulum**. This is not continuous with the rough endoplasmic reticulum and its cavities are tubes rather than flattened sacs. It is seen particularly in cells of the liver, gut and certain glands, and is concerned with the synthesis and transport of lipids and steroids.

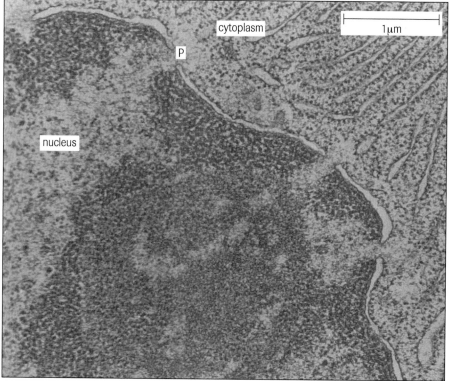

Figure 3.8 Pores (**P**) in the nuclear envelope as seen under the electron microscope in section.

Cytosol

At one time the cytosol was thought to be little more than a fluid. However, it has now been shown to contain a three-dimensional network of extremely fine protein filaments, a mere 5 or 6 nm wide, rather like a spider's web. These filaments connect the various organelles such as the mitochondria with the endoplasmic reticulum, holding them in place. They are part of the **cytoskeleton** to which we shall return shortly.

Golgi apparatus

With special staining techniques the **Golgi apparatus** can be detected under the optical microscope as a particularly dense part of the cytoplasm, and it has exercised the minds of biologists ever since it was discovered by the Italian physician Camillo Golgi at the end of the 19th century. **Secretory vesicles** are closely associated with the Golgi apparatus, suggesting that it may be concerned with the production of substances by the cell.

Figure 3.9 shows what the Golgi apparatus looks like in the electron microscope. It consists of a stack of flattened cavities lined with smooth ER, close to which are numerous secretory vesicles. Figure 3.10 summarises what is thought to happen. The Golgi cavities are formed by the fusion of vesicles which are pinched off the rough ER. Vesicles containing the secretory molecules then get pinched off the cavities of the Golgi apparatus. These vesicles move to the surface of the cell and discharge their contents to the exterior. So the Golgi apparatus is an assembly point through which raw materials for secretion are funnelled before being shed from the cell.

This hypothesis is supported by experiments in which the distribution of radioactively labelled substances taken up by the cell is followed by autoradiography (*page 120*). Nearly all cell secretions are **glycoproteins**, i.e. proteins conjugated with a carbohydrate (*page 58*). Newly synthesised proteins are found in the channels of the rough ER. From here they move to the Golgi apparatus where the carbohydrate is added to them. They then leave the cell. Thus, the function of the Golgi apparatus is to add the carbohydrate component to the protein and package the finished product before it leaves the cell.

An example of a glycoprotein produced by the Golgi apparatus is **mucus**, the slimy substance which serves as a lubricant in animals. The Golgi apparatus also produces materials for making plant cell walls and the cuticles of insects. It also performs the incidental function of replenishing the plasma membrane: when one of its vesicles empties its contents to the exterior, the membrane lining the vesicle fuses with, and thus becomes part of, the plasma membrane. In addition certain Golgi vesicles contain digestive enzymes and become lysosomes.

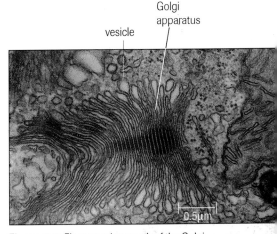

Figure 3.9 Electron micrograph of the Golgi apparatus. Notice the vesicles pinched off from the ends of the flattened cavities.

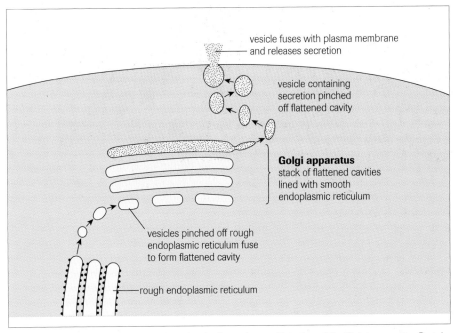

Figure 3.10 Schematic diagram illustrating the formation and function of the Golgi apparatus. Protein and carbohydrate derived from the channels of the rough endoplasmic reticulum are combined in the Golgi apparatus to form a glycoprotein secretion which is discharged from the cell as shown.

Microscopes and microscopy

To see cells you need to use a **microscope** which magnifies them. The main types of microscope which you need to know about are described here.

Light (optical) microscope

This was invented in the 17th century, and although it has been refined in many ways it is essentially the same now as it was then.

A modern light microscope is shown in illustration 1. Light rays from a light source beneath the stage are transmitted through two glass lenses in series, the objective and ocular (eyepiece) lenses. Depending on their strength, these two lenses together routinely provide magnifications of up to 400 times.

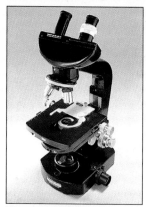

Illustration 1 A modern light microscope. Light rays from a source beneath the stage are transmitted through a glass condenser lens, through the specimen and then through two glass lenses; the objective and eyepiece lenses.

The light microscope has had a profound influence on biology, but there is a limit to the amount of detail which it can show. This limit is set by its **resolving power**.

The resolving power is the minimum distance by which two points must be separated in order for them to be perceived as two separate points rather than as a single fused image. For the light microscope this distance is approximately 0.2 μm. In theory it might seem possible to magnify an object indefinitely by means of glass lenses in series, but in practice this only produces a larger, fuzzier picture; the resolution is not improved and no more detail is visible.

The limited resolution of the light microscope is imposed by the wavelength of visible light, and it means that little can be gained by magnifying an object more than 1500 times. This puts a limit on the amount of structural detail that can be detected within a cell. Higher magnifications with good resolution can be achieved by using a special objective lens with a fluid situated between the lens and the objective (**oil immersion**). But even then it is not possible to achieve effective magnifications of more than 2000 times.

Electron microscope

Since the 1950s, microscopic studies have been revolutionised by the development of the **electron microscope**. This instrument uses an electron beam instead of light, and electromagnets instead of glass lenses. The electrons are recorded on a photographic plate, which then forms a viewable image on a fluorescent screen.

The electron beam has a much shorter wavelength than light, with the result that a modern electron microscope has a resolving power of 1nm or even less. This means that objects can be magnified greatly without loss of clarity.

As we have seen, a good light microscope can only magnify an object effectively about 1500 times. The electron microscope can give clear pictures of objects that are magnified 500 000 times. It is important to appreciate what this means in practice: with the electron microscope an object the size of a pinhead can be enlarged to the point at which it has a diameter of well over a kilometre; a cell with a diameter of 10 micrometres finishes up with a diameter of five metres.

It is difficult to exaggerate the impact that this instrument has had on biology.

Materials which were formerly described as structureless have been shown to have an elaborate internal organisation, and so-called homogeneous fluids are now known to contain a variety of complex structures. The electron microscope has opened up a new world whose existence was barely realised 60 years ago.

But there are problems. One snag is that the material for examination has to be mounted in a vacuum, and is therefore dead, before it can be viewed. This, coupled with the preliminary treatment to which the material has to be subjected, may distort the delicate structures inside cells and create images that are not 'real'. These are called **artefacts** (literally 'of artificial making'). The electron microscopist is always on the look-out for such artefacts and uses every means to prevent them occurring.

Illustration 2 A high resolution electron microscope currently used in biological research. Such an instrument has a resolving power of as little as 0.2 nm and achieves magnifications of about 240 000 times. The operator inserts into the microscope a tiny copper grid on which an ultra-thin section of the specimen has been placed. The section is made by embedding the tissue, suitably fixed and dehydrated, in plastic, then slicing it with an ultramicrotome which cuts very thin sections less than 100 nm thick. After mounting the section on the grid it is treated with heavy metal stains which scatter the electrons in such a way that individual structures can be distinguished.

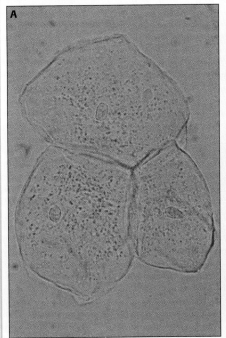

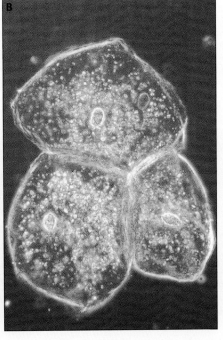

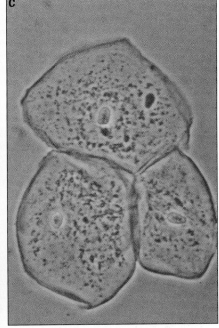

Illustration 3 Three kinds of light microscopy were used to photograph the same cheek cells:
A conventional light microscope with bright ground illumination.
B dark ground illumination.
C phase-contrast. Magnifications ×1500.

Other kinds of microscope

To some extent these problems can be overcome by using other types of microscopy in addition to the electron microscope. The **phase-contrast microscope**, for example, enables transparent objects to be seen, and is ideal for studying unstained living cells. Special illumination techniques can also be employed for increasing the contrast between the object and its background; for example, **dark-ground illumination**, in which the object is illuminated from above against a dark background, enables tiny structures inside cells to be seen clearly. Another technique is to examine the object in polarised light: the **polarising microscope** is useful for differentiating between different types of material embedded in another substance.

The kind of electron microscope shown in illustration 2 is called a **transmission electron microscope** because the electrons pass through the specimen. In the **scanning electron microscope**, solid specimens are bombarded with a beam of electrons which causes secondary electrons to be emitted from the surface layers of the specimen. These electrons are recorded on a photographic plate and the image is viewed on a screen, as with the transmission electron microscope. The scanning electron microscope enables details of the surface to be seen very clearly as, for example, in illustration 4. However, it can only magnify up to about 80 000 times.

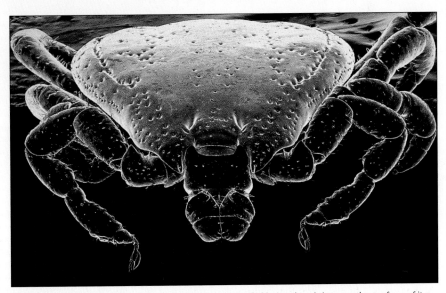

Illustration 4 A scanning electronmicrograph of a tick. Notice the pittings on the surface of its cuticle. Magnification ×80.

▶ Micrometre (μm) and nanometer (nm), page 8

Mitochondria

Embedded in the cytosol are variable numbers of **mitochondria**. Under the phase-contrast microscope, or light microscope with dark-ground illumination, they appear as minute rods, but under the electron microscope their internal structure becomes apparent. A typical cell contains about 1000 mitochondria, though some cells have more than this. Their shape and size vary, but generally they are sausage-shaped with a diameter of approximately 1.0 μm and a length of about 2.5 μm.

The wall of the mitochondrion consists of two thin membranes separated by a narrow fluid-filled space. The inner membrane is folded, giving rise to an irregular series of partitions, or **cristae**, which project into the interior (*figure 3.11*). The interior contains an organic **matrix** containing numerous chemical compounds.

The mitochondrion is one of the cell's most important organelles: it is here that most of the chemical reactions of aerobic respiration take place with the synthesis of **adenosine triphosphate** (**ATP**) (*Chapter 9*). Some of these reactions take place in the matrix of the mitochondrion, while others occur on the inner membrane and in the cytosol. The cristae have the effect of increasing the surface area so that more ATP can be produced.

Cells whose function requires them to expend particularly large amounts of energy contain unusually large numbers of mitochondria. These are often packed close together in the part of the cell where the energy is required. This is seen dramatically in

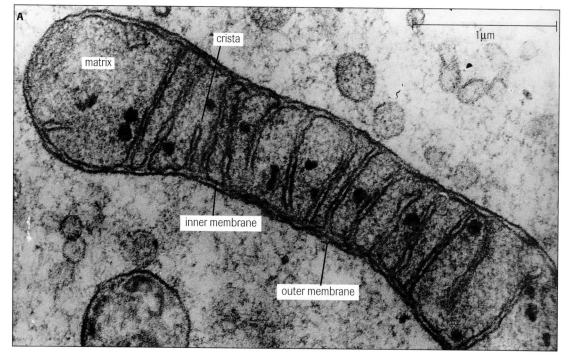

Figure 3.11 Structure of a mitochondrion.
A Electron micrograph of a large mitochondrion in longitudinal section from the oocyte of a bird. Notice the cristae projecting into the hollow interior.
B Cutaway view showing the inside of a mitochondrion. Many of the chemical reactions involved in the transfer of energy (respiration) take place in the matrix and on the cristae. Tiny stalked particles attached to the surface of the cristae, of diameter approximately 8 nm, are the site of ATP synthesis. They are shown in **C**.

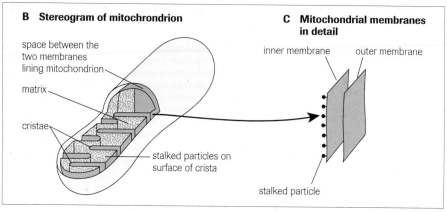

spermatozoa, where the mitochondria are tightly packed at the base of the motile tail (*page 502*). Mitochondria are also found alongside the contractile fibrils in muscle, and at the surface of cells where active transport occurs. In some cases the cristae may be very close together, thus further increasing the surface area within each mitochondrion (*figure 3.12*).

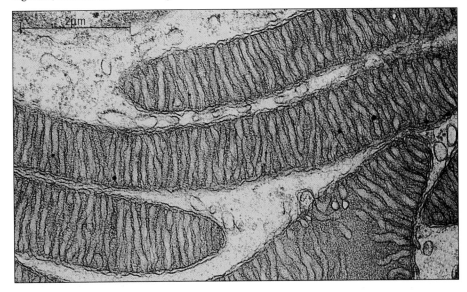

Figure 3.12 Electron micrograph of mitochondria in the heart muscle of a bird. Notice the numerous cristae packed close together inside the mitochondria, reflecting the high energy requirement of the muscle tissue.

Extension

Investigating the functions of cell organelles

To some extent the functions of organelles such as mitochondria may be tentatively surmised from their appearance in the electron microscope and from their reactions to various stains and so on. But to obtain reliable information it is necessary to isolate the individual organelles and test their properties separately.

The organelles can be isolated by **differential centrifugation**. First the cells are broken open, and their contents released. This is done by homogenising a tissue such as liver in a suitable isotonic solution that does not adversely affect the cells' contents. The solution is ice-cold so as to prevent the action of enzymes which might damage the organelles.

The homogenisation may be carried out in a blender of the type commonly used in the kitchen. The resulting suspension is then poured into a tube which is spun in a centrifuge at a speed of rotation that causes the heaviest organelles to be thrown to the bottom, forming a **sediment**. The other lighter organelles remain floating in the clear **supernatant fluid** above the sediment.

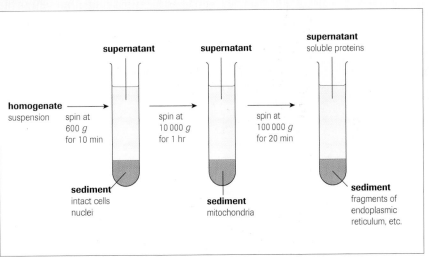

Differential centrifugation, the technique by which the organelles inside cells can be isolated. *g* is the unit of gravitational force: spinning at 600*g* means that the homogenate is subjected to a centrifugal force 600 times the force of gravity.

The supernatant fluid is then removed from the tube, leaving the sediment behind. The particular organelles in the sediment can then be investigated. Meanwhile the supernatant fluid is spun again at a higher speed so that another organelle is thrown down to form a new sediment. The supernatant fluid can then be re-spun at an even higher speed. In this way the different organelles can be collected and investigated separately.

The supernatant fluid finally contains only soluble proteins which may be analysed by techniques of the kind described on page 32. The whole procedure is summarised in the illustration.

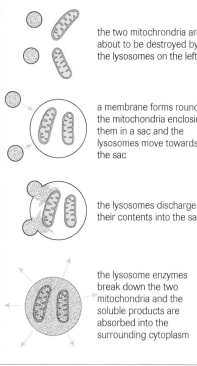

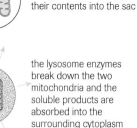

the two mitochrondria are about to be destroyed by the lysosomes on the left

a membrane forms round the mitochondria enclosing them in a sac and the lysosomes move towards the sac

the lysosomes discharge their contents into the sac

the lysosome enzymes break down the two mitochondria and the soluble products are absorbed into the surrounding cytoplasm

Figure 3.13 Diagrams to show how lysosomes destroy unwanted organelles in a cell. In this case two mitochondria are being broken down.

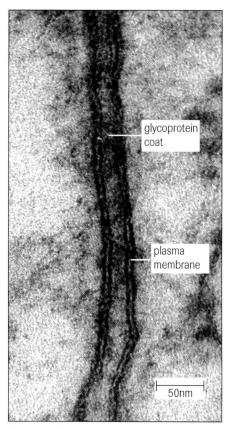

glycoprotein coat

plasma membrane

50nm

Figure 3.14 Electron micrograph of the plasma membranes of two adjacent epithelial cells.

Lysosomes

Also prominent in the cytoplasm of most cells are dark-staining spherical bodies called **lysosomes**. The word 'lysis' means to break apart, and lysosomes contain digestive enzymes responsible for splitting complex chemical compounds into simpler ones. Digestion is carried out in a membrane-bound vacuole with which the lysosomes fuse. This is discussed in more detail on page 115.

Another important function of lysosomes is to destroy worn-out organelles within the cell (*figure 3.13*). The unwanted structures, whether mitochondria, part of the endoplasmic reticulum or some other organelle, become enclosed in a membrane which forms a bag around them. This bag then fuses with one or more lysosomes. The organelles are broken down by the lysosome enzymes, and the soluble products are absorbed into the surrounding cytoplasm where they may be used in the construction of new organelles.

Sometimes lysosomes destroy the entire cell. In this case the lysosome membrane ruptures, liberating the enzymes which digest the contents of the cell, killing it in the process. This may seem rather disastrous but in certain instances it may be advantageous, as for example when old, damaged cells have to be replaced by new ones, or when certain embryonic tissues are discarded during development. Tadpole tails are destroyed this way during metamorphosis.

Microtubules and microfilaments

Tube-like structures with a diameter of about 20 nm are found in many cells. These are called **microtubules** and they are made of the protein **tubulin**. Microtubules are widely distributed in the cytoplasm where they may occur singly or in bundles. They are associated with cellular movements and transport inside cells.

Microtubules can be assembled in one part of the cell where they are needed, then taken apart and reassembled later in another part of the cell. In dividing root tip cells, for example, microtubules assemble to form the spindle. They then disintegrate and reassemble in the vicinity of the developing cell plate, and later still they are seen immediately beneath the cell wall, where they are involved in the deposition of cellulose (*page 42*).

Another place where we find microtubules is in cilia and flagella which will be described shortly.

Microfilaments are about a quarter of the diameter of microtubules (5 nm) and are solid, not tubular. Like microtubules, they are made of protein, in this case **actin**, and can be readily assembled and disassembled. They occur in bundles in the cytoplasm where they are associated with cell motility such as cytoplasmic streaming and muscle contraction (*page 407*).

Microfilaments and microtubules together make up the **cytoskeleton** referred to on page 46. However, because of their ability to disassemble and reassemble so rapidly, they form a dynamic system of moving parts which is much more than just a skeleton. The chemistry of microtubules and microfilaments is explained on page 30.

The cell surface

The thin plasma membrane as seen under the light microscope turns out to be rather more complex when viewed in the electron microscope. When viewed in section, as in figure 3.14, it appears to be made up of three layers: two dark layers, separated by a lighter region. The total thickness of the membrane is approximately 7.0 nm (*see page 56 for a detailed description of the plasma membrane*).

It used to be thought that the two dark layers were protein and the light region in between was lipid. The plasma membrane was therefore seen as a thin sandwich of lipid contained between two layers of protein. However, we now know that the two dark lines are caused by the deposition of heavy metal on both sides of the membrane during the staining of the sections. This is a good example of an artefact (*page 48*).

Beyond the plasma membrane of animal cells there is a **glycoprotein coat** of variable thickness. Cells touching each other are separated by this intercellular material. Materials pass through the glycoprotein coat as they flow in and out of cells.

Pinocytic and phagocytic vesicles

Various structures are associated with the surface of the cell. Of these, the most widespread are **pinocytic vesicles**, tiny flask-like invaginations of the plasma membrane. The neck of the flask eventually closes up so that the vesicle becomes sealed off from the outside and becomes entirely enclosed within the cell. They provide a means by which water and large molecules may be taken into the cell (*page 116*). It is thought that the large sap-filled **vacuole** characteristic of mature plant cells is formed by the fusion of numerous small vesicles derived from pinocytosis.

In some cells, larger flask-like invaginations are formed. These are called **phagocytic vesicles** and they provide a way of drawing food particles into the cell. The cells of certain animals and protoctists contain **food vacuoles** which are derived from the plasma membrane by phagocytosis. This is how, for example, *Amoeba* feeds (*page 115*).

Microvilli

It has already been mentioned that one function of the plasma membrane is to permit materials to enter the cell. Plainly, the larger the surface area of the plasma membrane the greater will be the exchange of materials across it. To this end, part of the plasma membrane of many cells bears numerous minute projections called **microvilli**.

Each microvillus is a very thin, finger-like process about 1.0 μm long and 0.08 μm wide. It is lined with plasma membrane and filled with cytoplasm which is continuous with that in the main body of the cell. Microvilli are only visible in the electron microscope though larger ones, if densely packed, may show up under the light microscope as a fuzzy line at the cell surface, the so-called **brush border** (*figure 3.15*).

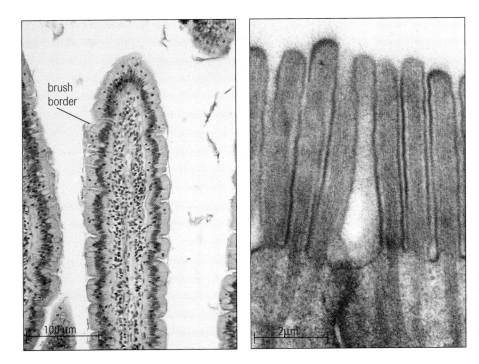

Figure 3.15 *Left* The brush border on the epithelial cells of the small intestine seen with a light microscope.
Right Electron micrograph of a small part of the brush border showing it to consist of microvilli. Notice the microfilaments inside each microvillus.

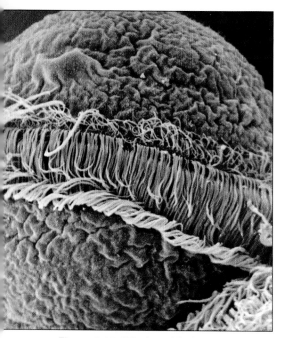

Figure 3.16 Side view of the larva of a mollusc showing the girdle of cilia by which it moves through the water. This is a scanning electron micrograph. Magnification ×1000.

Two places where microvilli abound are the epithelial lining of the convoluted tubules in the kidney and the lining of the small intestine. In both cases they increase the surface area of the epithelium, thereby aiding absorption of materials from the enclosed cavity. It has been estimated that a single epithelial cell may have 3000 microvilli and that in one square millimetre of intestinal lining there may be as many as 200 000 000, giving a 20-fold increase to the surface area. Some of these microvilli contain microfilaments and undergo squeezing, worm-like movements, thereby creating a pumping effect which may aid absorption. You can see microfilaments in the microvilli in figure 3.15 on the previous page.

Cilia and flagella

The surface of certain cells is drawn out to form elongated **cilia** or **flagella**. These organelles are fundamentally similar but cilia are usually shorter and more numerous than flagella (an average flagellum has a length of about 100 μm, a cilium 5 to 10 μm). Both are less than 0.3 μm in diameter. They have the ability to undulate or lash back and forth, and their functions depend on this.

Many unicellular organisms move by means of cilia or flagella. The surface of the freshwater protoctist *Paramecium*, for example, is covered with cilia which beat in a coordinated fashion, driving the organism through the water (*page 433*). Another freshwater protoctist *Euglena* has a single flagellum, which propels the organism by means of rapid undulations passing from the base to the tip. Many aquatic larvae have cilia for movement (*figure 3.16*).

Sometimes cilia occur on the surface of quite large animals such as flatworms and marine snails. Here their rapid beating, aided by muscular contractions of the body wall, enables the animal to glide on smooth surfaces.

Flagella are nearly always associated with locomotion, but cilia, which are found more widely, perform other functions as well. For example, they are often found lining ducts and tubules and other specialised surfaces, along which materials are wafted by means of their rapid and rhythmical beatings (*pages 319 and 507*).

Internal structure of cilia and flagella

The electron microscope has shown that cilia and flagella contain a bundle of microtubules which run longitudinally. These are arranged in a precise way: there are two in the centre surrounded by a ring of nine paired ones, called **doublets**. This arrangement is described as the **9+2 pattern**. The whole assemblage of microtubules is enclosed within a membrane which is continuous with the plasma membrane (*figures 3.17 and 3.18*).

At the base of the cilium or flagellum is an elaborate attachment apparatus consisting of a **basal body** from which **rootlet fibres** penetrate into the deeper layers of the cytoplasm. The basal body is composed of a ring of microtubules continuous with those in the cilium itself. However, the two central microtubules are absent, and the peripheral ones are in threes (**triplets**).

How do cilia and flagella move? Little arm-like processes project from the peripheral doublets. These are thought to be the site of ATP hydrolysis where energy is transferred for bending the flagellum or cilium. Bending is thought to be brought about by the peripheral microtubules sliding relative to one another, each doublet sliding past its next-door neighbour.

Other structures with the same organisation as cilia

As you can see in figure 3.5 on page 44, an animal cell has two rod-like **centrioles** situated at right angles to each other. Under the light microscope these appear as a single unit. Their behaviour in cell division is explained in Chapter 26 and for the moment we will concern ourselves only with their structure.

A discovery of great interest was that the centrioles have an internal structure similar to that of the basal body of cilia and flagella, each rod containing a ring of nine triplets, but no central microtubules. This is no coincidence, for centrioles are responsible for the formation of cilia and flagella. It is possible that the basal body is derived in evolution from a centriole which migrated towards the edge of the cell and became associated with the plasma membrane. It is now known that the centriole is the organising centre for all the microtubules in animal cells, including those inside the cilia and flagella.

Another surprising place where the ciliary structure appears is in the eyes of vertebrates. The light-sensitive cells in the retina have been shown to contain nine peripheral microtubules together with basal bodies and rootlet fibres just like ordinary cilia. These cells are certainly not concerned with movement, but their tell-tale internal structure suggests that they may have evolved from ciliated cells which lost their motility and became adapted for the reception of light stimuli.

It seems that the 9+2 pattern of microtubules arose at an early stage in evolution and, despite much modification, is now a basic feature of many eukaryotic cells.

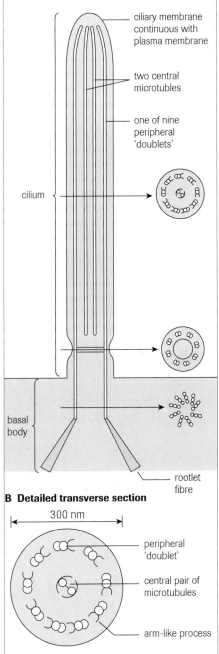

A Internal structure of cilium and basal body

ciliary membrane continuous with plasma membrane

two central microtubles

one of nine peripheral 'doublets'

cilium

basal body

rootlet fibre

B Detailed transverse section

300 nm

peripheral 'doublet'

central pair of microtubules

arm-like process

Figure 3.18 The detailed structure of cilia and flagella based on electron micrographs.
A Internal structure of cilium and basal body.
B Detailed transverse section. Note that the peripheral microtubules penetrate into the basal body where they may be attached to collagen rootlet fibres (not always present).

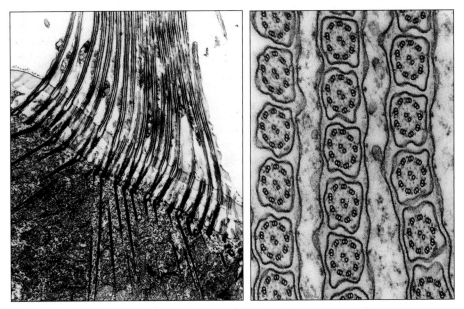

Figure 3.17 Fine structure of cilia and flagella as seen in the electron microscope.
Left Longitudinal section of a tuft of cilia from the larva of the marine annelid *Harmothoe*.
Right Transverse section through the flagella of the protoctist *Trichonympha*. Notice the 9+2 arrangement of microtubules within each flagellum.

Cell wall

The **cell wall** is unique to plants and certain other autotrophs. The electron microscope has confirmed earlier light microscope studies that it is not a uniform structure but is composed of **primary** and **secondary walls** as described on page 42. The cellulose itself is composed of ribbon-like **microfibrils** (*page 22*).

In places, the cell wall is absent altogether, giving rise to a **pit**. Where pits occur, two adjacent cells may be separated only by the primary wall (*figure 3.19*). The thinness of the wall in these regions facilitates movement of materials between adjoining cells. This function also applies to the **plasmodesmata**. The electron microscope has shown that the plasmodesmata contain endoplasmic reticulum which is therefore continuous from cell to cell (*figure 3.20*).

The fine structure of chloroplasts, page 203

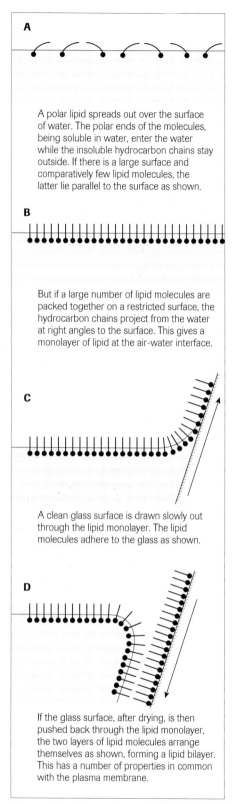

A

A polar lipid spreads out over the surface of water. The polar ends of the molecules, being soluble in water, enter the water while the insoluble hydrocarbon chains stay outside. If there is a large surface and comparatively few lipid molecules, the latter lie parallel to the surface as shown.

B

But if a large number of lipid molecules are packed together on a restricted surface, the hydrocarbon chains project from the water at right angles to the surface. This gives a monolayer of lipid at the air-water interface.

C

A clean glass surface is drawn slowly out through the lipid monolayer. The lipid molecules adhere to the glass as shown.

D

If the glass surface, after drying, is then pushed back through the lipid monolayer, the two layers of lipid molecules arrange themselves as shown, forming a lipid bilayer. This has a number of properties in common with the plasma membrane.

Figure 3.21 Diagrams illustrating the formation of a lipid bilayer. The polar ends of the lipid molecules are shown as solid dots, the hydrocarbon chains as bold lines.

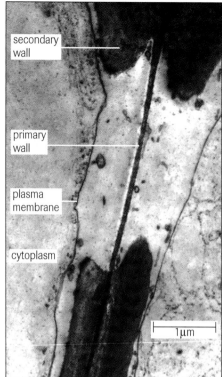

Figure 3.19 Electron micrograph of a pit between two cortical cells in the root of the pea plant *Pisum*. Notice the complete absence of the secondary cell wall, only the primary wall being present.

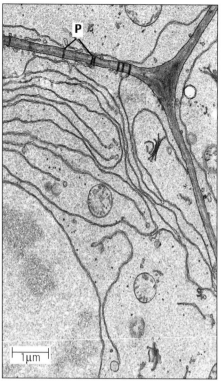

Figure 3.20 Plasmodesmata (**P**) linking adjacent cells in a root cap cell of maize. Notice that the plasmodesmata are connected to the endoplasmic reticulum and pass through the wall of the cell.

3.3 **Molecular structure of the plasma membrane**

We can make certain predictions about the structure of the plasma membrane from its physico-chemical properties. For example, substances that dissolve in oil penetrate it particularly rapidly, suggesting that it contains lipid. This is supported by the observation that its permeability properties are greatly influenced by treatment with lipid solvents.

How, then, are the lipid molecules arranged in the plasma membrane? A clue is provided by the properties of lipids. In certain lipids (**phospholipids**, for example) the long hydrocarbon chains which project from the glycerol part of the molecule are insoluble in water, whereas the glycerol end of the molecule is water soluble, because it contains polar groups (*page 11*).

When such a lipid is allowed to spread over the surface of pure water, the water-soluble ends of the lipid molecules are drawn into the water and the insoluble hydrocarbon chains, if the molecules are sufficiently tightly packed, point directly away from the surface of the water. Thus we get a single layer of lipid molecules with their hydrocarbon chains orientated at right angles to the surface, a so-called **monolayer**.

The lipid component of the plasma membrane cannot in fact be a monolayer for this is only formed where there is a water surface in contact with air, and the plasma membrane generally has water in contact with both sides. However, when the non-polar sides of two monolayers are brought into contact, the non-polar ends of the lipid molecules are attracted to each other to form a **lipid bilayer** (*figure 3.21*). Might the plasma membrane be similarly constructed?

Research has shown that the plasma membrane is indeed a lipid bilayer, but it is more than that for it also contains protein.

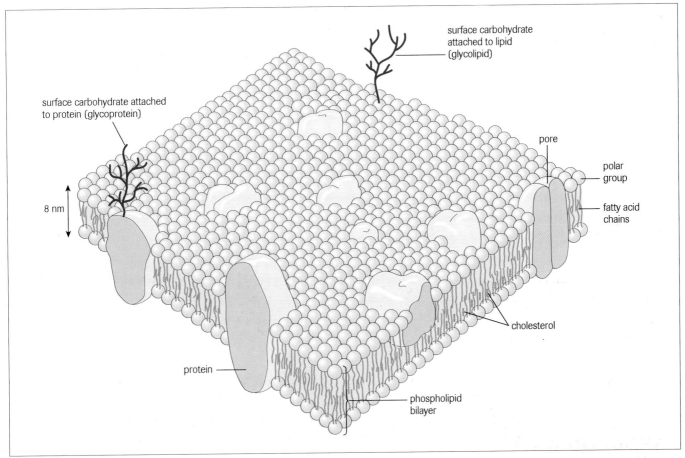

Figure 3.22 The fluid mosaic model of the plasma membrane proposed by Singer and Nicholson. The proteins exist in globular form and are either embedded in the lipid layer or extend right across it creating a mosaic pattern. Surface carbohydrates are shown attached to just one protein molecule and one lipid molecule whereas in reality they are attached to many more, and cholesterol is shown in just one small part of the membrane.

The fluid mosaic model

At one time it was thought that protein formed a continuous layer covering both sides of the membrane. However, it is now known that it takes the form of globules dotted about here and there in a mosaic pattern (*figure 3.22*). Some of the globules are attached to the surface of the membrane, while others penetrate into it to varying extents – indeed, some of them extend right through it and stick out on the other side.

The membrane is thought to be far less rigid than was originally supposed. Experiments on its viscosity suggest that it is of a fluid consistency rather like oil, and that there is considerable sideways movement of the lipid and protein molecules within it. On account of its fluidity and the mosaic arrangement of the protein molecules, this is known as the **fluid mosaic model**. The fluid mosaic model was put forward in the early 1970s by S.J. Singer of the University of California and G.L. Nicholson of the Salk Institute. There is now sufficient evidence for us to feel confident that it is correct. For example, pieces of plasma membrane have been treated on one side with chemicals which react with the proteins but cannot pass through the membrane. In some cases the reactions are confined to the side of the membrane to which the chemicals are applied, whereas in other cases they occur on both sides, suggesting that these particular proteins span the entire membrane.

Another piece of evidence comes from the technique of **freeze fracture**. In this process a piece of plasma membrane is frozen, then split down the middle longitudinally. If the inner surface is then viewed in the electron microscope, globular structures the same size as the membrane proteins can be seen scattered about as shown in figure 3.23.

The fluid mosaic model is thought to apply not just to the plasma membrane but to all biological membranes, and it is seen as a dynamic, ever-changing structure. The proteins serve as enzymes catalysing chemical reactions within the membrane, and as pumps moving ions and molecules across it. We shall return to this in Chapter 7.

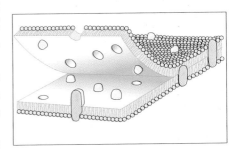

Figure 3.23 The three-dimensional structure of the membrane as deduced from the freeze-fracture technique. The membrane is split down the middle, exposing the globular proteins.

Cholesterol and the plasma membrane

Cholesterol has had a bad press: it is claimed to be a major cause of heart disease (*page 24*). But in relatively small quantities it is essential because it helps to maintain the fluidity of the plasma membrane. It interacts with the hydrocarbon chains of the phospholipid molecules just behind the polar heads. This enhances the mechanical stability and flexibility of the membrane.

Evidence that cholesterol strengthens the plasma membrane comes from studying cultured mutant cells that cannot synthesise cholesterol. Such cells readily break open and release their contents. However, if cholesterol is added to the culture medium, the cells remain intact.

Pores in the plasma membrane

That the plasma membrane is perforated by pores was predicted many years ago on the grounds that certain molecules, insoluble in lipid and therefore unable to get in between the lipid molecules, are still capable of penetrating the membrane. The pores are surrounded by protein and lined with hydrophilic groups (the polar groups of the protein molecules); this would make them readily penetrated by water-soluble substances.

By measuring the resistance of the membrane to the passage of such molecules, together with other methods of determining the diameter of small pores, it has been established that the pores must be less than 1.0 nm wide. As such they are too small to be seen even with the electron microscope. In Chapter 7 we shall see how they control the passage of molecules and ions in and out of cells.

Surface carbohydrates

An interesting discovery is that the plasma membrane contains not only lipid and protein but also carbohydrate. The carbohydrate component takes the form of short polysaccharide chains which project from the outer side of the membrane. Two such chains are shown in figure 3.22.

Some of the polysaccharides are attached to the lipids to form **glycolipids**. The function of glycolipids is not well understood, although it is known that in the plasma membrane of red blood cells they determine which blood group a person will have. They are also involved in certain diseases. For instance, in cholera and viral influenza the pathogens enter the target cell by first binding to surface glycolipids. This suggests that they act as some kind of receptor.

The vast majority of the polysaccharides are attached to the proteins to form **glycoproteins**. They make up, what has been graphically called, a 'forest' of glycoproteins at the cell surface (the **glycoprotein coat** referred to on page 53). The composition and branching pattern of these surface polysaccharides vary from one type of cell to another. This gives us a clue as to their function. When an organism is developing or a wound is healing, it is necessary that a given cell should 'know' whether it is in contact with another cell of the same type or with a cell of a different type. The surface carbohydrates enable cells to recognise each other in this way. They may also play a part in the way cells adhere together and interact, and in the mechanism by which specific hormones and foreign substances recognise, and in consequence associate with, particular types of cell. In short they are the key to cell signalling and recognition (*extension box on the next page*).

The diversity of cells

In this chapter we consider the basic features of cells in general. But this should not be taken simply to imply that all cells are identical.

Structures like chromosomes, mitochondria, endoplasmic reticulum and ribosomes are common to virtually all cells, but the shape, form and contents of individual cells show much variation. The structural characteristics of a particular cell are closely related to its functions.

The reason for this diversity is that in the course of evolution cells have become structurally specialised to perform particular tasks. In extreme cases specialisation may entail loss of the nucleus or cytoplasm, but in the majority of cases it involves modification of the shape and form of the cell, its basic features remaining unchanged.

An epithelial cell and a nerve cell may look very different, and perform different functions, but in their fundamental structure and chemistry they are remarkably alike. This is not surprising when we bear in mind that both are living entities and, whatever else they do, they must perform those functions which are necessary for the maintenance of life.

▶ Examples of different types of cells: epithelial, page 62; *Paramecium*, page 91; bone, page 67; stomatal guard cells, page 157; leaf cells, page 205, red blood cells, page 228; root hair cells, page 248; liver cells, page 276; white blood cells, page 321; nerve cells, page 348, sensory cells, page 380; muscle cells, page 69; eggs and sperm, page 502

Cell signalling

Biological phenomena involve transitions from one state to another. At the cellular level such transitions are initiated and controlled by various types of signal. Guest author Professor Anthony Campbell explains.

There are many types of cell and each has evolved to do certain things. Thus muscle cells contract, nerve cells transmit impulses, pancreatic beta cells secrete insulin, liver cells make glucose and lymphocytes make antibodies which kill invading bacteria. Cells also divide and differentiate, and defend themselves against stress and attack. Finally they die.

All these events, even death, have to be signalled by internal programming or various external agents. These **primary signals** are rather like traffic lights, telling the cell what to do. They include physical stimuli such as touch or light; chemical agents such as neurotransmitters, hormones, growth regulators and pheromones; and the biological agents such as bacteria and viruses. These all act on **receptors** on the cell surface, or within the cell, and trigger a sequence of chemical events which ends with a cell response. In addition, certain signals switch genes on or off. The receptors on the cell surface are plasma membrane proteins.

In most cases the external signal is linked to the response by a **second messenger**. Second messengers include **calcium** and a compound called **cyclic AMP** (*page 377*). They serve as internal (i.e. *intracellular*) signals and trigger a 'cascade' of chemical events in which a series of proteins are converted from an inactive to an active state, one after the other. The transformation between the two states often involves a change in covalent bonding, achieved by adding phosphate to certain amino acids in the protein. (Covalent bonding is explained on page 16.)

Calcium is one of the most widespread intracellular signals. An increase in cytosolic calcium triggers muscle contraction and secretion of hormones such as insulin, switches genes on or off, provokes key events in the cell cycle and induces changes in eggs after fertilisation. It also helps cells to defend themselves by removing damaged molecules from the cell surface, and can make unwanted cells 'commit suicide' (**apoptosis**).

Cell suicide is important in embryonic development. It enables organs such as our fingers to form properly, tadpole tails to disintegrate at metamorphosis and leaves to fall in autumn. It also helps our bodies to recover from infection by killing unwanted antibody-producing cells after they have done their job. Intracellular calcium is also involved in many bacterial events such as growth, chemotaxis, spore-formation and infectivity.

Why calcium? Outside our cells the concentration of calcium ions (Ca^{2+}) is about 1.3 millimoles per litre, but inside the cells it is a mere 0.1 *micro*moles per litre, lower than in fresh water. This huge (10 000-fold) gradient of Ca^{2+} across the plasma membrane is maintained mainly by a **calcium pump** which actively expels Ca^{2+} from the cells (*page 114*).

The calcium pump is vital because a high Ca^{2+} concentration inside cells is toxic: it inhibits ATP synthesis, causes breakage of DNA and protein molecules and can kill the cell. However, in cell signalling only a *small* increase in Ca^{2+} inside the cell (caused by the release of Ca^{2+} into the cytosol from the endoplasmic reticulum where calcium ions are stored, accompanied by a small influx through the plasma membrane) is needed to induce a change – far less than would harm the cell. For example, in a muscle fibre or at a nerve terminal the free Ca^{2+} rises to only 1–5 micromoles per litre, but this is 10–50 times as much as in the resting cell and is

enough to bring about contraction of the muscle or release of a neurotransmitter without in any way damaging the cell. The event is stopped by removing the Ca^{2+} from the cytosol.

Calcium ions provide a universal chemical signal in animal and plant cells and probably in many bacteria too. The key experiment establishing this idea has been to measure the rise in the Ca^{2+} concentration during a cellular event – the contraction of a muscle for example – and then to manipulate the Ca^{2+} signal and see if this stops the event occurring. The Ca^{2+} concentration is measured using a bioluminescent protein or, in more recent investigations, a small fluorescent organic molecule which is introduced into the cell where it binds with the calcium ions and glows or flashes according to the latter's concentration.

Cell signalling is central to all life. It is crucial to understanding most diseases such as cancer and rheumatoid arthritis, and is a major target in drug development. The key issue is how a graded change in the external signal activates an intracellular cascade which – when it occurs in the right cell at the right time and at the right level – causes the cell to cross a threshold and change in some way.

Anthony Campbell is Professor in Medical Biochemistry and Director of The Darwin Centre at the University of Wales, Cardiff.

Receptors on the cell surface, page 58. Examples of cell signalling: endocytosis, page 115; blood-clotting, page 228; nerve impulses, page 350; synaptic transmission, page 355; sensory cells, page 380 hormone secretion, page 370; muscle contraction, page 407; antibody-production, page 323; fertilisation, page 503

1. The cell may be regarded as the basic unit of an organism.

2. There are two types of cell. **Prokaryotic**, meaning 'before a nucleus', and **eukaryotic**, meaning 'good or true nucleus'. Prokaryotic cells have a simpler internal structure than eukaryotic cells and lack membrane-bound organelles.

3. A typical prokaryotic cell has a **plasma membrane**, **cell wall**, **nucleoid**, **plasmids**, **ribosomes**, **mesosome** and sometimes **chromatophores**, **capsule** and **flagella**. The prokaryotic flagellum is simpler than the eukaryotic flagellum and moves by rotating rather than bending.

4. The main parts of a typical eukaryotic cell are the **plasma membrane**, **cytoplasm** and **nucleus**. The nucleus contains the **nucleolus** and **chromosomes**, the latter carrying hereditary material. The cytoplasm is composed of the **cytosol** and **endoplasmic reticulum** and contains various membrane-bound organelles.

5. Organelles and inclusions in the cytoplasm of eukaryotic cells include: **glycogen granules** or **starch grains**, **ribosomes** and/or **polyribosomes**, **Golgi apparatus**, **secretory vesicles**, **mitochondria**, **lysosomes**, **centrioles**, **pinocytic** and **phagocytic vesicles**, **microfilaments** and **microtubules** (**cytoskeleton**), **chloroplasts** and – at the surface – **microvilli**.

6. Some eukaryotic cells possess **flagella** or **cilia** which contain microtubules in a **9+2 pattern**. They move by bending.

7. Typical plant cells differ from animal cells in lacking centrioles and in possessing **chloroplasts**, **starch grains** instead of glycogen, a **central vacuole** and a **cellulose cell wall**.

8. In plant cells, a **primary wall** of cellulose is laid down on the inside of the **middle lamella**. After the cell has expanded, a further **secondary wall** may be laid down inside the primary wall. The secondary wall may be absent locally giving rise to a **pit**, and **plasmodesmata** may link adjacent cells.

9. According to the **fluid mosaic model**, the plasma membrane consists of a **lipid bilayer** with globular protein molecules in or on it.

10. Some of the protein molecules associated with the plasma membrane are **glycoproteins** with carbohydrate chains projecting from them. They are important in cell signalling and recognition.

11. Though basically similar, cells show considerable diversity in their contents, shape and functions. In all cases, there is a close relationship between cell structure and function.

For general advice on these questions and advice on answering essay-type questions, see pages vii and viii.

1. The drawing shows an electron micrograph of part of an animal cell.

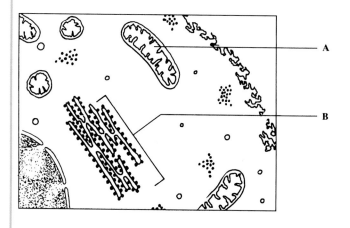

(a) Name one additional structure which would only be present in a plant cell. (1)

(b) Name the organelles labelled A and B. (1)

(c) Cell organelles can be separated using centrifugation. The cells are first broken open by homogenising the tissue in an ice-cold solution of a suitable water potential.

Suggest why the solution used when homogenising the tissue is

(i) ice cold; (1)

(ii) of a suitable water potential. (1)

(d) What difference between the organelles causes them to separate during centrifugation? (1)

(Total 5 marks)

NEAB 1997

2. (a) Explain why it is possible to see cell structure in more detail with an electron microscope than with an optical microscope. (2)

(b) The drawing shows a group of prokaryotic cells.

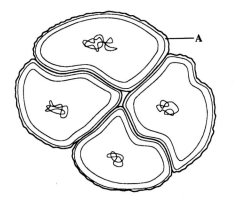

(i) Identify feature A. (1)

(ii) Give **two** pieces of evidence from the drawing to support the fact that these are prokaryotic cells. (2)

(Total 5 Marks)

AEB 1997

3. Chopped liver tissue was homogenised in salt solution. Cell organelles present in the homogenate were then separated by ultracentrifugation.

(a) Why was the salt solution of the same concentration as the liver tissue? (1)

(b) Copy and complete the table to show the order in which the mitochondria, nuclei and ribosomes would appear in the pellets at the bottom of the centrifuge tube after each centrifugation. (1)

Speed /g	Time /minutes	Organelles in pellet
500–1 000	10	
10 000–20 000	20	
100 000	60	

(c) (i) Explain why the pellet of mitochondria obtained would be unlikely to be pure. (1)

(ii) What could be measured to show that the mitochondria obtained were able to function? (1)

(d) Name **one** type of organelle that would be missing if the homogenate had been derived from a bacterial suspenslon instead of liver cells. (1)

(Total 5 marks)

AEB 1996

4. Write an essay on the structure and functions of cell surface membranes.

(Total 15 marks)

London 1997

5. The diagram represents a phospholipid molecule.

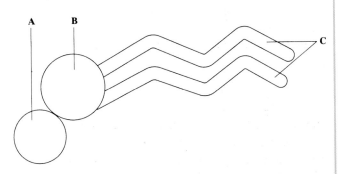

(a) (i) Name the parts of the molecule **A**, **B** and **C**. (1)

(ii) Explain how the phospholipid molecules form a double layer in a cell membrane. (2)

(b) Cell membranes also contain protein molecules. Give **two** functions of these protein molecules. (2)

(Total 5 marks)

NEAB 1998

I n Chapter 3 we considered cells as if they exist in isolation without any kind of contact with each other. This may be true of single-celled organisms, but the majority of organisms are **multicellular**, consisting of numerous cells. In such organisms, cells of one or more types are generally grouped together to form **tissues**.

The function of a tissue depends on what kind, or kinds, of cell it is composed of. Furthermore, in more complex organisms different tissues are combined to form **organs**. The study of tissues and the way they are arranged in organs is called **histology**. In this chapter we shall look at a range of tissues and organs, and discuss the part they play in the organisation of individual organisms.

Types of tissues

There are various ways of classifying tissues. We shall adopt a functional classification based on the jobs which the tissues do in the body. On this basis:

- Animal tissues may be divided into **epithelial tissue (epithelium)**, **connective tissue**, **skeletal tissue**, **blood tissue**, **nerve tissue**, **muscle tissue and reproductive tissue**.

- Plant tissues may be divided into **meristematic tissue**, **epidermal tissue (epidermis)**, **parenchyma**, **collenchyma**, **sclerenchyma**, **vascular tissue** and **cork**.

Our purpose in this chapter is not to describe all these tissues in detail but to look at the more basic ones, emphasising the principles underlying their construction.

4.1   Animal tissues

The following description is based mainly on the mammal. The tissues to be described also occur in other animals, though their detailed structure may differ in certain respects. We shall start with epithelial tissue – also known as epithelium – because this demonstrates how cells can be built up into multicellular structures of varying complexity.

Epithelium

Epithelium is *lining* tissue. It covers the surface of the animal and the organs, cavities and tubes within it. In its simplest form it consists of a sheet of cells which fit closely together, rather like crazy paving (*figure 4.1*). The cells rest on a **basement membrane** and have a **free surface** on the other side. The basement membrane is produced by the epithelial cells themselves and consists of a meshwork of fine protein fibres (**collagen**) embedded in a jelly-like matrix. It supports the epithelium and exercises some control over what passes through it.

The epithelium on the outer surface of an animal is called the **epidermis**. In some animals, for example arthropods, the epidermis secretes a protective **cuticle** of varying thickness and hardness. The epithelium which forms the inner lining of cavities and tubes inside the body, such as the heart, blood vessels and lymph vessels, is referred to as **endothelium**.

There are several ways of classifying epithelial tissues. None of them is entirely satisfactory because the demarcation between the different types is often blurred. However, a fundamental distinction may be made between epithelia that consist of only one layer of cells, and those that consist of many layers.

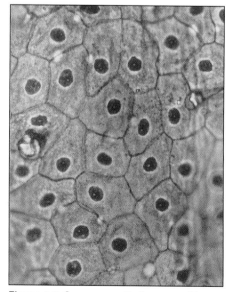

Figure 4.1 Squamous epithelium, one of the simplest animal tissues. Notice how the cells fit together. The nuclei of the cells are clearly seen. Magnification ×600.

Epithelia consisting of one layer of cells

This kind of epithelium can be divided into five main types on the basis of the shape and other features of its constituent cells (*figure 4.2*):

- **Squamous epithelium** is composed of cells which are flattened like paving stones – in fact an alternative name for it is **pavement epithelium**. The resulting sheet of cells is thin and delicate, often less than 2.0 μm thick. It is found in places where the protective covering needs to be readily permeable to molecules or ions in solution, for example the walls of blood capillaries and alveoli in the lungs.

- **Cuboidal epithelium** consists of cells whose height is approximately equal to their width, so when viewed in vertical section they appear square. The free surface is polygonal in shape and the cells fit together like a honeycomb. Many glands, and the ducts leading from them, are lined with cuboidal epithelium, as are the tubules in the kidney. Cuboidal epithelium may bear **microvilli** on the free surface. Such is the case with certain of the kidney tubules. The microvilli increase the surface area for the reabsorption of substances.

- **Columnar epithelium** consists of cells elongated at right angles to the basement membrane, so they appear to be column-shaped when viewed in vertical section. This kind of epithelium is found lining the small intestine. Like cuboidal epithelium, the cells may bear microvilli on the free surface. In the small intestine the microvilli increase the surface area for absorbing products of digestion.

- **Ciliated epithelium** has **cilia** on the free surface of the cells. The cilia can beat rhythmically. The cells themselves may be cuboidal or columnar in shape. Ciliated epithelium lines tubes and cavities in which materials are moved, for example the trachea and bronchial tubes. In certain animals, free-living flatworms for example, the underside of the body is covered with ciliated epithelium. The beating cilia drive the animal along, enabling it to glide on stones and weeds.

- **Glandular epithelium** has secretory cells as its main type of cell. A good example is seen in the lining of the rectum where the epithelium consists mainly of cells that secrete **mucus**. The rectal epithelium is greatly folded, thus increasing the surface area from which secretion takes place. Mucus is slimy and serves as a lubricant, easing the movement of faeces and protecting the delicate epithelial surface from abrasion.

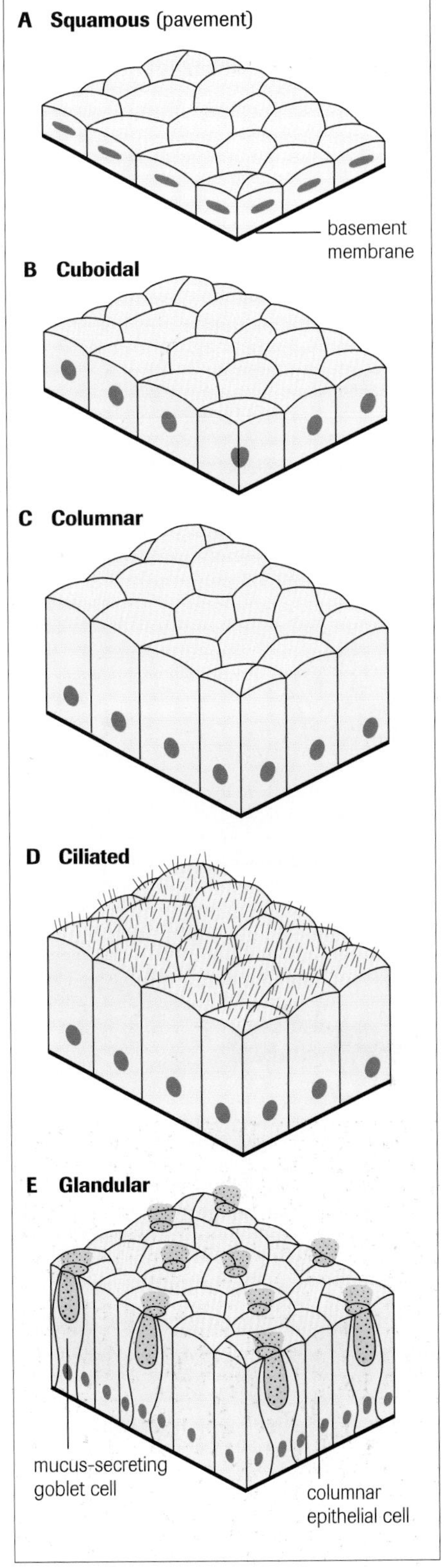

Support

Goblet cells and mucous membranes

Mucus-secreting cells usually have a bulbous top and a constricted base, like a wine glass. On account of their shape they are called **goblet cells** (*figure 4.2E*). After a goblet cell has discharged its mucus its bulbous top becomes slender until it fills up again.

A layer of moist epithelium containing goblet cells, together with the underlying connective tissue, is called a **mucous membrane** or **mucosa**. (Note that the noun is spelled *mucus*, the adjective *mucous*.) Mucous membranes are found lining cavities that are connected to the exterior, such as the gut and breathing tract. In some cases, including the breathing tract, the mucous membrane is ciliated. Mucus is slimy, and particles which are inadvertently inhaled get caught up in it. The mucus and particles are then driven by the beating cilia towards the throat.

A Squamous (pavement)

basement
membrane

B Cuboidal

C Columnar

D Ciliated

E Glandular

mucus-secreting
goblet cell

columnar
epithelial cell

Figure 4.2 Five types of single-layered epithelium.

Glands

Sometimes a patch of epithelium is folded inwards, forming an invagination. The cells lining the bottom of the invagination become secretory and develop into a gland.

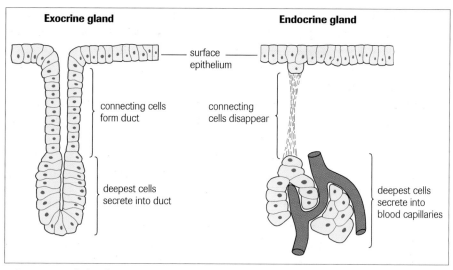

Figure 4.3 Diagram comparing an exocrine and endocrine gland. Both develop from invaginations (intuckings) of the surface epithelium. In the exocrine gland the connection with the surface epithelium becomes the duct into which the glandular cells shed their secretion. The endocrine gland loses its connection with the surface epithelium and develops a close association with blood capillaries into which it releases its secretion.

How glandular cells release their secretions, page 115

Two types of gland are recognised (*figure 4.3*):

- **Exocrine gland** The epithelial connection between the gland and the surface epithelium remains as a tube (**duct**) which carries the gland's secretion to wherever it has to go. The salivary glands are an example: they secrete saliva into the mouth cavity.

  The secretory part of an exocrine gland may be a spherical sack or a tube, and it may show various degrees of branching. Branching has the effect of increasing the area of the secretory surface.

- **Endocrine gland** The epithelial connection between the gland and the surface epithelium disappears, and the gland itself forms a close association with blood capillaries. Its secretion, instead of flowing along a duct, passes into the bloodstream. Endocrine glands secrete **hormones** about which we shall have much to say later in the book.

Tubules

In most animals, ourselves included, narrow tubes such as blood capillaries are created by a layer of epithelial tissue folding into a cylinder, rather like making a tube out of a sheet of paper. However, in some animals we find tubules which are constructed in a different way. They are made from **drainpipe cells**.

A drainpipe cell is a hollow cylinder, open at each end, with the nucleus situated in the 'wall' of the cylinder (*figure 4.4*). The tubule is formed by a row of such cells joining up end to end. Because its lumen is created from a cavity *inside* the cells, a tubule of this sort is described as an **intracellular tubule** (*intra* means 'within', *inter* means 'between' – an important distinction in biology). The fine breathing tubes (tracheoles) of insects and the excretory ducts of flatworms are intracellular tubules.

Epithelia consisting of many layers of cells

This kind of epithelium is called **stratified epithelium**. Only the bottom layer of cells rests on the basement membrane (*figure 4.5*). Obviously this type of epithelium is thicker than single-layered epithelia and more effective as a protective covering. It comprises the epidermis of the skin and the lining of certain cavities and tubes inside the body, for example the vagina and oesophagus.

The multi-layered nature of stratified epithelium derives from the fact that the cells of the bottom layer divide repeatedly in a plane parallel to the basement membrane, with the result that new cells are constantly being formed above the bottom layer of cells. As cell divisions continue, the older cells get pushed outwards as new cells are formed beneath them. As the cells move away from the dividing layer, they become flatter and eventually flake off, to be replaced by new ones from beneath.

Extension

Syncytia

Sometimes there are no plasma membranes between adjacent epithelial cells. The resulting epithelium consists of a multinucleate sheet of tissue. This is known as a **syncytium** (*syn* is Greek for 'together', referring to the fact that the cells are fused together). The villi in the placenta are lined with a syncytium (*page 508*).

Syncytia are found in other tissues besides epithelia. For example, skeletal muscle fibres are syncytia (*page 406*).

In human skin, the cells at the surface of the epidermis become transformed into a tough, non-living layer composed largely of the protein **keratin**. This greatly enhances the skin's efficiency as a protective covering. The epidermis lining internal organs such as the vagina and oesophagus does not normally become keratinised, at least not to anything like the same extent as the skin.

Exocrine glands often occur beneath stratified epithelia and their ducts run through the epithelium to the surface. Examples are sweat glands in human skin, and mucous glands in the skin of amphibians such as frogs.

There are several variants of stratified epithelium. For example, the lining of the trachea appears to be composed of several layers of cells but careful observation shows that all the cells rest on, or at least touch, the basement membrane. This is known as **pseudostratified epithelium**.

Another arrangement is found in the lining of the bladder. Here the cells are all approximately the same size, do not flake off, and can change their shape when the bladder wall is stretched as it fills up with urine. This is called **transitional epithelium**.

Connective tissue

Connective tissue binds organs and tissues together and fills the spaces between them. We would therefore expect this kind of tissue to be strong, and this indeed is often the case. It consists of a jelly-like **matrix (ground substance)** in which several types of cells and **protein fibres** are embedded. The matrix is similar in chemical composition to the basement membrane of epithelial tissue (*page 62*).

There are four main kinds of connective tissue, and their properties are determined by the type and number of protein fibres which they contain.

■ **Areolar tissue**, the most basic kind of connective tissue, is found all over the body: beneath the skin, connecting organs together, and filling spaces between other tissues. The matrix contains several types of cell and two types of protein fibre: bundles of unbranched **collagen fibres** and a network of branched **elastic fibres** (*figure 4.6*). The matrix and fibres are produced by cells called **fibroblasts**. Areolar tissue is quite easily torn and broken; what little strength it has is due to the fibres.

■ **Collagen tissue** (also called **white fibrous tissue**) contains mainly collagen fibres. It is flexible but relatively unstretchable and has great tensile strength. Tendons, attaching muscles to bones, are composed of collagen tissue (*figure 4.7*). Although

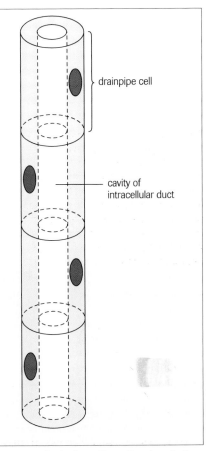

Figure 4.4 Drainpipe cells are like short, hollow cylinders. An intracellular tube may be formed from a row of such cells placed end to end as shown here.

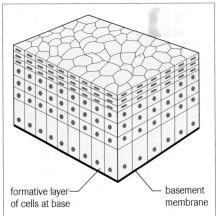

Figure 4.5 Stratified epithelium consists of layers of epithelial cells on top of each other. The cells are formed by cell divisions in the bottom layer.

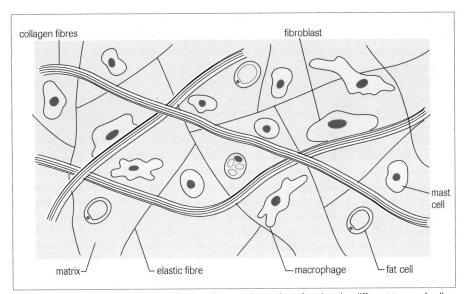

Figure 4.6 Areolar tissue as it appears in a microscopic section, showing the different types of cells and inclusions. The macrophages and mast cells help to defend the body against disease.

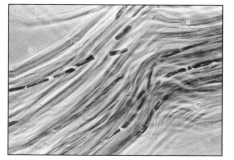

Figure 4.7 Longitudinal section of a tendon showing densely packed collagen fibres. The dark cigar-shaped objects are fibroblasts, which tend to occur in rows. Magnification ×500.

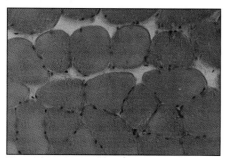

Figure 4.8 Section of adipose tissue showing closely packed fat cells. The red region inside each cell is fat. These cells are so full of fat that the nuclei (darkly stained) have been pushed against the plasma membranes. Magnification ×200.

collagen is relatively unstretchable, it does have a certain amount of elasticity. In fact considerable energy can be stored in stretched tendons, which is useful in locomotion.

■ **Elastic tissue** (also called **yellow elastic tissue**) contains mainly elastic fibres and the cells which produce them. It is flexible like collagen tissue, but less strong and more stretchable. It is found in ligaments, the tough strands which bind bones together across the joints, and in the wall of the bladder allowing it to stretch as it fills up with urine.

■ **Adipose tissue** contains large numbers of **fat cells** within a network of collagen and elastic fibres (*figure 4.8*). Normally the fat cells are full of fat, making adipose tissue an important energy store. In the skin it fulfils the additional function of insulation.

Extension

What gives connective tissue its properties?

Collagen and elastic fibres are both **fibrous proteins**. Their functional properties are related to their molecular structure.

X-ray analysis of collagen has shown it to consist of three polypeptide chains coiled round each other to form a **triple helix** (*page 30*). The chains are interlinked by strong covalent bonds, making the whole structure tough and inextensible like a plaited rope. Structures containing collagen fibres, such as the walls of arteries, can expand because in their resting state the collagen fibres are crinkled. Once the crinkles straighten out, further expansion is prevented.

Elastin consists of numerous short, randomly coiled polypeptide chains crosslinked by the same sort of covalent bonds as in collagen. This arrangement allows elastic fibres to stretch and recoil like a rubber band, as shown in the illustration.

Elastic structures such as ligaments contain a certain amount of collagen as well to stop them stretching so much that they tear.

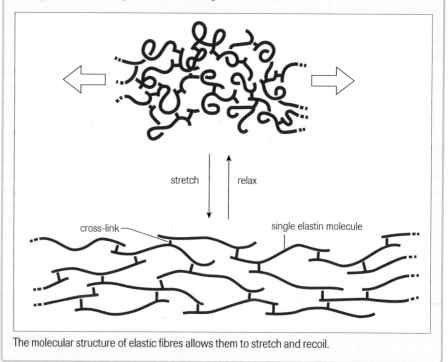

The molecular structure of elastic fibres allows them to stretch and recoil.

Skeletal tissue

Skeletal tissue supports the body and provides a strong framework whose rigid components can move against each other at smoothly articulating joints. Like connective tissue it consists of cells embedded in a matrix, but in this case the matrix is hard.

Two kinds of skeletal tissue occur in vertebrates: **cartilage** and **bone**. The skeleton of cartilaginous fishes, such as the dogfish, sharks and rays, is composed entirely of cartilage. The mammal, on the other hand, has a predominantly bony skeleton with cartilage at the joints and in the discs between the vertebrae.

Cartilage

Cartilage is softer than bone and you can slice through it quite easily with a sharp knife or scalpel. When pressed it 'gives' slightly, rather like hard rubber. This makes it useful as a cushioning material.

The matrix of cartilage, **chondrin**, consists mainly of a mucopolysaccharide in which are embedded spherical cells called **chondroblasts**. Bundles of collagen fibres and elastic fibres may also be present in varying amounts.

There are three types of cartilage:

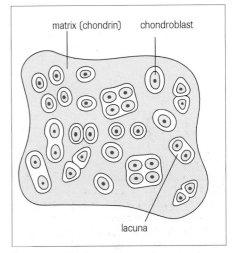

- **Hyaline cartilage** has a homogeneous matrix with chondroblasts dotted about either singly or in small groups (*figure 4.9*). This characteristic pattern is due to the way cartilage develops. Each chondroblast secretes some matrix and then divides first into two and then into four. As the daughter cells secrete matrix, they get pushed apart. The cells finish up imprisoned in little spaces called **lacunae** within the matrix which they themselves have produced.

  Hyaline cartilage is found in the wall of the trachea (windpipe) where its function is to prevent the wall caving in. It is also found in the ends (epiphyses) of limb bones where it is associated with the formation of bone tissue (ossification), and at the joints where it performs a cushioning function and provides a smooth articulating surface.

- **Fibrocartilage** (also called **white fibrous cartilage**) is like hyaline cartilage but it contains collagen fibres. It is found in the intervertebral discs of the vertebral column where it performs a cushioning function.

- **Elastic cartilage** (also called **yellow elastic cartilage**) contains elastic fibres. It is found in the pinna of the ear. Elastic cartilage is tough but bendable, as you will know from wiggling your ear.

Figure 4.9 Hyaline cartilage as it appears in a microscopic section. Notice the chondrocytes scattered about singly and in small groups.

Bone

Bone tissue, normally referred to simply as bone, consists of an organic matrix impregnated with mineral salts containing calcium and phosphate. These salts are in the form of tiny sub-microscopic crystals and they make bone extremely hard. The organic matrix contains densely packed collagen fibres which help to give bone its tensile strength, enabling it to bear heavy loads and withstand severe stresses without breaking.

Both the organic matrix and the mineral salts are produced by cells called **osteoblasts**. Projecting from these cells are slender processes which link up to form a network.

In a developing limb bone such as the femur, numerous osteoblasts arrange themselves in concentric rings around a series of channels called **Haversian canals**, each of which contains an artery and vein. Because of the concentric arrangement of the osteoblasts, the matrix is laid down in a series of layers (**lamellae**) encircling each Haversian canal. Each osteoblast finishes up in a space (**lacuna**) from which narrow channels called **canaliculi** traverse the lamellae. The canaliculi contain the fine processes of the osteoblasts during the development of the bone. Once imprisoned in the lacunae, the osteoblasts stop secreting matrix material and are known as **osteocytes**.

There are two types of bone tissue:

- **Compact bone** has Haversian canals and their surrounding lamellae packed tightly together, giving a very dense material.

- **Spongy bone** is of looser construction and forms a three-dimensional network of interconnected strands with spaces in between.

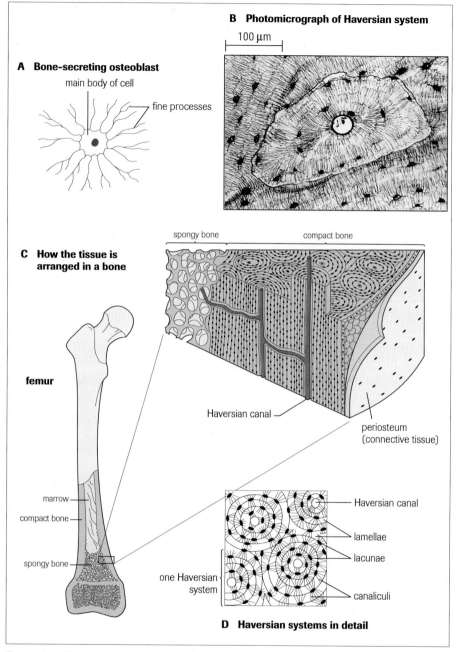

A **Bone-secreting osteoblast**

main body of cell

fine processes

B **Photomicrograph of Haversian system**

100 μm

C **How the tissue is arranged in a bone**

spongy bone   compact bone

femur

marrow

compact bone

spongy bone

Haversian canal

periosteum (connective tissue)

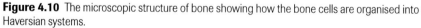

one Haversian system

Haversian canal

lamellae

lacunae

canaliculi

D **Haversian systems in detail**

Figure 4.10 The microscopic structure of bone showing how the bone cells are organised into Haversian systems.

In a limb bone such as the femur, the shaft contains compact bone whereas the two ends (epiphyses) contain spongy bone. The functional reason for this difference is explained on page 414. The microscopic structure of the femur is illustrated in figure 4.10.

Bone marrow

The centre of the femur and many other bones is filled with **marrow**. There are two types of marrow: **red** and **yellow**. Red marrow contains developing blood cells (hence its colour), whereas yellow marrow is mainly fatty tissue.

In an embryo only red marrow is found, but in the course of development some of it becomes replaced by yellow marrow. In the adult, red marrow is confined to parts of the axial skeleton and the upper ends of the femur and humerus (*page 415*). Here, inside the bones, blood cells – both red and white – are manufactured.

Although surrounded by skeletal tissue, red bone marrow is a tissue in its own right, its function being to make blood cells. Blood-forming tissue is also found in the lymphatic system which manufactures certain types of white blood cell.

Blood, page 227

Once released into the circulation, red and white blood cells become the main cellular components of **blood**.

Muscle tissue

Muscle tissue is unique in being able to **contract**, which allows it to change in length or develop tension. This is the basis of its main function which is to enable the body, or parts of it, to move.

Muscle tissue is composed of **muscle fibres**. It is classified into three types according to its location and structure:

- **Skeletal muscle** is attached to the skeleton.
- **Cardiac muscle** is in the wall of the heart.
- **Smooth muscle** is in the walls of the gut, blood vessels, bladder and other tubes and cavities in the body.

Skeletal and cardiac muscle are dealt with in later chapters, but smooth muscle will be described here because it illustrates the basic structure of muscle tissue and is widely distributed in the body.

The structure of smooth muscle is shown in figure 4.11. Each fibre is a single cell with a nucleus and cytoplasm. It is spindle shaped, typically about 0.2 mm long, and the cytoplasm contains thread-like **myofibrils** which are responsible for contraction.

In certain places, the skin for example, smooth muscle fibres occur singly or in small groups, mixed up with connective tissue. In the walls of cavities and tubes the smooth muscle fibres are concentrated into sheets with all the fibres running in the same direction.

In tubes such as the gut the sheets of smooth muscle fibres may be orientated circularly or longitudinally. When the circular fibres contract the tube narrows (**constricts**); when they relax the tube widens (**dilates**), an effect which may be enhanced by contraction of the longitudinal fibres. This principle applies not only to movements of internal organs such as the gut, but also to the locomotion of certain soft-bodied animals such as the earthworm (*page 431*).

At the ends of certain tubes in the body the circular smooth muscle fibres may be packed together to form a muscular ring called a **sphincter** which, by relaxing or contracting, opens or closes the tube. Examples are the **anal sphincter** which controls the opening and closing of the anus, and the **pyloric sphincter** which controls the passage of food from the stomach to the duodenum (*Chapter 11*).

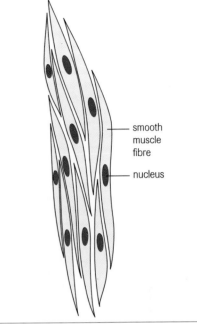

smooth muscle fibre

nucleus

Figure 4.11 Smooth muscle tissue consists of elongated muscle fibres, each of which is a single cell.

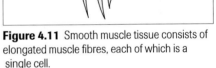
Cardiac muscle, page 233
Skeletal muscle, page 405
Nerve tissue, pages 348 and 362
Reproductive tissue, pages 500 and 501

4.2 Plant tissues

Some of the animal tissues which we have been looking at have their counterparts in plants, but plants also have certain unique tissues which may be related to their way of life. Here we shall concentrate on the tissues found in flowering plants.

Meristematic tissue

From a plant's meristematic tissue all other tissues are derived. It is found wherever growth occurs, for example in the tip of the stem and root. Meristematic cells are small and immature, with thin walls. The walls are thin because at this stage very little cellulose has been laid down. The cells lack chloroplasts and the large vacuole characteristic of mature plant cells, but they contain other organelles including undifferentiated plastids which are destined to give rise to chloroplasts or amyloplasts (*page 44*). Their important feature is the ability to divide by mitosis and subsequently differentiate into other types of cell.

Epidermal tissue

A plant's equivalent to epithelium is its **epidermis** which is located at the surface of, for example, stems and leaves (*figure 4.12*). Its cells are usually somewhat flattened, and often irregular when looked at in surface view. They fit together like a jigsaw, forming a protective layer covering the more delicate tissues beneath. With the exception of stomatal guard cells, plant epidermal cells lack chloroplasts. Their outer walls are frequently thick and covered with a waxy **cuticle** which is impermeable to water and prevents excessive evaporation in dry conditions.

Cork

Cork is a multi-layered tissue just under the epidermis of the stems and branches of shrubs and trees, where it forms the hard part of the **bark**. The cells are small and more or less spherical and, as they develop, their walls become impregnated with a fatty substance called **suberin** which renders them impervious to water and gases. Consequently the cells die and lose their contents. Cork is therefore a dead tissue. However, the tissues underneath it are very much alive. The function of cork is to protect these living tissues from cold, insect attack and physical damage. The detailed structure of cork and how it is formed are explained on page 542.

Being impervious and having a certain amount of 'give', this tissue is ideal for making corks for bottles. Commercial cork is obtained by stripping off large areas of bark from the cork oak (*Quercus suber*), native to Spain, Portugal and north Africa. Care is taken to avoid removing so much of the bark that the tree dies.

Parenchyma

Parenchyma is packing tissue, and its main function is to fill the spaces between other tissues. The cells are roughly spherical in shape, with flattened faces where they press against each other (*figures 4.13 and 4.14A*). If the cells are fully turgid and tightly packed, as they normally are, parenchyma helps to maintain the shape and firmness of the plant (*page 110*).

In certain regions of a plant, the parenchyma tissue may fulfil other more specialised functions. For example, in roots the cells frequently contain starch grains and thus serve a storage function. In leaves they contain chloroplasts and can therefore photosynthesise; this kind of tissue is known as **chlorenchyma**. Some aquatic plants contain parenchyma tissue with large, air-filled spaces between the cells; this is called **aerenchyma** and it helps to make the plant buoyant and provides a store of air for respiration.

Since parenchyma tissue contains nutrients, it is often used by humans for food. For instance the parenchyma cells in a potato tuber are full of starch, and those of sugar beet contain sucrose.

Collenchyma

Collenchyma tissue is composed of living cells whose cellulose walls are thickened at the corners (*figure 4.12*). Where several such cells lie in contact with each other, a tough rib of cellulose is created (*figure 4.14B*). Typically, collenchyma is found in the outer part of stems and in the midrib of leaves. Its function is to provide strength with flexibility.

Sclerenchyma

Sclerenchyma tissue is much stronger than collenchyma and plays a major part in support. It occurs in stems and in the midribs of leaves where it mainly takes the form of elongated **sclerenchyma fibres**, usually referred to simply as **fibres** (*figure 4.14C*).

The cells start off as living cells with cellulose walls. However, as the cells develop the cellulose becomes impregnated with **lignin**, a complex aromatic compound which makes

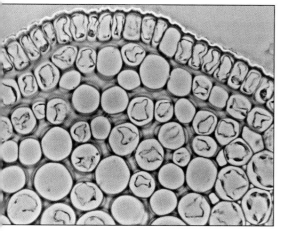

Figure 4.12 Photomicrograph of a transverse section of the stem of a deadnettle. Epidermal tissue can be seen lining the outer side of the stem (the topmost layer of cells in the photomicrograph). Notice the cuticle on the outer surface of the epidermis. Beneath the epidermis is a wad of collenchyma tissue which strengthens the stem. Magnification ×200.

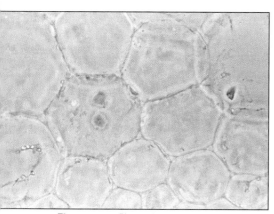

Figure 4.13 Photomicrograph of parenchyma tissue as seen in a section of the central region of a sunflower stem. Magnification ×400.

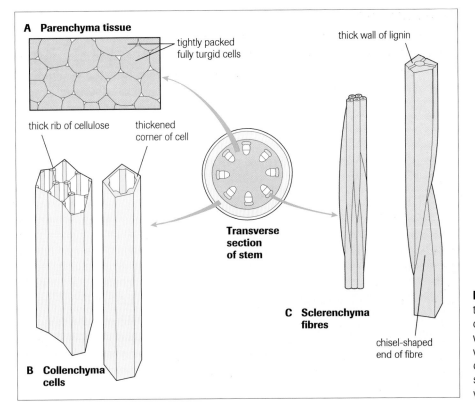

A Parenchyma tissue

tightly packed
fully turgid cells

thick rib of cellulose

thickened
corner of cell

thick wall of lignin

**Transverse
section
of stem**

**C Sclerenchyma
fibres**

chisel-shaped
end of fibre

**B Collenchyma
cells**

Figure 4.14 Three important strengthening tissues found in plants: parenchyma, collenchyma and sclerenchyma. Only the cell walls are shown. The transverse section shows where these tissues occur in a typical dicotyledonous stem. Collenchyma and sclerenchyma also occur in the midrib and veins of leaves.

the wall not only strong but also impervious to water, gases and solutes. Deprived of oxygen and nutrients, the cell contents die and degenerate, leaving a hollow fibre of lignin with tapering ends. Mature sclerenchyma tissue consists of tightly packed bundles of such fibres.

The strength and flexibility of sclerenchyma tissue varies from one type of plant to another depending on the length of the fibres, the thickness of their walls and the way they are arranged. Because of its properties, this tissue provides raw materials for the textile industry; it is used in the manufacture of linen (from the leaves of flax plants), rope (from hemp) and sacks, cheap cloth and twine (from jute). It is also used for making paper.

Vascular tissue

Vascular tissue is concerned with transport, and is functionally equivalent to the circulatory system of animals. However, that is where the similarity ends, for the two systems could not be more different.

There are two sorts of vascular tissue: **xylem** and **phloem**.

■ **Xylem tissue** consists of elongated, lignified tubes which may be either **vessels** or **tracheids**. Like sclerenchyma fibres, they begin as living cells but with the lignification of their walls lose their cell contents and die. They finish up as hollow tubes whose function is to transport water and mineral salts from the roots to the leaves.

■ **Phloem tissue** consists mainly of unlignified living cells called **sieve tubes** which, with the aid of adjacent **companion cells**, transport soluble food substances from one part of the plant to another.

Cork, page 542
Xylem, page 252
Phloem, page 258
Wood, page 540

Wood

Xylem tissue generally contains sclerenchyma fibres as well as vessels and/or tracheids. It is particularly abundant in shrubs and trees where it comprises the **wood**. Being lignified, wood is strong and is therefore important in support. Typically there is a lot of it in the trunk and branches which have to hold up the canopy. There is less in the roots, except in specialised roots which provide support such as the ones in figure 4.15.

Dense and flammable, wood makes a useful fuel and has the advantage of being a renewable resource. It is the basis of the timber industry and is used for many types of construction (*page 543*). It is also the main source of fibres for manufacturing paper.

Figure 4.15 A banyan tree. In the course of its growth large aerial roots have been let down from the larger branches. Well endowed with strengthening tissue, these prop roots form, in effect, supplementary trunks, providing extra support and enabling the tree to spread over a considerable area. It is said that Alexander the Great sheltered the whole of his army under a single Banyan tree.

Extension

Tissue culture

It is possible to remove individual tissues from an organism – animal or plant – and grow them on their own in the laboratory. This procedure is called **tissue culture**.

Having been removed, the sample of tissue – known as the **explant** – is placed in or on a **nutrient medium** which contains all the chemicals it needs for growth. The medium may be a solid substance such as agar or a saline solution such as Ringer's solution (*page 267*). Oxygen is supplied and waste products removed. The temperature, pH and other conditions are carefully controlled, and everything is kept sterile to avoid contamination with microorganisms such as bacteria. The tissue that develops usually takes the form of a flat sheet of cells.

Enormous advances in tissue culture have been made in recent years and it is now possible to grow entire plants and small organs such as blood vessels. As well as giving us important information on the way cells differentiate, the technique enables plants to be cultivated for commercial purposes, serves as a medium for culturing viruses and provides a source of tissues for replacement surgery.

Support

Animal and plant tissues compared

Animals and plants lead very different lives, so it is not surprising to find that their tissues show many differences. These differences stem from the very different ways that animals and plants feed.

Plants, unlike animals, can synthesise their own organic food. This relates to the fact that plants possess photosynthetic tissue whereas animals do not. But it explains other things too. For example, since animals cannot synthesise their own organic food, they have to obtain it in ready-made form, and this often means searching for it. This is why animals possess muscle and nerve tissue, as well as specialised epithelia for digesting and absorbing food. Photosynthesis renders such tissues unnecessary in plants.

All this can be summed up by saying that their method of feeding imposes on animals the necessity to move and respond rapidly, and this demands a greater range of specialised tissues than are necessary in plants. It is a curious paradox that the root cause of this is that animals lack the ability to perform a chemical process which plants are capable of performing, namely photosynthesis.

4.3 Organs and organ systems

An **organ** is a structurally distinct part of the body which performs one or more specific functions. Organs are generally made up of several types of tissue which have a highly organised structural relationship with each other.

Take the mammalian stomach, for example. The wall of the stomach consists of smooth muscle, nerve tissue, connective tissue, blood and several different types of epithelia, all organised into a complex system of interrelated structures whose combined function is the storage and processing of food before it passes on to the small intestine.

In most animals different organs are interrelated to form **organ systems**. An organ system is made up of several organs which together perform a particular function. For example, the stomach is part of the digestive system which also includes the rest of the gut (alimentary canal), along with various accessory organs such as the pancreas and liver.

Sometimes an organ belongs to more than one system. The pancreas, for example, secretes hormones in addition to digestive enzymes, and therefore belongs to the endocrine as well as the digestive system.

We tend to associate organs with animals. However, plants have them too though they are generally less elaborate and fewer in number than in animals. One of the most obvious plant organs is the leaf, whose principal function is photosynthesis. The flower is a reproductive organ, and structures such as bulbs and corms are organs of perennation and vegetative reproduction.

► Examples of organs: lungs, page 166; stomach, page 183; heart and blood vessels, pages 231 and 236; kidney, page 280; brain, page 359; leaves, page 205; flowers, page 482; perennating organs, page 490

4.4 Whole organisms

So far in this chapter we have considered *parts* of organisms: cells, tissues, organs and organ systems. Now we turn our attention to the whole organism – the individual.

A distinction may be made between organisms which consist of only one cell (**unicellular organisms**) and those that consist of more than one cell (**multicellular organisms**). Some multicellular organisms are constructed mainly of tissues and have few, if any, organs. Others possess organs as the basis of their construction.

Because unicellular organisms consist of only one cell, it is tempting to think of them as simple. Nothing could be further from the truth. They can be highly complex. The reason is that within a single cell they have to carry out all the functions which a multicellular organism can divide between many different types of cell. This is well illustrated by the slipper animalcule *Paramecium* which is described in the extension box on the next page.

Most organisms are single entities and there is no difficulty in recognising an individual. Some organisms, however, are made up of numerous similar parts or **modules**. A rose bush, for instance, consists of lots of branches each bearing leaves and buds, and the cnidarian *Obelia* is composed of numerous hydra-like individuals. Organisms which are constructed on this sort of plan are described as **modular organisms**.

Certain modular organisms are regarded as **colonies** rather than single individuals. Such is the case with *Obelia*, a collection of hydra-like individuals attached to a central stalk, and its relative the Portuguese man of war (*figure 4.16*). The latter is a floating colony consisting of several types of individual, each specialising in a particular activity. The colony behaves as a single unit – a sort of 'super-organism' whose individuals are equivalent to the organs of other multicellular organisms. The phylum to which these animals belong, Cnidaria, is important ecologically: it includes the corals whose vast colonies, encrusted with calcium carbonate, make up coral reefs.

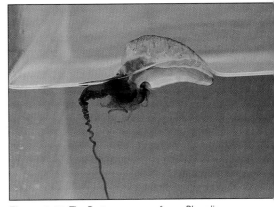

Figure 4.16 The Portugese man of war, *Physalia*, a complex floating colony. Different types of individual hang down from the underside of the gas-filled float. Some have long retractable tentacles armed with sting cells. The tentacles may be over 7 metres long and are used for defence and for catching prey such as fish. Other individuals have mouths and are for feeding, or produce gametes and serve a reproductive function.

Paramecium, a complex unicellular organism

Paramecium is a comparatively large freshwater protoctist whose internal structure can be observed under the light microscope. In addition to the usual organelles which one would expect to find in any cell (mitochondria, endoplasmic reticulum and so on), it has a number of special features (*illustration 1*).

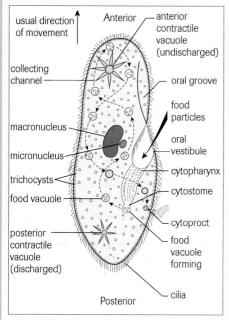

Illustration 1 Diagram of *Paramecium* showing structures visible under the light microscope. The arrows show the course taken by food particles which have been taken into the cell.

The cell is bounded by a protective **pellicle** from which protrude large numbers of **cilia**. By beating backwards and forwards the cilia 'row' the organism through the water. Just beneath the pellicle are numerous **trichocysts**: each is a tiny sac from which a needle-like thread can be discharged. Some species use these for defence.

There are two nuclei: the **macronucleus** controls metabolic functions, including growth, while the **micronucleus** is needed for reproduction. Two **contractile vacuoles**, one at each end, get rid of excess water (osmoregulation): water drains through the **collecting channels** into the contractile vacuole which, when full, discharges its contents to the outside through a hole in the pellicle.

Small particles of food, swept into the **oral vestibule** by ciliary action, are taken up into **food vacuoles** at the base of the **cytopharynx**. The food vacuoles circulate through the cytoplasm while the food is being digested, and any undigestible material is discharged through an opening in the pellicle called the **cytoproct**.

Perhaps the most intriguing aspect of *Paramecium* is the pellicle and associated structures. The electron microscope has shown this part of the organism to be surprisingly elaborate. The basal bodies of the cilia are interconnected by a system of threads (microtubules) situated immediately beneath the pellicle which

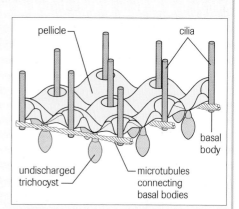

Illustration 2 Diagram of the surface region of *Paramecium* based on electron micrographs.

itself is elaborately sculpted (*illustration 2*).

The cilia beat in a beautifully coordinated manner in which each performs its backstroke slightly before the one in front, a **metachronal rhythm**. This ensures that the organism swims smoothly, rather than jerkily. If the organism bumps into an obstacle or swims into an unfavourable region, the cilia go into reverse and the organism backs away. It then alters its direction slightly, and swims forward again. By means of this **avoiding reaction** noxious stimuli are minimised.

So *Paramecium*, though unicellular, is by no means simple. This is true not only of its structure but also of the way it works. The cilia, for example are as coordinated as the legs of any multicellular organism.

The advantages of being multicellular

A single cell cannot grow indefinitely. When it reaches a certain size it either stops growing or divides into two smaller cells which then grow. Indefinite growth seems to be limited by the nucleus. It appears that a single nucleus can only exert control over a certain volume of cytoplasm. This means that for an organism to increase in size beyond a certain point it must become multicellular.

Becoming multicellular, then, allows an increase in size. With this comes the possibility of specialisation: instead of every cell carrying out all tasks, certain cells become specialised for one function, others for a different function. This **division of labour** permits greater efficiency and enables the organism to exploit environments that are denied to simpler forms. But, although it is an advantage to the whole organism, it means that individual cells are unable to exist on their own: the cells lose their independence and have to rely on one another's specialised activities.

With increased size and cell specialisation come all sorts of other advantages. For example, in animals better muscles and a skeleton can be developed. These give the animal greater strength and allow it to tackle larger prey, while at the same time enabling it to move faster towards prey or away from predators. Having specialised cells also means that more sophisticated physiological mechanisms can be developed which allow, for example, a constant body temperature to be maintained.

Although the multicellular state permits greater specialisation, the increased size that accompanies it can create difficulties. One of these difficulties concerns the acquisition of oxygen and food materials and their distribution to the cells. How this difficulty has been overcome is explained in later chapters.

Symmetry

If you examine an animal such as the toad in figure 4.17A, you will find that its external and internal structures are arranged symmetrically on either side of the midline. Now imagine bisecting the animal in two so as to produce two halves which are mirror images of each other. There is only one plane through which this is possible, and that is vertically down the middle. Such an animal is described as **bilaterally symmetrical**. Most animals, including the human, are bilaterally symmetrical at least in their external features.

Now think of an animal like the sea anemone (*figure 4.17B*). In this case the various structures are arranged round a central point like the spokes of a wheel. To get two mirror image halves, this animal could be bisected in more or less any plane that passes through the centre. Such an animal is described as **radially symmetrical**. Radial symmetry is seen in a number of invertebrate animals.

There is no sharp dividing line between these two types of symmetry. For instance, sea anemones are radially symmetrical externally but partially bilaterally symmetrical inside. Higher plants have radially symmetrical stems and roots, but bilaterally symmetrical leaves; and flowers may be either radially or bilaterally symmetrical depending on the type of plant (*page 483*). Animals such as mammals and birds are bilaterally symmetrical externally but show some degree of asymmetry internally.

Radial symmetry is found mainly in sedentary or slow-moving organisms. Bilateral symmetry, on the other hand, is associated with locomotion in a particular direction. A bilaterally symmetrical animal has a definite front and back end, and a top side and bottom side. These are known as **anterior**, **posterior**, **dorsal** and **ventral** respectively (*figure 4.18*).

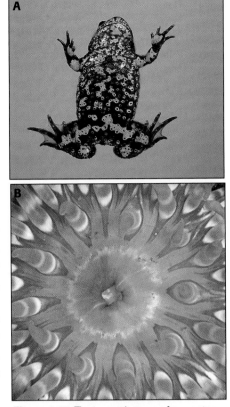

Figure 4.17 The two main types of symmetry found amongst organisms.
A Bilateral symmetry displayed here by the Oriental fire-bellied toad *Bombina orientalis*.
B Radial symmetry seen in the Dahlia sea anemone *Tealia felina*.

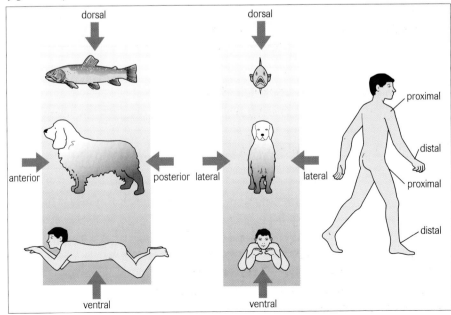

Figure 4.18 The principal terms used to describe the topography of animals.

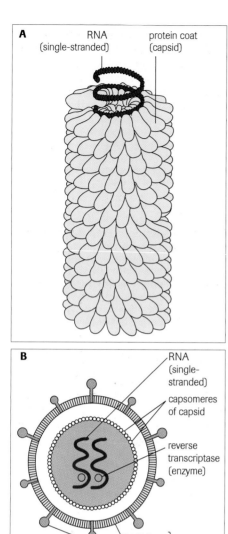

A   RNA   protein coat
(single-stranded) (capsid)

B
RNA
(single-
stranded)

capsomeres
of capsid

reverse
transcriptase
(enzyme)

lipid bilayer ⎱ envelope
glycoprotein ⎰

Figure 4.19 Structure of two well-known viruses.
A Part of a tobacco mosaic virus, the cause of mosaic disease in tobacco plants.
B Cross-section of human immunodeficiency virus (HIV) which causes AIDS. Proteins in the envelope, coded for by the viral RNA, enable the virus to bind to the host cell (*pages 328–9*).

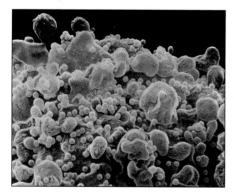

Figure 4.20 Human immunodeficiency viruses (HIV) (green), the causative agents of AIDS on the surface of a T-lymphocyte into which they inject their RNA. Magnification ×20 000.

Directional locomotion is associated with the development of a **head** at the leading end, with all the elaborations which that involves (*page 366*). Typically, such animals have **appendages** of one sort or another projecting from both sides of the body. Some or all of the appendages may be used as **limbs** for locomotion. The near end of an appendage (i.e. closest to the centre of the body) is described as **proximal**, the far end as **distal**.

4.5 Sub-cellular organisation: viruses and prions

Viruses

Viruses are the smallest objects to display some of the properties of life. Although they have no powers of active movement, they can reproduce, transmit characteristics to the next generation, and evolve by natural selection. However, they can only reproduce inside the cell of a living organism. In so doing they usually destroy the cell or at least affect its normal functioning. For this reason viruses are usually associated with disease. Smallpox, measles, poliomyelitis, AIDS and numerous plant diseases are all caused by viruses.

Viruses are so small that they can only be seen with the electron microscope. However, they were discovered before the electron microscope was invented by an ingenious experiment which is explained in the extension box opposite. Now, thanks to the electron microscope, many types of virus have been described, and chemical analysis of them has told us that they consist of little more than a coiled up strand of **nucleic acid** surrounded by a protein coat called the **capsid** (*figure 4.19*). The capsid is composed of protein subunits called **capsomeres**. The nucleic acid may be DNA or RNA depending on the type of virus. In some cases the nucleic acid is double-stranded; in other cases it is single-stranded. Certain RNA viruses contain an enzyme called **reverse transcriptase** which enables their RNA to be transcribed into DNA (*page 617*).

Viruses reproduce by entering, or injecting their nucleic acid into, living cells (*figure 4.20*). New viruses may be made inside the host cell, from which they are subsequently released either by the cell bursting open or in some cases by each virus budding off from the cell surface. When budding from the surface, a virus may take a small piece of the cell surface membrane with it, thereby acquiring a lipid–protein **envelope**.

Viruses are on the borderline between life and non-life: as someone has put it, you don't know whether to call them 'organules' or 'molecisms'. They are like living organisms in possessing replicable nucleic acid, but non-living in being unable to transfer energy and assimilate new materials without the participation of a living cell. Because they depend on *living* cells for their reproduction, they cannot be cultured on non-living material such as agar, as bacteria can. Instead they have to be grown on living material such as hens' eggs or tissue cultures (*page 72*).

Sir Peter Medawar has described a virus as 'simply a piece of bad news wrapped up in protein'. Certainly the damage they cause is out of all proportion to their size and structural simplicity.

Prions

Prions are just small glycoprotein molecules (*page 29*). They occur naturally in the brain, where their function is unknown, but occasionally they undergo a structural change which causes them to attack the brain tissue. Once a prion changes in this way it may cause other neighbouring prions to do so too, with the result that the brain is progressively destroyed.

Prions cause scrapie in sheep, bovine spongiform encephalopathy (BSE) in cattle ('mad cow disease') and Creutzfeldt–Jacob disease (CJD) in humans. All three diseases are fatal and the symptoms distressing.

Because sheep and cattle are part of the human food chain, intensive research has been going on into these disease-causing proteins, their mode of transmission and the possible ways they may be connected. Their scientific interest lies in the fact that they can attack cells without the participation of nucleic acid.

▶ Other aspects of viruses: classification, page 84; diseases caused by them, page 317; human immunodeficiency virus (HIV), pages 328, 506 and 743; structure and reproduction of bacteriophage, page 617; link with cancer, pages 467 and 618; as vectors in genetic engineering, page 630.

Extension

How viruses were discovered

Professor M.W. Beijerinck of Delft University, Holland, was a tyrannical head of department. He said that scientists should not get married, sacked an assistant for getting engaged and began his lectures with 'gentlemen and ladies'. But he was a superb research worker.

Beijerinck suspected that there might be disease-causing agents smaller than bacteria. To test this hypothesis he extracted some juice from a tobacco plant that had tobacco mosaic disease. He then passed the juice through a filter made of porous clay whose pores were too small to let through any known bacteria. When he applied the filtrate to a leaf of a healthy tobacco plant, he found that the plant developed tobacco mosaic disease.

Of course the filtrate might have been infective simply because it contained a toxic fluid produced by bacteria. So Beijerinck extracted and filtered some

juice from the second plant – the one he had infected – and applied it to a leaf of a third plant. This, too, developed the disease. Moreover, the filtered juice extracted from the third plant induced the disease in a fourth plant, and so on indefinitely. This suggested that the infective agent was multiplying, for otherwise it would have been rendered less and less effective by progressive dilution.

This was the first indication that disease-causing particles of sub-microscopic dimensions existed. Beijerinck himself thought he had obtained some kind of infectious fluid. He called it 'virus' which simply means poison.

That was at the beginning of the 20th century. It was not until the early 1930s that viruses were actually seen. Wendell Stanley, a young American scientist working at the Rockefeller Institute in New York, extracted, purified and crystallised the juice obtained from

diseased tobacco plants. The crystals proved to be highly infective when applied in solution to healthy tobacco plants. When the crystals were viewed in the then newly invented electron microscope, objects like the ones in the illustration were seen. These are tobacco mosaic viruses (TMV), the first type of virus to be isolated and characterised.

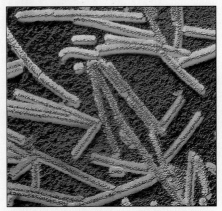

Tobacco mosaic viruses as seen in the electron microscope, magnified approximately 50 000 times.

Summary

1. Cells are massed together to form **tissues**, and different tissues are massed together to form **organs**. Different organs may be structurally and/or functionally united to form **organ systems**.

2. Animal tissues include **epithelium**, **connective tissue**, **skeletal tissue** (**cartilage and bone**), **blood**, **nerve tissue**, **muscle tissue** and **reproductive tissue**.

3. Plant tissues include **meristematic tissue**, **epidermis**, **parenchyma**, **collenchyma**, **sclerenchyma**, **vascular tissue** and **cork**.

4. The chief differences between animal and plant tissues (and between animals and plants in general) can be related to their different methods of nutrition.

5. In **unicellular organisms** all functions have to be carried out within one cell.

6. Most organisms are **multicellular**, and this carries with it certain advantages and disadvantages.

7. Some organisms, e.g. colonial animals and many types of flowering plants, are **modular organisms** composed of numerous similar parts (**modules**).

8. Organisms show various types of symmetry, the most common being **radial symmetry** and **bilateral symmetry**.

9. Terms used to describe the topography of animals include **anterior**, **posterior**, **dorsal**, **ventral** and **lateral**.

10. **Viruses** are sub-cellular particles of protein and nucleic acid, and are generally considered to be non-living. **Prions** are small protein molecules which are associated with certain diseases.

For general advice on these questions and advice on answering essay-type questions, see pages vii and viii.

1. The diagram of an electron micrograph shows some of the cells which form the lining of the mammalian small intestine.

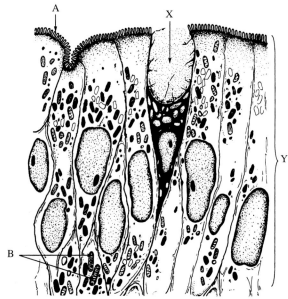

(a) What is the **general** name given to a tissue such as that labelled **Y**? (1)

(b) (i) Name the features labelled **A** and **B** in the diagram (2)

    (ii) Explain **fully** how A and B function in this tissue. (4)

(c) (i) Name the secretion labelled **X**. (1)

    (ii) State **two** functions of this secretion. (2)

(Total 10 marks)
WJEC 1997

2. The diagram below shows some cells from a plant tissue commonly used by humans.

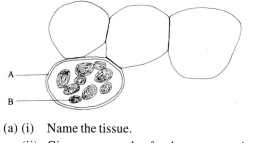

(a) (i) Name the tissue. (1)

    (ii) Give *one* example of a plant structure in which this tissue might be found. (1)

(b) Name the parts labelled A and B. (2)

(c) How is this tissue of importance to humans? (1)

(Total 5 marks)
London 1996

3. The diagrams below show *two* supporting tissues present in flowering plants.

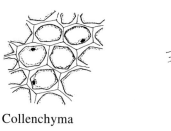

Collenchyma   Sclerenchyma

(a) Give *two* structural features shown in the diagram which are characteristic of collenchyma. (2)

(b) (i) Give *two* ways in which sclerenchyma differs from collenchyma. (2)

    (ii) Collenchyma is often present in the petiole and midrib of leaves. Suggest *two* reasons why collenchyma is more suitable than sclerenchyma for support in these locations. (2)

(c) Both tissues are shown in transverse section. Make a drawing of a sclerenchyma cell as it would appear in longitudinal section. (2)

(Total 8 marks)
London 1997

4. The diagram represents the structure of the human immunodeficiency virus (HIV).

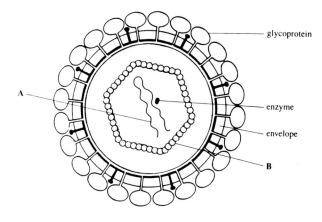

(a) Name (i) **A** and (ii) **B**. (2)

(b) Suggest how the lipid envelope of some viruses may assist entry into a cell. (1)

(c) One method of growing animal viruses is to inoculate them into susceptible animals. Give **two** other methods that can be used to grow animal viruses. (2)

(Total 5 marks)
NEAB 1996

Chapter 5

The principles of classification

It is estimated that there are at least 10 million, perhaps as many as 100 million, different kinds of organisms living on the Earth today, and an even greater number have become extinct. This great diversity has given rise to the branch of biology called **systematics**.

Systematics involves looking at the diversity of living organisms and the relationships between them. It embraces **taxonomy**, which is the science of naming an organism, and **phylogeny**, which is the grouping of organisms according to how recently they are believed to have diverged from a common ancestor.

Support

Why systematics is important

The Pinatubu people who live in the remote tropical forests of the Philippines can name and describe a large number of the many different organisms living there. They have names for at least 500 plants, about 100 birds, many of the mammals, snakes and insects and nearly 50 different fungi. They distinguish the different types of animals and plants on the basis of similarities and differences, and they can describe the habits of the animals and the plants with which they are associated.

Take the forest bats for instance: the Pinatubu people will tell you that the bat called litlit is found in bamboo clumps, whereas titidin is found on dry palm leaves, dikidik on the underside of wild banana leaves, and so on. These people have devised a system of classifying plants and animals in their surroundings which everyone agrees with and can use. There is an obvious practical use for this knowledge. These people depend on the natural environment for their food. In order to avoid mishaps they need to be able to tell each other which plants are edible and which are poisonous, and what to expect to find on each plant and behind each tree.

The Pinatubu people are not alone in devising a system of classifying the living things in their environment. Every culture has developed a taxonomy by which they can communicate to others about the organisms in their locality. Classifying things is a natural human activity which we acquire in early childhood, and indeed as the shelves of a supermarket demonstrate, it allows order to be brought out of chaos.

5.1 The taxonomic hierarchy

The basic unit of biological classification is the **species**. A species is a group of organisms which have numerous physical features in common and which are normally capable of interbreeding and producing viable offspring. Nowadays, biochemical, ecological, behavioural and life-cycle features are included with physical characteristics in helping to classify species.

Closely related species are grouped together into **genera** (singular: **genus**). Genera are grouped into **families**, families into **orders**, orders into **classes**, classes into **phyla** (singular: **phylum**) and phyla into **kingdoms**. (When classifying plants and bacteria, the term 'division' is sometimes used instead of phylum.) Intermediate categories are sometimes used: for example, a sub-phylum may be inserted between phylum and class, and sub-classes between class and order.

This ascending series of successively larger, more inclusive, groups makes up the **taxonomic hierarchy**. Each grouping of organisms within the hierarchy is called a **taxon** (plural: **taxa**) and each taxon has a rank and a name, for example class Mammalia or genus *Homo*.

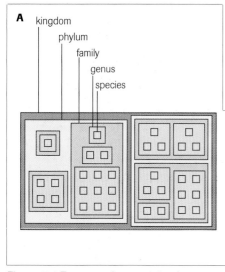

Figure 5.1 shows two ways of illustrating how the hierarchical arrangement of the taxa can be represented: a 'box-in-box' arrangement or a 'tree-like' arrangement (**dendrogram**). Table 5.1 shows how three well-known organisms fit into the system. The lowest three taxa (family, genus and species) are named according to strict internationally agreed rules. The names of the four highest taxa (kingdom, phylum, class and order) are often matters of opinion and are subject to the whims and fancies of individual taxonomists.

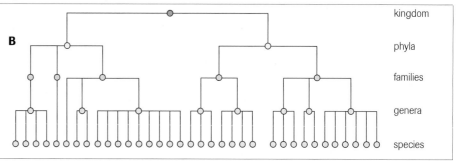

Figure 5.1 Two ways of representing the taxonomic hierarchy.
A box-in-box.
B dendrogram. Can you see how the 'box-in-box' relates to the dendrogram?

Table 5.1 In this table you can see how three well-known organisms are classified, one from the plant kingdom and two from the animal kingdom.

Taxonomic rank	Plant example	Animal examples	
Kingdom	Plantae	Animalia	Animalia
Phylum	Angiospermaphyta	Annelida	Chordata
Class	Dicotyledoneae	Oligochaeta	Mammalia
Order	Ranales	Terricolae	Primates
Family	Ranunculacae	Lumbricidae	Hominidae
Genus	*Ranunculus*	*Lumbricus*	*Homo*
Species	*R. acris*	*L. terrestris*	*H. sapiens*
Common name	meadow buttercup	earthworm	human

Figure 5.2 This illustration shows how humans are classified. As one proceeds down the taxonomic hierarchy from kingdom to species, the number of animals in each group decreases and the similarities between them increase. 'Ape-man' and 'primitive human' are popular terms covering a number of extinct forms known only from their fossil remains.

As you go down the hierarchy, the number of different organisms in each taxon usually decreases and the similarities between them increase (*figure 5.2*). Thus a phylum contains a large number of organisms which share several fundamental features but display quite a wide range of form. At the bottom of the hierarchy the differences within taxa are far less pronounced. This is particularly true of the species rank; indeed the various species in a genus may be so similar that only an expert can tell them apart (*figure 5.3*).

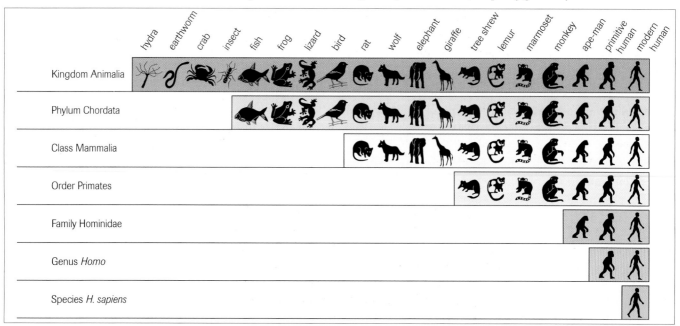

5.2 Naming organisms

It is customary to name an organism by its genus and species. This is known as the **binomial system** and was first introduced in 1753 by the Swedish naturalist Carolus Linnaeus. The **generic name** is written first and begins with a capital letter, followed by the **specific name** which begins with a small letter. Both names are written in italics or underlined. Closely related organisms, lion and tiger for example, have the same generic name (in this case *Panthera*) but different specific names. The lion is *Panthera leo* and the tiger is *Panthera tigris*.

If the organism belongs to a sub-species or variety, a further name is added. The British herring gull, for example, is *Larus argentatus argentatus*, and the American herring gull is *Larus argentatus smithsonianus* – both are sub-species of the same species.

When an organism's name has been referred to once in full it is acceptable to abbreviate the genus to its capital letter in all later references, for example the lion can now be referred to as *P. leo* and the tiger as *P. tigris*.

These **scientific names** are essential whenever precise identification is required, and they enable scientists to communicate accurately with each other. They are used the world over and have the merit that everyone knows exactly which organism is being referred to. However, in everyday language people generally use **common names**, such as the ones given at the foot of table 5.1. Common names, though, can be confusing (*support box below*).

Figure 5.3 Two species of the same genus, *Lysandra*, which are difficult to distinguish. *Top L. bellorgus* (Adonis blue butterfly) and *bottom L. cordon* (chalk blue butterfly).

Support

Why common names can be confusing

The trouble with common names is that a particular organism may be known by several different common names, and sometimes the same common name is used for two quite different organisms. For example, *Caltha palustris*, a flowering plant in the buttercup family Ranunculaceae, is known by at least 90 different names in Britain alone, including marsh marigold, king cup, golden cup, brave celandine, horse blob, butter-flower, mare blob, May blob, May bubbles, Mary-bud, grandfather's button, policeman's button, soldier's button, and when it grows alongside other buttercups, the mixture is called publicans and sinners. In parts of America it is called a cowslip, a name which in Europe is applied to *Primula veris*, a member of a completely different family, the Primulaceae.

Similarly, the British robin, *Erithacus rubecula* belongs to a totally different genus from the American robin, *Turdus migratorius* (*illustration*). The latter's scientific name tells us that it is more closely related to the British blackbird whose

scientific name is *Turdus merula*.

Top The British robin (*Erithacus rubecula*).
Bottom The American robin (*Turdus migratorius*).

Nowhere are precise names more important than in agriculture and medicine. For example, attempts have been made to develop new improved varieties of wheat by crossing wild forms. In plant breeding programmes of this kind it is essential to know the exact identity of the parent varieties. Similarly, if pests are to be controlled, whether by chemical or biological means, it is necessary to know precisely the organisms involved. And in medicine it is no use developing drugs and antibiotics unless you know which particular pathogenic organisms they are intended to destroy.

5.3 Different ways of classifying organisms

Suppose you are faced with a group of organisms. How do you classify them into groups and sub-groups?

One way is to place the organisms into groups according to the presence or absence of certain fundamental characteristics. Thus all land-living vertebrates are grouped together because they have a pentadactyl limb (*page 726*); they are subdivided into amphibians, reptiles, birds and mammals because each has certain features which are not found in any of the other groups.

The aim of such a classification is to show the evolutionary relationships between groups. This evolutionary (**phylogenetic**) approach to classification is discussed in Chapter 43. The important point to note at this moment is that in making the classification, particular weight is usually given to those features which are believed to be of evolutionary significance. In recent years, disenchantment with this idea has led to the growth of alternative approaches to taxonomy. We will look briefly at two other methods.

Numerical taxonomy and cladistics

Numerical taxonomy uses mathematical procedures and its aim is to construct precise unambiguous classifications. It is often thought of as a modern method of classification. In fact it was tried over 200 years ago. A French taxonomist called Adanson working in Senegal, could not fit all the species of plants he found into existing classifications, so he tried constructing his own. He did this by comparing as many characteristics as possible and considering them all to be of equal importance. Adanson's method of classification proved impractical because it involved comparing more characteristics than the human mind could cope with. Imagine classifying just a few species on the basis of, say, 100 different characteristics. However, with the advent of computers this method of classification has developed considerably.

Numerical classification uses equally weighted, observable features and is not based on any preconceived ideas about ancestry. However, some biologists feel that classification *should* be based on ancestry, and in particular on the points at which different groups have diverged from each other. This method of taxonomy is called **cladistics**, which is derived from the Greek word for 'branch'. Because branching of groups from a common ancestor to form distinct species is a central feature of evolutionary theory, cladists argue that this type of classification reflects evolutionary relationships and is therefore a *natural* classification.

Characteristics used in classification

When classifying a group of organisms, we have to choose certain features on which to base the classification. In doing this it is essential to select characteristics which are clear-cut and consistent. It is not much use selecting the characteristic 'short or long antennae' if individual specimens have antennae with all sorts of intermediate lengths. It is better to use the presence or absence of a particular structure, though even then problems can arise if in the course of evolution the structure has been severely reduced in some members of the group. Countable characteristics are often useful, particularly at the species level – for example, the number of spots on the wings of a butterfly or the number of stamens in a flower. However, one must avoid using features which are affected by the environment and may vary according to local conditions.

Nowadays all sorts of characteristics are used in classifying organisms. The main ones are as follows:

- **Gross structure** By gross structure we mean features that can be seen without the aid of a microscope. For example, chordates are classified into fish, amphibians, reptiles, birds and mammals on the basis of their skin and various other external and internal features, and deciduous trees can be classified according to the shapes of their leaves.

Microscopic structure Although gross structure is a convenient basis for classification, sometimes microscopic features have to be used. For example, studies with the transmission electron microscope have revealed that bacteria and what used to be called blue-green algae have a unique type of cell structure which is different from that of all other organisms. In this case microscopic observation of cell structure has been used to make a fundamental split in the classification of living things between prokaryotes and eukaryotes (*page 43*). Microscopic structure can be useful at the generic and species levels too. For example, the number of chromosomes can enable entomologists to classify locusts and grasshoppers, and the surface features of seeds and pollen grains, as revealed by the scanning electron microscope, can be used in classifying flowering plants (*figure 5.4*). Indeed, this sort of technique can show up differences between species or sub-species which are identical in every other respect.

Chemical constitution Sometimes it is impossible to classify organisms using structural criteria, even cellular ones, so one resorts to comparing the chemical substances which they contain. This is particularly useful when classifying organisms like bacteria, which may all look alike and have an identical cellular structure. Using techniques such as chromatography and electrophoresis, it is possible to compare the amino-acid sequence in the proteins of different organisms, or in the order of bases in their DNA. This is useful, not only in classifying organisms, but is indispensable when trying to establish evolutionary relationships (*page 729*).

Other characteristics used in classifying organisms include their immunological reactions, the types of symbionts with which they may associate, and various behavioural features such as responses to stimuli, nest-building or courtship.

Obviously characteristics which are used in classification can also be used for identification. If, for example, an animal is found to have a notochord, we know it must be a chordate, and the surface features of pollen grains can tell us the precise species or sub-species that a plant belongs to.

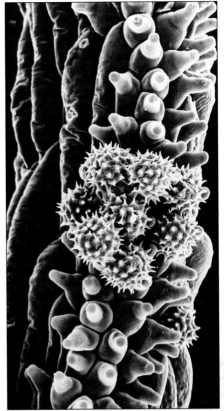

Figure 5.4 Pollen grains adhering to the stigma of a daisy, seen in the scanning electron microscope magnified approximately 1000 times. Notice the elaborate features of both the pollen grains and the stigma. Features like these help in the classification and identification of flowering plants at the species and sub-species level.

5.4 How many kingdoms?

One of the most difficult decisions to make in systematics is how to divide living organisms into kingdoms.

Until quite recently, organisms were divided into two kingdoms: the **animal kingdom**, which contained mainly motile organisms which fed heterotrophically, and the **plant kingdom** which contained mainly static organisms which fed autotrophically by photosynthesis. Unicellular heterotrophs (protozoans) were put in the animal kingdom, and unicellular autotrophs were put in the plant kingdom with the algae. Fungi and bacteria were attached to the plant kingdom mainly on the grounds that, like plants, they possessed a rigid cell wall.

There are a number of problems with having only two kingdoms. The first concerns unicellular flagellates like *Euglena* and its relatives (*figure 5.5*). These were put with the protozoans in the animal kingdom. However, some euglenoids, including *Euglena* itself, contain chlorophyll, feed autotrophically by photosynthesis and also swim and move in relation to light stimuli. Moreover, some flagellates can feed either autotrophically or heterotrophically depending on the conditions. With only two kingdoms, we have to contend with the fact that these organisms can, in effect, hop from one kingdom to the other!

Another problem concerns the fungi. Fungi are really very different from green plants. They lack chlorophyll and feed heterotrophically by an absorptive method, and their cellular structure differs from that of plants in several ways.

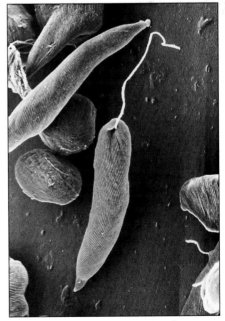

Figure 5.5 A spectacular scanning electron micrograph of *Euglena* showing the flagellum by which this unicellular organism swims through the water in which it lives. Magnification ×600.

▶ Differences between prokaryotic and eukaryotic cells, page 43

A third problem concerns bacteria. The electron microscope has revealed that bacteria and cyanobacteria (formerly called blue-green algae) have a simple **prokaryotic** cell structure (*page 43*). So bacteria and cyanobacteria appear to be similar to each other, and markedly different from all other organisms which are eukaryotic. Indeed, if living organisms have to be divided into just two kingdoms a division into prokaryotes and eukaryotes would probably be best. However, although it may be satisfactory for all prokaryotes to be in one kingdom, the rest would form a very large and unwieldy group.

The five kingdom system

To solve the problems outlined above, a number of different schemes of classification have been proposed. All have more than two kingdoms, and one has 18! The scheme that has gained most support was proposed in 1959 by an American biologist, Robert H. Whittaker. He based his classification on two main criteria: the level of organisation of the organisms, and their methods of nutrition. He recognised three levels of organisation: prokaryotes, unicellular eukaryotes and multicellular eukaryotes. The methods of nutrition were: heterotrophic (which could be subdivided into ingestive and absorptive) and photosynthetic. On this basis, Whittaker proposed the following five kingdoms:

- **Animal kingdom:** multicellular eukaryotes which feed heterotrophically by ingestion.
- **Plant kingdom:** multicellular eukaryotes which feed by photosynthesis.
- **Fungus kingdom:** multicellular eukaryotes which feed heterotrophically by absorption.
- **Protist kingdom:** unicellular eukaryotes which feed by a variety of different methods.
- **Prokaryote kingdom:** prokaryotes which feed by a variety of different methods.

Although Whittaker's scheme received widespread approval, it had one major snag. This relates to the protist kingdom which contained all unicellular organisms, including those that formerly had been regarded as animals (protozoans) and those that had been regarded as plants (unicellular algae). This in itself was no bad thing – indeed it solved the problem of awkward customers like *Euglena*. The problem was that it meant putting the unicellular and multicellular algae into two separate kingdoms. This was unfortunate because they share many common features. Indeed, some of the simpler multicellular algae are little more than aggregates of the unicellular forms. To this may be added the fact that the algae as a whole have rather little in common with the rest of the plant kingdom.

This led two other American biologists, Lynn Margulis and Karlene Schwartz, to put forward a modification of Whittaker's scheme. They suggested that the multicellular algae should be removed from the plant kingdom and placed, along with all unicellular organisms, in a new kingdom called the **protoctist kingdom** which would replace Whittaker's protist kingdom. This makes the plant kingdom a more natural group, and it brings the multicellular algae close to their unicellular relatives. However, it results in the protoctist kingdom being something of a 'ragbag' containing a wide range of unicellular and multicellular organisms. Indeed, it has been described as the kingdom that contains all those organisms which cannot be fitted into any of the other kingdoms!

In grouping organisms into kingdoms there are bound to be anomalies. The important thing is that the anomalies should be as few as possible and the classification consistent. Margulis and Schwartz's five-kingdom scheme offered this up to a point, and has therefore been commended until a more rational system is proposed. It is summarised in figure 5.6 and covered in detail in the next chapter.

Extension

The problem of viruses

Viruses are not included in the five kingdoms. The reason centres on the controversy, which has been going on ever since they were discovered, as to whether or not they should be regarded as living. A virus consists simply of nucleic acid surrounded by a protein coat, and it can only reproduce inside a living cell. For these reasons most biologists regard viruses, not as living organisms, but as aggregations of molecules similar to those normally found in living cells. That having been said, some viruses, such as the bacteriophage described on page 617, are surprisingly elaborate. This, together with the way they behave and reproduce, makes it difficult not to think of them as living. Is this yet another impossible conundrum? Not really. Just as there are awkward organisms that sit on the borderline between different kingdoms, so viruses appear to be on the borderline between the living and non-living worlds. They could probably form another kingdom if scientists felt like creating one. Certainly a great deal of time and effort has been spent classifying them. This is based on their physical and chemical properties and the way they reproduce, and is essential in diagnosing the many diseases which they cause.

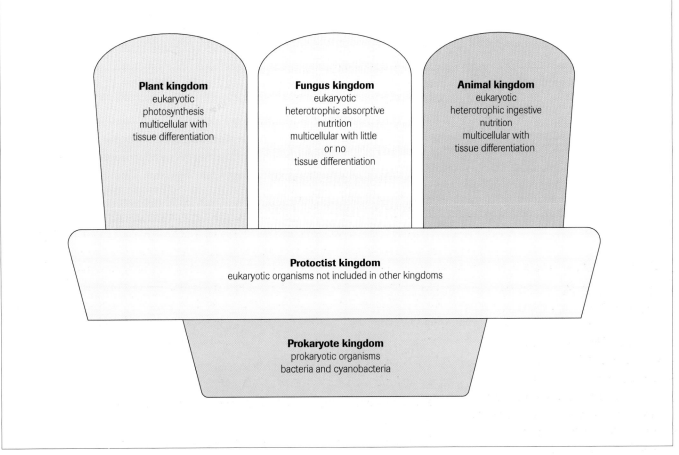

Figure 5.6 The five kingdom system of Margulis and Schwartz.

Summary

1. The number of species of living organisms which have been discovered runs into millions, so a system of classification is essential.

2. Systematics is the study of biological classification. It involves looking at the diversity of living organisms and the relationships between them. It embraces **taxonomy** which is the science of naming organisms.

3. A **species** is the smallest group in the taxonomic hierarchy and is defined as a group of organisms which have numerous physical and other features in common and are normally capable of interbreeding to produce fertile offspring.

4. Species are grouped together into **genera**, genera into **families**, families into **orders**, orders into **classes**, classes into **phyla**, and phyla into **kingdoms**.

5. As one progresses up the hierarchy the range of organisms within each group usually increases and the similarities between them decrease.

6. An organism's scientific name is composed of the name of the genus followed by the name of the species, e.g. *Homo sapiens*. This is called the **binomial system**.

7. Scientific names are essential where precise identification is required, e.g. in agriculture and medicine.

8. Phylogenetic systematics is based on supposed evolutionary affinities; **numerical taxonomy** uses equally weighted observable features; **cladistics** is based on the points at which different groups have diverged from each other. Cladists argue that this type of classification reflects evolutionary relationships and is therefore a *natural* classification.

9. A **five kingdom system** is used for the classification of living organisms. The kingdoms are **Prokaryotae**, **Protoctista**, **Fungi**, **Plantae** and **Animalia**.

10. Viruses are not included in the five kingdom system since many biologists consider them to be non-living. They could form a sixth kingdom.

For general advice on these questions and advice on answering essay-type questions, see pages vii and viii.

1. The classification system for living organisms is a hierarchy of phylogenetic groupings.

(a) Explain what is meant, in this context, by

   (i)   a hierarchy;   (2)

   (ii)   phylogenetic.   (2)

(b) Copy and complete the table to show the classification of the ocelot.

Kingdom	Animalia
	Chordata
Class	Mammalia
	Carnivora
Family	Felidae
	Leopardus
	pardalis

                                    (2)

                           (Total 6 marks)

                                NEAB 1997

2. The diagram shows the way in which four species of monkey are classified.

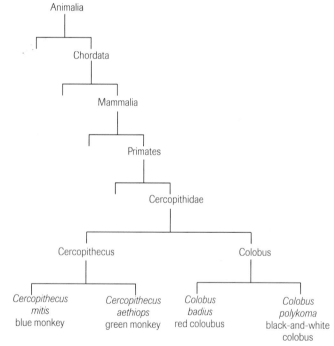

(a) This system of classification is described as hierarchical. Explain what is meant by a hierarchical classification.

                                    (1)

(b) (i)   To which genus does the green monkey belong? (1)

    (ii)   To which family does the red colobus belong?   (1)

(c) What does the information in the diagram suggest about the similarities and differences in the genes of these four species of monkey?   (2)

                             (Total 5 marks)

                              NEAB 1998

3. The box diagram below represents a classification hierarchy of the plant kingdom. Study the diagram and label boxes A to D using the most appropriate words from the following list: Class, Division, Family, Order, Phylum.

(a)

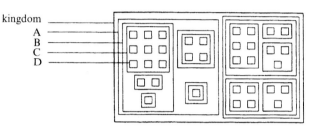

                                    (2)

(b) What is a species?   (2)

                             (Total 4 marks)

                              CCEA 1998

Chapter 6

The diversity of life

In the last chapter the scene was set for classifying living organisms into five kingdoms. In this chapter the general features of each kingdom are described. Only the major phyla within each kingdom are considered, and in most cases the classification does not go below the rank of class in the taxonomic hierarchy. Representative genera are used to illustrate the characteristics of each group, especially those that have an impact on human life.

6.1 Kingdom Prokaryotae

The members of this group have a **simple cell structure** typical of prokaryotic cells. Yet it is a very diverse group with varied methods of nutrition: autotrophic by photosynthesis and chemosynthesis, and heterotrophic by absorption. They all reproduce asexually but many reproduce sexually as well.

▶ Structure of prokaryotic cells, page 43

Extension

The classification of prokaryotes

The classification of prokaryotes has undergone a major revision in recent years. The evidence has come from the use of molecular techniques to sequence genes. As a result it is now recognised that prokaryotes are made up of two fundamentally different groups of organisms.

- **Archaea** (formerly **Archaebacteria**)
- **Bacteria**.

Present thinking is that Archaea are more closely related to eukaryotes than they are to bacteria even though they have superficial similarities such as the absence of a membrane-bound nucleus. There are good grounds therefore for giving Bacteria and Archaea kingdom rank.

Archaea

Archaea include a number of organisms which grow under extreme conditions such as extremely high salt concentrations (**halophiles**), very high temperatures (**hyper-thermophiles**) and in environments of very high or very low pH. As a result of this they have been nicknamed 'extremophiles' (lovers of extremes). Surveys of extreme environments, such as hot springs, continually reveal 'new' organisms. The group also includes the organisms that produce methane from hydrogen and carbon dioxide in the guts of ruminants, causing them to belch and break wind. On one spectacular occasion a farm in Holland was severely damaged by fire when a vet tested the gas from the anus of an uncomfortable cow with a lighted match. The cow was unhurt!

Bacteria

This is a very diverse group which many modern classifications divide into at least 15 phyla. Bacteria are classified on the basis of criteria which do not necessarily reflect evolutionary relationships. The technique of DNA sequencing may eventually provide a classification which reflects their true relationships. Until then, the classification tends to be one of convenience.

The characteristics used are both structural and metabolic. The main ones are as follows.

Classification by shape

The most obvious structural feature of bacteria is their shape. There are two basic shapes:

■ **Spherical** These are called cocci. Cocci occur singly or in pairs or they may form chains or be in clusters.

■ **Rod-shaped** These too occur singly or in chains. They may be straight, curved or spiral and may or may not have flagella. When flagella are present they lack the 9+2 structure.

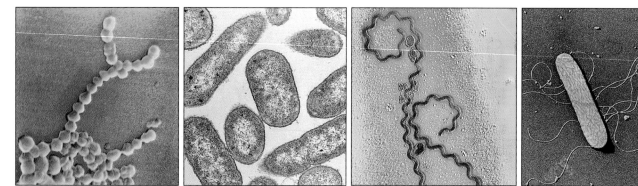

Figure 6.1 Scanning electron micrograph (SEM) of *Streptococcus*, a spherical bacterium. In this species the cocci are forming a chain. Magnification ×3000.

Figure 6.2 Transmission electron micrograph (TEM) of the straight, rod-shaped bacterium *Escherichia coli*. This is a Gram negative bacterium always found in the human gut. Magnification ×20 000.

Figure 6.3 SEM of a species of *Leptospira*. This is one of a group of bacteria which are in the form of long, thin spirals. They are called spirochaetes and include serious pathogens such as the bacteria which cause syphilis. Magnification ×4000.

Figure 6.4 TEM of a flagellated bacterium, *Listeria monocytogenes*, which causes the disease listeria. Magnification ×15 000.

Classification by staining reaction

The terms **Gram negative** or **Gram positive** are often used to describe bacteria. These terms refer to Gram's stain, named after a Danish doctor, Hans Christian Gram. Gram's stain is used universally to distinguish between different types of bacterial cell wall. Those which stain purple are called Gram positive while those which stain pink are Gram negative.

Classification by methods of nutrition

One of the most useful ways of classifying bacteria is based on their methods of nutrition, some of which are unique to bacteria.

■ **Autotrophic bacteria** build up their own organic food by photosynthesis or chemosynthesis. They are divided into two groups:

Photosynthetic bacteria use the energy of sunlight to convert carbon dioxide into carbohydrate. The process is basically similar to photosynthesis in plants but the details are different. Sulphur bacteria are an example.

Chemosynthetic bacteria do not require sunlight and use simple energy sources such as methane, ammonia or hydrogen sulphide. Nitrifying bacteria in the soil belong to this group.

■ **Heterotrophic bacteria** feed like animals and fungi on ready-made organic food. Some are parasites, others are saprobionts (*page 181*). The remarkable feature of the latter is the variety of organic compounds they can use as food. This is why they play such an important role in decomposition, and why only a few organic materials such as certain plastics are non-biodegradable.

Classification by methods of respiration

Another aspect of metabolism which can be used in the classification of bacteria is their need for oxygen in respiration.

- **Aerobes** require oxygen for respiration.
- **Anaerobes** respire without oxygen.

Some bacteria are killed in the presence of oxygen – they are called **obligate anaerobes**. Others use oxygen but can respire without it – they are called **facultative anaerobes**. Bacteria which can only survive with oxygen present are **obligate aerobes**.

Classification by biochemical characteristics

Use of only one of the characteristics just described does not result in a satisfactory classification of bacteria. If cell shape alone is used, each group will be made up of bacteria which look alike but exhibit very varied metabolic characteristics. If metabolic characteristics alone are used, all the different shapes may occur in one group.

The only way to achieve a more definitive classification of this group is to use biochemical characteristics, and already this approach has resulted in a substantial revision of their classification.

Extension

Cyanobacteria – the 'blue-greens'

Until the 1960s, cyanobacteria were called blue-green algae and were included in the plant kingdom. This was because, like plants, they contain chlorophyll and carry out photosynthesis. However, it was then discovered that they have a prokaryotic cell structure, so they are now included in the prokaryote kingdom with bacteria. They differ from plants in other ways too. For example, they possess chlorophyll *a* only, and although they carry out both photosynthesis and respiration they cannot do both at the same time, so they only respire in the dark.

The 'cyano-' refers to the characteristic blue-green appearance of many members of this group, which is caused by the presence of a blue pigment called **phycocyanin**. They may also contain a red pigment called **phycoerythrin**. They are responsible for the blue-green 'bloom' seen on the surface of ponds. **Gas vacuoles**, which they often contain, help them float on the surface of the water (*illustration 1*).

There are two sorts of cyanobacteria: those with round cells (cocci) and filamentous forms (*illustration 2*).

Illustration 1 Cyanobacteria forming a 'bloom' on the surface of a lake, giving the water the appearance of pea soup.

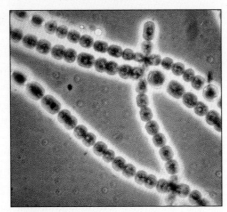

Illustration 2 Light micrograph of *Anabaena*, a filamentous cyanobacterium, showing the arrangement of single cells into filaments surrounded by a gelatinous sheath (×500).

Many cyanobacteria are able to fix atmospheric nitrogen and this, together with their ability to photosynthesise, means that their nutritional requirements are simple (mainly carbon dioxide and nitrogen from the air plus some minerals). For this reason they are often the first colonisers of moist soils.

Cyanobacteria are widespread, occurring in warm moist soils, and in marine and freshwater environments. Because of their ability to photosynthesise, they often form the basis of food chains and this, together with their nitrogen-fixing activity, means they fill an important role in many natural communities.

Role of cyanobacteria in natural communities, page 652

Bacteria and human life

Whatever the uncertainties of the classification of this diverse group, their impact in natural communities and on our lives is not in question. Bacteria are abundant everywhere, occurring in extremes of temperature from hot springs to freezing lakes. They are found in vast numbers in the soil and in our bodies. They are responsible for a great many processes which humans have exploited for many years and which form the basis of biotechnology.

Far too often, bacteria are given a negative image as troublemakers. But their positive value on this planet far outweighs the harm they do. The negative image arises from the fact that many of them cause **diseases** of humans and other organisms. These diseases include pneumonia, tetanus, cholera and syphilis in humans, anthrax in sheep, and plant diseases such as peach blight and carrot rot. Several bacteria are associated with food poisoning. Certain species of *Salmonella* cause mild food poisoning, while *Clostridium botulinum* causes a sometimes fatal form of food poisoning known as botulism. This can happen if sterilisation is not adequate when foods are canned and heat-resistant spores of the bacteria survive. *C. botulinum*

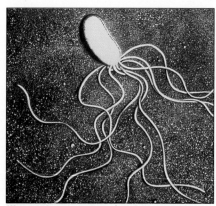

Illustration 1 A species of *Salmonella*, a common cause of food poisoning, magnified ×15 000.

▶ Food poisoning, page 318

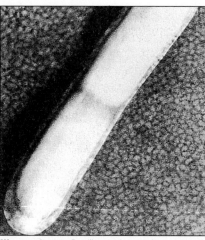

Illustration 2 *Bacillus anthracis*, the cause of anthrax, magnified ×20 000.

produces the most toxic substance known.

Against this must be balanced the fact that many bacteria are the means of *curing* diseases. **Antibiotics** such as streptomycin and chloromycetin, to name but two of the 50 or so available, are produced by bacteria, although the best-known antibiotic – penicillin – comes from a fungus.

Bacteria also play a vital part in **agriculture** because of their role in decomposition (decay) and recycling nutrients. It has been suggested that without nitrogen-fixing bacteria we would starve as a result of protein deficiency.

Sulphur bacteria are responsible for the huge deposits of **sulphur** found in some parts of the world. Bacteria are also essential in **sewage treatment**.

The **food industry** depends on bacteria to produce certain cheeses, yoghurts and other fermented foods such as sauerkraut.

Although other organisms may be involved in decomposition, if a substance is biodegradable it is almost certainly because there is a bacterium which can use it as a source of energy. More recently bacteria have come to play an important role in recombinant DNA research and **genetic engineering** (*page 629*).

▶ Eukaryotic cell structure, page 44

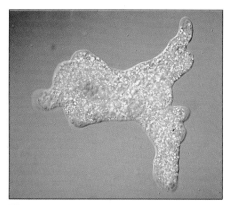

Figure 6.5 Light micrograph of a rhizopod, *Chaos carolinense*, just after ingesting a colonial flagellate, *Pandorina*, the green oval on the left. Magnification ×50.

6.2 Kingdom Protoctista

This kingdom contains all the eukaryotic organisms which are not fungi, plants or animals. It is rather a 'ragbag' of a kingdom, containing organisms which do not fit elsewhere. Their cellular structure is **eukaryotic** and they may be **unicellular** or **multicellular**. They are divided into about 30 phyla but only nine are listed here. These are the ones that you are most likely to encounter during your biology course.

Phylum Rhizopoda (rhizopods)

These are unicellular and have **pseudopodia** ('false feet') which are extensions of the flexible plasma membrane produced by flowing of the cytoplasm. Pseudopodia are used both for movement and to engulf food particles by phagocytosis. Their nutrition is heterotrophic and they reproduce asexually.

The most famous member of this group is *Amoeba proteus* but there are about 16 000 species showing great variety of form. Some are parasitic, for example *Entamoeba hystolytica* which causes amoebic dysentery.

Phylum Ciliophora (ciliates)

Ciliates are unicellular, heterotrophic organisms which move by the beating of numerous **cilia** which have the 9+2 structure. The cilia are also used for collecting food. Nearly all ciliates possess two nuclei – a large **macronucleus** and a smaller **micronucleus**. The micronucleus is used in a sexual process called **conjugation**. The group also reproduces asexually.

Ciliates are very common in freshwater and marine environments. *Paramecium* is probably the most familiar example (*page 74*). However, the group shows a wide range of form which includes sedentary stalked species.

Phylum Zoomastigina (flagellates)

These are unicellular, heterotrophic organisms which have one or more **flagella** for locomotion. The flagella, in keeping with those of all the eukaryotes, has a characteristic **9+2 structure** (*page 54*). They reproduce asexually or sexually. They may be free-living or parasitic. This group includes the genus *Trypanosoma* which causes African sleeping sickness and is transmitted by the tsetse fly.

Phylum Euglenophyta

Most of this group are unicellular and many are photosynthetic with chloroplasts containing chlorophylls *a* and *b*. Some are heterotrophic, lacking chloroplasts, and even the autotrophic ones can be heterotrophic at times. They move by using one of two large, conspicuous **flagella**, but they can also change their shape because their outer covering, called the **pellicle**, is made of a flexible protein. They reproduce asexually. They are very common in aquatic environments and the group includes colonial and parasitic forms. *Euglena* is a common genus in this group.

Some recent classifications include *Trypanosoma* amd *Euglena* in a single phylum called Discomitochondria. It is a diverse group, the members of which share the same ribosomal RNA sequences and have mitochondria with discoid cristae.

Phylum Apicomplexa (sporozoans)

All the members of this group are **spore-forming parasites** of animals. They are unicellular and heterotrophic and have **no locomotory structures**. They frequently have **complex life cycles** which involve several animal hosts, both invertebrate and vertebrate. They reproduce sexually and asexually.

The most familiar examples of this phylum are the malarial parasites (*Plasmodium* spp.) which are transmitted by the female anopheline mosquito (*page 708*).

Phylum Oomycota (oomycetes)

The oomycetes are fungus-like protoctists and may be parasites or saprobionts. Traditionally they have been classified with the Fungi and they resemble fungi in their mode of nutrition. Thread-like hyphae which secrete enzymes grow into the host's tissues which are digested and the soluble nutrients absorbed. Unlike fungi, the hyphae have cellulose walls, and sexual reproduction is by fertilisation between male and female gamete-like structures (**gametangia**) which never bear flagella. They also reproduce asexually by **spores** which, unlike fungal spores, have flagella.

The phylum includes *Pythium*, which causes 'damping off' of seedlings and *Peronospora*, a mildew which grows on grapes and various other plants. The most famous example is *Phytophthora infestans* which causes late blight of potatoes. This was responsible for the Irish potato famine in the 19th century (*page 707*).

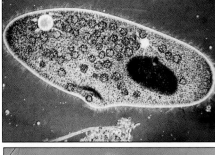
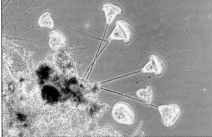

Figure 6.6 *Top* Light micrograph of the free-swimming ciliate *Paramecium caudatum*. Magnification ×100.
Bottom Light micrograph, in phase-contrast illumination, of several *Vorticella*, a sedentary stalked ciliate, shown here attached to a green alga. Magnification ×100.

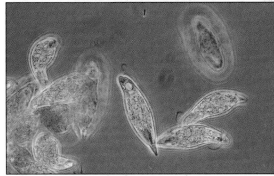

Figure 6.7 Light micrograph of *Euglena gracilis*. Magnification ×90.

Figure 6.8 Mildew, caused by an oomycete, on the surface of oak leaves.

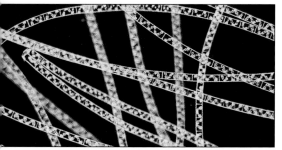

Figure 6.9 The filamentous green alga, *Spirogyra*, showing the spiral chloroplast. Magnification ×30.

Phylum Chlorophyta (green algae)

Green algae have many features in common with plants. They are **photosynthetic** and contain chlorophylls *a* and *b* as well as carotenes and xanthophylls. They have **cellulose** cell walls and store starch. They are mostly aquatic and include unicellular, colonial, filamentous and multicellular forms. They usually reproduce sexually and exhibit a wide variety of life cycles. Their spores and gametes usually have **two flagella**, though some like *Spirogyra* reproduce by conjugation and do not have flagella.

Other examples of this large and diverse group are the unicellular *Chlorella*, *Chlamydomonas* and *Acetabularia*, the colonial *Volvox*, and the multicellular green seaweed *Ulva* (sea lettuce).

Figure 6.10 Green, red and brown algae growing on a sea shore: brown serrated wrack, *Fucus serratus* (*top left*); green sea lettuce, *Ulva* sp. (*centre*); thin red alga, *Dumontia incrassata* (*centre*).

Phylum Rhodophyta (red algae)

The red algae are **multicellular** and mostly marine, being common inhabitants of rocky shores. They contain chlorophyll *a* and carry out **photosynthesis**. They also contain the red pigment **phycoerythrin** and the blue pigment **phycocyanin** of which the red predominates – hence their red colour. Reproduction is sexual, and their life cycles are complex although at no stage are flagella present.

They may be branched filaments or flattened sheets of cells. Sometimes they are encrusted with deposits of calcium carbonate. Agar, the jelly-like substance on which microorganisms are grown in the laboratory, is extracted from members of this group and some, called dulse, are eaten whole.

Phylum Phaeopthyta (brown algae)

The brown seaweeds are the largest protoctists. They are obvious on intertidal rocky shores and include all the wracks and kelps. They are all **multicellular** and show considerable cell differentiation. They reproduce sexually and many have alternation of haploid and diploid generations in their life cycles (*see page 475*). They carry out photosynthesis and contain chlorophyll pigments *a* and *c* (but never *b*). In addition they contain the brown pigment **fucoxanthin** which is responsible for their brown colour.

Various extracts from brown seaweeds are used in the manufacture of creams and ice cream. The wracks are also a source of iodine.

6.3 Kingdom Fungi

Fungi are **multicellular eukaryotes**. They are usually organised into a network (**mycelium**) of thread-like, multinucleate **hyphae** which sometimes have cross walls (**septa**). Their cell walls are not made of cellulose but usually contain **chitin**. There are no plastids and they **do not possess chlorophyll**. Their nutrition is **heterotrophic by absorption**. Some, including so-called 'moulds', are saprobionts; others are parasites. They reproduce by means of **spores** although most have a sexual method of reproduction (**conjugation**) as well. There are **no flagella** at any stage of the life cycle.

Many fungi cause diseases, especially of plants, and some produce powerful poisons. Some species form close associations with the roots of certain plants, particularly trees, where they seem to be essential for the absorption of nutrients. These are called **mycorrhizae** and are important in the forestry industry. The well-known antibiotic, penicillin, is obtained from the fungus *Penicillium chrysogenum*. Yeasts are used in the brewing and baking industries (*page 148*).

Phylum Zygomycota (zygomycetes)

This phylum takes its name from the **zygospore** which is produced when sexual reproduction by conjugation takes place. Certain hyphae function as gametangia and grow towards each other until they touch and join. Nuclei from both threads mingle and a thick-walled zygospore forms, inside which the nuclei fuse. Asexual reproduction also occurs by means of spores which develop inside **sporangia**. The hyphae do not have cross walls – in other words they are **non-septate**. Examples of this group are the common bread moulds, *Mucor* and *Rhizopus*.

Figure 6.11 The mould *Rhizopus*, showing thread-like hyphae and a mature zygospore (*left*). Two gametangia, just touching, can be seen on the right. Magnification ×125.

Phylum Ascomycota (ascomycetes)

This group takes its name from the sac-like **ascus** formed during sexual reproduction. Sexual conjugation and fusion of nuclei of two mating types (+ and –) results in the formation of eight **ascospores** inside an **ascus**. Sometimes, as in the mould *Sordaria*, the asci are grouped in a cup-shaped **perithecium**. Ascomycetes also reproduce asexually by fission, spores or budding.

The hyphae in this group have cross walls perforated by pores which allow continuity of the cytoplasm. Another well-known example in this group is the bread mould *Neurospora* which was used by George Beadle and Edward Tatum in their work on the one gene–one enzyme hypothesis (*page 614*).

Yeasts also belong to this phylum but differ from the other ascomycetes in normally being unicellular.

Figure 6.12 Asci of *Neurospora*. Each ascus contains eight ascospores. Magnification ×200.

Phylum Basidiomycota (basidiomycetes)

This group includes mushrooms, toadstools, puffballs and bracket fungi. They take their name from the **basidium**, a microscopic structure which bears sexually produced spores called **basidiospores**. The familiar mushrooms or toadstools are the fruiting bodies (called **basidiocarps**) on which the basidia are formed. The hyphae have cross walls, and many members of this group form associations with roots (mycorrhizae) which were mentioned earlier.

This phylum also includes rusts, parasitic fungi belonging to the genus *Puccinia* which attack cereal crops.

Figure 6.13 Sulphur tuft toadstools, *Hypholomo fasciculare*, growing on a rotting tree stump. The toadstools are the fruiting bodies on which the basidia are formed.

Extension

Lichens

A lichen is an association between an alga and a fungus (usually an ascomycete). Each member of the partnership is dependent on the other. The fungus makes up most of the lichen 'body' and shelters the alga which photosynthesises and passes food to the fungus.

Lichens are often the first colonisers of bare rock; they are slow growing and can live in cold, exposed regions, such as Antarctica, where hundreds of different species are found. They also colonise tree trunks. Because some species are very sensitive to air pollutants they are used as 'indicator species' for monitoring pollution in the atmosphere.

They reproduce by releasing structures which consist of small fragments of both the alga and the fungus. They are classified as a phylum of the Fungi.

Lichens in more detail, page 714

Several varieties of lichen growing on a gravestone.

Figure 6.14 The liverwort *Pellia epiphylla*, showing the flat thallus and spore capsules.

Figure 6.15 Photograph of the British pointed hair moss showing leaves and spore capsules.

Figure 6.16 The fern, *Polypodium vulgare*, showing the sori on the underside of the fronds.

Figure 6.17 The Douglas fir, *Pseudotsuga taxifolia*, showing cones and needle-like leaves.

6.4 Kingdom Plantae (plants)

All plants are **multicellular eukaryotes** with **photosynthetic nutrition** except for some parasites which lack chlorophyll. Their cell walls contain **cellulose**. The cells have green plastids called **chloroplasts** which contain **chlorophylls** *a* and *b* and other pigments. They reproduce by sexual and asexual means and have **alternating haploid and diploid generations** in their life cycle. The haploid generation is called the **gametophyte** and produces sex cells (gametes). The diploid generation is called the **sporophyte** and produces spores in special bodies called **sporangia**.

Phylum Bryophyta (bryophytes)

Bryophytes, which include mosses and liverworts, are mostly restricted to moist habitats. This is partly because the sperm, which bear flagella, must swim in water to fertilise the eggs. **The gametophyte is the most prominent phase in the life cycle**. Bryophytes are without xylem and phloem and have no roots. They are anchored by thin, filamentous structures called **rhizoids**. The sporophyte generation is small and derives nourishment from the gametophyte to which it is attached. Its most obvious feature is the sporangium which takes the form of a **spore capsule** carried at the end of a slender stalk above the gametophyte.

Class Hepaticae (liverworts)

The gametophyte is either flat and undifferentiated, called a **thallus**, or has a simple stem with **leaves in three ranks**, a so-called leafy liverwort. The rhizoids are unicellular and the short-lived spore capsules split into four valves when they open.

Class Musci (mosses)

The gametophyte has a stem and **spirally arranged leaves**. The rhizoids are multicellular and the spore capsules have an elaborate dispersal mechanism.

The remaining plant phyla are collectively called **tracheophytes** and differ from the previous plant phyla in having a **conspicuous sporophyte generation**. They show differentiation into tissues including **vascular tissues** – xylem and phloem. For this reason they are collectively described as **vascular plants**. They also have complex leaves with a waterproof cuticle.

Phylum Filicinophyta (ferns)

Ferns have **large prominent leaves (fronds)** with sporangia in clusters (**sori**) on the undersides. **The dominant phase is the sporophyte**. There is a free-living gametophyte stage which is much reduced and dependent on water. From it the sporophyte grows.

Phylum Coniferophyta (conifers)

These are **cone-bearing plants** which lack flowers or fruits. The cones carry spore-producing sporangia. The seed is 'naked' in that it is not enclosed by an ovary wall. The leaves are usually needle-like with a thick, waxy cuticle.

Coniferous trees are economically important because they are the source of 'soft wood' for the timber industry. Certain conifers such as firs and spruces provide Christmas trees, and pine nuts are increasingly used in cooking.

Phylum Angiospermophyta (angiosperms – flowering plants)

These are the familiar **flowering plants** and they are the predominant plant group of the modern world. They include all our major food plants and many of the flowers are valued for aesthetic reasons. As well as having flowers they have seeds which are enclosed in a **fruit** formed from the ovary wall. The flowers exhibit an infinite variety of mechanisms which ensure pollination, and the seeds and fruits have features which ensure the dispersal of the seeds.

Angiosperms are divided into two classes depending on the number of **seed leaves** (**cotyledons**) which they have in their seeds.

Class Monocotyledoneae (monocotyledons)

As the name suggests the embryo has **one seed leaf**. The leaves usually have **parallel veins**. The group includes grasses (and therefore cereals) and with the exception of palms and some bamboos they do not grow to a very large size. This is because cambium tissue is absent and so secondary growth cannot occur (*page 540*).

Figure 6.18 Two examples of monocotyledons. *Left* A British grass, brown bent, *Agrostis* sp., in flower. It grows on acid grassland and heaths. *Right Iris laevigata*, growing at the edge of a pond.

Class Dicotyledoneae (dicotyledons)

In this group the embryo has **two seed leaves** and the leaves are usually **net-veined**. They often grow to a large size because cambium is present in the stem and **secondary growth** can occur. The group includes many familiar trees (oak, horse chestnut, beech and birch) as well as shrubs like roses and familiar meadow and garden plants such as buttercups, daisies, dandelions, nettles, peas, cabbages and wallflowers.

Figure 6.19 Some examples of dicotyledons. *Left* Many garden plants are dicotyledons. Here, in Monet's garden at Giverny near Paris, herbaceous plants, mostly sweet rocket, are growing underneath rambler roses. *Right* Most trees are dicotyledons. This is a horse chestnut tree, *Aesculus hippocastanum*, in flower.

Sponges – a side issue

Sponges have been around for at least 570 million years. They, or rather their skeletons, were used by the ancient Greeks for scrubbing tables and floors and for padding their armour. The Romans made them into paintbrushes, tied them onto wooden poles to make mops, and on occasions used them as substitutes for drinking cups. Not so long ago they were found in most bathrooms but they have now been superseded by plastic varieties.

Some sponges are as small as a fingernail, while others are large enough for a diver to sit in. They may be flat and sprawling or compact and vase-like. These extraordinary organisms are placed in a sub-kingdom of the animal kingdom called Parazoa which means 'beside the animals'. This is because they lack tissues and organs and have no special shape. They interest taxonomists because they are thought to have had ancestors very similar to certain flagellated members of the Protoctist kingdom (*page 90*).

Whatever their form, the sponge body is organised in the same manner. It is made up of a collection of several distinct cell types which are organised into a system of pores, canals and chambers through which water circulates (*illustration*).

This cellular differentiation is a characteristic of sponges and allows different functions to be carried out within the organism. **Epithelial cells** cover the body and **porocytes** line the pores, but the **collar cells**, which line the inner chamber, are the most characteristic feature of these animals. They bear flagella whose beating creates a current of water flowing through the body from which food particles are collected.

There is a layer of jelly-like material between the epithelial cells and collar cells which is secreted by another type of cell called an **amoebocyte**. These cells wander through the jelly and carry food particles to the non-feeding cells. Amoebocytes also carry out sexual reproduction in suitable conditions by becoming eggs or sperm. The sperm are released in the outgoing current and may be collected by another sponge. If the latter contains eggs, these may be fertilised and then develop into a ciliated larva which swims away and develops into a sponge elsewhere.

The so-called skeleton is also deposited in the jelly layer. The skeleton may be made of a protein called **spongin** or of spicules of silica or calcium carbonate which often form delicate patterns.

We cannot leave the sponges without mentioning a demonstration carried out by Tom Humphreys and Aron Moscona in the 1960s. They took red and yellow coloured sponges and forced them through a fine sieve, producing single cells or tiny clumps of cells. They then swirled them about in a suitable nutrient medium and as they collided, red cells only stuck to red cells and yellow cells to yellow cells. The clusters grew and the cells arranged themselves into the characteristic body plan of the sponge. This experiment showed that a sponge is more than just a loose assemblage of cells. The cells are able to recognise each other and organise themselves in an orderly way.

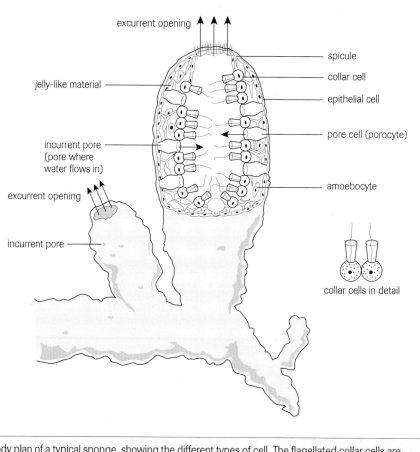

Body plan of a typical sponge, showing the different types of cell. The flagellated collar cells are similar to the single-celled protoctists called collar flagellates. It is possible that sponges have evolved from such collar flagellates.

6.5 **Kingdom Animalia (animals)**

Part 1

Animals are **multicellular eukaryotes** with **nervous coordination**. They do not possess photosynthetic pigments or plastids and their nutrition is **heterotrophic**. Most of them can move from place to place. Their cells do not have cell walls or a vacuole, and they have a high level of tissue differentiation, often with **specialised organs** as well. Reproduction is mainly sexual, with the only haploid stage of the life cycle being the eggs or sperm.

Phylum Cnidaria (cnidarians)

These animals have two cell layers to their body (**diploblastic**): an outer **ectoderm** and an inner **endoderm**. These two layers are separated by a jelly-like **mesogloea** in which lies a network of nerve cells. Two body forms exist: **polyp** and **medusa**, both of which exhibit **radial symmetry** and possess **tentacles**. The tentacles bear stinging cells called **nematoblasts**, some of which can pierce and poison prey. Examples of this group are the freshwater *Hydra*, and the marine jellyfish, sea anemones and corals.

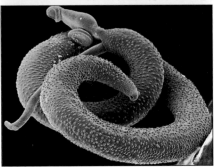

Figure 6.20 The two body forms of cnidarians.
Top The sea anemone, *Tealia* sp. illustrates the polyp form.
Bottom The medusoid form illustrated by the jellyfish, *Chrysaora hyocella.*

> The remaining animal groups mentioned in this chapter have three layers of cells to their bodies: an inner endoderm, outer ectoderm and between them – a **mesoderm**. They are **bilaterally symmetrical** with distinct anterior and posterior ends. They also have a dorsal ('back') and a ventral ('belly') side. Usually the anterior end forms a **head**.

Phylum Platyhelminthes (flatworms)

These are **flat** unsegmented animals, with a **mouth but no anus** (tapeworms are an exception). They have a rudimentary head. They are usually **hermaphrodite** and have a **complex reproductive system**. There are three classes:

Class Turbellaria (turbellarians)

These are **free-living** aquatic flatworms. Their outer surface is covered with **cilia** with which they glide over the surface of stones. They are scavengers and carnivores.

Class Trematoda (trematodes or flukes)

Flukes **do not have cilia** on their outer surface. They are **ecto-** or **endoparasites** and have one or more **suckers** for attachment to their hosts. The life cycle typically involves two hosts. Examples include the blood fluke *Schistosoma* and the liver fluke *Fasciola*.

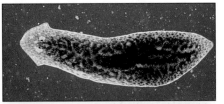

Figure 6.21 *Top* The free-living flatworm, *Dugesia gonocephala.*
Bottom The blood fluke, *Schistosoma*. Notice the mouth and the ventral sucker.

Class Cestoda (cestodes or tapeworms)

Tapeworms are **endoparasites**. They have a flattened, elongated body with a distinct head or **scolex** which bears hooks and suckers for attachment to the host. The body is usually divided into a chain of sexually reproducing parts, called **proglottids**. There is **no mouth or gut**, the host's digested food being absorbed directly through the integument. As with trematodes the life cycle typically involves two hosts.

Phylum Nematoda (nematodes or roundworms)

Roundworms have a slender, cylindrical body with tapering ends. In contrast to flatworms they are **rounded in cross-section**. They have a mouth and anus, and the sexes are separate. They are abundant in water and soil and are common parasites of plants and animals.

The threadworms of cats, dogs and children belong to this group. Elephantiasis is a distressing condition caused by a parasitic roundworm: the lymph system becomes blocked causing expansion of the limbs so that they look like an elephant's legs.

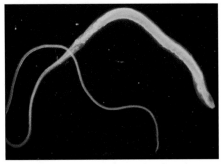

Figure 6.22 The roundworm, *Trichuris trichiuras* (female). Commonly called whipworms, they are spread as a result of poor sanitation and infest the large intestine of humans.

Figure 6.23 The free-swimming ragworm, *Nereis*, showing the well-developed head and the flap-like parapodia, bearing the chaetae, all along the body.

Figure 6.24 The sedentary peacock worm, *Sabella pavonina*, attached by its tube to a rock on the sea bed and showing the fan made up of tentacles for filter-feeding.

Figure 6.25 The earthworm, *Lumbricus* sp. on a lawn. Note the clitellum.

Figure 6.26 The medicinal leech, *Hirudo medicinalis*, showing posterior sucker.

Figure 6.27 The brown garden snail, *Helix aspersa*, showing most of the features typical of gastropods.

Members of the remaining animal groups outlined in this chapter possess a **coelom**, which is a fluid-containing body cavity surrounded by the mesoderm (*page 527*).

Phylum Annelida (annelids or segmented worms)

The body of the segmented worms is divided into a series of units (**segments**) which are separated from each other internally by partitions called **septa**. They have a circulatory system with distinct blood vessels in which blood, often containing an oxygen-carrying pigment, circulates. Typically, annelids possess bristles called **chaetae** and excretory organs called **nephridia** in each segment. This serial repetition of structures is called **metameric segmentation**.

Class Polychaeta (polychaetes or marine worms)

This is an entirely marine group. Their name means 'many bristles' and refers to the numerous **chaetae** which project from the body wall. The chaetae are borne on flap-like extensions of the body wall called **parapodia**. There is a distinct head. The sexes are separate and some members of the group show remarkable synchronisation in the release of eggs and sperm, thus increasing the chances of fertilisation.

The free-swimming ragworms and burrowing lugworms familiar to fishermen are examples, as are the beautiful fan and peacock worms which live a sedentary life in tubes.

Class Oligochaeta (oligochaetes or earthworms)

Although commonly called earthworms, some members of this group are found in fresh water. They have relatively **few chaetae**, no parapodia and a less distinct head than members of the previous group. They are hermaphrodites and during copulation an exchange of sperm takes place. Fertilisation and development take place in a cocoon which is produced by the **clitellum** ('saddle'), a characteristic feature of earthworms.

Class Hirudinea (leeches)

Leeches have no chaetae or parapodia, and no distinct head. Their distinguishing feature is a **sucker** at each end of the body. Many are free-living and carnivorous, and some are ectoparasites. The most famous, though not the most numerous, are those which suck the blood of animals including that of humans.

Phylum Mollusca (molluscs)

Members of this group have a soft, flexible body with little trace of segmentation. A **head, muscular foot** and **visceral hump** are often distinguishable. The principal body cavity is represented by a blood-filled **haemocoel**. Many of them have a **shell. Gills** are often present and are located in a chamber called the **mantle cavity**.

The phylum is divided into a number of classes but the most common representatives belong to just three of them:

Class Gastropoda (gastropods)

The members of this group have a head, which bears eyes and sensory tentacles, and a large, flat, muscular foot. The shell, into which the animal can withdraw, is single and often coiled (in slugs the shell is reduced to a trace). A rasping tongue-like structure, the **radula**, is used for feeding. Snails, slugs, limpets and whelks are members of this class.

Class Pelycopoda (formerly bivalves)

In this group the head is reduced and there are no tentacles. The **shell consists of two halves** which are hinged. Bivalves burrow in sand and mud with a muscular foot, or attach themselves to rock or driftwood. The gills are used for collecting food particles (filter-feeding) as well as for gaseous exchange. Cockles, mussels, clams and oysters belong to this class.

Figure 6.28 The spiny cockle, *Acanthocardia echinata*, showing the muscular foot protruding from the hinged shell as it burrows into the sand.

Class Cephalopoda (cephalopods)

Cephalopods are the largest and most complex molluscs. They have a conspicuous head into which the foot is incorporated, with large **sucker-bearing tentacles** for catching prey. The shell may be absent but if present it is reduced and internal. (The exception is *Nautilus* which is the only living species with a fully developed shell.) They have a **beak** and radula which are used in feeding. They are active, fast-swimming animals and have **well-developed sense organs**, including eyes, and nervous system. The octopus, squid and cuttlefish belong to this class.

Figure 6.29 The common octopus, *Octopus vulgaris*, showing the suckers on its tentacles and its well-developed eyes.

Phylum Arthropoda (arthropods)

Arthropods are segmented animals with a hard chitinous **exoskeleton** (cuticle) and **jointed limbs**. The coelom is much reduced, and the body cavity is a blood-filled **haemocoel**. Arthropods are a very successful group and contain most of the world's species of organisms. There are five main groups:

Superclass Crustacea (crustaceans)

There is such a wide variety of form among crustaceans that they are now usually given the rank of superclass and then subdivided further into classes, the details of which need not concern us here. Crustaceans are mainly aquatic and although the head is not clearly defined, they are distinguished by possessing **two pairs of antennae** and many have compound eyes. They include *Daphnia*, a free-swimming water flea; barnacles which are sessile and attached to rocks by the head; crabs, lobsters, crayfish and woodlice. Woodlice are the only fully terrestrial crustaceans.

Figure 6.30 The lobster, *Homarus vulgaris*, showing most of the features typical of crustaceans.

Class Chilopoda (centipedes)

Centipedes are terrestrial and have a distinct head with a pair of **jaws**. The legs are similar along the length of the body, and each segment bears one pair. They are mainly carnivorous, feeding on insects and other small animals.

Class Diplopoda (millipedes)

Millipedes are also terrestrial but they have two pairs of legs on each apparent segment of the body. They are herbivorous and some species damage plant roots.

Figure 6.31 *Lithobius*, a centipede common in garden soil. Note the single pair of legs per segment.

Figure 6.32 The orb web spider, *Araneus alsine*, hanging in its web and showing its four pairs of legs.

Figure 6.33 The brown hawker dragonfly, *Aeshna grandis*, in flight, showing three pairs of jointed legs and two pairs of wings attached to the thorax.

Figure 6.34 A starfish lying on a bed of seaweed. The five-way symmetry is clearly visible.

Figure 6.35 The bony fish, *Leuciscus leuciscus*, commonly called dace, showing the scales on the skin, the operculum and the fins.

Class Arachnida (arachnids)

This is a terrestrial group. They have **four pairs of legs** which are attached to what appears to be a combined head and thorax (**cephalothorax**). The latter is separated from the abdomen by a waist-like constriction. They do not have compound eyes. Spiders, scorpions, mites and ticks are all arachnids.

Class Insecta (insects)

Insects are terrestrial, although some of them have an aquatic larval stage in their life cycle. The body is divided into **head**, **thorax** and **abdomen**. Compound eyes are usually found on the head, and **three pairs of legs** and usually **two pairs of wings** are attached to the thorax.

Insects are a very large and diverse group. Many have complex life cycles involving **metamorphosis** (*page 533*). They have a great impact on humans as ectoparasites such as bugs and lice, and as carriers of diseases such as malaria. Some are serious pests of food crops and stored food. Others are valuable pollinators of crop plants. Examples include dragonflies, mosquitoes, fleas, locusts, bees, butterflies and stick insects.

Phylum Echinodermata (echinoderms)

This is an exclusively marine group. They show **five-way radial symmetry**, although the larvae are bilaterally symmetrical. They have a **water vascular system** with **tube feet** which are primarily for locomotion but are also used for feeding. The skin has **spines**.

Starfish, brittle stars, sea urchins, sea cucumbers and sea lilies are examples of echinoderms.

Phylum Chordata (chordates)

Chordates are united by the possession of certain internal and developmental characteristics which are present at some stage of their development. These are the presence of a **notochord**; a **hollow dorsal nerve cord**; **visceral clefts** (which usually take the form of gill slits) and a **post-anal tail**.

Most chordates have a **vertebral column** and are therefore referred to as **vertebrates**. However, some lack a vertebral column: they, and all the other animal groups which we have covered so far, are described as **invertebrates**. The vertebrate chordates are divided into the following classes:

Class Chondrichthyes (cartilaginous fish)

This class includes sharks, skates and rays. They have a skeleton which is made of **cartilage**, and two pairs of **fleshy fins**. The mouth is in a ventral position, and the gill slits open separately to the exterior.

Class Osteichthyes (bony fish)

Most fish belong to this group which includes coelacanths and lungfish as well as the more familiar herring, cod, mackerel and trout. Their skeleton is made of **bone** and the paired fins are supported by **bony rays**. The mouth is terminal (at the extreme front end of the body) and the gills are covered by a bony flap called the **operculum**.

Class Amphibia (amphibians)

Adult amphibians are usually terrestrial with simple lungs ventilated by the throat muscles, while the larvae (**tadpoles**) are aquatic and have gills. They have a **soft moist skin** which is used for gaseous exchange to supplement the lungs. The eggs are fertilised externally in water where they also develop. Adult amphibians suffer readily from desiccation if deprived of water for a long period. Newts, salamanders, frogs and toads are all amphibians.

Class Reptilia (reptiles)

Reptiles are a mainly terrestrial group and have a **dry skin with scales**. They have lungs for gaseous exchange, and these are ventilated by ribs (**costal ventilation**). The eggs are fertilised internally, covered by a **leathery shell** and laid on land. Lizards, snakes, crocodiles and alligators, turtles and tortoises are present-day reptiles, and extinct forms include the dinosaurs.

Class Aves (birds)

Birds are similar to reptiles in many ways. Differences between them are mainly associated with the birds' power of flight: **skin with feathers** and forelimbs developed as **wings**. Birds, unlike any group mentioned so far, are **endothermic** which means they can generate heat energy and maintain their body temperature by physiological means. Lungs are used for gaseous exchange and extensions called **air sacs** penetrate into the long bones. Birds develop from eggs which have a **hard shell**.

Class Mammalia (mammals)

Mammals have **skin with hair**, the hair growing in pits called **hair follicles**. They are mostly **viviparous** and the young are fed on **milk** produced by **mammary glands**. They are **endothermic** and have lungs for gaseous exchange with costal ventilation supplemented by a diaphragm. There are two generations of teeth in most mammals and the wide variety of dentition reflects their varied diets. There are two subclasses:

- **Prototheria** are the **egg-laying mammals** of Australia: the spiny anteater (*Echidna*) and the duck-billed platypus (*Ornithorhynchus*). They lay (large-yolked) eggs but like other mammals they suckle their young.

- **Theria** are **non-egg laying mammals** and are further divided into two groups:

    Metatheria (**marsupials**) are those mammals such as kangaroos, wallabies and koala bears which have pouches in which the young are suckled for most of their development, having been born in a very immature state.

    Eutheria (**placental mammals**) are all other mammals, including humans. Their young undergo considerable development inside the mother's uterus, receiving nourishment via the **placenta** before they are born. After birth they are nourished by suckling from the mother.

Figure 6.36 The glass frog, *Centrolenella buckleyi*, which lives in the Andes. It sticks its eggs to the underside of leaves which overhang water. The tadpoles then drop into water when they hatch.

Figure 6.37 The common lizard, *Lacerta vivipara*, lying on a rock and showing the scales on its dry skin.

Figure 6.38 A fairy tern, *Sterna alba*, in flight.

Figure 6.39 *Left* to *right* The egg-laying duckbilled platypus, *Ornithorhynchus anatinus*; a kangaroo with joey hanging out of the pouch; a lioness, *Panthera leo*, suckling her cubs. *Below* A Shetland pony with newly born foal.

Summary

1. The **Prokaryote kingdom** has undergone a major revision in recent years, and a division of prokaryotes into two fundamentally different groups is now recognised: **Archaea** and **Bacteria**.

2. The **Protoctist kingdom** contains all the eukaryotic organisms which do not fit elsewhere. They may be unicellular or multicellular and are divided into about 30 phyla which include the algae.

3. The **Fungus kingdom** contains multicellular eukaryotes which have heterotrophic nutrition. Some are parasites and are important medically.

4. The **Plant kingdom** contains multicellular eukaryotes which are usually sedentary and have autotrophic nutrition by photosynthesis. Phyla include mosses, ferns, conifers and flowering plants.

5. The **Animal kingdom** contains multicellular eukaryotes which are usually motile and feed heterotrophically. Phyla include various types of worms, molluscs, arthropods and chordates.

Practice questions

For general advice on these questions and advice on answering essay-type questions, see pages vii and viii.

1. The diagram represents a bacterial cell.

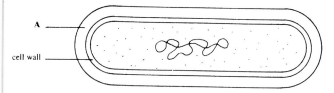

  (a) Name:

    (i)   the feature used to classify this bacterium as a bacillus;

    (ii) structure **A**.   (2)

  (b) Give a function of structure A.   (1)

  (c) Bacteria are prokaryotes whereas fungi are eukaryotes. Copy and complete the table to show **three** structural differences between these two groups of organisms.

Prokaryote	Eukaryote

                        (3)
           (Total 6 marks)
             NEAB 1996

2. What features do a fish and a mammal have in common? Discuss why they are placed in different classes.

           (Total 20 marks)
             O&C 1998

3. Copy and complete the table below by stating **one** external feature characteristic of the group.

Group	Characteristic external feature
Cnidarians	
Mosses	
Arthropods	
Ferns	

           (Total 4 marks)
             London 1996

4. The diagrams below show *three* organisms. Each belongs to a different phylum (major group).

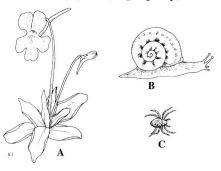

In the table below, fill in the name of the phylum to which each belongs and give *one* external feature, shown in the diagram, which is characteristic of this phylum.

Organism	Phylum	*One* visible external feature
A		
B		
C		

           (Total 6 marks)
             London 1998

In Chapter 3 we explained that the plasma membrane is composed of a double layer of phospholipid molecules whose hydrocarbon chains are hydrophobic – that is, they repel water molecules. This enables the membrane to hold in the water-soluble contents of the cell and prevent them leaking out. However, this same property makes it difficult for water-soluble substances to pass in and out of cells – at least it would be difficult were it not for special mechanisms which make it possible. In this chapter we shall look at these mechanisms and their consequences on the functioning of cells.

In general, substances pass in and out of cells by four main processes:

- **diffusion**;
- **facilitated diffusion**;
- **osmosis**;
- **active transport**;
- **endocytosis** and **exocytosis**.

We shall consider each in turn.

7.1 **Diffusion**

If you drop a crystal of potassium permanganate into a beaker of water it dissolves. Gradually the purple colour of the permanganate spreads through the water until eventually it is uniformly distributed. The explanation is that, as the crystal dissolves, the permanganate ions move away from the crystal through the water.

What causes the ions to behave in this way? The answer is that they are in a state of continual random motion. They can move in any direction, but the fact that initially there are far more of them in the vicinity of the crystal increases the probability that they will move away from the crystal. In other words, there is a *net* movement of ions away from the crystal. This process is called **diffusion**.

Diffusion is the net movement of molecules or ions from a region of their higher concentration to a region of their lower concentration.

The difference in concentration between the two regions is called the **concentration gradient** or **diffusion gradient**. Diffusion will always take place wherever such a gradient exists, and it will continue until eventually the particles are uniformly distributed throughout the system. When that happens **equilibrium** is said to be reached.

Diffusion is a passive process which takes place by random motion. It does not require energy from metabolism and will take place equally readily in living and non-living systems.

Why is diffusion important in biology?

Think of a cell in your own body. To stay alive the cell takes up oxygen. Because the oxygen is continually being used up in respiration, its concentration inside the cell is lower than in the blood and tissue fluids. This concentration gradient results in oxygen molecules diffusing into the cell from outside.

The same thing applies to carbon dioxide but in the other direction: its concentration is higher inside the cell, where it is continually being formed, than outside. This causes the carbon dioxide molecules to diffuse out of the cell.

Anything that increases the concentration gradient, i.e. makes it steeper, will speed up diffusion. This is one function of a circulatory system. By quickly carrying away the diffused substance, the circulation helps to maintain a steep concentration gradient, thus encouraging further diffusion. Similarly, the conversion of the diffused substance into another substance will help to maintain a concentration gradient, favouring continued diffusion. For example, when glucose enters a cell it is rapidly converted into glucose 6-phosphate (*page 142*), thus sustaining the gradient and encouraging more glucose to diffuse into the cell.

If diffusion is to take place, any membranes or partitions in the system must be readily permeated by the molecules or ions in question. Such is the case with the plasma membrane in relation to oxygen and carbon dioxide: the membrane is permeable to both these gases, as indeed it is to any small, uncharged particles. They pass between the lipid molecules as shown in figure 7.1.

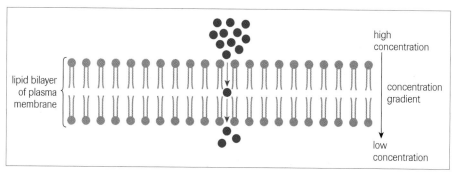

Figure 7.1 Simple diffusion through the plasma membrane of a cell. Small uncharged particles pass between the lipid molecules down a concentration gradient.

Extension

What determines the rate of diffusion?

The rate of diffusion, that is the quantity of the substance which diffuses from one region to another in a certain time, depends on a number of things, including:

- The difference in the concentration of the substance in the two regions, that is the concentration gradient. The steeper the gradient, the faster the rate of diffusion.

- The surface area across which the substance is diffusing. The greater the surface area, the faster the rate of diffusion.

- The distance over which the substance has to diffuse (the diffusion distance). The greater the diffusion distance, the slower the rate of diffusion.

In other words, *the rate of diffusion is directly proportional to the concentration difference and surface area, and inversely proportional to the diffusion distance:*

$$\text{rate of diffusion} \propto \frac{\text{surface area} \times \text{concentration difference}}{\text{diffusion distance}}$$

This is known as **Fick's Law** and it is relevant in all biological situations where diffusion is responsible for moving molecules or ions – gaseous exchange in the alveoli of the lungs for example (*page 167*).

Diffusion through channel proteins

Charged particles (ions) do not readily pass through the plasma membrane because they are relatively insoluble in lipid. Within the plasma membrane, certain proteins assist such particles to diffuse in or out of the cell. They are called **channel proteins**.

Figure 7.2 illustrates a channel protein. The protein molecule is arranged so that it forms a water-filled pore in the membrane. You can see one in figure 3.22 on page 57. Unlike the interior of the lipid bilayer, the lining of the channel is hydrophilic ('water-loving'), so water-soluble substances, and water itself, pass through it relatively easily.

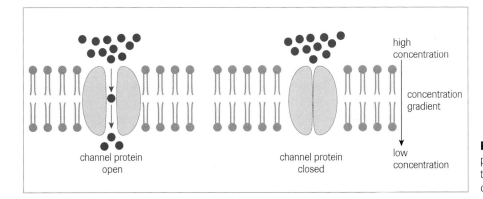

Figure 7.2 Diffusion via a channel protein in the plasma membrane of a cell. As with any other type of diffusion, the diffusing particles move down a concentration gradient.

Channel proteins are particularly concerned with transporting ions into and out of cells. The channels are selective, allowing certain ions to pass through but not others. Some of the channels can open and close rather like gates. These **gated channels** open only when they receive an appropriate signal such as a mechanical disturbance of the membrane, a change in the voltage across it, or the binding of another molecule or ion with the protein.

Channel proteins speed up the rate at which ions diffuse across the plasma membrane. However, like simple diffusion, the movement is passive and does not involve the transfer of metabolic energy. Consequently it can only take place down a concentration gradient.

7.2 Facilitated diffusion

▶ Movement of ions in nerves, page 352

In this case a diffusing molecule combines with a **carrier protein** which transports it across the membrane and deposits it on the other side. Figure 7.3 shows how this happens. It is called **facilitated diffusion**. As with simple diffusion, the movement occurs *down* a concentration gradient and does not require metabolic energy.

Facilitated diffusion is the main way by which glucose and amino acids are taken up into cells. Their molecules, being polar, cannot diffuse through the lipid bilayer, and they are too large to pass through channel proteins, so they are transported by carrier proteins.

Carrier proteins have been likened to enzymes. The relationship between the protein and the transported molecule is specific, and the mode of attachment is similar to that between the active site of an enzyme and its substrate (*page 128*). Carrier proteins are susceptible to poisons, just as enzymes are, and several different molecules may compete for transport by the same carrier.

We shall meet carrier proteins again in connection with active transport (*page 113*).

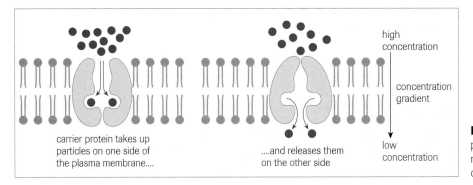

Figure 7.3 Facilitated diffusion via a carrier protein in the plasma membrane of a cell. Again, notice that the particles move down a concentration gradient.

Telling the difference between simple and facilitated diffusion

How can you tell if a chemical is moving across a plasma membrane by simple diffusion or facilitated diffusion? One way is to investigate the effect of increasing the concentration of the chemical on the rate at which it is taken up into the cell.

The results of such an investigation are shown in the illustration. If the process is simple diffusion, the relationship is linear, the rate of uptake rising steadily as the concentration increases. If the process is facilitated diffusion, the rate of uptake

rises more rapidly to begin with and then slows down, eventually reaching a plateau when all the membrane proteins are working to full capacity and therefore limit the process.

Graph showing the effect of increasing the concentration of a chemical on the rate of its uptake into a cell.

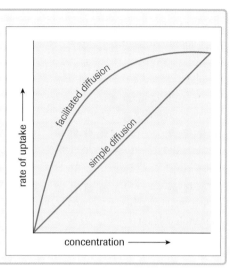

Diffusion and the structure of organisms

Organisms rely on diffusion to fulfil many of their needs, and this has a profound effect on their structure. For example, the way an organism undergoes gaseous exchange is related to its size. An organism's oxygen requirements (its needs) are approximately proportional to its volume, i.e. the bulk of respiring tissue which it possesses. Its exchanges, however, are proportional to the surface area over which diffusion of oxygen takes place – an aspect of Fick's Law (*page 104*).

In any organism the surface area over which diffusion takes place must be sufficient to fulfil the needs of the respiring tissues. It is a simple mathematical rule that as an object

increases in volume, the ratio of its total surface area to its volume decreases. In other words, the larger the object, the smaller is its **surface–volume ratio** (*illustration*).

The significance of this principle is as follows. In small organisms like *Amoeba*, flatworms and earthworms, the surface–volume ratio is large enough for diffusion across the general body surface to satisfy the organism's respiratory needs. However, in larger organisms the surface–volume ratio is too small for this to be the case. Such organisms have developed special surfaces for gaseous exchange. These surfaces are usually greatly folded, thus increasing the surface

area for diffusion. Lungs and gills are examples. The general strategy of increasing the surface area for diffusion is also shown by cells that have microvilli.

The bulkier the tissue, the slower the rate at which oxygen reaches the cells furthest from the surface – another application of Fick's Law. In small organisms the diffusion distance is short and there is no problem. However, in larger organisms like ourselves the distance is far too great for oxygen to diffuse to the innermost tissues quickly enough – and if the organism is active with a high demand for oxygen, diffusion is even less likely to suffice. In many organisms this problem is overcome by having a circulatory system with an oxygen-carrying pigment such as haemoglobin.

In addition to respiration, diffusion affects another important life process: the distribution of food materials. In most animals the circulatory system transports soluble food substances as well as oxygen. However, animals without a circulatory system have to rely on diffusion for distributing soluble food substances to the cells.

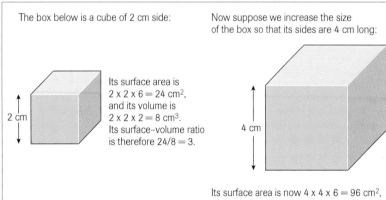

The box below is a cube of 2 cm side:

2 cm

Its surface area is
$2 \times 2 \times 6 = 24$ cm^2,
and its volume is
$2 \times 2 \times 2 = 8$ cm^3.
Its surface–volume ratio
is therefore $24/8 = 3$.

Now suppose we increase the size of the box so that its sides are 4 cm long:

4 cm

Its surface area is now $4 \times 4 \times 6 = 96$ cm^2,
and its volume is $4 \times 4 \times 4 = 64$ cm^3.
Its surface–volume ratio is therefore $96/64 = 1.5$,
only half that of the smaller box.

7.3 Osmosis

Look at the experiment in figure 7.4. The mouth of a thistle funnel is covered with a membrane such as cellophane. The funnel is then filled with a concentrated solution of sucrose and immersed in a beaker of pure water. What happens? Quite quickly the level of the solution in the tube begins to rise. This is because water passes into it from the surrounding beaker.

To explain why this happens it is necessary to appreciate that the membrane is permeable to the water molecules but impermeable to the much larger sucrose molecules. In other words the membrane is **partially permeable**.

Now consider the situation on either side of this partially permeable membrane. In the beaker there is nothing but water molecules; in the funnel there are water molecules plus sucrose molecules. The presence of the sucrose molecules means that the concentration of water molecules in the funnel is less than in the beaker. The result is that in a given time more water molecules diffuse from the beaker to the funnel than from the funnel to the beaker. In other words there is a net movement of water molecules from the beaker into the funnel. This movement of water molecules is what is meant by **osmosis**, and plainly it is a special case of diffusion applied to water.

Osmosis is the net movement of water molecules from a region of their higher concentration to a region of their lower concentration through a partially permeable membrane.

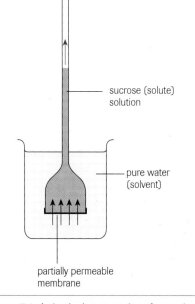

Figure 7.4 A simple demonstration of osmosis. The apparatus is called an **osmometer**. The black arrows indicate the net flow of water (solvent) into the sucrose (solute) solution. The membrane, being partially permeable, allows water molecules to pass from the beaker into the thistle funnel but prevents sucrose molecules passing from the thistle funnel into the beaker. As a result of water flowing into the funnel, the solution rises up the tube as indicated by the red arrow.

When will osmosis take place?

In the experiment in figure 7.4 the beaker contains pure water. However, osmosis would still occur from the beaker to the funnel if the beaker contained another sucrose solution, provided that the concentration of water molecules was greater than in the funnel.

If the concentration of water molecules is the same in the beaker and the funnel, there will be no net movement of water into or out of the funnel; and if the concentration of water molecules is greater in the funnel than in the beaker, there will be a net movement of water from funnel to beaker. In general terms, osmosis will occur whenever two solutions containing different concentrations of water molecules are separated by a partially permeable membrane.

Of course the solution does not have to be sucrose – it could be any substance soluble in water, salt for example. The general term for a substance dissolved in water is **solute**, and the liquid that it is dissolved in (water in this case) is called the **solvent**. Many types of solute occur in living organisms and exert osmotic action. In biological situations the solvent is almost always water.

The membrane in figure 7.4 is permeable only to water; in other words it is an *ideal* partially permeable membrane. In practice, partially permeable membranes need not be completely impermeable to the solute molecules. Many naturally occurring membranes permit the passage of solutes as well as water, though not at the same rate. All that is necessary for osmosis to occur is that the water molecules move more rapidly than the solute molecules.

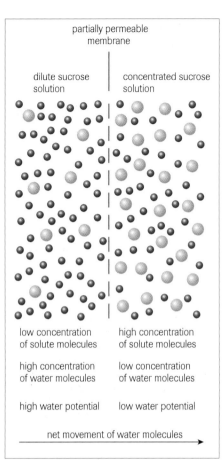

partially permeable membrane

dilute sucrose solution | concentrated sucrose solution

low concentration of solute molecules | high concentration of solute molecules

high concentration of water molecules | low concentration of water molecules

high water potential | low water potential

net movement of water molecules →

Water potential

Look at figure 7.5. You will appreciate that there will be a net movement of water molecules from the left of the partially permeable membrane to the right.

The reason, in thermodynamic terms, is that the potential energy of the water molecules on the left is greater than the potential energy of the water molecules on the right. The potential energy of the water molecules is called the **water potential**. Water will diffuse from a region of high water potential to a region of lower water potential, and the steeper the water potential gradient the greater will be the tendency for water to diffuse in this direction. We can therefore look upon water potential as the capacity of a system to *lose* water.

At sea level and standard temperature and pressure (in this case 25°C and approximately 100 kPa) pure water is given a water potential of zero. Adding solute molecules to the water *lowers* the water potential, making it negative. This is because the presence of the solute molecules lowers the concentration of the water molecules, thus reducing the number of water molecules that can diffuse out of it (remember, water potential is the capacity of a system to lose water). If you go on adding solute, the water potential gets lower and lower, i.e. more and more negative.

The symbol used for the water potential and other energy potentials in cells is ψ (the Greek letter psi). It is customary to express ψ in kilopascals (kPa) or megapascals (MPa). When water flows down a water potential gradient, the net movement of water molecules is always from a less negative value (e.g. –500 kPa) to a more negative value (e.g. –600 kPa). If you find these negatives confusing, read the support box below left.

Figure 7.5 Diagram summarising the conditions on the two sides of a partially permeable membrane, and the terms used to describe them. The large orange blobs represent sucrose molecules, the smaller blue blobs represent water molecules. The terms 'high' and 'low' are relative.

Extension

Water potential and osmotic pressure, two alternative approaches

We have just explained the movement of water across a partially permeable membrane in terms of water potential. Another way of explaining it is in terms of **osmotic pressure**. For practical purposes this can be regarded as the tendency of a solution to *gain* water across an ideal partially permeable membrane.

The osmotic pressure of a solution depends on its solute concentration: the greater the solute concentration, the greater the osmotic pressure. This is because the concentration of water molecules in the solution is relatively low, so water will tend to diffuse into the solution. It follows that a solution with a *high* osmotic pressure has a *low* water potential.

One can use either water potential or osmotic pressure to explain the movement of water. Animal and medical physiologists generally use osmotic pressure, whereas plant biologists use water potential. This is rather unfortunate, but until agreement is reached we have to get used to both systems. In this book the water potential concept is used throughout. One of its advantages is that it need not be restricted to osmotic situations: it can be applied to any situation where water is present, including soil and air, and this is particularly important in plant studies.

Osmosis and cells

Cells owe many of their properties to the fact that the plasma membrane is partially permeable. We can distinguish between three different situations:

- If a cell is surrounded by pure water, or by a solution whose solute concentration is lower, and water potential higher, than that of the cell's contents, water flows into the cell by osmosis and the cell swells up. The external solution is said to be **hypotonic** to the solution in the cell (*hypo* means 'lower than' and applies to the solute concentration).

In contrast, if the cell is surrounded by a solution whose solute concentration is higher, and water potential lower, than that of the cell's contents, water flows out of the cell and the cell shrinks. In this case the external solution is said to be **hypertonic** to the solution in the cell (*hyper* means 'higher than' and again applies to the solute concentration).

Finally, if the cell has the same solute concentration and water potential as the surrounding solution, there will be no net flow of water into or out of the cell so the cell stays the same size and neither swells nor shrinks. In this case the external solution is said to be **isotonic** with the solution in the cell (*iso* means 'the same as').

The terms hypertonic, hypotonic and isotonic are relative. What is isotonic for one cell – a red blood cell say – will not necessarily be isotonic for another cell – a kidney cell for instance. This is because the relative concentrations of solutes inside and outside the cell are not the same for all cells.

The effect of osmosis on animal cells

Figure 7.6 illustrates the effect of immersing red blood cells in hypotonic and hypertonic solutions. As you can see, both situations can be disastrous.

It follows that if a cell is to maintain its normal size and shape it must either exist permanently in a medium with which it is isotonic or have special mechanisms enabling it to survive in a hypertonic or hypotonic medium. These mechanisms are the business of **osmoregulation** which is immensely important in the lives of animals. For example, if water flows into an organism by osmosis, as it does in freshwater fish, the surplus water must be expelled as quickly as it enters (*page 292*).

The only other way of solving the problem is for the organism to adjust the solute concentration inside its cells so that it equals the solute concentration of the external medium. The water potentials inside and outside the organism will then be the same so there will be no net flow of water in or out. Certain animals do this, as is explained in Chapter 17.

The effect of osmosis on plant cells

Plant cells generally have a water potential which is markedly lower than that of their immediate surroundings. Their lower water potential is mainly due to the presence of various solutes in the fluid within the vacuole (the cell sap). The plasma membrane, and the tonoplast membrane surrounding the vacuole, are both partially permeable, letting water through but not solutes. The cell wall, however, is fully permeable to both water and solutes.

Now consider what happens when such a cell is immersed in pure water or a solution whose water potential is higher than that inside the vacuole. As you might expect, water flows through the plasma membrane and tonoplast into the vacuole by osmosis. As a result the cell swells. However, it does not burst. This is because the cellulose cell wall stretches and develops tension, resisting further expansion of the cell.

As water flows into the vacuole by osmosis, the tension developed by the cell wall causes an internal hydrostatic pressure to develop. This is called the **pressure potential**, and it opposes the continued uptake of water into the cell by osmosis. The pressure potential reaches its maximum when the cell wall is stretched as much as it can be and the cell cannot take in any more water. At this point the cell is described as **fully turgid**, or, to put it another way, **full turgor** is achieved.

Now consider what happens if the cell is immersed in a solution whose water potential is lower than that inside the vacuole. First the volume of the cell decreases as water flows out of the vacuole by osmosis. Then the cytoplasm starts to pull away from the cell wall, leaving a perceptible gap between the wall and the plasma membrane. This withdrawal of the cytoplasm from the cell wall is called **plasmolysis** (*figure 7.7*). The point when the cytoplasm just starts pulling away from the cell wall is called **incipient plasmolysis**; full

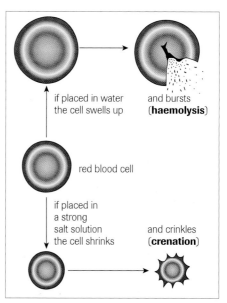

Figure 7.6 The effect of osmosis on red blood cells. In an isotonic solution, the cell neither swells nor shrinks. In water or a hypotonic solution, the cell swells and – if the solution is sufficiently dilute – bursts. The bursting of red blood cells is called **haemolysis** (meaning literally 'blood splitting'). In a hypertonic salt solution the cell shrinks and the plasma membrane crinkles. This is known as **crenation**.

Osmoregulation in detail, page 288

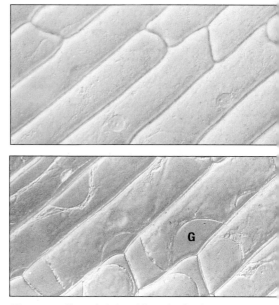

Figure 7.7 Plasmolysis in epidermal cells of an onion bulb. A small piece of the epidermis is mounted in a drop of water on a slide. The top photomicrograph shows a group of such cells in a fully turgid state. A drop of concentrated sucrose solution is then added to the water. The bottom photomicrograph shows the result of doing this: the cells have become plasmolysed and gaps can be seen between the cytoplasm and cell walls. One such gap is labelled **G**.

plasmolysis is reached when the cytoplasm has completely withdrawn from the cell wall. Plasmolysis rarely occurs in nature. However, when induced by experiment it can help us to understand the water relations of plant cells, as we shall see in a moment.

The effect of osmosis in plant cells is summarised in Figure 7.8.

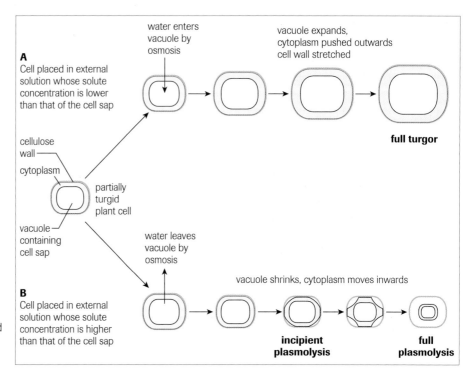

Figure 7.8 The effect of immersing a partially turgid plant cell in **A** pure water and **B** a solution whose solute concentration exceeds that of the cell sap in the vacuole. Because the cell wall is fully permeable to both water and solutes, the external solution passes through the cell wall and fills the space between the cell wall and the cytoplasm

Turgor

Provided there is plenty of water in the environment, a plant's cells are usually surrounded by a watery solution whose solute concentration is lower than that inside the cells – indeed, the cell walls will be saturated with such a solution. Water therefore tends to enter the cells by osmosis, making them turgid.

Turgor is important in supporting and maintaining the shape and form of plants. The stems of non-woody herbaceous plants are kept erect by being filled with turgid cells packed tightly together. Turgor also helps to hold leaves in a flat, opened-out position. If turgor is lost or reduced, the plant droops.

Certain plant cells undergo quite rapid changes in their solute concentration with consequent changes in turgor. This allows the cells to change their shape. Stomatal guard cells behave in this way, as do the cells responsible for the leaf movements of carnivorous plants such as the Venus fly-trap.

7.4 **Water relations of plant cells**

This is an important topic because it explains many aspects of how plants work. In considering it we need to take into account the following three pressures:

■ The water potential of the whole cell – we shall refer to this simply as the **water potential**.

■ The water potential of the solution in the vacuole – we shall call this the **solute potential**.

■ The hydrostatic pressure caused by the cell wall pressing inwards against the cytoplasm – this is called the **pressure potential**.

Suppose we plasmolyse a plant cell by placing it in a concentrated sucrose solution. We then take the cell out of the solution and immerse it in pure water. What happens?

Water immediately flows into the vacuole by osmosis, and the cell starts to expand. At this stage the cell wall is not pressing against the cytoplasm, so the pressure potential is zero and the water potential equals the solute potential. To begin with the water and solute potentials have a low value (i.e. very negative), but as water enters the cell the value gradually increases (i.e. becomes less negative).

As the influx of water continues, the cell goes on expanding until the cytoplasm starts pushing against the cell wall. At this point a pressure potential starts to develop. This raises the water potential, making it even less negative. This is understandable when you think about it: the water potential is the cell's capacity to lose water, and the pressure of the cell wall against the cytoplasm tends to force water out of the cell, rather like a hand squeezing a wet sponge. The water potential now exceeds the solute potential by the amount of the pressure potential.

As the cell continues to expand, the pressure potential gets steadily greater. At the same time the water potential increases, becoming less and less negative. Eventually full turgor is reached: the cell can expand no more and the water potential reaches zero. When this point is reached the solute potential (negative) and pressure potential (positive) become equal in value, exactly counterbalancing each other.

We can summarise the water relations of a plant cell by this equation:

water potential = solute potential + pressure potential
(usually negative)   (always negative)   (usually positive)

or in symbols:

$$\psi = \psi_s + \psi_p$$

In a plasmolysed cell ψ_p is zero and $\psi = \psi_s$. At full turgor ψ_p is equal and opposite to ψ_s, so $\psi = 0$. These relationships are summarised in figure 7.9.

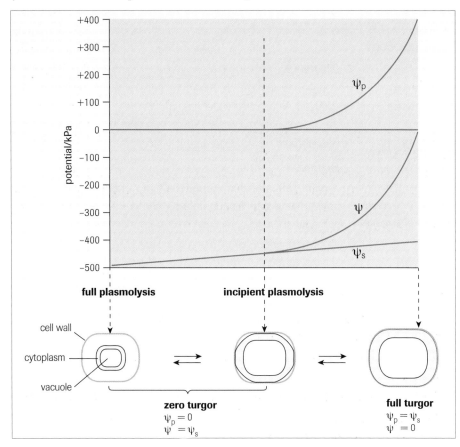

Figure 7.9 Graph showing the relationship between the water potential (ψ), solute potential (ψ_s) and pressure potential (ψ_p) of a plant cell at different stages of turgor and plasmolysis.

Measuring the water and solute potentials of plant cells

We can compare the water and solute potentials of a plant tissue by means of two experiments.

To measure the water potential, pieces of tissue of known mass or volume are placed in a series of solutions of different solute concentrations. The solution which produces no change in mass or volume of the tissue has a water potential equal to that of the tissue. Some class results are shown on the right.

Measuring the solute potential is slightly more difficult because one has to eliminate effects caused by the pressure potential. One method is to find the concentration of an external solution which causes the cells *just* to begin to plasmolyse (incipient plasmolysis). With the cell walls no longer pressing in on the cells' contents, we may assume that the water potential of the external solution is equal to the solute potential of the sap. In practice, the individual cells tend to

plasmolyse at different rates, and for practical purposes incipient plasmolysis is taken as the point when 50% of the cells are visibly plasmolysed.

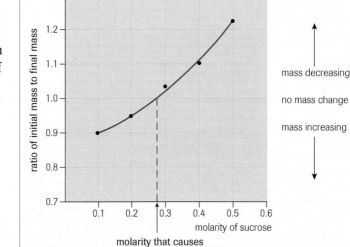

Results of an experiment to determine the water potential of potato tuber cells. Samples of potato tissue were placed in a series of sucrose solutions of different molarities, and the change in mass was measured. As you can see from the graph, the concentration of sucrose causing no change in mass has a molarity of 0.27M. If this is converted to the corresponding pressure reading using a suitable table, the value of the water potential of the potato tissue can be found.

Worked examples of the water potential concept

Example 1

A plant cell with a water potential of –700 kPa is immersed in a sucrose solution whose water potential is –350 kPa. In which direction will water flow?

Water will flow from the sucrose solution into the cell. This is because the water potential of the cell is lower than (i.e. more negative than) the sucrose solution, and there is always a net flow of water from a region of high water potential to a region of lower water potential, i.e. down the water potential gradient.

Example 2

A plant cell has a solute potential of –1240 kPa and a pressure potential of 350 kPa. What is the water potential of the cell?

The water potential of the cell is –890 kPa. This is calculated from the relationship between the water potential of the cell (ψ), the solute potential (ψ_S) and the pressure potential (ψ_P)

$$\psi = \psi_S + \psi_P$$
$$\psi = -1240 + 350$$
$$= -890 \, kPa$$

Example 3

A plasmolysed cell is found to have a solute potential of –960 kPa. What is the water potential of the cell?

The water potential of the cell is –960 kPa. This is because in a plasmolysed cell ψ_p is zero, so $\psi = \psi_S$.

Example 4

A plant cell, after being immersed in pure water for several hours, has a solute potential of –800 kPa. What is the water potential of the cell, and what is its pressure potential?

The water potential of the cell is zero. This is because, after several hours in pure water, the cell will be fully turgid and therefore ψ is zero. The pressure potential is 800 kPa. This is because in a fully turgid cell ψ_p is equal and opposite to ψ_S. (Note that ψ_S is negative and ψ_p positive.)

Example 5

Two plant cells, A and B, are next to each other in a tissue. The water potential of cell A is –700 kPa, and the water potential of cell B is –550 kPa. In which direction will water flow, from A to B or from B to A?

Water will flow from B to A. This is because water flows down a water potential gradient, just as in Example 1.

What effect will the flow of water have on the solute and pressure potentials of cells A and B?

The solute and pressure potentials of cell A will increase because the cell has gained water. The solute and pressure potentials of cell B will decrease because it has lost water. Eventually an equilibrium will be reached and there will be no net flow of water from one cell to the other.

Example 6

Two cells, C and D, are next to each other in a tissue. Their solute and pressure potentials are as follows:

	Cell C	Cell D
ψ_S	–630	–650
ψ_p	380	320

In which direction will water flow, from C to D or from D to C?

To arrive at the answer to this question we have to calculate the water potential of each cell from the relationship $\psi = \psi_S + \psi_P$
For cell C:

$$\psi = -630 + 380$$
$$= -250 \text{ kPa}$$

For cell D:

$$\psi = -650 + 320$$
$$= -330 \text{ kPa}$$

Water flows down a water potential gradient, so there will be a net flow of water from cell C to cell D.

Wilting

We have seen that water can be removed from plant cells by osmosis. It can also be removed by evaporation. If the cells in the stem and leaves of a plant lose more water by evaporation than they can absorb, the plant suffers from **water stress**. The most obvious result of this is that turgor is reduced and the plant droops. This is called **wilting**.

Of course water does not evaporate from *all* the cells of the plant, only from those that are exposed to the atmosphere, namely the ones in the immediate vicinity of the stomata. As water evaporates from these cells, the water potential gradient steepens and water passes from the cells in the centre of the plant to the peripheral cells from which water is evaporating. Some plants respond to water stress by closing their stomata, so wilting is prevented or at least slowed down.

Wilting can sometimes be observed in garden plants on hot dry days, or in indoor plants kept by absent-minded owners. Such plants usually recover quite quickly when given water (*figure 7.10*). However, if the roots are kept unwatered for too long, permanent wilting may occur and the plant dies.

Although wilting is generally disadvantageous to plants, it can serve as a form of temperature regulation by removing leaves from the direct rays of the Sun (*page 314*).

7.5 Active transport

There are certain biological situations where molecules or ions appear to break the laws of physics and move *against* a concentration gradient – that is, from a region of low concentration to a region of higher concentration. A spectacular example is provided by certain seaweeds which take up iodide ions so vigorously that they are more than two million times more concentrated inside the cells than in the surrounding water. This movement of molecules or ions against a concentration gradient is called **active transport** and, in contrast to diffusion, it requires energy.

Active transport is the energy-requiring movement of molecules or ions against a concentration gradient.

The energy for active transport comes from respiration. Respiration involves the synthesis of ATP (*page 140*). Anything that inhibits the synthesis of ATP, or prevents it being used, stops active transport. Cyanide, for example, prevents ATP being synthesised and therefore

Figure 7.10 The top photograph shows a tomato plant which has wilted due to lack of water. Below is the same plant 90 minutes after watering.

Active transport in stomatal guard cells, page 158; roots, page 258; phloem tissue, page 264; kidney, page 284; fish gills, page 292

inhibits active transport. Another interesting observation is that cells which are known to engage in active transport on a large scale have exceptionally large numbers of mitochondria, the site of aerobic respiration.

Active transport involves the use of carrier proteins coupled with a source of energy (ATP) which enables them to move molecules or ions against a concentration gradient (*figure 7.11*). Ion gradients created by active transport can in turn be used to provide energy for the transport of other ions and molecules (*see page 145 for an example*).

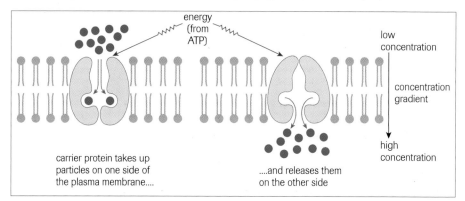

Figure 7.11 Active transport via a carrier protein in the plasma membrane of a cell. Energy is transferred to the carrier protein from the hydrolysis of ATP. This enables the protein to move the particles against a concentration gradient.

Active transport allows cells to take up nutrients even when their concentration outside the cell is very low. It also enables cells to get rid of unwanted substances when their concentration is much greater outside the cell. We shall meet examples later in the book. The carrier proteins work in only one direction so, although there may be some leakage in the other direction, they effectively act as one-way valves.

Indirectly, active transport provides a way of transporting water across cell membranes. The active pumping of chemicals such as sodium ions into or out of a cell creates a concentration gradient of solute across the plasma membrane and the water molecules follow passively by osmosis.

Two important active transport processes are described in the extension boxes.

Extension

The calcium pump

The concentration of calcium ions inside cells is generally much higher than outside. This unequal distribution of calcium ions is maintained by a **calcium pump** which actively expels calcium ions across the plasma membrane of the cell. If the calcium pump ceases, calcium ions diffuse rapidly into the cell down the steep concentration gradient. Momentarily stopping the pump is nature's way of transmitting signals into cells across the plasma membrane.

One of the best known instances of the calcium pump is in the sarcoplasmic reticulum of skeletal muscle where it plays a key role in bringing about contraction (*page 411*).

Some calcium ion pumps, and certainly the one in skeletal muscle, are **ATPases** (*page 140*). They catalyse the hydrolysis of ATP for providing the energy as well as carrying the calcium ions across the membrane.

Cell signalling, page 59

Extension

The sodium–potassium pump

Active transport is responsible for the well-established observation that cells contain relatively high concentrations of potassium ions but low concentrations of sodium ions. The mechanism responsible for this is the **sodium–potassium pump** which moves these two ions in opposite directions across the plasma membrane.

Is this two-way movement of potassium and sodium ions performed by the same carrier or by two different ones? This was investigated by following the passage of radioactively labelled ions across the plasma membrane of certain cells. It was found that the concentrations of sodium and potassium ions on the two sides of the membrane are interdependent, suggesting that the same carrier transports both ions. It is now known that the carrier is an ATPase and that it pumps three sodium ions out of the cell for every two potassium ions pumped in.

The sodium–potassium pump was discovered in the 1950s by a Danish scientist, Jens Skou, who was awarded a Nobel Prize in 1997. It marked an important step forward in our understanding of how ions get into and out of cells, and it has a particular significance for excitable cells such as nerve cells, which depend on it for responding to stimuli and transmitting impulses (*page 351*).

7.6 Exocytosis and endocytosis

So far we have discussed how small molecules and ions get in and out of cells by traversing the plasma membrane. But sometimes larger objects are taken into, or expelled from, cells by a process which relies on the versatility of the plasma membrane mentioned in Chapter 3.

- **Exocytosis** A vesicle containing the material to be expelled moves towards the surface of the cell and fuses with the plasma membrane. The vesicle then opens to the exterior and its contents leave the cell as shown in figure 7.12A. The vesicle membrane then becomes part of the plasma membrane. Exocytosis provides a means by which enzymes, hormones, antibodies and cell wall precursors are released from cells. The vesicles are often derived from the Golgi apparatus (*page 47*).

- **Endocytosis** The plasma membrane invaginates to form a flask-shaped depression which envelops the material. The 'neck' of the flask then closes, and the invagination becomes sealed off to form a vesicle which moves into the body of the cell as shown in figure 7.12B. The vesicle membrane, derived from the plasma membrane, remains intact. Any substances absorbed into the cytoplasm from the vesicle must traverse the membrane first before they can be regarded as being fully inside the cell. Endocytosis is therefore not a substitute for transport across the plasma membrane, but a supplementary process helping it. How the contents of the vesicle are absorbed into the cytoplasm will become clear in a moment.

There are two types of endocytosis, which differ in the size of the vesicles:

Phagocytosis

Phagocytosis literally means 'cell eating' and it involves relatively large particles being taken up into correspondingly large vesicles – usually more than 250 nm in diameter. In this process, which can be seen under the light microscope, the plasma membrane invaginates to form a **phagocytic vesicle** enclosing the particles. The vesicle then fuses with a lysosome whose enzymes digest the particles (*figure 7.13*). Because the particles are digested inside the cell, this is called **intracellular digestion**. The soluble products of digestion (glucose, amino acids and the like) are then absorbed into the surrounding cytoplasm. Any indigestible material may be got rid of by the vesicle moving to the surface of the cell and fusing with the plasma membrane (exocytosis).

One of the best places to see phagocytosis is in *Amoeba*, which feeds on small organisms (*figure 7.14*). It also occurs in cells, collectively called **phagocytes**, which ingest bacteria and other foreign bodies, thus helping to defend the body against disease (*page 321*).

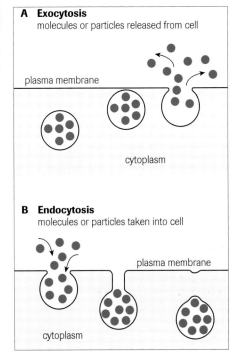

Figure 7.12 Exocytosis and endocytosis are ways of releasing particles from, and taking particles into, a cell.

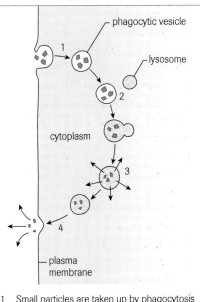

1. Small particles are taken up by phagocytosis to form a phagocytic vesicle.

2. A lysosome fuses with the vesicle and discharges its contents into it.

3. The lysosome enzymes digest the particles and the products of digestion are absorbed into the surrounding cytoplasm.

4. The vesicle membrane fuses with the plasma membrane and any indigestible matter is voided.

Figure 7.13 Diagram showing the phagocytic intake and digestion of particles inside a cell.

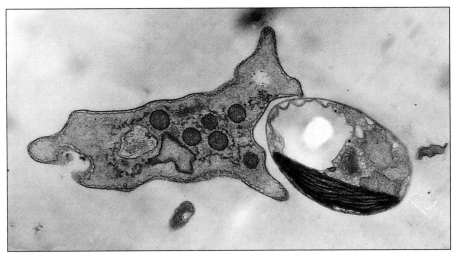

Figure 7.14 In this remarkable electron micrograph, an amoeba (left) appears to be ingesting a unicellular alga by phagocytosis. Magnification ×250.

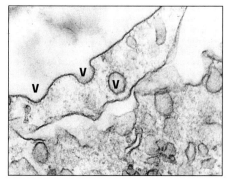

Figure 7.15 Electron micrograph of a cell showing vesicles (**V**) being fomed by pinocytosis. Three vesicles can be seen in different stages of formation. The one on the left has just started to be formed by invagination of the plasma membrane; in the middle one the invagination has pushed further into the cytoplasm; and the one on the right has become completely sealed off. Magnification × 20 000.

Cells can discriminate between different kinds of particle. *Amoeba*, for example, ingests particles of nutritional value but usually rejects particles that are of no food value. Similarly phagocytes only attack certain types of bacteria.

Pinocytosis

Pinocytosis literally means 'cell drinking'. It was first observed in *Amoeba* where tiny channels, formed by invagination of the plasma membrane, pinch off small vesicles which then pinch off even smaller ones. These **pinocytic vesicles** provide a means by which liquids can be brought into the cell and distributed within it.

Pinocytosis, as described above, can be seen under the light microscope. However, much smaller invaginations of the plasma membrane are visible in the electron microscope (*figure 7.15*). They become sealed off from the outside of the cell, forming minute pinocytic vesicles which are usually less than 150 nm in diameter.

Invagination can be induced by the attachment of certain materials to the cell surface, and it provides a means by which molecules may be selectively taken up into cells. The process is highly specific, involving the binding of the molecules with corresponding receptor molecules in the plasma membrane. In this way a cell can take up substances it needs and ignore others.

Judging from electron micrographs, pinocytosis is widespread in cells. Once the vesicles have become sealed off from the exterior, they may fuse with neighbouring lysosomes and have their contents digested as in phagocytosis. Alternatively the membrane surrounding the vesicle may break down, releasing the enclosed molecules which are then incorporated into the cytoplasm.

Summary

1. Materials move in and out of cells by **diffusion, active transport, osmosis, endocytosis** and **exocytosis**.

2. **Diffusion** is the net movement of particles down a concentration gradient, i.e. from a region of higher concentration to a region of lower concentration.

3. In **facilitated diffusion** particles are helped to move rapidly down a concentration gradient by **channel proteins** or **carrier proteins** in the plasma membrane.

4. **Osmosis** is the net movement of water molecules across a **partially permeable membrane**. The plasma membrane is partially permeable and osmosis may occur across it.

5. Osmotic influx of water into a red blood cell may burst the cell (**haemolysis**). Osmotic loss of water from the cell makes the cell shrink and crinkle (**crenation**).

6. Osmotic influx of water into a plant cell causes the cell to become **turgid**. Osmotic loss of water from the cell may induce **plasmolysis**.

7. The behaviour of water molecules in organisms may be expressed in terms of **water potential** (ψ).

8. The water potential of a plant cell depends on the **solute potential** (ψ_S) and **pressure potential** (ψ_p) as summarised by the equation:

$$\psi = \psi_S + \psi_P$$

9. Water potential is measured in kilopascals (kPa). There is always a net flow of water from a higher (less negative) to a lower (more negative) water potential.

10. In **active transport**, particles are moved *against* a concentration gradient by carrier proteins in the plasma membrane. This process requires energy from respiration.

11. Particles which cannot pass through the plasma membrane may be taken into cells by **endocytosis** or released from them by **exocytosis**.

12. There are two types of endocytosis: **phagocytosis** (uptake of large particles) and **pinocytosis** (uptake of small particles).

For general advice on these questions and advice on answering essay-type questions, see pages vii and viii.

1. The graph shows the effects of oxygen concentration on the rates of respiration and bromide ion uptake in carrot root discs.

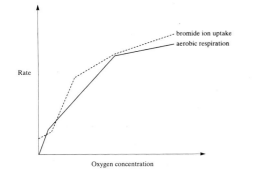

(a) Explain what these data suggest about the way in which bromide ions enter carrot root cells
   (i) in the absence of oxygen;
   (ii) at higher concentrations of oxygen. (4)

(b) Cyanide is a poison which completely inhibits aerobic respiration. Sketch a line on a copy of the graph to show the rate of bromide ion uptake in the presence of cyanide. (1)
   (Total 5 marks)
   NEAB 1998

2. (a) Give **two** differences between osmosis and active transport. (2)

(b) Samples of red blood cells were placed in a series of sodium chloride solutions of different concentrations. After three hours, the samples were examined to find the percentage of cells which had burst. The results are shown in the graph.

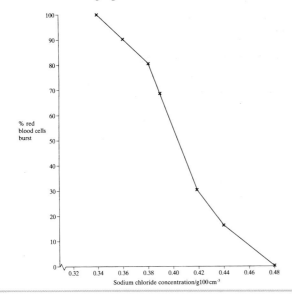

(i) Explain why all the red blood cells burst when placed in a 0.34% sodium chloride solution. (3)

(ii) The red blood cells burst over a range of sodium chloride concentrations. Suggest a reason for this. (1)

(c) When cells from an onion were placed in the same range of sodium chloride solutions, none of the cells burst. Explain why. (1)
   (Total 7 marks)
   NEAB 1998

3. A turgid plant cell was placed in a solution of sucrose. The diagram shows the appearance of the cell after one hour.

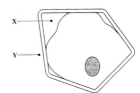

(i) From the diagram, what is the evidence which shows that the water potential of the cell sap must be higher than that of the sucrose solution? (1)

(ii) Explain why the water potential at point **X** is equal to that at point **Y**. (1)
   (Total 2 marks)
   AEB 1997

4. The diagram below shows a plant cell, immersed in a sucrose solution. The pressure potential (Ψ_p) of the cell and the solute potential (Ψ_s) of the cell and of the sucrose solution are shown in the diagram.

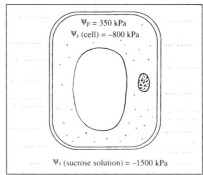

(a) Calculate the water potential of this cell (Ψcell). Show your working. (2)

(b) State whether water will move into or out of the cell. Explain your answer. (2)

(c) State the water potential of this cell at the point of incipient plasmolysis. Assume that changes in Ψ_s (cell) are negligible. (1)
   (Total 5 marks)
   London 1998

In previous chapters reference has been made to the many chemical substances found in cells. In this chapter we shall consider the reactions in which they take part.

The chemical reactions that occur in cells constitute **metabolism**, and the participating molecules are called **metabolites**. Some of these metabolites are synthesised within the organism, others have to be taken in from the environment.

Metabolism is a basic characteristic of all living organisms – indeed it is the metabolic reactions, particularly those that transfer energy, which keep the organism alive. It is only the truly dead parts of organisms, such as the hair and nails of mammals, the shells of molluscs and the lignified fibres of plants, which do not metabolise – and it is because they do not metabolise that they are dead.

8.1 Metabolism: some basic principles

Two types of chemical reaction occur in cells: **synthetic** and **breakdown**. Synthetic reactions include those in which molecules are linked together by chemical bonds to form more complex compounds:

$$A + B \rightarrow AB$$

A and B are the **substrate molecules** or **reactants**. AB represents the **product**. Examples of this kind of reaction are given in Chapter 2, for instance the bonding together of two monosaccharide molecules to form a disaccharide; of fatty acids and glycerol to form a lipid; and of a pair of amino acids to form a dipeptide.

Breakdown reactions are those in which a complex compound is split into simpler molecules:

$$AB \rightarrow A + B$$

In this case AB is the substrate, and A and B are the products. Examples are the hydrolysis of a disaccharide into its constituent monosaccharide molecules; of a lipid into fatty acids and glycerol; and of a dipeptide into its constituent amino acids.

Both synthetic and breakdown reactions occur in cells. Synthetic reactions comprise **anabolism**, and breakdown reactions **catabolism**. The important difference between them is that anabolic reactions generally require (i.e. absorb) energy, whereas catabolic reactions generally release energy.

Energy-absorbing reactions are termed **endergonic**, energy-releasing reactions **exergonic**. These terms are derived from the Greek word *ergon* meaning 'work'. The terms endothermic and exothermic are sometimes used for these two types of chemical reaction, but they are less suitable because they imply that the energy is always thermal, i.e. heat energy. Later we shall see that this is not always the case.

The relationship between these two types of biochemical reaction in a cell of a typical heterotroph such as the human is shown in figure 8.1. Anabolic reactions are concerned with synthesising substances in the cell: starch, glycogen, lipids and proteins are all products of anabolic pathways. Catabolic reactions, on the other hand, are mainly concerned with making energy available in cells.

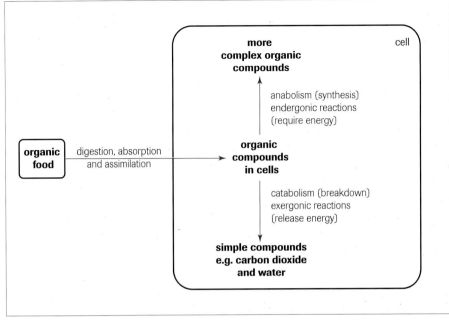

Figure 8.1 The fate of organic food substances in a generalised animal cell. The food substances may be either built up into more complex molecules (anabolism) or broken down into simpler molecules (catabolism).

What is energy needed for?

Energy is required for three main purposes:

- **Synthesis** – for example, the synthesis of proteins, storage compounds, etc.

- **Work** – for example, contraction of muscles, transmission of nerve impulses and secretion by glands.

- **Maintenance** – for example, maintaining a constant body temperature, keeping the tissues and organs in a state of health and repair.

Small steps and gentle reactions

Metabolites are not converted into products in single, rapid reactions. Such reactions would create unfavourable conditions – high temperatures for example – which would be incompatible with life. Instead metabolites are converted gradually, step by step, through a series of small reactions which together comprise a **metabolic pathway**. Each reaction, though small in itself, brings the raw material closer to the end product.

There are five main reasons why metabolism proceeds in small steps.

- It allows the overall process to be controlled so that everything happens in the right place and at the optimum rate.

- Energy can be derived from small catabolic reactions in a usable form. How this is achieved is explained in Chapter 9.

- Substances can be partially broken down so as to provide raw materials for other reactions. Certain intermediate compounds in a catabolic pathway may have functions in their own right.

- It is not possible to synthesise, in one step, complex organic compounds from simple raw materials in the gentle conditions prevailing in cells.

- Having small steps in an anabolic pathway increases the cell's ability to control what products are made.

Living cells have the unique ability to perform numerous individual reactions in dilute aqueous solution at low temperatures and within a narrow range of pH. However, the sheer number of reactions requires a fantastic degree of organisation in the cell. Much of this organisation is achieved by enzymes which control the individual reactions. We shall have more to say about enzymes later.

Anabolism in plants and animals

Plants and other autotrophic organisms synthesise complex organic molecules from simple inorganic sources such as carbon dioxide and water. They have much greater synthetic powers, and their anabolic pathways are therefore more extensive, than those of animals and other heterotrophs.

But even animals have to synthesise complex substances from simpler *organic* raw materials – for example, glycogen has to be synthesised from glucose molecules, and proteins from amino acids. Anabolic reactions are therefore a feature of all living organisms, but are particularly extensive in autotrophs.

To reinforce this idea, try reconstructing figure 8.1 so that it applies to a generalised *plant* cell.

Reconstructing metabolic pathways

Suppose you are a biochemist and you want to reconstruct a metabolic pathway. How do you set about this task, bearing in mind that over 1000 different reactions occur in an individual cell, an object only 20 μm in diameter?

The first step is to grind up the organ that you are interested in – the liver for example – and extract its juices. This is done by homogenising chunks of it in a **Waring blender**, a machine similar to those used for liquidising food in the kitchen. This separates the cells from each other and breaks them open. The resulting suspension is then filtered to separate the juice from the solid fragments and particles. Finally, the juice is centrifuged to separate the various fractions (*page 51*). Experiments can then be performed on the individual fractions – the mitochondria, for example, or the cytoplasmic matrix.

Each step in a metabolic pathway is catalysed by a specific enzyme. If a particular enzyme is inactivated by a specific poison, the substance on which the enzyme normally acts will accumulate, and the product(s) will decline. By systematically blocking the various enzymes that are believed to participate in a particular process, metabolic pathways can be pieced together.

Isotope labelling

A technique which is often used in reconstructing metabolic pathways is isotope labelling. This technique depends on the fact that the atoms of a particular element are not all identical but exist in several different forms or **isotopes**. The isotopes of a particular element share the same atomic number and chemical properties but are distinguished from each other by their relative atomic masses. Moreover, some of them are unstable, emitting characteristic radiations such as alpha particles or gamma rays. Radioactive carbon, ^{14}C, is an example of such an isotope, the 14 indicating that it

has a relative atomic mass of 14 compared with the normal carbon atom ^{12}C with its relative atomic mass of 12. Radioactive isotopes can be detected, and the amount of radiation accurately measured, by means of a Geiger–Müller tube or some other monitoring device sensitive to the radiations being emitted.

The development of cyclotrons and nuclear reactors has made available to biologists an artificial source of isotopes which can be used in biochemical research. The organism is supplied with a specially prepared compound in which one of the elements is replaced with its radioactive isotope. For example, plants can be put in an atmosphere containing $^{14}CO_2$, that is carbon dioxide in which the normal carbon, ^{12}C, is replaced with the radioactive isotope, ^{14}C. The radioactive carbon is described as a **tracer**, and we say that the carbon dioxide has been **labelled**. Such labelled compounds, though easily detected with great sensitivity, are indistinguishable chemically from normal compounds, and are treated by the organism in exactly the same way.

Having supplied an organism with a labelled compound such as carbon dioxide, an analysis can be carried out to find out which parts of the organism have come to contain the radioactive element. To do this the relevant parts of the organism are placed on a photographic film in the dark. As radioactivity has the same effect on photographic film as does light, subsequent development of the film reveals the exact whereabouts of the radioactive material. The pictures obtained are called **autoradiographs**, and the way they are produced is summarised in illustration 1.

If you want to identify the particular cells or organelles which have taken up a radioactive isotope, you have to cut sections of the organ or tissue and expose them to a photographic film. In this way photomicrographs or electron micrographs

can be made, showing the precise location of the radioactivity.

However, none of this tells us much about metabolic pathways. To do that you have to identify the particular compounds that the radioactive isotopes have become incorporated into. This is done by homogenising the organ or tissue and then separating the chemical constituents

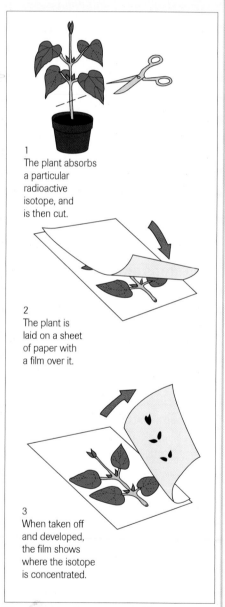

1
The plant absorbs a particular radioactive isotope, and is then cut.

2
The plant is laid on a sheet of paper with a film over it.

3
When taken off and developed, the film shows where the isotope is concentrated.

Illustration 1 How an autoradiograph is made. This particular autoradiograph shows that the isotope has got into the buds of the plant but nowhere else.

by **chromatography** (*page 32*). If paper chromatography is used, the chromatogram is exposed against a photographic film and the radioactive compounds identified in the resulting autoradiograph.

Not all isotopes are radioactive. Some are stable and do not emit radiations. The only way of distinguishing this kind of isotope from the usual one is by the fact that it has a different mass. Examples are the heavy isotopes of oxygen, ^{18}O (oxygen is usually ^{16}O), and nitrogen, ^{15}N (nitrogen is usually ^{14}N). These isotopes can be detected, and their amounts determined very accurately, by means of a **mass spectrometer**, an instrument which separates them according to their relative atomic masses.

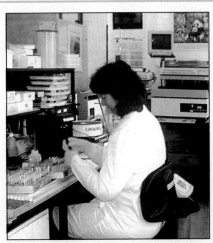
A biologist working with radioactive tracers.

Examples of reconstructing metabolic pathways: respiration, page 143; photosynthesis, page 213

8.2 Energy

If you burn a sample of sugar, the sugar reacts with oxygen and is broken down into carbon dioxide and water with the release of heat energy. The same sort of thing happens inside cells in **respiration**. However, the process is much more complex, taking place in a step by step metabolic pathway. In fact, the glucose never reacts with oxygen directly. Nor is all the energy simply released as heat energy; at least some of it is transferred to other molecules and used for the purposes outlined at the beginning of the chapter.

Support

Energy from breaking down sugar

Biologists often talk about energy being made available by the breakdown of sugar, implying that the breaking of chemical bonds in the sugar molecules releases energy. And yet in chemistry we learn that energy is released, not when chemical bonds are *broken*, but when they are *formed*. In fact respiration supplies energy, not by the breaking of bonds in the substrate, but by the formation of strong bonds in the products. However, the overall result of the process is to yield energy, and it is in this sense that biologists talk about the breakdown of sugar giving energy.

Potential energy and free energy

Think of a boulder sitting in a hollow at the top of a hill (*figure 8.2*). While at rest, the boulder has **potential energy** (or, more precisely, gravitational energy). If, however, it is pushed over the hump so that it rolls down the hill, its potential energy is transferred to the energy of motion, i.e. **kinetic energy**.

In the same kind of way, the glucose and oxygen molecules have potential energy which is transferred when they react together. Respiration transfers energy because the reactants (glucose and oxygen) are thermodynamically less stable than the products (carbon dioxide and water). The energy so transferred is capable of doing useful work. Energy which is released by a reaction and capable of doing useful work is described as **free energy**.

The boulder analogy can usefully be taken a step further. When the boulder reaches the bottom of the hill and comes to rest, it has less potential energy than it did at the top of the hill. In order to restore its potential energy it must be raised to its former position, and this requires energy.

Similarly, there is far less potential energy in the carbon dioxide and water resulting from the oxidation of glucose than there is in the more unstable glucose and oxygen molecules. The

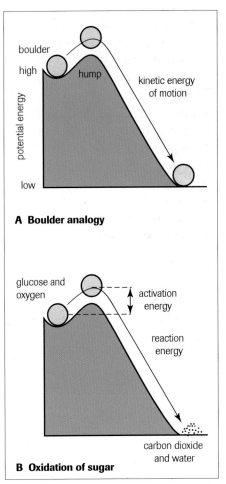

Figure 8.2 The concept of energy. Just as kinetic energy is released when the boulder rolls down the hill, so also energy is released when glucose and oxygen react to form carbon dioxide and water.

Figure 8.3 Two examples of energy transfer in organisms.

Top Weight-lifting and power-lifting are extreme examples of muscle contraction where chemical energy is transferred to the mechanical process of contraction. This process enables a trained weight-lifter to lift more than three times his body mass.

Bottom Lights at the ends of the tentacles of these coral polyps are an example of bioluminescence, the ability of an organism to emit visible light as a result of chemical energy being transferred to light energy. The energy transfer in bioluminescence is exceptionally efficient, hardly any heat energy being produced in the process.

potential energy can be restored only if the carbon dioxide and water are built up again into glucose, a process which requires the input of energy and can only be performed by autotrophs such as plants. They obtain the necessary energy from sunlight in the process of **photosynthesis**.

The idea that glucose can be broken down in respiration and built up again in photosynthesis is the basis of the **carbon cycle** (*page 667*). This recycling of matter depends of course on the continual trapping of solar energy by plants and other autotrophs. This requires the participation of the green pigment **chlorophyll**. Chlorophyll is therefore of enormous importance in the living world.

Energy transfer

The idea of energy being transferred is an obvious fact in our daily lives. For example, if you light a match, chemical energy in the match head is transferred to heat energy and light energy. Similarly, an organism (or certain specialised cells within it) can transfer energy from one situation to another. For example, the photosynthetic cells of a plant can transfer light energy from the Sun into chemical energy within the sugar molecules. Chemical energy in turn may be transferred to other processes (*figure 8.3*).

This fundamental idea is summed up in the **First Law of Thermodynamics** which states that when energy is transferred, there is no net loss or gain of energy. In other words, the total amount of energy which we are left with at the end is equal to the amount we start off with. However, this does not mean that all the energy transferred manifests itself in the same way. The examples given above show clearly that this is not the case.

Let us return to our boulder for a moment. As the boulder rolls down the hill, only a proportion of the potential energy is transferred to the kinetic energy of motion – the rest is used to overcome friction and is transferred to the surroundings as heat energy. This is summed up in the **Second Law of Thermodynamics** which includes the idea that when energy is transferred a proportion of it becomes heat energy. This, too, is an obvious fact of everyday life. The internal combustion engine generates energy for powering a car, but most of the energy simply heats up the engine and is lost to the surroundings.

This principle is of great importance in biology. It means that when sugar is metabolised in respiration, not all the energy can be used for synthesising more complex molecules or driving biological processes such as growth and movement. Most of it is transferred to heat energy and lost. Of course it does not follow that this heat energy is of no use to the organism; indeed it helps many animals to maintain a constant body temperature. But from a thermodynamic standpoint this proportion of the transferred energy has no direct metabolic use. The same applies to a car: the heat energy generated by the motor, though useless for powering the car, may help to keep the driver warm.

Activation energy

The boulder analogy illustrates yet another important concept. You will recall that the boulder rests in a slight hollow at the top of the hill and it is necessary to push it over the hump before it can start rolling down the hill. The hump represents an **energy barrier**, and energy is required to push the boulder over this barrier. Much the same applies to our glucose and oxygen molecules: they are not naturally reactive – indeed they are rather *un*reactive – and a small amount of energy must be applied, by heating them for example, before the process of oxidative breakdown can get underway. This is called the **activation energy**.

Clearly any factor, physical or chemical, that helps the glucose molecule over the energy barrier and decreases the activation energy necessary to get the reaction going will facilitate the process and speed up the reaction. This brings us to the question of what determines the rate of biological reactions.

The rate of biological reactions

Consider the type of chemical reaction in which two substrate molecules, A and B, react to form a product, AB – the sort of reaction that unites two monosaccharide molecules to form a disaccharide. What factors might influence the rate of such a reaction?

To answer this we must bear in mind that the substrate molecules are in a state of continual random motion. Only when they collide can they react. Clearly any factor that increases the frequency of collision will increase the rate of the reaction. In general three factors achieve this effect:

- the concentration of the substrate molecules;
- the temperature of the reaction mixture;
- the presence of a **catalyst**.

The first two need little explanation. It is obvious that the more concentrated (i.e. the closer together) the substrate molecules are, the more likely they are to collide and react. Raising the temperature speeds up the random motion of the molecules, thereby increasing the probability that they will collide. It also raises their energy levels, so they are more likely to react when they do collide.

Any factor which, directly or indirectly, raises the concentration of the substrate molecules will obviously speed up the reaction. Increasing the pressure has this effect, as does removal of some of the water in which the substrate molecules are dissolved. But the most effective way of concentrating the substrate is to supply a catalyst. The substrate molecules are absorbed onto the surface of the catalyst where, having been brought into close proximity, they react. The product then leaves the catalyst, which is unchanged by the process and may be used again.

Catalysts have the effect of lowering the activation energy required to get the reaction going, and as such they are very important. Many inorganic catalysts are known – for example iron, platinum and nickel – and they are important in industrial processes. Catalysts are also important in biological systems, but these are *organic* substances and operate in a slightly different way from the surface catalysts described above. The catalysts found in living systems are called **enzymes**, to which we now turn.

8.3 Enzymes and their properties

The word enzyme literally means 'in yeast' and it was coined for the active ingredient in yeast cells that causes fermentation (*extension box alongside*). It is now used as the collective name for the thousands of organic compounds that have been extracted from cells and found to speed up the chemical reactions which occur in organisms. As with other types of catalyst they achieve their effect by lowering the activation energy.

Why are enzymes important?

Without enzymes, the reactions that occur in living organisms would be so slow as hardly to proceed at all, and this would be incompatible with the maintenance of life. Of course the speed of the reactions could be increased by raising the temperature, but this would kill the organism by denaturing the proteins and disrupting the membranes, as well as being very expensive energetically. Enzymes therefore enable metabolic reactions to proceed rapidly but at low temperatures.

But enzymes do more than merely speed up the reactions. They also control them. It was mentioned earlier that over 1000 different reactions take place in an individual cell. The functional organisation which this demands is achieved by each individual reaction being catalysed by a specific enzyme in a particular place within the cell. It is this which ensures that metabolism proceeds by small, gentle steps in an orderly fashion.

Extension

How enzymes were discovered

Enzymes were discovered by the German chemist, Eduard Büchner, towards the end of the 19th century. His discovery is an example of one of those fortuitous accidents by which advances are sometimes made in science.

Büchner had been trying to obtain a fluid of medicinal use from yeast. However, his extracts kept going bad. To prevent this he tried adding sugar to one of the extracts, sugar being well known as a preservative of fruit. To his surprise the sugar was converted into alcohol – in other words it fermented.

Now there was nothing new about the discovery that yeast promotes fermentation – in fact this had already been demonstrated by Louis Pasteur some 20 years before. But Pasteur believed that fermentation was brought about by the *living* yeast cells. Büchner showed that it was not the living yeast cells that were responsible for fermentation, but the juice extracted from them.

Naming enzymes

Normally an enzyme is named by attaching the suffix -ase to the name of the substrate on which it acts. Thus **carbohydrases** act on carbohydrates, **lipases** on lipids, **proteases** on proteins and **nucleases** on nucleic acids. Within each of these major groups certain enzymes act on particular substrates. For example, carbohydrases include **maltase** which acts on maltose, and **sucrase** which acts on sucrose. The '-ase' rule does not always apply. For example, **pepsin** and **trypsin**, both found in the mammalian gut, act on proteins. They were discovered and named before the '-ase' idea was introduced.

In recent years enzymes have become important for a quite different reason: making products that are useful to humans. This is an aspect of biotechnology about which we shall have more to say at the end of the chapter.

Where do enzymes occur?

Enzymes are divided into two main groups: **intracellular** and **extracellular**. Intracellular enzymes occur inside cells where they speed up and control metabolism. Extracellular enzymes are produced by cells but achieve their effects outside the cell; they include **digestive enzymes** that break down food in the gut.

Some intracellular enzymes float around freely in the fluid parts of the cell. Others – probably the majority – are fixed to the plasma membrane or to membranes inside the cell.

Different types of enzymes

Following the recommendation of the International Union of Biochemical Societies, enzymes are divided into six main categories according to the type of chemical reaction which they catalyse:

- **Oxidoreductases** are involved in biological oxidation and reduction reactions. They include **dehydrogenases** which catalyse the removal of hydrogen atoms from a substrate, and **oxidases** which catalyse the addition of oxygen to hydrogen with the formation of water. These enzymes play an important part in the final stages of respiration.

- **Transferases** catalyse the transfer of groups of atoms from one substance to another. The groups transferred include, for example, amino groups (NH_2). Enzymes which specifically transfer amino groups are called **transaminases**. They enable organisms to synthesise certain amino acids (*page 31*).

- **Hydrolases** catalyse the addition of water to, or its removal from, certain substrates. The carbohydrases, lipases, proteases and nucleases mentioned earlier are all examples of this category of enzyme. They play an important part in the building up (**condensation**) and breaking down (**hydrolysis**) of storage compounds such as starch and other polymers.

- **Lyases** break chemical bonds by means other than hydrolysis, thereby creating double bonds. They include **decarboxylases** which remove carboxyl groups (COOH) from intermediates in respiration, with the formation of carbon dioxide.

- **Isomerases** catalyse the transfer of atoms from one part of a molecule to another. The new molecule and the original one are **isomers**, i.e. they each contain the same atoms but arranged differently. That's why these enzymes are called isomerases. In an early stage of respiration an isomerase enzyme rearranges the atoms in the sugar molecules so that they can enter the metabolic pathway.

- **Ligases** catalyse the joining together of two molecules, coupled with the breakdown of ATP. They include **phosphokinases** which catalyse the addition of phosphate groups to glucose in respiration, and **DNA ligase** which is involved in the synthesis of DNA.

Properties of enzymes

Enzymes are nearly always proteins, though as we shall see later they may contain a non-protein component. Their properties, and the way they work, are intimately bound up with their shape as determined by the tertiary structure of globular proteins (*page 29*).

Following the course of an enzyme-controlled reaction

To study the properties of enzymes, one must be able to follow the course of enzyme-controlled reactions in the laboratory. This can be done by estimating *either* the rate at which a substrate is used up *or* the rate at which a product accumulates.

This is not the place to go into practical details, but the principle is quite simple: you measure the amount of substrate still left, or product formed, at different times after the start of the experiment. This usually involves taking samples of the reaction mixture at intervals and analysing them chemically. Nowadays all sorts of techniques are available for doing this, depending on the particular substances involved. The results are best shown in a graph, with the amounts of substrate or product plotted against time.

To get a true picture of how the reaction proceeds it is necessary that the temperature, pH and other variables should be kept as constant as possible, and the reaction mixture should be stirred or agitated so that the contents are evenly distributed.

The main properties of enzymes are as follows:

- They generally work very rapidly.
- They are not destroyed by the reactions which they catalyse.
- They can work in either direction.
- They are usually inactivated by high temperatures.
- They are sensitive to pH.
- They are usually specific to particular reactions.

Let us look at each of these properties in detail.

The speed of action of enzymes

An enzyme's speed of action is expressed as its **turnover number**. This is the number of substrate molecules which one molecule of the enzyme turns into product per minute.

The turnover numbers of different enzymes vary from about 100 to several million, though for the majority it is around several thousand. One of the fastest enzymes is **catalase**. This enzyme is found in a number of organs and tissues, including the liver, where its job is to speed up the decomposition of hydrogen peroxide (H_2O_2) into oxygen and water:

$$2H_2O_2 \rightarrow 2H_2O + O_2$$

Hydrogen peroxide is a toxic by-product of metabolism, and its rapid conversion to water removes its toxicity. Catalase is therefore a very important enzyme. It has a turnover number of approximately six million, increasing the speed of the reaction by 10^{14} compared with what it would be in the absence of the enzyme. Its action can be demonstrated by dropping a small piece of liver into a beaker of hydrogen peroxide. The fizzing and bubbling that ensues as oxygen is given off is a dramatic demonstration of an enzyme in action (*figure 8.4*).

In their speed of action, enzymes are much more efficient than inorganic catalysts. Finely divided platinum or iron filings will also speed up the decomposition of hydrogen peroxide, but nothing like as quickly as a piece of liver. The reason is that the enzyme achieves a greater lowering of the activation energy.

There is an even faster enzyme than catalase, and that is **carbonic anhydrase**. This enzyme catalyses the combination of carbon dioxide and water in red blood cells (*page 220*). It has a turnover number of 36 million.

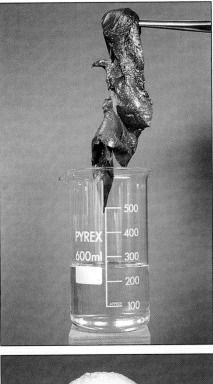

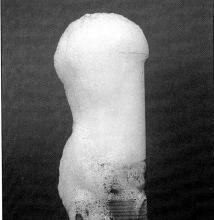

Figure 8.4 An enzyme in action.
Top A piece of liver (approximately 35 g) is dropped into a beaker of hydrogen peroxide.
Bottom The result after three minutes. Liver contains catalase, one of the fastest-acting enzymes known.

Enzymes can be used again

Enzymes are not altered by the reactions they catalyse, so they can be used again. The explanation of this will become clear when we discuss how enzymes work. This is not to say that a given molecule of an enzyme can be used indefinitely, for the action of an enzyme depends critically on its shape and this is readily affected by changes in temperature, acidity and so on. In this respect enzymes differ from inorganic catalysts which can be used over and over again almost indefinitely. Because enzymes wear out, they have to be constantly replaced.

Enzymes work in either direction

Consider this hypothetical enzyme-controlled reaction:

$$A + B \rightleftharpoons C + D$$

The enzyme which catalyses this reaction works in such a way that the reaction can proceed from left to right or from right to left, depending on circumstances – hence the two-way arrow.

The direction in which the reaction proceeds at any given time depends on the relative amounts of substrates and products present, that is, on the equilibrium conditions. If there is a lot of A and B compared with C and D, the reaction will go from left to right until an equilibrium between substrates and products is reached. If, on the other hand, there is a lot of C and D compared with A and B, the reaction will go from right to left, again until an equilibrium is reached.

Enzyme-controlled reactions are generally reversible, at least in theory. In practice though a particular reaction may only go in one direction because the equilibrium conditions always favour that.

Extension

The equilibrium constant

In the reaction $A + B = C + D$, equilibrium is reached when there is a particular ratio between the concentrations of $(A + B)$ and $(C + D)$. This ratio is always the same for a particular reaction but varies from one reaction to another. It is called the **equilibrium constant**. We can sum up the relationship like this:

$$K = \frac{[C]\,[D]}{[A]\,[B]}$$

where K is the equilibrium constant and [ ] means concentration. An enzyme has no effect on the value of the equilibrium constant; it merely speeds up the reaction until equilibrium is reached.

Effect of temperature on enzymes

Figure 8.5 shows the effect of temperature on the rate of a typical enzyme-controlled reaction. Up to about 40°C the rate increases smoothly, a ten degree rise in temperature being accompanied by an approximate doubling of the rate of the reaction – the normal temperature rule for chemical reactions in general. Above this temperature the rate begins to fall off and then declines rapidly, ceasing altogether at about 60°C. This is because heating changes the shape of the enzyme molecules, preventing them from working. This is called **denaturation** (*extension box on next page*).

In fact enzymes denature at any temperature – it is one of the reasons why they cannot be used over and over again indefinitely. However, the higher the temperature, the less time it takes for denaturation to occur.

Because of the susceptibility of enzymes to heating, few cells can function properly at temperatures higher than approximately 45°C. Organisms that live in environments where the temperature exceeds 45°C either have heat-resistant enzymes or are able to regulate their body temperature. Some examples of heat-tolerant organisms are given on pages 310 and 315.

Effect of pH on enzymes

Every enzyme has it own range of pH in which it functions best. Most intracellular enzymes have their optimum function round about neutral (pH 7). Excessive acidity (pH markedly less than 7) or alkalinity (pH markedly greater than 7) denatures them and renders them inactive. This is one of the reasons why the pH of the cells and body fluids needs to be regulated (*page 267*).

Digestive enzymes behave differently. Some of them work optimally in a distinctly acidic or alkaline environment. Thus the protease enzyme pepsin functions most effectively in an acid medium at a pH of about 2.0. It is found in the stomach where conditions are markedly acidic. Trypsin, on the other hand, functions most effectively in an alkaline medium at about pH 8.5. It is found in the duodenum where conditions are alkaline.

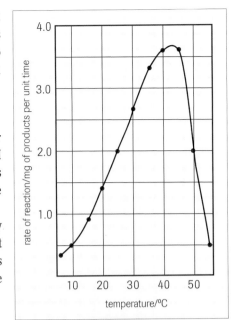

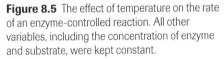

Figure 8.5 The effect of temperature on the rate of an enzyme-controlled reaction. All other variables, including the concentration of enzyme and substrate, were kept constant.

Part 2

Extension

What happens when an enzyme is denatured?

Enzymes, like other proteins, consist of polypeptide chains held in a particular position by cross-links (*page 29*). When an enzyme is denatured, the cross-links are broken and the polypeptide chains open up and become randomly arranged. As a result the protein loses its normal shape and becomes biologically inactive.

Denaturation is brought about by heating, extremes of pH and excessive amounts of certain chemicals such as urea, alcohol and detergents. It is normally irreversible.

Specificity of enzymes

Most enzymes catalyse only one reaction, or type of reaction. The degree of specificity varies, and some enzymes are less restricted in their choice of substrates than others. Most intracellular enzymes work only on one particular substrate. Catalase, for example, acts only on hydrogen peroxide. However, pancreatic lipase, an extracellular digestive enzyme in the duodenum, will digest a variety of different fats.

The specificity of intracellular enzymes helps to explain why metabolism proceeds in such an orderly way. Each enzyme molecule, fixed to a particular place on one of the membranes within the cell, catalyses a specific reaction in a particular metabolic pathway.

8.4 How enzymes work

We can explain the properties of enzymes by suggesting that when an enzyme-controlled reaction takes place the enzyme and substrate molecules bind together for a short time. As well as being consistent with the known properties of enzymes, this hypothesis is supported by other lines of evidence. One important piece of evidence comes from studying the effect on the rate of an enzyme-controlled reaction of altering the substrate concentration.

A graph summarising the results of such studies is shown in figure 8.6. Curve A shows the effect on the reaction rate of gradually increasing the concentration of substrate, the enzyme concentration being kept constant. As you can see, the reaction rate rises with increasing substrate concentration until, at a certain substrate concentration, it reaches a maximum and levels off.

These results fit in with the idea that the substrate molecules collide with the usually much larger enzyme molecules and then bind with them. Obviously the more substrate

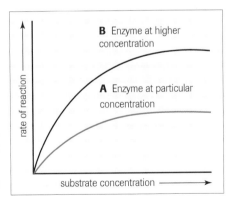

Figure 8.6 The effect of substrate concentration on the rate of an enzyme-controlled reaction at two different enzyme concentrations. The temperature was kept constant at an optimum value. Notice that when the concentration of the enzyme is increased the reaction proceeds at a faster rate and reaches a higher plateau.

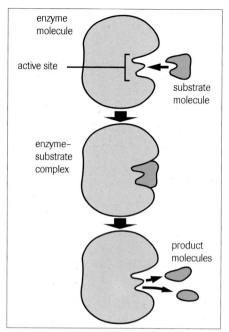

Figure 8.7 The lock and key mechanism proposes that the substrate fits into an active site on the surface of the enzyme, where the reaction takes place.

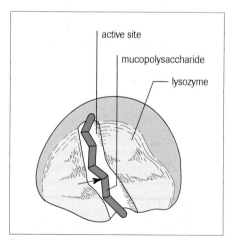

Figure 8.8 Greatly simplified diagram, based on X-ray diffraction studies, of the lysozyme molecule, showing part of the amino sugar chain of the mucopolysaccharide in the active site. The amino sugars (blue) are held in place within the active site by hydrogen bonds and various other types of attraction. The chain becomes broken at the position indicated by the red arrow.

molecules there are, the greater are the chances that the substrate and enzyme molecules will collide. The plateau in the graph can be explained by hypothesising that when the substrate concentration reaches a certain level, the system becomes saturated: all the enzyme molecules are working flat out and adding more substrate makes no difference to the rate of the reaction. When this point is reached the only way to increase the reaction rate is to raise the concentration of the enzyme, and curve B shows the result of doing just this.

The lock and key mechanism

Studies of this sort, together with other lines of evidence, led scientists to propose that in an enzyme-controlled reaction the substrate molecules bind with the enzyme to form an **enzyme–substrate complex**. The reaction then takes place and the product leaves the enzyme. The enzyme, unchanged by the reaction, can then be used again:

enzyme + substrate → enzyme–substrate complex → enzyme + product

It is thought that each enzyme molecule has a particular place on its surface to which the substrate molecules become attached. This is called the **active site**. Every protein has a particular shape, and this applies to enzymes no less than to other proteins. We can picture the active site of an enzyme molecule as having a distinctive shape into which only certain specific substrate molecules will fit. The shape of the active site, and the positions of the various chemical groups and bonds within it, ensure that only those substrate molecules with a complementary structure will combine with the enzyme. Thus we have an explanation of the specificity of enzymes: the enzyme and substrate molecules fit together like a lock and key. This explanation of enzyme action is known as the **lock and key mechanism**, and it is illustrated in figure 8.7.

Evidence for the lock and key mechanism

Over the years much progress has been made in elucidating the molecular structure of enzymes and the way they interact with their substrates. One enzyme which has been particularly studied is **lysozyme**. This enzyme is found in tears and other secretions where its function is to destroy pathogenic bacteria by dissolving their cell walls. The bacterial cell wall is a polysaccharide consisting of chains of amino sugars (*page 22*). Lysozyme destroys the cell wall by breaking the glycosidic bonds between certain of the amino sugars.

Lysozyme is a globular protein and X-ray diffraction studies have shown that there is a groove on one side of the molecule into which the polysaccharide chain fits (*figure 8.8*). Further analysis has shown that part of the amino sugar chain (six amino sugars to be exact) fits into the groove. The chain is held in place by hydrogen bonds and ionic attraction, and becomes broken at a specific point (indicated by the arrow in figure 8.8). This therefore seems to be the active site.

The lock and key mechanism helps to explain why enzymes are inactivated by high temperatures and changes in pH. Heating denatures the enzyme, bringing about a change in shape that prevents the substrate fitting into the active site. Changes in pH break the bonds which maintain the three-dimensional shape of the enzyme, and alter the ionic charges on the side groups within the active site itself.

The induced fit hypothesis

The lock and key mechanism, as originally proposed, suggested that there is an exact fit between the substrate and the active site of the enzyme. However, more recent research has suggested that the active site may not necessarily be exactly the right shape to begin with. It is believed that when the substrate combines with the enzyme it causes a small change to occur in the shape of the enzyme molecule, thereby enabling the substrate to fit more snugly into the active site. This is called the **induced fit hypothesis** and it is illustrated in figure 8.9.

Michaelis constant

The way the substrate concentration affects the rate of an enzyme-controlled reaction is summed up by the **Michaelis constant**. This is the concentration of substrate required to make the reaction go at half its maximum rate (*illustration*).

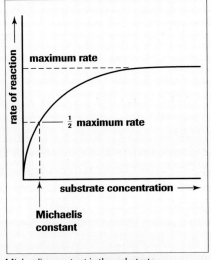

Michaelis constant is the substrate concentration which enables an enzyme-controlled reaction to proceed at half its maximum rate.

The Michaelis constant is always the same for a particular enzyme, but varies from one enzyme to another. It tells us how readily the enzyme reacts with its substrate – in other words it is a measure of the affinity of the enzyme for its substrate. A low Michaelis constant means that there is a high affinity between the enzyme and substrate, the substrate molecules reacting readily with the enzyme molecules. On the other hand, a high Michaelis constant means that there is a relatively low affinity between the enzyme and substrate, the substrate molecules reacting less readily with the enzyme molecules.

The importance of this in the cell is that some reactions proceed quickly even when there is very little substrate present, whereas others require a much higher concentration of substrate. By comparing the Michaelis constants of different enzymes we can learn much about the

reactions which they catalyse and their functions in the body. Moreover, the Michaelis constant of a particular enzyme can be changed by certain types of enzyme inhibitors, and this can give us important information about how these inhibitors work.

The Michaelis constant was developed in 1913 by Leonor Michaelis and Maud Menten (it is sometimes called the Michaelis–Menten constant). They derived the constant from mathematical considerations, and it enabled them to predict that the substrate combines with the enzyme. This prediction was borne out by later experimental observations which led to the development of the lock and key hypothesis.

The induced fit hypothesis is supported by X-ray diffraction studies. Scientists have compared the detailed shape and molecular configuration of certain enzyme molecules on their own and when combined with their substrates, and have found that they are not the same. Significant changes in shape do indeed take place, both to the enzyme molecule and also to the substrate, improving the fit and helping to lower the activation energy.

The fact that a substrate can, in effect, mould the enzyme to its own shape means that several different substrates may be able to react with the same enzyme. This would account for the relatively broad specificity of some enzymes, lipase for example.

8.5 Inhibition of enzymes

Certain substances inhibit enzymes, thereby slowing down or stopping enzyme-controlled reactions. These enzyme inhibitors are of special interest for three main reasons.

- They give us important information about the shapes and properties of the active sites of enzymes.

- They can be used to block particular reactions, thereby enabling biochemists to reconstruct metabolic pathways (*page 120*).

- They have important medical and agricultural uses as, for example, drugs and pesticides.

Later we shall see that inhibitors also play a natural part in the way enzymes are controlled in cells. But first, let us look at the two main types of enzyme inhibition that can occur.

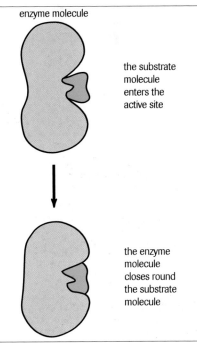

Figure 8.9 The induced fit hypothesis. When the substrate molecule enters the active site it causes (i.e. *induces*) the enzyme molecule to change its shape so that the two molecules fit together more snugly.

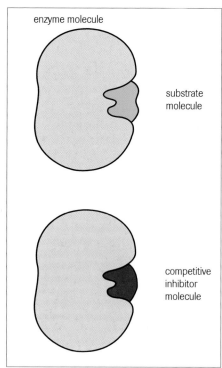

Figure 8.10 In competitive inhibition of an enzyme, an inhibitor molecule (red), similar in structure to the substrate molecule (blue), competes with the substrate molecule for the active site.

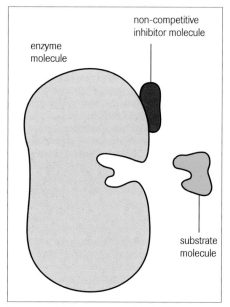

Figure 8.11 In non-competitive inhibition of an enzyme, an inhibitor molecule (red) combines with the enzyme molecule outside the active site, changing its shape and thus preventing the substrate molecule from interacting with the enzyme.

Competitive inhibition

In this type of inhibition another molecule, similar to the substrate, competes with the substrate for the active site of the enzyme. Once in position the inhibitor stays in the active site. It is like putting the wrong key in a lock: the key fits the lock but will not open it – instead it gets stuck. Competitive inhibition is illustrated diagrammatically in figure 8.10.

A classic illustration of competitive inhibition is provided by one of the metabolic steps in respiration. The reaction involves the oxidation of succinate (*page 142*). The enzyme which catalyses it is succinate dehydrogenase. Another substance called malonate has a molecular configuration similar to that of succinate, and if it is added to the system the reaction is slowed. The malonate molecule is so similar to the succinate molecule that it fits into the active site of the enzyme. It thus competes with the normal substrate.

Many antibiotics and sulphonamide drugs are competitive inhibitors. These compounds are used to destroy, or prevent the growth of, pathogenic bacteria. They exert their action by combining with enzymes essential for the normal functioning of the bacteria.

Non-competitive inhibition

In this type of inhibition the inhibitor molecule, instead of entering the active site, attaches itself to some other part of the enzyme molecule. Once in position, it exerts an effect on the enzyme molecule, preventing it from working (*figure 8.11*).

A well-known non-competitive inhibitor is cyanide. It inactivates cytochrome oxidase which is responsible for the transfer of electrons in respiration (*page 144*). Cyanide therefore prevents the organism respiring. This makes it a deadly poison.

Other non-competitive inhibitors include organophosphate insecticides and certain types of nerve gases. Both work in the same way. They combine with the enzyme cholinesterase which controls the transmission of nerve impulses across the junctions (synapses) in the nervous system (*page 356*). How they achieve their toxic effects is explained on page 358.

Heavy metals such as arsenic, mercury and lead are also non-competitive inhibitors. They combine covalently with sulphydryl (–SH) groups in the enzyme molecule, thereby breaking the sulphur bridges that hold the polypeptide chains together (*page 29*). This makes the enzyme incapable of reacting with its substrate.

Variations on the theme

Classifying enzyme inhibitors into competitive and non-competitive can be useful. However, there is considerable variation in the way different inhibitors achieve their actions, and rigid categorisation is not always possible.

Some inhibitors combine, not with the enzyme, but with the enzyme–substrate complex. The substrate gets jammed in the active site and products are not formed.

Another variation is seen in those enzymes which require a metal ion for their action (*page 132*). Inhibitors of such enzymes often work by combining with the metal ion rather than with the enzyme. Cyanide works this way – it combines with a metal ion (Fe^{3+}) associated with cytochrome oxidase.

Inhibitors also vary in the tenacity with which they bind with the enzyme. Some of them form a relatively loose association with the enzyme, becoming detached if and when circumstances permit. This sort of inhibition is described as **reversible**. The action of malonate on succinate dehydrogenase, mentioned at the top of the page, is an example of reversible inhibition. Other inhibitors combine permanently with the enzyme, making it impossible for the substrate to react with it at all. This kind of inhibition is **irreversible**. Nerve gases are irreversible inhibitors.

Telling the difference between competitive and non-competitive inhibition

How can you tell if an enzyme inhibitor is competitive or non-competitive? After all, you can't *see* if the inhibitor enters the active site or attaches itself to some other part of the enzyme molecule.

To tackle this problem you have to adopt an indirect approach. First you find the effect on the rate of the reaction of increasing the substrate concentration at a particular concentration of the enzyme. You then repeat the experiment in the presence of the inhibitor. The sort of results you get are shown in the illustrations.

Look carefully at the graphs. You will see that at low substrate concentrations both types of inhibitor slow down the reaction to the same extent. But look what happens at high substrate concentrations. If the inhibitor is competitive, the reaction rate eventually reaches almost the same maximum value that it did before. The reason is that at high substrate concentrations, the substrate molecules compete with the inhibitor so effectively that the reaction rate is almost as fast as it would be if the inhibitor was not there.

If, on the other hand, the inhibitor is non-competitive, the reaction rate never comes close to the maximum value that it reached before. The reason is that the inhibitor puts a certain proportion of the enzyme molecules out of action, so in effect the enzyme concentration is lowered. At this lower enzyme concentration the original maximum reaction rate can never be reached, however much you increase the substrate concentration.

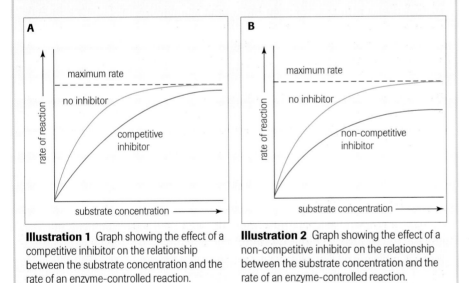

Illustration 1 Graph showing the effect of a competitive inhibitor on the relationship between the substrate concentration and the rate of an enzyme-controlled reaction.

Illustration 2 Graph showing the effect of a non-competitive inhibitor on the relationship between the substrate concentration and the rate of an enzyme-controlled reaction.

Natural inhibitors

By now you may have got the impression that enzyme inhibition is always unnatural and disastrous. Far from it. Cells contain many natural inhibitors which ensure that particular enzymes do not function until they are needed. The inhibition is often removed by another enzyme which serves as an activator.

Here is an example. The digestive enzyme trypsin is secreted by the pancreas as an inactive precursor, trypsinogen. The active site is masked by a polypeptide chain which is stripped off only when the enzyme reaches the small intestine. The removal of the polypeptide chain is catalysed by an enzyme called enterokinase which is present in the small intestine (*page 189*). So, the polypeptide chain *inhibits* the enzyme and enterokinase *activates* it.

Inside cells, variations in the rate of metabolism are brought about by non-competitive enzyme inhibitors. For example, suppose a metabolic pathway becomes overactive and too much end product is produced. In these circumstances the end product inhibits one of the enzymes that catalyses an early step in the metabolic pathway, so less product is formed. This is called **end product inhibition**, and it is an example of negative feedback (*page 272*). Sometimes inhibition is achieved not by the end product but by one of the intermediates in the pathway.

Enzymes that are inhibited in this way often exist in two different forms, one inactive and the other active. The inactive form of the enzyme – induced by the inhibitor – is shaped in such a way that the substrate will not fit into the active site. For the enzyme to become active, its shape must be altered so that the substrate will fit into the active site. This is brought about by an **activator**. Amongst the many important activators in biological systems are calcium ions (Ca^{2+}) which we shall meet in later chapters.

Enzymes that exist in two different forms are described as **allosteric** (meaning 'different shapes'). Such enzymes can be switched on or off, depending on circumstances, so metabolism as a whole can be regulated and adjusted to suit the needs of the organism.

8.6 Cofactors

Some enzymes only work in the presence of another chemical which serves as a 'helper'. Such chemicals are called **cofactors**.

In some cases the cofactor is a metal ion such as zinc (Zn^{2+}), iron (Fe^{2+} or Fe^{3+}), magnesium (Mg^{2+}) or copper (Cu^{2+}). The metal ion may help to bind the enzyme and substrate together, or it may serve as the catalytic centre of the enzyme itself. For example, iron is the catalytic centre of catalase. Indeed, iron on its own will catalyse the decomposition of hydrogen peroxide, though not as effectively as when it is associated with the enzyme.

In other cases the cofactor is a complex, non-protein organic molecule known as a **coenzyme**. Often the coenzyme functions as a carrier, transferring chemical groups or atoms from the active site of one enzyme to the active site of another. An example is **nicotinamide adenine dinucleotide** (**NAD**) which carries hydrogen atoms in respiration (*page 144*).

Sometimes the function of a coenzyme is carried out, not by a separate substance, but by a non-protein group of atoms attached to the enzyme. This is called a **prosthetic group**. The function of the prosthetic group is to transfer atoms or chemical groups from the active site of the enzyme to some other substance. The prosthetic group can therefore be regarded as a kind of built-in coenzyme. For example, in respiration the enzyme cytochrome oxidase has a prosthetic group which transfers hydrogen atoms to oxygen with the formation of water. This too is explained on page 144.

There is no hard and fast distinction between coenzymes and prosthetic groups. They simply represent different degrees of attachment to the enzyme: coenzymes are loosely bound to the enzyme whereas prosthetic groups are tightly bound. In both cases the active centre is often a metal ion such as iron or copper. In cytochrome oxidase the metal is iron but copper is also required for the catalytic action of the enzyme.

Prosthetic groups are not confined to enzymes – they are essential components of certain other proteins as well. For example, haemoglobin and other blood pigments contain a prosthetic group (the haem part of the molecule) whose role is similar to that of enzyme prosthetic groups, namely to carry atoms or chemical groups from one place to another. In the case of blood pigments it is oxygen that is carried.

Humans and other animals obtain cofactors, or the raw materials for making them, from their food. Metal ions come from the mineral component of the food, while coenzymes are derived mainly from vitamins. For example, NAD is synthesised from nicotinamide, one of the B vitamins (*page 35*).

Metabolic process involving end-product inhibition, page 146

Extension

Investigating cofactors

How can we find out if a cofactor is needed for a particular enzyme to work? One way is to put a solution of the enzyme in a sealed bag made of a partially permeable membrane such as cellophane. The bag is then suspended in distilled water.

The membrane allows small molecules and ions to pass through, but holds back the larger protein molecules. In the course of the next few hours, metal ions and coenzymes leave the enzyme molecules and diffuse through the membrane to the surrounding water. To make sure that all such cofactors diffuse through, the distilled water should be changed several times.

The bag now contains a solution of the enzyme, minus any cofactors that may have been present. The enzyme solution is now tested for its enzyme activity. If the activity is reduced, we conclude that one or more factors necessary for the working of the enzyme have been lost. If we put the missing factors back and find that the enzyme's activity is restored, our conclusion would seem to be confirmed.

This is one reason why vitamins and minerals are so important in the diet. However, only very small amounts of them are needed because the cofactors themselves are required by cells in such tiny quantities.

8.7 Putting enzymes to use

Many of the reactions catalysed by enzymes have commercial uses, the conversion of starch to sugar being just one example. These reactions can be made to happen without enzymes, for example by heating or by the use of strong acids. Indeed in the past this has been the main approach used in industry. However, enzymes with their fast but gentle action provide an attractive alternative.

There are three main advantages of using enzymes in industrial processes, and they are directly related to the properties of enzymes.

- They are specific in their action and are therefore less likely to produce unwanted by-products.
- They are biodegradable and therefore cause less environmental pollution.
- They work in mild conditions, i.e. at low temperatures, neutral pH and normal atmospheric pressure, and are therefore energy-saving.

The main disadvantage of enzymes is that they may be denatured by an increase in temperature and are susceptible to poisons and changes in pH. This means that the conditions in which they work must be stringently controlled. In particular the enzyme–substrate mixture must be uncontaminated with other substances that might affect the reaction, and the equipment should be scrupulously clean.

The production process

To be effective in a production process, the enzyme molecules must be brought into maximum contact with the substrate molecules. This is achieved in one of two ways. One way is simply to mix solutions of the enzyme and substrate in suitable concentrations. The other way is to **immobilise** the enzyme molecules by binding them chemically to a bonding agent, trapping them in a gel, or attaching them to an inert surface such as plastic beads. The immobilised enzymes are then brought into contact with a solution of the substrate. Immobilisation has the advantage of enabling the same enzyme molecules to be used over and over again, so that only a small amount of the enzyme is needed to make a lot of product. Moreover, enzymes are often more stable when immobilised and are easier to separate from the end product.

Commercial enzymes are produced by microorganisms such as yeasts and bacteria. Although intact cells can be used for driving enzyme-controlled reactions, it is better to extract and isolate the particular enzyme required because its concentration is then higher and unwanted substances are absent. Sometimes naturally occurring microorganisms are used, but increasingly nowadays special strains, developed by genetic engineering, are used to produce not only specific enzymes but other substances as well, such as human insulin or growth hormone. The microorganisms themselves are cultured in **fermenters** from which their enzymes or other products are removed as and when required (*extension box over page*).

Genetic engineering, page 629

When choosing microorganisms for culturing, a number of things need to be taken into account. Ideally their enzymes should work over as wide a temperature range as possible, i.e. they should be **thermostable**, and they should withstand the effects of chemicals that would normally inhibit enzymes. Fortunately the enzymes of many microorganisms are surprisingly resilient, some of them working at temperatures of 100°C or more.

What are enzymes used for?

Approximately 2000 enzymes have been identified, and of these over 150 are used in industrial processes. For example:

- **Amylases**, which convert starch to sugars, are used for making syrups, fruit juices, chocolates and other food products.

- **Cellulases** and **pectinases**, which break down cellulose and pectin respectively, are used for softening vegetables, removing the seed coat from cereal grain, and extracting agar jelly from seaweed.

- **Lipases**, which break down fats and oils, are used for ripening blue cheese and as constituents of washing powders.

- **Proteases**, which break down proteins, are used for tenderising meat, skinning fish, removing hair from hides and as constituents of washing powders.

Extension

Industrial fermentation

For producing enzymes and other products, microorganisms such as bacteria and fungi are cultured on a large scale in **industrial fermenters** (also called **bioreactors**). Technically, fermentation means anaerobic respiration such as occurs in yeast cells in the production of alcohol (*page 147*). However, in the present context the term is extended to include the vigorous metabolism and growth of microorganisms in any conditions, aerobic as well as anaerobic.

There are many types of industrial fermenter. Some are quite small like the one in the photograph below, others are huge. The one illustrated in the diagram consists of a large stainless steel vessel which, after being thoroughly cleaned and sterilised, is filled with a suitable medium. The medium consists of a sugar solution to which other nutrients such as proteins, vitamins and minerals are added, as required by the particular type of micro-organism to be cultured.

Illustration 2 A scientist at work in a commercial fermentation plant where genetically engineered strains of bacteria, yeasts and other microorganisms are cultured for various industrial uses.

A sample of the microorganisms is then added to the medium and allowed to multiply. Paddle-like stirrers keep the contents of the vessel moving, and – if the microorganisms are aerobic – air from a pump (aerator) is bubbled through the mixture.

As the microorganisms multiply and respire, considerable energy is released which heats up the medium. Small fermenters can be kept cool by being surrounded by a cooling jacket; larger fermenters have a cooling coil inside.

When fermentation is complete, the contents of the vessel are collected from a tap at the bottom. The required product is then separated from the rest of the mixture and purified by a process called **downstream processing**.

In the method of fermentation described above, the process is started, the products are collected and then you begin again. This is called **batch culture** and it is the traditional method used in industrial fermentation.

A more modern approach is to use a fermenter with an overflow, rather like that in a bath. Once the process has got underway, the contents of the fermenter trickle into the overflow and the product is extracted continuously. As fast as the culture overflows, more medium is added to keep pace with the loss. This is called **continuous culture**. Continuous culture systems are fully automated and go on working day and night. The production rate can be phenomenal!

▶ Growth of microorganisms, page 470

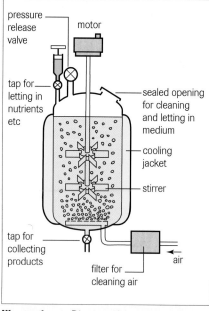

pressure release valve
motor
tap for letting in nutrients etc
sealed opening for cleaning and letting in medium
cooling jacket
stirrer
tap for collecting products
filter for cleaning air
air

Illustration 1 Diagram of a generalised fermenter.

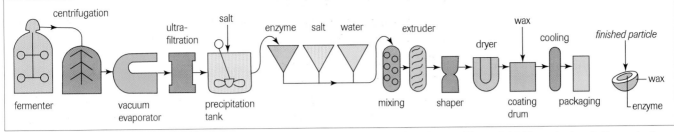

Figure 8.12 The main steps in the production of a biological washing powder. The enzyme is produced by bacteria in a **fermenter**. The bacterial cells are separated from the culture medium by **centrifugation**, and water is removed by **vacuum evaporation** and/or **ultrafiltration**. Any bacterial cells still present are filtered out by **ultrafiltration**. The enzyme is then separated from the liquid by **precipitation** with, for example, a salt. Next the enzyme is granulated with common salt which acts as a preservative, and mixed with water to form a paste. The paste is then **extruded** and shaped into spheres in a **shaper**. Finally the spheres are **dried** and coated with a layer of **wax**, then **cooled**. The finished particles are added to the other ingredients of the washing powder and **packaged**. The wax subsequently melts in the wash, releasing the enzyme.

Biological washing powders

A biological washing powder contains enzymes, mainly proteases, which remove 'biological' stains such as food, blood and so on. The first attempt to make such a product was carried out by Otto Röhm in Germany in 1913. He used the protease trypsin which he extracted from the pancreas of animals.

Since then biological washing powders have had a chequered history. They have been beset with manufacturing problems, and people suspected that the products were not as effective as they were trumped up to be. More important, many people turned out to be allergic to them. Today, however, they have regained their popularity. After being subjected to considerable scrutiny, the claims of the manufacturers have been found to be justified (or reasonably so), and the allergic reactions have been reduced by encapsulating the enzymes in wax from which they are released only when in the wash. The result is that biological washing powders are now manufactured on a very large scale (*figure 8.12*). Modern brands include lipase which removes grease stains.

The advantage of these modern biological washing powders is that they are effective at relatively low temperatures, and are therefore energy saving as well as gentler on the clothes. However, as with any other novel product, possible health hazards – particularly to those who are involved in their manufacture – need to be constantly considered and investigated. After all, protease enzymes break down proteins, one of the major constituents of the body, and it may be unwise to let them come into contact too much with the skin and mucous membranes.

Using enzymes as analytical reagents

Because of their affinity with specific substrates, enzymes can be used to detect, or measure the amounts of, particular substances in a mixture. For example, the enzyme glucose oxidase is used to measure the concentration of glucose in body fluids such as blood and urine. The device used for this is called a **biosensor**. It consists of a probe to which the immobilised enzyme molecules are attached. When the chemical whose concentration is being measured comes into contact with the probe, its molecules bind with those of the enzyme and the number of times this happens is turned into an electronic signal which can be monitored.

Biosensors can be extremely sensitive and respond even when the test chemical is very dilute or unstable. Moreover, they are highly specific, responding only to a single chemical, and they give quantitative data quickly which can, if necessary, be collected over a period of time. This makes them ideal for monitoring the course of chemical reactions in organisms and industrial processes, and for medical diagnosis. For example, they provide a quick way of measuring the blood glucose level of people with diabetes (*page 269*).

Summary

1. Chemical reactions in cells constitute **metabolism**. Metabolic processes proceed in small steps which together make up a **metabolic pathway**.

2. Metabolic pathways can be reconstructed by various techniques such as **isotope labelling, chromatography** and the use of **enzyme inhibitors**.

3. Metabolic reactions may build up substances (**anabolism**) or break them down (**catabolism**). The former absorb energy (**endergonic**), whereas the latter release energy (**exergonic**).

4. The energy transferred by catabolic reactions is required for synthesis, for work, e.g. muscular contraction and active transport, and for maintaining the tissues in a state of health and repair.

5. Oxidative breakdown of sugar yields carbon dioxide, water and energy (**respiration**). The chemical products of this catabolic process can be resynthesised into sugars by autotrophs such as plants (**photosynthesis**).

6. To initiate chemical reactions such as the oxidative breakdown of sugar, a small amount of **activation energy** must be supplied.

7. Chemical reactions in living organisms are catalysed by **enzymes**. Enzymes speed up reactions by lowering the amount of activation energy required to get them going.

8. Enzyme-controlled reactions can be speeded up by raising the temperature or by increasing the concentration of the substrate.

9. Enzymes are nearly always proteins, and this is reflected in some of their properties which are that they generally work rapidly, are not destroyed by the reactions they catalyse, can work in either direction, are sensitive to heating and pH, and are usually specific.

10. Enzymes work by combining with substrate molecule(s) to form an **enzyme–substrate complex**. The enzyme molecule has an **active site** where the substrate molecules become temporarily attached.

11. When a substrate molecule enters the active site, it may induce the enzyme molecule to change its shape, thereby ensuring a closer fit (**induced fit hypothesis**).

12. Enzymes are prevented from working by various inhibitors. Enzyme inhibition may be **competitive** or **non-competitive**.

13. The product of a metabolic pathway may itself act as an inhibitor, slowing down its own production by a negative feedback process (**end product inhibition**).

14. Enzymes controlled by end-product inhibition are usually **allosteric**, that is they have two different shapes, one active and the other inactive. An inhibitor makes the enzyme inactive, an activator makes it active.

15. Some enzymes are assisted in their action by non-protein **cofactors**. These include metal ions, coenzymes and prosthetic groups.

16. Enzymes are used commercially for speeding up various processes. One of their best-known uses is in biological washing powders. The enzymes, or other products, are obtained from microorganisms which are cultured on a large scale in **industrial fermenters**.

17. On account of this specificity, enzymes can be used as **analytical reagents** in industrial processes and medical diagnosis.

Practice questions

For general advice on these questions and advice on answering essay-type questions, see pages vii and viii.

1. (a) Define the term 'enzyme'. (2)

(b) Give **two** reasons why enzymes are essential for metabolism. (2)

(c) The following diagram shows the influence of substrate concentration on the rate of an enzyme controlled reaction working at its optimum temperature.

Explain **fully** the shape of the curve. (2)

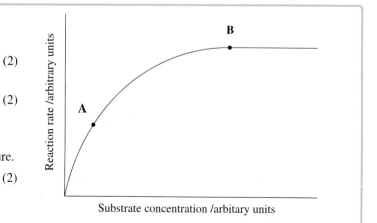

(d) (i) If the temperature was slightly increased at point **A**, draw a line on a copy of the graph to show how the plotted curve would change. (1)

(ii) Explain this change. (1)

(e) (i) If a small additional amount of enzyme was added to the reaction mixture at point **B**, draw on the graph a line to show how the plotted curve would change. (1)

(ii) Explain this change. (1)

(Total 10 marks)
WJEC 1998

2. The diagrams below illustrate one model of enzyme action.

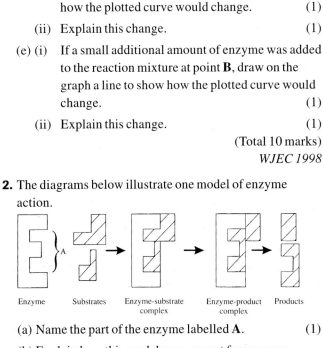

Enzyme   Substrates   Enzyme-substrate   Enzyme-product   Products
                          complex   complex

(a) Name the part of the enzyme labelled **A**. (1)

(b) Explain how this model can account for enzyme specificity. (2)

(c) With reference to this model, explain the effect of a competitive inhibitor on an enzyme-catalysed reaction. (2)

(Total 5 marks)
London 1998

3. The graph shows the results of an investigation into the effect of a competitive inhibitor on an enzyme-controlled reaction over a range of substrate concentrations.

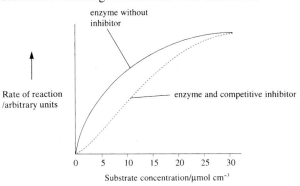

(a) Give **one** factor which would need to be kept constant in this investigation. (1)

(b) (i) Explain the difference in the rates of reaction at the substrate concentration of 10 μmol cm^{-3}. (2)

(ii) Explain why the rates of reaction are similar at the substrate concentration of 30 μmol cm^{-3}. (1)

(c) The diagram represents a metabolic pathway controlled by enzymes.

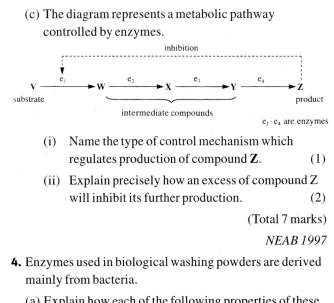

(i) Name the type of control mechanism which regulates production of compound **Z**. (1)

(ii) Explain precisely how an excess of compound Z will inhibit its further production. (2)

(Total 7 marks)
NEAB 1997

4. Enzymes used in biological washing powders are derived mainly from bacteria.

(a) Explain how each of the following properties of these enzymes suits them for use in washing powders.

(i) The enzymes split polymers into their constituent monomers. (1)

(ii) They are stable over a wide range of temperatures. (1)

(b) (i) Enzymes used in biological washing powders are produced by batch fermentation. What is meant by batch fermentation? (2)

(ii) The bacteria secrete the enzymes into the culture medium. Suggest how these enzymes might be obtained from the culture medium. (2)

(Total 6 marks)
NEAB 1998

5. The answer to this question should be illustrated by large, clearly labelled diagrams wherever suitable. Up to 2 additional marks are awarded for quality of expression.

(a) Explain how the structure of an enzyme is responsible for its mode of action. (9)

(b) Discuss the effect of **three** factors which affect the rate of an enzyme-catalysed reaction. (9)

(Total 18 marks)
UCLES 1997

6. More than 1000 chemical reactions may take place in a single cell. How are confusion and chaos prevented?

(Total 5 marks)

nergy is made available to cells by the metabolic breakdown of organic compounds, principally carbohydrates. The reactions involved comprise **respiration**. Oxygen is normally required, and carbon dioxide and water are produced.

Respiration occurs in all organisms and in every living cell, for it is the only way a living system can obtain usable energy. This applies to plants as well as animals. The fact that a plant can absorb energy from sunlight does not exempt it from the necessity to respire. A plant uses the energy of sunlight to build up organic compounds which it then breaks down in order to obtain energy for use by the cells.

9.1 The general nature of respiration

Respiration usually involves the oxidation of glucose. The process may be summarised by the following well-known equation:

$$C_6H_{12}O_6 \quad + \quad 6O_2 \quad \rightarrow \quad 6H_2O \quad + \quad 6CO_2 \quad + \quad Energy$$
$$\text{glucose} \qquad\qquad \text{oxygen} \qquad \text{water} \qquad \text{carbon dioxide}$$

This simplified equation is misleading for a number of reasons. For example, it gives the impression that respiration occurs in a single chemical reaction, a notion which is far from the truth as we shall see. It also suggests that some of the oxygen used in respiration finishes up in the carbon dioxide molecules, which we shall see later is not true. And there is also the implication that oxygen reacts directly with the glucose, which is not the case. But despite its shortcomings the equation is useful as an overall summary of the process, and its general validity can be demonstrated by various experiments such as those described in the support box below.

Support

Experiments confirming the respiration equation

To confirm the respiration equation we need to demonstrate that oxygen is used, carbon dioxide produced and energy transferred.

Oxygen usage and carbon dioxide production

That oxygen is used in respiration can be demonstrated in small organisms by means of a **respirometer** (*illustration 1*).

In humans, oxygen consumption can be studied by means of an apparatus called a **spirometer**, which can also be used to record the depth and frequency of breathing (*page 170*). Spirometry enables us to compare the oxygen consumption of a human subject in different conditions, such as when the person is at rest or taking exercise.

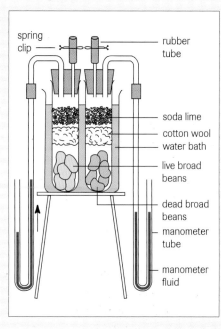

spring clip — rubber tube — soda lime — cotton wool — water bath — live broad beans — dead broad beans — manometer tube — manometer fluid

Illustration 1 A simple respirometer for measuring the oxygen uptake by small organisms such as woodlice or germinating beans. The organisms are placed in a pair of large test tubes as shown. The test tube containing dead organisms serves as a control. Carbon dioxide is absorbed by soda lime placed in the respiration chamber so that a movement of the manometer fluid will be caused only by the uptake of oxygen. As oxygen is used, the level of the fluid rises in the manometer tube, as indicated by the arrow. You can estimate the rate of respiration by timing how long it takes for the manometer fluid to rise through a certain distance. The fluid can be returned to its original level by opening the spring clip. The water bath should be kept at a constant temperature.

That carbon dioxide is produced can be demonstrated in humans by breathing out through **lime water** which turns milky in the presence of carbon dioxide. For small organisms a more sensitive reagent is needed. The organism is placed in a sealed chamber containing a **hydrogencarbonate indicator solution** sensitive to small traces of carbon dioxide; this indicator, normally red, turns yellow if the carbon dioxide concentration exceeds that of atmospheric air.

The oxygen and carbon dioxide content of atmospheric and exhaled air can be measured quantitatively by means of **gas analysis**. In this procedure a small sample of the air is brought into contact, first with potassium hydroxide which absorbs carbon dioxide, then with potassium pyrogallate which absorbs oxygen. The decrease in volume of the air sample when subjected to each reagent tells us how much carbon dioxide and oxygen are present. Details of this and other techniques will be found in standard practical manuals.

More modern methods of investigating respiration involve the use of machines which measure the total volume of air expired and draw off small samples for analysis. The samples are fed into a device which makes a continuous record of the oxygen and carbon dioxide present.

These and many other experiments indicate that organisms take in oxygen and give out carbon dioxide, but how do we know that this is connected with the oxidation of glucose? This has been shown by the use of **radioactive tracers** (*page 120*). For example, mice have been fed with glucose in which the normal carbon (^{12}C) was replaced with its radioactive isotope (^{14}C). The radioactive carbon subsequently appeared in the carbon dioxide which the mice breathed out, confirming that the carbon dioxide comes from the breakdown of glucose.

Energy release

That respiration releases energy can be demonstrated by means of a **calorimeter**. A calorimeter suitable for use with living organisms consists of a chamber with insulated walls which prevent heat energy being lost. The size of the chamber depends on the type of organism being investigated. For human subjects the calorimeter chamber may be the size of a small room. Energy released by the occupant is estimated by measuring the rise in temperature of a current of water circulated through the chamber.

If the release of energy is connected with respiration it should proceed at the same rate as oxygen consumption. This can be shown by collecting a person's expired air at rest and during muscular activity, and comparing their oxygen content. Exercise can conveniently be taken by pedalling a **bicycle joulometer**, the kind of bicycle that people use indoors for keeping fit. The bicycle is fixed in a stationary stand, the back wheel being replaced by a flywheel working against a frictional resistance. In this way the mechanical work done can be measured while the subject breathes in and out of a spirometer or some other comparable device from which the oxygen consumption can be measured (*illustration 2*). From experiments of this sort it can be shown that oxygen consumption is directly proportional to the work done by the subject.

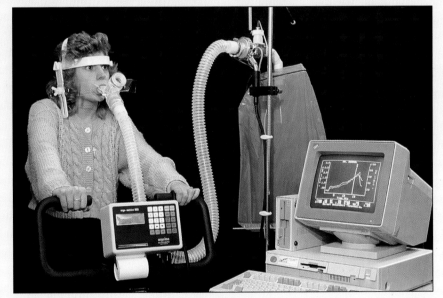

Illustration 2 Investigating the connection between respiration and energy expenditure. While pedalling the bicycle joulometer a continuous record is made of this woman's energy expenditure and oxygen consumption.

The spirometer and how it can be used to measure oxygen consumption, page 170
A calorimeter for use with human subjects, page 309

Such experiments indicate that respiration really is associated with energy transfer in the body. However, the energy that comes from oxidising glucose cannot make a muscle contract. The link between the oxidation of glucose and the body's energy-requiring activities is provided by another substance: **adenosine triphosphate** (**ATP**). What is ATP and what does it do?

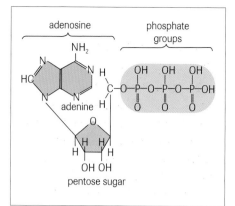

Figure 9.1 The structural formula of adenosine triphosphate (ATP), the universal supplier of energy in cells.

Figure 9.2 Albert Szent-Gyorgyi, who discovered the energetic role of ATP in muscle. 'Genius', Szent-Gyorgyi used to say, 'is seeing what everyone else has seen, and thinking what no one else has thought'.

9.2 ATP: the vital link

ATP is the universal currency of energy in all living organisms, from bacteria to humans. Chemically it is a nucleotide, a group of organic substances which form the building blocks of nucleic acids (*page 603*). Its structural formula is shown in figure 9.1. Notice that it consists of an organic component called adenosine to which is attached a chain of three inorganic phosphate groups.

In the presence of the right enzyme, ATP is readily hydrolysed. This is an exergonic reaction and free energy is released. Some of the energy is transferred to the surroundings as heat energy, but a proportion of it is normally transferred to other molecules and systems and used directly for driving biological activities such as muscle contraction.

Catalysed by the enzyme ATPase, the hydrolysis of ATP yields adenosine diphosphate (ADP) and inorganic phosphate, usually abbreviated to Pi.

$$\underset{\substack{\text{adenosine}\\\text{triphosphate}}}{\text{ATP}} + \underset{\text{water}}{H_2O} \xrightarrow{\text{ATPase}} \underset{\substack{\text{adenosine}\\\text{diphosphate}}}{\text{ADP}} + \underset{\substack{\text{inorganic}\\\text{phosphate}}}{\text{Pi}} + \underset{\text{energy}}{34\,kJ}$$

In this reaction the terminal phosphate group is detached from the end of the ATP molecule.

ATP was first isolated in the early 1930s, having been extracted from muscle tissue. Its function in muscles was subsequently demonstrated in America by Albert Szent-Gyorgyi (*figure 9.2*). He showed that isolated muscle fibres contract when ATP is placed on them but not when glucose is placed on them. This suggested that ATP rather than glucose is the immediate source of energy for muscle contraction.

Since then ATP has been shown to be the immediate source of energy for many other biological processes including nerve transmission, active transport and biosynthesis.

Extension

Detecting ATP

Luminescence can be used as a quantitative test for ATP. When solutions of ATP are added to a standard preparation of ground-up firefly tails, the tissue glows and the amount of light emitted is a measure of the amount of ATP present. Preparations of firefly tails are produced commercially for this purpose. It is a good example of how an organism can be used to estimate the amount of a biochemical substance present in a system.

Providing energy for ATP synthesis

If ATP is the immediate source of energy in cells, it follows that there should always be a ready supply of it for use when required. This is where respiration comes in. The purpose of oxidising glucose is to provide a continual source of energy for making ATP.

The synthesis of ATP involves attaching a phosphate group (derived from phosphoric acid) to ADP, the reverse of what happens when ATP is hydrolysed. This is an endergonic reaction, and the energy for it comes from the oxidation of glucose. The oxidative breakdown of glucose is thus coupled with the synthesis of ATP:

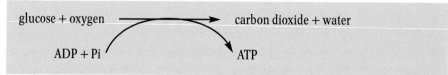

In humans and other vertebrates, phosphate groups for making ATP from ADP are stored in a compound called **creatine phosphate**. (Invertebrates use a similar compound called **arginine phosphate**.) Creatine phosphate is found particularly in muscles, where its function is to provide a ready source of phosphate groups for rephosphorylating ADP.

ATP is not stored – in fact there is barely enough of it in a typical muscle to sustain contraction for more than a second or so. This means that ATP has to be synthesised 'on the go', and the rate of synthesis must keep pace with the demand. To see how this is achieved we need to look at what happens when glucose is oxidised in respiration.

9.3 The breakdown of glucose in respiration

The glucose which is broken down in respiration is derived from the hydrolysis of polysaccharides such as **starch** and **glycogen**. These storage compounds provide a continual supply of glucose molecules for use when required.

As with other biochemical processes, the breakdown of glucose does not happen in one jump but in a series of small steps. The pathway can be divided into two parts, **glycolysis** and the **Krebs cycle**. Glycolysis takes place first, and its products are then fed into the Krebs cycle. Each step is catalysed by a specific enzyme. The overall process is summarised in figure 9.3, to which you should refer as you read the following account.

Glycolysis

Glycolysis literally means 'sugar splitting'. As you know, glucose is a **hexose sugar** with six carbon atoms (*page 16*). During glycolysis the hexose sugar is converted through a series of steps into **pyruvic acid** which has three carbon atoms. (Pyruvic acid, in keeping with other organic acids in the cell, usually occurs as the anion of a salt and is therefore better referred to as **pyruvate**.)

Before glycolysis can get underway the hexose sugar has to be **phosphorylated**. In this process, which takes place in several steps and is catalysed by phosphokinase enzymes, two phosphate groups are added to the sugar molecule. The reactions are endergonic and the necessary energy comes from the hydrolysis of two molecules of ATP, which also donate their terminal phosphate groups to the sugar. This initial phosphorylation activates the sugar and maintains a steep concentration gradient favouring the diffusion of more glucose into the cell.

The scene is now set for the breakdown of the sugar to commence. First, the phosphorylated 6-carbon sugar is split into two molecules of phosphorylated 3-carbon sugar (**triose sugars**). These two trioses can both enter the pathway leading to pyruvate. The first step of the pathway involves dehydrogenation: two hydrogen atoms are removed from the triose by a dehydrogenase enzyme. These hydrogen atoms are taken up by a hydrogen carrier which, for reasons explained later, leads to the synthesis of ATP from ADP and Pi.

Meanwhile, the triose, now deprived of two of its hydrogen atoms but still phosphorylated, is converted via a series of 3-carbon compounds, all acids, to pyruvate. Two of the steps are directly coupled with ATP synthesis: in each case the substrate is at a much higher energy level than pyruvate, and sufficient energy is transferred for the synthesis of a molecule of ATP from ADP and inorganic phosphate. The substrates also provide their phosphate groups for the ATP molecules.

The events leading to the formation of pyruvate take place in the cytosol. The pyruvate now moves into a mitochondrion where it is converted into a 2-carbon compound called **acetyl coenzyme A** (**acetyl CoA** for short). In this reaction carbon dioxide is given off, and the pyruvate loses a pair of hydrogen atoms which again results in the synthesis of ATP.

Acetyl CoA is a complex molecule incorporating a coenzyme (coenzyme A), a derivative of pantothenic acid (vitamin B_5). Acetyl CoA is a very important intermediate in respiration. It links glycolysis with the Krebs cycle, for which reason it is called the **link reaction**.

Creatine phosphate

When creatine phosphate gives its phosphate group to ADP for making ATP, it becomes creatine. When ATP loses its terminal phosphate group for providing energy, the phosphate group recombines with creatine to form creatine phospate. Thus the hydrolysis of ATP is coupled with the rephosporylation of creatine which therefore provides a continual source of phosphate groups for making ATP.

Improving athletic performance

Understanding the way energy is made available for muscular activity is of particular significance for athletes and others who engage in vigorous exercise. There are two main ways of improving performance:

- Eating a large quantity of carbohydrate before the event increases the amount of glycogen in the muscles. This is called **glycogen loading**. The glycogen is subsequently broken down into glucose and respired during the event. Sucking glucose tablets just before or during the event provides an even more immediate source of energy.

- Taking **creatine phosphate** before the event provides a source of phosphate groups for synthesising ATP. Many professional athletes take large amounts of creatine phosphate to enhance performance. This has not been banned by international athletic federations despite uncertainty as to its possible long-term health effects.

Figure 9.3 The metabolic pathway in which sugar is broken down in respiration. The process starts with phosphorylation of 6-carbon sugar (glucose). In the diagram this is shown happening in one step but in fact it involves several steps. In the first, a phosphate group is added to the glucose molecule, resulting in the formation of **glucose 6-phosphate**, so-called because the phosphate group is attached to the glucose molecule at position 6 (*page 17*). A second phosphate group is then attached to the sugar which is subsequently split into two molecules of 3-carbon sugar. These are in equilibrium with each other and normally both are converted into pyruvic acid (pyruvate) and fed into the Krebs cycle. The one that leads directly to pyruvic acid is called **glyceraldehyde 3-phosphate**. As quickly as this compound enters the pathway leading to pyruvic acid, the other 3-carbon sugar is converted into it.

The overall function of the pathway is to produce ATP molecules. Energy is transferred to ATP mainly as a result of the removal of pairs of hydrogen atoms from intermediate compounds in the pathway. The diagram shows the stages at which hydrogen atoms are removed, together with the numbers of ATP molecules synthesised. The ATP molecules circled are produced via the hydrogen carrier system which is explained on page 144. Usually three ATP molecules are synthesised every time two hydrogen atoms pass through the carrier system. However, in the conversion of succinate to fumarate only two ATPs are produced because in this case the initial carrier is FAD rather than NAD (*page 144*).

One of the most important intermediates in the pathway is **acetyl CoA** because it links glycolysis with the Krebs cycle. Coenzyme A is a complex molecule derived from the vitamin pantothenic acid (*page 35*). Its function is to transfer an acetyl group (CH_3CO) from pyruvate to oxaloacetate. In this way two carbon atoms are added to the oxaloacetate with the formation of citrate.

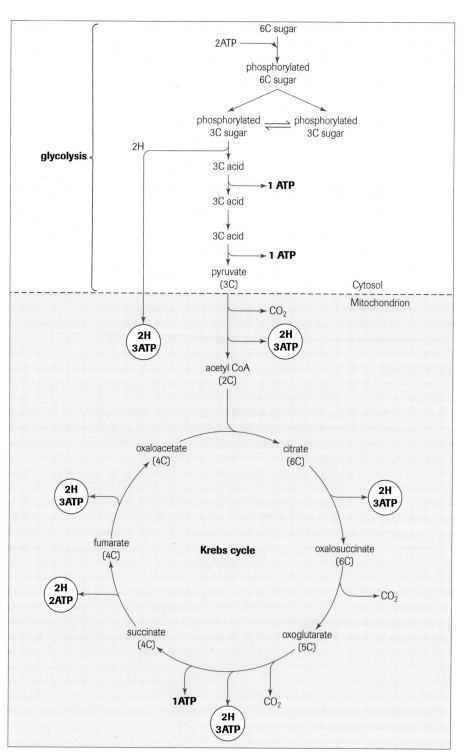

The Krebs cycle

Acetyl CoA has two carbon atoms and it reacts with a 4-carbon organic compound called **oxaloacetate** to form citrate with six carbon atoms. What's really happening here is that coenzyme A carries two carbon atoms from pyruvate to oxaloacetate, thereby converting the latter to citrate. This is a nice example of a coenzyme carrying out its function of transferring chemicals from one compound to another (*page 132*).

There now follows a series of reactions in which the citrate is gradually converted back to oxaloacetate, step by step. If you look at figure 9.3 you will see that two of the steps involve decarboxylation with the formation of carbon dioxide. More importantly, four of the steps involve the removal of pairs of hydrogen atoms (dehydrogenation, catalysed by a

The Warburg manometer and how it helped to unravel respiration

To find out what happens to sugar during respiration, it is necessary to study the rate of respiration of small pieces of tissue in different conditions. This can be done using a **Warburg manometer**. This apparatus was designed by the German chemist Otto Warburg in the 1940s.

A homogenised suspension of tissue is placed in the flask shown in illustration 1. The flask is connected to a U-shaped manometer tube. A compartment in the centre of the flask contains a small piece of filter paper soaked in potassium hydroxide (KOH). This absorbs any carbon dioxide produced so that movement of the fluid in the manometer tube is caused only by oxygen uptake.

The rate of oxygen uptake is determined by timing how long it takes for the fluid to rise through a certain distance in the right-hand side of the tube. The flask is kept at a constant temperature by being shaken continuously in a thermostatically controlled water bath.

Connected to the side of the flask are one or more side arms from which various reagents such as enzymes and inhibitors can be added to the tissue sample in the course of the experiment. This is done by tilting the flask so that the reagent flows in from the side arm. In this way different factors that might influence the rate of respiration may be investigated.

Establishing a step in the Krebs cycle

How can this apparatus be used to establish a step in the metabolic breakdown of sugar? Suppose we suspect that the following reaction occurs (it is one of the reactions in the Krebs cycle):

succinate → fumarate

and suppose we have identified the enzyme which catalyses this reaction (succinate dehydrogenase). If the proposed reaction does occur in cells, and if it is part of respiration, then inhibiting the enzyme should have certain predictable results, namely an accumulation of succinate, a decline in the amount of fumarate and a fall in the rate of oxygen uptake.

Predictions of this sort can be tested with the Warburg apparatus. Two flasks are set up, one to serve as a control. A tissue sample is placed in each flask, and the enzyme is added. It so happens that succinate has a specific inhibitor: malonate (*page 130*). This is let into one of the flasks. The effect on the rate of oxygen consumption is determined and compared with that of the control. The contents of the flasks can be analysed at the end of the experiment to find out how much substrate and product are present.

Illustration 2 shows a Warburg apparatus. Notice the two manometers. The flasks are inside the cylindrical chamber which contains the thermostatically controlled water bath. On the left is Sir Hans Krebs, whose discovery of the citric acid cycle owes much to the Warburg apparatus. Krebs was educated in Germany where he was a pupil of Warburg. Later he emigrated to England and, after a brief period at Cambridge, he became Professor of Biochemistry at Sheffield University and later at Oxford. In 1953 he won the Nobel Prize for Medicine for his work on carbohydrate metabolism.

Illustration 2 Sir Hans Krebs with a Warburg apparatus. Notice the two manometers which are used to measure the uptake of oxygen by the tissue samples.

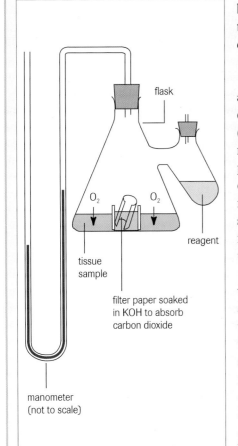

Illustration 1 Warburg flask used for measuring oxygen uptake by small samples of tissue.

Alternative names for the Krebs cycle

Because citric acid is the first acid formed in the Krebs cycle, the pathway is often called the **citric acid cycle**. If you were to look at the chemical formulae of citric acid and several other intermediates in the cycle, you would see that they possess three carboxyl (COOH) groups. For this reason the cycle is also called the **tricarboxylic acid cycle** or **TCA cycle** for short.

dehydrogenase enzyme) leading to the synthesis of ATP from ADP and Pi. We shall see how these hydrogen atoms lead to the synthesis of ATP in a moment. In addition, one of the steps in the cycle is coupled directly with the synthesis of ATP.

Piecing together the steps in this complex pathway was one of the early triumphs of modern biology, much of it derived from the brilliant work during the 1940s and 50s of Sir Hans Krebs, whose name is given to the cycle. An important piece of equipment which Krebs used in his work was a special kind of respirometer devised by his teacher, Otto Warburg. It is called a **Warburg manometer** and is described in the extension box on the previous page.

Careful auditing has shown that the complete oxidation of one molecule of the 6-carbon sugar can yield a net total of 38 molecules of ATP. Of these, 30 are produced by the Krebs cycle and the conversion of pyruvate to acetyl CoA compared with only eight by glycolysis. You can check this for yourself by adding up the ATPs in figure 9.3. Don't forget that two molecules of the 3-carbon sugar go through the process, and two molecules of ATP are required for the initial phosphorylation of the 6-carbon sugar.

9.4 The electron transport system

In the foregoing account of glycolysis and the Krebs cycle we have talked about pairs of hydrogen atoms, removed from various intermediates, leading to the synthesis of ATP. How do these hydrogen atoms generate ATP?

The answer centres on what happens to them. As soon as they are released, they are taken up by a **hydrogen acceptor** in the inner membrane of the mitochondrion. Two such acceptors are involved: one is called **nicotinamide adenine dinucleotide (NAD)**, derived from the vitamin nicotinic acid; the other is **flavine adenine dinucleotide (FAD)**, derived from vitamin B2.

Having been taken up by the acceptors, the hydrogen atoms separate into their constituent electrons and protons (hydrogen ions). The electrons then pass along a series of **electron carriers** in the inner mitochondrial membrane. These carriers belong to a complex of protein pigments called **cytochrome**. The pigments have iron-containing prosthetic groups, rather like haemoglobin, and they are responsible for transferring the electrons. The electron carriers make up the **electron transport system** (or **electron transport chain**). At the beginning of the system the electrons have a high potential energy. At each step in the transport process the electrons fall to a lower energy state, and energy is released which leads to the synthesis of ATP.

When the electrons have been through the electron transport system they rejoin the protons to form hydrogen atoms again. The hydrogen atoms are then transferred by the enzyme **cytochrome oxidase** to oxygen with the formation of water. The synthesis of ATP that occurs as a result of this process is called **oxidative phosphorylation** and it is summarised in figure 9.4.

What happens where?

Where do all the reactions which we have been describing take place? This has been investigated by isolating the different components of cells and finding out what happens in each one. First a chunk of liver is homogenised in a Waring blender and made into a suspension by mixing it with a saline solution. The components of the suspension are then separated by differential centrifugation as explained on page 51.

This, together with research using radioactive tracers, has shown that glycolysis takes place in the cytosol whereas the Krebs cycle takes place in the matrix of the mitochondria. The electron carriers are located in the inner membrane of the mitochondria, and ATPase – which catalyses the synthesis of ATP from ADP and Pi – is associated with the stalked particles which jut out from the inner membrane into the matrix.

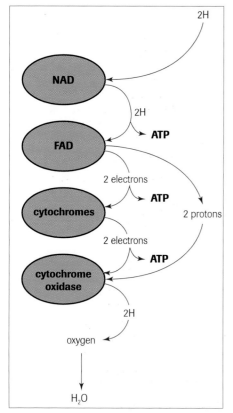

Figure 9.4 Simplified diagram of the hydrogen carrier system and electron transport chain.

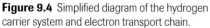
Structure of mitochondria, page 50.

The reactions in electron transport

The electron transport system is really a succession of linked reduction and oxidation reactions (**redox reactions**). When the first carrier accepts an electron it is reduced, and when it passes the electron to the second carrier the first one is reoxidised and the second one reduced – and so on. The final carrier is oxygen itself which, when reduced, forms water. The enzymes involved are **oxidoreductases** (*page 124*). The process is summarised in the illustration.

Because hydrogen atoms enter the system at the beginning, and leave it at the end, the whole process is sometimes called the **hydrogen transport system**.

Diagram illustrating the linked reduction and oxidation reactions in the electron transport system

How does the electron chain result in ATP synthesis?

Many years ago it was discovered that the pH – i.e. the hydrogen ion concentration – in the mitochondrial matrix is considerably lower than the pH in the space between the inner and outer mitochondial membranes, the so-called intermembrane space. This, together with other data on mitochondria, led in the early 1960s to the development of a theory to explain how the electron transport system – or electron chain as it is often called – generates energy for ATP synthesis.

The basic idea is summarised in figure 9.5. Hydrogen atoms, released from the Krebs cycle, are picked up by the initial carrier (usually NAD) on the side of the mitochondrial membrane that lies against the matrix. After the hydrogen atoms have split into electrons and protons, the electrons go through the electron chain as already described. However, the protons – driven by the energy released from the electron chain – are actively moved to the other side of the membrane and deposited in the intermembrane space. This is why the pH is higher in the intermembrane space than in the matrix, and it creates a steep electrochemical gradient across the inner membrane.

Having been pumped into the intermembrane space, the protons then diffuse down the gradient back into the matrix via the stalked particles. As the protons move, energy from them is used to make ATP from ADP and Pi, this reaction being catalysed by ATPase in the stalked particle. Once they reach the matrix, the protons reunite with the electrons and the resulting hydrogen atoms combine with oxygen to form water.

This explanation of how ATP is produced is called the **chemiosmotic theory** – 'chemi' because it is a chemical process, 'osmotic' because it involves movement (*osmos* is Greek for thrust). For many years it was very controversial, but enough evidence has now accumulated for it to become generally accepted. It was originally put forward by the English scientist Peter Mitchell, who was awarded the Nobel Prize in 1978.

Since then further pieces have been added to the jigsaw, particularly with regard to the enzymes involved, by – amongst others – John Walker, a Cambridge scientist who was awarded a Nobel prize in 1997.

Figure 9.5 Summary of the chemiosmotic theory.

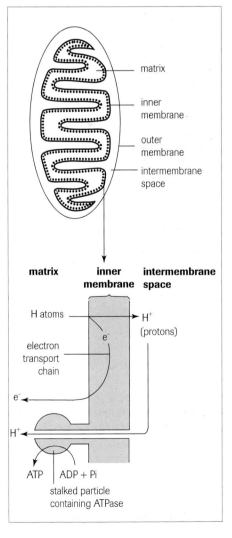

How the rate of respiration is controlled

It is important that sugar should be respired and energy released at the right rate. In practice the rate is determined by the amount of ATP which has been synthesised. If ATP synthesis has been going on apace and there is a lot present in the cells, then respiration is automatically slowed down. This is achieved by **end product inhibition** (*page 132*).

The key factor controlling the rate of sugar breakdown is the ratio of ATP to ADP. A high concentration of ATP relative to ADP inhibits one of the enzymes which catalyses the initial phosphorylation of the sugar. This enzyme is one of the first in the metabolic pathway, so it sets the pace of the whole process. Modulating the activity of the enzyme by this feedback process is therefore an effective way of controlling the overall rate of respiration.

The enzyme is allosteric, that is, it can exist in different shapes (*page 132*). Whether the enzyme is active or inactive depends on its shape and this in turn is determined by the concentration of ATP relative to ADP.

Because of the way it is controlled, very little ATP need be stored. Feedback control ensures that it is synthesised at the same rate as it is used. In fact the amount of ATP in the body remains remarkably constant – at about 50 g in a normal person. However, the amount synthesised in the course of a day can be as much as 100 kg. The turnover is therefore colossal. Indeed the constancy of ATP, and the fact that it is held in steady state, has led some biologists – principally Barbara Banks of University College, London – to suggest that ATP's main energy function is to serve as a phosphorylating agent which, by being held in steady state, controls the rate of metabolism.

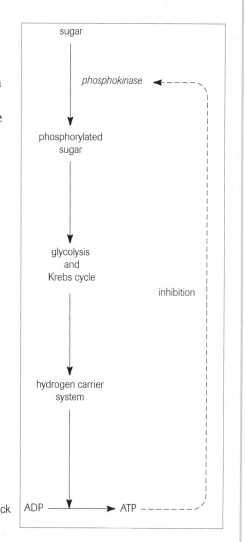

Simplified scheme showing how respiration is controlled. An excess of ATP relative to ADP inhibits the phosphokinase enzyme, thereby slowing down the rate at which glucose is respired. This is an example of negative feedback (*Chapter 21*).

9.5 Respiration without oxygen

From the foregoing account you will realise that the bulk of useful energy yielded by metabolism comes from the transfer of hydrogen atoms or electrons. For this to work oxygen must be available to accept the hydrogen atoms from the final carrier. This kind of respiration – involving the participation of oxygen – is called **aerobic respiration**, and organisms which engage in it are described as **aerobes**.

Most organisms are aerobes. However, a small but significant minority of organisms can obtain energy by breaking down sugar in the absence of oxygen. This is known as **anaerobic respiration**, and the organisms which do it are called **anaerobes**. Many microorganisms, including yeast and some bacteria, can respire anaerobically. So can certain species of annelids that live in oxygen-deficient mud, and gut parasites such as tapeworms. Sometimes particular tissues respire anaerobically if conditions make this necessary. For example, vertebrate skeletal muscles respire anaerobically during vigorous activity when they run short of oxygen, and so do the roots of certain plants when the soil is waterlogged.

Two kinds of anaerobe are recognised:

- **Obligate anaerobes** live permanently in oxygen-deficient conditions, and have no need at all for oxygen. Indeed, in some cases they may be poisoned by oxygen, even in small concentrations.

- **Facultative anaerobes** respire aerobically when oxygen is present, but if oxygen happens to be absent or in short supply they resort to anaerobic respiration. The majority of anaerobes fall into this category.

Types of anaerobic respiration

In anaerobic respiration sugar, instead of being oxidised to carbon dioxide and water, is converted into either **lactic acid** or **ethanol**. Lactic acid is the end product of anaerobic respiration in animals, ethanol in plants and yeast. The latter process is called **alcoholic fermentation**. Anaerobic bacteria can produce both end products, depending on the species. The overall equations for these two types of anaerobic respiration are as follows:

Anaerobic respiration with ethanol formation (alcoholic fermentation):
$$C_6H_{12}O_6 \rightarrow 2CH_3CH_2OH + 2CO_2 + 210\,kJ$$
$$\text{ethanol}$$

Anaerobic respiration with lactic acid formation:
$$C_6H_{12}O_6 \rightarrow 2CH_3CH(OH)COOH + 150\,kJ$$
$$\text{lactic acid}$$

Aerobic respiration (for comparison):
$$C_6H_{12}O_6 + 6O_2 \rightarrow 6H_2O + 6CO_2 + 2880\,kJ$$

Notice that in anaerobic respiration the sugar is not broken down as completely as it is in aerobic respiration. The consequence is that less energy is released than in aerobic conditions; the meagre yield of a couple of hundred kilojoules in anaerobic respiration contrasts sharply with the 2880 kJ produced in aerobic conditions.

The chemistry of anaerobic respiration

Why is sugar not broken down completely in anaerobic respiration? The answer is that in anaerobic conditions there is no oxygen to accept the hydrogen atoms produced by the Krebs cycle. This means that in anaerobic conditions the Krebs cycle cannot take place – nor of course can the electron transport system. Glycolysis though occurs in the usual way, and indeed is much speeded up, but the pyruvate, instead of being converted into acetyl CoA and fed into the Krebs cycle, is converted into lactic acid or ethanol. How this conversion takes place provides a nice example of the neatness of biological systems.

You will recall that the first step in the conversion of the 3-carbon sugar to pyruvate involves dehydrogenation: two hydrogen atoms are removed. In aerobic conditions these two hydrogen atoms are taken up by NAD after which they enter a mitochondrion and bring about the synthesis of ATP. However, in anaerobic conditions the NAD hands the hydrogen atoms to *pyruvate* which is thereby reduced and converted into ethanol or lactic acid. One effect of this is that it prevents hydrogen ions accumulating in the cell and raising the acidity. This would undoubtedly happen otherwise, for anaerobic respiration takes place at a much faster rate than aerobic respiration.

Figure 9.6 shows in detail how pyruvate is converted into lactic acid and ethanol. Notice that lactic acid is formed simply by adding the two hydrogen atoms to the pyruvate. Ethanol, however, is formed by taking away a molecule of carbon dioxide (decarboxylation) and then adding the two hydrogen atoms. This is why alcoholic fermentation is accompanied by the evolution of carbon dioxide.

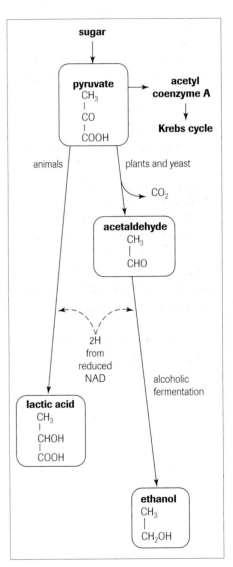

Figure 9.6 In anaerobic conditions pyruvic acid (pyruvate) is converted into either lactic acid or ethanol. The two hydrogen atoms which reduce the pyruvate come from the dehydrogenation of the 3-carbon sugar at the beginning of glycolysis. In aerobic conditions these two hydrogen atoms are shunted into a mitochondrion where they are sent through the hydrogen carrier system, but in anaerobic conditions the two hydrogen atoms are used to reduce the pyruvate.

Thus in anaerobic respiration glycolysis continues but the Krebs cycle is omitted. The consequence is that far fewer ATP molecules are produced than in aerobic conditions. In fact the anaerobic breakdown of a single molecule of the 6-carbon sugar yields only two molecules of ATP compared with the possible 38 molecules produced in aerobic conditions. Aerobic respiration is therefore much more effective, and the ability of organisms to utilise oxygen must have been an important step in the evolution of life (*page 763*).

To some extent the shortcomings of anaerobic respiration are compensated for by the fact that it can occur at a greatly accelerated rate, at least for short periods. So, although inefficient in energy terms, it can be useful as a short-term measure and undoubtedly has contributed to the survival of many species, particularly those that rely on sudden bursts of muscular activity for catching prey or escaping from predators. We ourselves use it when, for example, we perform a 100 metre sprint (*page 244*).

Commercial aspects of anaerobic respiration

In Britain alone over 6000 million litres of beer are drunk every year. The **brewing** and **wine-making** industries depend on yeast. In both cases sugar, traditionally obtained from barley in the case of beer and from grapes in the case of wine, is metabolised by yeast in conditions which maximise the production of ethanol (*illustration*).

Yeast is a classic example of an anaerobe, but in fact yeast cells grow much better in aerobic than in anaerobic conditions. If too little oxygen is present the ethanol concentration rises so much that the yeast cells are killed. The secret in making beer and wine is therefore not to let conditions become too anaerobic. It is useful commercially to develop new strains of yeast which are tolerant to high concentrations of ethanol. This has been a major occupation of microbiologists working for brewery companies.

Beer fermenting in a large vat in a brewery. The froth is caused by the evolution of carbon dioxide from the yeast.

Although alcohol can be abused, it does provide the body with energy, and this can be useful in parts of the world where food is scarce. It has been estimated that some Spanish peasants derive a third of their dietary energy from wine!

Alcoholic fermentation is also accompanied by the evolution of carbon dioxide, a fact which is made use of in **baking**: yeast is added to the flour and water and, when the mixture is warmed, the carbon dioxide gas causes the dough to rise. When the dough is baked the yeast cells are killed and any ethanol present evaporates. If this didn't happen one might become mildly intoxicated from eating a slice of bread!

Ethanol is of course flammable and can be used as a fuel. In some countries, notably Brazil, yeast is used to convert sugar into ethanol which is used as a motor fuel called **gasohol**. The sugar is obtained from sugar-cane or from starch-containing crops such as maize. Although gasohol production is expensive, it has the advantage of being made from a renewable resource (unlike normal petrol made from oil) and its combustion is less polluting – for example it does not produce carbon monoxide.

Lactic acid is produced by various anaerobic bacteria, notably lactobacilli. This is made use of in producing **yoghurt** and **cheese**, both of which are produced from milk. In the first stage of the production process, lactic acid from the bacilli coagulates the milk, and at a later stage the bacteria help to flavour the product.

Another product of fermentation by lactobacilli is **sauerkraut** which is made by fermenting shredded cabbage. The lactic acid formed by the bacteria creates a pH of 5 or less and this preserves the food from bacterial decomposition, enabling it to be stored for longer.

Some fermentations are carried out by mould fungi such as *Rhizopus* (*page 93*). For example, they ferment soya beans to **soy sauce** which is used to flavour foods such as rice and fish, particularly in oriental dishes.

Anaerobic microorganisms are also used in the **disposal of sewage** (*page 682*). They give off methane (CH_4) as well as carbon dioxide, the methane comprising 50–80 per cent of the mixture. Though the economics are questionable, this **biogas** is used as a fuel for providing energy in the home and in industry, particularly in developing countries.

Finally a word about **rice**, one of the world's most important cereal crops. Rice is normally cultivated in paddy fields with the roots under water. Aerenchyma tissue helps them to obtain oxygen for aerobic respiration (*page 70*). However, the roots can also respire anaerobically, producing ethanol to which the tissues are tolerant. If you drive past a paddy field you can sometimes smell the ethanol – it's like passing a brewery!

Extension

Fireflies can prevent food poisoning

Testing food to see if it has become contaminated with bacteria traditionally takes several days. However, a new technique has been developed which produces the same result within minutes.

All living cells contain ATP. If ATP is mixed with two compounds extracted from fireflies – luciferin and luciferase – light is released. If a sample of food is taken, it can be treated with an enzyme, apyrase, which breaks down any eukaryotic ATP, but has no action on prokaryotic ATP because it cannot get into the intact cells. Any ATP left over may therefore be assumed to be prokaryotic in origin. So if a sample of food, having been treated with apyrase, gives off light when mixed with luciferin and luciferase, bacteria must be present.

The food industry has been extremely interested in this technique because it is almost impossible routinely to test foods for bacterial contamination before they leave the factory. In 1986 more than 40 cases of *Salmonella* poisoning resulted after baby food from a factory in Cumbria became contaminated by bacteria. The plant had to close and the parent company lost an estimated £25 million.

What happens to the products of anaerobic respiration?

In anaerobic respiration a lot of energy remains locked up in the ethanol or lactic acid molecules. In animals, this energy can be released by subsequent conversion of the lactic acid back into pyruvate which is then oxidised in the usual way. This requires oxygen. In humans, the lactic acid that accumulates during muscular activity subsequently can be reconverted into carbohydrate or broken down with the release of energy when oxygen becomes available. Any lactic acid not disposed of in this way is excreted.

Plants, however, cannot make use of ethanol. It cannot be reconverted into carbohydrate, nor can it be broken down in the presence of oxygen. As it is toxic it must not be allowed to accumulate, and this is probably why very few plants are complete anaerobes. Many plants (or parts of plants) can respire anaerobically for a short time – germinating seeds for example, and roots living in waterlogged soil. But before the concentration of ethanol reaches a certain level they must revert to aerobic respiration, otherwise they will be poisoned by the ethanol. This is even true of yeast and has to be taken into account when making beer or wine (*extension box on previous page*).

9.6 Energy from non-carbohydrate sources

Carbohydrates are not the only substances which give energy. Energy can also be derived from the oxidation of fats and proteins. The metabolic pathways involved are closely linked with carbohydrate metabolism, as you can see in figure 9.7. Notice that most of them lead to acetyl CoA. Acetyl CoA is thus a kind of crossroads in metabolism. It is formed during the oxidation of fats and proteins as well as carbohydrates and represents a common pathway by which the products of all three are fed into the Krebs cycle.

Most of the reactions are reversible. This is important because it means that carbohydrates can be converted into fat for storage or used for the synthesis of certain fatty acids and amino acids.

Now let us look in a bit more detail at how energy is obtained from fat and protein.

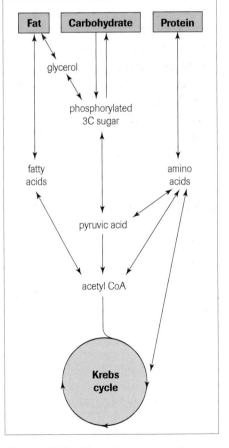

Figure 9.7 Simplified scheme showing how carbohydrate, fat and protein metabolism are interconnected. Notice that all three pathways converge on the Krebs cycle.

Ketone bodies

The fatty acid spiral takes place in the liver where the necessary enzymes are located. However, so much acetyl CoA may be formed that the liver cannot use it all. The liver converts the excess acetyl CoA into acids known collectively as **ketone bodies**. These are released into the bloodstream and taken to other tissues. Once inside the cells, they are reconverted into acetyl CoA and fed into the Krebs cycle with the release of energy. In this way the rapid oxidation of fats in the liver can supply the needs of the whole body.

Energy from fat

Fat is used as a source of energy when carbohydrate is in short supply or when the demand for energy is particularly great.

First the fat is split into fatty acid and glycerol. The latter is phosphorylated and converted into triose sugar which is then converted into pyruvate and fed into the Krebs cycle. Meanwhile the fatty acid goes through a series of reactions in which carbon atoms are split off its hydrocarbon chain, two at a time. Each 2-carbon unit is actually an acetyl group (CH_3CO). This combines with coenzyme A to form a molecule of acetyl CoA. The acetyl CoA then enters the Krebs cycle.

The process in which each 2-carbon unit is split off the fatty acid takes place in the mitochondria. It occurs in a series of steps, some of which involve the removal of hydrogen atoms. The latter pass through the carrier system with the synthesis of ATP. When eventually a molecule of acetyl CoA has been formed, the fatty acid, now containing two fewer carbon atoms in its hydrocarbon chain, goes through the same series of reactions again. This process is repeated, using the same enzymes, until the hydrocarbon chain has been completely dismantled. It is called the **fatty acid spiral**. The whole sequence transfers a lot of energy for ATP synthesis. Still more ATP molecules are produced every time an acetyl CoA molecule is fed into the Krebs cycle.

Exactly how many ATP molecules are produced by the complete oxidation of a fatty acid depends on the number of carbon atoms it contains. A fatty acid with a long hydrocarbon chain will obviously give more molecules of acetyl CoA, and therefore more ATP molecules, than one with a relatively short chain. The complete oxidation of a molecule of stearic acid with 16 carbon atoms in its hydrocarbon chain yields a net total of about 150 molecules of ATP. This is nearly four times as many as are given by the oxidation of a single glucose molecule.

The respiratory quotient

The respiratory quotient (RQ) is the amount of carbon dioxide produced, divided by the amount of oxygen used, in a given time:

$$RQ = \frac{CO_2 \text{ produced}}{O_2 \text{ used}}$$

The importance of the RQ is that it can tell us what kind of substance is being oxidised, i.e. the substrate being used in respiration. Theoretical RQs for the complete oxidation of carbohydrate, fat and protein can be worked out from the appropriate chemical equations. The figures are as follows:

Substrate	RQ
Carbohydrate	1.0
Fat	0.7
Protein	0.9

In theory we might expect an organism to give one of these three RQs, or a close approximation to it, depending on the type of food being respired. However, this rarely happens in practice because many factors influence the values obtained by experiment. For example, a respiratory substrate is rarely oxidised completely, and often a mixture of substrates is used in the body. Most animals have an RQ in resting conditions of between 0.8 and 0.9. A human's is generally around 0.85. As protein is normally not used to a great extent, an RQ of slightly less than 1.0 can be taken to mean that fat and carbohydrate are being respired.

As well as giving us some indication of the type of food being used, the RQ can tell us what sort of metabolism is going on. For example, high RQs (exceeding 1.0) are often obtained from organisms, or

tissues, which are short of oxygen. Under these circumstances they resort to anaerobic respiration, with the result that the amount of carbon dioxide produced exceeds the amount of oxygen used.

High RQs also result from the conversion of carbohydrate to fat, because carbon dioxide is liberated in the process. This is most noticeable in organisms that are laying down extensive food reserves – in animals preparing to hibernate, for example, and in fattening livestock.

A very low RQ, on the other hand, may mean that some (or all) of the carbon dioxide released in respiration is being put to some sort of use by the organism. In plants it may be used for photosynthesis, in animals for the construction of calcareous shells, and so on.

Energy from protein

Proteins are not stored as such, so our only reserves are the tissues themselves. Only if an organism is starving is its tissue protein used as a source of energy, but a certain amount of energy is always derived from excess dietary protein.

The protein is first split into its constituent amino acids. Each amino acid is then **deaminated**: its amino (NH_2) group is split off with the formation of **ammonia**. The ammonia is quickly converted into **urea** which is later excreted (*page 274*).

Meanwhile, the carbon fragment left after the removal of the amino group is fed into carbohydrate metabolism. Depending on the particular amino acid in question, it may enter the carbohydrate pathway by being converted into pyruvate, acetyl CoA or one of the Krebs cycle intermediates. Whatever the route, once the carbon fragment gets into the carbohydrate pathway, ATP molecules are synthesised in the usual way.

9.7 The metabolic rate

The metabolic rate is the amount of energy expended by an organism in a given time, and it is a measure of the rate at which the energy-yielding reactions take place.

An individual's metabolic rate depends on the amount of physical work done. But even when an organism is at rest and doing nothing, a certain amount of energy is still needed for basic functions such as breathing, beating of the heart, keeping up the body temperature and so on – in short for maintaining the life of the cells. This is the minimum amount of energy on which the body can survive, and it is called the **basal metabolic rate (BMR)**.

The BMR does not remain constant throughout life, but changes as growth, development and ageing take place. In a newborn baby the BMR is low: about 100 kJ m^{-2} h^{-1} (kilojoules per square metre of body surface per hour). It then rises rapidly, reaching a maximum of about 220 kJ m^{-2} h^{-1} by the end of the first year. This corresponds to the child's period of most rapid growth. The BMR then gradually declines as the rate of growth decreases, and continues to do so even after growth has ceased altogether (*figure 9.8*).

The BMR also varies with the sex and health of the individual. For a healthy young woman it is about 150 kJ m^{-2} h^{-1}, and for a healthy young man it is about 167 kJ m^{-2} h^{-1}. Although it is customary to express the BMR per unit of body surface, for general purposes it is sufficient to give the total energy output per day. For an average-sized woman this comes to about 5850 kJ per day, and for a man about 7500 kJ per day.

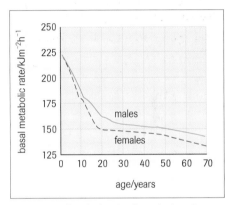

Figure 9.8 Graph showing how the basal metabolic rate of the human declines with age.

Support

Estimating a person's basal metabolic rate

A person's metabolic rate can be related to the surface area of the body. For this reason the BMR is normally expressed as kJ per m^2 per hour.

To estimate a person's BMR experimentally you measure his or her heat energy loss in a given time, using a human calorimeter of the kind described on page 309. Obviously the person must be completely at rest, a state which is not always easy to achieve in a laboratory situation.

The person's surface area can be estimated by encasing him or her in a tight wax-impregnated garment rather like a 'wet suit'. This is then removed, flattened out and its surface area measured. Such measurements have led to the development of a formula from which a person's approximate BMR can be calculated:

$$\text{surface area} = M^{0.425} \times H^{0.725} \times 0.007184$$

where M is the body mass and H the height in metres. Using this formula avoids having to subject the person to the indignity of being, in effect, incarcerated in a wax mould. To make life even easier, nomograms based on this formula are available from which you can read off the person's surface area (*question 5 on page 156*).

Table 9.1 Energy expenditure in relation to different kinds of activity.

Activity	Energy expenditure /kj min⁻¹	
	Woman	**Man**
Sleeping	3.8	4.2
Sitting	5.0	5.8
Light work	15.0	17.0
Sawing	34.0	38.0
Maximum work	57.0	63.0

Figure 9.9 Humming birds, in common with many other small birds and mammals, have a high food requirement to meet the demands of their metabolism, much of which is concerned with keeping up their body temperature. The picture shows a male rufus humming bird feeding on the nectar of a flower.

Variations in the metabolic rate

The basal metabolic rate applies to a person lying at rest. It does not even include the energy required to feed oneself, and therefore as an indication of a person's normal energy expenditure it is hardly applicable to everyday life. The moment you stand up and walk across the room, your metabolic rate increases – and if you engage in any sort of strenuous activity, such as lifting a heavy suitcase or running for the bus, your metabolic rate increases even more. In fact the energy expended by the body may increase more than ten times during muscular activity, as table 9.1 makes clear.

Amongst animals, the metabolic rate varies considerably between different species. For example, the metabolic rate of a humming bird at rest is over 5000 times that of a freshwater mussel (*figure 9.9*). Many small birds and mammals have high metabolic rates, mainly to keep up their body temperature, and their food requirements are correspondingly high. A classic case of this is the shrew: its staple diet consists of earthworms which it eats almost incessantly day and night.

9.8 Food and energy

The energy expended by the body comes from the oxidation of food, and it is therefore useful to know the contribution made by different types of food to our energy needs. This can be found by measuring the amount of energy transferred to the surroundings when a known quantity of food is burned. The apparatus used for this is called a **food calorimeter** (*figure 9.10*).

The sample of food is dried so as to remove all traces of water, and then weighed. It is then placed in a strong steel chamber which is filled with oxygen and tightly sealed. The calorimeter is surrounded by a jacket containing a known volume of water whose temperature is recorded. The food is ignited by means of a small electric heating coil, and

Figure 9.10 A food calorimeter. A sample of dry food of known mass is ignited, and the rise in temperature of the water is noted. The stirrer ensures that the temperature of the water is even. The energy content of the food is calculated knowing that 4.2 kJ of energy is required to raise the temperature of 1.0 kg of water by 1°C. In some circles the energy value of food is expressed in an older unit, the kilocalorie. One kilocalorie is approximately equal to 4.2 kilojoules. The term 'calorimeter' is derived from this older unit.

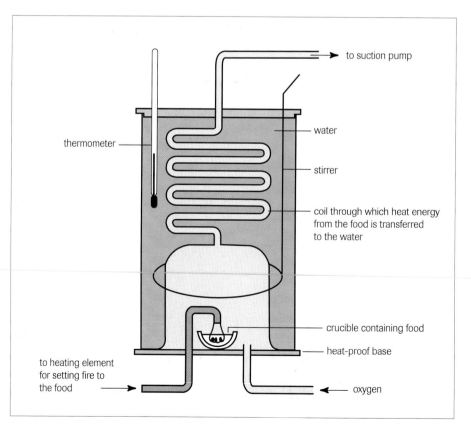

to suction pump

thermometer

water

stirrer

coil through which heat energy from the food is transferred to the water

crucible containing food

heat-proof base

to heating element for setting fire to the food

oxygen

the amount of heat energy transferred to the surroundings is calculated by measuring the rise in temperature of the water.

From food calorimetry, the **energy values** of the three main types of food substance have been established (table 9.2). Predictably, these figures are more or less proportional to the number of ATP molecules produced by the oxidation of these three types of substance in the body.

Carbohydrate and fat are the body's main sources of energy, and any excess can be stored for use later. Protein is required for growth and repair and is not a primary source of energy. However, if there is an excess of protein in the diet, as there often is in affluent countries, then the excess will be oxidised with the release of energy. If carbohydrate and fat are in short supply and the body's reserves have been used up, proteins from the tissues are used for supplying energy. This is what happens with people who are starving. The less vital organs are used first, such as the skeletal muscles, which is why starving people look so thin and emaciated. The heart and brain remain relatively unaffected.

Alcohol, as well as being socially popular, can be a supplementary source of energy. However, it cannot be stored and therefore can only be used as an immediate source of energy. Moreover, much of it is excreted, exhaled or incompletely oxidised, thus reducing its energy contribution.

If the total energy content of a person's food is estimated over a period of time, it is found to be equal to the person's energy expenditure plus the energy contained in the body's tissues and any lost in materials such as urine and faeces. This is in accord with the First Law of Thermodynamics, which states that energy is neither gained nor destroyed when it is transferred.

Human energy requirements

Unless the body is to draw heavily on its reserves, the energy we require must be provided by the diet. What then are our energy requirements?

It goes without saying that we must receive sufficient energy-giving food to sustain the basal metabolic rate. This means that a woman must receive at least 5850 kJ, and a man 7500 kJ, per day. But in practice we need much more than this, in order to meet the requirements which our daily activities demand. For example, a woman's energy requirements increase during pregnancy, and a coal miner's are much greater than those of a high-court judge. Table 9.3 gives approximate daily energy requirements according to gender, age and occupation.

While recognising these individual variations, attempts have been made to work out the daily energy requirements of an 'average person', one who spends a normal proportion of time sleeping, sitting, standing, walking and performing the sundry activities which most people do in their daily lives. This works out at about 9600 kJ per day for a young woman, and about 13 400 kJ per day for a young man.

These figures are recommended by the United Nations Food and Agriculture Organisation (FAO) and other official bodies. In view of these generally agreed figures, it is disturbing to realise that over two-thirds of the world's population receive less energy than the recommended minimum. In many parts of the world the daily energy intake is only just sufficient to maintain the basal metabolic rate. Tragically, millions of people receive even less than this and are in a state of **starvation**.

On the other hand, the daily energy intake of people living in affluent countries is often far more than they need. If you take in more energy than you use, the excess will be stored as fat. This causes an increase in body mass, a condition known as **obesity**. Obesity and its attendant problems are characteristic features of an affluent society, and they can only be countered by sensible eating habits and regular exercise (*extension box on next page*).

Information on the eating disorders anorexia nervosa and bulimia can be found on page 363.

Table 9.2 Energy values of the three main food groups.

Substance	Energy value/kJ g^{-1}
Carbohydrate	17.2
Fat	38.5
Protein	22.2

▶ Dietary reference values (DRVs), page 31

Extension

Efficiency of the human body

It is obviously important to any organism that it should transfer the energy of its food to the energy of muscular contraction with maximum efficiency, i.e. with minimum loss as heat energy. Knowing the energy input and output, the organism's efficiency can be calculated. For humans, the efficiency of the body as a whole turns out to be approximately 23 per cent, a figure that compares favourably with machines such as cars.

Although the efficiency of the human body may seem rather low, it must not be forgotten that the heat energy, though lost in the metabolic sense, is not all wasted. At least some of it may be used to warm the body and maintain a constant body temperature. This is one reason why shrews and humming birds have such high metabolic rates, and it necessitates having a high food intake.

Table 9.3 Approximate amounts of energy required daily by different types of people.

Type of person	kJ per day
Newborn baby	2000
Child 1 year	3000
Child 2–3	6000
Child 5–7	7500
Girl 12–15	9500
Boy 12–15	12 000
Girl 16–18	10 000
Boy 16–18	15 000
Office worker	11 000
Factory worker	12 500
Heavy manual worker	15 000
Pregnant woman	10 000
Woman breast-feeding	11 000

Obesity and dieting

Obesity is the most common nutritional disease in Britain and other affluent societies. Guest author Dr James Parkyn discusses this condition and how it can be remedied.

If you persistently take in more kilojoules in your food than your body uses, your body mass will increase and you will become 'overweight' (**obese**). So obesity is caused by the **energy input** exceeding the **energy output** over a prolonged period of time.

In Britain, about 10% of children are obese and by adolescence the proportion has risen to between 13 and 23%, the majority being adolescent girls. In the adult population some 20 to 30% are above the 'desirable' weight for their height.

Why are so many people obese? Although genetic factors may play a part, the two main reasons are:

- **Overeating**: A person who takes in 1260 kJ (about 10%) more energy each day than he or she uses undergoes a net gain of 420 kJ daily after allowing for the extra energy loss caused by extra heat energy production. This amounts to 153 300 kJ in a year, leading to the deposition of about 4 kg of fat in the body tissues.

- **Lack of exercise**: Most people take far less exercise now than they did 30 years ago, mainly because of television and the car. If the average Briton spent as much time each week walking or gardening as watching TV, the equivalent of at least one day's energy intake would be used up. Walking to school can use up eight times as much energy as going by car.

Assessing obesity

The current method for assessing obesity is to calculate the **body mass index** (**BMI**). This is the body mass in kilograms divided by the height (in metres) squared. So a person whose mass is 68.5 kg and height 1.7 metres will have a BMI of $68.5/1.7^2 = 23.6$. BMIs correlate quite closely with the amount of fat in the body as determined by, for example, estimating the thickness of the skin.

The World Health Organisation (WHO) considers people whose BMI is 30 or more to have a serious health risk. Ideally, the BMI should be between 20 and 25.

The dangers of obesity

Obesity shortens lives. This fact, based on statistical investigations, is well known to life insurance companies which therefore raise their premiums for clients who are overweight. Obese people are more likely to develop certain disabling diseases, including diabetes (five times more common amongst obese people), gall stones, high blood pressure, strokes (twice as common amongst obese people) and coronary heart disease.

In women, obesity can be associated with heavy menstrual periods and failure to ovulate (causing infertility), and complications in childbirth. An obese person is also more likely to have problems during surgical operations. Other effects include loss of libido and depression caused by lowered self-esteem.

Reducing obesity

Obesity can be reduced by increasing the energy output of the body and/or decreasing the energy input.

Increasing the energy output means taking exercise. About 30% of the energy used each day in a normal person goes into muscular activity, though in a labourer doing strenuous muscular work the figure may be as high as 75%. Engaging in muscular work is therefore an important aspect of reducing one's body mass. To be effective, regular exercise of the kind suggested in the box on page 425 should be taken. However, any exercise is better than no exercise: a recent American study suggests that even fidgeting can help.

Decreasing the energy input means consuming less energy-containing foods, and this may necessitate going on a **weight-reducing diet**. The following guidelines are based on recommendations by the American Heart Association for a healthy adult diet. Not all the recommendations are directly related to combating obesity; some are aimed at promoting general health and reducing the risk of heart disease.

- Total energy intake per day should not exceed total energy output. Indeed, an overweight person embarking on a slimming diet should arrange for his or her energy intake to be *less* than the output, so that the body fat will be utilised.

- Carbohydrates should comprise about 50% of the total energy intake, with emphasis on complex carbohydrates such as starch, from which we gain less net energy than we do from simple carbohydrates like glucose. Bread, potatoes, pasta and breakfast cereals are therefore recommended in moderation.

- Fibre (cellulose) is highly recommended because it provides no energy at all and helps to maintain the gut in good working order. High-fibre foods include fruit, vegetables, wholemeal bread and breakfast cereals with a high bran content.

- Sugar and sugary foods should be reduced, not only because they provide so much energy, but also because the action of bacteria on sugar in the mouth produces acids which cause tooth decay.

- Fat should comprise less than 30% of the total energy intake, with the emphasis on polyunsaturated fats (vegetable fats and oils as in margarine for example) rather than saturated fats (animal fats as in butter and meat).

- Cholesterol intake should not exceed 300 mg per day. Cholesterol, particularly in the oxidised form, is a major factor in heart disease. It is found in animal fats and is particularly abundant in eggs. Antioxidants, such as vitamin C, help to counteract its harmful effects.

- The remaining energy will be provided by protein which is required for health

but is a less fattening food than either carbohydrate or fat.

- Salt (sodium chloride) should not exceed 3 g per day because of its possible connection with heart disease.

- Alcohol should not exceed 3 units per day for a man, 2 units per day for a woman. (A unit of alcohol is 10 cm^3 which is the amount of alcohol in half a pint of beer, a standard glass of wine or a single measure of spirits.) Alcohol in moderation is said to be beneficial to

the heart but in excess it can lead to obesity and other health problems (*page 274*).

Provided all the necessary vitamins and minerals are included, a diet based on the above principles will be effective in the long-term control of obesity.

Dr Parkyn is a physician whose career has spanned clinical medicine, research and teaching.

Summary

1. Energy is transferred by **respiration** which occurs in all living cells. It generally involves the oxidation of glucose with the formation of water and carbon dioxide.

2. Experiments can be carried out to demonstrate the general validity of the respiration equation. For example, oxygen consumption, measured with a **respirometer**, can be related to energy expenditure.

3. The immediate source of energy for biological functions is **adenosine triphosphate** (**ATP**) which can be hydrolysed into **adenosine diphosphate** (**ADP**) and inorganic phosphate with the transfer of free energy.

4. The purpose of breaking down glucose in respiration is to provide energy for the synthesis of ATP.

5. In aerobic respiration glucose is broken down in two main stages: **glycolysis** followed by the **Krebs cycle**.

6. Most of the energy for ATP synthesis is derived from the **hydrogen carrier system** which involves **electron transport**. The hydrogen atoms for the carrier system are supplied mainly by the Krebs cycle.

7. Glycolysis takes place in the cytoplasm, Krebs cycle in the matrix of the mitochondria, and electron transport in the inner mitochondrial membrane.

8. According to Mitchell's **chemiosmotic theory**, the movement of electrons in the inner mitochondrial membrane provides energy for pumping protons (hydrogen ions) across the membrane outwards, resulting in an electrochemical gradient. Subsequent diffusion of the protons inwards releases energy which is used for ATP synthesis.

9. In anaerobic respiration glucose is converted into **ethanol** or **lactic acid**. Because the Krebs cycle is omitted, less energy is transferred than in aerobic respiration.

10. Fat and protein breakdown, as well as carbohydrate, feed into the Krebs cycle and provide energy for ATP synthesis.

11. The **respiratory quotient** (**RQ**) is the amount of carbon dioxide produced divided by the amount of oxygen consumed in a given time. The RQ can give useful information about the nature of the food being respired, and the kind of respiration that is taking place.

12. The minimum rate of energy transfer for the maintenance of life is called the **basal metabolic rate** (**BMR**). Actual metabolic rates usually exceed the BMR and depend on the activity of the individual.

13. The rate of glucose breakdown is controlled by a feedback system which enables the amount of ATP in the body to be held in steady state.

14. The energy value of different food substances can be determined by means of a **food calorimeter** which measures the amount of heat energy transferred to the surroundings when a known quantity of food is burned.

15. People's daily intake of energy falls short of the recommended minimum in many poorer parts of the world, whereas in more affluent regions it is often well in excess of what is needed.

16. If energy input exceeds energy output over a prolonged period of time, **obesity** results. This can be remedied by taking regular exercise and/or going on a weight-reducing diet.

For general advice on these questions and advice on answering essay-type questions, see pages vii and viii.

1. The diagram below shows an outline of anaerobic respiration in muscle.

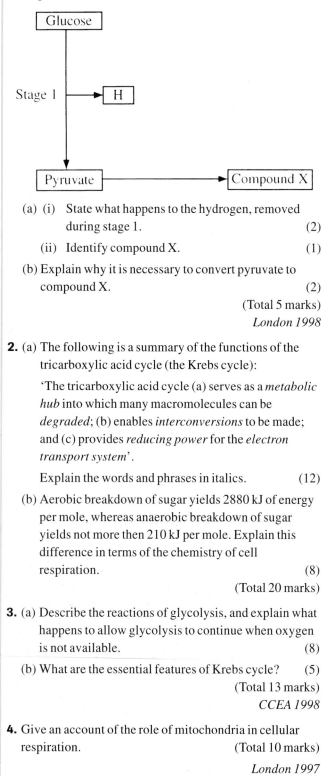

(a) (i) State what happens to the hydrogen, removed during stage 1. (2)

    (ii) Identify compound X. (1)

(b) Explain why it is necessary to convert pyruvate to compound X. (2)

                                        (Total 5 marks)

                                              London 1998

2. (a) The following is a summary of the functions of the tricarboxylic acid cycle (the Krebs cycle):

'The tricarboxylic acid cycle (a) serves as a *metabolic hub* into which many macromolecules can be *degraded*; (b) enables *interconversions* to be made; and (c) provides *reducing power* for the *electron transport system*'.

Explain the words and phrases in italics. (12)

(b) Aerobic breakdown of sugar yields 2880 kJ of energy per mole, whereas anaerobic breakdown of sugar yields not more then 210 kJ per mole. Explain this difference in terms of the chemistry of cell respiration. (8)

                                      (Total 20 marks)

3. (a) Describe the reactions of glycolysis, and explain what happens to allow glycolysis to continue when oxygen is not available. (8)

(b) What are the essential features of Krebs cycle? (5)

                                      (Total 13 marks)

                                            CCEA 1998

4. Give an account of the role of mitochondria in cellular respiration. (Total 10 marks)

                                              London 1997

5. The diagram below is a nomogram, which can be used to determine body surface area using values for height and mass. A straight line ruled from body mass to height intersects the central scale at the corresponding value for surface area. This value is of interest because the basal energy requirements of a human (at rest) depend on the body's surface area.

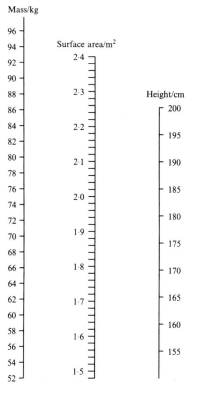

(a) Use the nomogram to determine the body surface area of person **A**, a male of height 185 cm and mass 78 kg. (1)

(b) Explain why basal energy requirements depend on body surface area. (2)

(c) Basal energy requirements for a male are 167 kJ m^{-2} per hour. Calculate the energy content of the food required to sustain person **A** at rest for 24 hours. (1)

(d) Person **B**, also a male, of height 175 cm and mass 85 kg was found to have exactly the same basal energy requirements as person A. Suggest an explanation. (1)

                                      (Total 5 marks)

                                            CCEA 1998

Chapter 10

Gaseous exchange

All living organisms exchange gases with the environment. This is necessary to allow the cells to obtain the gases needed for metabolic processes and to facilitate the removal of gaseous metabolic waste. Exchange of gases, whether it is with the atmosphere or in an aquatic medium, is therefore very important.

Most living cells require a supply of oxygen to carry out **respiration**. Carbon dioxide is a metabolic waste product of respiration. In addition plants require carbon dioxide for **photosynthesis** and produce oxygen in the process. We shall therefore concentrate on the exchange of carbon dioxide and oxygen.

Efficient gaseous exchange in all organisms depends on three conditions being met. These are:

- the maintenance of a **diffusion gradient** to sustain the exchange process;
- the provision of a **large surface area** across which the supply and removal of the gases can take place;
- the presence of a **moist surface membrane** so that the gases can go into solution before they pass across.

With these three requirements in mind let us look at gaseous exchange in plants and animals.

10.1 Gaseous exchange in plants

The living cells in the roots, stems and leaves of plants respire aerobically most of the time and yet there is no special system within plants for the transport of oxygen or carbon dioxide. These gases move entirely by **diffusion**. It is therefore not surprising to find that plant tissues are either permeated by air spaces through which gases can diffuse freely and/or have their respiring cells close to the surface. For example, the cells in a leaf are interspersed with many air spaces (*page 207*). However, there is a problem. The leaves and stems of flowering plants are usually covered with a **cuticularised epidermis** which reduces water loss but at the same time prevents any significant exchange of gases. How, then, do gases get in and out of plants? The answer is via **stomata**.

Stomata

Stomata (singular: *stoma* = mouth) are pores in the epidermis of the leaves and stems of plants, which can open and close (*figures 10.1 and 10.2*). The pore itself is bordered by a pair of modified epidermal cells called **guard cells** which can draw apart or close together rather like sliding doors.

The stomata are usually most numerous in the lower epidermis of the leaf, where there may be as many as 860 per mm^2 (sycamore) though more usually the number is around 200 per mm^2. In most trees and shrubs they are absent from the upper epidermis, but in water plants with floating leaves, such as water lilies, they are only present in the upper epidermis. Grasses and other monocotyledons in which the leaves are held more or less vertically have stomata on both surfaces.

In woody stems of shrubs and trees the epidermis is replaced by an impervious layer of densely packed **corky cells**. Gaseous exchange in these circumstances takes place in localised regions called **lenticels** where the corky cells are loosely packed (*page 542*).

In 1900, a discovery was made by two researchers, H.T. Brown and F. Escombe, which helps to explain why stomata are good at allowing gases to move in and out of leaves. They

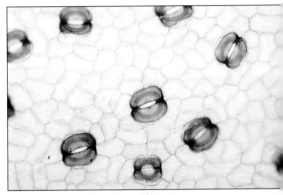

Figure 10.1 Photomicrograph of the lower epidermis of a privet leaf, showing stomata in surface view. Magnification ×200.

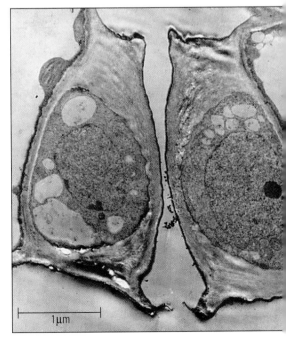

1μm

Figure 10.2 Electron micrograph of a section through a stoma of a French bean leaf. The guard cells have been sectioned transversely.

showed that a greater volume of gas will pass through numerous small holes in a given time than through a single hole of the same total area. This is because diffusion is faster at the perimeter than in the centre of a hole, and the combined perimeter of many small holes is greater than the perimeter of a few large ones. Stomata are therefore ideal for gaseous exchange.

Allowing the exchange of carbon dioxide and oxygen between the inside of the leaf and the surrounding atmosphere is only one function of stomata; another is to allow water to evaporate from the leaf, thus cooling the plant (*page 314*). However, the plant faces a conflict. If the stomata are open, carbon dioxide is available for photosynthesis but water loss may exceed water uptake. If they are closed, less water vapour is lost, but the cooling effect of the evaporation of water is reduced. The state of the stomata can therefore be crucial in the life of a plant, especially in dry conditions.

The opening and closing of stomata

In order to understand how stomata open and close we must look at their structure. In figure 10.3 you will notice that the guard cells are sausage-shaped and, unlike other epidermal cells, contain chloroplasts. There is a large, sap-filled vacuole and, a point of great importance, the inner cellulose wall (i.e. the wall lining the pore itself) is thicker and less elastic than the outer wall.

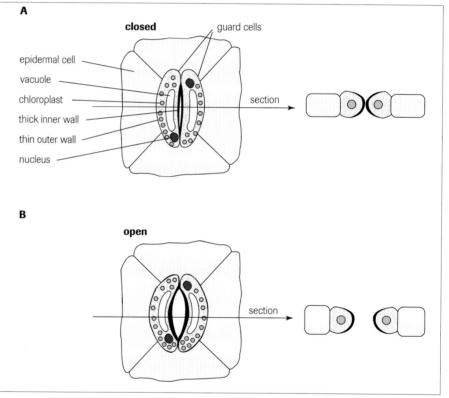

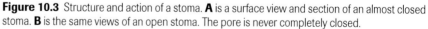

Figure 10.3 Structure and action of a stoma. **A** is a surface view and section of an almost closed stoma. **B** is the same views of an open stoma. The pore is never completely closed.

Stomatal opening and closing depends on changes in turgor of the guard cells. If water flows into the guard cells by osmosis, their turgor increases and they expand. But they do not expand uniformly in all directions. The relatively inelastic inner wall makes them bend and draw away from each other as shown in figure 10.3 B. The result is that the pore opens. If the guard cells lose water the reverse happens: their turgor decreases and they straighten, thus closing the pore.

We now know that the guard cells increase their turgor by actively accumulating potassium ions (K^+), thus lowering their water potential and causing the inflow of water by osmosis from the surrounding epidermal cells.

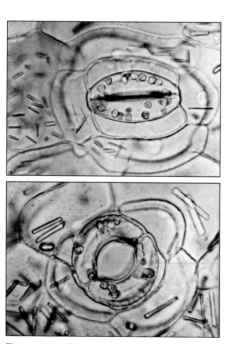

Figure 10.4 Photomicrographs of stomata of *Commelina* (dayflower) *top* closed, *bottom* open. Notice that chloroplasts are present in the guard cells but absent from other epidermal cells. Magnification ×300.

When potassium ions are lost from the guard cells, their water potential increases. Water flows out, causing them to become flaccid, and the stomata close. Table 10.1 shows the potassium ion concentration in the open and closed guard cells of some common plants.

The accumulation of potassium ions in the guard cells requires the expenditure of energy. The necessary energy is provided by the transfer of electrons during photosynthesis, which generates ATP (*page 210*). This is why the guard cells contain chloroplasts.

Diffusion inside the stoma

Once inside the leaf, the gases in the sub-stomatal air chambers diffuse through the intercellular spaces between the mesophyll cells. When the gases come into contact with the wet surfaces of the cells, carbon dioxide and oxygen go into solution. In addition, some carbon dioxide dissolves to form carbonic acid (H_2CO_3) which dissociates to give hydrogencarbonate ions (HCO_3^-). In either case the carbon dioxide diffuses through the plasma membrane to the chloroplasts. It then enters the photosynthetic process. As a result, the diffusion gradient of carbon dioxide from the atmosphere to the chloroplast is maintained.

Table 10.1 Potassium ion concentrations in open and closed stomata.

Species	Potassium (mM) in guard cells that are	
	open	closed
Vicia faba (broad bean)	645	138
Nicotiana tabacum (tobacco)	500	219
Commelina communis (dayflower)	448	95
Zea mais (maize)	400	150

Support

When do stomata open and close?

The timing of the opening and closing of stomata depends on the environment. Under natural conditions, stomata open at daybreak and close at night, so light appears to be the main factor which initiates opening (*illustration 1*).

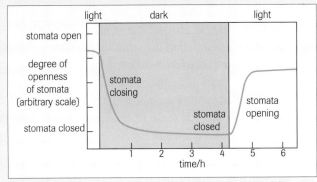
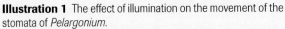

Illustration 1 The effect of illumination on the movement of the stomata of *Pelargonium*.

There are, however, situations in which other conditions override the effect of light. For example, on a warm sunny day as the temperature rises, more and more water vapour is lost through the open stomata. If the water loss exceeds the uptake of water from the soil, the water content of the plant falls and the plant suffers from **water stress**. Eventually the guard cells lose their turgor and close the stomata. In such conditions, photosynthesis may also be reduced, resulting in a rise in the concentration of carbon dioxide in the leaf. This too causes the stomata to close with the result that, for the moment, no further carbon dioxide diffuses in.

Conversely, a fall in the internal concentration of carbon dioxide promotes the opening of the stomata, thus encouraging more carbon dioxide to diffuse in.

Water stress is now known to cause the concentration of the plant growth regulator **abscisic acid** to rise quite quickly in the leaves, and this results in closure of the stomata. When water is again available, the concentration of abscisic acid falls and the stomata reopen (*illustration 2*).

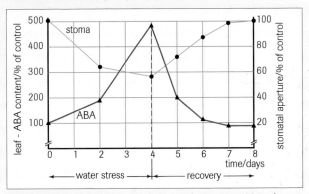

Illustration 2 The relationship between the concentration of abscisic acid (ABA) and stomatal opening in leaves of tobacco plants during a period of water stress followed by recovery.

The events which control the opening and closing of stomata are an example of **negative feedback**. In the case of drought, partial closure of the stomata is maintained until turgor is restored, at which time the stomata will open again. In the case of photosynthesis, a reduction in the concentration of carbon dioxide inside the leaf opens the stomata, resulting in an increase in the concentration of carbon dioxide inside the leaf.

▶ Negative feedback, page 272

▶ Abscisic acid, page 551

Carbon dioxide and oxygen may also diffuse from the cells into the sub-stomatal air spaces and thence out through the open stomata. The direction of diffusion depends on environmental conditions and the requirements of the plant. It is the net exchange of carbon dioxide and oxygen in relation to respiration and photosynthesis which matters.

10.2 Gaseous exchange in animals

Most animals carry out aerobic respiration, so their cells must receive an adequate supply of oxygen, and the carbon dioxide produced has to be removed. Land animals get their oxygen direct from the atmosphere. Most aquatic animals, such as fish, use oxygen dissolved in the water. Others, such as mosquito larvae, water spiders and whales, get their oxygen from the air above the water surface. In all cases gaseous exchange depends on a concentration gradient between the medium and the sites where oxygen is required and carbon dioxide is released.

In small animals, the surface–volume ratio is large enough for diffusion across the external surface to satisfy their respiratory needs. This is the case in the unicellular protoctists such as *Amoeba*. However in larger animals, especially active ones, the surface–volume ratio is too small for this to be so and a special **gaseous-exchange surface** is needed.

Animals that use the external body surface for gaseous exchange include the freshwater *Hydra*, free-living flatworms and earthworms. For the most part these animals are small enough not to require a special surface for gaseous exchange. Some of them are comparatively inactive and their sluggishness considerably reduces their need for oxygen (sea anemones, for example, are sedentary, catching their prey by moving their tentacles). The free-living flatworms are interesting in this context. They glide over stones and leaves in streams and lakes which are well aerated. The smallest species are almost cylindrical, but the larger species are flattened which has the effect of increasing the surface–volume ratio and decreasing the distance over which gases have to diffuse.

These adaptations are summarised in figure 10.5. They help to solve the problem of gaseous exchange. However, the overall size of an animal is limited if the only area available for gaseous exchange is the external body surface. This limit does not apply to animals which have special surfaces for gaseous exchange.

Specialised gaseous exchange surfaces

Most animals have special surfaces for gaseous exchange. Some are shown diagrammatically in figure 10.6. In all cases they consist of numerous flaps, sacs or tubes which provide a large area for diffusion.

The simplest devices are **external gills**, epidermal outgrowths from the body surface found in aquatic animals such as lugworms and young tadpoles. In contrast, **internal gills**, found in fish, are enclosed in cavities within the body where they are protected from damage and in which blood can be brought very close to the surrounding water.

Air-breathing vertebrates have **lungs** which are sac-like outgrowths of the pharynx in which air is brought close to the blood. A quite different arrangement is found in insects. Here, air pores at the surface open into a system of branching **tracheal tubes** which ramify through the body, coming into close association with all the tissues.

Although these various devices might seem rather different, they all have one essential feature in common: the exposure of a large surface area to whatever medium the animal happens to live in. This, we saw earlier in the chapter, is a basic requirement for efficient gaseous exchange.

We shall now look in detail at gaseous exchange systems in insects, fish and mammals.

Fick's Law, page 104

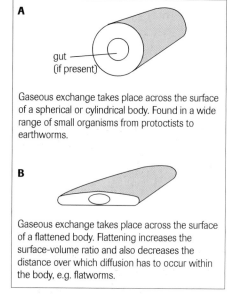

A

gut (if present)

Gaseous exchange takes place across the surface of a spherical or cylindrical body. Found in a wide range of small organisms from protoctists to earthworms.

B

Gaseous exchange takes place across the surface of a flattened body. Flattening increases the surface-volume ratio and also decreases the distance over which diffusion has to occur within the body, e.g. flatworms.

Figure 10.5 Organisms which undergo gaseous exchange across the entire surface of the body are either small or flattened.

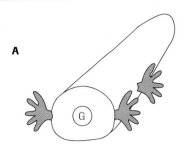

A

External gills. These increase the surface area but they are unprotected and therefore easily damaged. Gaseous exchange usually takes place across the rest of the body surface as well as the gills, e.g. lugworm.

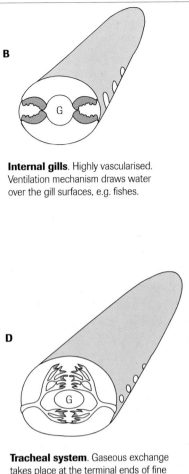

B

Internal gills. Highly vascularised. Ventilation mechanism draws water over the gill surfaces, e.g. fishes.

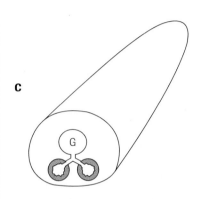

C

Lungs. Highly vascularised. The lungs are sacs connected to the pharynx. Air is drawn into them by a ventilation mechanism. Found in all air-breathing vertebrates.

D

Tracheal system. Gaseous exchange takes place at the terminal ends of fine **tracheal tubes** which ramify through the body and penetrate into all the tissues. Found in insects and other arthropods.

Figure 10.6 Diagrams showing different kinds of surfaces for gaseous exchange. In each case the gaseous exchange surface is shown in pink and the gut is labelled G.

Extension

Some adaptations of invertebrates to living in fresh water

Gaseous exchange is one of the problems facing animals living in fresh water. This is largely because the oxygen content of a body of fresh water fluctuates. One of the reasons for this is that the amount of oxygen dissolved in water is inversely proportional to temperature, so there is more oxygen available in water at low temperatures than at higher temperatures.

In order to carry out gaseous exchange, totally aquatic invertebrates exhibit a variety of structural, physiological and behavioural modifications. Some have a large surface–volume ratio (*page 106*) and a body covering through which

gaseous exchange is possible, e.g. flatworms. Larger animals such as leeches have a low metabolic rate and are able to maintain an adequate exchange of gases through the body wall, and small crustaceans like the water flea (*Daphnia*), because they have an impermeable cuticle, create a current of water with their limbs which flows over the soft part of their bodies where gaseous exchange can occur.

Many invertebrates living in fresh water, however, possess some kind of gill. An example of this is the nymph of the mayfly, found in still water at all times of year. Pairs of plate-like gills on the

abdomen vibrate and create a current of water which passes backwards until it meets the last pair, which are stationary and deflect the current to each side so that a fresh current of water is brought into use. If the water is highly oxygenated the gill movement is slow, but if the water is low in oxygen the gills vibrate much more rapidly (*illustration 1*).

Some freshwater snails have thread-like and/or feathery gills which can be protruded from their shells and waved about in the water for gaseous exchange (*illustration 2*). Freshwater mussels have gills enclosed within their shells, and as they lie in the mud, water is drawn into

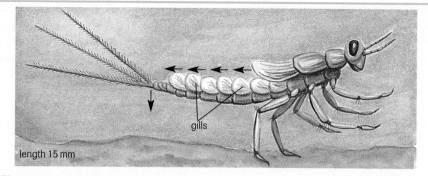

Illustration 1 Nymph of a mayfly showing the plate-like gills on the abdomen which create a current of water (shown by the arrows).

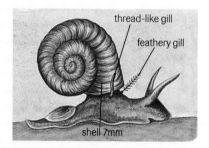

Illustration 2 A freshwater snail showing a thread-like and a feathery gill which protrude from the shell and wave in the water.

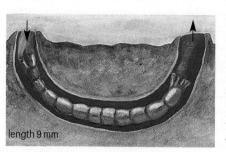

Illustration 4 A midge larva lying in its tube through which water is drawn (shown by the arrows).

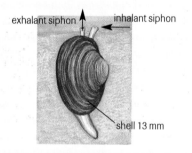

Illustration 3 A freshwater mussel showing the inhalant and exhalant siphons. The gills bearing cilia are enclosed within the shell.

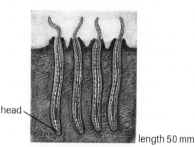

Illustration 5 Sludge worms, *Tubifex*, head down in mud tubes with 'tails' protruding.

an inhalant siphon and passed over the gills which are covered with cilia. The beating of the cilia aids the flow of water, which is then passed out of an exhalant siphon (*illustration 3*).

At the bottom of ponds, in the sediment, the oxygen content of the water is greatly reduced as a result of the decaying animal and vegetable matter (*eutrophication, page 682*). Some of the animals which live in this environment, certain midge larvae for example, possess haemoglobin which is capable of combining with oxygen and greatly increases the oxygen-carrying capacity of the blood. It has been calculated that the volume of haemoglobin in a midge larva could not store more oxygen than would last about 12 minutes without being replenished. But they are very sluggish animals and lie in 'silk' lined burrows into which a current of water is drawn – carrying with it, oxygen (*illustration 4*). The presence of haemoglobin allows the larvae to remain in their tubes for greater lengths of time and thereby escape predation.

Several annelid worms living in these conditions also possess haemoglobin – *Tubifex*, the sludge worm, is an example. It lives, head downwards, in a mud tube. The 'tail' protrudes and waves about , so it is used as a gill. The less oxygen there is in the water, the further the tail extends from the tube, so exposing a greater length of body in which blood containing haemoglobin is circulating (*illustration 5*).

10.3 **Gaseous exchange in insects**

In insects, the cuticle on either side of the thorax and abdomen is perforated by a series of segmentally arranged pores or **spiracles** which open into a system of **tracheal tubes** or **tracheae** (singular **trachea**) (*figure 10.7*). The spiracles are guarded by **valves** or **hairs** to prevent excessive evaporation through them. The tracheae are arranged in a regular pattern, some of them running longitudinally, some transversely. The larger tracheae are about a millimetre in diameter in some insects, and are kept permanently open by spiral or annular thickenings of hardened chitin, the same material that makes up the cuticle.

The function of the spiracles and tracheae is to permit the passage of air to a further

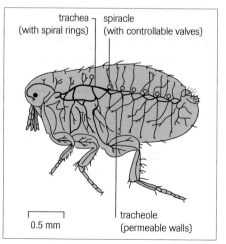

Figure 10.7 The tracheal system of a flea. The tracheal tubes convey oxygen to all tissues of the body, and carbon dioxide from the tissues to the exterior. Only the left half of the system is shown.

system of tubes, the **tracheoles**. These are very fine intracellular tubes, a mere 1 μm in diameter. They are extremely numerous and penetrate deep into all the tissues, particularly the muscles. Unlike the tracheae, they are not lined with a cuticle, gaseous exchange occurring freely across their walls.

The mechanism of gaseous exchange in insects is in marked contrast to most other animals. Instead of being picked up by blood at the gaseous exchange surface and then conveyed to the tissues, oxygen passes directly to the tissues via this system of ramifying air tubes.

How does oxygen get to the tissues along these tubes? In most insects, diffusion is the answer, which may be one reason why insects are generally rather small in size. However, in some species diffusion is aided by rhythmical movements of the thorax or abdomen. Such ventilation is seen, for example, in the locust where it has been demonstrated that air is drawn into the body through the thoracic spiracles and leaves via the abdominal spiracles. In all flying species ventilation is aided by muscular movements during flight.

Insects can control the rate at which oxygen reaches the tissues. The mechanism depends on the fact that the tracheoles contain varying amounts of watery fluid. In vigorous muscular activity (flight, for example), lactic acid accumulates in the tissues. This raises the solute concentration of the tissue fluids, with the result that water is drawn out of the tracheoles into the tissues by osmosis. This has the effect of opening up the air passages, facilitating the diffusion of oxygen to the tissues (*figure 10.8*).

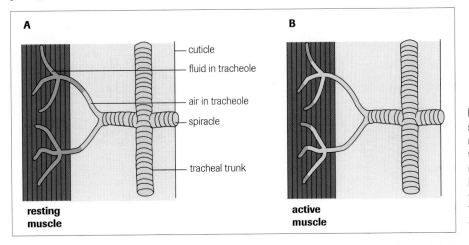

Figure 10.8 A A small part of the tracheal system of an insect. The spiracles open into a main longitudinal tracheal trunk on each side of the body. Branches of the tracheal trunks break up into numerous tracheoles which penetrate into the tissues. **B** shows withdrawal of the fluid from the tracheoles during muscular exercise. This facilitates diffusion of oxygen to the muscle tissue.

The tracheoles are extraordinary structures whose pattern of growth can be modified according to the needs of the tissues. If a body segment is deprived of oxygen because its main trachea is damaged, the tracheoles of neighbouring segments respond by growing towards the deprived segment. In this way uniform distribution of oxygen to the tissues is ensured.

10.4 Gaseous exchange in fish

If you look at table 10.2, you will see that water is denser and more viscous than air. The concentration of oxygen in water is lower, and it diffuses more slowly, than in air. As far as gaseous exchange is concerned, this presents fish with certain difficulties and it is one of the reasons why they are generally less active than mammals.

The properties of water as compared with air mean that the surface for gaseous exchange and the ventilation mechanism in fish need to be quite different from those of mammals. The idea of a fish propelling water in and out of sac-like lungs, such as mammals have, would not provide them with oxygen quickly enough. In fish, gaseous exchange takes place across the surface of highly vascularised **gills** over which a one-way current of water is kept flowing by a specialised pumping mechanism. The density of the

Table 10.2 Comparison of a sample of fresh water and air. The oxygen content is in cm³ per litre; other figures are in arbitary units.

	Air	Water
Density	1	777
Viscosity	1	100
Oxygen content	210	8
Diffusion rate	10 000	1

water prevents the gills from collapsing and lying on top of each other, which is what happens when a fish is taken out of water.

In Chapter 6 we saw that there are two classes of fish – those with a skeleton made of cartilage (chondrichthyes) and those in which the skeleton is made of bone (osteichthyes). The principles of gaseous exchange are the same in both groups, though the arrangement of the gills and the way they open to the exterior is different. We will describe one group in detail – bony fish.

Gaseous exchange in bony fish

In bony fish, like cod and whiting, the entire gill region is flanked by a muscular flap of skin, the **operculum**, which can be seen in figure 10.9. This encloses an **opercular cavity** into which the gills project (*figure 10.10*). Water is drawn into, and pumped out of, the **pharynx** by movements of the operculum. The ventilation cycle maintains a continuous stream of water over the gills at all times.

In figure 10.11, the way the gills are arranged is shown in detail. The gills are constructed in such a way that a large surface area of highly vascularised epithelium is exposed to the water as it flows through. Each gill is composed of two piles of leaf-like **filaments** which project from a solid base strengthened by a bony **branchial arch**. On the upper and lower surfaces of the filaments are numerous vertical **gill lamellae** which greatly increase the surface area of the gill.

Figure 10.9 The head of a perch, *Perca fluviatilis*, a bony fish, showing the operculum covering the gills. An operculum is typical of bony fish.

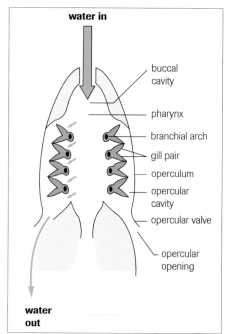

Figure 10.10 Diagram of a horizontal section through the pharynx and gill region of a bony fish. The muscular operculum covers the entire gill region on either side of the body. The way the water flows through the system is shown on the left by the blue arrows. Water is sucked in through the mouth by expansion of the buccal cavity and then flows into the opercular cavity by outward movement of the operculum accompanied by contraction of the buccal cavity. Water is expelled through the opercular openings by inward movement of the operculum and continued contraction of the buccal cavity.

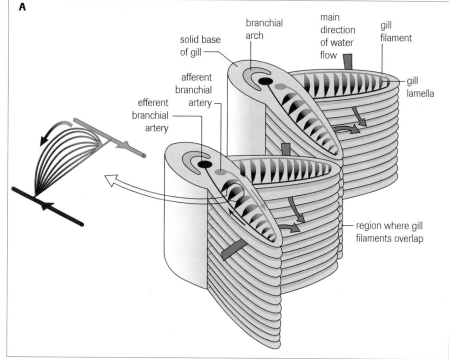

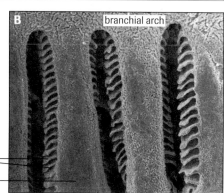

Figure 10.11 Detailed structure of the gills of a bony fish. **A** Notice that the gill filaments project outwards at approximately right angles to each other, an arrangement which allows for more efficient gaseous exchange. Deoxygenated blood, blue; oxygenated blood, red.
B A scanning electron micrograph of the gill filaments and lamellae of the cod. Magnification ×30.

The base of each gill contains an **afferent branchial artery** which brings deoxygenated blood to the gill from the ventral aorta beneath the floor of the pharynx. The base of the gill also contains an **efferent branchial artery** which carries oxygenated blood *away from* the gill to the dorsal aorta above the roof of the pharynx.

The afferent and efferent branchial arteries are interconnected within each filament and its gill lamellae by an extensive system of capillaries. Gaseous exchange takes place as the blood flows through the capillaries in the lamellae. The barrier between the blood and the water consists of only two thin layers of epithelium with a total thickness of about 0.5 μm, so diffusion readily takes place across it.

The orientation of the gaseous-exchange surfaces means that as water passes from the pharynx into the opercular chamber, it inevitably flows between the gill lamellae in a direction opposite to the blood flow, an arrangement known as **counterflow** (*extension box below*). This system is certainly efficient, about 80 per cent of the oxygen being extracted from the water as it flows over the gills compared with 10 per cent when the flow was experimentally reversed. Moreover, the free ends of adjacent gills touch each other, and this means that no water can avoid passing between the filaments as it flows from the pharynx to the opercular chamber.

Extension

Parallel flow and counterflow

In gill systems, water and blood flow close to each other and gaseous exchange takes place from one to the other. If the blood and water flow in the *same* direction at the *same* speed (**parallel flow**), the concentration difference in dissolved oxygen would be great at first, but would steadily decrease as the blood and water flowed together across the gaseous exchange surface (*illustration 1*). On leaving the gaseous exchange surface, the oxygen in the blood would be in equilibrium with the oxygen in the water at a point well below its maximum saturation with oxygen. Parallel flow is not therefore very efficient.

For *maximum* gaseous exchange to take place, it is best for the blood and water to flow in opposite directions (**counterflow**). This ensures that as blood flows across the gaseous exchange surface, it meets water which has had less and less oxygen extracted from it (*illustration 2*). By the time the blood is about to leave the gaseous-exchange

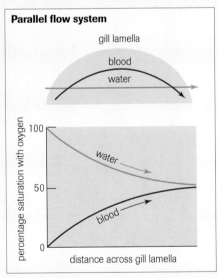

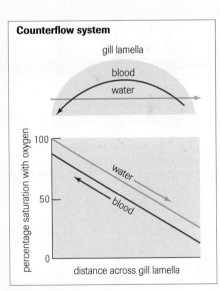

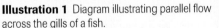

Illustration 1 Diagram illustrating parallel flow across the gills of a fish.

Illustration 2 Diagram illustrating counterflow across the gills of a fish.

In both diagrams it is assumed that the blood and water move at the same speed and have equal oxygen capacities.

surface it will have almost the same partial pressure of oxygen as the inhalant water. In other words the same steep diffusion gradient is maintained throughout the gaseous-exchange surface.

In bony fishes the structural arrangement of the gills is such as to make the counterflow system more certain.

10.5 Gaseous exchange in mammals

The medium for gaseous exchange in mammals is air. Most mammals are terrestrial and need to conserve water. They are endothermic and usually active, so their demand for oxygen is high.

The mammalian **lung** is a remarkably efficient structure which fulfils the function of gaseous exchange with minimum water loss and heat energy transfer. To illustrate this, let us look at the human system.

The human gaseous exchange system

The human lungs and associated structures are shown in figure 10.12. The lungs are situated in the **thorax**, the walls of which are formed by the **ribs**, **sternum** and **intercostal muscles**, and the floor by the **diaphragm**. The lungs are surrounded by a very narrow **pleural cavity** lined by **pleural membranes**. The pleural cavity contains a thin layer of lubricating fluid (**pleural fluid**) which allows the pleural membranes to slide easily over each other as the thorax expands and contracts during breathing.

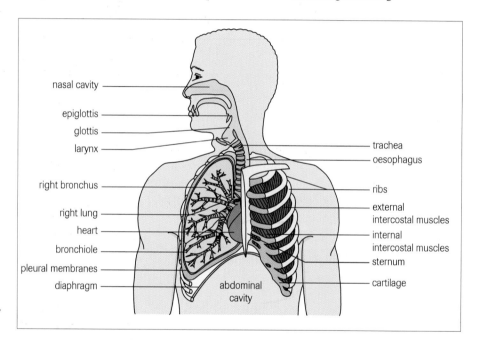

Figure 10.12 The human gaseous exchange and ventilation system. Expansion of the thorax draws air down the trachea and bronchi into the lungs. Incomplete rings of cartilage keep the trachea and bronchi permanently open. The right-hand side of the diagram shows the ribs and intercostal muscles in position. On the left-hand side the ribs and intercostal muscles have been removed and the lungs opened up to show the bronchial tubes.

Air is drawn into the lungs via the **trachea** and **bronchi**. The expansion of the thoracic cavity is brought about by the upward and outward movement of the ribs and forward movement of the sternum, accompanied by flattening of the diaphragm. The rib movements are achieved by the contraction of the external intercostal muscles, and the flattening of the diaphragm by contraction of its muscles which are arranged mainly in a radial direction. All this constitutes **inspiration** (*figure 10.13A*). The process then goes into reverse, air being expelled from the lungs in the act of **expiration** (*figure 10.13B*).

Expiration is a mainly passive process resulting from elastic recoil of the tissues that have been stretched during inspiration. However, in forced breathing or when the breathing tubes are blocked, expiration is aided by contraction of the internal intercostal muscles and **abdominal muscles**. Contraction of the latter raises the pressure in the abdominal cavity, forcing the diaphragm upwards.

The pressure and volume changes that occur during the ventilation cycle are shown in figure 10.14. At rest the pressure in the lungs is the same as atmospheric pressure, but because the lungs are elastic and tend to pull away from the walls of the thorax, the pressure in the pleural cavity is slightly less than atmospheric.

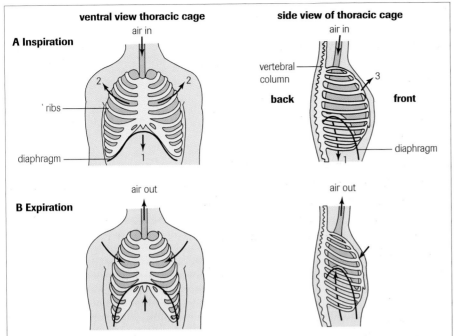

Figure 10.13 A Diagrams showing how the thorax expands. Expansion in the downwards direction takes place by descent of the diaphragm (arrow 1), in a sideways direction by upward and outward movement of the ribs (arrow 2), and in a back-to-front direction by upward and forward movement of the sternum (arrow 3). **B** The reverse movements occur during expiration.

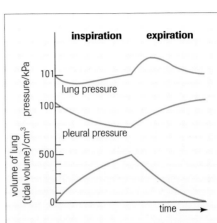

Figure 10.14 Pressure and volume changes during the ventilation cycle of a human. Volume changes are measured by means of a spirometer (*extension box on page 170*); pressures are measured by running a fine tube from the appropriate cavity to a suitable manometer. For practical purposes the pleural pressure can be estimated by measuring the pressure in the oesophagus.

During inspiration, when the walls and floor of the thorax are moving outwards and downwards respectively, the pleural pressure falls. This has the immediate effect of lowering the lung pressure to below atmospheric, so that air enters the lungs. This increases their volume and returns the lung pressure to atmospheric.

On expiration, the pressure of the thoracic wall and the diaphragm against the pleural cavity raises the pleural pressure. This is transmitted to the lungs where the pressure increases and volume decreases as air is expelled.

Structure of the lungs

The lungs are spongy in texture, and consist of a tree-like system of tubes which ramify from the two **bronchi**. Each tube eventually becomes a very narrow **bronchiole** which terminates as a bunch of tiny sac-like **alveoli** (*figure 10.15*).

Although a certain amount of gaseous exchange can take place across the walls of the smaller bronchioles, it is the alveoli which play the leading role in this respect. The efficiency of the mammalian lung as a gaseous exchange surface depends on the fact that a vast number of alveoli come into very close association with an extensive capillary system.

The alveolar epithelium is covered with a thin layer of fluid in which the oxygen dissolves before it diffuses into the cells. If this fluid had a normal surface tension it would pull the alveolar walls inwards, making it difficult to expand the lungs and possibly causing the alveoli to collapse. However, the fluid contains a 'surfactant', a detergent-like lipoprotein which reduces the surface tension and prevents this happening.

In humans, the two lungs contain approximately 700 million alveoli, giving a total surface area of over 70 m²; if the lungs were opened out into a continuous sheet they would just about cover a tennis court! The capillary network in the lungs has a total area of about 40 m². In the lungs, therefore, an enormous surface area for gaseous exchange is packed into a comparatively small space. This general principle also applies to other terrestrial vertebrates such as amphibians and reptiles. However, in these animals the total surface area of the lungs relative to their size is nothing like as great.

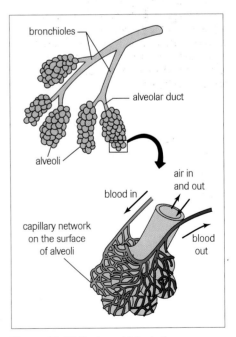

Figure 10.15 The bronchioles in the mammalian lung terminate as numerous alveoli, across whose much folded and highly vascular walls, gaseous exchange takes place.

Squamous epithelium, page 63

The relationship between the alveoli and the capillaries is extremely intimate. The walls of the capillaries and alveoli both consist of a single layer of flattened squamous epithelial cells which are extremely close to each other (*figure 10.16*). The resulting barrier between the alveolar cavity and the blood is a mere 0.3 μm thick in its thinnest part. As such it offers minimum resistance to the diffusion of gases from one side to the other.

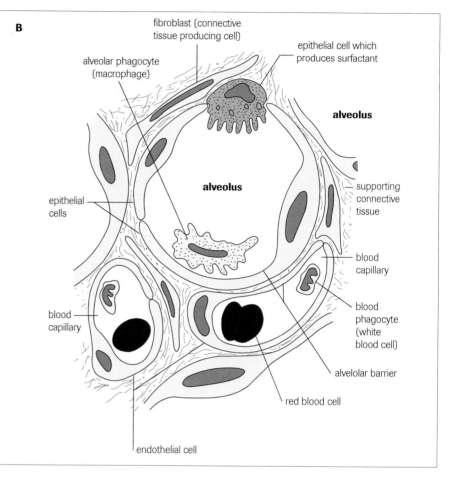

Figure 10.16 The relationship between the alveoli and capillaries in a mammalian lung. **A** Photomicrograph of a section through several alveoli and capillaries, magnified ×200. The alveoli are separated from the bloodstream by a very thin alveolar barrier consisting of only two layers of pavement epithelial cells, as shown in **B**. The phagocytes are important in defence against disease.

The ventilation cycle

A person breathing normally at rest takes in, and expels, approximately half a litre of air during each ventilation cycle. This is known as the **tidal volume**, and it can be recorded and measured by means of a **spirometer** (*extension box on page 170*).

The rate at which a person breathes is expressed as the **ventilation rate**. This is usually expressed as the volume of air breathed per minute and is called the **minute volume**. Thus:

**ventilation rate = tidal volume × number of breaths per minute
(minute volume)**

The ventilation rate changes according to the circumstances: in muscular exercise, for example, both the frequency and depth of breathing increase, resulting in a higher ventilation rate. We shall return to this later. The important point is that the lungs have a much greater potential volume than is ever realised in resting conditions, and this permits the ventilation rate to adapt to changing needs.

If you take a deep breath, you can take into your lungs about three litres of air over and above the tidal volume. This is called the **inspiratory reserve volume**, and is brought into use when required. If at the end of a normal expiration you expel as much air as you possibly can, the extra air expired is about one litre, and is called the **expiratory reserve volume**.

The total volume of air that can be expired after a maximum inspiration (i.e. the tidal volume plus inspiratory and expiratory reserve volumes) is known as the **vital capacity**. The vital capacity of an average person lies between 4 and 5 litres but in a fit athlete it may exceed 6 litres. Even after maximum expiration, about 1.5 litres of air remain in the lungs. This is known as the **residual volume**. The various lung volumes just described are shown in figure 10.17.

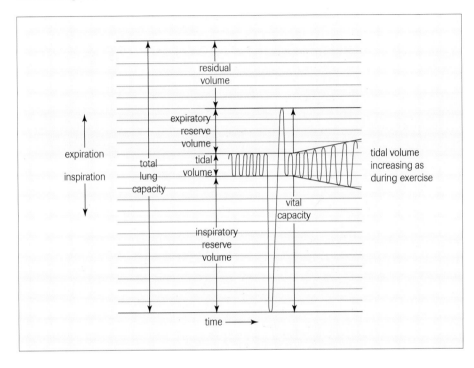

Figure 10.17 Diagram showing typical human lung volumes. The tracings are based on spirometer recordings obtained from a large number of individuals. The horizontal divisions correspond to 250 cm^3. There is considerable variation between different individuals in the tidal volumes and vital capacity. These tracings emphasise how little air is drawn into the lungs in resting conditions. The reserve volumes are brought into action only when necessary.

How much of the air taken in is actually used in gaseous exchange? Of the half litre or so inspired in quiet breathing, only about 350 cm^3 gets into the parts of the lung where gaseous exchange is possible. The rest remains in the trachea and bronchial tubes, collectively known as the **dead space**, where no gaseous exchange takes place. If the capacity of the lungs is about 6 litres, it is clear that in resting conditions only a small fraction of the total volume of air present in the lungs and associated tubes is actually used in gaseous exchange.

At each inspiration during normal quiet breathing, about 350 cm^3 of inspired air mixes with some 2.5 litres of air already present in the alveoli. With so little new air mixing with so much air already present, it is probable that the composition of the air in the depth of the lungs remains relatively constant during resting conditions. Through this air, situated between the inspired air and the blood, gases diffuse to and from the alveolar surface.

Exchanges across the alveolar surface

Table 10.3 compares the composition of inspired (i.e. atmospheric) and expired air. This indicates the exchanges that take place in the lungs: oxygen is taken up and carbon dioxide given out.

Analysis of the blood flowing to and from the alveoli gives us an insight into what happens at the gaseous-exchange surface itself. Blood reaching the alveoli has a lower partial pressure of oxygen, and a higher partial pressure of carbon dioxide, than the alveolar air. There is thus a concentration gradient favouring the diffusion of these two gases in opposite directions.

Table 10.3 A comparison of the oxygen, carbon dioxide and nitrogen in atmospheric and inspired air in a resting human at sea level.

	Atmospheric air/%	Expired air/%
Oxygen	20.95	16.4
Nitrogen	79.01	79.5
Carbon dioxide	0.04	4.1

Spirometry

In humans, a spirometer can be used to record and measure lung volumes and oxygen consumption (*illustration 1*).

Spirometers come in various shapes and forms but they all operate on the same principle. The person breathes in and out of an airtight chamber consisting of a light Perspex 'lid' floating in water. As the person inhales the lid goes down, and when the person exhales it goes up. These movements can be recorded by a pen writing on a revolving drum, by a chart recorder or by a computer acting via an interface device. In the photograph, a kymograph is being used.

To use the spirometer, the chamber is first filled with oxygen from a cylinder. The person is then connected to it by a mouthpiece at the end of a flexible tube. Between the tube and the oxygen chamber there is a canister containing a substance such as soda lime, which absorbs carbon dioxide. This ensures that all the carbon dioxide expired by the person is absorbed before the air is breathed in again. A nose clip must be worn so that the lungs, bronchi and trachea form a closed system with the spirometer.

The lung volumes and ventilation movements shown in figure 10.17 were measured with a spirometer. The apparatus can also be used to measure how much oxygen is used in a given time. As oxygen is used up, the spirometer 'lid' slowly sinks and the distance the top or bottom of the trace falls represents the volume of oxygen used (marked x in illustration 2).

Illustration 1 A spirometer in use. The trace is being recorded on a kymograph.

In order to calculate volumes, the recording paper has to be calibrated for time and volume so that the depth and frequency of the person's inspirations and expirations can be measured. From these measurements the rate of oxygen consumption can be calculated. Illustration 2 shows a spirometer trace of human ventilation.

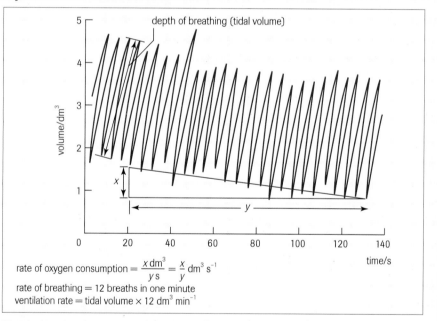

$$\text{rate of oxygen consumption} = \frac{x \, \text{dm}^3}{y \, \text{s}} = \frac{x}{y} \, \text{dm}^3 \, \text{s}^{-1}$$

rate of breathing = 12 breaths in one minute
ventilation rate = tidal volume $\times$ 12 dm^3 min^{-1}

Illustration 2 A spirometer trace of human ventilation.

As blood flows past an alveolus, oxygen diffuses into it and carbon dioxide out, so that by the time the blood leaves the alveolus, it has almost the same partial pressure of oxygen and carbon dioxide as the alveolar air (*figure 10.18*). During this equalisation of partial pressures, the percentage saturation of the blood rises from about 70 per cent to over 90 per cent. The composition of alveolar air, however, remains relatively unchanged because of exchanges between it and the inspired air.

In fact the process is not quite as efficient as it may seem because some alveoli are inevitably under-ventilated. Moreover, a proportion of the blood which goes to the lungs

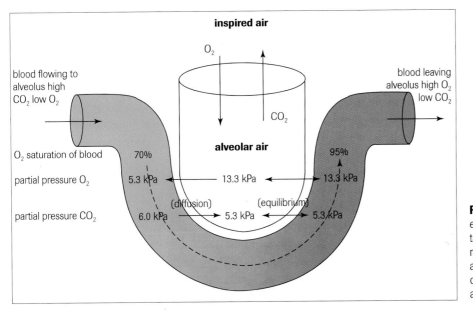

inspired air

O_2

blood flowing to
alveolus high
CO_2 low O_2

blood leaving
alveolus high O_2
low CO_2

CO_2

alveolar air

O_2 saturation of blood	70%		95%
partial pressure O_2	5.3 kPa	13.3 kPa	13.3 kPa
partial pressure CO_2	6.0 kPa	(diffusion) 5.3 kPa (equilibrium)	5.3 kPa

Figure 10.18 Diagram summarising the exchange of oxygen and carbon dioxide that takes place as blood flows past an alveolus in the mammalian lung. By the time the blood leaves the alveolus it has the same partial pressure of oxygen and carbon dioxide as the alveolar air, and it is almost fully saturated with oxygen.

does not go through any alveolar capillaries and therefore never gets oxygenated. The result is that the blood leaving the lungs is not as fully oxygenated as it might be.

The effects of fluctuations in oxygen and carbon dioxide

It is important to realise that conditions in the human body change all the time and yet it still manages to function adequately. This is particularly so in an active person. At the moment you are probably sitting reading this book; if you get up and walk, changes immediately occur in your body to which adjustments must be made. The changes will be even greater if you exert yourself further. But even with very slight exertion, there is bound to be a momentary increase in the metabolic rate. This will result in an increase in the amount of oxygen used and carbon dioxide produced. The oxygen content of the blood will therefore fall and carbon dioxide will rise.

The significance of these changes can best be appreciated by considering the effects that follow if these respiratory gases fluctuate badly. To take oxygen first, a deficiency of oxygen (**hypoxia**) deprives the tissues of a vital requirement for metabolism. The consequence is that the senses, particularly vision, are impaired, as is the brain. This results in the adoption of a slap-happy state of mind. Aircraft pilots experience this if their oxygen apparatus breaks down, and can result in gross misjudgements of situations – something which fortunately happens more often in films than in real life! The trouble is that the person may be unaware that anything is wrong, and so does nothing about it. Unconsciousness occurs suddenly, followed by paralysis (caused by irreparable damage to nerve cells) and death.

What about excess oxygen? Breathing pure oxygen at atmospheric pressure presents no problems. The saturation of our arterial blood with oxygen is about 96 per cent under normal circumstances, and breathing pure oxygen will not appreciably increase the amount of oxygen delivered to our tissues. However, if breathed at pressures greater than atmospheric, as in diving, excess oxygen can be very dangerous. At first, the tissues metabolise very rapidly, keeping pace with the extra oxygen supply. As the oxygen builds up, however, it inhibits certain enzymes involved in the Krebs cycle, thus interfering with cell respiration.

Cells are even more susceptible to changes in the level of carbon dioxide. An accumulation of this gas increases the acidity of the blood and tissue fluids, inhibits enzymes and stops essential metabolic processes. This is why breathing air rich in carbon dioxide is so dangerous. Re-breathing one's own expired air can be fatal very quickly.

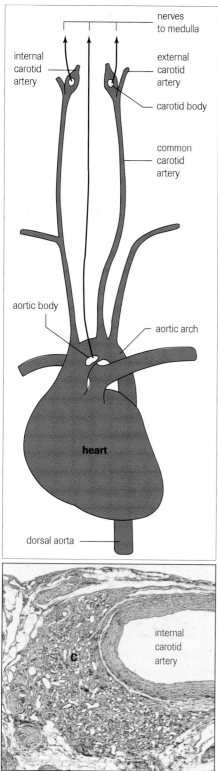

Figure 10.19 *Top* Diagram showing the positions of the aortic and carotid bodies, ventral view. *Bottom* Photomicrograph of a section of the carotid body (C). The carotid body consists of a mass of epithelial-type cells and nerve fibres which are sensitive to excess carbon dioxide or insufficient oxygen in the blood. The clear areas in the carotid body are blood spaces. The nerve fibres are stimulated as the blood flows through these spaces. Magnification ×25.

10.6 **The control of breathing**

As long ago as 1905, J.S. Haldane and J. Priestley showed that in humans, the ventilation rate can be doubled by increasing the carbon dioxide in the air from its usual 0.04 per cent to 3.0 per cent. In humans and other mammals, the overall control of ventilation involves groups of nerve cells comprising a **ventilation centre** in the posterior part of the brain called the **medulla oblongata** (*page 361*). The ventilation centre responds to the level of carbon dioxide, and to a lesser extent oxygen, in the bloodstream. If the partial pressure of carbon dioxide rises, the centre responds by increasing the ventilation rate. If it falls, the centre responds by decreasing the ventilation rate.

The chemical control of breathing

We now know that a change in the level of carbon dioxide in the blood is the effective stimulus initiating a change in ventilation rate. A small change in the amount of carbon dioxide is more effective than even a large change in the amount of oxygen. For this reason, the partial pressure of oxygen in the blood may vary considerably, but the partial pressure of carbon dioxide only shows very small deviations.

How is the ventilation centre informed of the level of carbon dioxide in the blood? In the walls of certain arteries there are receptor cells which are sensitive to chemical changes in the blood flowing past them. They function as **chemoreceptors**, detecting changes in pH and the partial pressure of carbon dioxide. They are found between the internal and external carotid arteries on each side of the neck, where they form the carotid bodies, and in the wall of the aorta close to the heart where they form the aortic body (*figure 10.19*).

If the partial pressure of carbon dioxide rises, the chemoreceptors are stimulated and impulses are sent to the ventilation centre in the brain, increasing its activity. In addition, there are chemoreceptors in the brain near the ventilation centre itself. They too detect changes in the pH and partial pressure of carbon dioxide – indeed this is probably the main pathway by which the ventilation centre is stimulated.

The chemoreceptors are situated in two ideal locations. Those near the ventilation centre in the brain monitor the cerebrospinal fluid so that instant responses can be given. Those in the carotid arteries and the aorta monitor the blood flowing to the head and to all organs of the body except the lungs.

The role of the brain

It is in the ventilation centre that overall control of breathing is brought about. The ventilation centre receives impulses from three sources:

- **stretch receptors** in the smooth muscle within the walls of the bronchial tubes;
- **chemoreceptors** in the carotid artery and aorta;
- the higher centres in the brain (**cerebral cortex**) which control voluntary changes in breathing.

These three sources of nerve impulses are shown in figure 10.20. Let us look at each in turn.

Impulses from stretch receptors

Sensory branches of the vagus nerve carry impulses from the stretch receptors in the wall of the bronchial tubes to the ventilation centre. If impulses from the vagus nerve are recorded with an oscilloscope, it can be shown that as the lungs inflate, the frequency of impulses increases – an effect known as the **Hering–Breuer reflex**. The job of these stretch receptors is to signal to the ventilation centre the degree of expansion of the lungs. As inspiration proceeds, the impulses eventually reach such a frequency that they inhibit inspiration, thereby initiating expiration which is largely a passive process.

Cessation of inspiration is therefore caused by expansion of the lungs themselves. However if the vagus nerves are cut, rhythmical breathing will still continue, though deeper and slower than before. It is therefore evident that the ventilation centre possesses an **intrinsic rhythmicity** which can bring about regular breathing. Impulses reaching the ventilation centre from the stretch receptors in the lungs keep this intrinsic mechanism under control and prevent the lungs being over-expanded.

Impulses from chemoreceptors

If the partial pressure of carbon dioxide in the blood rises, the chemoreceptors in the carotid and aortic bodies are stimulated and impulses are conveyed via sensory nerves to the ventilation centre in the brain. The latter responds by sending impulses to the external intercostal muscles and diaphragm muscle, thereby bringing about an increase in the ventilation rate.

This has been confirmed by experiments. In one experiment the carotid body was perfused with blood containing different levels of carbon dioxide. It was found that increasing the carbon dioxide content of the blood had the effect of speeding up the rate of breathing. Cutting the carotid nerves abolished this response.

The ventilation centre, then, is influenced by impulses from various receptors which can alter the normal pattern of breathing. In addition it is itself sensitive to carbon dioxide in the blood.

Impulses from the cerebral cortex

The ventilation centre is also under the influence of higher centres in the brain, that is, the cerebral cortex: if this were not so, voluntary changes in breathing would not be possible and the American, Robert Foster, would not have been able to hold his breath for 13.72 minutes submerged in a swimming pool!

Homeostatic control of breathing

The control of ventilation is an example of homeostasis, in which a system acts to maintain a steady state (*Chapter 16*). Figure 10.21 summarises how, when the normal level of carbon dioxide in the blood changes (an *error*) the chemoreceptors detect this and a sequence of events takes place which *correct* the error. This is an example of **negative feedback**.

In responding to changes in the partial pressure of carbon dioxide in the blood, the body not only prevents an accumulation of this poisonous gas but also ensures that sufficient oxygen is delivered to the tissues at all times.

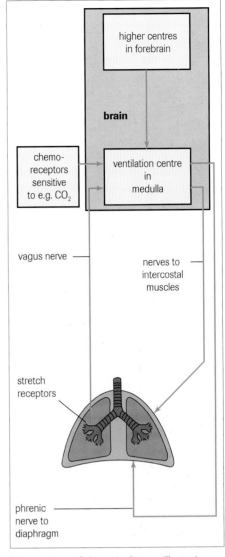

Figure 10.20 Schematic diagram illustrating the nervous control of ventilation in the mammal. The ventilation centre receives nerve impulses from various sources, while it sends out impulses to the inspiratory muscles in a rhythmical manner.

Negative feedback, page 272

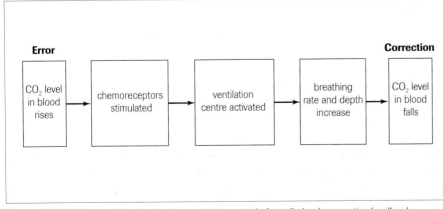

Figure 10.21 Diagram showing the homeostatic control of ventilation by negative feedback.

Figure 10.22 Sherpa Tenzing (left) and Edmund Hillary on the slopes of Everest,1953. Notice that they are not using oxygen apparatus. Hillary and Tenzing were the first climbers ever to reach the summit of Everest, 8848 m above sea level.

▶ Survival at high altitudes, page 243
▶ Acclimatisation to high and low temperature, page 310

Breathing at high altitudes

We have seen how the body responds when the partial pressure of carbon dioxide rises, but what happens if an abnormally low partial pressure of oxygen is experienced?. This is precisely what happens at high altitudes where the atmospheric pressure, and hence the partial pressure of oxygen, is considerably lower than at sea level. How does a person adjust to such conditions?

The answer depends on how high the altitude is and how quickly the person gets there. High is taken to mean above 3000 m. An aircraft pilot flying straight up to a great height without oxygen apparatus develops symptoms of **hypoxia** at about 4000 m, and becomes unconscious at about 8000 m. On the other hand a mountaineer who ascends slowly over a period of days or weeks has time to get used to the progressively rarefied atmosphere. At about 4000 m, he or she begins to develop signs of oxygen lack – breathlessness, headache, nausea and fatigue (**mountain sickness**). But these unpleasant symptoms wear off as one becomes **acclimatised**.

Adjustments to high altitude occur in both the ventilation and circulatory systems as the homeostatic responses to oxygen lack get pushed to their limit. The ventilation rate increases temporarily and this, together with parallel adjustments in the circulatory system, causes the rate of oxygen delivery to the tissues to go up. The circulatory aspects of this are dealt with in Chapter 14.

In the Himalayan expedition of 1953, Edmund Hillary and Sherpa Tenzing spent three hours at a height of over 8000 metres without oxygen apparatus, levelling snow and pitching a tent (*figure 10.22*). It was not easy, but the fact that they managed to do it at all indicates the importance of acclimatisation as a physiological process. An unacclimatised person at such a height would be unconscious within five minutes. Since then, many other mountaineers have climbed Everest without the use of oxygen apparatus.

People living permanently at high altitudes have special adaptations. They have, for instance, larger tidal volumes at each breath rather than an increased ventilation rate – in other words they breathe more deeply rather than faster. They also tend to be 'barrel-chested' and this may be because they have an increased lung surface area. They certainly have a larger vital capacity and residual volume than people living nearer to sea level.

Extension

Smoking and health

Research on smoking and its link with disease is a classic example of how biology impinges on society. Guest author Ann McNeill looks at some of the issues.

There are over 4000 chemicals in cigarette smoke, including 40 known carcinogens. Smoking is the largest single preventable cause of death in Britain, killing more people than all other avoidable dangers added together including fires, drugs, alcohol and road accidents.

If cigarettes were introduced today, there is little doubt that they would be banned outright. However, back in the early 16th century when tobacco was first discovered by Spanish explorers in America and then brought back to Europe, the dangers were unknown. Since then, people have sniffed, chewed or smoked tobacco. At first it was smoked in pipes, and it was not until the mid-19th century, when cigarettes were invented as a convenient way to smoke tobacco, that the habit really increased in popularity.

In 1936 an American doctor, Alton Ochsner, was intrigued by an outbreak of lung cancer cases, a condition so rare in those days that he had only encountered it once before – in 1919. He investigated the patients and found that all of them were cigarette smokers. This led to epidemiological studies being carried out in the UK and the USA. These studies concluded independently that smoking was correlated with lung cancer. Committees on smoking and health were set up in both countries, leading eventually to the first reports of the Royal College of Physicians in 1962 and the United States Surgeon General in 1964. These reports detailed the risks of smoking, and in the UK there was an immediate five per cent drop in cigarette sales. However, to the surprise and disappointment of the medical profession, the reports did not lead to political action to stem the epidemic.

Since then, further reports have been produced by the UK, the USA, the World Health Organisation and other international bodies. World conferences

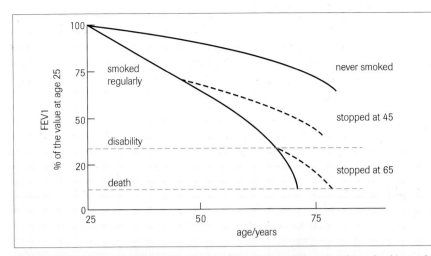

Illustration 1 In chronic lung disease, lung function declines with age as shown by this graph. Lung function is measured as the forced expiratory volume in one second (FEV1). Notice that lung function declines more rapidly in smokers than in non-smokers, but that the decline can be slowed by stopping smoking.

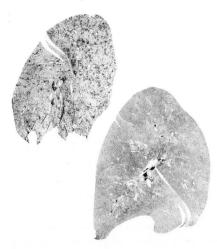

Illustration 2 The photographs compare the appearance of the lungs of a smoker (left) and a non-smoker (right). The smoker's lung is blackened with the tar from cigarettes.

on the subject take place every two years. It is now known, based on prospective and retrospective studies, clinical studies, autopsy studies and experimental studies in animals, that smoking causes a number of other diseases in addition to lung cancer. These include cancer of the bladder, kidney and stomach; circulatory diseases such as heart disease, stroke and atherosclerosis; respiratory diseases such as chronic obstructive lung disease, emphysema and pneumonia; digestive diseases such as stomach and duodenal ulcers; pregnancy complications and long-term, irreversible effects on the babies of women who smoke such as miscarriages, stillbirths and early

neonatal deaths, smaller and lighter babies, cot deaths, asthma and glue ear; reduced fertility in men and women.

The exact mechanisms by which cigarette smoking causes many of these conditions are not yet fully understood. Cigarette smoke affects the structure and function of the lungs. Toxins in cigarette smoke alter the airways, alveoli and the capillaries, and the immune system of the lung. Abnormal lung function has been demonstrated even in teenage smokers. Illustration 1 indicates a well-established smoking-related condition, chronic lung disease and illustration 2 compares the lungs of a smoker and non-smoker.

Symptoms of lung cancer are coughing up sputum and blood, breathlessness and chest pain. Symptoms of emphysema and chronic bronchitis are shortness of breath, wheezing, coughing and production of sputum.

Why do people still smoke?

In 1996, 28 per cent of adults in the UK were smokers. Smokers do not appear to have accepted the simple statistic that if they continue to smoke, their cigarettes have a one in two chance of killing them.

Why do people ignore the evidence about smoking? One reason centres on **nicotine** which is contained in tobacco smoke (*illustration 3*). Nicotine is a very powerful drug which affects nearly every organ in the body. It does not itself cause lung cancer – the aromatic compounds collectively called 'tar' cause cancer. Nicotine is addictive, but not to the extent that it is impossible to give up smoking.

The second reason is that the tobacco industry, which consists of powerful multinational companies, makes money out of cigarettes. It is in their commercial interests to keep people smoking. In the United Kingdom alone the tobacco industry needs to recruit 300 new smokers every day just to replace those who die of smoking-related diseases.

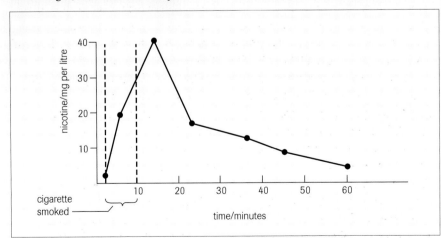

Illustration 3 Arterial concentration of nicotine before, during and after smoking a cigarette. The effects of nicotine on the body are varied and complex but it increases the heart rate, raises blood pressure and promotes blood clotting.

Anxiety, irritability and the craving for a cigarette are classic drug withdrawal symptoms. The cigarette – or rather the inhalation of nicotine – relieves these symptoms, thus appearing to have a positive effect. Young people are often reluctant to associate the act of smoking with disease because the symptoms take years to appear. Smoking has therefore been likened to slow motion suicide. The damage builds up slowly, almost imperceptibly, and often the warning signs are ignored. For example, the early morning cough and shortness of breath are readily written off as minor inconveniences. Death, when it comes, can be slow, drawn-out and painful. Anyone who has watched a person die of lung cancer will testify to this.

Smoking and society

Everyone should have the right to breathe smoke-free air. We now know that **passive smoking**, i.e. breathing other people's smoke, causes lung cancer and other respiratory diseases. It may also cause heart disease and chronic middle-ear disease, amongst other conditions. The risk of contracting lung cancer from passive smoking is some 50 to 100 times greater than the risk of getting it from exposure to asbestos. The smoke issuing from the lit end of a cigarette can contain greater amounts of the substances mentioned earlier than smoke which has been inhaled, because it has not gone through a filter.

Governments have attempted to reduce the damage done by smoking but too often their actions are piecemeal and ineffective against the powerful tobacco industry. Much more needs to be done before the epidemic can be eradicated. Cigarette advertising needs to be banned, the price of cigarettes should be increased annually, smoking in public places should be banned, public education programmes aimed at teenagers and adults are needed, methods of stopping smoking should be offered routinely by health professionals, and proven effective treatments such as nicotine replacement therapy should be made more widely available and accessible.

Giving up smoking has immediate and long-term effects. There is good evidence for secondary prevention of heart disease if a smoker can quit, even following a cardiac infarction (*page 243*). Most cigarette smokers want to stop, and as with other drug dependencies, they should be given assistance in doing so.

Dr McNeil is Research Addictions Advisor at the Health Education Authority, London.

Summary

1. All living organisms exchange gases with the environment. The two main gases exchanged are **oxygen** and **carbon dioxide** which participate in aerobic respiration and photosynthesis.

2. In plants, carbon dioxide is taken up through **stomata** which are located on the surfaces of leaves and stems.

3. The **guard cells** bordering stomata are controlled by an osmotic mechanism, dependent on the active transport of potassium ions, which ensures that stomata are generally open during the day and closed at night.

4. In small or flattened animals, the **surface–volume ratio** is large enough for gaseous exchange to take place by diffusion across the body surface. Larger animals, with a smaller surface–volume ratio, possess special **gaseous exchange** surfaces.

5. In insects, gaseous exchange occurs in the **tracheal system**. Air reaches the tissues by diffusion, aided in some species by rhythmical movements of the thorax and abdomen.

6. In fish, water is pumped over much folded and vascularised **gills** which present a large surface area to the water.

7. For gaseous exchange in aquatic animals, a **counterflow system** is more efficient than **parallel flow**. The gills of bony fish achieve a counterflow.

8. In mammals, air is drawn into the **lungs** by expansion of the thorax; here gaseous exchange occurs by diffusion across a very extensive and highly vascularised **alveolar surface**.

9. Lung volumes and oxygen consumption in humans can be measured by means of a **spirometer**.

10. In mammals and other vertebrates, rhythmical breathing movements are coordinated by the **ventilation centre** in the medulla oblongata of the brain.

11. The ventilation centre is informed of the concentration of carbon dioxide, and to a lesser extent oxygen, by **chemoreceptors** in the **aortic** and **carotid bodies**. The ventilation centre is also stimulated directly.

12. Experiments suggest that carbon dioxide is the most important stimulus initiating changes in the ventilation rate.

13. An alteration in the concentration of oxygen and carbon dioxide in the blood results in an appropriate change in the ventilation rate.

14. The effects of a slowly diminishing oxygen supply, such as occurs when ascending a mountain, are offset by **acclimatisation**, a series of responses to the low partial pressure of oxygen.

1. (a) (i) Give **one** similarity between the way in which oxygen from the atmosphere reaches a muscle in an insect and the way it reaches a mesophyll cell in a leaf. (1)

(ii) Give **one** difference in the way in which carbon dioxide is removed from a muscle in an insect and the way in which it is removed from a muscle in a fish. (1)

The diagram shows the way in which water flows over the gills of a fish. The graph shows the changes in pressure in the buccal cavity and in the opercular cavity during a ventilation cycle.

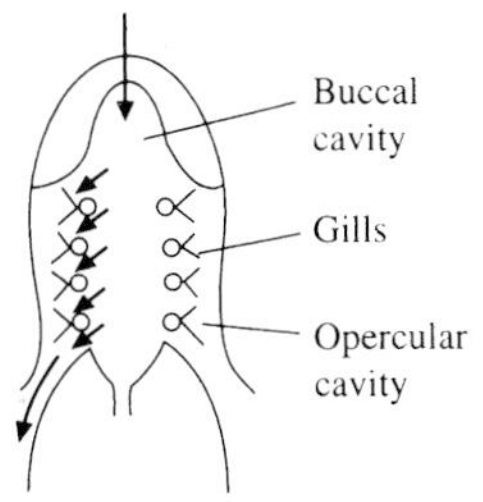

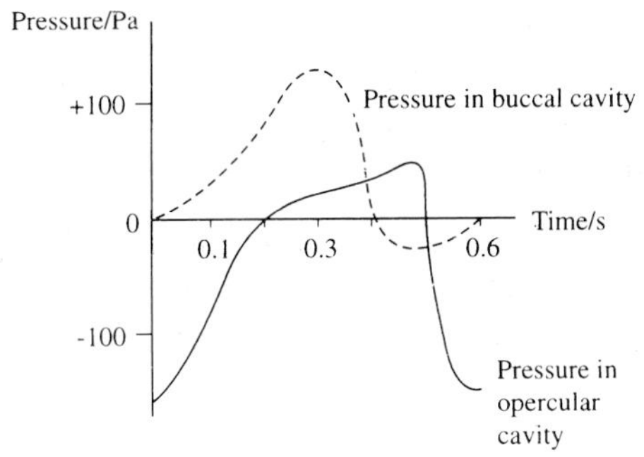

(b) Use the graph to calculate the rate of ventilation in cycles per minute. (1)

(c) For most of this ventilation cycle, water will be flowing in one direction over the gills. Explain the evidence from the graph that supports this. (2)

(d) Explain how the fish increases pressure in the buccal cavity. (2)

(Total 7 marks)

NEAB 1997

2. (a) Describe the functions of cilia, goblet cells and elastic fibres in the gaseous exchange system. (6)

(b) Discuss the short-term and long-term effects of tar and carcinogens in tobacco smoke on the gaseous exchange system. (12)

(Total 18 marks)

UCLES 1997

3. (a) The table below shows the effect of different types of breathing on ventilation.

breathing type (all at rest)	tidal volume /cm^3	resp.rate /breaths min^{-1} breath^{-1}	dead space volume/ cm^3	pulmonary ventilation /cm^3 min^{-1}	alveolar ventilation /cm^3 min^{-1}
quiet	500	12	150	6 000	4 200
deep, slow	1 200	5	150	6 000	5 250
shallow, rapid	150	40	150	6 000	0

(i) Suggest what is meant by the term dead space volume (1)

(ii) Pulmonary ventilation = Tidal volume x Respiratory rate. Using the data above, derive a similar word equation to show how the rate of alveolar ventilation has been calculated. (1)

(iii) Explain why alveolar ventilation decreases with shallow rapid breathing. (1)

(iv) What will happen to a person who continues to ventilate by shallow, rapid breathing? (2)

(b) Three types of cells are found in the alveolus. Type 1 cells are thin and flat. Type 2 cells are secretory and first activated in the foetus, late in pregnancy. Finally, the alveoli also contain some white blood cells called macrophages.

(i) Using the information above and your own knowledge, explain the roles of the three cell types in the alveolus.

Type 1 cells (2)

Type 2 cells (2)

Macrophages (2)

(ii) Sometimes babies born prematurely display breathing difficulties, a condition know as Respiratory Distress Syndrome (RDS). Without treatment they may become exhausted and die. Suggest the cause of this condition and explain why they become exhausted. (2)

(Total 13 marks)

O & C 1997

4. Compare the mechanisms for gas exchange in flowering plants and mammals. (Total 10 marks)

London 1996

Chapter 11

Heterotrophic nutrition

All living organisms need a source of energy. In Chapter 9 we saw that for most organisms this is provided by the oxidation of food (respiration). Food and oxygen are therefore essential requirements for living organisms. In this chapter we shall look at the food requirement.

Some organisms can manufacture their own food substances from simple, inorganic raw materials. Most plants and some prokaryotes are able to do this. They are said to have **autotrophic nutrition** and are called **autotrophs**. Their nutrition is the subject of the next chapter. Animals, fungi, many prokaryotes and protoctists are unable to synthesise organic compounds to use as food. They have **heterotrophic nutrition** and are called **heterotrophs**.

Heterotrophic organisms have to acquire and take in all the organic substances they need in order to survive. The examples shown in figure 11.1 illustrate how varied heterotrophic organisms are, both in their sources of food and how they obtain it.

Figure 11.1 A variety of heterotrophic organisms. .
Top A bracket fungus growing on a tree. It absorbs nutrients from the wood.
Bottom A zebra grazing on grass.
Right A leech sucking blood from a person's leg.
Far right A tree frog catching an insect.

A heterotroph feeding on organic substances in solution (such as a parasite in the human gut) can simply absorb the substances across its integument. Most animals, however, have a means of obtaining food and taking it into a gut (**alimentary canal**). This is called **ingestion**. All heterotrophs (except gut and blood parasites) have to convert solid food into soluble compounds capable of being **absorbed**. This process is **digestion**.

When the soluble products of digestion are absorbed they are distributed to various parts of the organism where they are either built up into complex materials (**assimilation**) or broken down for the release of energy (**respiration**).

11.1 Different ways of feeding

A convenient way of classifying heterotrophic organisms is in terms of the type of food they eat:

- **Herbivores** feed on plants.
- **Carnivores** feed on animals.
- **Omnivores** eat food of plant and animal origin.
- **Liquid feeders** consume a variety of animal and plant juices.
- **Microphagous feeders** live on small particles suspended in water.

In each case the method of feeding can be related to the type of food.

Herbivores

The problem facing all herbivores is that the concentration of nutrients in their food is low, and a large proportion of it is not digested. They therefore have to spend a great deal of time eating if their energy requirements are to be met. Cellulose in plant cell walls makes plant material tough and, as we shall see later, difficult to digest.

Herbivores have to grind their food, and the necessary apparatus for doing this is confined mainly to three groups of animals: mammals, molluscs and insects. Herbivorous mammals such as the horse or elephant use their **premolar** and/or **molar** teeth for grinding. These have a large surface area with ridges which are formed as the result of the uneven wear of the hard enamel and the softer dentine and cement (*figure 11.2*). The way the ridged premolars and molars in the upper and lower jaws grind against each other sharpens them. They also continue to grow throughout much of the animal's lifetime so as to keep pace with their wear and tear.

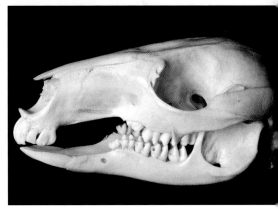

Figure 11.2 The inside of an Indian elephant's mouth showing two molar teeth. Notice the ridges of enamel alternating with cement and dentine. As a tooth wears down it moves forward in the jaw and when none of it is left another grows forward to replace it. During its lifetime an elephant may wear down as many as 24 molar teeth, each one of which is about the size of a house brick, although only four are in use at any one time. An elephant has only a certain number of teeth, and when all of them are worn out the animal will die of starvation.

In addition to the ridged molars, herbivorous mammals have other adaptive features in their dentition. These include long **incisor teeth** for cutting or pulling grass and other such plants. Also they lack canine teeth, thus creating a gap called the **diastema** where food can be held (*figure 11.3*).

Herbivorous insects like the locust have a pair of **mandibles** with a jagged edge for cutting through leaves of grass and other plants (*figure 11.4*).

Figure 11.3 The skull of a kangaroo, showing its long incisors for tearing grass and the gap (diastema) between the incisors and premolars.

Figure 11.4 A locust eating grass. Jaw-like mandibles are used for cutting and crushing plant food.

Figure 11.5 This Rock python is swallowing a Thompson's gazelle.

Figure 11.6 A shore crab, *Carcinis maenas*, feeding on a lugworm.

Figure 11.7 A dog's skull showing the canine and carnassial teeth. On each side of each jaw are three incisors, one canine and four premolars; there are two molars on each side of the upper jaw and three on each side of the lower jaw. The dental formula of a dog is therefore: i ⅜ c ⅟₁ pm ⁴⁄₄ m ⅔.

We shall consider how herbivores digest the cellulose in their plant food at the end of the chapter (*page 191*).

Carnivores

The problem here is not so much digesting the food as obtaining it. So we find that carnivores are adapted for catching prey. These adaptations take various forms, for example the great cats have **high speed locomotion**, sharp **claws** and dagger-like **canine teeth**.

Once captured, the prey is dealt with in one of three ways. It may be swallowed whole, chewed up and then swallowed, or digested externally outside the body and then ingested.

Ingesting the food whole, without breaking it up first, is the method used by pythons and boa constrictors, and also by sharks and sea anemones. The problem is that this puts a tremendous strain on the digestive system. Pythons and boas can tackle animals as big as goats and antelopes. The process of swallowing may take several hours, and the digestion of a complete antelope or goat can take weeks (*figure 11.5*).

The majority of carnivores chew their prey first. This is achieved by the **mouth parts** in carnivorous arthropods like crabs and crayfish. In the latter, the food, generally soft, is held by the pincers, then torn by the shredding action of manipulative structures called **maxillipeds**. Chewing is carried out by the **mandibles** (*figure 11.6*).

In mammals, the sharp **incisor teeth** are used for biting pieces of flesh and pulling it off the bone. In some mammals, the last pair of premolars in the upper jaw and the first pair of molars in the lower jaw are enlarged and have sharp ridges for shearing flesh (*figure 11.7*) As any dog owner knows, these **carnassial teeth** are very effective at scraping flesh off bones.

Animals that digest their food outside their bodies and then ingest it, do so in a variety of ways. Digestion is rarely completed outside the body, but it breaks the food up sufficiently for it to be drawn into the gut by suction or ciliary action. For example, blowflies, which feed on the carcasses of dead animals, pump saliva containing digestive enzymes onto the flesh and suck the fluid food into their stomachs (*figure 11.8*).

Carnivorous plants

Early reports that there were man-eating trees growing in remote parts of the world have faded into legend, but there are over 400 known species of plants which can trap and digest small animals, particularly insects.

These carnivorous plants live in nitrogen-deficient soils. Only a few such plants – sundews, butterworts and bladderworts – are found in Britain, and they are restricted to wet heath and moorland. Most species are tropical or sub-tropical, like the Venus fly-trap and pitcher plants. All have green leaves and obtain their carbohydrate by photosynthesis; they obtain their nitrogen from the bodies of their victims. The insect is attracted by colour, scent or sugary bait, then trapped, killed and digested by a fluid containing **proteases** (protein-digesting enzymes). The resulting amino acids are absorbed into the plant.

The method of trapping the insect varies from one species to another: sticky leaves in butterwort, adhesive hairs in sundew and an elaborate underwater trap in bladderworts. The Venus fly-trap has infolding leaves with spikes along the free edges and a hinge-like midrib (*figure 11.9*). Pitcher plants have leaves which are modified to become flask-like containers containing digestive fluid. Insects are attracted to the lips of the pitcher by nectar and fall into the fluid where they die and are digested.

Figure 11.8 A blowfly feeding on a slice of bread and honey. The expanded tip of the proboscis down which digestive enzymes flow is in contact with the food. After partial digestion outside the body, the semi-liquid food is sucked up into the stomach.

Omnivores

Omnivores include pigs and humans. As omnivores eat food of plant and animal origin it is not surprising to find that their teeth are well suited to this mixed diet by being less specialised. Figure 11.10 shows the skull and teeth of a human. The **incisors** and **canines** are for cutting the food, the **premolars** and **molars** for crushing it. The canines are less dagger-like than in carnivores, and the distinction between premolars and molars is less clear cut than in most other mammals.

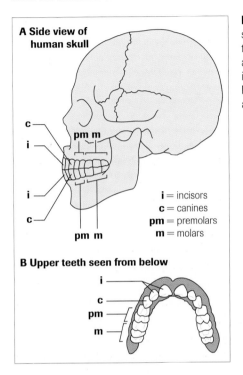

Figure 11.10 A Side view of a human skull showing the teeth. On either side of each jaw there are two incisors, one canine, two premolars and three molars. Thus the dental formula is: i 2⁄2 c 1⁄1 pm 2⁄2 m 3⁄3.
B A plan of the upper jaw showing the shape and arrangement of the various teeth.

Figure 11.9 Venus flytrap *Dionaea muscipula*, a carnivorous plant native on marshlands in parts of the USA. The modified leaf snaps shut on a fly. The teeth on the edge of the leaf interlock, trapping the creature while the inner surface secretes digestive enzymes. The leaf then absorbs the soluble products of digestion.

Liquid feeders

Liquid feeders fall into two groups: **absorbers** and **suckers**.

Absorbers include gut parasites such as tapeworms, which live in the small intestine of mammals. They feed on the digested food of the host, absorbing it straight through the integument. They therefore need no gut or digestive enzymes of their own.

Many prokaryotes, protctists and fungi feed on dead animals and plants. These **saprobionts** penetrate the material, secreting a variety of enzymes, including proteases, which break down the solid components of the material into soluble products. The dissolving of solid organic matter by saprobiontic bacteria and fungi is the first step in the decay of dead bodies, as a result of which the elements present in the organic compounds are ultimately recycled.

Saprobionts are not the only organisms to digest their food outside their bodies. Many parasitic bacteria, fungi and protoctists feed on the tissues of their hosts and also do this. The potato blight 'fungus' is an example (*page 71*).

The sucking forms are mainly insects such as mosquitoes, aphids, and butterflies and moths. They possess various types of **proboscis** which are adapted for obtaining the food. (*figure 11.11*).

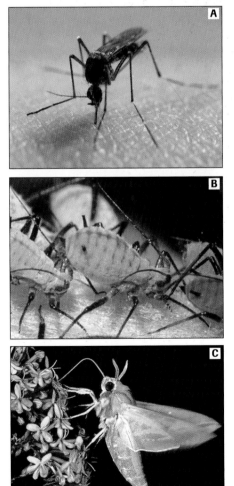

Figure 11.11 A A mosquito pierces the skin with its sharp proboscis, down which anti-clotting enzymes flow before blood is sucked into the stomach. **B** Aphids pierce plants and suck up their juices. **C** A sphinx moth feeding on nectar from a flower through its long, flexible proboscis.

Figure 11.12 A freshwater mussel *Anodonta* showing the inhalant (frilled) and exhalant (smooth) siphons. Water is drawn in through the inhalant siphon, flows through the perforated gills and then leaves by the exhalant siphon. Small particles suspended in the water are collected on the gills by ciliary action and passed to the mouth.

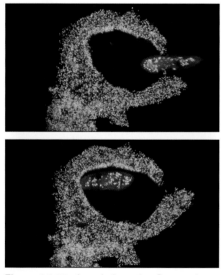

Figure 11.13 *Amoeba* ingesting *Paramecium*. The prey is taken into the cup-shaped phagocytic vesicle where it is digested.

Microphagous feeders

Microphagus feeders are always aquatic and feed on tiny particles suspended in water. Since their food is already 'broken up', the physical part of digestion is a relatively simple matter. The problem facing a microphagous feeder is collecting, sorting and concentrating the particles, and conveying them to the mouth.

Generally water is drawn towards the body either by the flapping of appendages as in various crustaceans, or by the beating of cilia. The water then goes through some kind of sieve which filters out the particles. For this reason microphagous feeders are also known as **filter-feeders**.

A typical filter feeder is the freshwater mussel *Anodonta* which uses sheet-like gills for sorting and straining food particles (*figure 11.12*).

11.2 Principles of digestion

Consider the problem faced by the Venus flytrap in figure 11.9. Its food is solid and in the form of large, complex molecules which are insoluble and relatively inert chemically. These molecules are too large to pass into the cells of the plant. Digestion is the process by which these molecules are turned into soluble products which can be absorbed.

Where does digestion take place?

Many animals digest their food completely before taking it into the cells. This is called **extracellular digestion** and the gut is where it usually takes place. In contrast to this, solid food particles may be taken into the cells by **phagocytosis** (*page 115*) and then digested within the cells. This is called **intracellular digestion**.

One of the best-known examples of intracellular digestion is provided by the single-celled protoctist *Amoeba*. This organism has a very thin, flexible plasma membrane, enabling it to change its shape as a result of cytoplasmic streaming within the cell. When the cytoplasm streams towards one particular point a projection called a **pseudopodium** is formed. When a pseudopodium comes into contact with a small particle of nutritional value – a diatom or green flagellate for example – it responds by forming a cup-shaped invagination which engulfs the food particle. Eventually the 'lips' of the cup seal, and the food becomes enclosed in a **phagocytic vesicle** (*figure 11.13*). Digestive enzymes are now secreted into the vesicle and the soluble products of digestion are absorbed into the surrounding cytoplasm. The entire process of digestion is therefore carried out inside the cell.

In some animals, digestion is divided into extracellular and intracellular phases. Extracellular enzymes secreted into the gut break the food down into small particles. These are then taken up by phagocytosis into the cells lining the gut (or in some cases a special digestive gland) where digestion is completed by intracellular enzymes.

In evolution, the tendency has been for intracellular digestion to be replaced by extracellular digestion. It would appear that in the early stages of animal evolution, the function of extracellular digestion was to break the food into particles small enough to be taken into the cells by phagocytosis. This would be important to an animal like a sea anemone which has no physical means of breaking up its food.

In subsequent evolution, extracellular digestion seems to have gradually replaced intracellular digestion. However, as we shall see later, even in mammals the final stages of protein and carbohydrate digestion are intracellular.

Physical and chemical digestion

The physical part of digestion in mammals is achieved by the cutting and/or crushing action of teeth, or their equivalent, followed by rhythmical contractions of the gut which pound the food into a semi-solid state. To fulfil this function the gut wall, particularly the

How digestive enzymes work

It is useful to look at the action of digestive enzymes in general terms before getting involved with the details. This can be illustrated by the digestion of proteins (*illustration*).

A protein is generally attacked first by enzymes that break the peptide links in the interior of the molecule. Such enzymes, called **endopeptidases**, have the effect of splitting proteins into polypeptides. Pepsin and trypsin are examples in the human gut.

The polypeptides are then attacked by enzymes which break off their terminal amino acids. These enzymes are called **exopeptidases**. Some exopeptidases, known as **aminopeptidases**, will only attack the end of a polypeptide chain which has a free amino (–NH$_2$) group. Others, known as **carboxypeptidases**, only attack the end of a polypeptide chain with a free carboxyl (–COOH) group.

Either way, the result is the liberation of free amino acids.

The same principles apply to the digestion of carbohydrates. Certain enzymes break the glycosidic links in the interior of polysaccharide chains, forming disaccharides such as maltose. Carbohydrate digestion is completed by enzymes which attack the disaccharides, liberating free monosaccharides.

In the case of fats, triglycerides are attacked by an enzyme called **lipase** which breaks the bonds between the glycerol and hydrocarbon chains. This yields a mixture of (mainly) monoglycerides and free fatty acids. (A monoglyceride is glycerol linked to a single hydrocarbon chain.)

Illustration How a protein is digested. Endopeptidases break the bonds between amino acids in the interior of the molecule, and exopeptidases (aminopeptidase and carboxypeptidase) liberate the terminal amino acids.

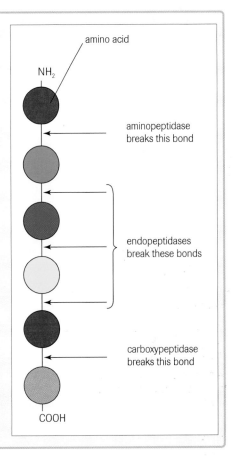

stomach, is well-endowed with muscle tissue. This is responsible for mixing the food and pushing it along the gut.

The chemical part of digestion is achieved by the secretion of **digestive enzymes**. The physical action increases the surface area over which enzymes can act. Some enzymes are secreted by glands situated outside the gut: salivary glands and pancreas, for example. Others come from glands located in the gut wall itself. Copious quantities of **mucus**, secreted along with the digestive enzymes, protect the delicate lining of the gut and facilitate the passage of food along it. Variable quantities of **acid** or **alkali** are also secreted to provide the correct pH for optimum functioning of the enzymes.

11.3 Digestion in humans

In the human, as in most animals, digestion takes place in the **gut** or **alimentary canal**. This is essentially a long tube connecting the mouth with the anus. However, the tube is not uniform all along its length: in some places it is quite narrow, being either straight or coiled. In other places it is wider and more capacious.

One of the straightest stretches of the alimentary canal is the **gullet** (**oesophagus**) which connects the pharynx with the **stomach**. It does not need to be coiled as its function is simply to convey food to the stomach. It runs straight through the thorax where it is located close to the trachea on the ventral side of the heart and lungs.

In the abdomen, however, the alimentary canal becomes highly coiled. It is here that most of digestion takes place and the products of digestion are absorbed into the bloodstream. Coiling has the effect of increasing the surface area for digestion and absorption. This part of the gut has a very good blood supply. Blood is drained away from it by the **hepatic portal vein** which carries the absorbed food to the **liver**.

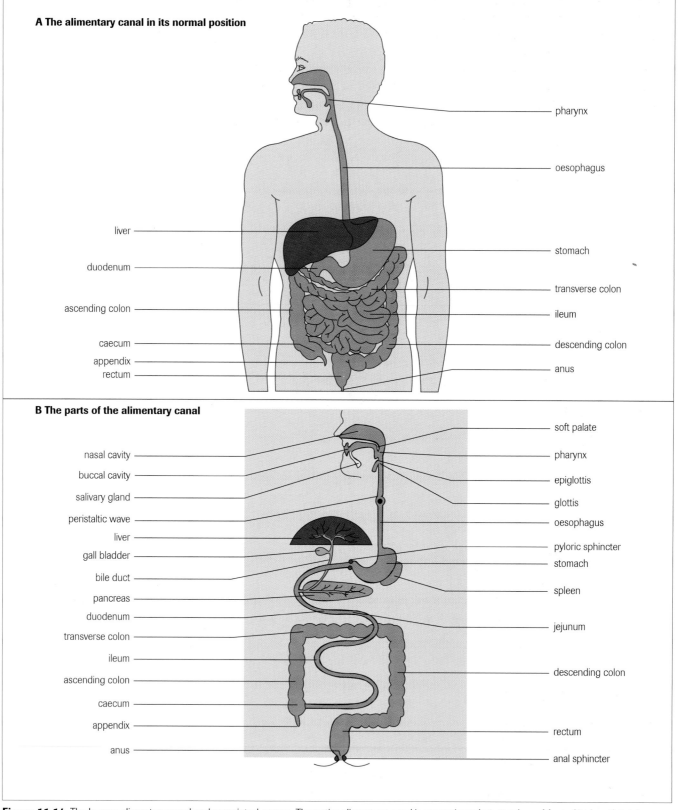

A The alimentary canal in its normal position

pharynx

oesophagus

liver

stomach

duodenum

transverse colon

ascending colon

ileum

caecum

descending colon

appendix

anus

rectum

B The parts of the alimentary canal

soft palate

nasal cavity

pharynx

buccal cavity

epiglottis

salivary gland

glottis

peristaltic wave

oesophagus

liver

pyloric sphincter

gall bladder

stomach

bile duct

spleen

pancreas

duodenum

transverse colon

jejunum

ileum

ascending colon

descending colon

caecum

appendix

rectum

anus

anal sphincter

Figure 11.14 The human alimentary canal and associated organs. The entire alimentary canal is approximately 8–9 m long. Most of its length is taken up by the small intestine (duodenum, jejunum and ileum) which is roughly 6 m long. In the course of its passage along the gut, food spends 3 to 5 hours in the stomach, about 4 hours travelling along the small intestine and from 6 to 20 hours in the large intestine. Digestion takes place mainly in the stomach and small intestine, the latter also being where most absorption takes place. Indigestible material (dietary fibre, roughage) passes on to the large intestine (caecum, appendix, colon and rectum). By the time it reaches the rectum much of the water has been removed. The contents of the rectum (faeces) consist mainly of indigestible cellulose, water, various salts, discarded epithelial cells and large numbers of bacteria, particularly the colon bacillus *Escherichia coli.*

The human alimentary canal is shown in figure 11.14. Various glands open into it. Some of the glands are embedded in the wall of the gut itself, others are located some way from the gut. The glands secrete **digestive enzymes** into the cavity of the gut (i.e. its **lumen**). They also secrete **sodium hydrogencarbonate** (or, in the case of the stomach, **hydrochloric acid**) which gives the contents of the gut an optimum pH for the action of the digestive enzymes. **Mucus** is also secreted to ease the passage of materials along the gut and protect its inner lining.

The wall of the alimentary canal contains muscle tissue (mainly smooth muscle) and its inner surface is lined with **mucosa** (*page 63*). The general plan is the same in all regions of the gut with a fairly constant arrangement of circular and longitudinal muscle layers. There are, however, variations in the amount of folding and the glands present in different regions (*figure 11.15*).

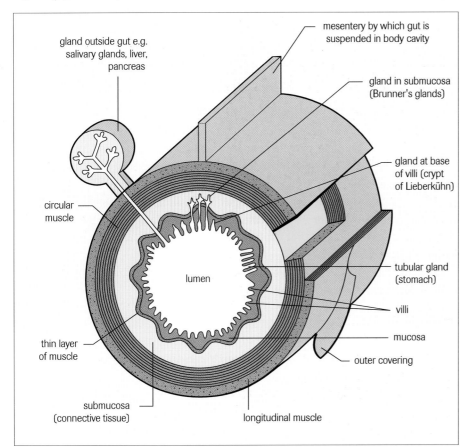

Figure 11.15 General structure of the wall of the mammalian gut showing the muscle layers and the different kinds of glands. Notice also the folding of the mucosa which greatly increases the surface area.

It takes at least 13 hours for food to travel the length of the gut, although the time varies tremendously according to the type of food eaten. With a high dietary fibre intake it may take less time.

Let us now consider what happens to a meal as it passes along the human gut.

In the buccal cavity

The first part of the digestive process begins in the **buccal cavity** where the food is broken up into smaller pieces by the chewing action of the teeth (**mastication**) and moistened by **saliva** from the **salivary glands**.

As you know, teeth are extremely hard. The **crown**, which projects into the buccal cavity, is covered with **enamel**. Enamel is the hardest substance in the body. It consists of mineral-salt crystals bound together by keratin. Beneath the enamel is a layer of **dentine** which is similar to bone but with a higher mineral content, thus making it harder. The dentine is perforated by fine channels called **canaliculi** which contain the cytoplasmic

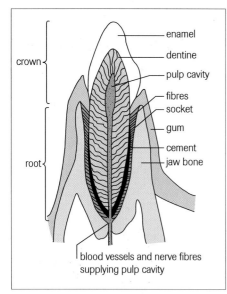

Figure 11.16 Section through a generalised mammalian tooth, the structure of which is described in the text.

Labels: enamel, dentine, pulp cavity, fibres, socket, gum, cement, jaw bone, crown, root, blood vessels and nerve fibres supplying pulp cavity

processes of the tooth-forming cells (**odontoblasts**). The central **pulp cavity** contains a network of blood capillaries and many sensory nerve endings. The **root** is embedded in a **socket** in the bone of the jaw. The root is covered with a bone-like substance called **cement** which is attached, securely but not inextricably, to the socket by tough fibres. All these structures can be seen in figure 11.16.

While being chewed, the food is mixed with saliva secreted by the **salivary glands**. There are three pairs of major salivary glands and numerous minor ones. The minor ones secrete continuously whereas the major ones, controlled by the parasympathetic nervous system, are stimulated by the sight, smell, taste or thought of food. Saliva is a watery mixture of **mucus**, mineral salts and the enzyme **salivary amylase**.

Salivary amylase is traditionally associated with the hydrolysis of the polysaccharide **starch** to the disaccharide **maltose**, but its primary role is more likely to be the removal of starch debris left around the teeth after eating a meal. Saliva is generally neutral or very faintly alkaline, this being the optimum pH for the action of the enzymes.

The watery part of saliva moistens the food as it is being chewed, and the mucus helps to bind the food together and lubricate it. The action of the tongue shapes the food into a **bolus**.

From the buccal cavity to the stomach

The bolus is forced through the pharynx into the oesophagus in the act of **swallowing**. Triggered by tactile stimulation of the soft palate and the wall of the pharynx, swallowing is a reflex in which contraction of the tongue forces the bolus against the soft palate, thus closing the nasal cavity. The opening into the larynx, the **glottis**, is closed by the valve-like **epiglottis**, so the bolus enters the oesophagus. While all this is happening, breathing is momentarily inhibited to prevent food entering the trachea ('going down the wrong way'). The nerve centre responsible for controlling this swallowing reflex is located in the posterior part of the brain.

The bolus is propelled down the oesophagus by a localised contraction of the circular muscles which sweeps along it, a process called **peristalsis**.

In the stomach

The stomach is a dilated part of the gut where the food remains for two hours or more. Once in the stomach, the food is acted on by **gastric juice** secreted by **gastric glands** in the stomach wall (*figure 11.17*).

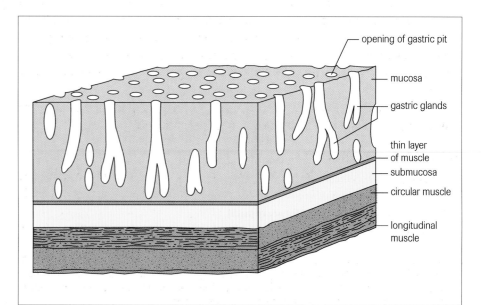

Labels: opening of gastric pit, mucosa, gastric glands, thin layer of muscle, submucosa, circular muscle, longitudinal muscle

Figure 11.17 The thick wall of the stomach contains tubular gastric glands. There are about 35 million gastric glands in the human stomach.

Gastric juice is a watery secretion containing **hydrochloric acid** and the enzyme **pepsin** which breaks down proteins into short polypeptide chains. Pepsin is secreted by the **peptic** (or **chief**) **cells** which are clustered at the base of the gastric glands (*figure 11.18*).

Pepsin is secreted as an inactive precursor **pepsinogen**. Why is pepsin secreted in an inactive form? The reason is that it is a protein-digesting enzyme and this prevents the gastric gland being destroyed by its own enzyme (**autodigestion**). It remains inactive until it reaches the lumen of the stomach where it is activated by hydrochloric acid, and also by pepsin itself – in other words the reaction is **autocatalytic**. Once secreted, the active form of the enzyme is prevented from attacking the tissues by the mucus lining the stomach wall; this is secreted by cells situated towards the neck of the gastric glands.

Not only does the hydrochloric acid contribute to the activation of the pepsinogen, but it also provides the **optimum pH** for the functioning of the enzyme; more importantly it kills microorganisms which may have been taken in with the food.

The acid is secreted by special **oxyntic cells** in the middle regions of the gastric glands and it gives the gastric juice a pH of less than 2.0. The production of hydrochloric acid by the oxyntic cells is a remarkable process, and bears certain similarities to the way carbon dioxide is carried in red blood cells. Inside the oxyntic cell, the enzyme **carbonic anhydrase** catalyses the formation of carbonic acid (H_2CO_3) from carbon dioxide and water. The carbonic acid dissociates into hydrogencarbonate (HCO_3^-) and hydrogen (H^+) ions. The latter then combine with chloride ions (Cl^-), derived from the dissociation of sodium chloride, to form HCl which is then secreted by the cell.

Control of gastric secretion

What brings about the secretion of gastric juice? At the beginning of the 20th century, the Russian physiologist Ivan Pavlov (1849–1936) carried out some classic experiments on digestion in dogs (*extension box on next page*). He showed that gastric juice, like saliva, will flow as the result of the sight, smell, taste or expectation of food. But this reflex production is relatively slight in humans compared with the copious secretion that occurs when the food arrives in the stomach. Here mechanical and chemical stimulation of the stomach lining by the food itself causes secretion.

There is another method by which gastric secretion is controlled. In the **pyloric region** of the stomach (the part just before the **duodenum**) enzyme-secreting cells are absent, although mucus is still secreted to lubricate the pyloric sphincter at the entrance to the duodenum. Scattered amongst the mucus-secreting cells are some special cells which secrete a hormone called **gastrin** into the bloodstream. The presence of food in the stomach stimulates the secretion of gastrin. Gastrin then stimulates the secretion of pepsin and hydrochloric acid. It also stimulates the muscular movements of the stomach. So the secretion of gastric juice is controlled by the nervous system *and* by a hormone (*figure 11.19*).

While the digestive enzymes are acting, the rhythmical muscular contractions of the stomach wall pound the food into a semi-fluid state called **chyme**.

In the small intestine

The **duodenum** is the first loop of the small intestine. The passage of food into the duodenum is controlled by a ring of muscle, the **pyloric sphincter**, situated immediately between the far end of the stomach and the beginning of the duodenum. By alternately contracting and relaxing, the pyloric sphincter can hold food back or let it through. The

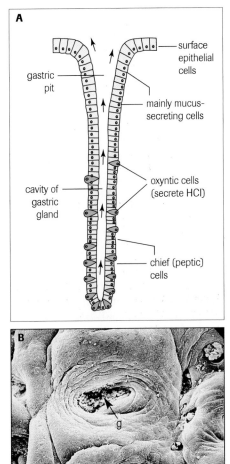

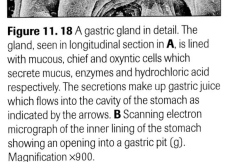

Figure 11. 18 A gastric gland in detail. The gland, seen in longitudinal section in **A**, is lined with mucous, chief and oxyntic cells which secrete mucus, enzymes and hydrochloric acid respectively. The secretions make up gastric juice which flows into the cavity of the stomach as indicated by the arrows. **B** Scanning electron micrograph of the inner lining of the stomach showing an opening into a gastric pit (g). Magnification ×900.

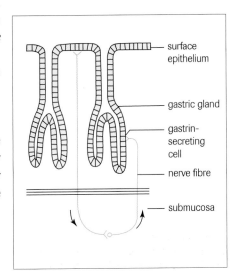

Figure 11.19 The hormone gastrin is released into the bloodstream as a result of a local reflex in the stomach wall. Following a meal, distension of the stomach, together with chemical substances in the food, stimulate nerve endings beneath the surface epithelium. Nervous impulses are then transmitted via the nerve pathway to gastrin-secreting cells in the gastric gland.

Pavlov's experiment

Ivan Pavlov's famous experiment was carried out in 1902. An operation was performed on an anaesthetised dog in which the oesophagus was diverted so that it opened to the exterior in the neck, and a small part of the stomach (called a 'Pavlov pouch') was separated from the main part without disturbing its innervation and then connected to the exterior by a tube so that its secretions could be collected.

Pavlov found that gastric juice is secreted when food is eaten without getting into the stomach (*arrow 1*) and when food gets into the stomach without passing through the mouth (*arrow 2*).

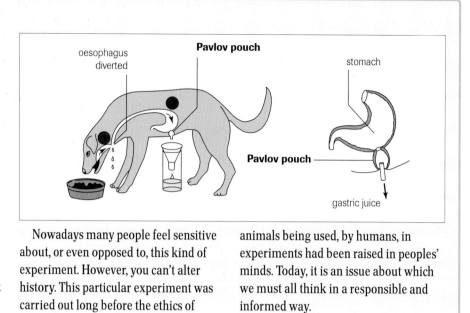

Nowadays many people feel sensitive about, or even opposed to, this kind of experiment. However, you can't alter history. This particular experiment was carried out long before the ethics of animals being used, by humans, in experiments had been raised in peoples' minds. Today, it is an issue about which we must all think in a responsible and informed way.

emptying of the stomach is carefully controlled and small quantities of chyme are let through intermittently.

The inner surface of the small intestine is covered with numerous finger-like projections called **villi**, between which are glands called **crypts of Lieberkühn** (*figures 11.20 and 11.21*). A great deal of digestion takes place in the small intestine. The agents of digestion come from three sources: the **liver**, the **pancreas** and the **wall of the small intestine**.

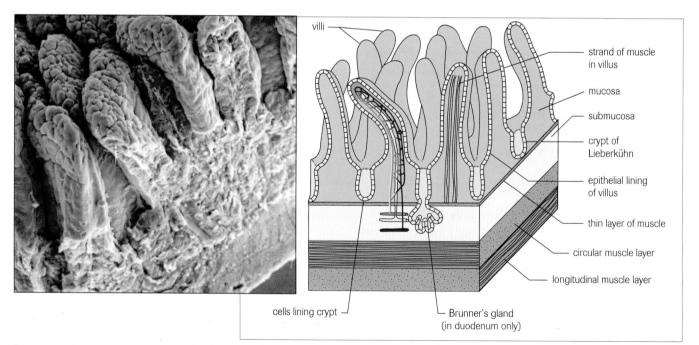

Figure 11.20 Diagram of part of the wall of the mammalian small intestine showing glands and villi. Note Brunner's glands opening into crypts of Lieberkühn. Crypts are present in all parts of the small intestine whereas Brunner's glands are restricted to the duodenum. The epithelial cells lining the villi are of two main kinds: goblet cells which secrete mucus, and columnar epithelial cells which are involved in digestion and absorption. Blood and lymph capillaries are included in the second villus from the left; they are shown in more detail in figure 11.23 on page 192. To the left of the diagram is a scanning electron micrograph of villi on the inner side of the wall of the small intestine. Magnification ×50.

The liver and bile

The liver produces **bile** which, after storage in the **gall bladder**, flows along the **bile duct** into the duodenum. Bile is a mixture of substances, not all of which are involved in digestion. Those which are – the **bile salts**, sodium taurocholate and sodium glycocholate – **emulsify** fats by lowering their surface tension, causing them to break up into numerous tiny droplets. This increases the total surface area of the fat, thereby facilitating the digestive action of the enzyme **lipase** (*see below*). The bile salts themselves are not enzymes; they are not even proteins and have no chemical effect on the fats, only the physical effect of emulsifying them.

Bile is also rich in sodium hydrogencarbonate ($NaHCO_3$) which, together with that from the pancreas, neutralises the acid from the stomach. The pH of the small intestine is therefore distinctly alkaline, which favours the action of the various enzymes.

Pancreatic juice

The pancreas produces **pancreatic juice** which flows into the duodenum from the pancreas via the pancreatic duct. The main pancreatic enzymes are:

- **pancreatic amylase** which breaks down starch to the disaccharide maltose;
- **pancreatic lipase** which breaks down triglycerides in the emulsified fat into monoglycerides and fatty acids;
- **proteases** (protein-splitting enzymes) which include **trypsin**, **chymotrypsin**, **carboxypeptidase** and **elastase**.

The four proteases are secreted as inactive precursors: **trypsinogen**, **chymotrypsinogen**, **procarboxypeptidase** and **proelastase**. As with pepsin in the stomach, this prevents autodigestion. Trypsinogen is converted into trypsin by the action of the enzyme **enterokinase**, secreted by the wall of the small intestine. The trypsin then activates the other three proteases. These pancreatic proteases break down proteins and polypeptides into tripeptides and dipeptides.

Pancreatic juice also contains **nucleases** which break down nucleic acids into nucleotides, and a variety of **peptidases** which release some free amino acids from polypeptide chains.

Intestinal enzymes

Various enzymes, associated with the epithelial lining of the small intestine, complete the digestion of carbohydrates by breaking down disaccharides into monosaccharides. These enzymes include:

- **maltase** which hydrolyses maltose to glucose, thus completing the digestion of starch;
- **sucrase** which hydrolyses sucrose (cane sugar) to glucose and fructose;
- **lactase** which hydrolyses lactose (milk sugar) to glucose and galactose.

The end products of carbohydrate digestion are all monosaccharides. The final stage of carbohydrate digestion is intracellular, as disaccharides are absorbed by the plasma membrane of the epithelial cells before being broken down into monosaccharides.

The epithelial cells also absorb tripeptides and dipeptides which are then broken down into amino acids by various peptidases. Thus the final stages of protein digestion are also intracellular.

Nucleotidases are also present in the epithelial cells of the small intestine. They split nucleotides into their constituent subunits.

Brunner's glands, found in the wall of the duodenum, secrete an alkaline mucus which helps to neutralise the acid from the stomach and protects the duodenal lining from autodigestion. These glands do not produce any enzymes.

The enzymes are present in the epithelial cells which originate at the bottom of the

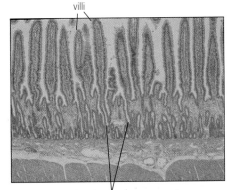

villi

crypts of Lieberkühn

Figure 11.21 Microscopic section of the wall of the ileum showing villi and crypts of Lieberkühn. Magnification ×20.

▶ Structure and functions of the liver, page 273
▶ Structure and functions of the pancreas, page 269

Extension

Lactase

The enzyme **lactase** (also known as β-galactosidase) hydrolyses lactose to its constituent monosaccharides. This enzyme is found in all human babies, but is only found in adults from northern Europe (and their descendants, for example, in North America) and a few African tribes. Most other human groups, including Orientals, Arabs, Jews, most Africans, Indians and Mediterranean peoples produce little or no lactase as adults and as a result may show lactose intolerance. This condition is characterised by diarrhoea and pains in the large intestine, and is caused by ingesting large amounts of milk in the absence of the enzyme that would otherwise break it down.

crypts of Lieberkuhn. These cells are constantly dividing and the daughter cells move slowly up the sides of the crypt and then the villus, until after a few days they reach the tip. They are then shed into the lumen of the intestine and are replaced by new ones which move up behind them. The entire epithelial lining is replaced every three to five days in this way. It has been shown that as the cells move up the sides of the villus, they mature and acquire the capacity to carry out the final stages of digestion described above, and to absorb the products into the blood.

Table 11.1 Summary of the main enzymes associated with the mammalian gut, together with their source, site of action and functions. The products in italics are soluble. Rennin is secreted only by young ruminants such as cattle, and possibly by human babies. It has the effect of coagulating milk protein (casein), turning it into a semi-solid which is then digested by pepsin. The reason why milk is coagulated is that otherwise it would pass through the stomach too quickly for digestion to take place.

Secretion	Source	Site of action	Flow induced by	Enzymes etc.	Substrate	Products
Saliva (neutral or slightly acid)	Salivary glands	Mouth cavity	Expectation and reflex action	Salivary amylase	Starch	Maltose
				Lysozyme	Bacteria	Dead bacteria
Gastric juice (distinctly acid)	Stomach wall (gastric glands)	Stomach (lumen)	Expectation, reflex action, contact with stomach lining, and hormone (gastrin)	Pepsin	Proteins	Polypeptides
				Rennin	Soluble casein	Insoluble casein
Bile (alkaline)	Liver	Duodenum (lumen)	Reflex action and hormones	Bile salts (not enzymes)	Fats	Fat droplets
Pancreatic juice (alkaline)	Pancreas	Duodenum (lumen)	Reflex action and hormones	Pancreatic amylase	Starch	Maltose
				Proteases (e.g. trypsin)	Proteins and polypeptides	Tripeptides and dipeptides
				Peptidases	Polypeptides	*Amino acids*
				Pancreatic lipase	Fats	*Monoglycerides and fatty acids*
				Nucleases	Nucleic acids	Nucleotides
Intestinal enzymes (intracellular)	Microvilli	Small intestine (epithelial cells)	Mainly contact with intestinal lining	Maltase	Maltose	*Glucose*
				Sucrase	Sucrose	*Glucose + fructose*
				Lactase	Lactose (milk sugar)	*Glucose + galactose*
				Peptidases	Dipeptides and tripeptides	*Amino acids*
				Nucleotidases	Nucleotides	*Pentose sugars + phosphoric acid + organic base*

Control of intestinal secretion

How is the flow of secretions in the small intestine controlled? In the case of bile and pancreatic juice, control is partly by nervous reflexes triggered by the sight, smell and taste of the food, and also by hormones. The presence of acidified chyme in the duodenum stimulates certain cells scattered throughout the mucosa of the duodenum to secrete two hormones into the bloodstream. These two hormones are known as **secretin** and **cholecystokinin-pancreozymin (CCK-PZ)**.

Secretin acts on the liver and pancreas, causing the liver to secrete bile and the pancreas to secrete the fluid (non-enzymatic) components of the pancreatic juice. CCK-PZ stimulates the pancreas to secrete its enzymes, and it also acts on the smooth muscle in the wall of the gall bladder, causing it to squirt bile into the bile duct. Another hormone called **enterogastrone** inhibits any further secretion of acid by the stomach.

Digestion of cellulose

We mentioned earlier that the problem facing all herbivores is that the nutrient content of their food is low and a high proportion of it is difficult to digest. This is due to the large amount of cellulose in their diet. If maximum value is to be derived from plant food, cellulose must also be digested. This requires the enzyme **cellulase**, a powerful carbohydrase which breaks β-glycosidic links and so splits cellulose into its constituent monosaccharides (*page 21*).

A variety of microorganisms, mainly bacteria and protoctists, are able to secrete cellulase; so can fungi which use it to dissolve plant cell walls so as to penetrate the cells. But apart from this, cellulase is extremely rare, and is practically unheard of in the animal kingdom.

Mammals cannot produce cellulase themselves and yet many of the meat and milk producers such as cattle, sheep, goats and camels are herbivores, and cellulose is certainly digested in their guts. Cellulose is also digested in other herbivores such as horses and rabbits. How do they do it?

Ruminants

Ruminant (cud-chewing) mammals like the cow have an enlarged 'stomach' at the lower end of the oesophagus (*illustration*). This is divided into four chambers. Grass and other plant food is ground up by the molars and then passed down the oesophagus into the

first chamber, the **reticulum**. Here it is formed into balls of cud which are regurgitated into the buccal cavity and chewed again when the cow is not actually feeding.

When it is swallowed for the second time, the food passes into the **rumen**, by far the largest chamber. Here it is mixed with vast numbers of cellulose-digesting bacteria and with copious quantities of saliva from the salivary glands. A cow may produce as much as 100 to 190 litres of saliva a day! The rumen is a fermenting chamber and in anaerobic conditions the cellulose is broken down into ethanoic, propionic and butyric acids, with the evolution of carbon dioxide and methane gas. These gases are released from both ends of the digestive tract. Meanwhile the contents of the rumen pass through the **omasum** into the **abomasum** (the true stomach) and thus to the duodenum where the soluble products of digestion are absorbed.

As well as cellulose-digesting bacteria, other bacteria are present which synthesise proteins from ammonia. These bacteria are ingested in the rumen by protoctists, which are therefore a rich source of protein. The protoctists pass out of the rumen into the rest of the gut where they are digested by the ruminant's own enzymes, and the protein is made available to the host. This makes a significant contribution to the protein requirements of the animal.

The reason why urea is added to cattle feed is that it is broken down to ammonia which is then used by the protein-synthesising bacteria, further supplementing this source of protein. The other nutritional value of rumen bacteria is in the synthesis of B-vitamins. Cows obtain all the vitamin B_{12} they need from these mutualistic microorganisms.

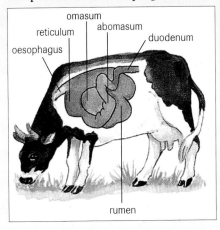

Illustration The 'stomach' of a cow showing the positions of the four chambers. The rumen makes up 80 per cent of the volume.

omasum
reticulum
oesophagus
abomasum
duodenum
rumen

Non-ruminants

Non-ruminant herbivorous mammals also possess fermentation chambers where microorganisms digest cellulose. In horses and rabbits they are the **caecum** and **appendix**, a blind-ending diverticulum of the gut situated at the junction of the small and large intestines. However, having a fermentation chamber near the end of the gut has disadvantages. Food cannot be regurgitated and the products of digestion cannot efficiently be shunted forwards into the small intestine for absorption to take place. You have only to compare the appearance of horse dung and cowpats to see which method is more efficient.

To make up for this deficiency, rabbits and hares form two distinct types of faeces. The first are soft and are eaten directly from the anus, a phenomenon known as **coprophagy**. The soft faeces contain significant amounts of digested food which is absorbed when it passes through the gut a second time. If rabbits are prevented from eating their soft faeces they show signs of nutritional deficiency. The second type of faeces is the familiar form of hard pellets which are dropped and contain relatively little food material.

What about humans? Humans do not possess a rumen or a large caecum, and the appendix is apparently without function. Yet we eat significant quantities of plant material in our diet and are constantly encouraged to eat more fibre. High-fibre diets are known to prevent diverticulitis of the colon and are thought to reduce the incidence of bowel cancer and colitis (inflammation of the colon). Bacteria are present in the human colon but until recently their fermenting activity was considered to be insignificant. However, it is now thought that the action of these bacteria on carbohydrate in the colon can contribute to as much as 10 per cent of our energy requirements.

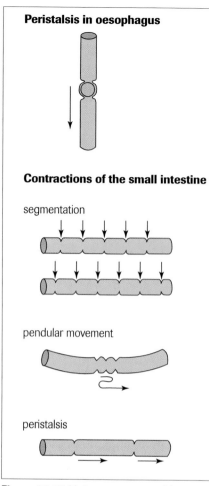

Figure 11.22 Various movements of the gut brought about by localised contractions of the circular muscle.

Movements of the small intestine

Muscular contractions of the gut wall keep the food moving along the small intestine and mix it thoroughly with the various juices secreted into it. The movements are of three main kinds (*figure 11.22*).

■ **Segmentation**, circular constrictions at 1 to 2 cm intervals, divide the gut contents into segments. Each contraction lasts about a second and is followed by a similar constriction in a different place. This mixes the chyme with the digestive enzymes.

■ **Pendular movement** causes the chyme to move back and forth along 15–20 cm lengths of small intestine. This type of movement both mixes the chyme and increases the flow of blood to the intestinal lining thus aiding absorption.

■ **Peristalsis**, similar to that which occurs in the oesophagus, occurs over long lengths of the small intestine. It is brought about by contraction and relaxation of the circular muscles and causes waves of contraction to push the food along towards the large intestine.

As a result of all these activities, the food in the small intestine is converted into a watery emulsion called **chyle.** It is from this that the products of digestion are absorbed.

11.4 Absorption, assimilation and defecation

In humans, digestion begins in the buccal cavity and is completed in the small intestine. The small intestine is therefore the logical site for the absorption of the products of digestion.

The structures in the small intestine responsible for absorption are the **villi**. The detailed structure of a villus is shown in figure 11.23. Villi contain smooth muscle, enabling them to contract and expand, thus bringing them into contact with newly digested food. Running the length of each villus is an arteriole and a venule interconnected by a network of capillaries.

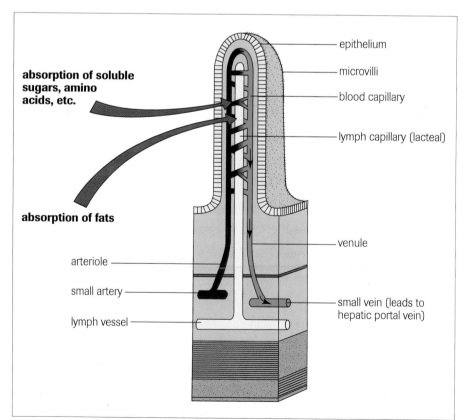

Figure 11.23 Detailed structure of a villus showing the epithelial lining with microvilli on the outside and the blood vessels and lacteal inside.

Monosaccharide sugars (mainly glucose) and amino acids are absorbed by a combination of facilitated diffusion and active transport from the epithelial cells, where the final stages of digestion have been completed, into the capillaries. The blood from the venules, which contains the dissolved nutrients, eventually reaches the **hepatic portal vein** whence it flows to the liver.

Fat is dealt with rather differently. In the centre of each villus is a blind-ending **lymph capillary**. Fat is absorbed into the epithelial cells lining the villi as little droplets called **micelles** which contain monoglycerides, bile salts and free fatty acids. Triglyceride fat is then resynthesised and shed into the lymphatic vessels as a white emulsion of minute globules. This gives the lymphatic vessels a milky appearance, for which reason they are known as **lacteals**. As the lymphatic system ultimately opens into the veins, the fat eventually finds its way into the circulatory system which distributes it around the body. Most absorption of fat is thought to take place by this route, although some short-chain fatty acids are reabsorbed directly into the bloodstream.

The villi greatly increase the surface area over which absorption can occur. The surface area is further increased by the fact that the epithelial cells lining each villus bear numerous microvilli (*figure 11.24*).

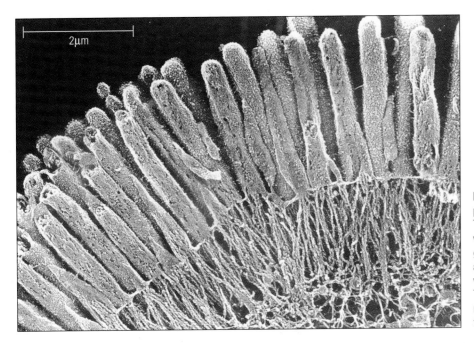

Figure 11.24 Scanning electron micrograph of part of an epithelial cell from the small intestine. This particular cell comes from the lining of a villus. Notice the closely packed microvilli. They give the cell a large surface area for absorption and also for enzyme action, at least the part which takes place on the membrane lining them. There is evidence that some intestinal microvilli may undergo contractile movements, thereby facilitating mixing and absorption.

The epithelial cells also contain large numbers of mitochondria, reflecting the high energy requirements of active absorption.

Inorganic salts, vitamins and water are absorbed in the small intestine, and also in the **colon** whose wall is likewise much folded. Thus by the time it reaches the **rectum**, indigestible food is in a semi-solid state ready to be **egested** through the **anus** as **faeces**. This process is called **defecation** and is facilitated by the lubricative effect of large amounts of mucus secreted by numerous goblet cells in the lining of the rectum.

The processes of digestion and absorption are now complete. Through the bloodstream, the soluble nutrients are distributed to the tissues where they are either **assimilated** (built up into complex materials) or used in **respiration** for the transfer of energy.

1 Organisms which feed on organic food are said to have **heterotrophic nutrition** and are called **heterotrophs**.

2. The problem facing any heterotroph is how to acquire and take in organic food and then break it down into soluble products capable of being absorbed.

3. In most heterotrophs, food is successively **ingested, digested**, **absorbed**, **distributed** and then either **assimilated** or **respired**. The functions of digestion and absorption are carried out in a gut (**alimentary canal**). Indigestible remains are **egested**.

4. Heterotrophic organisms can be classified in terms of the type of food they eat, as **herbivores**, **carnivores**, and **omnivores**.

5. Herbivores have special adaptations for ingesting and digesting plants, e.g. the ridged **molar teeth** of horses and elephants and the **mandibles** of locusts.

6. Carnivores have adaptations for catching and killing prey (e.g. **claws** and **canine teeth**) and for crushing and slicing their food (e.g. **carnassial teeth**).

7. Carnivorous plants have adaptations for trapping and digesting small animals, particularly insects. In this way the nitrogen requirements of these plants are supplemented by heterotrophic means.

8. Omnivorous mammals such as humans have a relatively unspecialised dentition which reflects their mixed diet of plant and animal food.

9. Liquid feeders include **absorbers** (e.g. tapeworm) and **suckers** (e.g. mosquito). The mouth parts of sucking insects are adapted in different ways to form various types of **proboscis**.

10. Microphagous feeders feed on small particles suspended in water which are collected and filtered. They are hence also known as **filter feeders** (e.g. bivalve molluscs).

11. Digestion, the breaking down of food into soluble substances, is either **extracellular** or **intracellular**. It may be entirely intracellular as in *Amoeba*, or both extracellular and intracellular as in humans.

12. Digestion takes place by physical and chemical means. In mammals, physical digestion is achieved by teeth, gut muscles, and the action of bile on fats. Chemical breakdown is the result of the action of **digestive enzymes**.

13. Digestive enzymes work by splitting specific chemical bonds in the molecules of the food substances.

14. The mammalian gut is differentiated into a series of specialised regions, each showing a close relationship between structure and function.

15. Chemical digestion is achieved by enzymes secreted by the stomach wall, the pancreas and the wall of the small intestine. The final stage of digestion of carbohydrates and proteins is intracellular.

16. Secretion of digestive enzymes is initiated by expectation, reflex stimulation, hormones or direct mechanical stimulation, depending on the source of the enzymes.

17. The digestion of cellulose requires the enzyme **cellulase**, which very few animals secrete. Herbivores harbour mutualistic cellulase-secreting microorganisms in special parts of their gut.

18. To aid absorption, the surface area of the absorptive epithelium is increased by the presence of **villi** and **microvilli**.

Practice questions

For general advice on these questions and advice on answering essay-type questions, see pages vii and viii.

1. (a) Digestion in the mammalian gut relies on enzymes. Copy and complete the table opposite, which shows the sites of origin, sites of action and the reactions catalysed for various digestive enzymes. (8)

Enzyme	Site of origin	Site of action	Reaction
salivary amylase	salivary glands	mouth	
pepsin	stomach		proteins to peptides
		small intestine	fats to fatty acids and glycerol
carboxy-peptidase	small intestine		peptides to peptides and amino acids
		small intestine	lactose to glucose and galactose
sucrase	small intestine	small intestine	

Lactose sugar cannot be utilised in the absence of the appropriate digestive enzyme. Most mammals cease to secrete this enzyme as they grow to maturity, but in many human groups the enzyme is still secreted in adulthood. The table below compares the persistence of the production of the enzyme into adulthood among selected human groups.

Group	Population able to utilise lactose /%
Eskimos (Arctic region)	15
Bantu (Africa)	0
Danes (Europe)	98
Aborigines (Australia)	15

(b) (i) Why is lactose not utilised in the absence of the enzyme? (1)

(ii) Suggest why the populations shown in the table differ in their ability to utilise lactose. (2)

(c) (i) Explain the role of bile in fat digestion. (3)

(ii) Outline the mechanisms by which the products of fat digestion are absorbed into the blood. (4)

(Total 18 marks)

O&C 1998

2. The drawing shows the human digestive system.

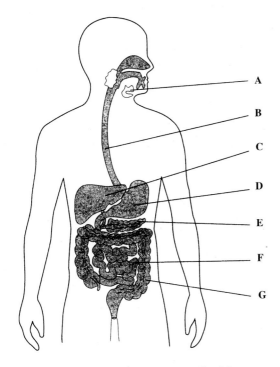

(a) Give the letter of an organ where each of the following is produced.

(i) endopeptidase

(ii) maltase (2)

(b) Name the compounds which are produced by the digestion of triglyceride. (1)

(c) Describe **one** role of bile in digestion of triglycerides. (2)

(d) (i) Name the hormone which causes the gall bladder to contract. (1)

(ii) What is the stimulus that initiates the release of this hormone? (1)

(Total 7 marks)

NEAB 1998

3. The diagram shows how protein can be digested in the human gut.

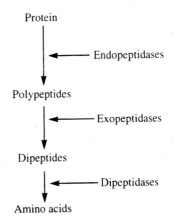

(a) (i) Describe the main difference between the mode of action of an endopeptidase and an exopeptidase. (1)

(ii) Give the name of the endopeptidase produced by the pancreas. (1)

(b) Where precisely is the site of action of dipeptidases in the small intestine? (1)

(c) Ruminants such as cattle need considerable quantities of protein yet they can survive on diets which contain very little. Explain how they obtain the extra protein that they need. (2)

(Total 5 marks)

AEB 1996

4. Describe the mechanisms and control of the digestion of carbohydrates.

(Total 10 marks)

London 1996

Chapter 12 — Autotrophic nutrition

The previous chapter considered those organisms that depend on an external source of organic compounds for their food supply – the heterotrophs. Other organisms are able to manufacture organic compounds from simple molecules such as carbon dioxide (CO_2) and water (H_2O). These organisms are called **autotrophs**. The type of feeding they employ is therefore called **autotrophic nutrition** and is the subject of this chapter.

The manufacture of complex molecules from carbon dioxide and other simple molecules requires large amounts of energy, and two main types of autotrophic organisms are distinguished depending on their source of energy:

- **Chemoautotrophs** Certain bacteria synthesise organic compounds from carbon dioxide and water, using energy supplied by special methods of respiration involving the oxidation of various inorganic materials such as hydrogen sulphide, ammonia, nitrites and iron(II). This method of synthesis, which does not require sunlight, is called **chemosynthesis**. Chemautotrophs are considered briefly at the end of the chapter.

- **Photoautotrophs** These organisms, which include green plants, some protoctists and certain bacteria, synthesise sugars from carbon dioxide and water using sunlight as the source of energy. The green pigment **chlorophyll** is used for trapping the light energy. This process is, of course, **photosynthesis**.

12.1 The importance of photosynthesis

Heterotrophs, including humans, depend on photosynthesis for their food. As a means of manufacturing sugar the contribution of photosynthesis is astounding. A hectare (2.47 acres) of maize (*Zea mais*) can convert as much as 10 000 kg of carbon from carbon dioxide into the carbon of sugar in a year, giving a total yield of 25 000 kg of sugar per year.

Although it is difficult to arrive at a total world figure for photosynthesis, one biologist has calculated that 3.5×10^{16} kg of carbon are fixed by plants per year. Our ability to solve the world's food problem will depend, at least in part, on agriculturalists increasing these figures still further.

Extension

Photosynthesis and the energy crisis

Hardly a day passes without our attention being drawn to the fact that people in many parts of the world do not have enough to eat. Shortage of food is essentially an energy problem. All living organisms require energy in order to grow, maintain themselves and reproduce. Plants, some protoctists and certain bacteria can manufacture their own food by trapping energy from sunlight. These organisms – **producers** as they are called – are therefore the basis of **food chains** (*page 670*).

The world's food problem arises from the fact that in global terms the producers cannot manufacture food fast enough to keep pace with the demands of an ever-increasing human population. But it is not just a matter of supply and demand. A more immediate problem is how to distribute the food. Some countries have food surpluses while others are experiencing severe food shortage and famine as a result of crop failures.

We can extend the idea of supply and demand to **fossil fuels**. Coal, natural gas and oil were formed from land plants and marine organisms millions of years ago. These organisms captured energy from the Sun and subsequently became the fossil fuels which we so relentlessly remove from the Earth's crust today. You could say that when we burn these fuels we are using 'fossil sunshine'. Regrettably, this invaluable source of energy is being used up far faster than it could ever be replaced by natural means.

But there is another reason why photosynthesis is important. It created the Earth's oxygen-containing atmosphere in the geological past and helps to regulate the concentration of carbon dioxide in it. The concentration of carbon dioxide in the atmosphere remains almost constant, in spite of the fact that it is continually being removed by photosynthesis. This is because most organisms produce carbon dioxide when they respire.

Oxygen which is added to the atmosphere as a result of photosynthesis is removed during respiration and the carbon dioxide in the air is replenished. These two processes – photosynthesis and respiration – create a cycling of carbon dioxide and oxygen in the atmosphere which is summarised in figure 12.1. The ecological significance of this **carbon cycle** is explained on pages 667 and 677. A detailed understanding of photosynthesis can help us to understand the cycling of oxygen and carbon dioxide on Earth.

12.2 Demonstrating photosynthesis

For photosynthesis to take place a plant requires **carbon dioxide**, **water**, **light**, **chlorophyll** and a **suitable temperature**. The necessity for these factors can be demonstrated by simple experiments either on whole plants or single leaves (*support box on next page*).

The main product of photosynthesis is **monosaccharide sugar**, although this is often built up into **starch** for storage. As an indication of whether or not photosynthesis has been taking place, leaves are tested for starch. First you have to **destarch** a plant by placing it in the dark for at least 48 hours. This prevents photosynthesis from taking place so the starch reserves are used up. After de-starching, one of the leaves is tested for starch to check none is present. The plant is then returned to the light and after a period of time one of the leaves is again tested for starch. Its presence indicates photosynthesis has been going on. The test for starch is as follows: the leaf is boiled gently in water until it is flaccid and immersed in 90 per cent ethanol until decolourised. When placed in dilute iodine solution any parts of the leaf containing starch turn dark blue colour.

The other product of photosynthesis is **oxygen**. To show that photosynthesis has taken place you need to demonstrate that oxygen is produced. It is much easier in practice to collect oxygen from an aquatic plant than from a land plant. For this reason, Canadian pondweed, *Elodea*, from whose cut stem gas may be seen emerging as a stream of bubbles, is commonly used in this experiment. The number of bubbles given off in a given time can be counted or, to be more accurate, the volume of gas given off in a given time can be measured (*support box below*).

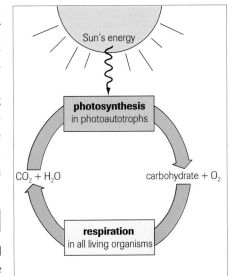

Figure 12.1 Photosynthesis plays an important part in the cycling of carbon dioxide and oxygen in the atmosphere.

Part 2

Support

Measuring the rate of photosynthesis

The illustration shows the apparatus for measuring the rate of photosynthesis of a water plant such as *Elodea*. Gas from the cut end of the stem is allowed to collect in the flared end of the capillary tube for a known period of time. The bubble of gas is then drawn into the straight part of the capillary tube by means of the syringe, and its length is measured. The bubble is then drawn on into the reservoir, after which a new bubble can be admitted into the capillary tube as before. The procedure is repeated as many times as is necessary to obtain consistent results with the plant in a given set of conditions.

This apparatus may be used to investigate the effect of various factors, for example light intensity and wavelength, on the rate of photosynthesis. By calibrating the capillary tube the actual volume of gas given off can be determined.

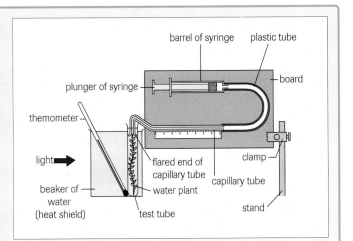

Apparatus for investigating the effect of light intensity on the rate of photosynthesis of a water plant such as *Elodea*.

The conditions required for photosynthesis

Carbon dioxide

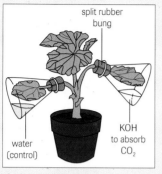

split rubber bung

water (control)

KOH to absorb CO₂

Illustration 1 One way of demonstrating that carbon dioxide is required for photosynthesis.

The necessity for carbon dioxide can be demonstrated by the arrangement shown in illustration 1. A plant such as geranium (*Pelargonium*) is well watered and then destarched (*page 197*). One of the green leaves is then deprived of carbon dioxide by enclosing it in a flask containing a small volume of potassium hydroxide (caustic potash), which absorbs the carbon dioxide from the air in the flask. A second leaf is enclosed in a separate flask containing water, to serve as a control. The flasks must be made completely airtight.

The plant is placed in a well-lit place for several hours, after which the two leaves are removed and tested for starch. The control leaf is usually found to have formed a significant quantity of starch, the other leaf little or none.

Water

The necessity for water is difficult to demonstrate by a simple experiment. Depriving a plant of water will certainly kill it but this might be due to any number of reasons, not necessarily connected with photosynthesis. The only way of showing that water is required for photosynthesis is to trace what happens to it after it has been taken into the plant. Such an experiment is described on page 210 and it shows that water is required for photosynthesis.

Light

The importance of light can be demonstrated by covering part of both surfaces of a previously destarched leaf with opaque paper and then exposing the leaf to light for several hours. On testing the leaf with dilute iodine solution it is found that the dark blue

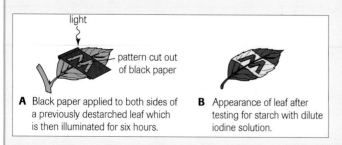

light

pattern cut out of black paper

A Black paper applied to both sides of a previously destarched leaf which is then illuminated for six hours.

B Appearance of leaf after testing for starch with dilute iodine solution.

Illustration 2 A simple demonstration to show the necessity for light in photosynthesis. No starch is formed in the covered part of the leaf.

colour, signifying the presence of starch, is confined to the illuminated parts of the leaf. The covered part does not turn dark blue, indicating the failure of this part of the leaf to form starch. The completed test gives a **starch print** (*illustration 2*).

Although this is a striking demonstration of the importance of light in photosynthesis, it is not an ideal scientific experiment. What are its shortcomings? Can you think of a better way of finding out if light is needed for starch formation?

Chlorophyll

That chlorophyll is required for photosynthesis can be shown by studying the distribution of starch in a **variegated leaf**. A variegated leaf is one which lacks chlorophyll in some parts, giving it a cream appearance wherever the green pigment is absent. This is quite common in geranium and ivy plants.

If a variegated *Pelargonium* plant, previously destarched, is exposed to light and one of its leaves is then tested for starch, the dark blue colour develops only in those parts of the leaf that were green. In fact the distribution of the dark blue colour corresponds exactly to the distribution of chlorophyll (*illustration 3*).

In the case of variegated ivy, this experiment may be taken a step further. Some varieties of this plant have four different shades of colour in their leaves: dark green towards the centre, then two zones of progressively paler green, and at the edge a yellow rim. If after a period of illumination, one of these leaves is tested for starch, the intensity of the blue colour follows exactly the same pattern as the chlorophyll.

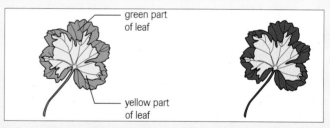

green part of leaf

yellow part of leaf

Illustration 3 A variegated *Pelargonium* leaf before and after testing for starch with dilute iodine solution. Notice that the dark colour indicating starch corresponds to the green areas where chlorophyll is

Temperature

Photosynthesis proceeds by a series of chemical reactions controlled by enzymes which are sensitive to temperature. It can be shown, by comparing a plant's rate of photosynthesis at different temperatures, that the optimum temperature for photosynthesis in most plants growing in temperate regions is around 30°C. At lower temperatures the rate is slowed. If the temperature exceeds about 45°C the process stops altogether because cell membranes are affected and the enzymes become denatured (*page 126*).

12.3 Interaction of factors controlling photosynthesis

Consider the following experiment. A plant is subjected to a series of increasing light intensities. The rate of photosynthesis is determined at each intensity, and the results plotted on a graph (*figure 12.2*). The temperature and carbon dioxide concentration are kept constant, the temperature at 20°C, the carbon dioxide concentration at 0.04 per cent – its normal value in the atmosphere. The experimental details need not concern us; let us concentrate on what happens and why.

As you can see from figure 12.2, the rate of photosynthesis rises steadily as the light intensity increases, and then levels off as the process reaches its maximum rate. What causes the rate of photosynthesis to stabilise at high light intensities?

Here are three possible answers (you may think of others):

■ The photosynthetic process is going at the fastest possible rate and no amount of additional light will make it go any faster, whatever the circumstances.

■ There is insufficient carbon dioxide available to allow the process to speed up any further.

■ The temperature is too low for the chemical reactions to go any faster.

How can we decide between these three possibilities? The simplest way is to raise either the temperature or carbon dioxide concentration and repeat the experiment. The result of doing this is shown in figure 12.3. Curve A is the same one as we obtained before (*figure 12.2*). If the experiment is now repeated at the same carbon dioxide concentration but at a higher temperature (30°C instead of 20°C), curve B is obtained which is virtually identical to curve A. This shows that it cannot be temperature that is preventing the process going any faster.

However, if the temperature is kept the same and the carbon dioxide concentration is increased to 0.13 per cent, curve C is obtained: the rate of photosynthesis rises to a maximum which is more than double that achieved at the lower carbon dioxide concentration.

This shows that our second hypothesis is the correct one; carbon dioxide is limiting the rate of photosynthesis in the first experiment.

What is limiting the process where curve C flattens out? Curve D shows that in this case the rate of photosynthesis is increased by raising the temperature, thus indicating that temperature is the limiting factor where curve C flattens out.

The facts demonstrated by this experiment can be put into a general statement, called the **law of limiting factors**.

> *When a chemical process depends on more than one essential condition being favourable, its rate is limited by that factor which is nearest its minimum value.*

In figure 12.3, light is the limiting factor where the curves are rising. When the curves flatten out we know that some other factor, such as temperature or carbon dioxide concentration, is limiting the process.

Photosynthesis and the environment

Limiting factors are important to plants in their natural surroundings. On a warm summer day, light and temperature are generally well above their minimum value for plants living in the open, and carbon dioxide is the factor limiting photosynthesis. But in the cool of the early morning or evening, light or temperature may become limiting factors as they do in winter.

Habitat is also important: for plants living in shady places such as the floor of a forest or wood, light will be the limiting factor most, if not all, the time.

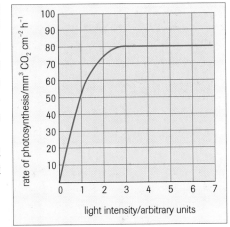

Figure 12.2 The results of an experiment showing the effect of different light intensities on the rate of photosynthesis of cucumber plants. The temperature was kept at 20°C and the carbon dioxide concentration at 0.03 per cent. The rate of photosynthesis was determined by measuring the volume of carbon dioxide taken up per square centimetre of leaf per hour.

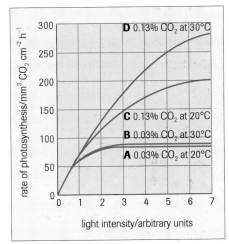

Figure 12.3 The results of an experiment investigating the effect of different light intensities on the rate of photosynthesis of cucumber plants at two temperatures and two carbon dioxide concentrations.

Figure 12.4 Adaptations shown by three different plants for obtaining light in dimly lit places. **A** Black bryony showing twining stems and leaf presented towards light. **B** Dog's mercury growing under trees in early spring before the tree leaves have formed a canopy. **C** Violets growing in quite dense shade in a wood.

Plants often compete for light. Tall plants will get plenty of light while those growing beneath them may not always get enough. Tallness is most clearly seen in trees although herbaceous plants like nettles and willowherbs also have sturdy, erect stems with leaves in a well-lit position for photosynthesis. Their great height makes taller trees like beech and oak the dominant plants of a temperate woodland community, though for sheer size the jackpot must go to the California coastal redwoods (*Sequoia sempervirens*) which can reach heights of over 100 metres.

Plants which live in the shadow of taller trees and shrubs exhibit various strategies for obtaining sufficient light. Climbing plants like black bryony have **twining stems** and others have **tendrils** enabling them to 'scramble' towards light. Certain woodland plants grow to maturity and flower in early spring before the leaves come out on the trees, for example dog's mercury. Other woodland plants, such as violets, photosynthesise very slowly in conditions of very low illumination and thus survive in relatively dark places (*figure 12.4*).

Controlling the environment in glasshouses

Good agricultural and horticultural methods of increasing the yield of plants growing in fields have been practised for years. Weeding, watering, addition of fertilisers, variety of seed used and optimum space between plants have all contributed to achieving higher yields. When a crop is grown in a glasshouse it is possible to control other factors as well.

The most usual factors to be controlled are **carbon dioxide**, **temperature**, **water** and **light**.

Carbon dioxide concentration of the atmosphere

Enrichment of the atmosphere in glasshouses with extra carbon dioxide has been used since the 1960s. The concentration of carbon dioxide in the air is normally 0.03 per cent. Increasing the level to 0.1 per cent boosts tomato yields, for example, by about 40 per cent. Above this level there is often not enough light for the plants to use the extra carbon dioxide unless the light is also enhanced (*limiting factors, page 199*). At much higher levels of carbon dioxide photosynthesis stops altogether.

The carbon dioxide is produced by burning methane and the amount pumped into the glasshouses is carefully monitored. As this costs money, it has to be shown to be economically worth while and considerations such as the best time of year and the best time of day to supplement the atmosphere have to be taken into account.

Temperature

For tomato plants to benefit from extra carbon dioxide they must also be grown at controlled temperatures. A minimum night temperature of 16°C is usually recommended, and a day temperature of 20°C with the ventilators open for cooling at 22 to 25°C. (This is why carbon dioxide enrichment is usually carried out only from November to May.)

Water and nutrients

In order to avoid stress in the plants, which would limit their growth, water and nutrients also need to be monitored. The system normally used is called **hydroponics (solution culture)** and the modification used for tomatoes is called **Nutrient Film Technique (NFT)**. The roots of the plant simply grow out into the nutrient solution in a polythene trough. The nutrient solution contains all the elements required for optimum plant growth and both the composition and the pH are monitored and adjusted automatically.

Light

Whilst it is not difficult to add extra lighting to a glasshouse, it is costly, so additional lighting is used sparingly. If it is used, it is normally for the first three or four weeks after germination, when a large number of plants can be packed together under a single light source. With extra carbon dioxide as well, a much sturdier plant is produced quickly, giving it a good start.

Enhancement of the environment in glasshouses is just one example of the application of science making a contribution to an increased production of good quality crops at lower prices.

Figure 12.5 Leaf mosaic formed by the leaves of a beech tree. Notice that the leaves are arranged in such a way that they do not cast shade on each other.

In large plants the leaves may cast shade on each other. You will often find that the leaves of such plants fit together in a sort of mosaic pattern, leaving few gaps between one leaf and the next, a condition called **leaf mosaic**. This is seen, for example, in beech trees and is the reason why they cast so much shade. Next time you are lying in a beech wood, look up at the canopy and notice how dense it is. Leaf mosaic makes beech woods very dark and the ground flora is sparse as a result (*figure 12.5*).

12.4 The absorption of light

It is useful to think of light travelling in distinct packets called **photons**. When a photon strikes a molecule of a pigment such as chlorophyll it may bounce off (i.e. be reflected), or, it may be absorbed by the chlorophyll molecule. The absorption of light is the first step in any process dependent on light as a source of energy. What happens to this light energy will be explained presently.

Only certain wavelengths of light (i.e. colours) are absorbed by chlorophyll. This can be shown by projecting a beam of daylight through a solution of extracted chlorophyll and then a prism which separates it into its different wavelengths. After passing through the prism, the light is projected on to a screen and any colours absent from the normal spectrum are those that have been absorbed by the chlorophyll. This gives us a **transmission spectrum** for chlorophyll (*figure 12.6*). It turns out that the red and blue ends of the spectrum are much reduced in intensity, showing that light of these colours is absorbed to varying extents by the chlorophyll. However, the middle part of the daylight spectrum, green light, is hardly absorbed at all: most of it is reflected or transmitted, which is why chlorophyll looks green.

Figure 12.6 *Top* The visible spectrum obtained by passing white light through a prism so that it is split into its different colours.
Bottom The transmission spectrum of chlorophyll obtained by passing light through a chlorophyll extract and a prism.

But are the wavelengths absorbed actually used in photosynthesis? That they are can be shown by exposing leaves to different coloured lights and then determining the amount of carbohydrate or oxygen formed in each case. This gives us an **action spectrum** for photosynthesis. Red and blue light turn out to be the most effective wavelengths in

The structure of chlorophyll

Chlorophyll belongs to a group of organic compounds known as **carotenoids** (a subset of lipids). The head of the chlorophyll *a* and *b* molecules consists of a **porphyrin**. Haemoglobin and the cytochromes also contain porphyrin molecules. A characteristic feature of porphyrins is that they form complexes with metal ions. In the case of chlorophyll the metal is magnesium, located at the centre of the porphyrin head of the molecule (*illustration*). A long chain alcohol called **phytol** is attached to the porphyrin head. It is only after the phytol 'tail' has been added to the porphyrin that photosynthesis can take place.

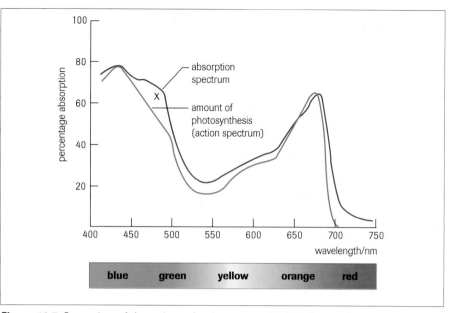

Figure 12.7 Comparison of absorption and action spectra of a plant shows a close correspondence between the two, indicating that most of the wavelengths of light absorbed by chlorophyll are used in photosynthesis. The graphs are based on data obtained from the sea lettuce *Ulva taeniata*. In this particular alga, efficiency in blue light is unusually high. The marked non-correspondence of the two curves at X is because of absorption of this wavelength by carotenes which are not used in photosynthesis.

photosynthesis; green is only used to a slight extent. There is thus a considerable similarity between the absorption and action spectra, as can be seen in figure 12.7.

The chloroplast pigments

What we have been calling chlorophyll is in fact a mixture of various pigments. These pigments can be extracted from leaves with a solvent such as propanone and separated by chromatography (*figure 12.8*). At least five pigments can be identified: **chlorophyll *a*** (blue-green), **chlorophyll *b*** (yellow-green), **xanthophyll** (yellow) and **carotene** (yellow). The fifth pigment, **phaeophytin** (grey), is a breakdown product of chlorophyll.

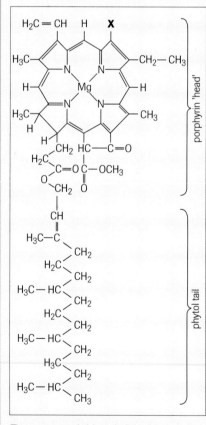

The structure of chlorophyll. In chlorophyll *a*, X is CH_3 and in *b* it is CHO. The arrangement of the porphyrin 'head' and phytol 'tail' is important in determining the orientation of the molecules in the chloroplast membranes.

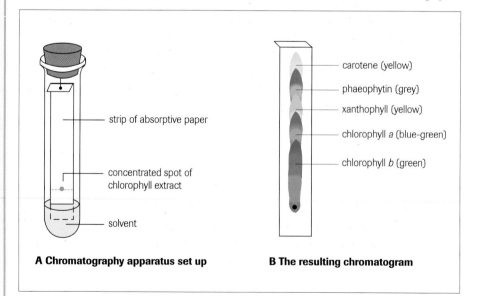

Figure 12.8 Different pigments in a leaf can be separated by paper chromatography. **A** A strip of absorptive paper carrying a concentrated spot of the leaf extract is dipped into a suitable solvent, for example a mixture of propanone and petroleum ether. The solvent rises up the paper, sweeping the pigments with it. The pigments travel at different speeds, thus becoming separated as shown in **B**.

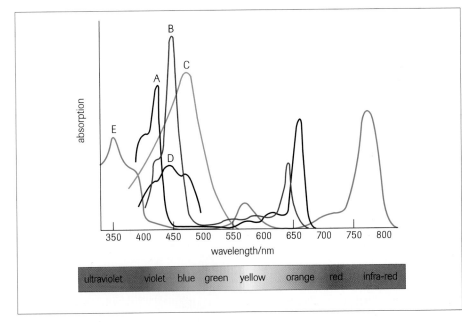

Figure 12.9 Absorption spectra of various photosynthetic pigments: **A** chlorophyll *a*; **B** chlorophyll *b*; **C** xanthophyll; **D** carotene; **E** bacteriochlorophyll of purple sulphur bacteria. Note the differing abilities of the various pigments to absorb different wavelengths. Chlorophyll *a* absorbs at longer and shorter wavelengths than either chlorophyll *b* or xanthophyll, and bacteriochlorophyll can absorb in the infra-red and ultraviolet parts of the spectrum.

By making separate solutions of each pigment and determining the absorption spectrum of each, it can be shown that chlorophyll *a* and *b* absorb light from both the red and blue/violet parts of the spectrum, whereas xanthophyll and carotene absorb light only from the blue/violet part (*figure 12.9*).

Chlorophyll *a* is the most abundant pigment and is of universal occurrence in all photosynthesising plants. Its function is to absorb light and use it in the manufacture of carbohydrate. The other pigments do this too and then hand on the energy to chlorophyll *a*.

Why are these accessory pigments necessary? Would not chlorophyll *a* alone be sufficient? To answer this look again at figure 12.9. Chlorophyll *a* utilises light from only limited parts of the spectrum. The other pigments utilise light from other parts of the spectrum, so they effectively increase the range of wavelengths from which the plant can obtain energy.

The amount of energy which the pigment can absorb from the light depends on two things: its **intensity** and its **wavelength**. The greater the intensity of the light, the greater will be the amount of energy that falls on, and is absorbed by, the pigment in a given time. The wavelength is important because it determines the frequency with which the light waves strike the pigment. The shorter the wavelength of the light, the more energy it contains. Thus there is more energy in blue light at 450 nm wavelength than there is in red light of the same intensity at 750 nm. This is why the pigments illustrated in figure 12.9 absorb more light at the blue end of the spectrum.

12.5 The site of photosynthesis

The distribution of starch in a variegated leaf demonstrates that photosynthesis can only take place in the green parts of a plant, and this suggests that the process is closely associated with chlorophyll. Chlorophyll is normally contained within **chloroplasts** so it is logical to conclude that photosynthesis takes place in or close to the chloroplasts.

Structure of the chloroplast

A typical chloroplast is biconvex in shape, about 5 μm across at the widest part. Studies with the electron microscope show it to have an elaborate internal structure which can be related to its function.

Detecting the site of photosynthesis

The German botanist T.W. Engelmann realised that it was no use trying to detect the site of photosynthesis in an ordinary cell filled with densely packed chloroplasts. It was necessary to find a large cell containing a localised chloroplast. It so happens that the filamentous alga *Spirogyra* fills the bill nicely. The filaments of *Spirogyra* are composed of comparatively large cylindrical cells placed end to end. Each contains a ribbon-like chloroplast which describes a spiral around the edge, just under the cell wall.

Engelmann chose *Spirogyra* for his experiments and used the evolution of oxygen as an indication that photosynthesis was proceeding. His method of detecting oxygen illustrates the ingenuity of this remarkable biologist. He had previously discovered that certain bacteria (*Pseudomonas*) move vigorously in the presence of oxygen, clustering together where the oxygen concentration is highest. A filament of *Spirogyra* was mounted on a microscope slide in a drop of water containing numerous bacteria. The slide was first put in darkness which prevented photosynthesis, stopped the evolution of oxygen and immobilised the bacteria. The slide was then exposed to light and viewed under a microscope. Motile bacteria were seen to cluster around the edge of the cells adjacent to the chloroplast, indicating that oxygen was being given off at that point (*illustration*).

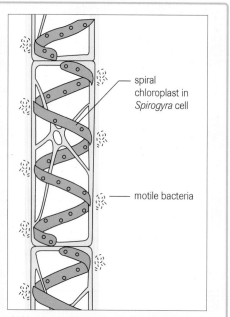

In his classical experiment, Engelmann used bacteria of the genus *Pseudomonas* to demonstrate that oxygen is given off during photosynthesis by the filamentous alga *Spirogyra*. After oxygen deprivation, motile bacteria are seen only in the immediate vicinity of the chloroplast.

The fine structure of the chloroplast is shown in figures 12.10 and 12.11. As you can see, it is bounded by a double membrane within which are numerous structures called **thylakoids**. Each thylakoid consists of a pair of membranes close to each other with a narrow space between. In places the thylakoids are arranged in neat stacks, rather like a pile of coins. Each stack is called a **granum** (plural **grana**). Its diameter is about 600 nm. The grana are connected to each other by a less regular arrangement of **inter-granal thylakoids**.

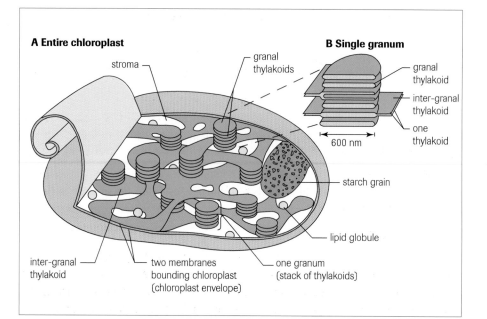

Figure 12.10 The structure of a chloroplast. **A** Stereogram showing the internal structure of the whole chloroplast. **B** Section of a single granum, showing that it consists of a stack of thylakoids.

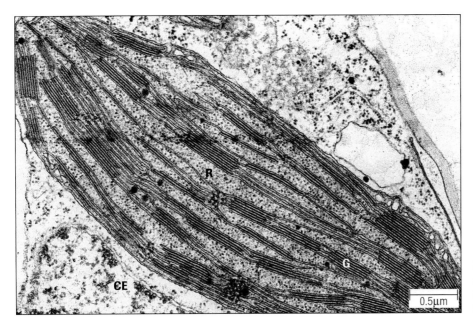

Figure 12.11 Electron micrograph of part of a chloroplast in a mesophyll cell of a leaf. The chloroplast envelope (**CE**), grana (**G**) and ribosomes (**R**) can all be distinguished.

The thylakoids are surrounded by a protein-rich matrix, the **stroma**. This contains the enzymes responsible for the reduction of carbon dioxide, together with starch grains and numerous ribosomes.

One function of the thylakoid membranes is to hold the chlorophyll molecules in a suitable position for trapping the maximum amount of light energy. In its internal organisation the chloroplast appears to achieve this admirably. A typical chloroplast contains approximately 60 grana, each consisting of about 50 thylakoids. The chlorophyll molecules are, as it were, laid out on shelves stacked on top of each other with considerable economy of space. This provides a large surface area without taking up too much room.

Figure 12.12 shows how the chlorophyll molecules and related structures are arranged in the thylakoid membrane. The stalked particles contain enzymes for catalysing the synthesis of ATP and the electron carriers transfer energy from the chlorophyll molecules after they have absorbed light – more about that shortly.

Next, we have to consider where the chloroplasts are in relation to the whole plant and how light, carbon dioxide and water get to them. In some organisms, like the alga *Spirogyra*, all the cells contain chloroplasts and carry out photosynthesis. But most plants possess organs specialised for photosynthesis. These are the **leaves**.

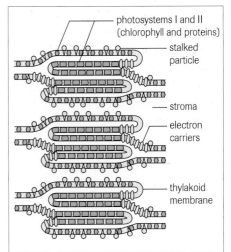

Figure 12.12 Diagram illustrating the possible arrangement of chlorophyll and related molecules within the thylakoid membranes, based on studies of isolated grana.

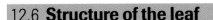

12.6 Structure of the leaf

Leaves are generally thin and flat and collectively present a large surface area to the light. Their thinness minimises the distance over which the diffusion of carbon dioxide has to take place. Of course being thin and flat makes them liable to sag, but their shape is maintained by the turgor of the living cells inside them, and by the **midrib** and **veins** which contain strengthening tissue. Their large surface area, while allowing maximum gaseous diffusion, increases evaporative water loss but this is reduced by the impermeable cuticle on the leaf surface and the closure of the stomata at night.

Internal structure

We will consider the structure of a leaf of a dictyledonous flowering plant (*page 95*). The leaf is covered on both sides by a layer of **epidermal cells**, on the outer surface of which is a waxy **cuticle**. The cuticle is generally thicker on the upper surface of the leaf than on the lower surface because the upper surface is more susceptible to evaporative water loss.

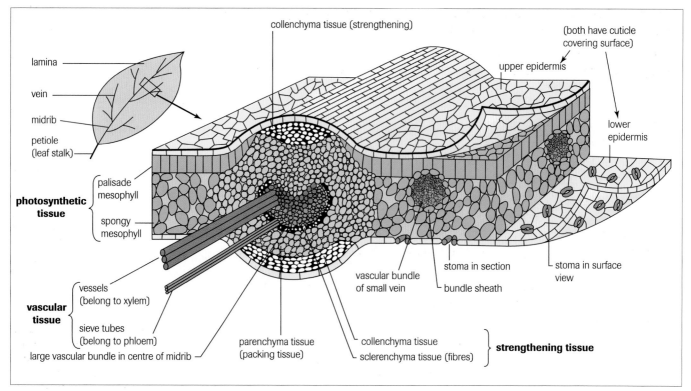

Figure 12.13 The leaf is a complex organ for photosynthesis. The photosynthetic cells are held in the best position for gaining maximum light. Strengthening tissue maintains the shape of the leaf. Stomata allow the entry of carbon dioxide whilst the cuticularised epidermis prevents excessive water loss. Vascular tissues in the midrib and veins bring water and mineral salts to the leaf, and remove the products of photosynthesis from it.

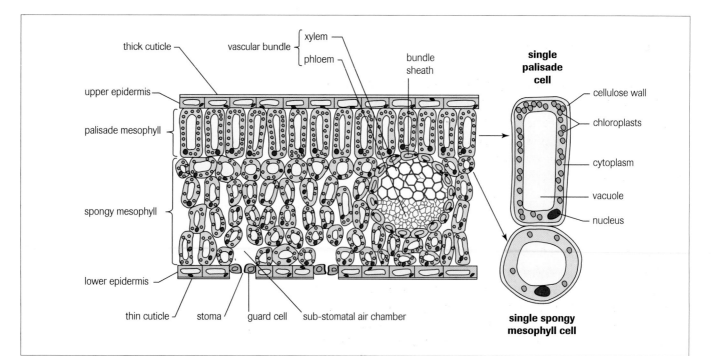

Figure 12.14 Photosynthetic cells in a leaf as seen in a diagrammatic transverse section. Note the intercellular air spaces allowing free diffusion of carbon dioxide, and the close proximity of the photosynthetic cells to the vascular tissues.

The inside of the leaf is illustrated in figures 12.13, 12.14 and 12.15. It is filled with cells containing chloroplasts. These cells are of two types:

- Those immediately beneath the upper epidermis, called the **palisade cells**, are elongated with their long axes perpendicular to the surface. They are separated from each other by **narrow air spaces** and are densely packed with chloroplasts. The chloroplasts tend to be in the upper part of the cell, which receives maximum illumination. The palisade cells collectively form the **palisade mesophyll** which may be one or several cells thick.

- Filling the leaf between the palisade layer and the lower epidermis is the **spongy mesophyll**. Its cells are irregular in shape and arrangement; they also contain chloroplasts but fewer than the palisade cells, which is why the lower side of a leaf usually looks paler than the upper side. Assuming that the plant is well supplied with water, the thin cellulose walls of the spongy mesophyll cells are permanently saturated with moisture. Between the spongy mesophyll cells are **large air spaces** which connect with each other and with the much narrower air spaces between the palisade cells. This system of air spaces allows gases to diffuse freely between the cells within the leaf and the cell walls of the spongy mesophyll present a large surface area to the air for the uptake of carbon dioxide.

The lower epidermis is pierced by numerous pores called **stomata** (singular **stoma**). The upper epidermis may have some too, but they are usually fewer than in the lower epidermis. Each stoma opens into a **sub-stomatal air chamber** which connects with the intercellular air spaces described above. Bordered by **guard cells** which can open or close the stomata, the passage of carbon dioxide and water vapour into and out of the leaf is regulated. How they open and close is explained on page 158.

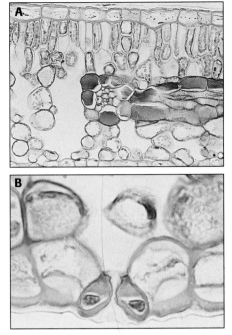

Figure 12.15 Stained photomicrographs of a dicotyledonous leaf in transverse section. **A** The whole leaf from upper to lower epidermis including a small vein, ×70. **B** A stoma and sub-stomatal air chamber on the lower side of the leaf, ×500. Use figure 12.14 to help you identify the structures in these photomicrographs.

Part 2

The midrib and veins

The diagram in figure 12.13 includes the central midrib as well as two smaller veins. The veins consist of conducting tissue specialised for transporting materials to and from the leaf.

- The **xylem** brings water and mineral salts from the roots in elongated conducting tubes called **vessels** and **tracheids**.

- The **phloem** carries soluble food materials, such as sucrose, from the leaf in specialised rows of cells called **sieve tubes**.

The xylem and phloem together constitute a **vascular bundle**. The xylem elements, being lignified (woody), also provide the flexible leaf with mechanical strength (*page 251*).

The midrib is basically similar to the smaller veins except that there is more conducting tissue and, in addition, much specialised strengthening tissue (sclerenchyma and collenchyma) for supporting the leaf (*page 70*).

The leaf as an organ of photosynthesis

How does the leaf work as a photosynthetic organ? Carbon dioxide from the atmosphere diffuses through the stomata into the sub-stomatal air chambers and thence via the intercellular air spaces to the chloroplasts in the spongy mesophyll and palisade cells.

Water, drawn up from the soil via the conducting tissues of the roots and stem, passes out of the xylem elements in the veins to the surrounding cells. Maintenance of this flow is discussed in Chapter 15. Its importance in the present context is that it supplies water for photosynthesis. With the water come mineral salts (including nitrates, sulphates and phosphates) required for the synthesis of proteins and other compounds.

The importance of the stomata

The stomata play a vital part in photosynthesis. When they are open, the rate of photosynthesis may be 10 or 20 times as fast as the rate of respiration. Under these circumstances, although the plant may use all of the carbon dioxide from its respiration for photosynthesis, the bulk of its carbon dioxide must be brought in from the atmosphere. If the stomata are closed photosynthesis can still continue, albeit at a slower rate, using the carbon dioxide from respiration.

In fact an equilibrium can be reached between photosynthesis and respiration, photosynthesis using carbon dioxide from respiration, and respiration using oxygen from photosynthesis. This is the principle underlying a 'bottle garden' (*illustration*). However, the rate of photosynthesis under these circumstances will be much slower than when an external source of carbon dioxide is available.

Plants can be kept indefinitely in an illuminated sealed container ('bottle garden'). The carbon dioxide from respiration is used for photosynthesis, and the oxygen from photosynthesis is used for aerobic respiration.

Oxygen and excess water vapour diffuse out of the leaf via the intercellular air spaces and stomata. Sugar and other soluble products of photosynthesis are moved to other parts of the plant in the sieve tubes.

12.7 The chemistry of photosynthesis

In the process of photosynthesis, energy from sunlight is trapped by chlorophyll and used for the manufacture of carbohydrate from carbon dioxide and water. The process can be summarised by the following equation:

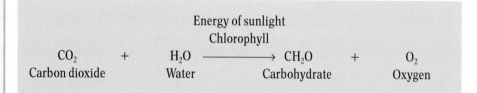

$$CO_2 + H_2O \xrightarrow[\text{Chlorophyll}]{\text{Energy of sunlight}} CH_2O + O_2$$

Carbon dioxide + Water → Carbohydrate + Oxygen

Though useful as an overall summary of the process, this simplified equation is misleading because it may give the impression that the oxygen evolved comes from the carbon dioxide, which we know is not true (*extension box on page 210*). It also suggests that photosynthesis takes place in a single photochemical reaction, whereas it occurs in many steps, not all of which require light.

If photosynthesis consisted only of photochemical reactions we would not expect the process to be influenced by temperature since photochemical reactions are temperature insensitive. But in fact the rate of photosynthesis is strongly influenced by temperature, provided of course that other factors are not limiting it. A 10°C rise in temperature approximately doubles the rate. This is typical of ordinary chemical reactions, and it would therefore seem that photosynthesis proceeds in more than one stage, each with different light and temperature requirements.

We can see these two factors, light and temperature, operating in curve C in figure 12.3 (*page 199*). Over the first part of the curve, when it is rising steeply, light is influencing the rate of photosynthesis and temperature has no effect on it, i.e. a light-requiring reaction is setting the pace. However, when the curve flattens out temperature controls the rate, suggesting that at least some of the reactions are not limited by light.

Photosynthesis as a three-stage process

Photosynthesis takes place in three main stages:

- **light harvesting**
- **electron transport**
- **reduction of carbon dioxide**.

The first two stages require light and take place in the thylakoids of the chloroplast. These are known as the **light-dependent reactions**. The reactions of the third stage do not require light. They take place in the stroma and are **light-independent reactions**.

The three stages are summarised in figure 12.16. Although they take place simultaneously it is convenient to study them separately, and as the primary event of photosynthesis is the capture – or harvesting – of light, this is where we shall begin.

Stage 1: Light harvesting

Pigment molecules, arranged in specific association with protein and lipid molecules in the thylakoid membranes of the chloroplasts, form the light-harvesting system. It acts like a funnel, collecting photons of light and transferring the energy to special molecules of chlorophyll *a* in a **reaction centre** (*figure 12.17*).

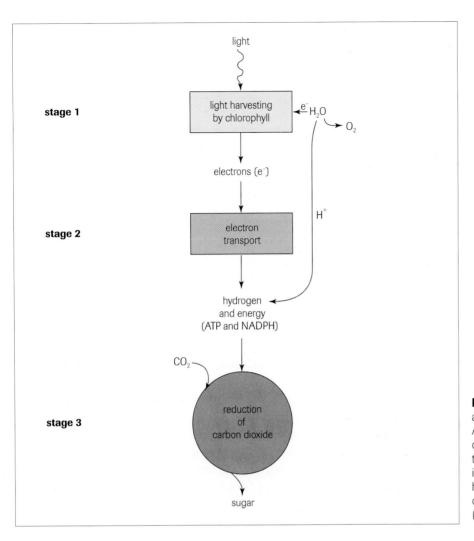

Figure 12.16 In photosynthesis, light energy is absorbed (harvested) by chlorophyll (stage 1). As a result, electrons are released from the chlorophyll and transferred through an electron transport system (stage 2). This process, which is associated with the splitting of water, provides hydrogen and the necessary energy for reducing carbon dioxide with the formation of sugar (stage 3).

The transfer of the energy to a reaction centre is achieved in the following way. When a chlorophyll molecule absorbs light, the energy is passed to an electron and this raises its energy level. The chlorophyll molecule goes from the 'ground' state to an 'excited' state. An 'excited' chlorophyll molecule can immediately pass its energy to a neighbouring chlorophyll molecule which itself becomes 'excited', while the original one returns to the 'ground' state. In this way energy can be transferred very rapidly from one chlorophyll molecule to another in a manner which has been described as a 'random walk'. This is indicated by the arrows in figure 12.17. The other pigments act rather like 'antennae', collecting energy and transferring it to chlorophyll *a*.

An 'excited' chlorophyll *a* molecule is very unstable and will dissipate its energy as fluorescent light and return to its ground state in a tiny fraction of a second. However, the transfer of energy from an excited molecule of chlorophyll *a* to a special molecule of chlorophyll *a* in a reaction centre takes place even faster, so at least some of the energy is transferred.

There are two kinds of reaction centre in plants called **photosystem I** (**PS I**) and **photosystem II** (**PS II**). While many chlorophyll molecules are involved in the capture of light energy, only a few make up the reaction centres. PS I absorbs light at 700 nm and PS II at 690 nm. These two centres differ not only in the structure of their chlorophylls but also in their functions, as we shall see. The transport of electrons through these two centres comprises the second stage of photosynthesis, which we must now consider.

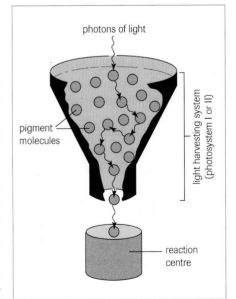

Figure 12.17 The light-harvesting system is here likened to a funnel. Photons of light are collected and passed in a random manner from pigment molecule to pigment molecule until they reach the reaction centre.

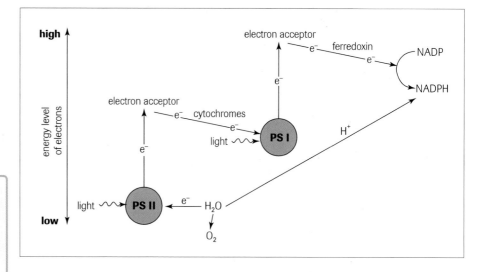

The Hill reaction

In 1938, Robert Hill demonstrated that isolated chloroplasts, when illuminated in the presence of an electron acceptor, produce oxygen and acquire reducing properties. He used a coloured dye called dichlorophenol-indophenol (DCPIP) as the electron acceptor. This dye is blue in the oxidised state but becomes colourless when reduced. As carbon dioxide was not involved in this reaction, Hill concluded that water had been split into hydrogen and oxygen – what is now known as the **Hill reaction**.

The source of oxygen in photosynthesis

S. Ruben and M. Kamen and their co-workers established that the oxygen evolved in photosynthesis comes from the water and not from carbon dioxide. In an experiment carried out in 1941 they placed the green protoctist *Chlorella* in water in which the oxygen atom had been replaced by the heavy isotope of oxygen, ^{18}O. By using a mass spectrometer they found that ^{18}O was present in the oxygen given off by the organism. If, however, the protoctist was given normal water but the carbon dioxide was labelled with ^{18}O, the oxygen given off contained no ^{18}O, thus confirming that the oxygen formed in photosynthesis comes only from the water.

Stage 2: Electron transport

The way electrons are transported through PS I and PS II is shown in figure 12.18. We shall start with PS I.

When light is absorbed by a chlorophyll molecule in PS I an electron is displaced and transferred to an electron acceptor, which in turn donates it to a protein called **ferredoxin**. The latter then passes the electron to **nicotinamide adenine dinucleotide phosphate** (**NADP**) which is thereby reduced to NADPH.

Obviously for this process to continue the electron displaced from PS I must be replaced. This is where PS II comes in. When PS II absorbs light, an electron is displaced from it and passed along a chain of electron carriers, which include the cytochromes. Eventually the electron replaces the electron displaced from PS I which is thus returned to its ground state.

In order for this process to continue, the PS II molecule must be restored to its ground state. This is brought about by a process in which water is split and an electron donated to PS II. As light is associated with this reaction, it is called **photolysis of water** and it results in the release of molecular oxygen. It is summarised by the following equation:

$$2H_2O \longrightarrow O_2 + 4e^- + 4H^+$$

From this equation we can see that the photolytic splitting of water supplies the oxygen evolved during photosynthesis, the electrons to reduce carbon dioxide and the hydrogen ions (H^+) for ATP synthesis or carbon dioxide reduction. It is called the **Hill reaction** after the scientist who discovered it, and it is one of the principal events of photosynthesis.

Photophosphorylation

The electron transport system just described does more than simply release NADPH, it also produces ATP. How is the ATP produced? You will recall from your study of respiration that for ATP to be synthesised, ADP and inorganic phosphate must be present (*page 141*). As a result of the splitting of water and the electron flow from PS II to PS I in the thylakoid membranes, hydrogen ions (H^+) accumulate inside the thylakoid, creating a steep electrochemical gradient. The subsequent passage of H^+ out of the thylakoids provides the energy for ATP to be synthesised in the presence of ATPase. This is called **non-cyclic photophosphorylation** (*figure 12.19*).

Sometimes the electrons follow a different route. In this case PS I is both the donor and acceptor of electrons. There is again an accumulation of H^+ inside the thylakoid and ATP is synthesised as before. Because there is a cyclical flow of electrons in this pathway, it is

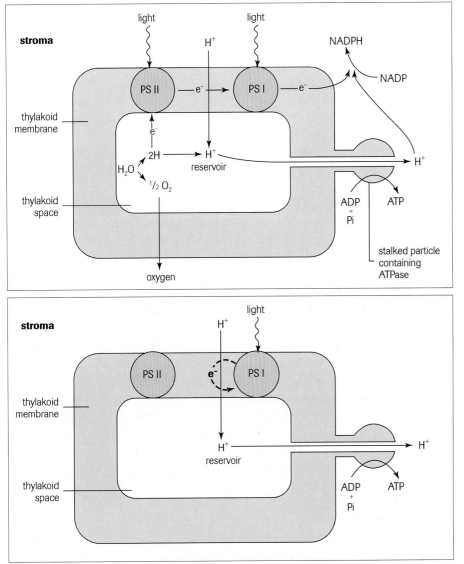

stroma

light   light

H^+

PS II — e^- → PS I — e^-

NADPH

NADP

thylakoid
membrane

e^-

2H → H^+
reservoir

H_2O

$\frac{1}{2} O_2$

thylakoid
space

ADP
+
Pi

ATP

H^+

stalked particle
containing
ATPase

oxygen

Figure 12.19 How ATP and NADPH are formed in photosynthesis. As a result of the splitting of water and the flow of electrons in the thylakoid membrane, hydrogen ions accumulate in the thylakoid space. The movement of electrons in the thylakoid membrane releases energy which enables hydrogen ions to be pumped by active transport from the stroma into the thylakoid space. As a result the hydrogen ion concentration is about 1000 times greater in the thylakoid space than in the stroma, creating a steep electrochemical gradient. Hydrogen ions (H^+) then diffuse out of the thylakoid via the stalked particles and this provides energy for the synthesis of ATP in the presence of ATPase. It also provides the hydrogen for reducing NADP with the formation of NADPH. The passage of electrons from PS II to NADP via PS I occurs as shown in figure 12.18. The whole process is called **non-cyclic photophosphorylation**.

stroma

light

H^+

PS II e^- PS I

thylakoid
membrane

H^+
reservoir

thylakoid
space

ADP
+
Pi

ATP

H^+

Figure 12.20 If ATP rather than NADPH is needed, the plant automatically switches to **cyclic photophosphorylation**, as shown here. Electrons from PS I, instead of being passed to NADP, return to PS I. The movement of electrons releases energy which results in hydrogen ions accumulating in the thylakoid space with the consequent synthesis of ATP just as in non-cyclic photophosphorylation.

called **cyclic photophosphorylation** (*figure 12.20*). NADPH is not formed by this method.

Insofar as energy is derived from an electrochemical gradient resulting from the movement of hydrogen ions (i.e. protons) across the thylakoid membrane through stalked particles, the production of ATP by cyclic and non-cyclic photophosphorylation is an application of the chemiosmotic theory explained on page 145 in connection with mitochondria. There are, in fact, many similarities between what happens in the thylakoids and what happens in mitochondria. However, one *difference* is that, whereas in mitochondria protons are moved inwards, in the thylakoids they are moved outwards.

We now turn to the third stage of photosynthesis, namely the reduction of carbon dioxide to form carbohydrate.

Stage 3: Reduction of carbon dioxide

The events described so far have taken place in the thylakoids. The scene now shifts to the stroma of the chloroplast. Here the NADPH and ATP formed in the previous stages provide the reducing power and the energy for synthesising sugars from carbon dioxide.

The reduction of carbon dioxide and subsequent synthesis of carbohydrate takes place in a series of small steps, each controlled by a specific enzyme. The individual steps were established by Melvin Calvin and his associates at the University of California (*extension box on page 213*).

From their investigations it emerged that the chain of reactions is cyclical, now known as the **Calvin cycle** or the **light-independent reactions** (*figure 12.21*). In the first step, (bottom left in figure 12.21) the carbon dioxide combines with a 5-carbon organic compound called **ribulose bisphosphate** (abbreviated to **RuBP**). This serves as a carbon dioxide acceptor and fixes the carbon dioxide, i.e. incorporates it into the photosynthetic machinery of the plant. The enzyme needed for this is called **RuBP carboxylase**. This enzyme is the most abundant protein on Earth, accounting for about half of the protein in most leaves or 10 kg for every human being on Earth.

The combination of carbon dioxide with RuBP gives an unstable 6-carbon compound which splits immediately into two molecules of a 3-carbon compound, **glycerate 3-phosphate** (**GP**).

The next step is crucial: the GP is reduced to form a 3-carbon sugar, **glyceraldehyde 3-phosphate** (**GALP**). The hydrogen for this reduction comes from NADPH which also supplies most of the energy, the rest coming from ATP. The 3-carbon sugar is now built up to a 6-carbon sugar which can be converted into starch for storage.

Not all the 3-carbon sugar is converted into 6-carbon sugar. Some of it (the majority in fact) enters a series of reactions, driven by ATP, which results in the regeneration of RuBP. This is very important because only by ensuring a supply of RuBP can the continued fixation of carbon dioxide take place.

Because the 3-carbon compound **glycerate 3-phosphate** (**GP**) is the first product of carbon dioxide fixation in the Calvin cycle, the pathway just described is known as the **C$_3$ pathway** and plants which have it are called **C$_3$ plants**. The C$_3$ pathway is typical of plants in temperate areas. Most temperate crops such as wheat and potatoes are C$_3$ plants.

Figure 12.21 The main steps in the Calvin cycle. The details of how the 3-carbon sugar (GALP) leads to the regeneration of ribulose bisphosphate as well as giving the 6-carbon sugar are complicated, but basically what happens is this. Say we have 12 molecules of 3-carbon sugar. Two of these combine with each other to give one molecule of 6-carbon sugar. The remaining 10 molecules of 3-carbon sugar go through a complex series of reactions from which six molecules of 5-carbon ribulose bisphosphate eventually emerge. These then react with six molecules of carbon dioxide, giving a total of 12 molecules of 3-carbon glycerate 3-phosphate which in turn yield 12 molecules of 3-carbon sugar. This brings us back to where we started. Note that no carbon atoms are 'lost' in this process.

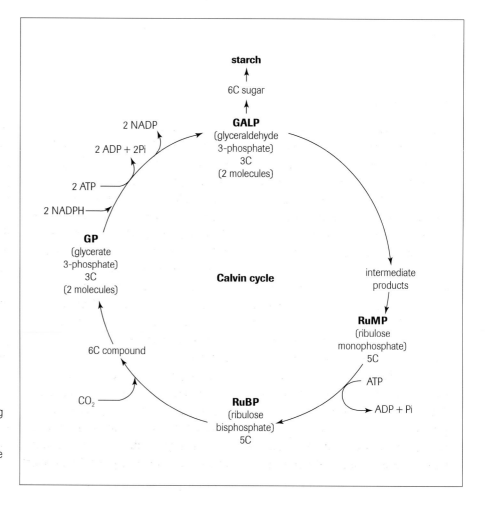

Calvin's experiments

Calvin and his co-workers carried out their original experiments in the 1950s. They illuminated the unicellular green alga *Chlorella* in the presence of carbon dioxide labelled with the radioactive isotope of carbon, ^{14}C (*see illustration*). The algae were allowed to photosynthesise for a certain period of time after being given the labelled carbon dioxide. They were then quickly killed with boiling ethanol which inactivated all their enzymes and stopped the reactions instantaneously. The radioactive compounds which had been formed were then extracted from the organisms and separated by paper chromatography. Autoradiographs were made and the amount of radioactivity in the different compounds was determined. The algae were killed at intervals after initial fixation of the carbon dioxide,

Left Melvin Calvin, who discovered how carbohydrates are made in photosynthesis.
Right Calvin's 'lollipop' apparatus. The 'lollipop' refers to the thin, transparent vessel containing a suspension of *Chlorella*. Carbon dioxide labelled with radioactive ^{14}C is bubbled through the suspension, and subsequent analysis of the radioactive compounds formed enables the path taken by carbon in photosynthesis to be traced.

from a few seconds to a few minutes. By identifying the intermediates formed after different periods of time and determining the amount of radioactivity in each one, the pathway through which carbon compounds are built up was established.

C_4 and CAM plants

Since Melvin Calvin and his colleagues established the C_3 pathway, another pathway has been found in some plants in which a different compound is used as the substrate for fixing carbon dioxide. This compound is **phosphoenol pyruvate** (**PEP**). In this case the immediate product of carbon dioxide fixation is not 3-carbon GP but the 4-carbon compound **oxaloacetic acid**. Because of this, these plants are called **C_4 plants**. The carbon dioxide fixed in this way is then released and fed into the Calvin cycle to form carbohydrate.

What is the point of this? The enzyme which catalyses the fixation of carbon dioxide in the **C_4** system is **phosphoenolpyruvate carboxylase** (**PEP carboxylase**) and it has an exceptionally high affinity for

carbon dioxide even when it is in low concentration. It is also a very rapid reaction and operates particularly efficiently at high temperatures and in bright light. Plants which utilise this pathway are mainly tropical and it allows them to close their stomata and thus reduce water vapour loss. This would normally result in a shortage of carbon dioxide for photosynthesis, but because of the high affinity of PEP carboxylase for carbon dioxide at low concentrations, carbon dioxide does not become a limiting factor.

The **C_4** pathway therefore enables tropical crop plants such as maize and sugar cane to combine high levels of photosynthesis with a low loss of water.

There is yet another mechanism which allows plants to survive in hot, arid desert

conditions. These are called **CAM plants**. (CAM stands for **crassulacean acid metabolism**, named after the plants of the family Crassulaceae in which it was first discovered). They also use PEP carboxylase for fixing carbon dioxide just like C_4 plants. While C_4 plants fix carbon dioxide in the daytime, CAM plants fix carbon dioxide at night. They keep their stomata closed during the hot daylight hours and open them only at night when the loss of water vapour is greatly reduced. Carbon dioxide is then fixed using PEP carboxylase. During the day the carbon dioxide is released and fed into the Calvin cycle in the usual way. The CAM pathway is found in many succulents such as prickly pear and in pineapple.

Starch is not the only end product of photosynthesis. This is shown by the fact that in Calvin's experiments radioactive carbon was eventually identified in other compounds, including amino acids and fatty acids. For amino acids to be formed, nitrates are required. These are converted to ammonium ions which are used for the formation of the amino acid glutamine. From this other amino acids are made by transamination (*page 31*).

12.8 Autotrophic bacteria

Autotrophic bacteria are divided into two groups: **photosynthetic** and **chemosynthetic**. Both can build up organic compounds from simple inorganic raw materials. They differ in the way they obtain the necessary energy. Let us look at each in turn.

Photosynthetic bacteria

Like green plants, these bacteria are able to build up carbon dioxide and water into organic compounds using energy from sunlight. The energy is trapped by a pigment called **bacteriochlorophyll** which is similar to, though somewhat simpler than, chlorophyll. They differ from green plants in their source of hydrogen for reducing the carbon dioxide. Instead of obtaining it from water, they get it from hydrogen sulphide, for which reason they are known as **sulphur bacteria**.

Sulphur bacteria live at the bottom of lakes, ponds and rock pools, where hydrogen sulphide is supplied by the mechanism of anaerobic decay bacteria. The residual sulphur resulting from the splitting of hydrogen sulphide is deposited in the bacterial cells.

$$CO_2 + 2H_2S \xrightarrow[\text{bacteriochlorophyll}]{\text{light}} CH_2O + 2S + H_2O$$

Bacteriochlorophyll comes in two closely related forms, green and purple, giving the so-called **green** and **purple sulphur bacteria** respectively. The absorption spectrum of the purple form is included in figure 12.9, from which it will be seen that it absorbs light of wavelengths on either side of those absorbed by chlorophyll and related pigments. This enables sulphur bacteria to survive underneath green seaweeds in rock pools on the seashore. Much of the light that can be used by the bacteria passes straight through the algae and is then absorbed by the bacteria.

Chemosynthetic bacteria

The chemosynthetic bacteria can also synthesise organic compounds from inorganic materials but instead of using sunlight, they obtain the necessary energy from special chemical processes which generally involve the oxidation of compounds other than sugar. Thus **iron bacteria**, living in streams that run over iron-containing rocks, oxidise divalent iron salts. The **colourless sulphur bacteria** (not to be confused with green and purple bacteria discussed in the last section) live in decaying organic matter and oxidise hydrogen sulphide to water and sulphur. There are even **hydrogen bacteria** which can oxidise hydrogen with the formation of water.

Nitrifying and other bacteria in the nitrogen cycle, page 669

A particularly important group of chemosynthetic organisms are the **nitrifying bacteria** found in the soil. These are dealt with in Chapter 38.

1. Autotrophic nutrition, the synthesis of organic compounds from inorganic sources, takes place by **photosynthesis** and **chemosynthesis**.

2. An understanding of photosynthesis is very important to agriculturalists in the provision of enough food to meet the needs of an ever-increasing world population.

3. Photosynthesis plays a vital role in the balance of gaseous oxygen and carbon dioxide in the atmosphere.

4. The raw materials of photosynthesis are **carbon dioxide** and **water**; the major products are **carbohydrate** and **oxygen**. **Light** from the Sun is the source of energy which is trapped by the green pigment **chlorophyll**, and the process requires a **suitable temperature**.

5. Photosynthesis is subject to the **law of limiting factors**, i.e. its rate is limited by whatever factor is nearest its minimum value.

6. The yield of crop plants can be increased by enhancing the environment of glasshouses in a carefully controlled and monitored manner.

7. When photosynthesis and respiration proceed at the same rate so that there is no net loss or gain of carbohydrate, the plant is said to be at its **compensation point**.

8. The **transmission spectrum** of chlorophyll indicates that red and blue light are absorbed most, and the **action spectrum** for photosynthesis shows that these are the most effective wavelengths in photosynthesis.

9. The photosynthetic pigments in a leaf are **chlorophyll *a*** and **chlorophyll *b*** plus the accessory pigments **xanthophyll** and **carotene**. The function of the accessory pigments is to increase the range of wavelengths from which energy can be harvested.

10. Photosynthesis occurs in the **chloroplasts**. Inside the chloroplasts chlorophyll is located on numerous pairs of parallel membranes called **thylakoids**.

11. The chloroplasts are mainly in the leaves whose anatomy shows a close relationship between structure and function.

12. Photosynthesis is a three-stage process. The first two stages occur in the **grana** of the chloroplasts and the third stage in the **stroma**. The first stage involves the **harvesting of light energy** by specialised pigments and the splitting of water, releasing oxygen.

13. In the second stage, **electrons are transferred** by **electron carriers** as a result of which **reduced NADP** (i.e. **NADPH**) and ATP are formed (**non-cyclic photophosphorylation**).

14. Sometimes the electrons follow a different route when only ATP is formed (**cyclic phosphorylation**).

15. In the third stage, **carbon dioxide** is **reduced** to form sugars in the Calvin cycle. Hydrogen for the reduction, and energy to drive the process, come from the second stage.

16. Because the 3-carbon compound **glycerate 3-phosphate** (**GP**) is the first product of carbon dioxide fixation in the Calvin cycle, it is known as the **C_3 pathway**.

17. Some plants fix carbon dioxide into a 4-carbon compound, oxaloacetic acid; this is known as the **C_4 pathway**.

18. Some C_4 plants living in arid conditions take up carbon dioxide at night, and during the day the stomata close and the carbon dioxide is released for photosynthesis. These are known as **CAM plants**.

19. In **chemosynthesis**, organic compounds are synthesised from inorganic raw materials; the necessary energy coming from the oxidation of, e.g. iron salts, nitrates and nitrites.

For general advice on these questions and advice on answering essay-type questions, see pages vii and viii.

1. (a) Explain the meaning of the term 'limiting factor'. (2)

(b) The graph shows the results of three experiments, **K**, **L** and **M**, investigating the effect of carbon dioxide concentration on the rate of photosynthesis at maximum, medium and minimum light intensity. The experiments were all performed at 16°C and the plants were well watered.

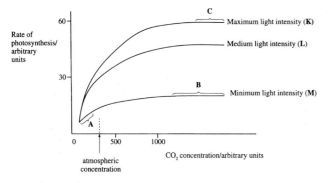

(i) Using only the information in the graph state **one** factor which limited the rate of photosynthesis in experiment **M** in the regions labelled **A** and **B**. (2)

(ii) Suggest **one** factor which limits the rate of photosynthesis in experiment **K** in the region labelled **C** on the graph. (1)

(c) Describe **two** ways in which the data in the graph might be helpful to growers of greenhouse crops. (2)

(Total 7 marks)

WJEC 1998

2. (a) Explain how a plant can use the light energy reaching a chlorophyll molecule to make ATP. (2)

(b) The diagram shows the light-independent stage of photosynthesis.

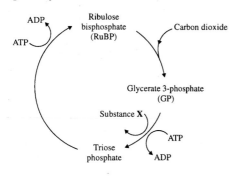

(i) Substance **X** is oxidised during the reduction of glycerate 3-phosphate to triose phosphate. Give the name of substance **X**. (1)

(ii) A plant was placed in the light for a period of one hour and allowed to photosynthesise. At the end of this time the light was switched off and the plant left in the dark. Explain why there would be a decrease in the amount of RuBP in the leaf cells of the plant when the light was switched off. (2)

(Total 5 marks)

AEB 1998

3 A cell suspension of a species of *Chlorella*, an alga, was supplied with carbon dioxide, initially at a concentration of 3%. This was then reduced to 1% after 100 seconds, and then to 0.03% after a further 200 seconds. The levels of RuBP and GP (PGA) present were determined at intervals. The graph shows the results obtained.

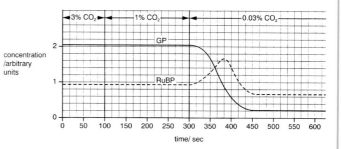

(a) With reference to the graph , state the effect on

(i) the concentration of GP when the carbon dioxide concentration is reduced from 3% to 1%; (1)

(ii) the concentration of GP when the carbon dioxide concentration is reduced from 1% tio 0.03%; (2)

(iii) the concentration of RuBP when the carbon dioxide concentration is reduced from 1% to 0.03%. (3)

(b) Explain the observed change in the concentration of RuBP during the 100 seconds immediately after the carbon dioxide concentration was reduced to 0.03%. (4)

(c) State the evidence provided by the graph which indicates that the concentration of carbon dioxide may not be a limiting factor. (3)

The results of such experiments have contributed to work on plant productivity in field crops.

(d) Explain how GP contributes to plant productivity in a field crop. (3)

(e) Suggest **one** condition which might cause the carbon dioxide concentration in a crop to fall below atmospheric level. (1)

(Total 17 marks)

UCLES 1997

Chapter 13

The principles of transport

A ll organisms need a way of distributing the raw materials for metabolism, and its products, to the appropriate parts of the body. For small organisms, where distances are short, **diffusion** will suffice for doing this. However, large organisms, in which distances may be far greater, need special **transport systems**.

Such transport systems usually involve some kind of **mass flow**. Mass flow occurs when all the particles in a liquid or gaseous medium move in the same direction at more or less the same speed. In this chapter we shall look at some of the general principles underlying mass flow transport systems, first in animals and then in plants.

▶ Fick's Law, page 104

13.1 Transport in animals

One of the simplest mass flow transport systems is seen in aquatic animals such as sponges and jellyfish which use the surrounding water as the medium (*figure 13.1*). However, in most animals the mass flow system has become enclosed in tubes or vessels which have no connection with the exterior and contain their own distinctive fluid. In such systems the fluid usually circulates around the body and is known as the **circulatory system**.

Most circulatory systems have the following features:

■ a transport medium, usually called **blood**, capable of carrying dissolved materials such as food, oxygen and carbon dioxide;

■ tube-like **vessels** to convey the medium to all parts of the body;

■ some kind of muscular **pump**, to propel the medium in the vessels;

■ one-way **valves** to keep the medium flowing in one direction;

■ a close association between the tissues and the medium so that the cells can obtain the required substances from the medium and deliver their products (including waste products) to it.

The transport medium

A few animals have a type of blood which is more or less like sea water. One of the substances to be transported is oxygen. Now, 100 cm³ of sea water can carry about 0.5 cm³ of oxygen, which is not very much, and such animals are therefore sedentary or slow-moving. More active animals usually have a **blood pigment**, the function of which is to increase the oxygen-carrying capacity of the blood. In most species the pigment is contained in special **blood cells**, but in some species it is free in the fluid part of the blood – the **plasma**.

Haemoglobins are the most common oxygen-carrying pigments. They are made up of two parts: a prosthetic group and a protein. The protein part consists of four polypeptide chains known as **globin**, each associated with a complex iron-containing prosthetic group called **haem** (*figure 13.2*). It is with the haem group that the association with oxygen takes place.

Haemoglobins are found in all vertebrates and some invertebrates, and each species has its own distinct form. In the account that follows we shall refer to them simply as haemoglobin.

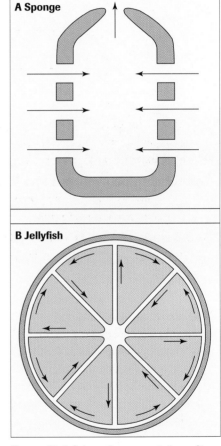

Figure 13.1 Schematic representations of two simple transport systems found in animals.
A In a sponge the body is perforated by many pores. A current of sea water is drawn in through the pores by the concerted action of numerous flagellated cells. The cells collect food particles from the water which then leaves through a hole at the top (*page 96*).
B In a jellyfish, a series of canals link the gut cavity to a peripheral circular canal. Cilia lining the canals cause sea water, drawn in through a mouth in the centre, to circulate, distributing digested food to all parts of the body. In both **A** and **B** the movement of water is indicated by the arrows.

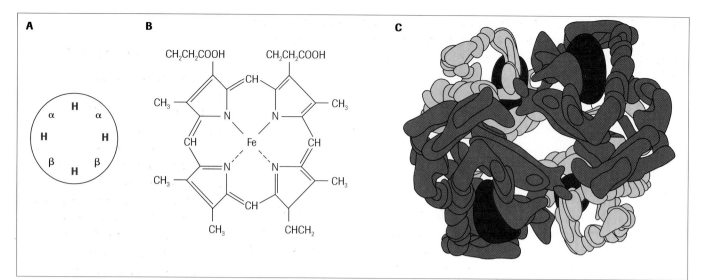

Figure 13.2 The chemical nature of haemoglobin. **A** A simple representation of human haemoglobin. The Hs stand for four haem groups, each of which contains an iron atom, and the α and β stand for two types of polypeptide chain. Each chain is associated with one of the four haem groups. **B** The structure of haem, the prosthetic group of haemoglobin. Haem, a porphyrin, is the part of the haemoglobin molecule that combines with oxygen. Note that the iron at the centre of the haem is in the divalent (iron (II)) state. It remains in this state while oxygen is being transported. **C** A model of the haemoglobin molecule as deduced from X-ray diffraction studies. In this model the α globin chains are brown and the β chains are grey. The haem groups are represented by the red discs.

Extension

The haemoglobin molecule as a carrier

Research by Max Perutz at Cambridge helps us to understand haemoglobin's affinity for oxygen.

When one of the four polypeptide chains in the haemoglobin molecule receives an oxygen molecule in the lungs, its structure is altered in such a way that the remaining three polypeptide chains accept oxygen more readily. In the tissues the reverse occurs: one of the polypeptide chains loses its oxygen molecule and this causes the others to give up their oxygen more readily. In other words haemoglobin takes up oxygen more rapidly if it already possesses one or more oxygen molecules, and conversely it releases oxygen more rapidly if it has already released one or more oxygen molecules.

The chemical explanation of this depends on the fact that each of the four polypeptide chains is associated with an iron-containing **haem group** (*figure 13.2*). It is thought that when an oxygen molecule joins on to the iron atom in the first haem group, the position of the polypeptide chains is altered slightly. This has the effect of exposing the iron atoms of the remaining haem groups to oxygen molecules, which are then readily taken up. Thus, although the oxygen is actually carried by the haem, its ability to do so is influenced by the associated polypeptide chains.

It is thought that hydrogen ions, derived from the carriage of carbon dioxide, lower haemoglobin's affinity for oxygen by binding to the polypeptide chains, thereby influencing the haem groups and reducing their tendency to take up oxygen.

13.2 **Carriage of oxygen by haemoglobin**

We have already said that most oxygen-carrying pigments are contained in special blood cells. In mammals, haemoglobin is found inside the **red blood cells** which are dealt with in Chapter 14 where we consider the structure of the blood. For the moment it is sufficient to note that oxygen diffuses into the red blood cell across its plasma membrane and combines with the haemoglobin to form **oxyhaemoglobin**. It has already been explained that each of the four haem groups in the haemoglobin molecule can combine with a molecule of oxygen, so a single haemoglobin molecule can carry a total of four oxygen molecules. The attachment of the oxygen does not involve chemical oxidation of the iron which remains in the iron(II) state throughout the process. The union is a loose one, the oxygen molecules being attached to the haemoglobin in the lungs and equally readily detached in the tissues:

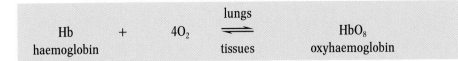

$$\text{Hb} + 4O_2 \underset{\text{tissues}}{\overset{\text{lungs}}{\rightleftharpoons}} HbO_8$$

haemoglobin   oxyhaemoglobin

Oxygen dissociation curve

The ability of the blood to transport enough oxygen to meet the needs of the body is largely attributable to the affinity of haemoglobin for oxygen. This can be demonstrated experimentally by subjecting samples of blood to different partial pressures of oxygen, and then determining the percentage saturation of the blood with oxygen in each case (partial pressures are explained in the support box alongside).

In practice, the blood samples are placed in a series of cylindrical glass containers into which air mixtures of known oxygen partial pressure are introduced. Each sample of blood is given time to come to equilibrium with the air mixture, and then its percentage saturation is determined. If the percentage saturation is then plotted against the oxygen partial pressure, an **oxygen dissociation curve** is obtained.

You will notice in figure 13.3 that the curve is S-shaped (sigmoid). This is very appropriate for a blood pigment. Over the steeply rising part of the curve, a small increase in the partial pressure of oxygen achieves a relatively high percentage saturation of the blood. The flat part of the curve at the top corresponds to the situation in the lungs: over this range a high saturation is maintained even if the partial pressure of oxygen in the alveoli falls. So the oxygen dissociation curve favours the loading of haemoglobin with oxygen in the lungs.

The oxygen dissociation curve, as well as facilitating the loading of haemoglobin with oxygen in the lungs, also facilitates unloading in the tissues. The steep part of the curve corresponds to the range of oxygen partial pressures found in the tissues. Over this part of the curve, a small drop in oxygen partial pressure will bring about a comparatively large fall in the percentage saturation of the blood. So if the partial pressure of oxygen falls as a result of the tissues utilising oxygen at a faster rate, the haemoglobin gives up more of its oxygen.

The shape of the oxygen dissociation curve therefore ensures that the red blood cells take up oxygen in the lungs and release it in the tissues. The points where loading and unloading of oxygen typically occur are indicated in figure 13.3 as the arterial and venous pO_2 respectively.

The effect of carbon dioxide on the oxygen dissociation curve

In the experiment just described all factors, apart from the partial pressure of oxygen, were kept constant. Consider now what happens if the experiment is repeated at three different partial pressures of carbon dioxide. The results are shown in figure 13.4. You will notice that increasing the partial pressure of carbon dioxide has the effect of shifting the oxygen dissociation curve to the right. This is called the **Bohr effect** after the scientist who first discovered it, Christian Bohr. (He was the father of the eminent Danish physicist, Niels Bohr, who proposed a structure for the hydrogen atom in 1913.)

When the Bohr effect is operating, the haemoglobin must be exposed to a higher partial pressure of oxygen in order to become fully saturated. But equally it will release its oxygen at higher partial pressures of oxygen. In other words carbon dioxide makes the haemoglobin less efficient at taking up oxygen, but more efficient at releasing it.

What is partial pressure?

The partial pressure of a gas is a measure of its concentration and is expressed in kilopascals (kPa). For example, at sea level the total atmospheric pressure is 101.3 kPa and because the atmosphere contains approximately 21 per cent oxygen, this gas contributes 21 per cent of the total pressure, which is 21.2 kPa. In other words, the partial pressure of oxygen in the atmosphere is a measure of how much of the whole atmospheric pressure is due to the oxygen present in it. (The partial pressure of oxygen is written pO_2.)

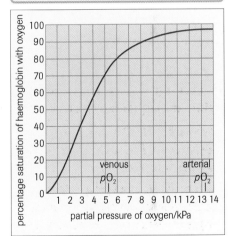

Figure 13.3 Oxygen dissociation curve for human haemoglobin. The sigmoid shape indicates haemoglobin's affinity for oxygen.

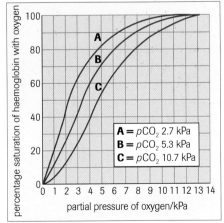

Figure 13.4 The influence of three different concentrations of carbon dioxide on the oxygen dissociation curve for human haemoglobin. Notice that the effect of a high concentration of carbon dioxide is to shift the curve to the right, i.e. it lowers the affinity of haemoglobin for oxygen.

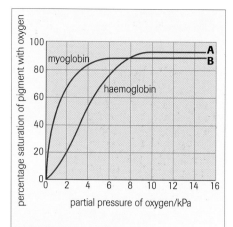

Figure 13.5 Oxygen dissociation curves for myoglobin and haemoglobin. Notice that the myoglobin curve is well to the left of the haemoglobin curve, indicating its much higher affinity for oxygen.

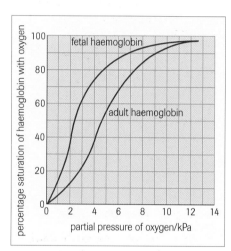

Figure 13.6 The oxygen dissociation curves for adult and fetal human haemoglobin. Notice that the fetal haemoglobin curve is well to the left of the adult haemoglobin, indicating its much higher affinity for oxygen.

The release of oxygen is therefore favoured in the tissues where the partial pressure of carbon dioxide tends naturally to be high as a result of its continual release from the respiring cells. On the other hand in the lungs the partial pressure of carbon dioxide is relatively low owing to its continual escape into the atmosphere, and this favours oxygen uptake.

Oxygen dissociation curves of myoglobin and other blood pigments

From the discussion so far, the fact emerges that the further an oxygen dissociation curve is to the left, the more firmly the pigment absorbs and holds on to its oxygen. There are certain types of blood pigment which readily take up oxygen even when the partial pressure of oxygen is very low. Such is the case with **myoglobin**, which has an oxygen dissociation curve situated well to the left of haemoglobin (*figure 13.5*).

Closely related to haemoglobin chemically, myoglobin is found in muscles where it remains fully saturated with oxygen at partial pressures well below that required for haemoglobin to give up its oxygen. Myoglobin *stores* oxygen, releasing it when the partial pressure of oxygen falls very low, as in severe muscular exertion. Myoglobin is responsible for the colour of 'red muscles', and is particularly abundant in animals which are liable to suffer from oxygen shortage, for instance very active animals and diving mammals such as seals.

Interestingly, the haemoglobin of animals like the lugworm, which burrow in oxygen-deficient mud, is functionally similar to myoglobin. The oxygen dissociation curve of lugworm haemoglobin is situated well to the left of human haemoglobin and reflects its unusually high affinity for oxygen at low partial pressures.

Not only do the haemoglobins of different species vary widely in their affinities for oxygen, but they may even change during the life cycle of a single individual. For instance, the haemoglobin of the human fetus (**fetal haemoglobin**) has an oxygen dissociation curve situated to the left of adult haemoglobin. The reason is that fetal blood has to pick up oxygen from the mother's blood across the placenta, and this can only take place if the fetal haemoglobin has a higher affinity for oxygen than the mother's haemoglobin (*figure 13.6*).

The explanation of the Bohr effect, the shifting of the oxygen dissociation curves by carbon dioxide, is to be found in the mechanism by which carbon dioxide is transported in the blood.

> **Extension**
>
> ### Haemoglobin and carbon monoxide
>
> An unfortunate property of haemoglobin is that it combines even more readily with carbon monoxide than with oxygen. The result of this union is **carboxyhaemoglobin**. The carbon monoxide combines with the haemoglobin at the sites normally occupied by the oxygen molecules, thus preventing the latter from taking up their normal position. This makes carbon monoxide a powerful 'respiratory poison'. Carbon monoxide is a constituent gas of vehicle exhaust and cigarette smoke, and indeed is formed whenever combustion is incomplete, such as in gas-fired central heating boilers.

13.3 **Carriage of carbon dioxide**

Carbon dioxide diffuses from the tissues into the red blood cells where it combines with water to form carbonic acid, H_2CO_3. This is normally a very slow reaction, but in the red blood cell it is greatly accelerated by the presence of the fast-acting enzyme **carbonic**

anhydrase (*page 125*). Because of this enzyme, most of the carbon dioxide enters the red blood cells rather than remaining in the plasma. The carbonic acid then dissociates into hydrogencarbonate and hydrogen ions.

If the hydrogen ions were allowed to accumulate they would increase the acidity of the cell and kill it. However, they are **buffered** by the haemoglobin itself. Their presence encourages the oxyhaemoglobin to dissociate into haemoglobin and oxygen. The latter diffuses out of the cell to the tissues, and the haemoglobin takes up the hydrogen ions forming a very weak acid, **haemoglobinic acid** (HHb). It is therefore clear that the Bohr effect is due not to carbon dioxide as such, but to the hydrogen ions resulting from its presence. These chemical events are summarised in figure 13.7.

The carriage of carbon dioxide as just explained results in an accumulation of hydrogencarbonate ions in the red blood cell, but the plasma membrane is highly permeable to these negative ions, which therefore readily diffuse out into the plasma. However, the membrane is relatively impermeable to positive ions, so the inside of the cell tends to develop a net positive charge. Electroneutrality is maintained by an inward movement of chloride ions from the plasma, the so-called **chloride shift**.

Although most of the carbon dioxide is carried in this way, some of it combines with amino groups in the haemoglobin molecule, forming **carbaminohaemoglobin** (HbCO$_2$). A very small amount of carbon dioxide, probably not more than 5 per cent, never gets into the red blood cells at all but dissolves in the plasma and is carried in solution.

When the red blood cells reach the lungs, the partial pressure of oxygen is high and the partial pressure of carbon dioxide is low. With this sudden change in the equilibrium conditions, the reactions described above go into reverse. As a result oxygen is taken up by the red blood cells and carbon dioxide is released.

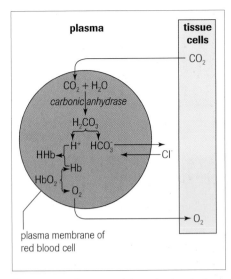

Figure 13.7 Summary of the main chemical events that take place in a red blood cell on reaching the tissues. The uptake of carbon dioxide results in the formation of hydrogen ions (H$^+$) whose presence aids the dissociation of oxygen from oxyhaemoglobin (HbO$_8$). The haemoglobin combines with the hydrogen ions, forming haemoglobinic acid (HHb). This promotes oxygen dissociation.

Part 2

Extension

Other oxygen-carrying pigments

There are several other groups of blood pigments and they differ mainly in the nature of the prosthetic group. **Chlorocruorin** and **haemoerythrin** both contain iron, and **haemocyanin** contains copper. These three pigments are confined to invertebrate groups, particularly annelids and molluscs. Blood pigments are compared in the table.

From the table you can see that the pigments differ in their oxygen-carrying capacities and that in some cases they are dissolved in the plasma rather than contained inside cells.

A comparison of oxygen-carrying pigments found in different groups of animals.

	Haemoglobin	**Chlorocruorin**	**Haemocyanin**	**Haemoerythrin**
Colour of pigment	red	green	blue	red
Metal in prosthetic group	iron	iron	copper	iron
Molecule of oxygen carried per atom of metal	1:1	1:1	1:2	1:3
Location in blood	cells or plasma	plasma	plasma	cells or plasma

Other substances carried in the blood

Other materials are also transported in blood. For example, soluble food materials, waste products and hormones are all conveyed from one place to another in the plasma. Cells are constantly shedding things into the blood which flows past them, and removing things from it. Blood provides the medium through which this continual exchange takes place.

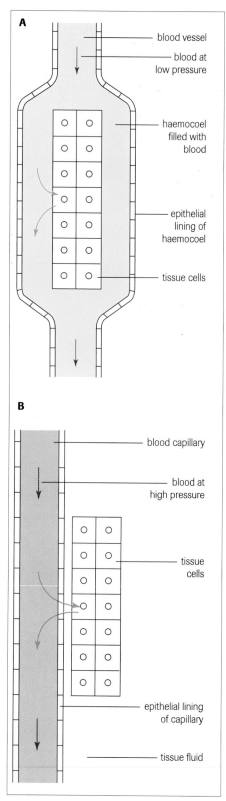

A

- blood vessel
- blood at low pressure
- haemocoel filled with blood
- epithelial lining of haemocoel
- tissue cells

B

- blood capillary
- blood at high pressure
- tissue cells
- epithelial lining of capillary
- tissue fluid

Figure 13.8 A An open circulation. **B** A closed circulation. Notice the close relationship between the blood and the tissue cells. The green arrows signify exchanges between the tissue cells and the blood.

13.4 Pumps and circulations

If the transport medium is to be efficient at moving substances around the body, some kind of pump is required. Certain animals, nematodes for example, depend on contractions of the body wall to move the blood around. However, such contractions alone will not keep the blood moving in a particular direction, so this is not very efficient.

If, however, the blood is enclosed in a tubular vessel, contraction of the muscle in the wall of that vessel may produce a **directional flow** which is what is needed if the blood is to **circulate**. In annelids such as the earthworm, the dorsal vessel contracts: waves of contraction pass from the posterior end of the vessel towards the anterior end, sweeping the blood forward. However, in most animals there is a specialised pumping device – the **heart**.

Open and closed circulations

There are two kinds of circulatory systems in animals: **open** and **closed**. They both allow the transported materials to be exchanged between the blood and the cells, but there is a different relationship between the blood and the surrounding tissue in each case (*figure 13.8*).

- In **open systems**, the blood circulates in large open spaces. The cells are in contact with the blood and materials are exchanged by direct diffusion through the plasma membranes. Arthropods and most molluscs have this kind of circulatory system. In insects, for example, the body cavity is filled with blood, and is called a **haemocoel**. Here, the blood seeps around amongst the organs which are literally bathed in blood.

  Because the blood is in large spaces and the heart is only weakly muscular, the blood pressure can never be very high. This limits the efficiency of the open system. Open blood systems are therefore not found in large animals.

  In insects, gaseous exchange takes place through the tracheal system (*page 162*). The insect circulatory system is not therefore concerned with transporting oxygen and carbon dioxide. Accordingly, it lacks an oxygen-carrying pigment. However, it does play an important part in distributing food substances and eliminating nitrogenous waste matter.

- In **closed systems**, the blood is entirely enclosed within tubular vessels. Gaseous exchange occurs across the wall of blood **capillaries** which ramify through the organs and come into close association with all the cells. This sort of system is typical of vertebrates, including humans, and of annelids and cephalopod molluscs.

  In animals with a closed system, the heart is more muscular and higher blood pressures can be developed, which makes closed systems much more efficient than open ones. Animals with closed systems are generally larger, and often more active, than those with open systems. We shall look in detail at the closed system of the mammal in Chapter 14.

  A disadvantage of a closed circulatory system is that the blood is in vessels and their walls form a barrier between the blood and the surrounding tissue cells. Oxygen and other substances have to cross this barrier into the surrounding tissue fluid and thence into the cells. At the same time, waste products diffuse from the cells into the **tissue fluid** and so to the blood capillaries.

From this you can see that simple diffusion is the main way of getting substances into and out of the cells, even in animals with closed circulatory systems. The circulation simply moves the transport medium (blood) as near to the tissue cells as possible. So diffusion, which is the only method of transport in small organisms, is also important in large animals even though they have a transport system to move materials over long distances.

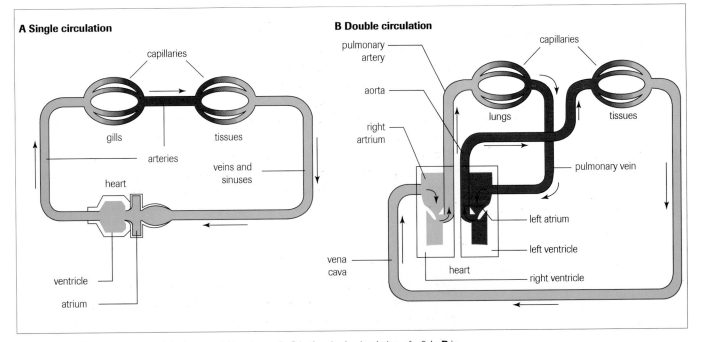

A Single circulation

capillaries

gills

tissues

arteries

veins and sinuses

heart

ventricle

atrium

B Double circulation

pulmonary artery

aorta

right artrium

vena cava

capillaries

lungs

tissues

pulmonary vein

left atrium

left ventricle

heart

right ventricle

Figure 13.9 The arrangement of the heart and blood vessels **A** in the single circulation of a fish; **B** in the double circulation of a mammal. The arrows indicate the direction of the blood flow. Oxygenated blood, red; deoxygenated blood, blue.

Single and double circulations

Animals with closed circulations have two fundamentally different systems which are illustrated in figure 13.9. The simpler of the two is seen in fish.

In fish, deoxygenated blood is pumped by the heart to the gills, from which the oxygenated blood flows to various parts of the body and then returns to the heart. The blood flows only once through the heart for every complete circuit of the body; this is called a **single circulation** (*figure 13.9A*).

The problem with this arrangement is that blood has to pass through two capillary systems, the capillaries of the gills and then those of the rest of the body, before returning to the heart. Capillaries offer considerable resistance to the flow of blood, and this means that in fish there is a marked drop in blood pressure before the blood completes a circuit. For this reason the blood flow tends to become sluggish as the venous blood returns from the tissues to the heart. This is overcome to some extent by the fact that fish have wide **sinuses**, which offer minimum resistance to blood flow, in place of narrow veins. Nevertheless the problem of getting blood back to the heart is an acute one and probably imposes severe limitations on the activities of many species of fish.

In mammals, this problem has been overcome by the development of a **double circulation** in which deoxygenated blood is pumped by the heart to the lungs, after which the oxygenated blood returns to the heart and is then pumped to the rest of the body. So the blood flows twice through the heart for every complete circuit of the body (*figure 13.9B*).

Returning to the single circulation, some fish are able to swim very fast in spite of the fact that the amount of oxygen which can be delivered to the tissues is limited by the relatively low blood pressure. The explanation lies partly in the fact that fish are ectotherms and their metabolic rate is sufficiently low for the limited oxygen supply to satisfy their needs.

A higher metabolic rate demands a higher oxygen supply and this is only possible if the pressure in the vessels carrying the oxygenated blood to the tissues is also higher. Birds and mammals, being endotherms, have a higher metabolic rate than fish. An increased

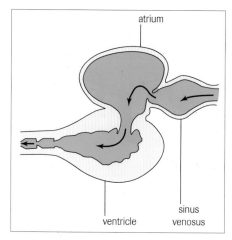

Figure 13.10 The two-chambered heart of a fish viewed from the side. The blue tint represents deoxygenated blood.

Extension

Do plants have a circulatory system?

The xylem transports water and mineral salts from the roots to the leaves, and the phloem transports sugars and other products of photosynthesis from the leaves to the roots. These photosynthetic products are in solution, the water having come from the xylem. At the root end of the system sugars are removed by the cells for use in metabolic processes, and water flows out by osmosis into the intercellular spaces.

Some of the water which flows out in the roots is taken up into the xylem, and is transported up to the leaves again where it may be used in photosynthesis, lost by evaporation through the stomata or drawn into the phloem whence it may return to the roots again.

So although there are two distinct transport systems, xylem and phloem, it is possible for water to be transported between leaves and roots in a closed loop, travelling up in the xylem and down in the phloem. Plants, therefore, may be said to have a circulatory system.

oxygen supply could in theory be achieved by having a higher pressure in a single circulation, but in animals with lungs the necessary pressure would be so high that it would drive fluid through the capillary walls, causing the lungs to become waterlogged. In mammals, blood is pumped to the lungs at a much lower pressure than that at which it is pumped to the rest of the body. In humans, the pressure in the pulmonary artery is about one sixth of that in the aorta.

Separation of oxygenated and deoxygenated blood

In the single circulation of a fish, only deoxygenated blood flows through the heart. The heart has two main chambers, the **atrium** and the **ventricle**, the ventricle being more muscular than the atrium. It is an S-shaped structure and there is a chamber before the atrium called the **sinus venosus** from which the heartbeat originates (*figure 13.10*).

In mammals, with a double circulation, the heart is divided into right and left sides with two atria and two ventricles. This division of the heart prevents the oxygenated blood on the left side mixing with the deoxygenated blood on the right side. The structure of the mammalian heart is dealt with in detail in the next chapter so there is no need here to elaborate on it further except to emphasise that oxygenated and deoxygenated blood are kept completely separate.

The general principle being illustrated is that if a double circulation is to be developed, it must be coupled with some kind of mechanism for keeping the deoxygenated and oxygenated bloodstreams apart. The mammalian heart, being divided into completely separate right and left sides, achieves this admirably. It is really two pumps joined together which work simultaneously and send out blood at different pressures to different places.

Having a double circulation is only one way of overcoming the pressure problem. An alternative solution would be to have a single circulation with two hearts, one for pumping deoxygenated blood to the gaseous-exchange surface and another one for pumping the oxygenated blood to the rest of the body. This is what happens in squids and octopuses. Octopuses are on a quite different evolutionary line from vertebrates, but like vertebrates they are active creatures. Comparing their circulations shows us how the same physiological problem can be solved in two quite different ways and is one reason why studying animals other than the mammal can be so interesting.

13.5 Transport in plants

Vascular plants have two distinct transport systems, both of which consist of tubes. One system is concerned with the movement of water and mineral salts which are obtained from the soil, the other with transporting sugars and other soluble products of photosynthesis from the leaves to other parts of the plant.

Plants are relatively inactive and their metabolic needs are such that they do not need the dynamic type of transport system characteristic of most animals. However, the distances over which substances need to be moved can be far greater than in animals – think of the size of a redwood tree for example. As plants have no pump, like the heart, the question we have to ask is: how are the contents of their transport systems moved?

We shall look at the detailed structure and functioning of the transport systems of plants in Chapter 15. It is sufficient here to note that the system of tubes in which water and mineral salts are transported is the **xylem**, while the system of tubes conducting dissolved food substances is the **phloem**.

The fascinating thing is that the two systems employ quite different principles. Xylem transport is essentially a passive process, depending mainly on water potential gradients within the plant. Indeed, the xylem tissue in which it takes place is composed of dead cells. Phloem transport, on the other hand, is an active energy-requiring process which takes place in living tissue.

Summary

1. There is a need for the distribution of raw materials and the removal of metabolic products in all organisms.

2. In small organisms, the transport of materials can take place by **diffusion**. However, larger organisms generally require special **transport systems**.

3. Transport systems usually involve **mass flow**, which is the movement of particles in a gaseous or liquid medium in the same direction and at the same speed.

4. The transport systems of animals range from water-filled canals to blood-filled **circulatory systems**.

5. Essential features of most circulatory systems include a **transport medium** (**blood**), tubular **vessels** to carry the medium, a muscular **pump** to propel the medium, a system of **valves** for keeping the medium flowing in one direction, and a close association between the medium and the tissue cells.

6. In many animals, the oxygen-carrying capacity of the blood is increased by the presence of a **blood pigment**. **Haemoglobin** is the most common pigment but there are others. The pigments may be free in the plasma or in blood cells.

7. Haemoglobin's affinity for oxygen is lowered by the presence of carbon dioxide. Thus loading of haemoglobin with oxygen is favoured in the lungs, whereas unloading is favoured in the tissues.

8. **Myoglobin** and **fetal haemoglobin** have a higher affinity for oxygen than adult haemoglobin, and this is related to their functions.

9. The carriage of carbon dioxide in the blood depends on the presence in the red blood cells of the enzyme **carbonic anhydrase**.

10. There are two kinds of circulatory systems in animals, **open** and **closed**. Open systems are typical of arthropods and molluscs; closed systems are typical of vertebrates.

11. In open systems, the blood is in a cavity called the **haemocoel** which contains the organs. In closed systems, the blood is enclosed within vessels which separate it from the tissues; exchange of materials takes place via **tissue fluid**.

12. In most animals blood is pumped around the circulatory system by means of a **heart**.

13. A circulatory system in which blood flows only once through the heart for every complete circuit of the body is called a **single circulation**. A **double circulation** is one in which the blood flows through the heart twice for every complete circuit of the body.

14. Fish have a single circulation with an undivided heart. A double circulation requires that oxygenated and deoxygenated blood are kept separate, so in mammals the heart is divided into right and left sides.

15. Plants have two transport systems, both consisting of tubes: the **xylem** transports water and mineral salts, and the **phloem** transports the products of photosynthesis.

16. Xylem and phloem transport involve quite different principles: xylem transport is essentially passive whereas phloem transport is active.

17. Because of the closed system that seems to exist between the xylem and phloem, plants may be said to have a circulatory system.

Practice questions

For general advice on these questions and advice on answering essay-type questions, see pages vii and viii.

1. (a) The oxygen capacity of an animal's blood is the amount of oxygen carried in the blood when it is saturated. The table on the right gives the oxygen capacity of the blood of various vertebrates. In all cases the blood contains haemoglobin. Comment on the figures. (8)

    (b) Most invertebrates have blood with low oxygen capacities (generally ranging from 0.1 to 2.5 cm^3 O_2 per 100 cm^3) but there are two notable exceptions: the lugworm *Arenicola* has a capacity of 8.0 and the cuttlefish *Sepia* has the capacity of 7.0 cm^3 O_2 per 100 cm^3. Comment. (2)

Animal	Oxygen capacity (cm^3 O_2 per 100 cm^3 of blood)
human	20.0
seal	29.3
llama	23.4
crocodile	8.0
frog (*Rana esculenta*)	9.8
carp	12.5
mackerel	15.7
electric eel	19.75

(Total 10 marks)

2. The graph below shows the oxygen dissociation curve for the pigment haemoglobin in a human. The loading tension is the partial pressure of oxygen at which 95% of the pigment is saturated with oxygen. The unloading tension is the partial pressure at which 50% of the pigment is saturated with oxygen.

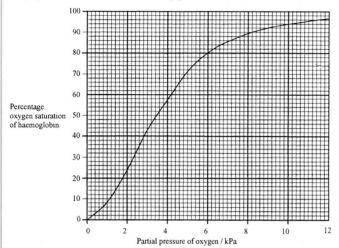

(a) Explain why haemoglobin is an efficient respiratory pigment. (2)

(b) (i) From the graph determine the difference between the loading and unloading tensions of the haemoglobin. Show your working. (2)

(ii) Give one location in the human body where partial pressures lower than the unloading tension may be reached. Give a reason for your answer. (2)

(c) Suggest what effects increasing concentrations of carbon dioxide in the blood would have on the loading and unloading tensions of human haemoglobin. Give reasons for your answers. (4)

(d) The oxygen dissociation curve for fetal haemoglobin lies to the left of the curve for adult haemoglobin. Suggest an explanation for this difference. (2)

(e) State *three* ways in which carbon dioxide is transported in the blood. (3)

(Total 15 marks)

London 1996

3. A small amount of oxygen diffuses from the blood into the small intestine of a mammal. Some parasitic platyhelminths living in the small intestine can make use of this oxygen.

The graph shows oxygen dissociation curves for human haemoglobin and for the haemoglobin of a parasitic platyhelminth which lives in the human small intestine.

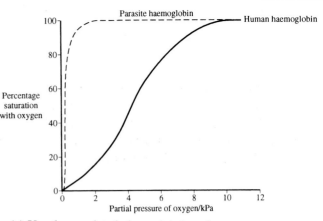

(a) Use the graph to help explain how human haemoglobin releases oxygen when it reaches the cells of the wall of the small intestine. (3)

(b) Explain one advantage to the parasite of having haemoglobin with an oxygen dissociation curve like that shown on the graph. (2)

(Total 5 marks)

AEB 1996

4. The graph shows the results of an experiment in which the effect of temperature on the oxygen dissociation curve of human blood was investigated.

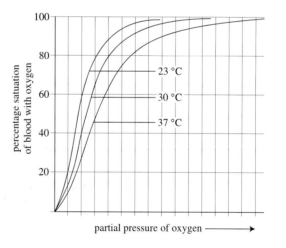

(a) How would you explain these results? (2)

(b) Suggest one other condition which would have the same kind of effect as temperature on the oxygen dissociation curve, and explain its effect. (3)

(Total 5 marks)

5. What sort of organisms require a transport system, and why? Support your answer with examples. (5 marks)

6. What is meant by mass flow? Explain the importance of mass flow in transporting substances inside organisms. (5 marks)

hapter 13 was concerned with the general features of transport systems in animals and plants. In this chapter we shall look specifically at the transport system of the mammal. The composition and functions of blood will be considered, followed by the structure and dynamics of the circulatory system. Adjustments to unusual conditions and disorders of the heart and circulation are also discussed.

14.1 Blood

Mammalian blood is a specialised tissue consisting of several types of cell suspended in a fluid medium called **plasma** (*figure 14.1*). The cellular constituents consist of:

- **red blood cells** (**erythrocytes**), which carry oxygen;

- **white blood cells** (**leucocytes**), which have an important role in the immune system (*Chapter 19*);

- **blood platelets**, cell fragments involved in blood-clotting (*page 228*).

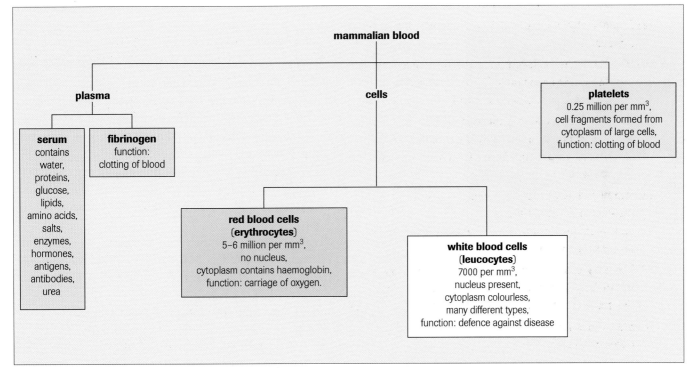

So, blood has a varied structure and performs a wide range of functions. As far as transport is concerned, its two important components are the red blood cells and plasma.

Plasma

Plasma is mainly water containing a variety of dissolved substances which are transported from one part of the body to another. Thus food materials (such as glucose and amino acids) are conveyed from the small intestine to the liver, urea from the liver to the kidneys, hormones from various endocrine glands to their target organs, and so on. Cells are constantly shedding substances into the blood which flows past them, and removing other substances from it. Plasma provides the medium through which this continued exchange takes place.

Figure 14.1 Chart summarising the constituents of mammalian blood. The two components responsible for transport are the red blood cells and the plasma. The white blood cells are responsible for defence against disease and are considered in Chapter 19. The red cells are manufactured in the red bone marrow in the centre of certain bones, from which they pass into the general circulation. The numbers of the different types of cells in the blood are approximate.

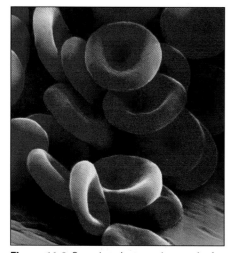

Figure 14.2 Scanning electron micrograph of red blood cells showing their biconcave surfaces. Magnification ×4000.

 Blood groups, page 337

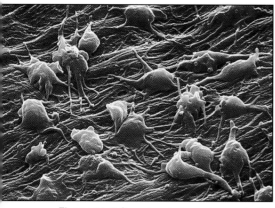

Figure 14.3 Scanning electron micrograph of activated platelets showing their thin extensions. Magnification ×3500.

Red blood cells

The prime function of the red blood cells is to carry oxygen from the lungs to the tissues, and their structure is adapted accordingly; they also play a part in transporting carbon dioxide. If you look at a smear of human blood on a slide under a microscope, you will see that the red blood cells are small and numerous. There are approximately five million per cubic millimetre, each about 8 μm across at its widest part.

The red blood cell has a unique structure. There is no nucleus, and other organelles are absent. The cell is sunk in on each side giving it the shape of a **biconcave disc** (*figure 14.2*). Surrounded by a thin, flexible plasma membrane, the inside of the cell is filled with the red pigment **haemoglobin** (*page 218*). The lack of a nucleus permits more haemoglobin to be packed into the cell.

The red blood cell has a limited life span of about 120 days. The red bone marrow manufactures new ones at the rate of about $1\frac{1}{2}$ million per second to replace those destroyed. A single red blood cell contains 250 million molecules of haemoglobin, each of which can carry four molecules of oxygen. It is therefore possible for 1000 million molecules of oxygen to be carried by a single cell. The biconcave disc provides a large surface–volume ratio for the absorption of oxygen. Details of the carriage of gases are described in the previous chapter.

14.2 Blood clotting

We are all familiar with the way our blood congeals when we cut ourselves. This is called **blood clotting**.

When a blood vessel is damaged, speed is vital in order to prevent loss of blood, so the clotting system has to come into action quickly. Within the first few seconds, small bodies in the bloodstream called **platelets** stick to the damaged tissue and send out chemical messages which trigger a series of changes terminating in the formation of a gel-like **clot**.

Platelets are fragments of cells, shaped like flattened discs, which arise in the bone marrow. During their short life of five to seven days they circulate in the blood until they detect damage to a blood vessel, which may be a puncture from outside or damage to the inner side of the wall. Very quickly they become sticky and change from flattened discs to spheres with long thin projections (*figure 14.3*). They then stick to the damaged surface of the blood vessel.

These activated platelets attract **clotting factors** from the plasma and also release certain clotting factors themselves. In addition they release ADP which causes more platelets to become sticky, with the result that a large number of platelets clump together at the site of the damage.

Most of the clotting factors are plasma proteins. They exist in a soluble and inactive state in the blood and are activated by the breaking of one or more of their peptide bonds. They are mostly given Roman numerals (up to XII), and when one factor acts on the next it turns it into its active state. Some of them are enzymes. However, factor V and factor VIII (lack of which causes the inherited blood-clotting deficiency disease, haemophilia) are not enzymes but help to bind enzyme and substrate molecules together. The factors act one on another in a kind of 'cascade' (*figure 14.4*).

Calcium ions, phospholipids and vitamin K also play a part in the clotting process. The phospholipids are associated with the membrane surrounding the platelets. Many of the factors are dependent for their formation or action on vitamin K, a group of quinone compounds found in abundance in vegetables.

What activates the first clotting factor in the cascade? There is, as yet, no certain answer, though contact of the platelets with an unfamiliar surface seems to be an important stimulus triggering the process. Also important in initiating clotting is a protein called **thromboplastin** which is released from damaged tissues.

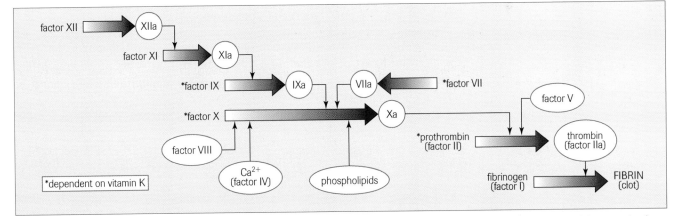

This cascade of factors leads to the formation of factor X. This causes a protein called **prothrombin** to form **thrombin**. Thrombin then acts on the soluble plasma protein **fibrinogen**, causing it to turn into solid threads of **fibrin**. The fibrin threads tangle together and trap protein and water molecules, forming the clot itself. When this happens, the long arms of the platelets shorten and draw back into the centre of the platelet. This has the effect of pulling together the edges of the cut and reducing the loss of blood and entry of microorganisms. At the same time the platelets secrete a substance which causes the local capillaries to constrict, further reducing blood loss.

Why should the clotting process be controlled by such a complex succession of factors? There are two main reasons. Firstly, it allows an initially small stimulus to generate a relatively large response – in other words, it *amplifies* the response. Secondly, by controlling the individual steps in the cascade, the final response can be finely tuned so as to meet precisely the requirements at the place where the clot occurs.

Of course it is imperative that clotting should not occur inside normal healthy blood vessels. An anticoagulant called **heparin** is secreted by mast cells in the walls of the blood vessels, and this may help to prevent clotting occurring inside the blood vessels. Heparin has the effect of inhibiting thrombin, so fibrinogen cannot be converted into fibrin. In addition, mechanisms exist which quickly remove any fibrin that may be formed in the blood. In this way the blood is maintained in a fluid state. The building up of plaque in the walls of the vessels can disrupt these mechanisms and cause clotting to occur inside a vessel. This is what happens in a heart attack (*page 240*).

Figure 14.4 Diagram of the cascade of factors required for blood clotting. Each factor, which has a Roman numeral, is converted to its activated form, e.g. factor XI to XIa, which then activates the next factor down the pathway.

Part 2

Extension

Haemophilia, factor VIII and HIV

One of the most common blood-clotting disorders is **haemophilia A** which is caused by a deficiency or complete absence of factor VIII. Haemophilia A is a sex-linked disorder which affects approximately 5000 males in the United Kingdom (*page 589*).

During the 1960s it became possible to concentrate factor VIII from donated blood and give it to males suffering from haemophilia A. As a result the quality of life for many haemophiliacs improved greatly. To a large extent haemophilia ceased to be a life-threatening condition.

A single donor never gives more than a pint (500 dm³) at any one time, and this contains only a minute amount of factor VIII. As a result, each haemophiliac receives factor VIII from thousands of different donors. It had long been realised that this put haemophiliacs at a significant risk of developing viral hepatitis, as only one of these thousands of donations needed to come from someone with this disease for the recipient to become infected too. In 1985 it became apparent that HIV (human immunodeficiency virus) was spreading among haemophiliacs in the same way. By then a total of 1200 of the 5000 haemophiliacs in the UK had become infected with HIV. By January 1990 over 100 of them had died from AIDS.

Since 1985, donated factor VIII has been heat-treated so as to destroy the virus. Infection with HIV by this route is therefore no longer a risk for haemophiliacs. In the long term, genetically engineered microorganisms may be used to produce factor VIII, so eliminating altogether the need for blood donation.

14.3 **The mammalian circulation**

The general layout of the mammalian circulatory system is shown in figure 14.5. Basically, the muscular **heart** pumps the blood into a system of **arteries** which branch into **arterioles**. Within the tissues the arterioles branch into **capillaries** where exchange of materials between blood and cells takes place. From the capillaries, blood is collected up into a series of **venules** which join up to form **veins** in which the blood returns to the heart.

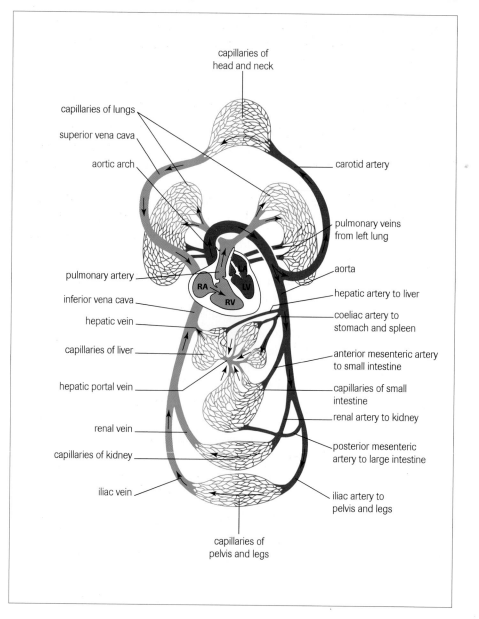

Figure 14.5 General plan of the mammalian circulation. Arteries to the arms are not shown: they arise from the aortic arch shortly after it leaves the heart. Bilaterally disposed organs such as the arms, legs and kidneys have paired arteries and veins, i.e. one on each side of the body. Median organs such as the gut have unpaired arteries and veins. Most of the veins carry blood straight back to the heart, but the hepatic portal vein is an exception: it carries blood from the gut to the liver and is unique in having capillaries at both ends. **RA**, right atrium; **LA**, left atrium; **RV**, right ventricle; **LV**, left ventricle. Oxygenated blood, red; deoxygenated blood, blue.

The heart is divided into four chambers: **right** and **left atria**, and **right** and **left ventricles**. Blood returning to the heart from all parts of the body, except the lungs, enters the right atrium, whence it passes into the right ventricle, and then via the **pulmonary artery** to the lungs. This is relatively deoxygenated blood, oxygen having been removed from it and carbon dioxide added to it during its passage through the tissues. As this blood flows through the capillaries in the lungs it unloads its carbon dioxide and takes up oxygen.

The oxygenated blood now returns via the **pulmonary vein**s to the heart, entering the left atrium. From this chamber it passes into the left ventricle, and thence to the **aorta**, the main artery of the body. From this, numerous arteries, some single and some paired, convey blood to the capillary systems in the organs and tissues, where gaseous exchange takes place. Corresponding veins convey the deoxygenated blood to the **venae cavae** (great veins) by which it is returned, once again, to the right atrium.

The walls of the arteries and veins are elastic, and the heart and veins are equipped with **valves** which prevent blood flowing backwards.

From a functional point of view, the two most important parts of the circulatory system are the heart and the capillaries. As the organ responsible for pumping the blood, the heart is of the utmost importance in maintaining the tissues in a state of health and efficiency. The capillaries represent the place where exchange of materials takes place, and as such provide the *raison d'être* for the circulatory system. We will deal with these two parts of the circulatory system in more detail later.

14.4 The heart

The heart undergoes contraction (**systole**) and relaxation (**diastole**) rhythmically throughout the animal's life. Its performance is prodigious: in the course of a normal human life span the heart beats over 2.5×10^9 times, pumping a total of more than 1.5×10^6 litres of blood from each ventricle.

Figure 14.6 shows the mammalian heart, and the passage of blood through it. As we have already seen, blood returning via the venae cavae enters the right atrium. The resulting pressure in this chamber forces open the flaps of the **atrioventricular valve** (also known as the **tricuspid valve** because it consists of three flaps). The result is that blood flows through the atrioventricular opening into the right ventricle.

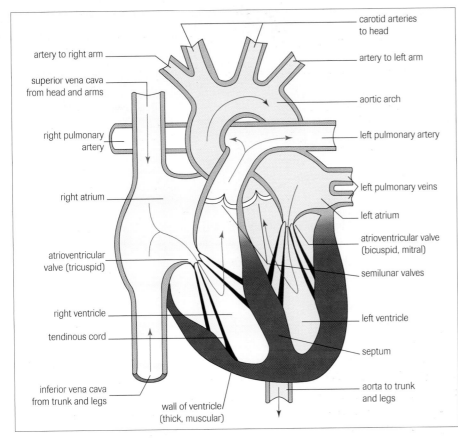

Figure 14.6 Ventral view of the mammalian heart and the blood vessels connected to it. Oxygenated blood, red; deoxygenated blood, blue. The arrows indicate the direction of blood flow. The atrioventricular valve on the right side of the heart consists of three flaps or cusps (tricuspid valve); the atrioventricular valve on the left side of the heart consists of two flaps (bicuspid or mitral valve). The semilunar valves at the entrance to the pulmonary artery, and at the entrance to the aortic arch, consist of pocket-like flaps which catch the blood if it tries to flow back into the heart. They are called semilunar valves.

When the atrium and ventricle are full of blood, the atrium suddenly contracts, propelling the remaining blood into the ventricle. The contraction spreads from the right atrium over the rest of the heart. Atrial systole is relatively weak but the ventricles, whose thick walls are particularly well-endowed with muscle, contract more powerfully. As a

Figure 14.7 Atrioventricular valves and tendinous cords in a sheep's heart. The tendinous cords prevent the flaps of the valve being pushed inside out by the pressure of blood when the ventricle contracts.

result, blood is forced from the right ventricle into the pulmonary artery.

The blood is prevented from flowing back into the atrium by the flaps of the atrioventricular valve, which closes tightly over the atrioventricular opening. The atrioventricular valve is prevented from turning inside out by tough strands of connective tissue, the **tendinous cords** ('heart strings') which run from the underside of each flap to the wall of the ventricle (*figure 14.7*).

Once in the pulmonary artery, blood is prevented from flowing back into the ventricle by **semilunar valves** guarding the opening of the artery. Semilunar means 'half moon' and each valve consists of three half-moon shaped pockets which fill with blood and close if the blood should start to flow backwards.

From the lungs, oxygenated blood returns to the left atrium via the pulmonary veins. It flows into the left ventricle and so into the **aortic arch** which leads to the aorta. This flow of blood takes place in the same way as on the right side of the heart. A minor difference is that the atrioventricular valve consists of two flaps rather than three, for which reason it is called the **bicuspid valve**. It is also known as the **mitral valve** because its two flaps are rather like a bishop's mitre.

Although systole starts at the right atrium, it quickly spreads to the left so that the whole heart appears to contract synchronously. Thus deoxygenated blood is pumped from the right ventricle into the pulmonary artery at the same time as oxygenated blood is pumped from the left ventricle into the aortic arch. Figure 14.8 shows the flow of blood through the heart and the actions of the valves.

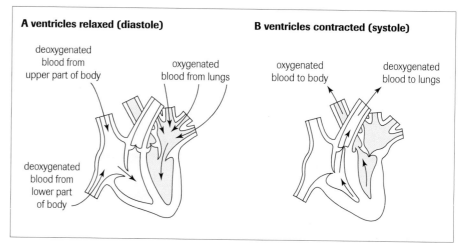

Figure 14.8 Flow of blood through the heart during diastole and systole and the action of the valves. Ventricles relaxed: atrioventricular valves open, semilunar valves closed. Ventricles contracted: atrioventricular valves closed, semilunar valves open. Oxygenated blood, red; deoxygenated blood, blue.

Systole is followed by diastole, during which the heart refills with blood again. The entire sequence of events is known as the **cardiac cycle**, and is accompanied by electrical activity in the wall of the heart and by 'sounds' corresponding to the closing of the various valves. The mammalian cardiac cycle is summarised in figure 14.9.

The output of the heart

The rate at which blood flows through the heart varies according to the body's need for supplies of oxygen and glucose, and for the need to remove metabolic products. The total volume of blood expelled from the heart per minute is called the **cardiac output** and it depends on two things:

▩ the **stroke volume**, that is the volume of blood expelled from the heart at each beat; and

▩ the **cardiac frequency**, the number of beats per minute.

When you are at rest, the cardiac output is approximately 5 litres per minute. During exercise, the stroke volume and cardiac frequency both increase to such an extent that the cardiac output may reach over 20 litres per minute.

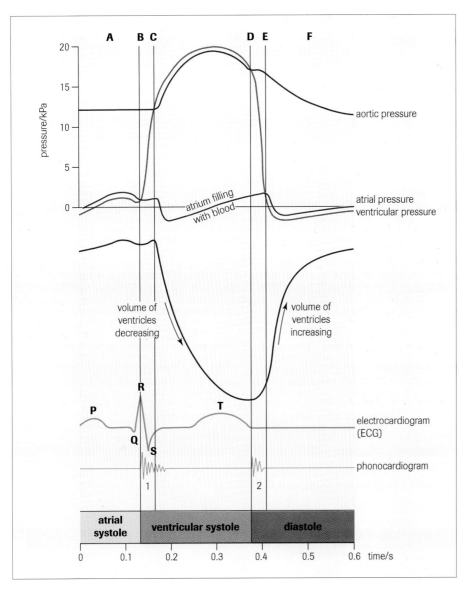

Part 2

Figure 14.9 Graphs illustrating the pressure and volume changes that occur during the mammalian cardiac cycle. Pressure changes were measured in the left atrium and ventricle, and the aorta. Volume changes were measured for both ventricles. The electrical activity in the heart wall (electrocardiogram) and heart sounds (phonocardiogram) as recorded in a human subject are also shown. The actions at different points on the graphs are as follows:
A Atrium contracting: blood flows into ventricle.
B Ventricle starts to contract: ventricular pressure exceeds atrial pressure so atrioventricular valve closes.
C Ventricular pressure exceeds aortic pressure, forcing semilunar valve open: blood therefore flows from ventricle into aorta, and ventricular volume falls.
D Ventricular pressure falls below aortic pressure resulting in closure of semilunar valve.
E Ventricular pressure falls below atrial pressure so blood flows from atrium to ventricle; ventricular volume rises rapidly.
F Atrium continuing to fill with blood from pulmonary vein: atrial pressure exceeds ventricular pressure so blood flows from atrium to ventricle.
Electrocardiogram (ECG): P wave corresponds to wave of excitation spreading over atrium; QRS and T waves correspond to wave of excitation spreading over ventricle.
Phonocardiogram: the first and second heart sounds (labelled 1 and 2 in the diagram) are due to sudden closure of atrioventricular and semilunar valves respectively.

Cardiac muscle

One of the most remarkable things about the heart is that it can contract rhythmically throughout our lives without fatiguing. It owes this property to the muscle tissue in its wall. Known as **cardiac muscle**, it consists of a network of interconnected **muscle fibres** (*figure 14.10*). The fibres are divided up into uninucleate cells containing fine contractile **myofibrils**. The muscle fibres show the same kind of cross-banding as skeletal muscle, and the mechanism of contraction is substantially the same (*Chapter 23*). The interconnections between the fibres ensure a rapid and uniform spread of excitation throughout the wall of the heart, which in turn gives rise to a synchronous contraction.

The blood supply to the heart

It is, of course, essential for cardiac muscle to have its own good blood supply and this is provided by the **coronary circulation**. The blood carrying oxygen and glucose is delivered to the cardiac muscle by the right and left **coronary arteries** which are the first blood vessels to arise from the aorta. They divide into branches which encircle the heart and lead to an extensive capillary network.

The greater thickness of the walls of the ventricles compared to the walls of the atria is related to the difference in the contraction forces of the two chambers. The relatively weak

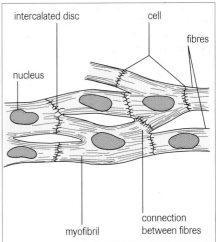

Figure 14.10 Network of cardiac muscle fibres as seen under the light microscope. Notice the connections between adjacent fibres. These facilitate the spread of excitation over the heart and cause synchronous contraction of the muscle. The intercalated discs are reinforced plasma membranes and serve as tough junctions between the myofibrils of successive cells.

William Harvey – an English physician

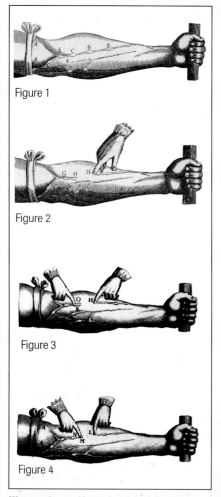

Figure 1

Figure 2

Figure 3

Figure 4

Illustration 1 Harvey's original drawings demonstrating that blood flows towards the heart in the cutaneous vein of the arm.
Figure 1 On tying a ligature around the upper arm, the veins in the arm show up as small swellings at B, C, D, etc.
Figure 2 If blood is pushed down with the finger from O to H, blood does not flow back through valve O.
Figure 3 If an attempt is made to push the blood through valve O, the valve becomes swollen but the part of the vein between O and H remains empty.
Figure 4 If a finger is put at L and another finger M pushes the blood towards and beyond the valve N, the part of the vein from N to L remains empty because the blood cannot pass back through the valve at N. When the finger at L is removed, the vein fills with blood again.

Illustration 2 Harvey demonstrates his famous experiment on the circulation in the arm to a group of physicians in London.

At one time it was thought that blood was pumped from the heart and subsequently drawn back into it via the same vessels, a sort of ebb-and-flow system. This kind of thing does happen in certain invertebrate animals, but not in vertebrates. That the blood circulates was first discovered by the 17th century physician, William Harvey (1578–1657). By meticulous dissection and ingenious experiments, Harvey showed beyond all reasonable doubt that blood flows away from the heart in certain vessels (arteries), and returns to it in different vessels (veins).

In 1628, William Harvey published an account of his experiments, *Anatomica de mortu cordis et sanguinis in animalibus* (On the anatomy and motions of the heart and blood in animals) – a book which has been described as the most important publication in the history of medicine. It is remarkable to find a book published so long ago in which the anatomical detail is so accurate.

One of Harvey's experiments is shown in illustration 1 – a simple experiment to be sure, but a masterpiece of deductive reasoning. The painting in illustration 2 shows Harvey demonstrating his technique to a group of physicians in London. The conclusion to be drawn is that blood flows in only one direction in the arm vein, and is prevented from flowing in the other direction by the valves.

Although Harvey discovered that the blood circulates in mammals, he was unable to demonstrate the existence of vessels connecting the arteries and veins. This was left to the Italian physiologist, Marcello Malpighi, who, towards the end of the 17th century, saw and described capillaries and demonstrated that they form the link between the arteries and veins.

contraction of the atrial walls sends blood into the ventricles, but the contraction of the walls of the ventricles is much greater, sending blood either to the lungs (right ventricle) or to the rest of the body (left ventricle). The greater thickness of the walls of the left ventricle relates to the greater force needed to send blood to all parts of the body except the lungs.

The blood is returned from the heart muscle to the right atrium of the heart in the **coronary veins**.

What makes the heart beat?

Most muscles contract as a result of impulses reaching them from nerves. This is not, however, true of the heart, which will continue beating rhythmically even after its nerve supply has been cut. Indeed the heart will go on beating for a short time after it has been entirely removed from the body, a fact which is of importance in heart transplant operations. Cardiac muscle is, therefore, **myogenic**: its rhythmical contractions arise from within the muscle tissue itself.

What then initiates this rhythm? The mammalian heart has a specialised plexus (network) of fine cardiac muscle fibres embedded in the wall of the right atrium, close to where the venae cavae enter it. This is called the **sinoatrial node** (**SAN**), and experiments have shown that it serves as a **pacemaker**. If cut out, it will continue to beat at the normal rate. Other pieces of excised atrium will also beat on their own, but at a slightly slower rate. Pieces of excised ventricle contract very much more slowly – at about a third of the normal rate.

So, different parts of the heart are capable of beating at their own intrinsic rate. However, in the intact heart the beating of the ventricles is dependent on the atria, and the atria on the SAN. In other words the SAN, the region of the heart with the fastest intrinsic rhythm, sets the rate at which the rest of the heart beats.

Confirmation that the SAN is the pacemaker has come from recording electrical activity from various parts of the heart wall. It has been found that contraction of the heart is preceded by a wave of electrical excitation, similar to the nerve impulse discussed in Chapter 20. This starts at the SAN and then spreads over the two atria, accompanied by contraction (*figure 14.11*). When the wave reaches the junction between the atria and ventricles, it excites another specialised group of cardiac muscle fibres called the **atrioventricular node** (**AVN**). Continuous with the AVN is a strand of modified cardiac muscle fibres, called the **bundle of His**. This runs down the interventricular septum and fans out over the walls of the ventricles where it breaks up into a network of fibres called **Purkinje tissue** (also called **Purkyne tissue**) just beneath the endothelial lining.

When the AVN receives excitation from the atria, it sends impulses down the bundle of His to the Purkinje tissue. The impulses then spread out to the cardiac muscle tissue in the walls of the ventricles, making it contract. The role of the Purkinje tissue is not to contract, but simply to transmit excitation over the ventricles, and its microscopic structure bears this out (*figure 14.12*). The most remarkable aspect of the whole performance is that the

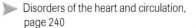 Disorders of the heart and circulation, page 240

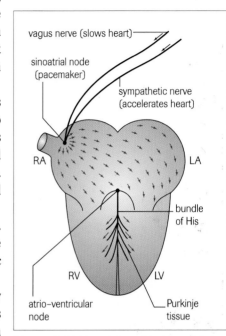

Figure 14.11 Ventral view of the heart showing the spread of electrical excitation that causes contraction. The rhythmical beating of the heart is initiated by the pacemaker, the nerves merely serving to speed up or slow down its rate. The Purkinje tissue transmits impulses relatively slowly, so as to ensure that the ventricles contract after the atria. The Purkinje tissue is named after a Czechoslovakian physiologist.

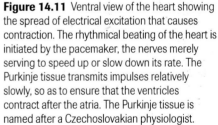

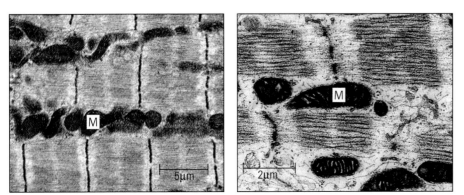

Figure 14.12 Microscopic structure of the heart wall. *Far left* Electron micrograph of part of a cardiac muscle cell. The cell contains numerous myofibrils of which several can be seen here in longitudinal section. Note the densely packed mitochondria (M) between the fibrils, for providing energy. The banding pattern in the fibrils has the same basis as in skeletal muscle (*page 405*). *Left* Conducting tissue in the wall of the ventricle. This consists of modified cardiac muscle fibres which, instead of contracting, conduct electrical impulses like nerves. Compare this electron micrograph with the appearance of cardiac muscle seen in the far left picture. Notice that the conducting tissue has fewer myofibrils and mitochondria.

rhythmical initiation of the excitatory waves by the pacemaker is quite independent of nervous control.

Not only is the rhythmical beating of the heart independent of nervous control, but the heart automatically pumps into the arteries the same amount of blood as it receives from the veins, even when the latter varies. This is because the extent to which the cardiac muscle contracts is proportional to the initial length of the muscle fibres. In other words, the more the muscle is stretched during diastole, the greater is the subsequent systolic contraction.

Innervation of the heart

The fact that the pacemaker initiates the rhythmical beating of the heart does not mean it has no nerve supply. On the contrary, it receives two nerves, a **sympathetic nerve** which is part of the sympathetic nervous system, and a branch of the **vagus nerve** which belongs to the parasympathetic nervous system (*page 366*). These do not initiate the beating of the heart, but can modify the activity of the pacemaker, speeding up or slowing down the rate at which the heart beats.

The roles of the two nerves have been demonstrated by attaching a heart to a lever that writes on a slowly revolving drum. The sympathetic and vagus nerves are hooked on to fine electrodes through which weak electrical stimuli can be delivered. In this way impulses can be generated in one or other of the two nerves. The results of such an experiment are shown in figure 14.13. If the sympathetic nerve is stimulated, the heart speeds up; if the vagus is stimulated, it slows down.

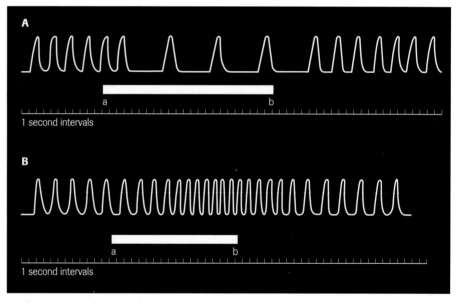

Figure 14.13 The effect on a heart of stimulating **A** the vagus nerve and **B** the sympathetic nerve with high-frequency stimuli. In each case the period of stimulation was from a to b. The recordings were made by attaching the heart to a lever which wrote on a revolving drum (kymograph). Note that impulses in the sympathetic nerve speed up the heart rate, whereas impulses in the vagus slow it down.

The vagus and sympathetic nerves are therefore antagonistic in their effects. This double innervation makes an animal's transport system much more versatile than would otherwise be the case. It means that the cardiac output can be modified to suit the needs of the animal as occasion demands.

14.5 Arteries and veins

Blood is expelled from the heart only when it contracts. Blood flow through the arteries is therefore intermittent, the blood flowing rapidly during systole and slowly during diastole. However, by the time the blood reaches the capillaries it is flowing evenly (*figure 14.14*). The gradual change from intermittent to even flow is made possible by the elasticity of the arterial walls which contain much elastic tissue and smooth muscle (*figure 14.15*).

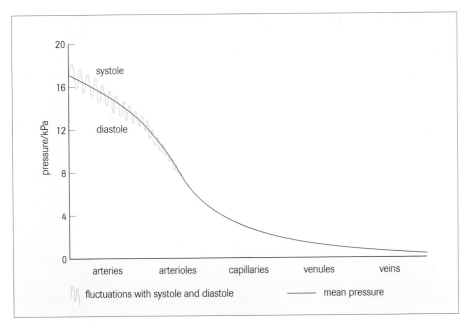

Figure 14.14 Changes in blood pressure in different parts of the circulatory system of a human subject. The fluctuations in the flow of blood in the arteries, caused by contraction and relaxation of the heart (systole and diastole), gradually decline as blood flows from the arterioles into the capillaries and so to the veins.

When blood is pumped into the aorta, the semilunar valves at the entrance prevent the back-flow of blood to the heart and the wall of the first part of the artery therefore becomes distended. As the heart relaxes, the distended section of the artery recoils, which distends the next section – and so on. Thus a wave of distension followed by recoil (the **pulse wave**) progresses along the artery. The blood itself flows more slowly than the pulse wave, falling to 1 mm per second by the time it reaches the capillaries. To some extent the blood is kept flowing by wave-like contractions of the smooth muscle in the walls of the smaller arteries.

Veins have thinner walls and a larger lumen than arteries. In the limbs, blood flow through them is assisted by contraction of the skeletal muscles which squeezes the blood along (*figure 14.16*). Back-flow is prevented by valves, and by the relatively large diameter of the veins which minimises the resistance to forward flow. Also the negative pressure developed in the thorax during inspiration will tend to draw blood back to the heart. Contraction of the smooth muscle in the walls of the veins can also facilitate the return of blood to the heart.

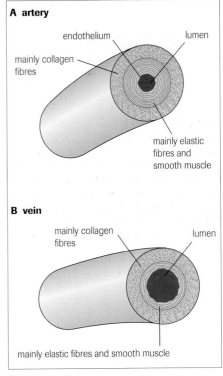

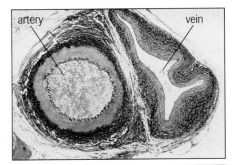

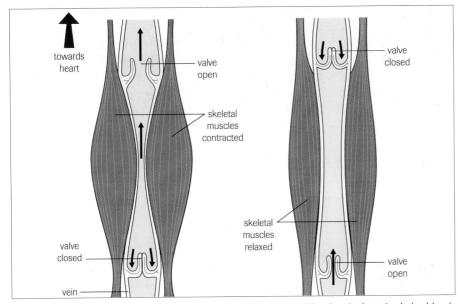

Figure 14.16 The contraction of skeletal muscles in conjunction with valves in the veins helps blood to return to the heart. If blood flows backwards it is caught in the pocket-like valves as indicated by the downward-pointing arrows.

Figure 14.15 The structure of an artery and a vein. The walls contain elastic and collagen fibres and smooth muscle. They are therefore tough but stretchable and can constrict or dilate. The vein has a thinner wall and wider lumen than the artery. The diagrams show the arrangement of the different types of tissue in the walls.

14.6 Capillaries

As a transport system, the job of the circulation is to take up substances in one part of the body and deliver them to another. There must therefore be an intimate relationship between the circulatory system and the tissues. This is achieved by the **capillaries**.

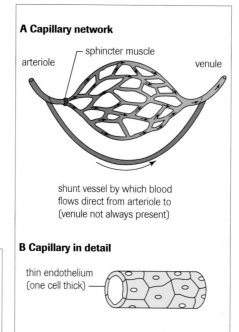

A Capillary network

arteriole — sphincter muscle — venule

shunt vessel by which blood flows direct from arteriole to (venule not always present)

B Capillary in detail

thin endothelium (one cell thick)

Figure 14.17 Diagram of a capillary network. The capillaries provide a vast irrigation system which supplies the cells with their needs. It is said that if all the body's capillaries were placed end to end they would extend for over 80 000 km! The bore of the capillaries averages about 10 μm, just wide enough to permit the passage of red blood cells in single file. The single layer of lining epithelial cells is, at its thinnest, less than 0.1 μm thick, thus facilitating rapid exchange of materials between the blood and tissue cells. No cell is more than 25 μm from the nearest capillary. The capillaries have no muscle layer and are incapable of changing their diameter to any extent. Blood flow through them is controlled by constriction or dilation of the arterioles, whose walls contain smooth muscle, and of the sphincter muscles at the ends of the arterioles. Oxygenated blood, red; deoxygenated blood, blue.

Figure 14.17 shows a small part of a capillary network. In contrast to arteries and veins, the capillaries are narrow (an average of 10 μm in diameter) and thin walled. The wall consists of a single layer of very thin **squamous epithelium** which allows rapid diffusion of dissolved substances into or out of the capillary (*page 63*). The cells are bathed in **tissue fluid** derived from the blood plasma which provides a medium through which diffusion can take place. The close proximity between the capillaries and the tissue cells, and the thinness of the barrier between them, facilitates exchange of materials.

The flow of blood through the capillaries can be regulated locally. Rings of muscle surround the ends of the arterioles at the points where they break up into capillaries. Under the influence of nerves, hormones or local conditions, these **sphincter muscles** contract or relax, thereby decreasing or increasing the flow of blood through them.

In some parts of the body larger vessels form a direct connection between arteries and veins, and so bypass the capillaries. By constricting or dilating, these **shunt vessels** can regulate the amount of blood which flows through a particular set of capillaries at any given time. This occurs in parts of the body where the blood flow needs to be adjusted from time to time (*page 305*).

The capillaries are like a vast irrigation system, different parts of which can be opened or closed according to local needs and conditions. This, coupled with the fact that the heart can vary its rate of beating, makes the mammalian circulation a highly adaptable transport system.

14.7 Blood pressure

Blood pressure is the term used to describe the pressure in the aorta and major arteries. It is highest when the ventricles contract (**systolic pressure**) and lowest when the ventricles relax (**diastolic pressure**). It is normally measured in the brachial (arm) artery by means of a **sphygmomanometer**, an inflatable arm-band connected to a manometer.

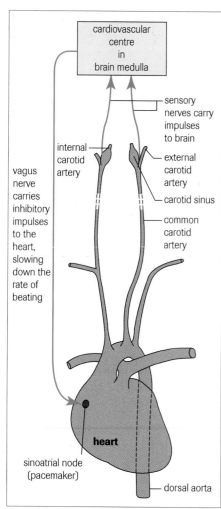

cardiovascular centre in brain medulla

sensory nerves carry impulses to brain

internal carotid artery

external carotid artery

carotid sinus

common carotid artery

vagus nerve carries inhibitory impulses to the heart, slowing down the rate of beating

heart

sinoatrial node (pacemaker)

dorsal aorta

Figure 14.18 How changes in blood pressure bring about changes in the heart rate. An increase in arterial pressure stimulates stretch receptors in the walls of the carotid sinuses which leads to a slowing of the heart.

The lymphatic system

In Chapter 16, the interchange of materials between capillaries and tissue fluid, the formation and reabsorption of tissue fluid and the formation of lymph are described. In this box we are concerned with the **lymphatic system** which makes up a drainage system for tissue fluid, returning it, as lymph, to the blood.

The lymphatic system is shown in the illustration on the right. It consists of **lymphatic capillaries** into which the lymph drains. They are similar to blood capillaries but with thinner walls which reflects their greater permeability. The capillaries converge to form the larger **lymphatic vessels** which are similar in structure to veins but with more numerous valves. The movement of lymph is also similar to the movement of blood in the venous system. Lymphatic vessels may be distinguished from veins by the lack of red blood cells. These vessels ultimately form two main ducts – the **thoracic duct** into which most of the lymph from the left side of the body drains, and the **right lymphatic duct** which receives the rest. These vessels return lymph to the blood via the left and right subclavian veins . The subclavian veins bring blood back to the heart from the arms via the superior vena cava (*page 230*).

The lymph enters numerous **lymph nodes** during its course through the lymphatic vessels; the function of these is described on page 322.

The lymph vessels in the villi of the small intestine are called **lacteals**. They play an important part in the absorption of fat (*page 193*).

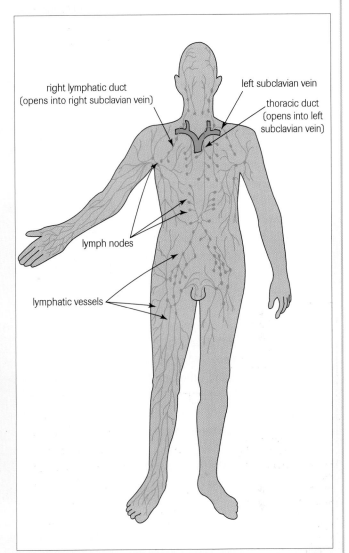

The lymphatic system in the human showing the main vessels (the vessels in the left limbs have been omitted).

You might expect it to be expressed in kilopascals but it is medical practice to express it in millimetres of mercury, the normal healthy values being around about 120 mm Hg for systolic pressure and 80 mm Hg for diastolic pressure.

A rise in blood pressure means that the heart is overworking and this can put a strain on the circulatory system. A fall in blood pressure can affect the functioning of organs such as the kidneys. It is therefore important that blood pressure should be maintained within normal limits.

How is the blood pressure controlled? The main mechanism is summarised in figure 14.18. At the base of the internal carotid artery, on each side of the neck, is a small bulbous swelling called the **carotid sinus**. In its walls are sensory cells sensitive to stretching. If the arterial pressure rises, the walls of the carotid sinus are distended and the stretch receptors stimulated. Impulses are then transmitted via sensory nerves to a group of nerve cells in the medulla of the brain called the **cardiovascular centre**. This responds by sending out impulses in the appropriate effector nerves which reduce the cardiac output and dilate the peripheral blood vessels, thereby lowering the arterial pressure.

If the arterial pressure falls too much, the stretch receptors will stop being stimulated; the cardiac output will then increase and the peripheral blood vessels will constrict, resulting in a rise in arterial pressure. The carotid sinus is thus a sensitive pressure gauge, detecting changes in arterial pressure and signalling these to the cardiovascular centre. The latter then brings about appropriate adjustments. This is an example of a homeostatic system whose principles are discussed in Chapter 16.

Disorders of the heart and circulation

Disorders of the heart and circulation are called **cardiovascular disorders**. (Cardiovascular is a collective term describing anything which relates to both the heart and the circulation.)

In the United Kingdom, the number of deaths from cardiovascular disorders is amongst the highest in the world and is about twice the number of deaths from cancer. Caring for people with painful cardiovascular problems puts a very heavy demand on medical resources in terms of medical staff, equipment and drugs. The high death rate and the millions of working days lost every year make this almost certainly the most costly illness in this country.

It is a salutory fact that many of the factors associated with cardiovascular disorders are avoidable. Before addressing this aspect we will consider briefly the major types of cardiovascular disorder.

Coronary heart disease

When the flow of blood in the coronary arteries is interrupted, the heart muscle is partially or completely deprived of its supply of oxygen and other nutrients so it cannot function normally. The blocking of a main coronary artery is the commonest cause of sudden death in middle-aged and elderly people. If a branch of a coronary artery is blocked, the area of heart muscle supplied by that branch dies. This is called a **cardiac infarction** or **'heart attack'**. The usual symptoms are severe chest discomfort, which may spread to the neck and arms, accompanied by breathlessness. Another condition called **angina** results when the artery is narrowed so that the blood flow is reduced. This causes the same sort of

discomfort as that just described but it is less severe and tends to occur when people with this condition exert themselves.

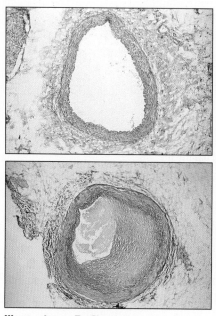

Illustration 1 *Top* Photomicrograph of normal coronary artery and *bottom* one showing an extensive plaque.

The two most common causes of a blockage of the coronary arteries are **atherosclerosis** and **coronary thrombosis**. Atherosclerosis is a thickening of the artery walls as a result of the deposition of fat and cholesterol in the inner lining of the artery. The deposit is called an **atheroma**. Calcium salts and fibrous tissue also accumulate and lead to the formation of hard, uneven patches called **plaques** which cause a narrowing of the artery and interfere with the even flow of blood (*illustration 1*).

The second cause of blockage – coronary thrombosis – is a blood clot (**thrombus**) in the coronary circulation which often forms when the surface of a

plaque breaks away. The clot then blocks the lumen of the blood vessel. If the clot becomes dislodged and travels through the bloodstream it is called an **embolus**.

Coronary artery disorders can also cause irregular or abnormal heart rhythms, a condition called **arrhythmia**. Some arrhythmias are normal, such as bradycardia (*page 244*) and tachycardia (a heart rate above 100 beats per minute which occurs normally during exercise and stress). But if the right coronary artery becomes blocked the sinoatrial node may be affected, leading to a slowing of the heart rate. In severe cases the heart may stop beating altogether and the person suffers a **cardiac arrest**. A blockage which severely affects the atrioventricular node or associated conducting tissue will lead to the atria and ventricles beating independently – a condition known as a **complete heart block** which is potentially fatal.

Arrhythmias and coronary atherosclerosis can be diagnosed by several procedures including **stress electrocardiograms (ECGs)** which record the electrical activity of the heart while exercising on a treadmill. **Angiography** is another technique used which involves injecting a dye into the bloodstream and then taking X-rays of the arteries called an **angiogram** (*illustration 2*). Anyone who suffers a heart attack and survives will have the heart function monitored by being connected to an electrocardiograph.

High blood pressure

High blood pressure (**hypertension**) is caused by a gradual increase in resistance to blood flow in the small arteries so that a high pressure is

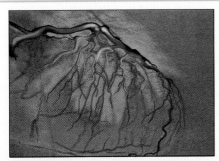

Illustration 2 Angiogram of a coronary artery showing narrowing (the pinched part at the top). The green/brown area shows where loss of blood flow has caused part of the heart muscle to die.

sustained even when the person is resting. This makes the heart work harder and, in time, it may enlarge and fail to pump effectively. Many people are unaware that they have high blood pressure because it may be symptomless. For this reason it is sometimes called the 'silent killer'. It is an increasing problem from middle-age onwards and contributes to the development of other cardiovascular disorders. A resting diastolic pressure of 130 mm of mercury is considered serious (*page 238*).

Arteriosclerosis

This is commonly referred to as 'hardening of the arteries', a condition in which the artery walls thicken and lose their elasticity. Fibrous deposits are laid down and deposits of calcium occur, giving rise to calcified plaques. In such arteries a thrombus is likely to develop and the vessel may rupture. Although it may be associated with atherosclerosis, it is essentially a condition that takes a long time to develop and is connected with ageing.

Treatment of cardiovascular disorders

There are several methods of treating cardiovascular disorders. Probably the best-known way of dealing with a blocked coronary artery is to have a **heart bypass** or – more accurately – a **coronary artery bypass**. Surgeons take a piece of a vein or artery from some other part of the body, a leg or arm for

example, and use it to bypass the blocked artery. During this operation the heart has to be stopped so the patient needs to be kept on a **heart–lung machine**.

Angioplasty is another technique, in which a tube made of plastic with a small balloon on the end containing a flexible metal guide wire, about the diameter of a human hair, is passed into the blocked coronary artery (*illustration 3*). The balloon is then inflated at the region of the blockage, pushing the plaque that is blocking the artery out of the way. The balloon and guide are then removed.

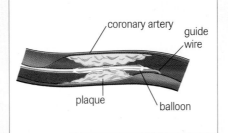

coronary artery

guide wire

plaque

balloon

Illustration 3 A drawing showing a balloon in a blocked artery ready to be inflated.

In cases of complete heart block and disturbance of the conducting system of the heart (the His–Purkinje system), an artificial **pacemaker** may be inserted. Pacemakers come in different types. In one type an insulated wire with an electrode at the end is inserted into a vein in the shoulder and guided into the right atrium and/or ventricle. The pacemaker itself consists of a battery which is placed under the skin in one shoulder, just below the collar bone.

Finally, drugs called **beta blockers** are used to prevent and treat angina and arrhythmia and to lower high blood pressure. A Scotsman, Sir James Black, received a Nobel Prize for Medicine in 1988 for his contribution in developing beta blockers. Briefly, they decrease the activity of the heart by inhibiting the so-called **beta receptors** at the ends of the sympathetic nerves supplying the heart. It is the activation of these receptors which increases the rate and force of the heartbeat during exercise, excitement or

anxiety. In a healthy heart these changes result in more blood being delivered to all parts of the body. When the blood vessels which supply the heart itself are narrowed, the heart muscle runs short of oxygen. Anaerobic respiration then occurs with an accumulation of lactic acid which contributes to the pain. Sir James Black realised that blocking these receptors would limit the increase in heart rate and reduce the need to switch to anaerobic respiration.

Risk factors

The main risk factors in cardiovascular disorders are as follows:

- **High level of cholesterol in the blood:** because of the link between high levels of cholesterol in the blood and heart attacks, it has seemed logical to suggest that people should reduce the intake of cholesterol in their diet. However, it has been established more recently that the cholesterol we eat is not the same cholesterol that plays a role in causing coronary heart disease. In fact the liver manufactures the cholesterol which causes the damage. It now seems to be more important to reduce the fat content of our diet, particularly **saturated fats**. Even this probably only reduces blood cholesterol level by about 10 per cent. It may not be long before products are available which actively lower cholesterol levels in the blood (*page 24*).

- **Obesity:** obese people run the risk of developing high blood pressure, atherosclerosis and diabetes among other problems (*page 154*).

- **Smoking:** smoking is a major contributing factor to the development of coronary heart disease as well as other problems (*page 175*).

- **Lack of regular exercise:** there has been a tendency in recent years for young people to become 'couch potatoes' and to sit around watching television. It has been shown that even half an hour of brisk exercise a day lessens the risk of coronary heart disease and it is encouraging that jogging and fitness programmes have become popular with people of all ages.

- **High blood pressure:** high blood pressure is more difficult to avoid as several factors may contribute to it. Heredity may play a part, so might diet, since a high salt intake can raise blood pressure in those predisposed to it. It is therefore desirable that blood pressure should be checked on a regular basis

and treated if it is found to be consistently raised.

- **Stress:** some heart disorders are accepted now as having a link to stress. There are many sources of stress in daily living. Strategies for coping with stress include aerobic exercises and mental relaxation.

- **Diabetes:** atherosclerosis can be a long-term complication of diabetes.

- **Family history:** a genetic predisposition to some cardiovascular disorders is recognised.

- **Age and sex:** coronary artery disease is much more common in middle-aged and old people than in younger people. It is also more common in men than women until about the age of 50. After the menopause in women there is little difference between the sexes.

Advice for avoiding cardiovascular disorders should certainly include the following:

- **don't smoke**
- **eat little fat**
- **take regular, brisk exercise.**

14.8 Control of the circulation

In Chapter 10 we saw that the ventilation centre in the medulla of the brain controls the rate of breathing. In a similar kind of way the cardiovascular centre controls the rate at which the heart beats. A number of reflexes are involved including the carotid sinus reflex already described (*page 238*). Another reflex occurs if the pressure in the right atrium increases. This causes impulses to pass to the cardiovascular centre, which then sends impulses along the sympathetic nerve to the heart. The heart rate is thus increased. This is called the **Bainbridge reflex**. So, depending on circumstances, the cardiovascular centre sends impulses along the sympathetic nerve to the heart, increasing its rate of beating; or along the vagus nerve, decreasing its rate of beating.

As with the ventilation centre, the cardiovascular centre is connected by nervous pathways to higher centres in the brain. It can therefore be influenced by impulses reaching it from the cerebral cortex. However, although we can exercise voluntary control over our rate of breathing, we cannot change the rate of our heartbeat at will.

Most people have experienced the increased pulse rate that accompanies excitement, shock and various other emotions. In this case impulses are conveyed from the higher centres to the sympathetic nervous system and thence to the **adrenal glands**. The latter respond by secreting the hormone **adrenaline** into the bloodstream. The effects of adrenaline are almost the same as those produced by the sympathetic nervous system, and their joint function is to prepare the body for coping with demands that may be made on the circulatory system, before they actually happen.

This is achieved by an increase in cardiac output which is brought about by an increase of heart rate and/or stroke volume (exercise, of course, increases both). This causes general constriction of arterioles except for those serving vital structures such as the skeletal muscle and heart itself. As a result there is a general rise in blood pressure, and blood is diverted to those places where it is needed most. This diversion of blood is enhanced by various local responses. For example, carbon dioxide tends to accumulate in the active muscles. This causes the arterioles serving these particular muscles to dilate, thereby increasing the blood flow through them.

Response to oxygen deprivation

What happens if an animal is suddenly deprived of oxygen? For most species the result is disastrous, death occurring within a matter of minutes. But certain animals, notably those

Surviving at high altitudes

A shortage of oxygen is experienced by people who visit, or live at, a high altitude (about 3000 metres) where the partial pressure of oxygen is less than at sea level (*page 174*). At this altitude unacclimatised people will experience breathlessness, severe fatigue, headache and often nausea.

People who live permanently at such an altitude, for example in the Himalayas and the Andes, possess certain adaptations which allow them to live there successfully. The inhabitants of the Peruvian mining community of Auconquilcha (called Quechuas) live at an altitude of 5330 metres and climb 450 metres each day to work but refuse to sleep at this height. There seems, therefore, to be a critical height at around 5500 metres above which permanent acclimatisation does not take place.

Among the adaptations possessed by these people are:

- **More haemoglobin:** in the Quechuas the haemoglobin concentration in the blood is 200 mg cm^{-3} compared with a sea level normal of 150 mg cm^{-3}. This is because the red blood cell count is 6.4×10^{12} dm^{-3} compared with a sea level value of 5.1×10^{12} dm^{-3}.

- **More myoglobin:** the myoglobin content of the body is around 25 per cent greater than at sea level.

- **More capillaries:** there is some evidence that the number of capillaries per unit volume of muscle is 25 per cent greater than at sea level. This increases the blood flow and reduces the distance over which oxygen has to diffuse to the tissue cells.

- **Hyperventilation:** the tidal volume is greater, which results in a 25 to 35 per cent increase in the volume of air breathed per minute than is normal at sea level.

- **Increased lung surface area:** the barrel-like chests of people living permanently at high altitude permit an increased lung size and greater vital capacity.

- **Larger and more numerous mitochondria:** there is an increase in both the size and number of mitochondria in the cells.

Mountaineers experience a shortage of oxygen when climbing at high altitudes and in the past many of them carried their own oxygen supply, but now it has become the norm to climb even Mount Everest without the use of extra oxygen. This is possible because a mountaineer who ascends slowly over a period of days or weeks has time to get used to the progressively rarefied atmosphere. At about 4000 m, he or she begins to develop signs of **mountain sickness** (breathlessness, headache, nausea and fatigue). However, these unpleasant symptoms wear off as one becomes **acclimatised**.

At high altitudes the heart works remarkably well; there is an initial increase in cardiac output but this eventually settles to sea-level values. However, people who ascend suddenly to high altitudes in balloons, aircraft and spacecraft, reach altitudes where oxygen is scarce or absent. In commercial aircraft the cabin pressure and oxygen content is increased to that which prevails at around 2500 metres, and astronauts only leave their pressurised cabins in space suits. High-altitude balloonists such as Richard Branson and others who attempt to go around the world would lose consciousness at around 6000 metres if they did not have an oxygen supply and/or a pressurised capsule (*illustration*).

Richard Branson's hot air balloon near Mount Fuji, Japan. The capsule was pressurised and an oxygen supply was available.

▶ Acclimatisation to temperature, page 310

▶ Breathing at high altitudes, page 174

Figure 14.19 The Weddell seal can remain submerged for an hour or more while diving. During the dive the blood flow to all parts of the body, except the central nervous system and heart, is restricted. The heart rate and output are reduced, but sufficient to maintain the blood pressure.

capable of diving, can survive for much longer. For example, the Weddell seal and certain species of whales can remain under water for an hour or more (*figure 14.19*). How is this achieved?

By recording the heartbeat, blood pressure and other variables in a variety of diving mammals, it has been found that very soon after the dive commences the cardiac frequency decreases dramatically. This is called **bradycardia** ('brady' is derived from the Greek word *brados*, meaning slowness). At the same time the arterioles of all but the vital organs constrict. This rapid reflex results in the body's oxygen store, derived from its haemoglobin and myoglobin, being sent to those organs that are least able to endure oxygen deprivation, namely the heart and brain. The lowered cardiac frequency is just enough to keep the tissues ticking over.

It is now known that this response is not restricted to diving mammals like seals and whales but is shown by many other animals, diving ducks for example, when confronted with sudden oxygen deprivation. It also occurs in humans – a human diver will develop bradycardia within 30 seconds after the beginning of a dive – and in fish it occurs when they are taken *out* of water. It therefore seems to be a life-saving response of general importance.

14.9 Adjustments during exercise

Let us now look at how changes in the circulatory and other systems enable an athlete to run a 100 m sprint. Here they are, in roughly the order in which they occur.

1. Before and during the early stages of the sprint, the sympathetic nervous system is alerted and adrenaline is secreted into the bloodstream. Triggered by impulses received from the brain in anticipation of the race, there is an increase in the cardiac output and general constriction of arterioles except for those serving vital organs, so that blood under high pressure is diverted to the active muscles. Anticipation of the race also brings about an increase in the ventilation rate so that oxygen can be delivered to the muscles more quickly.

2. During the sprint the metabolic rate increases. This is caused by shortage of ATP. We only have enough ATP in our muscles at any one time to provide for several seconds maximal exertion. ATP is therefore manufactured on the go. A decrease in the amount of ATP relative to ADP activates the enzyme which initiates the further breakdown of glucose or muscle glycogen (*page 146*).

3. The increased metabolic rate results in carbon dioxide building up in the skeletal muscle tissues. This causes local dilation of the arterioles, leading to an increased blood flow through the muscles. It has been found that the increase in body temperature (which may be up to 2°C after a game of squash and up to 4°C in a marathon) renders the tissues more sensitive to carbon dioxide, thereby accentuating this mechanism.

4. Rapid movement of the limbs stimulates stretch receptors in the skeletal muscles and tendons. These transmit impulses to the cardiovascular centre leading to a further increase in the cardiac output.

5. Any fluctuations in the level of carbon dioxide in the bloodstream are monitored by the chemoreceptors in the carotid and aortic bodies and medullary centre, leading to appropriate adjustments in the ventilation rate (*page 172*).

6. Despite the mechanisms described above, insufficient oxygen is delivered to the muscles to keep pace with their demands. As a result the muscles start respiring anaerobically with the formation of lactic acid (*page 147*). This accumulates during the race, but afterwards it is oxidised via the Krebs cycle or circulated to the liver where it is

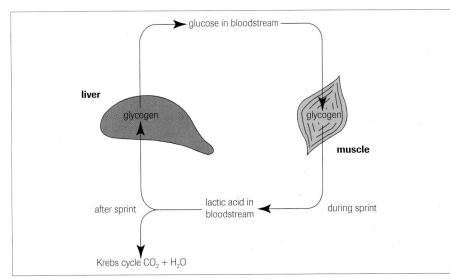

Figure 14.20 Scheme summarising carbohydrate metabolism during and after a sprint. As a result of the conversions shown here, energy is made available for the race, and the glycogen store in the muscle is replenished afterwards.

converted back to glycogen (*figure 14.20*). For this to happen oxygen is required. Constituting the so-called **oxygen debt**, it accounts for the heavy panting that ensues after the race.

7. The lactic acid which accumulates during the sprint has the same effect on the arterioles as carbon dioxide, i.e. it causes local vasodilation. It also stimulates the aortic and carotid bodies, thereby accentuating the ventilation responses initiated by the carbon dioxide.

8. Carbon dioxide itself will continue to increase, partly because of the oxidation of lactic acid in the Krebs cycle, but also because of the way lactic acid is buffered in the bloodstream. In this process lactic acid dissociates into lactate and hydrogen ions:

$$\text{lactic acid} \rightarrow \text{lactate} + H^+$$

The hydrogen ions then combine with hydrogencarbonate ions to form carbonic acid:

$$H^+ + HCO_3^- \rightarrow H_2CO_3$$

The carbonic acid then splits into water and carbon dioxide:

$$H_2CO_3 \rightarrow H_2O + CO_2$$

9. While all this has been happening, the greatly increased metabolic rate results in a rise in body temperature. This is offset by the body's cooling processes described in Chapter 18.

The same kind of adjustments occur in longer races. One difference, however, is that the oxygen debt may be paid on the run, an equilibrium being established between oxygen supply and oxygen usage. When this point is reached **second wind** is said to be acquired.

For the short period involved in a sprint, the muscles can function perfectly efficiently under anaerobic conditions, provided of course that the oxygen debt is paid immediately afterwards. This enables an athlete to hold his or her breath during the sprint. Under these circumstances circulatory and metabolic adjustments occur as described above, but changes in breathing are temporarily suspended until after the race.

Many complex physiological changes occur during muscular activity. What this brief and simplified account shows is that several different systems cooperate in bringing about appropriate adjustments, which together maintain the continued efficiency of the body.

Extension

Effects of athletic training

The aim of training for an athlete is, of course, to improve his or her performance. This is a specialised subject and we will only note the general effects on the ventilation and cardiovascular systems.

In general, training has the effect of increasing most lung volumes (*page 169*). They are larger in athletes than non-athletes of the same sex and body size. Athletes also have a greater diffusion capacity at the alveolar–capillary surface in the lungs, which may be because they have larger lung volumes. Training also results in an increase in the volume of oxygen consumed per minute.

Aerobic training refers to prolonged, usually continuous exercise of fairly low intensity which is undertaken by endurance athletes, such as distance runners. The effects of this on the cardiovascular system include an increase in the size of the heart (particularly the size of the left ventricle), a slowed heart rate (**bradycardia** - *page 244*) and an increased **stroke volume** (*page 232*). There is usually an increase in blood volume and in haemoglobin content. All these changes contribute to increasing the volume of oxygen consumed as more oxygen is extracted from the blood by the muscles, during exercise.

Summary

1. Mammalian blood is composed of **red blood cells** (**erythrocytes**), **white blood cells** (**leucocytes**) and **platelets** suspended in **plasma**. Dissolved food substances are transported in the plasma; oxygen by the red blood cells.

2. Mammalian red blood cells are non-nucleated, biconcave discs which contain the red pigment **haemoglobin** that carries oxygen.

3. The mammalian circulation with its **heart**, **arteries**, **capillaries** and **veins** is well adapted for delivering oxygen to the tissues at high speed.

4. The heart is divided into four chambers: two **atria** and two **ventricles**. Blood is propelled through the heart by a series of events which constitute the **cardiac cycle**. The ventricles have thick, muscular walls, and **valves** prevent blood flowing in the wrong direction.

5. The heartbeat is initiated by the **sinoatrial node** (**pacemaker**) which, though it has an innate rhythm, is influenced by its nerve supply. The **sympathetic nerve** accelerates the beating of the heart and the **vagus nerve** slows it.

6. Despite variations in the frequency with which it beats, the heart automatically pumps into the arteries the same amount of blood that it receives from the veins.

7. **Cardiac muscle** has a similar microscopic structure to that of skeletal (striated) muscle but adjacent fibres are interconnected. It contracts repeatedly without fatigue. The mechanism of contraction is similar to that of skeletal muscle.

8. Arteries and veins are adapted in their structure and properties for carrying blood away from, and back to, the heart respectively.

9. Capillaries are narrow, thin-walled vessels which come into intimate association with the tissue cells. Exchanges take place between the capillary blood and the neighbouring tissues.

10. The **lymphatic system** enables tissue fluid to be returned as **lymph** to the circulation.

11. The circulation is controlled by the **cardiovascular centre** in the medulla of the brain. It responds to, amongst other things, changes in blood pressure as monitored by stretch receptors in the walls of the carotid sinuses.

12. The higher centres in the brain, a variety of reflexes and the hormone adrenaline are also involved in the initiation of cardiovascular responses.

13. **Cardiovascular disorders** are a major cause of deaths in the United Kingdom and could be greatly reduced by avoiding certain well-established risk factors.

14. When facing total oxygen deprivation many animals, particularly diving mammals and birds, undergo **bradycardia**: the cardiac frequency falls and blood is redistributed to the vital organs.

15. Appropriate adjustments take place in the circulatory and ventilation systems as people become **acclimatised** to living at high altitudes where oxygen is limited. There is, however, a critical altitude above which further acclimatisation cannot take place.

16. People who live permanently at high altitudes have various **adaptations** which enable them to live there successfully.

17. Before, during and after a bout of heavy exercise, various adjustments take place in the ventilation and circulatory systems. In bringing about these adjustments, the nervous and endocrine systems play an important part.

18. Training brings about effects on the ventilation and cardiovascular systems which generally improve the efficiency and performance of athletes.

For general advice on these questions and advice on answering essay-type questions, see pages vii and viii.

1. The graphs below show the changes in pressure in the aorta and in the left and right ventricles of the heart, during the cardiac cycle. Time 0 indicates the start of atrial contraction.

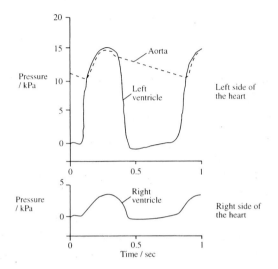

(a) Compare the changes in pressure in the left ventricle with those in the right ventricle, giving reasons for the differences. (4)

(b) Compare the changes in the pressure in the aorta with those in the left ventricle, giving reasons for the differences. (3)

(c) On the graph of changes in pressure in the aorta and left ventricle, show by means of an arrow when the aortic semilunar valve closes. (1)

(d) Cardiac muscle is described as myogenic. Explain how the cardiac cycle is coordinated within the heart. (4)

(Total 12 marks)

London 1998

2. Give an account of the cardiac cycle. 16 marks are allotted for scientific content and 4 marks for orderly presentation and quality of English. Diagrams may be used to assist your account but are not essential.

(Total 20 marks)

O & C 1998

3. Write an essay on risk factors in coronary heart disease.

(Total 20 marks)

London 1997

4. The diagram shows a vertical section through a human heart. The arrows represent the direction of movement of the electrical activity which starts muscle contraction.

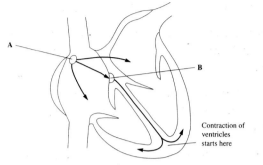

(a) Name structure **A**. (1)

(b) Explain why each of the following is important in the pumping of blood through the heart.

(i) There is a slight delay in the passage of electrical activity that takes place at point **B**. (1)

(ii) The contraction of the ventricles starts at the base. (1)

(c) Describe how stimulation of the cardiovascular centre in the medulla may result in an increase in heart rate. (2)

(d) Arteries may become blocked by the formation of fatty material on the walls. An operation called balloon angioplasty may be used to correct this. The procedure is shown in the diagram.

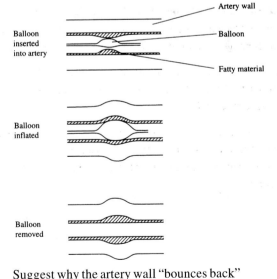

(i) Suggest why the artery wall "bounces back" when the balloon is removed. (1)

(ii) Explain why the ability of the artery wall to bounce back is important in a normal, healthy artery. (2)

(Total 8 marks)

NEAB 1997

Chapter 15

Transport in the flowering plant

Figure 15.1 Scanning electron micrograph of root hairs on a root of a wheat seedling. The root hairs greatly increase the surface area over which water and mineral salts can be absorbed.

In Chapter 13, the systems by which substances are transported in plants were introduced briefly. In this chapter we shall take a closer look at the uptake of water and mineral salts from the soil, their transport in the xylem and the loss of water vapour from the leaves. We shall also discuss the transport of organic compounds in the phloem.

15.1 Uptake and transport of water

Plants and animals require water for essentially the same reasons. It is the medium in which all metabolic reactions take place, it is needed for hydrolysis and for the transport of solutes around the organism and it keeps it cool when it evaporates from its surface. In plants it performs the additional function of generating a pressure potential in the cells which helps to support the plant (*page 110*).

Uptake of water by roots

As well as anchoring the plant, the **roots** provide the surface through which water is taken up. The surface area is greatly increased by the presence, just behind the tip of each root, of thousands of tiny **root hairs** (*figure 15.1*). A plant's roots may present an enormous surface for the absorption of water. For instance, at four months the root system of a single rye plant, including the root hairs, was found to have a total surface area of 639 m², which is about 130 times greater than the surface area of its shoot system.

To follow what happens to the water that is taken up by the roots, we must examine the internal structure of a typical root.

Internal structure of the root

Figure 15.2 shows the arrangement of the tissues in the root of a typical dicotyledon. The root hairs belong to the outer layer of cells, the **epidermis** – each root hair is a slender extension of a single epidermal cell up to 4 mm long.

The root hairs are confined to the part of the epidermis immediately behind the tip where they comprise the **piliferous layer**. Further back, in the older part of the root, the

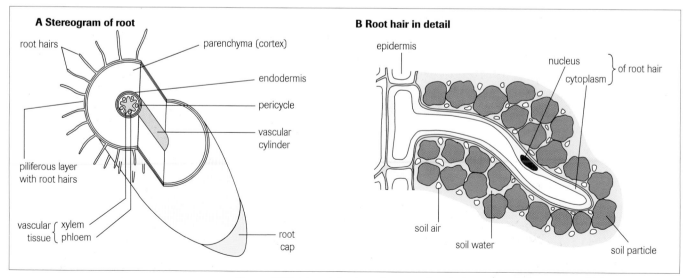

A Stereogram of root

root hairs
parenchyma (cortex)
endodermis
pericycle
vascular cylinder
piliferous layer with root hairs
vascular tissue { xylem phloem
root cap

B Root hair in detail

epidermis
nucleus
cytoplasm } of root hair
soil air
soil water
soil particle

Figure 15.2 Internal structure of a young dicotyledonous root. **A** Stereogram of the root showing the positions of the various tissues. **B** A root hair in detail, showing its close association with the soil from which it absorbs water and mineral salts.

piliferous layer sloughs off and is replaced by the layer of cells immediately underneath. This becomes the functional epidermis.

The root hairs penetrate between the soil particles and are in close contact with the soil water. It has been found that the cells towards the tip of the root, including the root hairs, take up water as much as six times faster than the cells in the older regions of the root further back.

Beneath the epidermis, large, thin-walled **parenchyma** cells make up the **cortex**, which constitutes the main body of the root. In the centre there is a core of vascular tissues, referred to as the **vascular cylinder**. The vascular cylinder of a young root consists of several groups of lignified **xylem cells** between which are distinct groups of **phloem cells**.

The centre of the vascular cylinder consists of parenchyma tissue to begin with, but as the root of a dicotyledonous plant develops this changes into xylem. So, when viewed in transverse section, the xylem finishes up looking like a star with several 'spokes'. A typical pattern can be seen in figure 15.3.

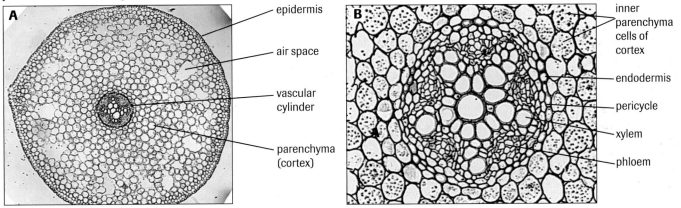

The vascular cylinder is bounded by a layer of parenchyma cells called the **pericycle**, where **lateral roots** originate. In older roots the pericycle becomes lignified. Outside the pericycle is a layer of cells called the **endodermis**. The endodermis and the tissues inside it are known as the **stele**.

Figure 15.3 Photomicrographs of a buttercup root. **A** Transverse section of the root. **B** The vascular cylinder at higher magnification.

The pathway taken by water

Most of the water probably enters the root, from the soil, down a gradient of water potential. Inside the root the water follows three pathways:

■ The **apoplast pathway**: this consists of the interconnected cellulose cell walls of adjacent cells which are in contact with each other and therefore form a continuous system. The water flows in the spaces between the cellulose microfibrils (*page 22*).

■ The **symplast pathway**: this consists of the cytoplasm which is continuous from cell to cell via the **plasmodesmata** (*page 55*). To reach the symplast, water has to cross the partially permeable plasma membrane by osmosis.

■ The **cell-to-cell pathway**: water passes across the epidermal cell wall, plasma membrane and tonoplast, then into the vacuole. From there it continues into the next cell in the same fashion.

All three pathways are probably used, though the relative extents to which water flows through each one is uncertain. Once the water reaches the endodermis, its flow is thought to be barred by an impermeable thickening of suberin in the walls of the endodermal cells. This **Casparian strip**, as it is called, diverts the water from the cell walls, forcing it to take the symplast pathway through the endodermal cells (*figure 15.4*).

What is the significance of this diversion? It is thought that the endodermal cells actively transfer salts from the cortex to the pericycle. The resulting high concentration of salts in the pericycle cells creates a low water potential which causes water to move into

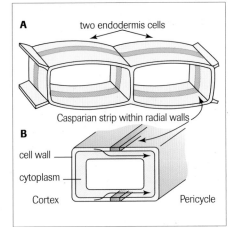

Figure 15.4 A Endodermal cells of the root showing the suberised Casparian strip in the radial walls. **B** Diagram showing how the Casparian strip diverts the water from the cellulose wall (apoplast pathway) to the cytoplasm (symplast pathway).

them by osmosis from the cortex through the partially permeable plasma membranes of the endodermis cells. In other words, the salts are actively transferred across the endodermis and the water follows passively. Once in the pericycle, the water flows into the xylem down a water potential gradient in both the symplast and apoplast pathways.

Figure 15.5 summarises the passage of water from the soil to the xylem in the root.

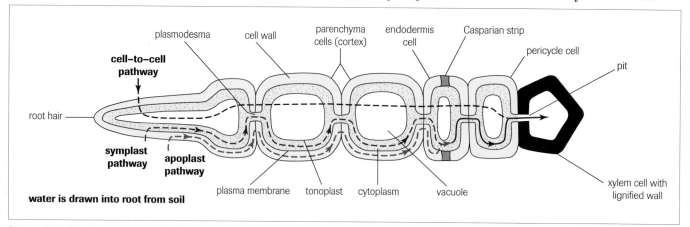

Figure 15.5 The three routes by which water may pass from the soil to the xylem in the centre of the root. The apoplast pathway which consists of the cell walls, the symplast pathway which consists of the cytoplasm, and the cell-to-cell pathway.

From root to leaf

Water is transported from the roots to the leaves via the **stem**. To understand how this happens we must first look at the internal structure of the stem, particularly the vascular tissues (*figure 15.6*).

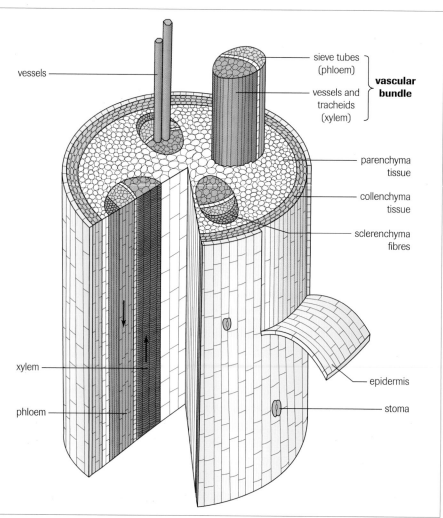

Figure 15.6 Internal structure of a dicotyledonous stem. The peripheral part of the parenchyma (outside the ring of vascular bundles), together with the collenchyma, make up the cortex; the central parenchyma (inside the ring of vascular bundles) comprises the medulla; and the parenchyma between the vascular bundles comprises the medullary rays. The terms cortex, medulla, medullary ray and vascular bundle are topographical terms, signifying different regions of the stem. The terms collenchyma, parenchyma, xylem and phloem refer to the different types of tissue in the stem. The arrows signify the upward flow of water and mineral salts in the xylem and the predominantly downward flow of soluble food substances in the phloem.

Internal structure of the stem

In the stem, the vascular tissue is found in a series of **vascular bundles**. In dicotyledons, the vascular bundles are arranged in a ring (*figure 15.7*). They run the entire length of the stem, connecting with the vascular cylinders in the roots and with the vascular bundles in the midrib and veins of the leaves.

The vascular bundles are embedded in **parenchyma tissue** which forms the bulk of a young stem. This is surrounded by a layer of **collenchyma tissue** whose unevenly thickened cellulose walls provide the stem with strength, while allowing it to be flexible (*page 70*). The outermost collenchyma cells may contain chloroplasts, giving the stem a green colour and enabling it to photosynthesise.

The surface of the stem is covered with a layer of **epidermis** which usually possesses a **cuticle** like that of leaves, and may be pierced by a number of **stomata**. The parenchyma cells, when fully turgid, press against each other and against the surrounding collenchyma and epidermis. This contributes to the mechanical strength of the stem, helping to maintain its erect form and preventing it from drooping.

Also important in providing mechanical strength is the **pericycle**, which is located on the immediate outside of the vascular bundles. It consists of **sclerenchyma tissue** which is made up of tightly packed, lignified **fibres**. This lignified tissue, along with that of the xylem, helps to make the stem relatively rigid.

If we examine vascular bundles more closely (*figure 15.8*) we see that there is a clear demarcation between the xylem and phloem. The xylem is towards the inner side of the vascular bundle, the phloem towards the outside.

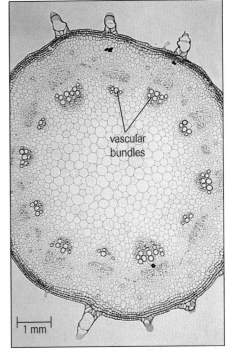

Figure 15.7 Photomicrograph of a transverse section of a buttercup stem showing the stem structure of a typical dicotyledon. Notice that the vascular bundles are arranged in a regular ring towards the outside of the stem.

Extension

The roots and stems of monocotyledons

The structure of the root and stem of dicotyledons is described in the main text. How do monocotyledons differ from dicotyledons in this respect?

The roots of monocotyledons are much the same as dicotyledons, except that the xylem has many more 'spokes' and surrounds a permanent core of parenchyma cells. The vascular bundles too, are similar, with the xylem towards the inner side and the phloem towards the outside.

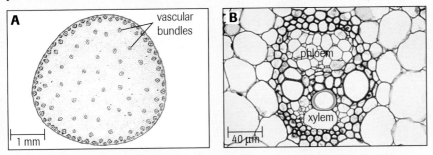

A Photomicrograph of a transverse section of a maize stem showing the vascular bundles scattered throughout the stem. This arrangement is typical of monocotyledons.
B Photomicrograph of a single vascular bundle of maize. This shows the typical arrangement of xylem and phloem cells in cereals which is often likened to a monkey's face!

It is in the arrangement of the vascular bundles within the stems that the difference lies. Instead of being arranged in a ring about a central core, the vascular bundles in most monocotyledons are scattered throughout the stem (*illustration*). The individual bundles run the entire length of the stem, as they do in dicotyledons, connecting with the vascular cylinders in the roots and with the vascular bundles in the veins of the leaves.

➤ Other differences between monocotyledons and dicotyledons, pages 95 and 534

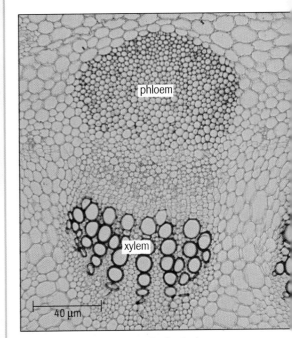

Figure 15.8 Photomicrograph of a single vascular bundle in a buttercup stem showing the large, thick-walled xylem cells and the thinner walled phloem cells.

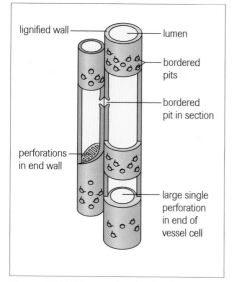

Figure 15.9 Diagram showing the detailed structure of vessels. Each vessel is a long tube with a lignified wall. It starts off as a chain of cylindrical cells whose end walls become perforated by a single large opening or by a number of parallel, slit-like openings. With the lignification of the walls, the cells die and lose their contents so the tubes become empty except for the water and mineral salts which they transport from the roots to the leaves.

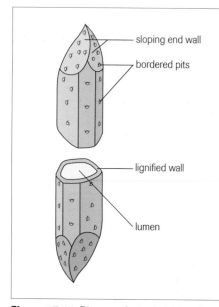

Figure 15.11 Diagram of a tracheid showing the tapered ends and pits.

Xylem tissue

Xylem contains two types of conducting cells: **tracheids** and **vessels**. These are dead cells and they form a system of pipes through which water can travel. The cells are dead because once they have reached their full size, their cellulose cell walls become impregnated with **lignin** which is impermeable to water and solutes. The living contents of the cells die, leaving the cell walls surrounding a water-filled cavity (lumen).

Vessels are characteristic of angiosperms and are absent from the xylem tissue of conifers. Tracheids occur in a few angiosperms and all conifers. The detailed structure of vessels is shown in figure 15.9. Water moving up the plant encounters little resistance as it moves along them. This is because vessels are formed from a chain of cylindrical cells, the end walls of which break down so that the cells are in open communication with each other. Alternatively, there may be ladder-like bars extending across the end, forming a **perforation plate** (*figure 15.10*). In tracheids, on the other hand, the end walls remain intact, and are perforated only by small holes called **pits** (*figure 15.11*). Because there is less resistance, water moves up a plant 10 times faster in vessels than in tracheids.

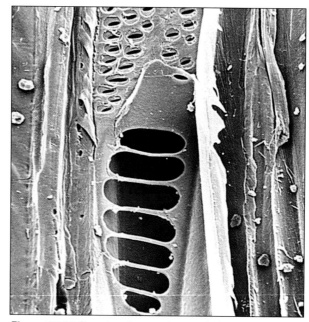

Figure 15.10 Scanning electron micrograph showing the perforations in the end wall of a vessel cell. Magnification ×300.

Pits occur in the walls of both tracheids and vessels. Where a pit occurs, lignin fails to be deposited and only the cellulose cell wall remains. The pits match up with the pits of neighbouring cells, so the cell cavities are connected to adjacent cell cavities on either side and, in the case of tracheids, above and below as well. This permits the passage of water sideways as well as upwards. The pits are frequently bordered by a lignified rim. These **bordered pits** sometimes have a central 'plug' or **torus** (*figure 15.12*). The torus may act as a control valve, safeguarding the system as a whole if the water column in one of the xylem tubes should collapse.

As xylem cells develop, **lignified thickenings** of various kinds, often rings or spirals, are laid down on the immediate inside of the walls (*figure 15.13*). They strengthen the walls. Wood is mainly composed of tracheids and vessels, which gives some idea of the strength of these water-conducting cells and the role they also have in support (*Chapter 30*).

Xylem tissue is found in all mature parts of the plant. The vessels and tracheids of the roots, stems and leaves connect to form a continuous system of water-conducting channels serving all parts of the plant.

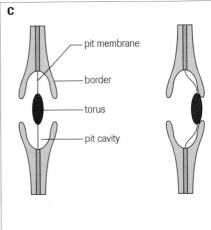

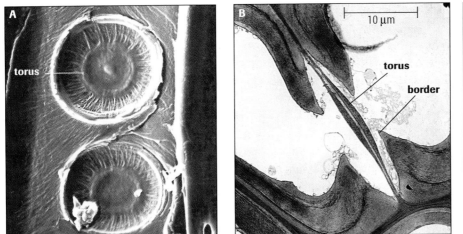

Figure 15.12 Scanning electron micrograph of a bordered pit, **A** in surface view and **B** in section. Bordered pits are found in both flowering plants and conifers. The torus is common in conifers but comparatively rare in flowering plants. When there is an unequal pressure in two adjacent tracheids, the torus may be pushed over to one side, thus acting as a valve as shown in **C**.

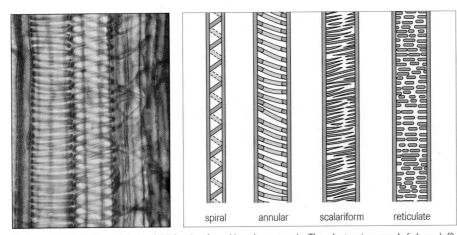

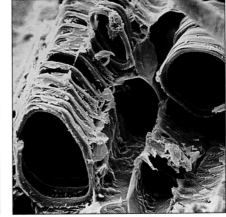

Figure 15.13 Different kinds of thickening found in xylem vessels. The photomicrograph (*above left*) is a longitudinal section of xylem magnified 300 times. Annular and spiral thickening can be seen in longitudinal stem sections which have been treated with acidified phloroglucinol, which stains lignin red. The scanning electron micrograph (*above right*) shows two vessels magnified 550 times.

The ascent of water up the stem

Measurements have shown that there is a gradient of **water potential** through the whole plant, highest in the soil surrounding the roots and lowest in the atmosphere surrounding the leaves. This creates a flow of water through the plant as shown in figure 15.14. Moreover, the evaporation of water from the leaf cells would lower their hydrostatic pressure, further facilitating the flow of water through the plant.

Although this water potential gradient provides the basic mechanism by which water flows through plants, for a full explanation we need to examine some other forces that exist in plants.

Root pressure

If the stem of a plant is severed, the cut end will exude copious quantities of water for a considerable time, suggesting that there is a force pushing water up the stem from the

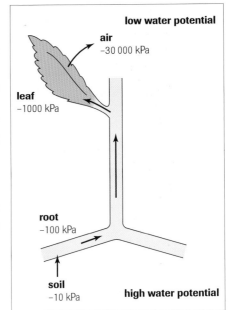

Figure 15. 14 Estimated water potentials of soil water, root, leaf and air. There is much variation. These figures are based on a typical mesophyte growing in good soil. The steepest gradient is between the leaf and the air. Why do you think this is? The arrows indicate the flow of water through the plant.

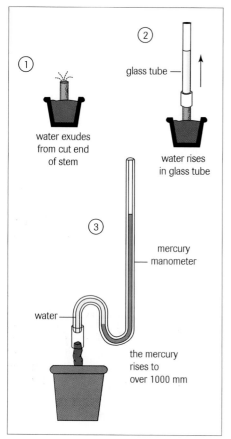

Figure 15.15 Three ways of demonstrating root pressure in a potted plant.

Labels in figure:
1. water exudes from cut end of stem
2. glass tube — water rises in glass tube
3. mercury manometer — water — the mercury rises to over 1000 mm

roots. This force is known as **root pressure**, and it was discovered by Stephen Hales in 1727. Hales found that it could raise water to a height of over 6.4 m in a vine. He noticed, however, that it only occurred at certain times of the year and never in winter.

Root pressure can be measured by attaching a suitable mercury manometer to the cut end of the stem (*figure 15.15*). In this way it has been found that sizeable pressures can be set up by the roots of some plants: a stump of *Fuchsia*, for example, can develop a pressure of over 90 kPa.

We now know that root pressure is the result of osmotic flow across the endodermis, the necessary water potential gradient being created by the active transport of salts referred to on page 114. Anything that inhibits active transport, such as metabolic inhibitors, low temperatures or shortage of oxygen, also reduces root pressure – which is why Hales saw no root pressure in winter.

Root pressure provides a force which, in effect, pushes water up the stem. We must now turn to the leaves to see what contribution they make to the upward flow of water.

Forces generated by the leaves

Water evaporates from the leaves by a process called **transpiration** which is discussed in detail later. The water lost this way is replaced by water drawn up through the xylem tubes in what is called the **transpiration stream**. Continuous columns of water therefore hang from the top of the plant. Two forces hold them there: **adhesion** and **cohesion**. Let us look at these two forces in turn.

Adhesion

Water tends to adhere to the walls of any container. This is because there are forces of **adhesion** between the water molecules and the molecules comprising the material lining the container. Adhesion is defined as the force of attraction between unlike molecules. The narrower the container, the greater will be the proportion of water molecules in contact with its walls. This results from the fact that the smaller the container, the greater the area of its wall in comparison with the volume of water enclosed, i.e. the surface-volume ratio is greater.

Now let us see to what extent a plant complies with this. The effective evaporating surface of a plant consists of the cellulose walls of the leaf mesophyll cells. Studies on the fine structure of the cellulose wall have shown it to be perforated by numerous channels of molecular size which open at the surface as minute pores. Being very narrow, considerable adhesive forces will be expected to develop in these. These forces must be sufficient to 'hold up' a considerable mass of water.

Cohesion

The problem, however, is not only to hold up the column of water, but also to prevent it breaking in the middle. What is responsible for this? The answer is the force of **cohesion**. Cohesion is defined as the force of attraction between *like* molecules, in this case the water molecules. Experiments carried out by Josef Böhm in 1893 and by Dixon and Joly in 1895 provided evidence for the tensile strength of water that results from the force of cohesion. These experiments are described in the extension box on the next page.

The **cohesion–tension theory**, as it is called, offers an explanation of the rise of water in the xylem of all plants including tall trees. Cohesive forces between water molecules hold the continuous columns of water together, and when water transpires from the leaf the whole of the water column moves up the xylem.

However, there's a problem. If you suck water up a straw, the walls collapse if you suck too hard, and the column of water breaks. In the xylem, the thickened walls normally prevent this happening. The tension in the xylem of a very tall redwood tree must be colossal, but the tensile strength of the water columns must be sufficient or such trees could not exist.

Further evidence that the water in the xylem is under tension comes from taking measurements of the diameter of tree trunks over 24 hours with an instrument called a **dendrograph**. The measurements show that the diameter of a tree trunk decreases during the day. The diameter reaches the minimum size in the afternoon, after which it increases again to reach a maximum in the early morning (*figure 15.16*). The decrease during the day occurs because water loss (transpiration) exceeds water uptake and this puts the xylem contents under tension; at night, transpiration is greatly reduced and the water deficit is replenished from the soil.

Part 2

Extension

Experimental evidence for the tensile strength of water

The tensile strength of water was demonstrated by the Austrian botanist Josef Böhm in 1893 using the apparatus shown in the illustration. The porous vessel and tube were filled with water and the end of the tube inserted into a bottle of mercury. The evaporation of water vapour through the porous vessel caused water to move up the capillary tube, pulling the mercury behind it to a height of one metre.

This was a physical model of the movement of water up the xylem. If an air bubble had got into the water column in Böhm's apparatus, the mercury would have fallen back. This is because the water column, being broken, would no longer have the same tensile strength as it had before.

Just two years later in 1895, the Irish botanist H.H. Dixon and his co-worker J. Joly modified Böhm's experiment, using a pine twig instead of a porous pot. Transpiration from the pine needles also lifted a column of mercury, again demonstrating the tensile strength of a column of water. As a result of this experiment Dixon and Joly proposed

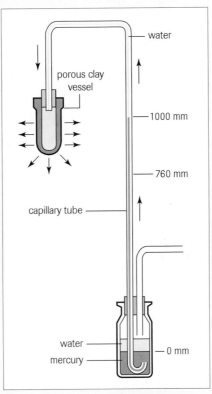

Böhm's apparatus for demonstrating the tensile strength of water

what is now known as the **cohesion– tension** theory of the rise of water in the xylem.

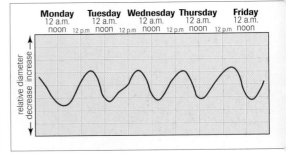

Figure 15.16 Daily variations in the diameter of the trunk of the Monterey pine, *Pinus radiata*.

In dry weather, however, when there is a shortage of water in the soil, the tension gets so high that the water columns do break and are said to make a distinct cracking sound as they do so. This is called **cavitation** and it results in a 'bubble' of gas forming in the tracheid or vessel. The bordered pits mentioned earlier act as valves, ensuring that only a few vessels or tracheids are affected, thus safeguarding the system as a whole. The pits also allow the transpiration stream to find a way round an air bubble by moving into an adjacent vessel, past the bubble and then back into the original vessel chain. The additional xylem vessels which are produced each year in secondary growth also help to compensate for the vessels blocked by air bubbles.

From leaf to air

The stomata, as well as permitting the entry of carbon dioxide, allow the evaporation of water from the plant, the phenomenon known as **transpiration** which was referred to earlier. Transpiration is by no means restricted to the leaves, for there are generally a number of stomata in the stem epidermis as well. However, the leaves, with their large surface area and abundant stomata, are the main source of water loss. To a small extent evaporation also takes place through the cuticle of the epidermal cells (**cuticular transpiration**) but this rarely exceeds 15 per cent of the total water loss.

The rate at which water is transpired from a plant may be considerable, particularly if the atmosphere is warm and dry. In one hour during a hot summer day a leaf may lose more water than it contains at any one moment. An oak tree may transpire as much as 680 litres of water in a day. It has been estimated that a sunflower plant may transpire over 200 litres of water during its life of six months. These figures give some idea of the scale of transpiration. They also emphasise how essential it is for a plant to have an adequate system of water uptake, for the water which is lost must be replaced.

How transpiration can be measured and the factors which affect the rate of transpiration are discussed in the support box on the next page.

The evaporating surface

In figure 12.14 on page 206 you can see that each stoma opens into a small **sub-stomatal air chamber** which is lined with **spongy mesophyll cells**. The effective evaporating surface of a leaf consists of the saturated walls of these spongy mesophyll cells. The water evaporates from the walls and moves down a gradient of water potential from the plant to the atmosphere. As evaporation proceeds, water vapour accumulates in the sub-stomatal chambers from which it escapes through the open stomata. Provided the plant has an adequate supply of water, the water which evaporates from the cell walls of the spongy mesophyll cells is replaced by water from the xylem vessels in the leaf (*figure 15.17*). The water flows in the apoplast, symplast and cell-to-cell pathways. However, as in the root, the relative extents to which each of these three pathways is used is uncertain.

Water stress

When a plant loses more water through transpiration than it can take up into its roots, it **wilts** and is said to suffer from **water stress**. The loss of water from the leaves raises the tension of the water columns in the xylem, and the water potential gradient from the soil to the xylem increases. Nevertheless, if the soil is dry the roots will not be in contact with continuous films of water between the soil particles so the flow of water to the roots stops. The stomata then close rapidly, thereby reducing water loss to a minimum. There is evidence that this rapid stomatal response is brought about by a plant growth regulator, probably **abscisic acid** (**ABA**), which is synthesised in the root and passed up to the leaf in the xylem.

The closing of the stomata reduces the rate of photosynthesis. This is one of the most noticeable side-effects of water stress. However, it is brought about not by the shortage of water as such but by the closing of stomata which then reduces the uptake of carbon dioxide.

The functions of transpiration

Transpiration is the inevitable result of the inside of the leaf being open to the atmosphere for the uptake of carbon dioxide. As such, it might be regarded as more of a nuisance than a help. But it does have a positive function, namely that it cools the leaves, an important effect in hot conditions (*page 314*). In addition, the transpiration stream provides the pathway through which mineral salts are transported in the plant. To that topic we now turn.

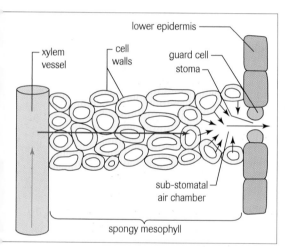

Figure 15.17 Water movement in a leaf. Continual evaporation through the open stoma (black arrows) encourages the further movement of water from the xylem towards the surface of the leaf (red arrow). The water may follow the apoplast, symplast or cell-to-cell pathways which are not shown individually in this diagram. Water moves up the xylem vessel (blue arrow) to replace the water lost from the leaf.

▶ The structure of leaves in the context of photosynthesis, pages 205–7

▶ Abscisic acid, page 551

Factors affecting the rate of transpiration

To find out which factors affect the rate of transpiration we must be able to measure its rate. This can be done in various ways. A commonly used method is to measure the rate at which the plant takes up water; the assumption being that this is the same rate at which water evaporates from the leaves and other exposed surfaces. The apparatus for doing this is called a **potometer**.

There are various types of potometer but they all work on the same principle. The cut end of the stem of a leafy shoot is attached by a short length of rubber tubing to a capillary tube full of water. There must be no air locks: the water in the stem and the capillary tube should form a continuous system. The rate of water uptake is measured by introducing an air bubble into the capillary tube and timing how long it takes for the bubble to travel a certain distance along the tube.

What factors, then, affect the rate of transpiration? For convenience we can divide them into internal and external factors.

Internal factors

The most important internal condition affecting transpiration is the state of the stomata: their number, distribution, structural features and how open they happen to be. Any factor that influences the opening and closing of the stomata will obviously affect transpiration. In some plants the stomata and other features are modified to prevent excessive water loss (*page 296*).

External factors

External conditions affecting transpiration include:

- **Temperature**: a high temperature provides latent heat of vaporisation and therefore encourages evaporation from the mesophyll cells.

- **Relative humidity**, the degree to which the atmosphere is saturated with water vapour, is important because it determines the **saturation deficit**, i.e. the humidity difference between the inside and outside of the leaf. Normally the relative humidity in the sub-stomatal chambers is very high. (Why should this be so?) The lower the relative humidity of the surrounding atmosphere, the greater will be the saturation deficit and the water potential gradient, and the faster will water vapour escape through the stomata.

- **Air movements**: water vapour tends to build up close to the surface of the leaf as it diffuses out of the stomata. Obviously

the atmosphere will be most highly saturated immediately outside each stoma and become progressively less saturated as water vapour diffuses away. Water vapour molecules are deflected by the perimeter of a stoma, and the closer they are to the perimeter the greater is the deflection. The diffusion paths of the water vapour molecules therefore describe a hemisphere around the stoma, called a **diffusion shell** (*illustration*). If the air is still, diffusion shells build up around the stomata and the rate of evaporation from the mesophyll cells inevitably decreases. Air movements blow away these diffusion shells, thereby increasing the rate of evaporation from the leaf.

Diagram of a diffusion shell. Points of equal water potential (joined by broken lines) form a series of hemispheres over the pore. As a result, the paths of diffusion of molecules along the water potential gradient are curved (shown by the arrowed lines). This means that the molecules near the edge of the pore escape more readily than those in the centre.

- **Atmospheric pressure**: the lower the atmospheric pressure, the greater is the rate of evaporation. For this reason alpine plants, which live at high altitudes where the atmospheric pressure is lower than at sea level, are liable to have a high rate of transpiration, and many of them therefore have adaptations which prevent excessive loss of water.

- **Light**: if the light intensity is increased, the rate of evaporation from a plant increases. The reason is not that light affects evaporation as such, but that it causes the stomata to open, thereby increasing water loss from the plant.

- **Water supply**: transpiration depends on the walls of the mesophyll cells being thoroughly wet. For this to be so the plant must have an adequate water supply from the soil. If for some reason the plant cannot take up water from the soil (for example if it is too dry) sooner or later the stomata close, thus reducing the rate of transpiration.

▶ How plants survive dry conditions, page 296

15.2 Uptake of mineral salts

In addition to carbon dioxide and water, plants require a variety of mineral elements (*page 15*). These are absorbed as the appropriate ions from the surrounding water in the case of aquatic plants, and from the soil water in the case of terrestrial plants.

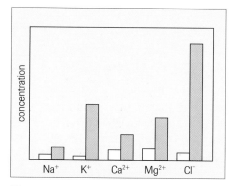

Figure 15.18 Bar chart showing the relative concentrations of different ions in pond water (clear boxes) and in the cell sap of the green alga *Nitella* (shaded boxes). The much greater concentration of ions in the cells suggest that their absorption involves active transport.

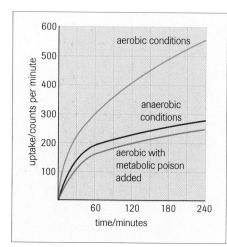

Figure 15.19 The influence of oxygen deprivation and metabolic poison on the uptake of sulphate ions by intact barley plants. The plants were provided with sulphate labelled with radioactive ^{35}S and the amount taken up by the plants was measured by means of a Geiger–Müller tube. The much-reduced uptake in anaerobic conditions and with addition of a metabolic poison suggests that active transport is involved. (Data kindly supplied by Dr Richard Gliddon.)

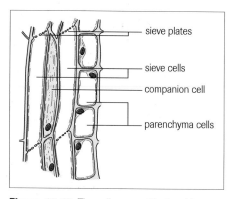

Figure 15.20 The cells present in the phloem as seen in a longitudinal section of phloem tissue under the light microscope.

The concentration of certain ions may be many times greater in the cells of aquatic plants than in the surrounding water (*figure 15.18*). This indicates that they enter the plant against a concentration gradient. Moreover certain ions are more concentrated than others. These observations suggest that ions are selectively absorbed by active transport, involving the expenditure of energy.

There are good reasons to believe that in terrestrial plants, mineral ions are absorbed by similar means. It has been found, for instance, that the uptake of certain ions by young barley roots is increased by raising the temperature, and decreased by oxygen deprivation or treatment with a metabolic poison, all strong indications that active transport is involved (*figure 15.19*).

Like water, mineral ions are taken up into the root hairs and other surface cells in the young parts of the root. Active transport occurs across the plasma membranes of the root hairs and the cortex cells, and the ions move inwards via the symplast through plasmodesmata. There is evidence that the endodermis may actively secrete salts into the pericycle, from which they diffuse into the vascular tissues (*page 249*).

Once inside the vessels and tracheids, the ions are carried up the stem along with the water in the transpiration stream. This has been shown by **ringing experiments**. All the living tissues are removed in a ring from around the central core of vessels and tracheids in a woody stem, and the plant is then placed in a solution containing radioactive phosphate, $^{32}PO_4^{3-}$. Removal of the living cells in no way impedes the upward movement of the radioactive phosphate, which can subsequently be detected in the leaves by means of a Geiger–Müller tube.

From the xylem vessels the ions are conveyed, probably by a combination of diffusion, mass flow and active transport, to their two main destinations: the photosynthetic cells of the leaf and the various growing points in the plant. Here they are put to their sundry uses, for example the building up of amino acids and proteins (*page 26*).

15.3 Transport of organic substances

So far we have considered the uptake and transport of water and mineral salts in plants. They are needed as raw materials for various metabolic processes. Now we must consider how the products of metabolism are transported. In particular, the products of photosynthesis (sugars, amino acids and the like) have to be moved from the leaves where they are formed to the parts of the plant where they are needed. All the cells that are unable to photosynthesise need a share of these materials, especially those in the apices of the roots, stem and branches where cell division and growth are taking place.

Transport of food materials to these **growing points** is greatest in the spring and summer when growth is most prolific. Later in the year many plants form **perennating organs** (such as tubers, bulbs and corms) to which food materials are transported for storage until the following season. When the next season arrives the stored food is transported in soluble form to the growing points of the new plant.

Transport of the soluble products of photosynthesis in a plant is called **translocation**, and a number of experiments have been done showing that it occurs in the part of the vascular tissue known as the **phloem**. We must start by looking in detail at this tissue.

Phloem tissue

When the phloem tissue of a flowering plant is observed under a microscope, three main types of cell may be seen: **sieve cells**, **companion cells** and **parenchyma cells** (*figure 15.20*).

Sieve cells lack nuclei, which disintegrate during development. The cells are aligned end to end to form long **sieve tubes** running up and down the plant. It is the sieve tubes which form the channels for translocation.

Special methods of obtaining nutrients

Some soils are deficient in mineral salts, and plants living in them have special means of obtaining nitrogen and other essential elements.

For example, the roots of many plants which live in soil rich in humus but deficient in mineral salts, possess a **mycorrhiza**, an association between their roots and a fungus. Birch and beech trees are examples of plants which have such an association. The fungus consists of a network of fungal threads (**hyphae**). In some cases the fungal hyphae are located on the surface of the root, in others it is internal. Either way, the fungus has the ability to break down the humus into soluble nutrients, some of which are absorbed and utilised by the host.

The majority of plants with mycorrhizal roots only obtain phosphorus, and perhaps nitrogen, compounds from the fungus. They can photosynthesise normally and can therefore manufacture their own carbohydrates, some of which are absorbed by the fungus. The association is therefore one in which both partners benefit, an example of **mutualism** (*page 714*).

Although most plants with mycorrhizal roots can photosynthesise, there are some that lack chlorophyll and cannot do so. An example is the bird's nest orchid, *Neottia nidus-avis*, an unusual inhabitant of beech woods (*illustration*). Because it has no chlorophyll it is a pale brown colour. Such

The bird's nest orchid, *Neottia nidus-avis*. It has no chlorophyll so it cannot photosynthesise and depends on its mychorrhiza for carbohydrates and proteins. It lives under beech trees where little light penetrates and where few other plants are found.

plants depend upon their mycorrhiza for carbohydrates as well as nitrogen compounds.

Another special adaptation is seen in leguminous plants such as peas, beans, gorse and clover, which harbour **nitrogen-fixing bacteria** in their roots (*page 669*).

Plants living in nitrogen-deficient soil sometimes resort to feeding on animals as a means of obtaining nitrogen. These **carnivorous plants** trap small animals, mainly insects, in a modified leaf where they are subjected to the action of protease enzymes and digested. The products of digestion are absorbed into the leaf and transported to wherever they are needed (*pages 180 and 658*).

Each sieve cell has perforated end walls known as **sieve plates**. The perforations between one cell and the next are perfectly matched and allow the passage of materials from one to another (*figure 15.21*).

Slender **cytoplasmic filaments** extend from one sieve cell to the next through the pores in the sieve plate. The cytoplasm of these filaments is structurally very simple: it contains no endoplasmic reticulum, mitochondria, plastids or other organelles. All these disintegrate during development. A few such organelles persist immediately adjacent to the cellulose wall, but elsewhere they are absent.

Closely applied to the side of each sieve cell are one or more **companion cells**, which possess a nucleus, dense endoplasmic reticulum, ribosomes and numerous mitochondria.

Figure 15.21 A Photomicrograph of sieve cells from the phloem of a flowering plant, showing the sieve plate. **B** Electron micrograph of part of a sieve tube and neighbouring companion cell showing the pores in the sieve plate. The micrograph also shows plasmodesmata piercing the cellulose wall between the sieve tube and companion cell.

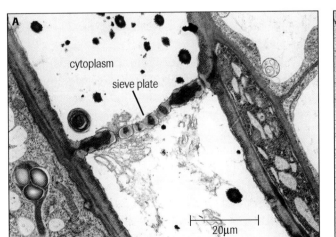

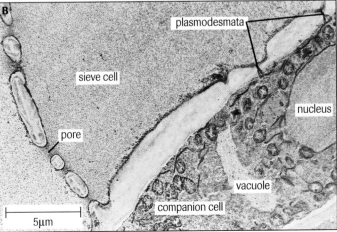

Plasmodesmata connect each sieve cell with its adjacent companion cell or cells (*figure 15.22*). The latter are the site of intense metabolic activity. On purely structural grounds we might predict that translocation of food materials takes place along the sieve tubes, with the adjacent companion cells providing the necessary energy for some part of the process and the pathway by which compounds enter and leave the sieve tubes.

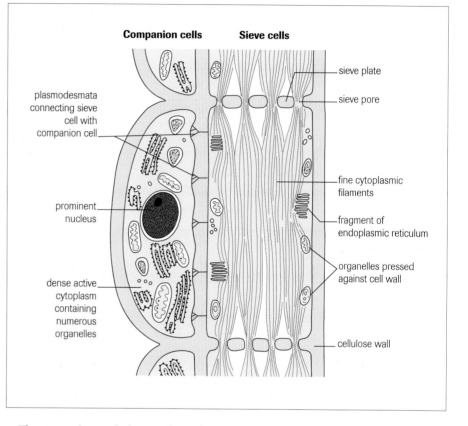

Figure 15.22 Diagram of a sieve cell and companion cell. The sieve cell has no nucleus and not many organelles, what few there are being pushed to one side. In contrast the companion cell has a prominent nucleus and dense cytoplasm containing numerous mitochondria, abundant endoplasmic reticulum and ribosomes.

The sieve tubes with their perforated sieve plates seem to be well suited for transport. However, the perforations are often blocked with protein and, during dormancy, with carbohydrate. This gives the plant some protection from leakage of the phloem contents during grazing by herbivores.

Establishing the site of translocation

How do we know that translocation occurs in the phloem? Some of the earliest investigations involved **ringing experiments** of the type described on page 258. It so happens that in a mature tree trunk the phloem is confined to the inner part of the bark. If a ring of bark is stripped off a tree trunk it can be shown that the sugar concentration increases immediately above the ring and decreases below it, indicating that the downward movement of sugars is blocked at that point.

More critical investigations have been carried out with **radioactive tracers**. If a plant is exposed to carbon dioxide labelled with radioactive ^{14}C, the ^{14}C becomes incorporated into the products of photosynthesis which are subsequently detected in the parts of the plant that are served by the intact phloem. If the phloem is removed by ringing, the photosynthetic products cannot get through (*figure 15.23*). That these substances are confined to the phloem can be shown by cutting sections of the stem, placing the sections in contact with photographic film and making **autoradiographs**. It is found that the sites of radioactivity correspond precisely to the positions of the phloem. These experiments indicate that organic food materials are transported in the phloem. In fact one can imagine that the sieve tubes carry a constant stream of materials from the leaves to the rest of the plant.

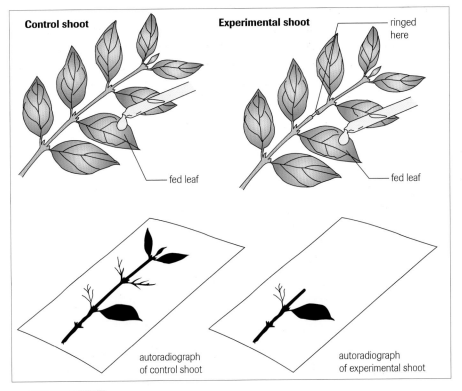

Control shoot
Experimental shoot
ringed here
fed leaf
fed leaf
autoradiograph of control shoot
autoradiograph of experimental shoot

Figure 15.23 An experiment to test the hypothesis that translocation of food substances occurs in the phloem. Two privet shoots were prepared. One of them (the experimental shoot) was ringed – that is, the outer part of the stem including the phloem tissue (but not the xylem) was removed. The other shoot (the control) was left intact. A drop of sucrose solution containing radioactive carbon dioxide ($^{14}CO_2$) was applied to one leaf of each shoot (fed leaf). Both shoots were given water and left in the light for 24 hours. They were then dried and placed flat on a piece of photographic film and left for four to five days in the dark. The radiation from the plants was recorded on the film and the resulting autoradiographs showed the distribution of the ^{14}C. Notice that in the control shoot the ^{14}C has spread to the leaves at the top of the shoot, but in the experimental shoot the ^{14}C has been blocked at the ringing site where the phloem was removed.

Extension

Parasites of plants

A number of **parasites** make use of the phloem of certain plants as a source of food. They tap into the sieve tubes and feed on their contents.

For example, several parasitic plants send out sucker-like processes which pierce the roots or stem of the host plant and link up with the sieve tubes. Dodder, a climbing plant belonging to the convolvulus family, attaches itself to the stems of various host plants in this way. Broomrapes and toothwort go for the roots (*illustration*). In all these cases the fact that the parasite acquires ready-made organic food means that it does not require chlorophyll. Accordingly it lacks the green colour characteristic of most plants and may be either yellow in appearance or more highly coloured as a result of the presence of other pigments.

A striking example of an animal parasite that feeds on the contents of the phloem is that enemy of every gardener – the aphid. Aphids include green-flies, white-flies and black-flies. They obtain plant juices by means of a sharp proboscis rather like a hypodermic needle, which is inserted into the stem or one of the leaf veins. The plant juices then pass up the proboscis to the aphid's gut (*figure 15.24*).

The toothwort *Lathraea squamaria* is a parasite on the roots of hazel, elm and poplar. It has no chlorophyll and obtains its food from the phloem of the host plant.

Tom Mittler of the University of California has made use of aphids to locate the site of translocation. His method is beautiful for its simplicity and ingenuity. An aphid alights on a stem or leaf and inserts its proboscis into the tissue (*figure 15.24*). A stream of carbon dioxide is then passed over the animal to immobilise it. The proboscis is then cut as close to the head as possible, and left sticking into the plant. It is found that fluid exudes from the cut end of the proboscis and may continue to do so for days, providing a perfect technique for tapping the contents of the phloem with minimum injury to the plant. The fluid is collected with a micropipette, and chemical analysis shows that it contains sucrose and a wide range of amino acids.

Figure 15.24 This photograph shows an aphid with its proboscis inserted into the phloem tissue of a leaf.

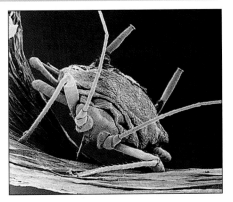

Figure 15.25 Electron micrograph of a section through a leaf vein showing the proboscis of an aphid inserted into a sieve cell (**S**) in the phloem. The food canal of the proboscis is full of material, presumably phloem protein (**pp**). Above the food canal is one of the sharp maxillary stylets (**mx**) which enables the proboscis to pierce the plant tissue The plasma membrane (**Pl**) surrounding the sieve cell is clearly visible. Below the sieve cell you can see part of an adjacent companion cell (**CC**) and one of the plasmodesmata (**Pd**) which connect it to the sieve cell.

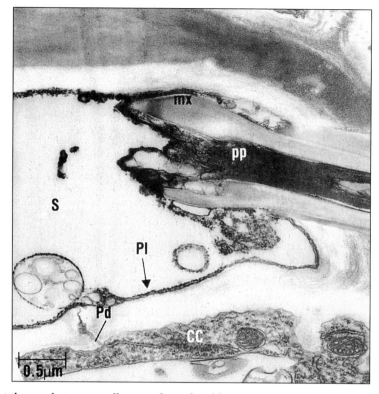

That these substances really come from the phloem can be confirmed by cutting thin sections of the part of the stem or leaf which has the proboscis in it. In this way it has been demonstrated that the tip of the proboscis pierces a single sieve tube (*figure 15.25*).

The rate at which fluid exudes from a sieve tube through an aphid proboscis may exceed 5 mm^3 per hour, which must delight the aphid as it means that it does not even have to suck in order to get a plentiful supply of food – the pressures in the plant are sufficient to force out the fluid. For a plant scientist this provides a means of calculating the speed of translocation. An exudation rate of 5 mm^3 per hour means that an individual sieve tube cell must be emptied and refilled between three and ten times per second. From this it can be calculated that the speed of translocation in a sieve tube is of the order of 1000 mm^3 per hour, a figure which is about twice that obtained from work with radioactive tracers.

Loading and unloading the sieve tubes

We come now to the way sugars and other soluble products of photosynthesis are fed into the sieve tubes in the leaf and removed from them in the roots and other parts of the plant where they are needed. In some flowering plants, the cells which surround the sieve tubes in the phloem include, in addition to the companion cells, specialised parenchyma cells called **transfer cells**.

Transfer cells differ from ordinary parenchyma cells in possessing irregular intuckings of the primary cell wall and plasma membrane which increase the surface area. Numerous plasmodesmata link the cytoplasm of the transfer cells with that of adjacent mesophyll cells and sieve tubes of adjacent cells. In the leaf, the transfer cells are responsible for actively moving the products of photosynthesis from the mesophyll cells to the sieve tubes. They also carry water and salts from the xylem vessels to the mesophyll cells and indeed to the sieve tubes too.

The transfer cells are metabolically active and, together with the companion cells, they supply the necessary energy for loading the sieve tubes. In the roots, storage organs and growing points, similar cells are responsible for retrieving solutes from the sieve tubes and moving them to the cells that need them. However, not all species possess transfer cells, and in those that lack them the energy comes from the other cells.

Transfer cells are not confined to the phloem. They are found in a number of other places where active transport is thought to occur, for example in the secretory tissues inside **nectaries** and in the **hydathodes** at the edges of certain leaves. They also occur in **salt-secreting glands** in the leaves of the saltbush *Atriplex*, a halophyte which lives in dry, saline soil.

▶ Salt glands of plants, page 298

▶ Hydathodes, page 298

▶ Nectaries, page 482

The mechanism of translocation

We have seen that the sieve tubes are loaded with sugars by active transport, but what maintains the flow of the sugars once they have entered the sieve tubes? Of course it would be possible for sugars and other substances in the sieve tubes to move by diffusion along concentration gradients, but the relatively rapid speed at which they travel (40 000 times greater than simple diffusion) rules this out. The truth is that there is, as yet, no certain answer to this question.

The mass flow hypothesis

Among the many mechanisms proposed over the years, one which has gained some support from experimental work is the **mass flow hypothesis** put forward in 1927 by Ernst Münch. The way mass flow is believed to occur in the sieve tubes may be illustrated by the model in figure 15.26 which Münch himself used for demonstrating his hypothesis. If set up correctly, water enters the left-hand funnel by osmosis through the partially permeable membrane. The hydrostatic pressure so developed causes the sugar solution to flow into the right-hand funnel and forces water out through the partially permeable membrane on that side. There is therefore a flow of solution from left to right which will cease when the concentrations in the two funnels are equal.

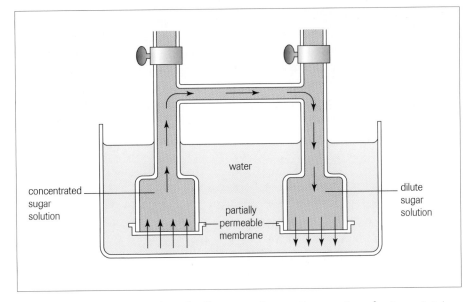

Figure 15.26 Ernst Münch's demonstration of how mass flow might occur in the phloem. Water flows through the system from left to right, carrying the sugar molecules with it. Full explanation in the text.

Of course in the living plant the flow must be *continuous*. In order to maintain a continuous flow, sugars would have to be loaded into the sieve tubes at one end (the **source**) and off-loaded at their destination (the **sink**). The loading of sugars into the phloem is achieved in the leaf by active transport, as we have seen. This creates a high sugar concentration at the source, which draws water into the sieve tubes by osmosis.

At the root end of the system, sugars are removed for use in metabolic processes, so water flows out into the intercellular spaces. The continual input of sugars and water at the top of the system and their removal at the bottom creates a pressure gradient which maintains the downward flow of fluid in the sieve tubes.

If the mass flow hypothesis is correct, we would expect there to be a pressure in the sieve tubes. That such a pressure exists is supported by the aphid experiment mentioned earlier.

Other possible mechanisms of translocation

The mass flow hypothesis is an attractive way of explaining the movement of substances in the sieve tubes. There is, however, a problem with it. If it occurs we would expect different substances to move at the same speed, but it is known from tracer experiments that sugars and amino acids can move at different speeds, and even in opposite directions within the same group of sieve tubes.

Electro-osmosis

There is another objection to the mass flow hypothesis. Calculations indicate that the pressure gradients which actually exist would be insufficient to overcome the considerable resistance imposed by the sieve pores, particularly if they are partly filled with the filaments mentioned earlier. This has led to the suggestion that mass flow might be aided at the sieve plates by a mechanism known as **electro-osmosis** which is the passage of water across a charged membrane.

It is argued that an electrical potential might be maintained across the sieve plate, the lower side being negative relative to the upper side. Such a potential could be maintained by an active pumping of positive ions in an upward direction. A charged solution in a sieve element would be expected to flow through the sieve plate towards the negative side in a manner similar to that which occurs in electrophoresis (*page 32*). Although theoretically possible, there is little experimental evidence that this actually happens, though some researchers using fine electrodes have measured a potential difference across the sieve plates.

Surface spreading

Another mechanism which has been put forward is **surface spreading**. The idea here is that solute molecules might spread over the interface between two different cytoplasmic materials, just as oil spreads at a water–air interface. The molecular film so formed could be kept moving by molecules being added at one end and removed at the other. A major objection here is that the films would be so thin that a very large number of them would need to be formed to account for the known rates of translocation. However, sieve tubes do contain numerous membranes and filaments which collectively might provide the necessary surface.

Active mechanism

Independent movement of different substances strongly suggests that translocation involves some sort of **active mechanism**. This is supported by other lines of evidence. For example, phloem tissue has a high rate of respiration, and there is a close correlation between the speed of translocation and the metabolic rate. Again, lowering the temperature and treatment with metabolic poisons both reduce the rate of translocation, suggesting that it is an active energy-requiring process which cannot be explained by physical forces alone.

Streaming

In their search for a mechanism of translocation, plant scientists nowadays attach increasing significance to the fine protein filaments which span the sieve cells from end to end. As shown in figure 15.22 (*page 260*), these filaments are continuous from one sieve cell to the next via the pores in the sieve plates. High magnification electron micrographs suggest that in the vicinity of the sieve plate the protein filaments take the form of microtubules approximately 20 nm wide, but as they traverse the sieve cell they break up into finer strands. It has been suggested that solutes might be transported by **streaming** along these protein filaments, the necessary energy coming from the sieve tubes themselves or the companion cells. It is envisaged that some strands convey solutes downwards, while others convey them upwards, thus accounting for the bi-directional flow of materials that is known to occur in the sieve tubes. Some investigators claim to have seen cytoplasmic streaming in sieve tubes.

How exactly this streaming occurs is unknown, but one suggestion is that the protein is contractile, rather like that found in muscle, and material is swept along by some kind of wave-like movement of the filaments. But this is highly speculative and the reader is advised to consult recent articles on the subject for the latest views.

Whatever the details of the mechanism, streaming of the cytoplasm has been observed in many different plant cells. You may have observed it yourself in the cells of Canadian pondweed, *Elodea*, where sometimes the chloroplasts circulate round and round the perimeter of the cells (**cyclosis**). It is possible that a similar kind of cytoplasmic streaming occurs in sieve cells, at least in young ones which still contain active cytoplasm.

1.   Roots are adapted for the uptake of water by the possession of a permeable epidermis whose surface area is increased by **root hairs**.

2.   Water moves through the living tissues of the root via the **apoplast** (cellulose cell walls), **symplast** (cytoplasm) and/or the **cell-to-cell pathway**. The **Casparian strip** in the radial walls of the **endodermal cells** diverts the water through the cytoplasm of the endodermis cells; the water then travels to the **xylem**.

3.   The **stem** is adapted for carrying water and mineral salts from roots to leaves. The water and salts are transported in lignified **xylem elements** (**tracheids and vessels**) within vascular bundles, which are continuous with the vascular tissues in the roots and leaves. Lateral movement occurs through **bordered pits** which in some species contain a **torus** which serves as a valve.

4.   **Root pressure** contributes to the rise of water up the stem. It requires energy from aerobic respiration.

5.   Water evaporates from leaves by **transpiration** to the air, down a water potential gradient. This water is replaced by water which moves down a water potential gradient from the soil, to the root, and thence to the leaf, via the xylem in the stem.

6.   The rise of water in tall stems is thought to be helped by two physical properties of water: **adhesion** and **cohesion**. These forces hold up the water columns in the xylem and prevent them breaking (**cavitation**).

7.   In the leaves, water evaporates from the surfaces of the **spongy mesophyll** cells into the **sub-stomatal chambers**, whence it diffuses through the **stomata** to the outside.

8.   The rate of transpiration can be estimated indirectly by measuring the rate of water uptake by a cut leafy shoot using a **potometer**.

9.   The rate of transpiration depends on temperature, relative humidity, air movements, atmospheric pressure, light and water supply.

10.   Mineral salts are taken up as ions by active transport in the root epidermis and cortex, and are carried in the transpiration stream through the xylem to the leaves.

11.   Some plants have special methods of obtaining essential elements, particularly nitrogen. They may harbour mutualistic **mycorrhizal fungi** or **nitrogen-fixing bacteria** in their roots, or they may adopt a parasitic or carnivorous habit.

12.   Organic compounds manufactured in the leaves are **translocated** to the rest of the plant in **sieve tubes** in the **phloem** within the vascular tissues. The structure of the sieve tubes shows adaptations for this function.

13.   The mechanism of translocation is not fully understood, although **mass flow** is one possibility. Considerable controversy still surrounds this aspect of plant physiology and various additional mechanisms have been suggested.

Practice questions

For general advice on these questions and advice on answering essay-type questions, see pages vii and viii.

1.   Water is a liquid because of the large number of hydrogen bonds linking adjacent water molecules. Hydrogen bonds also play a vital role in the transport of water through the xylem of plants. Water moves up the xylem vessels in a stem because of water potential differences between living cells at the top and those at the bottom of the stem. In addition, the structure of xylem vessels aids water transport.

Sometimes the forces involved in the transport of water through xylem vessels may cause problems by breaking the water columns, resulting in the presence of air bubbles. This process, cavitation, often occurs.

(a) Explain

   (i)   why water movement in the xylem depends on transpiration;   (2)

   (ii)   how hydrogen bonds play an important role in the transport of water up the xylem.   (3)

(b) Describe how the structure of xylem vessels aids the transport of water.   (3)

(c) Suggest how plants overcome the problem of cavitation.   (1)

Two cuttings, X and Y, were taken from shoots of the same plant and their cut ends placed into water. Both shoots wilted after about 40 minutes. The shoot of cutting X was then cut under water 5 cm above the original cut. Cutting X recovered from wilting but cutting Y did not.

(d) Explain these observations.   (3)

          (Total 12 marks)

UCLES 1997

2. The diagram shows the main pathways by which water moves through a plant.

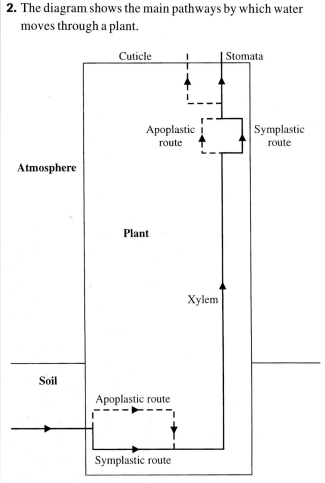

(a) Explain how water moves from the soil into the xylem of the root. (6)

(b) Explain how water moves through the xylem in the stem of the plant. (5)

(c) Explain how the structure of a leaf allows efficient gas exchange but also limits water loss. (6)

Quality of language (3)

(Total 20 marks)

AEB 1998

3. (a) Describe the processes by which carbohydrates are transported through a plant. (4)

(b) The drawing shows an outline of a young morning glory plant.

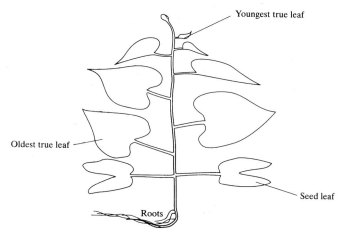

(Reproduced from *Plant Physiology*, Salisbury and Ross, by permission of Wadsworth Publishing Co.)

Autoradiograms are images produced on X-ray film. In six different morning glory plants, **A–F**, identical to the plant above, the leaf marked **a** was allowed to photosynthesise in the presence of radioactive carbon dioxide ($^{14}CO_2$) prior to autoradiograms being produced. Drawings **A–F** show autoradiograms of the six plants. The dark area on each autoradiogram indicates radioactivity.

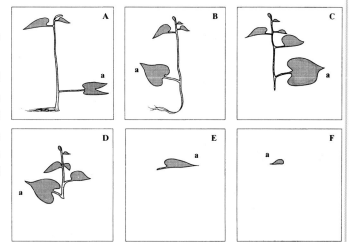

Give **two** conclusions that can be drawn from the autoradiograms about the transport of the carbohydrates produced by photosynthesising leaves in the morning glory plant. (2)

(Total 6 marks)

NEAB 1998

Chapter 16

Homeostasis and the control of glucose

An important generalisation to emerge from physiological studies over the last century or so is that the conditions in which cells can function properly are narrow. Even quite small fluctuations in the physical and chemical surroundings of cells can disrupt their biochemical processes and in extreme cases kill them.

This basic idea was first recognised by the French physiologist Claude Bernard (*figure 16.1*). In 1857 he wrote *La fixite du milieu interieur est la condition de la vie libre* ('The constancy of the internal environment is the condition for free life').

Claude Bernard's famous statement will form the theme of this chapter. First we shall examine the term 'internal environment'. Then we shall look at the principles underlying the mechanisms by which 'constancy' is maintained. We shall also see what Claude Bernard meant by 'free life'.

16.1 The internal environment

In mammalian tissues the cells are surrounded by tiny spaces filled with **tissue fluid**. The tissue fluid contains a whole range of chemical substances derived from the blood (*extension box below*). It provides the cells with the medium in which they have to live; from it they take up all the substances they need, and into it they release unwanted substances.

The tissue fluid is Claude Bernard's 'milieu interieur'. It is this that must be kept constant, or at least held within narrow limits, if the cells are to function properly. And since tissue fluid is formed from the blood, it is the blood which must be kept constant. Much of an animal's physiology is concerned with doing just this.

Figure 16.1 Claude Bernard, 1813–1878, has been described as the father of modern experimental physiology. He was the first person to appreciate the importance of the 'internal environment' in the functioning of organisms. Born in Villefranche in the Rhone Valley, France, Bernard studied medicine. However, he abandoned the idea of medical practice in favour of scientific research and eventually became Professor of General Physiology at the Sorbonne in Paris. From all accounts he was a harsh man who worked relentlessly in his laboratory and expected the same of others. 'One must live in the laboratory', he once said.

What must be kept constant?

The most important features of the blood and tissue fluid that must be kept constant are:

- the concentration of **glucose**;
- the concentration of **various ions**, e.g. sodium, potassium and calcium;
- the concentration of **carbon dioxide**;
- the **water potential**, as determined by the relative concentrations of water and solutes (**osmoregulation**);
- temperature (**thermoregulation**);
- pH (**acid–base balance**).

Support

Keeping tissues alive outside the body

If tissues are removed from an animal and subjected to conditions markedly different from those prevailing in the body, they will die, but if maintained under the correct conditions, they will survive.

This was appreciated by the 19th century physiologist Sidney Ringer, who perfected the art of keeping tissues and organs alive outside the body. He found, for example, that the heart of a frog or mammal would continue to beat for a long time outside the body if kept in a mixture of sodium, potassium and calcium salts, provided of course that it was adequately oxygenated.

It is now known that virtually all tissues can be kept alive in a suitable mixture of ions similar to the tissue fluids. Such solutions, which vary according to the species, are known as **physiological salines** or **Ringer's solutions**.

Physiological salines have particular significance in transplant operations (*page 334*). The organ to be transplanted may be taken from a donor a long way away and then transported in an ice-cold saline solution to the hospital where the operation is to take place.

PART 3   REGULATION AND DEFENCE

How tissue fluid is formed

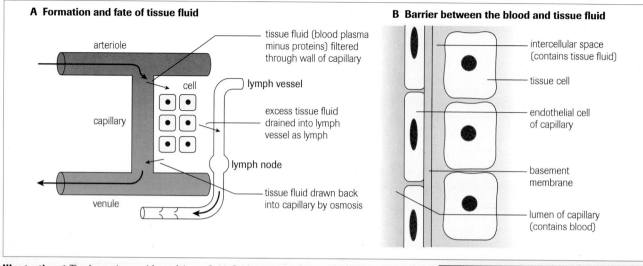

A Formation and fate of tissue fluid

arteriole

cell

capillary

venule

tissue fluid (blood plasma minus proteins) filtered through wall of capillary

lymph vessel

excess tissue fluid drained into lymph vessel as lymph

lymph node

tissue fluid drawn back into capillary by osmosis

B Barrier between the blood and tissue fluid

intercellular space (contains tissue fluid)

tissue cell

endothelial cell of capillary

basement membrane

lumen of capillary (contains blood)

Illustration 1 The formation and fate of tissue fluid. **A** shows very diagrammatically how tissue fluid is formed, and what happens to it subsequently. **B** Greatly magnified view of the wall of the capillary showing the basement membrane through which tissue fluid is filtered from the blood.

Tissue fluid is formed from the blood by a process of **ultrafiltration**. Analysis of tissue fluid shows that it consists of blood plasma minus the proteins. The walls of the capillaries act as a filter, holding back the comparatively large plasma protein molecules and cellular components of the blood, but allowing water and other constituents of the plasma to pass through. Research has shown that the actual filter is not the capillary endothelial cells themselves but the **basement membrane** on which they rest (*illustration 1*).

How does this process of ultrafiltration take place? When blood reaches the arterial end of a capillary it is under pressure because of the pumping action of the heart and the resistance to the blood flow offered by the narrow capillaries. The hydrostatic pressure

forces the fluid part of the blood through the capillary walls into the intercellular spaces.

Once formed, the tissue fluid circulates amongst the cells and eventually returns to the blood system. At the venous end of the capillary system the hydrostatic pressure of the blood is relatively low because the capillaries open into the much wider venules which offer less resistance to the blood flow. Moreover, the water potential of the blood is now low due to the high concentration of plasma proteins. The net result is that the tissue fluid flows back into the capillaries by osmosis and returns to the circulation.

Not all the tissue fluid flows straight back into the circulation. Some of it drains into the **lymph vessels**, where it becomes **lymph** which eventually passes into the veins.

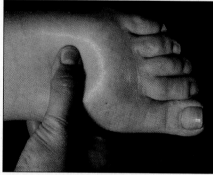

Illustration 2 A case of oedema in the foot. Oedema tends to occur if the mean blood pressure in the capillaries is consistently too high, or if the concentration of plasma proteins in the blood is too low. A common cause medically is a high pressure at the venous end of the capillaries due to heart failure.

Normally tissue fluid returns to the blood system at the same rate as it is formed. If for some reason tissue fluid is formed faster than it can be removed, it accumulates in the tissues. As a result the tissues swell up, a condition called **oedema** (*illustration 2*).

In addition, certain **toxic substances** must be eliminated altogether or at least kept at a concentration which the cells can tolerate. These include certain nitrogenous products of protein metabolism.

Maintenance of a constant internal environment is called **homeostasis**, a Greek word meaning 'staying the same'. Many physiological processes are homeostatic in that they are responsible, directly or indirectly, for regulating the internal environment. It is impossible to exaggerate their importance. Without them life would be impossible. As an example let us take the control of glucose in the human body.

16.2 The control of glucose

The normal concentration of glucose in human blood is approximately 90 mg per 100 cm³, and even after the heaviest carbohydrate meal rarely exceeds 150 mg per 100 cm³. What keeps it constant? Before trying to answer this question, let us briefly consider the various things that can happen to glucose in the body:

- It may be broken down into carbon dioxide and water (respiration), particularly in active tissues such as the muscles.
- It may be built up into glycogen and stored.
- It may be converted into fat and stored in the body's fat depots.
- If glucose is in short supply, glycogen may be broken down into glucose.
- In prolonged deficiency, glucose may be formed from non-carbohydrate sources, including fat and protein. This is called **gluconeogenesis**.

The concentration of glucose in the blood and tissue fluids at any given moment is determined by the relative extent to which these five processes are occurring in the body. For instance, if there is too much glucose – for example, after you have digested a large stodgy meal – the cells convert the surplus glucose into glycogen. If there is a deficiency of glucose, the cells convert glycogen into glucose, thereby raising the glucose concentration in the body.

The role of the pancreas

The cells cannot regulate the concentration of glucose unaided. They have to receive instructions telling them what to do. The instructions are provided by the hormone **insulin** which is secreted into the bloodstream by special cells in the **pancreas**.

Insulin increases the uptake of glucose by the cells, and facilitates the conversion of glucose to glycogen and fat. At the same time it inhibits the formation of glucose from glycogen and non-carbohydrate sources. The overall effect of insulin is therefore to lower the concentration of glucose in the bloodstream (*figure 16.2*). In the absence of insulin, the reverse happens and the glucose concentration rises.

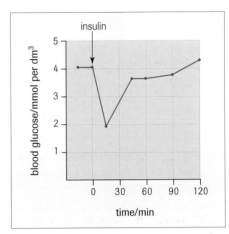

Figure 16.2 Changes in the concentration of blood glucose following the injection of a small quantity of insulin into the bloodstream of a human subject. The moment when the insulin was injected is indicated by the arrow. Notice the sharp fall in the glucose concentration immediately afterwards.

▶ The pancreas is a dual-function organ: as well as secreting hormones it secretes digestive enzymes, page 189.

Part 3

Diabetes, causes and treatment

Guest author Patricia Kohn explains the causes of diabetes and what can be done about it.

In certain individuals the insulin mechanism is faulty. The result is a condition known as **diabetes mellitus** – usually just called **diabetes**. After a meal there is an abnormally large increase in the blood glucose concentration (**hyperglycaemia**), and glucose appears in the urine (**glycosuria**). The production of urine increases and the patient may suffer from intense thirst. Later symptoms include severe loss of body mass, muscular waste and skin lesions. If untreated, the patient goes into a **diabetic coma** and may die.

There are two main types of diabetes:

- **Late onset diabetes** comes on gradually, usually in late middle age, often in people who have been overweight for years. Persistent overeating of sugary foods, and the resulting high levels of insulin, reduces the sensitivity of the target cells to insulin. (Target cells are the cells on which hormones act.) This type of diabetes can often be controlled by altering the diet: simply cutting down carbohydrate intake reduces insulin secretion and allows the target cells to recover. Taking exercise also helps.

- **Early onset diabetes** usually starts early in life, often quite suddenly. It is caused by a loss of insulin-secreting cells in the pancreas and can only be controlled by regular injections of insulin. (Insulin cannot be taken by mouth as it is a protein and is digested in the gut.) The amount and timing of the injections have to be tailored to the needs of each individual. As diabetes is for life, patients must learn to manage their own treatment. They learn how to inject themselves and how to juggle their diet and insulin dosage to keep their blood glucose reasonably normal. This means that they must recognise the symptoms of having either too much or too little glucose in the blood and know what action to take.

Dr Kohn was a research physiologist in the Department of Biomedical Science at the University of Sheffield.

How insulin was discovered

Insulin, and its role in regulating glucose and preventing diabetes, was discovered in the early 1920s by two Canadian physiologists, Frederick Banting and Charles Best. They removed the pancreas from dogs, thereby inducing diabetes with the inevitable rise in the blood glucose concentration. At the same time they extracted substances from the pancreases of other dogs. They then injected the pancreatic extracts into the bloodstream of the depancreatised dogs. Although their research was beset with difficulties, they eventually found that an extract of the pancreas, suitably prepared, reduced the high blood glucose levels of diabetic dogs. This extract contained the substance we now call insulin.

By 1922 insulin was being produced commercially and used to treat human diabetics. The results were dramatic and patients who had suffered misery for years suddenly had their lives transformed. Although their use of animals in their experiments would be questioned today, Banting and Best's discovery stands as a landmark in the history of physiology and clinical medicine.

There are enough diabetics in the world to make insulin production an extremely important part of the pharmaceutical industry. A premium is placed on the mass production of pure and cheap insulin. Traditionally, insulin has been obtained from the pancreases of slaughtered animals, but now human insulin can be produced by genetic engineering.

▶ Production of human insulin and its advantages over animal insulin in treating diabetes, page 631

Which particular tissues respond to insulin? The main ones are the liver, skeletal muscles and adipose tissue. The liver is particularly important in the control of blood glucose, as indeed it is in other aspects of homeostasis.

Clearly insulin plays a crucial role in the regulation of blood glucose. Its importance can be illustrated by considering what happens when the insulin mechanism goes wrong. The result is **diabetes**, which you can read about in the extension box on the previous page.

Glucagon, a second pancreatic hormone

A second pancreatic hormone was discovered In the 1950s. It is called **glucagon**. Like insulin, glucagon is involved in the control of blood glucose, but whereas insulin lowers the blood glucose concentration, glucagon raises it. Glucagon therefore opposes insulin in its action. Moreover, each hormone inhibits the other's release from the pancreas.

Glucagon prevents the blood glucose level falling too low following the secretion of insulin. A sub-normal blood glucose concentration (**hypoglycaemia**), if uncorrected, can cause a person to go into a coma. Hypoglycaemia is particularly liable to occur during fasting, and one of glucagon's main functions is to counteract this. It also occurs when diabetics inject themselves with too much insulin.

Glucagon raises the blood glucose level mainly by stimulating the liver to convert glycogen into glucose. It also promotes the formation of glucose from non-carbohydrate sources.

Which cells secrete insulin and glucagon?

Insulin and glucagon are secreted by special groups of cells in the pancreas called **islets of Langerhans** after a German medical student, Paul Langerhans, who discovered them in 1869. No one knew what their function was. They were called 'islets' because they looked like little islands in a sea of otherwise uniform tissue. If you look at a section of the pancreas under the light microscope, you can see the islets dotted about here and there, embedded in the tissue that secretes the digestive enzymes (*figure 16.3A*).

By suitable staining techniques, two types of secretory cells can be distinguished in the islets: **alpha cells** and **beta cells** (*figure 16.3B*). The alpha cells secrete glucagon, whereas the beta cells secrete insulin. Both hormones are secreted into blood capillaries within the islet, from which they pass into the general circulation.

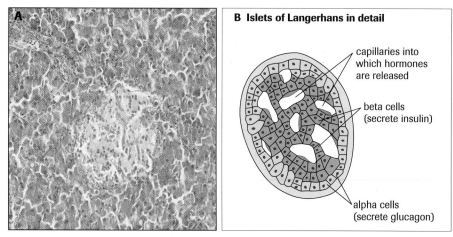

Figure 16.3 Insulin and glucagon are secreted by the islets of Langerhans in the pancreas.
A Section of the pancreas as seen under the light microscope showing an islet of Langerhans surrounded by the tissue that secretes digestive enzymes. The spaces which you can see inside the islet are blood capillaries. Magnification ×100.
B Diagram of an islet of Langerhans showing the insulin- and glucagon-secreting cells and their close proximity to the capillaries into which they release their secretions. The alpha cells are located towards the edge of the islet; the beta cells are towards the centre.

How is secretion of the islet cells controlled?

How do the islet cells know when to secrete insulin and glucagon? The control agent is the concentration of glucose in the blood. If the blood glucose concentration rises above a certain value (the **norm**), this stimulates the islet cells to produce correspondingly more insulin and less glucagon. As a result, the glucose concentration falls. Conversely, if the blood glucose concentration falls below the norm, the islet cells secrete less insulin and more glucagon and the glucose concentration rises. We have here a control system in which the glucose itself switches on the mechanism by which it is itself regulated. The sequence of events is summarised in figure 16.4.

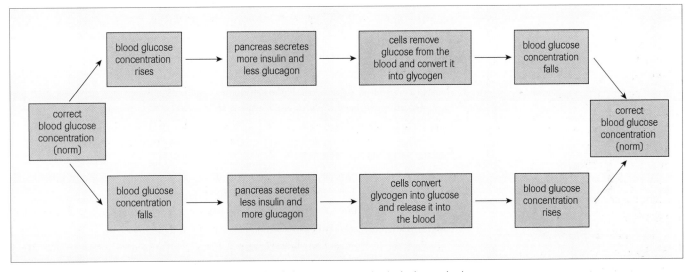

Figure 16.4 Homeostatic scheme for the control of the blood glucose concentration in the human body.

Part 3

Extension

Other factors which control the blood glucose concentration

Although insulin and glucagon are the main hormones that control the concentration of blood glucose, other hormones also influence the blood glucose level at any given time. For example, **adrenaline** and **thyroxine** both increase the usage of glucose and thus lower its concentration in the blood. On the other hand, **cortisol** and **growth hormone** raise the blood glucose level. These hormones interact in such a way that in normal circumstances the concentration of blood glucose is kept reasonably constant.

The time when the blood glucose concentration is most likely to rise is immediately after a meal. When you eat, the gut itself secretes hormones which stimulate the pancreas to release insulin, so insulin secretion has already got underway *before* the blood glucose concentration starts to rise. This is an example of how the body sometimes anticipates a change before it actually takes place, and it is an important way of increasing the efficiency of homeostatic mechanisms.

Another factor that affects the blood glucose concentration is **dietary intake**. Obviously if you are feeling hungry and eat a lot of food, your blood glucose level will increase. On the other hand, if you are full (**satiated**) you will stop eating and your blood glucose level will fall. How hungry you feel is determined by a number of factors, including the blood glucose concentration itself. The control centres involved are in the **hypothalamus** and other parts of the brain (*page 361*).

Extension

How do the target cells respond to insulin and glucagon?

Insulin and glucagon, in common with many other hormones, induce their effects by binding to specific receptors in the plasma membrane of the target cells. This triggers a series of enzyme-controlled events inside the cells which leads to an increase in the rate at which glucose is taken up into, or expelled from, the cells by facilitated diffusion (*page 105*).

> How hormones affect their target cells, page 377

> Hormones are dealt with in detail in Chapter 21

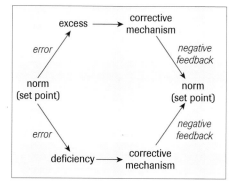

Figure 16.5 Generalised scheme summarising any homeostatic control process. A deviation from the norm (set point) starts up the appropriate corrective mechanism which restores the norm. Because the deviation triggers a *return* to the norm, i.e. an *opposite* effect, it is called negative feedback.

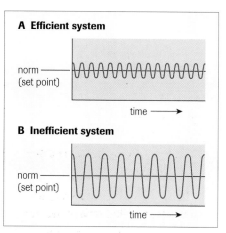

Figure 16.6 Graphs comparing an efficient homeostatic system with an inefficient one. In both graphs the vertical axis represents the magnitude of the particular feature under consideration, for example the concentration of blood glucose or the body temperature. Notice the much larger fluctuations in the inefficient system. In reality the fluctuations would be less regular than in these theoretical graphs.

➤ Other examples of homeostatic systems and negative feedback:
lung ventilation, page 173;
osmoregulation, page 288;
ionic regulation, page 289;
temperature regulation, page 308;
blood pressure, page 239;
sex hormones, page 514;
population control, page 694;
constancy of species, page 750

16.3 Some generalisations about homeostasis

The glucose story illustrates an important principle of homeostasis: **negative feedback**. Negative feedback means that when something changes, the *opposite* effect is instigated. In the case of glucose regulation, an increase in the concentration of glucose sets into motion the processes which *decrease* it. Conversely a decrease in the glucose concentration sets into motion the processes which *increase* it. The result is that, whatever the direction of the change (i.e. the **error**), the concentration of glucose automatically returns to its optimum value. This optimum value (norm) represents the **set point** in the homeostatic process.

To counteract a change in the concentration of blood glucose, some kind of **corrective mechanism** must be involved. The corrective mechanism is triggered by the very thing which is to be regulated. In other words the system is self-adjusting.

For the corrective mechanism to work there must be **receptors** capable of detecting the change, and **effectors** that carry out the corrective measures. We may also predict that there must be some kind of **control centre** for coordinating the overall response. In many homeostatic processes the control centre is in the brain. These general principles are summarised in figure 16.5.

Reducing fluctuations

Another generalisation emerging from the control of blood glucose is that homeostasis necessarily must involve fluctuations, small though these may be. In the case of glucose regulation, when the concentration of blood glucose falls it overshoots the norm, thus triggering the corrective processes which cause it to rise again.

The secret of an efficient homeostatic system is to minimise the overshoot, thus dampening down the fluctuations (*figure 16.6*). This is achieved mainly by:

- gradually cutting off the corrective mechanism as the glucose concentration approaches the norm, by secreting an antagonistic hormone (glucagon);

- having a system whose components (receptors, control centre and effectors) respond quickly with the minimum delay.

The way homeostasis works means that it is impossible for anything to be absolutely constant. Fluctuations, however small, are inevitable. It is therefore more accurate to talk about things being held near constant rather than constant.

The scope of homeostasis

We have seen how homeostasis works in the regulation of glucose. Later we shall apply it to the regulation of osmotic pressure and body temperature. However, it is by no means confined to physiological situations. The size of a population of animals or plants is kept under control by homeostatic means, and essentially the same mechanism maintains the constancy of species over long periods of time.

Nor are homeostatic processes restricted to biology. To take an everyday example, the thermostat in an oven or central heating system operates on a homeostatic basis, switching itself on or off according to the temperature. Many machines involve similar principles, as do industrial processes and economic systems. For example, in supermarkets the ordering of merchandise for stocking the shelves is regulated by the demand.

Positive feedback

Sometimes a deviation from the norm is not corrected. Instead it leads to a further deviation. The result is a 'runaway' situation in which a change triggers more change in the same direction. This is known as **positive feedback**.

At first sight positive feedback would appear to be damaging, even destructive. Think, for example, how harmful it would be if an increase in body temperature led not to a decrease but to a further increase in temperature. This is in fact what happens in **heat stroke** (*page 307*). However, in certain circumstances positive feedback is useful.

An example of useful positive feedback is seen in amphibians such as frogs and toads. Their development is controlled (as ours is) by the thyroid hormone, **thyroxine**. In the tadpole the secretion of thyroxine is kept in steady state by negative feedback. However, just before the tadpole is due to undergo metamorphosis into the adult, negative feedback is replaced by positive feedback. In consequence the concentration of thyroxine rises, and this triggers metamorphosis (*page 534*).

What is happening here is that a homeostatic system is jumping into a new gear. A new set point is established and thereafter negative feedback takes place around the new set point. We shall come across other examples of this in later chapters.

The ecological advantage of homeostasis

Consider two animals, A and B:

- **Animal A** has no homeostatic mechanisms and therefore cannot maintain a constant internal environment. For example, if the surrounding temperature rises, its body temperature rises too. The result is that it can only live in places where the external environment is itself pretty constant.

- **Animal B**, on the other hand, has evolved an impressive repertoire of homeostatic mechanisms which enable it to maintain a constant internal environment even when the external environment varies. So, instead of being restricted to a specific external environment, animal B can move with ease from one environment to another.

There are many animal species like B – for example, mammals whose powers of temperature regulation allow them to be equally at home in temperate or tropical regions, and fish such as salmon and eels whose efficiency at controlling their internal osmotic pressure allows them to migrate from sea to freshwater or vice versa.

This ability to exploit widely differing external environments is what Claude Bernard meant by 'free life'. It has been made possible by the development of homeostatic mechanisms of the kind we shall be looking at in the next few chapters.

16.4 The mammalian liver

We have seen that the liver plays a key part in the regulation of glucose. This is only one of several homeostatic functions performed by this vital organ. The rest of this chapter will be devoted to looking at the liver with its homeostatic role in mind.

Functions of the liver

It has been estimated that the liver performs over 500 specific functions. For our purposes they can be reduced to ten broad categories.

1 **Metabolism of carbohydrates, lipids and proteins** Along with certain other tissues, the liver controls the concentration of glucose in the bloodstream, supplying it when it is needed and removing it when it is in excess. It removes lipids from the blood and either oxidises them with the transfer of energy, or modifies them chemically before they are sent to the body's fat depots for storage (*extension box alongside*). It can also synthesise lipids from excess carbohydrate and protein, and synthesises non-essential amino acids by **transamination** (*page 31*). It also gets rid of unwanted protein, as we shall see in the next point.

2 **Detoxification** The liver renders harmless (**detoxifies**) many drugs and poisons by changing them chemically. For example, hydrogen peroxide, a toxic by-product of metabolism, is rapidly split into water and oxygen by the enzyme **catalase** which occurs in high concentration in the liver (*page 125*).

How the liver cells deal with surplus fat

After meals the liver converts any excess carbohydrate and protein into triglyceride fat. This, together with any surplus fat that the liver has not oxidised (respired), is converted into low density **lipoproteins**. The lipoproteins then pass from the liver cells into the bloodstream which carries them to the adipose tissue in the body's fat depots. Here the lipoproteins are converted back into triglycerides which are stored in fat cells.

If the liver cells are damaged, excess fat cannot be converted into lipoproteins and fat accumulates in the liver cells as droplets of triglyceride. A 'fatty liver' is one of the many complications resulting from excessive drinking of alcohol.

Triglycerides, page 24; lipoproteins, page 29; adipose tissue and fat cells, page 66

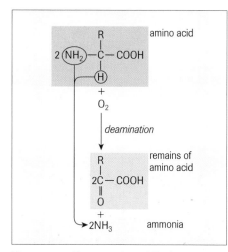

Figure 16.7 How an amino acid is deaminated. The ammonia is subsequently converted into urea and excreted.

An important detoxification function of the liver is the disposal of ethanol (alcohol). The ethanol is first converted into **acetaldehyde** which is then metabolised. There is, however, a limit to the capacity of the liver to cope with this poisonous substance. If taken in excess over a long time, ethanol may kill the liver cells which become replaced with useless fibrous tissue. This condition is called **cirrhosis of the liver** and is a contributing cause of death in alcoholics. Ethanol can also damage the brain.

3 **Excretion of nitrogenous waste** The body is unable to store proteins or amino acids as such, and much of the surplus is got rid of by the liver. First the liver cells remove the amino (NH_2) group from the amino acid, with the formation of ammonia. This process is called **deamination** (*figure 16.7*). The rest of the amino acid is then fed into carbohydrate metabolism and respired.

Meanwhile the ammonia, which is highly toxic and must not be allowed to accumulate, reacts with carbon dioxide to form the less toxic nitrogenous compound urea. The details, if you want them, are explained in the extension box below.

Finally the urea is released from the liver cells into the bloodstream, and taken up by the kidneys which eliminate it from the body (*Chapter 17*).

Extension

How urea is formed

The formation of urea from ammonia and carbon dioxide can be summarised by this equation:

$$2NH_3 + CO_2 \rightarrow CO(NH_2)_2 + H_2O$$

ammonia   urea

There is no shortage of carbon dioxide for this reaction as it is continually being produced by respiration.

The reaction, however, does not take place in a single step as suggested by the above equation. Instead it takes place by a series of reactions which together make up the **urea cycle** (also called the **ornithine cycle**) (*illustration*).

The urea cycle was worked out by Hans Krebs and a medical student called Kurt Henseleit in 1932. It was the first cyclical metabolic pathway ever discovered. The citric acid cycle followed later.

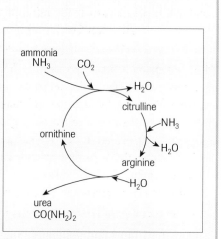

The urea cycle (ornithine cycle).

Although urea is regarded as an excretory product to be got rid of from the body, there is always a certain amount of it in the bloodstream and it does have certain functions in humans and other animals as we shall see in the next chapter.

---

4 **Inactivation of certain hormones after they have achieved their effects**
Insulin, glucagon, thyroxine and various steroid hormones (including the sex hormones) are dealt with in this way.

5 **Thermoregulation** Its consistently high metabolic rate, coupled with its large size and excellent blood supply, make the liver ideal for the steady transfer of heat energy. Of course other organs transfer heat energy too – skeletal muscles for example – but the liver does this even when the body is resting and the general metabolic rate is low. This helps to maintain the body temperature.

6 Production of bile Bile is produced by the liver and stored in the gall bladder. From the gall bladder it passes down the bile duct to the duodenum. The **bile salts** are synthesised from cholesterol and play an important part in digestion by emulsifying fats in the small intestine (*page 189*).

In addition the bile contains **bile pigments**, the principal one being a brown pigment called **bilirubin**. The bile pigments are the breakdown products of haemoglobin resulting from the destruction of used red blood cells by phagocytes in the liver, spleen and bone marrow. Once in the gut, bilirubin is converted into another closely related pigment which is responsible for giving the faeces their brown colour.

7 Formation of cholesterol Cholesterol is an important constituent of plasma membranes (*page 58*). It is synthesised in the liver by a metabolic pathway that leads from acetyl coenzyme A. Excess cholesterol is excreted in the bile. If there is a surplus, it may precipitate in the gall bladder or bile duct as **gall stones** (*figure 16.8*). These sometimes block the bile duct, leading to **obstructive jaundice** in which the skin goes yellow due to retention of bilirubin in the blood.

The amount of cholesterol in the blood is largely determined by dietary intake in conjunction with the metabolic activities of the liver. If you take in more cholesterol than you need, a negative feedback process occurs and the liver stops synthesising it.

If there is persistently too much cholesterol in the blood, some of it may be deposited in the walls of certain arteries, obstructing the smooth passage of blood and often leading to **cardiovascular disease** (*page 240*). The elimination of excess cholesterol is therefore an important function of the liver.

8 Formation of red blood cells In the fetus the liver is responsible for the formation of red blood cells, but gradually this function is taken over by the bone marrow. However, the adult liver still plays an important part in the production of red blood cells for it stores **vitamin B_{12}**, a porphyrin with cobalt in the centre, which is required for the formation of red blood cells in the bone marrow.

Lack of vitamin B_{12} results in **pernicious anaemia**, characterised by a drastic reduction in the number of red cells and therefore in the amount of haemoglobin in the blood. If untreated, pernicious anaemia is fatal.

9 Synthesis of the plasma proteins fibrinogen, globulins and albumen
Fibrinogen is responsible for the clotting of blood (*page 228*). In fact most of the factors needed for blood clotting are made by the liver. The other plasma proteins have a number of functions connected with homeostasis and defence against disease (*Chapter 19*).

10 Storage of certain vitamins and minerals We have already seen that the liver stores vitamin B_{12}. Most of the other B-vitamins are also stored by the liver, as are vitamins A and D. Minerals stored by the liver include iron and copper.

Reviewing these functions of the liver, one is struck by the extent to which it controls the internal environment. Each of the functions listed above is in some way connected with homeostasis. We can summarise the role of the liver by saying that it synthesises certain vital substances required by the body, stores compounds which are of no immediate use, ensures that the blood has the right glucose concentration and generally regulates the internal environment.

Structure of the liver

The liver has been described as the body's metabolic centre. As such, it must have a good blood supply from which it can take up raw materials, and into which it can shed products.

The structure of the liver is directly related to its functions. It is the largest organ in the body, in the human adult weighing about 1.5 kg, 3–4 per cent of the total body mass. It has an excellent blood supply, receiving more blood per unit time than any other organ. It has

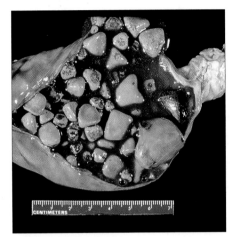

Figure 16.8 A sample of gall stones in the gall bladder of a person who had been suffering from obstructive jaundice. Gall stones consist of cholesterol and calcium salts.

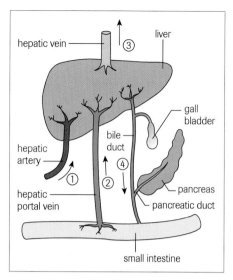

Figure 16.9 Schematic diagram of the liver and its connections.
Arrow 1: oxygenated blood.
Arrow 2: blood from the gut containing soluble food substances.
Arrow 3: blood containing all the products of the liver except bile.
Arrow 4: bile.

been calculated that the blood flow through the liver is well over a litre per minute, which is marginally greater than that of the kidneys.

The connections of the liver are summarised in figure 16.9. Its blood supply is derived from two sources:

- the **hepatic artery**, which brings oxygenated blood from the heart via the dorsal aorta;
- the **hepatic portal vein**, which brings blood rich in food materials from the gut – as much as three-quarters of the blood reaching the liver does so via the hepatic portal vein.

The liver releases its products (except bile) into the **hepatic vein**: glucose, amino acids, lipids, plasma proteins, urea, cholesterol and of course carbon dioxide from the respiration of its cells. Bile is secreted into the **bile duct**.

The liver's microscopic structure

Examination of the liver with the light microscope shows it to be composed of numerous **lobules**, roughly cylindrical in shape and approximately one millimetre in diameter. Each lobule is filled with a large number of small polygonal cells called **hepatocytes** ('liver cells') which are arranged in rows radiating outwards from the centre. You can see the pattern of these cells in the photomicrograph in figure 16.10.

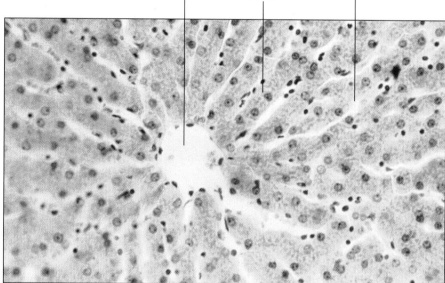

Figure 16.10 Photomicrograph of a transverse section of a lobule of the liver. Notice the rows of hepatocytes (liver cells) radiating out from the central vein, and the blood capillaries (sinusoids) between them. Magnification ×200.

Running alongside each lobule are branches of the hepatic artery, hepatic portal vein and bile duct (*figure 16.11A*). The first two are referred to as **interlobular vessels** since they lie between adjacent lobules. In the centre of each lobule is a branch of the hepatic vein, referred to as the **intralobular** or **central vein**.

The interlobular vessels are connected to the central vein by a system of blood capillaries, called **sinusoids**, which lie between the chains of liver cells and follow the same radiating pattern. They can be seen clearly in figure 16.10. The sinusoids have a flattened endothelial lining across which substances pass to and from the liver cells.

Also between the chains of liver cells are fine channels called **canaliculi** which connect up with the branches of the bile duct at the edge of the lobule. The canaliculi have no endothelial lining – they are simply intercellular spaces.

So, the liver cells have an intimate relationship both with the sinusoids and with the canaliculi. This is made clear in figure 16.11B.

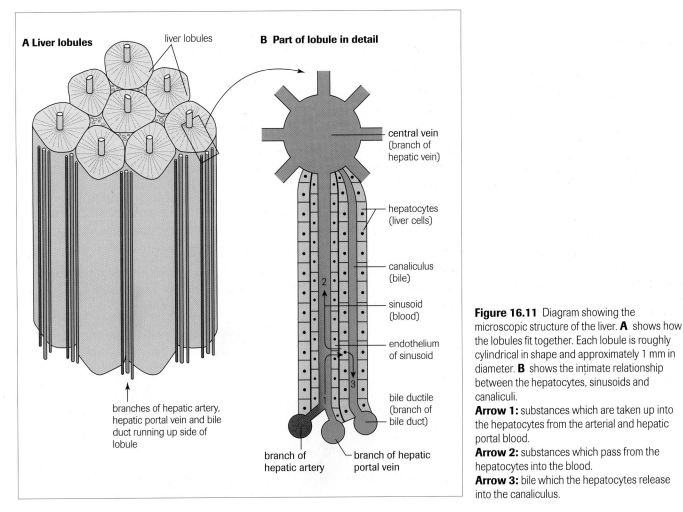

A Liver lobules

liver lobules

branches of hepatic artery, hepatic portal vein and bile duct running up side of lobule

B Part of lobule in detail

central vein (branch of hepatic vein)

hepatocytes (liver cells)

canaliculus (bile)

sinusoid (blood)

endothelium of sinusoid

bile ductile (branch of bile duct)

branch of hepatic artery

branch of hepatic portal vein

Figure 16.11 Diagram showing the microscopic structure of the liver. **A** shows how the lobules fit together. Each lobule is roughly cylindrical in shape and approximately 1 mm in diameter. **B** shows the intimate relationship between the hepatocytes, sinusoids and canaliculi.
Arrow 1: substances which are taken up into the hepatocytes from the arterial and hepatic portal blood.
Arrow 2: substances which pass from the hepatocytes into the blood.
Arrow 3: bile which the hepatocytes release into the canaliculus.

Blood reaches each lobule via the interlobular vessels: oxygenated blood arrives in the branches of the hepatic artery, blood rich in food materials in the branches of the hepatic portal vein. The blood then flows along the sinusoids towards the central vein. As it does so, the hepatocytes take up from the blood what they require, and shed their products into it. The only exception is the bile which is secreted, not into the sinusoids, but into the canaliculi from where it trickles to the bile duct.

Attached to the walls of the sinusoids are phagocytic **macrophages** which destroy old red blood cells and remove bacteria and foreign particles from the blood flowing through the liver. All other functions of the liver are carried out by the hepatocytes.

The fine structure of the hepatocytes

The electron microscope shows the hepatocytes to have a prominent Golgi apparatus, abundant mitochondria and numerous glycogen granules (*figure 16.12*). These are features we would expect to find in any cell whose principal activities are secretion and the storage and transfer of energy.

They also have prominent bodies called **peroxisomes**. Peroxisomes are found in all eukaryotic cells but are exceptionally large in the liver. They contain catalase and other oxidative enzymes responsible for detoxification. Much of the ethanol that a person drinks is disposed of by the peroxisomes.

Otherwise the hepatocytes show no special features. If they appear rather nondescript, this is more than made up for by what they do. For sheer metabolic versatility, this unremarkable looking cell is probably unrivalled anywhere else in the body.

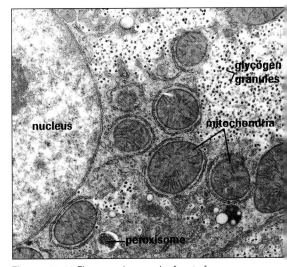

glycogen granules

nucleus

mitochondria

peroxisome

Figure 16.12 Electron micrograph of part of a hepatocyte. Magnification ×14 000.

Summary

1. 'The constancy of the internal environment is the condition for free life.' This principle was first put forward by Claude Bernard in 1857. Maintenance of a constant internal environment is called **homeostasis**.

2. By 'free life' is meant the ability of a species to inhabit a wide range of environments.

3. The 'internal environment' is the immediate surroundings of the cells. In animals, this consists of **tissue fluid** which bathes the cells.

4. Tissue fluid consists of plasma minus proteins and is formed by ultrafiltration from the blood capillaries. Excess tissue fluid passes into the **lymph vessels** where it constitutes **lymph**.

5. The main features of an animal's internal environment which need to be controlled are its **chemical composition**, **osmotic pressure**, **pH** and **temperature**. In addition, nitrogenous waste products and other toxic substances are either eliminated altogether or at least kept to a minimum.

6. The principles of homeostasis can be illustrated by the control of **blood glucose** in the mammal. A rise in the glucose level results in the secretion of **insulin** from the **islets of Langerhans** in the **pancreas** and this brings about the metabolic disposal of excess blood sugar in the liver and certain other organs.

7. Insulin's effects are opposed by another hormone, **glucagon**, also secreted by the islets of Langerhans.

8. Failure of the pancreas to secrete sufficient insulin results in **diabetes mellitus**.

9. In general, homeostatic control processes work as follows: any deviation from the **norm** (**set point**) sets into motion the appropriate **corrective mechanism** which restores the norm (**negative feedback**).

10. Various mechanisms help to minimise deviations from the set point, thereby dampening down fluctuations and improving the efficiency of the homeostatic system.

11. In certain circumstances a deviation from the norm may result in a further deviation (**positive feedback**).

12. One of the most important homeostatic organs in the body is the **liver**. Its homeostatic functions include the production of bile, the regulation of carbohydrates, lipids and amino acids, the elimination of haemoglobin from used red blood cells and the transfer of heat energy.

13. The microscopic structure of the liver, showing an intimate association between the **liver cells** (**hepatocytes**) and bile channels and blood capillaries, is directly related to its functions.

Practice questions

For general advice on these questions and advice on answering essay-type questions, see pages vii and viii.

1. The diagram below shows values for the pressure potential and solute potential of the blood plasma in a capillary and of the surrounding tissue fluid. The pressure potential is the pressure exerted by the fluid in a confined space (hydrostatic pressure), while the solute potential is caused by the presence of solute molecules, particularly ions and plasma proteins.

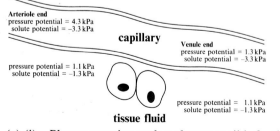

Arteriole end
pressure potential = 4.3 kPa
solute potential = –3.3 kPa

capillary

Venule end
pressure potential = 1.3 kPa
solute potential = –3.3 kPa

pressure potential = 1.1 kPa
solute potential = –1.3 kPa

pressure potential = 1.1 kPa
solute potential = –1.3 kPa

tissue fluid

(a) (i) Plasma proteins are largely responsible for the solute potential of the plasma. Suggest why the solute potential of the plasma remains the same along the length of the capillary. (1)

(ii) Suggest a reason for the fall in the pressure potential (hydrostatic pressure) along the length of the capillary. (1)

(b) The formula below is used to calculate the water potential of the plasma and the tissue fluid.

Water potential = pressure potential + solute potential
(Ψ) (Ψ_p) (Ψ_s)

(i) Use the equation, and the information in the diagram, to calculate values for the water potential of plasma and tissue fluid at each end of the capillary.

Write your answers in a table like the one below. (2)

	at the arteriole end	at the venule end
Water potential (Ψ) of the plasma		
Water potential (Ψ) of the tissue fluid		

(ii) Use your calculated values to explain why water moves out of the plasma at the arteriole end, and into the plasma at the venule end of the capillary. (3)

(c) A lack of plasma proteins can lead to swelling in various parts of the body as tissue fluid accumulates. Suggest a reason for the accumulation of the tissue fluid. (3)

(d) The thin capillary wall consists of flattened cells, whereas the cells lining the ileum are columnar and contain many mitochondria. Account for these structural differences with reference to the types of transport which take place through the cells. (3)

(Total 13 marks)

CCEA 1998

2. A person fasted overnight and then swallowed 75 g of glucose. The graph shows the resulting changes in the concentrations of insulin and glucose in the blood.

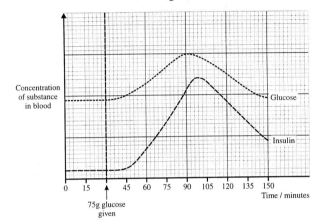

(a) (i) Explain the relationship between the concentrations of glucose and insulin in the blood in the first 30 minutes after the glucose was swallowed. (2)

(ii) Use information from the graph to explain what is meant by the term *negative feedback*. (1)

(b) Explain why the concentration of glucagon in the blood rises during exercise while that of insulin falls. (2)

(Total 5 marks)

AEB 1998

3. People with diabetes have blood glucose levels higher than normal. The blood glucose levels can be monitored by glucose tolerance tests.

The graph above right shows typical results of glucose tolerance tests for normal and diabetic people. The reading at time 0 minutes shows the fasting blood glucose level. The other points show the changes in blood glucose level over a period of 150 minutes after consuming a high glucose drink.

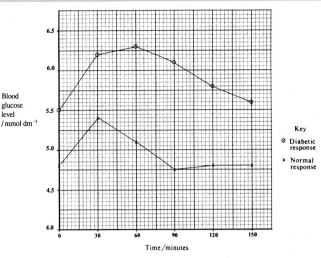

(a) Calculate the difference in the fasting blood glucose level of normal and diabetic people expressed as a percentage of the normal fasting level. Show your working. (2)

(b) Comment on the similarities and differences between the curves. (5)

(c) Explain why diabetics are advised to eat foods rich in starch but low in sugars. (2)

(d) Explain why a carefully regulated diet is essential for juvenile-onset diabetics whose illness is controlled by insulin injections. (2)

(Total 11 marks)

London 1996

4. (a) Describe the role of the pancreas and the liver in the control of blood sugar. (6)

(b) Describe the role of the liver in the metabolism of proteins and amino acids. (6)

(Total 12 marks)

NEAB 1998

5. Answers should be illustrated by large, clearly labelled diagrams whenever suitable. Up to 2 additional marks in this section are awarded for quality of expression.

(a) Describe the blood supply of the liver. (7)

(b) Discuss the role of the liver in protein metabolism. (11)

(Total 18 marks)

UCLES 1997

6. Answers should be illustrated by large, clearly labelled diagrams whenever suitable. Up to 2 additional marks in this section are awarded for quality of expression.

(a) Discuss the **principles** of homeostasis. (7)

(b) Explain how the blood glucose concentration is regulated. (11)

(Total 18 marks)

Chapter 17

Excretion and water balance

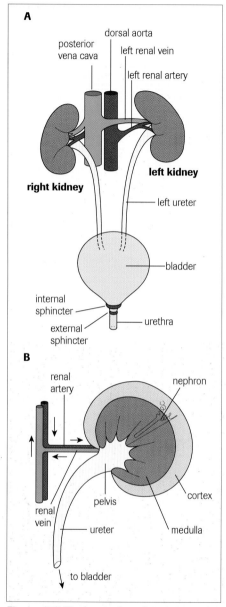

Figure 17.1 The mammalian urinary system.
A Ventral view of the whole system. The sphincters and their role in urination are explained on page 288.
B Section through a kidney showing the position of the nephron in relation to the cortex and medulla.

Excretion is the removal from the body of the waste products of metabolism. The term is generally taken to mean **nitrogenous waste** such as urea and ammonia, but the removal of other waste products of metabolism like carbon dioxide and the bile pigments are also part of excretion. The term is also extended to include toxic substances such as drugs, though these are not products of metabolism. In this chapter we shall be concerned mainly with nitrogenous excretion.

The blood and tissue fluid contain a variety of solutes (glucose, salts and the like) dissolved in water. The concentrations, relative and absolute, of these solutes have to be regulated, as does their total concentration relative to water. The latter gives the blood and tissue fluids a particular **solute concentration**, and this too must be kept constant. Maintaining the correct balance between the water and solutes in the body is called **osmoregulation**.

These two processes, excretion and osmoregulation, are both aspects of homeostasis, and the physiological mechanisms involved are bound up with each other. Indeed, in the mammal the same system performs both functions. This is the **urinary system** to which we must now direct our attention.

17.1 The mammalian urinary system

The mammalian urinary system is shown in figure 17.1A. Its principal organs are the **kidneys** of which there are two, one on each side of the abdomen. If you put your hands on your hips, your kidneys are just under your thumbs.

The kidneys control the composition of the body fluids by selectively removing unwanted substances from the blood. To this end they have an exceptionally good blood supply.

Blood is conveyed to each kidney by the **renal artery**, a branch of the dorsal aorta. After flowing through the kidney, the blood is collected into the **renal vein** from which it flows to the posterior vena cava. Meanwhile, substances which have been removed from the blood in the kidneys pass into a space inside each kidney called the **pelvis** and thence, via the two **ureters**, to the **bladder**.

The fluid which enters the bladder is called **urine**, and every now and again it is expelled to the exterior via the **urethra** in the process of **urination**.

The kidney

Each of our kidneys contains between one and two million microscopic structures called **nephrons**. The nephron can be regarded as the basic unit of the kidney, performing all its regulatory functions. It is the nephron that produces urine.

Figure 17.1B shows how a typical nephron is positioned in relation to the kidney as a whole. The kidney consists of two main regions: an outer **cortex** and inner **medulla**. Part of the nephron lies in the cortex, and part of it in the medulla.

To understand how the nephron works, we must first examine its structure.

Structure of a nephron

Figure 17.2 shows the detailed structure of the nephron. At its inner (proximal) end there is a spherical structure called the **Malpighian body**. This is about 200 μm in diameter, and is located in the cortex of the kidney. The Malpighian body consists of a cup-shaped **Bowman's capsule** which is like a hollow rubber ball that has been pressed in on one side. The invagination contains a dense network of capillaries called a **glomerulus**. The inside of the capsule, the **capsule space**, is separated from the lumen of the capillaries by only two layers of cells: the epithelium of the capsule and the endothelium of the capillaries. These two layers of cells are highly specialised. Their significance will become clear presently.

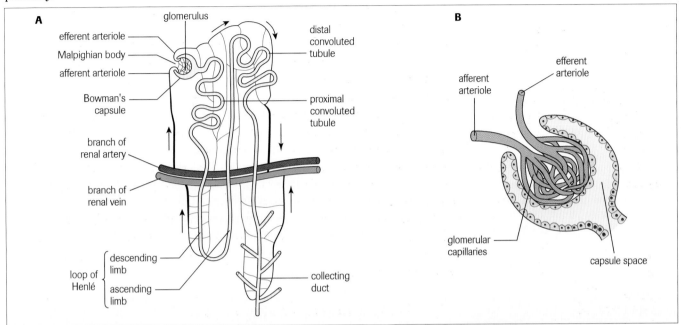

Figure 17.2 Microscopic structure of the mammalian kidney. **A** Single nephron with its blood supply. **B** Malpighian body enlarged to show its internal structure.

Leading from the Bowman's capsule is a tubule, about 60 μm in outer diameter, whose lumen is continuous with the capsule space. The first part of the tubule is located in the cortex of the kidney and is coiled: it is called the **proximal convoluted tubule** (*proximal* because it is the first part, *convoluted* because it is coiled). You can see the beginning of it in figure 17.3.

The proximal convoluted tubule leads to a U-shaped **loop of Henlé**, named after the German microscopist F.G.J. Henlé, who discovered it in the 19th century. It consists of a straight **descending limb** which plunges down into the medulla, where it does a hair-pin bend and returns to the cortex as the **ascending limb**. The ascending limb of the loop of Henlé leads to the final part of the nephron, the **distal convoluted tubule**. This, as the name implies, is coiled and it opens into a **collecting duct**. Several nephrons share the same collecting duct.

The collecting ducts converge at the pelvis of the kidney, emptying their contents into the ureter which conveys them to the bladder as urine. The tubules and collecting ducts are lined with a single layer of epithelial cells, mainly of the cuboidal type.

Each nephron has its own blood supply. Blood from the renal artery is carried to the glomerulus by an **afferent arteriole** and leaves it by an **efferent arteriole**. The latter splits up into a capillary network which envelops the tubule of that particular nephron. Blood from the capillaries drains into the renal vein. So blood flows first to the glomerulus and then to the capillaries surrounding the tubules before leaving the kidney.

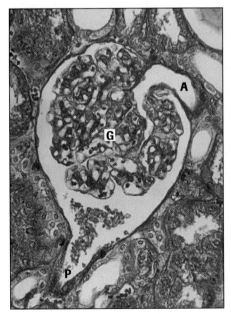

Figure 17.3 Photomicrograph of Bowman's capsule and associated structures. **A** arteriole; **G** glomerulus; **P** proximal convoluted tubule. Magnification ×550.

17.2 How the kidney works

The kidney accomplishes its regulatory functions by three separate but related processes: **filtration**, **reabsorption** and **secretion**. The fluid part of the blood is *filtered* from the glomerulus into the capsule space. As the resulting fluid flows along the tubules, useful

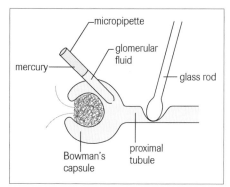

Figure 17.4 Micropuncture technique for removing a sample of fluid from a Bowman's capsule. The proximal tubule is blocked by pressing on it with a fine glass rod. A micropipette, filled with mercury, is inserted through the wall of the capsule into the capsule space beneath. The mercury is then slowly withdrawn from the pipette, and as a result fluid is withdrawn from the capsule. The fluid is then analysed and compared with the composition of the blood. The glass rod and pipette are operated by micromanipulators, mechanical devices which scale down the movements of the experimenter. When the experimenter's hand moves through a distance of, say, one centimetre, the pipette moves only a fraction of a millimetre.

substances are *reabsorbed* back into the bloodstream in the amounts required by the body. In addition certain unwanted substances in the blood are actively *secreted* into the tubules. Let us examine each of these processes in turn.

Filtration in Bowman's capsule

Our knowledge of what happens in Bowman's capsule, and indeed the entire nephron, is based on **micropuncture experiments** pioneered by Alfred Richards at the University of Pennsylvania in the 1930s, and repeated since then with ever-increasing sophistication by other research workers. The technique involves inserting a micropipette into an individual capsule and drawing off a small quantity of fluid from the capsule space (*figure 17.4*). The fluid is then analysed and its composition compared with that of the blood.

It turns out that the fluid in the capsule space has the same composition as blood plasma *minus the plasma proteins*. It seems that the capsule fluid is formed by a process of filtration from the glomerular capillaries. The filtrate (called **glomerular filtrate**) contains all the constituents of blood except the blood cells and plasma proteins. These are held back because they are too large to pass through the barrier between the glomerular capillaries and the capsule space. This barrier therefore functions as a **dialysing membrane**, separating the plasma proteins from the other components of the plasma. This is filtration at the molecular level, and it is called **ultrafiltration**.

For ultrafiltration to occur there must be sufficient pressure in the glomerular capillaries to force fluid through their walls. In fact the blood pressure in the glomerular capillaries is considerably higher than in the capillaries of other organs. The reason is that the efferent arteriole in which blood leaves the glomerulus is markedly narrower than the afferent vessel (*see figure 17.2B*). The resulting high pressure tends to force the fluid constituents of the blood into the capsule space (*extension box below*).

The structure of the filter

The filter must be constructed in such a way as to retain molecules above a certain size while allowing smaller molecules (and ions) to pass through.

The electron microscope has provided information on the structure of the filter (*figure 17.5*). It is made up of two cell layers: the epithelium of the capsule and the endothelium of the glomerular capillaries. Between these two cell layers is the basement membrane.

The capsule epithelial cells are quite unlike ordinary epithelial cells (*figure 17.5A*). Instead of fitting together to form a continuous sheet, they are arranged in an irregular network rather like a net curtain. The cells are called **podocytes**, which literally means 'footed cells'. Each podocyte has about six arm-like **major processes** from whose lower side much finer **minor processes** project. The minor processes – the 'feet' of the podocyte – lie between similar processes of neighbouring podocytes and extend to the basement membrane. Between adjacent minor processes are narrow spaces, about 0.1 μm wide. These **filtration slits**, as they are called, are large enough to allow the passage of all the constituents of blood plasma, including the proteins, but not the blood cells.

On the other side of the basement membrane are the endothelial cells of the glomerular capillaries. The electron microscope has shown these cells to be perforated by numerous **pores**. These pores, like the filtration slits, hold back the blood cells but are large enough to allow the passage of all the constituents of blood plasma (*figures 17.5B and C*).

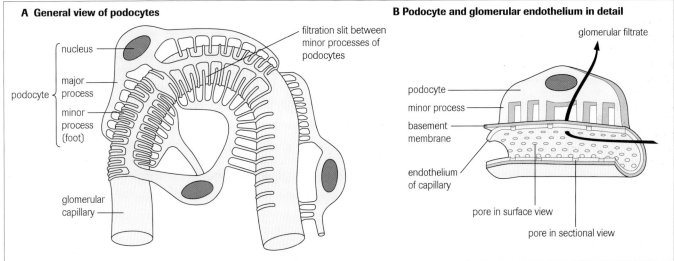

A General view of podocytes

nucleus

major process

podocyte

minor process (foot)

glomerular capillary

filtration slit between minor processes of podocytes

B Podocyte and glomerular endothelium in detail

glomerular filtrate

podocyte

minor process

basement membrane

endothelium of capillary

pore in surface view

pore in sectional view

Figure 17.5 Structure of the glomerular barrier through which ultrafiltration occurs in the Bowman's capsule.
A Realistic diagram showing how the epithelial cells (podocytes) of the capsule fit together to form a perforated covering over a glomerular capillary.
B Schematic diagram of a single podocyte showing the way it relates to the endothelium of the capillary.
C Electron micrograph of a section through a glomerular capillary and adjoining podocytes. Magnification ×8000.

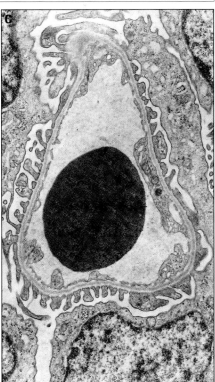

If the pores and slits let through all the constituents of blood plasma, which component of the barrier serves as the dialysing membrane holding back the plasma proteins? There is only one answer: the basement membrane. This is the only *continuous* structure between the blood and the capsule space, the only part of the barrier which has not got holes in it large enough to let through the plasma proteins. So the basement membrane must be the dialysing membrane responsible for ultrafiltration.

Reabsorption from the tubules

After the glomerular filtrate has been formed, it flows along the tubule of the nephron and eventually emerges from a collecting duct as urine. Researchers have compared the volumes and composition of glomerular filtrate and urine, and have found that for most substances the amount excreted is considerably less than the amount filtered (*table 17.1*). It is therefore clear that these substances are reabsorbed back into the bloodstream as they flow along the tubule.

Whereabouts in the nephron does reabsorption take place? This, too, has been investigated by micropuncture experiments (*figure 17.6*). These studies have shown that all the glucose and most of the water and salt (sodium and chloride ions) are reabsorbed in

Table 17.1 The relative amounts of various substances filtered, reabsorbed and excreted by the kidney of an adult human on a normal diet.

Substance	Filtered	Reabsorbed	Excreted
Na⁺	26 000	25 850	150
Cl⁻	19 000	18 800	200
Urea	870	460	410
Glucose	800	800	nil
Amino acids	400	400	nil
Water	180 000	179 000	1000

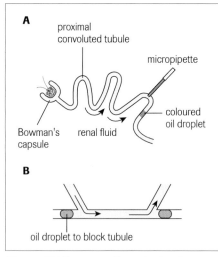

Figure 17.6 Two ways of investigating the functions of the kidney tubules by micropuncture techniques.
A A tiny drop of coloured oil is injected into a tubule. A fine micropipette is inserted into the tubule in front of the oil droplet. Fluid is then withdrawn from the tubule at a rate that keeps the oil droplet stationary. The fluid is then analysed and compared with glomerular filtrate.
B An artificial fluid of known composition is injected into one end of an isolated length of tubule and withdrawn from the other end. It is then analysed to find out if any changes have occurred in its composition.

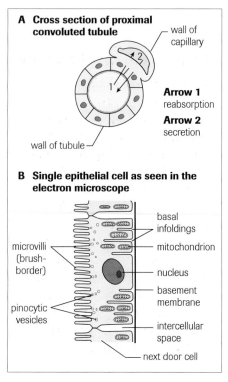

the proximal convoluted tubule. The remaining water is mainly reabsorbed in the collecting duct by a mechanism which depends on the loop of Henlé – more about that in a moment. In general, most reabsorption is completed in the proximal tubule, the distal tubule being mainly for fine adjustment.

Reabsorption of glucose and salts takes place at least partly by **active transport** and can therefore occur against a concentration gradient. In the case of salt, sodium ions are reabsorbed actively and the chloride ions then follow passively. Water is reabsorbed passively by osmosis following the active reabsorption of sodium ions.

You will notice in table 17.1 that all the glucose which is filtered is reabsorbed. The concentration of glucose in the blood is controlled, not by the kidney, but by other homeostatic processes, principally the insulin–glucagon mechanism described in Chapter 16. Only if the blood glucose concentration exceeds a certain critical value does the kidney fail to reabsorb it all and glucose starts appearing in the urine. This is what happens in people who have diabetes. In fact, testing the urine for sugar is how doctors find if a person has diabetes; in the old days they used to taste it!

Glucose is not the only substance to be completely reabsorbed by the kidney. Amino acids are too. As with glucose, the reabsorption of amino acids involves active transport and takes place in the proximal convoluted tubule.

Secretion into the tubules

Certain substances that escape being filtered are actively transferred (secreted) into the tubules from the surrounding blood capillaries.

There is evidence that in some mammals a certain amount of urea is actively secreted in this way. Ammonia and uric acid are certainly secreted, as are hydrogen ions (*page 290*). Potassium ions are secreted *and* reabsorbed: their final concentration in the bloodstream depends on the balance between these two opposing processes.

Structure of the tubule cells

The tubules that make up the nephron are lined with a single layer of mainly cuboidal epithelium which lies close to the endothelium of adjacent blood capillaries. There is therefore a close relationship between the tubules and the surrounding blood vessels, which correlates well with their functions of reabsorption and secretion (*figure 17.7A*).

The structure of the individual epithelial cells lining the tubules can also be related to their functions (*figure 17.7B*). The free surface of each cell (i.e. the surface bordering the lumen of the tubule) bears numerous **microvilli**, each about 1 μm in length. There are so many of them that in humans the total surface area achieved by the proximal convoluted tubules of the two kidneys is of the order of 50 m². Between the microvilli are numerous **pinocytic vesicles** which help to draw substances into the cell.

Figure 17.7 Microscopic structure of the proximal convoluted tubule.
A In this low-magnification view notice how the epithelial lining is closely associated with an adjacent capillary.
B Detail of an individual epithelial cell based on electron micrographs. The inner side of the epithelial cell bears numerous microvilli between which pinocytic vesicles can be seen. The outer side is greatly folded, with mitochondria between the folds.

The surface area of the other side of the epithelial cell (i.e. the surface bordering the capillary) is increased by infoldings of the plasma membrane. Between these **basal infoldings** lie numerous mitochondria which supply energy for active transport.

Another interesting feature of these tubule epithelial cells is the presence of large **intercellular spaces** between adjacent cells. Only towards the free surface are the cells in contact. They are involved in the transfer of sodium and chloride ions, and water, into the adjacent capillary.

The role of the loop of Henlé

It is in the interests of terrestrial animals to be able to conserve water. In mammals, this function depends on the loop of Henlé. Mammals are the only vertebrates whose kidneys can produce a urine with a markedly higher solute concentration than that of the blood plasma. Desert mammals, which produce a particularly concentrated urine, have an extra-long loop of Henlé.

What exactly does the loop of Henlé do? In brief, it concentrates salt in the medulla of the kidney. The high salt concentration then causes a vigorous osmotic flow of water out of the collecting ducts, thereby concentrating the urine.

In achieving this the loop of Henlé employs the principle of a **hair-pin countercurrent multiplier** (*figure 17.8*). Imagine that renal fluid has just gone down the descending limb and is starting to flow up the ascending limb. As the fluid flows up the ascending limb, salt is actively removed from it and deposited in the surrounding tissue fluid. From there the salt equilibrates with the fluid in the descending limb.

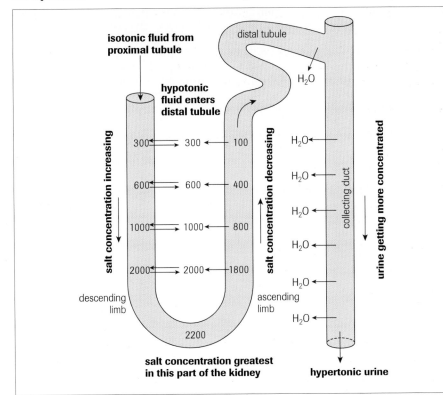

Figure 17.8 Diagram to show the role of the loop of Henlé in the reabsorption of water. The numbers in the descending and ascending limbs, and in the tissue in between, represent osmolarity values in milliosmoles per kilogram of water. The shunting of sodium ions from the ascending to the descending limb creates a high salt concentration in the medullary tissue of the kidney, and this results in water flowing out of the collecting duct by osmosis.

Extension

The blood vessels in the medulla

The blood vessels are also involved in the countercurrent mechanism. The capillaries in the medulla are arranged differently from those in the cortex. Instead of being coiled, they are U-shaped and run parallel with the loops of Henlé. Only about one per cent of the blood that flows through the kidney goes through these vessels, so the blood flow is sluggish. Moreover, their U-shape means that they have a countercurrent system similar to that which occurs in the loop of Henlé itself. This helps to ensure that the high salt concentration in the medulla is not rapidly dissipated by the blood.

This active transfer of salt takes place at all levels of the loop of Henlé. At any given level, the effect is to raise the salt concentration in the descending limb above that in the adjacent ascending limb. The effect at any one level is slight, but the overall effect is multiplied by the length of the hair-pin. As the renal fluid flows down the descending limb towards the apex of the loop, it becomes more and more concentrated; as it flows up the ascending limb it becomes more and more dilute.

The result of this process is to produce a region of particularly high salt concentration in

The term hypertonic is explained on page 109

the deep part of the medulla. The collecting duct passes through this region before opening into the pelvis. As fluid flows down the collecting duct, water may pass out of it by osmosis. This raises its solute concentration, resulting in the production of a markedly hypertonic urine. Meanwhile, the water which has been reabsorbed is taken away in the bloodstream.

What we have been calling salt is in fact sodium and chloride ions. Sodium ions are actively moved, the chloride ions following passively. It is now known that urea, as well as salt, is retained in the medulla and this helps to build up the high solute concentration necessary for the osmotic withdrawal of water from the collecting ducts. So urea, traditionally regarded solely as a waste substance, has a positive function in the body.

Extension

Renal dialysis

People with kidney failure can be treated by renal dialysis. Guest author Patricia Kohn explains what this is and how it has developed.

The kidney performs its functions of excretion and osmoregulation by ultrafiltration followed by selective reabsorption and secretion. Renal dialysis relies solely on passive diffusion to carry out these functions.

Renal dialysis is commonly carried out by a **kidney machine** of the sort shown in illustration 1. The patient's blood is passed along numerous narrow tubes made of a partially permeable **dialysing membrane**. The tubes are immersed in a specially prepared dialysis fluid which contains the desirable components of blood plasma at the same concentration as in the blood itself. These chemicals include sodium ions and glucose. Unwanted substances such as urea are absent from the **dialysis fluid**.

The lining of the tubes holds back the blood cells and plasma proteins but allows all the other chemicals to diffuse through freely (*illustration 2*). As the desirable substances are present in equal concentrations on both sides of the membrane, no net change in their concentrations will occur. However, there will be a net loss from the blood of unwanted substances such as urea because they are not present in the dialysis fluid, and any excess of normal plasma constituents such as potassium or phosphate will also be lost. The dialysis fluid is replaced frequently so that a steep concentration gradient is maintained,

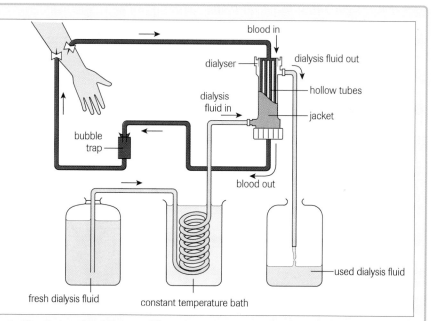

Illustration 1 A modern kidney machine.

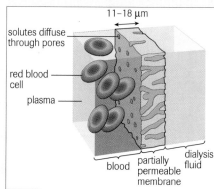

Illustration 2 Detail of the dialysing membrane in a kidney machine. The membrane is partially permeable, allowing the passage of all the components of blood except for the blood cells and plasma proteins.

favouring the continued diffusion of these unwanted substances.

The osmoregulatory function of the kidney is also performed during renal dialysis. Net water loss from the blood can be induced by raising the solute concentration of the dialysis fluid by adding a solute such as dextran to which the dialysing membrane is impermeable. Water will then flow out of the blood by osmosis.

Finding the right membrane

The key piece of technology which makes renal dialysis possible is the dialysing membrane. The principle of dialysis was discovered in the 1860s, but it was not until 1924 that it was applied to the removal of unwanted substances from human blood. The dialysing membrane used then was celloidin, a cellulose-based synthetic material. However, the celloidin membrane was very fragile and few patients were treated.

Then, in the 1930s a breakthrough occurred. Seamless cellophane tubing was developed for the sausage industry and became available in large quantities.

Cellophane is much tougher than celloidin, and the sausage skins provided a source of ready-made dialysis tubing. In Holland, a young physician called Willem Kolff found that sausage skin cellophane was an efficient dialysing membrane for separating urea from blood.

In 1945, using a machine with such a membrane, he succeeded in saving the life of an elderly woman with acute renal failure.

After the war, modern methods of renal dialysis were developed. Today it is a routine procedure. The cellophane membrane was used for many years but has now been replaced by membranes based on other cellulose esters and different polymers. The membranes take the form of a coiled tube, parallel sheets or numerouus hollow tubes, depending on the type of machine.

The problem of pressure

A problem that faced the early pioneers was that efficient dialysis requires a very high rate of blood flow through the machine – between 200 and 300 cm^3 per minute. The only blood vessels that will deliver blood at this pressure are arteries, so every time treatment was given an artery had to be pierced. Arteries are narrower and deeper down than veins, so this procedure was difficult and risky. Clearly, if treatment was to be lifelong, some easier form of access to the circulation had to be developed so that dialysis could be carried out at home.

The modern solution to this problem, first used in 1966, is to join an artery to a nearby vein, creating an **arteriovenous fistula** (*illustration 3*). The blood passes from the artery to the vein at a high flow rate, and is then drawn off from the vein by means of a needle inserted through the skin. Two puncture sites are needed, one to take the blood to the machine, the other to return it to the patient.

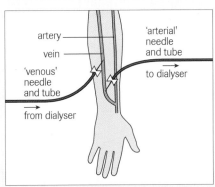

Illustration 3 The arteriovenous fistula provides a convenient way of attaching a person to a kidney machine.

A machine that filters the blood

Modern dialysing membranes are sufficiently strong to withstand pressures high enough to separate particles of different sizes by an ultrafiltration process analogous to that used by the kidney itself. In fact it has become possible to treat patients by a system which relies solely on ultrafiltration to remove toxic solutes.

The water and desirable solutes filtered are not reabsorbed as in the kidney, but are replaced by the correct volume of a specially prepared substitution fluid which is added to the blood as it returns to the patient's body. This technique has certain advantages over conventional dialysis. In the future it may offer an improved quality of life for people with renal failure.

Peritoneal dialysis

As an alternative to being put on a kidney machine, a person may be given **peritoneal dialysis** in hospital. Between one and two litres of sterile dialysis fluid are let into the abdominal cavity via a tube inserted through the body wall. The fluid is left in the abdominal cavity for several hours and then siphoned out and replaced by a fresh lot.

The principle underlying peritoneal dialysis is quite simple. The abdominal cavity and all the organs in it are lined with a membrane called the **peritoneum**. This membrane covers a total area of about 2 m^2 and it has its own extensive blood supply. While the dialysis fluid is in the abdominal cavity, equilibration takes place between the fluid and the surrounding blood. Since the dialysis fluid is changed regularly, toxic substances such as urea are lost from the blood just as they are in a kidney machine.

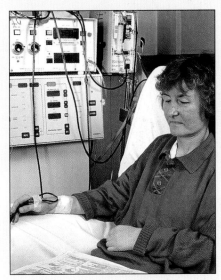

Illustration 4 A kidney machine in use.

Dr Kohn was a research physiologist in the Department of Biomedical Science at the University of Sheffield.

17.3 **The bladder and urination**

The result of all the processes described so far is the production of a fluid, urine, which contains substances the body does not want. The urine trickles out of the collecting ducts into the pelvis of the kidney from which it is conveyed to the bladder by regular waves of muscular contraction which pass down the ureters.

The wall of the bladder is lined on the inside by **transitional epithelium** which is stretchable (*page 65*). Outside the epithelium is a layer of **smooth muscle** which relaxes as the bladder expands. Because the bladder muscle relaxes, the pressure in the bladder does not increase greatly until the bladder is almost full. The urethra is kept closed by two rings of muscle, the **internal** and **external sphincters** (*figure 17.1 on page 280*). The expulsion of urine from the bladder is called **urination**. For urination to occur, the two sphincters open and the bladder muscle contracts.

Though we learn to control it, urination is basically a reflex which is triggered by the filling of the bladder itself. Impulses reaching the brain from the bladder wall create an awareness of the presence of urine in the bladder which later gives way to a feeling of urgency. Eventually urination becomes inevitable.

Innervation of the bladder and sphincters

The nerves that supply the bladder muscle and internal sphincter belong to the autonomic (involuntary) nervous system (*page 366*). The external sphincter, however, is innervated by the voluntary nervous system. When the bladder is filling up with urine, impulses in the involuntary system make the bladder muscle relax and internal sphincter contract. When urination occurs, impulses in the involuntary system make the bladder muscle contract and internal sphincter open. At the same time the external sphincter opens voluntarily, so urine flows out.

17.4 Osmotic regulation

In its treatment of water, the kidney shows its use as an osmoregulator. The amount of water reabsorbed is geared to the body's needs, and it is upon this that the solute concentration of the blood and tissue fluids depends. The question is: how does the kidney know how much water to reabsorb? The answer is that the solute concentration of the blood itself determines the reabsorptive activities of the kidney. Briefly, the mechanism is as follows.

In the brain there are groups of cells sensitive to a rise in the solute concentration of the blood, such as might occur if the person loses a lot of water or takes in an excessive amount of salt. These **osmoreceptors** are situated in the hypothalamus region of the brain at the base of the pituitary gland (*page 361*). When the receptors are stimulated, a hormone is released from the posterior lobe of the pituitary gland into the bloodstream. The hormone is carried to the kidneys where it speeds up the rate at which water is reabsorbed. As a result, less urine is produced per unit time and it has a higher solute concentration. Stimulation of the osmoreceptors also makes the person feel thirsty, so he or she drinks. The overall effect is that the solute concentration of the blood falls.

Drinking, particularly if excessive, results in the solute concentration of the blood falling below its normal value. The osmoreceptors are now less stimulated than before. As a result less hormone is produced, less water is reabsorbed by the kidney, and a more copious and dilute urine is produced. Result? The solute concentration of the blood rises.

The production of a large quantity of watery urine is known as **diuresis**, and clearly the hormone counteracts this condition. It is therefore known as **antidiuretic hormone**, or **ADH** for short. Its role is summarised in figure 17.9.

You can appreciate the importance of ADH by considering what happens to someone who has a faulty pituitary which fails to produce the hormone. The person permanently produces large quantities of dilute urine and has to make good the loss by drinking a lot of water, otherwise the body quickly becomes dehydrated.

How does ADH exert its effect on the kidney? Research suggests that it makes the cells lining the collecting ducts more permeable to water, thus facilitating the osmotic movement of water into the surrounding tissues. The distal convoluted tubule is also affected, so this too reabsorbs some of the water.

Effects of dehydration on the human body, page 307
Oral rehydration therapy, page 340

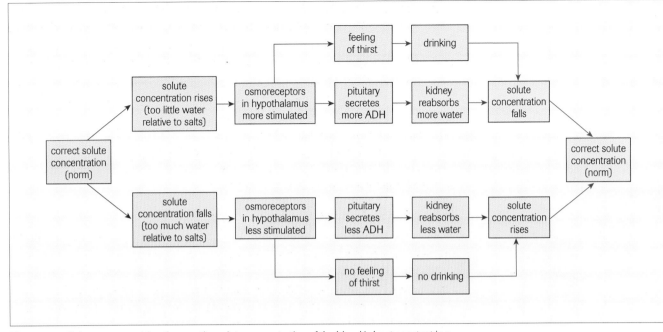

Figure 17.9 Scheme summarising the way the solute concentration of the blood is kept constant in a mammal. The process works in essentially the same way as other homeostatic mechanisms, deviations from the norm (set point) being corrected by negative feedback.

17.5 The control of ions

We have just seen how the kidney fulfils its osmoregulatory role by controlling the amount of water expelled in the urine. Controlling the concentration of ions is also an important aspect of osmoregulation. It is particularly important that sodium and chloride ions should be controlled because they make up the bulk of the salt in the blood.

But there is another reason for controlling ions which was touched on in Chapter 16. Cells will function efficiently only if they are bathed in a solution with the correct ionic composition. Not only does the total quantity of all the ions have to be right, but their relative concentrations must be right too.

Ionic regulation in animals is complex, but the principles are quite simple. In general terms, the concentration of a particular type of ion – sodium for example – in the blood and tissue fluid is regulated by one or more hormones which may affect three things:

■ the uptake of the particular ions into the bloodstream from the gut;

■ their removal from the blood by the kidneys and elimination in the urine;

■ their release into the bloodstream from organs (if any) which contain them in high concentrations.

By adjusting the balance between these three processes, the concentrations of ions in the blood and tissue fluid are held in steady state. The result is that the cells are bathed in a fluid whose ionic composition is suited to their needs.

To illustrate these principles, consider how calcium ions are controlled. A hormone called **parathormone** increases the uptake of calcium ions by the gut and their reabsorption in the kidneys. It also encourages the release of calcium ions from the bones. The overall effect of this hormone is therefore to raise the concentration of calcium ions in the blood.

▶ Parathormone and the parathyroid glands, pages 370 and 371

The control of sodium ions is explored in detail in the extension box on the next page. It illustrates the role of homeostatic feedback in ionic regulation.

How sodium ions are controlled

The concentration of sodium ions in the blood and tissue fluid is controlled by a hormone called **aldosterone** secreted by the **adrenal cortex** (*page 371*).

Aldosterone increases the uptake of sodium ions by the gut and their reabsorption in the kidney. The result is that the concentration of sodium ions in the blood rises.

The main method of control depends on a negative feedback process. If the concentration of sodium ions is too high, the adrenal cortex becomes inhibited with the result that it secretes *less* aldosterone. If the concentration of sodium ions is too low, the inhibitory influence is removed with the result that the adrenal cortex secretes *more* aldosterone.

The way the sodium ion concentration feeds back to the adrenal cortex is indirect and involves an enzyme called **renin** (not to be confused with the digestive enzyme rennin). Renin is released from special cells lining the afferent glomerular arterioles in the kidneys.

If the sodium ion concentration *falls*, the blood volume and pressure fall too because water is lost with the sodium ions. The fall in blood pressure causes renin to be released into the bloodstream where it catalyses the conversion of one of the plasma proteins into a substance called **angiotensin**. This then stimulates the adrenal cortex to secrete aldosterone.

A *rise* in the sodium ion concentration has the reverse effect: the blood volume and pressure increase, less renin and angiotensin are produced, so less aldosterone is secreted by the adrenal cortex. The sequence of events is summarised in the illustration.

The control of sodium ions is bound up with that of potassium ions. In the kidneys the reabsorption of sodium ions is accompanied by the loss of potassium ions. This is because of the sodium–potassium pump which moves these ions in opposite directions (*page 114*). The result is that as the sodium ion concentration in the blood rises, the potassium ion concentration falls. The mechanisms that control the sodium ion concentration therefore also control the relative concentrations of sodium and potassium ions. This is called the **sodium–potassium balance**, and holding it in steady state is essential for the normal functioning of cells.

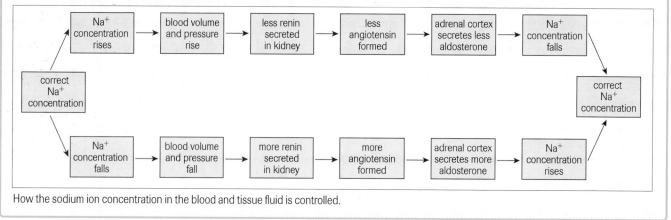

How the sodium ion concentration in the blood and tissue fluid is controlled.

How the pH is controlled

The blood and tissue fluid normally have a pH of about 7.4. The pH does not alter very much, which is just as well because even quite small deviations in pH can be fatal. This constancy is maintained despite the fact that excess hydrogen ions, which increase the acidity (lower the pH), are always being formed as by-products of metabolism.

One of the main sources of hydrogen ions is the reaction between water and carbon dioxide (from respiration). This results in the formation of carbonic acid which then dissociates into hydrogen ions and hydrogencarbonate ions:

$$CO_2 + H_2O$$
$$\downarrow$$
$$H_2CO_3$$
$$HCO_3^- \qquad H^+$$

Keeping the pH constant depends on controlling the relative concentrations of acid and base, the **acid–base balance**. This is achieved in three main ways.

- The lungs expel carbon dioxide in the process of breathing, which greatly reduces the amount of carbonic acid that would otherwise be formed.

- The buffering mechanisms in the blood lower the hydrogen ion concentration (*page 221*).

- The kidneys reabsorb hydrogen-carbonate ions and actively expel hydrogen ions which, after being buffered, are excreted in the urine.

17.6 Excretion and osmoregulation in aquatic animals

If a freshwater fish finds itself in sea water it will die. Sea water contains about twice as much salt as the blood of the fish, with the result that water is drawn out by osmosis. Although the scaly skin is relatively impermeable, the lining of the mouth cavity and gills acts as a partially permeable membrane. So the fish behaves like an osmometer, losing water if it is in a medium more concentrated than that of its blood and tissue fluid, and gaining water if it is in a medium more dilute than that of its blood and tissue fluid.

From this an important generalisation emerges, namely that most aquatic animals cannot tolerate appreciable fluctuations in the salinity of their external medium. This is not to say that they are incapable of osmoregulation. Indeed many aquatic animals can maintain a solute concentration which is different from that of their surroundings, but their ability to do so breaks down if the concentration of the external medium deviates too far from its normal value.

From the point of view of osmoregulation animals fall into two groups: those that cannot osmoregulate at all, and those that can – at least to some degree. The former are all marine invertebrates, and as they are thought to represent the starting point in an evolutionary sequence we shall consider them first.

Marine invertebrates

There is good reason to suppose that life began in the sea. Many animals, notably marine invertebrates such as sea anemones, jellyfish, spider crabs and starfish, have remained in the sea throughout their evolutionary history (*figure 17.10*). Their body fluids have the same solute concentration as sea water – indeed in animals like the starfish the tissues are perfused with sea water itself.

Since their internal solute concentration is equal to the external solute concentration, there is no need for these animals to osmoregulate so long as they remain in the open sea.

Figure 17.10 Marine invertebrates, such as the sea anemones and starfish in this picture, have body fluids with the same solute concentration as sea water.

> ### Extension
>
> #### Living in estuaries
>
> Living in an estuary presents particular problems because the salinity of the water changes with the tide, increasing when the tide comes in and decreasing when it goes out.
>
> There are three ways of coping with this problem:
>
> - The animal may osmoregulate and thus maintain a solute concentration which is independent of that of the surrounding water. Fishes do this, as do certain species of crab.
>
> - The animal may possess tissues that can tolerate a wide range of salinities. This is true of the lugworm *Arenicola* and the ragworm *Nereis*.
>
> - The animal may avoid the effects of dilution by behavioural means. For instance, the estuarine snail *Hydrobia* burrows into the mud when the tide is going out, thus escaping the twice-daily dilution of its external medium with fresh river water.

Freshwater fish

The problem facing any freshwater animal is that the internal solute concentration is greater than the external solute concentration. The danger here is dilution of the tissues resulting from the osmotic influx of water across the exposed partially permeable surfaces of the body.

The contractile vacuole

This device is found in *Amoeba*, *Paramecium* and other unicellular protoctists that live in fresh water. It is a small membrane-lined sac located in the cytoplasm.

The plasma membrane surrounding the organism is partially permeable, so water flows into the cell by osmosis. To counter this, water is collected up into the contractile vacuole as fast as it enters the cell. The contractile vacuole gradually expands as it fills up with water, and eventually discharges its contents to the exterior through a small pore in the plasma membrane as shown in the illustration. The cycle is then repeated.

To be effective as an osmoregulatory device, the contractile vacuole must eliminate water but not salts. The electron microscope shows the contractile

vacuole of *Amoeba* to be surrounded by mitochondria and tiny vesicles. It is thought that the vesicles collect fluid from the cytoplasm and then pump salts back into the cytoplasm by active transport, energy being provided by the mitochondria. The vesicles, now containing water, fuse with the contractile vacuole which gradually expands.

Treating *Amoeba* with a metabolic poison puts the contractile vacuole out of action: the cell can no longer get rid of surplus water so it swells up and dies.

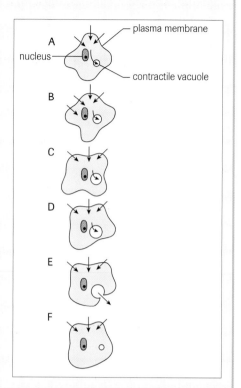

Osmoregulation in *Amoeba*. The arrows indicate the flow of water. Water which enters the cell by osmosis collects in the contractile vacuole and is discharged to the exterior.

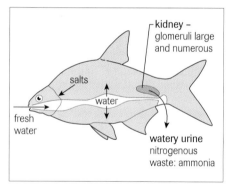

Figure 17.11 Summary of osmoregulation in a freshwater bony fish such as a trout.

Freshwater bony fish such as carp, trout and stickleback are liable to osmotic influx of water across the gills and the lining of the mouth cavity and pharynx. The fish solves this problem by getting rid of water and conserving salts. This is achieved in three main ways (*figure 17.11*):

■ The rate of filtration in the kidney (**glomerular filtration rate**) is high. This is achieved by the glomeruli being exceptionally large and numerous.

■ As the renal fluid flows along the kidney tubules, salts (i.e. sodium and chloride ions) are extensively reabsorbed back into the bloodstream with the result that the urine has a lower solute concentration than the blood.

■ The gills take up sodium and chloride ions from the water and move them against the concentration gradient into the bloodstream. This function is carried out by special **chloride secretory cells** in the gills. The result is that chloride is some 800 times more concentrated in the animal's blood than in the surrounding water. This active transport of salts requires energy.

Thus, to summarise, the osmotic problem facing freshwater fish is solved by combining the expulsion of water with the active uptake of salts. The same applies to amphibian larvae (tadpoles).

One problem which freshwater animals do *not* have is getting rid of nitrogenous waste. They have lashings of water with which to dilute their main excretory product, ammonia.

Marine fish

Marine bony fish such as mackerel and cod have the opposite problem to their freshwater relatives: their internal solute concentration is lower than that of the surrounding sea water. The result is that water tends to leave the body by osmosis, leading to dehydration of the tissues. So the animal must save water and get rid of salts.

This is achieved by a combination of three processes (*figure 17.12*):

- The glomerular filtration rate in the kidney is relatively low. The glomeruli are small and few in number compared with freshwater species.

- Salts are actively *expelled* by chloride secretory cells in the gills, the reverse of what happens in freshwater species.

- Nitrogenous waste is excreted in a form which requires relatively little water for its elimination. Ammonia, which is highly toxic and has to be diluted with a lot of water, is replaced by **urea** which is considerably less toxic and a compound called **trimethylamine oxide** which is totally non-toxic.

So the osmotic problem of marine bony fish is solved by saving water and getting rid of salts. Marine cartilaginous fish such as sharks and rays get round the same problem in a different way. They retain urea in the body with the result that their internal solute concentration is slightly higher than that of the surrounding sea water. The result is a slight influx of water which is readily expelled by the kidney. This is another instance of where urea serves a useful purpose.

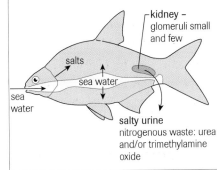

Figure 17.12 Summary of osmoregulation in a marine bony fish such as a mackerel.

Extension

Why do turtles cry and penguins have runny noses?

Marine birds and reptiles face the same osmotic problem that confronts marine bony fish, namely a surplus of salt. How do they get rid of it?

Marine reptiles have **salt-secreting glands** in the head. In turtles the glands are located behind the eyes, from which the salty fluid emerges – hence the turtle 'shedding tears'. In the marine iguana lizards of the Galapagos Islands the glands open into the nasal cavity. Every now and again the lizard gives a powerful exhalation and the salty fluid is expelled as a fine spray.

Salt-secreting nasal glands are also found in marine birds such as penguins, gulls and cormorants. The fluid trickles out of the nasal openings, giving the impression that these birds have runny noses.

Comparing marine bony fish with these other vertebrates is interesting because it shows how the same physiological problem is solved by different groups of animals in essentially the same way. We can even extend the comparison to plants. A land plant living in salty water may excrete surplus salt from salt glands on the leaves (*page 298*).

17.7 Excretion and osmoregulation in terrestrial animals

Like marine bony fish, terrestrial animals are liable to lose water, but whereas in a fish this is caused by osmosis, in a terrestrial animal it is caused by evaporation from permeable surfaces exposed to the atmosphere. Terrestrial animals have a number of features which help them to overcome this problem.

How animals survive dry conditions

In the list that follows, a distinction can be made between passive and active (i.e. metabolic) methods.

They have a waterproof integument

This passive way of reducing water loss is particularly evident in reptiles, birds and mammals whose skin is protected by structures which contain the protein **keratin**. The **scales** of reptiles, **feathers** of birds and **hair** of mammals all contain keratin, as does the

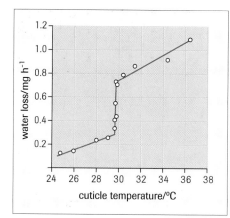

Figure 17.13 The results of an experiment designed to test the hypothesis that the wax on the surface of an insect cuticle makes the cuticle waterproof. A cockroach nymph was gradually warmed up and the rate of water loss from its body was measured at a series of temperatures. Below about 30°C there was very little increase in water loss as the temperature was raised, but as the temperature approached 30°C the rate of water loss suddenly increased dramatically. It was found that at this temperature the arrangement of the wax molecules changed and the cuticle became permeable to water.

upper part of the epidermis. Keratin makes these structures hard, thus providing protection from physical damage. It also makes them waterproof, a property which is enhanced in birds and mammals by the presence of **oil** on the surface of the skin. The impermeability of the skin is one reason why these animals can live successfully in hot, dry places such as the desert.

Amongst invertebrates, insects have developed waterproofing to a remarkable degree. Insects have a hard **cuticle** whose surface is covered with a microscopically thin layer of **wax**. The wax, in common with lipids generally, is impermeable to water and confers on the cuticle its waterproofing properties (*figure 17.13*).

An animal cannot insulate itself entirely from the outside world; it must be able to breathe, and a certain amount of water will always evaporate from the gaseous-exchange surfaces. Insects breathe through small holes in the cuticle called **spiracles**. These are guarded by **hairs** or, in some species, by **valves** which can open and close. In this way evaporative water loss is reduced to a minimum.

They have a low glomerular filtration rate

It was explained earlier that marine bony fish have a low filtration rate because the glomeruli in their kidneys are small and few. The same adaptation is found in certain terrestrial vertebrates, particularly reptiles, which live in hot dry habitats.

They produce a non-toxic nitrogenous waste

Marine bony fish excrete nitrogenous waste in the form of urea or trimethylamine oxide, an adaptation for conserving water. Similar trends are found in terrestrial animals. For example, amphibians and mammals excrete **urea** which, being less toxic than ammonia, requires less water for its removal.

Reptiles, birds and insects have taken this a step further and excrete nitrogenous waste as **uric acid**. Uric acid is insoluble in water. This means that water can be removed from it before it leaves the body, the uric acid being excreted in a semi-solid form. In insects the uric acid is produced by the **Malpighian tubules**, a bunch of narrow tubes leading off the gut (*figure 17.14*).

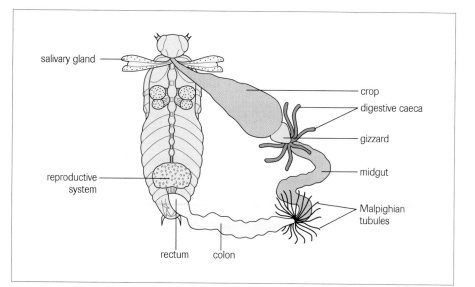

Figure 17.14 The inside of an insect with the gut unravelled and deflected to one side. Notice the Malpighian tubules. Each tubule opens into the gut at its inner end, while its closed outer end floats freely in the blood-filled body cavity. Soluble nitrogenous waste in the blood is absorbed by the tubules and converted into uric acid which passes along the tubules into the gut and out with the faeces. Water is reabsorbed back into the blood in the colon and rectum, particularly the rectum.

Desert frogs

Of all terrestrial vertebrates, the least well adapted are amphibians such as frogs and toads. The skin of most amphibians is thin and moist, with the result that water readily evaporates from it. This is one reason why amphibians are generally restricted to damp places.

There are some notable exceptions though. For example, the Australian desert frog *Chiroleptes* has a very low glomerular filtration rate and retains urine in its bladder for use during the dry season. So much urine may be retained that the animal swells up like a ball (*illustration*). The Aborigines use these frogs as a source of water.

The Australian desert frog *Chiroleptes*.

Desert frogs in general show many interesting adaptations for living in hot, dry places. For example, some species have a waterproof skin and excrete uric acid instead of urea.

Figure 17.15 The kangaroo rat *Dipodomys*, a desert rodent which lives in the North American desert, shows many adaptations to life in a hot, dry environment. It is amazingly good at conserving water. This is achieved by not sweating, by producing a highly concentrated urine and very dry faeces, and by staying in its burrow during the heat of the day thereby reducing evaporation from the lungs.

They reabsorb water

Insects reabsorb water mainly in the **rectum**. Uric acid, produced by the Malpighian tubules, moves into the rectum where water is reabsorbed so vigorously that, in some species, the material which finally passes out of the anus is solid.

Desert mammals have an extra-long loop of Henlé and produce a more concentrated urine in consequence. For instance, the kangaroo rat, an animal that shows all sorts of adaptations for living in the desert, produces urine four times as concentrated as the human's, a feat which is made possible at least partly by its long loop of Henlé. You can see this cute little animal in figure 17.15.

In birds, as in many other vertebrates, the ureters and rectum open into a common cavity called the **cloaca**. *Cloaca* is the Latin word for sewer, which is apt because it receives excretory waste and faeces. Water is extensively reabsorbed from the faeces and excretory waste by the wall of the cloaca. What passes out is a semi-solid mixture of faeces (black or brown) and uric acid (white) which birds, with singular disregard for anti-litter laws, deposit on pavements and buildings.

They avoid exposing themselves to the atmosphere

Many terrestrial animals behave in such a way as to avoid, or at least reduce, the problem of water loss. Earthworms, for example, burrow deeper when the surface soil is dry.

Some species of earthworm respond to very dry conditions such as may occur in summer by going into a state of dormancy, a phenomenon called **aestivation**. The worm coils up into a tight ball in a pocket of air and surrounds itself with mucus which then dries. The metabolic rate falls and the worm goes into a state of suspended animation from which it is aroused when the soil becomes wet again.

Another animal that aestivates is the garden snail *Helix*. In dry conditions it retreats into its shell, the opening of which becomes covered by a tough membrane secreted by the foot.

Aestivation can also be useful to aquatic animals in drought conditions. For example, the African and South American lungfishes can survive even if the water dries up completely. The fish burrows into the soft mud which later dries and hardens into a 'cocoon' with the animal inside. Here it remains until the arrival of the next rainy season six or seven months later.

The pocket mouse

Although a correlation between water conservation and a long loop of Henlé makes sense, it is not the whole story.

The most 'powerful' kidney known is that of the pocket mouse *Perognathus*, a nocturnal rodent found in the south-western desert of North America. Its urine is six times as concentrated as that of humans, but its loops of Henlé are much shorter.

It seems that the pocket mouse can maintain exceptionally steep gradients across its loops of Henlé, possibly by producing a much higher concentration of ATP to power the active transport involved.

The strange case of the camel

Camels thrive in the desert. Among their many adaptations is the ability to go for long periods without drinking. They store fat in the hump, and produce water by metabolising it. However, a camel cannot produce more metabolic water than it loses by evaporation. How then does it survive without drinking?

Camels are well adapted to living in the hot, dry desert.

The answer was discovered by the American physiologist, Knut Schmidt-Nielsen. He found that a camel's tissues are exceptionally tolerant to dehydration. As the days go by, more and more water is lost and the body fluids become more and more concentrated, and yet the animal survives. In fact it will survive water loss that reduces its body mass by as much as 30 per cent, 10 per cent more than would be fatal to a human. Little wonder that when camels *do* drink, they do so with great gusto. Schmidt-Nielsen reports that a camel which was given water after 16 days without it, drank 40 litres in ten minutes!

Figure 17.16 The desert in bloom, the result of a shower of rain.

They make use of metabolic water

As you know, one of the products of respiration is water (*page 138*). Some desert animals rely on this **metabolic water** as a source of water.

The amount of water yielded by respiration depends on the food substance being metabolised. For example, one gram of fat yields almost twice as much water as the same amount of carbohydrate. For this reason a desert animal such as the kangaroo rat tends to metabolise fat rather than carbohydrate.

In most animals, breathing to obtain the necessary oxygen for metabolising fat entails losing more water than can be gained from metabolic water. However, the kangaroo rat can produce more water by metabolism than it loses. How it achieves this is explained in the caption to figure 17.15 on the previous page. In fact this remarkable animal produces and retains metabolic water so efficiently that it never needs to drink.

17.7 Water regulation in plants

Plants can be divided into three groups according to how much water is available to them in their natural environment.

- **Hydrophytes** live partially or completely submerged in fresh water. Examples are water lilies and the Canadian pondweed *Elodea*. Obviously such plants have no difficulty getting enough water.

- **Mesophytes** grow in normal, well-watered soil. Most land plants in temperate regions belong to this category. Usually the water which they lose by transpiration is readily replaced by uptake from the soil, so they require no special means of conserving water.

- **Xerophytes** live in dry places such as the hot desert where the water potentials in the soil and air are very low. These plants face the possibility of drastic dehydration and have ways of preventing this.

How plants survive dry conditions

It is amazing how resilient many plants are when faced with dry conditions. Here are some of the main adaptations which enable them to survive. They are called **xerophytic** (or **xeromorphic**) **adaptations**.

Their tissues tolerate water loss

In general, plants are better than animals at tolerating fluctuations in the water content of their tissues. Those that live in dry places are particularly tolerant to desiccation. Indeed, some species are so adaptable that their tissues can, to all intents and purposes, be completely dried out and yet resume normal functioning later when water becomes available. This is seen in certain desert species and also in many mosses and ferns.

Their life cycles are adapted

Most species can survive dry periods as **seeds** or **spores**. The living contents are generally in a highly dehydrated state and protected within a hard case. Metabolism proceeds at a very slow rate. In this condition a seed or spore may remain viable for a long time, germinating into a new plant when water becomes available and other conditions are suitable.

The use of seeds for surviving dry conditions is well illustrated by small desert ephemerals. Germination, growth and flowering – the entire life cycle in fact – take place during the few weeks following a burst of rain. Suddenly the arid desert landscape is turned into a spectacular carpet of colour (*figure 17.16*). After the seeds have been dispersed, the parent plants die and the seeds remain dormant in the dry soil until the next rains come.

They have special ways of obtaining water

Some plants that live in dry places have extremely long **vertical roots** which absorb water from deep down in the soil. Many Mediterranean trees and shrubs, such as *Acacia* and *Oleander*, do this. Other plants, including most cacti, have **superficial roots** which grow out horizontally just beneath the surface of the soil. This puts them in the best position to absorb water quickly before it has a chance to evaporate.

The mesquite tree, which grows in the arid regions of the south-western United States, has a deep taproot and numerous horizontal fibrous roots. The taproot may grow down as far as 20 metres below the surface, reaching the water table, and the fibrous roots extend over a wide area.

They store water

Certain plants store water in large parenchyma cells contained within swollen stems, branches or leaves. This makes the tissues wet and juicy, for which reason these kinds of plants are called **succulents**.

Two well-known succulents are the giant Saguaro cactus of the North American desert and the prickly pear cactus (*figure 17.17*). In both these plants water is stored in the thick stems and branches from which sharp spines project to deter thirsty animals that might otherwise tap the valuable juices.

They have a reduced rate of transpiration

A problem facing land plants is that the rate of transpiration may exceed the rate of water uptake from the soil (*page 256*). Many species have adaptations which reduce the rate of transpiration.

One method is to have **fewer stomata**, an adaptation seen in many desert plants including the prickly pear.

Some plants, for example the evergreen shrub *Hakea* of the Australian desert, have **sunken stomata**: the stomata are at the bottom of little pits in the epidermis. Humid air accumulates in the pits, reducing the rate of transpiration from the leaves. Other plants achieve the same thing by having a **hairy epidermis** which holds humid air against the leaf surface. These devices are accompanied in some species by **folding of the leaves**, an adaptation seen in marram grass which thrives on dry coastal sand dunes (*figure 17.18*).

In mesophytic plants transpiration is not confined to the stomata; a certain amount of water evaporates through the cuticle as well. This cuticular transpiration is reduced by having **small leaves** with a small surface area, and by having a **thick cuticle** which is impermeable to water. This is particularly well seen in desert plants, but it is also shown by many evergreen trees and shrubs in temperate regions – pine trees for example.

Certain plants face the possibility of water shortage in the winter because the soil water freezes. One way of getting round this problem is to **shed the leaves** before winter sets

Figure 17.17 Two desert succulents. The Saguaro cactus (*left and rear*) grows in the desert of Arizona and Northern Mexico. The prickly pear (*foreground*), though native to the North American desert, is now found in desert regions all over the world. In both these plants water is stored in the thick stems and branches. Excessive transpiration is prevented by having an epidermis with a thick cuticle and very few stomata. A superficial root system ensures that after a shower of rain, water is quickly absorbed before it has time to evaporate.

Figure 17.18 Marram grass, *Ammophila arenaria*, is adapted to growing on sand dunes. **A** The whole plant in its natural environment. **B** Photomicrograph of a cross section of one of the leaves in the folded position. Stomata occur only in the furrows on the inner side of the leaf where the photosynthetic tissue is located. Large, thin-walled epidermal cells at the bases of the furrows shrink when they lose water from excessive transpiration. This causes the leaf to fold. The stiff, interlocking hairs help to hold in water vapour. The epidermis on the outer side of the leaf has a thick cuticle and lacks stomata. Magnification ×20.

Do plants excrete?

Plants produce a wide variety of substances which at first sight seem to be excretory products. However, many of them have been found to have a function, for example in defence against herbivores and parasites (see page 339).

Even the salt secreted by halophytes may have a function. It has been shown that in some species the salt crystals trap water vapour from the surrounding air, which may then be absorbed by the leaf cells as liquid water. Thus what seems at first to be excretion may in fact be an ingenious mechanism enabling the plant to obtain water.

Trees produce various gums, resins and latexes. Whether we regard these compounds as excretory or not, once collected they have wide-ranging industrial applications. From them we get such products as turpentine, paints, varnishes, soaps, cosmetics, surgical goods, foods, golf balls, bubble gum and rubber.

in, thereby reducing the leaf surface to nil and preventing transpiration altogether. This is what deciduous trees do.

Although there are many other reasons for leaf-fall, there is no doubt that it is an effective way of cutting down transpiration. A spectacular example is shown by *Ocotillo*, the 'vine cactus' of the North American desert, which comes out in leaf every time it rains and sheds its leaves immediately afterwards. This may happen five or six times a year.

The stomatal rhythm may be reversed

The adaptations mentioned so far are essentially structural ones, but the water problems of some plants are solved by physiological means. For example, certain succulents reverse the normal stomatal rhythm: instead of the stomata opening by day and closing at night, they open at night and close by day.

As a means of preventing excessive water loss reversing the stomatal rhythm seems an excellent idea, but what happens about photosynthesis? Such plants take up carbon dioxide at night, when the stomata are open, and fix it into malic acid. When daybreak comes, the stomata close and the carbon dioxide is released for photosynthesis. This is called **crassulacean acid metabolism** after the group of plants, the Crassulaceae, in which it was first observed (*page 213*).

Halophytes

Some plants live on mud flats and salt marshes around the coast. They are called **halophytes**, meaning 'salt plants'. An example is *Salicornia europaea*, a species of glasswort. Their roots are surrounded by water which has a higher salt concentration, and therefore lower water potential, than the contents of the cells.

How do these halophytes prevent osmotic loss of water? They do so by actively absorbing salts into their roots, with the result that the solute concentration of their tissues is higher than that of the surrounding water. They can then take up water by osmosis in the usual way.

But there is a problem: the plants may absorb salt so vigorously that it becomes toxic to them. They get round this by isolating the surplus salt and storing it in their cells, or by secreting it from salt glands on the leaves. An example of a halophyte with **salt glands** is the sea heath *Frankenia*.

Figure 17.19 Guttation occurring at the edges of a leaf of lady's mantle, *Alchemilla vulgaris*. This plant is found around streams and in moist pastureland, particularly in hilly situations where at times the rate of water uptake exceeds the rate of transpiration.

Getting rid of surplus water

Excessive uptake of water, potentially so dangerous for animals, is not a problem for plants because the cellulose cell walls impose a natural limit on the amount of water that can be taken in. However, in certain conditions more water may be taken up by a land plant than is lost by transpiration. Pressure builds up and water may exude from the leaves, either through the stomata or from special structures called **hydathodes**. This process is called **guttation** (*figure 17.19*).

Guttation is particularly common in tropical rain forests where, because of the high rainfall and humid atmosphere, plants have a plentiful water supply but a low rate of transpiration. One botanist remarked that standing under a guttating tree in the rain forest is like being out in a gentle drizzle! Even in a temperate country like Britain you can sometimes see water dripping from the leaves of trees on humid evenings in summer, especially in damp places such as close to a river or stream.

Guttation may be useful to plants in that it keeps the transpiration stream on the move and ensures a continued supply of nutrients even when normal transpiration cannot take place.

Summary

1. Excretion is the elimination from the body of the waste products of metabolism. **Osmoregulation** is the process by which the solute concentration of the blood and tissue fluid is kept constant.

2. In mammals, excretion and osmoregulation are carried out by the **urinary system** of which the principal organ is the **kidney**.

3. Each kidney contains approximately 1.5 million **nephrons** which perform the functions of excretion and osmoregulation by a combination of **ultrafiltration**, **reabsorption** and **secretion**.

4. The **dialysing membrane** responsible for ultrafiltration is the basement membrane in the part of the nephron known as **Bowman's capsule**.

5. In the tubules of the nephrons, water is reabsorbed by osmosis, and glucose and salts by diffusion and active transport. Ammonia, uric acid and hydrogen ions are secreted into the tubules.

6. Further water is reabsorbed osmotically from the collecting ducts as the result of a special part of the nephron known as the **loop of Henlé** conserving salts on the principle of a hair-pin countercurrent multiplier.

7. Reabsorption of water by the kidney is controlled by **antidiuretic hormone** (**ADH**) from the posterior lobe of the pituitary gland.

8. Ionic regulation in animals is achieved by hormones which regulate the uptake of ions in the gut and their elimination by the kidneys.

9. In animals, the **acid–base balance**, and hence pH, is controlled by the lungs, blood and kidneys.

10. Freshwater animals, including freshwater fish, eliminate excess water by means of a kidney or comparable device. In some cases salts are taken up actively from the surrounding water by the gills.

11. Marine vertebrates, including most marine fish, eliminate excess salts and retain as much water as possible. Their nitrogenous excretory waste tends to be relatively insoluble and non-toxic.

12. Terrestrial animals are liable to lose water by evaporation from exposed surfaces. They possess a variety of adaptations for preventing excessive water loss.

13. Depending on the availability of water, plants may be classified into **hydrophytes**, **mesophytes** and **xerophytes**. A wide range of water-conserving devices are seen in land plants, particularly xerophytes.

14. Land plants which live in places where the water is salty are called **halophytes**. They have adaptations for getting rid of excess salt.

15. Land plants living in humid conditions may gain more water than they can lose by transpiration. The surplus water is lost by **guttation**.

Practice questions

For general advice on these questions and advice on answering essay-type questions, see pages vii and viii.

1. (a) Give **one** difference between the composition of glomerular filtrate and blood plasma. (1)

(b) In the renal capsule, the effective filtration pressure depends on the hydrostatic pressure in the capillaries of the glomerulus which tends to force fluids out and the osmotic pressure of the blood proteins which tends to draw fluids back into the blood.

   (i) If the hydrostatic pressure in the capillaries is 5.5 kPa and the osmotic pressure of the blood proteins is 4.2 kPa, calculate the effective filtration pressure. (1)

   (ii) Describe **one** structural feature of the blood vessels associated with the glomerulus and explain how it helps to maintain a high effective filtration pressure. (2)

   (iii) Suggest an explanation for the fact that the urine of patients suffering from hypertension may contain protein. (2)

(c) The diagram summarises the mechanism by which sodium is reabsorbed from the first convoluted tubule.

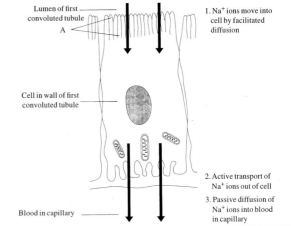

Lumen of first convoluted tubule

A

Cell in wall of first convoluted tubule

Blood in capillary

1. Na⁺ ions move into cell by facilitated diffusion

2. Active transport of Na⁺ ions out of cell

3. Passive diffusion of Na⁺ ions into blood in capillary

(i) What is the function of the structures labelled **A**? (2)

(ii) Sodium ions move into the tubule cell by facilitated diffusion and out into the blood by active transport. Give **two** differences between facilitated diffusion and active transport. (2)

(iii) Explain the importance of the active transport mechanism in enabling diffusion of sodium ions into this cell. (1)

(d) Explain why, although large amounts of glucose and sodium ions are reabsorbed from the liquid in the first convoluted tubule, its overall solute concentration remains constant. (2)

(e) The graph shows how the rates of filtration of glucose by the glomerulus and its reabsorption from the first convoluted tubule vary with plasma glucose concentration.

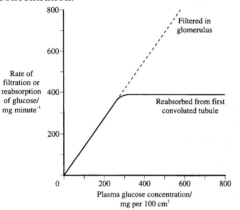

(i) Describe and explain the difference in the shape of these two curves at plasma glucose concentrations greater than 300 mg per 100 cm³. (3)

(ii) Sketch a curve on a copy of the graph to show how the amount of glucose in the urine would vary with plasma glucose concentration. (2)

(f) Explain why, in a non-diabetic individual, glucose does not normally appear in the urine. (2)

(Total 20 marks)

AEB 1997

2. Give an account of nitrogenous excretion in mammals.

(Total 10 marks)

London 1998

3. (a) (i) Name **two** surfaces permeable to water in both freshwater and marine fish. (2)

(ii) In which direction will water move by osmosis between fish and the environment in the case of:

1 a freshwater fish;

2 a marine bony fish? (2)

(b) The diagram below represents the nephrons of a freshwater fish and a marine bony fish.

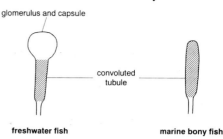

How do the structures of such nephrons relate to the work they must do for osmoregulation in:

(i) freshwater fish; (2)

(ii) marine bony fish? (2)

(c) (i) Describe the osmotic problem faced by a young salmon migrating from freshwater to the sea. (1)

(ii) What change in kidney structure and output would you expect to take place in such a fish after a few days in the sea? (2)

The diagram below represents longitudinal sections of the kidneys of three species of mammal drawn to the same scale.

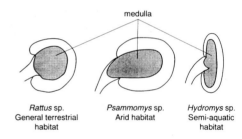

(d) Suggest reasons to explain the relationship between the size of the medulla of each animal and the habitat in which it lives. (3)

(Total 14 marks)

O&C 1998

4. Describe how the xeromorphic features of plants help them to survive in arid habitats.

(Total 10 marks)

I t is well known that irrespective of fluctuations in the temperature of the environment, the temperature of the human body remains at about 37°C. Many of the body's organs and physiological processes contribute towards the maintenance of this constant body temperature. The process by which the body temperature is kept constant (or, to put it more accurately, near-constant) is called **thermoregulation**.

Why is thermoregulation necessary?

A body temperature of about 37°C is the optimum temperature for the action of most enzymes upon which all aspects of our metabolism depend. If the temperature rises much above 45°C, enzyme action goes into a sharp decline. This is because enzymes are proteins, and become denatured (*page 126*).

Temperature also affects the structure and functioning of cell membranes, including the plasma membrane. If the body temperature gets too high or too low, processes involving the plasma membrane – active transport for example – shut down with disastrous consequences on ionic and other regulatory mechanisms.

Support

Measuring body temperature

The body temperature is normally taken by means of a clinical thermometer placed under the tongue. This **oral temperature** is normally about 37°C but is quite variable. The temperature in the centre of the body, the **core temperature**, is about 0.5°C higher than the oral temperature and is less variable. The easiest reasonably accurate way of measuring the core temperature is to take the **rectal temperature**.

18.1 Types of temperature regulation

Organisms can be divided into two types on the basis of their ability to regulate their body temperature (*figure 18.1*):

- **Homoiothermic** This word, derived from Greek, means *having the same temperature*. Homoiothermic animals are popularly described as 'warm blooded': their body temperature is independent of the environmental temperature, so in cold conditions their blood is at a higher temperature than that of their surroundings. They achieve this by generating heat energy by metabolism within the body, and keeping it there. For this reason they are described as **endothermic**. Mammals and birds belong to this category, and their success is often attributed at least in part to this important feature.

- **Poikilothermic** This word means *having a variable temperature*. Poikilothermic animals are described as 'cold blooded': their body temperature changes with fluctuations in the environmental temperature. If the environment is cold, so are they. Their main way of keeping warm is to absorb heat energy from their surroundings by, for example, basking in the Sun. For this reason they are described as **ectotherms**. All organisms apart from mammals and birds fall into this category.

The above terms have their limitations. For example, the body temperature of a poikilotherm is not necessarily variable. Indeed, many so-called cold-blooded animals maintain a surprisingly constant body temperature, as we shall see later.

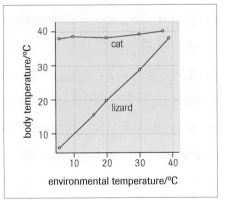

Figure 18.1 Relationship between the body temperature and environmental temperature for a cat and a lizard. The environmental temperature is the air temperature immediately outside the body. Notice that the cat maintains a more or less constant body temperature irrespective of changes in the environmental temperature. In contrast, the lizard's body temperature is the same as the environmental temperature.

Nor is the distinction between endotherm and ectotherm always clear cut. For example, the heat energy from an ectotherm's metabolism must inevitably help to keep the body warm. And most endotherms (including ourselves) supplement their metabolic production of heat energy by absorbing heat energy from their surroundings. More about this later.

Diurnal fluctuations in body temperature

If you take a person's temperature at regular intervals over several days, you find that the body temperature falls at night and rises during the day, like this:

Because the variations occur on a daily (i.e. 24 hour) basis, they are an example of a **diurnal rhythm** (*page 440*).

The rise in body temperature during the day is caused by the increased release of heat energy from metabolism. At night, when the person is sleeping, the metabolic rate decreases and less heat energy is released, so the body temperature falls. There is also evidence that when a person is asleep the temperature-regulating mechanisms are less efficient. It's not surprising that people who, for one reason or another, get up at around 4 a.m. report that they feel ghastly.

In people who are active at night and sleep during the day – nurses on night duty for example – the diurnal rhythm is reversed, the body temperature rising at night and falling during the day.

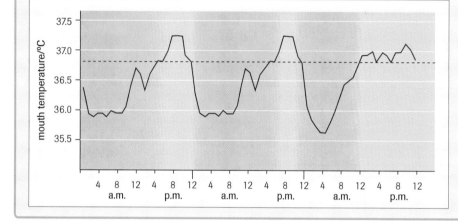

How heat energy is lost and gained

An organism whose body temperature exceeds the temperature of its surroundings may lose heat energy by four physical processes (*figure 18.2*):

- **Conduction** is the transfer of heat energy from the hotter to the cooler of two objects in contact with each other. A person sitting on a cold chair will lose heat energy to the chair. Heat energy can also be conducted to the surrounding medium, air or water as the case may be.

- **Radiation** is the transfer of heat energy from a body to colder objects that are not in contact with it. The heat energy is transferred by infra-red waves. As much as 60 per cent of the total heat energy lost by a person sitting in a room at 21°C may be caused by radiation.

- **Evaporation** is the change of a liquid to a vapour, and it is accompanied by cooling. As much as 25 per cent of the total heat energy lost by a person at 21°C can be caused by evaporation of water from the surface of the skin, and it explains the cooling effect of sweating (*see below*).

- **Convection** is the movement of air resulting from local pockets of warm air being replaced by cooler air, and vice versa. These air movements can help to spread heat energy through the environment, and they speed up the loss of heat energy from objects by conduction and evaporation.

Of course conduction, radiation and convection can work both ways. If the environmental temperature is higher than the body temperature, heat energy will be gained by these processes. However, a body cannot gain heat energy by evaporation – it can only lose it.

We also gain heat energy from **metabolism**, and as metabolism goes on all the time we cannot fail to gain at least *some* heat energy this way.

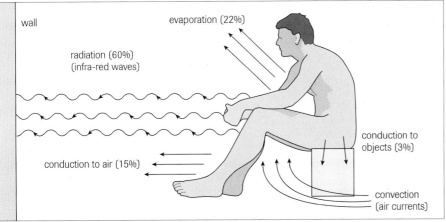

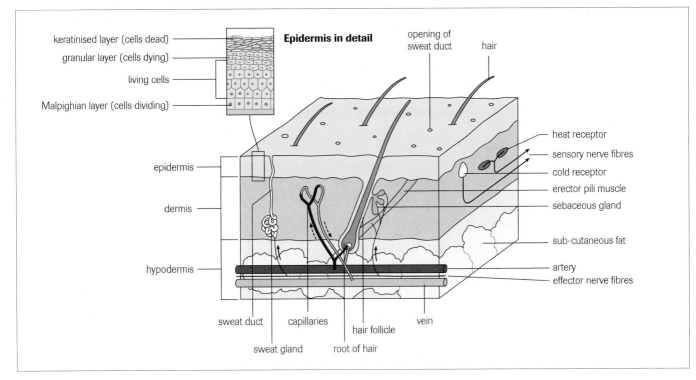

To sum up, the body is continually gaining and losing heat energy. When these two processes proceed at exactly the same rate, the person is said to be in **thermal balance**. The purpose of temperature regulation is to keep the body in thermal balance. In endothermic animals the key structure involved in this is the **skin**.

18.2 The skin and its role in thermoregulation

The structure of mammalian skin is shown in figure 18.3. Nearly all the structures seen in this picture play some part in temperature regulation.

Figure 18.2 Physical mechanisms by which heat energy may be lost from a naked person. The percentages show how much heat energy may be lost by each mechanism when the room temperature is 21°C.

Figure 18.3 Diagram of a small part of the skin. Nearly all the structures shown are involved directly or indirectly with temperature regulation. Broken arrows, blood flow; solid arrows, nerve impulses.

The skin is divided into two main layers, the **epidermis** at the surface, and the **dermis** beneath. Below the dermis is another layer, not strictly part of the skin, called the **hypodermis**.

The epidermis is composed of **stratified epithelium** (*page 64*). The bottom-most layer of cells, the **Malpighian layer**, contains variable amounts of the black pigment **melanin** which protects the body from the harmful effects of ultraviolet rays from the Sun.

The cells of the Malpighian layer divide repeatedly in a plane horizontal to the surface of the body. As new cells are formed, the older ones get pushed outwards towards the surface, flattening as they do so. After a time, the cytoplasm becomes full of granules and the cells die. Finally they become converted into scales of **keratin**, giving rise to the **keratinised layer** at the surface of the epidermis.

Keratin is a tough fibrous protein (*page 30*). It gives the skin its protective properties and makes it waterproof. This dead tissue constantly flakes off or is worn away. In parts of the body where the skin is subjected to constant pressure, such as the soles of the feet, the keratinised layer becomes very thick.

Oil is secreted on to the surface of the epidermis by **sebaceous glands** which open into the **hair follicles**, the deep pits from which the **hairs** project. The oil (known as **sebum**) affects the texture of the hair and enhances the skin's waterproofing properties.

The roots of the hairs are embedded in the dermis or hypodermis. Running from the side of each hair follicle to the base of the epidermis is an **erector pili muscle**. When this muscle contracts, the hair is pulled into a more vertical position.

The dermis contains **sweat glands** which secrete a salty solution, **sweat**. The sweat passes along the **sweat ducts** to the surface of the epidermis. There are approximately two million sweat glands in a person's skin, and evaporation of the sweat cools the skin and the blood flowing through it.

The hypodermis is permeated by arteries and veins. Blood flows from the arteries towards the surface of the skin in arterioles which split into capillaries below the epidermis. The blood is drained from the capillaries in venules which lead to the veins. There is thus a continuous flow of blood towards the surface of the skin and then away again. The way this flow can be modified is important in temperature regulation.

In the dermis there are **receptors** sensitive to touch, pressure, pain and temperature. Evidence suggests that the temperature receptors (**thermoreceptors**) are of two types, one sensitive to warmth and the other to cold. They enable us to detect changes in the temperature of our surroundings. Sensory nerve fibres lead from the receptors, and effector nerve fibres supply the erector pili muscles and sweat glands.

The structures described above are embedded in a loose connective tissue made mainly of collagen fibres but containing some elastic fibres too. This makes the skin soft and pliant. The hypodermis consists mainly of fat tissue. This **subcutaneous fat** serves as an insulator, helping to prevent heat energy being lost from the body. However, this is a purely structural adaptation and endotherms have more dynamic means of keeping warm, as we shall now see.

How do endotherms respond to cold conditions?

In cold conditions heat energy is liable to be lost from the body, but this is counteracted by the following responses:

- **The hairs are raised into a more vertical position by contraction of the erector pili muscles**. Air gets trapped in the spaces between the hairs and, being a poor conductor of heat, it creates an insulatory layer round the animal. This response is involuntary, and is brought about by the autonomic nervous system (*page 366*).

   In humans the body hair is much reduced, its place being taken by clothes. Even so, the erector pili muscles contract just the same, resulting in 'goose pimples'. In birds the feathers serve the same function as the hair of mammals, being raised in cold weather.

- **The arterioles leading to the superficial capillaries constrict**. As a result the blood flow to the surface of the skin is reduced, thereby cutting down the loss of heat energy from the blood to the surroundings. This vasoconstriction is brought about by the sympathetic nervous system and is particularly powerful in exposed structures such as the ears, which are particularly susceptible to cold.

- **The metabolic rate increases, heating the inside of the body**. A general increase in the metabolic rate is brought about by the hormones **adrenaline** and **thyroxine** which are produced in extra large amounts in cold conditions. The main organ to respond to these hormones is the liver, but the muscles – activated by the nervous system – also play a part. There is a general increase in muscle tone, and this may be followed by spasmodic contractions (**shivering**).

  In winter as much as 40 per cent of the food we eat may be used for generating heat energy in resting conditions. And of course we may augment these involuntary responses by voluntary actions, such as rubbing our hands together or stamping our feet.

How do endotherms respond to hot conditions?

Responses of endotherms to hot conditions include the following:

- **The hairs are lowered by relaxation of the erector pili muscles, so they lie flat against the surface of the skin**. Less air is trapped between the hairs, insulation is therefore reduced, and heat energy can be lost more readily by conduction, radiation and convection.

  However, heat energy will be lost only if the external temperature is lower than the body temperature. If the external temperature is higher than the body temperature, the hair becomes important in insulating the body against overheating from outside. This is of special significance to large animals like the camel which, in the open desert, cannot escape the heat of the Sun.

- **The arterioles leading to the superficial capillaries dilate**. As a result the blood flow to the surface is increased and more heat energy can be lost to the surroundings. In exposed extremities such as the ears additional vessels and blood plexuses, which are constricted in cool conditions, dilate so that extra blood flows to the surface of the skin.

- **Sweating occurs**. Evaporation of sweat from the surface of the skin cools the blood as it flows through the superficial vessels. As a means of cooling the human body, sweating is extremely important. Indeed when the external temperature exceeds the body temperature there is no other way of doing it. Sweating is an involuntary response brought about by the sympathetic nervous system.

  The cooling effect of sweating depends not only on the temperature of the surrounding air but also on its relative humidity, i.e. the degree to which it is saturated with moisture. When the relative humidity is low, evaporation and hence cooling are rapid. When the relative humidity is high, evaporation and cooling are slow. This is why a temperature of 35°C in the desert with a relative humidity of only 20 per cent is more comfortable than a temperature of 25°C in a tropical swamp with a relative humidity of 90 per cent. At very high humidities a large proportion of the sweat does not evaporate at all but drips from the skin or sinks into the clothes, creating conditions which many people find intolerable.

  The evaporating power – and hence cooling effect – of the atmosphere is greatly increased by air movements. A gentle breeze will disperse the layer of humidity that builds up around the body after a long period of sweating. As well as cooling the body this encourages further evaporation to take place. The use of electric fans in hot weather is based on this principle.

- **Panting occurs**. In dogs and cats there are no sweat glands except in the pads of the paws. These animals make up for this deficiency by panting. This speeds up evaporation from the lungs, pharynx and other moist surfaces, helping to cool the blood.

■ **The metabolic rate decreases, so less heat energy is generated by the body**. This is why animals are generally less active, and require less food, in hot weather than in cooler weather. However, there is a limit to how far the metabolic rate can fall. In normal circumstances metabolism must continue at least at the basal rate, and some heat energy will always be generated as a result.

So we see that when the temperature of the environment changes, the body responds in such a way as to maintain its temperature at a constant level. But how does the body know when to 'switch on' its heating or cooling devices? The answer is that the brain tells it to do so.

Extension

Cold stress

Exposure of localised regions of the body to cold, particularly extremities such as the hands or feet for example, can result in **cold injury**. What happens is that the superficial blood vessels constrict for so long that the skin cells become deprived of oxygen. Mild cases, though painful, can be remedied by gentle warming of the affected part. Cold injury often afflicted the feet of soldiers serving in the trenches during the First World War and was known as **trench foot**.

If exposure of the extremities to cold is more severe, **frost bite** may occur: the tissues are permanently damaged to an extent which depends on how low the temperature is and how long the body is exposed to it.

Hypothermia

If the whole body is subjected to prolonged cold, when for instance a person wears inadequate clothing, heat energy is lost from the body more rapidly than it can be produced and the body temperature falls below normal. This is called **hypothermia**.

Humans are surprisingly good at tolerating a decrease in body temperature, but if the decrease is too great or goes on for too long, problems arise. One of the first organs to be affected is the brain, resulting in the person becoming clumsy and mentally sluggish. Since brain function is impaired, the victim may not realise that

anything is wrong and so does nothing about it such as putting on more clothes. Indeed, there are cases of people in this condition taking *off* some of their clothes!

As the body temperature falls, the metabolic rate falls too and that makes the body temperature fall even further – a case of **positive feedback**. Death usually occurs when the body temperature drops to about 25°C, though people have been known to survive lower body temperatures than this. The cause of death is usually **ventricular fibrillation**, a condition in which the normal beating of the heart is replaced by uncoordinated tremors.

People most at risk from hypothermia are babies and the elderly: babies because of their undeveloped thermoregulatory mechanisms and small size (high surface–volume ratio), the elderly because their thermoregulatory mechanisms may have deteriorated through old age. Of these two groups the elderly are the more susceptible. Human babies are remarkably tolerant and have been known to survive core temperatures as low as 9°C.

Hypothermia is associated with inadequate clothing, lack of heating in the home and poor diet. It is therefore a social problem afflicting, in particular, people on low incomes. Old people living on their own are particularly vulnerable.

Healthy young adults are prone to hypothermia if, for some reason, they are

exposed to the cold for a long time. Most at risk are hikers, climbers and pot-holers, especially if their clothes get wet. Matters are made worse if mental impairment causes them to make mistakes or lose their bearings. Fatal accidents have been caused this way.

The effects of the cold are exacerbated by wind. Wind increases the rate of heat energy loss from the body, so it has the same effect as a lower temperature. This is called the **wind chill factor**.

To prevent hypothermia the correct sort of clothing is essential. Ideally, the clothes should be the sort which – like the fur of animals – trap air, for it is the air which insulates the body.

Hypothermia and surgery

Artificial hypothermia is sometimes used in surgical operations on the heart. By cooling the patient the metabolic rate is reduced and the demand for oxygen by the brain and other tissues is lowered. This allows the heart to be stopped while the operation is performed without the risk of the patient suffering brain damage through lack of oxygen. But the patient must not be cooled for too long or the tissues may be permanently damaged.

Lowering the body temperature to 25°C allows about ten minutes for the operation. The patient is cooled either by circulating the blood through a cooling machine or by placing ice packs or some equivalent device in contact with the body.

Heat stress

The human body is poor at tolerating even a small increase in the body temperature.

The body temperature increases during disease and when the environmental temperature and/or humidity are so high that the body gains more heat energy than it can lose. As a result, the body's cooling mechanisms break down and the metabolic rate becomes subject to the temperature rule, increasing steadily as the temperature rises (*page 126*). Moreover, every time the metabolic rate increases, more heat energy is produced which raises the metabolic rate even more – and so on. This is another example of **positive feedback** (*page 272*).

The events outlined above culminate, when the body temperature exceeds about 40°C, in **heat stroke**. This is a complex condition which takes a number of different forms depending on its severity. The brain is the main organ affected. The

person feels giddy and develops flu-like symptoms which may lead to convulsions and unconsciousness. If nothing is done about it, the person will die.

It is impossible to give an exact figure for the *environmental* temperature at which death occurs because it depends on so many things. However, the *body* temperature at which death occurs is about 42°C for most humans, though some people have endured higher body temperatures than this and lived to tell the tale. The record is held by a man with heat stroke whose body temperature rose to 46.5°C!

A side effect of heat stress is **dehydration** and **loss of salt** (sodium and chloride ions) resulting from excessive sweating. Dehydration, of course, can be remedied by drinking water. However, the water dilutes the body fluids, exacerbating the effects of salt loss.

Salt loss from sweating affects the

circulation and other body systems, and causes muscular cramps (**heat cramps**). It can be put right by drinking a salty drink or eating salt tablets, a remedy used by miners and others who work in hot places.

Effects of dehydration on the human body

Moderate:
- thirst, difficulty swallowing;
- concentrated urine;
- mild confusion and muscle weakness.

Severe:
- intense thirst;
- concentrated urine;
- confusion, coma, muscle weakness;
- low blood volume and pressure; increased heart rate.

▶ Oral rehydration therapy, page 340

18.3 The role of the brain in temperature regulation

For a long time, since about 1912 in fact, it was suspected that the brain was responsible for controlling the body temperature, and experiments have narrowed down the site of action to the **hypothalamus** (*page 361*). Electrical stimulation of a specific part of the hypothalamus brings about thermoregulatory responses, and nerve impulses can be recorded from this region when the environmental temperature is changed. It seems therefore that the hypothalamus contains a **thermoregulatory centre**.

Evidence suggests that the hypothalamic centre functions as a **thermostat** (*extension box on page 309*). It senses the temperature of the blood flowing through it, and responds by sending nerve impulses to the appropriate effectors.

In addition, the skin contains millions of **thermoreceptors** which are connected to the central nervous system by sensory nerves. Through these nerves the thermoreceptors signal changes in the skin temperature to the hypothalamic centre.

The information which passes to and from the brain in temperature regulation is summarised in figure 18.4.

The role of the thermoreceptors in the skin

If the hypothalamus detects changes in the temperature of the blood as well as initiating appropriate responses, what part do the thermoreceptors in the skin play in temperature regulation?

The answer is that while the hypothalamus detects temperature changes *inside* the body, the skin receptors detect temperature changes at the *surface*. They enable you to *feel*

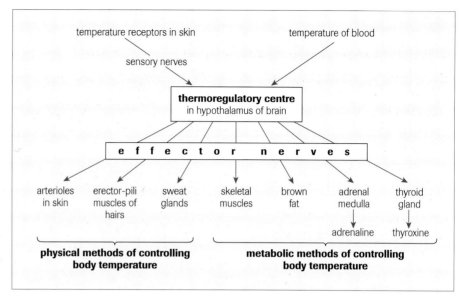

Figure 18.4 Summary of the structures involved in the reflex control of body temperature in a mammal. Increases in the general metabolic rate are brought about by the hormones adrenaline and thyroxine which are secreted in larger amounts in cold conditions.

whether the external environment immediately outside your body is hot or cold. This information, acting via the thermoregulatory centre, initiates voluntary activities such as taking exercise in severe cold, or moving into the shade if it is very hot.

The homeostatic control of body temperature

We can summarise the way our body temperature is controlled like this. If the temperature of the blood is higher than normal, the thermoregulatory centre detects this and sets into motion the various processes that cool the body. On the other hand, if the temperature of the blood is below normal, the centre initiates the processes that warm the body. So we have here yet another homeostatic system involving negative feedback (*figure 18.5*).

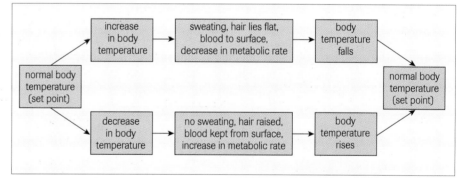

Figure 18.5 The homeostatic control of body temperature in a mammal. The physiological mechanisms outlined here may be aided by behavioural ones (*page 312*).

Because it is controlled by negative feedback, the body temperature fluctuates on either side of the norm or set point (*page 272*). The fluctuations are very slight, a mere 0.1°C or so, and each one takes about a minute. Although they are happening all the time, they are far too small for us to notice them. (Don't confuse these very small minute-to-minute fluctuations with the much larger diurnal fluctuations shown in the box on page 302.)

When the body temperature increases during a fever it is probable that the set point of the hypothalamic thermostat is raised to a new level. The rise in body temperature may be a useful adaptation for destroying the pathogens.

Evidence that the thermoregulatory centre is a thermostat

It was pointed out in Chapter 16 that for any homeostatic process to work, there must be a receptor, a control mechanism and an effector.

The question is: does the thermoregulatory centre in the hypothalamus serve only as a control device, or is it a receptor as well? In other words, does it simply relay information which it has received from the skin thermoreceptors to the appropriate effectors, or is the centre itself sensitive to changes in body temperature? If the latter is true, then the centre is functioning like a thermostat in a central heating system.

To answer this question, an ingenious experiment was carried out by T.H. Benzinger and his team at the Naval Medical Research Institute in Maryland, USA. They put a volunteer in a special form of calorimeter which enabled simultaneous measurements to be made of the temperatures of the hypothalamus and the skin, together with the loss of heat energy from the body by radiation, convection and sweating (*illustration 1*). The temperature of the hypothalamus was recorded by placing a thermocouple in the outer ear close to the ear drum. Previous tests had shown that the temperature measured at this point was the same as that of the hypothalamus itself.

The subject, lying in the calorimeter at a constant temperature well above that of his body, was asked to consume a large quantity of iced sherbet at 30 minute intervals. The results are shown in illustration 2. On each occasion, immediately after taking the iced sherbet, three changes occurred:

- The temperature of the hypothalamus fell, owing to the cooling of the blood by the ice in the gut.
- Less heat energy was lost from the skin because of decreased sweating.

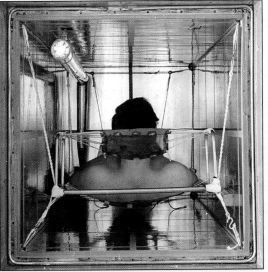

Illustration 1 Benzinger's calorimeter with a volunteer inside. The lining of the chamber is interlaced with thousands of thermoelectric junctions which measure heat energy loss from the skin.

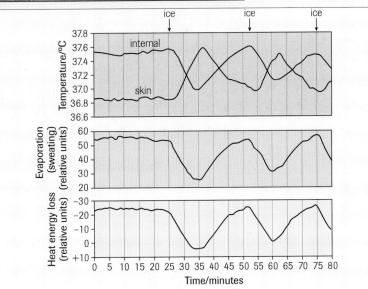

Illustration 2 The results of Benzinger's experiment are shown in these recordings.

- The skin temperature rose due to reduced heat energy loss from it.

The important thing to emerge was a close correlation between the fall in temperature of the hypothalamus and the decrease in the rate of sweating. We can explain this by suggesting that the decreased temperature of the blood is in some way detected by the hypothalamus, which then causes a decrease in the rate of sweating.

That the skin receptors play little or no part in the response is indicated by the fact that the skin temperature rose during this period. If the temperature changes were detected by the receptors in the skin, a rise in the skin temperature would switch on the body's cooling processes – exactly the reverse of what actually happened.

More recent experiments have confirmed the idea that the thermoregulatory centre functions as a thermostat. Moreover, within the centre certain areas are responsible for switching on the body's cooling mechanisms, others for switching on the warming mechanisms.

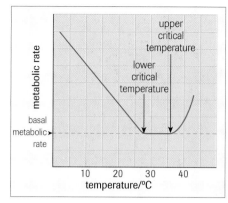

Figure 18.6 The effect of environmental temperature on the metabolic rate of a human.

▶ Acclimatisation to high altitudes, pages 174 and 243

How does the camel survive in the hot desert?

A camel can survive for days without water and be active in the full heat of the Sun. How does it manage it? Part of the answer is that it saves water by not sweating, at least not until its body temperature reaches about 40°C.

The trouble is that by not sweating, the camel is deprived of its most effective means of keeping cool. The result is that during the day its body temperature gradually increases, rising as high as 40°C by sundown. In the cool of the desert night, heat energy is lost from the body to such an extent that the body temperature falls as low as 34°C. This is important because it means that during the following day the temperature climbs from an abnormally low starting point. This prevents the body temperature reaching the lethal level by the end of the day.

Not only are the camel's tissues tolerant to daily fluctuations in temperature but they are also exceptionally tolerant to dehydration (*page 296*). The camel is reputed to be a bad-tempered animal – perhaps that's why.

Consider what happens to a naked person if the air temperature is gradually lowered from a pleasant 29°C to freezing point.

To begin with, the physical mechanisms - insulation and so on - keep the body temperature at its normal level, and the metabolic rate remains unchanged. However, at about 27°C (the exact temperature varies from person to person) the physical mechanisms are no longer able to keep the body temperature constant, and the metabolic rate starts rising. The environmental temperature at which this happens is called the **lower critical temperature**.

As the environmental temperature is lowered further, the metabolic rate continues to rise until eventually it can no longer generate enough heat energy to maintain the body temperature. When this point is reached, the body temperature and metabolic rate fall, and the subject is liable to die. Of course the experiment is not normally taken to this extreme! However, it is important to realise that this is essentially what happens when people suffer from **hypothermia** (*extension box on page 306*).

Now consider the result of *increasing* the air temperature from about 29°C. To begin with, the body's physical mechanisms – sweating and so on – keep the body temperature at its normal level. However, there comes a point when the physical mechanisms can no longer cope, and the body temperature starts rising with the environmental temperature. The environmental temperature at which this happens is called the **upper critical temperature**. If the upper critical temperature is exceeded, **heat stroke** may occur (*extension box on page 307*).

To summarise, between the upper and lower critical temperatures the metabolic rate remains unchanged and physical mechanisms alone keep the body temperature constant. Above the upper critical temperature and below the lower critical temperature the metabolic rate increases. These observations are shown graphically in figure 18.6.

Adaptation and acclimatisation

The lower critical temperature varies from one person to another. It is lowest in people who are adapted, or have become acclimatised, to living in cold conditions. A naked European, unless acclimatised, starts shivering when the air temperature falls below about 27°C. In contrast, Australian Aborigines and Kalahari Bushmen are adapted to the cold and can sleep almost naked without shivering at air temperatures as low as 4°C. This is achieved mainly by blood being diverted from the surface of the skin, with the result that the body temperature stays at about 28°C.

The upper critical temperature depends on the humidity of the atmosphere as well as the environmental temperature and, as with the lower critical temperature, it varies from person to person. It is highest in people who are adapted, or have become acclimatised to, living in hot places such as in the tropics. Their cooling mechanisms, particularly sweating, are particularly efficient.

The lower critical temperature and the environment

Our lower critical temperature of about 27°C is quite high compared with other mammals, and it supports the view that the human is essentially a tropical species whose origins are to be found in the warmer parts of the world.

The lower critical temperature has been determined for different mammals, and it has been found to be lower for species living in cold places than for those which live in warm places. For example, the desert kangaroo rat *Dipodomys* has a lower critical temperature just below 30°C, whereas the Arctic fox's is about –40°C. Moreover, below the lower critical temperature the metabolic rate rises more slowly in cold-dwellers than in warm-dwellers (*figure 18.7*).

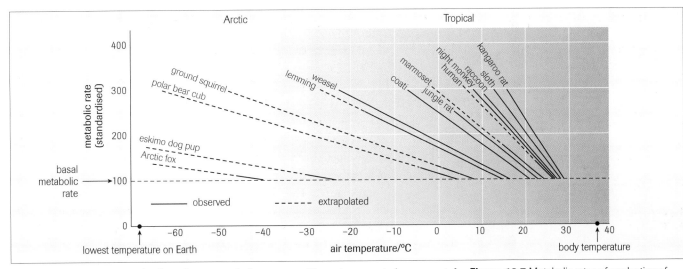

Figure 18.7 Metabolic rates of a selection of mammals as a function of the environmental (air) temperature. Notice that the lower critical temperature at which the metabolic rate starts to rise is much lower for 'arctic' animals than for 'tropical' animals.

These findings reflect the fact that animals living in cold environments have special adaptations for keeping warm. Let us look briefly at some of these adaptations.

Adaptations for living in cold environments

In cold-dwellers the **hair is usually thicker** and better at holding air around the body than it is in warm-dwellers. In many mammalian species the hair thickens as winter approaches and becomes sparser in summer (*figure 18.8A*).

Figure 18.8 Two well-known animals with special adaptations for preventing loss of heat energy.
A The polar bear has a thick layer of subcutaneous fat and a dense coat of hair, both of which insulate it efficiently against heat energy loss. The polar bear inhabits some of the coldest places on Earth and it does not hibernate.
B The Cape seal, a marine mammal whose distribution extends to the Antarctic, has an exceptionally thick layer of subcutaneous fat (blubber) which helps to insulate it against heat energy loss.

Animals living in cold climates, polar bears and seals for example, have a particularly **thick layer of sub-cutaneous fat**. In the seal and other marine mammals such as whales, the fat is called the **blubber** (*figure 18.8B*).

Because of its relatively large surface–volume ratio, a small animal loses heat energy more quickly than a larger animal. Being large may therefore be regarded as an adaptation for living in cold places (*extension box below*).

Extension

Large is warm

Gordon Grigg and his colleagues at the University of Queensland in Brisbane, Australia, measured the body temperatures of 11 crocodiles by the ingenious method of feeding them with chicken carcasses fitted with temperature-sensitive radio transmitters – crocodiles don't take kindly to having their oral or rectal temperatures taken!

The largest crocodile weighed over 1000 kg, the smallest ones a mere 50 kg. The body temperature of the largest crocodile was on average 3.7°C higher in summer, and 1.9°C higher in winter, than that of the smallest ones. Moreover, the body temperatures of the large crocodiles fluctuated daily by only 2°C compared with 10°C for the small ones.

These findings support the general principle that heat energy exchanges across the body surface are less for large animals than for small ones.

It was observed many years ago that extremities such as the ears tend to be smaller in animals that live in cold regions than in their relatives living in warm regions. An example is given in figure 18.9. The small ears of the Arctic fox minimise heat energy loss from the exposed surface. On the other hand, the large ears of the desert fox, richly supplied with blood vessels, serve as cooling devices like the radiator of a car.

It has been found that certain mammals, including humans, possess patches of a special kind of fat tissue, called **brown fat**, in various parts of the body, particularly between the shoulder blades. Brown fat cells contain enormous numbers of mitochondria and the tissue has a very rich blood supply. Controlled by the sympathetic nervous system, it has an exceptionally high metabolic rate and generates a lot of heat energy very quickly.

Brown fat is particularly useful in newborn babies because their temperature control mechanisms have not yet developed and their large surface-volume ratio makes them particularly susceptible to heat energy loss. Because it takes the place of shivering, the production of heat energy from brown fat is called **non-shivering thermogenesis**. It is also important in animals coming out of hibernation, where rapid warming of the tissues is essential.

Another interesting adaptation is seen in the flippers of dolphins and the legs of ducks, both of which are highly susceptible to loss of heat energy, particularly if they are in cold water. In the limbs the arteries and veins are very close to each other (*figure 18.10*). As blood flows down the artery, heat energy passes from it to the cooler blood which is returning in the opposite direction in the vein. This achieves two things. Firstly it means that the arterial blood has already been cooled by the time it reaches the end of the limb, so that relatively little heat energy is lost from it. Secondly it warms the venous blood before it gets back to the main part of the body. This **countercurrent heat exchange system** is an efficient way of conserving heat energy, and is widespread amongst animals. It even occurs in the legs of humans to some extent, and the same principle is used by heating engineers.

As an endotherm, the human is in a rather embarrassing position. Our lower critical temperature of about 27°C is not much below that of the desert kangaroo rat, and equips us for little else than running around naked in the tropics. We owe this to the scantiness of our hair, a deficiency for which we compensate by **wearing clothes**. Had we not developed the ability to make and wear suitable clothes, humans would never have been able to exploit the temperate regions of the world, let alone the poles. The wearing of clothes is an example of behavioural control of body temperature, to which we now turn.

Figure 18.9 The Arctic fox of the northern tundra has small ears whereas Blanford's fox of the Middle East desert has large ears.

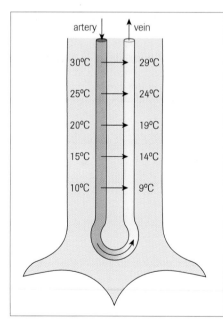

Figure 18.10 Diagram showing the countercurrent heat exchange system in a limb. The artery and vein run parallel with each other. At each level, heat energy is transferred from the artery to the vein, so that by the time the venous blood leaves the limb it is almost as warm as the arterial blood. In some cases the veins may be wrapped around the arteries in a most intimate way.

18.5 Behavioural control of body temperature

When an animal finds itself in a particularly hot environment it may behave in such a way as to cool itself. When cold it behaves so as to warm itself up. Such adaptive behaviour is seen in our own species when, for example, we put on extra clothes or switch on the central heating.

Behavioural control is particularly important for ectothermic organisms, in which it is usually the only effective method of temperature regulation. Even unicellular organisms such as *Paramecium* will seek out a region in their environment (freshwater) which provides the optimum temperature. Similar responses are shown by other ectothermic animals such as insects and fish. However, it is in reptiles that the behavioural control of temperature is most apparent.

Many lizards and snakes gain heat energy by lying in the Sun, or absorbing it from rocks and sand. By absorbing heat energy from, or losing it to, the surroundings, the animal maintains its body at a near constant temperature of about 36°C (*figure 18.11*).

Reptiles cannot sweat but alligators cool themselves by opening their mouths and letting water evaporate from the moist surfaces in the buccal cavity (*figure 18.12*).

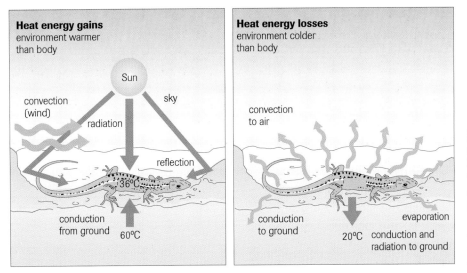

Figure 18.11 Heat gains and losses by an ectotherm such as a lizard. The body is warmed by radiation from the Sun, convection currents in the air, reflection from nearby surfaces, and conduction from the ground. The body is cooled by comparable processes working the other way round, together with evaporation from the lungs and mouth cavity. As a result the animal maintains a near-constant body temperature of approximately 36°C.

Figure 18.12 At temperatures above about 38°C, alligators open their mouths and evaporation of moisture from the buccal cavity cools their blood.

Approximately 65 per cent of metabolic heat energy can be lost by this **thermal gaping**. Iguana lizards enhance the cooling effect of thermal gaping by breathing rapidly and protruding the tongue, which has a rich blood supply. Tortoises employ a different strategy: they salivate over their neck and front legs, and the evaporation of the water cools the body.

At night, when it can be extremely cold, a desert lizard may burrow or seek out a crevice in which to build up a warm atmosphere from the heat energy generated by its metabolism. These animals are not insulated as a mammal is, but by shifting from one place to another they do the next best thing, which is to make sure that the temperature of their immediate surroundings is always agreeable.

Although we tend to associate behavioural thermoregulation with ectotherms, endotherms show similar responses and use them to augment their physiological mechanisms. My dog used to lie in front of the fire until he became unbearably hot, then he would move behind the settee to cool off.

Temperature and hibernation

Keeping warm in cold conditions requires a plentiful food supply to provide the fuel for generating the necessary heat energy. In winter, when the environmental temperature is low and food is scarce, this can be difficult so the animal may **hibernate**.

Hibernation occurs in many temperate and Arctic animals, and is usually stimulated by cold. The animal responds by going into a deep sleep: the metabolic rate falls to the minimum required to keep life ticking over. The body temperature also falls, and is maintained at a much lower level than normal, often about 18°C but as low as 2°C in the hamster. Generally, temperature regulation does not stop altogether but operates at a lowered set point. It is comparable to saving fuel in a central heating system by turning the thermostat down to a lower setting.

There is of course another way of saving fuel, and that is by switching the thermostat off altogether. Bats do this, their body temperature following that of the environment during hibernation. The danger here is that if the environmental temperature falls too low, the animal may die of cold. However, some bats are remarkably resilient. A horseshoe bat can become frozen almost solid and yet remain alive.

Because of its larger surface–volume ratio, the rate of heat energy loss is greater for a small animal than for a large one. If this loss of heat energy is to be made good by metabolism, a very high metabolic rate may be required. In winter, a small animal simply cannot eat sufficient food quickly enough to supply the fuel for maintaining such a high metabolic rate. For this reason it is mainly small animals that hibernate.

18.6 Temperature control in plants

Plants can tolerate fairly wide fluctuations in temperature. This is what one would expect of ectothermic organisms that are rooted to the ground and incapable of getting out of the Sun's rays. Plants of different regions are adapted to different temperature ranges. Temperate species thrive best between about 25 and 30°C, whereas the optimum temperature for Arctic and alpine plants may be as low as 15°C. However, there are limits to the range which each group can tolerate, and experiments suggest that plants may be better at controlling their temperature than was once thought.

Plants gain or lose heat energy by the same physical mechanisms as animals do: conduction, radiation and convection, and they lose heat energy by evaporation. In fact **transpiration**, the evaporation of water through (mainly) the stomata of the leaves, is the principal way that plants keep cool. If the air temperature exceeds about 30°C, transpiration keeps the plant at a temperature lower than that of the air, often considerably lower, even when the leaves are in full sunlight. For this to be possible the plant must have a reasonably good water supply. The California palm tree, *Washingtonia filifera*, an accomplished temperature regulator by plant standards, flourishes in the hot desert but is restricted to oases (*figure 18.13*).

It has been shown that when the temperature of certain plants approaches danger-point, a sudden increase in transpiration cools the plant sufficiently to save it from disaster. Such is the case with the California monkey flower, *Mimulus cardinalis* (*figure 18.14*). When the leaf temperature reaches 41.5°C, the stomata suddenly open right up and the transpiration rate increases by four times. The cooling effect of this is enough to keep the leaf temperature at 42°C even when the air temperature exceeds 60°C!

Plants have other ways of preventing overheating. For example, a **shiny cuticle** reflects heat radiation, and having a **small leaf area** reduces the uptake of heat energy from the Sun.

Another helpful process is **wilting** (*page 113*). The drooping of the plant removes the leaves from the direct rays of the Sun. A plant which has wilted may remain in this condition without untoward effects until sunset.

Figure 18.13 The California palm tree, *Washingtonia filifera* thrives in the hot desert so long as it has a reasonable water supply.

Figure 18.14 The California monkey flower, *Mimulus cardinalis.* responds to high environmental temperatures by opening its stomata and transpiring rapidly.

Surviving extremes of temperature

Organisms which cannot control their body temperature may have to withstand freezing temperatures, at least at certain times of the year. Others may have to survive in intense heat.

Surviving very low temperatures

In general terms there are four main methods:

■ **Supercooling** Supercooling is the lowering of the temperature of a fluid to below its freezing point without the formation of ice. Ice crystals can damage tissues, and supercooling provides a way of avoiding this. Experiments have shown that certain reptiles can be supercooled to as low as –8°C without freezing. Plants and fishes also go in for supercooling.

■ **Freezing tolerance** Some organisms, notably plants and insects, can tolerate the formation of ice in their tissues.
Certain insect larvae can recover after as much as 90 per cent of the body has been frozen. In these organisms ice crystals form between, rather than inside, the cells. The cells themselves shrink and recover later when the ice melts. In some species of fish, ice damage is lessened by the presence of **glycerol** in the tissues. Glycerol is used in human blood banks and sperm banks to prevent injury to cells that are frozen for storage.

■ **Using an antifreeze** The antifreeze in the radiator of a car lowers the freezing point so that the water does not freeze in winter. A similar substance has been found in the blood of certain Antarctic fish. Of course the presence of solutes in the blood means that the freezing point of any animal's blood will be slightly lower than that of pure water. However, in these fish a special antifreeze – a glycoprotein – is present which lowers the freezing point even further and keeps the blood in an unfrozen state even in the coldest water.

■ **Protecting cell membranes** The membrane lipids of hibernating animals undergo a chemical change before hibernation starts. This lowers the temperature at which the lipids solidify, thus ensuring that ionic regulation and other functions involving cell membranes are not impaired.

Surviving very high temperatures
The main adaptation here is **heat tolerance**. This enables certain types of algae to flourish in hot springs at temperatures of 55 to 60°C (*illustration*). However, it is prokaryotes that show the greatest tolerance. There are many reports of bacteria growing in boiling hot springs in North America and New Zealand, but the jackpot must go to certain bacteria which have been discovered in the hot water rising from sulphide-encrusted vents in the deep ocean floor. Some of these bacteria were living at temperatures of 350°C. It is claimed that in the laboratory they reproduced enthusiastically in sea water at 250°C, doubling in number every 40 minutes!

Heat-tolerant bacteria possess membranes which are more heat-stable than those of other prokaryotes, and their enzymes work optimally at temperatures well above those that would denature the enzymes of other organisms. For example, *Thermophilus*, a bacterium which lives in hot springs, possesses enzymes that work best at 80°C.

Green algae flourishing in hot water in Waimangu Thermal Valley, New Zealand.

Part 3

Summary

1. Organisms cannot withstand fluctuations in body temperature beyond that which is compatible with the functioning of their cells. In many cases this necessitates some form of **thermoregulation**.

2. On the basis of their ability to thermoregulate, animals are classified into **homoiothermic** (or **endothermic**) and **poikilothermic** (or **ectothermic**).

3. Heat energy is gained by **metabolism**, lost or gained by **conduction**, **radiation** and **convection**, and lost by **evaporation**. The problem in temperature regulation is to counteract, control or make use of these processes.

4. Endothermic animals (e.g. mammals) have various structural and physiological ways of coping with low or high environmental temperatures, many of them involving the **skin**.

5. Structures in mammalian skin important in temperature regulation include the **blood vessels**, **hairs**, **sweat glands**, **thermoreceptors** and **subcutaneous fat**.

6. Thermoregulatory responses are controlled by a **thermoregulatory centre** in the **hypothalamus** of the brain. The centre serves as a **thermostat** and responds to changes in the temperature of the blood.

7. In endotherms, physical (non-metabolic) mechanisms alone maintain a constant body temperature so long as the environmental temperature ranges between an **upper** and a **lower critical temperature**.

8. The lower critical temperature is significantly lower for 'Arctic' than for 'tropical' animals. Humans may be **adapted**, or become **acclimatised**, to living in particularly hot or cold situations.

9. Some endothermic animals reduce excessive loss of heat energy by special adaptations, e.g. a **countercurrent heat exchange system**.

10. Many animals regulate their body temperature by means of **behaviour**. In ectothermic animals this is the only method. **Hibernation** and **migration** are ways of avoiding unfavourable environmental temperatures.

11. Plants have a number of structural features which help them to withstand high temperatures. To some extent plants are cooled by **transpiration**, in some cases markedly so.

12. Some organisms can survive in extremely hot or cold environments. Their adaptations include **supercooling**, using an **antifreeze** and **tolerance** to very low or very high temperatures.

For general advice on these questions and advice on answering essay-type questions, see pages vii and viii.

1. (a) Define the term *homeostasis*. (2)

(b) (i) State **three** advantages to mammals of being able to maintain a constant body temperature. (3)

(ii) State **two** disadvantages of maintaining a constant temperature. (2)

(c) Outline **one metabolic** change that may occur if the peripheral body temperature falls. (3)

(d) In 1961 Benzinger measured the core and skin temperature of a human volunteer before and after ingesting ice. He also measured heat loss to the environment over the same period. His results are shown below.

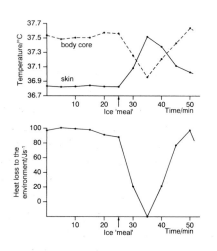

Give an explanation of these results. (5)

(Total 15 marks)

O&C 1998

2. The diagram shows the way in which temperature is regulated in the body of a mammal.

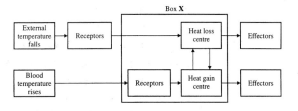

(a) Which part of the brain is represented by box **X**? (1)

(b) (i) How does the heat loss centre control the effectors which lower the body temperature? (1)

(ii) Explain how blood vessels can act as effectors and lower the body temperature. (3)

(Total 5 marks)

AEB 1997

3. *Liolaemus* is a reptile which lives at a high altitude in the mountains of South America. In an investigation, the air temperature and the body temperature of this lizard were measured at intervals during one morning. The results are shown in the table below.

Time of day (24 hour clock)	Air temperature / °C	Body temperature of lizard / °C
07.10	−3.0	2.5
07.20	−1.0	10.0
07.30	−2.0	19.0
08.00	1.0	31.0
08.20	1.5	33.0
08.45	5.0	34.0
10.00	9.0	35.0
11.00	13.0	36.0

Adapted from Schmidt-Nielsen, Animal Physiology, 1983

(a) Describe the changes in air temperature and body temperature during the following time intervals.

(i) 07.10 to 08.00 (2)

(ii) 08.00 to 11.00 (2)

(b) Suggest how the lizard increases its body temperature during the early morning. (2)

(c) Suggest how the lizard controls its body temperature between the hours of 08.45 and 11.00. (2)

(d) Explain why it may be an advantage for this lizard to be able to control its body temperature. (2)

(Total 10 marks)

London 1997

4. Humans show patterns of physiological activity or behaviour which follow a circadian cycle of about 24 hours.

Plan an investigation which you could personally carry out to find out if there is a relationship between the time of day and body temperature.

Your answer should include details under the following headings.

(a) Plan of the investigation to be carried out (9)

(b) Presentation of results and methods of data analysis (7)

(c) Limitations of your method and an indication of further work which could be undertaken (5)

(Total 21 marks)

London 1997

5. Give an account of the adaptations shown by human populations to life in extremes of temperature.

(Total 10 marks)

London 1998

hat exactly do we mean by disease? It is a word that most people think they understand. The majority will probably think of it as an infectious illness, like chicken pox. But a disease is not a 'thing', rather it is a reaction between the individual body and its environment. For example, some of the worst effects of tuberculosis and leprosy are not caused by the infectious microorganisms themselves, but by our defence system's persistent but fruitless attacks on them, which destroy healthy tissue.

Any attempt at a definition is therefore remarkably difficult. What can be said is that disease is a structural and/or functional disorder of the body which results in the development of discernible signs called **symptoms**.

19.1 Types of disease

For practical purposes, diseases can be grouped into categories although, as you will see, some diseases fit into more than one category. The following classification shows one way in which diseases may be grouped, but others could be used.

- **Infectious diseases** These are passed from person to person and are caused mainly by bacteria and viruses. Amongst these are common childhood diseases such as rubella (German measles) and mumps. Other examples are tuberculosis, influenza, poliomyelitis, meningitis, glandular fever, AIDS and other sexually transmitted infections. Diarrhoea, which you may consider is a symptom rather than a disease, could be included here when it is caused by water- or food-borne microorganisms such as *Salmonella* and *E. coli*. Infectious diseases are responsible for the majority of deaths in developing countries today.

- **Non-infectious diseases** These are not passed directly from one person to another and include many of the diseases in the categories which follow. Malaria and diseases caused by larger parasites such as parasitic worms, although caused by infective agents, are not passed from person to person directly.

- **Degenerative diseases** These are associated with ageing (*page 634*) and include coronary heart disease, arthritis, Alzheimer's disease and some cancers. Unfortunately degenerative diseases are becoming increasingly common in younger age groups in industrialised countries as a result of sedentary lifestyles, smoking and high alcohol consumption.

- **Deficiency diseases** Shortage of food or lack of particular constituents of the diet gives rise to deficiency diseases such as scurvy and beri-beri, and kwashiorkor (protein deficiency disease) in children. These diseases are the result of persistent poverty such as is found in some parts of developing countries.

- **Inherited diseases** These are disorders passed to children from their parents in the genes, and include haemophilia, cystic fibrosis and Huntingdon's chorea.

- **Self-inflicted diseases** Diseases which develop as a result of certain types of behaviour or habits are in this group. For example, emphysema and lung cancer may be the outcome of smoking cigarettes, and cirrhosis of the liver may result from excessive consumption of alcohol.

- **Mental diseases** There are two recognised kinds of mental illness: relatively mild disorders called **neuroses**, often connected with stress, which result in anxiety and phobias (irrational fears); and more serious **psychoses** such as schizophrenia, for

Support

Influenza

Influenza is a highly infectious illness caused by a virus. The initial symptoms, after a short incubation period, are a headache, aching in the limbs, shivering, sore throat, cough and fever. These symptoms do not usually last long (1–2 weeks). Afterwards a person may experience a longer period of feeling generally weak and depressed – a condition sometimes called post-viral syndrome. So influenza has a mental as well as a physical component.

Influenza is caused by two main types of virus: **influenza A** and **influenza B**. Both undergo genetic changes as they spread and give rise to variants, usually named after their place of origin, hence Asian flu and Hong Kong flu. It is for this reason that immunisation is often ineffective because new vaccines have to be developed for each new strain that emerges. The influenza virus enters and leaves the body through the nose and mouth. It is spread by direct and indirect contact, and certainly includes droplet infection (*figure 19.1 on page 320*).

▶ Immunisation, page 330

which medical treatment with drugs or psychotherapy is required. Mental disorders are increasing throughout the world; it is estimated that one person in six is affected by mental illness such as depression at some point in their lifetime.

■ **Social diseases** Diseases tend to reflect social conditions which means that diseases associated with poverty are in this group. Cholera, an infectious diarrhoeal disease, spreads in overcrowded living conditions when water and food supplies are contaminated with cholera bacteria.

■ **Environmental diseases** Disorders which result from the external environment are in this group. Air pollution in some cities (Athens, Bombay and Los Angeles, for example) can cause long-term lung damage, and excessive exposure to ultraviolet rays from the Sun may cause skin cancer. Asbestosis, caused by asbestos dust, causes permanent damage to the body; and the effects of nerve gas, pesticides and the contaminants released from motor vehicles all qualify for inclusion in this group.

The rest of this chapter will be concerned mainly with infectious diseases and how they are controlled.

19.2 Infectious diseases

The body of an animal is constantly being invaded by **microorganisms**, particularly **bacteria** and **viruses** but also certain **protoctists** and **fungi** which includes **yeasts**. They enter the body through its openings, particularly the nose and mouth, and thus gain entry to the lungs or gut. They may also enter the reproductive system during sexual intercourse – indeed, some only get into the body this way. Another mode of entry is via the skin when it is broken as a result of a cut or bite.

Most of these microorganisms are harmless or even beneficial – for example, some enable certain mammals to digest plants. However, a minority of them either feed the tissues or release poisonous substances (**toxins**) into the bloodstream, thereby bringing about disease.

Toxins are of two types:

■ **Exotoxins** These are produced by bacteria and released into the surrounding medium, causing cell and tissue damage. Among the bacteria known for exotoxin production are *Corynebacterium diphtheriae* (which causes diphtheria) and *Clostridium tetani* (which causes tetanus). In these cases the illness is caused by the toxin and the effects are better treated as chemical poisoning rather than disease caused by growth of the bacteria. Food poisoning is a consequence of exotoxin produced by staphylococci; in the same way the diarrhoea associated with cholera is caused by the exotoxin produced by the bacterium *Vibrio cholerae*. Botulism, a very serious type of food poisoning, is the result of the exotoxin produced by *Clostridium botulinum*.

The body can produce antibodies to these toxins called **antitoxins**, which provide protection against future infection (*page 323*). In addition, exotoxins can be modified chemically so that they no longer cause the disease, but induce the body to produce antitoxins which are also active against the original toxin. These modified toxins are called **toxoids** and are used to produce immunity to diphtheria and tetanus.

➤ Bacteria and human life, page 90

■ **Endotoxins** These are also produced by bacteria, but the effects of endotoxins only become apparent when the bacteria die and release them. They do not promote the formation of antitoxins, nor can they be converted into toxoids. All endotoxins produce similar symptoms, such as fever and general weakness seen in many diseases. *Salmonella typhi*, which causes typhoid fever, is a notable producer of endotoxin.

As mentioned at the beginning of this chapter, the symptoms of a disease may be the result of the body's counter-attack against the causative microorganism. Diseases caused by viruses include influenza, poliomyelitis and the common cold; typhoid, diphtheria and tuberculosis are caused by bacteria; while malaria and amoebic dysentery are caused by unicellular protoctists. The activities of these disease-causing microorganisms – or **pathogens** as they are called – are not, of course, confined to humans. All animals and plants are susceptible, though the particular microorganisms that infect them may be different.

In destroying the tissues and liberating toxic substances, these pathogenic microorganisms change the internal environment and upset the smooth running of the body. The control by the body's natural defence mechanisms in mammals is thus an aspect of homeostasis.

The body's defences against disease can be divided into those which *prevent* the entry of microorganisms, and those which *destroy* them once they manage to get in. We will deal with each in turn. Since we know more about these defence mechanisms in mammals than in other organisms, our discussion will be mainly confined to them.

Part 3

Extension

Koch's postulates

The fact that a certain microorganism is found in the body of someone with a particular disease does not necessarily mean that it is the cause of the infection. Traditionally, confirmation that a microorganism causes a given disease is based on four fundamental concepts put forward in the 19th century by Robert Koch.

The concepts are known as **Koch's postulates** and are as follows:

1. The microorganisms must be observed in every case of the disease.

2. The microorganisms must be isolated from the diseased host and grown in culture.

3. The disease must be reproduced when a pure culture is introduced into a disease-free susceptible host.

4. The microorganism must be recovered from the experimentally infected host and its identity confirmed.

Koch's postulates have been confirmed for the vast majority of infectious microorganisms. There are, however, some notable exceptions, either because of failure to culture the microorganism thought to be responsible, as is the case with *Microbacterium leprae* which is present in people with leprosy, or because not all cases of a particular disease show evidence of the microorganism being present. The latter applies to the association of *Helicobacter pylori* with duodenal and gastric ulcers, although it is found in the vast majority of cases.

Nevertheless, Koch's postulates do provide a useful framework for establishing that a particular microorganism is the infective agent in a given disease.

19.3 Preventing entry

The **skin** with its hard, keratinised outer layer serves as an effective barrier to most microorganisms. However, much as an animal might like to envelop itself in an impenetrable barrier, this is patently impossible.

The alimentary tract and gaseous-exchange surfaces are major pathways through which microorganisms can get into the body. To some extent access to the gaseous-exchange surface is prevented by **cilia** lining the trachea and bronchi. Microorganisms and undesirable particles get caught up in **mucus** secreted by numerous goblet cells and are carried by the beating cilia towards the glottis and thence to the throat where they are swallowed.

Figure 19.1 Short-duration flash photograph of a sneeze. Notice the vast number of droplets emitted from the mouth and nose This is one way in which pathogenic microorganisms are transferred from one person to another.

Coughing and **sneezing** help to expel foreign bodies from the breathing tract as figure 19.1 makes only too clear. The **acid in the stomach** kills many of the bacteria that come in with the food and from the breathing tract; in more extreme cases **vomiting** and **diarrhoea** expel undesirable bacteria from the gut.

Areas of the body not covered by skin such as the eyes, nose and mouth are particularly vulnerable to invasion by bacteria. An enzyme called **lysozyme**, present in tears, nasal secretions, saliva, urine and other body fluids, is capable of destroying certain bacteria by making them burst. It works by splitting molecules that occur only in bacterial cell walls. It is a powerful enzyme, effective even in low concentrations, and undoubtedly plays a part in keeping bacteria out of the body. (Don't confuse lysozyme with lysosomes – *page 52*).

In the vagina, certain beneficial (mutualistic) bacteria produce **lactic acid**. This makes the vagina acidic, creating an unfavourable environment for many pathogenic yeasts, bacteria and viruses.

The entry of microorganisms through wounds is a major cause of infection. To some extent this is prevented, or at least cut down, by the **clotting of blood** which not only plugs up the wound and stems the flow of blood but is the first step in the healing process.

Figure 19.2 summarises the body's barriers to infection. The structure of skin is described on page 303, and the blood-clotting mechanism on page 228.

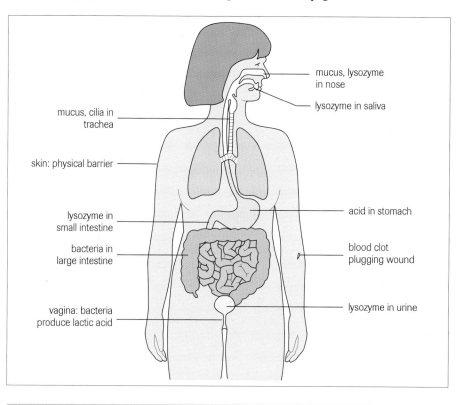

mucus, lysozyme in nose

lysozyme in saliva

mucus, cilia in trachea

skin: physical barrier

lysozyme in small intestine

bacteria in large intestine

vagina: bacteria produce lactic acid

acid in stomach

blood clot plugging wound

lysozyme in urine

Figure 19.2 The body's barriers to invasion by pathogenic microorganisms. The bacteria in the large intestine occur naturally, and by competing with other bacteria they help to prevent pathogens from gaining a foothold if they manage to get into the gut. One disadvantage of antibiotics is that they tend to kill off the useful bacteria as well as the pathogenic ones.

19.4 **The immune response**

Once microorganisms get into the body they multiply prodigiously, attack cells and/or release toxins into the bloodstream (*page 318*). The body must somehow distinguish them from its own cells and destroy them in a way that limits damage to its own tissues. This task is carried out by the **immune system** and is called the **immune response**.

All animals have to defend themselves against microorganisms. During the evolution of the immune system certain cells - notably **white blood cells (leucocytes)** - have emerged to produce a complex defence system which reaches its peak in mammals. In the past it has been customary to call the defensive cells in the immune system white blood cells. However, they are by no means confined to the bloodstream; in fact many are found outside the blood vessels, in the lymphatic system and various tissues. For this reason it is becoming common practice to refer to them simply as **white cells**.

The simplest components of the immune system are cells which engulf and digest foreign material in the blood and tissues in the same way as *Amoeba* engulfs and digests its food – by **phagocytosis** (*page 115*).

Phagocytosis in the immune system

Phagocytosis is carried out by white cells called **phagocytes**. There are two main types of phagocyte; neutrophils and macrophages.

- **Neutrophils** are cells with an irregular, many-lobed nucleus and granular cytoplasm. They are the commonest type of immune cell and make up about 60 per cent of all white cells in the bloodstream. The bone marrow produces 80 million of these cells every minute and their number increases during an infection. They move about in contact with the endothelium of the blood vessels where they ingest bacteria (*figure 19.3*). Once taken up, the bacteria are digested by lysosomes as described on page 320.

  The neutrophils can squeeze between the cells lining the capillaries and migrate into the tissues. They wander through the tissues to the site of an infection, attracted by chemicals released by the microorganisms and the local tissue cells (chemotaxis). Neutrophils survive for only a few days.

- **Macrophages** are larger cells with a regular, horseshoe-shaped nucleus and non-granular cytoplasm. They develop from another type of white cell called **monocytes** which make up only 6 per cent of the white blood cells. Monocytes are made in the bone marrow and, after circulating in the blood for one or two days, they squeeze through the cells lining the capillaries and migrate into the tissues where they become macrophages (*figure 19.4*).

  The macrophages wander around the tissues collecting up 'rubbish', which may be microorganisms or other foreign bodies (in the lungs, dust particles as well as microorganisms are collected in this manner). They are particularly numerous in the lungs, liver, kidney, spleen and lymph nodes (lymph nodes are explained in the support box on the next page). Although the neutrophils are the first cells to arrive at a site of infection, the longer-lived macrophages take over at any major site.

Phagocytes are an efficient means of defence but they must identify correctly which cells to engulf. They could do untold damage if they engulfed the body's own cells. So how do phagocytes recognise which cells to engulf? Certain chemicals are common to the cell walls of bacteria but do not occur on mammalian cells. Phagocytes have receptor molecules on their surfaces which bind to these unique bacterial chemicals because they have complementary shapes – like two pieces of a jigsaw puzzle fitting together. Other

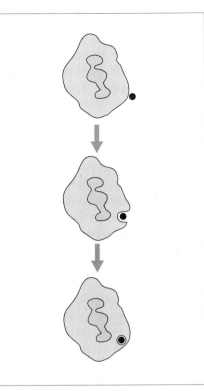

Figure 19.3 A neutrophil ingests a bacterium. When the bacterium (red blob) comes into contact with the surface of the phagocyte, a cup-shaped indentation is formed and the bacterium is taken into a vesicle where it is digested. Fully engorged, a single neutrophil may contain as many as 20 visible bacteria, many of them still alive and moving.

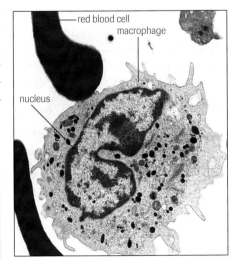

Figure 19.4 Electron micrograph of a phagocytic macrophage in a capillary. Notice the amoeboid shape of the cell and phagocytic vesicles in the cytoplasm. Magnification ×5000.

Part 3

Inflammation

One effect of a local infection, which we have all experienced, is **inflammation**. This is caused by **mast cells** releasing inflammatory substances such as **histamine**, which dilate the blood vessels and make them leaky, so that plasma and white cells flow out into the infected area. Hot, red, swollen and painful, the inflamed area contains numerous bacteria and phagocytes, many of which die and form **pus**. Sometimes the inflamed area forms a **boil**. The host's cells form scar tissue around the boil, whose head may eventually burst open as a result of the pressure of pus inside it.

▶ Mast cells, page 65
▶ The role of prostaglandins in the inflammatory response, page 375
▶ Histamine in allergies, page 333

Lymph nodes

The **lymph nodes** are our so-called 'glands' which sometimes swell up when we are suffering from an infection. They are widely distributed in the body, particularly the groin and armpits.

Each lymph node consists of a network of delicate fibres through which **lymph** percolates. Lymph is a colourless fluid, derived from the blood by a filtration mechanism which is explained on page 268. It is brought to the node and drained away from it by **lymph vessels**. Lymph vessels leaving the nodes lead ultimately to a vein in the neck where the lymph rejoins the bloodstream (*page 239*).

The lymph nodes contain phagocytic macrophages which remove pathogens and foreign particles from the lymph. These phagocytes are mainly fixed to the fibrous network, though they can move out of the lymph node to nearby tissues.

The lymph nodes also contain large numbers of lymphocytes. These are explained in the main text.

Lymphoid tissue is found in other places besides the lymph nodes – the **spleen** and **tonsils** for example. These organs are therefore particularly important in defence against disease.

▶ Lymphatic system, page 239

▶ Formation of tissue fluid, page 268

Larger invaders

Not all invaders of the mammalian body are as small as bacteria and viruses. Some parasites are multicellular and are too large to be engulfed by phagocytes. Examples are nematode worms, flukes and tapeworms.

Special cells exist to deal with these larger invaders. These include a type of white cell called **eosinophils** which produce a protein which is capable of punching holes in the surface cells of flukes and other such parasites. At the same time **basophils** (another type of white cell) and mast cells produce chemical substances which stimulate the immune system to mount an attack against these invaders at the site of infection.

cells in the immune system produce molecules which bind to the bacteria and 'label' them as targets for the phagocytes (*extension box on the next page*).

Phagocytosis, however, has distinct limitations: it does not act against all bacteria and is not very effective against viruses because they reproduce inside the body's own cells where they are protected from attack.

Natural immunity

The type of resistance to infection described so far provides what is called **natural** or **innate immunity**. Similar mechanisms are found throughout the animal kingdom, even in simple invertebrates such as sponges. The key features of this kind of immunity are that it is:

- **inborn**: that is, the response is genetically programmed and not acquired during the individual's lifetime;
- **non-specific**: that is, the cells responsible for it (phagocytes, eosinophils, mast cells and the rest) cannot distinguish between one type of microorganism and another. Phagocytes, for example, will engulf any foreign cell they encounter provided that it is 'labelled' for them;
- **non-adaptive**: that is, the response is the same no matter how many times an individual is infected with the same type of microorganism. Natural immunity does not improve if the same microorganisms get into the body a second time or more.

Adaptive immunity

Mammals, birds and some other vertebrates have an additional line of defence called adaptive or acquired immunity. The special features of adaptive immunity are that it is:

- not inborn but is **acquired** during the individual's life;
- **specific**: that is, different types of the cells responsible for it can distinguish between different types of microorganism;
- **adaptive**: that is, its cells produce an enhanced response to repeated infection by the same type of microorganism.

It is the task of another kind of white cell, called **lymphocytes**, to bring about this type of response to infection. Lymphocytes make up about 24 per cent of the white cells in the bloodstream. They are called lymphocytes because they are abundant in the lymphatic system, particularly the lymph nodes (*support box above*).

There are two types of lymphocytes in the blood and lymph: **B lymphocytes** and **T lymphocytes** (also called **B cells** and **T cells** for short). Each is responsible for a different kind of immune response. These are truly remarkable cells and we shall look at them in turn.

B lymphocytes

The B lymphocytes originate in the bone marrow (B stands for *bone-marrow derived*). Any substance that initiates an adaptive immune response is called an **antigen** – it may be a pathogen or its toxic products, or various non-harmful cells and molecules such as pollen and penicillin. When a B lymphocyte encounters an antigen to which it can bind, it produces an **antibody**, a specialised protein molecule called **immunoglobulin (Ig)** of which there are five main types (*extension box below*). The antibody binds to the antigen and 'labels' it for destruction by phagocytes and other white cells.

Sequence analysis and X-ray diffraction studies have shown that each antibody molecule consists of four polypeptide chains, two heavy and two light (*figure 19.5*). The antibody molecule has two binding sites, each of which binds to an antigen molecule. The regions of the antigen and antibody molecules which bind together have matching shapes, like jigsaw puzzle pieces fitting together.

It is now possible to make large quantities of antibodies in the laboratory and this has provided scientists with a source of antibodies for research into their structure and properties.

What makes B lymphocytes so remarkable is that, between them, they can produce highly specific antibodies against a vast number of different types of antigen. However, each B lymphocyte can only produce one type of antibody which binds to one type of antigen. To understand how this comes about we must consider how the B cells are formed in the bone marrow.

Formation of the B lymphocytes

During embryonic development, large numbers of B lymphocytes are formed in the bone marrow. Each one undergoes rapid cell division to form a **clone** of identical B cells. (A clone is a population of identical cells formed by mitotic cell division – *page 470*.) At birth, each clone consists of a small number of cells programmed to recognise just one type of antigen and to respond to it by secreting antibodies which bind to that antigen alone. A

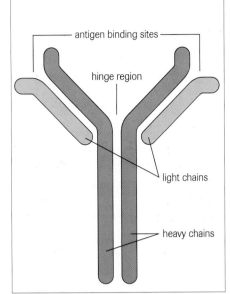

Figure 19.5 Diagram showing the structure of an antibody molecule. Each antibody has four polypeptide chains, two heavy and two light. There are two antigen binding sites. The hinge region allows flexibility when the antibody binds to the antigen, enabling both binding sites to make contact with a matching area of the antigen, thus prolonging the interaction.

Part 3

Extension

Immunoglobulins

The five main types of immunoglobulin are known as **IgG, IgM, IgA, IgD** and **IgE**. Although there are structural differences between them, we shall confine ourselves to their roles in the immune response.

- **IgG** is the most abundant antibody. It diffuses out of blood vessels where it neutralises bacterial toxins, and assists phagocytosis by coating bacteria and making it possible for the phagocytes to engulf them. It can cross the placenta from mother to fetus, and protects the offspring during the first few weeks after birth. This transfer to the fetus does not occur until the last three months of pregnancy, which explains why premature babies are so vulnerable to infection.

- **IgM** is mostly confined to the blood and it too facilitates phagocytosis by coating bacteria. It is particularly good at binding to several antigens at the same time, sticking them together in clumps (*illustration*). This is called **agglutination**.

- **IgA** is found in secretions of parts of the body exposed to the external environment, such as the nose, mouth, vagina and gut. It assists the barrier provided by the mucous membranes in preventing the entry of bacteria and viruses.

- **IgD** exists at very low levels in children and is barely detectable in adults; at present its function is unknown.

- **IgE** is concerned with allergic reactions; it binds to mast cells and can trigger inflammatory responses.

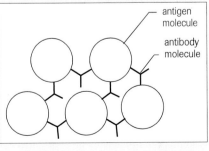

Diagram showing how the two antibody binding sites cause agglutination (clumping together) of antigens.

---

newborn baby's immune system contains at least 100 million different clones of B cells, with the potential between them to recognise any antigen that is likely to get into the body.

Antigen recognition

How does each B lymphocyte recognise its unique antigen? The way it does so is rather neat. The B cell carries on its surface the same kind of antibodies that it is capable of producing. These surface antibodies act as **receptors**. When an appropriate antigen comes along, it combines with one of the receptors. This activates the B cell, causing it to start making antibodies which are then released into the blood and lymph (*figure 19.6*).

Although each B cell has the ability to produce large quantities of its own specific antibody, it does so only if it is needed – that is, if it encounters the right kind of antigen. The particular type of antibody that each B cell produces binds only to one specific type of antigen – or, at the most, several closely related antigens such as the smallpox and cowpox antigens. When a particular antigen gets into the body, it is recognised by the matching

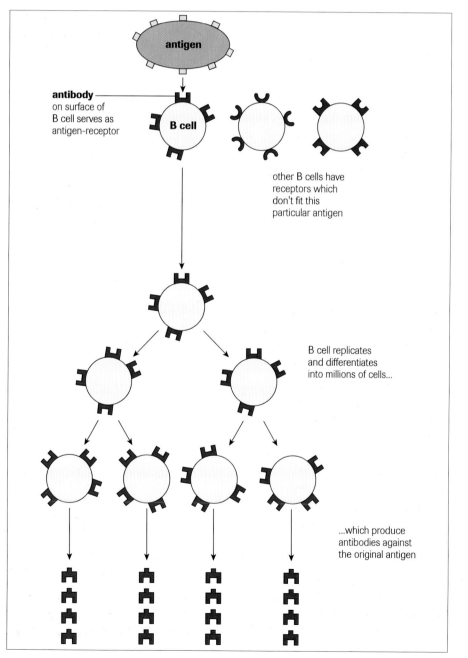

Figure 19.6 When a B cell meets an appropriate antigen it proliferates into millions of identical cells (clones) which produce antibodies against the antigen. Not all the clones produce antibodies straight away; some of them become memory cells which quickly produce antibodies if the person receives another dose of antigen at a later date.

clone and the B cells from that clone bind to it; these cells then divide rapidly to make millions more identical B cells, all secreting antibodies that bind to that specific antigen.

Clonal selection

The process described above is called **clonal selection** because the antigen 'selects' the appropriate clone of B cells from among the millions in the body. The clonal selection theory was first put forward in the 1950s by the Australian scientist Sir Macfarlane Burnet, who was subsequently awarded a Nobel Prize for his work. Since then much evidence has been obtained to support it (*page 336*).

A microorganism is complex chemically and its structure is likely to include not just one antigen but several different types of antigens. These will activate several different clones of B cells to produce appropriate antibodies. This is known as **polyclonal activation** and it produces a mixture of different antibodies, each of which binds to a different type of antigen on the same microorganism.

The B cell clones are, in effect, 'antibody factories' and the B cells show a number of features which fit in with this idea. For example, they are particularly rich in ribosomes, indicative of the high rate of protein synthesis necessary for producing large numbers of antibodies. The mature antibody-producing cells are called **plasma cells** (*figure 19.7*).

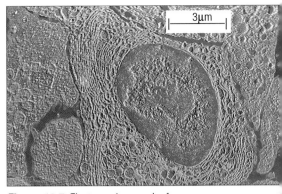

Figure 19.7 Electron micrograph of an antibody-producing plasma cell. Notice the dense endoplasmic reticulum (yellow). This bears numerous ribosomes characteristic of a cell which is engaged in rapid protein synthesis.

Part 3

Monoclonal antibodies

When a microorganism gets into the body, or when a vaccine is administered, antibodies are always produced. For certain sorts of laboratory research it is useful to have a pure preparation of antibodies with single specificity

Until comparatively recently it was impossible to obtain such pure cultures. However, in 1975 Cesar Milstein and Georges Kohler at Cambridge succeeded in fusing antibody-secreting cells with tumour cells. The resulting cells, called **hybridomas**, secrete antibodies, and are immortal – a property of tumour cells.

Single hybridoma cells can be cultured in a vessel where they replicate to form a pure clone, from which their antibodies are collected. Antibodies produced this way are, like the cells that produce them, all identical and they are called **monoclonal antibodies**.

Milstein and Kohler were awarded a Nobel Prize for their work in 1984. Their technique is summarised in the illustration.

Monoclonal antibodies have a number of uses. For example, when directed towards tumour antigens and coupled to cytotoxic ('cell-killing') drugs they could comprise a 'magic bullet' which would target tumour cells but leave healthy cells unaffected. This heralds an exciting prospect for the future of cancer treatment.

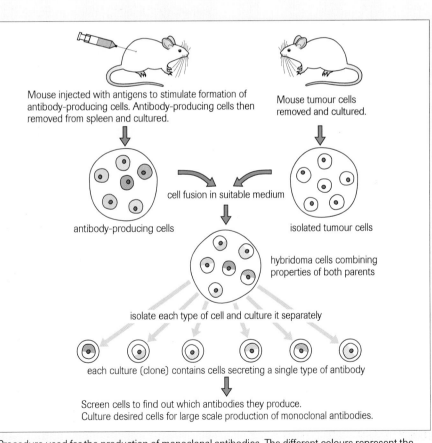

Mouse injected with antigens to stimulate formation of antibody-producing cells. Antibody-producing cells then removed from spleen and cultured.

Mouse tumour cells removed and cultured.

cell fusion in suitable medium

antibody-producing cells

isolated tumour cells

hybridoma cells combining properties of both parents

isolate each type of cell and culture it separately

each culture (clone) contains cells secreting a single type of antibody

Screen cells to find out which antibodies they produce. Culture desired cells for large scale production of monoclonal antibodies.

Procedure used for the production of monoclonal antibodies. The different colours represent the different kinds of antibodies which the cells produce.

▶ Use of monoclonal antibodies in pregnancy testing, page 517

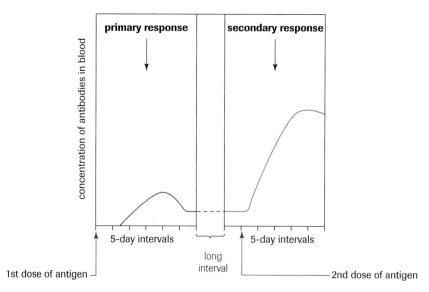

Figure 19.8 The effect of two successive doses of antigen on antibody production. The first dose of antigen triggers the production of a relatively small number of antibodies (primary response). The second dose results in a larger, more rapid and sustained production of antibodies (secondary response). Immunity against some diseases (e.g. measles and poliomyelitis) can last a lifetime; but for other diseases (e.g. typhoid, cholera and tetanus) further doses of antigen ('boosters') are needed from time to time. The enhanced response to a second dose of antigen is due to the presence of memory cells.

Humoral immunity and memory

The type of immunity provided by B lymphocytes and their antibodies is called **humoral immunity** – *humoral* refers to the blood and lymph in which the antibodies circulate. (Because it involves the use of antibodies, it is also called **antibody-mediated immunity**.) The strength of this system lies in its ability to respond to specific antigens which were previously unknown to the body. Its weakness is that if challenged by a massive dose of antigen – the measles virus for example – antibodies cannot be produced quickly enough to prevent illness. This is because, with so many B cells needed, only a few of each type can be present at the outset, and the body needs time for these to proliferate into enough antibody-producing cells to fight the disease.

Fortunately, after an infection, so-called **memory cells** develop from the clone which produces the antibodies, and these memory cells may survive for months or even years. If the body is subjected to another attack by the same antigen – the measles virus for example – it is quickly recognised by the memory cells, which divide repeatedly to form a large clone of antibody-producing cells. As a result, the required level of antibody is built up very quickly and the pathogens are destroyed so rapidly that no symptoms appear. This is how we become **immune** to diseases (*figure 19.8*).

We have seen that the B lymphocytes work by producing specific antibodies when the appropriate antigens get into the body. However, the B lymphocytes respond in this way only if they receive the right signals. These signals come from the T lymphocytes which we must now consider.

T lymphocytes

The T lymphocytes also originate in the bone marrow but they have to pass through the **thymus gland** during their maturation (T stands for *thymus derived*). In the thymus gland they undergo a complex 'education' process without which they cannot take part in the immune response. They differentiate during maturation into three functionally distinct types (*see next page*).

Evidence for the involvement of the thymus gland in the adaptive immune response comes from experiments on mice. If the thymus is removed from newborn mice, the animals develop a wasting disease characterised by retarded growth: the lymph nodes are much reduced in size and there is a reduction in the number of lymphocytes in the blood, the immune response does not develop and antibodies fail to be produced.

T lymphocytes look exactly like B lymphocytes but they do not produce antibodies and are responsible for what is called **cell-mediated immunity**. They are more varied in their action than B lymphocytes, but, like B lymphocytes, they have to make contact with their matching antigen before they can proliferate into clones of effective cells. There are special receptors on their surface which enable them to recognise the correct antigen, and – like B cells – each T lymphocyte responds to only one type of antigen. This enables the adaptive immune response to be targeted specifically at whichever pathogens have invaded the body. The process of clonal selection, proliferation and memory cell formation is exactly like that already described for B cells (*figure 19.6 on page 324*).

Types of T lymphocyte

Three main types of mature T lymphocyte exist, each with particular functions:

- **Helper T cells** assist other cells in the immune system. For example, they stimulate B lymphocytes to divide into antibody-producing cells. If these helper cells are not present, the B lymphocytes cannot go into action. They also enhance the action of phagocytes. It is primarily the helper T cells which are invaded by HIV (human immunodeficiency virus) and this explains why people with AIDS are susceptible to infections (*extension box on page 328*).
- **Suppressor T cells** inhibit other cells in the immune system. For example, they inhibit the production of antibodies by the B lymphocytes and suppress the action of phagocytes. They act as brakes in the immune system, dampening it down and preventing it from over-reacting.
- **Killer T cells** (also known as **cytotoxic T cells**) destroy body cells infected with viruses and other intracellular pathogens (such as the bacteria that cause tuberculosis, *Mycobacterium tuberculosis*) before the pathogens have time to proliferate. They also attack cells from other individuals if they get into the body, so they cause the rejection problems associated with skin grafts and transplant surgery (*page 333*). The killer T cells are regulated in the same way as B cells, by the helper and suppressor T cells.

Overall control of the immune response

Together, the helper and suppressor T cells regulate and control the production of antibodies by the B cells, and enhance or suppress the action of phagocytes. The T cells also secrete short-lived messenger proteins called **lymphokines**, which activate or suppress every aspect of the immune response. One of their functions is to stimulate macrophages to engulf other cells much more readily. This enables the macrophages to attack bacteria which have invaded the immune system and to fight fungal infections and certain types of tumour which are caused by infections.

One group of lymphokines are called **interferons**. These are effective against a wide range of viruses and they work by inhibiting the protein-making machinery of the infected cell so that the virus cannot proliferate. They also stimulate changes in uninfected cells which makes them resistant to the virus.

Summary of the cells in the immune system

In the course of the last few pages we have encountered no less than 10 different types of immune cell, and you have every reason to feel confused. It would therefore be helpful at this point to pause for a moment and draw the threads together. To help you, two illustrations are provided.

Figure 19.9 summarises the origin and fate of the B and T lymphocytes. Although this is a useful diagram, it does not show the complex interactions that occur between the different types of cell. The arrows suggest that the B and T lymphocytes are completely separate, whereas we have seen that they are functionally interconnected.

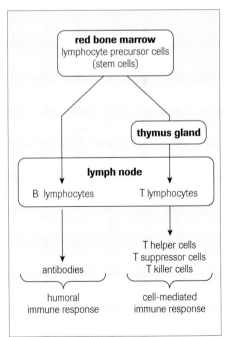

Figure 19.9 Simplified summary of the origin and fate of B and T lymphocytes. T lymphocytes perform many functions, and the way they interact with one another and with the B lymphocytes is highly complex. Both types of lymphocyte can produce memory cells which recognise and respond to later doses of antigen which they have previously encountered.

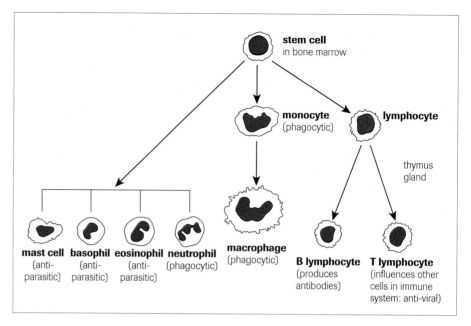

Figure 19.10 Diagram summarising the cells of the immune system.

Figure 19.10 shows the cells of the whole immune system. You will see that all the cells come from a common **stem cell** in the bone marrow. This divides repeatedly and the daughter cells then differentiate into all the kinds of immune cell which we have been considering.

Interestingly, red blood cells and platelets are also derived from these same stem cells. It is the stem cells therefore that hold the key to repopulating a person's entire blood and immune system following a bone marrow transplant.

Extension

AIDS: how HIV damages the immune system

Research on AIDS and its causative agent, HIV, has shed light on other conditions and on how the immune system works. Guest author Professor Anthony Pinching explains.

In the early 1980s, some astute doctors noticed that they were starting to see patients with evidence of severe **immunodeficiency** for no previously recognised reason. Immunodeficiency is a state where part of the body's immune defence against disease becomes defective, leading to an increased susceptibility to certain infections. These infections are described as **opportunistic** because they take advantage of the host's impaired defences, causing problems that would not normally arise. The pattern of infection in these new cases indicated that this particular defect mainly affected the cell-mediated part of the immune system.

Previously, immunodeficiency had been confined to relatively uncommon congenital disorders where a person was born without part of the immune system, and to situations where a previously normal immune system had become damaged or suppressed by disease or drug therapy, such as that used to prevent rejection of transplanted organs. The new cases were occurring in people whose immune system had shown no previous signs of damage or suppression. The condition became known as **AIDS (acquired immune deficiency syndrome)** and the cause turned out to be a virus, now known as **human immunodeficiency virus**, **HIV** (*page 76*).

HIV is a small virus consisting of RNA genes surrounded by a lipid coat. The RNA codes for its own specific proteins, one of which is an enzyme called **reverse transcriptase**. This enzyme reverses the usual process of gene transcription so that a DNA copy of the viral genes can be made from its RNA (*page 617*). This DNA copy is then spliced into the DNA of the infected human cell, so the viral genes become incorporated into the human genome. Thus protected, the viral genes issue instructions to the cell to make thousands of new viruses, causing persistent infection and turning the host cell into a factory for HIV replication.

One of the virus proteins that the viral genes code for is a glycoprotein in the viral coat, called **gp120**. This is vital in targeting the virus to cells of the immune system which thus become infected and damaged.

An early finding in people with AIDS was that they have a greatly reduced number of **helper T lymphocytes**. These cells are characterised by a molecule on their surface membrane called **CD4**, which is central to communication between cells of the immune system. The viral gp120 molecule has a region that binds to a part of the lymphocyte CD4 molecule, rather like a key fitting into a lock (*illustration*). In this way the virus is able to recognise the lymphocyte and attach itself to it. The virus then binds to a second molecule on the host cell's surface and then the membrane surrounding the virus fuses with the membrane of the lymphocyte, allowing the viral RNA to enter the host cell.

Other cells of the immune system, notably macrophages and related cells, also carry CD4 and can become infected in a similar way. Such cells are important because they seem to act as a reservoir of HIV infection.

Helper T lymphocytes (and other CD4-bearing lymphocytes) and their interactions with macrophages are at the very heart of cell-mediated immunity, so their role as HIV targets fits well with the susceptibility of AIDS patients to infections that affect this part of the defence mechanism. Tests on people with AIDS have shown that they have many defects in their immune system, but most striking and consistent is a reduction in the number and functioning of their helper T lymphocytes.

Infection of the helper T lymphocytes by HIV leads to their premature death. This may be caused by the virus itself, or by killer T cells attempting to eliminate the virus-infected cells, or both. Moreover, helper T cells that are not infected by HIV show defects in their functioning.

The loss of helper T lymphocytes and their functional impairment has knock-on effects on many other cells. For example, macrophages cannot be properly activated to kill certain organisms, B lymphocytes are unable to develop new antibody responses, and killer T cells show impaired function. Some of these effects are the result of reduced signals which

normally come from helper T lymphocytes.

All this leads to progressive impairment of the cell-mediated immune system and, to a lesser extent, the humoral system. The net result is the development of increasing susceptibility to certain bacteria, fungi, protoctists and viruses and to some rather unusual virus-induced tumours such as Kaposi's sarcoma.

If this sounds like bad news, the *good* news is that combinations of anti-HIV drugs can now suppress the virus enough to allow significant repair and recovery in the immune system, with greatly

improved life expectancy.

In parallel with immunodeficiency, HIV can damage the nervous system. The main cells in the nervous system that harbour HIV are macrophages. It seems that HIV infection of these cells causes the release of virus proteins or macrophage products which in turn damage or alter the function of neighbouring nerve cells.

Anthony Pinching is Professor of Immunology at St Bartholomew's Hospital and The Royal London School of Medicine and Dentistry, London.

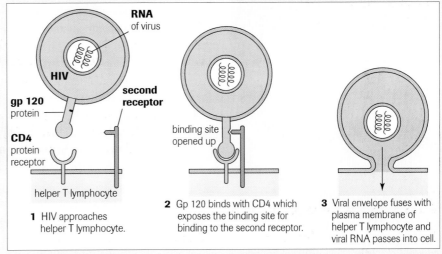

1 HIV approaches helper T lymphocyte.

2 Gp 120 binds with CD4 which exposes the binding site for binding to the second receptor.

3 Viral envelope fuses with plasma membrane of helper T lymphocyte and viral RNA passes into cell.

Sequence of events in the infection of a helper T lymphocyte with HIV.

Symptoms of AIDS

Most people with HIV infection can remain very well for many years, though some have slight enlargement of their lymph nodes. When immune deficiency starts to develop, they may show non-specific symptoms such as tiredness, sweats, rashes and diarrhoea. Minor infections such as shingles, caused by a herpes virus, and thrush (*Candida*) in the mouth, caused by a fungus, may occur.

Symptoms of AIDS itself are the symptoms of the specific opportunistic infections which result from an impaired immune system. So for example **pneumocystis pneumonia**, caused by a protozoan which attacks the lungs, results in a dry cough, breathlessness and fever; **cryptosporidiosis**, an intestinal infection caused by another type of protozoan, brings about weight loss and severe watery diarrhoea; **cryptococcal meningitis**, caused by a yeast-like fungus that affects the brain, gives rise to confusion and fever with some headache; and **cytomegalovirus**, a herpesvirus, may cause loss of vision.

Kaposi's sarcoma can show up as purplish lumps on the skin and in the lining of the gut, and lymphoma may cause greatly enlarged lymph nodes or lumps in the gut or brain. HIV brain disease can result in a form of dementia, paralysis, loss of sensation or fits.

The type of immunity provided by antibody production is called **active immunity** because the body makes its own antibodies in response to the arrival of an antigen.

During the development of a mammal, a certain number of antibodies pass from the mother to the fetus via the placenta or, after birth, via the milk. This confers **passive immunity** on the young animal, at least for a short time after birth. The human infant, for example, may be protected from diseases such as measles and poliomyelitis as a result of passive immunity, and this is undoubtedly one of the advantages of breast-feeding. However the number of antibodies conferred in this way is limited, and such immunity is short-lived.

Active artificial immunity

In immunity, as in so many other aspects of homeostasis, we have augmented nature's methods with our own. **Active artificial immunity** can be established by introducing a small quantity of antigen, a **vaccine**, into the body (**immunisation**). This activates the appropriate antibody-producing and cell-mediated systems which are then at the ready if and when that particular microorganism gets into the body. For example, protection against poliomyelitis may be secured this way (*figure 19.11*).

Vaccines used today usually consist of weakened (**attenuated**) forms of the virus or bacterium. An attenuated microorganism will not cause the disease but it stimulates the immune system to produce antibodies against it. The oral polio vaccine and the BCG vaccine are examples. The BCG vaccine gives protection against tuberculosis and is named after two French scientists, Calmette and Guerin. In 1908 they discovered, by accident, that after 13 years in a special culture medium, the bacillus causing tuberculosis had become attenuated. Attenuated live microorganisms are also used in the combined vaccine against measles, mumps and rubella (MMR), whereas killed virulent microorganisms are used in the vaccine for whooping cough.

Many vaccines are now prepared by growing and treating pathogenic microorganisms in such a way that they lose their capacity to cause the disease but not their ability to stimulate the production of the appropriate antibodies. Generally two successive doses of the vaccine need to be given. The reason for this is explained in figure 19.8 on page 326. In some cases it is necessary to keep up the immunity by giving 'booster' doses of the vaccine at regular intervals. However, some of the most common infections affecting humans and domestic livestock still cannot be reliably controlled by vaccination. Although new technologies using genetically modified microorganisms or genetically engineered antigens show promise, there aren't, as yet, effective vaccines against major food- and water-borne infections such as *Salmonella, E. coli* and *Vibrio cholerae*. Nor are there effective vaccines against HIV, malaria and certain strains of meningitis. One problem is that new strains of some pathogens (e.g. HIV, influenza) are continually emerging by genetic mutation, so vaccines become out of date.

Passive artificial immunity

A quite different technique is to give a person antibodies from another individual. In this **passive artificial immunity** the recipient is not induced to produce his or her own antibodies but is supplied with them, ready-made as it were, from an outside source. The antibodies are usually prepared by injecting antigens responsible for the disease into a suitable animal, or by extracting the antibodies from the bloodstream of a person who is already making them.

The drawback with this procedure is that the protection, though immediate, is relatively short-lived, lasting only as long as the antibodies persist. As antibodies are proteins, and proteins are continually being broken down and replaced, they may last for only a few

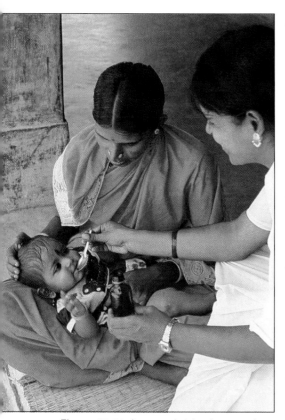

Figure 19.11 A nurse administering an oral vaccine against polio to a child in India. The oral vaccine is of a live attenuated type: the virus is cultured under special conditions so that it loses its virulence but retains its ability to stimulate antibody production.

Edward Jenner

Immunisation techniques were first developed in the 18th century by the Gloucestershire physician Edward Jenner. He observed that people who contracted the mild disease, cowpox seemed to be resistant to the much more serious disease, smallpox. He carried out what today would be considered a highly risky and unethical experiment. He introduced, into an eight-year-old boy, the pus from a cowpox pustule which he obtained from a dairy-maid. Jenner predicted that this would protect the boy against smallpox. A few weeks later he inoculated the boy with smallpox lymph. The boy did not develop smallpox. The cowpox virus had stimulated his body to manufacture antibodies against the much more virulent smallpox virus.

The cowpox and smallpox viruses are structurally very similar, so the cowpox virus triggers production of antibodies which can also bind to the smallpox virus. Jenner's was a

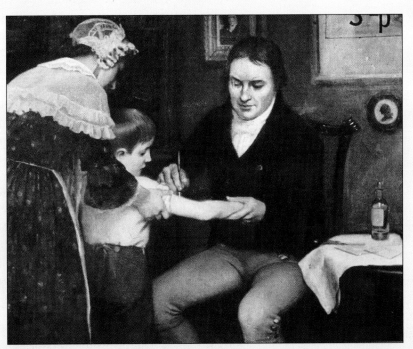

Edward Jenner inoculating a child against smallpox. Using a thorn mounted on a holder, he scratched the boy's skin and introduced the pus from a cowpox vesicle into his bloodstream.

momentous discovery in the history of medical science, for it paved the way to development of immunisation against all sorts of diseases. He used a thorn for his inoculation (*illustration*) whereas nowadays a sterile needle is used. Jenner's discovery led to the eventual worldwide eradication of smallpox in 1980.

days or weeks. On the other hand, active immunity, where the individual is induced to manufacture his or her own antibodies, can last a lifetime. The passive method is normally used only in emergencies when it is too late for active immunisation to work quickly enough.

19.6 Chemotherapy and antibiotics

If disease-causing microorganisms manage to avoid the body's defence mechanisms, both natural and artificial, further efforts to combat the disease can be employed. The methods include **chemotherapy**. This is the administration of chemical substances, natural or synthetic, that kill or prevent the reproduction of microorganisms. The term is now extended to include the inhibition of dividing malignant cells in cancer (*page 468*). The chemical substances used are called **chemotherapeutic agents** or, in common parlance, drugs. Some of these substances were originally derived from secretions of microorganisms which are selectively toxic to other microorganisms. Such substances are called **antibiotics**.

The first antibiotic to be discovered was **penicillin** (*support box on the next page*). Since the 1940s penicillin has saved countless millions of lives. It proved to be effective against numerous bacterial infections including pneumonia, meningitis, gangrene, gonorrhoea, syphilis and anthrax. Penicillin kills bacteria by preventing the synthesis of **peptidoglycan**, a constituent of the cell wall; this has the effect of making them 'burst' (lysis). However, it is not effective against viruses as they have a completely different structure.

Since the discovery of penicillin, many more antibiotics have been isolated from microorganisms, both bacteria and fungi. These include erythromycin, streptomycin and chloramphenicol. Also, a number of synthetic antibiotics have been developed, including penicillins. Not all antibiotics act by preventing cell-wall formation. Some inhibit protein synthesis (e.g. streptomycin) and others inhibit DNA replication.

It is important that a particular disease is treated with the most suitable antibiotic. Although beyond the scope of this book, it is worth noting that antibiotics generally fall into one of two groups – **broad spectrum antibiotics** (e.g. tetracycline), which are effective against a wide variety of microorganisms, and **narrow spectrum antibiotics**, which are limited in their effectiveness to only a few microorganisms. Penicillin comes under this category, although from the list above you might be forgiven for thinking otherwise.

Non-antibiotic drugs include **sulphonamides**, complex organic ring compounds with a powerful anti-bacterial action. Sulphonamides are similar in their chemical structure to para-aminobenzoic acid, an essential metabolite in the reproduction of certain bacteria. They are believed to compete with para-aminobenzoic acid for the active site of an enzyme (*page 128*). In this way, though they do not actually kill the bacteria, they stop them reproducing.

Support

Sir Alexander Fleming and the discovery of penicillin

Penicillin was discovered by the British bacteriologist Alexander Fleming in 1928, as the result of a fortuitous accident. Fleming had been working on the bacterium *Staphylococcus aureus*, and it happened that one of his plates became contaminated with some spores of a mould which are believed to have floated into his laboratory through an open window. Fleming noticed that the bacteria were absent in the vicinity of the mould (*illustration*).

Fleming reasoned that the mould had secreted a chemical which was toxic to the bacteria. The mould was subsequently identified as *Penicillium notatum*, for which reason the active substance was named penicillin.

The discovery was not widely noticed at the time and Fleming himself was unable to isolate pure penicillin. It was the need for better anti-bacterial drugs during the Second World War that led to renewed interest in penicillin. In 1940 two Oxford scientists, Howard Florey and Ernst Chain, succeeded in isolating and purifying the active substance, thereby enabling it to be injected into patients. A programme of research was then carried out in the USA and large-scale production of penicillin commenced within three years. The maufacturers used *Penicillium chrysogenum* which gave a higher yield than the original *P. notatum*.

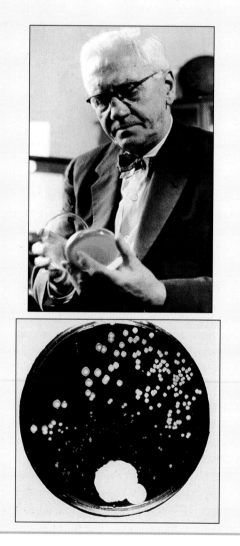

The top picture shows Fleming examining the Petri dish which led to his discovery of penicillin. Below is a photograph of the contaminated Petri dish (culture plate). Notice the absence of staphylococcal (bacterial) colonies (small white blobs) in the vicinity of the *Penicillium* colony (large white blob). Fleming, a Scotsman, worked at St Mary's Hospital in London. In 1945 he, together with Howard Florey and Ernst Chain were awarded the Nobel Prize for medicine.

Although chemotherapeutic agents have had an enormous influence on the control of disease, they have one serious drawback. Every time a new one is used, resistant strains of microorganisms arise (*page 752*). Further drugs then have to be developed. New drugs should therefore be used with restraint and discrimination.

19.7 The importance of the immune system

The immune system is essential for survival. Even with the aid of medical science, the longest time anyone has survived without an effective immune system is 12 years. In order to achieve this doctors in Houston, Texas, had to provide a microbe-free environment for a boy who was born with a severely impaired immune system. He was enclosed in a 'plastic bubble' soon after birth. He breathed filtered air and ate sterilised food and had no direct contact with anyone (*figure 19.12*).

The doctors hoped to cure the boy by giving him a bone-marrow transplant, but the operation was unsuccessful. This illustrates how much we need an immune system and one that works – which, thankfully, it does most of the time. The plight of people with AIDS has also made this abundantly clear, for the symptoms which they develop are attributable to a collapse of the immune response (*extension box on page 328*).

Gene therapy is being developed to help people born without an effective immune system (*page 633*).

Figure 19.12 This little boy has an immune deficiency condition. He needs to be protected from possible infection because his immune systems are impaired. This is achieved by enclosing him in a sterile, germ-free atmosphere. He has a plastic head cover and is wearing a protective suit which keeps out pathogens but allows him to move freely and lead a more or less normal life.

19.8 Problems arising from the immune system

Occasionally the immune system over-reacts to a harmless foreign substance that enters the body, and sometimes it responds when we don't want it to, such as when foreign tissue is introduced into the body in transplant surgery. Let us look at these situations in detail.

Allergy

Every year millions of people suffer bouts of sneezing, running noses and itchy eyes during the pollen season – all of which are symptoms of **hay fever**. These unpleasant symptoms are the result of an excessive immune response (**hypersensitivity**) and they constitute an **allergy**. Allergies can be induced by a variety of harmless proteins such as grass pollen, cat fur, house-dust, mites, fungal spores, certain drugs and wasp or bee venom.

People who are genetically susceptible to allergies react to these harmless proteins by producing antibodies of the IgE type (*extension box on page 323*). IgE binds to mast cells, which are abundant in the skin and mucous membranes in the respiratory tract and around the eyes. The IgE molecules have their antigen-binding sites facing outwards, so the next time that the same antigen comes along it will be trapped on the mast cell by IgE. This causes the mast cells to produce potent chemical substances such as **histamine** which are responsible for the unpleasant symptoms.

Histamine causes dilation of the capillaries, flushing of the skin, itching, and constriction of the bronchi. It also increases the permeability of the capillaries which results in an increase in the rate of formation of tissue fluid, causing swelling of the organs and tissues. One method of treating allergies is to give the patient **anti-histamine** drugs. The normal function of histamine in the body, if it has one, is obscure.

Transplantation surgery

Transplantation surgery is an important field of medicine in which great advances have been made in recent years. Indeed, **organ transplantation** is now a common operation in many hospitals (*extension box on next page*).

Cortisol as an anti-stress agent

Inflammation and allergy impose **stress** on the organism, for example by diverting energy from other important functions. Stress is combated by the secretion of the hormone cortisol from the **adrenal cortex**. Cortisol causes shrinkage of the lymph nodes, lowers the number of white cells and combats inflammation. In short it adapts the animal to stress and prevents its anti-infection mechanisms from being too pronounced and widespread.

The production of cortisol is triggered by **adrenocorticotrophic hormone** (**ACTH**) from the anterior lobe of the pituitary gland, which is acted on by various stress agents such as bacteria. Cortisol controls its own production by a negative feedback mechanism.

Cortisol also combats the stressful effects of shock. In a shock situation adrenaline is released from the adrenal medulla. One of adrenaline's effects is to increase the flow of ACTH from the pituitary, thereby promoting the secretion of cortisol from the adrenal cortex.

The problem is that, despite the increasing skills of the surgeons and the use of the most up-to-date surgical techniques, transplanted organs may be **rejected**. This is because the recipient's immune system attacks and destroys the foreign cells. For success, the tissues of the donor and recipient must be as genetically similar as possible, which is why rejection is never seen between identical twins.

How compatible the cells of the recipient and donor are can be determined beforehand by **tissue matching**. But however closely the tissues match, all transplant patients receive controlled doses of various **immunosuppressive drugs**. These drugs suppress the body's normal immune response and so increase the chances of the graft being accepted.

However, it is as well to remember that organ transplantation is an unnatural event which never occurs in nature. The fact that transplanted organs are rejected is the result of individual genetic diversity, and rejection is part and parcel of the body's normal defence against disease. The immune system cannot be expected to distinguish between invading pathogenic microorganisms and useful tissue introduced by a surgeon.

Organ transplantation

Sir Roy Calne, a leading transplant surgeon, explains some of the problems and achievements in transplantation surgery.

Since the first transplant operations were carried out in the 1960s, organ grafting has emerged from being a perilous final attempt at saving life to become the standard treatment for many major diseases of vital organs. More than 30 000 organ grafts have been performed world wide, and results continue to improve.

The problem of rejection

The greatest problem facing the transplant surgeon is rejection of the transplanted organ. Unless special treatment is given to suppress the patient's immune system, a graft between members of the same species is rejected after 5 to 14 days. The body destroys the foreign tissue as it would a bacterium or virus. The speed of rejection depends on how closely matched the tissues of the donor and recipient are. Thus, grafts

between identical twins are accepted permanently, since identical twins have the same genes and are perfectly matched. In grafts between siblings, there is a one in four chance that the main tissue types will match each other. In grafts between unrelated people, the chance of the tissues matching is remote.

The chief factors that determine rejection are the ABO blood groups and the tissue-typing of the white blood cells. However, even if these are matched, rejection may still occur because there are minor tissue groups that we cannot yet identify. Therefore, in all cases except identical twins, drug treatment to prevent rejection is necessary after a transplant operation. The drugs prevent the recipient's lymphocytes attacking the graft. Their dosage needs to be carefully watched: too low a dose results in the graft being rejected; too high a dose suppresses the immune system to such an extent that the patient readily succumbs to infection.

The surgical procedure

We can now transplant all vital organs except the brain – and even if it were possible to transplant the brain so that it functioned, the outcome would be a body grafted to the brain rather than the other way around.

Of course, the grafted organ must continue to function properly after the transplantation operation. It is therefore necessary to join up the arteries and veins of the donor organ to those of the recipient, and if the organ has a duct this must also be dealt with. Speed is essential, for the circulation to the organ must be re-established before the cells die.

Donors

For paired organs such as the kidneys, a volunteer – usually a close relative – can be a donor, provided the blood group and tissue match are satisfactory. The donor can manage with the one remaining organ. In the same way, a lobe of the liver can be removed for grafting without jeopardising the donor's health. It is even possible for a donor who happens to be receiving a combined heart–lung transplant to give his or her own heart to another patient, the so-called 'domino' operation.

However, most human transplants are taken from recently dead donors. Organs from patients dying of cancer or an infectious disease cannot be used for fear of transmitting the disease to the

Illustration 1 A human liver being transported before being used in a transplant operation.

Illustration 2 Pearl Cameron had a heart transplant in 1995. In 1996 she was leading a very active life and is here seen rock climbing.

recipient. In practice, most donors are people who have died from brain injury caused by trauma or haemorrhage following a ruptured brain artery. In such donors the heart can be kept beating only by ventilating the lungs with a machine. When tests make it absolutely certain that the donor's brain is irreversibly damaged, the ventilator should be stopped, since to continue resuscitation in these circumstances would be fruitless and very distressing for the relatives. If permission has been given, organs may then be removed for transplantation.

Which organs are transplanted?

Vital organs commonly grafted to replace those that have become diseased are the following:

■ **Kidney** This was the first organ to be transplanted. The donor kidney is usually placed on one side of the lower abdomen. The current success rate is encouragingly high: in cases where the donor and recipient are unrelated, 80 per cent of transplanted kidneys are functioning after one year; and in cases where the kidney comes from a matched sibling, the figure is over 90 per cent. The longest survivor with graft function is in good health, over 30 years after his transplant operation. Should a kidney graft fail, the patient can be kept in a reasonable state of health by repeated dialysis until another kidney becomes available for transplantation. Some patients have had as many as five or six kidney transplants.

- **Heart and lungs** These are grafted in their normal positions after removal of the diseased organs. They may be grafted together or separately. Heart transplants are more successful than lung transplants since the latter are more prone to infection and rejection. Approximately 70 per cent of heart grafts, and 60 per cent of lung grafts, are functioning after one year, whether they are grafted separately or together.

- **Liver** This is the most difficult organ to transplant because of its multiple connections and complex blood supply. Moreover, in liver disease blood clotting is impaired and serious bleeding can occur, making surgery difficult. However, the procedure has improved and 80 per cent of liver grafts are now functioning after one year. The longest survivor had the operation 28 years ago.

Suppressing the immune system

In principle, all recipients of organ grafts receive the same drugs to inhibit rejection, whatever the transplanted organ. Each drug has particular advantages and disadvantages. Their combined action is to inhibit the production or action of lymphocytes.

Patients generally receive small doses of azathioprine, corticosteroids and cyclosporin. This **triple therapy** combines the effectiveness of all three drugs but avoids most of the more serious side effects. If rejection starts to occur, extra doses of corticosteroids or anti-lymphocyte proteins usually reverse the rejection.

For the majority of patients who respond well, their quality of life can be virtually normal. They can participate in active sports and have children, but they need to continue taking immunosuppressive drugs in low doses indefinitely. As a result, they are more susceptible to infection and cancer than are normal people.

The future

Most transplant failures are caused by the graft being rejected, or from infection resulting from excessive immunosuppression. No doubt safer and more effective drugs will be developed. As the results of organ grafting within the human species improve, efforts may be made to use organs taken from other animal species. This will introduce new moral dilemmas.

Another development will be the grafting of non-vital organs. Already, more than 3000 pancreas grafts have been performed to combat diabetes, but there is controversy over whether this treatment is better than insulin injection. The first successful bowel grafts have been reported. Grafts of testes and ovaries will raise new ethical debates!

But whatever the ethical problems, organ grafting is now an established and preferred treatment for many previously fatal diseases and its continued development will form one of the main branches of surgery.

Sir Roy Calne is Professor of Surgery and a Fellow of Trinity Hall, Cambridge.

Immunological tolerance

Will the body not accept foreign tissue under any circumstances? The answer is that it will, provided that the formation of antibodies against it is first prevented. One way of achieving this is to introduce some of the foreign tissue into the recipient before, or very soon after, birth – i.e. at the time when, according to Burnet's clonal selection theory, immune responsiveness (both humoral and cell-mediated) against the individual's own antigens is being abolished.

The key experiment establishing this was conducted in 1953 by Sir Peter Medawar, who injected cells obtained from an adult black mouse into a newborn white mouse. He found that, after birth, the recipient accepted, permanently, grafts of skin and other tissues from the donor. The recipient had been made **immunologically tolerant** to the donor's tissues by receiving a prenatal injection of the donor's cells (*figure 19.13*).

Medawar's discovery fits in with the clonal selection theory and helps to explain why we do not normally mount an immune response against antigens on our own cells. It is argued that any lymphocytes, B or T, which come into contact with matching antigens during embryonic life, are rendered incapable of forming clones of active immune cells. So any lymphocytes that might potentially attack the individual's own antigens are inactivated before birth.

For his achievement Medawar, together with Burnet (the originator of the clonal

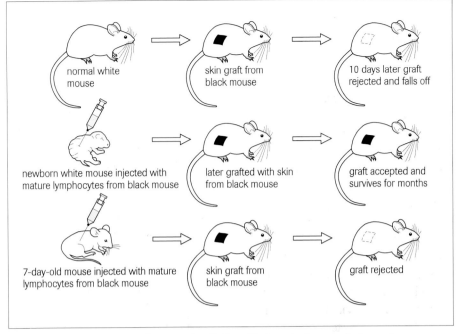

Figure 19.13 An experiment demonstrating Sir Peter Medawar's discovery that a newborn mouse will accept a skin graft if it is given a dose of the donor's cells. (In many other species, the exposure has to occur before birth.)

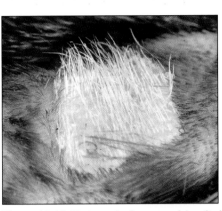

Figure 19.14 Photograph of a successful graft of rat tail skin (white hairs) about four months after transplantation to an adult mouse. Normally such a graft would be rejected, but in this case the adult mouse was rendered immunologically tolerant by means of anti-lymphocytic serum.

selection theory), were awarded the Nobel Prize for medicine in 1960. Since then a number of agents capable of inducing immunological tolerance have been developed. These include a preparation made by introducing lymphocytes into a horse and then collecting and purifying the antibodies produced. The resulting **anti-lymphocytic serum** is capable of destroying the original lymphocytes to such an extent that an animal treated with the serum will subsequently accept grafts from another individual (*figure 19.14*). There is a problem though: because the horse serum is 'foreign protein' the graft recipient makes anti-horse antibodies. So such sera cannot be used to induce long-term tolerance and have no value in sustaining human organ transplants.

19.9 Blood groups

We have seen that living material introduced deliberately into the body may be treated by the recipient as 'foreign' and rejected by the immune system. The same sort of thing occurs when blood is transferred from one person to another.

The ABO system

The entire human population can be divided into four groups on the basis of the reaction between the blood of different individuals when mixed together. These groups are called **A, B, AB** and **O** and they are known collectively as the **ABO system**. The capital letters stand for different types of glycoproteins present on the surface of the person's red blood cells. These glycoproteins are antigens, similar to those found on the surface of bacteria. We all make antibodies against foreign antigens, but not of course against those on our own red blood cells.

The antibodies are called **anti-A** and **anti-B**. If an individual has a particular antigen on his or her red cells, the corresponding antibody is not present in that person's own plasma. Thus a person belonging to blood group **A** has red cells with **A** antigens on them; the plasma does not then contain **anti-A** antibodies, but it does contain **anti-B** antibodies. A person belonging to blood group **B** has **B** antigens on the red cells and the plasma contains **anti-A** antibodies only. In a person with blood group **AB**, the red cells

▶ Inheritance of the ABO blood group system, page 596

Table 19.1 Summary of reactions that occur when bloods of different groups are mixed. + agglutination; – no agglutination. The capital letters refer to antigens on the red blood cells, small letters to antibodies in the plasma. A universal donor (group **O**) can give blood to a recipient of any group without causing agglutination. A universal recipient (group **AB**) can receive blood from a donor of any group without agglutination. In practice, blood transfusions are normally carried out using blood which belongs to the same group as that of the recipient. The group to which a sample of blood belongs is determined by a compatibility test.

		recipient			
		O ab	**A** b	**B** a	**AB**
donor	**O** ab	–	–	–	–
	A b	+	–	+	–
	B a	+	+	–	–
	AB	+	+	+	–

universal donor (arrow pointing to **O** row)
universal recipient (arrow pointing to **AB** column)

carry both antigens **A** and **B** and neither antibodies are present in the plasma. Group **O** blood has neither antigen but both antibodies.

Table 19.1 summarises what happens when bloods of different groups are mixed together in a transfusion. All is well, provided the recipient's blood does not contain antibodies that will bind to the donor's red-cell antigens. If it does, the donor's red cells become linked together by the antibodies, forming clumps which may block the recipient's blood vessels. This is called **agglutination**. For example, if blood of group **A** is given to a patient of blood group **B**, the **anti-A** antibodies in the patient's blood will cause agglutination of the donor's red cells because they carry the **A** antigen. It does not matter that the donor's antibodies (**anti-B**) are incompatible with the recipient's antigens (**B**) because the recipient receives relatively little blood and the dilution effect minimises agglutination.

The Rhesus system

In addition to the ABO system there are many other antigens on human red blood cells. One of these is the **Rhesus antigen**, so-called because it was first discovered by injecting rabbits with red blood cells obtained from the Rhesus monkey. The majority of people possess red blood cells with the Rhesus antigen present, and they are known as **Rhesus positive (Rh+)**. The remainder lack the Rhesus antigen and are called **Rhesus negative (Rh–)**.

Unlike the ABO system, Rhesus-negative blood does not already contain anti-Rhesus antibodies. However, if Rhesus-positive blood finds its way into a Rhesus-negative recipient, the latter responds by producing the corresponding anti-Rhesus antibodies.

Fortunately it takes about a week for the antibodies to appear in the bloodstream, by which time all the donated red cells will have died – so no harm results. But if a Rhesus-negative recipient subsequently receives another dose of Rhesus-positive blood, the anti-Rhesus antibodies already present will bring about a much faster and more intense response, causing agglutination of the donor's red cells, often with fatal results (*figure 19.8 on page 326 gives an explanation*). This can occur during pregnancy.

The trouble starts when a Rhesus-negative mother bears a Rhesus-positive child. Sometimes during labour, fragments of the fetus's red blood cells, containing the Rhesus antigen, pass across the placenta into the mother's bloodstream. The mother responds by producing anti-Rhesus antibodies which pass back across the placenta into the fetal circulation. Generally the antibodies are not formed quickly enough or in sufficient quantities to affect the first child, but a subsequent Rhesus-positive child will suffer from massive destruction of red blood cells.

This condition is known as **haemolytic disease of the newborn**. The newborn baby suffers from acute anaemia and is very breathless as a result of shortage of oxygen; the baby's skin also appears yellow because of the breakdown of its haemoglobin into other pigments.

Haemolytic disease used to be a major cause of death in newborn infants and was treated by replacing the child's blood with a complete transfusion of Rhesus-negative blood. A more modern method of prevention is explained in the extension box on the left.

Plant defences against disease

Plants do not possess phagocytes or an immune system. However, that does not mean that they have no means of protection against disease. Just like animals, they have all sorts of protective devices (thick cuticle, hairs, thick bark and the like) which make it difficult for microorganisms to get in.

If a vascular plant is damaged, the wound becomes plugged by a mass of undifferentiated parenchyma cells called **callus tissue** and/or by protective chemicals such as **resins** which prevent the entry of microorganisms. In fact plants produce a bewildering array of chemicals. At one time they were thought to be excretory products but many of them are now known to have defence functions.

Infectious diseases such as wheat rust and potato blight are the cause of serious losses in yield. One way of overcoming these diseases is to produce strains of the crop which are resistant to the causative microorganisms. This is the job of plant breeders and genetic engineers, and considerable success has been achieved in this area.

Many plants, however, possess a natural resistance to fungal infection and this may be connected with the presence of protective chemicals within their cells. One of these natural fungicides has been identified and given the name **wyerone** as its structure was established at Wye College in Kent. Many other such substances occur naturally and may play a part in disease resistance in plants.

Active defence

In the 1940s, the first evidence for an active defence mechanism in plants was found. Substances were discovered which were produced in response to fungal attack, and they were given the name **phytoalexins**. In recent years about 20 phytoalexins have been identified and most of them are phenolic ring compounds. Each species of plant produces one or two particular phytoalexins which, unlike antibodies, are not specific and will attack a wide range of fungal infections.

One of the first phytoalexins to be characterised was called **pisatin** as it was extracted from peas (*Pisum* sp). Healthy pea tissues do not contain pisatin. However, when inoculated with a spore suspension of a fungus and incubated, pisatin was found to be present in the pea tissues. Phytoalexins are certainly produced in response to infection and the indications are that they are an important aspect of defence in plants. The illustration shows the effect of one of them.

Phytoalexins in plants are analogous to antibody production in animals, in which chemicals are produced in response to infection. Defence against disease in plants is a complex subject in which much research is being undertaken at the present time.

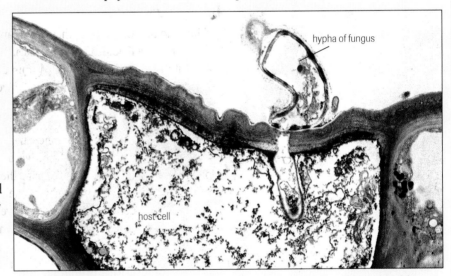

A cell of French bean following attempted infection by a pathogenic fungus. The growth of the fungus has been totally inhibited by phytoalexins produced by the cell. Magnification ×900.

19.10 Being healthy

While we might agree that our **health** is important to us, we would probably disagree about the exact meaning of the word 'health'. The World Health Organisation (WHO), founded in 1948 by the United Nations, defined health in their Constitution of 1958 as *'a state of complete physical and mental well-being, and not merely the absence of disease or infirmity'*. The achievement of 'complete well-being' is a desirable objective but is it possible for health to be given an absolute value?

The WHO has since set a goal which has become known as '**health for all by the year 2000**'. This aimed to make possible *'the attainment by all citizens of the world by the year 2000 of a level of health that will permit them to lead a socially and economically productive life'*.

Was this a realistic aim when almost one-fifth of the world's population is caught up in a daily struggle for survival because of poverty and malnutrition? Most of these people live in the rural areas and urban slums of the least developed countries of Africa, Asia and South America. For them the basic needs of enough food, a safe water supply and sewage disposal, adequate housing, medical care and a basic education in numeracy and literacy are of major importance if they are to understand their problems and take responsibility for their own health.

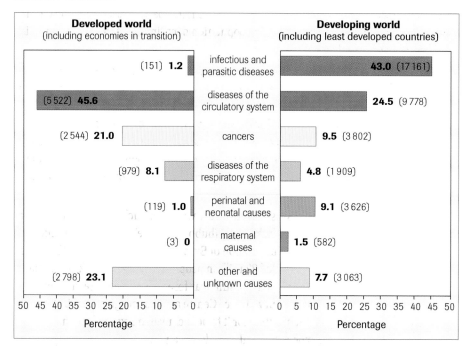

Figure 19.15 The causes of death in the developed and developing world in 1996. A comparison of the two graphs emphasises the inequality of the state of health that exists between the two. The bold figure alongside each bar is the percentage of deaths; the figure in brackets is the number of deaths in thousands.

Diarrhoea and oral rehydration therapy

One-quarter of all deaths in the world occur in children under the age of five, and 99 per cent of these are in the poorer countries. Diarrhoea is the single largest cause of death, mostly from water-borne bacteria in contaminated drinking water. Diarrhoea results in severe dehydration which can kill children very quickly. Oral rehydration therapy was introduced by the WHO in 1980 and consists of giving a prepared mixture of salts, sugar and uncontaminated water by mouth. Because it is simple, inexpensive and easy to administer, it is used by over one-third of families in poorer countries. Statistics suggest its use is saving over a million lives a year and this could soon rise to two million.

In contrast, people living in the rich industrialised nations of Europe, North America, Australasia and Japan are generally more affluent and in a position to make choices about the quality of their lives and their health. This does not mean that the *right* choices are always made, as the high incidence of coronary heart disease and lung cancer demonstrates. Figure 19.15 shows the causes of death in the developed and developing world which reflect some of the inequalities that exist between them.

World health

The WHO, with its headquarters in Geneva, gives advice and information to all countries on problems concerning health. For this to be effective it must be based on reliable statistics collected and analysed by experts. Once the principles of controlling infectious disease were understood, the WHO set as two of its goals the eradication from the world of malaria and smallpox. Now, more than half a century later, only one of these diseases – smallpox – has been completely eradicated (*extension box on page 342*).

The failure to eradicate malaria is disappointing, but it does not mean that other diseases will not be eradicated in the future. Indeed, poliomyelitis may be the next infectious disease to go as a result of a world-wide campaign of immunisation.

When eradication fails, the next best approach is to develop cheap and effective methods of treatment which improve health and the quality of life. Eradication is hugely costly and unrealistic for all but a very few infectious diseases, so 'containment' is the main WHO goal. An example is the use of **oral rehydration therapy** for treating diarrhoea.

In addition, public education campaigns about food preparation, domestic hygiene, safe disposal of refuse, siting latrines away from water supplies, and the provision of water treatment and sanitation plants, is having a major impact on food- and water-borne infections.

19.11 **Global patterns of disease**

The incidence and extent of particular diseases varies from time to time and from place to place throughout the world. Sometimes a disease sweeps through a community causing terrible destruction, only to recede and not to occur again for years. This has been recognised since ancient times and we still use the names coined by the Greeks to describe these patterns – endemic, epidemic and pandemic.

- An **endemic** disease is one which is always present in a particular area and of which a substantial number of cases occur in the population over time. Malaria, for example, is endemic in parts of Africa.

- An **epidemic** is an outbreak of a disease in a localised area which affects a lot of people. In the 19th century there were three epidemics of cholera in England in a space of 20 years. During one such epidemic in 1854, Dr John Snow plotted the location of this disease on a map of London and saw that there was a concentration of cases around a public water pump in Broad Street. The handle of the pump was removed so people had to go elsewhere for their water and the epidemic soon ended. This was the first indication that cholera was spread from person to person through contaminated drinking water.

- A **pandemic** occurs when a disease covers a very wide area such as a whole country, a continent or even the globe. The 'Black Death' (bubonic plague) killed 17–28 million people – well over one third of the population of Europe – between 1347 and 1350. The influenza pandemic in 1918–19 killed 22 million people, more than were killed in the whole of the First World War. Each year we still hear forecasts of widespread outbreaks of influenza. The WHO Influenza Surveillance Centre aims to recognise and isolate any new strain of the influenza virus in time for it to be included in a vaccine, so that hopefully the world never experiences a flu pandemic again.

Figure 19.16 The impressive headquaters of the World Health Organisation in Geneva, seen here in the mid-1960s shortly after completion, symbolised society's confidence in the future of world health. However, although there has been spectacular progress in controlling disease and pandemics of the kind that used to afflict the world are now confined to history, WHO's goal of 'health for all by the year 2000' has not been achieved. The eradication of smallpox, described in the extension box on the next page, shows what can be done and provides hope for the future.

Smallpox: the rise and fall of a disease

Smallpox has been known for thousands of years. It is described in the earliest literature and at one time occurred, often in epidemic proportions, throughout the world. First recorded in Britain in the 13th century, there were particularly severe outbreaks in Britain and her North American colonies during the 18th century. In 1796 a breakthrough in the control and prevention of the disease was achieved by Edward Jenner with his discovery of a vaccine (*page 331*). At first his ideas were derided by the medical establishment, but Jenner persisted and vaccination was eventually adopted first in Britain and soon afterwards in other countries. Napoleon had all his troops vaccinated, the Empress of Russia decreed that her subjects should receive universal vaccination and Thomas Jefferson, President of the United States, had his family vaccinated.

The disease is caused by a virus called Variola, of which the most virulent type, Variola major, was responsible for killing up to 25 per cent of sufferers before vaccination got underway. The symptoms were rather like those of influenza: high temperature, headache and muscle pains. This was accompanied by an outbreak of pus-filled blisters on the skin (*illustration 1*). These pustules erupted, discharged and then scabbed over within about three weeks. Survivors of smallpox were often left with permanent disfiguring pock marks.

A highly infectious disease, smallpox was spread in a number of ways, not all of them fully understood. The virus was present in the patient's urine and faeces as well as in the skin pustules and throat, and one of the main routes of infection was through inhalation. Without vaccination everyone was vulnerable. In Britain, if a case of smallpox was diagnosed the area medical officer of health had to be notified and the patient confined in an isolation hospital (*illustration 2*). Anyone in contact with a smallpox case had to be quarantined and vaccinated.

Babies were particularly susceptible to the disease and in Britain compulsory vaccination of all children under the age of three years was instituted in 1853 and continued until 1948. This certainly produced results: in 1901 there were 356 deaths from smallpox in Britain, in 1956 there were none.

During the 1950s, a world-wide vaccination programme was established by the World Health Organisation, its aim being to provide everyone with lifelong immunity from smallpox. This led to a dramatic fall in the incidence of the disease. In May 1980 the World Health Organisation announced officially that smallpox had been eradicated from the world.

The conquering of smallpox is a success story in public health, involving the use of freeze-dried stable vaccines, new needles, inoculation 'guns' and intensive advertising. It is ironic that only a year after it was declared extinct, the first case of AIDS, a *new* disease, was reported. The struggle to combat disease, in all its formidable complexity, continues.

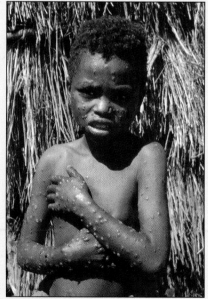

Illustration 1 A child with smallpox, showing the pustules typical of this disease. The head and limbs are particularly affected by the pustular rash which has also spread into the mouth and throat.

Illustration 2 Isolation hospitals were built well away from the general population. The picture shows a floating hospital on the River Thames around 1900. Buildings were erected on barges to house the sick.

WARNING
SMALLPOX HOSPITAL
THE PUBLIC ARE REQUESTED TO
KEEP AWAY FROM THIS ROAD

Illustration 3 The public were kept away from areas where there were cases of smallpox. The picture shows a public road in England during an outbreak of the disease in the early 1950s.

1. **Disease** can be defined as a structural and/or functional disorder of the body which results in the development of **symptoms**.

2. The control of disease by the body's natural defence mechanisms in mammals is an important aspect of homeostasis.

3. The body of an organism is defended from infection by preventing the entry of pathogenic organisms and/or destroying them after they have entered.

4. Preventing entry is achieved by means of **barriers**, e.g. skin and clotting of blood; **expulsion**, e.g. coughing; and **destruction**, e.g. lysozyme in external secretions.

5. Destruction of microorganisms, once they are inside the body, is the responsibility of the **immune system**.

6. Phagocytosis is carried out by phagocytic white cells and contributes to **natural (non-specific) immunity**.

7. Another type of immunity called **adaptive** or **acquired immunity**, is the function of white cells called **lymphocytes**.

8. There are two kinds of lymphocyte. **B lymphocytes** give rise to **humoral immunity** and this involves the production of **antibodies** in response to **antigens**.

9. B lymphocytes divide to form **clones**. Each clone produces one type of antibody which recognises, and attacks, a specific antigen.

10. Large quantities of **monoclonal antibodies** can now be made in the laboratory and have various uses.

11. T lymphocytes give rise to **cell-mediated immunity**. There are three types of mature T lymphocytes with different functions. They mature in the **thymus gland**.

12. **Artificial immunity** may be conferred on an animal by **active** or **passive** means depending on whether the animal is stimulated by a **vaccine** to produce its own antibodies or receives ready-made antibodies from an external source.

13. **A primary adaptive immune response** to an antigen takes about a week to develop. An enhanced **secondary adaptive immune response** occurs if the body receives a second dose of antigen at a later date.

14. Sometimes an inappropriate immune response occurs to a harmless antigen, causing damage to the tissues. This is called an **allergy**. Allergies are counteracted by anti-stress agents such as cortisol.

15. An unfortunate aspect of the cell-mediated immune response is that foreign tissue introduced into a recipient in an **organ transplantation** operation is usually rejected. The use of **immunosuppressive drugs** increases the chance of a transplant being accepted.

16. A graft is accepted by the recipient if cells from the donor are introduced into the recipient before, or soon after, birth. The recipient then becomes **immunologically tolerant** to the donor's cells.

17. An immune reaction occurs when bloods belonging to two incompatible groups in the **ABO system** are mixed.

18. An immune response is also seen when **Rhesus-positive** and **Rhesus-negative** bloods come into contact. In certain situations this occurs during pregnancy, resulting in **haemolytic disease of the newborn**.

19. Other efforts to combat disease include the use of **chemotherapeutic agents** such as antibiotics.

20. Plant defences against disease-causing microorganisms include various protective devices (e.g. cuticle), the formation of **callus tissue** and the production of **phytoalexins**.

21. The WHO has defined health as a state of complete physical and mental well-being, and has set a goal of *health for all* by the year 2000. The differences between the poorer developing countries of the world and the wealthier developed ones pose problems for achieving this aim.

22. Global patterns of disease are described in terms of **endemic**, **epidemic** and **pandemic**.

23. The WHO's aim to eradicate smallpox and malaria has been achieved in the case of the former but not the latter. Although the ultimate goal must always be eradication, the prevention and control of diseases play an important part in the aim of 'health for all'.

For general advice on these questions and advice on answering essay-type questions, see pages vii and viii.

1. (a) Describe how natural defence mechanisms prevent the entry of disease-causing organisms in the body. (6)

   (b) Describe how each of the following protects the body from disease.

   (i)   Fibrinogen (4)

   (ii) Phagocytes (2)

   (Total 12 marks)

   NEAB 1996

2. (a) Copy and complete the table below by stating **two structural** differences and **one functional** difference between phagocytes and lymphocytes. (3)

difference	phagocytes	lymphocytes
structural	1.	1.
	2.	2.
functional		

   (b) (i)   State the site of origin of lymphocytes. (1)

   (ii) State the site of maturation of T cells. (1)

   (iii) Describe briefly what happens to T cells as they mature. (3)

   (c) Distinguish between the responses of phagocytes and lymphocytes on **first** and **repeated** infections of the same antigen. (4)

   (Total 12 marks)

   UCLES 1997

3. Measles is caused by a viral infection. The virus is spread by droplet infection, and it gains entry to the body through the respiratory organs. Children who catch measles normally recover completely within two to three weeks of being infected.

   (a) Describe how the natural defence systems of the body overcome the measles infection. (6)

   (b) A person who has had measles is normally immune for life, whereas some diseases can be caught several times. Explain how one exposure to measles can provide lifelong immunity. (4)

   (c) A person with measles is most infectious about 8 to 16 days after first infection. Suggest why. (2)

   (Total 12 marks)

   NEAB 1998

4. (a) Outline **one** function of each of the following in defending the human body against bacterial infection.

   Skin   Tear fluid   Gastric juice (3)

   (b) In vaccination against tuberculosis (TB), children are injected with a weakened strain of TB bacteria.

   (i)   Explain how this procedure can result in long-term defence against TB. (4)

   (ii) Suggest why sufferers from AIDS may contract TB, even though they have been vaccinated against it. (2)

   (c) The body's defence system may cause problems, if a blood transfusion is carried out without pre-testing for the compatibility of the blood groups of the donor and the recipient.

   (i)   Explain clearly the cause of failure of a transfusion of blood of Group A into an individual of Group O. (4)

   Among North American Indians, 75% of the population belong to Group O and the remainder to Group A.

   (ii) Calculate the percentage risk of failure of random transfusion (without pre-testing of blood groups) in this population. (1)

   (Total 14 marks)

   CCEA 1998

5. Write an essay on the following statement:
   The body's immune response can **cause** medical or health problems.

   (Total 10 marks)

6. Why is transplantation surgery beset with so many difficulties?

   (Total 6 marks)

7. Write a short essay on B and T lymphocytes, explaining their respective roles in the body's defences against disease.

   (Total 10 marks)

Chapter 20

Nervous communication

It is important that in a complex animal like the human, changes in the external environment should be detected instantly and appropriate signals sent quickly to the relevant parts of the body. It is also important that within the body, different organs should be able to communicate with each other rapidly. This rapid communication is achieved by the **nervous system**.

The nervous system is composed of **nerve cells** (**neurones**) which transmit messages, or impulses as they are called, from **receptors** to **effectors**. In general terms, the receptors detect changes in the environment (**stimuli**), and the effectors – usually muscles – produce a **response**.

Receptors and effectors are dealt with in Chapters 22 and 23. In this chapter we shall look at the nervous system and how it works.

20.1 General organisation of the nervous system

The main parts of the human nervous system are shown in figure 20.1 and summarised in table 20.1. As with the nervous system of other vertebrates, the system is subdivided into two main parts:

■ **Central nervous system** (**CNS**) consisting of the **brain** inside the cranium, and the **spinal cord** inside the vertebral column.

■ **Peripheral nervous system** consisting of numerous **nerves** which link the CNS with the receptors and effectors.

The nerves are subdivided into two groups: **spinal nerves** connected to the spinal cord, and **cranial nerves** connected to the brain. The spinal nerves are associated with receptors and effectors in the trunk, including the arms and legs, whereas all but one of the cranial nerves are associated with receptors and effectors in the head and neck.

Each nerve splits into branches which serve the receptors and effectors in that region of the body. In the trunk the spinal nerves are gathered together to form large compound nerves which go to the limbs: the **brachial nerves** to the arms, and the **sciatic nerves** to the legs.

The cranial nerves are fewer in number than the spinal nerves; humans, in keeping with other mammals, have twelve on each side. Those supplying the mouth and jaws are like the spinal nerves in that they serve receptors *and* effectors. The other cranial nerves serve either receptors or effectors, but not both. For example, the **optic nerves** are connected only to the **eyes**, and the **auditory nerves** to the ears.

The only cranial nerve that serves structures outside the head and neck is the **vagus**, the 'wandering' nerve. This nerve emerges from the posterior part of the brain and passes down the neck to the thorax and abdomen, giving off branches to various receptors and effectors. The vagus is part of the **autonomic nervous system** which controls involuntary actions such as the circulation of the blood. We shall discuss this part of the nervous system at the end of this chapter. For the moment let us concentrate on how the nervous system enables us to respond to stimuli.

20.2 Reflex action

A **reflex action** is an immediate, short-lived response to a stimulus, brought about by the nervous system. In humans the withdrawal of the hand from a hot object is an example.

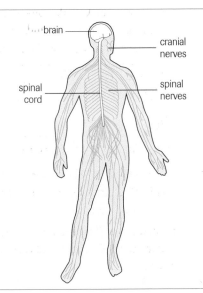

Figure 20.1 General plan of the human nervous system. In reality the brain is encased within the cranium (part of the skull) and the spinal cord is surrounded by the vertebral column. In this diagram the skeletal structures are not shown, so the central nervous system is exposed to view.

Table 20.1 Structural subdivisions of the nervous system of a vertebrate.

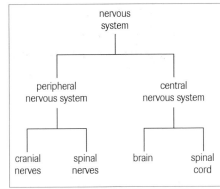

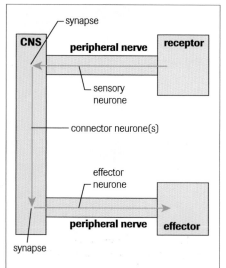

Figure 20.2 Schematic diagram showing the basic components of a typical reflex arc. There is much variation in the number of neurones between the receptor and effector. In the simplest reflexes a sensory neurone connects directly with an effector neurone, but in most cases sensory and effector neurones are linked by at least one connector neurone.

Figure 20.3 Diagrammatic cross-section of the spinal cord to illustrate the main reflex arc involved in the response to treading on a nail. The arrows indicate the direction in which impulses are transmitted through the nervous system.

Another example is the rapid straightening of the leg when the tendon just below the knee is tapped. This familiar **knee jerk** is important clinically; abnormalities of it are used for diagnosing certain disorders of the nervous system.

The structural basis of reflex action is the **reflex arc**. This is the series of structures along which impulses travel when they bring about a reflex response.

The structure of a generalised reflex arc

A generalised reflex arc is shown in figure 20.2. It starts with a **receptor** which leads to a **sensory neurone** in a peripheral nerve. Inside the CNS the sensory neurone is linked to a **connector neurone**. This in turn is linked to an **effector neurone**. The effector neurone extends into a peripheral nerve and goes to an **effector**, usually a muscle or gland. The point where one neurone links up with the next one is called a **synapse**.

To bring about a reflex action, impulses have to travel through the reflex arc from the receptor to the effector via the structures in between, including the synapses. There is always a very slight delay between the moment that a receptor is stimulated and the onset of the response. This is due to the time that it takes for impulses to travel through the reflex arc.

This general description of a reflex arc applies to any animal with a CNS, namely all vertebrates and most invertebrates including annelids, arthropods and molluscs. Of course there are variations on the theme. For example, there may be several connector neurones, one after the other, between the sensory neurone and effector neurone; and in the human knee jerk there is no connector neurone at all: the sensory neurone is linked directly to the effector neurone.

A human reflex arc

Suppose you tread on a nail. You respond by quickly pulling your leg away. The reflex arc involved in this response is illustrated in figure 20.3. The neurones are located in one of the spinal nerves serving the leg. This nerve, in common with other spinal nerves, is attached to the spinal cord by two connections, a **dorsal root** and a **ventral root**.

The receptors in this reflex are **nerve endings** in the skin of the foot, just under the epidermis, and they give rise to the sensation of pain. They are usually referred to simply as **pain receptors**. The main effector is the **flexor muscle** at the back of the leg – when it contracts the leg bends (flexes) at the knee. The neurones in this reflex arc possess a **cell**

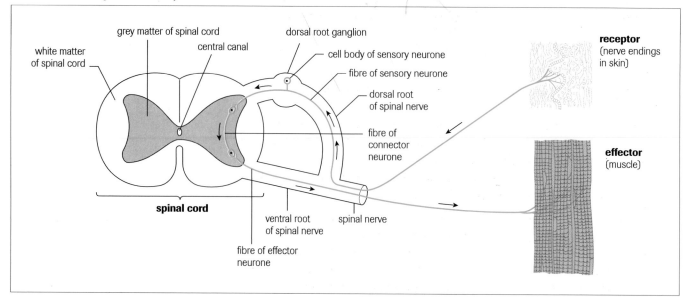

body and an elongated **nerve fibre** which transmits the impulses. We shall look at the detailed structure of these neurones in a moment – here we are simply concerned with the course they take in the reflex arc.

The fibre of the sensory neurone enters the spinal cord via the dorsal root. The cell body of this neurone is located in the **dorsal root ganglion**, a swelling of the dorsal root. The ganglion contains the cell bodies of many other sensory neurones besides this one, which is why it is swollen. In the **grey matter** of the spinal cord the sensory neurone makes synaptic connection with the connector neurone. This in turn makes synaptic connection with the effector neurone, which passes out of the spinal cord in the ventral root and supplies the flexor muscle.

▶ Other human reflexes: lungs (Hering–Breuer), page 172; pupil, page 385

Part 4

> **Support**
>
> ### What is a ganglion?
>
> A **ganglion** (plural: **ganglia**) is a localised part of the nervous system which contains a concentrated collection of nerve cells. The dorsal root ganglion referred to in the text contains nerve cell bodies, but many other ganglia contain synapses too. A ganglion may be a swelling associated with a nerve or it may be a collection of nerve cells within the central nervous system.

Many other reflex arcs share the same route as that outlined above, so the spinal nerve and its dorsal and ventral roots are packed with nerve fibres, and the grey matter in the spinal cord contains numerous synapses.

What happens, then, when you tread on a nail? Stimulation of the pain receptors in the skin fires off impulses in the sensory neurone. The impulses enter the spinal cord, travel along the connector neurone, and leave the cord in the effector neurone. Very quickly the impulses reach the flexor muscle which then contracts.

Some complications

Think for a moment about the response to treading on a nail. Three things about it give us important information about reflex action in general and the nerves responsible for it.

- **The response involves the contraction of other muscles in the leg besides the flexor**. For example, certain muscles bend the leg at the hip, and others flex the foot. These muscles augment the action of the knee flexor and make the overall response more effective. Obviously impulses must be sent to these muscles at the same time as they are sent to the knee flexor.

- **The muscles in the leg are in pairs and the action of one opposes the action of the other**. Thus the flexor muscle which bends the leg is opposed by an **extensor muscle** which stretches the leg. Plainly when the flexor contracts, the extensor must relax, and vice versa. So, when impulses are sent to the flexor they must stop being sent to the extensor. The excitation of one muscle and simultaneous inhibition of its opposing muscle (or muscles – there may be more than one) is called **reciprocal innervation**. This principle is explored more widely in Chapter 24.

- **The response may involve muscles in other parts of the body besides the leg**. For example, you might jump back and let out a cry. This would involve the muscles of the back, arms and larynx, necessitating the spread of impulses to reflex arcs other than those that deal with the leg. More importantly, various muscles will adjust your **posture** so that you do not fall over when your leg is withdrawn from the ground.

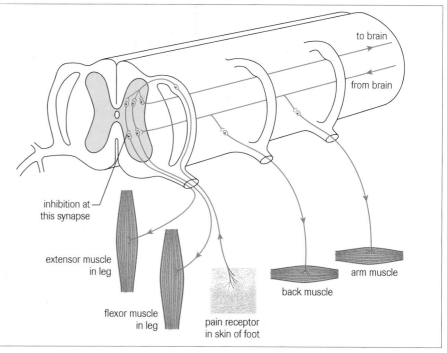

Figure 20.4 Simplified diagram of part of the spinal cord showing the pathways through which impulses are transmitted in bringing about a full response to treading on a nail. The arrows indicate the direction of transmission of impulses. Transmission occurs across all the synapses shown except for the one in the pathway leading to the extensor muscle. This synapse is temporarily blocked (inhibited) while the reflex is in progress.

Figure 20.5 A very high level of nervous coordination is needed by these ballet dancers.

▶ More about the coordination of locomotion, page 423

From these observations we may conclude that different reflex arcs are connected with each other. Careful examination of the nerve pathways in the spinal cord show that this is indeed the case (*figure 20.4*).

Different reflex arcs are interconnected by neurones whose fibres run longitudinally in the **white matter** of the cord. These neurones form nerve pathways which not only connect different reflex arcs together but also connect them with the brain. Some of the pathways carry impulses up the spinal cord to the brain; others carry impulses down the cord from the brain.

In bringing about a full response the synapses play a crucial part, for they determine which particular muscles will contract. For example, when you flex your leg, a synapse in the pathway leading to the extensor muscle is automatically inhibited. This ensures that when the flexor muscle contracts, the extensor relaxes (*figure 20.4*).

The brain ensures that the correct muscles contract or relax at the right moment. This process is called **coordination**. If a relatively simple reflex like withdrawing your foot from a nail requires coordination, think how much more is needed for activities like walking and running – or ballet dancing (*figure 20.5*). We shall have more to say about the coordinating role of the brain later.

20.3 Structure of neurones

An effector neurone can be taken to illustrate the structure of a typical neurone (*figure 20.6A*). The **cell body** contains the nucleus which is surrounded by cytoplasm. Slender processes called **dendrites** extend from the cell body, like the branches of a tree, and make synaptic contact with other neurones. Also extending from the cell body is a long nerve fibre which transmits impulses to the effector. A **nerve fibre** which transmits impulses away from the cell body, as this one does, is called an **axon**. A human axon can be over a metre long, so the axon adds greatly to the total volume of the cell.

Despite its specialised shape, the neurone possesses the same basic features as other animal cells. The cell body is enclosed within a plasma membrane, and the cytoplasm contains the usual range of organelles. Ribosomes are particularly prominent and, as in other cells, they are the site of protein synthesis. The cell body has a high rate of protein synthesis because it has to supply proteins to the axon.

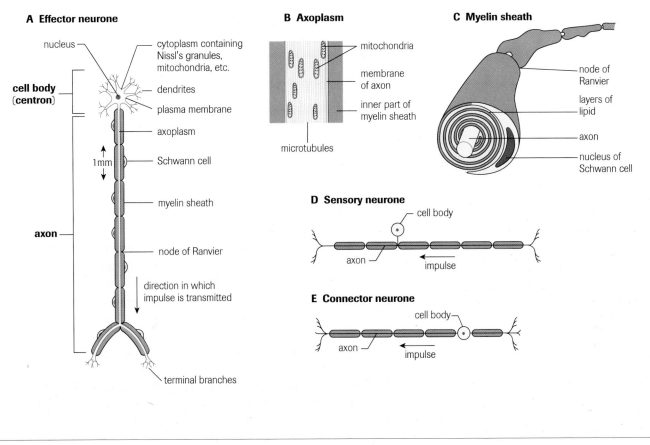

A Effector neurone

nucleus

cytoplasm containing Nissl's granules, mitochondria, etc.

dendrites

plasma membrane

cell body (centron)

axoplasm

1mm

Schwann cell

myelin sheath

axon

node of Ranvier

direction in which impulse is transmitted

terminal branches

B Axoplasm

mitochondria

membrane of axon

inner part of myelin sheath

microtubules

C Myelin sheath

node of Ranvier

layers of lipid

axon

nucleus of Schwann cell

D Sensory neurone

cell body

axon

impulse

E Connector neurone

cell body

axon

impulse

The axon is filled with cytoplasm, here called **axoplasm**, which is continuous with the cytoplasm in the cell body. The axoplasm lacks ribosomes, so it cannot make its own proteins; instead, the cell body makes the proteins which are then transported along the axon to where they are needed. The axoplasm contains numerous microtubules which are involved in this transport process (*figure 20.6B*).

The axon is bounded by a plasma membrane continuous with that of the cell body. Outside the plasma membrane there is usually a fatty **myelin sheath**. This is not part of the nerve cell itself, but is formed by a series of accessory cells called **Schwann cells**. Each Schwann cell wraps itself around the axon like a Swiss roll (*figure 20.6C*). Where one Schwann cell ends and the next one begins, the myelin sheath is absent and the axon is covered only by its plasma membrane. These points occur at regular intervals along the axon and are called **nodes of Ranvier**. They are approximately one millimetre apart. The function of the myelin sheath is to insulate the axon and speed up the transmission of impulses along it (*page 354*).

Many other types of neurone are found in the nervous system. They vary in shape and the number of dendrites, but their basic structure is similar to the effector neurone just described. Figure 20.6 includes a sensory and connector neurone from the spinal cord for comparison with the effector neurone.

In addition to the Schwann cells already mentioned, various other accessory cells are found in the nervous system. The collective name for these is **glia**. Some, like the Schwann cells, form myelin sheaths around the axons. Others support and protect the neurones, or form scar tissue following damage.

From a functional point of view, the most important part of the neurone is the nerve fibre, for it is this that carries the impulses upon which the functioning of the nervous system depends. What exactly is a nerve impulse and how is it transmitted?

Figure 20.6 The structure of neurones (nerve cells).
A Effector neurone. The dendrites make contact with other neurones in the spinal cord. The terminal branches at the far end of the axon are connected to an effector.
B Detail of the axoplasm as seen in the electron microscope. Proteins synthesised in the cell body are transported along slender microtubules.
C Detail of the myelin sheath. The electron microscope shows the sheath to consist of layers of lipid, formed by an extension of the plasma membrane of the Schwann cell which wraps itself around the axon.
D Sensory neurone. The cell body is at the end of a short stalk to one side of the main conducting fibre. The branches at the right-hand end are connected to the receptor.
E Connector neurone. The branches at both ends are connected to other neurones.

It gradually became clear many years ago that the impulse transmitted by an axon is an electrical phenomenon and that in certain respects an axon is like an electric cable. In fact nerve impulses can be recorded and measured using an apparatus which is sensitive to small electrical changes.

Such an instrument is the **cathode ray oscilloscope**. Impulses are picked up from the nerve through a pair of **recording electrodes** placed in contact with it, then fed into an oscilloscope where they appear as 'spikes' on the screen. The oscilloscope incorporates an **amplifier** which enlarges the signals. This is necessary because the electrical change associated with a typical nerve impulse is very small – a mere 50 millivolts (mV) or less.

The oscilloscope has been used extensively by neurophysiologists to measure the magnitude and speed of transmission of impulses, and to analyse their occurrence in different parts of the nervous system. But useful though this information is, it tells us little about the fundamental nature of the nerve impulse.

What we really need to know is what happens to an axon when an impulse passes along it. This has proved a difficult question to answer mainly because most axons are very fine, rarely exceeding 20 µm in diameter. This makes them too small to see, let alone do experiments on. Fortunately certain animals possess axons which are exceptionally large – so large in fact that they are called **giant axons**. One such animal is the squid. The largest of its giant axons is about a millimetre in diameter – still small, but big enough for a neurophysiologist to do something with. Moreover, they are close to the inner surface of the body wall and are therefore easy to get at, and the impulses they carry are relatively large.

Most of the experiments on how these giant axons transmit impulses were carried out by two Cambridge scientists, Alan Hodgkin and Andrew Huxley, in the 1940s and 50s. Sir Andrew tells the story himself in the extension box on page 352.

Basically what they did was to insert a very fine microelectrode into the axon, and place another one outside the axon close to the membrane (*figure 20.7*). This enabled them to record differences in electrical potential *across* the membrane. The electrodes were connected to an oscilloscope for recording the potentials. The following account of the nerve impulse is based on Hodgkin and Huxley's discoveries.

The electrical nature of the nerve impulse

When the axon is at rest, that is when it is not transmitting an impulse, a potential difference of approximately 70 mV exists between the inside and the outside of the axon, the inside being negative relative to the outside. As this is the situation when the axon is at rest, it is called the **resting potential**. It shows that the membrane is **polarised** – that is, it is able to maintain a potential difference between its two sides.

When an impulse passes the electrodes, the resting potential is momentarily reversed and the inside becomes positive relative to the outside. This sudden reversal of the resting potential is called the **action potential** and it means that for a brief moment the membrane has been **depolarised**.

The resting and action potentials, as recorded with an oscilloscope, are shown in the top part of figure 20.8. As you can see from the time scale, the action potential is extremely short-lived. It lasts about a millisecond (one thousandth of a second), after which the resting potential is restored.

The ionic basis of the impulse

Later experiments provided an ionic explanation of the electrical events described above. The results of these investigations are summarised in the lower part of figure 20.8. When the axon is at rest, the concentrations of ions on the two sides of the membrane are different. There is an excess of potassium ions inside the axon and of sodium ions outside. This difference is

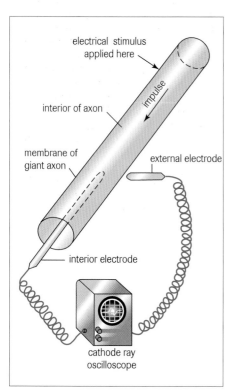

Figure 20.7 How the nerve impulse was investigated by Hodgkin and Huxley. One microelectrode is inserted into the interior of the giant axon of a squid. The other microelectrode is placed outside the membrane surrounding the axon. The electrodes are connected to a cathode ray oscilloscope. Electrical activity is recorded when the axon is resting and also when it transmits impulses generated by applying an electrical stimulus to the right-hand end.

The use of invertebrates

Often in the history of biology, major advances in our understanding of life processes have come from research, not on humans but on invertebrates and other relatively lowly animals. This is one of the reasons why studying such animals is so important. Without the squid we might not understand the nature of the nerve impulse even now.

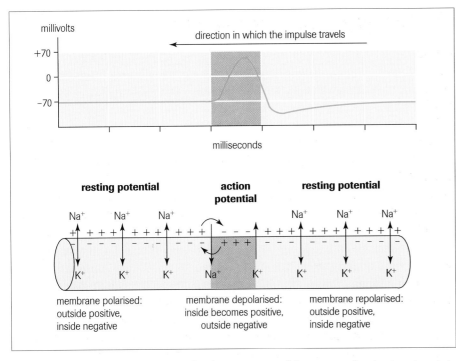

Figure 20.8 Summary of the events that occur in the giant axon at rest (yellow) and during passage of an impulse (pink). The top part of the picture shows the resting and action potentials as they appear on the screen of an oscilloscope. The lower part shows the electrical charges inside and outside the membrane, together with the movements of sodium and potassium ions, corresponding to the resting and action potentials. Notice that the entry into the axon of sodium ions, which initiates the action potential, is followed by a loss of potassium ions. This causes the resting potential to be restored. Depolarisation of the membrane corresponds to the rising phase of the action potential, repolarisation to the falling phase.

maintained by the active pumping of sodium ions out of the axon and potassium ions into it. We have met this process before – it is called the **sodium–potassium pump** and it is what happens in other animal cells (*page 114*).

The sodium-potassium pump works in such a way that three sodium ions are expelled for every two potassium ions admitted. Moreover, some of the potassium ions leak back out again. The result is that there is a slight surplus of negative ions inside the axon, making the inside of the axon negative relative to the outside: this is the resting potential. Only a very slight excess of negative ions inside the axon is required to create the resting potential, though in practice it may be enhanced by the presence inside the axon of negative organic ions to which the membrane is impermeable.

When an impulse passes along the axon, the membrane suddenly becomes permeable to sodium ions which, being about ten times more concentrated outside the membrane, begin to diffuse into the axon. This depolarises the membrane and reverses the resting potential. The inside of the axon now becomes positive and the outside negative: this is the action potential.

As sodium ions enter the axon, potassium ions begin to leave. This marks the beginning of the recovery process in which the inside of the axon regains its negative charge. However, we now have some sodium ions inside the axon which must be got rid of sooner or later or the system will run down. This is achieved by the sodium–potassium pump, which expels the sodium ions and brings in potassium ions, thus restoring the distribution of ions which normally exists when the axon is at rest.

So we see how an action potential develops in an axon, but what causes it to pass along the axon from one end to the other? The answer lies in the distribution of ions at the leading end of the action potential. Here, as you can see in figure 20.8, positive and negative ions lie alongside each other on each side of the membrane. This creates local electrical currents which depolarise the next section of the membrane. In this way the action potential passes along the axon rather like fire spreads along a trail of gunpowder.

20.5 Properties of nerves and impulses

Having discussed the nature of the nerve impulse, we can go on to consider some important properties of nerves and their impulses.

How do the ions move in an axon?

The ability of a nerve to transmit impulses depends ultimately on the sodium–potassium pump which is responsible for the resting potential. How does it work? Basically the process is the same as that which occurs in other animal cells: a single **carrier protein** in the membrane transports sodium ions out of the axon and potassium ions into it.

As the sodium ions are being moved against an electrochemical gradient, the process must involve the expenditure of energy. Treating an axon with a metabolic poison such as dinitrophenol inactivates the sodium–potassium pump and

prevents the expulsion of sodium ions. Their expulsion will, however, start up again if the poison is washed away. This confirms that the pump requires energy. Moreover, when treated with a poison which prevents ATP formation, the axon loses ATP at about the same rate as the sodium–potassium pump runs down, suggesting that the two are connected. When the poisoned axon is given some ATP, the sodium–potassium pump starts up again and the resting potential is at least partly restored.

What causes sodium ions to enter the axon during the passage of an impulse?

In the membrane there are specific **channel proteins** which open up and allow the sodium ions to pass through. The opening of these **gated channels** is triggered by the change in potential across the membrane resulting from the local currents at the leading end of the action potential. Once depolarisation is complete, the channels close and the influx of sodium ions ceases. This mechanism is in accord with what we know about membrane transport in general.

▶ Carrier proteins and channel proteins, Chapter 7

Unravelling the nature of the nerve impulse

Guest author Sir Andrew Huxley describes how he and Sir Alan Hodgkin discovered the nature of the nerve impulse.

Alan Hodgkin, four years older than I, was well known in nerve research by the time I completed my undergraduate work in the summer of 1939. We had met at Trinity College, Cambridge, where he was a Fellow and I was a student. He invited me to join him in August 1939 at the Laboratory of the Marine Biological association in Plymouth, where he was planning some experiments on the giant nerve fibres of the squid. We had to leave Plymouth earlier than we had intended because of the imminent prospect of war, but we did manage to record both the resting and action potentials with electrodes pushed down inside the nerve fibres. So, for the first time, it was possible to measure directly the potential difference across the surface membrane of a nerve fibre.

The striking and unexpected thing we found was that the inside of the fibre, which was electrically negative to the external solution in the resting state,

became electrically positive during the action potential. This was an important discovery because up till then it had been thought that during the action potential the potential difference across the membrane would be abolished and approach zero. What we found was that the potential was *reversed*.

For most of the war Hodgkin was engaged in the development of short-wave airborne radar and I in gunnery research, first for Anti-Aircraft Command and later for the Navy. We met a good many times and discussed plans for collaborating again after the war. Meanwhile, I had been elected to a Research Fellowship at Trinity, so when released from our war duties we both returned to Cambridge and got down to our experiments again.

What we wanted to do was to analyse the permeability changes that occurred during the action potential. This could only be done with internal electrodes, which meant using squids – and the only laboratory in Britain where they were available was the laboratory at Plymouth.

So back we went to Plymouth in the summers of 1948 and 1949, Bernard Katz

of London University joining us for some of the earlier experiments. Most of our research was done at night. This was because the squids were caught in a trawl during the day, and we used them as soon as they were brought in because they did not survive well in captivity. A successful experiment would go on into the small hours of the morning, and often dawn was breaking by the time we returned to our boarding house.

We hoped to correlate the action potential with permeability changes in the membrane. First we applied changes of membrane potential to the giant fibre and analysed the time course of the permeability changes. The next stage was to see if these would account for the time course of the potential change that occurred when an action potential passed along the nerve fibre. This involved some heavy computation requiring the repeated solving of four simultaneous differential equations, three of them non-linear. For each solution a value for the transmission velocity had to be guessed and, depending on the outcome, an improved value chosen for the next solution.

The first electronic computer in Cambridge (EDSAC I) was not then running, so I spent the best part of a year in 1950–51 doing the computations with a hand calculating machine. Later, I ran the equations on EDSAC I (programmed entirely in machine language) and then on EDSAC II and other computers. Fortunately they confirmed the hand calculations. This came as a great relief because the first solutions on an electronic computer, carried out in the United States, had shown a serious discrepancy from our results. This was later traced to a programming error.

Our findings were published in 1952. Hodgkin and I could not see how to take the analysis further, so we turned to other problems. Since then, new methods have become available which have confirmed our results and have led to an understanding of the molecular mechanism by which permeability changes occur in the nerve membrane.

In 1963 Sir Alan Hodgkin and Sir Andrew Huxley were awarded a Nobel Prize for their work on the nerve impulse. Subsequently, each became Master of Trinity, Hodgkin from 1978 to 1984, Huxley from 1984 to 1990. Bernard Katz, who collaborated with them in some of the experiments, received a Nobel Prize in 1970 for showing how nerve impulses make muscle fibres contract. Sir Alan died in December 1998.

Methods of stimulation

What sort of stimuli generate nerve impulses? In natural circumstances impulses are generated as a result of the stimulation of receptors. But impulses can be set up in nerves by directly applying any stimulus which opens the sodium channels and causes local depolarisation of the membrane. For example, this can be done by pinching a nerve.

In the laboratory, nerves are usually stimulated by applying weak electrical shocks through **stimulating electrodes**. Such stimuli are useful experimentally because their strength, duration and frequency can be controlled and they do not damage the nerve fibres.

All-or-nothing law

Suppose you stimulate one end of an axon with a series of electrical stimuli of gradually increasing intensity, and record action potentials from the other end. Figure 20.9 shows what happens.

If the intensity of the stimulus is below a certain value, called the **threshold**, no action potential is evoked. However, if the intensity of the stimulus exceeds this value, a full-sized action potential is given and any further increase in the intensity of the stimulus, however great, does not give a larger potential.

This is called the **all-or-nothing** law which states that *the response of an excitable unit (in this case an axon) is independent of the intensity of the stimulus.* In other words, the size of the impulse is independent of the size of the stimulus. All that is necessary for a full-sized action potential to be produced is that the stimulus is above the threshold.

The all-or-nothing law is an important concept on which much of the functioning of the nervous system depends. It means that the 'quantity' of information sent through the nervous system is determined not by the size of the impulses but by their number and frequency.

Refractory period

After an axon has transmitted an impulse, it cannot transmit another one straight away. The axon has to recover first. The membrane has to be repolarised and the resting potential restored before another action potential can be transmitted.

The period of inexcitability following the transmission of an impulse is called the **refractory period**, and typically it lasts about 3 milliseconds. It can be divided into an **absolute refractory period** during which the axon is totally incapable of transmitting an impulse, followed by a somewhat longer **relative refractory period** during which it is possible to generate an impulse in the axon provided that the stimulus is stronger than usual (*figure 20.10*).

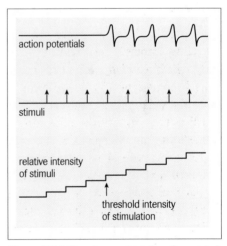

Figure 20.9 The all-or-nothing law. One end of an axon is stimulated with eight electrical shocks of gradually increasing intensity, and action potentials are recorded from the other end. The results, shown above, indicate that a stimulus either evokes a full-sized action potential or no action potential at all.

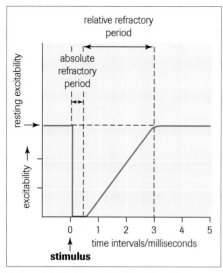

Figure 20.10 The graph shows how the excitability of an axon changes following the application of an above-threshold stimulus. The excitability is the ease with which the axon can be stimulated: the greater the excitability, the lower the intensity of stimulation required to generate an action potential. Notice that, following the transmission of an action potential, the excitability of the axon falls to zero (absolute refractory period) after which it gradually returns to normal (relative refractory period).

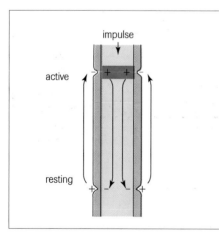

Figure 20.11 Diagram showing how an impulse is transmitted along a myelinated axon. The sheath (orange) insulates the axon, preventing currents crossing the membrane, so action potentials only develop at the nodes where the sheath is absent. Suppose an action potential develops at the node shaded red. When this node becomes depolarised, currents flow along the inside and outside of the axon as shown by the arrows. These currents depolarise the next node. The same thing then happens at successive nodes all along the axon, so the impulse leaps from node to node.

The importance of the refractory period is that, together with transmission speed, it determines the maximum frequency at which an axon can transmit impulses. For most axons the maximum frequency is about 500 per second, though some neurones can reach 1000 per second.

Transmission speed

If the nervous system is to be efficient as a means of communication, its neurones must transmit impulses quickly. In fact transmission speeds vary enormously, depending on the type of neurone and the animal in question. The slowest neurones transmit at speeds of about 0.5 metres per second, the fastest ones at over 100 metres per second.

What enables neurones to transmit impulses at such high speeds? In vertebrates like ourselves the **myelin sheath** is responsible. Experiments have shown that when a myelinated axon transmits an impulse, depolarisation occurs only at the **nodes of Ranvier**. Between one node and the next the myelin sheath insulates the axon, so currents cannot flow across the axon membrane in these regions. But when a node becomes depolarised, the juxtaposition of positive and negative ions between that node and the next creates currents which depolarise the next node (*figure 20.11*). These currents are equivalent to the local currents at the leading end of the action potential in figure 20.8. The difference is that in the myelinated axon the currents occur over a longer distance. The result is that the impulse leaps from node to node, thereby increasing the overall transmission speed. This is called **saltatory transmission** (from the Latin word *saltus,* a leap).

Certain invertebrates achieve high transmission speeds in a different way. Instead of having myelin sheaths they have very thick axons which transmit impulses exceptionally rapidly. We have already met these **giant axons** in the squid, but other invertebrates have them too, for example earthworms, fan-worms and lobsters. High speed impulses in their giant axons bring about rapid **escape responses** which enable these animals to retreat quickly from danger.

20.6 **The synapse**

The cell body and dendrites of a typical neurone in the brain or spinal cord are covered with numerous **synaptic knobs** derived from other nerve cells (*figure 20.12*). Each knob is the swollen end of a dendrite, and as many as 50 000 of them may be in contact with a single neurone. The computing facility of the nervous system depends on the complex interconnections which these synapses permit.

It has long been known that transmission across synapses occurs not by electrical but by chemical means. One of the earliest experiments supporting this notion is described in the extension box on page 357. In more recent years this idea has received support from the electron microscope which has been used to study the fine structure of synapses.

The fine structure of the synapse

The synaptic knob contains numerous **mitochondria** and **synaptic vesicles**. Between the knob and the adjoining neurone there is a small but definite gap, the **synaptic cleft**. The membrane on the near side of the cleft (belonging to the knob) is called the **presynaptic membrane**, and the membrane on the far side (belonging to the adjoining neurone) is called the **postsynaptic membrane**. The space between the two membranes is approximately 20 nm across (*figure 20.13*).

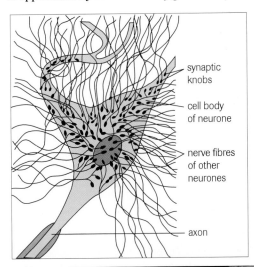

Figure 20.12 Synaptic knobs on the surface of a motor neurone. A single neurone may have on it as many as 50 000 synaptic knobs derived from many different neighbouring neurones.

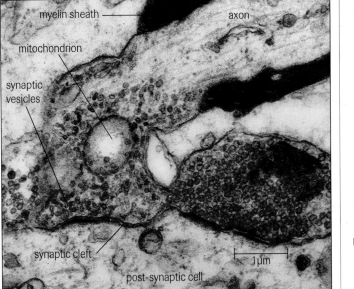

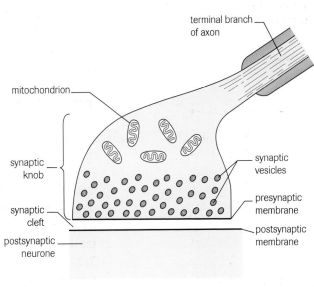

Figure 20.13 Structure of the synapse.
Left Electron micrograph of a section through a synaptic knob in the spinal cord of a fish.
Right Diagram of a synaptic knob. The synaptic cleft separating the presynaptic and postsynaptic membranes is approximately 20 nm wide.

How the synapse works

When an impulse arrives at a synaptic knob it causes calcium ions to diffuse into it from the surrounding tissue fluid. These ions cause some of the synaptic vesicles to move to the presynaptic membrane and discharge a **neurotransmitter substance** into the cleft. This is an example of exocytosis (*page 115*). The neurotransmitter substance then diffuses across the cleft to the postsynaptic membrane, which consequently becomes partially depolarised.

How does this partial depolarisation occur? The postsynaptic membrane contains specific **protein receptors** with which the transmitter molecules combine. Once this has happened, **protein channels** open up in the membrane, allowing sodium ions to diffuse from the cleft into the postsynaptic neurone. If the membrane becomes sufficiently depolarised, an action potential is fired off in the axon of the postsynaptic neurone (*figure 20.14*).

Inevitably this method of transmission results in a slight delay – usually about one millisecond – so synapses have the cumulative effect of slowing down transmission in the nervous system. However, the effect is negligible.

Synapses prevent impulses going in the wrong direction. An impulse can pass along an axon in either direction, but it can only cross a synapse in one direction. This is because synaptic vesicles are confined to the presynaptic side of the cleft, and protein receptors to the postsynaptic side.

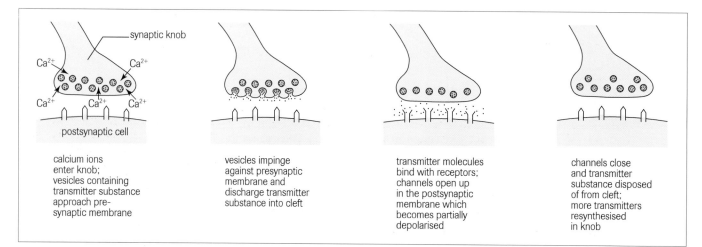

calcium ions enter knob; vesicles containing transmitter substance approach pre-synaptic membrane

vesicles impinge against presynaptic membrane and discharge transmitter substance into cleft

transmitter molecules bind with receptors; channels open up in the postsynaptic membrane which becomes partially depolarised

channels close and transmitter substance disposed of from cleft; more transmitters resynthesised in knob

Figure 20.14 This diagram shows how transmission across a synapse is thought to occur.

The neuromuscular junction

The point where a motor neurone makes contact with a muscle fibre is called the **neuromuscular junction**. The electron microscope has shown its internal structure to be similar to that of a synaptic knob, so we can regard it as a special kind of synapse (*figure 20.15*). The main difference relates to the postsynaptic membrane: in the neuromuscular junction this is folded to form a **muscle end plate**.

Transmission at the neuromuscular junction takes place in the same way as at synapses between neurones. When an impulse arrives at the neuromuscular junction, a neurotransmitter substance is released from synaptic vesicles into the synaptic cleft. The neurotransmitter substance diffuses across the cleft and depolarises the muscle end plate. An **end plate potential** develops and, once it has built up sufficiently, an action potential is generated in the muscle fibre.

Neurotransmitter substances

One of the most widespread neurotransmitter substances is an ammonium base called **acetylcholine**. It occurs at synapses and neuromuscular junctions in the voluntary nervous system and in certain parts of the involuntary system (*page 368*). If you move your arm or leg, it is acetylcholine which activates the muscles.

Acetylcholine must not be allowed to remain in the synaptic cleft after it has depolarised the postsynaptic membrane. If it did, the postsynaptic neurone would go on firing off impulses indefinitely. This is prevented by an enzyme called **acetylcholinesterase** (or **cholinesterase** for short) which is present in the cleft. As soon as acetylcholine has done its job, it is hydrolysed by cholinesterase and rendered inactive. The products of the hydrolysis pass back into the synaptic knob where they are resynthesised into acetylcholine, using energy from ATP. One of the functions of the mitochondria in the synaptic knob is to provide energy for replenishing the supply of ATP.

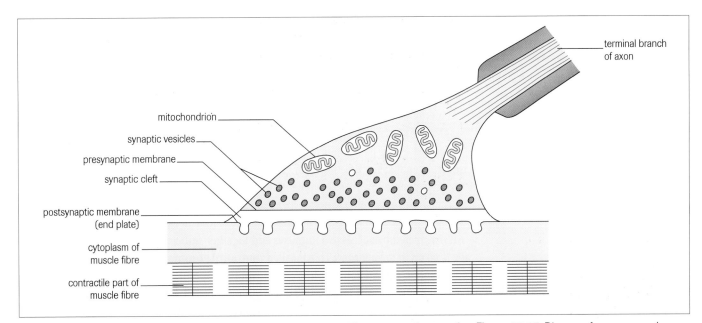

Labels on diagram:
- terminal branch of axon
- mitochondrion
- synaptic vesicles
- presynaptic membrane
- synaptic cleft
- postsynaptic membrane (end plate)
- cytoplasm of muscle fibre
- contractile part of muscle fibre

Another widespread transmitter substance is **noradrenaline**. This occurs, along with acetylcholine, in the involuntary nervous system. It works in the same way as acetylcholine but is inactivated differently: after it has depolarised the postsynaptic membrane it is taken up into the synaptic knob where its action is terminated.

Synapses that have acetylcholine as the transmitter substance are described as **cholinergic**. Those that have noradrenaline as the transmitter are described as **adrenergic**. Both are found in the peripheral nervous system. The brain contains synapses which use other transmitter substances in addition to acetylcholine and noradrenaline (*page 364*).

Figure 20.15 Diagram of a neuromuscular junction. The postsynaptic membrane, formed from the plasma membrane (sarcolemma) surrounding the muscle fibre, is folded to form the muscle end plate. Notice that the neuromuscular junction is essentially the same as the interneural synapse in figure 20.13.

Extension

How chemical transmission was discovered

Guest author Patricia Kohn describes a classic experiment which led to the discovery of chemical transmission.

In the mid-19th century it was well established that nerve and muscle action both involved electrical phenomena, and it was assumed that neuromuscular transmission was also an electrical process.

Then along came an Austrian physiologist called Otto Loewi. In 1921 he carried out an experiment which was so simple in conception and so easy to perform that one wonders why nobody had done it before.

The experiment involved using a frog's heart. The heart has a dual nerve supply: impulses in the **sympathetic nerve** speed up the rate at which it beats, whereas impulses in the **vagus nerve** slow it down. Loewi removed the heart from the body,

with the vagus nerve intact, and immersed it in Ringer's solution (*page 267*). He then stimulated the vagus nerve repetitively for 15 minutes. As expected, the heart rate slowed. He then transferred the Ringer's solution to a second heart from which the vagus nerve had been removed. The result was that the second heart also slowed.

Loewi concluded that vagal stimulation of the first heart had released a substance, some of which had found its way into the Ringer's solution. The effect of vagal stimulation was then mimicked when the Ringer's solution was applied to the second heart.

The inspiration for this experiment came to Loewi in a dream. Apparently he woke up in the middle of the night and wrote it down, but in the morning he could not read what he had written. Fortunately the next night he had the

same dream again. He decided to take no risks this time, so he got up and did the experiment in the middle of the night!

Loewi demonstrated that chemical transmission occurs at the junctions in the autonomic nervous system. What about the voluntary system? This problem was resolved in 1936 by Sir Henry Dale, who managed to detect minute amounts of acetylcholine at the skeletal neuromuscular junctions. Loewi and Dale shared a Nobel Prize in 1936.

The discovery of chemical transmission was hugely significant, not only for pure research but also because it led to an understanding of how drugs affect the nervous system.

Dr Kohn was a research physiologist in the Department of Biomedical Science at the University of Sheffield.

Helping synapses

The local potential which develops in a postsynaptic neurone when the neurotransmitter substance impinges upon it is known as an **excitatory postsynaptic potential** (**EPSP**). If enough neurotransmitter substance is released, the EPSP may get large enough to generate an action potential in the neurone.

Usually neurones only fire when excited through several synapses simultaneously. A single synapse fails to produce enough transmitter substance for an action potential to be generated in the postsynaptic neurone. However, sufficient transmitter is produced by several synapses acting together. The EPSPs produced by the different synapses add together, generating an action potential. This is called **spatial summation**.

A neurone may fail to generate an action potential when only one impulse arrives at the synapse, but does so when two or more impulses arrive in quick succession. In this case the EPSPs created by successive impulses add together sufficiently for an action potential to be fired off in the neurone. This is called **temporal summation**.

Temporal summation involves a process called **facilitation**. The first impulse cannot cross the synapse but it leaves an effect which makes it easier for the next one to do so. How would you explain this in terms of the neurotransmitter substance?

Hindering synapses

Certain synapses inhibit postsynaptic neurones, making it more difficult for excitatory impulses to get across. The transmitter released at these inhibitory synapses causes the inside of the postsynaptic neurone to become more negative than usual, creating an **inhibitory postsynaptic potential** (**IPSP**). This makes it harder for the postsynaptic membrane to become depolarised, so action potentials are not fired in the neurone.

If an excitatory synapse is continually bombarded with impulses at high frequency,

---

Extension

Drugs and synapses

Any substance that prevents the action of a neurotransmitter substance will stop transmission at synapses which use that particular transmitter. On the other hand, any substance that prevents the transmitter being disposed of after it has done its job will prolong the action of the transmitter.

A substance that prevents the action of acetylcholine is **curare**, a poison which can be extracted from certain tropical trees. Curare's molecules have a similar shape to those of acetylcholine and they fit into receptors on the postsynaptic membrane, blocking neuromuscular junctions in the voluntary part of the nervous system. So curare stops the skeletal muscles contracting. At high enough concentrations it causes paralysis and death. South American Indians put it on their arrowheads, and some snakes have a similar compound in their venom. Controlled doses of such substances are used by surgeons to make the patient's muscles relax during operations.

Another acetylcholine inhibitor is **atropine** which occurs in the juice of the deadly nightshade, *Atropa belladonna*. Atropine blocks certain synapses in the involuntary nervous system by preventing acetylcholine depolarising the postsynaptic membrane. Its effect on the eye is explained on page 385.

The opposite effect is produced by **organophosphate insecticides** and **nerve gases**. They inhibit cholinesterase. Without cholinesterase, acetylcholine remains in the synaptic cleft and causes repeated firing of the postsynaptic neurone or, if it is a neuromuscular junction, repeated contractions of the muscle. The result is that the nervous system becomes overactive and muscles contract uncontrollably, in some cases with fatal results.

Prolonged synaptic transmission is also caused by certain chemicals that mimic the action of the real transmitter substance but are not inactivated afterwards. Such a substance is produced by certain types of algae resulting from eutrophication (*page 682*). Its molecules are similar in shape to acetylcholine's and they fit into the postsynaptic receptors and trigger impulses in the usual way. However, they are not inactivated by cholinesterase so impulses continue to be discharged, causing excessive responses. One of its effects is to cause the secretion of large amounts of saliva.

Chemicals that mimic natural transmitter substances are described as **agonists**. Those that prevent transmitter substances from working are described as **antagonists**.

The effect of drugs on synapses in the brain, page 366

---

there comes a time when the postsynaptic neurone stops responding and action potentials are no longer generated in it. It is as if the synapse gets tired. What actually happens is that the transmitter substance runs out, and its resynthesis cannot keep pace with the rate at which impulses reach the synapse. The synapse has become **fatigued**.

Synapses vary in how quickly they fatigue. Some do not fatigue at all, whereas others do so after transmitting only a few impulses. A fatigued synapse must be given time to regenerate a new supply of transmitter substance before it can transmit again.

Rapidly fatiguing synapses are a feature of relatively inactive animals such as sea anemones. The synapses of more active animals such as ourselves are generally slow to fatigue.

The role of synapses in the nervous system

Synapses influence the ease with which impulses are transmitted through the nervous system. An impulse reaching a synapse may facilitate the passage of other impulses or it may inhibit them. Sometimes an impulse may cross the synapse unimpeded, at other times it may be blocked. The pattern of facilitation and inhibition of the synapses therefore determines the flow of impulses within the nervous system as a whole.

What decides whether a particular synapse should be open or closed? One of the most important deciding factors is the brain, to which we now turn.

20.7 The brain

In all vertebrates, the central nervous system develops as a longitudinal tube of nerve tissue towards the dorsal side of the embryo (*page 527*). The anterior end of the tube, situated in the head, expands to form the **brain**. The rest of the tube becomes the spinal cord.

When fully formed, the human brain consists of two main parts, a large bulbous **cerebrum** consisting of a pair of **cerebral hemispheres** at the anterior end and, immediately behind, a narrow **brain stem**. Associated with the brain stem are various structures which you can see in figure 20.16.

Having been formed originally from a tube, the brain is hollow. Its cavities, called **ventricles**, are continuous with one another and with the central canal of the spinal cord. The cavities are filled with **cerebrospinal fluid** which is similar to tissue fluid.

Figure 20.16 Diagram showing the different parts of the human brain. The thalamus forms the roof and sides of the brain stem immediately behind the cerebral hemispheres and is not visible in this sectional view.

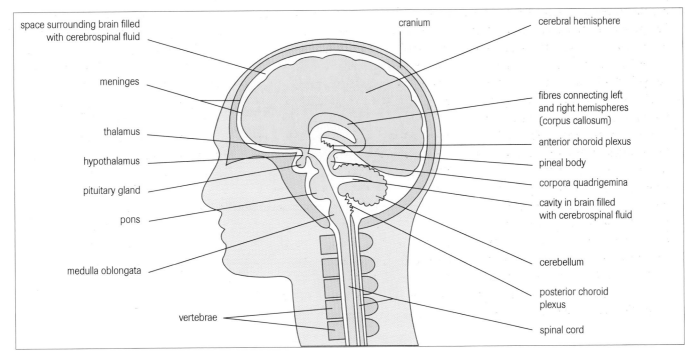

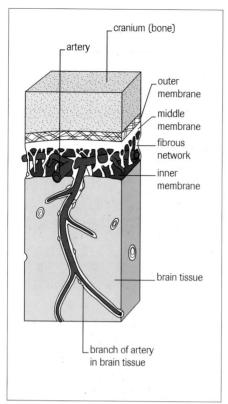

Figure 20.17 The brain is protected by the cranium and meninges which are shown here in three-dimensional view. The space between the inner and middle meninges is traversed by the fibrous network and filled with cerebrospinal fluid. Inflammation of the meninges, caused by viruses, bacteria or fungi, is called **meningitis** and can be fatal.

The brain contains at least ten billion (10^{10}) neurones together with supporting glial cells, and each neurone may be connected by synapses to as many as 25 000 others.

Protection and nourishment of the brain

Brain tissue is soft with the consistency of a ripe avocado pear, so it needs to be protected. It is enveloped by the bony **cranium**, part of the **skull**, on the inner side of which are three connective tissue membranes called **meninges** (*figure 20.17*):

- The **outer membrane** is relatively tough and merges with the bony tissue of the cranium.
- The **middle membrane** is a thin delicate sheet from which a network of fine fibres projects across a narrow space to the inner membrane.
- The **inner membrane** is also a thin delicate sheet in contact with the brain tissue itself.

The space between the fibres in the middle membrane is filled with cerebrospinal fluid which cushions the brain and prevents it jarring. Amongst the fibres are arteries which penetrate into the brain tissue and supply it with oxygen and nutrients.

The membranes surrounding the brain are continuous with similar membranes enveloping the spinal cord which is enclosed by the vertebral column. Small holes (**foramina**) in the cranium allow the entry and exit of blood vessels and nerves.

Cerebrospinal fluid is produced by two areas of concentrated blood capillaries called **choroid plexuses** in the roof of the brain. At these points the brain tissue is very thin so the capillaries lie just above the ventricles. They produce cerebrospinal fluid by active transport, possibly aided by ultrafiltration.

Arteries that enter the brain itself break up into capillaries from which the neurones and glial cells receive oxygen and nutrients. If a capillary bursts, or becomes obstructed by a blood clot, the brain cells in the region served by that capillary may die, resulting in a **stroke**. The likelihood of this happening increases in old age, and the severity depends on the location and extent of the damage. A major stroke can cause partial paralysis and may be fatal.

The overall role of the brain

In a word the overall function of the brain is **coordination**. To accomplish this, different parts of the brain deal with specific functions such as locomotion, breathing and so on. Neurones and synapses are particularly concentrated in these centres, and they are connected with the spinal cord and peripheral nerves by tracts of nerve fibres.

Collectively the brain:

- receives impulses from receptors;
- integrates these impulses;
- sends out new impulses to appropriate effectors.

By **integration** we mean that if impulses arrive simultaneously from several different receptors, the centre interprets and correlates the incoming information before sending impulses to the effectors. In addition certain parts of the brain, particularly the cerebral hemispheres, are responsible for higher functions such as memory and intelligence.

Extension

Investigating brain function

Various techniques can be used to determine the functions of particular regions of the brain. One method is to study the behaviour of people suffering from wounds or lesions in which certain identifiable regions of the brain have been damaged.

Another approach is to stimulate different regions of the brain with carefully controlled electrical stimuli, and observe the results. Alternatively, one can stimulate individual receptors such as the eye, and record electrical activity from various parts of the brain.

The above techniques involve experimenting on the brain itself. A quite different approach is to study the responses and behaviour of human subjects, and then attempt to explain them in terms of brain function. This method is used by psychologists.

In recent years advances have been made in understanding the structure and functioning of the brain, in health and disease, by computerised imaging techniques which scan the brain and produce detailed three-dimensional pictures of it.

Functions of the main parts of the human brain

Let us start at the back and work forward.

Medulla oblongata

Usually abbreviated to **medulla**, this is the most posterior part of the brain and is continuous with the spinal cord.

Suppose the whole of a person's brain in front of the medulla is destroyed in a car accident. All voluntary movement ceases, but breathing and the circulation continue. This is because the medulla contains the **ventilation** and **cardiovascular centres** (*pages 172 and 242*).

Other actions controlled by the medulla include swallowing, salivation and movements of the gut including vomiting. They are controlled by the autonomic nervous system which presides over the body's involuntary actions – more about that shortly.

Plainly a person with only the medulla intact, though unconscious and incapable of voluntary actions, can – with the necessary support – remain alive indefinitely. Such a person is described as being in a **persistent vegetative state**. The question of whether or not the support should be withdrawn so that the person can die peacefully is one that all too often faces the families of car accident victims. It also raises the question of what we mean by death.

Cerebellum

This is a greatly folded expansion of the roof of the brain just in front of the medulla.

A person with a badly damaged cerebellum finds it difficult to make precise movements. If, for example, he or she tries to pour cream into a cup of coffee, most of the cream is likely to go into the saucer. These kinds of observations indicate that the cerebellum is responsible for the fine adjustment of intentional movements, particularly those that have to be learned. We owe our manual dexterity to the cerebellum.

The cerebellum is particularly important in the performance of complicated physical actions that involve coordination and balance. For example, suppose you want to jump over a gate. The cerebellum, working in conjunction with other parts of the brain, integrates the motor impulses required to bring about the muscular response with sensory information from the eyes, balancing organs and muscle spindles, so that the whole enterprise is carried out in a fully coordinated manner.

Pons

This is a bulbous protuberance on the ventral side of the part of the brain just in front of the medulla. It contains a dense mass of neurones and fibres called the **reticular formation**. This helps to integrate the information travelling up and down the brain so that fully coordinated responses are given.

The reticular formation extends back to the medulla where it contains the ventilation and cardiovascular centres (*see above*).

Thalamus and associated structures

The next part of the brain, as we move forward, contains the **thalamus** above and at the sides, and the **hypothalamus** below.

The thalamus integrates sensory information and relays it to the higher centres of the brain. The hypothalamus contains centres controlling such functions as sleep, aggression, feeding, drinking, osmoregulation, temperature regulation and sexual activity. There is a fairly precise localisation of function in this part of the brain. Electrical stimulation of the appropriate regions will induce specific responses such as sleep or drinking.

Projecting downwards from the hypothalamus is the **pituitary gland**. This is an endocrine gland and secretes a wide range of hormones. There is a close connection –

Development and evolution of the brain

In vertebrates the CNS develops as a longitudinal tube of nervous tissue towards the dorsal side of the embryo (*page 527*). The anterior end of this **neural tube**, that is the portion of it contained in the head, expands greatly to form a swelling which then becomes subdivided into three regions: the **forebrain**, **midbrain** and **hindbrain**.

Each of these main regions of the embryonic brain gives rise to specific structures. The anterior end of the forebrain expands dorsally to form the cerebral hemispheres, whilst further back it forms the pineal body dorsally and the hypothalamus and pituitary gland ventrally. The midbrain gives rise to the corpora quadrigemina dorsally and the pons ventrally. The hindbrain expands dorsally to form the cerebellum, the ventral and posterior part becoming the medulla oblongata. Meanwhile the rest of the CNS, that is everything posterior to the brain, remains as a uniform tube, the spinal cord.

It is thought that in the early evolution of the vertebrates the forebrain was mainly responsible for the sense of smell, the midbrain for vision and the hindbrain for motor coordination together with various automatic functions such as breathing and the circulation. We see this clear-cut functional demarcation in present-day fish. However, in the course of vertebrate evolution this distinction has become obscured by the fact that these and other functions have gradually been taken over by the forebrain.

The third eye of the Tuatara

The only existing animal that has a third eye is the lizard-like tuatara (*Sphenodon*) which is found on the offshore islands of New Zealand. In this intriguing reptile the pineal body – situated in the top of the head – has a lens, pigmented retina and optic nerve which passes through a hole in the cranium. Though covered with a layer of skin and incapable of forming an image, there is evidence that the tuatara's pineal body is sensitive to light.

functionally as well as structurally – between the pituitary gland and the hypothalamus, as is explained in the next chapter.

Immediately in front of the pituitary gland is the **optic chiasma**. At this point the two optic nerves, one from each eye, cross each other on their way into the brain. The routes taken by the nerve fibres in the optic chiasma are such that impulses from each eye go to both sides of the brain.

The dorsal side of this part of the brain bears a slender stalk called the **pineal body**, a relic of a third eye that is believed to have existed on top of the head in certain extinct vertebrates. In amphibians such as frogs it produces a hormone called **melatonin** which causes constriction of the pigment cells in the skin. In mammals, the same hormone helps to control the reproductive state of seasonal breeders such as sheep. In humans, it may be involved in the onset of puberty and in the control of the body's circadian rhythms (*extension box below*).

The pineal body and melatonin

For many years the function of the pineal body in humans was a mystery. With the discovery of the fact that it secretes melatonin, experiments could be carried out to investigate its function.

It has been found that the secretion of melatonin is stimulated by darkness and inhibited by light, so its concentration is higher at night than during the day. This suggests that it may be involved in controlling the body's **circadian rhythms**, the approximate 24 hour changes that occur in our physiology and behaviour (*page 440*).

Interestingly, administration of melatonin at the right time and in the right dosage can reduce the feeling of malaise which occurs when a person's normal pattern of light and dark is interrupted by, for example, **shift work** or travelling rapidly through several different time zones (**jet lag**). Melatonin may also be associated with **winter depression**, the lowering of some people's mental state caused by the reduced amount of daylight in winter.

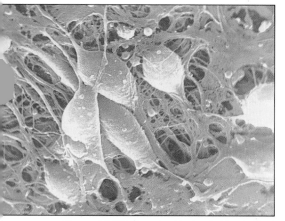

Figure 20.18 Scanning electron micrograph of a very small part of the human cerebral cortex. The human brain contains approximately 10 000 million neurones of which over 9000 million are in the cerebral cortex.
Magnification ×1500.

Cerebral hemispheres

In the human, the cerebral hemispheres are the largest and most prominent part of the brain. The two hemispheres are separated by a deep cleft down the middle, but they are linked together at their base by a transverse band of nerve fibres called the **corpus callosum**.

The superficial part of the cerebral hemispheres, called the **cerebral cortex**, is greatly folded, like a sheet of crumpled paper. This enables a large number of neurones to be packed into a relatively small space. Of the ten billion neurones in the human brain, over nine billion are in the cerebral cortex (*figure 20.18*).

The synaptic interconnections in this part of the brain are exceedingly numerous and complex. Moreover, new synapses can be formed by learning and repetition, and the pattern of connections can change. This structural versatility may help to explain how we acquire special skills like reading, writing and playing a musical instrument. It may also be the basis of memory (*page 442*).

The cerebral cortex is the least understood part of the brain. However, its importance is in no doubt. A person with a badly damaged cortex cannot see, hear, think or speak properly and is unable to move in a coordinated fashion. In severe cases the person may be unconscious and fail to respond to normal stimuli.

Localisation in the cerebral cortex

Experiments have been carried out to discover which regions of the cortex are responsible for particular functions. These investigations suggest that the cortex can be divided into three different types of area (*figure 20.19*):

- **Sensory areas** receive impulses from receptors via cranial and spinal nerves. Particular sensory areas are associated with specific senses – sight, hearing and so on. Stimulation of a receptor such as the eye results in electrical activity in the appropriate sensory region of the cortex, and damage to that region abolishes that sense.

- **Motor areas** send out impulses to the voluntary muscles via cranial and spinal nerves. There is considerable localisation of function. Electrical stimulation of a particular area will initiate a precise response such as flexing of the little finger or movement of the lips.

- **Association areas** sort out, integrate and, where appropriate, store information before sending it to the relevant motor areas. For example, when a person sees an object and says what it is, the association areas translate the visual experience into a spoken word.

Within each of the areas shown in figure 20.19 there is further localisation of function. Take the visual association area for example. When we see an object, certain groups of neurones within the visual association area process its shape, others its colour, position, movement and so on. Other areas may also be involved: for example, we may talk about, or describe, the object and that will involve the comprehension and speech areas.

Speech is a particularly complex function. It was shown many years ago that in adults, loss of speech can be caused by damage to the left cerebral hemisphere. It is now known that the production of speech is dealt with mainly by the speech area in this hemisphere whereas the understanding of words is a function of the comprehension area further back.

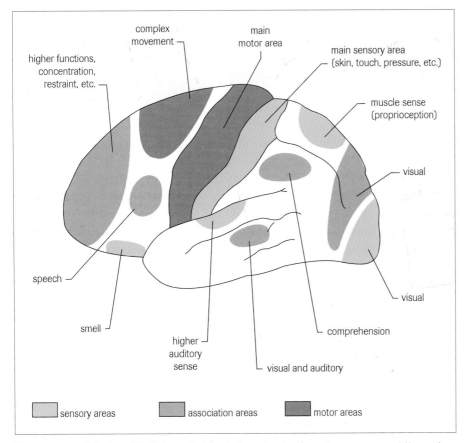

Figure 20.19 Side view of the left cerebral hemisphere showing the main sensory, association and motor areas of the cerebral cortex. The front of the brain is to the left.

Most of the nerve tracts leading from the cerebral hemispheres cross over in the brain stem, so the right hemisphere is connected to the left side of the body, and the left hemisphere to the right side. This means, for example, that the left hand is controlled by the right hemisphere, and the right hand by the left hemisphere.

Experiments have shown that the two cerebral hemispheres supervise different skills. The right hemisphere is primarily responsible for spatial and musical sense, whereas the left hemisphere is more concerned with mathematical ability, language and deductive reasoning. Thus artists depend mainly on the right hemisphere, accountants on the left. This applies to right-handed people – it is the other way round with left-handers!

Although we can make a broad functional distinction between the two hemispheres, they do not work in isolation from each other. The corpus callosum, which links them together, allows impulses to cross from one to the other and ensures that they cooperate in carrying out their functions.

Again, other areas may be involved, for speaking is often accompanied by gesticulations and a range of facial expressions.

There is considerable variation in the sizes of the different areas. Broadly speaking, an area's size is related to the number of neurones it contains and the complexity of their interconnections.

Localisation in the cerebral cortex is not as clearly defined as it may seem. There are many cases of people with head injuries losing a particular function of the brain and then regaining it later. Brain tissue is notoriously poor at repairing itself, so the lost function is probably taken over by neighbouring regions of the brain. Some parts of the cortex have no obvious role, and it is possible that they take over the functions of other areas if and when necessary.

The higher functions of the brain

The largest and most complex association area is in the anterior part of the cerebral hemispheres – the **frontal lobes**. This part of the brain is particularly well developed in humans.

People whose frontal lobes have been badly damaged are unable to think in an organised way, to concentrate and to correlate different pieces of information. Abstract thought is particularly difficult. At one time surgical cutting of nerve fibres in the anterior part of the frontal lobes was done to relieve extreme mental anxiety. Sometimes, this operation (known as **leucotomy**) led to a lowering of the patient's mental state and finer judgements.

One might be tempted to conclude that the frontal lobes are the seat of higher functions such as memory, imagination, thought and intelligence. However, it is not as simple as that. Although the frontal lobes are undoubtedly involved in these processes, other parts of the cerebral hemispheres also play a part.

Brain chemistry

Parkinson's disease is characterised by uncontrolled contractions of the voluntary muscles: the limbs tend to become rigid and a characteristic tremor develops in the hands, particularly when the person intends to do something with them. Research has shown that these symptoms are caused by degeneration of particular neurones in the brain which use **dopamine** as their transmitter substance. These dopamine synapses are part of a subtle mechanism whereby the brain translates our desire to make a particular movement into the necessary instructions for making it happen.

Dopamine is just one of about 20 neurotransmitter substances which have been discovered in the brain. Some have an excitatory effect on synapses, others an inhibitory effect.

An example of an excitatory transmitter is **acetylcholine** (*page 356*). Lack of it, caused by degeneration of cholinergic neurones in certain regions of the brain, is associated with

Restoring brain function

The functional versatility of the brain is remarkable. In one case a boy's brain was damaged by a pitch fork which went through his head. The result was that he could no longer read. However, he was re-taught how to read as though he was a child all over again.

Not everyone is as lucky as this and many people with brain damage never regain the skills they have lost, at least not fully. But brain research proceeds apace and new forms of treatment are constantly being developed. A promising discovery is that a certain protein, called

nerve growth factor, can stimulate neurones to form new connections. This offers hope to people with degenerative brain disorders such as Parkinson's disease and Alzheimer's disease.

➤ Alzheimer's disease, page 636

Electrical activity in the brain

Guest author Patricia Kohn describes the electrical activity that goes on in the brain and explains its significance.

In 1875 an English physician, Richard Caton, showed for the first time that the brain possesses its own electrical activity. He recorded what he called 'feeble currents of varying direction' from the cerebral cortex. Today the recording of these 'feeble currents' is a routine procedure. Electrodes are placed on the scalp, and the electrical signals are fed into a recording device. The trace so obtained is called an **electroencephalogram (EEG)**.

The EEG in activity and rest

The EEG appears as an irregular wavy line ('brain wave') whose frequency, amplitude and pattern vary with the type of activity going on in the brain. If you are alert and struggling with a difficult mental problem, your EEG will be irregular with small, high-frequency waves. On the other hand, if you are relaxed with your eyes closed, your EEG will be more regular with larger waves of lower frequency. This pattern is called the **alpha rhythm** and it changes as soon as you open your eyes.

What causes the EEG and how is it related to brain function? The EEG is recorded as the potential difference between two electrodes placed on the scalp. Beneath the electrodes are millions of neurones. Each neurone is covered with thousands of synapses derived from other neurones. As the incoming signals induce postsynaptic potentials, the cell becomes positively charged at one end and negatively charged at the other end. If this happens to sufficient neurones at the same time, the electrical field generated is large enough to be detected by the electrodes.

The more in synchrony the neurones are, the larger and more regular will be the waves in the EEG. The more unsynchronised the neurones, the smaller and more irregular will be the waves. Mental activity therefore seems to be associated with the cortical cells becoming less synchronised.

The EEG during sleep

At one time it was thought that during sleep the brain shuts down and becomes inactive. The EEG shows that this is not the case.

The wave pattern depends on how deeply asleep we are. In deep sleep (judged by how hard it is to wake the person up) the EEG is highly synchronised and the waves are large and slow (**slow-wave sleep**). However, at intervals during sleep the waves become highly unsynchronised and an observer would notice that our eyes are moving under their lids – which is why this is called **rapid eye movement sleep (REM sleep)**. There may be other signs of activity too: for example, the fingers may twitch and the teeth grind, in males the penis may become erect, and dreaming is likely to occur. Despite the active-looking EEG, we are still profoundly asleep and our muscles are totally relaxed.

While asleep we alternate between slow-wave and REM sleep, passing from one to the other and back again four or five times during a full night's sleep.

As well as telling us how active the brain is, EEGs are useful for diagnosing certain types of brain disorders. For example, doctors can distinguish between different types of epilepsy from EEG patterns, and the EEG can also be used to locate brain tumours.

Dr Kohn was a research physiologist in the Department of Biomedical Science at the University of Sheffield.

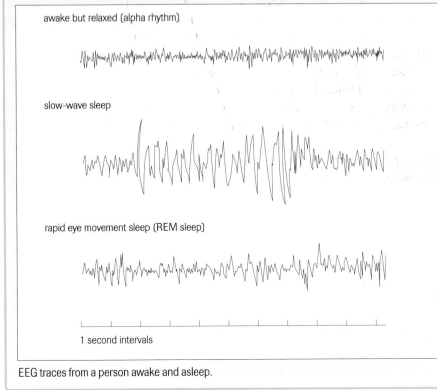

awake but relaxed (alpha rhythm)

slow-wave sleep

rapid eye movement sleep (REM sleep)

1 second intervals

EEG traces from a person awake and asleep.

Heads, brains and the environment

The brain is an integral part of the head, which is itself a fundamental feature of most animals. The development of a head in evolution is known as **cephalisation**. Why have heads developed in animals, and why is the head always associated with some kind of brain?

The head appears to have developed as a result of **directional locomotion**. Most animals move in a definite direction with the anterior end in the lead. Since this is the end to come into contact with new environmental situations first, it is not surprising to find that it has become equipped with highly sensitive receptors for receiving stimuli and monitoring the environment. In some animals these receptors take the form of elaborate **sense organs** such as eyes, nose and ears.

With the development of the head as the main region for stimulus reception, the flow of impulses into the anterior end of the nervous system increases. In relatively simple animals, such as flatworms and annelids, the function of the brain is primarily to receive this 'sensory information' and relay the appropriate signals to the rest of the body. In more complex animals, such as insects and vertebrates, the brain is also important as an integrating centre for coordinating movement and controlling more advanced types of behaviour.

The head is further complicated by the fact that it contains the mouth and associated feeding structures. It is logical that these should be at the leading end of the body. The necessity for them to be properly coordinated results in further elaboration of the nervous system in the head region.

Alzheimer's disease, a distressing age-related condition characterised by memory loss and confusion (*page 636*).

More and more evidence is coming to hand which suggests that the state of the brain synapses, as determined by these transmitter substances, plays an important part in determining a person's mental state and behaviour. For example, an excess of dopamine is associated with **schizophrenia**, a mental disorder characterised by personality changes which can give rise to episodes of abnormal behaviour.

Another substance, called **serotonin**, determines mood. In general, having too little serotonin can result in anxiety and depression, whereas too much may cause irresponsible exuberance. Knowing the underlying cause of human behaviour is the first step towards developing effective treatment, which includes the use of drugs.

Drugs and the brain

Certain **psychoactive drugs** affect brain function by interfering with synapses. Some of them have an excitatory effect, others an inhibiting effect.

- **Excitatory psychoactive drugs** include caffeine (present in coffee, tea and cola), nicotine (in tobacco), amphetamines (of which 'ecstasy' is a derivative) and cocaine ('crack' is a crude form of cocaine). All these drugs stimulate the brain, producing effects which range from the barely noticeable to intense euphoria and hallucinations. Prolonged use of such drugs can lead to mental illness.

- **Inhibitory psychoactive drugs** include alcohol, cannabis, opiates (derivatives of opium which include the powerful painkillers morphine and heroin), benzodiazepines (a group of tranquillisers which include valium and librium) and the hallucinatory drug LSD (lysergic acid diethylamide). Alcohol may *appear* to be a stimulant but in fact it is a depressant and achieves its effects by suppressing our normal inhibitions.

Much research has been done on how these drugs exert their actions. To take just one example, **nicotine** works by binding to acetylcholine receptors and opening up ion channels in postsynaptic neurones in the brain.

Needless to say, some drugs are extremely dangerous. This is not surprising when you bear in mind that they are interfering with the normal working of the brain. They can be habit-forming or addictive to varying degrees, and stopping them may cause severe withdrawal symptoms. Those that are prescribed medically have to be taken in carefully controlled dosages.

Interestingly, substances with effects similar to those of certain drugs occur naturally in the brain. For example, the brain contains a group of small polypeptides called **endorphins** and **enkephalins** which reduce the sensation of pain. (Endorphin is short for 'endogenous morphine-like substance'.)

20.8 The autonomic nervous system

The autonomic nervous system is divided into two distinct parts: the **sympathetic** and **parasympathetic systems**. Both contain nerve fibres serving structures over which the body normally has no voluntary control, and which are not innervated by the voluntary part of the nervous system. In both cases nerve fibres emerge from the brain and spinal cord and pass to the organs concerned. Both systems have many such pathways. At certain points in the pathways there are **ganglia** containing synapses (*ganglia are explained on page 347*). The positions of the ganglia differ in the two systems (*figure 20.20*).

The sympathetic system consists of a **sympathetic chain** which runs down the body on each side of the vertebral column just below the spinal nerves. The chain consists of a series of ganglia strung together like a string of beads. The ganglia are linked to the ventral roots of the spinal nerves by slender connections; and from each ganglion **sympathetic**

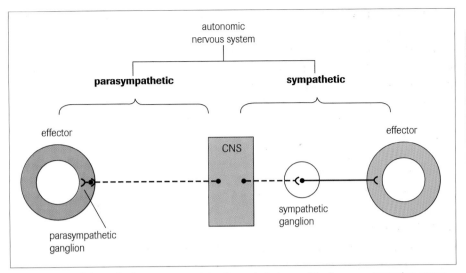

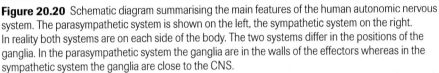

Figure 20.20 Schematic diagram summarising the main features of the human autonomic nervous system. The parasympathetic system is shown on the left, the sympathetic system on the right. In reality both systems are on each side of the body. The two systems differ in the positions of the ganglia. In the parasympathetic system the ganglia are in the walls of the effectors whereas in the sympathetic system the ganglia are close to the CNS.

nerves pass to the various organs, either directly or via further ganglia. The synaptic connections inside the ganglia ensure that impulses spread rapidly to all the appropriate effectors. For example, in the main ganglion in the neck there are about ten thousand incoming nerve fibres and a million outgoing fibres.

The parasympathetic system consists of the **vagus nerve** and its branches, together with certain other cranial and spinal nerves. In this case the ganglia are located in the walls of the effectors.

The functions of the sympathetic and parasympathetic systems are summarised in table 20.2. Notice that, in the main, their effects oppose each other.

Table 20.2 Summary of the main responses produced by the two parts of the mammalian autonomic nervous system. Note that the effects produced by the sympathetic generally oppose those produced by the parasympathetic. It should also be noted that the sympathetic system, while causing general vasoconstriction, dilates those arterioles serving vital organs such as skeletal muscle. In addition to the functions listed, the sympathetic system causes secretion of adrenaline from the adrenal medulla (*page 372*). The actions of this hormone are similar to those initiated by the sympathetic nervous system.

Effector	Parasympathetic system	Sympathetic system
Heart	slows down	speeds up
Arterioles	–	constrict
Bronchioles	constrict	dilate
Iris	constricts	dilates
Tear glands	secrete	–
Salivary glands	secrete	–
Gut	movements speed up	movements slow down
Anal sphincter	relaxes	contracts
Bladder sphincter	relaxes	contracts
Bladder wall	contracts	relaxes
Erector pilli muscle	–	contracts
Sweat glands	–	secrete

Gaining control over involuntary responses

Bearing in mind that the autonomic system is in charge of involuntary responses, it may surprise you that it controls the emptying of the bladder and the opening of the anal sphincter. After all, these are actions over which we have very definite *voluntary* control.

However, other animals cannot control these functions voluntarily, at least not without training, and even we have to learn to do so. The interconnections in the nervous system as a whole are such that voluntary control can be imposed on the autonomic system but only through **conditioning** (*page 440*).

Does this mean that a person could, by a stupendous act of perseverance, learn to bring about peristalsis of the gut or slow down the beating of the heart? The answer is 'yes' provided that one is prepared to enter upon a long and rigorous programme of mental and physical 'training'. This is essentially what mystics do when undertaking the art of yoga. It is interesting to speculate what is going on in the nervous system during these activities.

The overall function of the sympathetic system is to prepare the body for emergency: widening of the pupils, acceleration of the heart, tightening of the anal and bladder sphincters, contraction of the erector pili muscles and secretion of sweat are all responses associated with a sudden shock or preparing for action.

The parasympathetic system, on the other hand, tends to calm the body. This part of the nervous system is probably at its most active in a person snoozing after Sunday lunch.

Neurotransmitters in the autonomic nervous system

Two neurotransmitters occur in the autonomic nervous system. The ends of the parasympathetic nerves – the vagus nerve for example – produce **acetylcholine**, the same transmitter that is found in the voluntary part of the nervous system.

The ends of the sympathetic nerves produce mainly **noradrenaline**. This is almost identical chemically with the hormone adrenaline, and many of the responses produced by the sympathetic system are also produced by this hormone.

This demonstrates the close connection between nerves and hormones. Hormones are the subject of the next chapter.

Summary

1. In most animals the nervous system consists of a **central nervous system** (**CNS**) which is subdivided into the **brain** and **spinal cord**, and **peripheral nervous system** which is subdivided into **cranial** and **spinal nerves**.

2. The simplest type of response produced by the nervous system is **reflex action**. The structural basis of reflex action is the **reflex arc** which consists of a **receptor**, a series of **neurones**, and an **effector**.

3. An **effector neurone** possesses a **cell body** from which arise a variable number of **dendrites** and a long **axon**. The axon generally has a **myelin sheath**.

4. At rest, the inside of an axon is negative with respect to the outside (**resting potential**) but during the passage of an **impulse** this situation is momentarily reversed to give an **action potential**.

5. The resting potential is maintained by the **sodium–potassium pump** which expels sodium ions and takes in potassium ions. During the passage of an action potential, sodium ions enter the axon whose membrane thus becomes **depolarised**.

6. The size of an action potential is independent of the strength of stimulation. This is the **all-or-nothing law**.

7. For a brief period after it has transmitted an impulse, an axon is totally inexcitable (**absolute refractory period**). This is followed by a slightly longer period during which the axon is partially excitable (**relative refractory period**).

8. High speeds of transmission are achieved in vertebrates by having **myelinated axons** in which action potentials leap from one node of Ranvier to the next (**saltatory transmission**), or in certain invertebrates by having **giant axons**.

9. Neurones are interconnected by **synapses**. Transmission across a synapse is achieved by a **neurotransmitter substance** which diffuses across the gap and depolarises the membrane of the next neurone. **Neuromuscular junctions** work in the same kind of way.

10. Important properties of synapses include **summation**, **inhibition** and **fatigue**. Synapses ensure that impulses travel through the nervous system in only one direction and they play a major part in **coordination**.

11. Synapses are affected by certain drugs and poisons. Synapses in the brain are affected by **psychoactive drugs** which can have a profound effect on feelings and behaviour.

12. **Coordination** is a particularly important function of the brain. The **medulla** and **hypothalamus** coordinate various automatic functions, the **cerebellum** and **pons** coordinate movement, and the **cerebral hemispheres** supervise all voluntary responses as well as being responsible for memory, intelligence and other higher functions.

13. Involuntary responses are dealt with by the **autonomic nervous system**. This is subdivided into the **sympathetic** and **parasympathetic systems**. The overall role of the sympathetic system is to prepare the body for an emergency, an effect which is generally opposed by the parasympathetic system.

14. The brain is an integral part of the **head** which in the course of evolution has become progressively more and more elaborate, a process known as **cephalisation**.

For general advice on these questions and advice on answering essay-type questions, see pages vii and viii..

1. (a) Describe the structure and functions of (i) a sensory neurone, and (ii) a motor neurone. (8)

(b) Explain the transmission of an action potential along a myelinated neurone. (10)

(Total 18 marks)

UCLES 1997

2. The graph shows the changes in membrane potential which occur during the transmission of a nerve impulse.

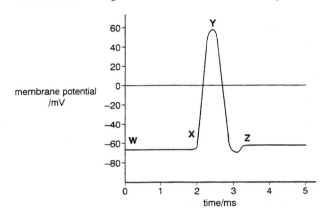

(a) (i) State which letters on the diagram correspond with the process of depolarisation of the axon membrane. (1)

(ii) State the direction in which sodium ions will move across the membrane during depolarisation. (1)

(iii) Explain how the impermeability of the axon membrane to sodium ions helps to maintain the resting potential at **W**. (2)

Mammals have myelinated axons whereas invertebrates, such as squids, have non-myelinated axons.

(b) Explain the advantage of having myelinated axons. (2)

The table shows the relationship between axon diameter and speed of conduction in an axon of a squid and that of a cat.

axon	diameter /µm	conduction velocity /m sec⁻¹
squid	650	24
cat	4	26

(c) Suggest why it is possible for both animals to conduct impulses with similar velocity. (3)

(Total 9 marks)

UCLES 1997

3. (a) Describe the sequence of events that takes place when a nerve impulse arrives at a synapse. (4)

(b) The diagrams below show the changes in membrane potential in a presynaptic neurone and postsynaptic neurone when an impulse passes across a synapse.

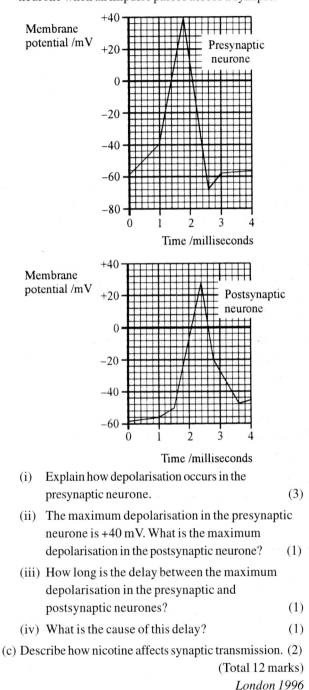

(i) Explain how depolarisation occurs in the presynaptic neurone. (3)

(ii) The maximum depolarisation in the presynaptic neurone is +40 mV. What is the maximum depolarisation in the postsynaptic neurone? (1)

(iii) How long is the delay between the maximum depolarisation in the presynaptic and postsynaptic neurones? (1)

(iv) What is the cause of this delay? (1)

(c) Describe how nicotine affects synaptic transmission. (2)

(Total 12 marks)

London 1996

4. Outline the arrangement of the main regions in the mammalian brain, briefly indicating the functions of each. (Total 10 marks)

WJEC 1998

Chapter 21

Hormonal communication

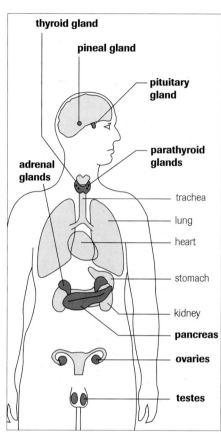

thyroid gland

pineal gland

pituitary gland

parathyroid glands

adrenal glands

trachea

lung

heart

stomach

kidney

pancreas

ovaries

testes

Figure 21.1 The main endocrine glands in the human body. The glands are coloured red. The adrenal glands consist of two parts: the adrenal medulla in the centre, and the adrenal cortex round the edge. Each secretes its own hormone or hormones. The pancreas is an exocrine as well as an endocrine gland; the endocrine part consists of the islets of Langerhans.

The following hormones are covered in detail in other parts of the book:

➤ gut hormones, pages 187 and 190
➤ insulin and glucagon, pages 269–71
➤ antidiuretic hormone, page 288
➤ parathormone, page 289
➤ aldosterone, page 290
➤ melatonin, page 362
➤ sex hormones, pages 512–19
➤ growth hormone, page 364
➤ thyroxine in amphibians, page 566

N erves, the subject of the last chapter, are not the only means of communication in the body. Communication is also achieved by chemical substances called **hormones**.

A hormone is a chemical substance produced in one part of the body, from which it is transported – usually in the bloodstream – to another part where it brings about a response. A minute quantity of a hormone may have a profound effect on the organism's development, structure or behaviour. Hormones are always organic compounds, some of them complex.

21.1 Introducing hormones

In the human and other vertebrates, hormones are secreted into the bloodstream by **endocrine glands**. The word endocrine means 'internal secretion'. Since endocrine glands shed their secretions directly into the bloodstream, they have no ducts. This contrasts with **exocrine glands**, such as the salivary glands, whose secretions are carried by ducts to specific destinations (*page 64*). The pancreas is an example of an organ which is both an exocrine *and* endocrine gland. Its exocrine function is to secrete digestive enzymes, its endocrine function is to secrete insulin and glucagon (*Chapter 16*).

Once in the bloodstream, hormones are carried around the body and bring about responses in specific **target organs**. A hormone's target organ or organs (there may be more than one) may be situated a long way from the gland that secretes the hormone.

The main endocrine glands of the human body are shown in figure 21.1. The fact that they are widely separated from one another spatially does not mean that they work in isolation. Some of them cooperate with, or are influenced by, other hormones as we shall see presently.

Functions of mammalian endocrine glands

Table 21.1 summarises the hormones secreted by the endocrine glands of a mammal. Hormones occur in other animals too, invertebrates as well as vertebrates, and comparable substances occur in plants as explained in Chapter 31.

In the present chapter we shall look at the principles of hormonal communication and its role in controlling various processes that go on inside the human body – metabolism, growth, sexual development and so on. In regulating these activities hormones are serving a coordinating role. As such they bear certain resemblances to the nervous system, and it is instructive to compare the two systems from a functional point of view.

Hormonal and nervous communication compared

Hormones and nerves both involve transmission of messages which are triggered by stimuli and produce responses. The target organs of a hormone are equivalent to a nerve's effectors.

The main difference between the two systems is in the nature of the message. In the endocrine system the message is a chemical substance (a **chemical messenger** as it is sometimes called) which is conveyed through the circulatory system to all parts of the body. In the nervous system the message is a discrete, all-or-nothing **action potential** which is transmitted along a nerve fibre to (usually) a specific part of the body.

Despite this difference, there is one fundamental similarity between the two systems: both involve **chemical transmission**. In the last chapter we saw that transmission at

Table 21.1 The principle endocrine glands of a mammal, together with their hormones and main functions. The hormones secreted by the gut and the placenta are not included – they are explained on pages 187–8, 190 and 517.

Gland	Hormone	Chemical structure	Main functions
Thyroid	Thyroxine	Amino acid (tyrosine) with iodine-containing group attached	Raises basal metabolic rate
	Calcitonin	Polypeptide	Opposes action of parathormone (*see below*)
Parathyroids	Parathormone	Polypeptide	Controls concentration of calcium and phosphate ions in blood
Pancreas (islets of Langerhans)	Insulin	Protein	Lowers blood sugar concentration
	Glucagon	Polypeptide	Raises blood sugar concentration
Adrenal medulla	Adrenaline	Ring compound with short side chain	Prepares body for emergency: metabolic rate increases, blood diverted to vital organs, etc.
Adrenal cortex *adrenal cortical hormones*	Aldosterone	Steroid	Controls concentration of sodium and potassium ions in blood
	Cortisol	Steroid	Prevents excessive immune response (anti-stress)
	Androgens	Steroids	Promote development of testes and secondary sexual characters of male
Pineal body	Melatonin	Hydroxy-indol	Causes concentration of melanin in frog's skin; promotes sexual development in mammals, and controls circadian rhythms
Testes	Androgens	Steroids	Promote development of testes and secondary sexual characters of male
Ovaries	Oestrogens	Steroids	Promote development of ovaries and secondary sexual characters of female; control menstrual cycle and pregnancy
	Progesterone	Steroid	Controls menstrual cycle and pregnancy
Pituitary (anterior lobe)	Thyroid stimulating hormone (TSH)	Polypeptide	Causes thyroid gland to secrete thyroxine
	Adrenocorticotrophic hormone (ACTH)	Protein	Causes adrenal cortex to secrete adrenal cortical hormones
	Growth hormone	Protein	Stimulates growth
	Prolactin	Protein	Causes mammary glands to secrete milk
gonadotrophic hormones	Follicle stimulating hormone (FSH)	Glycoprotein	Controls testes and ovaries
	Luteinising hormone (LH)	Glycoprotein	Controls testes and ovaries
Pituitary (posterior lobe)	Antidiuretic hormone (ADH)	Polypeptide	Causes reabsorption of water in kidneys
	Oxytocin	Polypeptide	Causes contraction of uterus at birth
Thymus	Thymosin and thymulin	Polypeptides	May promote proliferation and maturation of T lymphocytes but little is known about their actions

Comparing the nervous and endocrine systems, an analogy

In comparing the nervous and endocrine systems as means of communication, you may find this analogy helpful.

You are stranded on a desert island. How do you communicate with the outside world? Fortunately there are 200 empty beer bottles on the island. So you write letters, put them in the bottles and float them out to sea, confident that sooner or later at least one of them will be washed up on the mainland. This is equivalent to the endocrine system.

But there is another possibility. It so happens that there is a telephone box on the island. So you ring home. This is equivalent to the nervous system.

Can you see any flaws in this analogy? If so, what are they?

synapses and neuromuscular junctions is achieved by a chemical substance – a neurotransmitter. The latter is equivalent to a hormone in the endocrine system. The main difference between them is that the neurotransmitter substance has to travel a mere fraction of a micrometre to reach its destination, whereas a hormone may have to travel the full length of the body.

Three other differences flow from this:

- **Hormonal responses are produced more slowly than nervous responses.** It takes longer for a hormone to reach its destination and produce a response than it does for a nerve impulse. The hormone is limited by the speed at which blood flows through the arteries.

- **Hormonal responses are usually more widespread than nervous responses.** A single hormone may act on target organs far removed from each other. In contrast, nervous responses may be very localised, involving the contraction of only one muscle in a particular part of the body.

- **Hormonal responses frequently continue for much longer than nervous responses.** Hormones tend to be secreted continuously in a steady 'trickle'. Examples of such long-term responses are growth and metabolism. Nervous responses, however, are usually brought about by sporadic bursts of nerve impulses and are therefore short-lived, such as the contraction of a muscle in a reflex action.

The close connection between the endocrine and nervous systems

Despite the differences between them, the endocrine and nervous systems are closely connected. This is best illustrated by the **adrenal glands**. The middle part of these glands, the **adrenal medulla**, secretes the hormone **adrenaline**. This is almost identical chemically to the neurotransmitter substance **noradrenaline** which is produced at the ends of the sympathetic nerves.

The hormone adrenaline evokes many of the same responses as impulses in the sympathetic nerves: acceleration of the heart, redistribution of the blood and so forth. The combined effect of the adrenal medulla and sympathetic nervous system is to prepare the body for emergency. The nervous system produces an instant response with no delay. The response is then reinforced and sustained by the slower action of the hormone.

The adrenal medulla

The connection between the adrenal medulla and sympathetic nervous system is so close that one cannot help suspecting that the two share a common evolutionary origin. Innervated by the sympathetic nervous system, the adrenal medulla can be looked upon as a conglomeration of modified neurones which, far removed from the effectors, shed their transmitter substance into the bloodstream.

During embryonic development the secretory cells of the medulla are derived from the same group of cells that elsewhere give rise to sympathetic ganglion cells, but as they differentiate they become rounded and thoroughly unlike nerve cells in their appearance, so their final form belies their origin.

21.2 An endocrine gland in detail: the thyroid

We will take the **thyroid** to illustrate the main features of an endocrine gland. This gland is situated in the neck close to the Adam's apple which is part of the larynx. It secretes **thyroxine**, a complex organic compound containing iodine. This is why we need iodine in our diet (*page 15*).

The microscopic structure of the thyroid gland is shown in figure 21.2. It demonstrates the essential requirement of any endocrine organ, namely a close association between the hormone-producing cells and the bloodstream. The secretory cells are arranged round a series of hollow **follicles** in which an inactive precursor of the hormone, **thyroglobulin**, is stored before being converted into thyroxine and released into the bloodstream. Numerous capillaries lie between the follicles, their thin walls in close contact with the thyroid cells.

Figure 21.3 shows how thyroxine is produced. From the blood flowing through the capillaries the thyroid cells take up the raw materials they need for synthesising the hormone. These include **iodide ions** which the cells take up from the blood by active transport. So efficient is this process that iodide is several hundred times more concentrated in the follicle cells than in the blood. Once inside the cells, the iodide is oxidised to iodine and incorporated into thyroglobulin.

Thyroglobulin is transferred by exocytosis into the follicle, where it is stored. When needed it is taken up by endocytosis into the thyroid cells where it is converted into thyroxine and secreted into the bloodstream.

The whole process is like a production line: the product is manufactured in a factory (the thyroid cell), stored in a warehouse (the follicle) and then dispatched by a transport system (the blood).

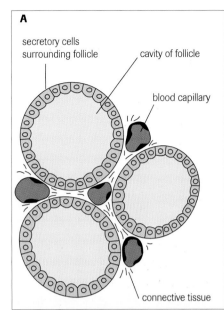

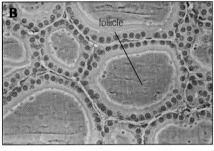

Figure 21.2 Microscopic structure of the thyroid gland.
A Diagram showing the close relationship between the follicles and blood capillaries.
B Photomicrograph of a thin section through part of the thyroid gland. Notice the follicles in which thyroglobulin is stored before being shed into the bloodstream.
Magnification ×350.

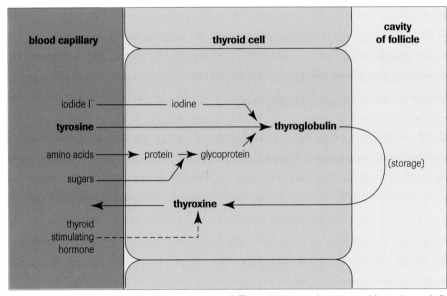

Figure 21.3 How thyroxine is made in a thyroid cell. The cell takes up the amino acid tyrosine and all other necessary raw materials from the blood in the adjacent capillary, stores the inactive thyroglobulin in the follicle, and sheds the hormone into the capillary as instructed by thyroid stimulating hormone from the pituitary gland. Thyroglobulin consists of thyroxine conjugated with a protein; a protease enzyme in the thyroid cell removes the protein, thus allowing the free hormone to be released.

The function of thyroxine

Thyroxine controls the basal metabolic rate, and is therefore important in growth. Under-secretion of it during development (**hypothyroidism**) causes arrested physical and mental development, a condition called **cretinism**. At the age of 14 or 15 years, cretins are stunted and pot-bellied, and so mentally retarded that they may not even be able to feed themselves.

In adults, hypothyroidism is not so serious since by this time growth is complete. The condition is called **myxoedema**. The symptoms are a decreased metabolic rate, increase in the amount of subcutaneous fat, coarsening of the skin and general physical and mental sluggishness.

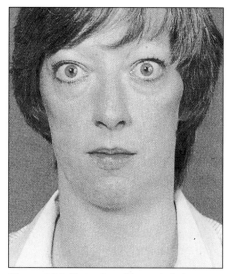

Figure 21.4 Protrusion of the eyeballs is a symptom of exophthalmic goitre, caused by persistent over-secretion of thyroxine by the thyroid gland in an adult human. The soft connective tissue in the eye socket swells, pushing the eyeball forward and forcing the eyelids apart, resulting in a staring appearance.

Over-production (**hyperthyroidism**) leads to **exophthalmic goitre** (*figure 21.4*), so called because of the characteristic protrusion of the eyeballs (exophthalmia) and swelling of the thyroid gland in the neck (**goitre**). Other symptoms include a greatly increased metabolic rate, loss of body mass and an accelerated heartbeat, all this being accompanied by a general physical and mental restlessness.

Plainly the thyroid is important in determining its owner's general mental and physical state. It is interesting to speculate on the extent to which our personalities may be altered by minor fluctuations in thyroid activity.

A deficiency of thyroxine in the body may be caused either by the thyroid gland failing to work properly, or to a shortage of iodine in the diet. Dietary shortage of iodine used to be common in certain iodine-deficient regions of the world – for example, parts of Switzerland, the Great Lakes in North America and Derbyshire in England where goitre cases were referred to as 'Derbyshire neck'. In such areas the problem can be overcome by adding iodine to the drinking water or by supplying the inhabitants with iodised salt. The remedy for myxoedema used to be to take thyroid orally; the old prescription was one fried sheep's thyroid weekly with redcurrant jelly. Nowadays carefully regulated quantities of thyroxine are administered to the patient.

An excess of thyroxine is generally caused by an overactive, often excessively large thyroid gland. In the old days, the remedy was for a surgeon to remove part of the thyroid and hope for the best. If severe myxoedema resulted, small pieces of the thyroid were grafted back. Nowadays surgical removal of thyroid tissue is carried out with much greater precision.

Sometimes surgery is avoided altogether by injecting controlled doses of radioactive iodine into the patient's bloodstream. This is taken up by the thyroid cells, killing those in which it accumulates above a certain concentration.

Control of thyroxine production

There are two problems here, and they apply to most endocrine glands. First, at any given time it is important that thyroxine should be secreted at a steady level so that its concentration in the bloodstream is held more or less constant. Second, it must be possible to vary the amount secreted at certain times to fit in with the changing needs of the body.

Keeping the concentration of thyroxine near-constant is an example of homeostasis and is achieved by a negative feedback process of the kind outlined in Chapter 16. The mechanism is summarised in figure 21.5.

The secretion of thyroxine into the bloodstream is triggered by a hormone produced by the anterior lobe of the **pituitary gland**. This is called **thyroid stimulating hormone (TSH)**. The production of TSH is regulated by thyroxine itself. A slight excess of thyroxine inhibits the anterior lobe of the pituitary which responds by secreting less TSH. This in turn reduces the activity of the thyroid gland, leading to a drop in the amount of thyroxine produced. This then removes the inhibitory influence on the pituitary so that more TSH will be produced and so on.

Figure 21.5 How the production of thyroxine is controlled. If too much thyroxine is present in the bloodstream, it inhibits its own production by the negative feedback mechanism shown here.

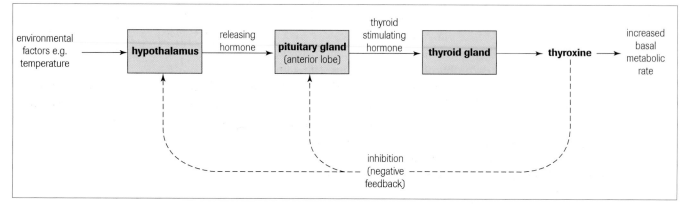

The second problem – changing the amount of thyroxine secreted – is dealt with by the brain. The production of TSH by the pituitary gland is controlled by the **hypothalamus** – we shall see how in a moment. The hypothalamus itself is subject to environmental influences such as temperature, so that in some animals the secretion of thyroxine – and hence metabolism and growth – can be geared to the seasons. The hypothalamus is subject to feedback inhibition by thyroxine so that excessive secretion is prevented.

Part 4

Extension

How hormones were discovered

Guest author Patricia Kohn puts hormones into historical perspective.

The more obvious endocrine organs like the thyroid and pituitary were described as long ago as the second century AD. Diseases which we now know to be caused by endocrine abnormalities were described by the ancient physicians, and their accounts make it clear that they were familiar with diabetes mellitus, goitre, cretinism and several other endocrine disorders, though their cause was unknown.

Many functions, some of them highly fanciful, were ascribed to these mysterious organs. For example, the pituitary was once thought to serve as a drain through which excess mucus from the brain could flow to the back of the nose!

In the latter half of the 19th century experiments were carried out on animals in which endocrine glands were removed and the effects compared with the symptoms of known diseases. This was followed by attempts to treat patients with extracts of various glands, even though in many cases the functions of the glands were not understood. On occasions this kind of therapy got out of hand. For example, one notorious endocrinologist claimed that testicular extracts produced amazing rejuvenating effects on elderly men – including himself!

During the early part of the 20th century a more systematic approach was adopted. The principle was to remove the gland from an experimental animal, study the effects and then remedy them by treating the animal with extracts of the gland. This eventually led to the identification of the functions of most of the endocrine glands.

Once the extracts were shown to be biologically active, the chemists moved in. They purified the extract down to a single chemical which still showed the same properties. This was the actual hormone. With the hormone available in a pure form, chemical analysis could be carried out to reveal its structure. In some cases it then became possible to synthesise the substance artificially and use it to treat people with hormone deficiency diseases.

All this painstaking work laid down the foundations for the modern molecular approach which aims to show how hormones bring about their effects on individual target cells.

Extension

Prostaglandins

Prostaglandins provide another means of communication in the body. Guest author Patricia Kohn explains.

Until relatively recently it was thought to be characteristic of hormones that they travel via the circulation to distant target organs. However, it is now known that some chemical messengers act locally. Certain fatty acids called **prostaglandins** are an example of these 'local hormones'.

The effects of prostaglandins vary, but one effect is common to all tissues and organs: when the body is injured or infected, prostaglandins help to initiate and strengthen the **inflammatory response** which occurs (*page 321*). The pain which accompanies inflammation is caused by the stimulating effect of prostaglandins.

Sometimes the immune system mistakenly identifies certain of the body's own tissue antigens as foreign. When this happens, the inflammatory response does not quickly die down, as happens after an acute infection is defeated. Instead it persists, giving rise to chronic and sometimes painful diseases such as

rheumatoid arthritis. These conditions are treated with **anti-inflammatory drugs**, such as aspirin which suppress the production of prostaglandin.

Recently, it has been found that prostaglandins are involved in the control of mammalian reproduction (*page 514*).

Dr Kohn was a research physiologist in the Department of Biomedical Science at the University of Sheffield.

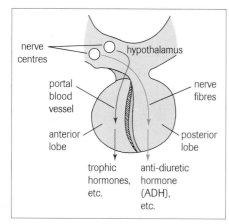

Figure 21.6 Diagram of the pituitary gland viewed from the side, showing its blood and nerve connections with the hypothalamus.

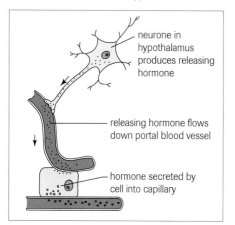

Figure 21.7 How the anterior lobe of the pituitary gland produces its hormones. The anterior lobe receives releasing factors (dots) which reach it from the hypothalamus via the portal blood vessels. The releasing factors then cause the cells in the anterior lobe to secrete their hormones (circles) into the bloodstream.

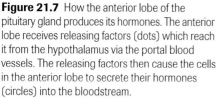

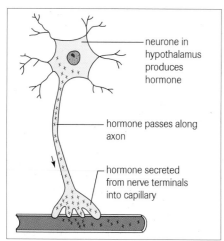

Figure 21.8 The posterior lobe receives its hormones (crosses) from the hypothalamus via axons (neurosecretion). The hormones are stored in the expanded nerve terminals until the arrival of nerve impulses from the hypothalamus triggers their release into the bloodstream.

21.3 The role of the pituitary gland

The production of thyroid stimulating hormone illustrates one of the most important functions of the pituitary gland, namely to regulate the activity of other endocrine glands. The pituitary secretes other stimulating hormones (known collectively as **trophic hormones**) which activate such endocrine glands as the adrenal cortex and gonads. The pituitary is in turn inhibited by the hormones secreted by these target organs (negative feedback).

The pituitary gland is closely influenced by the brain and, through the brain, by the receptors. In this way environmental changes, as well as the animal's general mental state, can influence hormonal activity. We saw this a moment ago in the way the brain controls the thyroid gland. The same sort of mechanism ensures that certain mammals breed in the spring. They are brought into season by **gonadotrophic hormones** which are secreted by the anterior lobe of the pituitary gland. With the approach of spring the brain senses, through the eyes, that the amount of daily light is increasing. As a result, the hypothalamus sends messages to the pituitary gland instructing it to secrete these hormones.

The brain and the pituitary gland

Figure 21.6 shows the close relationship between the pituitary gland and the brain. The gland projects down from the floor of the brain and is divided into an **anterior** and a **posterior lobe**, each of which secretes certain hormones.

In the hypothalamus there are two groups of nerve centres. One is connected to the anterior lobe, the other to the posterior lobe. These centres send instructions to their respective lobes telling them whether or not to release their hormones into the bloodstream.

The centres communicate with the anterior and posterior lobes of the pituitary in different ways:

■ **Anterior lobe** (*figure 21.7*). The nerve centres in the hypothalamus are connected to the anterior lobe by a **portal blood vessel**. (A portal blood vessel is one with capillaries at both ends.) When the hypothalamic centres are stimulated, **releasing hormones** are secreted into the portal vessel by the nerve cells. These releasing hormones are then carried by the blood in the portal vessel to the anterior lobe where they regulate the secretion of its various hormones. An example of a releasing hormone is **thyrotrophin releasing hormone** (**TRH**) which causes the release of thyroid stimulating hormone.

■ **Posterior lobe** (*figure 21.8*). The nerve centres in the hypothalamus are connected to the posterior lobe not by blood vessels but by **neurones**. The axons of these neurones perform two functions: they carry hormones from the nerve centre to the posterior lobe where they are stored in the nerve terminals, and when appropriate they transmit impulses from the nerve centre to the posterior lobe, causing the hormones to be released into the blood.

Neurosecretion

It may surprise you to find axons carrying hormones as well as nerve impulses, but in fact it is quite common and is yet another indication of the close connection between the nervous and endocrine systems. The process is called **neurosecretion**, and the cells that do it are called **neurosecretory cells**.

An example of a hormone which is secreted this way is antidiuretic hormone (ADH) (*page 288*). In this case the stimulus which causes impulses to be sent to the posterior lobe is a rise in the osmotic pressure of the blood. The stimulus is detected by osmoreceptors in the hypothalamus, and in consequence ADH is released from the posterior lobe into the bloodstream.

The production of ADH is a good example of neurosecretion in mammals, but neurosecretion is also found in other animals such as crustaceans and insects.

21.4 How hormones control cells

Let us suppose that a hormone has reached its target organ. How does it cause the cells to respond? Some light has been thrown on this question by the discovery that many animal cells contain a compound called **cyclic adenosine monophosphate (cyclic AMP)**.

Cyclic AMP is similar to ATP, which we have already met in connection with energy transfer, except that it contains only one phosphate group instead of three, and this phosphate group is attached to the adenosine part of the molecule in the form of a ring. Cyclic AMP is formed from ATP by the enzyme **adenylate cyclase** which is found in the plasma membrane.

Cyclic AMP occurs in extremely low concentration inside the cell (approximately one part per million), but it has been found that its concentration increases if the cell is brought into contact with the appropriate hormone. This has led to the suggestion that cyclic AMP may serve as a **second messenger** linking the hormone with the cell's response.

A model for hormone action

When a hormone molecule reaches the target cell, it binds to a specific **receptor protein** on the outer surface of the plasma membrane. The receptor protein is associated with a molecule of adenylate cyclase. The binding of the hormone to the membrane increases the activity of adenylate cyclase, causing ATP on the immediate inside of the membrane to be converted into cyclic AMP. The cyclic AMP then activates specific enzymes which bring about the appropriate response within the cell (*figure 21.9*).

The extent of the particular response is determined by the concentration of cyclic AMP, which in turn depends on a delicate balance between adenylate cyclase, responsible for its synthesis, and another enzyme – a phosphodiesterase – which destroys it.

Although cyclic AMP was the first second messenger to be discovered, others are now known. They include calcium ions which are becoming seen as more and more important in this role. A common feature of these second messengers is that the enzymatic changes which occur on the inner side of the plasma membrane lead to a rise in the concentration of the second messenger inside the cell. In other words the second messenger amplifies the response, a very small amount of hormone producing a disproportionately large effect.

Hormones which bind to receptor proteins on the plasma membrane and utilise a second messenger include adrenaline and peptide hormones such as glucagon and ADH. In these cases the second messenger is cyclic AMP. Insulin also binds to receptors on the plasma membrane but the internal events that follow are somewhat different.

Another model for hormone action

Some hormones, for example thyroxine and steroid hormones such as progesterone, are fat-soluble and can diffuse through the plasma membrane into the cell. In the cytoplasm the hormone binds to a specific receptor protein which carries it into the nucleus. It then activates, or in some case inhibits, appropriate genes in the DNA. The genes direct the synthesis of enzymes which bring about the appropiate response (*figure 21.10*).

What the two models have in common

There are variations on the two models outlined above, but one feature is common to them all, namely that the hormone molecules have to bind to specific receptor proteins, either on the cell surface or inside the cell, before they can produce an effect. There is a complimentary configuration between the hormone molecule and its receptor, just as there is between an enzyme and its substrate. This explains why a given hormone acts only on certain target organs. A cell will respond to a hormone only if it possesses the 'right' receptors.

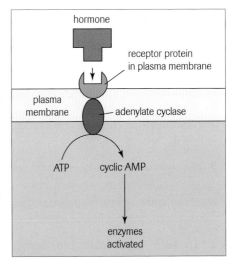

Figure 21.9 Schematic diagram showing how a hormone such as adrenaline is believed to affect its target cell. The hormone molecule binds to a receptor site on the plasma membrane. This activates adenylate cyclase which catalyses the conversion of ATP to cyclic AMP. The latter then activates specific enzymes in the cytoplasm.

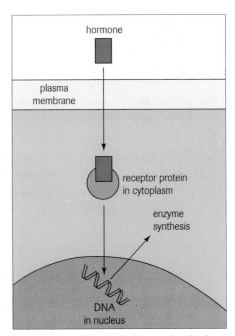

Figure 21.10 Schematic diagram showing how a steroid hormone such as progesterone is believed to affect its target cell. The hormone molecule enters the cell and binds with a specific protein which carries it to the nucleus where it switches on the appropriate genes in the DNA.

▶ Cell signalling, page 59

1. **Hormones** are chemical substances which are secreted into the bloodstream by **endocrine glands** and which produce a response in specific **target organs**.

2. The **endocrine system** may be compared with the **nervous system**. Both provide a means of communication within the body, but they work in different ways.

3. The close connection between the endocrine and nervous systems is illustrated by the **adrenal medulla** whose principal hormone, **adrenaline**, is similar to the neurotransmitter substance **noradrenaline** produced by sympathetic nerves.

4. The basic requirement of any endocrine gland is a close association between the secretory cells and blood capillaries. This is demonstrated by the **thyroid gland** whose cells absorb the raw materials for making the hormone from the bloodstream and shed the hormone into it.

5. The thyroid gland also illustrates how the production of a hormone may be controlled by **negative feedback**, in which process the **pituitary gland** plays an important part.

6. Failure of the control mechanism may result in an excess or deficiency of the hormone. Excess is associated with **exophthalmic goitre**, deficiency with **cretinism** and **myxoedema**.

7. The pituitary gland provides another example of the close connection between the endocrine and nervous systems. The pituitary gland is attached to, and controlled by, the **hypothalamus** of the brain.

8. The hypothalamus communicates with the anterior lobe of the pituitary by means of **releasing hormones**.

9. The hypothalamus communicates with the posterior lobe of the pituitary by means of neurones. The neurones secrete hormones (**neurosecretion**) as well as transmitting impulses.

10. Some hormones affect their target cells by activating the appropriate enzymes via **cyclic AMP**. Others work by influencing the cells' genes (DNA). In both cases the hormone binds to a specific **protein receptor** before it can exert its effects.

11. **Prostaglandins** are chemical messengers which are secreted by most types of cell and exert their effects locally.

Practice questions

For general advice on these questions and advice on answering essay-type questions, see pages vii and viii.

1. The following table shows the distribution of membranes in two types of cells, a liver cell and a hormone secreting cell from the pancreas. For each organelle, the amount of membrane is expressed as a percentage of the total amount of membrane in the cell.

Membrane type	% of total cell membrane	
	Liver cell	Pancreatic cell
Plasma membrane	2	5
Rough endoplasmic reticulum	35	60
Smooth endoplasmic reticulum	16	1
Golgi	9	10
Mitochondria outer membrane	7	4
Mitochondria inner membrane	28	16
Others	3	4

(a) Explain why there is a difference between the rough endoplasmic reticulum values for the two cell types. (3)

(b) (i) What is the ratio between inner membrane and outer membrane values for the mitochondria of the cells? (1)

(ii) Give a **structural** explanation for this ratio. (1)

(iii) Give a **functional** explanation for this ratio. (2)

(c) The cells of the liver play an important part in lipid metabolism and in the detoxification of foreign molecules. Give **one** piece of evidence from the table which appears to confirm this role. (1)

(d) Suggest a reason for the **similarity** in the values for Golgi. (1)

(e) (i) If the table had included a prokaryotic cell, within which of the following ranges would the value for plasma membrane lie?

0 – 20   20 – 40   40 – 60   60 – 80   80 – 100 (1)

(ii) Explain your choice. (1)

(Total 11 marks)
WJEC 1998

2. The menstrual cycle is controlled by the endocrine system whilst the cardiac cycle is controlled mainly by the nervous system. Suggest the advantages of using different control systems for the two cycles.

(Total 6 marks)

NEAB 1998

3. (a) Adrenaline increases the rate of conversion of glycogen to glucose.

    (i) Under what conditions is adrenaline normally secreted? (1)

    (ii) Explain how the release of adrenaline during exercise is of benefit to the body. (2)

(b) The diagram shows how adrenaline affects a target cell.

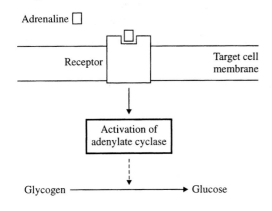

(Adenylate cyclase is also known as adenyl cyclase.)

    (i) Explain how proteins are suited to their function as receptors. (2)

    (ii) Describe the precise function of adenylate cyclase. (2)

    (iii) Explain how a single molecule of adrenaline can lead to the formation of many molecules of glucose. (3)

(Total 10 marks)

AEB 1998

4. The following questions relate to the mammalian endocrine system.

(a) Name **two** hormones which have the effect of raising the metabolic rate. (2)

(b) Give **one** example of a pair of hormones which produce opposite effects. (2)

(c) Give **one** example of opposite effects being produced by different concentrations of the same hormone. (2)

(d) Name **one** hormone which controls the concentration of a named ion. (1)

(e) Name **one** hormone which affects the retention or expulsion of water by the kidney. Briefly explain how it achieves this effect. (2)

(f) Name **one** hormone which brings about a rise in blood pressure. Briefly explain how it achieves this effect. (2)

(g) Name an endocrine organ which is an exocrine gland as well as an endocrine gland. (1)

(h) A trophic hormone is one which stimulates another endocrine gland to secrete. Name **two** such hormones and in each case state its target organ. (4)

(i) The pituitary gland is often described as the 'master gland' of the endocrine system. Briefly justify this title. (2)

(j) Give **two** examples of diseases caused by under-secretion of a hormone. (2)

(Total 20 marks)

5. Endocrine glands do the secreting in the endocrine system; neurones do the secreting in the nervous system. Explain this statement. (Total 5 marks)

6. Give a brief illustrated account of how hormones are believed to affect their target cells. (Total 6 marks)

Chapter 22

Reception of stimuli

It is obviously important that organisms should be aware of conditions around them so as to respond appropriately to any changes that may occur. These changes, or stimuli, may be local, such as a prick with a pin, or more general, such as the intensity of illumination.

In animals, stimuli are registered by **receptors** from which impulses pass to the nervous system. The receptors consist of **receptor cells** (also called **sensory cells**) which may be single, scattered more or less uniformly over the whole body, or concentrated to form a **sense organ**. In some animals the sense organs reach a high degree of elaboration – the mammalian eye and ear for example.

In this chapter we shall consider the structure and functioning of individual receptor cells, and then explore how these are integrated to form complex sense organs.

Support

Types of receptors

There are four main types of receptor, distinguished by the type of stimulation to which each responds:

- **Chemoreceptors** are stimulated by chemicals, for example receptors mediating the senses of smell and taste, and receptors that detect changes in the concentration of carbon dioxide or oxygen in the blood.

- **Mechanoreceptors** are sensitive to mechanical deformation, for example receptors sensitive to touch, pressure, tension (stretch), sounds (ear) and displacement of the body. Mechanoreceptors specifically concerned with giving details of position and movement are termed **proprioceptors**, and they are important in balance and locomotion.

- **Photoreceptors** are stimulated by light, for example the eyes of vertebrates and the scattered light-sensitive cells of invertebrates such as the earthworm.

- **Thermoreceptors** are stimulated by temperature, for example receptors located in mammalian skin, sensitive to warmth and cold.

A distinction can be made between receptors at or near the surface of the body which detect changes in the external environment and receptors inside the body which register internal changes such as the concentration of carbon dioxide in the blood, the degree of tension in the muscles, or the position of the head relative to gravity. These two types of receptor are known as **exteroceptors** and **interoceptors** respectively.

22.1 Receptor cells

The essential job of receptor cells is to transfer energy associated with a stimulus to an electrical change in a nerve, i.e. the nerve impulse. For example, photoreceptor cells transfer energy from light to nerve impulses, and thermoreceptor cells transfer heat energy to nerve impulses.

Each type of receptor cell is specialised in position and structure to respond to one kind of stimulus. For example, receptor cells in the nose have tufts of sensory processes which are sensitive to odorous airborne molecules that impinge upon them (*figure 22.1*).

A receptor cell may be a specialised cell which makes synaptic contact with a sensory neurone, or it may be part of the sensory neurone itself – the cell body perhaps or the ends of dendrites leading from it. The receptor cells in the nose, for example, are the cell bodies of sensory neurones whose axons go straight to the brain.

20 μm

Figure 22.1 Scanning electron micrograph of sensory processes projecting from a receptor cell in the olfactory epithelium in the nose. The receptor cell is coloured blue. These particular receptor cells are chemoreceptors, responsible for our sense of smell (olfaction). Their processes are stimulated by odorous airborne molecules that impinge upon them. The receptor cell is surrounded by supporting epithelial cells with microvilli. The microvilli are exceptionally clear in this picture.

What do receptor cells do?

The job of a receptor cell is to respond to a specific stimulus by discharging an action potential in the sensory nerve fibre. This has been demonstrated in a wide range of animals by exposing sensory nerve fibres and placing them in contact with recording electrodes connected to an oscilloscope (*page 350*), When the receptor cells are stimulated by appropriate stimuli, action potentials appear on the screen of the oscilloscope.

The sensitivity of some receptors is astonishing. For example, the hair-like mechanoreceptors of certain insects will respond to a deflection of as little as 3.6 nm, a property which makes them highly sensitive to airborne sounds. Similarly, the chemoreceptors on the antennae of certain moths are stimulated by a single molecule of scent. So sensitive are these chemoreceptors that males of the Chinese saturnid moth *Arctias selene* can locate females as far as 10 km away.

It is easier to demonstrate what a receptor does than to show how it does it. Small and often inaccessible, most receptor cells defy investigation by standard physiological techniques. However, certain receptor cells are sufficiently large and accessible for physiologists to carry out experiments on them. These include **muscle spindles** and a type of receptor in the skin called a **Pacinian corpuscle** (*extension box below*). Physiologists have inserted microelectrodes into such receptors and have recorded the electrical changes which take place when they are stimulated.

Part 4

Extension

The skin as a sense organ

We are literally encased in our largest sense organ, the skin. One of the skin's most important functions is to inform us of changes in our immediate surroundings. This it does with the help of five main types of receptor shown in the illustration and summarised below.

- **Touch receptors** Several types of mechanoreceptors, located in the more superficial part of the skin, are sensitive to touch. Those sensitive to light touch are concentrated in certain regions such as the fingertips and the tip of the tongue. In addition, nerve endings wrapped round the bases of the hair follicles are stimulated by movements of the hairs.

- **Pressure receptors** These are located in the deeper part of the skin. The one shown in the illustration (a Pacinian corpuscle) consists of the end of an axon encased in a capsule made of concentric layers of connective tissue, rather like an onion. Stimulation is caused by distortion of the capsule when pressure is applied to the skin.

- **Pain receptors** Free nerve endings below, and in places within, the epidermis are sensitive to excessive stimulation or damage to the skin. They send impulses to the brain which give rise to the sensation of pain. This sequence protects the body from potential harm by initiating avoiding reactions such as the withdrawal reflex described on page 346.

- **Warmth receptors** Thermoreceptors consisting of branched nerve endings surrounded by loose connective tissue, are sensitive to skin temperatures between about 30 and 43°C. The rate of discharge of impulses from these receptors increases as the temperature rises.

- **Cold receptors** Thermoreceptors consisting of branched nerve endings surrounded by a connective tissue capsule, are sensitive to skin temperatures between about 20 and 35°C. Their rate of discharge of impulses increases as the temperature falls.

The distinction between the different kinds of skin receptor is not always clear cut. For example, touch receptors may be stimulated by pressure, and pressure receptors by touch (pressure is really just prolonged touch).

Other functions of the skin and its role in temperature regulation, page 303

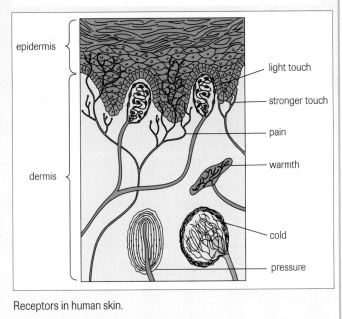

Receptors in human skin.

How is a generator potential created?

Research on Pacinian corpuscles has shown how the generator potential is created. Mechanical distortion of the receptor cell causes channels to open in the plasma membrane. Sodium ions then enter the cell and produce the generator potential. It is thought that the greater the intensity of the stimulus, the greater the number of channels that are opened.

Of course, the fact that Pacinian corpuscles work this way does not mean that all receptor cells do so too. In fact it is known that certain receptor cells, such as those in the eye, work differently (*page 388*).

How receptor cells work

On receiving a stimulus, the sensitive part of the receptor cell develops a local non-conducted positive charge called the **generator potential**. The generator potential is caused by depolarisation of the membrane surrounding this part of the cell, brought about by movement of ions similar to that which takes place in the transmission of nerve impulses (*page 350*).

The size of the generator potential depends on the intensity of the stimulus. If the stimulus is weak, only a slight potential develops. However, if the stimulus is strong enough, the generator potential may build up to such an extent that it reaches the necessary level, or **threshold**, to fire off an **action potential** in the nerve fibre (*figures 22.2 and 22.3*).

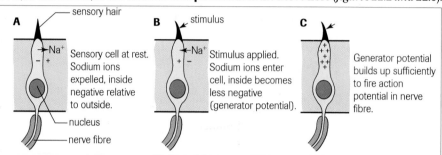

Figure 22.2 These schematic diagrams show the development of a generator potential and firing of an action potential (impulse) when a receptor cell is stimulated. In the hypothetical receptor cell shown here, stimulation is achieved by a slight deflection of the sensory hair.

If the generator potential is maintained after an action potential has been conducted away, a second one will be fired off. Generally action potentials will continue to be discharged as long as the generator potential remains above the threshold (*figure 22.4*).

Frequency of discharge

Since the generator potential was discovered, a number of interesting facts about it have emerged.

In the first place it has been found that the larger the generator potential, the shorter the interval between successive action potentials. In other words the size of the generator potential (which itself depends on the intensity of stimulation) determines the frequency of action potentials discharged from the receptor. Thus a weak stimulus brings about a comparatively small generator potential and a low-frequency discharge of impulses in the nerve fibre; a stronger stimulus produces a larger generator potential and a higher frequency discharge of impulses.

And there is a further point. The larger the generator potential, the longer it takes to fall below the firing threshold after stimulation has ceased. This means that the total number of impulses fired off in a nerve fibre is greater with stronger stimuli.

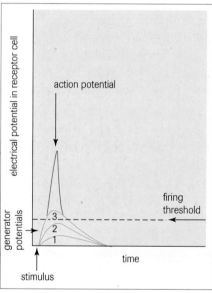

Figure 22.3 The electrical changes which develop in a receptor cell when stimulated with three separate stimuli of increasing intensity. The generator potentials produced by the first two stimuli are too small to reach the firing threshold, so they fail to initiate action potentials. However, the third stimulus produces a generator potential which reaches the firing threshold and causes an action potential to be discharged.

Figure 22.4 When a receptor cell is stimulated with a prolonged stimulus, action potentials continue to be discharged for as long as the generator potential remains above the firing threshold.

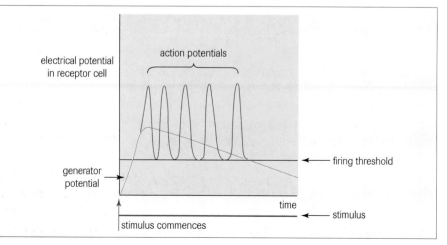

These facts provide an explanation of the everyday experience that strong stimuli produce larger, more prolonged responses than weak stimuli. For example, you would respond more violently if you were hit by a tennis ball than if a fly landed on you. There is more about these graded responses in Chapter 23.

Adaptation

If a steady stimulus is maintained, the generator potential gradually declines and the frequency of action potentials decreases. Eventually the generator potential may fall below the firing threshold and no further action potentials are discharged. When this state is reached the receptor is said to be **adapted**. You can see this in figure 22.4.

The speed at which a receptor adapts depends on the size and duration of its generator potential in relation to the firing threshold. These in turn depend on the properties of its membrane. Some receptors adapt rapidly, others slowly or not at all. The one in figure 22.4 is a rapidly adapting receptor and only five action potentials are discharged.

Adaptation protects the organism from excessive discharge of impulses in its sensory nerves. To illustrate the usefulness of this, think what happens if you put on a coarse shirt. At first the tickling sensation is almost intolerable, but within half an hour or so the unpleasant feeling disappears. This is because the tactile receptors in your skin stop firing impulses.

Of course it is not only receptors that adapt in this way. Synapses do so too (*page 359*), and it is sometimes difficult to decide whether an animal's failure to respond to repeated stimulation is due to adaptation of its receptors or failure of synapses in the nervous system.

▶ Habituation, page 440

Fusion of stimuli

If a receptor cell is stimulated repetitively, the stimuli can be detected separately only if the frequency is not too great. To be detectable individually, the frequency must be sufficiently low for the generator potential produced by each stimulus to die down before the next stimulus is received.

If the frequency of stimulation is increased, there comes a point when the generator potentials fuse, resulting in a continual stream of action potentials being discharged from the receptor. When this point is reached the stimuli, instead of being detected separately, fuse into one continuous stimulus.

The initial events in the reception of a stimulus

We have seen that sensory cells do their job by developing a generator potential which fires off action potentials. But how does a stimulus create a generator potential in the first place? In the case of mechanoreceptors, physical disturbance of the cell opens up ion channels in the plasma membrane which depolarise the membrane locally, just as happens in nerve cells. For example, bending of the sensory hair in the hypothetical tactile receptor cell in figure 22.2 depolarises the membrane in that region of the cell.

In other receptors the mechanism may be less direct. In the photoreceptors of the eye, for example, the stimulus sets into motion a chain of chemical reactions which depolarises the plasma membrane.

But whether the mechanism is direct or indirect, the generator potential provides the link between the stimulus and the impulse which is fired off in the nerve. In other words the generator potential transduces the stimulus into a propagated electrical signal.

To carry out this transduction efficiently, receptor cells are often massed together to form localised **sense organs**. A typical sense organ includes many supplementary structures in addition to the receptor cells themselves. These supplementary structures protect the receptor cells and ensure that they receive the kind of stimuli to which they are adapted to respond. To illustrate this let us look briefly at two of our sense organs, the eye and ear.

The structure of the human eye is shown diagrammatically in figure 22.5. The eyes of other mammals conform to this general plan.

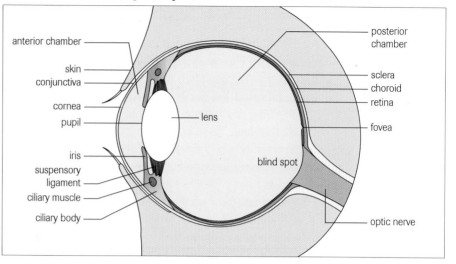

Figure 22.5 Diagrammatic section of the human eye. The light-sensitive photoreceptor cells are located in the retina which lines most of the inside of the eyeball. All the other parts of the eye (lens, cornea, iris, etc.) protect the retina and ensure that it receives the right kind of stimulation.

The photoreceptor cells are concentrated in the **retina** which lines most of the interior of the eyeball. The spherical shape of the eyeball is maintained by the jelly-like **vitreous humour** which fills the **posterior chamber**. The retina is nourished by the **choroid** layer which is highly vascular and protected by a thick layer of connective tissue, the **sclera**. Heavy pigmentation in the choroid layer shields the retina and prevents light being reflected within the eye.

The front of the eye is protected by the thick, transparent **cornea** which is continuous with the sclera. The cornea is covered by a delicate and highly sensitive membrane called the **conjunctiva**. Behind the cornea is the **anterior chamber** which is filled with watery **aqueous humour**. Projecting into the anterior chamber is the **iris**, a circular structure just in front of the **lens**.

The anterior part of the eye is mainly concerned with refracting (i.e. bending) light rays and bringing them to focus on the retina. The structures which do the refracting are the lens and the cornea. The posterior part of the eye, with the retina, is concerned with transducing the light rays into nerve impulses which are transmitted to the optic nerve and thence to the brain.

The lens and cornea

The lens is like a transparent rubber balloon filled with fluid. It is held in position by slender fibres which make up the **suspensory ligament**. The fibres are attached to the **ciliary body** which encircles the lens. The ciliary body contains smooth muscle fibres arranged mainly in a circular direction and controlled by the autonomic nervous system.

In its normal state, the lens is more or less spherical. When the ciliary muscle relaxes, the edge of the lens is pulled outwards, giving it a flattened shape; when the ciliary muscle contracts, the tension on the lens is released so that it returns to its more spherical shape. By changing its shape, the lens can alter its refractive power and thus **accommodate** for near and far objects. It becomes flatter for distant objects and rounder for closer objects. In this way an object can be kept in focus whatever its distance from the eye, provided it is not *too* close (*figure 22.6*).

The shortest distance from the eyes at which an object can be seen in focus is called the **near point**. An object viewed closer than this gives a blurred image because the lens cannot increase its refracting power any more. You can see this for yourself by moving a pencil closer and closer to your eyes. (Be careful!)

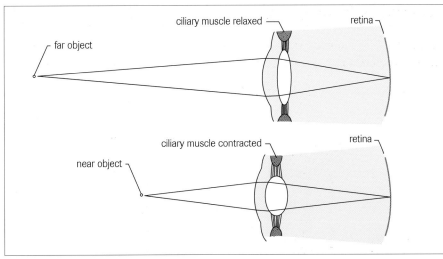

Figure 22.6 Accommodation of the eye.
A When a far object is viewed, the lens is flattened by *relaxation* of the ciliary muscle, which springs outwards, increasing the tension on the lens.
B When a near object is viewed, the curvature of the lens is increased by *contraction* of the ciliary muscle, which releases the tension on the lens, allowing it to adopt a more spherical shape. In its more spherical state the lens bends (refracts) the light rays more strongly, ensuring that they come to a focus on the retina.

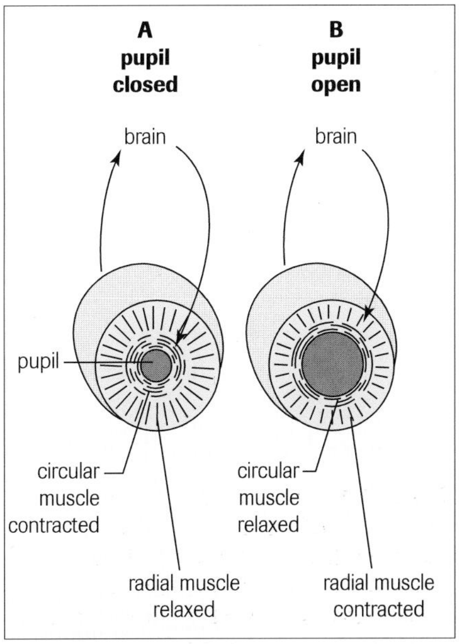

The cornea refracts light rays too: in fact most of the eye's refraction takes place at the air–cornea interface, as this is where the largest change in refractive index occurs. That is why you cannot see very clearly under water without goggles. However, the cornea cannot *vary* its refractive power and therefore plays no part in accommodation.

The iris

The iris surrounds the aperture, or **pupil**, of the eye. It contains two sets of smooth muscle fibres, one circular and the other radial. Differential contraction of these two sets of muscles has the effect of varying the size of the pupil, like opening and closing the iris diaphragm of a microscope or camera. Closure of the pupil is triggered by light, so excessive light is prevented from falling on the retina. This **pupil reflex** is summarised in figure 22.7.

The iris muscles, like those of the ciliary body, are controlled by the autonomic nervous system. Atropine, which stops the action of acetylcholine, prevents the circular muscles of the iris from contracting. To dilate the pupils opticians sometimes put a few drops of atropine into their patients' eyes before examining the retina with an opthalmoscope. Film stars sometimes do the same thing to keep their pupils open in bright light.

Figure 22.7 The opening and closing of the pupil is controlled by a reflex.
A If the illumination is increased, nerve impulses are transmitted from the retina to the brain and thence to the iris, making the circular muscle contract and the radial muscle relax, so the pupil constricts.
B If the illumination is decreased, the opposite occurs: the radial muscle contracts and the circular muscle relaxes, so the pupil dilates.

How atropine works, page 358

Extension

Seeing in depth

In common with other primates, both our eyes are at the front of the head and face forward. Each eye sees a slightly different aspect of the same object. In the brain the two images are fused to give us a single three-dimensional view of the object.

Seeing a single object through two eyes is called **binocular vision** and it enables us to see in depth and judge distances. Other factors help with this, for example our knowledge (from experience) of the relative sizes of everyday objects, shadows and, in the case of moving objects, their apparent movement relative to each other. For example, when you move in a particular direction, near objects seem to move in the opposite direction whereas distant objects move in the same direction.

Seeing in depth is believed to have been important in evolution as an adaptation for living in trees. Obviously accurate judging of distances is essential for an animal whose livelihood depends on swinging from branch to branch.

Some common defects of the eye

The most common defects of the eye are **short-sightedness** and **long-sightedness**.

■ Short-sighted people can focus on objects close to, but not far away from, the eye. This is caused by the eyeball being too long (or the lens too strong) with the result that the point where the light rays converge is in front of the retina. The condition can be corrected by wearing spectacles with concave lenses which bend the light rays outwards before they reach the eye (*illustration 1*) or by contact lenses which alter the shape of the cornea.

■ Long-sighted people can focus on objects far away from, but not close to, the eye. This is caused by the eyeball being too short (or the lens too weak) with the result that the point where the light rays converge is behind the retina. The condition can be corrected by wearing spectacles with convex lenses which bend the light rays inwards before they reach the eye (*illustration 2*) or by contact lenses which alter the shape of the cornea.

In elderly people, the lens tends to harden so its shape cannot be changed. Accommodation for near objects becomes difficult, so the person becomes long-sighted. This is why elderly people sometimes hold the book they are reading a long way away. Again, the remedy is to

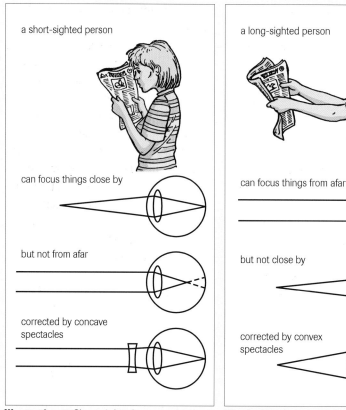

Illustration 1 Short-sightedness

Illustration 2 Long-sightedness

wear spectacles with convex lenses. Some people have a defect of the eye called an **astigmatism**. This is caused by the cornea or lens (or both) being unevenly curved, with the result that light rays in one plane may converge in front of the retina whereas in another plane they converge behind the retina. In other words the person is short-sighted in one plane and long-sighted in another. Astigmatism

can be corrected by wearing spectacles with specially made lenses, or by contact lenses.

Another defect of the eyes is **cataract.** In this condition the lens becomes opaque, resulting in blurred vision. It has a number of different causes, the most common being ageing. It is usually treated by removing the lens surgically and replacing it with an artificial one made of plastic.

The retina

The retina contains two types of photoreceptor cells: cones and rods.

■ **Cones** are found over most of the retina but are particularly concentrated in the centre, directly behind the lens. This is called the **fovea**, and it is the part of the retina that we use when we look directly at an object.

The cones enable us to perceive the environment in conditions of good illumination. In other words they are responsible for **daylight vision**. They enable us to see things clearly and sharply, and in colour. However, they are relatively insensitive to low light intensities, and this is why they will only work in good light.

Image inversion

Suppose you look at a person. The illustration shows how light rays reflected from the person, are transmitted through your eye. Notice that the light rays from the head cross the light rays from the feet. The result is that the image is upside down on the retina. The same thing happens when light rays pass through the lens of a camera.

Why then don't we see everything upside down? The answer lies with the brain. The brain analyses and interprets information which it receives from the retina in such a way that we see things the right way up.

The remarkable thing is that the brain can modify its interpretation of the retinal image according to circumstances. This was demonstrated some years ago by a fascinating experiment. A human volunteer was given a pair of specially made spectacles fitted with prisms which caused him to see everything upside down. However, after a few hours the brain started to make the necessary adjustment and he began to see things the right way up again.

The brain did not make the adjustment all at once. To begin with the subject saw things the right way up for a short while, and then upside down again. It was a week or more before the adjustment was complete and things appeared the right way up all the time. Apparently some visual anomalies still occurred and individual objects tended to look peculiar. However, the adjustment was sufficiently good for the person to do such things as catching balls and riding a bicycle.

There was an interesting sequel to this experiment. When the person eventually took the spectacles off, everything went upside down again and the process of adjustment had to be repeated.

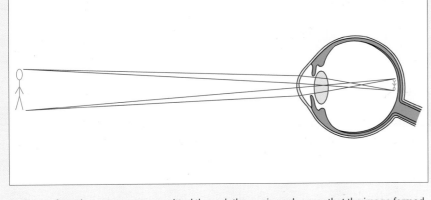

Light rays from the person are transmitted through the eye in such a way that the image formed on the retina is upside down.

- **Rods** lie outside the foveal region in the more peripheral part of the retina. We use this part of the retina when we look at an object out of the corner of our eyes.

  The rods enable us to perceive the environment in conditions of low illumination. In other words they are responsible for **night vision**. They are sensitive to very small intensities of light, which is why they can operate at low levels of illumination. However, they do not register things as clearly and sharply as the cones, and they cannot respond to different colours, so they only allow us to see things in black, white and various shades of grey.

When do we use our rods, and when do we use our cones? Here is a very rough guide:

- When you are reading comfortably in a good light you are using your cones.
- When you are reading with difficulty in a poor light you are using your cones *and* rods.
- When you are looking at the countryside on a moonlit night you are using your rods.

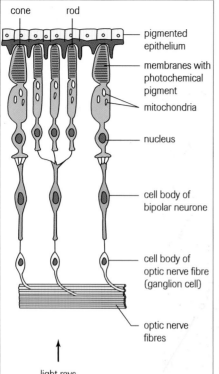

cone rod

pigmented epithelium

membranes with photochemical pigment

mitochondria

nucleus

cell body of bipolar neurone

cell body of optic nerve fibre (ganglion cell)

optic nerve fibres

light rays

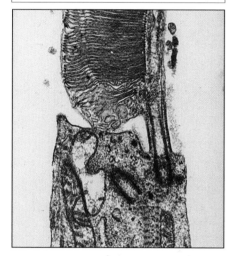

Figure 22.8 Structure of the retina.
Top Simplified diagram of a small part of the retina. Rods and cones make synaptic connection with bipolar neurones, which in turn synapse with nerve fibres that form the optic nerve. Notice that the photoreceptor cells lie towards the outer part of the retina, and the bipolar neurones and optic nerve fibres lie towards the inside where the light rays come from. This means that light rays have to traverse a thin layer of nerve fibres and cell bodies before they reach the light-sensitive cells.
Bottom Electron micrograph of the upper end of a rod showing numerous parallel membranes on which the molecules of the photochemical pigment rhodopsin are located, and, further back, prominent mitochondria which provide energy for the resynthesis of rhodopsin after it has been broken down. Magnification ×15 000.

Interactions between the photoreceptors

The way the rods and cones are arranged in the retina is shown in figure 22.8. Each one makes synaptic connection with a **bipolar neurone**, so called because two dendrites extend from its cell body. The bipolar neurones make synaptic connection with nerve fibres which run over the surface of the retina and converge at the blind spot, where they pass through the back of the eye as the optic nerve (*Figure 22.5 on page 384*).

The diagram in figure 22.8 is greatly simplified. In reality the photoreceptor cells are interconnected by horizontal neurones, as are the bipolar neurones and ganglion cells. This allows considerable interaction to take place between neighbouring photoreceptors. For example, when you look at a view, the photoreceptor cells in one region of the retina may inhibit the photoreceptor cells in an adjacent region. Indeed, the photoreceptor cells in the two regions may inhibit each other, but to different degrees. This is called **lateral inhibition**.

The importance of this from the visual point of view is that it can heighten the contrast at light–dark boundaries and therefore enhance contours, an effect which is often accentuated by artists in their drawings and paintings. A similar process occurs in other receptors. For example, in the human ear it may lead to a sharpening of the sense of pitch.

How does light stimulate the rods and cones?

For a generator potential to develop in a rod or cone, the light must first be absorbed by a **photochemical pigment**. Rods contain a reddish photochemical pigment called **rhodopsin** (also called **visual purple**). Briefly, when light strikes a rod the photochemical pigment is broken down, and this leads to the development of a generator potential. The pigment is then rapidly resynthesised and can be used again. Details are given in the extension box below.

This resynthesis is experienced when we enter a dimly lit room from bright light. At first nothing can be seen, but gradually we begin to make out our surroundings. Vision becomes possible when the photochemical pigment, previously broken down by the bright light, has been regenerated. This is known as **dark adaptation**.

The rod is structurally adapted to carry out its functions. Stacks of sheet-like membranes in the receptive part of the cell increase the surface area for holding the pigment molecules, and numerous mitochondria just behind this region supply the necessary energy.

Though the details are different, cones operate on the same principle as the rods. The initial process in the receptor mechanism involves the splitting of a photochemical pigment similar to rhodopsin. There are several forms of this pigment, known collectively as **iodopsin**. The cone pigment is less readily broken down than rhodopsin and it regenerates more slowly. That is why the cones only function in conditions of good illumination.

Having discussed the way rods and cones work, we can use this information to explain three important properties of the eye: its sensitivity, precision and colour discrimination.

> **Extension**
>
> ### How rhodopsin excites the rods
>
> Rhodopsin is a complex protein, **opsin**, conjugated with a comparatively simple light-absorbing component called **retinene**.
>
> Retinene, an aldehyde of vitamin A (retinol), can exist in two different isomeric forms known as '**cis**' and '**trans**' **isomers**. When a quantum of light strikes a molecule of rhodopsin, the retinene changes from the 'cis' form to the 'trans' form. This initiates the splitting of the rhodopsin into opsin and retinene, which in turn triggers a chain of further reactions leading to the excitation of the rod.
>
> The resynthesis of rhodopsin from opsin and retinene takes place by a series of energy-requiring reactions.

Visual sensation and the brain

Our eyes monitor the environment and send signals to the brain. The brain integrates the signals and produces the appropriate visual image.

The actual visual sensation which we experience is not always an exact representation of what is registered by our eyes. This is because the brain, susceptible to all sorts of influences past and present, modifies the image so that we see what our brain is conditioned to see.

The brain affects what we see in five main ways:

- **It interprets retinal images**, and in so doing may prejudice us to see objects in a particular way. A well-known example of this is shown in illustration 1.

- **It fills in gaps**, enabling us to recognise objects which would otherwise be unrecognisable. It is remarkable how imprecise an object can be for us to recognise it.

- **It creates images** which may mislead us into thinking that we have seen something when we have not. Sometimes a visual experience may arise entirely within the brain and have no basis in reality at all.

- **It filters out unnecessary images** so that much of what we see is barely registered by the conscious brain. A driver, concentrating on what is in front of the car, is aware of only a tiny fraction of what he or she actually sees.

- **It distorts things**, giving rise to optical illusions and other visual aberrations. Some examples are given in illustration 2. Optical illusions are fun and can sometimes be useful. For example, they are used by stage designers and advertisers to create visual effects, and by architects to overcome restrictions in the scale and dimensions of their buildings.

Illustration 1 Do you see a young girl or an old woman? Can you switch from one to the other? What sort of influences determine what you see?

Illustration 2 This picture of a living room contains four well-known optical illusions. The guitar at the front looks smaller than the one behind; the rear edge of the carpet looks much shorter than its front-to-back dimension; the front edge of the carpet looks shorter than the bottom width of the back wall; and the vertical lines on the wallpaper on either side of the fireplace don't look parallel.

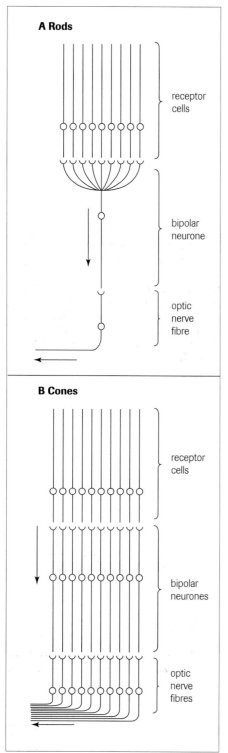

Figure 22.9 The greater sensitivity of rods, compared with cones, can be explained by their connections in the retina.
A shows how a group of rods converge onto a single optic nerve fibre. This allows summation to occur and increases overall sensitivity.
B shows how the cones are arranged. In the central part of the fovea each cone has its own optic nerve fibre.

Sensitivity

High sensitivity is a property of the rods; this is what makes the eye capable of seeing in low illumination. The sensitivity of the rods is achieved partly by the fact that a single sensory cell can be excited by a very small amount of light.

However, there is more to it than this. In the human eye there are about 150 million sensory cells (about 7 million cones, the rest being rods) but only one million fibres in the optic nerve. This means that a large group of rods must share, or converge onto, a single optic nerve fibre. Microscopic examination of the retina shows that this is indeed the case (*figure 22.9A*). Numerous rods make synaptic contact with a single bipolar neurone which in turn connects with a single optic nerve fibre. This is known as **retinal convergence**.

The importance of retinal convergence is that it enables the eye to be more sensitive than it would otherwise be. Look at it this way. A faint beam of light hitting a single rod may not stimulate the rod sufficiently to generate an action potential in the bipolar neurone attached to it. However, several rods stimulated together combine to excite the bipolar neurone.

On the basis of extremely careful experiments it has been estimated that six rods stimulated simultaneously are enough to fire an impulse in an optic nerve fibre. We have met this process of summation before in connection with synaptic transmission (*page 358*), and now we see how it can effectively increase the sensitivity of a receptor. It is interesting that the cones, which operate in daylight and therefore do not need to be so sensitive, show far less convergence. Indeed, in the centre of the fovea each cone has its own optic nerve fibre (*figure 22.9B*).

Precision

Imagine yourself looking at two black dots on a piece of paper which is gradually moved further and further away. There comes a point when the two dots can no longer be distinguished, or *resolved*, as separate entities so they appear as one. The ability of the eye to resolve two or more stimuli separated spatially is known as its **visual acuity**. The vertebrate eye has particularly high visual acuity, a property that it owes to the cones. What is it about the cones that makes this possible?

To answer this question consider what must happen if two dots are to be distinguished. If their images fall on the same cone they will obviously not be perceived separately. Even if they fall on next-door cones they cannot be distinguished, for the result will be the same as a single image falling on both cones. To be seen as two separate dots their images must fall on two different cones separated by at least one between. This principle is illustrated in Figure 22.10.

From this it follows that the closer together the cones, the higher will be the acuity of the eye. The structure of the retina fits in exactly with this idea. Most of the 7 million cones are concentrated in or around the fovea in the centre of the retina. The fovea is not much more than a millimetre across and the cones in it are thinner than elsewhere, enabling more of them to be packed into this small area.

If the cones are to send two separate signals to the CNS, they must obviously connect with different optic nerve fibres. Plainly they would lose their identity if they were to share the same sensory pathway. For this reason cones show little or no convergence. In the central part of the fovea each cone has its own bipolar neurone which connects with a single optic nerve fibre. This, coupled with the close proximity of the cones to each other, enables the eye to discriminate between closely spaced objects. In other words it increases the resolving power of the eye. The same principle applies to the sense of touch.

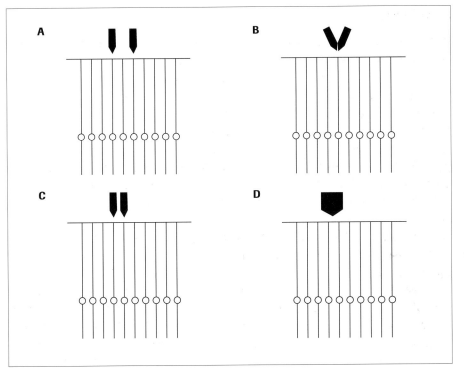

Figure 22.10 The principle of visual acuity.
A For two dots to be distinguished (resolved) their images must activate two cones separated by at least one in between.
B If the images fall on a single cone, the dots cannot be distinguished and will appear as a single dot. **C** The dots cannot be distinguished if their images fall on next-door cones, as this is no different from a single image falling on the two cones (**D**).

Colour vision

The generally accepted theory of colour vision, the **trichromatic theory**, depends on the principle that all colours can be produced by mixing the primary colours (blue, green and red) in various proportions.

The theory proposes that in the retina there are three functionally distinct types of cone, each sensitive to one of these three wavelengths. It is thought that a particular colour is perceived by its wavelengths stimulating one, two or all three cone types to a particular extent. In other words the sensation, the colour 'seen', is determined by the relative excitation of the three types of receptor cells.

Can it be shown that there are in fact three types of cone in the retina? The answer is yes. To mention one experiment, the particular wavelengths of light absorbed by single cones have been determined by projecting very fine beams of light of known wavelength through an isolated retina placed on a slide on a microscope stage. After passing through the eyepiece, the intensity of light is measured by means of an extremely sensitive photomultiplier. The results are compared with light passing through a control tissue lacking photoreceptors.

These experiments, originally carried out by George Wald and his collaborators at Harvard University, have shown that there are three types of cone in the retina of humans and monkeys, each containing a different pigment with maximum absorption in, respectively, the blue, green and red parts of the spectrum (*figure 22.11*). The three pigments are different forms of iodopsin, which was mentioned on page 388.

The *intensity* of colour is determined by the absolute frequency at which impulses are discharged from the three receptors, the *type* of colour by the relative frequency of discharge from each. The brain also plays a vital part because it interprets the pattern of incoming signals.

Some people have red and green absorption curves that are so close together that they cannot distinguish between these two colours. They are **red-green colour blind**, a sex-linked inherited condition (*page 588*). In another type of colour blindness one of the three types of cone may be missing altogether. A person with this defect can only see colours formed by mixing *two* primary colours – the ones whose cones are present.

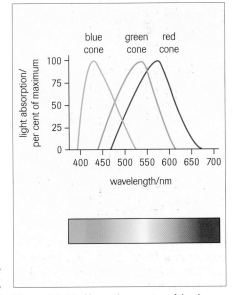

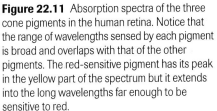

Figure 22.11 Absorption spectra of the three cone pigments in the human retina. Notice that the range of wavelengths sensed by each pigment is broad and overlaps with that of the other pigments. The red-sensitive pigment has its peak in the yellow part of the spectrum but it extends into the long wavelengths far enough to be sensitive to red.

The insect eye

Insects have a type of eye that contrasts interestingly with the vertebrate eye. There are some basic similarities – for example, there are photoreceptor cells which work in much the same way as ours. However, the way the photoreceptor cells are arranged is quite different.

The insect eye is composed of numerous 'mini-eyes', for which reason it is called a **compound eye**. The 'mini-eyes' are called **ommatidia**. Each ommatidium contains a group of photoreceptor cells which functions as a single unit (*illustration 1*).

Insects have a much lower visual acuity than vertebrates. The honey bee, for example, has an acuity about a hundredth of that of the human. It is said that an insect's view of the world is rather like looking at a newspaper photograph through a magnifying glass – dotty.

On the other hand, the ommatidia are extremely sensitive and the compound eyes cover a substantial area of the head which makes them very good at detecting movement over a wide field (*illustration 2*). This, aided by rapid transmission of impulses in the nervous system, means that an insect's reactions are usually very rapid – as is well known to anyone who has tried to swat a fly.

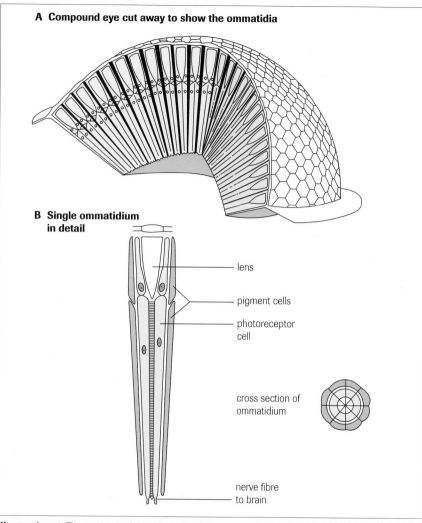

A Compound eye cut away to show the ommatidia

B Single ommatidium in detail

lens

pigment cells

photoreceptor cell

cross section of ommatidium

nerve fibre to brain

Illustration 1 The compound eye of a honey bee.

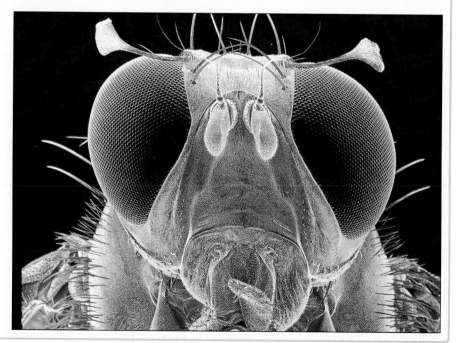

Illustration 2 In this photograph of the head of a fruit fly, notice how much of the head is covered by the compound eyes.

22.3 The ear and how we hear

Figure 22.12 shows the main parts of the human ear. It consists of three parts:

- an air-filled **outer ear**;
- an air-filled **middle ear**;
- a fluid-filled **inner ear**.

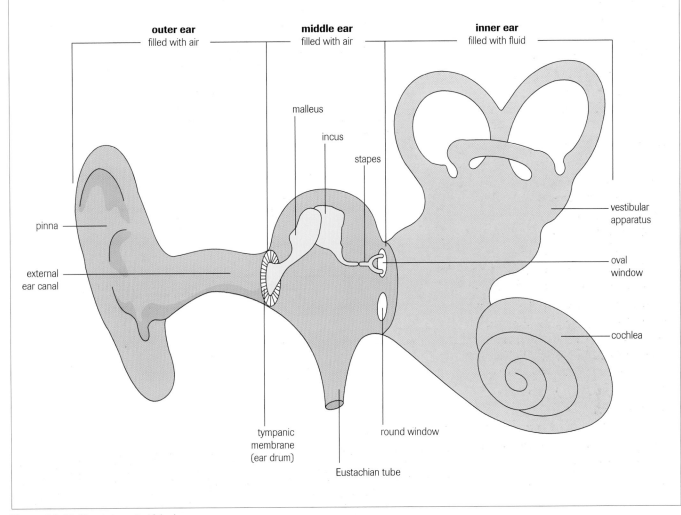

Figure 22.12 The main parts of the human ear.

The outer ear consists of the **pinna** ('ear flap') and **external ear canal** which leads to the **tympanic membrane (ear-drum)**. The middle ear is separated from the outer ear by the tympanic membrane and from the inner ear by an **oval window** and **round window**, each covered by a membrane.

Spanning the middle ear chamber from the tympanic membrane to the oval window are three tiny **ear ossicles** called the **malleus**, **incus** and **stapes**, or more colloquially **hammer**, **anvil** and **stirrup**. They are the smallest bones in the body and are held in place by slender ligaments and muscles. The **Eustachian tube**, which connects the middle ear with the pharynx, ensures that the air pressures on the two sides of the tympanic membrane are equal.

The inner ear, embedded in the side of the cranium, is made up of two main parts, the **vestibular apparatus** and a coiled tube called the **cochlea**. These are continuous with each other and filled with a lymph-like fluid derived from the blood. The vestibular apparatus is responsible for our sense of balance – more about that later. The cochlea is for hearing.

The cochlea

The inside of the cochlea is shown diagrammatically in figure 22.13. It is divided longitudinally into three parallel canals: the **vestibular canal** (connecting with the oval window), **the middle canal**, and the **tympanic canal** (connecting with the round window). The three canals are separated from each other by membranes: **Reissner's membrane** between the vestibular and middle canals, and the **basilar membrane** between the middle and tympanic canals. All three canals are filled with fluid: **endolymph** in the middle canal, and **perilymph** in the other two canals (*endo* means 'inner' and *peri* means 'outer').

Into the middle canal projects a shelf, the **tectorial membrane**, which runs parallel with the basilar membrane for the full length of the cochlea. Receptor cells span the gap between the basilar and tectorial membranes. Their bases are rooted in the basilar membrane where they are connected to nerve fibres that join the **auditory nerve**. At the other end they bear fine sensory hairs which just reach the tectorial membrane. This part of the cochlea, the part that actually responds to sound, is the **organ of Corti** (*figure 22.14*).

Figure 22.13 Highly schematic diagram illustrating the basic structure and mode of action of the auditory part of the human ear. The cochlea has been sectioned transversely close to its base so that its internal structure can be seen. The receptor cells are located in the organ of Corti which runs along the length of the cochlea. As with the eye, the purpose of the other structures is to protect the receptor cells and ensure that they receive the right kind of stimulation, which in this case is mechanical disturbance resulting from sound waves hitting the tympanic membrane. The arrows indicate the path taken by the sound waves through the ear.

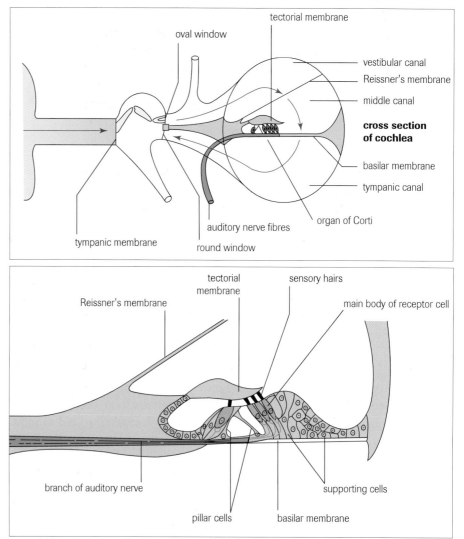

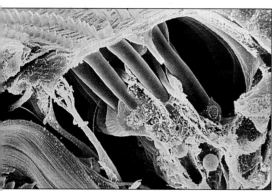

Figure 22.14 Structure of the organ of Corti. *Right* The organ of Corti as seen in a transverse section of the cochlea. The receptor cells are shown in pink, their sensory hairs extending to the tectorial membrane. It is possible that the pillar cells augment the stimulation process in some way. *Above* Scanning electron micrograph of a small part of an organ of Corti. The tectorial membrane has been removed, exposing the tufts of sensory hairs (orange) which project from the upper ends of the receptor cells (pink). Each receptor cell possesses up to 100 sensory hairs. Magnification ×700.

Hearing

How, then, do we hear? In simple terms what happens is this. Sound waves, amplified and directed by the pinna into the ear canal, impinge on the tympanic membrane which vibrates accordingly. The movements of the tympanic membrane are transmitted by the three ear ossicles to the oval window. This results in displacement of fluid in the vestibular canal, which in turn causes movement of Reissner's membrane. This displaces fluid in the middle canal which moves the basilar membrane, thereby displacing fluid in the tympanic canal. Displacement of this latter fluid is taken up by the elasticity of the membrane covering the round window.

Thus vibrations of the tympanic membrane, set up by sound waves hitting it, are transmitted via a series of ossicles, membranes and fluid-filled canals, to the basilar membrane. Here, deep in the inner ear, sensory stimulation takes place. Movement of the basilar membrane distorts the receptor cells of the organ of Corti, resulting in impulses being fired in the auditory nerve.

Intensity

The intensity, i.e. loudness, of a sound is related to the amplitude of the sound waves impinging upon the tympanic membrane. This in turn determines the amplitude with which the basilar membrane vibrates. Loud sounds, that is sound waves of large amplitude, bring about greater displacement of the basilar membrane than softer sounds. The result is that the receptor cells are stimulated more strongly, and larger volleys of impulses are discharged in the auditory nerve.

The human ear can only detect sounds within a certain range of intensities. The intensity of a sound is measured in decibels (dB). Figure 22.15 shows the range of sound intensities that a human being can tolerate, from the threshold to the loudest sound. Sounds above 120 dB can be painful and may cause immediate damage to the cochlea receptors. Long-term exposure to sounds over 85 dB can also damage the receptors, leading to partial loss of hearing, as has happened to workers in noisy industries and members of pop groups.

Pitch

The pitch of a sound is set by the frequency of the sound waves. High notes are caused by sound waves of high frequency, low notes by sound waves of lower frequency. The pitch of a sound determines the frequency at which the basilar membrane vibrates. Careful experiments on the inner ear have shown that the receptor cells in different regions of the cochlea respond to different frequencies. Those towards the apex respond to low notes while those towards the base respond to high notes.

How is this localisation of response in the cochlea accomplished? The mechanism depends on the fact that the basilar membrane gradually decreases in stiffness from the base of the cochlea to the apex. It is thought that movement of the ear ossicles sets up a travelling wave which passes along the basilar membrane for a certain distance, and then dies out. How far it gets depends on the frequency. High-frequency waves travel only a short distance, low-frequency waves much further. So, in effect, different parts of the cochlea respond to different frequencies. The sensation produced in the brain is determined by the pattern of impulses generated in the many fibres of the auditory nerve.

The human ear is only capable of detecting sounds within a certain range of frequencies. The frequency of a sound, i.e. the pitch or note, is measured in sound-wave cycles per second, one cycle per second being a Hertz (Hz). At its best, the human ear can detect sounds ranging in frequency from about 20 to 20 000 Hz. Within this range the average person can distinguish between approximately 2000 different pitches (notes), though trained musicians can do much better than this. Pitch discrimination is best between 1000 and 3000 Hz, which corresponds to the range encompassed by normal human speech.

Some animals have a much wider frequency range than we do. For example, dogs and cats can hear high-pitched sounds which are inaudible to humans, and bats can hear the ultrasonic squeaks which they make in order to locate objects in the dark. Changes occur with age: a young child can hear sounds at the top of the human range (about 20 000 Hz), but this ability is lost progressively as we get older.

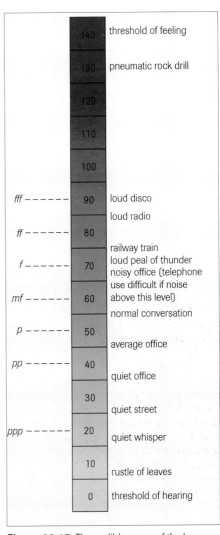

Figure 22.15 The audible range of the human ear expressed in decibels (dB) above the threshold of hearing. The threshold of hearing is the quietest sound which can just be heard by an average young person. This is a logarithmic scale – the loudest tolerable sound (120 dB) is actually one million million times as loud as the threshold sound. On the left are the approximate values for the markings on musical scores made by the conductor Leopold Stokowski: *ppp* extremely quiet, *pp* (pianissimo) very quiet, *p* (piano) quiet, *mf* (mezzo forte) moderately loud, *f* (forte) loud, *ff* (fortissimo) very loud: *fff*, extremely loud.

What do the ear ossicles do?

The ear ossicles are the smallest bones in the body. When pressure changes associated with sound waves reach the tympanic membrane, the latter vibrates in sympathy with the sound waves. The movements of the tympanic membrane are transmitted to the ear ossicles which vibrate in sympathy. The consequence is that the foot of the stapes moves backwards and forwards in the oval window at the same frequency as the movements of the tympanic membrane. In this way movements of the tympanic membrane are faithfully transmitted to the fluid in the inner ear.

But the ear ossicles do more than just transmit the movements – they also increase their force. This is necessary because the pressure changes created by the sound waves have to pass from air to water, and water is a much denser medium than air. The three ossicles articulate with each other in such a way as to form a lever system which increases the force sufficiently to move the fluid in the inner ear. The foot of the stapes fits neatly into the oval window, and when it moves forward it displaces the fluid in the inner ear. The fluid is, of course, incompressible and the pressure wave

thus created is taken up by the membrane covering the round window.

Muscles are attached to the ossicles. They run from the malleus and stapes to the wall of the middle ear chamber. When there is a loud sound the muscles contract and the movements of the ossicles are dampened down. This helps to prevent the receptor cells in the cochlea being damaged by excessive noise. However, the time-lag of this reflex is rather long, and it cannot cope with sudden loud sounds which rarely occur in nature but are all too common in our artificial environment.

Hearing loss – how technology can help

Guest author Geoffrey Curtis, a hearing-aid consultant, describes some recent advances in hearing-aid technology.

There are two main causes of hearing loss:

- **Conductive loss** is caused by a defect in the hearing process up to, but excluding, the receptor cells and sensory nerve.

- **Sensorineural loss** is caused by a defect in the receptor cells and/or sensory nerve fibres in the cochlea.

Nearly four million people in the United Kingdom have a degree of hearing loss which is, or could be, helped by a suitable **hearing aid**, and over 90 per cent of these cases have a sensorineural cause brought on by wear and tear within the cochlea as a natural part of the ageing process.

The problem is most severe at the high-frequency end of the auditory range. The reason for this is understandable when you think how the cochlea works. According to the travelling wave theory (*page 395*), all sound signals enter the cochlea at the high-frequency end and then travel along it to their own points of registration.

Imagine a pianist picking out a tune with one finger but doing so by dragging the finger across every note, depressing but not sounding it, from the top end of the keyboard down to the specific note required. Plainly there would be excessive wear and tear in the top range, but relatively little at the lower end.

It was originally thought that hearing aids could only help people with conductive loss. However, modern advances in hearing-aid technology have meant that now the majority of sensorineural cases can also be helped.

Early attempts at overcoming hearing problems included ear trumpets, speaking tubes and, more recently, rather cumbersome devices consisting of a microphone and power source pinned to the clothes in the chest area and connected to the ear by an electrical cord. However, thanks to miniaturisation, most hearing aids can now be worn either behind the pinna (**post-aural**) or inside it (**intra-aural**), though for very severe deafness powerful chest aids are still used.

The post-aural aid

A compact unit containing a power source and one or two microphones is placed immediately behind the pinna so as to pick up sound as close as possible to its normal reception point (*illustration 1*). The sound signals are then amplified by the instrument and passed down a plastic tube held inside the pinna by a moulded ear fitting. Advanced instruments have controls which enable the hearing-aid technician to tune the performance to the maximum benefit of the user. Further variations in the response can be made by modifying the ear mould so that maximum assistance is gained from the natural resonance of the ear canal.

Acoustic feedback tends to occur, as it does in any amplified sound system, when the amplified sound escapes and is picked up by the microphone and reamplified. In a hearing aid this can cause a high-pitched whistle which can be annoying for users and disconcerting for their friends. Otherwise this type of aid is very good and has improved the quality of life of many deaf people.

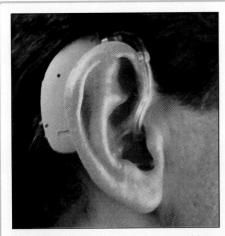

Illustration 1 A post-aural hearing aid. Volume and tone controls are at the back of the unit.

The intra-aural aid

In this case a microphone is placed within the pinna close to the opening of the ear canal (*illustration 2*). Indeed, the latest microchip and transistor technology enables very effective instruments to be worn entirely inside the ear canal with the microphone where the natural ear opening is located. Both positions ensure that sound signals are collected and amplified by the person's own pinna before they are picked up by the microphone.

These instruments are prescription-built to fit the exact contours of the person's ear, and they contain circuits which have been individually designed to give a response that makes maximum use of the user's residual hearing. Modern technology allows miniaturisation to such an extent that even the smallest intra-aural aids have enough controls to allow fine tuning by the technician.

An advantage of the canal type of instrument is that it leaves the inside of the pinna virtually empty. Recent research has shown that considerable amplification (particularly in the frequency range 3000 to 5000 Hz) is achieved by the pinna before the sound arrives at the microphone. This natural amplification has been found to be between 8 and 20 dB, depending on the exact configuration of the pinna, and it is therefore clear that this part of the ear acts as an effective pre-amplifier. This boost at the beginning of the hearing process means

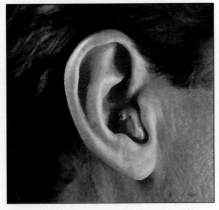

Illustration 2 An intra-aural hearing aid in position within the ear.

that the hearing aid does not have to amplify sounds so much, thus reducing distortion.

Latest developments

The mid-1990s saw the arrival of the **digital hearing aid** as opposed to the traditional analogue instrument. Both types of aid described above are now available in digital form.

The advantage of the digital aid is that it can sample the incoming signal efficiently before the sound is presented to the listener. The digital circuit is able to tell the difference between background noise and speech patterns, making it possible for the hearing-impaired person to comprehend speech in a wide variety of circumstances such as in a pub or on a bus.

Geoffrey Curtis is a Hearing Aid Consultant for Broom, Reid and Harris, Exeter.

22.4 The vestibular apparatus and balance

The vestibular part of the inner ear consists of an assemblage of interconnected sacs and canals continuous with those of the cochlea. Like the cochlea, they are filled with fluid and contain receptor cells. However, instead of being sensitive to sound, the receptor cells are proprioceptors which give us our sense of balance (*figure 22.16*).

The semicircular canals

The vestibular apparatus includes three **semicircular canals** in planes at right angles to each other. At one end of each semicircular canal is a cavity called an **ampulla** which contains a receptor. The semicircular canals are connected to two further cavities, the **utricle** and **saccule**, both of which contain receptors.

The ampulla receptors consist of groups of receptor cells with hairs, rather like those in the cochlea. However, in this case the hairs are embedded in a dome-shaped gelatinous cap, the **cupula**.

The ampulla receptors are sensitive to movements of the head, and the fact that the three semicircular canals are in different planes ensures sensitivity to movement in any

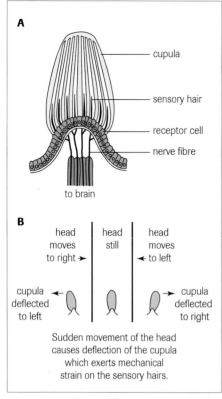

Figure 22.17 The ampulla organ is stimulated by movements of the head.

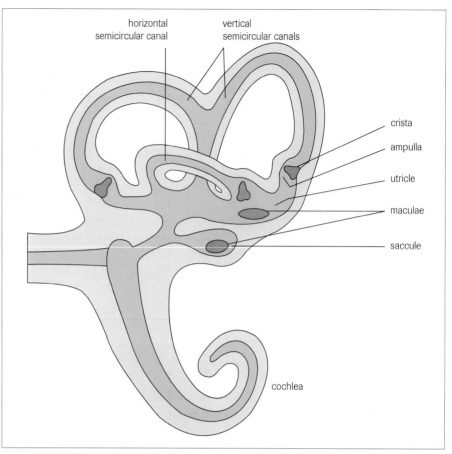

Figure 22.16 The vestibular apparatus in the inner ear, showing the location of the two main types of receptor (cristae and maculae) responsible for our sense of balance.

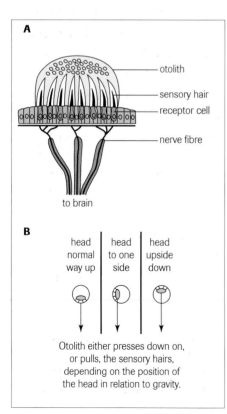

Figure 22.18 The utricle organ is stimulated according to the position of the head relative to the force of gravity.

plane. Thus, if you shake your head the horizontal canal is activated; if you nod your head one of the vertical canals is brought into play, and so on. Because of the inertia of the fluid in the semicircular canals, the cupula gets deflected in a direction opposite to that in which the head is moving. This puts a mechanical strain on the receptor cells, causing them to fire impulses in the sensory nerve fibres (*figure 22.17*).

Which particular receptor cells are stimulated most depends on the direction in which the cupula is deflected, and this in turn determines the pattern of impulses discharged in the sensory nerve fibres. This pattern is interpreted by the brain which therefore enables you to know the direction in which your head has been moving. An increase in the speed of movement increases the frequency of the impulses. So the overall function of the semicircular canals is to register directional acceleration.

The utricle and saccule

The utricle and saccule give information on the *position* of the head. The receptors consist of a group of receptor cells whose free ends are embedded in a gelatinous substance containing a concretion of densely packed particles of calcium carbonate, called an **otolith** (*figure 22.18*).

According to the position of the head, the pull of gravity on the otolith will vary. Thus, when your head is upright, the otolith will press down on the sensory hairs. With the head tilted sideways the otolith will exert an oblique pull on the hairs, and if the head is upside down the otolith will pull the hairs downwards (*figure 22.18*).

The differential distortion of the receptor cells resulting from the head being in different positions determines the pattern of impulses discharged in the sensory nerve fibres. This is interpreted by the brain which thus makes you aware of the position of your head.

Other receptors important in balance

The vestibular apparatus is not the only structure in the body sensitive to position and movement. Other proprioceptors such as **muscle spindles** are also important (*page 422*), as are our **eyes**, and also **pressure receptors** in the skin on the soles of the feet.

The importance of these other receptors can be seen in simple tests which you can do on yourself. For example, stand up straight with your eyes open. Then raise one foot off the ground and note how you keep your balance. Now repeat with your eyes closed. Do you find it less easy to keep your balance with your eyes closed?

Or try this test. Stand up straight with your feet close together, arms at your sides and eyes open. Notice the way the body sways slightly from side to side (postural swaying).

Now slowly lean forward and note how your feet respond in helping you to retain your balance.

Warning! If you try these tests, please be careful not to lose your balance and fall down.

Summary

1. Receptors may consist of isolated **receptor cells** or multicellular **sense organs**. They can be classified into **chemoreceptors**, **mechanoreceptors**, **photoreceptors** and **thermoreceptors.**

2. The function of receptors is to transfer the energy associated with the stimulus to nerve impulses.

3. In general, sensory cells, when stimulated, develop a local **generator potential** which, if it builds up sufficiently, elicits propagated **action potentials** in a sensory neurone.

4. If a stimulus is maintained, the generator potential usually declines and the action potentials decrease in frequency until they cease altogether (**adaptation**).

5. For repetitive stimuli to be detected separately, the generator potential produced by each stimulus must fall below the firing threshold before the next stimulus is delivered.

6. In the mammalian eye the receptor cells, **cones** and **rods**, are located in the **retina** on which light rays are brought to a focus by the **cornea** and an adjustable **lens**.

7. The cones, which are particularly concentrated in the **fovea**, are responsible for high acuity colour vision in conditions of good illumination (**daylight vision**), the rods for black-and-white vision at low levels of illumination (**night vision**).

8. The efficiency of the rods in night vision is due to their sensitivity and rapid resynthesis of photochemical pigment, and to the fact that they show **retinal convergence**.

9. The acuity of the cones is due to their high density in the fovea, and to their one-to-one relationship with the optic nerve fibres.

10. According to the **trichromatic theory**, colour vision is achieved by differential stimulation of three types of cone, each of which contains a different photochemical pigment.

11. Common defects of the eye include **short-sightedness**, **long-sightedness** and **astigmatism**, all of which can be remedied by using appropriate spectacles or contact lenses.

12. A **cataract** is caused by the lens becoming opaque. It is rectified by replacing the lens with an artificial one.

13. The mammalian ear performs two functions: **hearing** and **balance**. Hearing is dealt with by receptor cells in the **organ of Corti** in the **cochlea**, to which sound waves are transmitted via a series of membranes, ossicles and fluid-filled canals.

14. The cochlea can discriminate between sounds of different intensity and pitch.

15. Hearing loss may have a **conductive** or **sensorineural** cause, both of which may be remedied by wearing a **post-aural** or **intra-aural hearing aid**.

16. Balance is dealt with by the **vestibular apparatus**. Receptor cells associated with the **semicircular canals** are sensitive to directional acceleration of the head. Receptor cells in the **utricle** and **saccule** are sensitive to the position of the head relative to gravity.

Part 4

For general advice on these questions and advice on answering essay-type questions, see pages vii and viii.

1. The eyeball consists of the following three layers: a tough fibrous layer made up of the transparent cornea and the white sclera; a vascular layer comprising the choroid, iris and ciliary body; the retina containing several million light-sensitive cells.

Light stimulation of the retina's photoreceptor cells triggers a chain of events leading to the transmission of electrical impulses to the brain via the optic nerve.

Inside the eyeball, suspended from the ciliary body, is the lens - a transparent structure the shape of which can be changed so that it becomes more or less convex depending upon the tension exerted on it. The lens and suspensory ligaments separate the eye into two compartments, one anterior to the lens and the other posterior to it.

(a) (i) Give one function of each of the following:
The choroid The iris (2)

(ii) Make a labelled sketch of a section through the eye to show the relationship between all the structures mentioned in the passage above. (6)

(iii) The anterior compartment of the eye contains the fluid aqueous humour whereas the posterior compartment contains a jelly-like substance, the vitreous humour. Suggest one function of the jelly-like vitreous humour. (1)

The graph below shows how the near point of focus increases with increasing age in humans.

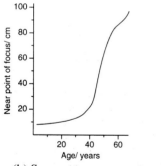

(b) Suggest two reasons to explain these changes. (2)

(c) Nerve impulses generated in the retina are transmitted to the brain across a number of synapses. Explain briefly how a synapse works. (5)

(Total 16 marks)

O&C 1998

2. Give an account of the structure and functioning of the retina.

(Total 10 marks)

London 1997

3. The graph shows the distribution of rods and cones across part of the retina of a human eye.

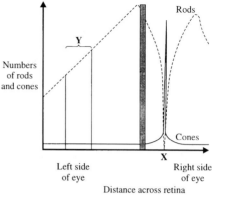

(a) (i) Which part of the retina does point **X** represent? (1)

(ii) Give a reason for your answer. (1)

(b) (i) Give **one** difference between the connections that a rod cell and a cone cell make with other neurones in the retina. (1)

(ii) Explain why the part of the retina in region **Y** is very sensitive to dim light. (2)

(Total 5 marks)

AEB 1998

4. The figure below shows the wavelengths of light absorbed by certain cells in the retina.

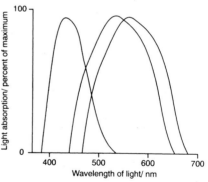

(i) Why are three separate curves shown in the figure? (1)

(ii) Use the information provided in the figure to help you explain how humans see in colour. (4)

(iii) About 8% of males have a defect in the retina which causes red-green colour blindness. Sketch another graph to show the likely absorption of light wavelengths by the colour sensitive cells of such an individual. (1)

(iv) Suggest how people who have red-green colour blindness can tell when traffic lights show red. (2)

(Total 8 marks)

O&C 1997

Chapter 23

Muscles and other effectors

A s the body's principal **effectors**, muscles respond when they receive impulses from nerves. In this chapter we shall look at the structure of muscle and relate this to the way it contracts. We shall concentrate mainly on skeletal muscle because it was this that first engaged the attention of physiologists. But first we must look briefly at the different types of muscle that are found in the body.

23.1 Different types of muscle

All muscles have one thing in common: they are composed of numerous contractile **muscle fibres** which together make up **muscle tissue** (*page 69*). The muscle fibres are usually orientated in a particular direction and when they contract the whole muscle shortens or develops tension.

Vertebrate muscle tissue can be divided into three types:

- **Skeletal muscle** This is attached to the skeleton. It is innervated by the voluntary part of the nervous system and is therefore also known as **voluntary muscle**. When viewed under the microscope its fibres are seen to have stripes running across them, for which reason it is called **striated muscle**. Characteristically it contracts, and fatigues, rapidly.

- **Smooth muscle** This is found in the wall of the gut, blood vessels and various cavities, and is innervated by the autonomic (involuntary) nervous system, for which reason it is also known as **involuntary muscle**. Its fibres do not have stripes running across them, in other words they are unstriated – that's why it is called smooth muscle. In contrast to skeletal muscle, it contracts, and fatigues, slowly.

- **Cardiac muscle** Situated in the wall of the heart, its fibres are striated and joined by cross-connections to form a network. Like smooth muscle, it is innervated by the autonomic nervous system. However, it can contract on its own without receiving impulses from its nerves, i.e. its contractions are **myogenic**. It contracts over and over again rhythmically, without fatigue. The function of its nerves is to speed up or slow down the frequency of the contractions.

The fundamental question is: how do muscles contract? In attempting to answer this we shall focus our attention, as physiologists have done, on skeletal muscle. But first let us look briefly at what skeletal muscle is capable of doing.

23.2 Properties of skeletal muscle

When a muscle is activated it either shortens or, if it is attached to a rigid skeleton, develops tension. Its properties can be investigated by attaching it to a movable lever that writes on a revolving drum (**kymograph**).

For this kind of work the **calf (gastrocnemius) muscle** of the frog has been much used. The muscle is removed from the leg and set up as shown in figure 23.1. The muscle is stimulated with single or repetitive stimuli, either directly or through its nerve, and the resulting contractions are recorded on the drum.

Let us now look at some recordings, and discover some of the properties of skeletal muscle from them.

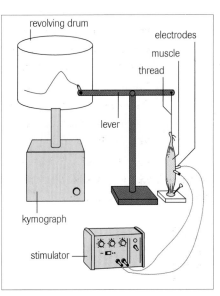

Figure 23.1 Investigating the properties of skeletal muscle by means of a gastrocnemius muscle preparation. One of the tendons is pinned to a fixed piece of cork, the other to a recording lever. The muscle is kept permanently moist by pipetting Ringer's solution onto it. A pair of electrodes is placed in contact with the muscle. When the experimenter activates the stimulator an electrical stimulus is sent into the muscle through the electrodes and the muscle responds by contracting. When it contracts it pulls the lever which makes a tracing on the revolving drum (kymograph). The stimulator can deliver single stimuli or repetitive stimuli at a range of frequencies.

Smooth muscle, page 69;
cardiac muscle, page 233

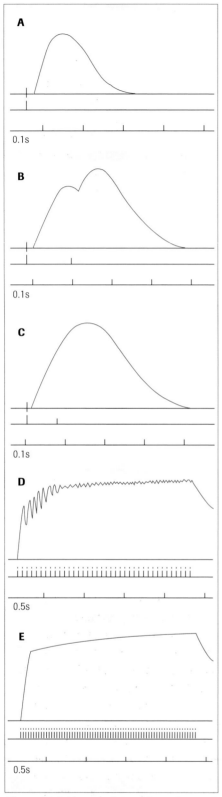

Figure 23.2 Kymograph recordings of responses obtained by stimulating a muscle with electrical stimuli. In all cases the stimuli are dotted and a time scale is shown below each recording.

The simple twitch

If a single stimulus of sufficient strength is applied to the muscle, the latter responds by giving a quick contraction or **twitch** (*figure 23.2A*). It takes about a tenth of a second (0.1 s) for the contraction to reach its height, and a further 0.2 s for relaxation to be complete. The entire response is therefore over in approximately 0.3 s. These figures are typical of a frog calf muscle, but in animals as a whole there is much variation between different muscles.

There is a short delay between the application of the stimulus and the onset of the muscular contraction. This is called the **latent period**. It is caused partly by the inertia of the apparatus but also by the time taken for the electrical response to be translated into a contraction. Typically the latent period lasts about 0.02 s.

Summation

Now consider what happens if two stimuli are delivered in succession (*figure 23.2B and C*). If the interval between the stimuli is long enough, two separate twitches are given by the muscle, one after the other. However, if the interval is gradually shortened there comes a point when the two twitches fuse (**summate**) to give a single smooth contraction. Each impulse initiates a contraction, but the second contraction starts before the muscle begins to relax, so that the summated response is larger and lasts longer than the simple twitch (*figure 23.2C*).

Tetanus

We can take the above experiment a stage further. Instead of stimulating the muscle with only two stimuli, we send a train of stimuli into the muscle. If the frequency of the stimuli is not too great, separate twitches can be discerned (*figure 23.2D*). If, however, the frequency is great enough, the muscle goes into a sustained contraction called a **tetanus**, relaxing only when the stimuli are switched off (*figure 23.2E*). Numerous twitches have fused, as it were, to give a single prolonged response. To produce a smooth tetanus in a frog calf muscle, a minimum frequency of approximately 20 stimuli per second is required.

When a muscle contracts under natural conditions it normally undergoes a tetanus rather than a simple twitch. For example, if you bend your arm, the flexor muscle undergoes a sustained tetanic contraction as a result of a train of high-frequency impulses reaching it from the brachial nerve. How long the contraction goes on for depends on the duration of the train of impulses, and that depends on you. Just as an experimenter can stop tetanising a muscle by switching off the stimuli, so you (using your brain) can voluntarily stop your flexor muscle contracting by 'turning off' the impulses streaming down to it.

> **Support**
>
> ### Muscles are just one kind of effector
>
> Important though they are, muscles are not the only effectors found in the body. **Glands** are effectors too, and they occur in virtually all animals. Less widespread, but no less important to the animals possessing them, are **pigment cells** which enable some animals to change colour, **light-producing organs** which enable organisms to communicate in the dark, and **electric organs** which emit electrical pulses (*page 405*).
>
> Most effectors are controlled by the nervous system and respond when they receive impulses from nerves. However, certain effectors, such as glands in the wall of the small intestine, can respond to direct stimulation. The **sting cells** of cnidarians such as sea anemones and jellyfish are also independent of nervous control and respond directly when touched.

Tetanus, the disease

Although tetanic contractions are a natural process, the term tetanus is also used for a bacterial disease characterised by sustained contractions (spasms) of certain muscles. The first to be affected are the jaw muscles, for which reason the disease is called lockjaw. If untreated, the spasms become violent and spread to other muscles including those of the neck, back and abdomen.

The bacteria that cause this disease enter the body through wounds inflicted by dirty objects such as nails or barbed wire. The symptoms are caused, not by the bacteria themselves, but by a toxin produced by them which acts on effector neurones and nerve endings. Immediate help is needed, and this may necessitate being given a dose of ready-made antibodies (*page 330*).

Though rare in developed countries like Britain, tetanus is a major killer in developing countries where the mortality rate from it may exceed 40 per cent.

Fatigue

A tetanic contraction cannot go on indefinitely. If stimulation is continued, the muscular responses gradually decline and eventually disappear altogether. This **fatigue** is brought about by various factors operating within the muscle, such as shortage of muscle glycogen and a build-up of lactic acid with a resulting increase in the pH.

If, instead of being stimulated directly, the muscle is excited through its nerve, the responses decline even more quickly. This is due to exhaustion of the transmitter substance (acetylcholine) at the neuromuscular junctions.

Graded contractions

By varying the frequency of the stimuli (the number per unit time) delivered to a muscle, contractions of different strengths can be produced. Low frequencies produce relatively weak contractions, whereas high frequencies produce more powerful contractions. Such graded contractions are very important in the normal functioning of our muscles. A high-frequency tetanic contraction may be 20 times more powerful than a single individual contraction.

Electrical activity in muscle

Recording contractions with a kymograph involves using a whole muscle. More detailed investigations may be carried out on single muscle fibres which are teased out of the whole muscle, isolated, and experimented on individually. Microelectrodes are inserted into the muscle fibre and its electrical as well as mechanical responses are recorded with an oscilloscope (*page 350*).

What emerges from these experiments is that the membranes of muscle fibres are basically similar to those of nerve cells (*page 350*). When not active they have a **resting potential**, and when activated this is momentarily reversed to give an **action potential**. This generally lasts longer, and is transmitted more slowly, than that of a nerve cell, but otherwise the two are similar and have essentially the same ionic basis.

Like nerves, muscle fibres obey an **all-or-nothing law**. By stimulating an isolated muscle fibre with stimuli of gradually increasing intensity, it can be shown that the size of the action potential, and the resulting contraction, are independent of the intensity of stimulation. If the strength of a stimulus is below the threshold required to excite the fibre, no action potential and no contraction are given. If the stimulus is above this threshold, an action potential and contraction are given, and further increase in the intensity of the stimulus will not enhance this response.

Muscles also have a **refractory period**. After contraction there is a brief period of complete, followed by partial, inexcitability – the **absolute** and **relative refractory periods** respectively. They are generally slightly longer than for a nerve.

From an electrical standpoint, nerves and muscles are therefore very similar. The main difference is that in a muscle, the action potential is accompanied by a contraction. How the electrical and mechanical events are coupled together will be discussed later.

There is another way of grading contractions, and that is by varying within the muscle the number of fibres that contract. The motor nerve that supplies a particular muscle contains numerous axons, each of which supplies a group of fibres within the muscle. The group of muscle fibres supplied by a single axon is called a **motor unit**. Graded contractions can be produced by varying the number of motor units which are brought into play. If only a few motor units are activated, a weak contraction is given. If all the motor units are activated, a much more powerful contraction is given.

Muscles differ in the size of their motor units. In some muscles the motor units consist of only a few fibres, whereas in other muscles the motor units may consist of several hundred fibres. Predictably, muscles with small motor units give rise to more delicate movements than muscles with large motor units.

Extension

Fast and slow twitch muscle fibres

Guest author Patricia Kohn explains these two kinds of muscle fibre and discusses their significance in athletic events.

There are two main types of fibre in human skeletal muscles, distinguished by how quickly they contract.

Slow twitch fibres predominate in those muscles involved in sustained but relatively low levels of activity, such as the maintenance of posture and long-distance running. In these activities the oxygen supply keeps pace with the demand for ATP, so aerobic respiration can provide the necessary energy and anaerobic respiration is not needed.

The fuel molecules, e.g. glucose, are broken down via glycolysis and the Krebs cycle. The latter takes place in the mitochondria which are particularly plentiful in slow twitch fibres. These fibres have a good blood supply and contain lots of myoglobin to serve as an oxygen store (*page 220*). The high myoglobin and blood content give muscles with a lot of slow twitch fibres a brownish red colour ('red muscles').

Fast twitch fibres are the exact opposite. They are adapted for sudden bursts of maximum activity, such as occur in sprinting, throwing, jumping and lifting. These activities may consume ATP at such a rate that the supply of oxygen for aerobic respiration cannot keep up with demand. The energy need is

therefore met by very high rates of anaerobic respiration which, you will recall, involve glycolysis but not the Krebs cycle (*page 147*).

This is reflected in the characteristics of this kind of muscle: enzymes of the glycolysis pathway are plentiful but there are relatively few mitochondria, the myoglobin content is low and the blood supply unexceptional. Muscles with a high proportion of fast twitch fibres are therefore 'white muscles'.

All human muscles contain both types of fibre though in differing proportions. However, the muscles of some other animals are composed almost exclusively of one or other type. For example, a trout has mainly fast twitch fibres with only a narrow band of slow twitch muscle on either side of the body. The slow twitch fibres propel the fish while it is cruising along slowly, but if the need for swift escape arises, the fast twitch muscle is activated and the fish darts to safety.

Different types of muscle in athletes
It has been found that trained sprinters have a high proportion of fast twitch fibres, whereas marathon runners have a high proportion of slow twitch fibres.

Is this difference inborn or the result of the different training which these two kinds of athlete undergo? Studies on identical twins suggest that basically the fibre composition of our muscles is

genetically determined. However, there is evidence that training can bring about changes in the proportions of the different types of fibre. This may be due to conversion of one type to the other or to the presence of unspecialised fibres which can form either type when given the appropriate stimulus.

The maximum work rate of muscles rich in fast twitch fibres cannot be sustained for long. The 400 metres sprint is notoriously difficult, and great fatigue is felt if anaerobic respiration continues at a high rate for long. This is probably due to the fall in pH that occurs in the muscle fibres as lactic acid, the end product of anaerobic glycolysis, accumulates.

In contrast, fatigue in slow twitch fibres is probably caused by a switch to fatty acids as the main fuel when glycogen runs out. This occurs towards the end of the marathon and is known in the trade as 'hitting the wall'.

Dr Kohn was a research physiologist in the Department of Biomedical Science at the University of Sheffield.

➤ Changes in the body during exercise, page 244
➤ Effects of training on muscles, page 425

Electric organs

Adaptation often involves the modification of a structure so that it performs a new, highly specialised, function. Nowhere can this be better seen than in certain species of fish in which some of the muscles have been turned into **electric organs**.

In the South American electric eel and the Mediterranean electric ray, these organs consist of stacks of sheet-like **electroplates**. They are modified muscle fibres which, instead of contracting when they receive impulses from their nerves, send out electric pulses. The total discharge from all the plates simultaneously can exceed 600 volts, more than enough to immobilise quite sizeable prey and give an unsuspecting human a nasty shock.

Many species of fish emit much weaker electric pulses which are used, not for killing prey, but for locating objects in their immediate vicinity. The fish is sensitive to disturbances of the electric field surrounding it, providing it with a kind of radar system. This is particularly useful to fish living in the murky waters of tropical rivers where visibility is low.

Each species has its own characteristic pattern of pulses. Hans Lissmann, a Cambridge biologist, used to wade through rivers in South America, a loudspeaker strapped to his back and a pair of electrodes in his hands, identifying the different kinds of fish from the electric pulses recorded when he dipped the electrodes in the water.

The elephant fish, *Gnathenemus petersi*, emits low voltage electric pulses. It has been used by Thames Water to monitor the quality of river water. The rate of emission of pulses changes when the water contains chemical pollutants.

23.3 Structure of skeletal muscle

A whole muscle is made up of many hundreds of **muscle fibres** varying in length from 1 to 40 millimetres (*figure 23.3A*). If an individual fibre is sectioned longitudinally, stained and examined under the microscope, the structures shown in figure 23.3B may be seen.

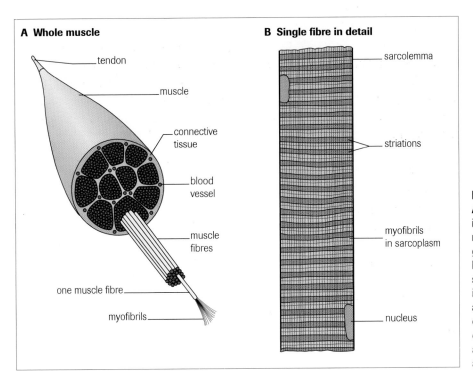

A Whole muscle

- tendon
- muscle
- connective tissue
- blood vessel
- muscle fibres
- one muscle fibre
- myofibrils

B Single fibre in detail

- sarcolemma
- striations
- myofibrils in sarcoplasm
- nucleus

Figure 23.3 Structure of skeletal muscle.
A A whole muscle sliced transversely to show its internal structure. The muscle is composed of numerous muscle fibres bound together in groups by connective tissue.
B Diagram of part of a single muscle fibre as seen under the high power of a light microscope in ideal conditions. Myofibrils can just be seen, as can detail of the striations, but note that no clue is given as to the possible mechanism of contraction. Muscle fibres vary in diameter from about 10 to 20 μm depending on the type of animal they come from.

The fibre is filled with a specialised cytoplasm called **sarcoplasm** in which about 100 nuclei are spaced out evenly just beneath the bounding membrane or **sarcolemma**. The nuclei are not separated from each other by plasma membranes – in other words they are not in separate cells – so the fibre is a **syncytium** (*page 64*). Numerous slender threads called **myofibrils** run along the length of the fibre, and a series of parallel **striations** traverse it.

Until the early 1950s, this was all that was known about the structure of muscle, and a frustrating picture it was for it gave no clue as to how contraction takes place. However, since then the electron microscope has revealed a wealth of information about muscle that helps to explain how it works.

The fine structure of muscle

Under the light microscope the myofibrils appear as extremely thin lines. However, in the electron microscope their internal structure shows up clearly, and the reason for the striations becomes apparent. This is shown in figure 23.4. Notice that each myofibril is divided up into alternating **light** and **dark bands** (known as the **I** and **A** bands respectively). The light and dark bands of adjacent myofibrils lie alongside each other, and this is why when you look at an entire fibre you see striations running across it.

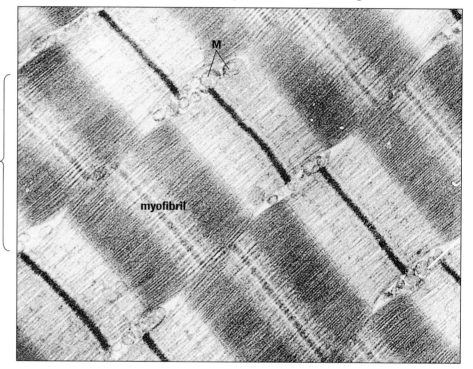

one myofibril (width)

Figure 23.4 Low magnification electron micrograph of part of a skeletal muscle fibre in longitudinal section. Parallel myofibrils can be seen with their characteristic pattern of alternating dark and light bands. Notice the mitochondria (**M**) between adjacent myofibrils. Magnification ×30 000.

Now let's examine the bands in more detail. First look at figure 23.5A which shows a short length of a single myofibril. You can see that the dark band has a relatively light region in the middle. This is called the **H zone**, and it has darker regions on either side. Running across the middle of the H zone is a dark **M line**, and traversing the middle of the light band is an even darker **Z line**. The region of a myofibril from one Z line to the next is called a **sarcomere**. For descriptive purposes the sarcomere can be regarded as the basic unit of the myofibril; the whole myofibril consists of a long chain of such units placed end to end.

The explanation of the banding pattern is made clear in figure 23.5B. The myofibril is composed of numerous longitudinal filaments of two types: thick and thin. The **thick filaments** are confined to the dark band. The **thin filaments** occur in the light band, but extend in between the thick filaments into the dark band. The areas on either side of the H zone are therefore particularly dark because they contain both thick and thin filaments.

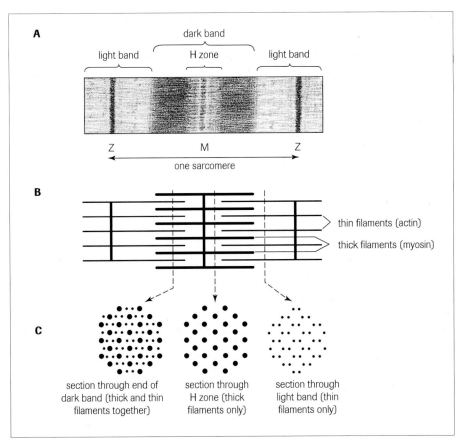

Figure 23.5 The detailed structure of individual myofibrils has been worked out with the electron microscope. The light and dark bands seen in low magnification electron micrographs (**A**) are due to the presence of alternating groups of thick and thin filaments which interdigitate between each other as shown in **B**. The groups of filaments are held in alignment at the Z and M lines. The arrangement of the filaments has been confirmed by examining cross sections of myofibrils in the electron microscope as shown in **C**.

The H zone consists of thick filaments only, which is why it is slightly lighter than the two ends of the dark band.

Cross-sections through the myofibril at different levels give the appearance shown in figure 23.5C. This confirms the idea that the thick and thin filaments overlap and shows how they relate to each other spatially.

What are the filaments made of? Research on the chemistry of muscle has shown that the thick filaments are composed of the protein **myosin**, the thin filaments of the protein **actin**.

So, to summarise, myofibrils consist of alternating sets of thick myosin and thin actin filaments which overlap with each other. What, then, happens when the muscle contracts?

23.4 How muscle contracts

From the structure of the myofibril it would seem reasonable to propose that contraction occurs by the thick and thin filaments sliding between each other. The thin filaments in each light band are held together at the Z line, and the thick filaments are held together at the M line, so each set of filaments would be expected to slide as a unit. The orderly arrangement of the filaments would therefore be maintained during the contraction process.

This **sliding filament hypothesis** was first put forward in the early 1950s by Hugh Huxley and Jean Hanson of London University, on the basis of observations using light microscopy. They argued as follows. If it is true that the filaments slide, the banding pattern in the myofibril should change as contraction occurs. When the muscle contracts, the light bands and H zones would be expected to get shorter, as would the overall length of each sarcomere. However, the dark bands should stay the same length, and the particularly dark regions on either side of the H zone should get longer.

Part 4

Extension

The chemistry of muscle

How do we know that that the thick filaments are made of myosin and the thin filaments of actin?

This question was investigated by treating muscle tissue with chemicals that selectively dissolve one or other of these proteins, and then examining the myofibrils under a phase-contrast microscope.

It was found that when a muscle is treated with a solution that dissolves myosin, all the dark bands disappear. If, however, the muscle is treated with a solution that dissolves actin, all the light bands disappear.

When actin and myosin are extracted from muscle fibres and placed in a solution of ATP, contraction occurs. This means that from a purely biochemical standpoint all that is required for contraction to occur is a mixture of actin, myosin and ATP.

This is precisely what Huxley and Hanson found. Using the most advanced light microscopes then available, they studied the appearance of isolated myofibrils contracting in a solution of ATP and found the change in the banding pattern to be exactly as they had predicted.

In fully contracted muscles, the light bands and H zones disappear altogether and new bands appear at the positions occupied by the M and Z lines. These new bands can be interpreted by suggesting that when a muscle contracts to this extent the filaments meet and then crumple or overlap.

Confirmation of the sliding hypothesis was obtained by comparing the appearance of stretched and contracted myofibrils in the electron microscope. As living material cannot be viewed in the electron microscope it is impossible to watch the sliding process actually taking place, but examining electron micrographs of muscle in different states of contraction is the next best thing (*figure 23.6*).

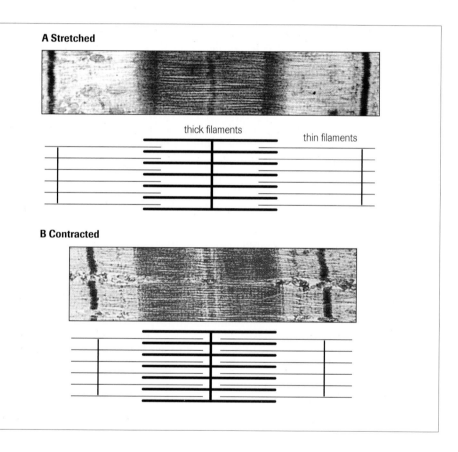

Figure 23.6 The sliding filament hypothesis proposes that when a myofibril shortens, the thick and thin filaments slide between each other, as shown here. The hypothesis predicts that when contraction takes place the banding pattern should change, and the sarcomere should shorten. This does in fact happen, as you can see in the two electron micrographs.

How do other types of muscle contract?

Since Jean Hanson and Hugh Huxley did their research on skeletal muscle, it has been discovered that cardiac and smooth muscle also contract by actin and myosin filaments sliding between each other. In fact, cardiac muscle, which is striated like skeletal muscle, is almost identical with skeletal muscle in the way it contracts (*page 233*).

Smooth muscle is slightly different because the actin and myosin filaments are not aligned as they are in skeletal and cardiac muscle. That's why smooth muscle is unstriated. There are no distinct myofibrils and the filaments, although orientated longitudinally in the muscle fibres, are more loosely arranged. Contraction, though, still takes place by actin and myosin filaments sliding past each other.

What propels the filaments?

We are now faced with the question: how do the two sets of filaments move between each other? A clue comes from studying high-magnification electron micrographs of myofibrils such as the one in figure 23.7.

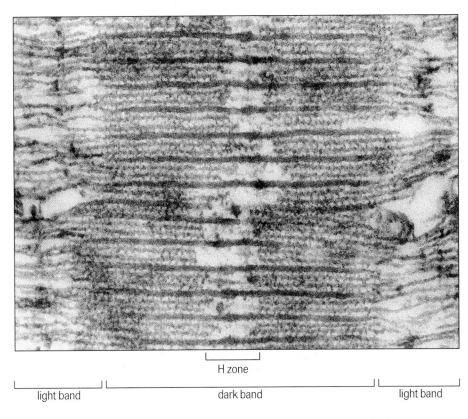

H zone

light band | dark band | light band

Figure 23.7 High magnification electron micrograph (×75 000) of one complete sarcomere in a myofibril. Notice the thick and thin filaments between each other and the bridges that connect them together.

In this micrograph you can see cross-connections between the thick and thin filaments where they overlap. These **bridges** are side branches of the thick filaments and are made of myosin. They project from the thick filaments at roughly 6 nm intervals, and careful analysis has shown that they describe a spiral pathway around the filament. In the region of overlap each thick filament is surrounded by a hexagonal array of six thin filaments (*figure 23.5C on page 407*). Successive bridges projecting from the thick filament are attached to each of these thin filaments in turn so the spiral pattern of bridges repeats itself once every six bridges, a distance of about 40 nm.

The ratchet mechanism

The bridges bring about contraction. During shortening of the muscle, each bridge attaches itself to a thin filament, and then swings through an arc. The concerted action of many bridges all doing this together has the effect of pulling the thin filaments past the thick ones. After it has completed its movement, each bridge detaches from the thin filament, swings back to its original position and re-attaches at another site further along. The cycle is then repeated. Shortening of the muscle is thus brought about by the bridges going through a kind of **ratchet mechanism** (*figure 23.8*).

To account for the known rate at which muscles contract, it has been estimated that each bridge goes through its cycle between 50 and 100 times per second. This figure, together with measurements of the rate of respiration of contracting muscle, indicate that for each bridge to go through a complete cycle, the hydrolysis of one molecule of ATP is required. The ATP consumption of contracting muscle is therefore considerable, which explains why the gaps between adjacent myofibrils contain numerous mitochondria. You can see them in figure 23.4 on page 406.

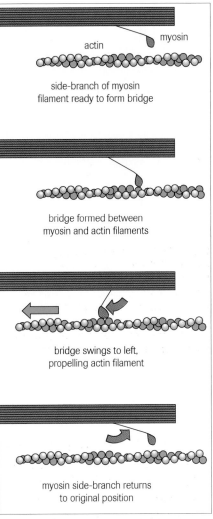

actin   myosin

side-branch of myosin
filament ready to form bridge

bridge formed between
myosin and actin filaments

bridge swings to left,
propelling actin filament

myosin side-branch returns
to original position

Figure 23.8 These diagrams summarise the ratchet mechanism by which the thick (myosin) and thin (actin) filaments are pulled towards each other by a myosin bridge.

Evidence for the ratchet mechanism

The ratchet hypothesis is supported by various lines of evidence. Special techniques in electron microscopy have shown the detailed structure of the actin and myosin filaments, and X-ray analysis supports the view that the bridges undergo substantial movement during contraction. The ratchet idea also explains many facts about muscle which have been known for a long time, and is consistent with more recent research on the molecular structure of the filaments. In fact, these molecular studies not only support the ratchet hypothesis but also show us how it is controlled. Calcium ions play a key role in this, and they trigger the contraction process. The details, if you want them, are given in the extension box below.

Extension

How the bridges are controlled

Research on the molecular structure of the actin filaments has shown that, in addition to actin itself, the filaments contain two other proteins known as **tropomyosin** and **troponin** (*illustration*).

An actin filament consists of two chains of globular protein molecules twisted around each other (*page 30*). When the muscle is at rest, the tropomyosin is disposed in such a way that it covers the sites on the actin chain where the heads of the myosin bridges become attached. When the muscle is required to contract, calcium ions bind with the troponin molecules and cause them to move slightly. This has the effect of displacing the tropomyosin and exposing the binding sites for the myosin heads. Once the myosin head has become attached to the actin filament, ATP is hydrolysed and the bridge goes through its cycle.

From the above account you will appreciate that ATP is needed to break the link between the myosin bridge and the actin. After death, the amount of ATP in the body falls. Under these circumstances the bridges cannot be broken and so they remain firmly bound. This results in the body becoming stiff, a condition known as *rigor mortis*.

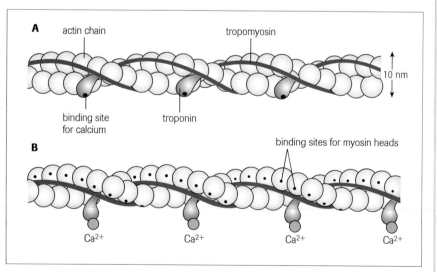

How the ratchet mechanism is controlled.
A When the muscle is relaxed, tropomyosin covers the sites where the myosin bridges will bind with the actin filament.
B When contraction is about to take place, calcium ions combine with troponin which displaces the tropomyosin and uncovers the binding sites.

23.5 Activation of muscle fibres

In natural conditions muscles contract when they receive impulses from the nerves that supply them. When a muscle is activated through its nerve, an action potential consisting of a wave of depolarisation sweeps along the plasma membrane (sarcolemma) of each muscle fibre, and this is quickly followed by a contraction. How is the electrical activity in the muscle fibre linked to the mechanical process of contraction?

The link is provided by a specialised form of smooth endoplasmic reticulum in the muscle fibre called the **sarcoplasmic reticulum**.

The sarcoplasmic reticulum

The sarcoplasmic reticulum consists of a network of flattened membrane-lined cavities which envelop each myofibril like a net stocking. Part of it is shown in figure 23.9. Basically it consists of a series of **transverse tubules** flanked by relatively large cavities called **vesicles** which are interconnected by **longitudinal tubules**. The transverse tubules are continuous with the sarcolemma.

What does the sarcoplasmic reticulum do? The vesicles contain calcium ions in high concentration. As an action potential sweeps along the sarcolemma, electrical signals are transmitted to the interior of the muscle fibre via the membrane lining the transverse tubules. This causes the membrane surrounding the adjacent vesicles to become permeable to calcium ions, which diffuse down the steep concentration gradient into the surrounding cytosol. The calcium ions then make the muscle contract as described in the extension box on the previous page.

Immediately after contraction, the calcium ions are actively pumped from the cytosol into the longitudinal tubules. This lowers their concentration in the cytosol and allows the muscle to relax. Meanwhile the calcium ions diffuse back to the vesicle where they may be used again.

The action potential travels very quickly over the sarcolemma and transverse tubules so it reaches all the sarcomeres at the same moment, resulting in a synchronous contraction of the whole muscle fibre.

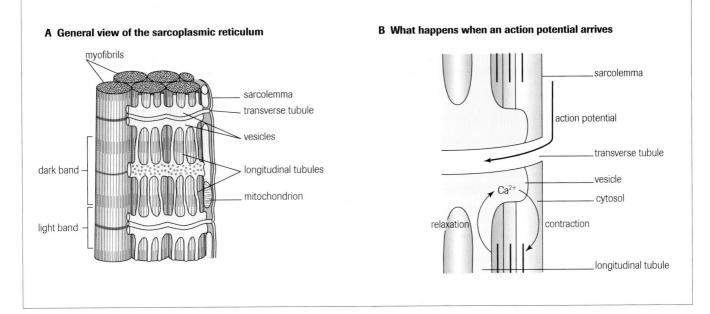

Figure 23.9 Part of the sarcoplasmic reticulum of an amphibian. The transverse tubules are invaginations of the sarcolemma (plasma membrane) which surrounds the whole muscle fibre. The sarcoplasmic reticulum envelopes all the individual myofibrils.

1. Effectors are structures which respond directly or indirectly to stimuli. The body's principal effectors are **muscles** and **glands**.

2. Other effectors, besides muscles and glands, include **chromatophores** (pigment cells), **electric organs** and **light-producing organs**.

3. Vertebrate muscles are classified into **skeletal** (voluntary, striated), **smooth** (involuntary, unstriated), and **cardiac** (heart) muscle. Each possesses certain characteristic properties.

4. Generally, muscles contract when impulses reach them through the nervous system but sometimes, as in the case of cardiac muscle, contractions are **myogenic**.

5. Vertebrates have two kinds of skeletal muscle fibres: **fast twitch fibres** and **slow twitch fibres**. The former are for short bursts of activity, the latter for more prolonged activity.

6. When a skeletal muscle receives a single electrical stimulus or a single impulse through the nerve that innervates it, it responds by giving a simple **twitch**.

7. With repetitive stimuli at a sufficiently high frequency, muscle twitches summate to produce a **tetanus**, whose duration depends on how long the stimulation is continued.

8. A skeletal muscle is made up of groups of **fibres**, each group being innervated by a single axon: this comprises a **motor unit**. By varying the number of motor units activated, weak or stronger contractions can be produced.

9. Contraction of a muscle fibre is initiated by an impulse (action potential) whose ionic basis is similar to that of a nerve impulse. The **muscle action potential** obeys the **all-or-nothing** law and is followed by an absolute and relative **refractory period**.

10. Muscle fibres contain numerous **myofibrils** which are made up of alternating sets of thick myosin and thin actin **filaments**. The way the filaments are aligned gives skeletal muscle its striated appearance.

11. Studies on the microscopic structure of skeletal muscle indicate that when a muscle contracts, the thick and thin filaments slide between one another, propelled by **cross bridges** acting as **ratchets**.

12. The ratchet mechanism depends on two other proteins, **troponin** and **tropomyosin**, which are associated with the actin filaments. Slight movement of these protein molecules, initiated by calcium ions, exposes the binding sites on the actin molecules to which the bridges become attached.

13. The calcium ions which initiate the above mechanism are released from the **sarcoplasmic reticulum** on the arrival of a muscle action potential.

For general advice on these questions and advice on answering essay-type questions, see pages vii and viii.

1. A muscle and its attached nerve were set up as shown in the diagram so that muscle contraction in response to electrical stimulation could be investigated.

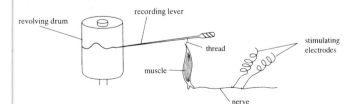

A stimulus was applied to the nerve by the electrodes, and the contraction of the muscle was recorded on the paper of the revolving drum. The trace obtained is shown opposite.

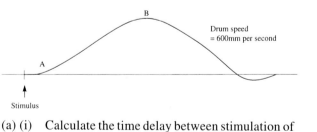

(a) (i) Calculate the time delay between stimulation of the nerve and the onset of muscle contraction. Show your working. (2)

(ii) Give **two** factors which would contribute to the delay before the muscle contracts. (2)

(b) Describe the changes which occur to the filaments in the muscle fibres as the muscle contracts. (4)

(Total 8 marks)

NEAB 1997

2. The diagram represents a longitudinal section through part of a striated muscle.

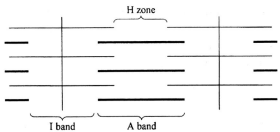

H zone

I band   A band

(a) The diagram shows the **A** band, the **I** band and the **H** zone. Which one or more of these:

   (i)   contains actin but not myosin;   (1)

   (ii) shortens when the muscle contracts?   (1)

(b) Describe the part played by each of the following in muscle contraction:

   (i)   ATP;   (2)

   (ii) calcium ions.   (1)

(Total 5 marks)

AEB 1997

3. Explain how the processes which occur at synapses lead to contraction in striated muscle.   *(Total 20 marks)*

O&C 1997

4. The diagrams below, (labelled 1, 2, 3, 4, and 5), show five possible states of a sarcomere from striated muscle. The relative positions of some actin and myosin filaments are shown.

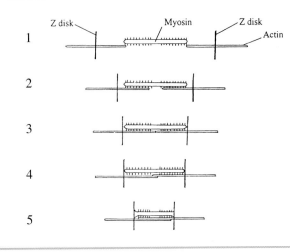

The graph below shows the relationship between sarcomere length and the amount of tension generated during the contraction. The letters A, B, C, D and E on the graph correspond to the different positions of the actin and myosin filaments, shown on the diagrams above, during the contraction.

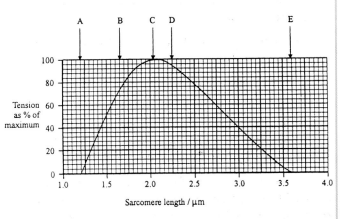

(a) (i)   State the letter of the stage on the graph which corresponds to the greatest length of the sarcomere shown in the diagrams.   (1)

   (ii) State the length of the sarcomere when the maximum tension is generated during contraction.   (1)

   (iii) Which diagram of the sarcomere shows the position of the actin and myosin filaments when the maximum tension is generated?   (1)

(b) (i)   Describe *two* ways in which the positions of structures in the sarcomere you have identified in (a) (iii) differ from those in the sarcomere at its greatest length.   (2)

   (ii) Explain how a sarcomere in a contracting muscle would change between the state shown in diagram 1 and that in diagram 3.   (4)

(c) Suggest why the maximum tension is not achieved when the sarcomere length is at its shortest.   (2)

(Total 11 marks)

London 1998

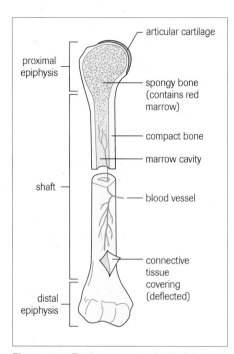

Figure 24.1 The humerus, a typical limb bone. The top half has been sectioned longitudinally to show the inside.

Microscopic structure of bone and cartilage tissues, page 67

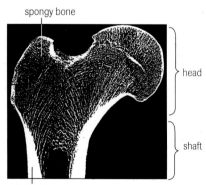

Figure 24.2 X-ray photograph of the top part of the femur showing the network of bony fibres that makes up the spongy bone in the epiphysis.

I n Chapter 23 we saw how muscles contract. There we were looking at muscles on their own, in isolation from the rest of the body. In this chapter we shall see how muscles move the body. To achieve this, muscles work in conjunction with the skeleton. Indeed the muscles and skeleton are so inextricably bound up with each other that it is customary to regard them as a single functional system: the **musculo-skeletal system**.

The aim of this chapter is to analyse movement and locomotion in terms of the musculo-skeletal system. But of course muscles cannot work without nerves and receptors, so we shall have occasion to refer to them too. We begin with the skeleton.

24.1 **The human skeleton**

The skeleton is composed of numerous incompressible **bones**. In some places adjacent bones are firmly connected, but usually they articulate with each other at **joints**.

Bones are constantly subjected to severe compression, tension and shearing forces, and in their composition and structure they are adapted to withstand these forces.

The human skeleton, in common with that of most other vertebrates, is constructed of two main types of tissue: **bone** and **cartilage** (*page 67*). Cartilage is softer than bone and is found mainly between the bones where it serves as a shock absorber, preventing jarring. The cartilage discs between successive vertebrae are particularly important in this respect, and they also give the vertebral column a certain degree of flexibility.

Although a large bone like the femur is extremely hard and strong, it does have a certain amount of flexibility. When you jump from a height, the bones in the leg bend slightly and then spring back to their usual shape.

Structure of a limb bone

A typical limb bone is shown in figure 24.1. The slender middle part is called the **shaft**, and the two swollen ends are called the **epiphyses**. The entire bone has a connective-tissue covering, beneath which is a layer of extremely hard **compact bone**. This is particularly thick in the shaft region where it consists of tightly packed Haversian systems disposed longitudinally. Compact bone is located here because this is where the greatest stress occurs. The centre of the shaft contains soft **bone marrow**.

The epiphyses contain a network of bony fibres called **spongy bone** (*figure 24.2*). This makes the ends of the bone very strong and helps them to withstand forces imposed upon them in a variety of different directions. For example, the head of the femur, which sticks out sideways from the main axis of the bone, is able to bear the weight of the body acting downwards. The spongy bone inside it is comparable to the crisscross fret in a crane.

Although we may think of bones as inert structures, they are really very much alive. They have a blood and nerve supply and contain living tissues with metabolic needs just like those of other tissues.

Functions of the human skeleton

The skeleton performs four basic functions:

■ **Movement** In conjunction with the muscles, it brings about movement, and is therefore the basis of locomotion.

■ **Support** Again in conjunction with the muscles, it supports the body, holding it up and maintaining its shape and form.

- **Protection** It protects the soft organs, particularly the brain, spinal cord, heart and lungs.
- **Production of blood cells** Blood cells are produced by cell division in the bone marrow of certain bones.

Structure of the human skeleton

The human skeleton is shown in figure 24.3. For convenience it can be divided into two parts: the **axial skeleton** and the **appendicular skeleton**.

The axial skeleton

This comprises those components of the skeleton which lie along the main axis of the body, namely the **skull**, **vertebral column** and **rib cage**. The vertebral column is composed of a chain of **vertebrae** (singular: **vertebra**). The ribs run from the vertebrae to the **sternum** which guards the front of the chest.

The function of the vertebral column is to carry the weight of the body, and this is reflected in the structure of the vertebrae. The main body of a vertebra is stout and strong, the mode of articulation with its neighbours is firm and secure, and from the upper part,

Relating the structure of the skeleton to its functions

Nowhere can the close relationship between structure and function be better seen than in the skeleton. Every cavity, hole and knob has a specific job to do. For example, the large space inside the cranium contains the brain, and the aperture at the back – the **foramen magnum** (meaning 'large hole') – is where the brain stem connects with the upper end of the spinal cord. Holes (**foramina**) on either side of the cranium and between successive vertebrae permit the cranial and spinal nerves to leave the brain and spinal cord en route to their destinations.

The vertebrae show the relationship between structure and function particularly well. A **lumbar vertebra** is illustrated in figure 24.4 on the next page. However, not all the vertebrae are like this. The **thoracic vertebrae**, for example, have additional processes for articulation with the **ribs**. The ribs have two processes at the dorsal end and these articulate with small depressions called **facets** on the vertebrae: typically one of the facets is on the underside of the transverse process and the other one is at the side of the body of the vertebra (the **centrum**).

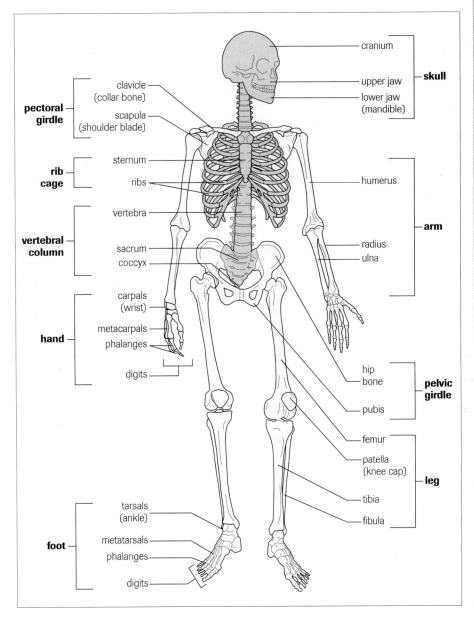

Figure 24.3 The human skeleton, showing its constituent parts in their normal positions. Axial skeleton, brown; appendicular skeleton, yellow.

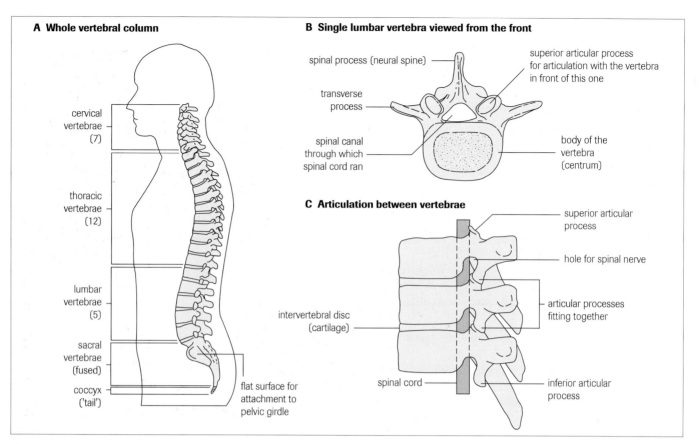

A Whole vertebral column

cervical vertebrae (7)

thoracic vertebrae (12)

lumbar vertebrae (5)

sacral vertebrae (fused)

coccyx ('tail')

flat surface for attachment to pelvic girdle

B Single lumbar vertebra viewed from the front

spinal process (neural spine)

transverse process

spinal canal through which spinal cord ran

superior articular process for articulation with the vertebra in front of this one

body of the vertebra (centrum)

C Articulation between vertebrae

intervertebral disc (cartilage)

spinal cord

superior articular process

hole for spinal nerve

articular processes fitting together

inferior articular process

Figure 24.4 The vertebral column of the human.
A The whole vertebral column viewed from the side.
B A typical vertebra from the lumbar region of the vertebral column, viewed from the front.
C Three lumbar vertebrae showing how they fit together.

various processes project for the attachment of ligaments and tendons which hold the vertebral column together (*figure 24.4*).

The appendicular skeleton

Appendicular comes from the Latin word 'to hang', and it refers to those components of the skeleton which are attached to, or articulate with, the axial skeleton. They include the bones of the arms and legs (**limb bones**) together with the **pectoral** and **pelvic girdles**.

The pectoral girdle is made up of two shoulder blades (**scapulae**) which are joined to the sternum by the collar bones (**clavicles**). The pelvic girdle is more massive: its two sides are fused with each other and with the sacral region of the vertebral column. This provides a firm base for the articulation of the thigh bone (**femur**).

In figure 24.3 notice the large number of bones in the hands and feet. For the variety of movements which they can make, the hands are particularly versatile, an attribute which has been very important in our evolution (*page 774*).

Types of bones

As you can see, the bones in the body are many and varied. It is therefore helpful to classify them, and the most useful way to do this is according to their shapes. On this basis bones fall into four groups:

- **Long bones** have a greater length than width and are found mainly in the limbs. Their ends are specially adapted to articulate with each other or with the girdles.

- **Short bones** are shaped like small cylinders and are found, for example, in the wrists and ankles where they allow considerable freedom of movement.

- **Flat bones** have a large surface area for attachment of muscles or for protecting underlying structures. Examples are the pelvis, scapula and cranium.

- **Irregular bones** have complex shapes related to particular specialised functions. They include the vertebrae and jaw bones.

Christy Brown

Our hands, with their numerous bones and elaborate musculature, have amazing dexterity, as evidenced by musicians and others who use their hands for creative purposes. Though the digits are shorter, our feet too have considerable *potential* dexterity which is developed by those who for one reason or another are unable to use their hands.

Christy Brown was born with severe paralysis of many of his muscles, particularly those of his arms and right leg. However, he overcame his disability with remarkable determination, learning to use his left foot to do all sorts of things which other people do with their hands. The picture shows him at the age of 19, writing with his foot. He went on to become an accomplished artist and author. Many other people have learned to cope with similar disabilities.

Christy Brown writing with his left foot.

How do bones develop?

The skeleton of a human embryo is composed of cartilage. As the embryo develops, the cartilage is gradually replaced by bone in a process called **ossification**. The developing bone tissue hardens by becoming impregnated with minerals. The main mineral is **calcium**, and this is why growing children need plenty of this element in their food (*page 15*). If you remove the calcium from a bone by treating it with an acid, the bone becomes soft and flexible like rubber.

Some bones, such as those of the cranium, develop directly from connective tissue just under the skin. However, most bones start off as cartilage. Such is the case with a long bone like the femur. The cartilage is produced by cartilage cells (**chondroblasts**). Soon the cartilage becomes invaded by blood vessels, and then bone cells (**osteoblasts**) start producing bone tissue: spongy bone in the epiphyses and compact bone in the shaft surrounding the marrow cavity.

As new bone tissue is laid down, the bone grows in length and girth. Meanwhile, old bone tissue towards the centre of the bone is resorbed by specialised macrophages called **osteoclasts** formed in the bone marrow. Consequently the marrow cavity gradually expands as the bone grows.

The remodelling of bone

The macrophages in a bone such as the femur are important throughout the time the bone is developing. Their eroding activities enable the bone to be continually changed and remodelled to meet the stresses and strains to which the limb is subjected. They also cut channels in the bone, enabling blood vessels to grow into it. These channels become the Haversian canals of mature bone (*page 64*).

The process of remodelling continues even after the bone reaches full size. Bone tissue is laid down or resorbed in response to the mechanical demands made upon it: it is formed where it is needed and resorbed where it is not, so it becomes concentrated in the main lines of load bearing. This makes the skeleton incredibly versatile and efficient. By minimising the amount of material necessary to carry out its mechanical functions, its mass and metabolic costs are kept to a minimum.

24.2 Ligaments and tendons

The bones that make up the skeleton are connected to each other by tough connective tissue **ligaments** which, being elastic, are well suited to bear sudden stresses. They are composed of tightly packed bundles of **elastic fibres**.

The bones are moved relative to one another by an elaborate system of **skeletal muscles**. The muscles are attached to the bones by **tendons**, tough connective-tissue strands consisting almost entirely of **collagen fibres**.

▶ Structure and properties of elastic and collagen fibres, pages 65 and 66;

Tendons, being composed of collagen, are less elastic than ligaments. This makes sense when you think about it. If tendons were highly elastic, they would simply stretch when the muscle contracted. However, they do have a certain degree of elasticity and this allows them to store energy during locomotion.

Skeletal muscles have their **origin** on one bone (the bone nearer to the centre of the body) and their **insertion** on another, so they span the joints. Ligaments too span the joints. The stresses and strains to which the ligaments and tendons are subjected can be considerable, so they need to be firmly attached to the bones: their collagen and elastic fibres run into the connective tissue surrounding the bone, securing a firm attachment which is difficult to break.

Extension

Fractures and replacement surgery

Guest author Glyn Evans, an orthopaedic surgeon, describes some of the problems that can arise with our bones and how they can be remedied.

Fractures

Sometimes accidents happen, resulting in a **fracture**. Fractures vary in shape, extent and where they occur. In severe cases a bone, the femur for example, may break in two with accompanying damage to the surrounding tissues. Fractures are particularly common in elderly people who, as a natural consequence of the ageing process, develop **osteoporosis**. Bone tissue and calcium are lost, resulting in the bones becoming fragile. To some extent this condition may be prevented by taking extra calcium in the food (for example, by drinking more milk) or by hormone replacement therapy (*page 513*), but the incidence of fractures in the elderly is still very high.

If an animal in the wild, or a person living in an isolated community, breaks a bone, the fracture heals by a natural process without the assistance of an orthopaedic surgeon. First the cut surfaces of the bone bleed, then the blood

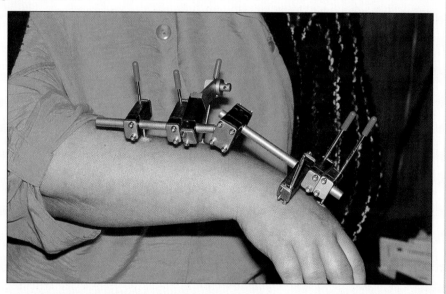

Illustration 1 A fixator may be used for holding bones in place following a fracture. The pins can be inserted using a power tool with wire-driving attachment.

clots and solidifies. Blood vessels grow into the clot and a **repair tissue** develops which holds the cut ends of the bone together. This tissue then slowly hardens and calcium salts are deposited in it, converting it into bone tissue which joins the two parts of the bone together.

Although nature is superbly equipped to heal fractures, fractures that heal naturally nearly always do so with the

bone in a crooked position. This may be due to the pull of the muscles, or to a deformity caused by the injury itself. The role of the orthopaedic surgeon is not normally to bring about healing, which would happen anyway, but to keep the bone in the correct alignment while healing takes place.

In many cases the bone is held in the correct position by a **cast**, which acts as a splint while the fracture heals. However, this does not always work, and it may be necessary to fix the broken pieces of bone together in some way. In some cases we make use of the marrow cavity and insert a stainless steel rod into it to act as an internal splint. If this is not possible, we can attach a plate to the surface of the bone with stainless steel screws.

If the skin over the fracture site is broken, some kind of external fixation may be necessary: pins are inserted through the skin into the bone and then linked together by a rod outside the skin. An example is shown in illustration 1.

On rare occasions the healing process fails and the pieces of bone do not knit together. One way of getting round this problem is to take a piece of bone from another part of the body, usually the pelvis, and insert it into the fracture site. Such a **bone graft** helps the fracture to heal.

Replacement surgery

Like any mechanical device, the joints in the skeleton undergo wear. Unlike the hinges of a door, however, our joints are normally able to repair any damage that occurs. However, if the joint surfaces wear faster than they can be repaired, the joint as a whole wears out. This results in

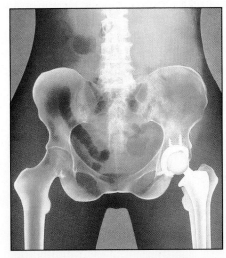

Illustration 2 X-ray image of the pelvic area following surgery to replace a patient's right hip joint, seen here in white on the right of the picture.

osteoarthritis. Another thing that may happen is that the joint surfaces get destroyed by disease, giving rise to **rheumatoid arthritis**.

In severe cases of arthritis a **joint replacement** may be necessary. The commonest joint that requires replacing is the hip joint. We remove the head of the femur (the ball) and replace it with a stainless steel ball attached to a rod inserted into the marrow cavity. Usually a small plastic cup is placed in the acetabulum, the natural socket in the

pelvis (*illustration 2*).

In most cases the plastic cup and metal rod are held in place by an acrylic cement. However, in younger patients hip replacements can be carried out without the use of a cement. For this to be possible the components have to be exceptionally well engineered so that they lock into place in their respective bones.

At one time **bone cancer** generally required amputation of the affected limb. These days the entire femur can be removed and replaced with a custom-made metal one. This is inserted into the leg with a hip replacement at the top and a knee replacement at the bottom.

Technology has enabled great advances to be made in treating disorders of the skeleton but of course problems do occur. The biggest enemy is infection. We also have to contend with the fact that metal components tend to work loose after a time, and metal fatigue sometimes occurs. However, the development of new materials may one day prevent these problems arising.

Glyn Evans is a Consultant Orthopaedic Surgeon at the Royal Isle of Wight County Hospital and a frequent writer on medical topics.

24.3 **Joints**

Joints vary in the amount of movement they permit. Some joints, such as those between the vertebrae, permit very little movement; whereas others, such as those between the different limb bones, allow considerable movement.

The latter type is called a **synovial joint** (*figure 24.5*). It is enclosed within a connective tissue capsule which is lined with a **synovial membrane**. The synovial membrane secretes **synovial fluid** which fills the cavity inside the joint and serves as a lubricant. The articulating surfaces are covered with a layer of **articular cartilage** which, being relatively soft, serves as a shock-absorber preventing jarring. The articular cartilage, synovial membrane and synovial fluid provide an exceptionally smooth surface against which the bones move with the minimum of friction.

Ligaments run between the two bones both inside the joint (i.e. inside the capsule) and outside it. Together with the capsule itself, they hold the joint together and prevent the bones coming apart. The muscles and tendons also help to strengthen the joint.

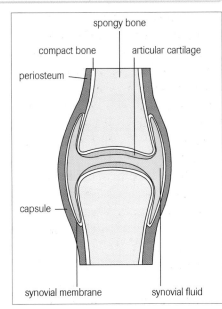

Figure 24.5 The structure of a typical synovial joint.

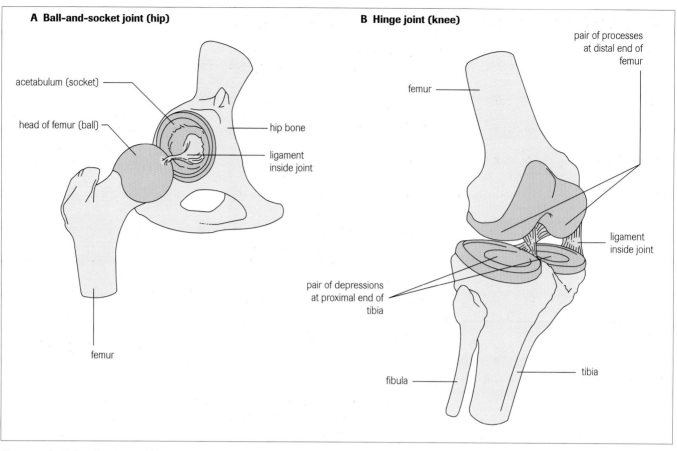

A Ball-and-socket joint (hip)

acetabulum (socket)

head of femur (ball)

hip bone

ligament inside joint

femur

B Hinge joint (knee)

pair of processes at distal end of femur

femur

ligament inside joint

pair of depressions at proximal end of tibia

fibula

tibia

Figure 24.6 Ball and socket and hinge joints illustrated by the hip joint and knee joint respectively. In both diagrams the fibrous capsule has been removed and the articular cartilage is coloured orange. Notice that the *single* articulation at the hip joint permits movement in any plane, whereas the *double* articulation at the knee joint restricts movement to only one plane.

Types of joint

All synovial joints have the same basic structure, but they differ in the shape of the articulating surfaces. This has important consequences, for it determines the freedom of movement at the joint. Synovial joints are of two main kinds:

- **Ball and socket joints** permit extensive movement in any plane, including rotation. Examples are the shoulder and hip joints (*figure 24.6A*).

- **Hinge joints** permit extensive movement in only one plane. Examples are the elbow and knee joints (*24.6B*).

You can test these joints for yourself by moving your arms and legs and seeing what sort of movement is possible at each one.

> **Extension**
>
> ### Accidents affecting joints
>
> Joints are the weak points of the skeleton and are therefore susceptible to damage.
>
> Most people **sprain** a joint sometime during their lives. A sprain is caused by wrenching the joint, and the wrench may be sufficiently severe to displace or tear one or more of the ligaments or tendons. Sprains can be painful and the affected structures must be given time to heal. Muscles spanning the joint are also liable to tearing, all the more so for being relatively soft.
>
> In more severe accidents the ends of two articulating bones may be forced apart at the joint, resulting in **dislocation**. For example, the head of the femur may come right out of the socket (acetabulum), tearing ligaments and/or tendons in the process. The remedy is to push the two articulating surfaces together again and, if necessary, keep them in position by means of a cast.

24.4 Muscles and the skeleton

To fulfil its function of supporting the body and permitting movement, the skeleton works in conjunction with muscles. To gain an insight into how they work together let us look at the arm.

The **lower arm bones** (the radius and ulna) are moved by two muscles, the **biceps** and **triceps**. Figure 24.7 shows the origin and insertion of these muscles and what happens when they contract.

Notice that they produce opposite effects: the biceps bends the arm at the elbow, and the triceps straightens it. A muscle such as the biceps, which pulls two limb bones towards each other, i.e. closes the joint, is called a **flexor**; a muscle such as the triceps, which pulls two limb bones away from each other, i.e. opens the joint, is called an **extensor**. The biceps and triceps are the main flexor and extensor muscles in the arm.

The bones which are pulled by the muscles act as **levers**. A lever is a solid bar which is turned about a fixed point or **pivot**. Levers are common in everyday life: you are using a lever when you prize open the lid of a box, or when you propel someone up and down on a seesaw. In any lever system two opposing forces operate on one or other side of the pivot: a **load** and an **effort**. Different kinds of lever are recognised depending on the positions of the load and the effort relative to the pivot. Figure 24.7 shows the lever systems which operate when the arm is flexed and extended.

Antagonistic and synergistic muscle action

Plainly the biceps and triceps (indeed all flexors and extensors) oppose each other in their actions. Such muscles are described as **antagonistic**. Other muscles assist each of these muscles to achieve their effects in a smooth and efficient manner. For example, when the biceps flexes the arm, other muscles hold the arm in a steady position so that the flexing action is more effective. These muscles are said to be **synergistic** to the flexor.

It is obviously necessary that when a muscle such as the biceps contracts its antagonist – in this case the triceps – should relax, and vice versa. This is achieved by the coordinating action of the central nervous system, operating via synapses in the spinal cord (*page 348*). This principle applies to any pair of antagonistic muscles, not only in the human but in other animals as well. We shall return to it in a moment.

A muscle which moves two parts of the skeleton relative to each other, for example when you bend your arm, shortens without developing tension. This kind of contraction is described as **isotonic** and it is obviously important in locomotion. In contrast, a muscle which contracts without moving the skeleton, as happens when the body – or part of it – is in a fixed position, develops tension without shortening. This kind of contraction is described as **isometric** and it is important in the maintenance of posture.

When your body is in a fixed position, for example when you are standing still, all your postural muscles are in a state of slight contraction. This is largely due to the presence in our muscles of **stretch receptors** which are explained in the extension box on the next page.

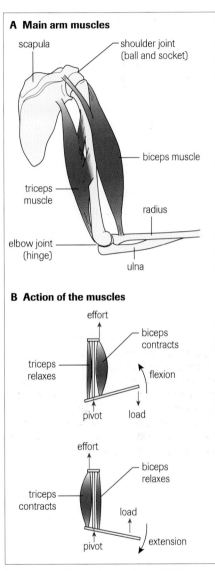

A Main arm muscles

scapula — shoulder joint (ball and socket)

biceps muscle

triceps muscle

radius

elbow joint (hinge)

ulna

B Action of the muscles

effort

biceps contracts

triceps relaxes

flexion

pivot — load

effort

biceps relaxes

triceps contracts

load

pivot — extension

Figure 24.7 The main muscles which flex and extend the arm at the elbow joint, and their actions.

24.5 Locomotion on land

In considering the locomotion of any animal, three things must be taken into account:

- **Propulsion:** the animal must be propelled with sufficient force in the appropriate direction.

- **Support:** the animal must be supported by its body acting against the particular medium in which it lives.

- **Stability:** the animal may become temporarily unstable while moving, but eventually stability must be restored.

Stretch receptors

A stretch receptor is a sensory device found inside muscles and tendons which is stimulated by being stretched. It is a type of **proprioceptor** (*page 380*). Together with other proprioceptors, such as those in the vestibular apparatus in the inner ear, they play an important part in the maintenance of posture and control of movement. In fulfilling this function they work in conjunction with the brain, particularly the **cerebellum** (*page 361*).

There are two main types of stretch receptor: **muscle spindles** and **tendon organs**.

Muscle spindle

It is helpful to understand what muscle spindles achieve before considering how they do it. If a muscle is stretched (for example by its antagonist) the muscle spindle initiates a reflex which causes that muscle to contract. In other words *when a muscle is stretched it responds by contracting*. This is called a **stretch reflex** and, insofar as the stimulus evokes a corrective response, it is an example of negative feedback.

The muscle spindle is embedded in the muscle and runs parallel to the ordinary muscle fibres. The central part of it consists of spiral nerve endings wrapped round a slender bundle of modified non-contractile muscle fibres (*illustration*). The spiral nerve endings are branches of a sensory nerve which leads to the CNS. The two ends of the spindle are composed of contractile muscle fibres which receive effector nerves from the CNS.

The muscle spindle works like this. As soon as the muscle is stretched, nerve impulses are discharged from the spiral nerve endings to the CNS. This results in impulses being transmitted via the appropriate effector nerves to the muscle, making it contract. The nerve pathway in this stretch reflex is shown by the broken arrow in the illustration. It has been found that the more the spindle is stretched, the greater is the frequency of impulses discharged in the nerve and the harder the muscle contracts.

The contractile ends of the spindle set the tone of the receptor so that it is not slack when the muscle is stretched. This is

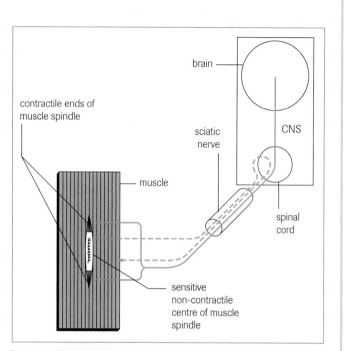

Diagram of a muscle spindle and the reflex pathway by which it achieves its effects.

particularly important if the muscle is liable to considerable stretching, such as when a heavy load is lifted or during the maintenance of posture. Under these circumstances contraction of its two ends increases the stretch on the spindle and so augments the response. The nerve pathways through which this is achieved are shown by the solid arrows in the illustration.

Tendon organs

A tendon organ consists of branched nerve endings which, when stretched, discharge impulses to the CNS. Experiments show that the tendon organ only responds when the tension is extreme. This is because it has a high threshold, much higher than the muscle spindle. Excitation of the tendon organ triggers a reflex which inhibits the muscle, thereby preventing it from contracting so powerfully that it might get damaged.

Most land-living vertebrates are **tetrapods** (**quadrupeds**), i.e. they have four limbs all of which are used for locomotion. Humans, however, are **bipeds**. This difference does not affect propulsion but it does affect support and stability, as we shall see.

Propulsion

The legs of land-living vertebrates contain numerous muscles, most of which are directly or indirectly involved in propulsion. The muscles can be divided into seven groups according to their actions (*figure 24.8*).

- **Protractors** pull the limb forward.
- **Retractors** pull the limb backwards.
- **Adductors** pull the limb inwards.

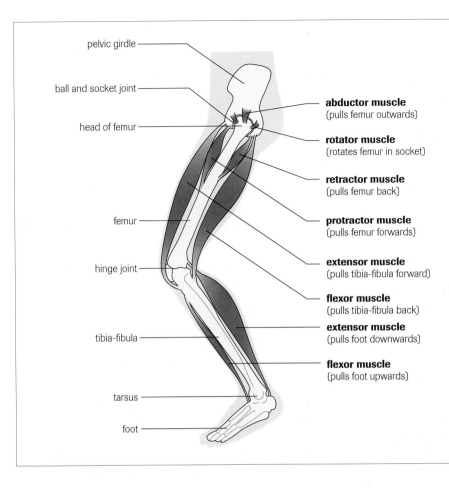

pelvic girdle

ball and socket joint

head of femur

femur

hinge joint

tibia-fibula

tarsus

foot

abductor muscle
(pulls femur outwards)

rotator muscle
(rotates femur in socket)

retractor muscle
(pulls femur back)

protractor muscle
(pulls femur forwards)

extensor muscle
(pulls tibia-fibula forward)

flexor muscle
(pulls tibia-fibula back)

extensor muscle
(pulls foot downwards)

flexor muscle
(pulls foot upwards)

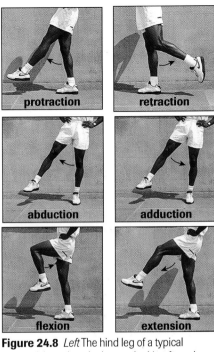

protraction

retraction

abduction

adduction

flexion

extension

Figure 24.8 *Left* The hind leg of a typical mammal, based on the human looking from the outside. Only a small selection of the muscles is shown; there are at least 30 in the human leg. Adductor muscles are found on the inner side of the leg and are therefore not visible in this diagram. They pull the femur inwards.
Above The main actions produced by the muscles, illustrated here by a young athlete.

■ **Abductors** pull the limb outwards.

■ **Flexors** pull two parts of the limb towards each other.

■ **Extensors** pull two parts of the limb away from each other.

■ **Rotators** swivel the whole, or part, of the limb.

Some of these muscles are **extrinsic**, that is they have their origin outside the limb itself, i.e. on the limb girdles. The rest are **intrinsic**, having both their origin and insertion within the limb.

Some of the muscles are synergistic, contracting together to produce a particular action. For example, if you raise your foot off the ground and bend your knee at the same time, as in picture 5 in figure 24.8, your protractor and flexor muscles contract together. Other muscles are antagonistic, opposing each other in their actions. Thus protractors are antagonistic to retractors, adductors to abductors, and flexors to extensors.

The different muscles are supplied by axons from the main nerve serving the limb – the **sciatic nerve** in the case if the hind limb. Different axons, or bundles of axons, go to each muscle. By sending impulses down the appropriate axons, the central nervous system ensures that the various muscles contract at the right moment, synergists at the same time, antagonists at *different* times.

The mechanism in the nervous system which ensures that antagonistic muscles do not contract simultaneously is called **reciprocal innervation** and is explained on page 347.

Propulsive action of the muscles

In propelling the body forward the most important muscles are the retractors and extensors. When they contract the limb acts as a lever. The foot presses downwards and backwards against the ground, resulting in an equal and opposite force which is

Support

Walking

We take walking for granted, but have you ever thought how complicated it is?

Using figure 24.8 to help you, try to describe the actions of the various muscles in *one* of your legs during a complete walking cycle, that is from the moment you lift your foot off the ground to the moment you lift it off the ground again.

Explain how your nervous system ensures that each muscle contracts, or relaxes, at the right time.

Now do the same thing for *both* legs together. In other words, consider what's happening in your right leg when your left leg goes through a complete cycle.

Easy though it may seem, we have to *learn* how to walk, suffering all sorts of mishaps on the way. How do you think a toddler learns how to walk?

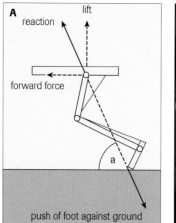

Figure 24.9 These diagrams illustrate the action of the limb in propelling the body forward.
A Model of a limb, showing the retractor and extensor muscles (red). The extent to which the body is propelled forwards rather than upwards depends on the size of the angle, a.
B For a sprinter the angle a should be small so as to gain maximum forward thrust.

transmitted along the length of the limb against the body (*figure 24.9A*). This force can be resolved into a vertical component and a horizontal component. The former lifts the body off the ground, the latter propels it forward.

The relative magnitude of these two forces will depend on the angle between the ground and the main axis of the limb (*angle a in figure 24.9A*). If this angle is 90°, with the point of contact of the foot with the ground directly below the centre of gravity, there will be a lift force but no forward force, with the result that the body is thrust vertically upwards. This is what high-jumpers try to achieve then they leave the ground.

On the other hand, if the angle is small and the foot is a long way behind the centre of gravity, the forward force will be considerable but the upward lift force relatively small. This is what sprinters aim to achieve when they take their positions at the starting blocks (*figure 24.9B*).

Support

The limbs must hold the body off the ground both when the animal is in motion and when it is standing still. For maximum efficiency the limbs should be directly beneath the body.

To appreciate this, we have only to compare the limbs of a mammal such as a horse with a reptile such as a lizard. Figure 24.10 compares their forelimbs. In the lizard the limbs splay out from the body, giving the animal a bow-legged appearance. Holding the body off the ground necessitates the contraction of powerful adductor muscles running from the ventral side of the pectoral girdle to the humerus. One cannot help thinking that, for a heavy reptile like a crocodile, walking must be a great strain, like push-ups for a human. No wonder such animals spend so much of their time lying on their bellies.

In mammals, this problem has been overcome by bringing the limbs into a straight line beneath the body. The result is that the load is transmitted along what are essentially four straight struts. Predictably, the adductor muscles are considerably reduced and the ventral part of the pectoral girdle is absent altogether.

Figure 24.10 *Right* Diagrammatic end-on views of a primitive and an advanced tetrapod to show their respective stances. Note that the primitive condition requires the development of powerful adductor muscles to hold the body off the ground. *Below* Photograph of a lizard, showing the primitive splayed-out position of the limbs.

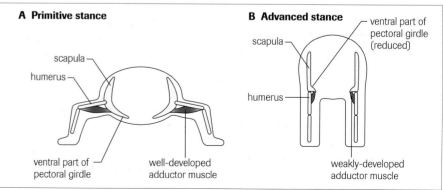

The vertebral column as a bridge

In most tetrapods, the vertebral column bridges the gap between the forelimbs and hind limbs. The tetrapod skeleton can, in fact, be regarded as a bridge in which the limbs represent the piers and the vertebral column the span.

What kind of bridge is it? This question was investigated many years ago by the great zoologist D'Arcy Thompson. On the basis of mathematical considerations, he came to the conclusion that the vertebral column is comparable to a **cantilever bridge** like the Forth railway bridge in Scotland.

Though extravagant in its use of materials, the cantilever is a strong construction and there is no risk of it breaking in the middle. This is important when you think of the load it has to bear. In an elephant, for example, the entire weight of the abdomen acts downwards at right angles to the vertebral column.

In humans, being bipedal, the vertebral column is more like a tower than a bridge. The weight of the body is transmitted down the main axis of the vertebral column, each vertebra pressing against the one below. Here the problem is not so much to prevent the vertebral column breaking in the middle as to withstand the downward pressure. The intervertebral discs, being made of cartilage, are particularly vulnerable in this respect. If the pressure suddenly becomes unevenly distributed, one of the discs may burst on one side, giving what is called a **slipped disc** *(support box on the right)*.

Support

What causes a slipped disc?

The centre of each intervertebral disc consists of hyaline cartilage which is soft and rubbery. The outer part of the disc consists of fibrocartilage and is relatively hard and tough. (*The microscopic structure of these two types of cartilage is described on page 67.*)

In a 'slipped disc' the outer fibrous layer of the disc splits and the softer inner material bulges out. Great pain may be caused if the extruded material presses on one of the spinal nerves.

Slipped discs are often caused when people try to lift a heavy load by bending forward with the legs straight. If the bulge is small it may regress after a few weeks. Otherwise physiotherapy or surgery may be necessary.

Extension

Musculo-skeletal fitness

To get the best out of our muscles and skeleton we need to be fit. This applies not only to the parts of the musculo-skeletal system concerned with locomotion, but also to those that deal with non-locomotory actions such as chest movements. Fitness is acquired by taking regular exercise of the right kind, which can have a number of beneficial effects.

Effects on the muscles

- The muscles get larger and stronger. This is because the individual muscle fibres thicken rather than because they become more numerous.
- More actin and myosin are produced because the rate of protein synthesis increases. There is also an increase in the amounts of metabolic enzymes and stored nutrients such as glycogen.
- The amount of connective tissue in the muscles increases, strengthening the connective-tissue framework.
- The muscles become more taut. This is useful for maintaining posture as well as bringing about movement. Flabby muscles are inefficient because the first part of their contraction simply tightens them without producing any useful effect.

Effects on the skeleton

- Bones get stronger because their mineral content increases, assuming of course that the diet contains sufficient nutrients such as calcium. Bone tissue becomes concentrated in the main lines of load bearing (*extension box on page 417*).
- Ligaments and tendons get tougher because the amount of connective tissue in them increases. This helps to protect joints and muscles from injury.
- Joints become more mobile as a result of increased elasticity of the ligaments. This makes the body more flexible.

How much exercise do you need to take to achieve the benefits outlined above? The answer, according to the Medical Research Council, is a minimum of 3 times a week for 20 minutes at 70 per cent of the maximum heart rate. (The maximum heart rate in beats per minute = 220 minus your age in years.)

▶ Effects of exercise on body mass, page 154

▶ Effects of exercise on metabolism, breathing and the circulation, page 244

▶ Effects of exercise on fast and slow twitch muscles, page 404

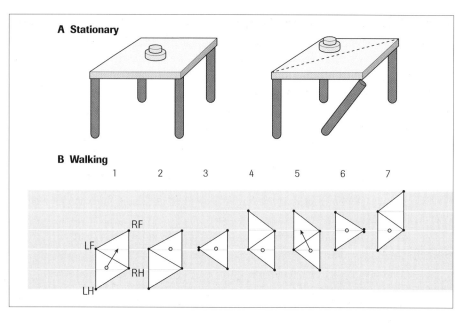

Figure 24.11 The problem of stability in a tetrapod.

A A stationary tetrapod is like a table. If all four legs are in contact with the ground, the table will remain stable if the centre of gravity is anywhere within the area delineated by the four legs. If one leg is taken off the ground the table will fall over unless the centre of gravity is shifted into the triangle delineated by the three legs that remain in contact with the ground.

B Successive stages in the diagonal locomotory pattern of a walking tetrapod. The order in which the feet are raised off the ground is: left hind, left fore, right hind, right fore. Note that a foot can be raised only if the centre of gravity (represented by the circle) is first shifted into the triangle delineated by the three feet that remain in contact with the ground.

Stability

For a tetrapod at rest, with its four legs planted fairly and squarely on the ground, stability is not a major problem. The animal is like a four-legged table with the centre of gravity falling inside the area delineated by its four legs (*figure 24.11A*).

However, when the animal is in motion, problems arise because periodically at least one leg must be taken off the ground. When this happens, the tetrapod changes to being a tripod. If the animal is to remain stable when it takes a foot off the ground, it must first shift its centre of gravity into the triangle delineated by the three legs that are still in contact with the ground. If it fails to do this, it will topple over.

The sequence of events that occurs during tetrapod locomotion is based on this simple fact of mechanics. Look at figure 24.11B. Imagine a slow-moving tetrapod with its legs in the positions shown in diagram 1. In order to progress, the first thing it must do is to move its weight forward so that its centre of gravity falls within the triangle delineated by the right fore, right hind and left forelimbs (diagram 2). It then lifts the left hind limb and brings it up behind the left forelimb (diagram 3). It then lifts its left forelimb and places it out in front (diagram 4). The centre of gravity is now shifted into the new triangle delineated by the left fore, left hind and right forelimbs (diagram 5). The right hind limb can now be raised and brought up behind the right forelimb (diagram 6).

The animal thus progresses in a **diagonal pattern** in which the order of leg-raising is: left hind, left fore, right hind, right fore – and so on.

The diagonal pattern is clearly seen in slow-moving tetrapods like newts and salamanders, but even in a galloping horse, as slow-motion films show, the diagonal pattern can still be detected, the legs being slightly out of phase with each other during the locomotory cycle.

The importance of the centre of gravity

Plainly the position of the centre of gravity plays an important part in an animal's life. In an animal like a horse the centre of gravity lies towards the front of the body, so the animal can raise one of its hind limbs with no risk of instability. But if it is to raise one of its forelimbs, it must first move its weight back so that its centre of gravity is nearer the hind legs.

In squirrels, bears and kangaroos the centre of gravity lies towards the rear, so the forelimbs can be lifted off the ground without loss of stability. This enables such animals to sit on their haunches, a useful thing to be able to do for it enables the animal to survey its surroundings from an elevated vantage point. In the kangaroo, the centre of gravity is so far back that it would fall over backwards were it not for the strong muscular tail acting as a support. In this way the kangaroo can rest on a tripod whilst surveying its surroundings (*figure 24.12*).

Humans of course are bipedal and can stand – and move – permanently on the hind limbs. The development of bipedalism was a most important step in our evolution (*page 774*). Care is needed though, for if the centre of gravity falls outside the area delineated by our feet we run the risk of falling over. Fortunately mechanical stability is augmented by reflexes arising from proprioceptors such as the muscle spindles and vestibular apparatus in the inner ear, from pressure receptors in the soles of the feet, and of course from the eyes. If it were not for these reflexes, gymnasts and ballet dancers would not be worth watching.

Figure 24.12 The kangaroo uses its strong muscular tail to provide support when in the upright position. In doing so it becomes a tripod.

24.6 Locomotion in water

Water, being much denser than air, offers far more resistance to the movement of objects through it. In many aquatic animals such as fish and porpoises, this disadvantage is minimised by streamlining.

On the credit side, water provides more support than air and is a relatively thick medium on which propulsive devices can gain a purchase.

Propulsion in fish

In most fish propulsion comes from side-to-side lashing of the tail which is equipped with a **caudal fin** for increasing its surface area (*figure 24.13*). The movements are brought about by contraction of segmentally arranged blocks of muscle called **myotomes** which extend from the transverse processes of one vertebra, and the connective tissue septum

Figure 24.13 Locomotion in a fish.
A The powerful myotome muscles on either side of the vertebral column swing the tail from side to side.
B The muscles contract alternately on either side, bending the vertebral column as shown.
C The forces set up as the tail moves through the water.

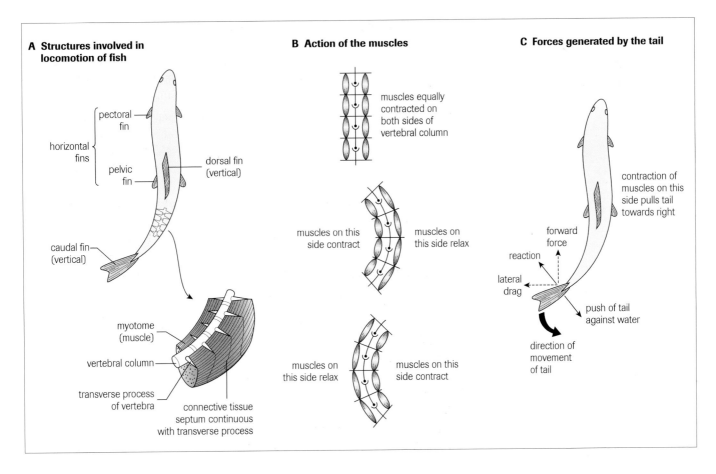

A Structures involved in locomotion of fish

horizontal fins
pectoral fin
pelvic fin
dorsal fin (vertical)
caudal fin (vertical)
myotome (muscle)
vertebral column
transverse process of vertebra
connective tissue septum continuous with transverse process

B Action of the muscles

muscles equally contracted on both sides of vertebral column

muscles on this side contract
muscles on this side relax

muscles on this side relax
muscles on this side contract

C Forces generated by the tail

contraction of muscles on this side pulls tail towards right
forward force
reaction
lateral drag
push of tail against water
direction of movement of tail

The eel-like method of locomotion is not confined to aquatic animals. Snakes move by lateral undulations which pass along the body from front to rear, as in eels. So long as there is something reasonably firm for the body to push against, the animal can glide forward.

A striking demonstration of this is seen in eels themselves. An eel placed on a flat slippery surface makes little or no progress, but if placed on a peg-board it progresses quickly and efficiently by gaining a purchase on the pegs. In effect, the animal is swimming on land. This enables eels to move overland if necessary as they migrate up rivers to fresh water. It also means that, from a locomotory point of view, an animal like a grass snake is as adept in water as it is on land. Grass snakes are in fact excellent swimmers.

continuous with it, to the next. The tail sweeps from side to side by alternate contractions of the myotomes on each side of the body. The myotomes on the left and right sides are, of course, antagonistic and their contractions are coordinated by the CNS.

When the fish is swimming, forces are set up as shown in figure 24.13C. As the tail sweeps across towards the right it pushes against the water, as a result of which it experiences a force which can be resolved into a forward and a sideways component. The forward component drives the fish through the water. The sideways component tends to swing the tail towards the left and the head towards the right. How this **lateral drag** is minimised will be explained presently.

In the type of fish just described propulsion is achieved by the tail lashing from side to side. Most other fish use the same basic method of propulsion, though different amounts of the body may be involved. In eels, for example, the entire body is thrown into lateral undulations which progress from front to rear, exerting forces similar to those exerted by the tail of other fish.

In bony fish, the pectoral and pelvic fins are small fan-like appendages on either side of the body. They can be pulled into the side or stuck out at will, and are used for steering and braking. In some species the pectoral and pelvic fins are very mobile, making these fish astonishingly agile as you will know if you have ever kept tropical fish.

Support in fish

Bony fish such as trout are made buoyant by a gas-filled **swim bladder** situated towards the dorsal side of the body. There are two types of swim bladder:

- An **open swim bladder** is connected to the pharynx by a duct, and air is taken into it, or expelled from it, through the mouth. So by 'blowing bubbles' a goldfish can make itself heavier and sink to a lower level in the water. On the other hand, to occupy a higher level in the water it must first swim to the surface and gulp air into its swim bladder.

- A **closed swim bladder** is not connected to the pharynx. Gas, mainly oxygen, is secreted into it, or withdrawn from it, by specialised blood vessels in its lining. By this means the density of the fish can be adjusted with minimum inconvenience to the animal, enabling it to stay at the required depth without having to swim up to the surface. The majority of bony fish have swim bladders of this type.

Cartilaginous fish such as sharks do not possess a swim bladder of any kind. They sink if they stop swimming, and support comes from the process of swimming itself. As the fish swims along, its large flap-like **pectoral fins** and to a lesser extent the smaller **pelvic fins** – held at a slight angle to the body – provide a lift force. Posteriorly the tail provides lift as well as a propulsive forward force.

Stability in fish

A fish is liable to the same kinds of instability that affect boats: yawing, pitching and rolling.

- **Yawing** is the side-to-side swinging of the anterior part of the body resulting from the propulsive action of the tail. It is counteracted by the general massiveness and inertia of the head and by the pressure of water against the side of the body and the vertical fins. In many bony fish the stabilising effect of the fins is enhanced by lateral flattening of the body.

- **Pitching** is the tendency of the anterior end to plunge vertically downwards. It is counteracted by the flap-like pectoral fins. The larger the surface area of these fins, the more effective they are as stabilisers.

- **Rolling** is the rotation of the body about its longitudinal axis. It is counteracted by the vertical and horizontal fins rather like the feathers at the back of an arrow.

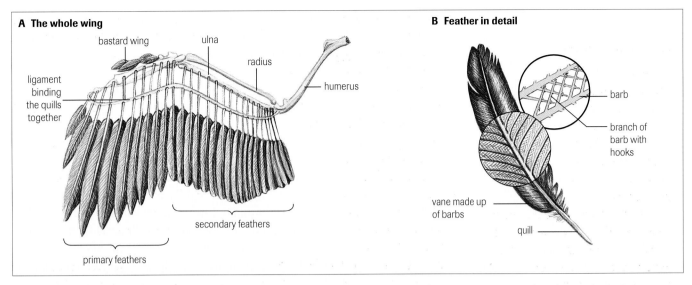

A The whole wing

bastard wing

ulna

radius

humerus

ligament binding the quills together

secondary feathers

primary feathers

B Feather in detail

barb

branch of barb with hooks

vane made up of barbs

quill

Figure 24.14 The wing of a bird showing the main feathers involved in flight.

24.7 Locomotion in air

The technical problems connected with movement in air are considerable. This is due to the thinness of the medium which, compared with water, provides little support and negligible purchase for the propulsive devices. On the other hand, resistance to movement is less than in water.

Active flight has been successfully developed in three groups of animals: birds, bats (an order of mammals) and insects. In all three cases the flight mechanism depends on the possession of **wings**.

Flight in birds

The bird wing consists of a row of **feathers** projecting from the forelimb (*figure 24.14*). The number of digits is reduced compared with the human, and the feathers give the wing a large surface area. The feathers themselves are extremely light and are arranged rather like the slats of a Venetian blind with the result that air can pass between them as the wing goes up but not when the wing goes down.

A bird can fly either passively by gliding or actively by flapping its wings.

Passive flight

When a bird glides, the wings act as **aerofoils**. An aerofoil is any smooth surface which moves through the air at an angle to the airstream. The main properties of an aerofoil, as applied to the wing of a bird, are summarised in figure 24.15.

The air flows over the wing in such a way that the bird is given lift, the amount of lift depending on the angle at which the wing is held relative to the airstream, that is the **angle of attack**. Turbulence, which could cause the bird to lose height, is prevented by the **bastard wing** which smoothes the flow of air over the top side of the wing. The same

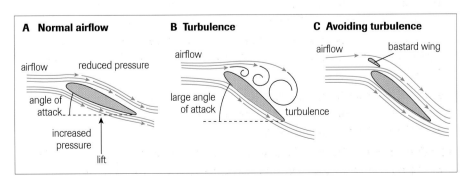

A Normal airflow

airflow

reduced pressure

angle of attack

increased pressure

lift

B Turbulence

airflow

large angle of attack

turbulence

C Avoiding turbulence

airflow

bastard wing

Figure 24.15 The bird wing as an aerofoil.
A The air flows faster over the upper surface of the wing than the lower surface. This creates a reduced pressure above the wing and an increased pressure below it, thereby providing the bird with lift. The lift force can be increased by holding the wing at a greater angle to the airstream, i.e. by increasing the angle of attack.
B If the angle of attack is too large, turbulence may occur above the wing.
C Turbulence is normally prevented by the bastard wing and by the end-feathers which serve as slots, smoothing the flow of air over the upper surface of the wing.

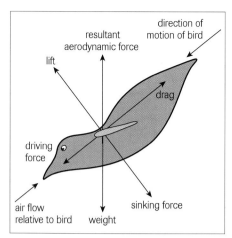

Figure 24.16 Diagram illustrating the forces operating on a bird gliding in still air. The weight of the bird acting downwards can be resolved into two components: a sinking force and, at right angles to this, a driving force propelling the body obliquely downwards. Assuming that the bird is moving at constant speed, these two forces are opposed by equal forces acting in the opposite direction. The sinking force is opposed by a lift force acting obliquely upwards, and the driving force by a drag force. The resultant of these two forces is the aerodynamic force, and is equal and opposite to the weight.

Figure 24.17 In this photo of a gliding albatross notice the enormous wing span compared with the size of the body. The wing span of the wandering albatross, *Diomedea exulans*, may exceed three metres.

Figure 24.18 The musculo-skeletal basis of flight in birds.
A The skeleton of a pigeon showing the deep keel on the lower side of the sternum for the attachment of the large wing muscles.
B Diagrammatic front view of the skeleton showing the origin and insertion of the wing muscles. The large and powerful muscle that lowers the wing gives the bird lift during active flight. The tendon of the muscle that raises the wing passes through the foramen triosseum (a small hole bounded by the scapula, coracoid and clavicle) and has its insertion on the top side of the humerus. When it contracts it pulls the wing upwards, like a pulley.

effect is achieved by the feathers at the far end of the wing which separate from each other during flight.

The flow of air over the wings as the bird moves forward sets up the forces shown in figure 24.16. Consequently, the bird does not drop like a stone but glides along an inclined path.

The speed of gliding depends on the bird's weight and the size and shape of its wings. A heavy bird with small wings glides faster than a light bird with large wings. The distance a bird can glide in still air depends on the height from which it starts gliding and on the angle between its downward path and the horizontal. For an expert glider such as an albatross this angle is small and the bird can glide almost horizontally (*figure 24.17*). This is achieved by holding the wings at an angle of attack that ensures that drag is minimised and lift maximised.

Even the best gliders cannot maintain an absolutely horizontal path in still air, but if the air is rising the bird can maintain its level or even climb. Birds are constantly using upward air currents for gaining height. These upcurrents arise in several ways – for example when air, warmed by the Earth's surface, rises and is replaced by cooler air (**thermal upcurrents**) or when horizontal wind hits a vertical obstruction such as a cliff (**obstructional upcurrents**). When you see gulls gliding on the windward side of a cliff they are making use of such obstructional upcurrents.

By making use of natural air currents, a bird such as the albatross in figure 24.17 can glide for over 50 km.

Active flight

When little or no support can be gained from upward air currents, the same effect can be achieved by flapping the wings (**active flight**). The flapping of the wings creates an airflow over them which produces much the same system of forces as in gliding flight. At the completion of the each downstroke, the wings are returned to their original position, front edge first, so as to minimise downward drag.

The wings are raised and lowered by powerful muscles rich in myoglobin (*page 220*). The way these muscles are attached to the skeleton is shown in figure 24.18. To provide an adequate surface for their attachment, the sternum of birds is greatly expanded and has a deep **keel** to increase its surface area. Birds such as the ostrich, which do not fly, have less extensive wing muscles and lack a sternal keel.

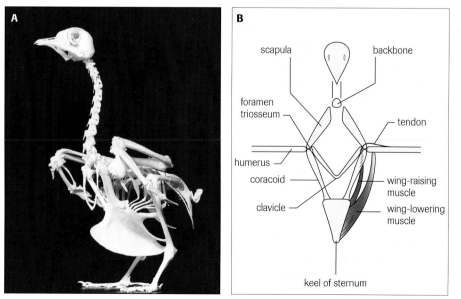

24.8 Movement in other animals

The type of skeleton which we and other vertebrates possess is called an **endoskeleton**. This name derives from the fact that the skeletal elements, bone or cartilage as the case may be, are internal to the muscles which are attached to them. Thus in our own limbs the bones are ensheathed by the muscles that move them.

Exoskeleton

A different arrangement is found in arthropods such as insects and crustaceans. Here the hard cuticle performs the function of a skeleton. As the cuticle is *outside* the muscles that move it, it is called an **exoskeleton**.

Figure 24.19 shows the inside of an arthropod leg. Notice that the flexor and extensor muscles are enclosed within the box-like exoskeleton to which they are attached. Bending occurs at the **joint**, where the hard exoskeleton is replaced by a flexible membrane like the concertina connection between the coaches of a train. The muscles are attached to inward projections of the exoskeleton called **apodemes**. The muscles are antagonistic – the flexor bending the leg and the extensor straightening it.

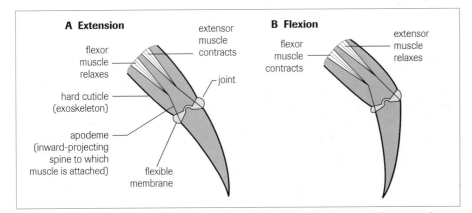

Figure 24.19 The distal part of the leg of an arthropod showing the extensor and flexor muscles. Notice that the muscles are internal to the skeleton, which is therefore called an exoskeleton.

Hydrostatic skeleton

A totally different system is found in soft-bodied invertebrates such as sea anemones and earthworms. In these animals there is no hard skeleton at all, its place being taken by a fluid under pressure. The fluid is surrounded by muscles which press against it, for which reason it is called a **hydrostatic skeleton**.

In the earthworm the muscular **body wall** contracts against the fluid in the **body cavity (coelom)**, creating a pressure which maintains the animal's shape in much the same way as a balloon's shape is maintained when full of air.

There are two antagonistic sets of muscle tissue in the body wall: **circular** and **longitudinal**. When the circular muscle contracts and the longitudinal relaxes, the body becomes long and thin; when the longitudinal muscle contracts and the circular relaxes, the body becomes short and fat.

Transverse partitions called **septa** divide the body cavity into a series of watertight compartments (**segments**). This means that a change in pressure in one part of the body does not immediately spread to other parts, so localised bulges can occur (*figure 24.20*). Locomotion is achieved by these bulges passing along the body from front to rear. This is an effective means of propulsion for a burrowing animal like the earthworm. Where the bulges occur, bristle-like **chaetae** protrude from the body wall and gain a purchase on the soil.

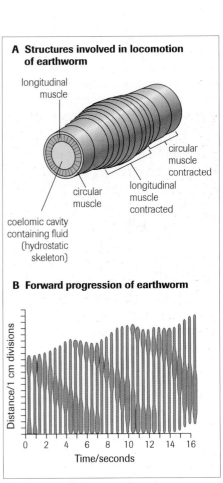

Figure 24.20 In the earthworm the body wall muscles contract against the fluid in the body cavity which acts as a hydrostatic skeleton.
A A bulge is formed by localised contraction of the longitudinal muscle.
B The worm progresses forward by bulges being propagated slowly from the anterior to the posterior end of the body.

'Static' in the word hydrostatic suggests an inert system in which the fluid is stationary. However, as we see in the earthworm, the hydrostatic skeleton provides the basis for a dynamic system of movement.

A system comparable to the hydrostatic skeleton is seen in situations where a fluid is forced into an extendable appendage. In humans such a system is responsible for making the penis erect (*page 504*), and in bivalve molluscs such as clams it enables the foot to be protuded from the shell for burrowing into mud or sand. The clam's foot extends by blood being forced into it; then it shortens, pulling the rest of the body into the sand. The process is usually quite slow but the West Indian surf clam *Donax denticulatus* is an exception: about 2 cm in length, it can bury itself in less than 5 seconds!

▶ Parenchyma tissue, page 70

In plants the parenchyma tissue in stems and leaves, when fully turgid, is eqivalent to (though far less dynamic than) the hydrostatic skeleton of animals.

Extension

Flight in insects

Insect flight obeys much the same aerodynamic principles as bird flight, but its musculo-skeletal basis is quite different. Instead of being attached to the wings, the flight muscles are attached to the inside of the hard cuticle surrounding the **thorax**. When the muscles contract they alter the shape of the thorax in such a way that the wings go up and down.

The mechanism is summarised in the illustration. It depends on the ingenious way the wings are attached to the thorax. The base of each wing is attached to both the roof and the walls (i.e. sides) of the thorax, the roof attachment being median to (i.e. slightly further in than) the wall attachment.

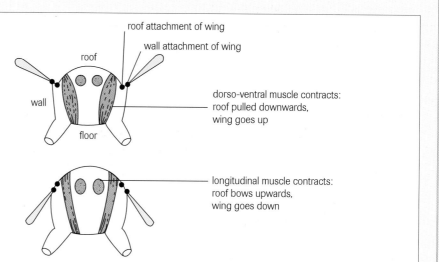

Diagrams of the thorax of an insect in cross-section showing how the muscles make the wings go up and down.

The thorax contains two sets of flight muscles: a pair of **dorso-ventral muscles** run from the roof to the floor of the thorax, and a pair of **longitudinal muscles** run from the anterior surface of the dome-like roof to the posterior surface. When the dorso-ventral muscles contract, the roof attachment of the wing is pulled downwards relative to the wall attachment, with the result that the wing goes up. When the longitudinal muscles contract, the top of the dome-like roof rises slightly and the roof attachment of the wing is pulled upwards relative to the wall attachment, with the result that the wing goes down. Only a tiny contraction is sufficient to produce a sizeable movement of the wing tip. In wasps, for example, a minuscule contraction moves the wings through an angle of 150°.

Since the muscles responsible for the wing movements are not actually attached to the wings, they are known as **indirect flight muscles**. There are, in addition, some muscles attached to the base of the wing itself. These **direct flight muscles** adjust the wing stroke and also fold the wings at rest.

A remarkable feature of insect flight is the frequency at which the wings can beat. Large insects like butterflies, locusts and dragonflies beat their wings comparatively slowly at frequencies ranging between about 10 and 50 per second. In these cases nerve impulses are sent to the muscles at the same frequency as the wing beat. But many insects beat their wings much faster than this: the housefly at 200 per second, mosquitoes at 600 per second, and certain midges at over 1000 per second!

The flight muscles achieve these astonishing frequencies because they do not need to receive an impulse for each contraction. In the blowfly, for instance, the muscles receive an impulse only once every 40 wing beats. Nerve impulses are needed to initiate flight, after which the muscles oscillate at their own natural frequency with occasional impulses to keep them going.

Amoeboid movement

Amoeboid cells, such as *Amoeba* itself and phagocytic white blood cells, can change their shape, and this is the basis of how they move. The plasma membrane, in keeping with that of other cells, is flexible. Inside the cell, the cytoplasm consists of fluid **endoplasm** in the centre surrounded by stiffer **ectoplasm** towards the periphery.

When the cell moves, the fluid endoplasm flows inside the 'wall' of ectoplasm to form a temporary projection called a **pseudopodium**. When it reaches the leading end of the advancing pseudopodium, the endoplasm everts, rather like a cuff being folded back, and is converted into the stiffer ectoplasm. At the other end of the cell the reverse happens: the ectoplasm inverts and becomes fluid endoplasm. So the cell moves by a fluid core flowing forward through a tube of its own making (*illustration*).

Despite years of research, the mechanism of amoeboid movement is still not fully understood. The current theory is based on the observation that

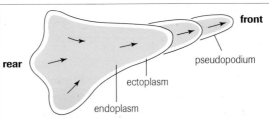

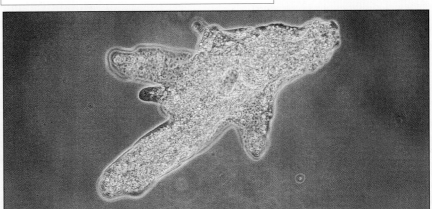

A pseudopodium being formed by an amoeba. The arrows indicate the direction in which the fluid endoplasm flows. The photomicrograph shows an amoeba in the process of forming a pseudopodium.

the cytoplasm contains numerous short **microfilaments** made of **actin**. Each filament is composed of a double helical chain of globular protein molecules which can readily be removed from, or added to, the ends of the filament (*page 52*). At the leading edge of a pseudopodium the

filaments are orientated at right angles to the plasma membrane. It is thought that the pseudopodium extends by globular protein molecules being added to the leading ends of the microfilaments and taken away from the other ends. ATP is needed for this process to occur.

Movement by means of cilia and flagella

Many small organisms swim by means of **cilia** or **flagella**.

Flagella, and flagella-like structures such as sperm tails, achieve their propulsive action using principles similar to (but not identical with) those involved in the swimming of fishes such as eels. Undulations pass along the flagellum from base to tip, driving the organism in the opposite direction.

Cilia, such as those of *Paramecium*, employ a different principle. Each cilium, held out straight from the body, swings back through an arc of about 180°, propelling the organism forward like the oars of a rowing boat (*illustration*). On completing its movement, the cilium

returns to its original position, bending as it does so. Then, held out straight once more, it repeats its backstroke.

The numerous cilia projecting from the surface of an organism like *Paramecium* beat in relays, giving an effect like waves passing over a cornfield in a gust of wind. This is called a **metachronal rhythm**. The combined effect of all the cilia of *Paramecium* is to propel the organism through the water at a speed of about 3 mm per second. The arrangement of the cilia and the way they are coordinated is explained on page 74.

How do cilia and flagella bend? The mechanism depends on the 9+2 array of microtubules found in these organelles

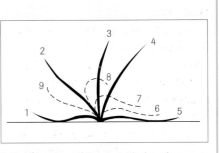

Action of a cilium. Cilia are rigid when they beat backwards (stages 1–5 in the diagram), but bend when they return to their original position (stages 6–9).

(*page 54*). The peripheral microtubules have little arms projecting from them. These arms are believed to serve as ratchets, causing the microtubules to slide relative to one another in the same kind of way as in muscles.

Part 4

1. Movement is brought about by **muscles** working in conjunction with a **skeleton**.

2. The human skeleton, as well as bringing about movement, supports the body, protects the soft structures and produces blood cells.

3. The skeleton can be divided into the **axial** and **appendicular skeletons**, both of which are composed of numerous **bones**.

4. The bones articulate with each other at **joints** and are held together by **ligaments** and **muscles**. Muscles are attached to the bones by **tendons**.

5. A limb bone such as the femur is composed of two types of bone tissue, **compact bone** and **spongy bone**, whose distribution can be related to the stresses and strains which the bone has to bear.

6. Most bones start off as **cartilage** which is then replaced by bone tissue. Bone is laid down by bone-forming **osteoblasts** and remodelled by bone-destroying macrophages.

7. **Synovial joints**, such as exist between successive limb bones, allow the bones to move against each other with minimum friction.

8. There are two main types of synovial joint: the **ball and socket joint** and **the hinge joint**. Their shapes dictate their freedom of movement.

9. Bones are susceptible to various types of **fracture** which are particularly common in elderly people suffering from **osteoporosis**. Joints are susceptible to **arthritis** which can be remedied by having a **joint replacement**.

10. The skeleton is operated by sets of **synergistic** and **antagonistic muscles** whose actions, coordinated by the nervous system, bring about movement and maintain posture.

11. **Muscle spindles** and **tendon organs** ensure that antagonistic muscles contract to just the right extent.

12. In maintaining posture and producing movement, the skeleton provides a system of **levers** which are worked by the muscles.

13. In considering the locomotion of an animal three things should be taken into account: **propulsion**, **support** and **stability**, and these can be applied to animals that move on land, in water or in the air.

14. The type of skeleton possessed by vertebrates is called an **endoskeleton**. Invertebrates have either an **exoskeleton** (e.g. insects) or a **hydrostatic skeleton** (e.g. the earthworm).

15. Some small aquatic organisms move by means of **cilia** or **flagella**. **Amoeboid movement** occurs in *Amoeba* itself and also in phagocytic white blood cells.

For general advice on these questions and advice on answering essay-type questions, see pages vii and viii.

1. The diagram shows a section through a human hip joint.

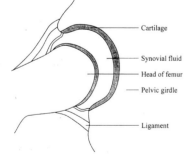

(a) Describe how the structure of this joint would be affected by osteoarthritis. (2)

(b) The table shows the percentage of women of different age groups reporting to the accident and emergency unit of a large hospital with fracture of the femur.

Age group/ years	Percentage of women in age group reporting with fracture of the femur
20 - 29	0
30 - 39	0
40 - 49	0.4
50 - 59	1.1
60 - 69	2.6
70 - 79	7.4

Apart from an increased likelihood of falling with age, suggest an explanation for the trend shown by the figures in this table. (3)

(Total 5 marks)

AEB 1997

2. (a) For a land animal lacking the buoyancy of water, strength and support are vital factors.

Give **two** ways in which a long bone, such as the humerus, provides the necessary supporting strength for a land vertebrate. (2)

(b) Comparing the humerus of a mammal with that of a bird, indicate:

(i) one structural feature which they have in common. (1)

(ii) one structural feature in which they differ. (1)

(c) The diagram below shows a typical mammalian lumbar vertebra from the lower back (lumbar) region.

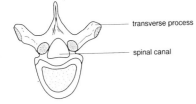

transverse process

spinal canal

(i) Copy the diagram and label:

the centrum (body) with the letter **A**; (1)

the prezygapophysis (superior articular process) with the letter **B**. (1)

(ii) Explain the part played by **A** and **B** in providing flexible support for the body. (2)

(d) The diagram below shows the muscles attached to the hind limb of a rabbit

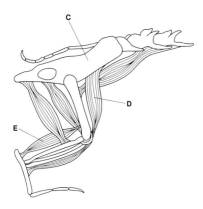

(i) Identify the part labelled **C**. (1)

(ii) What part do muscles **D** and **E** play in the movement of the rabbit's hind limb? (2)

(iii) Explain how the rabbit's hind limb and girdle are adapted to the animal's life on land. (4)

(Total 15 marks)

O&C 1997

3. The drawing shows some of the main flight muscles of a locust.

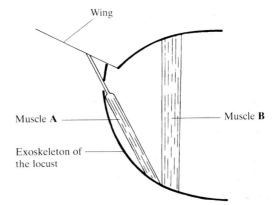

Wing

Muscle **A**

Muscle **B**

Exoskeleton of the locust

(a) Sketch the diagram then use a label line and the letter **X** to label the point about which the wing pivots. (1)

(b) (i) What name is used to describe the action of a pair of muscles such as **A** and **B**? (1)

(ii) Explain how the action of muscles **A** and **B** brings about movement of the wing. (3)

(c) Suggest one function of the exoskeleton in the movement of the wing. (1)

(Total 6 marks)

NEAB 1998

4. Write an essay on support and movement in animals. (Total 20 marks)

London 1996

5. (a) During swimming and running, flexor and extensor muscles in the leg work in opposition.

(i) Make an **unlabelled** diagram of the bones of the human leg from hip to foot.

(ii) To your diagram **add and label** an opposing flexor and extensor muscle.

(iii) Label on your diagram a ball and socket joint and a hinge joint.

(iv) Show by means of arrows the direction of the leg's movement during the operation of the muscles labelled. (5)

(b) Suggest why fractures of the hip become increasingly common in old age. (2)

(Total 7 marks)

O&C 1998

Behaviour

Figure 25.1 Courtship in the laysan albatross.

In nature, those organisms that respond appropriately to changes in their environment are more likely to survive and reproduce. The responses that an individual animal makes to the stimuli it receives are its **behaviour**. The stimuli may come from other organisms or from the physical environment. An animal's behaviour will help it to locate food, avoid predators and, in sexual species, find a mate with which to reproduce (*figure 25.1*).

In this chapter we shall look at various aspects of animal behaviour – or **ethology** as the study of animal behaviour is called – and discuss to what extent studies of animal behaviour tell us anything about human behaviour.

Natural selection, page 750

> ## Extension
>
> ### The scope of behaviour
>
> Although this chapter mostly confines itself to animal behaviour, other organisms behave too. Protoctists, such as *Amoeba* and *Euglena*, show various behavioural traits and some botanists have suggested that even plants can be thought of as behaving. For example, ground ivy sends out runners as it grows. The number of runners the plant produces, and the direction in which they grow, depend on the abundance of nutrients in the soil. Such behaviour is comparable to the foraging behaviour of certain animals.

25.1 **The development of behaviour**

How do lions become skilful hunters, terns agile fliers and otters graceful swimmers? To almost every behaviour there are two components, one **instinctive** and one **learned**. Otters instinctively swim when they first take to water. Instincts are genetically inherited from parents and handed down in evolution. In most cases they are common to all the members of a species and – like structural features such as eyes and limbs – they are subject to natural selection. However, although their ability to swim is instinctive, otters must also *learn* to swim effectively. When young they practise swimming and gradually become more skilful at it.

Interaction between genetic and environmental influences

Instinctive behaviour is sometimes referred to as **innate behaviour**, meaning that it is inborn and does not have to be learned. However, the distinction between innate and learned behaviour is by no means a sharp one. Take human speech, for example. At first one might think it is instinctive; after all, we all speak don't we? But in fact not everyone can speak. People who are born deaf have to be taught very patiently and skilfully to speak, otherwise they grow up deaf and dumb. Normally we learn to speak only by hearing others speak. This is why children in France speak French, while children in Germany speak German.

Clearly, the capacity for speech is inherited but what we speak is learned. Some people have wasted years trying to teach chimpanzees or gorillas to speak out loud. Usually the animals manage about two or three words after several years of training for several hours each day! These animals simply have not got the muscles nor the speech areas of the brain to enable them to speak proper words. However, the chimpanzee, Sarah, learned over a period of six years to associate some 130 differently shaped and coloured blocks of plastic with words which she had been taught (*figure 25.2*).

Figure 25.2 Chimpanzees can be trained to use symbols to stand for words, demonstrating their very considerable intelligence. From top to bottom, the six blocks on the magnetic board stand for: 'Sarah', 'insert', 'apple', 'pail', 'banana', 'dish'. After seeing this combination of symbols, Sarah would nearly always put the apple in the pail and the banana in the dish.

Here's another example of the interrelationship between innate and learned behaviour. Laughing gulls peck at their parents' bills for food from the first day of hatching. This is behaviour in a stereotyped fashion, in the sense that all laughing gull chicks peck in a similar manner. This suggests that the pecking is innate. However, the American ethologist Jack Hailman published a paper on the pecking of laughing gull chicks with the paradoxical title 'How an instinct is learned'. Hailman found that during the days after hatching the chicks learn to peck more accurately and become better at judging the distance between themselves and their parents' beaks.

Some ethologists have compared behaviour to a cake. A cake is the result of ingredients, a recipe and the cooking. No useful purpose is served by arguing about how much of the cake is due to the recipe or to the ingredients or to the cooking. In the same way it is impossible to classify some parts of a behaviour pattern as innate and other parts as learned. However, for purposes of analysis, it can be convenient to consider instinct and learning separately, as we shall do in the account that follows.

25.2 Instinct

Defined formally, instinctive behaviour is an innate, usually stereotyped, response to one or more environmental stimuli. Thus defined, it ranges from simple reflexes to complex behaviour patterns.

Reflexes

A **reflex** is a simple act of behaviour in which a stimulus produces a specific, short-lived response. The physiological basis of reflexes is discussed in Chapter 20. Here we are more concerned with their functions.

Escape response of the earthworm

On warm, wet nights, lots of earthworms may be observed lying on the surface of the ground. If you walk towards them, they quickly disappear into their burrows. The function of this behaviour is probably to reduce the chance of the earthworm being eaten by a badger, fox or other predator.

The escape response of an earthworm is a fairly simple behaviour and its physiological mechanism is well understood. Normally the posterior end of the worm remains in the burrow. On the detection of vibrations by touch receptors in the skin, the powerful **longitudinal muscles** contract, shortening the body. Meanwhile the bristle-like **chaetae** are protracted, enabling the posterior part of the worm to grip the sides of the burrow.

The key to a successful escape is speed, and the nerve impulses which elicit the earthworm's escape response are carried very rapidly by **giant axons** (*page 350*). A large **median giant axon** transmits impulses from receptors at the front of the worm to its rear. If it is attacked at its rear end, for instance by a subterranean mole, the worm may also escape. In this case a pair of **lateral giant axons**, each slightly narrower than the median giant axon, transmits nerve impulses from receptors at the rear end of the animal to its front. Chaetae at the front end grip tightly to the soil, the worm rapidly shortens and its rear is pulled forwards.

Kinesis

A **kinesis** is a behaviour pattern in which an animal responds to a change in stimulus intensity by increasing or decreasing its activity. A classic example is the response of woodlice to humidity. The lower the humidity, the more the woodlice move about.

Note that the woodlice do not move up a gradient of humidity. They simply move *more* in a drier environment. Eventually by sheer chance they are likely to reach a more humid environment; then they move less. The result is that woodlice spend most of their time in moist habitats which is where they thrive. The behaviour is therefore clearly adaptive.

Figure 25.4 A herring gull chick about to peck at the red spot on the beak of one of its parents. This causes the parent to regurgitate food for the chick.

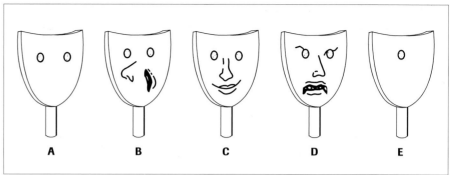

Figure 25.3 Models used in experiments to determine what causes smiling in babies aged one to two months. Models **A** to **D** are equally effective in triggering a smile when presented face-on to a relaxed baby of this age. Model **E** is consistently ineffective.

Taxis

A **taxis** is a movement that is oriented in relation to the direction of a stimulus. *Euglena* swims towards light (provided the light is not too intense). *Euglena* is therefore said to be **positively phototactic**. Earthworms move away from light and are therefore **negatively phototactic**. Many organisms are **chemotactic**, moving towards certain chemicals and away from others.

Sign stimuli

Animals typically respond to only some of the many stimuli detected by their sensory receptors. These are called **sign stimuli** or **releasers** and they produce selective stereotyped responses. Such selective behaviour is adaptive because it allows an animal to respond to *relevant* aspects of its environment, and to ignore others.

Everyone knows that babies smile at people. But what triggers the baby's smile? When a baby is about one to two months old, a pair of eyes is all that is necessary to trigger smiling (*figure 25.3*). The two eyes constitute the sign stimulus causing the baby to smile, which in turn may elicit a favourable response in the onlooker.

We shall now look in detail at two examples of behaviour in which sign stimuli play an important part.

Herring gull pecking

Shortly after it emerges from its egg, a herring gull chick begins to peck at the tip of its parent's beak. This causes the adult gull to regurgitate a mass of half-digested food which the chick eats. On close inspection it can be seen that the chick directs its pecks at the **red spot** on its parent's yellow beak (*figure 25.4*). In 1937 the German ornithologist F. Goethe discovered that newly hatched herring gull chicks would peck at the red spot on the beak of a dead herring gull held in his hand. When he painted over the red spot with yellow paint, the baby birds pecked less frequently.

Inspired by this result, Goethe reared some herring gull eggs in an incubator. When the chicks hatched they were presented with two types of beaks. Yellow beaks with a red spot received more than three times as many pecks as did uniformly yellow beaks. These isolated hand-reared birds would also sometimes peck at cherries or the red undersoles of tennis shoes if given the opportunity. Goethe's experiments suggested that the birds had an innate response to the contrast of red on yellow.

Subsequent work by the Dutch ethologist Niko Tinbergen showed that a red spot elicited more pecks than spots of other colours (*figure 25.5*). Evidently, the red spot functions as a sign stimulus.

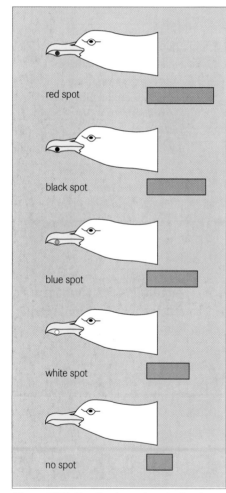

Figure 25.5 Results of experiments showing that the red spot on the beak is the most effective stimulus eliciting the begging response of herring gull chicks. The strength of the response was measured as the number of pecks directed at the model over a 30 second period. The length of the bar beneath each model indicates the strength of the response.

red spot

black spot

blue spot

white spot

no spot

Stickleback courtship and reproduction

In a series of experiments dating from the 1930s, Tinbergen and others investigated the reproductive behaviour of the three-spined stickleback, a small freshwater fish.

In the spring, male sticklebacks set up territories from which they chase away other sticklebacks. They then build nests out of weeds and stop chasing away females swollen with eggs. When a female appears, the territorial male moves towards her in a curious zig-zag fashion (the **zig-zag dance**). When she sees him, the female responds by swimming towards the male and presenting her swollen abdomen to him. The swollen abdomen acts as a sign stimulus. Tinbergen showed that realistic model females lacking a swollen belly are not courted, while crude model females provided with a swollen lower surface are *(figure 25.6)*.

Having displayed her swollen abdomen to the male, the female follows the male to the nest entrance which the male pokes with his snout. The female enters the nest and the male gives her rump several prods with a trembling motion. This stimulates the female to lay her eggs. After releasing the eggs, she leaves the nest and the male enters it and ejaculates over the eggs. He then chases the female away.

In order for stickleback courtship to proceed to fertilisation, a whole chain of behaviours needs to be completed *(figure 25.7)*. If any stage of the courtship fails to produce the appropriate sign stimulus, courtship ceases and the two fish separate.

Courtship leads to reproduction and a male may mate with as many as five females. Then he begins regular aeration of the eggs by fanning with his pectoral fins. The time spent fanning increases daily until the eggs hatch, at which point it stops.

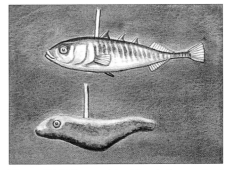

Figure 25.6 Two models of female three-spined sticklebacks. A detailed model (*top*) but lacking a swollen abdomen fails to elicit courtship from a territorial male with a nest. A crude model (*bottom*) which has a swollen abdomen is vigorously courted.

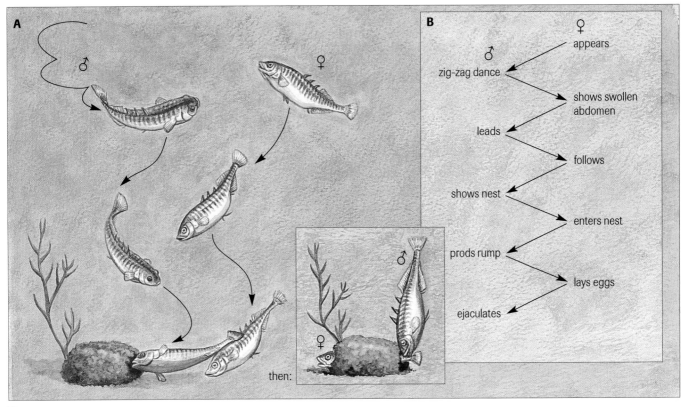

Figure 25.7
A Courtship and mating in the three-spined stickleback. The inset shows the female in the nest and the male is prodding her rump.
B The chain of stimuli which guide the sequence of events in courtship and mating of three-spined sticklebacks. If at any stage either sex fails to produce the appropriate sign stimulus, the chain of stimuli is broken and fertilisation is not achieved.

Diurnal and circadian rhythms

Many animals show behaviours on a daily (24 hour) basis. These are called **diurnal rhythms**. For example, diurnal animals sleep at night; in spring, song birds sing each dawn, and so on.

Interestingly, many such behaviours occur even if an organism is removed from the environmental cues, such as the alternation of night and day, that indicate the passing of each 24 hours. A hamster, for instance, continues its life on an *approximate* 24 hour cycle even if kept in permanent darkness. Such cycles are known as **circadian rhythms** from the Latin for 'about a day'.

25.3 Learning

Learning may be regarded as a more or less permanent change in behaviour which occurs as a result of experience. Animals vary in how much they are capable of learning. In general, the larger an animal's brain, the more it can learn, though in fact much of the brain has nothing at all to do with learning. The tremendous learning capacity of humans is due to our large cerebral hemispheres with their extensive cortical folding and organisation (*page 359*).

There is no universally accepted classification of learning, though the one that follows is widely adopted.

Habituation

If an animal is repeatedly given a stimulus which is neither beneficial nor harmful, it soon learns not to respond. This is called **habituation**. It involves the *loss* of a response. Birds soon ignore the scarecrow which frightened them when it was first placed in a field. They become habituated to it.

It is easy to see the function of habituation. An animal needs to respond to changes in its environment only when it is appropriate to do so. The rabbit that disappears down its burrow every time it hears the wind will have no time to feed. On the other hand, the rabbit that fails to disappear quickly when it hears an *unfamiliar* noise risks being caught by a predator. We usually continue to sleep through loud but familiar noises yet wake up at a quieter but strange sound.

Classical conditioning

At the turn of the 20th century, the Russian physiologist Ivan Pavlov studied the production of saliva by dogs in response to food. He found that the smell, sight and taste of food induced the flow of saliva. Pavlov mounted his dogs in a harness and collected their saliva in a tube leading from the salivary duct (*page 185*). When the dogs had got used to this, Pavlov rang a bell before each portion of food was presented. At first this stimulus caused no response, except that the dogs pricked up their ears. However, after about five or six such tests, the dogs salivated after the bell rang but *before* the food appeared.

In Pavlov's experiments the dogs had learned to associate the ringing of the bell with the delivery of food. This type of learning is called **classical conditioning**. The salivation response to the bell is a **conditioned reflex**.

To produce this conditioned reflex, the food must appear within about a minute of the bell being rung. However, rats and many other animals will learn to avoid a novel food that causes vomiting, even if vomiting only occurs hours after eating the food.

Trial and error learning

Suppose a hungry dog is allowed to roam around a room. As soon as it jumps onto a particular chair we give it some food. The dog soon learns to associate jumping onto the chair with a **reward**. If hungry it will go straight to the chair as soon as it enters the room. This is rather like classical conditioning but in this case the dog has learned to associate a reward not with a particular stimulus, but with its own behaviour. This sort of learning is known as **trial and error learning** (or **operant conditioning**).

The American psychologist B.F. Skinner devised a special piece of apparatus to investigate trial and error learning in rats and other animals. This apparatus is now known as a **Skinner box**. Its crucial feature is that it includes a lever. When an animal is put in the box it eventually presses the lever. As a result, a piece of food falls into the box. The animal therefore comes to associate pressing the lever with the arrival of food.

In the same kind of way, animals may learn *not* to do certain things by associating their behaviour with a **punishment**. Cats can (sometimes) be trained not to scratch the furniture, and dogs not to chew table legs.

There are many examples of trial and error learning in humans. Children are rewarded for good behaviour, and punished for bad behaviour. Experimental psychologists talk about particular behaviours being **positively reinforced**; this simply means that they are conditioned to occur.

Adults too can be conditioned. In one case the members of a class agreed, without their teacher knowing, to smile appreciatively only when he placed his hand on his chest. The professor soon became conditioned to spend the entire lecture imitating Napoleon!

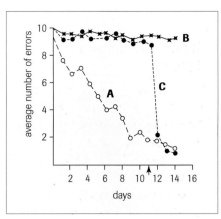

Figure 25.8 Performance of rats placed once a day in a maze in which there were 14 T-junctions at which the rats could turn either left or right.
A Rats given food at the end of the maze on each day. Note the improvement in their performance.
B Rats given no food at the end of the maze, and therefore having no motivation for improving their performance.
C Rats given food only at the end of the maze on day 11 and thereafter. Latent learning has occurred in the rats in group **C**.

Latent learning

If a rat is placed at the entrance to a maze, it typically enters the maze and runs here and there, busily sniffing and exploring. If such rats are rewarded with food when they find the end of the maze, they gradually learn, by trial and error, the quickest way through the maze. You can see this in curve A in figure 25.8. Note how this contrasts with curve B where no reward was given.

Now look at curve C in figure 25.8. This shows rats which were placed individually in a maze once a day for 10 days but were *not* rewarded for finding their way to the end. From day 11 they *were* rewarded on reaching the end. A rat which has had the opportunity to explore can find its way through a maze with fewer mistakes than a rat which has had no experience of that maze.

The implication is that the rat has learned something about the maze while exploring, even though it was not rewarded for reaching the end. What is learned remains hidden or *latent*, hence the term **latent learning**. For an animal in its natural environment, the benefit of latent learning is clear. For instance, a knowledge of the precise physical details of the area in which it lives may make the difference between life and death on the sudden appearance of a predator.

Insight learning

We sometimes solve new problems by trial and error. Often, though, we pause and try to work out a solution. **Insight learning** occurs when an animal solves a problem by looking at it, assessing the situation and then arriving at a solution.

The first experiments which demonstrated this type of learning in non-humans were done on chimpanzees by Wolfgang Köhler. Presented with a bunch of bananas too high to reach and a few boxes, some chimpanzees piled up boxes to make a stand for themselves (*figure 25.9*). Often they arrived at this solution quite suddenly (insight learning). However, they benefited from playing with boxes beforehand (latent learning) and showed considerable trial and error learning when actually building a stable pile of boxes.

To an observer watching their behaviour, these chimpanzees displayed what in everyday language we would call 'intelligence'.

Intelligence

Intelligence is notoriously difficult to define. One way of looking at it is to say that an animal is intelligent if it is good at solving problems it has not encountered before. On this understanding of the term, intelligence is closely related to insight learning.

Even if people agree on what is meant by intelligence, they may not agree on how to measure it. Considerable controversy surrounds the design and use of **IQ (Intelligence Quotient)** tests for humans. Some psychologists have even defined intelligence as that which is measured by IQ tests!

Figure 25.9 Chimpanzees may stack boxes on top of one another to reach bananas otherwise out of reach. This is an example of insight learning.

The neural basis of memory

Memory is the basis of learning and is therefore an aspect of behaviour. Guest author Patrick Bateson discusses the basis of memory and shows how behaviour and neurophysiology can connect.

The precise ways in which environmental information is processed and stored in the brain for future use are not known for any animal. However, it is plain that there are several jobs for which learning and memory are required. For instance, some memory is required for the recognition of familiar objects and social companions. Other sorts of memory are needed to store links between causally related events. These associative memories are particularly important in predicting the occurrence of important resources, such as food, and potential danger. In view of these various functions of memory, it is likely that more than one set of neural mechanisms are involved. Whether the differences in functions have been achieved during the evolution of brains by subtle rearrangements of essentially similar mechanisms or by entirely different processes is not yet known.

Despite uncertainties about the details, storage of information is likely to involve a change in the connections between neurones, some synapses being strengthened and others weakened. The starting point for the sequence of events that achieves this is whether or not the neurone which brings an input and the neurone it addresses are electrically active at the same time. If they are, the connection becomes stronger and, if they are not, it becomes weaker. The neurone providing the input sends its signal as a chemical transmitter. The strength of the connection depends on how many receptor sites, sensitive to that transmitter, are present in the neurone receiving the input. Steps in the strengthening process involve 'marking' the membrane of the junction between the two neurones for a limited period of time, possibly by changing temporarily the ease with which calcium ions can pass through channels in the membrane. Meanwhile, new protein is synthesised to make more receptors. These receptors are moved into place so that the junction between the two neurones ends up with more receptor sites than it had before. Conversely, the weakening process may lead to a reduction in the number of receptor sites.

Detection of a familiar but complex visual stimulus involves putting together a combination of features present in the stimulus, such as colour, shape and size. At one time it was supposed that the familiar face of one's grandmother might be localised in a single cell. However, the requirement to synthesise a pattern from such a complex object is more likely to involve a population of cells rather than a single one. On this view, the representation is formed at the strengthened (and weakened) connections between feature detectors and the next layer of neurones.

Computer models of neural nets have been constructed based on the properties of real neurones. In such models, connections are strengthened as the result of correlated activity, or weakened through uncorrelated activity. These models are helping us to understand how animals may learn and how objects are recognised. Some models are now being constructed to see how the neural rules that govern learning have evolved. If a rule is allowed to mutate, and the computer solves a problem more quickly as a result, then the new set of rules is used in future. In this sense the models not only mimic what happens in real brains, they also simulate the process of Darwinian evolution that gave rise to brains.

Patrick Bateson is Professor of Animal Behaviour and Provost of King's College, Cambridge.

➤ Synapses and chemical transmission, page 354; brain neurones, page 362

Imprinting

In his fascinating book, *King Solomon's Ring*, the Austrian zoologist and founder of ethology, Konrad Lorenz, describes how young geese follow the first moving object they see after they hatch. Generally, of course, the first mobile object they see is one of their parents, but Lorenz found they would **imprint** on almost anything that moved, including himself. He found, however, that newly hatched mallard ducks would not imprint on him. Until, that is, he started quacking! Lorenz describes how he crawled around his garden on his hands and knees followed by a batch of ducklings only to look up suddenly and find a group of tourists staring at him in horror, unable to see the ducklings in the tall spring grass.

It is now known that there is a **sensitive period** during which imprinting occurs. A number of mammals are born, and birds hatched, sufficiently mature to be able to move around very soon after birth. In these species imprinting on a parent occurs within a few days of birth or hatching. This allows the young animal both to recognise and follow its parents from an early age. Lorenz found that birds which had imprinted on other species of bird, or on humans or even on cardboard boxes, later attempted to court and mate with them.

During early childhood, humans, in common with a number of other species, become imprinted on their brothers and sisters and subconsciously learn *not* subsequently to mate with them. Evidence for this comes from studies of young adults raised on Israeli kibbutzim. Such young adults never marry within their rearing groups. The only exceptions are pairs who have been separated from one another for a large part of their childhood. The functional significance of this is that normally one grows up with one's brothers and sisters. Thanks to this learned behaviour, the risk of inbreeding is avoided (*page 643*).

Displacement activity

When an animal is confronted with two alternative courses of action, it may perform what appears to be an irrelevant behaviour. For example, if a bird sitting on its eggs is suddenly confronted by a predator, it may be torn between fleeing the nest and attacking the predator. So, it does neither. Instead, it preens its feathers! This is an example of a **displacement activity**.

Displacement activities are inappropriate behaviours which are sometimes seen when an animal is in a state of internal conflict. Examples in humans include biting one's nails (*figure 25.10*).

Figure 25.10 An example of a displacement activity. Phil is biting his nails while going through some accounts. Humans commonly display such displacement activities in tense situations.

25.4 Reproductive behaviour

For organisms that reproduce sexually, reproductive success depends on finding a mate. During the course of evolution an amazing diversity of patterns of courtship and mating have arisen. Here we shall focus on one particular problem which faces an organism reproducing sexually, namely choosing a mate.

Choosing a mate

The phrase 'choosing a mate' does not imply that organisms consciously try to decide with whom to mate. For almost all species the 'decisions' made are subconscious ones. Indeed, the extent to which humans are capable of exercising free will may be more limited than many of us realise.

Species-specific signals

At the most basic level, a mate must be an individual of the same species but the opposite sex. In many species what ensures that the 'right' individuals mate with each other is **courtship**, such as that which we have already seen in the stickleback (*page 439*).

Courtship conveys much more information than just the species and sex of the individuals performing. As females generally invest more time and energy in their offspring than do males, **mate choice** is particularly important for females. Males therefore make themselves attractive to females, advertising their fitness-enhancing characteristics, for example good genes, adaptive behaviour and possession of valuable resources such as a good territory.

Courtship may provide an opportunity for individuals to prove to each other that they can reproduce successfully. In the common tern, males bring fish to the females during courtship. The greater the number of fish the male brings to the female, the more likely she is to mate with him, and the more offspring subsequently survive (*figure 25.11*).

Courtship behaviour tends to be specific to each species. For example, males of the

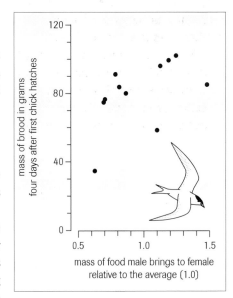

Figure 25.11 The relationship between the amount of food a male tern of the species *Stema hirundo* brings to his mate and the total mass of the brood shortly after hatching. Note that those females which have the most food brought to them subsequently produce the heaviest broods. The heavier the brood, the greater the number of chicks likely to survive to adulthood.

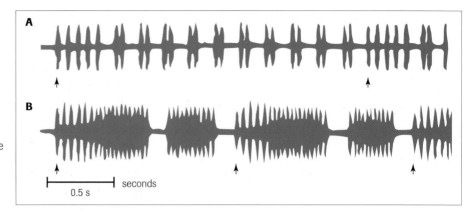

Figure 25.12 Sound spectrograms showing the calling songs of male crickets. **A** The song of *Teleogryllus oceanicus*. **B** The song of *T. commodus*. The arrows indicate the start of a single song.

closely related cricket species *Teleogryllus oceanicus* and *T. commodus* both sing songs to attract females, but the songs are different (*figure 25.12*). Interestingly, the difference between the songs is due to different alleles at a single locus in the two species (*alleles are explained on page 573*). Hybrid females prefer the songs of hybrid males.

25.5 Communication

The ability of animals to **communicate** with one another is fundamental to much of animal behaviour. Communication between two individuals involves the following:

- a **signal** – the message conveyed from one individual to another;
- a **sender** – the individual who transmits the signal;
- a **context** – the setting in which the communication occurs (e.g. courtship, aggression);
- a **channel** – the medium in which the signal is transmitted (e.g. chemical, auditory or tactile);
- a **receiver** – an individual who detects the signal;
- a **code** – the rules which enable the receiver to decipher the signal.

Communication may be either **intraspecific** (occurring between individuals of the same species) or **interspecific** (occurring between individuals of different species). Most communication is intraspecific and we shall concentrate on this type, starting with its importance in **territorial defence**.

Territorial defence

A **territory** is a more or less exclusive area defended by an individual or group. Not all species have territories, but in those that do, territories have a variety of functions. They may allow exclusive access to food. Some hummingbirds, for instance, defend patches of flowers, thus giving themselves exclusive access to the nectar produced by the flowers. In other species territories allow one sex, usually the male, to defend an area to which females are attracted for mating.

Many studies have been made of territorial behaviour, and territories can be advertised and defended by their owners in a variety of ways. Here we shall confine ourselves to sticklebacks and humans.

Sticklebacks

As described earlier, in spring, male sticklebacks defend territories from which they chase away intruders.

Tinbergen reported that the characteristic red patch on the belly of sexually mature males made them particularly likely to be chased away by territory holders. Tinbergen claimed that a realistically shaped but non-red model male stickleback provoked fewer attacks from a territorial male than extremely crude models painted red on their lower

Stickleback courtship and reproduction: a modern interpretation

Tinbergen's classic account of stickleback behaviour is still the one found in textbooks. However, several investigators have questioned either his observations or the details of his experimental procedure.

Perhaps the most remarkable challenge to the classic account is provided by W.J. Rowland. Rowland carefully repeated Tinbergen's experiments on the importance of stickleback colouration in territorial encounters between males. He found exactly the opposite of what Tinbergen had reported! Adding colour to a model stickleback male made it *less* likely to be attacked by a territorial male.

We can see the importance of proper experimental design. Rowland carefully replicated his experiments and tested his hypothesis using appropriate statistical tests (*pages 779–781*). Tinbergen merely described his observations. It may be unfair to criticise Tinbergen with the benefit of hindsight. Certainly he wasn't alone in not using statistics. Lorenz, with

whom Tinbergen and von Frisch shared the Nobel Prize, boasted that none of his publications contained any tables or graphs!

Rowland also claimed that his findings made more sense than Tinbergen's. He argued that it is difficult to imagine how the red colouration could have evolved if its effect was to release aggression from opponents.

Rowland's results contradict the classic stickleback story. A study by Li and Owings supplements it. Li and Owings considered the behaviour of the *female* sticklebacks. The earlier work by Tinbergen had concentrated on the male's behaviour to the extent that females were viewed merely as passive recipients of the males' attentions.

Unlike previous researchers, Li and Owings watched female sticklebacks for as long as they watched males. First of all Li and Owings compared the behaviour of six females in one tank with the behaviour of six males in another tank of

the same size and shape. They found that some females defended territories, and there were more aggressive encounters in the all-female groups than in the all-male groups.

What is the function of this female aggression? Aggression by dominant females helps them to reproduce successfully at the expense of subordinate females. On at least two occasions a dominant female poked or squashed a subordinate female, and repeated attacks led to the subordinate females prematurely shedding their eggs.

Li and Owings also studied tanks containing six females and six males. Female–female interactions were again important. On three occasions a subordinate female accepted a courting male before the dominant female. Each time this happened the dominant female disrupted courtship. On two other occasions a subordinate female attempted to disrupt the courtship of a dominant female, but the attempts failed.

surfaces. Indeed, he wrote that even a red mail van passing his window at a distance of 100 yards could make the males in the tank charge its glass side in that direction. The red colour would therefore seem to be a sign stimulus eliciting aggression (*page 438*).

In sticklebacks the territory functions as an exclusive area within which a male may build a nest and court females in comparative safety.

Humans

The English zoologist Desmond Morris points out that humans advertise their territories at three levels: at the level of the individual, the family and the larger group.

■ **Individual territory** Each of us is surrounded by a 'portable' territory called a **personal space** (*figure 25.13*). If people encroach on our personal space we feel uncomfortable. When we get jammed into a lift we are forced to abandon our personal space. Our response is to ignore the other people. We keep quiet, adopt a neutral expression and avoid eye contact. We can advertise our personal territory even in our absence. In an experiment carried out in a library, placing a pile of journals on a table by a seat successfully reserved the place for an average of 77 minutes. When a jacket was draped over the back of the chair, the place remained unoccupied for over two hours.

■ **Family territory** The family is the breeding unit. Morris argues that the family territory displays conspicuous boundary-lines such as garden fences and walls. Many families at the seaside set up a temporary territory, advertised by rugs, towels and a wind-break.

Figure 25.13 Personal space seen in the spacing behaviour of people in a queue. To invade people's personal spaces is to threaten them.

Figure 25.14 The round dance of the honeybee. The bee on the right at the top is dancing. The other three are picking up the cues she gives.

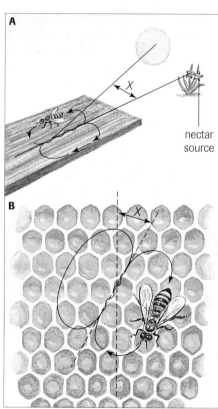

Figure 25.15 The waggle dance of the honeybee.
A The directional component of the dance is easiest to see when the dance is performed outside the hive on a horizontal surface. Here the bee repeatedly runs directly towards the food site.
B Inside the dark hive the dance is performed on a vertical comb and oriented with respect to gravity. The angle the dance makes clockwise from the vertical is the same as the angle of the food source clockwise from the Sun (the angle X in **A** and **B**).

■ **Group territory** Humans probably evolved as group-living animals with only a few dozen individuals at most in each group occupying a larger group territory. Patriotism can be considered as the endpoint of this, with national boundaries and frontier checkpoints. Most of us also belong to groups such as games clubs, music societies or groups of friends. Often such groups have territorial signals such as badges permitted only to members of the group.

Honeybees: communication by dances

Honeybees, despite their small size, have one of the most sophisticated communication systems of any species. More than 2000 years ago Aristotle found that although a source of food placed within flying distance of a hive might remain undiscovered for hours or even days, once a bee had located the food, many other bees soon appeared. In a series of classic experiments dating from the 1920s, the Austrian biologist Karl von Frisch investigated how honeybees communicate with each other, and other scientists have extended his work.

When worker honeybees collect food from a rich source within about 80 metres of the hive, they perform a **round dance** on their return (*figure 25.14*). It is dark inside a hive, so the other workers cannot watch the dance; instead they follow the dancing worker as she moves around on the comb. If, as a result of the round dance, workers fly out of the hive to look for the food, they search only within about 80 metres of the hive.

The round dance conveys no precise information about the distance to the food source, nor does it tell the bees in which direction to fly. Their search is helped by the fact that they pick up odour cues from the body of the dancing bee, and they may taste her regurgitated nectar. However, the round dance does convey information about the worth of the food source. The higher its worth, the more often the dancing bees change the direction of their dances.

If a bee finds a rich source of food more than about 80 metres from the hive, on her return she performs a **waggle dance** (*figure 25.15*). This conveys precise information about the distance to the food source in the range of roughly 80–1000 metres. The information seems to be conveyed in three different ways:

■ The greater the speed with which the bee completes a single dance circuit, the nearer the food.

■ The more abdominal waggles given during the straight-run portion of the dance, the nearer the food.

■ The higher the pitch at which sound bursts are produced while dancing, the nearer the food.

It is not known for certain whether all three types of signal are recognised by the other bees in the hive. The most important is probably the pitch at which the dancing bee produces sound bursts.

The waggle dance also conveys information about the direction of the food source. If the bee performs the dance on a horizontal surface outside the hive, the straight-run portion of the dance points directly to the food source. In the dark hive, on the side of the honeycomb, the angle which the straight-run portion of the waggle dance makes to the vertical equals the angle that the food source makes clockwise to the Sun (*figure 25.15*).

Language

Human language is vastly richer than the communication system of any other species. It involves **true language**. This means both the use of **symbols** (e.g. words) for abstract ideas, and an appreciation of **syntax**. Syntax means that the same symbol may convey different messages depending on its position relative to other symbols. (Consider, for example, the different uses of the word 'bow' as in 'I bow down before you' and 'I shoot with a bow'.)

It was mentioned earlier that the chimp, Sarah, learned to use different shaped and coloured blocks as word symbols. Another chimp, Washoe, learned over 100 signs of the

American sign language for the deaf. A major controversy has arisen over the extent to which chimpanzees and certain other primate species really can generate sentences and engage in true language. Whatever the outcome of this debate, *humans* obviously have an exceptionally rich and versatile communication system.

Charles Darwin pointed out the extent to which we have a system of **non-verbal communication**. This involves postures, gestures and facial expressions of considerable complexity and subtlety. Try moving the muscles of your face to indicate each of the following emotions: indignation, curiosity, amusement, approval, fear.

Non-verbal communication may or may not be conscious. Both men and women subconsciously register approval of objects they have seen by enlarging their pupils. This is why people prefer photographs of individuals whose pupils look large.

Extension

Chimpanzee behaviour in the wild

Research on animal behaviour does not necessarily involve elaborate equipment and techniques. A good pair of eyes and empathy with the animals under investigation can be just as valuable, as guest author Jane Goodall explains.

In 1960 I began a study of chimpanzees in the Gombe National Park, Tanzania, that is still in progress today. At first the chimpanzees were so shy that they would run off even if I was 500 yards away. However, I discovered a wonderful vantage point from which, using binoculars, I was gradually able to learn something of the chimpanzees' behaviour. And because I always wore the same-coloured clothes and never tried to get too close, they gradually got used to me. I'll never forget the day when two males, whom I had named David Greybeard and Goliath, continued to groom each other, only glancing briefly towards me, as I arrived just 20 yards away. I was accepted! Gradually the others also lost their fear and eventually I was able to follow some of them when they travelled through the forest.

I remember vividly the first time I saw a chimpanzee using a tool – David Greybeard fishing for termites with a twig – and when I observed chimpanzees cooperating to hunt a colobus monkey. Anthropologists were so excited by these things that we were able to get more money for the project.

For the first few months I had to have an African helper. Once I had proved my bush sense I was able to be alone. I soon learned that every chimpanzee has his or her own distinctive appearance and personality. At first I scribbled notes which I transcribed every evening. Later I used a tape recorder. A different chimpanzee was followed each day, from dawn to dusk, and his or her behaviour was noted in detail. I still spend as much time as possible at Gombe and even after 40 years, we are still continually learning new things.

I would like to emphasise that it is possible to record data objectively, despite feeling empathy with one's subjects. Yet implicit in much science education is the notion that a good scientist must be coldly distanced from his or her subject. This is not true – nor should it happen. Compassion must always come first.

Understanding chimpanzees helps us to understand ourselves. We are not as different from the rest of the animal kingdom as we used to think. Chimpanzees are like us not only physiologically, but behaviourally and emotionally also. And they possess many cognitive abilities we used to think unique to ourselves. They help us to cross the imagined gap between *us* and *them* and to develop a new attitude, a new respect, for all living creatures.

Dr Goodall founded the Gombe Stream Research Centre in Tanzania, where she has directed research on chimpanzees and baboons for many years.

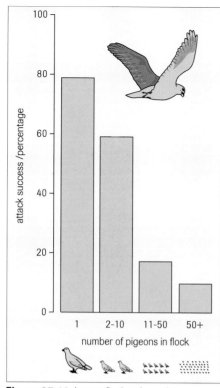

Figure 25.16 Larger flocks of woodpigeons are less likely to suffer from successful attacks by predators.

Figure 25.17

A Adult male lions have large manes which make them obvious to prey and therefore poor hunters. The males in a pride leave the hunting to the females and sleep about 20 hours a day.

B The adult females in a pride of lions cooperate in hunting and suckle any of the cubs. Here we see three adult females with their dependent young.

25.6 Social behaviour

In some species individuals are **social**, typically being found in groups; in others individuals are **solitary**, usually occurring on their own. To understand the reasons for this difference we need to consider the advantages and the disadvantages of being in a group. **Sociobiology** is the branch of biology devoted to studying the biological basis of social behaviour.

Advantages and disadvantages of sociality

In some species larger groups suffer less predation. Woodpigeons benefit from being in a large group because such groups are less likely to be attacked successfully by hawks (*figure 25.16*). Even if a predator succeeds in attacking a large group, each individual is safer simply because the chance of it being the unlucky one caught by the predator is smaller. If a predator takes just one prey individual at a time, the probability of an animal in a group of two being killed is 0.5; for an animal in a group of 10, the probability is only 0.1. (Note that this assumes that large groups are not attacked proportionately more often.)

Predators too may benefit from living in groups. Thus some species are more successful at catching large prey when hunting in **packs** than when hunting on their own. Classic studies in the African Serengeti have shown that this is so for lions, spotted hyenas and African wild dogs.

There are many other advantages of living in a group. Groups of woodlice huddle together and survive desiccation better. Group living may also allow individuals to do things they could never achieve on their own. Honeybees build hives with an internal air-conditioning system created by thousands of worker bees fanning with their wings. From late spring to autumn this keeps the colony between 34.5° and 35.5°C. In winter, the energy released by the bees means that the temperature never falls below 17°C. Collectively honeybees are **endothermic** (*page 301*).

However, being in a group has costs too. In particular, members of a group may compete for food, simply because they share the same area. The presence of even a few companions means that resident herbivores, such as rabbits, have to move further afield each day to feed. Moreover, living in a group gives dominant individuals, particularly males, the opportunity to monopolise the breeding. For a subordinate this is indeed a disadvantage.

Altruism and kin selection

Altruism is the word given to behaviour which is *disadvantageous* for the individual performing the behaviour, but *helpful* to another individual. Worker honeybees are altruistic in that they help their mother – the queen – to produce offspring rather than lay eggs themselves.

How has altruism evolved? One possible way is by **kin selection**. Kin selection occurs when a decrease in an individual's fitness, as measured by the number of offspring it produces, is more than compensated by an increase in the fitness of its relatives. We shall look at lions as an example of this.

Lions

Lions live in social groups, called **prides**, which usually consist of about half a dozen adult females, their dependent offspring and some two to four adult males (*figure 25.17*). Daughters born into the pride commonly remain there for life, while sons leave before they reach reproductive maturity. Because of this, the females within a pride are quite closely related.

Within the pride, cubs may suck from any adult female with milk. Such **communal suckling** is rare in mammals. In most species each female suckles only her own offspring.

As the females within a lion pride are related, kin selection has been invoked to explain the existence of communal suckling.

The adult males in a pride may be driven away by new males coming in from outside. The new males kill as many as possible of the young cubs. The function of this **infanticide** is more subtle than might appear at first sight. In common with many other mammals, female lions do not ovulate when they are producing milk. However, once their cubs have been killed, the females come back into oestrus. Infanticide therefore allows the new males to sire their own cubs more quickly. In the African Serengeti 25 per cent of all cubs die from infanticide.

Early data suggested that the adult males in a pride were full or half-brothers. Kin selection was therefore used to explain the cooperation between the males in a pride. It now appears that in some 40 per cent of prides, the adult males are not all related to one another. What then is the explanation for the cooperation between the adult males? The answer may lie in **reciprocal altruism**, to which we now turn.

Reciprocal altruism

As the phrase suggests, this is where one animal, A, helps another, B. At some later point B **reciprocates**, that is, helps A. The expression 'you scratch my back and I'll scratch yours' sums it up. Examples are given in the extension box below.

A fundamental difficulty in the evolution of reciprocal altruism is the possibility of **cheating**. Cheating occurs when B accepts help from A, but then fails to reciprocate! It seems that reciprocal altruism has evolved in those species where individuals can recognise each other. Individual recognition allows altruists to detect a cheat and ensure that they don't help it in future.

Having discussed the advantages and disadvantages of sociality and altruism in a number of species, we can now look in detail at the social behaviour of honeybees, chimpanzees and humans.

Extension

Two examples of reciprocal altruism

Vampire bats

Vampire bats are found in Central and South America. They live in groups whose membership changes little over the course of a year or longer. As is well known, vampire bats fly out at night to find animals from which to take blood. Usually they attack horses, cattle, goats or pigs, but occasionally they attack humans or wild animals. On some nights an individual bat is unsuccessful in its search for food and returns to the group without having obtained a meal. This is potentially very serious for the unsuccessful bat as it can only survive two consecutive nights without a meal. After that the bat usually starves to death.

Fascinatingly, a bat that fails to obtain a meal during the night is usually fed by another member of the group when it returns. The altruist regurgitates blood for the hungry bat. Careful observations show that bats which have received regurgitated blood meals subsequently reciprocate. Furthermore, the probability that a bat will regurgitate blood for a hungry bat is independent of the degree of relatedness between the two bats. This rules out kin selection. If kin selection was responsible for this kind of altruism, regurgitation would be restricted to close relatives.

Humans

It can be argued that reciprocal altruism is the basis of human society. We are very good at remembering people we have helped. If we are honest with ourselves, don't we usually expect such people to reciprocate in the future? People who give us presents on our birthday are more likely to get presents back from us. The bank that lends us money expects us to reciprocate, with interest, and banks have effective methods of dealing with cheats!

Reciprocal altruism is more likely to persist in groups where all the individuals know each other. Once humans started living in towns and cities, rather than in small bands, the risks involved in reciprocal altruism became greater. We would therefore expect altruism to be more common among people who know each other well. How often do we do something helpful, at a cost to ourselves, to people we are sure we will never meet again?

The social life of honeybees

At the peak of its numbers in summer, a healthy colony of honeybees consists of up to sixty thousand **workers** (sterile females), a few hundred **drones** (fertile males) and a single **queen** (a fertile female). In addition there are a number of combs whose compartments (**cells**) contain **eggs**, **larvae** and **pupae**, with stores of honey and pollen. There is a strict division of labour: the queen lays eggs, the drones fertilise queens, and the workers forage for food, rear the young and guard the hive.

The great majority of the eggs laid by the queen are diploid, the result of one of the haploid sperm she stores fusing with one of her haploid eggs (*support box on left*). These diploid eggs develop into females. Whether these females turn out to be workers or queens depends on the way they are looked after. Eggs that will develop into queens are laid in special large **queen cells**. For the first three days, queen larvae and worker larvae appear to be treated the same: they are fed on **royal jelly**, a highly nutritious food secreted by the hypopharyngeal and mandibular glands of the workers. After that, however, only the queen larvae continue to be fed on royal jelly. Worker larvae are switched from this to a mixture of pollen and nectar.

To produce males, the queen lays *unfertilised* eggs. Males are therefore haploid. Honeybees, in common with other bees, ants and wasps, are said to be **haplodiploid**, because males are haploid and females diploid. Males do not help in the hive – all the workers are females. Rather, they attempt during the **nuptial flight** to mate with newly emerged queens from other colonies.

The social life of chimpanzees

The chimpanzee is our closest relative. Humans and chimpanzees probably shared a common ancestor until only five to eight million years ago. Tragically chimpanzees are becoming increasingly rare in the wild as their habitat is destroyed, while many of them have been taken for medical research. The features of their behaviour which stand out are their intelligence and the flexibility of their behaviour (*figure 25.18*).

Chimpanzees are found in forested areas throughout equatorial Africa. Their basic social unit is a loose association of about 30 to 80 animals that tend to remain in the same area for many years. They spend 25–50 per cent of their time on the ground and the rest in trees. Chimpanzees feed on the fruit, leaves, bark and seeds of a wide variety of plant species. They also consume termites and ants and occasionally kill and eat small baboons and other monkeys.

A considerable amount of cooperation occurs between chimpanzees, though their social organisation is **hierarchical** with each individual knowing its place in the hierarchy.

Figure 25.18 Chimpanzees make and use tools. This type of behaviour was previously thought unique to humans. Here a chimpanzee is using a rock to crack open palm nuts.

The social life of African wild dogs

African wild dogs occur throughout Africa, chiefly in savannah woodland. Population densities are very low and there are probably fewer than 10 000 of them in existence.

A pack typically has 6 to 10 adults and up to a dozen or more pups. Hunting usually takes place around dawn or dusk, when it is cooler. The chief prey are impala, puku and Thomson's gazelle. African wild dogs can run at about 60 km per hour for 5 km or more and it is this ability that enables them to run down their prey.

When they close in for the kill, different individuals in the pack specialise in going for different regions of the body, so one animal typically attacks the nose, another tail and so on. After a successful hunt, any pups present are allowed to feed first. Pups too young to take part in the chase are fed on food regurgitated to them by any adult – not just their mother.

African wild dogs with pups.

The adult males and females in a pack have separate dominance hierarchies. About once a year the dominant male and female mate. On the rare occasions when two females in a pack attempt to rear pups, the dominant female may kill the other's pups.

So, females don't cooperate, quite the reverse. Indeed, mortality among females is higher than among males and adult males outnumber females by two to one.

Unusually among mammals, it is the females that disperse from the pack, which they do when aged between 14 and 30 months. Males remain in the pack throughout their lives (up to 10 years or so). This sex-specific dispersal prevents inbreeding from occurring but means that the males in the group are related to one another whereas the adult females are not.

The species is unusual among mammals in that at puberty the females disperse from the troops in which they were born. This means that within a group, males may be closely related to each other. This may account for the frequent grooming between males, their cooperation in hunting and subsequent begging and sharing of meat.

In both sexes there is a period of several years during which the young are dependent on their mothers. This long period gives the young chimpanzee time to learn a great deal from its mother. The relative abundance of food in their environment means that time is also available for extensive and complex social interactions between the members of a group.

Human society

Human societies have much in common with those of monkeys and apes. Kinship is important and certain individuals are more dominant than others. However, we differ in the precision and subtlety of our communication system, our distinctive intelligence and the tremendous capacity we have for learning from others. Our knowledge and beliefs are **cultural** and differ from one society to another. Much of our behaviour is socially rather than genetically transmitted.

Socialisation

The process by which each of us learns to become a member of our society is called **socialisation**. **Primary socialisation** refers to the learning that takes place during childhood, mainly within the family. We spend longer learning from our parents than does any other species. **Secondary socialisation** refers to the learning that takes place later, at school or in work for instance (*figure 25.19*).

Figure 25.19 Student nuns visiting Bhupaya Temple on a pilgrimage. This is an example of secondary socialisation.

Socialisation takes place without our consciously trying to fit into society. It is only when people attempt to live in a different society that they realise the extent to which they have been moulded by the society in which they grew up. **Resocialisation** may be necessary if we move home, change our job or get married.

Norms and roles

Every society has a set of **norms**. These are unwritten patterns of behaviour which are usually accepted without question by the members of that society. Norms may change over time, and this may be one reason for the existence of a 'generation gap'. What was thought appropriate behaviour for teenagers 20 years ago may be thought by the present generation to be boring or weird.

Every day each of us occupies several **roles**. The same person might be a teacher, a mother, a wife, a friend, a neighbour and a daughter. The way we behave depends on our role at a particular time. **Role conflict** occurs when an individual's expected behaviour in one role conflicts with his or her expected behaviour in another role. Having a boyfriend or girlfriend with whom one wants to spend a lot of time may conflict with getting the examination grades one needs. In one's role as a boyfriend or girlfriend, one may be expected to spend a lot of time together in the evening. But in one's role as a diligent student one may be expected to do two or three hours homework each night!

Gender differences

One result of socialisation is that boys and girls are 'expected' to behave differently. We hear a lot about equality of opportunity nowadays, but what would be your initial reaction to a girl who wanted to become a bricklayer (*figure 25.20*), or to a boy who wanted to be a midwife?

Stereotypes abound about male and female behaviour. Males are said to be more aggressive, more competitive and more prepared to take risks; girls to be more caring, more expressive and more affected by relationships. This may often be the case but these differences probably say more about the way society expects males and females to behave than about any innate differences between the sexes.

One reason for studying human behaviour is that it forces us to look objectively at why we do the things we do and like the things we like. That may be the first step to deciding if we are happy with the way we are, or would like to be different.

Figure 25.20 The norm is for bricklayers to be male. To what extent are the jobs we do dictated by society?

1. An animal's **behaviour** consists of the responses it makes to the stimuli it receives.

2. Most behaviours have two components, one **instinctive** and one **learned**; however, trying to disentangle the two is often very difficult.

3. Instinctive (**innate**) behaviour is inborn and does not have to be learned. It ranges from simple acts such as **reflexes**, to complex behaviour patterns such as courtship.

4. A behaviour pattern in which an animal responds to an alteration in stimulus intensity by changing its activity level is called a **kinesis**. A movement that is oriented in relation to the direction of a stimulus is called a **taxis**.

5. Animals respond to only some of the many stimuli detected by their sensory receptors. A stimulus that produces a selective stereotyped response is known as a **sign stimulus**.

6. **Learning** is a more or less permanent change in behaviour which occurs as a result of experience.

7. Types of learning include **habituation, classical conditioning, trial and error learning, latent learning, insight learning** and **imprinting**.

8. **Courtship** allows animals to mate with an individual of the right sex and species. It also enables the two individuals to gather information about each other's fitness and receptivity.

9. **Communication** between individuals requires a **signal**, a **sender**, a **context**, a **channel**, a **receiver** and a **code**.

10. A **territory** is a more or less exclusive area defended by an individual or group.

11. On her return to the hive from foraging, a worker honeybee can provide information for her fellow workers about the direction, distance and value of a food source. This information is largely encoded in the **round dance** or **waggle dance** she performs.

12. **True language** involves the use of **symbols** (e.g. words) for abstract ideas, and an appreciation of **syntax**.

13. True language is found almost exclusively in humans. However, humans also use a wide repertoire of **non-verbal communication**.

14. An organism may be **solitary** or **social**. There are advantages and disadvantages to being in a group.

15. Behaviour that is disadvantageous for the individual performing it, but helpful to another individual, is said to be **altruistic**.

16. Altruistic behaviour can evolve as a result of **kin selection**, when help is given only to close relatives, or as a result of **reciprocal altruism**, when the altruist subsequently receives aid in return.

17. The process by which humans learn to become members of a society is called **socialisation**.

Part 4

Practice questions

For general advice on these questions and advice on answering essay-type questions, see pages vii to viii.

1. The graph shows the effect of light on the locomotion of a free-living flatworm.

    (a) Describe the effect of light on the locomotion of the flatworm. (1)

    (b) (i)   Name this type of behavioural response. (1)

        (ii) Give a reason for your answer. (1)

    (c) Suggest how the pattern of behaviour shown in the graph helps to keep the flatworm in favourable conditions. (2)

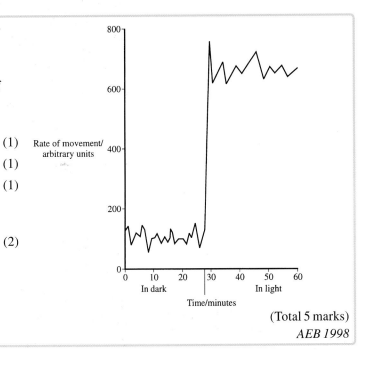

(Total 5 marks)

AEB 1998

2. The flow chart shows how light affects the reproductive activity of some birds.

Increased day-length

↓

Receptors stimulated

↓

Hormones released from anterior lobe of pituitary gland

↓

Sex organs increase in size and activity. Courtship behaviour begins.

(a) Suggest why day-length is a more appropriate stimulus to start courtship behaviour than temperature. (1)

(b) Give **two** reasons why courtship behaviour is important in birds. (2)

(c) Hens reared intensively for egg production are housed in large buildings without windows. Use the information in the flow chart to explain why, despite the expense, the lights are left on all the time. (2)

(Total 5 marks)

NEAB 1996

3. Two groups of rats were run through a maze every day for ten days. Group **A** always received food on reaching the end of the maze. Group **B** only received food for the last three days and not the first seven.

The average number of errors made by the rats in each group while finding their way through the maze is shown in the table below.

Day	Group A	Group B
1	9.8	10.2
2	8.3	9.1
3	7.5	8.2
4	6.2	8.0
5	5.9	8.0
6	4.0	7.0
7	3.9	6.6
8	3.8	6.1
9	3.7	3.8
10	2.9	3.0

(a) What type of behaviour was being investigated in this experiment? (1)

(b) Explain the difference in the results obtained on day 5 for the two groups. (2)

(c) (i) State in which group and during which period the greatest change was observed. (1)

(ii) Suggest an explanation for this sudden change. (2)

(d) Suggest, with explanation, a way in which the experiment could be modified in order to speed up the daily rate of change in the two groups. (2)

(Total 8 marks)

WJEC 1997

4. Copy and complete the following passage on bees, using the most appropriate word or words to fill in the blanks.

Eggs are laid in cells by the queen as she moves over the brood area. She lays .... eggs which develop into drones, and .... eggs which develop into workers or queens. The eggs hatch after .... days. Then, for the first three days, all the larvae are fed on .... which is rich in .... and which is .... secreted by the .... of the workers. Larvae which are destined to become workers and drones are then fed on .... until they are ready to pupate.

(Total 7 marks)

London 1996

5. (a) African Wild Dogs are social animals that inhabit the grassy plains of Eastern and Southern Africa. They usually hunt in packs and can therefore take prey that is several times larger than an individual dog. When out hunting the dogs approach a herd of grazing animals, select their victim and then run it down relying on their stamina rather than great speed to catch their prey.

The table gives data on the hunting success rate of these animals.

Prey	No. of hunts	No. of kills	% success rate
Thompson's Gazelle			
Adult	156	52	33
Adolescent	15	8	54
Half Grown	11	10	91
Infant	24	22	92
Wildebeest			
Adult	20	11	55
Yearling	16	10	
Infant	64	51	

(i) Calculate the two missing % success rate figures. (2)

(ii) Construct a suitable graphical representation of the % hunting success rate for different types of prey. (4)

(iii) What trend can be seen in the data? (1)

(iv) Suggest why the dogs made so many attacks on adult Thompson's Gazelle even though the success rate was only 33%. (2)

(b) Communication is important in maintaining social order. Describe how the dogs communicate with one another. (5)

(Total 14 marks)

O&C 1998

Growth, reproduction and replacement of old cells all involve the multiplication of cells. To multiply, cells undergo **cell division**: one divides into two, these two may divide into four and so on.

The phrase 'cell division' is misleading in some ways because it implies that the process involves halving the cell and its contents. In fact cell division is usually preceded by cell growth, so that when the parent cell divides, the two **daughter cells** are essentially similar to the parent cell. Understanding cell division is largely a matter of appreciating how this similarity is preserved.

In cell division, the action focuses on the **chromosomes**. As the vehicles of heredity they determine the characteristics of the cell and its progeny. It is essential that they are correctly distributed between the daughter cells. A cell may have each of its chromosomes in pairs of exactly the same length, in which case it is said to be **diploid**; or each chromosome may exist on its own without a partner of exactly the same length, in which case it is said to be **haploid**.

Two types of cell division can be recognised according to the behaviour of the chromosomes (*figure 26.1*):

- In **mitosis**, the daughter cells finish up containing exactly the same number of chromosomes as the parent cell. This is true whether the cell is diploid or haploid. Mitosis is the type of cell division which takes place when an organism grows, replaces old cells or reproduces asexually.

- In **meiosis**, each daughter cell ends up with exactly half the number of chromosomes as the parent cell. In this case, the parental cell is diploid and the daughter cells are haploid. This type of division is associated with sexual reproduction. It generally takes place in the formation of gametes, or in some cases spores. Note that haploid cells cannot divide by meiosis.

In this chapter we look at mitosis and meiosis in some detail. We also examine the causes of cancer, because cancers occur when cell division gets out of control. First, however, we shall see how cell division, particularly mitosis, fits into the life of a cell.

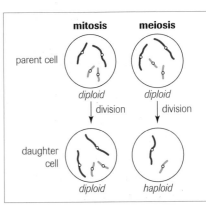

Figure 26.1 What do mitosis and meiosis achieve? A cell contains different types of chromosomes and usually there are two of each type, the diploid state (two large and two small chromosomes in the parent cells shown above). Mitosis results in daughter cells with the same chromosome complement as the parent cell. If a diploid cell divides by mitosis, it ends up diploid. Meiosis, however, results in daughter cells with only half the number of chromosomes of the parent cell. When a diploid cell divides by meiosis, it ends up in the haploid state.

26.1 The cell cycle

The entire sequence of events which takes place in a cell between one cell division and the next comprises the **cell cycle**. In eukaryotes it can be divided into four phases:

- **M phase** (**mitotic phase**);
- **G$_1$ phase** (**first gap phase**);
- **S phase** (**synthesis phase**);
- **G$_2$ phase** (**second gap phase**).

The sequence of these four phases is shown in figure 26.2. The **mitotic phase** consists of **nuclear division** (mitosis) and **cytoplasmic division**. During this phase cells make few new chemicals; in other words they have a low rate of synthesis. After the mitotic phase, the daughter cells enter the **first gap phase**, during which there is a great increase in the rate at which new cell components are made. The start of DNA synthesis marks the beginning of the **synthesis phase** which ends once DNA synthesis is complete. The cell then enters

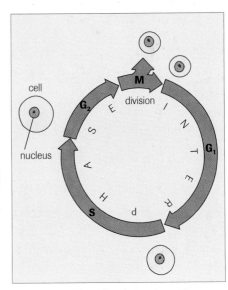

Figure 26.2 The cell cycle consists of four phases. The longest phase is nearly always the G$_1$ (first gap) phase in which a cell makes lots of biochemicals and increases the numbers of most of its organelles. The S (synthesis) phase is characterised by the replication of the genetic material. The short G$_2$ (second gap) phase is followed by the M (mitotic) phase in which nuclear and cytoplasmic division occurs, giving rise to two new cells.

the **second gap phase** during which a small amount of further growth takes place. With the completion of the second gap phase, the mitotic phase is entered once more.

Figure 26.2 shows the relative lengths of the four phases of the cell cycle for a population of cells which doubles in number every 24 hours. The period between successive cell divisions is called **interphase**. You can see that the M phase lasts only an hour or two and that interphase makes up the remaining 95 per cent of the time.

Each of us, when adult, has about 10^{13} cells, that is ten thousand thousand million of them. These cells differ greatly in the lengths of their cell cycles. Some, such as skeletal muscle cells, red blood cells and neurones, never divide, while others such as liver cells normally divide only once every year or two. At the other extreme, certain epithelial cells in the gut divide every 12 hours on average.

Despite this great variation in the length of the cell cycle, the time cells spend in the S, G_2 and M phases varies surprisingly little: typically, in humans, they take about 12 to 18 hours altogether. The G_1 phase, however, can last from a few hours to months or even years.

Interphase

It should be clear to you that the great majority of cells spend nearly all their time in interphase. During interphase the chromosomes are not visible as distinct bodies either under the light microscope or the electron microscope. Instead they are mostly strung out in the form of long **chromatin threads**. Not until the cell leaves interphase and enters mitosis do the chromatin threads condense to form visible chromosomes.

Interphase is sometimes described as a resting stage. This is very misleading. The first gap phase is in many respects the 'normal' active stage of the cell cycle. During this phase protein synthesis takes place, together with the formation of new organelles and all the countless processes which go on in an active cell, as a result of which the cell doubles in size. The synthesis phase is characterised by the replication of the genetic material (DNA).

Just before mitosis begins, the **centrioles** are among the most prominent organelles in the cell. Centrioles are found in the cells of all animals and most protoctists, but they are absent from cone-bearing and flowering plants. Their structure is described on page 42. Centrioles always come in pairs. Unlike other organelles, they replicate during the S phase, along with the DNA. This means that by the start of mitosis, each cell has two pairs of centrioles.

26.2 Mitosis

For the purposes of description mitosis is divided into four stages: **prophase**, **metaphase**, **anaphase** and **telophase**. At each of these stages certain crucial events take place, particularly in regard to the chromosomes. However, it is important to realise that mitosis is a continuous process and there are no sharp breaks between one stage and the next. Typically the entire process takes about an hour and is followed by cytoplasmic division, during which the cytoplasms of the two daughter cells separate.

Let us now follow what happens when a cell undergoes mitotic division. For convenience we shall consider a diploid cell which contains only four chromosomes: a pair of long ones and a pair of short ones. The events are summarised in figure 26.3.

Prophase

If interphase can be thought of as preparing the cell for division, prophase can be described as 'mobilisation for action' (*figure 26.3B and C*). Certain clearly visible events can be seen under the microscope. The most obvious is the condensing of the chromatin threads to form distinct chromosomes. Long and thin at first, they gradually become shorter and fatter. As the chromosomes shorten, it becomes increasingly clear that each chromosome consists of a pair of bodies lying close alongside each other. These are called **chromatids**. They tend to lie parallel along most of their length but are joined only in a specialised region called the **centromere**. The centromere holds the two chromatids together until later in mitosis. The two chromatids of one chromosome are usually referred to as **sister chromatids**.

It is essential to appreciate what the chromatids are. After mitosis is finished, each chromosome consists of a single very long thread of DNA accompanied by special proteins which protect the DNA and help to regulate its functioning. During the replication of the genetic material, an exact copy of this single thread is made. These two threads cannot be distinguished visually until prophase, when they make their appearance as the two chromatids. We shall consider the molecular basis of these events in Chapter 34, but for the moment it is sufficient to realise that the two chromatids making up a chromosome at the start of mitosis are identical. Except for the occasional mutation, they contain exactly the same genetic material point for point along their length.

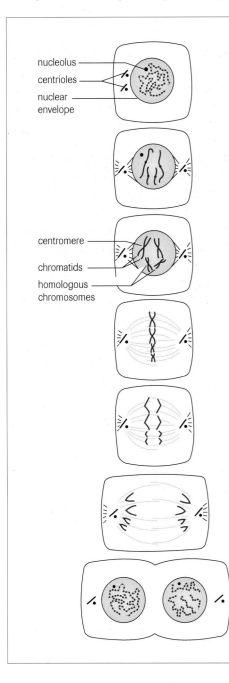

A Interphase
Cell has normal apperance of non-dividing cell. Chromosomes too thread-like for clear visibility.

B Early prophase
Chromosomes become visible as they contract, and nucleolus shrinks. Centrioles at opposite sides of the nucleus. Spindle fibres start to form.

C Late prophase
Chromosomes become shorter and fatter – each seen to consist of a pair of chromatids joined at the centromere. Nucleolus disappears. Prophase ends with breakdown of nuclear envelope.

D Early metaphase
Chromosomes arrange themselves on equator of spindle. Note that homologous chromosomes do not associate.

E Early anaphase
Chromatids part company and migrate to opposite poles of cell, the centromeres leading.

F Late anaphase
Chromatids, destined to become the chromosomes of the daughter cells, reach their destination.

G Telophase
Chromosomes unravel. Nuclear envelopes and nucleoli form.

Figure 26.3 Mitosis in a generalised animal cell. Two pairs of chromosomes are shown: a long pair and a short pair. Plant cells undergo mitosis in the same way except that there are no centrioles. For comparison a cell in interphase is drawn in **A**, although interphase is, strictly, not part of mitosis.

Condensing of the chromosomes is one of the most important events in prophase. If it failed to happen it would be impossible for the chromosomes to move around the cell without getting tangled up. While the chromosomes are getting shorter and thicker, other changes are happening. The cytoplasmic microtubules that are part of the cell's cytoskeleton disassemble and reassemble to form a structure known as the **spindle**, composed of **spindle fibres**.

In cells where centrioles are present, one pair is found at one end of the spindle and the other pair at the other end. This is achieved by one pair skirting the nuclear envelope so that it comes to rest at the opposite side of the nucleus. The two pairs of centrioles are now said to be at the **poles**, and the spindle fibres can be seen to go from one pole to the other. Also during prophase the nucleolus starts to disperse, so that it seems to disappear. Prophase ends, and metaphase begins, with the breakdown of the nuclear envelope.

Metaphase

As the nuclear envelope breaks down, it dissociates into vesicles which are indistinguishable from bits of endoplasmic reticulum. At the same time, the chromosomes migrate to the central plane of the cell and arrange themselves around the middle of the spindle, known as its **equator** (*figure 26.3D*). Finally, the chromosomes become attached to the spindle fibres at the centromeres.

Anaphase

For anyone who has watched a film of mitosis, this is the most spectacular part of the whole process (*figure 26.3E and F*). Suddenly, the chromatids belonging to each chromosome part company and move towards opposite poles of the spindle.

Anaphase begins with the splitting of the centromeres down the middle. This allows each chromatid to be pulled by one of the spindle fibres towards the pole it is facing. This takes only a few minutes. Anaphase is said to end once the separated daughter chromatids arrive at the two poles. The spindle fibres that draw them to the poles, like the proverbial Cheshire cat, become disassembled into nothingness (*extension box below*).

How do the chromatids separate during anaphase?

In recent years there has been a great deal of research on how the chromatids separate during anaphase. It is now believed that two related but distinct processes are going on. First, the chromatids are pulled towards the poles at a speed of about 1 μm per minute. This is accompanied by a shortening of spindle fibres that run from the chromatids to the poles. Secondly, the poles themselves separate. This is accompanied by a lengthening of pairs of overlapping spindle fibres that run from pole to pole.

Precisely how the chromatids are pulled towards the poles is still not known. However, spindle fibres are microtubules composed of **tubulin** (*page 52*). As the

chromatids move towards the poles, individual tubulin molecules are subtracted from the spindle fibres that run from the chromatids to the poles, causing them to shorten and so pull the chromatids to the poles.

Lengthening of the pole-to-pole fibres, on the other hand, is caused by the *addition* of tubulin molecules. At the same time, the microtubules that are joined to one pole push against the microtubules that are joined to the other pole. The result is that the two poles are forced apart, possibly by a ratchet mechanism comparable to that which occurs in muscle (*page 409*).

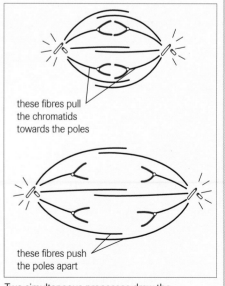

these fibres pull the chromatids towards the poles

these fibres push the poles apart

Two simultaneous processes draw the chromosomes to the poles and push the two poles apart.

Telophase

The end of anaphase marks the beginning of telophase, the last stage of nuclear division. The reverse of the various processes that occurred in prophase now take place. The condensed chromosomes begin to unravel, a new nuclear envelope forms around each group of daughter chromosomes and new nucleoli appear (*figure 26.3G*).

Mitosis is now at an end. However, the two new nuclei are still contained within the one cell. Mitosis is therefore followed by cytoplasmic division which starts even before telophase is finished. We shall look at this in a moment.

The essential principle underlying mitosis

The really important thing about mitosis is that the daughter cells receive precisely the same number and types of chromosomes as the original parent cell: two long ones and two short ones in the case illustrated in figure 26.3. In other words, the genetic constitution is maintained from one generation to the next.

Two salient features of mitosis ensure that the chromosome constitution is preserved:

- The fact that the DNA of the parent cell has replicated before mitosis begins.
- The arrangement of the chromosomes on the spindle.

As a result of DNA replication during the cell cycle, the parent cell contains twice the genetic information it normally does. The arrangement of the chromosomes on the spindle ensures that the chromatids are distributed evenly between the two daughter cells. This even distribution is illustrated in the photomicrographs in figure 26.4.

26.3 Cytoplasmic division

The cytoplasm divides by a process known as **cleavage**. In animal cells, the plasma membrane around the middle of the cell is drawn inwards to form a **cleavage furrow**. This gradually deepens until eventually the cell is cut in two and two cells result (*figure 26.5A*).

Cleavage is accomplished by the contraction of a ring composed mainly of actin filaments. These filaments are bound to the inner face of the plasma membrane (*figure 26.5B*). The mechanism by which they contract is still unknown, though the protein myosin is thought to be involved as it is in the contraction of muscle. Evidence that myosin is involved in cleavage comes from a number of sources. For instance, injecting anti-myosin antibodies into sea urchin eggs causes the cleavage furrow to relax.

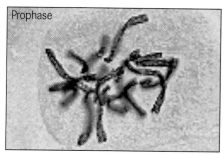

Prophase

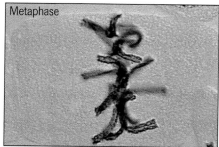

Metaphase

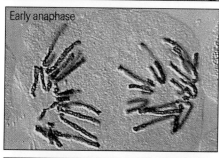

Early anaphase

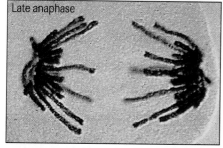

Late anaphase

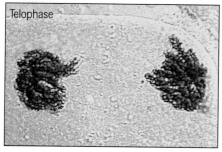

Telophase

Figure 26.4 Mitosis in the bluebell. The material was prepared in such a way that only the chromosomes are visible.

▶ How muscle contracts, page 407

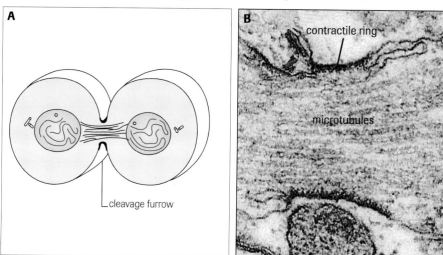

Figure 26.5 A Cytoplasmic division in a generalised animal cell.
B Electron micrograph showing the contractile ring of actin filaments responsible for the cleavage furrow at cytoplasmic division in an animal cell.

Observing mitosis

One of the easiest places to see the stages of mitosis is in the tip of a growing root. The root tip is cut off, sectioned or macerated and treated with a dye such as acetic orcein which stains the chromosomes. In good preparations the various stages of mitosis can be seen clearly. However, nothing is revealed of the movement of the chromosomes.

In 1957, an American (formerly Polish) biologist, Andrew Bajer, made the first successful film of mitosis. He used endosperm tissue, the nutritive tissue surrounding the embryo inside a seed. The cells divide rapidly and, being a rather runny tissue, a thin smear can be made on a microscope slide and filmed without harming the cells.

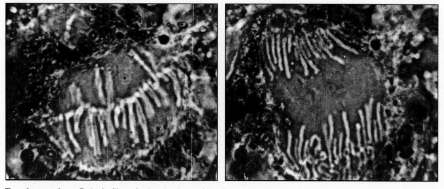

Two frames from Bajer's film of mitosis viewed in phase-contrast.

In plants, cytoplasmic division occurs in a very different way. A new cell wall, the **cell plate**, grows across the middle of the cell as a result of the Golgi apparatus depositing vesicles where the new cell wall is to be formed. These vesicles contain the pectins, hemicelluloses and cellulose which make up the primary cell wall. These cell wall precursors are deposited by the vesicles at the edge of the cell plate, causing it to extend outwards (*figure 26.6*).

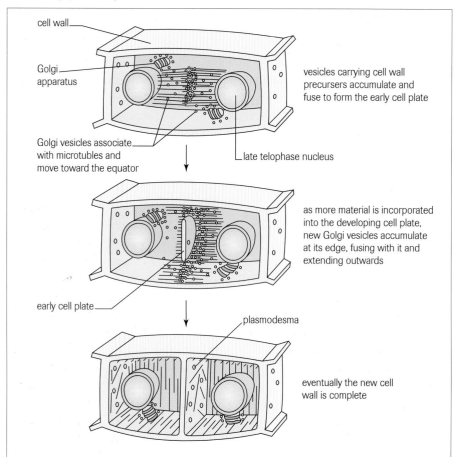

cell wall

Golgi apparatus

vesicles carrying cell wall precursers accumulate and fuse to form the early cell plate

Golgi vesicles associate with microtubles and move toward the equator

late telophase nucleus

early cell plate

as more material is incorporated into the developing cell plate, new Golgi vesicles accumulate at its edge, fusing with it and extending outwards

plasmodesma

eventually the new cell wall is complete

Figure 26.6 Diagrammatic representation of cytoplasmic division in a plant cell. As a result a new cell wall is formed between the two cells. Plasmodesmata provide connections between the two cells.

The role of mitosis

Mitosis is the type of cell division that takes place during the **growth** of an organism, for example in the development of a fertilised egg into an adult human being. The fact that these divisions are mitotic means that all the cells of the body have the same chromosome constitution, a total of 46 chromosomes (23 pairs) in our case.

Mitosis allows an organism to **replace old** or **damaged cells**. If you cut yourself, epithelial cells in the skin are stimulated to divide mitotically to cover up the cut. These epithelial cells continue to divide until they are surrounded by skin cells on all sides. In this way they know when to stop dividing, that is, when the cut is covered over by skin.

Mitosis is also the basis of **asexual reproduction**. This is the process that occurs when an *Amoeba* undergoes binary fission, when a bud develops in *Hydra* or when a new plant develops from a vegetative organ such as a corm or bulb. In each case mitosis ensures that the chromosome complement, and hence the genetic constitution, of the offspring is the same as the parent's.

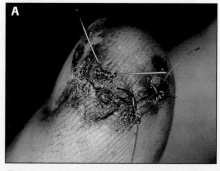
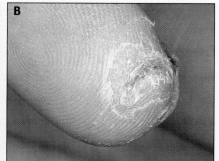

The repair of damaged tissue requires mitotic cell division, as in this cut finger where stitching has been used to speed recovery and reduce scarring.
A Index finger with stitches following an industrial accident with a bow saw.
B The same finger one week after the removal of the stitches showing fresh skin and a scab.

26.4 **Meiosis**

We have seen that mitosis conserves the parental complement of chromosomes. In meiosis, however, the number of chromosomes is halved, the daughter cells receiving only one of each type of chromosome instead of two – thus making them haploid (*page 475*).

The role of meiosis

In animals, meiosis occurs in the **formation of gametes** (sex cells), that is eggs and sperm, which are therefore haploid. A gamete is a cell which usually develops no further until it fuses with another gamete. Thus a sperm and an egg have no future unless they unite to form a zygote which then has the potential to develop into an adult organism.

In the process of fertilisation the nuclei of the two gametes fuse to form the nucleus of the zygote. Now if the gametes were to have two, rather than one, of each type of chromosome, the zygote would

have four of each type – twice the normal number. Let us assume that this zygote develops into an adult which itself produces gametes with the same number of chromosomes, that is with four of each type of chromosome. If two of these gametes were to unite, a zygote would be formed with eight of each type of chromosome, and so on. In other words, if gametes were formed by mitosis rather than by meiosis, the chromosome number would double with each succeeding generation. By halving the chromosome number prior to fertilisation, meiosis

ensures that this does not happen. When gametes with the haploid number of chromosomes unite, the normal diploid condition is restored.

In Chapter 27 we shall see that meiosis does not invariably happen in gamete formation; in some organisms it occurs in the **formation of spores**. In one sense this does not matter: it is immaterial *when* halving of the chromosome number occurs so long as it happens at some stage in the life cycle if sexual reproduction takes place.

The essential principle underlying meiosis

How does meiosis halve the chromosome number? The answer lies in the behaviour of the chromosomes during the division process. Meiosis consists of two successive divisions: the parent cell splits into two (**first meiotic division**) and the products then divide again (**second meiotic division**), giving a total of four daughter cells. There is no synthesis of genetic material between these two divisions, so each daughter cell ends up being haploid.

In a haploid cell, each chromosome is unique with respect to its length and the genes it contains. In a diploid cell, each chromosome has a partner of exactly the same length and with precisely the same genes. The two chromosomes in a pair are described as **homologous**. In the first meiotic division the homologous chromosomes of each pair line up together and then get separated from each other and go into different cells. The second division merely separates the chromatids.

With these basic ideas in mind, let us examine in detail the events that take place in meiosis (*figure 26.7*). As in mitosis, the process is divided for convenience into a series of stages. These are given the same names as in mitosis, but each is followed by I or II indicating whether it belongs to the first or second meiotic division.

Prophase I

In many respects this is similar to the prophase of mitosis: the chromosomes condense, the nucleolus disappears, the centrioles, if present, arrange themselves at opposite sides of the nucleus and a spindle forms (*figure 26.7B to D*). However, there is one fundamental difference. In mitosis, homologous chromosomes do not associate with each other in any way, but in meiosis they come to lie side by side, a process known as **synapsis**. In this condition each pair of homologous chromosomes constitutes a **bivalent**, so that in figure 26.7D there are two bivalents.

As prophase proceeds, the homologous chromosomes may become intimately coiled around each other. Later, they move slightly apart, but the chromatids remain in contact at certain points called **chiasmata** (singular **chiasma**). Extremely important genetic changes occur in association with the chiasmata, but we shall deal with these genetic aspects separately (*page 464*).

Although chiasmata are found in most meiotically dividing cells, we shall start by considering what happens in meiosis when chiasma formation does not occur. While such achiasmate divisions are uncommon, they are simpler to understand than divisions involving chiasmata.

Metaphase I

As in mitosis, the nuclear envelope breaks down and the chromosomes move to the equator of the spindle (*figure 26.7E*). The important difference from mitosis is that here homologous chromosomes do this together; in other words, each bivalent behaves as a unit. They arrange themselves in such a way that the centromeres of the two homologous chromosomes making up a pair orientate towards opposite poles. The cell is now poised ready for the separation of the homologous chromosomes.

Anaphase I

The homologous chromosomes, each made up of a pair of chromatids joined at the centromere, move towards opposite poles of the spindle (*figure 26.7F*). The sister chromatids also separate slightly from one another along their length, except at the centromere.

Telophase I

When the chromosomes reach their respective poles the cell starts to divide across its middle, and, as in mitosis, a nuclear envelope forms around each of the two new nuclei and the spindle breaks down (*figure 26.7G*).

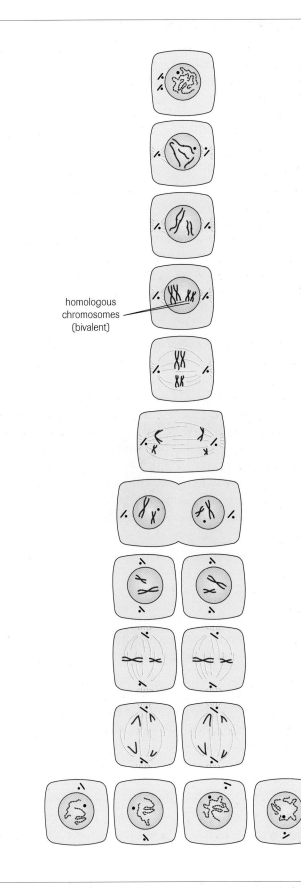

A Interphase
Cell in normal non-dividing condition
with chromosomes long and thread-like.

B Early prophase I
Chromosomes contract, becoming more
clearly visible. Nucleolus shrinks.

C Mid-prophase I
Homologous chromosomes come
together forming a bivalent.

D Late prophase I
Each chromosome seen to consist of a
pair of chromatids.

homologous
chromosomes
(bivalent)

E Metaphase I
Chromosomes arrange themselves on
equator of spindle.

F Anaphase I
Homologous chromosomes part company
and migrate to opposite poles of the cell.

G Telophase I
Nuclear envelopes and nucleoli form.

H Prophase II
The two daughter cells prepare for the
second meiotic division: centrioles have
replicated and a new spindle is formed.

I Metaphase II
Chromosomes arrange themselves on
the spindle in the usual way.

J Anaphase II
Chromatids part company and migrate
to opposite poles of the cell.

K Telophase II
Spindle apparatus disappears and the
chromosomes begin to regain their thread-like
form. New nuclear envelopes and nucleoli
form.

Figure 26.7 Meiosis in a generalised animal cell. As in the diagrams of mitosis only two pairs of chromosomes are shown: a long pair and a short pair. In **C** to **E** homologous chromosomes are shown diagrammatically lying side by side. Actually, the association is so intimate that at first the four chromatids cannot be distinguished from each other. For comparison a cell in interphase is drawn in **A**, although interphase is, strictly, not part of meiosis.

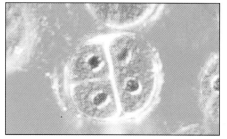

Figure 26.8 Tetrad of four haploid cells derived from a single parent diploid cell.

Interphase

At the end of meiosis I, a brief interphase usually occurs. The chromosomes expand somewhat, but they soon re-condense and prophase II begins. During this interphase no DNA synthesis occurs. Indeed in some organisms the cells go straight from telophase I to prophase II.

The second meiotic division

Separation of the homologous chromosomes that make up a bivalent is achieved by the first meiotic division. The purpose of the second division is to separate the chromatids from one another.

In prophase II (*figure 26.7H*) a new spindle is formed at right angles to the first one. In metaphase II (*figure 26.7I*) the chromosomes move to the equator of the spindle, the chromatids orienting towards opposite poles as in mitosis. Anaphase II (*figure 26.7J*) sees the chromatids separating and moving apart from each other. The chromatids become the chromosomes of the daughter cells. When they reach the poles, the cells enter telophase II (*figure 26.7K*). As is typical of telophase, the spindle apparatus disappears, the chromosomes begin to regain their thread-like form, and new nuclear envelopes and nucleoli form.

Meiosis is now complete. Cytoplasmic division follows so that four haploid have been formed from the original single diploid parent cell. Because of the way the spindle is orientated in anaphase II, the four daughter cells usually form a group called a **tetrad** (*figure 26.8*).

The importance of meiosis in bringing about variation

As well as halving the chromosome number, meiosis promotes genetic variation. This is partly because each chromosome making up a homologous pair carries different genetic material, with the result that the daughter cells are bound to be genetically distinct. Furthermore, the different pairs of homologous chromosomes arrange themselves on the spindle, and subsequently separate, independently of each other, so that the daughter cells finish up containing different combinations of chromosomes.

A further reason why meiosis promotes genetic variation is that it normally involves the formation of **chiasmata**, to which we must now turn.

The causes of genetic variation, page 740

Chiasmata

Towards the end of prophase I the intimate association between homologous chromosomes weakens and the four chromatids within a bivalent move slightly apart. It may now be seen that the chromatids are in contact with each other at certain points. These are the chiasmata.

The number of chiasmata in a bivalent varies considerably. There may be as many as eight and most bivalents have at least one, though sometimes, as in male *Drosophila* flies, none is found. Chiasmata can be formed between any two of the non-sister chromatids (*figure 26.9*).

As the cell moves from prophase I to metaphase I, the homologous chromosomes in a bivalent become increasingly separated from one another except at the chiasmata. This results in the bivalents adopting characteristic shapes, which vary according to the number and positions of the chiasmata:

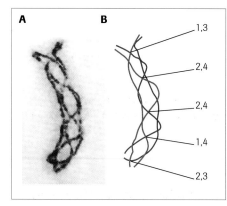

Figure 26.9 Chiasmata.
A is a photomicrograph of a bivalent at late prophase I from the testis of a locust.
B is an interpretative diagram. Chiasmata are numbered according to which chromatids are in contact. Note that chiasmata can be formed between any two non-sister chromatids.

■ A bivalent with only one chiasma looks like a cross.

■ A bivalent with two chiasmata looks like a ring.

■ A bivalent with three or more chiasmata looks like a series of interconnected loops. However, not all the loops need necessarily be visible because consecutive ones may be at right angles to one another like links in a chain.

The functions of chiasmata

Chiasmata have two functions, one genetic, the other mechanical. The less important of these is the mechanical one: chiasmata help to hold pairs of homologous chromosomes together while they manoeuvre themselves onto the spindle prior to separation.

The genetic function follows from the fact that the chiasmata represent places where non-sister chromatids break and rejoin, as shown in figure 26.10. When this happens, a portion of one chromatid changes places with the equivalent portion of another. This enables exchange of genetic material to occur between homologous chromosomes, a process known as crossing over. Since the two homologous chromosomes contain different genetic material, **crossing over** promotes genetic variety, which in turn plays an important part in the process by which evolution takes place (*page 741*).

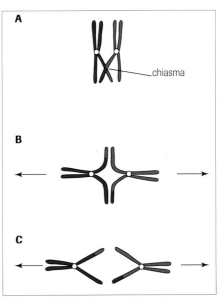

Figure 26.10 Crossing-over takes place during prophase of the first meiotic division. **A** shows a chiasma at mid-prophase I: notice that two of the chromatids of homologous chromosomes have broken and changed places. **B** shows the chromosomes separating at late prophase I. **C** shows the two chromosomes, each with its exchanged portion of chromatid separating during metaphase I. Later, at anaphase I, they will move apart.

Observing meiosis

To observe stages in meiosis one must choose a reproductive tissue in which gametes or spores are being produced. In flowering plants meiosis can be observed in developing pollen grains or embryo sacs. This means examining the contents of anthers or ovules respectively. In animals meiosis can be observed in the testes or ovaries.

In all these cases the tissues must be stained appropriately in order to show up the chromosomes, this being achieved either by sectioning or by making squash preparations. The photomicrographs shown in the illustration were obtained from the testis of a locust, a convenient choice because the chromosomes are large and comparatively few in number, enabling individual chromosomes to be seen and followed clearly.

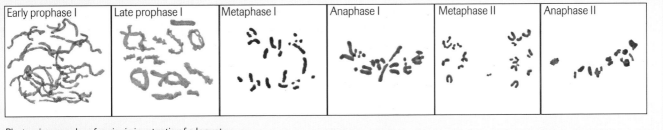

Photomicrographs of meiosis in a testis of a locust.

The differences between mitosis and meiosis

This brief account of cell division will have shown that there are many detailed differences between mitosis and meiosis. As we have seen, there are two central distinctions. The first is that in meiosis homologous chromosomes associate with one another, whereas in mitosis they do not. This is clearly seen in late prophase, when the chromosomes make their appearance as distinct bodies, and again at metaphase when they arrange themselves on the spindle. The second is that no DNA replication occurs between the first and second meiotic divisions. If you think about it, all the other differences between these two types of nuclear division stem from these fundamental differences in the behaviour of the chromosomes.

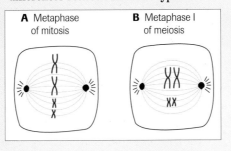

The essential difference between mitosis and meiosis lies in the behaviour of the chromosomes. This can be seen at metaphase when they arrange themselves on the spindle. In mitosis (**A**) homologous chromosomes do not associate with one another, whereas in meiosis (**B**) they come together and then segregate.

Cancer is not a single disease. There are hundreds of different sorts, and they attack different parts of the body. Despite these differences, all cancers have in common that they involve the uncontrolled growth of cells. In a cancerous cell something goes wrong with the control of the cell cycle and the cell starts to divide more often than it should. Eventually a mass of cancerous cells results, called a **tumour**, which may give rise to **secondaries** in other parts of the body (*figure 26.11*).

What causes cancer?

In a cancerous cell, specific changes or **mutations** have happened in the genetic material as a result of which the controls which prevent excessive cell division fail to work. Generalisations about cancer are difficult as there are so many different types, though the chances of developing most cancers increase with age. Apart from increasing age, there are three main causes of cancer: **chemicals**, **radiation** and **viruses**. As well as these environmental causes, some people **inherit** a greater likelihood of developing cancer.

Chemicals

In 1775, a London surgeon called Percival Pott noticed that boys who swept chimneys for a living had a very high incidence of cancer of the scrotum. Pott argued that the cancer was caused by contact with soot. Pott's theory led to a law being passed in Denmark, but not in Britain, requiring chimney sweeps to wear protective clothing and wash more regularly. The occurrence of scrotal cancer subsequently fell.

Following on from Pott's pioneering work, a number of industrial chemicals are now known to cause cancer, that is they are **carcinogenic**. Asbestos is an example. In most countries there are laws designed to reduce the risks associated with such substances. However, world-wide, the chemicals that cause the most cancers are those found in cigarettes.

Cigarette smoke is a complicated aerosol containing a suspension of millions of tiny particles. There are many different compounds in cigarette smoke but **tars** are the ones responsible for lung cancer. In Britain, **lung cancer** kills about 40 000 people a year and over 90 per cent of these deaths are due to smoking (*page 174*).

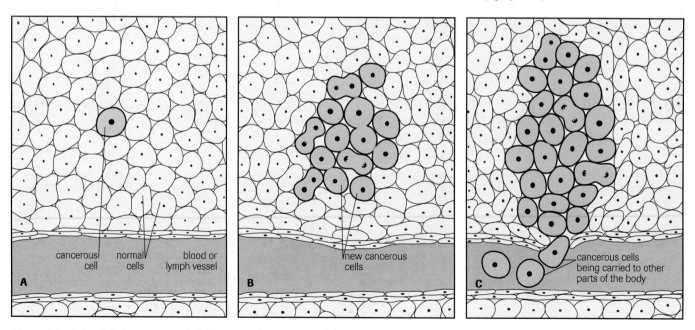

Figure 26.11 A and **B** A cancerous cell divides more often than normal cells and gives rise to a mass of cancerous cells called a tumour. **C** The tumour may be carried to other parts of the body via blood vessels or the lymphatic system. This can give rise to new (secondary) cancers some distance from the original one. A tumour which spreads in this way is described as malignant.

The extent to which our diet is responsible for cancer is less certain. Nevertheless, there is good evidence that a low fibre intake increases the chance of getting cancer of the bowel. It is also known that cancers of the breast and bowel are most common in countries where people eat a lot of fat. Although the precise causal links between these cancers and fat intake have yet to be established, the overall message is clear. In many Western countries our diet is too low in fibre and too high in fat.

▶ Coronary heart disease and diet, page 000

Radiation

Several sorts of radiation may also lead to cancer. Exposure to too much ultraviolet radiation in sunlight, especially if even mild sunburn results, may lead to **skin cancer** developing, sometimes many years later. With the damage to the ozone layer leading to more ultraviolet radiation reaching the Earth's surface, it is all the more important to prevent sunburn through the use of protective creams and appropriate clothing (*page 679*).

X-rays can damage the genetic material of a cell and cause cancer. The risks from X-rays are particularly great for the developing fetus, which is why pregnant women tend not to be given X-rays.

Nuclear power stations inevitably produce small amounts of radiation, just as coal mines produce coal dust. There is some evidence in Britain that the children of men who work in nuclear power stations may have a higher incidence of cancers of their white blood cells (**leukaemia**), though the evidence is still controversial.

The accident at the nuclear plant in Chernobyl on 26 April 1986 contaminated millions of people in the then USSR and northern Europe (*figure 26.12*). Mary Morrey, of Britain's National Radiological Protection Board, has estimated that Chernobyl will cause an extra 1000 deaths in the European Union, chiefly from cancer. The number of extra deaths in the former USSR is more difficult to estimate, but will undoubtedly be many times this number.

Viruses

Some cancers are now known to be caused by viruses. It appears, for example, that **cervical cancer** (cancer of the cervix) is associated with the presence of **human papilloma viruses** (**HPVs**). Some strains of these viruses may be passed on during sexual intercourse with an infected partner. In this sense cervical cancer behaves like a sexually transmitted infection. Some **liver cancers** are also believed to be caused by viruses.

Inherited cancers

Finally we come to those cancers where heredity is implicated. Often, no clear-cut pattern of inheritance is found. All we can say is that there is a tendency for certain cancers to run in families. In some cases, though, the underlying genetic causes are better understood. For example, a mutation in a certain gene (the BRCA1 gene) greatly increases a woman's chances of developing **breast cancer**. However, at least 15 per cent of women with this mutation do not go on to develop breast cancer while many women with a history of breast cancer in their family do not have a mutation in this gene.

Treating cancers

Treatments for cancer are improving all the time and nowadays many cancers can often be cured. A number of techniques are used, but their common aim is to destroy the cancerous cells, while leaving the normal healthy cells intact. Treatments are most effective if started early. This is why **screening** for cancers is becoming widespread. For example, regular screening for breast cancer cuts the chances of dying from breast cancer by locating tumours before they have spread. In the case of cervical screening, abnormal changes in cells lining the cervix can be spotted even before these cells become cancerous.

The most direct treatment is **surgery**. Obviously this is most appropriate if the cancer is localised and the aim is to remove the entire tumour. Surgical techniques have now

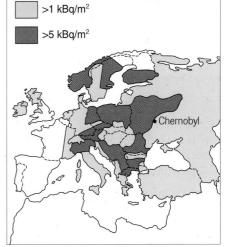

>1 kBq/m²

>5 kBq/m²

Chernobyl

Figure 26.12 A Aerial photograph of the Chernobyl nuclear power plant, near Kiev. Taken in 1991, five years after the accident that devastated the plant and released large quantities of radioactive contaminants into the environment.
B Radioactive contamination as a result of the nuclear accident at Chernobyl on 26 April 1986. The pattern of contamination is the result of wind and rainfall. The becquerel (Bq) is a unit of radioactivity. 1 kBq corresponds to 1000 decays per second.

improved to the point where the cosmetic effects of the operation may hardly be noticed. For instance, surgical treatment of breast cancer nowadays often does not require the removal of the entire breast. Instead only the tumour may be removed, leading to almost no disfigurement.

A second way of treating cancers is to use high-energy ionising radiation to destroy the cancerous cells. This is called **radiotherapy**. X-rays, gamma rays from a radioactive isotope such as cobalt, beams of electrons or beams of neutrons may be used depending on the type and position of the cancer.

A third technique involves the use of drugs, i.e. **chemotherapy**. To understand how chemotherapeutic drugs work, it helps to recall the details of the cell cycle. While a cell is in the first gap phase, its chromosomes are much less susceptible to these drugs than when they are in the other phases. Cancerous cells spend less time in the first gap phase than do non-cancerous cells, because they are so busy dividing. This means that chemotherapeutic drugs are more likely to kill cancerous cells than healthy ones. Can you now explain why chemotherapy may cause a patient's hair to fall out?

New ways of tackling cancers are being developed. Some cancers can now be treated using **lasers**. These can destroy the blood supply to the malignant cells, thus starving the tumour of oxygen and nutrients. **Radio waves** are also beginning to be used to destroy liver tumours by cooking them, just as a microwave cooks food.

Summary

1. Cell division is necessary for **growth**, **reproduction** and the **replacement of old or damaged cells**.

2. The sequence of events which takes place in a cell between successive cell divisions is known as the **cell cycle**.

3. Mitosis leads to the production of two **daughter cells**, each with the same number and types of chromosomes as the **parent cell**. The cells usually contain two of each type of chromosome (**diploid state**).

4. Mitosis can be divided into four stages: **prophase** in which the chromosomes condense, **metaphase** in which they arrange themselves on the equator of the spindle, **anaphase** when they separate and are pulled towards the two poles by spindle fibres, and **telophase** in which two new nuclear envelopes form.

5. In **meiosis**, the number of chromosomes is halved, the daughter cells receiving only one of each type of chromosome (**haploid state**).

6. Nuclear division (mitosis or meiosis) is followed by **cytoplasmic division**.

7. Meiosis occurs in the production of **gametes** or **spores** and is necessary for sexual reproduction.

8. Meiosis consists of two successive divisions with no intervening replication of the genetic material. As a result four haploid cells are formed from a single diploid one.

9. In the first meiotic division **homologous chromosomes** separate from one another and go into different cells. In the second meiotic division the sister chromatids of each chromosome segregate into different cells.

10. Meiosis promotes **genetic variation** in three ways:

- the two chromosomes of each homologous pair carry different genetic material and end up in separate cells;

- the different pairs of homologous chromosomes **segregate independently**;

- **chiasmata** result in the exchange of genetic material (**crossing-over**) between non-sister chromatids.

11. **Cancers** are due to a breakdown in the control of the cell cycle. Cancerous cells divide more often than they should and form **tumours**.

12. Cancers may be caused by **increasing age**, by certain **chemicals**, by various sorts of **radiation**, by some **viruses**, or they may have a **hereditary component**.

13. At present, cancers may be treated by **surgery**, high-energy ionising radiation (**radiotherapy**) or by certain drugs (**chemotherapy**). Regular **screening** can reduce the incidence of cancers and new methods of treatment are currently being developed.

For general advice on these questions and advice on answering essay-type questions, see pages vii and viii.

1. The flow chart shows one way in which a chromosome preparation may be obtained.

Sample of cells obtained.

↓

Sample incubated for 48 hours.

↓

Addition of colchicine and further incubation for 24 hours. Colchicine acts as a spindle inhibitor.

↓

Squash preparation made and chromosomes stained.

↓

Chromosomes examined under microscope.

(a) Explain why it was necessary to incubate the cells for 48 hours before adding colchicine. (2)

(b) (i) What is the function of the spindle in mitosis? (1)

(ii) Suggest why a spindle inhibitor like colchicine was added in making this preparation. (1)

(iii) The total amount of DNA in the nucleus of one of these cells immediately before cell division was 6.8 units. How much DNA would there be in this cell after treatment with colchicine? Explain your answer. (2)

(Total 6 marks)

AEB 1997

2. Copy and complete the following passage on the cell cycle and mitosis, using the most appropriate word or words to fill the blanks.

In the cell cycle, replication of DNA takes place during .... At the beginning of prophase the chromosomes become visible and can be seen to consist of two .... joined at the .... The .... and nuclear membrane disappear and a spindle develops in the cell. The chromosomes become attached to the spindle at the equator during .... At anaphase one copy of each chromosome is pulled towards each .... of the spindle. The final phase, called telophase, involves the formation of two new nuclei. In plant cells the two daughter cells are separated by the formation of a ....

(Total 7 marks)

London 1997

3. (a) During which phase of the cell cycle do the following events take place:

(i) the replication of DNA; (1)

(ii) the movement of daughter chromosomes to the poles of the cell? (1)

(b) The diagram shows a section through an onion bulb which is starting to grow.

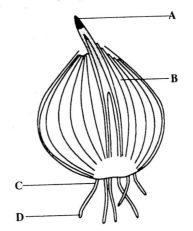

(i) Which of the parts **A** to **D** of this bulb would you use in order to prepare a slide showing mitosis? (1)

(ii) Give the name of the stain you would use to make this preparation. (1)

(iii) Describe the effect that this stain would have on the cells. (1)

(Total 5 marks)

AEB 1996

4. The drawings show four stages in mitosis.

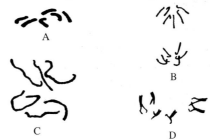

(a) Give the correct sequence of the four drawings. (1)

(b) Explain how mitosis results in daughter cells containing copies of genetic information identical to the parent cell. (3)

(c) Daughter cells produced by meiosis are genetically different from each other.

Give **two** processes occurring during meiosis which are responsible for the differences. (2)

(Total 6 marks)

NEAB 1997

Chapter 27

Types of reproduction and life cycles

I n Chapter 26 we looked at the cellular aspects of cell division and saw how cell division is necessary for reproduction as well as for growth and the replacement of old or damaged cells. In this chapter we shall look at the reproduction of whole organisms, concentrating on general aspects rather than details.

27.1 Asexual reproduction

Asexual reproduction does not involve combining genetic material from two different individuals. It therefore does not necessitate the production and fusion of gametes. Instead, one individual produces near-identical copies of itself. The descendants produced asexually from a single individual belong to a **clone**. Unless mutation occurs, all the members of a clone share the same genetic constitution.

Asexual reproduction probably evolved long before sexual reproduction. It still occurs today in many species. One reason is that it generally takes place very rapidly and so helps to maximise the production of offspring, particularly when environmental conditions are favourable.

For convenience, asexual methods of reproduction can be divided into six categories, which we shall look at in turn:

- fission
- spore formation
- budding
- fragmentation
- vegetative reproduction
- parthenogenesis.

Fission

In fission, the organism divides into two or more equal-sized parts. **Binary fission**, the division of the organism into two or more daughter cells, is characteristic of prokaryotes and many protoctists (*figure 27.1*). The rate of multiplication achieved in this way can be prodigious: for example, in favourable conditions bacterial cells may divide once every 20 minutes, which means that in 24 hours a single cell can theoretically give rise to a population exceeding 4000 million million million (4×10^{21}).

This astronomical figure is achieved because the increase is exponential (*page 691*): one cell divides into two, two into four, four into eight, and so on. In its early stages such exponential growth seems rather unimpressive, but it gains momentum as the numbers increase. Think of those bacteria dividing in two every 20 minutes: only eight exist at the end of the first hour, and only 512 by the end of the third hour. But by the end of a day...! The principle is the same in compound interest. If 1p had been invested at just 1 per cent interest per year when Jesus was born, it would be worth over £4 million today.

Even higher reproductive rates are achieved by **multiple fission** which is shown by various protoctists, particularly parasitic ones. In this case the nucleus divides repeatedly and each daughter nucleus breaks away, together with a small portion of the cytoplasm. This splitting process is termed **schizogony**, and a cell that does it is called a **schizont** (*page 708*).

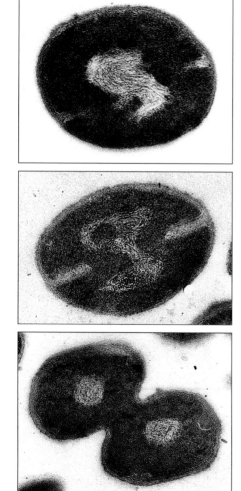

Figure 27.1 Electron micrographs showing three successive stages in the binary fission of the bacterium *Staphylococcus aureus*.

Spore formation

Spores are unicellular bodies formed by cell division in a parent organism. Having become detached from the parent they develop, directly or indirectly, into a new individual, provided environmental conditions are suitable. Spores are produced by prokaryotes, protoctists, fungi and many plants (though *not* flowering plants). They come in a wide range of forms, and are produced and dispersed in many different ways.

Spores are generally very small and light, which helps them to be dispersed by water, animals or wind (*figure 27.2*). Some spores have thick, resistant walls which enable them to survive unfavourable conditions for long periods of time. They are usually numerous. The ability of fungi to produce vast numbers of airborne spores explains why members of this important group of saprobionts and parasites manage to spread so quickly. Spore formation in mosses and ferns will be considered in more detail later in this chapter.

Figure 27.2 Puffball releasing a cloud of spores.

Budding

In this method of reproduction an organism develops an outgrowth which, on detachment from the parent, becomes a self-supporting individual. Budding is characteristic of yeast cells (*figure 27.3*) and a wide variety of animals including *Hydra*, certain flatworms and several annelid groups. In multicellular animals like *Hydra*, budding takes place by proliferation of undifferentiated cells which then develop into appropriate structures within the bud (*figure 27.4*).

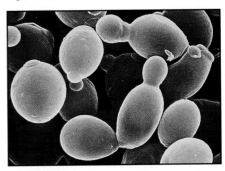

Figure 27.3 Scanning electron micrograph of yeast cells budding.

Fragmentation

Sometimes an organism may be broken into two or more pieces, each of which grows into a new individual. As a means of reproduction, fragmentation depends on the organism having good powers of regeneration. Sponges and hydroid coelenterates, for example, have astonishing powers of regeneration: if a sponge is macerated by passing it through fine gauze, the separated cells come together in groups and grow into new individuals. Given the right conditions, very small fragments of free-living flatworms will regenerate into new individuals, and in the marine nemertine worm *Lineus* dozens of individuals may be formed from a single worm.

▶ Vegetative reproduction, page 490

Vegetative reproduction

Vegetative reproduction is the form of asexual reproduction in plants where parts of the body become detached and develop into new self-supporting individuals. Scores of examples could be given.

Parthenogenesis

Parthenogenesis is the development of new individuals from an unfertilised egg. It is found in a number of plant and animal groups, including some lizards.

■ In **haploid parthenogenesis**, eggs are produced by meiosis in the usual way, and are therefore haploid. These develop, without being fertilised, into individuals whose cells are therefore haploid. An example of this is seen in ants, bees and wasps. In honeybees, for instance, haploid eggs laid by the queen develop into adult males (drones) (*page 450*).

■ In **diploid parthenogenesis** the eggs, instead of being formed by meiosis, are formed by mitosis, with the result that they are diploid instead of haploid. The egg then divides by mitosis to give rise to a diploid adult. This happens at certain stages in the life cycle of aphids. In the summer months, wingless females produce further generations of mainly wingless females by diploid parthenogenesis, a rapid and efficient way of increasing numbers without necessitating the presence of males.

In certain flowering plants an embryo may develop from a diploid cell in the ovule which has not undergone meiosis and remains unfertilised. As the embryo develops,

Figure 27.4 Budding in *Hydra*. A perfectly formed bud can be seen on the left.

Figure 27.5 Despite the fact that they have bright flowers, most dandelion plants result not from sexual reproduction, but from the mitotic growth of a single diploid cell in the ovule.

the surrounding tissues form the seed and fruit in the usual way (*page 487*). The formation of a plant embryo without the fusion of gametes occurs in several plants, including potatoes, citruses and dandelions (*figure 27.5*).

27.2 Sexual reproduction

In its broadest sense **sexual reproduction** is any process in which genetic material is transferred from one cell to another. It generally involves the fusion of specialised sex cells called **gametes** which are derived from two different individuals. Gametes are always haploid, and they cannot develop further unless they fuse appropriately.

How gametes may have evolved

The fusion of gametes is called **fertilisation**. Generally the gametes differ from each other in structure, size and behaviour. However, some organisms, such as protoctists and fungi, produce gametes that are identical with each other (**isogamy**) or are only very slightly different. In many unicellular organisms the gametes, as well as being identical with each other, are also structurally similar to the parent cells. At the simplest level there are no gametes at all, genetic material being transferred directly from one individual to another. This is essentially what happens in bacterial conjugation (*extension box on the next page*) and, with certain elaborations, in some protoctists. We can therefore envisage a progression from bacterial conjugation through isogamy to the situation where the male and female gametes differ from one another.

In most species fusion does not occur between gametes from the same parent. Even in isogamous species, the gametes, though structurally identical, can recognise whether or not they come from the same parent and react accordingly. In some protoctists and fungi, for example in pin mould (*Mucor*), it is possible to separate members of a single species into **plus** and **minus strains**: plus conjugates (fuses) with minus, but plus will not conjugate with plus, nor minus with minus. This foreshadows the existence of separate sexes which almost certainly arose later in evolution.

Some protoctists and fungi also show a tendency for one gamete to be migratory and the other stationary. This anticipates the existence of **sperm** and **eggs**. Fully differentiated eggs and sperm are found in organisms as different as seaweeds, mosses, cnidarians, insects and chordates. The sperm of different species differ somewhat in structure. However, all sperm share the same fundamentals of smallness, the ability to swim and the possession of a haploid nucleus. Similarly, eggs always have a haploid nucleus, but are relatively large and non-motile. An egg receives genetic material from a sperm and may provide nourishment for the developing embryo.

The pros and cons of sexual reproduction

Sex is a risky business. Consider, for example, a female toad. When she mates she risks being drowned by the onslaught of male toads fighting amongst themselves to mate with her (*figure 27.6*). Not only that but she depends on her eggs being penetrated by sperm that contribute nothing but another individual's genes! Why doesn't she simply produce the same number of diploid eggs and avoid males altogether? In that way she would side-step the dangers of mating, and produce offspring each of which would contain all her genes rather than only half her genes.

The answer is probably 'variation'. Although sex may be hazardous, it generates genetic variation. As we shall see in Chapter 43, much of this variation is harmful, but in the long run it provides the raw material for evolution. Organisms that reproduce asexually show less variation and evolve more slowly than organisms that reproduce sexually. They therefore run the risk of their descendants being outcompeted by organisms resulting from sexual reproduction.

Figure 27.6 The hazards of sexual reproduction. Several male toads are attempting to mate with a single female.

Sexual reproduction in bacteria

Until the 1940s, bacteria were thought to be capable only of asexual reproduction. However, in 1946 Joshua Lederberg and Edward Tatum showed that the colon bacillus *Escherichia coli* can also reproduce sexually. They discovered that on coming into contact with another bacterium of the same species, an individual may develop one or more specialised tubes called **sex pili** (singular **pilus**) (*illustration 1*). One of these pili allows some of the DNA from the first bacterium to pass into the second. Experiments have shown that the longer the two bacteria are in contact, the more DNA passes from one to the other. Because this form of sexual reproduction requires two individuals to be in contact with each other, it is known as **conjugation** (literally 'joined together').

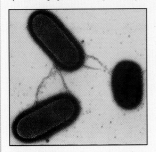

Illustration 1 Bacteria with sex pili. The pili allow DNA to pass between bacteria during conjugation.

All *E. coli* look identical, so we cannot really talk about males and females. However, only some of them can produce sex pili. These particular bacteria have a special bit of DNA called an **F factor** (F standing for fertility). This is not part of the main bacterial DNA but a separate structure called a **plasmid**. Plasmids are small circular pieces of DNA separate from the rest of a cell's DNA. They are found in bacteria and yeast and can replicate independently of the rest of the DNA. Some plasmids carry genes for resistance to antibiotics.

The F factor carries genes for producing pili and for the other functions needed to transfer DNA from the donor to the

recipient bacterium. What happens is that this F factor inserts into the rest of the DNA and then causes some of it to pass into the recipient cell. Once in the recipient cell, some of the donor's genes may change places with corresponding genes of the recipient. This **recombination** results in a bacterium with a new set of genes (*illustration 2*).

Another way in which sexual reproduction occurs in some bacteria is rather more straightforward. The bacterium simply takes up pieces of DNA from the environment across its cell wall in a process called **transformation**. On

entering the cell the foreign DNA may, as in conjugation, be integrated into the bacterial DNA by recombination. Transformation falls within our definition of sexual reproduction because genetic material is transferred from one cell to another. The DNA might come, for instance, from an individual that has died and released its DNA to the environment.

Certain viruses provide a third way of bringing the genes of different bacteria together. Essentially what happens is that the viruses carry bits of bacterial DNA from one bacterium to another. This process is called **transduction**.

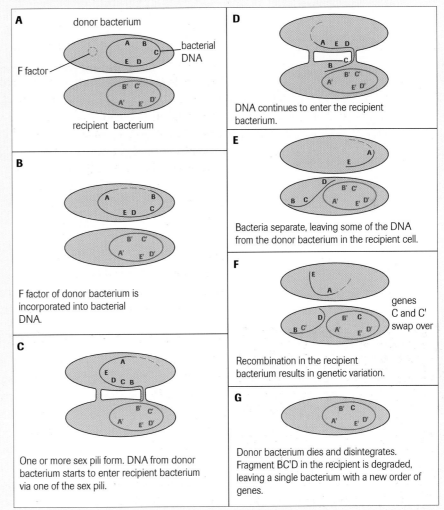

Illustration 2 Diagram to show the transfer of genetic material in bacterial conjugation. Each bacterium has a circular piece of DNA, shown here in the donor bacterium with genes ABCDE and in the recipient bacterium with genes A'B'C'D'E'. In addition, the donor bacterium has a small extra piece of DNA (a plasmid) known as an F factor.

Cross fertilisation and self fertilisation

Two sorts of fertilisation are found in sexual reproduction:

- **cross fertilisation** – the gametes come from two separate individuals;
- **self fertilisation** – both gametes come from the same individual.

If sexual reproduction is geared towards generating genetic variation, we should expect organisms to favour cross fertilisation rather than self fertilisation. By and large, this is what we see in nature. Some plants, such as certain violets, can reproduce by both self fertilisation and cross fertilisation. In such cases self fertilisation is used as a back up, adopted only if cross fertilisation fails to occur.

Details regarding self and cross fertilisation in relation to pollination can be found on pages 487–8.

Details regarding self and cross fertilisation in relation to pollination can be found on pages 487–8.

What's in an egg?

When we say that animals with internal fertilisation 'lay eggs', the object that is laid is not just an egg cell; if fertilised, it will have started dividing, so an embryo will be present inside the original egg covering (the egg shell in the case of birds). In egg-laying mammals (prototherians, *page 101*) the embryo has developed to quite an advanced stage by the time the 'egg' leaves the mother's body, and this foreshadows the development of viviparity in placental mammals.

Figure 27.7 Many mammals look after their young long after they are weaned. Here an adult female bear helps her two cubs learn how to fish.

27.3 Evolution of reproductive methods

Fundamental to sexual reproduction is the method by which gametes are brought together. At its simplest this takes place by the gametes of both sexes being liberated into the surrounding water as occurs, for instance, in seaweeds and many fish. In animals, this sort of fertilisation is known as **external fertilisation**. It is found in many aquatic organisms and in certain terrestrial ones, such as the toads in figure 27.6 that return to water for breeding. In most terrestrial animals, however, fertilisation occurs inside the body of the female (**internal fertilisation**). Generally, internal fertilisation necessitates the use of some kind of **intromittent organ** (e.g. a **penis**) to introduce the sperm into the female's body.

Internal fertilisation has three advantages over external fertilisation:

- It is a surer method since, from the point of view of both the male and the female, there is less chance of gametes being wasted.
- It means that in egg-laying (**oviparous**) animals the fertilised egg can be enclosed within a protective covering before it leaves the female's body. Such is the case with reptiles, birds and insects.
- It may enable the embryo to develop within the female parent and derive nourishment from her (**viviparity**). This reaches its greatest development in those mammals which nourish their developing young before birth by means of a placenta.

Comparable mechanisms occur in terrestrial plants. They may not possess intromittent organs as such, but special techniques have evolved for transferring the male gametes to the egg cells, after which early development of the embryo takes place within the body of the parent plant.

Many organisms desert their offspring as soon as they have been produced. Others provide some sort of parental care. For example, the male stickleback looks after the fertilised eggs in a defended territory and fans them, to provide oxygen, until they hatch and swim away (*page 439*).

By and large, the more parental care provided, the fewer the number of offspring produced. To take two extremes, certain types of fish produce over 100 million eggs at a spawning, whereas certain mammals, including ourselves, usually produce only one offspring at a time. Mammals continue to provide maternal care after birth in the form of milk production (**lactation**). Even after the offspring have been weaned, parental care may be provided by one or other parent, usually the mother, who protects the young as they grow up and helps them learn how to survive in their environment (*figure 27.7*).

An organism's **life cycle** is the sequence of events from fertilisation in one generation to fertilisation in the next generation. In the course of its life cycle, an organism normally produces a new generation of individuals which repeat the process. New generations are produced by **reproduction**, which we have seen may be either asexual or sexual.

We shall start by looking briefly at the life cycle of the human which, despite the structural complexity of the adult, is comparatively simple (*figure 27.8*).

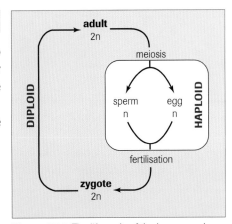

The life cycle of the human

An adult human produces either eggs or sperm. If these gametes fuse successfully, a **zygote** is formed which may develop into a new adult. The details of this complex process are discussed in Chapter 29. At present we are only concerned with the overall picture. All the nucleated cells of an adult human are diploid except for the gametes. These are formed by meiosis and are therefore haploid. When a sperm and an egg fuse as a result of fertilisation, a zygote results. Since it is formed by the union of two haploid gametes, the zygote is diploid; and as it divides mitotically, the adult to which it gives rise will also be diploid.

Meiosis and fertilisation divide the life cycle into two distinct phases: the **diploid phase**, which spans the zygote and the adult, and the **haploid phase**, containing only the gametes. This is shown in figure 27.8.

The majority of animals have life cycles which conform to the same general plan seen in humans, though there are a number of variations on the theme. For example, one or more **larval stages** may be interpolated between the zygote and the adult, as in amphibians, certain insects and a number of parasites. While the existence of larval stages increases the general complexity of the life cycle, it does not affect the overall pattern seen in figure 27.8.

Figure 27.8 The life cycle of the human and most other animals follows the plan outlined here. There is considerable variation in different animals as to the way the zygote develops into the adult, but the fundamental division of the life cycle into diploid and haploid phases is the same throughout. n = haploid; 2n = diploid.

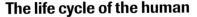
Larvae, page 533

Alternation of generations

An important departure from the basic life cycle described above is seen in certain seaweeds and in mosses, liverworts and ferns. In these organisms gametes are produced by *mitosis* from a haploid **gametophyte** (literally 'gamete plant'). The gametophyte is sexually mature and its gametes are haploid, as you would expect. These gametes fuse to produce a diploid zygote, but this cannot – being diploid – develop into a new gametophyte. Instead it grows (by mitotic cell divisions) into another individual which is quite distinct from the gametophyte.

The function of this individual is to produce **spores**, for which reason it is referred to as the **sporophyte** (literally 'spore plant'). Formed by meiosis, and therefore haploid, spores are small, light and readily dispersed. When they alight on a suitable surface, they germinate and grow by mitosis into a gametophyte, which then repeats the sequence of events. This kind of life cycle is summarised in figure 27.9.

From this brief account it is clear that the life cycle of a moss or fern contains two distinct stages, a haploid gametophyte and a diploid sporophyte, which alternate with each other within the life cycle. This phenomenon is known as **alternation of generations**.

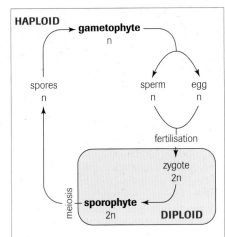

Figure 27.9 The life cycle of many plants, notably ferns and mosses, shows alternation of generations in which a haploid gamete-producing gametophyte alternates with a diploid, spore-producing sporophyte. Notice that, as in animals, meiosis and fertilisation divide the life cycle into haploid and diploid phases.

The life cycles of mosses and ferns

Figure 27.9 is a general outline of the life cycle of any organism showing alternation of generations and takes no account of the variations and complexities of individual species. Let us now see show how the life cycles of a common moss and fern conform to this general pattern. We advise you to concentrate on the overall picture to begin with, rather than the details.

In both mosses and ferns the gametophyte bears special gamete-forming organs:

- **antheridia** which produce sperm;
- **archegonia** which produce eggs.

By methods which are slightly different in mosses and ferns, sperm are released from the antheridia and brought into contact with the eggs. In both groups water is essential for this. The result of the union of a sperm with an egg is a diploid zygote which grows into a sporophyte. In mosses this is attached to, and dependent on, the gametophyte. In ferns, though, the sporophyte is a separate, self-supporting plant. In both cases the spores are formed in specialised spore-bearing structures called **sporangia** from which they are released by dispersal mechanisms which ensure that they are scattered over a wide area. The spores, if they germinate, grow into gametophytes.

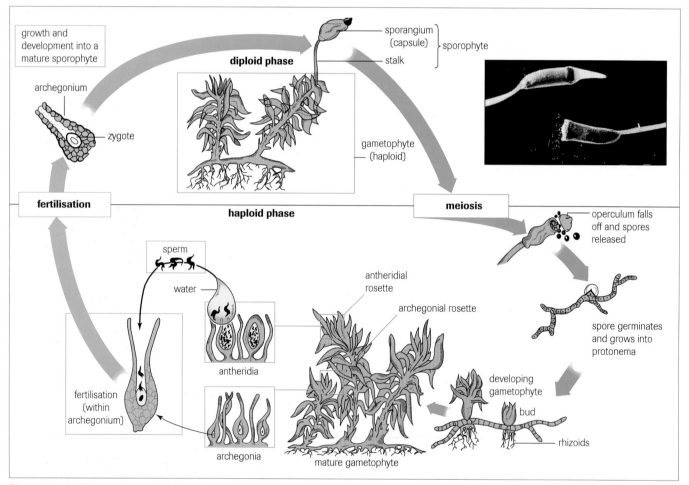

Figure 27.10 Life cycle of a moss such as *Funaria*. In spring, egg-containing archegonia and sperm-producing antheridia are found amongst the leaves of the haploid gametophyte. For fertilisation to occur, the antheridial and archegonial rosettes must contain water. Sperm are released by rupture of the antheridia. At the same time the necks of the archegonia open, creating an open passage through which the sperm can swim to the eggs. This movement of sperm from antheridia to archegonia is thought to be aided by splashing from rain. After fertilisation, the zygote grows into the sporophyte which remains attached to, and dependent on, the gametophyte. Spores develop by meiosis within a spore sac inside the sporangium (capsule). In dry weather the operculum falls off. The tissues near the opening of the capsule dry out and the haploid spores are released, to be dispersed by wind and air currents (*see photograph at top right*). On landing on moist ground, each spore germinates into a green, filamentous protonema which produces buds that grow into the gametophyte, thus completing the life cycle.

The two life cycles are therefore basically similar but differ in detail. You can see this by looking at figures 27.10 and 27.11. The most noticeable difference is the relative emphasis which each places on the gametophyte and sporophyte. In mosses the gametophyte is the dominant generation, the sporophyte being comparatively simple in structure, short-lived and dependent – almost parasitic – on the gametophyte.

In ferns it is the other way round. The sporophyte is the dominant generation: it is large (some tree ferns are over seven metres high), differentiated into leaf, stem and roots with vascular tissues and a complex internal organisation on a level with that of a flowering plant. By comparison, the gametophyte of a fern (or **prothallus** as it is called) is quite insignificant and needs a moist environment. A mere millimetre or two in diameter, it is a flat plate of photosynthetic cells anchored to the soil by thin, root-like rhizoids.

The gametophytes and sporophytes of mosses and ferns are compared in figure 27.12.

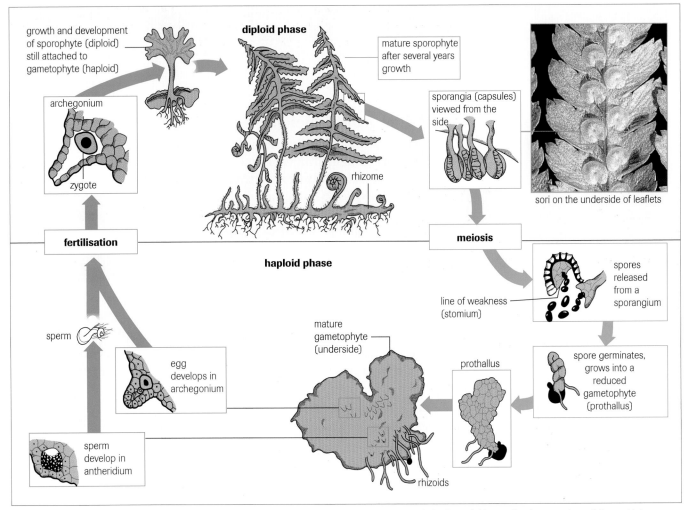

Figure 27.11 Life cycle of the fern *Dryopteris*. The prominent sporophyte (diploid) consists of a horizontal rhizome (underground stem) from which vertically-growing fronds (leaves) arise. The rhizome overwinters, new fronds being formed from it each year. On the undersides of sporophylls (spore-bearing leaflets), groups of sporangia (capsules) develop. Each group, protected by an umbrella-like shield, is called a sorus, and inside the sporangia haploid spores are formed by meiosis. The mature sporangium is topped by a row of cells which in dry weather readily lose water by evaporation. The resulting tension ruptures the sporangium at the stomium, thereby releasing the spores. If moisture is present, each spore germinates into a simple heart-shaped prothallus, a flat plate of photosynthetic cells anchored to the soil by filamentous rhizoids. The prothallus is a reduced gametophyte: antheridia and archegonia, located on its underside, produce sperm and eggs respectively. The gametophyte depends on a damp environment, not only to prevent it drying out, but also for transference of sperm. After rupture of the antheridium, the ciliated sperm swim to an egg cell at the base of an archegonium where fertilisation occurs. The zygote grows into a young sporophyte which, once it has established roots and leaves, becomes self-supporting, thus completing the cycle. Note that in contrast to the life cycle of the moss, in ferns the sporophyte is the dominant generation, the gametophyte being much reduced.

Figure 27.12 *Left* Moss showing diploid sporophytes growing out of the leafy gametophytes. *Right* Fern showing a haploid gametophyte from which a young diploid sporophyte is beginning to grow.

Reduction of the gametophyte

Alternation of generations is basic to the life cycle of almost all plant groups. It is most clearly seen in mosses, liverworts and ferns, where both generations can readily be seen. In other groups the pattern may be obscured by the gametophyte generation being reduced or absent and the sporophyte being correspondingly prominent.

We have already seen this to some extent in ferns, where the gametophyte is dwarfed by the sporophyte. But it is in conifers and flowering plants that the dominance of the sporophyte is seen most dramatically.

Flowering plants

Consider a flowering plant such as a buttercup or oak tree. The bulk of the plant is the sporophyte; the gametophyte is hidden away inside the sporophyte. We have seen that the function of a sporophyte is to produce spores, and this is precisely what happens in flowering plants.

Flowering plants, in common with conifers and certain fern-like groups, have two types of spores:

- very small **microspores** from which male gametes are derived;
- larger **megaspores** from which female gametes are derived.

The details of how these spores are produced and what happens to them are discussed in Chapter 28. Here it is sufficient to note that flowering plants represent the end product of a line of evolution in which the gametophyte, a prominent self-supporting plant in groups such as mosses, gradually degenerates until eventually it becomes incorporated into the body of the sporophyte. Meanwhile the sporophyte gains in structural importance, being very much the dominant generation in ferns, and even more so in flowering plants.

Why this evolutionary trend towards the dominance of the sporophyte generation has occurred is uncertain. It may be because the sporophyte, being diploid, is able to 'hide' the effect of harmful recessive alleles (*page 573*). Alternatively (or in addition) it may be an adaptation to life on land: the gametophyte, with its dependence on water, is suppressed and reproduction is based on the production of seeds. This is characteristic both of conifers and flowering plants.

Summary

1. Reproduction can be **sexual** or **asexual**. Asexual reproduction produces offspring which, in the absence of mutations, are genetically identical to one another and to their parent. Sexual reproduction, in contrast, confers genetic variation.

2. The descendants produced asexually from a single individual belong to a **clone**.

3. Asexual methods of reproduction include **binary** and **multiple fission**, **spore formation**, **budding**, **fragmentation**, **vegetative reproduction** and **parthenogenesis**.

4. Sexual reproduction involves the transfer of genetic material from one organism to another.

5. Three sorts of sexual reproduction are found in bacteria: **conjugation** in which contact between two bacteria is required; **transformation** in which a single bacterium picks up a bit of DNA from its environment; and **transduction** in which the passage of genetic information from one bacterium to another is mediated by a virus.

6. Sexual reproduction typically involves the union of haploid **gametes** to form a diploid **zygote**. Gametes may be identical (**isogamy**), or they may differ from each other with respect to their structure, size and behaviour.

7. In some cases of isogamy, individuals cannot be separated into males and females, but can be classified into **plus** or **minus strains**. Plus and minus strains can mate with each other but not amongst themselves.

8. The structure of **eggs** and **sperm** is related to their functions: sperm are motile vehicles for the male's genetic material; eggs receive genetic material from sperm and may provide nourishment for embryos.

9. Many aquatic animals show **external fertilisation**. Most terrestrial animals have **internal fertilisation** with **oviparity** or **viviparity**. In mammals, nourishment of the embryo is provided by a **placenta**, **lactation** occurs after birth and there may be subsequent **parental care**.

10. The progressive sequence of changes which a species goes through from fertilisation in one generation to fertilisation in the next is known as the **life cycle**.

11. In organisms with sexual reproduction, **meiosis** (halving of the chromosome number) and **fertilisation** (union of gametes) divide the life cycle into **haploid** and **diploid** phases.

12. In animals, the haploid phase is represented only by the gametes. However, in mosses, ferns and certain other organisms, the life cycle shows an **alternation of generations** between a haploid gamete-producing **gametophyte** and a diploid **sporophyte** that produces haploid spores.

13. In mosses, the gametophyte is the dominant generation, the sporophyte being attached to, and dependent upon, the gametophyte. In ferns, the sporophyte is the dominant generation, the gametophyte being reduced. In both groups wet conditions are needed for the gametophyte to reproduce.

14. Conifers and flowering plants continue the trend seen in ferns towards reduction of the gametophyte.

15. Alternation of generations is not known in the animal kingdom.

Part 5

For general advice on these questions and advice on answering essay-type questions, see pages vii and viii.

1. The diagram below illustrates the life cycle of the bean aphid, *Aphis fabae*.

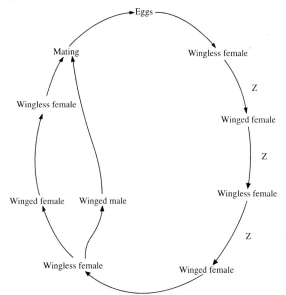

(a) Name the type of reproduction occurring at the stages labelled **Z** on the diagram. (1)

(b) State the importance of the winged stages in the life cycle. (1)

(c) Suggest an environmental stimulus for the production of male and female aphids in autumn. (1)

(d) Give one reason why aphids are pests of crop plants. (1)

(Total 4 marks)

London 1997

2. The diagram shows the life cycle of a moss.

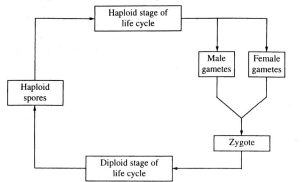

(a) Copy the diagram and mark with a cross to show where meiosis occurs. (1)

(b) A spore of this organism contains 16 chromosomes. How many chromosomes would you expect to find in:

(i) a female gamete;

(ii) a cell taken from the moss during the diploid stage of its life cycle? (2)

(c) Some DNA was extracted from cells during the haploid stage of the life cycle. It was found to contain 14% adenine.

(i) What percentage of thymine would you expect this DNA sample to contain? (1)

(ii) What percentage of cytosine would you expect to find in this DNA sample? (1)

(d) Suggest two ways in which the male gametes of this organism are likely to differ from female gametes. (2)

(Total 7 marks)

NEAB 1996

3. The diagram shows the life cycle of a water flea.

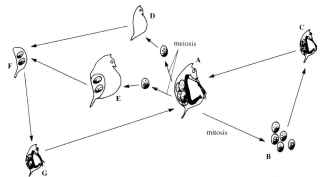

In favourable conditions all the animals in a population are females (**A**). These females produce eggs (**B**), by mitosis, which develop into young females (**C**) without being fertilised. In unfavourable conditions, eggs produced by meiosis develop directly without fertilisation into either males (**D**) or females (**E**). The eggs produced by females (**E**) are fertilised by sperm from the males, then released in a protective case (**F**) which enables them to survive unfavourable conditions. When favourable conditions return these eggs develop into young females (**G**).

(a) (i) Explain why the eggs in female **E** must be produced by mitosis. (1)

(ii) Copy and complete the table to show the number of chromosomes at each stage in the life cycle. (2)

Stage in life history	Chromosome number
A	2n
C	
D	
E	
G	

(b) Explain why the females **G** are genetically different from each other but females **C** are genetically the same. (3)

(c) Explain in terms of natural selecltion why it is advantageous to an organism to have a sexual stage as well as an asexual stage in its life history. (3)

(Total 9 marks)

NEAB 1997

Chapter 28

Reproduction of the flowering plant

In Chapter 27 we saw how, in the life cycles of many plants, a haploid gamete-producing gametophyte alternates with a diploid spore-producing sporophyte. The flowering plant represents the end product of a line of evolution in which the gametophyte, a self-supporting plant in groups such as mosses, gradually degenerates until eventually it becomes enclosed within the body of the sporophyte. The sporophyte is thus very much the dominant generation in flowering plants (*figure 28.1*).

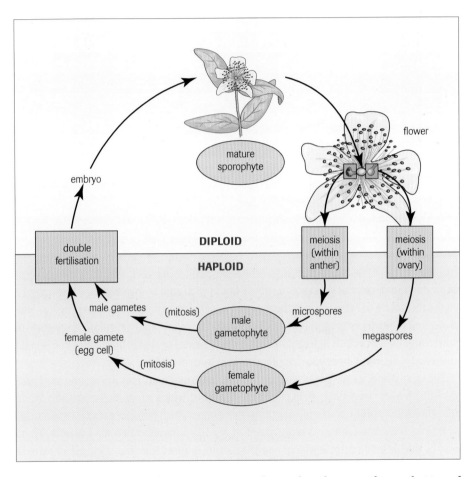

Figure 28.1 The life cycle of a flowering plant showing alternation of the gametophyte and sporophyte generations. The gametophyte generation is greatly reduced and incorporated into the sporophyte. Later we shall see what the microspores and megaspores represent and where the male and female gametophytes are found. We shall also see why fertilisation is described as 'double'.

The success of flowering plants as a group may be attributed to many factors, but two of the most important are undoubtedly the suppression of the gametophyte with its dependence on water and the development of that unique feature of the group – the **flower**.

28.1 The flower

A flower is best considered as a specially modified shoot, produced by the sporophyte, whose role is sexual reproduction. As we shall see later, the flower contains the relics of the gametophyte. Though their arrangement varies, flowers generally occur, either singly or in groups, in the angle (**axil**) between the main stem and a small reduced leaf called a **bract**.

Flowers show tremendous variety in their structure. There is therefore no such thing as a 'typical' flower. However, all flowers possess certain fundamental features which will now be described.

Structure of the flower

A flower typically consists of a series of modified leaves arranged in four circlets called **whorls** around a central **receptacle** at the apex of a **stalk** which is usually a branch of the main stem (*figure 28.2*).

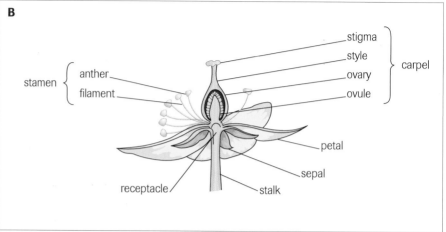

Figure 28.2 A *Hypericum* flower showing the parts of a typical flower.
B Drawing of a section of a *Hypericum* flower showing the arrangement of the four whorls of specialised leaves.

The outermost whorl is usually, but not always, composed of small, green, leaf-like **sepals**, which together constitute the **calyx**.

The next whorl of leaves may be modified in both shape and colour to form the **petals**, which together comprise the **corolla**. These two outer whorls together make up the **perianth**. Neither sepals nor petals are involved in the production of gametes; the function of the petals is to attract insects or other pollinating agents by their colour, scent or production of **nectar**. Nectar is a sugary liquid produced by **nectaries** which may be on the receptacle or other parts of the flower. The sepals and petals may also provide some protection to the more central parts of the flower. The sepals are particularly important in protecting the flower bud before it opens. In some cases the sepals have hairs and secrete gums and toxic substances which protect the bud from predators.

The next whorl, as we pass from the outside inwards, comprises the **stamens**. These modified leaves consist of a stalk called the **filament** which supports the **anther**. When ripe, the anther splits open to release the pollen grains which produce the male gametes.

Finally, the central whorl is represented by modified leaves called the **carpels**. There may be one or many carpels which may be separate or fused together. A carpel, or carpels, make up an **ovary**, which encloses one or more **ovules** inside which are the female gametes. The top of the ovary extends into the **style** which ends in a sticky and sometimes hairy **stigma** on which the pollen grains land during pollination.

Variations in flower structure

The flowers of different species show great diversity. For example, the number of parts in each whorl varies and sometimes the parts are fused together or indistinguishable from each other. In flowers such as lilies and tulips, both of the outer whorls are coloured and petal-like. Some of these variations are illustrated in figure 28.3.

In some species a whorl may be missing altogether. For example, the stamens or carpels may be absent, thus making the flower **unisexual**. If the stamens are missing and only the carpels are present, the flower is female. If only stamens are present, then the flower is male. When the male and female flowers are on the same plant, the species is described as **monoecious**. When the male and female flowers occur on different plants the species is

Figure 28.3 There are many variations in the basic four-whorl arrangement of the parts of a flower. **A** In the lily (*Lilium* sp.) the perianth is not distinguished into sepals and petals (a feature of monocotyledons), the six stamens are separate but the three parts to the stigma suggest that the styles have become fused. **B** In the hellebore (*Helleborus* sp.) the sepals look like petals, the petals are modified as nectaries and there are many separate stamens and carpels.

Figure 28.4 Holly trees (*Ilex sp.*) are usually dioecious which means that all the flowers on a tree are either male or female. This is why some holly trees never bear berries.
Left Male flowers with stamens but no carpels. *Right* Berries formed from female flowers.

dioecious. Examples of monoecious species are hazel and birch. Examples of dioecious species are willow and holly (*figure 28.4*).

Another variation is seen in the receptacle, the end of the stalk on which the parts are arranged. It may be flat, cup-shaped or cone-shaped (*figure 28.5*).

There is also much variation in the shape and symmetry of flowers. The parts of the flower may be arranged in a radially symmetrical way as in the buttercup: such flowers are described as **actinomorphic**. If the flower parts are arranged in a bilaterally symmetrical manner as in a foxglove, they are **zygomorphic** (*figure 28.6*).

The enormous diversity in the colour, size and shapes of flowers can be related to the way in which the pollen is transferred, a subject we shall return to later.

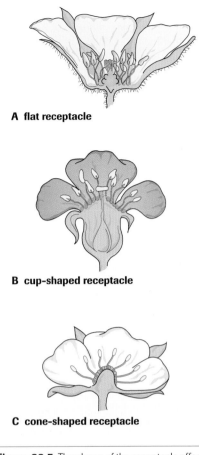

A flat receptacle

B cup-shaped receptacle

C cone-shaped receptacle

Figure 28.5 The shape of the receptacle affects the position of the ovary, or ovaries, in relation to the other parts of the flower. **A** The flowers of cinquefoils, *Potentilla* sp., have a flat receptacle. **B** In the cherry flower, *Prunus* sp., the receptacle is cup-shaped. **C** In the strawberry flower, *Fragaria* sp., the receptacle is cone-shaped.

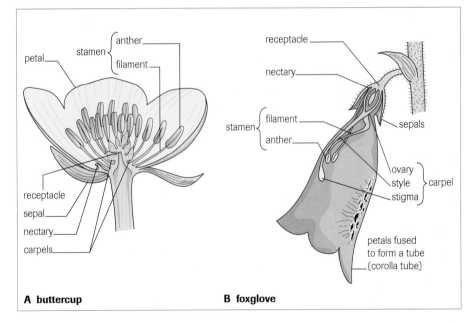

A buttercup   **B** foxglove

Figure 28.6 Sections of two flowers to illustrate different types of symmetry.
A A buttercup flower in which the arrangement of the parts shows radial symmetry.
B A foxglove flower in which the arrangement of the parts shows bilateral symmetry.

28.2 **Gamete formation**

The events that take place inside the male and female parts of a 'typical' flower are concerned with sexual reproduction, and we will start with the formation of the gametes.

Male gametes

The male gametes are formed in the anthers of the stamens. Each anther contains four pollen-producing chambers called **pollen sacs**. In terms of the life cycles of plants described in Chapter 27, the pollen sacs are **microsporangia**. Inside the pollen sacs a

Figure 28.7 A Diagram of a transverse section of a lily anther with the pollen grains inside.
B Photomicrograph of a single pollen sac showing the tetrad stage of pollen formation in a lily.

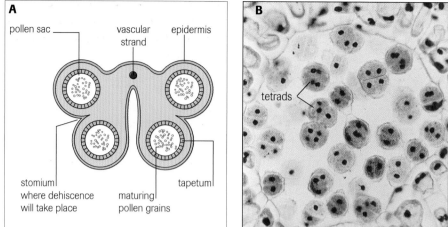

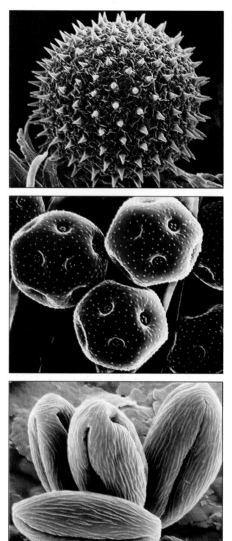

Figure 28.8 Scanning electron micrographs of the pollen grains of three different species. The outer wall is water-repellent and extremely resistant to decay. Pollen grains have been found in peat bogs after thousands of years, providing interesting information about which species existed there in the past.
Top Hollyhock ×1000. *Middle* Carnation ×2000. *Bottom* Cornflower ×1000.

large number of diploid **pollen mother cells** are produced as a result of a series of mitotic cell divisions. Each pollen mother cell then divides by meiosis to give a **tetrad** of four haploid cells which separate from each other and become the **pollen grains** (**microspores**) (*figure 28.7*). Each pollen sac is lined with a layer of cells called the **tapetum** which provides the developing pollen cells with nourishment. The filament which holds up the anther contains a vascular strand which supplies the anther with water and nutrients.

While these events are taking place an **inner wall**, made largely of cellulose, is formed around each pollen cell. By the time the cells of the tetrad have separated, various other substances, mainly proteins, are deposited on the surface of the inner wall to form an **outer wall**. The outer wall is often beautifully sculptured and its detailed features are unique to each species of plant (*figure 28.8*).

The proteins in the outer wall provide a recognition system whereby a stigma can recognise pollen of its own species or even from the same plant. This is crucial in preventing self-fertilisation and fertilisation by another species. These proteins are also responsible for the unpleasant allergic reaction we call hay fever.

The way the pollen grains develop is illustrated in figure 28.9. In the tetrad stage, each cell contains a single haploid nucleus. After separation, the nucleus of each cell divides by mitosis into a **generative nucleus** and a **tube nucleus**. These nuclei and the cytoplasm surrounding them represent the male gametophyte. So in flowering plants the male gametophyte is totally enclosed within the pollen grain.

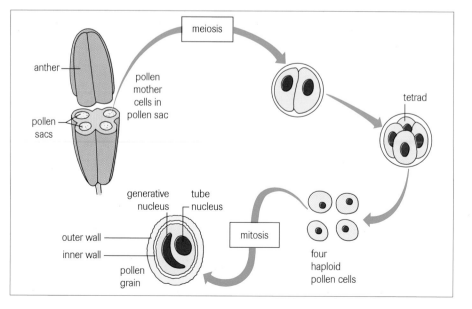

Figure 28.9 The development of a pollen grain. As a result of the meiotic division of the pollen mother cells the pollen cells are haploid.

When the anther dries out, it splits down both sides. This is known as **dehiscence** and it results in the pollen grains being released (*figure 28.10*). The pollen grains are not motile and depend on other agents, which we shall look at shortly, to carry them to the receptive stigmas of (usually) a different flower of the same species.

Female gametes

The formation of the female gametes takes place in the carpels of the ovary. The ovary is hollow and contains one or more ovules (*figure 28.11*). The ovule starts as a small bulge of tissue called the **nucellus** on the inside of the ovary wall. Two folds of tissue called **integuments** grow up and over the nucellus leaving a small pore, the **micropyle**, at one end (*figure 28.12*).

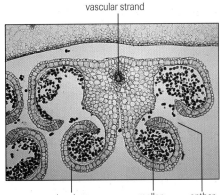

Figure 28.10 Photomicrograph of a transverse section of a lily anther which has split (dehisced), releasing the pollen grains from the pollen sacs.

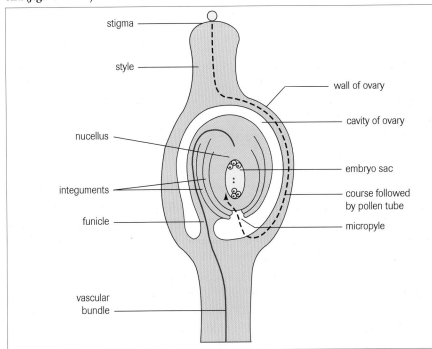

Figure 28.12 A mature ovary containing a single ovule, in the centre of which is the embryo sac. The ovule is attached to the wall of the ovary by a stalk, the funicle.

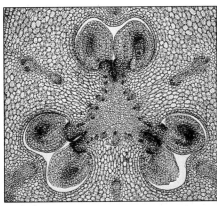

Figure 28.11 Photomicrograph of ovules in the ovary of a lily. Each ovule is attached to the ovary by a stalk (funicle) through which nutrients pass from the parent plant to the ovule. Many of these nutrients will be stored in the seed.

The ovule is a **megasporangium**. Inside it a single cell, called the **embryo sac mother cell**, undergoes meiotic cell division to form a row of four haploid cells (**megaspores**). Three of these cells usually disintegrate. The remaining one expands and its nucleus undergoes three successive mitotic cell divisions to form an immature **embryo sac** containing eight nuclei (*figure 28.13*).

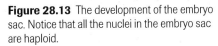

Figure 28.13 The development of the embryo sac. Notice that all the nuclei in the embryo sac are haploid.

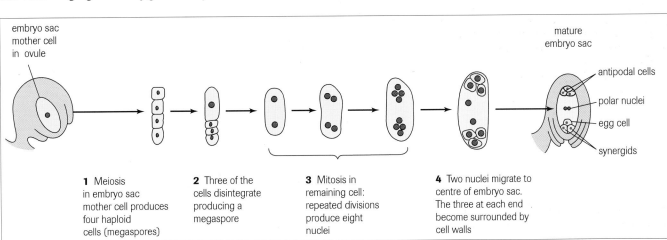

1 Meiosis in embryo sac mother cell produces four haploid cells (megaspores)

2 Three of the cells disintegrate producing a megaspore

3 Mitosis in remaining cell: repeated divisions produce eight nuclei

4 Two nuclei migrate to centre of embryo sac. The three at each end become surrounded by cell walls

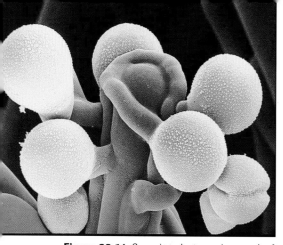

Figure 28.14 Scanning electron micrograph of pollen grains of poppy with tubes growing into a stigma. Magnification ×900.

Inside the embryo sac, the eight nuclei become arranged in a 3:2:3 pattern. Three remain at the micropylar end where they become separated from each other by cell walls and form one **egg cell** and two similar 'helper' or **synergid cells**. The three at the other end become the so-called **antipodal cells**. The remaining two nuclei occupy a central position and do not become surrounded by cell walls. They are called the **polar nuclei**.

The mature embryo sac represents the female gametophyte. It is surrounded by the ovule which in turn is enclosed within the ovary. So here, as in the male parts of the flower, the gametophyte is hidden away inside the sporophyte. The ovule is now ready for fertilisation. The style and stigma will have developed and the flower will usually be open so that pollination can take place.

Although the events just described are typical of many flowering plants, there are a number of variations. You will find details of these in botanical textbooks.

28.3 Pollination and the growth of the pollen tube

Pollination takes place when pollen is transferred from an anther to a stigma. Sometimes the pollen grains fall onto the stigma of the same flower or another flower on the same plant (**self-pollination**) but more often they are conveyed either by wind, insects or some other agent to a flower of another plant (**cross-pollination**).

When a pollen grain lands on a compatible stigma, it adheres to it because the stigma cells secrete a sticky, sugar solution. The sugar solution also promotes further development of the pollen grain. Because the embryo sac is embedded in the tissues of the ovule, a channel has to be provided to carry the pollen nuclei to it. In large flowers the distance may be as much as five centimetres. Fertilisation is therefore preceded by a process in which an outgrowth from the pollen grain, called the **pollen tube**, grows down to the embryo sac taking the pollen nuclei with it.

The pollen tube starts as a small outgrowth, lined by the inner wall of the pollen grain, which protrudes through the outer pollen wall. The pollen tube penetrates the surface of the stigma and then grows into the style, deriving nourishment from the surrounding tissues (*figure 28.14*). Exactly what causes it to do this is uncertain, but most pollen tubes are negatively aerotropic, i.e. they grow away from air where there is a higher concentration of oxygen. There is also some evidence that they are guided to the ovule by a chemical produced by the embryo sac.

When the pollen grain germinates, the tube nucleus occupies a position at the tip of the growing pollen tube. It controls the growth of the tube which is remarkably rapid: a rate of between 20 and 30 mm an hour has been recorded under laboratory conditions so that in some species the tube reaches the ovule in a matter of minutes.

By this time the generative nucleus has divided into a pair of **male nuclei** and these follow behind the tube nucleus as the pollen tube grows down the style (*figure 28.15*). On reaching the ovary, the pollen tube penetrates the ovule, usually through the micropyle. It then enters the embryo sac and releases its contents near the egg cell and polar nuclei. The tube nucleus now disintegrates and fertilisation follows. In ovaries with numerous ovules, each ovule is fertilised by a male gamete from a different pollen grain.

The pollen grain, with its ability to withstand dry conditions and deliver the male gamete to the female gamete via the pollen tube, has been of great significance in the evolution of angiosperms as it has freed them from a dependence on external water for fertilisation.

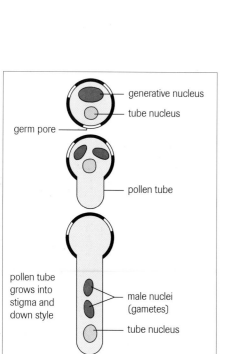

germ pore

generative nucleus

tube nucleus

pollen tube

pollen tube grows into stigma and down style

male nuclei (gametes)

tube nucleus

Figure 28.15 The germination of the pollen grain and growth of the pollen tube. The wall of the pollen tube is continuous with the inner wall of the pollen grain.

28.4 Fertilisation

Fertilisation is illustrated in figure 28.16. Recall, first, that two male nuclei have reached the embryo sac. One of these nuclei fuses with the egg cell to form a diploid zygote. This is the first cell of the new sporophyte and will give rise to the **embryo**.

The second male nucleus fuses with both polar nuclei to form a *triploid* nucleus. This will give rise to a tissue called the endosperm whose function will be explained in a moment.

The events just described constitute a **double fertilisation**, in the sense that *two* male nuclei fuse with female cells. This is unique to flowering plants.

After fertilisation

Following fertilisation, certain changes take place in the floral parts of the plant. Although the details vary from one species to another, the pattern is essentially the same in all flowering plants.

- The zygote divides mitotically to form the **embryo**, which differentiates into three main parts: a **radicle** (young root), **plumule** (young shoot) and either one or two **cotyledons** (seed leaves). The embryo is attached to the wall of the now expanding embryo sac by a row of cells called the **suspensor** through which it may derive nourishment (*figure 28.17*).

- The endosperm nucleus divides by mitosis into a mass of nuclei which eventually become separated from one another by thin cell walls. This forms the **endosperm**, a food storage tissue which surrounds the embryo and provides it with nourishment. In order to accommodate the developing endosperm the nucellus becomes crushed out of existence, so the embryo and endosperm come to fill the whole space inside the integuments.

  The endosperm tissue is very important because the food reserves of all cereals such as maize, wheat, rice, barley and oats are stored in it. Endosperm is, without question, the most important single source of food in the world. In the seeds of many dicotyledonous plants, however, the endosperm is absorbed by the developing cotyledons which then provide the main food reserve. This is the case in legumes (peas and beans, etc.).

- The ovule develops into the **seed**, the outer integument becoming the **seed coat**. While this is happening the ovary develops into the **fruit**. The wall of the fruit (**pericarp**) is derived from the ovary wall. The sepals, petals, styles and stamens often wither and fall off after fertilisation, although they may contribute to the formation of the fruit as may the receptacle and even the bracts. Fruits formed from parts of the flower other than the ovary are called **false fruits**, for example apple and strawberry in which the fleshy part of the fruit is formed from the receptacle.

Fruits come in a wide range of shapes and forms but they all have a common function, which is to protect the seeds and aid their dispersal. We shall return to this later.

The final transformation of the ovule into the seed involves the removal of water from an initial 90 per cent to a mere 15 per cent, thus forming a dormant, resistant structure that can withstand adverse conditions.

Self versus cross fertilisation

The majority of plants are **hermaphrodite**. This means that both male and female organs are present in the same flower. This has the advantage that every flower is a potential producer of fertilised eggs, which increases the chances of a large number of offspring being produced. The disadvantage is that the plant runs the risk of **self fertilisation**.

Self fertilisation is the most extreme form of **inbreeding** (*page 756*). It precludes the possibility of genetic mixing between different individuals, and if carried out on a large

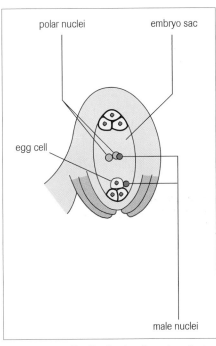

Figure 28.16 Fertilisation in a flowering plant. One male gamete fuses with the female gamete (egg cell) giving rise to a diploid zygote which develops into the embryo. The other male gamete fuses with the two polar nuclei giving rise to a triploid cell which develops into the endosperm tissue.

▶ Seeds as a source of food, page 535

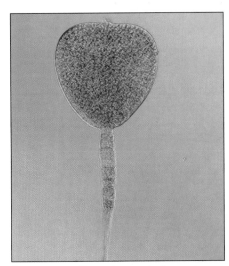

Figure 28.17 Photomicrograph of an embryo showing the row of cells called the suspensor by which it is attached to the wall of the embryo sac.

Figure 28.18 The male catkins of silver birch, *Betula pendula*. A catkin is a cluster of unisexual flowers and is found in many wind-pollinated plants. There are no petals and the stamens hang loosely, producing large amounts of smooth, light pollen which is easily carried by the wind.

Figure 28.19 Grass flowers are pollinated by wind. The long filaments with large anthers dangle in the wind, and the hairy stigmas are prominent and ideally placed for 'catching' pollen. In the photograph the dangling anthers are white, and some of them have split open. This particular grass is perennial rye, *Lolium perenne*.

Figure 28.20 A bumble bee foraging on a knapweed flower. Notice the pollen grains on the bee's legs.

scale over many generations it may lead to a decline of the species. In general, the offspring resulting from self fertilisation are less vigorous and productive than those resulting from cross fertilisation. It is not surprising to find that hermaphrodite organisms generally have anatomical and physiological mechanisms which promote **outbreeding** and prevent, or at least reduce, the chances of self fertilisation.

In flowering plants this means having mechanisms that encourage **cross pollination** and prevent **self pollination**. The surest way of preventing self pollination is to have male and female flowers on separate plants, as we have already seen in holly. In hermaphrodite flowers it is usual to find either the stamens maturing first and the carpels later or vice versa. When the stamens mature before the carpels as in ivy, it is called **protandry**. If the carpels mature before the stamens, as in plantain, it is called **protogyny**. Both conditions reduce the liklihood of self pollination.

Also, the relative positions of the stamens and stigma may be such that the chance of self pollination is reduced while cross pollination is increased. Some plants are self sterile, that is the plant's pollen fails to germinate on its own stigmas. As we shall see in the next section there are many devices which favour cross pollination.

28.5 Methods of pollination

Flowering plants are usually rooted in the soil and may be some distance from each other. Even if they are near to one another there is no way the male gametes can be transferred to another plant without the assistance of an outside agent. The agents which carry the pollen grains from one plant to another include wind, animal vectors (usually insects) and, in a few aquatic plants, water. The characteristics of flowers are closely related to the way their pollen is transferred.

■ **Wind-pollinated plants** have small, dry pollen grains which are produced in great abundance, and the flowers lack large, highly coloured petals or sepals. The stamens or the whole flower or inflorescence may hang in a pendulous fashion, as in hazel or birch catkins, which ensures that the pollen is scattered as far away from the parent plant as possible (*figure 28.18*). In grasses, the flowers are small but the anthers are borne on long flexible filaments (*figure 28.19*). The stigmas of wind-pollinated flowers usually have a large and hairy surface on which the smooth wind-borne pollen grains are trapped.

The disadvantage of wind as a vector is that the direction of pollen movement cannot be controlled; also, to be effective, the pollen must land on the stigma of the correct species. Much pollen is therefore wasted.

■ **Insect-pollinated plants** have special features which attract insects, for example, brightly coloured sepals and/or petals, the emission of scent and the secretion of nectar (*figure 28.20*). In some species a large number of small flowers are clustered together at the end of a shoot to form an **inflorescence**. This can provide a bright splash of colour and a concentrated source of scent and nectar for insect pollinators. The common shrub *Buddleia*, much visited by butterflies, is an example.

Amongst insect-pollinated flowers there are sometimes elaborate mechanisms for promoting cross pollination. In many flowers the stigma is higher than the surrounding stamens, thus making it impossible for pollen to fall onto the stigma of the same flower. Moreover, if a large insect, such as a bee, visits the flower, its body will brush against the stigma before it reaches the anthers. Any pollen the bee has picked up from another flower will therefore be deposited on the stigma. The pollen grains of insect-pollinated plants are usually sculptured or sticky, enabling them to adhere to the body of the insect.

Traps and trickery

The varied ways in which animals are involved in pollination include some of the most fascinating mechanisms in the living world. To the human onlooker some of the devices appear to trap or deceive the animal, usually an insect, in order to achieve pollination. Here we look at a few examples to illustrate the principles involved.

In Britain, a highly specialised insect-trapping mechanism is found in the wild arum, *Arum maculatum*. The inflorescence of this extraordinary plant consists of two main parts, the **spadix** which is the axis of the inflorescence, and the leaf-like **spathe** (*illustration 1*). The female flowers, which consist only of ovaries and stigmas, are at the base of the spadix. Immediately above them is a ring of hair-like sterile flowers. Above them is a mass of male flowers consisting of short-stalked stamens, the uppermost ones being hair-like and sterile. Above this the spadix extends as a club-shaped structure which is usually purplish in colour and generates much energy with the result that at times it feels warm.

The spathe opens about midday and a smell of rotting carrion is produced by the spadix. Certain species of flies which would normally lay their eggs in dung are attracted to the flowers by the smell. They crawl to the bottom of the spadix where the nectar is produced. There they are trapped, unable to climb out because of the hairs and the slippery surface of the spadix and spathe. If the insects happen to be covered with pollen from another *Arum*, they pollinate the female flowers. The stigmas then wither and become non-receptive. The next day the spadix no longer produces a smell, and the male flowers open and release their pollen with which the insects become covered. The hairs, which prevented escape, then wither and the insects fly to another inflorescence where the female flowers are ready for pollination. By this ingenious mechanism cross pollination is ensured and self pollination prevented.

Another strategy is found in orchids. In many species of orchids the stamen contains two curiously shaped structures called **pollinia** which consist of masses of pollen grains joined together by delicate threads. As soon as an insect alights on the flower and starts to search for nectar, a kind of explosion takes place and a small drop of sticky liquid is ejected which fixes the pollinia to the visiting insect. The liquid sets in a second or so, and the startled insect flies off, with the pollinia, to another flower. If the flower is more mature than the one just visited, the first structure it will encounter is the stigma. Pollen grains from the pollinia then become attached to the sticky stigma (*illustration 2*).

Illustration 2 A wasp pollinating a broad-leaved helleborine orchid. Notice the pollinia.

A further elaboration of this exists in the bee orchid and fly orchid. The males of certain species of insect (bees and flies) are tricked into copulating with the flower because the lip of the orchid flower resembles the female insect, and some of these flowers secrete pheromones identical to those secreted by the female insects (*page 450*). This happens before the female insects have emerged from pupation. In attempting to copulate with the flower the male insect removes pollinia from it. These pollinia are transferred to the stigma of the next flower of the same species with which the male tries to copulate. As soon as the female insects emerge, the males stop visiting the flowers. The visits of the male insects coincide exactly with the flowering of the orchid.

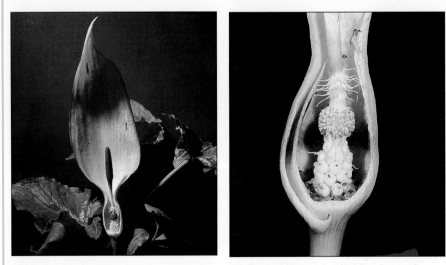

Illustration 1 The wild arum, *Arum maculatum*. *Left* The leaf-like spathe shielding the spadix. *Right* Close-up of the spadix cut open to show the specialised inflorescence. Trapped flies can be seen at the base.

- **Water-pollinated plants** are relatively rare. They usually have small petals and large, smooth stigmas. A familiar example is the Canadian pondweed, *Elodea canadensis* (*Figure 28.21*). This plant is unisexual and the pollen grains from the male flowers are dispersed across the water surface to the stigmas of the female flowers. However, the male plants are so rarely found in Britain that sexual reproduction is not known to occur, Instead this plant reproduces by an entirely different method which is the subject of the next section.

28.6 Asexual reproduction

There are two basic types of asexual reproduction in flowering plants. The first one occurs when new individuals are formed from tissues which are not normally involved in sexual reproduction. This is called **vegetative propagation**. In the second type, embryos are formed without prior fertilisation, that is by **parthenogenesis** (*page 492*).

Vegetative propagation

Vegetative propagation depends largely on the possession in various parts of the plant of **meristematic cells** which are capable of dividing and differentiating into new tissues. This is what happens in the plant embryo, so in a sense meristems represent a continuation of the embryonic stage in the adult plant.

Vegetative propagation in land plants often takes place by means of modified stems. For example, a side branch, known as a **runner**, can grow out from one of the lower axillary buds of the parent plant such as a strawberry. At its nodes, small axillary buds and **adventitious roots** grow and develop into new plants. (An adventitious root is a root that grows out of a stem.) Later the new plants become separated from the parent and each other by decay of the internodal portions of the runner.

Vegetative propagation may involve the formation of some sort of storage organ, which lies in the soil over the winter and develops into one or more plants the following year. Such devices are known as **perennating organs**. They may be formed from a modified stem, root or bud, depending on the plant in question. The potato is a swollen stem (**tuber**), as is the **corm** of a plant like the crocus and the **rhizome** of an iris. Like any normal stem, these structures have adventitious roots, apical buds and nodes with leaves and axillary buds. It is from the buds that new plants are formed. The basic principles involved in the formation and subsequent growth of a perennating organ are illustrated by the potato in figure 28.22.

Figure 28.21 Canadian pondweed, *Elodea canadensis*.

Meristematic tissue, page 69

Meristematic tissue, page 69

Extension

The vegetative success of *Elodea*

The spread in Britain of the Canadian pondweed, *Elodea canadensis*, is a classic example of how successful vegetative propagation can be. The slender stems of this plant are brittle and snap very easily, setting free pieces of stem which then grow and live independently. This simple but effective method of vegetative reproduction is called **fragmentation**. Its success as a method of propagation is demonstrated by the rapid spread of *Elodea* in the last century. The Curator of the Cambridge Botanic Garden was given a few sprigs of it in 1847 and introduced it into a tributary of the river Cam in 1848. By 1852 it had spread into the river to such an extent that it prevented fishing, swimming and rowing and even made the towing of barges difficult.

This plant spread so rapidly throughout parts of the country, along rivers and canals, that it was soon considered a pest. No successful plan was ever devised for dealing with it. However, by the beginning of the 20th century it had fortunately declined in vigour and was no more luxuriant than any other water plant, so it ceased to be a problem. This sort of decline is not unusual in water plants.

In warmer climates, Africa, for example, water hyacinth and water lettuce are even more vigorous examples of the rapid spread of species by vegetative means.

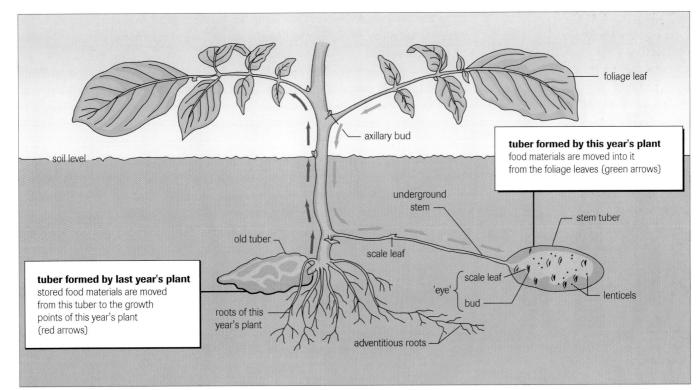

Labels in figure:
- foliage leaf
- axillary bud
- soil level
- old tuber
- scale leaf
- underground stem
- tuber formed by this year's plant — food materials are moved into it from the foliage leaves (green arrows)
- stem tuber
- scale leaf
- 'eye'
- bud
- lenticels
- tuber formed by last year's plant — stored food materials are moved from this tuber to the growth points of this year's plant (red arrows)
- roots of this year's plant
- adventitious roots

Bulbs are swollen buds in which food is stored in thick, fleshy leaves projecting from a much shortened, vertical stem. Apical and axillary buds, situated between the leaves, develop into new plants either directly or via further bulbs.

These are just a few examples of vegetative propagation; the main point to note is that many different parts of a plant can contribute towards this method of reproduction.

Vegetative propagation is very important from an ecological point of view. Some of the most pernicious weeds have creeping rhizomes and can spread into, and colonise, new areas extremely rapidly. Couch grass, *Elymus repens*, can produce a new plant every 14 days and ground elder, *Aegopodium podograria*, is a gardener's nightmare.

Parthenogenesis in flowering plants

In this type of asexual reproduction, embryos and seeds are formed without meiosis or fertilisation taking place. A familiar example is the production of viable seeds with asexual embryos identical to the parent in citrus fruits – oranges, grapefruits and tangerines, and their hybrids. It comes about either because a diploid embryo sac is formed or because the embryo develops from a diploid cell in the nucellus or inner integument of the ovule. In either case meiosis is side-stepped and an embryo develops without fertilisation.

Parthenogenesis has some of the same consequences as persistent self fertilisation in that the offspring are genetically similar to the parent and new genotypes are unlikely to occur. The flowers of parthenogenetic plants are apparently still able to function for pollination. However, in many cases it seems that the formation of the embryo takes place without any outside stimulus such as pollination. The method does, of course, have the advantage of retaining the same dispersal mechanism associated with sexual production of seeds.

Vegetative propagation in horticulture and agriculture

Humans exploit the natural vegetative propagation of plants in horticulture and agriculture, using in particular bulbs, corms and tubers as a means of propagating plants more rapidly than from seed. As the process is asexual, it ensures genetic uniformity and therefore consistent quality.

Figure 28.22 The general principle of the formation of perennating organs is illustrated by a potato plant. Towards the end of the growing season, the plant forms swollen tubers at the ends of horizontally growing underground stems. The tubers lie dormant in the soil until the following year when the axillary buds give rise to new plants. In the drawing only one new plant is shown growing out of the old tuber, but in fact all the axillary buds are potentially capable of producing new plants. The old tuber shrivels as the food store is depleted.

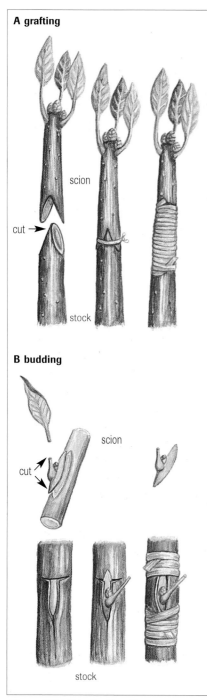

A grafting

scion

cut →

stock

B budding

scion

cut

stock

Figure 28.23 A Grafting. There are several ways of grafting. Here the scion and stock have been cut so that the two surfaces fit neatly together and the join is bound with tape.
B Budding. A scion bud is scooped out of the selected variety and inserted into a T-shaped cut in the bark of the stock which is bound with tape. The binding is loosened as growth begins.

In addition, we have developed artificial methods of vegetative propagation. For instance, the cut stems of plants (**cuttings**) can be induced to form roots if they are placed in well-watered soil.

Some of the most important methods of artificial vegetative propagation are **grafting** and **budding**. In these procedures, a twig or bud of one plant is attached to the stem or roots of another. The method is based on the principle that the cambium tissues of different plants will unite and give rise to normal conducting tissue. (Cambium tissue is explained on page 540.) The plant whose root is used is called the **stock**, and the twig or bud is called the **scion**. The way they may be joined is shown in figure 28.23.

These methods of propagation are of economic importance to the growers of fruit trees and roses because the desirable qualities of root stock and scion can be combined. For example, a scion of a good eating apple can be grafted to a dwarf root stock, making it a more suitable garden tree. Or the bud from a fragrant rose can be grafted to a disease-resistant root stock. Fortunately, the problem of rejection which bedevils grafting in animals does not apply to plants.

28.7 Dispersal

In the extension box on page 490 there is an example of the successful dispersal of a plant by vegetative means – Canadian pondweed. Another often quoted example of dispersal is that of the Oxford ragwort, *Senecio squalidus*, which was introduced to the Oxford Botanic Garden from Sicily in 1794. It is a vigorous weed and, with the coming of the railways to London, it spread on railway ballast. It is now seen in many parts of the country. The difference between its method of dispersal and that of Canadian pondweed is not just that it used railways instead of rivers and canals, but that it was dispersed by means of its fruits.

On 14 November 1963, a volcanic eruption occurred on the ocean floor several kilometres off the south coast of Iceland, and the new island of Surtsey was formed. The first flowering plant appeared there in 1965 and the island is still being colonised.

These examples show that mechanisms are built into the reproductive processes of flowering plants ensuring wide dispersal of the progeny. Plants are sessile and wide dispersal is important, otherwise the offspring may compete with one another, and indeed with the parents, thus lowering the survival rate. Moreover, wide dispersal enables the species to gain a foothold in new unexploited localities.

Seeds and fruits

Flowering plants may be dispersed as **seeds** and **fruits** by natural agents such as wind, water and animals. To this end they are adapted accordingly. For example, many seeds are extremely **small** and **light**, aiding airborne dispersal. Heavier seeds and fruits are equipped with devices such as **wings** and **hairy parachutes** which keep them airborne for longer (*figure 28.24*).

Figure 28.24 Wind dispersed fruits and seeds. *Left* The light, hairy seeds of rosebay willow herb, massed together like cotton wool. *Right* The winged fruits of sycamore.

Cloning the oil palm

Oil palm oil is used in large quantities in the manufacture of margarine and detergents. When grown under ideal conditions some oil palms (*Elaeis guineensis*) will yield 6 tonnes of oil per hectare. When seeds of high-yielding plants are sown, not all the plants are high yielding – there is a great deal of variation. The obvious solution is to **clone** the high-yielding oil palm plants.

There is nothing new about cloning plants. Indeed, it is an ancient art which was practised by the earliest horticulturists. It is usually quite easy and amateur gardeners do it when they want to increase the numbers of a valued plant, for example by taking cuttings.

There are now laboratory techniques by which parent plant tissue can be induced to form large numbers of new plants. It relies on the fact that certain cells in the plant remain unspecialised and are capable of further development. It is possible to stimulate these cells to undergo mitosis and form clumps of cells called a **callus** (*illustration 1*). All the cells in a callus are identical and each one can be grown by the technique of **tissue culture** into a new plant identical to the parent. In this way thousands of identical plants can be created, all belonging to the same clone (*illustration 2*).

The theoretical significance of this is explained on page 72. Here we are concerned with its commercial importance. It took scientists at Unilever 10 years to find a way of cloning oil palms by this method. Besides using a sterile technique, it is essential to have a culture medium on which the plant tissue will grow. It must contain the right nutrients in the correct amounts. Oil palms reared in this way are now growing in plantations in Cameroon, West Africa (*illustration 3*) and all the plants are capable of a producing a high yield of oil.

Other food plants, such as pineapples and bananas, are being cloned commercially, and attempts are being made to clone forest trees such as the Norway spruce, which is resistant to acid rain. For the gardener, orchids and roses and many other ornamental plants are being cloned using tissue culture.

▶ Tissue culture, page 72

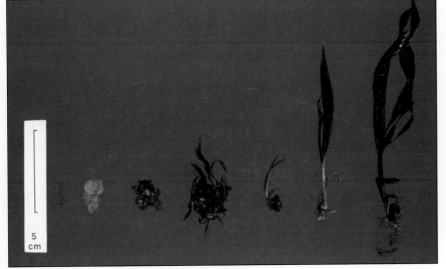

Illustration 1 Oil palm plantlets growing from a callus.

Illustration 2 Young cloned oil palms in Colombia.

Illustration 3 An oil palm plantation in Cameroon, West Africa.

Part 5

Figure 28.25 Pods of *Laburnum anagyroides* splitting open and dispersing the seeds.

Figure 28.26 The burrs of greater burdock clinging to a walker's sock. The hooks are modified bracts.

Figure 28.27 Shiny ripe fruits of a blackberry.

Figure 28.28 A fruit of the coconut palm (*Cocos nucifera*) washed ashore and starting to germinate

Dispersal is further aided by seeds being discharged from the parent plant by an 'explosive' mechanism involving the sudden splitting of the seed-containing body. This is called **dehiscence** (*figure 28.25*). Alternatively, they may be **scattered** from an ovary borne at the end of a long flexible stalk that sways in the wind or is knocked by passing animals. Such 'pepper-pot' mechanisms are seen in the dispersal of poppy seeds.

The role of animals in dispersal is equally varied. **Hooked fruits** such as cleavers may cling to their bodies as they brush past (*figure 28.26*). Other fruits are **edible**; they may be fleshy and often shiny or brightly coloured, making them attractive to birds (*figure 28.27*). The hard seeds are indigestible so they pass out with the faeces, unharmed and still capable of germination. In fact germination may be stimulated by the passage of the seed through the gut. The seeds may be dropped a long way from the parent plant.

Water is also important in the distribution of certain plants such as the coconut palm. The fruits have thick, fibrous walls containing **air pockets**, enabling them to float (*figure 28.28*). Undoubtedly this has been important in the colonisation of previously unoccupied land masses during evolution.

Despite these mechanisms to aid dispersal, most seeds do not get very far away from the parent plant. However, the occasional ones that do so have significant effects on the distribution of the species and the colonisation of new habitats.

1. In flowering plants, the reproductive organs are contained within the **flower**.

2. A flower typically consists of four whorls of modified leaves: **sepals, petals, stamens** and **carpels**. Flowers show great diversity in their structure.

3. The male gametes are formed within the anthers of the stamens. A meiotic division in each **pollen mother cell** gives rise to a **tetrad** of haploid **pollen grains**.

4. A mitotic division of the pollen grain nucleus gives rise to a **tube nucleus** and a **generative nucleus**; the latter divides again into two **male nuclei**.

5. The female gametes are formed in the ovules. The **embryo sac mother cell** divides meiotically to give four haploid cells, one of which develops into the **embryo sac**. The embryo sac contains an **egg cell** and several nuclei.

6. **Pollination** is the process by which pollen is transferred from the male to the female parts of flowers. Sometimes **self pollination**, but more often **cross pollination**, takes place.

7. After a pollen grain has landed on a compatible stigma, a **pollen tube** grows down to the embryo sac taking the male nuclei with it.

8. The pollen tube enters the ovule, and **fertilisation** takes place when one of the male nuclei fuses with the egg cell to give rise to the **zygote**.

9. The other male nucleus fuses with two **polar nuclei** in the embryo sac to form the triploid **endosperm nucleus** which develops into the **endosperm tissue**.

10. After fertilisation, the zygote develops into an **embryo** consisting of **radicle**, **plumule** and one or two **cotyledons**. Meanwhile the ovule develops into the **seed** and the ovary into the **fruit**.

11. Self fertilisation leads to **inbreeding** which may cause a decline in the species. Cross fertilisation leads to **outbreeding** and the offspring are generally more vigorous. Accordingly flowering plants usually have mechanisms which prevent **self pollination** and promote **cross pollination**.

12. Because plants are sessile they depend on outside agents to carry the pollen from one individual to another. The most usual agents are wind and insects, and plants show various adaptations for **wind pollination** or **insect pollination**.

13. Because plants possess meristematic tissue they are able to reproduce asexually by **vegetative methods** such as **tubers, runners, bulbs** and **corms**. In some cases embryos are formed **parthenogenetically**, i.e. without prior fertilisation.

14. In agriculture and horticulture, humans have exploited the natural vegetative reproduction of plants as well as developing artificial methods.

15. **Tissue culture** has enabled scientists to **clone** commercially important plants such as the oil palm.

16. Although plants may be dispersed by asexual structures, they are more usually dispersed by their **fruits** and **seeds**. Fruits and seeds have special features which aid their dispersal by agents such as wind, animals and water.

For general advice on these questions and advice on answering essay-type questions, see pages vii and viii.

1. The diagram shows the life cycle of a flowering plant.

    (a) Which stage(s) in the life cycle shown are the:

        (i)   sporophyte?   (1)

        (ii) gametophytes?   (2)

        (iii) spores?   (3)

    (b) How does this life cycle show alternation of generations?   (2)

    (c) At which points does meiosis occur in the cycle.   (2)

    (d) In this life cycle there is said to be 'double fertilisation'. What is meant by double fertilisation? (2)

    (e) Name two organisms which exhibit alternation of generations in which the gametophyte generation is dominant.   (2)

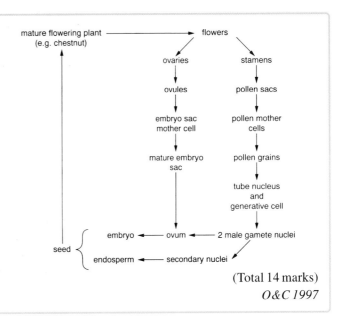

(Total 14 marks)

O&C 1997

2. (a) Distinguish between pollination and fertilisation in flowering plants. (1)

(b) Describe the development of a flowering plant embryo sac from an embryo sac mother cell. (4)

The diagram shows an embryo sac of *Epipactis helleborine*, within an unfertilised ovule. The chromosome number of this plant is 2n=40.

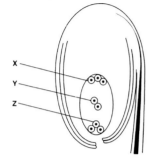

(c) State the number of chromosomes in structures **X** and **Y**. (1)

(d) Outline what happens to structures **Y** and **Z** at fertilisation. (4)

(Total 10 marks)

UCLES 1997

3. The diagram below shows a flower of the grass *Festuca pratensis*.

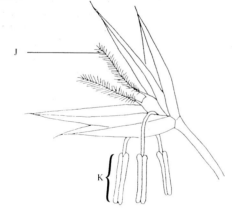

(a) Name the parts labelled **J** and **K**. (2)

(b) State **three** features, shown on the diagram, which indicate that this flower is wind-pollinated. (3)

(Total 5 marks)

London 1998

4. (a) Describe how artificial propagation may be used to produce plants commercially. (12)

(b) Discuss the advantages and disadvantages of such methods of propagation. (6)

(Total 18 marks)

UCLES 1997

5. The diagram below shows part of a potato plant. Structure **A** and structure **B** are stem tubers.

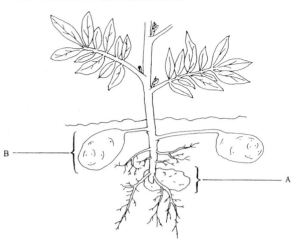

(a) (i) What is the function of structure **A** in the annual cycle of the plant? (1)

(ii) Explain how structure **B** is formed. (2)

(b) Give **one** advantage to the potato grower of using stem tubers rather than seeds to propagate the crop. (1)

(Total 4 marks)

London 1997

6. The diagram below shows a method of grafting.

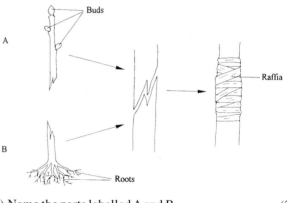

(a) Name the parts labelled A and B. (2)

(b) Give *two* reasons for the shape of the cuts made to A and B. (2)

(c) Explain why grafting is used to propagate fruit trees such as apple. (2)

(Total 6 marks)

London 1996

Chapter 29

Reproduction of the mammal

C hapter 27 was concerned with the general principles of reproduction as illustrated by a wide range of organisms. In this chapter we shall look at mammalian reproduction with particular reference to the human.

In considering how mammals reproduce, three issues need to be addressed:

■ How and where are the gametes produced and what is their structure?

■ How are the gametes brought into contact with each other?

■ What happens to the zygote?

These questions cannot be answered without a sound understanding of the anatomy of the **reproductive system**, so we shall start with that.

29.1 Anatomy of the human reproductive system

The male and female systems both consist essentially of a **genital tract**, which runs from the **gonads** (ovaries or testes) to the exterior. The parts of the reproductive system that are visible externally constitute the **external genitalia**.

The female system

This is shown in figure 29.1. The main structures are:

■ a pair of **ovaries** which produce eggs;

■ a pair of **oviducts** (Fallopian tubes) each of which opens by a **funnel** close to one of the ovaries and leads to

■ the **uterus** whose lower end, the **cervix**, opens into

■ the **vagina**, which runs to the exterior.

Primates are unusual in having a simple uterus of the sort depicted in figure 29.1. Most mammals have a Y-shaped uterus, with the two sides of the Y extending up towards the ovaries. The oviducts are correspondingly short. With its extra capacity, this kind of uterus

Figure 29.1 The reproductive system of the human female.
A General view from the ventral side. The ovary and oviduct are shown in their natural positions on the left side of the picture. On the right side the oviduct has been deflected upwards so as to expose the whole of the ovary, and the organs have been sliced horizontally so as to show their internal structure.
B The external genitalia with the hymen still intact.

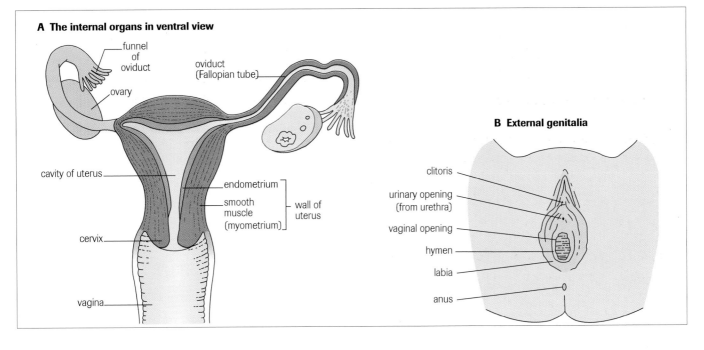

A The internal organs in ventral view

funnel of oviduct
oviduct (Fallopian tube)
ovary
cavity of uterus
endometrium
smooth muscle (myometrium)
wall of uterus
cervix
vagina

B External genitalia

clitoris
urinary opening (from urethra)
vaginal opening
hymen
labia
anus

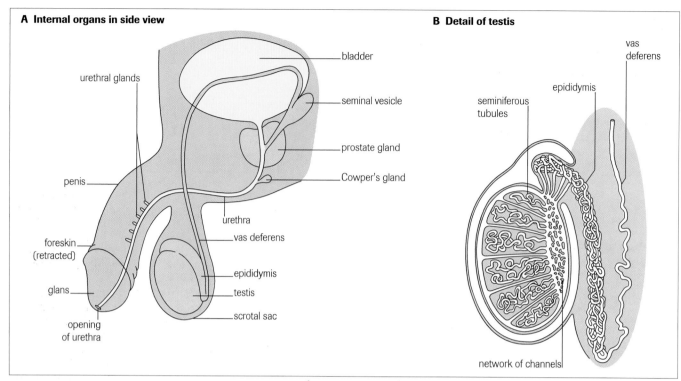

A Internal organs in side view

bladder

urethral glands

seminal vesicle

prostate gland

Cowper's gland

penis

urethra

vas deferens

foreskin
(retracted)

epididymis

testis

glans

scrotal sac

opening
of urethra

B Detail of testis

vas
deferens

epididymis

seminiferous
tubules

network of channels

Figure 29.2 The reproductive system of the human male.
A General view from the side. The bladder and urethra are central in position and unpaired. The testes, vasa deferentia and seminal vesicles are all paired but only those on the nearside are shown. The left and right vasa deferentia join the urethra in the middle of the prostate gland.
B Internal structure of a human testis. Far more seminiferous tubules exist than are shown here; each testis contains about 1000 of them.

Support

Why are the testes outside the abdominal cavity?

The external position of the penis is understandable, but why are the testes located in the scrotal sac rather than in the abdominal cavity where they would be more protected? In fact they do start off in the abdominal cavity, but before or soon after birth they descend into the scrotal sac. Because of their position outside the abdominal cavity, they are at a lower temperature than the general body temperature – about 5°C lower. Sperm can only be produced in sufficient numbers at this lower temperature. If the scrotal sac is kept too warm, fewer sperm are produced.

can accommodate numerous embryos at the same time and is therefore well suited to the production of litters.

The external genitalia consists of an area of skin called the **vulva** which is perforated by the **urinary** and **vaginal openings**. It is flanked on either side by folds of skin called **labia** (literally 'lips') and anteriorly by a small protuberance, the **clitoris**. In the young female the vaginal opening is partly covered by a fold of tissue, the **hymen**, which is usually lost during adolescence.

The male system

The male system is shown in figure 29.2. The main structures are:

- a pair of **testes** located in a **scrotal sac**;
- a pair of **vasa deferentia** (singlular: **vas deferens**), one from each testis, which join in the midline and enter
- the **urethra** which runs down the **penis** to the exterior.

Three important glands open into the vas deferens and urethra: they are the **seminal vesicles**, **prostate** (not 'prostrate'!) and **Cowper's glands**. We shall see what they do later.

The penis and scrotal sac make up the external genitalia. The head of the penis, called the **glans**, is covered by the **foreskin**. The foreskin may be removed, in the operation known as **circumcision**, for traditional, religious or medical reasons – for example, because the foreskin is tight.

Each testis is composed of numerous **seminiferous tubules** where the sperm are manufactured. The seminiferous tubules converge upon a network of channels which leads to a long, tightly coiled tube called the **epididymis**. The epididymis lies to one side of the testis and it leads to the vas deferens which leaves the scrotal sac and joins the urethra (*figure 29.2B*).

The total length of the seminiferous tubules exceeds 500 metres, which makes the rate of sperm production prodigious. In normal circumstances the seminiferous tubules and epididymis will be full of sperm. How they are produced and what happens to them will be explained next.

29.2 Formation of gametes

The formation of gametes is called **gametogenesis**. The overall sequence of events is essentially the same in both sexes. Three stages are recognised:

- **Phase of multiplication:** diploid cells in the embryo, destined to give rise to gametes, divide repeatedly by mitosis.
- **Phase of growth:** the daughter cells from the mitotic divisions increase in size.
- **Phase of maturation:** the products of the growth phase divide by meiosis, and the haploid daughter cells differentiate into the appropriate gametes (eggs or sperm).

Now let us look at the details of gametogenesis in the two sexes. Sperm formation is called **spermatogenesis**, egg formation **oogenesis**. Figure 29.3 shows the two processes side by side, so they can be compared.

In spermatogenesis, the products of the phase of multiplication grow into **spermatocytes**. The latter divide by meiosis to form haploid **spermatids** which differentiate into **spermatozoa** (or sperm for short). The way the sperm are formed by repeated cell divisions means that the total number produced is very great indeed.

Oogenesis is basically similar to spermatogenesis, but differs from it in detail. Most of the cells formed by the phase of multiplication degenerate, but some of them grow into **oocytes**. The amount of growth that takes place at this stage is much greater than in spermatogenesis – this is why eggs are so much larger than sperm. The oocyte now undergoes meiosis, but the divisions are unequal, resulting in four daughter cells that differ greatly in size. One of the cells remains large and becomes the **egg cell** (**ovum**). The other cells are small, non-functional **polar bodies** which eventually degenerate.

Figure 29.3 Summary of the way sperm and eggs are formed in a mammal (gametogenesis). Notice that the sequence of events is essentially the same in both cases. In spermatogenesis all the cells resulting from the phase of multiplication develop into spermatocytes. In oogenesis only some of the cells develop into oocytes; the rest degenerate. Also in spermatogenesis, all four products of meiosis become functional sperm, but in oogenesis only one becomes a functional egg. The polar bodies are the inevitable result of the fact that meiosis involves two successive divisions; they simply serve as a depository for unwanted chromosomes, thereby ensuring that the ovum is haploid. The second meiotic division in oogenesis usually occurs immediately after fertilisation.

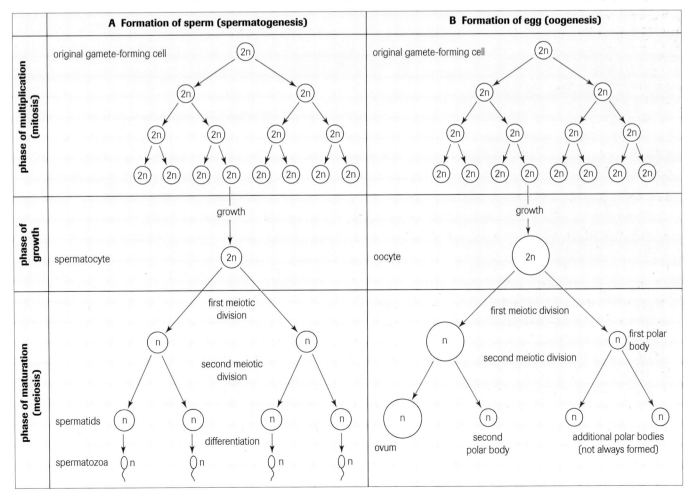

Gametogenesis takes place in the gonads: spermatogenesis in the testes and oogenesis in the ovaries. To see gametes at various stages of formation it is necessary to look at sections of these organs under the microscope.

Microscopic structure of the testis

The testis is packed full of seminiferous tubules, and spermatogenesis takes place in their walls (*figure 29.4*). Cell multiplication takes place in the outer part of the wall just beneath the surrounding connective tissue.

As cell divisions proceed, the daughter cells get pushed towards the lumen of the tubule, and spermatocytes can be seen undergoing meiosis into spermatids. The final transformation of spermatids to spermatozoa takes place in the part of the wall immediately adjacent to the lumen. At this stage the heads of the developing sperm are embedded in large **Sertoli cells**, and their tails project into the fluid-filled lumen of the tubule.

The Sertoli cells span the wall of the seminiferous tubule from the connective tissue envelope to the lumen. Their function is to nourish the sperm-forming cells and provide them with the right environment for undergoing meiosis. In addition, they secrete the fluid which fills the lumen, and they phagocytose foreign particles.

Eventually the mature sperm become detached from the Sertoli cells and are released into the lumen of the seminiferous tubule. They are not yet motile as their tails cannot wave, so they move passively along the seminiferous tubules towards the epididymis. Motility is gradually acquired, and by the time the sperm reach the epididymis the tails are waving vigorously.

Sperm have a limited life span; if they are not discharged from the male genital tract, they degenerate and are either resorbed or, more usually, lost via the urine.

For spermatogenesis to take place **male sex hormones** are needed. These are secreted into the bloodstream by prominent **interstitial cells** between the seminiferous tubules.

Figure 29.4 Microscopic structure of the mammalian testis.
A Scanning electron micrograph of a section of the testis. One complete seminiferous tubule is visible, with parts of several others around the edge of the section. Notice the sperm tails projecting into the lumen of the tubule. Magnification × 250.
B Part of the wall of a seminiferous tubule showing spermatogenesis. Sperm can be seen in various stages of development, nourishment coming from the Sertoli cells.
C Tissue between adjacent seminiferous tubules showing the interstitial cells which secrete male hormones (androgens).

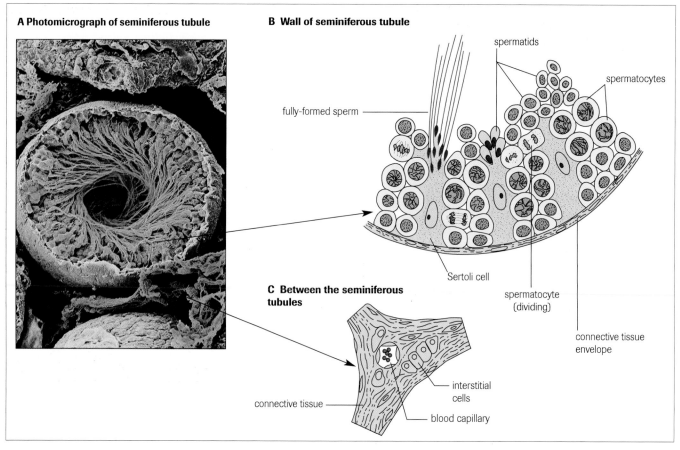

A Photomicrograph of seminiferous tubule

B Wall of seminiferous tubule

spermatids

spermatocytes

fully-formed sperm

Sertoli cell

spermatocyte (dividing)

connective tissue envelope

C Between the seminiferous tubules

connective tissue

interstitial cells

blood capillary

Microscopic structure of the ovary

In contrast to the testis, which is made up of numerous tubules, the ovary is a solid mass of tissue (*figure 29.5*). Oocytes, resulting from cell multiplication and growth in the embryo, may be seen towards the edge of the ovary. Each oocyte is surrounded by a layer of **follicle cells**. The whole structure, about 50 μm in diameter, is called a **primary follicle**. At birth there are millions of **primary follicles** – and therefore potential eggs – in each ovary. No further development takes place until puberty some 12 years later, when the viable follicles continue their development, one a month for the duration of the woman's reproductive life (*page 513*). Altogether, only about 400 complete their development; the rest degenerate.

You can follow what happens to one of the viable follicles in figure 29.5. First the follicle cells surrounding the oocyte proliferate to form a wall many cells thick. As this occurs, a fluid collects between the cells, forming little pools. As more and more fluid accumulates, the pools coalesce, eventually forming one large fluid-filled cavity called the **antrum**. The follicle grows and the oocyte finishes up embedded in a little hillock of follicle cells projecting into the antrum. Meanwhile, connective tissue inside the ovary forms a protective sheath around the follicle. It is called the **theca** and it has two layers: a vascular inner layer and a fibrous outer layer. The whole structure is called a **Graafian follicle** after the 17th century Dutch physician, Reinier de Graaf, who first described it.

As the Graafian follicle matures, it increases in size. From a mere 50 μm in diameter, it finishes up with a diameter of about 12 mm. As it grows, one side of it pushes against the edge of the ovary, causing a distinct bulge. When the time is ripe, the bulge ruptures and the oocyte is pinched off from its attachment to the wall of the follicle and extruded from the ovary, with some of the follicle cells still adhering to it. This process is called **ovulation**. In a woman who has reached puberty it occurs in one of her two ovaries approximately once every 28 days.

Shortly before ovulation the oocyte completes its first meiotic division. The second meiotic division into the ovum does not take place until fertilisation.

Figure 29.5 Microscopic structure of the mammalian ovary.
A Diagram of part of an ovary showing an oocyte developing into a Graafian follicle which, after ovulation, turns into a corpus luteum (yellow body) and then degenerates.
B Part of an ovary as it appears in a section under the microscope. Two developing Graafian follicles can be seen. Magnification ×150.

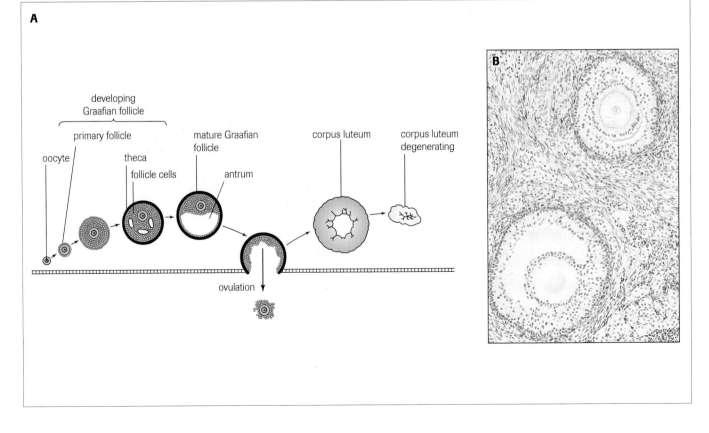

The role of the follicle is to protect the egg and provide a vehicle from which it can be shed from the ovary. The electron microscope has shown that the innermost follicle cells have fine processes which penetrate into the egg. Vesicles, pinched off the ends of these processes, are deposited in the egg cytoplasm and provide it with nourishment.

Structure of the sperm and egg

Before examining the sperm and egg in detail, let us recall their functions. The sperm simply has to convey genetic material from the male to the female. The egg, on the other hand, has to receive the genetic material from the sperm and then develop into a new individual. Most of the differences between eggs and sperm can be explained by the different jobs they have to do.

Sperm

The structure of a generalised mammalian sperm is shown in figure 29.6. It is differentiated into three main regions: **head**, **middle piece** and **tail**. The head is occupied by the **nucleus** which contains DNA conjugated with protein in a highly condensed form. In fact DNA accounts for most of the dry mass of the head. The amount of DNA in the sperm nuclei is half that of the body cells. This is because it is haploid. The nucleus is surmounted by a thin cap – rather like those woolly caps which you can pull down over your ears. It is called the **acrosome**, and it contains enzymes which play an important part in fertilisation.

The rest of the sperm is concerned with propulsion, and our understanding of its detailed structure is based largely on the electron microscope. Running down the centre of the middle piece and tail is an **axial filament** consisting of two central microtubules surrounded by a circle of nine peripheral ones. This is the **9+2 structure** characteristic of cilia and flagella (*page 54*). The sperm tail is therefore a modified flagellum. By lashing from side to side, it propels the sperm in the fluid medium through which it must swim to the egg. The microtubules are surrounded by a circle of solid fibres which provide strength, and the whole thing is enclosed in a sheath which is ribbed to permit flexibility.

Figure 29.6 Structure of a mammalian spermatozoon.
A The whole sperm. The tail is really much longer than shown here.
B Part of the tail in detail showing the 9+2 array of microtubules typical of eukaryotic flagella.
C Electron micrograph of a longitudinal section through the sperm of a bat, showing the dense nucleus in the head and the closely packed mitochondria in the middle piece. Magnification ×15 000.

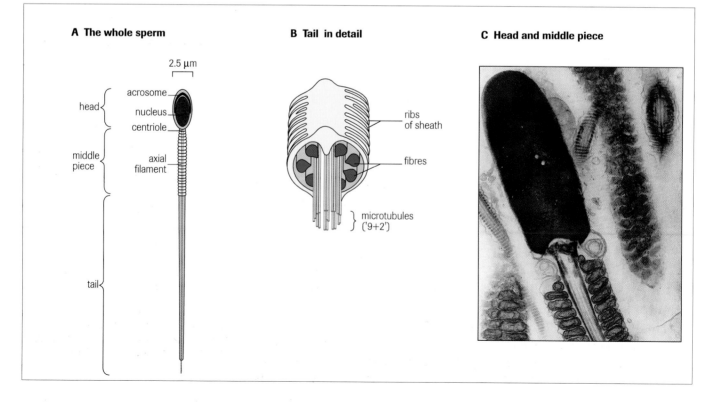

A The whole sperm

2.5 μm

head — acrosome, nucleus, centriole

middle piece — axial filament

tail

B Tail in detail

ribs of sheath

fibres

microtubules ('9+2')

C Head and middle piece

In the middle piece the microtubules and strengthening fibres are surrounded by closely packed mitochondria (*figure 29.6C*). Mitochondria are, of course, associated with energy transfer, and the function of the middle piece is to provide the motive power for making the tail wave.

Egg

Since the egg does not have to propel itself, it has a simpler structure than the sperm. On the other hand it has to contain nutrients and metabolites to help sustain itself through the earliest stages of its development. It is therefore much larger than the sperm. A human egg is just over 0.1 mm in diameter (100 μm), compared with the sperm whose head is only 2.5 μm across at the widest point.

Figure 29.7 shows a typical mammalian egg. A large haploid nucleus, situated slightly towards one end of the egg, is surrounded by cytoplasm which contains the usual organelles and enzymes found in cells generally. Just beneath the plasma membrane are numerous small **vesicles** whose function will be explained shortly.

Beyond the plasma membrane is a glycoprotein coat which, because of its jelly-like consistency, is called the **jelly coat**. A small fluid-filled space separates the jelly coat from the plasma membrane, and in this space one or two polar bodies may be seen.

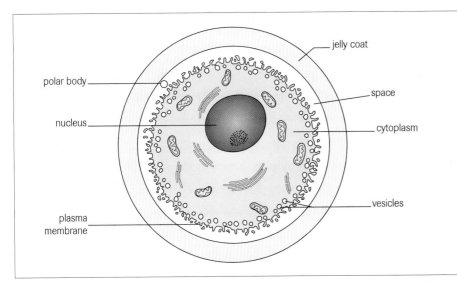

Figure 29.7 Structure of a mammalian egg. This picture, based on electron micrographs, is of an oocyte which is ready to be fertilised. Follicle cells have been omitted from the diagram.

29.3 Fertilisation

For a sperm to be capable of fertilising an egg, it must spend a certain amount of time in the female genital tract. This final part of the sperm's maturation process is called **capacitation** and it results in chemical changes on the surface of the sperm which enable it to penetrate the plasma membrane of the egg.

The sperm come into contact with the eggs by random movements. There is no convincing evidence that in mammals (or indeed in any animals) the sperm are attracted to the eggs. However, in some plants this certainly happens. For example, in bracken (bracken has sperm, believe it or not), the eggs secrete malic acid to which the sperm are attracted. This is an example of **chemotaxis** (*page 438*).

The sequence of events in fertilisation is illustrated in figure 29.8. Soon after the head of a sperm comes into contact with the jelly coat, the acrosome opens and releases its enzymes. The enzymes (which include a carbohydrase and a protease) soften the

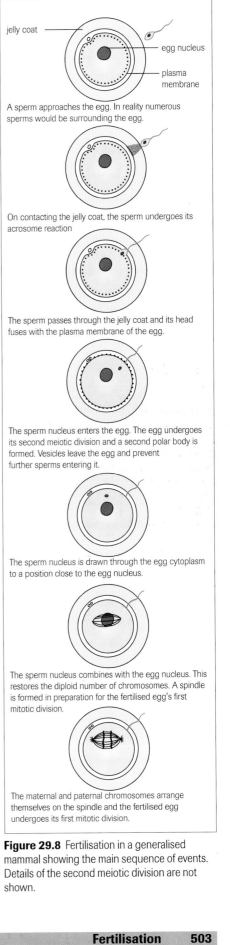

A sperm approaches the egg. In reality numerous sperms would be surrounding the egg.

On contacting the jelly coat, the sperm undergoes its acrosome reaction

The sperm passes through the jelly coat and its head fuses with the plasma membrane of the egg.

The sperm nucleus enters the egg. The egg undergoes its second meiotic division and a second polar body is formed. Vesicles leave the egg and prevent further sperms entering it.

The sperm nucleus is drawn through the egg cytoplasm to a position close to the egg nucleus.

The sperm nucleus combines with the egg nucleus. This restores the diploid number of chromosomes. A spindle is formed in preparation for the fertilised egg's first mitotic division.

The maternal and paternal chromosomes arrange themselves on the spindle and the fertilised egg undergoes its first mitotic division.

Figure 29.8 Fertilisation in a generalised mammal showing the main sequence of events. Details of the second meiotic division are not shown.

Specificity between egg and sperm

Normally eggs are only fertilised by sperm of the same species. What ensures that this happens? Research has shown that the sperm has a protein on its surface which binds to a specific protein-binding site on the surface of the jelly coat, in much the same way as hormones bind to specific binding sites on the surface of their target cells (*page 377*). In this way the sperm recognises the egg, and specificity between sperm and egg is achieved.

glycoprotein at the point of contact, allowing the sperm to pass through it. The whole process is called the **acrosome reaction** (*figure 29.9*).

The acrosome reaction enables the sperm to reach and penetrate the plasma membrane of the egg. As soon as this happens the vesicles in the outer part of the egg cytoplasm discharge their contents by exocytosis into the space between the plasma membrane and the jelly coat. This prevents any other sperm entering the egg.

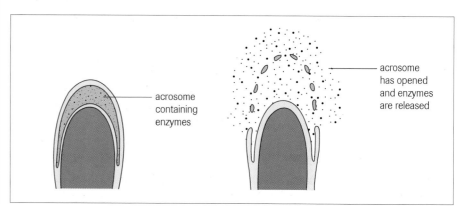

acrosome containing enzymes

acrosome has opened and enzymes are released

Figure 29.9 Acrosome reaction of a mammalian sperm. The acrosome breaks open, releasing enzymes which soften the jelly coat of the egg and enable the sperm to pass through it.

After a sperm has penetrated the egg membrane, its tail is usually discarded and the head and middle piece are drawn through the cytoplasm towards the nucleus. There is considerable variation in the way the two nuclei fuse. In many species the nuclear envelope breaks down, a spindle is formed, and the now visible sperm and egg chromosomes (the **paternal** and **maternal chromosomes** respectively) arrange themselves on the spindle as in mitosis. The diploid number of chromosomes is thus restored and the fertilised egg, or **zygote**, is ready for its first mitotic division.

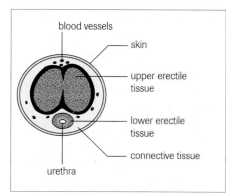

blood vessels

skin

upper erectile tissue

lower erectile tissue

connective tissue

urethra

Figure 29.10 Transverse section of a human penis showing the erectile tissue.

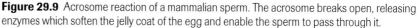

29.4 **Mating**

In aquatic animals the eggs and sperm are usually released into the surrounding water, and it is largely fortuitous whether or not they come into contact. Mammals, in common with most other terrestrial animals, have developed a more certain way of bringing the gametes together. This is achieved by the **penis**, through which the sperm are introduced into the female in the act of **mating (sexual intercourse)**.

The penis contains three cylindrical bands of **erectile tissue** consisting of a network of connective tissue and smooth muscle permeated by blood spaces, rather like a sponge (*figure 29.10*). The arteries and veins serving this erectile tissue are equipped with muscular valves. Under conditions of erotic excitement, the arterial valves dilate and the venous valves constrict. The resulting high blood pressure causes the penis to become **erect**, enabling it to be inserted into the vagina.

Rhythmical moving of the penis in the vagina stimulates tactile receptors in the glans, triggering a reflex which causes repeated contractions of muscle tissue surrounding the vasa deferentia and urethra. The contractions sweep the sperm along these tubes where they become mixed with secretions from the seminal vesicles, prostate and Cowper's glands, the greatest contribution coming from the seminal vesicles. The secretions activate the sperm and keep them in a viable and motile state. The resulting milky suspension, **semen**, is expelled from the penis in the process of **ejaculation**.

The reflex mechanism which brings about ejaculation also inhibits urination, so there is no chance of the sperm being contaminated with urine. Ejaculation comes as the climax of the mating process and is accompanied by a pleasurable feeling, the **orgasm**.

For mating to take place successfully, the erect penis needs to be lubricated. This enables it to move easily in the vagina, and prevents the epithelial lining of either being damaged by abrasion. Small amounts of a natural lubricant, secreted by the urethral glands, are discharged from the tip of the erect penis prior to ejaculation. Glands in the cervix secrete copious quantities of mucus which flows over the surface of the vagina and serves as an additional lubricant.

Movement of sperm in the female genital tract

Ejaculation usually occurs with sufficient force to propel the sperm to the upper end of the vagina and even into the cervix. They must now get from here to the upper part of an oviduct. By rhythmical undulations of the tail, they swim through the mucus. Round about the time of ovulation the mucus is thin and watery, and its glycoprotein chains run parallel with each other. This makes it easier for the sperm to swim through it.

It has been suggested that a sperm swimming the full length of the female genital tract would be equivalent to a human swimming across the Atlantic – in treacle! How the sperm propel themselves is still not fully understood but the densely packed mitochondria provide the necessary energy, and the sperm can respire anaerobically as well as aerobically.

Nevertheless, it is doubtful if the sperm could ever complete the journey without the aid of muscular contractions of the genital tract. In fact the vagina, cervix, uterus and oviducts all undergo contractions which help to sweep the sperm along. Sperm have been detected in oviducts within minutes of ejaculation, and these could not have swum there unaided. Even inert particles injected into the vagina get into the oviducts. It seems that contractions of the female genital tract provide the main force, the sperm propelling themselves unaided for only the last few millimetres.

Despite the help they receive, relatively few sperm reach the egg. A fertile man may produce as many as 500 million sperm in a single ejaculation. Of these, fewer than 500 ever get to the part of the oviduct where the egg is located – less than one in a million.

Extension

The orgasm

To describe an orgasm as a 'pleasurable feeling' is a masterpiece of understatement. It is a complex process whose physiological basis is still not understood. The female orgasm is particularly complex, but it is at least partly due to repeated tactile stimulation of the clitoris. Developmentally, the clitoris is equivalent to the penis and, like the latter, is highly sensitive and can become erect.

Accompanied by an almost explosive spread of excitation through the central nervous system, an orgasm involves almost every system in the body. For sheer extent, the only other response that comes anywhere near it is sneezing. The heart rate, blood pressure and breathing rate increase before and during an orgasm, and subside immediately afterwards.

It obviously takes a certain amount of time to reach an orgasm, and this may determine how long mating lasts. In this respect there are marked differences between species. For example, a chimpanzee may mate for less than ten seconds, the camel for 24 hours.

Extension

Sexually transmitted infections

Any infectious disease may be transmitted during intercourse, but certain bacteria and viruses are normally only transmitted by this route. The infections they cause are called **sexually transmitted diseases (STDs)** or – more aptly because they are not always diseases – **sexually transmitted infections (STIs)**. The agents responsible for them normally survive for only a very short time outside the body. It is therefore impossible to acquire them from, for example, a lavatory seat, convenient though this may be for explaining how one got infected!

STIs include syphilis, gonorrhoea and AIDS, all of which can be fatal and can be transmitted by pregnant mothers to their babies. Syphilis and gonorrhoea are both caused by bacteria and can be successfully treated with antibiotics such as penicillin. AIDS, however, is caused by a virus (HIV) which, like all viruses, cannot be destroyed by antibiotics. Although treatment with drugs can help, there is no cure for AIDS and a vaccine has not yet been developed against it.

Sexually transmitted infections have been called 'hidden diseases'. This is because, in the early stages of infection, the symptoms may be very slight or even non-existent. For example, approximately half of all women with gonorrhoea experience no symptoms at all. However, the causative agent is there, and can cause trouble months or years later. Meanwhile, the person is a **carrier** and may transmit the infection to his or her sexual partner or partners. This is why STIs can spread so quickly through the community, and why hospitals take pains to trace the partners of infected patients.

The term 'sexually transmitted infections' includes a number of infections which, though commonly transmitted by close sexual contact, can be caught in other ways too. They include chlamydia infection, genital herpes and viral hepatitis (the type of hepatitis known as hepatitis B can be fatal), and a number of less serious but troublesome infections such as thrush and genital warts.

Until the early 1980s most people were not unduly worried about STIs. Serious ones like syphilis could be cured if treated early enough, and the others were relatively rare and mainly curable. But then came AIDS. The only sure way of avoiding AIDS (and any other STI for that matter) is to not have sexual intercourse with anyone. But this is patently ridiculous. We are therefore faced with a dilemma. It may be impractical to avoid intercourse altogether, but at least one can be guided by the dictates of common sense and avoid having casual sexual encounters with numerous different partners. And if a lifelong one-to-one relationship is not possible, or casual sex is too tempting to resist, then one can take the precaution of practising 'safe sex'.

What is 'safe sex'?

Let us consider the basic principle. HIV, the virus that causes AIDS, is usually transmitted by the blood, semen or vaginal fluid of an infected person getting into another person's bloodstream. The amount of body fluid need only be very small for transmission to occur. This can happen during any kind of sexual activity which involves contact between delicate body surfaces that are, or might become, punctured. It is during intercourse that

this is most likely to happen. 'Safe sex' (or 'safer sex' as more cautious people prefer to call it) avoids direct contact between such surfaces. One way of achieving this is to wear a good quality **condom**, though even the manufacturer of one of the most reliable brands admits that no method of contraception can give 100 per cent protection against infection.

HIV has also been detected in saliva, tears and urine. However, the virus is extremely dilute in these fluids and there has never been a reported case of someone being infected through them. The main method of transmission is through blood, semen and vaginal fluid, and preventive measures are based on this fact.

Brief notes on four sexually transmitted diseases

- **AIDS:** Caused by human immuno-deficiency virus (HIV), which attacks cells in the immune system rendering the person susceptible to opportunistic infections such as pneumonia. Symptoms may take years to develop; no vaccine; no cure. Drugs have been developed which delay the progress of the disease but the side-effects can be unpleasant.

- **Syphilis:** Caused by a spiral bacterium, *Trepanoma pallidum*, which attacks the genital organs causing a sore on the penis or in the vagina (**primary syphilis**). Subsequent symptoms usually include skin rash and fever (**secondary syphilis**) and, years later, blindness, insanity, paralysis and heart failure (**tertiary syphilis**). Can be completely cured by antibiotics such as penicillin if treated early enough.

- **Gonorrhoea:** Caused by a spherical bacterium, *Neisseria gonorrhoea*, which attacks the genital organs causing discharge from the urethral opening and pain when urinating

(described by Boswell as 'a most exquisite pain'). Later symptoms include general ill health, arthritis, emphysema and inflammation of the pericardium. Responds well to antibiotics such as penicillin but resistant strains of the bacterium have evolved, necessitating the use of stronger doses and/or other antibiotics.

- **Chlamydia:** Virus-like bacterium, *Chlamydia trachomatis*, infects the genital tract. Very common, particularly in young women with multiple partners. Can cause pain in lower abdomen, vaginal discharge and abnormal menstruation, and in serious cases infertility and miscarriage. Difficult to diagnose because it is often symptomless. Can be cured with antibiotics. Incidence reduced by using a condom.

Sexually transmitted diseases present a formidable problem to the health service. In the United Kingdom the cost of diagnosing and treating chlamydia infection alone is at least £50 million a year (1997 figure).

▶ AIDS is described in detail on page 328

29.5 From ovulation to implantation

The oviduct and its funnel are lined with cilia. After ovulation, the beating of these cilia draws the egg into the funnel and propels it along the first part of the oviduct (*figure 29.11*). Follicle cells, still attached to the egg, provide a large surface on which the cilia can gain a purchase. Although the wall of the oviduct contains smooth muscle tissue, muscular contractions do not play much part, if any, in the transport of the egg at this stage, at least not in those species of mammal which have been studied.

Fertilisation usually occurs about a third of the way along the oviduct. After fertilisation, the zygote is pushed down the oviduct by gentle contractions of circular muscle in the oviduct wall. Once the egg has been fertilised, **conception** has been achieved and the woman is **pregnant**.

Figure 29.11 shows the progress of the zygote along the oviduct. In humans it takes about four days to reach the uterus. As it moves along, it divides to form a solid ball of cells which then becomes a hollow **blastocyst**. The follicle cells have disappeared by this time but the jelly coat is still present. Eventually the blastocyst breaks out of the jelly coat and becomes attached to the lining of the uterus, a process called **implantation**. In the human, implantation begins about eight days after fertilisation and takes about a week to complete.

The uterus prepares itself for implantation beforehand. Its wall consists of two main layers: a layer of smooth muscle called the **myometrium** towards the outside, and a soft inner lining called the **endometrium**. By the time the blastocyst arrives, the endometrium is thick and soft, like a cushion, and contains numerous blood vessels and glandular invaginations. The glands secrete a wide range of nutrients and other substances which help the blastocyst to survive and continue its development. One of the nutrients is glucose, from which the blastocyst obtains energy.

Figure 29.11 The events which take place from ovulation to implantation. In the human it takes about a week for an egg which has just been released from the ovary to develop into a blastocyst and begin to implant. So typically implantation begins on the 21st day of the menstrual cycle and ends around what would have been the 28th day. This is when menstruation would have taken place. It is usually the missing of a menstrual period that tells a woman that she is, or may be, pregnant.

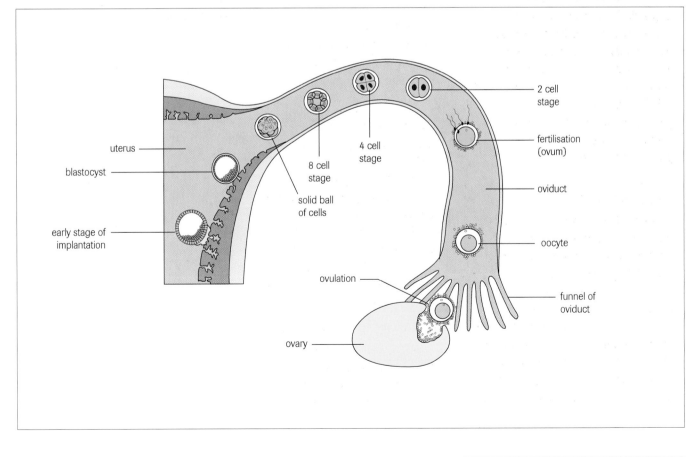

In the human species, the number of embryos that fail to survive is surprisingly high. Of 100 fertilised eggs, as many as 55 per cent fail to implant successfully. Some never implant at all, others are lost during the implantation process. Of the embryos that do implant successfully, approximately 10 per cent are spontaneously aborted at a later stage, usually between the 7th and 10th weeks of pregnancy.

Why should so many embryos be lost? The answer is not known, though it may be nature's way of getting rid of defective embryos. This idea is supported by the observation that approximately 50 per cent of all spontaneously aborted embryos carry major genetic defects such as chromosome mutations. On the other hand, only about 2 per cent of newborn babies carry major genetic defects.

The outermost layer of cells of the blastocyst is called the **trophoblast**. This sends out finger-like outgrowths which project into the endometrium. As well as providing anchorage, these **trophoblastic villi** increase the surface area for the absorption of nutrients. In this way the developing embryo is nourished and supported during the early stages of its development.

29.6 Pregnancy

Within a few weeks, the job of nourishing the embryo is taken over by the **placenta**. At the same time the embryo becomes enveloped by a membrane called the **amnion**. The space enclosed by the amnion (the **amniotic cavity**) is full of fluid.

The function of the fluid-filled amniotic cavity is to cushion the embryo and protect it from physical disturbance. The amniotic cavity gradually expands to accommodate the growing embryo, and eventually it fills the entire uterus. By this stage all the organs and systems of the body have been laid down and the embryo is referred to as a **fetus** (also spelled **foetus**). This is the stage reached in figure 29.12A.

The placenta

The placenta is intimately associated with the endometrium of the uterus, and is connected to the fetus by the **umbilical cord**. The cord contains two blood vessels: an **umbilical artery** which carries blood from the aorta of the fetus to the placenta, and an **umbilical vein** which carries blood from the placenta to the posterior vena cava of the fetus. Within the placenta numerous tree-like **chorionic villi**, containing capillary loops derived from the umbilical artery, project into a large **maternal blood space** in the wall of the uterus (*figure 29.12B*). This space is kept charged with blood from branches of the mother's uterine artery.

The fetal and maternal bloodstreams flow very close to each other. Exchange of materials takes place across the thin barrier which separates them:

- Soluble food substances, oxygen, water and salts pass from the mother's blood into the fetal blood.

- Carbon dioxide and nitrogenous waste pass from the fetal blood into the mother's blood.

- In addition, antibodies pass from the mother's blood into the fetal blood, thereby conferring on the fetus **passive immunity** against various diseases (*page 330*).

The placenta is therefore the fetus' gaseous exchange surface, source of food, excretory organ and source of antibodies.

Although the relationship between the fetal and maternal bloodstreams is extremely intimate, the bloods do not mix. The mother and fetus may belong to different blood groups, and if their bloods were to mix coagulation might occur (*page 337*). Moreover, the mother's blood pressure would be far too high for the fetus.

The placental villi

The placental villi are well adapted to their function. Their branched arrangement gives them a large surface area, and the capillary loops within them are extensive. The barrier between the blood in the capillaries and the mother's blood in a fully developed placenta is extremely thin. As shown in figure 29.12C, it consists of three layers:

- the wall of the fetal capillary (i.e. the endothelium);

- a thin layer of connective tissue;

- the wall of the villus (i.e. its epithelial lining).

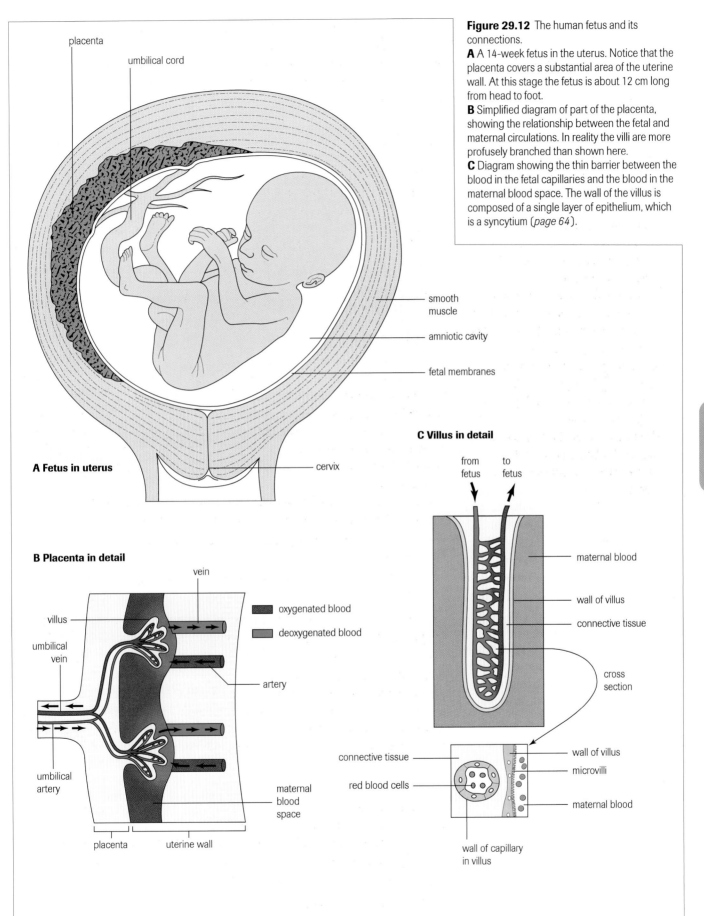

A Fetus in uterus

placenta

umbilical cord

smooth muscle

amniotic cavity

fetal membranes

cervix

Figure 29.12 The human fetus and its connections.
A A 14-week fetus in the uterus. Notice that the placenta covers a substantial area of the uterine wall. At this stage the fetus is about 12 cm long from head to foot.
B Simplified diagram of part of the placenta, showing the relationship between the fetal and maternal circulations. In reality the villi are more profusely branched than shown here.
C Diagram showing the thin barrier between the blood in the fetal capillaries and the blood in the maternal blood space. The wall of the villus is composed of a single layer of epithelium, which is a syncytium (*page 64*).

C Villus in detail

from fetus   to fetus

maternal blood

wall of villus

connective tissue

cross section

connective tissue

red blood cells

wall of villus

microvilli

maternal blood

wall of capillary in villus

B Placenta in detail

vein

villus

umbilical vein

umbilical artery

artery

maternal blood space

placenta   uterine wall

oxygenated blood

deoxygenated blood

In vitro fertilisation

In vitro *fertilisation (IVF) can help infertile couples to have children. The following account of the technique is based on detailed information provided by scientists who work in this field.*

In vitro fertilisation means fertilisation outside the body, and it leads to the production of what are popularly called 'test-tube babies'.

The term 'test-tube baby', coined by the media when the technique was first introduced, is misleading. Only fertilisation itself and the first few cell divisions take place outside the body, and the 'baby' that is placed back in the mother consists of eight cells at the most. From that point on, nature takes over and if all goes well the embryo will implant in the uterus and continue to develop in the normal way.

A key step in IVF is the removal of the egg. This has to be taken from the Graafian follicle in the ovary, for once ovulation has occurred and the egg has started its journey down the oviduct, it cannot be located. The aim is to collect the egg a few hours before ovulation. (At this stage it is, of course, an oocyte but for simplicity we shall refer to it as the egg.)

To increase the chance of success, doctors arrange for the woman to produce a larger number of eggs than the single one normally formed during each menstrual cycle. This is called **super-ovulation**. Having more than one egg means that:

- if one egg fails to get fertilised, another one may be successful;

- the most viable embryos can be selected for transfer back to the mother;

- more than one embryo can be transferred back to the mother, thereby increasing the chance of her becoming pregnant.

The procedure

The woman is made to super-ovulate by treatment with hormone-based drugs. This strategy not only increases the number of eggs produced but it also enables the doctors to control the time of ovulation so they know exactly when to collect the eggs.

Doctors achieve this control by first preventing the woman from producing her own hormones and then supplying FSH and then LH (*page 514*). The doses are tailored and timed to obtain an optimal response.

Collecting the eggs is a relatively simple matter. The ovaries are only about 2 cm from the wall of the vagina – they are normally further away than this but the presence of the follicles makes them heavier, so they drop down nearer the vagina. Just before ovulation each mature follicle is about 2 cm in diameter. The follicles are located by means of an ultrasound scanner.

Using ultrasound guidance, a hollow needle is inserted into the vagina and through its wall into one of the follicles. The egg is then sucked out, together with the follicular fluid, and placed in a test tube containing a special medium. This procedure is repeated for the other follicles. The eggs are then maintained in separate test tubes at 37°C in an incubator.

Meanwhile the sperm are prepared. As well as normal sperm, the seminal fluid contains a large proportion of dead and abnormal sperm which must be removed. The semen is placed in a test tube and a layer of special medium is carefully placed on top. Strong motile sperm swim up into the medium from which they are easily harvested.

A few hours after collection, about 100 000 of the prepared sperm are added to each egg in a small Petri dish. After 16 to 20 hours the eggs are checked to see if they have been fertilised. The embryos are then left in the incubator to develop for two or three days. By this time they will have reached the 4- or 8-cell stage and can be transferred back to the uterus. Up to three embryos are replaced, in the hope that one of them will implant successfully and develop into a new human being. Alternatively the embryos may be frozen and stored for future use. A substance such as glycerol is added first to protect the embryos from being damaged by ice crystals, then they are immersed in liquid nitrogen at –196°C.

Suppressing the pituitary

An important aspect of IVF is to stop the patient's pituitary secreting its own gonadotrophins, so that ovulation can be controlled entirely by the doctor. The current method of suppressing the pituitary is most ingenious. The theory behind it is as follows. In natural circumstances the secretion of gonadotrophins by the pituitary cells is triggered by **gonadotrophin releasing hormone** from the hypothalamus (*page 516*). When this hormone reaches the pituitary cells it binds to specific receptor molecules and causes the gonadotrophins to be released. To suppress the pituitary, drugs are used which mimic the action of the releasing hormone. They bind avidly with the receptors, preventing the releasing hormone from doing so.

The drugs block the receptor molecules for only a limited time, after which they and the receptor molecules disintegrate. The pituitary cells then produce new receptors and resume their normal functioning. Altogether it takes between a week and 10 days for the pituitary to function normally again. By then, hopefully, the IVF procedure will have been completed.

Effects of pregnancy on the fetus and mother

The mother and fetus are structurally and functionally joined together and it is hardly surprising that they have a profound effect on each other.

How the fetus affects the mother

The mother's body responds to being pregnant in various ways. For example, her body mass, appetite, thirst, metabolic rate, ventilation rate, cardiac output, blood volume and red blood cell count all increase, as do the release of calcium and blood glucose into the bloodstream. All this fits in with the fact that she has a developing human being inside her. Her thermal balance changes too and her food requirements increase, for she is in effect feeding two people.

Her diet must include plenty of carbohydrate (for energy), protein (for growth), iron (for blood), calcium (for bones) and various vitamins including folic acid. The effects of malnutrition on the fetus include retarded growth, possible learning difficulties and the risk of developing heart disease in later life. Absence of folic acid can cause neural defects.

Although being pregnant may be fulfilling, it has its bleak moments. For example, it can cause backache, and during the first three months the mother is liable to feel sick, particularly in the early morning. This **morning sickness** is probably caused by high levels of oestrogen and other hormones acting on the vomiting centre in the brain (*page 361*).

How the mother affects the fetus

Being incarcerated in the uterus affects the fetus in a number of ways. For example, since it receives its food and oxygen via the placenta, its lungs and gut are non-functional and its heart and circulation are organised differently from the adult's. The **fetal circulation**, and what happens to it at birth, is explained on page 532.

The mother's behaviour, diet and lifestyle can have a profound effect on the fetus. The placenta is a superbly efficient device for providing the fetus with everything it needs, but by the same token undesirable things can get across it too. This is why pregnant women are urged to avoid harmful drugs – including alcohol, nicotine and hard drugs such as heroin and cocaine. Bacteria and viruses can get across the placenta too, including those that cause sexually transmitted diseases (*page 505*). If the virus that causes rubella (German measles) crosses the placenta it can cause malformation of the fetus. For this reason girls in most countries are vaccinated against this disease before they reach puberty.

▶ Prenatal diagnosis including the use of ultrasound, page 748

The epithelium lining the villus bears **microvilli** which increase its surface area, and it contains numerous mitochondria which provide energy for active transport. Exchanges occur by a combination of diffusion, active transport and pinocytosis. The villi can pulsate, creating a stirring effect and bringing them into contact with substances in the mother's blood. Absorption of oxygen by the fetus is aided by **fetal haemoglobin** which has a higher affinity for oxygen than maternal haemoglobin (*page 220*).

29.7 Birth

During pregnancy, the uterus expands enormously to accommodate the steadily growing fetus. At the same time, the muscular part of the uterine wall thickens and the endometrium becomes more and more richly vascularised. When the fetus reaches a certain size relative to the uterus, birth (**parturition**) takes place.

Birth starts with rhythmical contractions of the uterine muscle ('going into labour'). Next, the amnion bursts and the amniotic fluid flows out through the vagina ('breaking of the waters'). Then the fetus is forced out through the cervix and vagina by powerful contractions of the uterine muscle. The placenta comes away from the uterine wall and is expelled as the 'afterbirth'. The now redundant umbilical cord is tied and cut in the human but in other mammals it may be chewed through by the mother. With the loss of the placenta as the source of oxygen, the baby starts breathing.

By this time the **mammary glands** in the breasts have developed greatly and at the time of birth they start secreting milk in the process known as **lactation**. This provides the newborn baby with nourishment and a continued source of antibodies until it builds up a supply of its own. The milk produced during the first few days of lactation is called

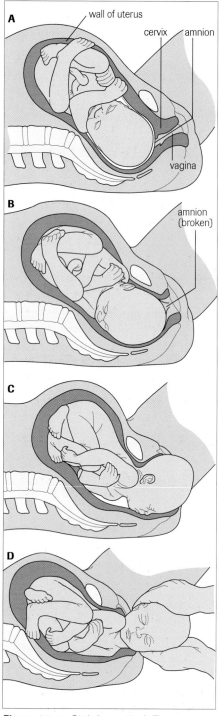

A — wall of uterus, cervix, amnion, vagina

B — amnion (broken)

C

D

Figure 29.13 Birth (parturition). The cervix dilates and the uterine muscle contracts, forcing the baby through the vagina ('birth canal').

colostrum (Latin for 'first milk'). It has a high protein content and is particularly rich in antibodies.

Milk is the baby's main source of food for about the first year of life. It contains all the necessary nutrients, including calcium and vitamin D which are needed for the development of bones and teeth. For a mother who is breast-feeding her baby it is essential that her diet should contain sufficient amounts of all these nutrients.

The time from conception to birth is called the **gestation period**. In the human it lasts approximately nine months, but in other mammals it ranges from as little as 18 days in mice to 22 months in elephants. Human birth is illustrated in figure 29.13.

29.8 The sexual cycle

The impressive thing about the female's reproductive physiology is that all the events are synchronised, so that each occurs at the right moment. For example, in the human, well before ovulation is due to take place the lining of the uterus starts to prepare itself for implantation, so that by the time the blastocyst arrives in the uterus the endometrium is ready to receive it. What controls the timing of these events?

The answer lies in the fact that the female's reproductive behaviour occurs in a cycle. This is called the **sexual cycle**. The events that occur in the course of the cycle follow a regular pattern which is controlled by hormones from the pituitary gland and ovaries. If pregnancy occurs, the normal cyclical pattern is interrupted and a third source of hormones comes into play: the placenta.

In the human female the most obvious outward sign of the sexual cycle is the monthly discharge of blood known as **menstruation**. Menstruation is characteristic of humans and certain other primates, for which reason their sexual cycle is called the **menstrual cycle**. In a woman, menstruation marks the end of a series of changes that have occurred in her body during the previous 28 days. To understand what has happened we must return to the ovary.

The ovary and uterus working together

During the first 14 days following the beginning of menstruation, a Graafian follicle develops in one of the ovaries, as described earlier. After ovulation, the empty follicle undergoes certain changes. The follicle cells enlarge considerably, and a yellow pigment accumulates in them. Eventually they fill the cavity of the original follicle, turning it into a solid **corpus luteum** ('yellow body') (*figure 29.5 on page 501*). If the egg is *not* fertilised, the corpus luteum remains in the ovary for the next week or 10 days and then degenerates.

While the Graafian follicle is developing, the wall of the uterus prepares itself for receiving a blastocyst. The endometrium thickens and becomes permeated by blood vessels and glands in readiness for implantation. If, however, fertilisation does not occur, the unfertilised egg simply degenerates. Under these circumstances the corpus luteum regresses, and the endometrium of the uterus breaks down and sloughs off. The discarding of the endometrial tissue, accompanied by the loss of blood, takes place intermittently over several days and constitutes menstruation. The amount of blood lost is usually quite slight but if for any reason it is severe the woman may need to increase her dietary intake of iron and other nutrients to make good the loss.

So, to summarise, the menstrual cycle is divided into two phases: a **follicular phase** during which a Graafian follicle develops, and a **luteal phase** during which the corpus luteum develops and then regresses.

Puberty, sex hormones and the menopause

Puberty

In a young child, the gonads, though present, do not function. This situation continues until the onset of **puberty** at the age of about 11–14 years in girls, 12–16 in boys, when eggs and sperm start being produced. Girls experience their first menstrual period towards the end of puberty (the **menarche**). Boys find that their external genitalia grow considerably, and ejaculation becomes possible.

At puberty the **secondary sexual characteristics** develop: breasts and wide hips in the female; body hair and broken voice in the male. Growth also speeds up, giving the well-known **adolescent growth spurt** (*illustration*). It is then that parents find themselves buying new clothes for their offspring more often than they may have bargained for.

Hormonal control of puberty

The changes which occur at puberty happen gradually over about a year. They are brought on by **sex hormones** secreted by the gonads: **androgens** (principally **testosterone**) by the testes, and **oestrogens** by the ovaries. The production of these hormones is in turn controlled by **gonadotrophic hormones** from the anterior lobe of the pituitary gland.

Although androgens are regarded as male hormones and oestrogens as female hormones, small amounts of each are found in the opposite sex. For example, androgens in women cause development of pubic hair. The function of oestrogen in males is not known.

The sex hormones continue to be produced in adult life. In the female they control the menstrual cycle. In the male they maintain the steady production of sperm, and they stimulate muscular growth.

Synthetic androgens have been used (illegally) by athletes to enhance their

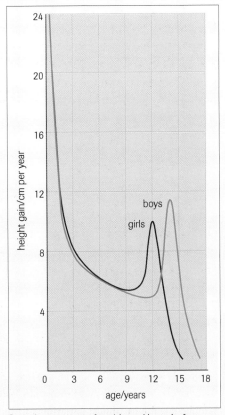

Growth rate curves for girls and boys before, during and after puberty.

performance, and by farmers to stimulate the growth of muscle in livestock. Some of these **anabolic steroids** are remarkably powerful and selectively stimulate the growth of skeletal muscle.

The menopause

Men can go on producing sperm well into old age, but women stop ovulating at the age of about 50 when they reach the **menopause**. During the preceding few years the secretion of sex hormones gradually declines until no more Graafian follicles are produced and menstruation ceases.

Although there is considerable variation between different women, the time leading up to the menopause can be accompanied by tiresome symptoms such as hot flushes, sweating, anxiety and irritability. In the longer term loss of bone tissue may occur, resulting in

osteoporosis (*page 418*). This is caused by shortage of oestrogen and is exacerbated by smoking, excessive alcohol and lack of exercise.

These problems can be alleviated by **hormone replacement therapy** (**HRT**). This involves taking carefully regulated doses of oestrogen and progesterone, either orally or from some other source such as patches attached to the skin. Treatment is continued for a year or two, the doses being gradually reduced. For prevention of osteoporosis, treatment is usually continued for at least five years. There is also evidence that HRT helps to prevent cardiovascular disease.

HRT does not stop the woman's ovaries declining and so it does not prolong her reproductive life. However, it can remove the stresses and strains of the menopause and improve health.

Why do humans take so long to reach puberty?

No other species of eutherian mammal takes as long to reach puberty as humans do. The reason probably has its roots in our evolution. The postponement of puberty and comparatively long period of growth mean that the young are dependent on their parents for much longer than would otherwise be the case. Ample opportunity is therefore provided for strong bonds to be forged between parents and offspring, promoting the family unit and enabling the young to learn from instruction (language, for example) and receive the experience necessary for successful integration into society. This must have been very important in our evolution from hunter–gatherers that lived in social groups, and probably contributed in large measure to our emergence as the dominant species.

▶ Human evolution, page 772

Sexual cycles of other mammals

In most mammals, the time of ovulation is marked by heightened sexual excitement and is called **oestrus**. Oestrus comes from the Greek word *oistros* meaning 'mad desire' and the animal is described as being 'on heat'. At this stage the female may produce various secretions which act as **pheromones**, inducing sexual activity in the male (*pheromones are explained on page 450*). This ensures that mating takes place at the right time. In some species, rabbits for example, ovulation is delayed until about 10 hours after mating has occurred, by which time the sperm will have reached the oviducts and will be ready to fertilise the eggs.

In humans and other primates, however, no such safeguards exist. Indeed, there is no evidence that women show greater sexual awareness at the time of ovulation, despite the hormonal changes that are taking place in her body. It is therefore largely fortuitous as to whether or not mating happens at the right time. However, in some species, notably cats and rabbits, mating stimulates ovulation to occur. This is called **induced ovulation**.

In the human female ovulation occurs approximately midway between one menstrual period and the next, and as the sexual cycle lasts about 28 days a woman will ovulate some 12 or 13 times in the course of a year – unless she is pregnant or lactating. In few other mammals is the frequency so low. Even in large mammals like cows, the sexual cycle only lasts about three weeks, and in small mammals like rats and mice, oestrus occurs at approximately four to five day intervals. Menstruation does not occur in these mammals and it is usual to refer to their sexual cycle as the **oestrous cycle** ('oestrus' is the noun, 'oestrous' the adjective).

Breeding seasons

Rats, mice, cows and women can reproduce at any time of the year, but in many other mammals there are definite **breeding seasons**. During the breeding season the female may come into oestrus once (e.g. hedgehogs, dogs) or many times (e.g. hamsters, sheep, horses). The number and timing of the breeding seasons are also variable: commonly there is only one, occurring in the spring or summer, but some mammals have two.

In bats, mating occurs in the autumn but fertilisation is delayed until the spring; in badgers and roe deer the blastocyst lies dormant in the uterus for weeks or even months. This **delayed implantation** ensures that the young are born at a suitable time of the year.

Breeding seasons are closely related to the environment. However, the natural pattern seen in animals in the wild may be severely disrupted by domestication. The environmental stimuli which bring wild animals into season may not apply to an animal that spends most of its time curled up on a hearth rug.

Oestrous cycle of the cow

The cow may be taken to illustrate the oestrous cycle of a commercially important domestic animal.

The cow's reproductive system is essentially the same as that of the human. The oestrous cycle normally lasts 21 days and, if the cow does not become pregnant, it is repeated over and over again. The cycle is divided into a short follicular phase followed by a relatively long luteal phase. The two phases are controlled by gonadotrophic and ovarian hormones in much the same way as in humans, though there are a number of detailed differences. For example, the corpus luteum is made to regress at the end of the luteal phase by the secretion of a prostaglandin by the uterus (*see page 375 for prostaglandins*).

It is important for farmers to know when oestrus – and therefore ovulation – is likely to occur, for it is then that the cow, if she is to become pregnant, should be impregnated either by a bull or by artificial insemination. As menstruation does not occur in cows, farmers cannot use that for predicting when oestrus will occur. However, various signs indicate its onset. The cow becomes restless, shows more attention to other animals, eats less and produces less milk if she is lactating. There are also changes in the appearance of the vulva.

How breeding is controlled by the environment, page 564; use of hormones in controlling the reproduction and growth of domestic animals, page 565

29.9 Hormonal control of the sexual cycle

The changes occurring in the ovary and uterus are synchronised by hormones. Basically two groups of hormones are involved:

- Hormones secreted by the anterior lobe of the pituitary gland, under the influence of the hypothalamus in the brain. They are called **gonadotrophic hormones** because they bring about changes in the gonads, in this case the ovaries. There are two such hormones: **follicle stimulating hormone** (**FSH**) and **luteinising hormone** (**LH**).

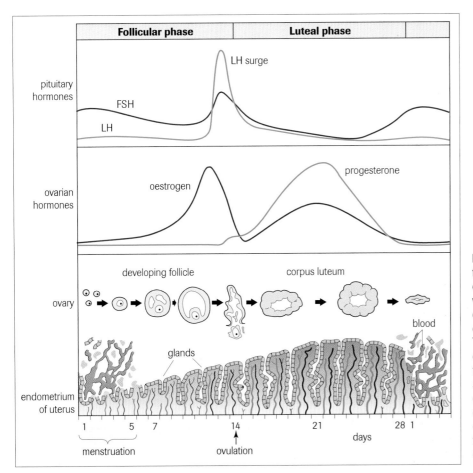

Figure 29.14 The menstrual cycle of a human female showing the events occurring in the ovary and endometrium of the uterus, together with the relative concentrations of pituitary and ovarian hormones in the blood. How these events are synchronised is explained in the text. The increase in the concentration of FSH coinciding with the LH surge is caused by the fact that oestrogen, at *high* concentrations, *stimulates* secretion of FSH, whereas at lower concentrations it inhibits it. The slight rise in the concentration of progesterone *before* the corpus luteum has been formed is due to the fact that the ovary itself secretes small quantities of progesterone at this time.

- Hormones secreted by the ovary itself. The two main ovarian hormones are **oestrogen** and **progesterone**, and they bring about changes in the uterus.

The details are summarised in figure 29.14. At about the time of menstruation, the anterior lobe of the pituitary gland secretes FSH. This causes a Graafian follicle to develop in the ovary, and stimulates the ovary and the wall of the follicle to secrete oestrogen, whose concentration therefore gradually rises.

Oestrogen's immediate effect is to bring about the repair of the uterine endometrium following menstruation. In the first half of the cycle the amount of oestrogen in the bloodstream steadily increases, slowly at first and then more quickly. Shortly before ovulation is due to take place, it reaches such a high concentration that it causes a large amount of LH to be suddenly released by the anterior pituitary (the **LH surge**). If you look at the curves in figure 29.14 you can see a perfect correlation between the moment when oestrogen reaches its peak and the onset of the LH surge. The LH surge causes ovulation, and makes the Graafian follicle change into a corpus luteum.

The corpus luteum secretes progesterone – in fact small quantities of this hormone have already started coming from the ovary itself. Progesterone, together with oestrogen which is also secreted, causes the continued thickening and vascularisation of the uterine endometrium in preparation for implantation. At the same time, the rising concentration of progesterone, in the presence of oestrogen, inhibits any further secretion of FSH by the pituitary (negative feedback). This ensures that another follicle does not develop in the ovary.

The rising concentration of progesterone also inhibits secretion of LH by the pituitary (negative feedback again). As a result, the corpus luteum degenerates and the concentrations of oestrogen and progesterone decrease. This decline starts about a week after ovulation. With the fall in the level of these two hormones, the uterine endometrium disintegrates and menstruation takes place. Meanwhile the anterior pituitary, freed from the inhibitory influence of progesterone, starts secreting FSH again, so immediately after menstruation the repair process begins and the cycle is repeated.

The hormonal interactions in the sexual cycle are illustrated in figure 29.15. We can sum up by saying that the two pituitary hormones, FSH and LH, stimulate the ovary to secrete oestrogen and progesterone respectively. These hormones, in turn, regulate the production of the pituitary hormones by feedback. How the feedback mechanism works is explained in the extension box below.

Figure 29.15 Scheme summarising the main interactions of hormones controlling the female sexual cycle. Solid arrows and positive sign signify stimulation, broken arrows and negative signs signify inhibition.

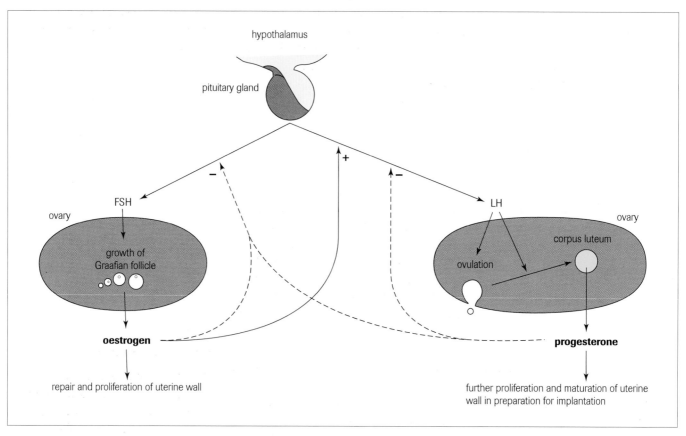

Extension

The role of the hypothalamus

In controlling the sexual cycle the anterior pituitary does not act alone. It receives instructions from the hypothalamus in the brain. The instructions take the form of a hormone called **gonadotrophin releasing hormone (GnRH)** which flows from the hypothalamus to the anterior pituitary, telling it to secrete its gonadotrophins. (*Releasing hormones are explained on page 376.*)

Do oestrogen and progesterone achieve their feedback effects by acting on the pituitary or the hypothalamus or both? The answer is both. They act on the hypothalamus by controlling the secretion of the releasing hormone, and they act on the pituitary by altering its responsiveness to the releasing hormone.

The details of these two levels of feedback – which ovarian hormone does what and when – need not concern us here. What you should appreciate, though, is the importance of the close association between the pituitary and the hypothalamus. In brief, it allows the environment, acting via sensory receptors and the brain, to exert control over sexual activity. There is more about this on pages 564 and 565.

Treating infertility

In some women the pituitary fails to produce enough FSH, with the result that Graafian follicles do not develop in the ovary and ovulation does not occur. This can be remedied by injections of FSH or a synthetic equivalent, the so-called **fertility drug**. So effective is this treatment that it may cause several eggs to be produced at the same time, resulting in twins, triplets, quadruplets or more (the record is nine, though none of the offspring survived).

Some women fail to ovulate because they secrete too much oestrogen which has the effect of inhibiting FSH secretion by the pituitary. They can be treated with non-steroidal drugs such as **clomiphene** which oppose the action of oestrogen, thus releasing the pituitary from inhibition.

In men, infertility is sometimes caused by the semen containing too few sperm (low sperm count). This may be remedied by treatment with natural or synthetic androgens such as testosterone. Another problem that some men face, particularly as they get older, is failure of the penis to become erect. The new drug **Viagra** (sildenafil), which can be taken orally, rectifies this condition. It is an enzyme inhibitor and indirectly causes the smooth muscle surrounding the main cavities in the penis to relax so that more blood can be pumped into them during the erection process.

Needless to say, all these treatments require consultation with doctors for they can produce side-effects and some carry health risks.

▶ *In vitro* fertilisation, page 510

29.10 Hormonal changes during and after pregnancy

The sequence of events described so far is what happens if fertilisation does not take place. If, however, the egg is fertilised and the woman becomes pregnant, a different course is followed. Under these circumstances the corpus luteum, instead of degenerating, persists. In humans this is due to a hormone called **human chorionic gonadotrophin** (**HCG**), a glycoprotein, which is secreted by the developing placenta. This hormone signals to the mother's body that an embryo is present in the uterus. It is the basis of **pregnancy tests**: excess chorionic gonadotrophin is excreted, and its presence in the urine is detected and used as an indication that the woman is pregnant.

HCG starts being produced soon after implantation, and its concentration in the bloodstream (and urine) increases until it peaks after about two months and then declines. At first very little is produced but, thanks to monoclonal antibodies, it can be detected in the urine within a month of the woman's previous menstrual period. Simple-to-use **pregnancy testing kits** are available from pharmacies.

The corpus luteum continues to secrete progesterone which, coupled with a small but steady secretion of oestrogen, maintains the continued development of the uterus and, of course, prevents menstruation. These hormones also inhibit the anterior pituitary from producing FSH, thus preventing further follicles developing in the ovary.

After the first three or four months of pregnancy the corpus luteum begins to regress and the job of secreting oestrogen and progesterone is taken over by the placenta. In this way the endometrium of the uterus is maintained in a suitable state throughout pregnancy.

Hormonal control of birth

Towards the end of pregnancy, the level of oestrogen in the blood rises while that of progesterone falls. This may play a part in bringing about birth. Certainly oestrogen promotes uterine contraction, and progesterone inhibits it. Premature births sometimes occur when the progesterone level falls too low, and if this happens before about the seventh month of pregnancy a **miscarriage** may occur. The chance of a miscarriage occurring during a subsequent pregnancy can be reduced by giving the mother injections of progesterone.

The contraceptive pill

The fact that during pregnancy oestrogen and progesterone prevent Graafian follicles developing in the ovary was exploited in developing the **contraceptive pill**. The 'combined' pill contains synthetic equivalents of these two hormones. It works by suppressing the development of follicles in the ovary.

Since the pill was first introduced in the 1960s, the amounts of oestrogen and progesterone in it have been steadily reduced. This has decreased its side-effects, one of which was to increase the risk of cardiovascular disease. The pill is now considered to be very safe and has the added advantage of preventing ovarian cancer.

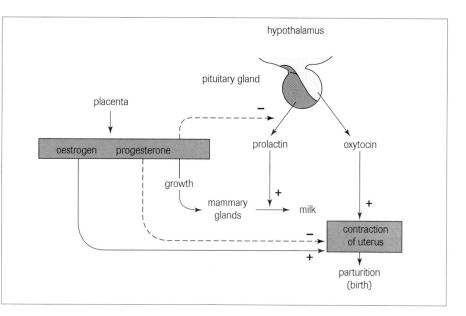

Figure 29.16 Actions of the female hormones during and immediately after pregnancy. Solid arrows and positive signs signify stimulation, broken arrows and negative signs signify inhibition.

But the most direct cause of birth is another hormone, **oxytocin**, secreted by the posterior lobe of the pituitary gland. This causes the uterine muscle to contract. Oestrogen achieves its effect on the uterus by making the uterine muscle more sensitive to oxytocin. Progesterone has the reverse effect. This is illustrated in figure 29.16.

Hormonal control of lactation

Figure 29.16 also shows how milk production (lactation) is controlled. During the latter part of pregnancy, oestrogen and progesterone stimulate the growth of the milk-producing **mammary glands**. After birth, milk production is induced by yet another hormone, **prolactin**, secreted by the anterior lobe of the pituitary.

Before birth, prolactin secretion is inhibited by oestrogen and progesterone. The sudden fall in the level of these two hormones with the loss of the placenta at the end of pregnancy permits a small but steady secretion of prolactin. Milk flow itself is induced by **suckling**. Stimulation of receptors in the nipples by the baby's mouth triggers a reflex which – acting via the hypothalamus – induces bursts of prolactin secretion.

29.11 Sex hormones in the human male

In the human male, the production of sperm by the testes is regulated by gonadotrophic hormones identical to those produced by the female. The anterior pituitary secretes FSH and LH. FSH promotes the growth of the seminiferous tubules in the testes and stimulates spermatogenesis. LH stimulates the interstitial cells between the seminiferous tubules to secrete male sex hormones (**androgens**). These are steroids, and the main one is **testosterone**. This is needed, along with FSH, for spermatogenesis.

Both FSH and LH are controlled by feedback mechanisms. LH is controlled directly by testosterone. FSH is controlled by a hormone called **inhibin** which is secreted by the Sertoli cells in the walls of the seminiferous tubules (*page 500*).

The way these hormones interact is summarised in figure 29.17. You will notice parallels with the female system. However, there is one fundamental difference. In the female the hormones are produced in waves, which give rise to the menstrual cycle. In the male they are produced more or less uniformly all the time. Consequently there is no sexual cycle in the male.

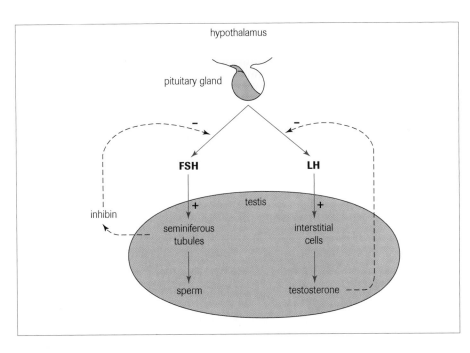

Figure 29.17 Actions of the male hormones. Solid arrows and positive signs signify stimulation, broken arrows and negative signs signify inhibition.

Extension

Family planning, principles and practice

There are times when couples may wish to prevent pregnancy. This can be achieved by **family planning** (**birth control**), and generally it involves some form of **contraception**. Contraception is any procedure which *prevents* conception.

There are many different methods of birth control. Some are easy to use, others more difficult; some are reliable, others less so; and some carry health risks or may be disapproved of by particular religious or cultural groups. Choosing the right method is therefore an important matter and depends on many factors – personal, medical and social. **Family planning clinics** provide advice on the different methods available.

From the biological point of view, birth-control methods fall into three categories:

- methods that prevent sperm reaching the egg;
- methods that prevent eggs being produced (ovulation);
- methods that prevent the blastocyst implanting.

The various methods are summarised in the table on the next page, from which you will be able to see the category that each method belongs to.

A distinction can be made between **barrier methods** and **chemical methods**. Barrier methods involve setting up a block in either the male or the female system which stops the sperm getting through. Chemical methods involve the use of substances, usually hormonal, which interfere with the body's normal physiology and either prevent ovulation or stop the blastocyst implanting.

Not all the methods shown in the table involve using artificial devices or procedures. Some of the methods are natural. They appeal to people who, for religious or other reasons, object to artificial methods. The main natural method is the **rhythm method**. As this illustrates some important biological principles, we shall look at it in detail.

The rhythm method

The time when a woman can conceive is around the time of ovulation, which is approximately 14 days after the beginning of the preceding menstrual period. The length of time during which fertilisation is possible depends on how long the egg and sperm remain viable in the female genital tract. The egg can survive in the oviduct for several days, but it is only capable of being fertilised successfully for up to about 24 hours after ovulation. Sperm can live in the oviduct for a week or more, but their ability to fertilise an egg declines after about 48 hours.

From this we may conclude that a woman should conceive only if she has intercourse within a day or so on either side of ovulation. The rhythm method of contraception is based on the premise that if a woman avoids having intercourse at this time, she should not become pregnant.

The rhythm method depends on knowing when ovulation is going to occur, but in some women this is very difficult to determine. A number of subtle changes occur in the body at or around the time of ovulation – for example, the basal body temperature increases very slightly (by about 0.2°C) and the cervical mucus becomes more copious and runny. If these and other changes are monitored over many months, they can be used to predict when ovulation is likely to occur in future menstrual cycles. Once this information has been obtained, a calendar can be drawn up indicating when the 'safe periods' are likely to be.

Unfortunately, variations in the time of ovulation make this an imprecise method of contraception. It can also be a source of stress to some couples, particularly if they are experiencing sexual or emotional difficulties. However, it does have the advantage of being a natural method and therefore appeals to people who have moral objections to artificial methods.

Abortion

Despite the wide range of contraceptive methods available, women sometimes become pregnant when they do not wish to. The only way of avoiding giving birth is to have an **abortion** or – in medical parlance – **termination of pregnancy**. Countries have strict laws on abortion. In Britain an abortion is permitted up to the 24th week of pregnancy so long as two doctors agree that by continuing the pregnancy the woman's physical or mental health is at risk.

Abortions are also given when the fetus is found to be severely abnormal or when the mother's life would be placed in jeopardy by having the baby. In such circumstances abortions up to the end of pregnancy may be permitted.

The moral and ethical issues involved in abortion are probably well known to you and we shall not go into them here, except to say one thing. A central question which must influence one's attitude to abortion is: when does a human life begin or, putting it another way, when does an embryo or fetus become a human being with rights? Is it at conception, or at a later stage? And if the answer is a later stage, then should it be 10 weeks, 24 weeks, at birth – or when? On this question biologists can make useful contributions based on their knowledge of the human embryo and how it develops. There is more about this in the extension box on page 529.

▶ Theory behind the oral contraceptive, page 517; contraceptive vaccine, page 530

Method	Description	Comments
METHODS WHICH PREVENT SPERM REACHING THE EGG		
Natural methods		
Coitus interruptus	Penis withdrawn from vagina before ejaculation	Very unreliable because pre-ejaculation lubricating fluid may contain sperm. Also it requires considerable self-control
Rhythm method	Intercourse avoided at times when ovulation is likely to occur	Unreliable except under expert guidance of doctor or counsellor
Artificial methods		
Vaginal douche	Vagina flushed out with soapy water after intercourse	Extremely unreliable because sperm may reach uterus before douche is given
Spermicide	Cream or pessary, available from pharmacy, placed in vagina before intercourse	Unreliable unless used with condom or diaphragm (see below)
Condom	Rubber sheath placed over penis	Very reliable *if used correctly*. Most condoms are coated with a spermicidal lubricant
Diaphragm	Rubber diaphragm placed over cervix	Very reliable so long as it stays in place and is combined with a spermicide
Male sterilisation	Vasa deferentia tied and cut by surgeon (vasectomy)	Very reliable but must be regarded as irreversible; semen still produced but without sperm
Female sterilisation	Oviducts tied and cut by surgeon (tubal ligation)	Very reliable but must be regarded as irreversible
METHODS WHICH PREVENT OVULATION		
Oral contraceptive (the 'pill')	Tablet (hormone preparation), prescribed by doctor, taken daily	Very reliable and decreases the risk of ovarian cancer
Injectable contraceptive (e.g. Depo-provera)	Single intramuscular injection, given by doctor, stops ovulation for three months	Very reliable but prolonged use may cause irregular bleeding and possibly other health hazards
METHODS WHICH PREVENT IMPLANTATION		
Intra-uterine device (IUD)	Plastic or metal object placed in uterus by doctor; normal fertility resumed when IUD is removed	Reliable without ill effects though menstrual bleeding may be more severe than usual
Morning-after pill	Tablet taken within three days after intercourse	Reliable but may cause nausea; normally used only as emergency measure
Intra-vaginal ring	Ring-shaped polymer placed in vagina, slowly releases progesterone-like substance	Very reliable though this is a new method and long-term health effects have yet to be fully assessed

1. Sexual reproduction starts with **gametogenesis**, the formation of gametes: **spermatogenesis** in the male and **oogenesis** in the female. Both involve mitosis, growth and meiosis.

2. The microscopic structure of the **testis** and **ovary** is directly related to their functions of producing eggs and sperm respectively. Eggs are shed from the ovary in the process of **ovulation**.

3. The structure of sperm and eggs can be related to their functions. The sperm conveys the genetic material of the male to the egg; the egg receives the male's genetic material and develops into an embryo.

4. In mammals, as in many other animals, internal fertilisation is achieved by **mating (sexual intercourse)**.

5. Certain **sexually transmitted infections** are associated with intercourse or close sexual contact.

6. In the process of **fertilisation**, a spermatozoon, aided by its **acrosome reaction**, penetrates the jelly coat and fuses with the plasma membrane of the egg. Its haploid set of chromosomes (**paternal chromosomes**) unites with those of the egg (**maternal chromosomes**) to form the **zygote**.

7. Childless couples may be helped to have children by *in vitro* fertilisation and various other methods.

8. After fertilisation, the zygote develops into a **blastocyst** which becomes **implanted** in the endometrium of the uterus.

9. In the human female, the **sexual cycle (menstrual cycle)** follows a monthly pattern, ovulation alternating with **menstruation**. The sequence of events is controlled by **gonadotrophic hormones** from the pituitary gland interacting with **ovarian hormones** from the ovary.

10. In the event of fertilisation and implantation, the hormonal balance is altered in such a way that menstruation and ovulation are temporarily suspended and the uterine endometrium continues to grow.

11. A **placenta** develops in association with the uterine endometrium. Connected to the fetus by an **umbilical cord**, it permits exchange of materials between the fetal and maternal bloodstreams.

12. During pregnancy, the placenta takes over the function of secreting the hormones formerly secreted by the ovary. They promote the continued growth of the uterine endometrium.

13. The placental hormones, together with certain hormones produced by the pituitary gland, ensure that **birth (parturition)** and **lactation** occur at the appropriate time.

14. In the male, **testosterone** (an **androgen**) stimulates spermatogenesis. Its secretion is maintained by pituitary hormones identical to those produced by the female.

15. As well as initiating egg and sperm production, the sex hormones cause the development of **secondary sexual characteristics** at **puberty**. Hormonal changes are also associated with the **menopause** whose unpleasant side-effects may be alleviated by **hormone replacement therapy** (**HRT**).

16. Some mammals, including the human, can reproduce at any time of the year. Others have specific **breeding seasons**, the timing of which is controlled by a combination of environmental and hormonal factors.

17. Various methods of **birth control**, natural and artificial, are available to those who want them.

For general advice on these questions and advice on answering essay-type questions, see pages vii and viii.

1. (a) Define the following terms:

    (i) *tissue*; (ii) *organ*   (4)

The diagram on the right is a transverse section through part of a mammalian testis.

  (b) (i) The cells in this tissue section are becoming differentiated (specialised). What is the name of this process of differentiation?   (1)

    (ii) Identify the structures labelled **A** to **D**.   (4)

    (iii) Use the appropriate letter(s) to identify which of the cells labelled A to D is/are haploid.   (2)

    (iv) What is the role of the interstitial cells shown in the diagram?   (1)

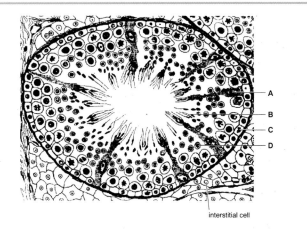

interstitial cell

(Total 12 Marks)

O&C 1998

2. Records of human fertility for the period 1930 to 1990 have shown changes in the sperm counts of normal men.

The table below summarises the changing percentages of men with high or low sperm counts over a period of sixty years.

High sperm count $> 100 \times 10^6$ sperm cm^{-3}
Low sperm count $< 20 \times 10^6$ sperm cm^{-3}

Time period	Men with high sperm counts / %	Men with low sperm counts / %
1930 – 1950	50	5
1951 – 1960	45	4
1961 – 1970	28	14
1971 – 1980	21	11
1981 – 1990	15	18

(a) (i)   Comment on the changes in the percentage of men with high sperm counts during the period 1930 to 1990. (2)

(ii)   Compare the figures for men with low sperm counts with those with high sperm counts over the same period. (3)

(b) Explain why it is necessary for large numbers of sperms to be produced when only one sperm is required to bring about fertilisation. (2)

(c) Exposure of pregnant women to high levels of certain oestrogens during early pregnancy can result in reproductive disorders in their male offspring.

It appears that a number of compounds in the environment can mimic the action of oestrogens when ingested. Such compounds, termed oestrogenic chemicals, are found in pesticides, such as DDT and PCBs, and also in the breakdown products of certain detergents. They accumulate in the fatty tissue and have the same effect as oestrogens, which play a major role in the menstrual cycle.

(i)   Describe the normal role of oestrogens in the menstrual cycle. (3)

(ii)   Suggest how the oestrogenic chemicals pass from the mother to the developing fetus. (3)

(Total 13 marks)
London 1996

3. Discuss how the human placenta is adapted to its role in maintaining the developing foetus.

Diagrams may be used to assist your account, but are not essential.

(Total 20 marks)
O&C 1997

4. The table below shows the timing of some of the aspects of puberty in a large sample of girls and boys.

Event	Average age at which event begins / years	Range of ages at which event begins / years	Average age at which event ends / years	Range of ages at which event ends / years
Height spurt in girls	10.5	8.5-14.0	14.0	12.5-15.5
Development of breasts	10.8	8.0-13.0	14.8	12.0-18.0
First menstrual period	13.0	10.5-15.5	not applicable	not applicable
Height spurt in boys	12.5	10.5-16.5	16.0	14.0-17.5
Growth of penis	12.5	10.5-14.5	14.5	12.5-16.5
Growth of testes	11.5	9.5-13.5	15.5	14.0-17.0

(a) Suggest **two** possible explanations for the variation in the age at which puberty begins in girls. (2)

(b) Use the information in the table to give

(i)   the earliest age at which a girl in the sample could have completed the aspects of puberty shown; (1)

(ii)   the range of ages when **all** boys in the sample were in the process of puberty. (1)

(c) Which hormone is mainly responsible for

(i)   the development of the breasts; (1)

(ii)   growth and development of the testes? (1)

(Total 6 marks)
NEAB 1998

5. (a) The mammalian oestrous cycle is controlled by hormones secreted from the pituitary gland and from the ovaries.

Describe the roles of the following hormones in the control of this cycle.

(i)   The pituitary hormones FSH and LH. (5)

(ii)   The ovarian hormones oestrogen and progesterone. (5)

(b) Rats can reproduce at any time of the year. Some other mammals, for example deer, have a specific breeding season. Suggest **one** advantage to each animal of its particular pattern of breeding. (2)

(Total 12 marks)
NEAB 1997

Chapter 30

Patterns of growth and development

I n the course of its life cycle an organism changes from a fertilised egg into an adult. As development proceeds, all sorts of changes take place. The most obvious change is **growth**. One has only to compare the hands of a human adult with those of a baby to appreciate the effectiveness of growth as a biological process (*figure 30.1*).

But development involves more than just growth. The egg gives rise first to a ball of cells that does not look at all like the adult organism. Somehow this ball of cells is transformed into a complex body with all the different tissues and organs arranged in the right positions. In other words, the cells become specialised and this involves **differentiation**.

The progressive changes which are undergone before an organism acquires its adult form constitute **embryonic development**. Studying the embryonic development of any animal or plant entails asking two basic questions: what changes take place, and how do they occur? In this chapter we shall be mainly concerned with the structural changes that occur, starting with growth.

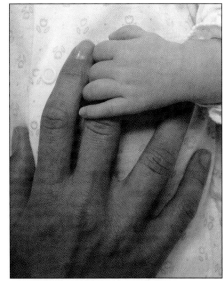

Figure 30.1 The hand of a ten-day-old baby compared with that of the mother.

30.1 Growth

Growth is the permanent and irreversible increase in size that occurs as an organism gets older. Although growth entails, first and foremost, an increase in mass, other parameters increase too, such as volume, length and so on. Growth does not include temporary increases in these parameters resulting from, for example, drinking a lot of water or eating a large meal.

How is growth achieved?

Three distinct processes contribute to growth: **cell division**, **assimilation** and **cell expansion**.

Cell division is the basis of growth in all multicellular organisms, but plainly to grow to the size of the parent cell, the daughter cells must be able to synthesise new structures from raw materials which they absorb from their surroundings. This is what is meant by assimilation, and it results in cell expansion.

In plants, cell expansion may be aided by vacuolated cells taking up water by osmosis and swelling up. This is the basis of how stems and roots increase in length, about which we shall have more to say later.

Measuring growth

Growth can be quantified by measuring a particular parameter such as height or mass, at suitable intervals over a known period of time. This is not always easy, because of difficulties in selecting the right feature. Commonly a linear dimension such as height or length is measured. Because growth usually takes a long time, a slowly revolving **kymograph** (*page 401*) or **time-lapse photography** may be used for making a continuous record of it. This also has the advantage of showing up any variations in the rate of growth that may occur at different times.

The drawback with measuring a single linear dimension such as height, is that it takes no account of growth in other directions, which in some cases may be considerable. One can sometimes get round this by measuring changes in volume. However, this may call for considerable mathematical ingenuity if the organism has an irregular shape.

Mass is often used, but this may vary because of fluctuations in the fluid content of the

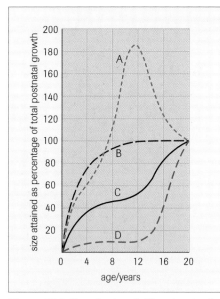

Figure 30.2 Growth rates of different parts of the human body between birth and maturity. The sizes on the vertical axis are expressed as percentages of the total gain between birth and maturity (20 years). Thus the size of any given part of the body is 100 per cent at age 20.
Curve **A**: lymph tissue.
Curve **B**: brain and head.
Curve **C**: general, i.e. legs, arms, lungs, kidneys, muscles, etc.
Curve **D**: reproductive organs.

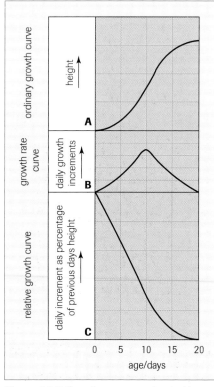

Figure 30.3 Growth curves constructed from data on lupins. The shape of the curve depends on how you express the growth. See text for details.

organism. To overcome this problem one may resort to estimating **dry mass**, that is the mass after all moisture has been driven off by heating. The trouble here is that it kills the organism, so measurements must be made on random samples of individuals taken at intervals from a large population. The latter should be the same age, growing under constant conditions, and preferably all identical genetically – that is members of the same clone. This technique is commonly adopted with plants.

Allometric growth

One problem with measuring growth is that different parts of the organism may grow at different rates and stop growing at different times. For example, in humans the head grows rapidly at first and then slows down, virtually stopping altogether soon after the age of about five years. However, the legs and arms continue to grow for another 15 years or so, as do most of the other organs (*figure 30.2*).

The growth of different parts of the body at their own particular rates, higher or lower than the growth rate of the body as a whole, is known as **allometric growth**. Most organisms show allometric growth to some extent. A full description of an organism's growth must obviously take this into account.

The growth curve

If an organism's measurements (height, mass or whatever) are plotted against time, a **growth curve** is obtained. Despite difficulties in measuring growth, the general pattern turns out to be the same for most organisms. If measured from an early enough stage, you get an S-shaped curve of the kind shown in figure 30.3A: growth is slow at first, then it speeds up, and finally it slows down as the adult size is reached.

In humans and certain other vertebrates, growth stops altogether when the adult size is reached (in the early 20s in most humans). However, in most organisms growth continues in adult life, though slowly.

Absolute growth rate

The growth curve enables us to work out the rate at which an organism grows. This can be done by estimating the increase in size that takes place during successive intervals of time. The increases (**growth increments**) are then plotted against time. This gives us the organism's **absolute growth rate**.

In an organism with a growth curve like the one in figure 30.3A, the growth rate increases steadily until it reaches a maximum, after which it gradually falls, giving the bell-shaped curve shown in figure 30.3B.

Relative growth rate

During the growth of multicellular organisms, each generation of new cells undergoes assimilation and expansion. In other words the products of the growth process are themselves capable of growing. This is quite different from, say, the growth of a crystal, in which new material is added to the surface of the existing crystal from the outside. Different, too, from the building of a house in which new bricks, obtained from an outside source, are added one by one to the existing structure.

In contrast, an organism's growth is essentially an internal process, taking place from within the organism. This means that the amount of growth which takes place at any one stage is dependent on the bulk of tissue already present, i.e. on how much growth has already occurred. This is taken into account by measuring the **relative growth rate**, in which the increase in growth over a period of time is expressed as a percentage of the amount of growing matter already present.

Let us take an example. Between the ages of one and two years, a baby's body mass might increase from 10 to 12 kg. The absolute increase is therefore 2 kg, but the relative

Measuring human growth

One problem that researchers on human growth do *not* have is finding large samples of individuals on which to carry out their studies. Baby clinics, nurseries and schools provide a particularly useful resource.

Suppose an investigator wants to study the growth of children, as measured by increase in mass, from birth until the age of 15 years. Basically there are two approaches depending on whether or not the investigator is in a hurry.

■ A single cohort of babies is selected and the mass of each individual is measured at regular intervals for the next 15 years. This is called a **longitudinal study** and, although it gives an accurate record of growth, it has the disadvantage in that it takes a long time.

■ Groups of individuals at a series of ages ranging from birth to 15 years are selected and their masses are measured. This is called a **cross-sectional study** and it is much quicker. Its main disadvantage is that it may be complicated by genetic and other differences between individuals and is therefore not an entirely accurate record of growth.

increase, expressed as a percentage, is $\frac{2}{10} \times 100 = 20$ per cent. Now, in the same period of time the mass of a teenager might go up from 50 to 55 kg, giving an absolute increase of 5 kg. However, the *relative* increase is only $\frac{5}{50} \times 100 = 10$ per cent, half that of the baby. So the baby, though it puts on less mass in a year, has a higher relative growth rate.

If relative increase is plotted against time, we get a curve of the sort shown in figure 30.3C. Represented this way, the growth rate does not rise and then fall. On the contrary, growth is fastest at the beginning of life (in the human while the fetus is in the uterus), after which it gradually slows down. This is true of most organisms, plants as well as animals.

You can see an example of this type of growth curve for humans on page 513. The curve shows the dramatic increase in the growth rate at puberty – the adolescent growth spurt.

Intermittent growth of arthropods

The smooth growth curve shown in figure 30.3A is typical of most organisms, but there is one notable exception: arthropods. Look at figure 30.4, for instance. This curve was obtained by plotting the body mass of an insect against time. Instead of increasing smoothly, growth takes place in a series of jumps. These correspond to the sequence of stages, or **instars**, in the insect's development (*page 533*).

This intermittent growth is made necessary by the **cuticle (exoskeleton)** which, because of its hardness, prevents the body from growing. Periodically the cuticle is shed, a process called **moulting (ecdysis)**. Only then – while the new cuticle underneath is still soft enough to allow the body to expand – can any significant amount of growth take place.

In some cases rapid expansion is achieved by the insect swallowing air or water. The waterboatman, from which the growth curve in figure 30.4 was obtained, expands by swallowing water – that is why its mass increases so abruptly each time it moults. The distension of the gut when water or air are swallowed pushes the new cuticle outwards. The cuticle then hardens and the tissues inside can grow to fill the space available. After that, further growth is impossible until the cuticle is shed again. At the final shedding of the cuticle, the wings expand.

30.2 The main stages in animal development

The changes that occur as an animal develops are brought about by the cells rearranging themselves and taking up new positions. This is achieved partly by cells migrating from one place to another, and partly by layers of cells folding in various ways.

Cell migration is possible because the embryonic cells are able to move about by a process similar to amoeboid movement (*page 433*) Once the cells have got into the right positions, they lose the ability to move. They then differentiate into particular types of tissue.

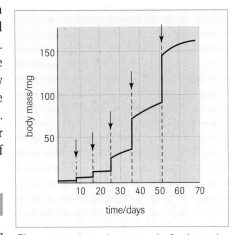

Figure 30.4 Intermittent growth of arthropods illustrated by increase in mass of a waterboatman, *Notonecta glauca*, with time. The times of moulting are indicated by the arrows. The reason why the mass rises so abruptly is that the animal swallows water when it moults.

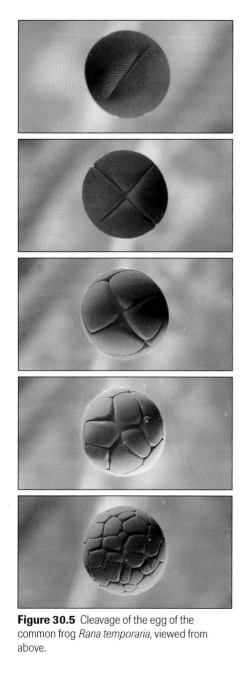

Figure 30.5 Cleavage of the egg of the common frog *Rana temporaria*, viewed from above.

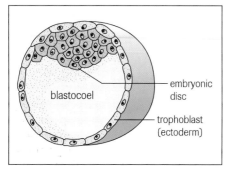

Figure 30.6 Vertical section of a human blastocyst on the sixth day after fertilisation.

Embryonic development is normally triggered by fertilisation. In vertebrates, including humans, the subsequent changes fall into four main stages:

- **cleavage**, the division of the zygote into daughter cells;
- **gastrulation**, the arrangement of these cells into distinct layers;
- **neurulation**, the formation of a central nervous system;
- **organogenesis**, the formation of organs and organ systems.

Development is, of course, a continuous process and to some extent these four stages may overlap. Let us look briefly at each of them. The descriptions that follow are based on the development of amphibians such as frogs which have been much studied.

Cleavage

During cleavage, the zygote divides repeatedly into progressively smaller cells (*figure 30.5*). The cell divisions are mitotic, so all the cells have the same genetic constitution. It is a highly organised process, the first two divisions being vertical and the third one horizontal. After that alternate vertical and horizontal divisions take place.

The end result of cleavage is a simple embryo consisting of a ball of cells which, as no assimilation and cell growth have yet taken place, is the same size as the original fertilised egg. At this stage the ball of cells is solid, but as cell divisions continue a fluid-filled cavity is formed in the middle. The resulting hollow ball of cells is known as a **blastula** and its cavity is called the **blastocoel**.

This is what happens in amphibians. In mammals, including humans, the process is essentially the same but the end product – the **blastocyst** – is rather different (*figure 30.6*). The wall of the blastocyst, known as the **trophoblast**, has on its inner side a localised patch of cells called the **embryonic disc** which will develop into the embryo itself. The region of the trophoblast beneath the embryonic disc is several cell layers thick and bears **trophoblastic villi** from which the embryo obtains nourishment after the

---

Extension

Embryo transfer and cloning

A mammalian embryo at the 8–16 cell stage looks rather like a blackberry. All the cells are alike, no differentiation having yet taken place, and each is potentially capable of developing into a new, but genetically identical, individual. Identical twins result from an embryo splitting at this early stage of development. As the cells are easily separated, this provides a way of **cloning** animals.

An embryo is removed from a **donor female** and broken down into its constituent cells. The individual cells are encouraged to grow and divide until they reach the blastocyst stage. They are then transferred to the uterus of a **recipient female** where, hopefully, they will implant and continue their development. Alternatively, they may be frozen and stored for future use. In this way several genetically identical offspring can be produced from one embryo.

A distinction should be made between cloning and **embryo transfer**. The latter simply involves removing an embryo from one female and placing it in the uterus of another. This procedure was first carried out on rabbits over 100 years ago. Today it is widely used in breeding as the best way of making use of a superior female, and it has the potential for saving endangered species such as the giant panda.

▶ *In vitro* fertilisation, page 508; embryo research, page 530; cloning by nuclear transplantation, page 620

blastocyst has implanted (*page 507*). The rest of the trophoblast consists of a single layer of cells which will give rise to the placenta and other structures associated with, but outside, the embryo.

Gastrulation

The key event in gastrulation is the formation of the gut (gastrulation means literally 'formation of a stomach'). The way this happens varies from one animal group to another. In amphibians the wall of the blastula invaginates at one end, rather like a hollow rubber ball being pushed in on one side. This has the effect of partially obliterating the blastocoel and creating an opening – which eventually closes up – at the future posterior end of the embryo.

As a result of the aforementioned process the embryo becomes two-layered, a sort of cup within a cup. The outer layer of cells, called the **ectoderm**, will give rise to the skin and associated structures. The inner layer, called the **endoderm**, lines the future gut.

Meanwhile, cells at the posterior end proliferate and migrate into what's left of the blastocoel. As a result the embryo acquires a third layer of cells which, because it is between the other two layers, is called the **mesoderm**. This is destined to give rise to various internal organs, as we shall see. At this stage the embryo is known as a **gastrula** (*figure 30.7*).

In mammals, including the human, the mesoderm is formed by an inward migration of cells on either side of a deep longitudinal indentation on the dorsal side of the embryo. This indentation is called the **primitive streak**. In the early 1980s the primitive streak hit the headlines in Britain because it was decided that its appearance in the human embryo should be taken as the point when embryo research should stop (*extension box on page 529*).

The ectoderm, endoderm and mesoderm are called the **germ layers**. Having three layers of cells like this is a fundamental feature of the ground plan of most animals. Indeed, the only major group of animals that do not have three cell layers are the cnidarians – *Hydra* and its relatives. They have only two layers – ectoderm and endoderm.

The appearance of the three germ layers in the right positions marks the end of gastrulation and paves the way towards the next important event: neurulation.

Neurulation

Neurulation, the formation of the central nervous system (CNS), is shown in figure 30.8. First, the cells in the mid-dorsal line immediately above the gut form a rod-like **notochord** which strengthens the embryo. In certain invertebrate chordates, notably a little fish-like animal called *Amphioxus*, the notochord persists in the adult. However, in the vertebrates it becomes replaced by the vertebral column.

If you follow the diagrams in figure 30.8 you will see that the ectoderm immediately above the notochord differentiates into a flat area called the **neural plate** which sinks downwards and folds up on either side to form a longitudinal **neural groove**. The folds on either side of the groove then grow towards each other until they meet in the mid-dorsal line. They then fuse together, forming a **neural tube** which is destined to give rise to the central nervous system.

By now the embryo – or **neurula** as it is called at this stage – has increased in length. A small indentation on the ventral side towards the posterior end breaks through to the gut as the **anus**, and a pouch-like invagination at the anterior end becomes the **mouth**.

The next step in development centres on the mesoderm, which by this stage has acquired a small internal cavity called the **coelom**.

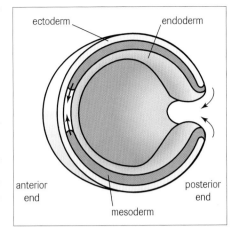

Figure 30.7 Diagrammatic horizontal section of a gastrula of an amphibian showing the endoderm and mesoderm migrating inwards from either side of the blastopore. This process obliterates the blastocoel and creates a new internal cavity which will become the gut.

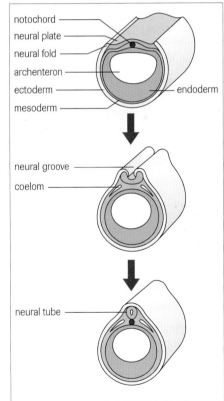

Figure 30.8 Neurulation in an amphibian. The diagrams are transverse sections of the developing neurula. In all chordates neurulation takes place by the neural plate on the dorsal side of the embryo sinking downwards and becoming first a groove and then a tube. Notice that by the time neurulation starts, the mesoderm completely fills the space between the ectoderm and endoderm.

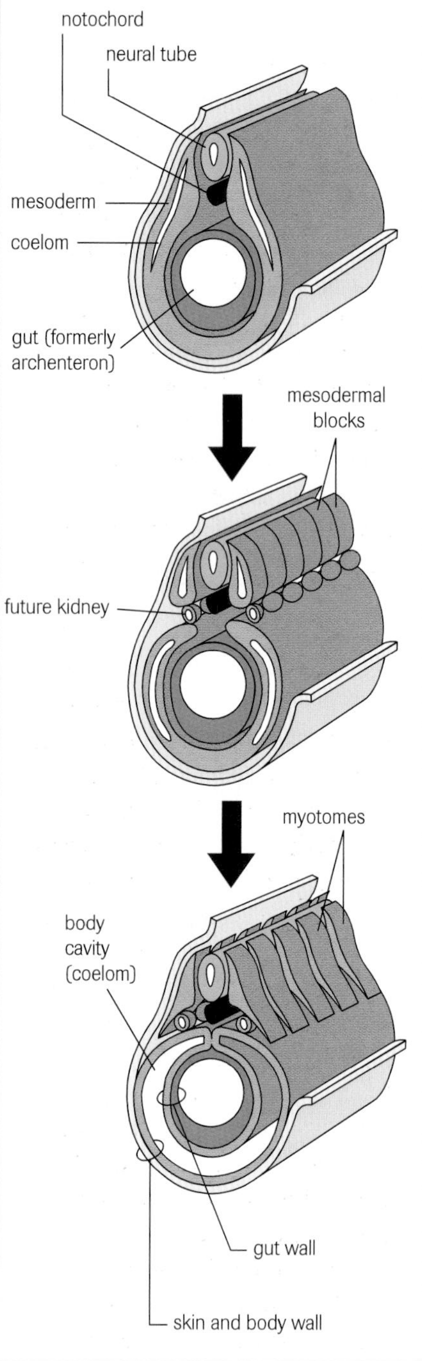
notochord
neural tube
mesoderm
coelom
gut (formerly archenteron)
mesodermal blocks
future kidney
myotomes
body cavity (coelom)
gut wall
skin and body wall

Figure 30.9 Development of the mesoderm as seen in transverse sections through the trunk region of amphibian embryos. The way the mesoderm develops is fundamentally the same in all chordates, including the human.

Development of the mesoderm and coelom

The way the mesoderm and coelom develop is illustrated in figure 30.9. Three important events occur:

- The part of the mesoderm on either side of the neural tube splits up transversely into a series of identical blocks called **somites** which will develop into skeletal muscles.
- The part of the mesoderm on either side of the notochord also becomes segmented and will give rise to the kidneys.
- The rest of the mesoderm remains unsegmented and the coelom inside it expands to form the body cavity in which the gut and other internal organs are suspended.

The mesoderm surrounding the body cavity develops into the body wall muscles and gut muscles. The superficial layer of mesoderm lining the body cavity itself forms the **peritoneum**. (This is made use of in **peritoneal dialysis** – *page 287*).

While the body cavity develops, the segmental blocks of mesoderm on either side of the neural tube lose their coelomic cavities and become solid blocks of muscle called **myotomes**.

In fishes and larval amphibians (tadpoles) the segmental pattern of the myotomes is very apparent, but in adult terrestrial chordates including humans, the segmental pattern is obscured by the development of limbs. Nevertheless, the serial repetition of body parts, imposed on the embryo by the way the mesoderm develops, is a fundamental feature of chordates. It is called **metameric segmentation**.

Organogenesis

By the late neurula stage, the basic organisation of the body is laid down. Subsequent development involves the differentiation of the three germ layers into specific organs. The main events are as follows:

- Cells migrate inwards from the segmental mesodermal blocks and surround the notochord, eventually replacing it with the **vertebral column**. The **limbs** develop as outgrowths from the sides of the body, their **muscles** being formed from mesodermal cells which migrate into them.
- The **gut** lengthens and becomes differentiated into various regions: pharynx, stomach, intestine and so on, and various accessory organs such as the **liver** and **pancreas** develop as outgrowths from it.
- The **trachea** and **lungs** arise as an outgrowth from the back of the pharynx, and **blood vessels** are moulded out of the mesoderm.
- The ventral mesoderm towards the anterior end of the body arranges itself into the shape of a large tube which expands to become the **heart**. The part of the coelom surrounding the heart becomes the **pericardial cavity**.
- The anterior end of the neural tube expands to form the **brain**. The rest of the neural tube remains narrow and becomes the **spinal cord**. The cavity inside the neural tube becomes the cavities in the brain and spinal cord.
- **Nerves** grow out of the brain and spinal cord, linking up with the body's receptors and effectors. **Special sense organs** (nose, eye and ear) develop in close association with the brain.

Why 14 days?

Research on human embryos is only permitted in the UK for 14 days following fertilisation. Here, guest author Baroness Mary Warnock explains why the committee which she chaired on this matter decided on 14 days.

There were good biological reasons for picking on this particular number of days. These reasons give grounds for a moral distinction which justifies our adopting a different attitude towards a human embryo before 14 days after fertilisation from that which we adopt towards later embryos or fetuses.

Let me explain our reasoning. Up to 14 days, the embryo consists of a collection of dividing cells which are loosely clustered together. These cells are not yet differentiated into particular tissues or organs. Nor will all of them become part of the embryo itself: some of them will become part of one of the extra-embryonic structures such as the placenta or the amnion. Moreover, it is possible at this stage for two or even three embryos to develop from the cluster of cells. It is in fact the last stage at which twins or triplets may be formed.

The pre-14 day embryo is therefore not yet a single individual living organism: it may be one or two or three individuals. Indeed, such is its lack of differentiation that it has been suggested that the cluster of cells should not be called an embryo, but a 'pre-embryo'. However, at about the 14th day a definite change takes place: a groove appears on the upper side of the embryo – the **primitive streak** (*page 527*). This marks the beginning of gastrulation. It is at this stage that the cells begin to differentiate into specialised types, some taking up their role as part of the placenta, others coming together to form what will become the brain or spinal cord of the embryo itself. From this time onwards we must recognise that the cluster of cells has become an individual embryo which will become a fetus and then a child.

Our committee sought evidence from many different quarters, and a range of opinions was expressed. For example, The Royal College of Obstetricians and Gynaecologists suggested that embryos should not be allowed to develop *in vitro* beyond a limit of 17 days, as this is the point when early neural development begins. The British Medical Association favoured a limit of 14 days whilst certain other groups, including the Medical Research Council and the Royal College of Physicians, suggested that the limit should be the end of the implantation stage – that is, about 15 days after fertilisation. Some groups suggested that the limit should be the beginning of the implantation stage – about eight days after fertilisation.

To summarise, although the pre-14 day embryo contains all the genetic material that the child will ultimately have, in another sense it is not the same individual as that child: indeed it is not an individual at all. It has the potential to develop into several individuals, and its nervous system has not yet started to develop. These were the main biological reasons why Parliament decided that research of certain kinds might be carried out on the early human embryo.

The law states that by the 14th day the embryo must either be placed in a woman's uterus to develop in the normal way, or be frozen so that it may be placed in the uterus later. In practice, embryo transfers are carried out by the fifth or sixth day at the latest, and usually by the second day. If transfer or freezing does not take place, the embryo may be used for research but must be destroyed by the 14th day. In practice any research will have been completed long before the 14th day.

Baroness Warnock, a philosopher, chaired the government committee on human embryo research and was Mistress of Girton College, Cambridge.

Organisers

In 1924 a remarkable experiment was carried out by two German scientists, Hans Spemann and Otto Mangold. They removed from one amphibian embryo a small piece of tissue that was destined to give rise to the notochord and grafted it into the ventral side of another embryo just under the epidermis. The result was that the ventral epidermis of the recipient invaginated to form a second neural tube. In fact eventually an almost complete second embryo was formed on the ventral side of the recipient. It seemed that the prospective notochord tissue had somehow influenced the adjacent epidermis to develop into nerve tissue which then led to the formation of all the other embryonic structures.

A tissue which induces an adjacent tissue to develop in a particular way is called an **organiser**. Prospective notochord tissue is a prime example of an organiser. However, it is now known that most embryonic tissues can exert an effect on their neighbours at *some* stage of development, after which they lose this ability. Equally, a tissue which responds to an organiser at a certain stage of development may lose its responsiveness later.

Spemann and Mangold's experiment was a milestone in the history of development biology for it was the first indication that cells can signal to each other and thereby control development. The nature of these signals and the way they orchestrate the changes that occur during development is the focus of considerable research at the present time.

▶ Cell signalling, page 59

Research on human embryos

Research on human embryos is permissible in the UK until the 14th day after fertilisation. Here guest author Professor Henry Leese explains the kind of research that is carried out.

The main types of research which are carried out on human embryos are:

Developing culture media for *in vitro* fertilisation

The development of a suitable culture medium in which to grow human embryos was a major hurdle facing early researchers in their pioneering work on *in vitro* fertilisation (IVF) (*page 508*). Improvements to the media have been made over the last 30 years, and continue today. Obviously embryos are needed to test the efficacy of the various culture media under trial.

Improving the success of embryo transfer

The major point of failure in IVF therapy is at the embryo transfer stage. Embryos are assessed for transfer on the basis of their appearance under the microscope and on how well they develop in culture. Many embryos show extensive cell fragmentation, a process that may occur by a type of programmed cell death known as **apoptosis**. Apoptosis is currently the focus of much attention, and research is also being carried out to devise more rigorous ways of assessing embryos.

One approach is based on the observation that those embryos which implant successfully have a higher glucose consumption than those which do not. The aim, then, would be to analyse the culture medium using ultra-sensitive techniques and choose those embryos which take up most glucose.

Improving methods of storing embryos

Further experiments are aimed at improving the procedures for freezing and storing embryos so that a woman can have the opportunity of receiving an embryo at a later date.

Research on assisted fertilisation

Over 30 per cent of infertile couples owe their infertility to some kind of disorder of sperm production or function, and until recently the problems were untreatable. Hope for infertile men has come from research which has led to the development of a new technique called **intracytoplasmic sperm injection** (**ICSI**) in which a single sperm is injected directly into the egg cytoplasm. This technique, devised by scientists in Belgium, is now used widely in human assisted conception clinics.

Development of a contraceptive vaccine

The sperm of a given species will only bind to the jelly coat of an egg belonging to the same species. This provides a key to developing an immunological method of contraception. The strategy would be to immunise the woman against the recognition proteins located on the egg or sperm. The antibodies against the egg or sperm would prevent fertilisation and act as a long-lasting contraceptive.

Research on chromosome abnormalities

Careful observation of human embryos created by IVF has revealed that about one third of the embryos have an abnormal chromosome content, preventing them developing into blastocysts capable of implanting, or leading to the births of abnormal babies. It is thought that these sorts of chromosome abnormalities are responsible for about 50 per cent of the 75 000 miscarriages that occur in the United Kingdom each year.

Diagnosis of genetic disease

Perhaps the most exciting area of human embryo research is that aimed at diagnosing genetic abnormalities.

About 14 000 babies are born in the United Kingdom each year with such defects as cystic fibrosis, haemophilia, Huntingdon's chorea and β-thalassaemia.

Half the babies born with genetic defects die in early infancy.

Embryo research offers the possibility of diagnosing genetic disorders at a very early stage of development.

Embryo screening

Diagnosis of many genetic disorders has been possible for some time by the techniques of **amniocentesis** and, more recently, **chorionic villus sampling** (**CVS**) (*page 748*). The trouble is that these procedures cannot be carried out until well into pregnancy. If the diagnosis of genetic disorders could be carried out before implantation occurs, affected embryos could be discarded and only the healthy ones put back in the uterus.

Currently, techniques are available which make it possible to remove one or more cells at an early stage of development – usually the 8-cell stage three days after fertilisation. The embryo is unharmed by this. In the meantime, the DNA in the isolated cell(s) is analysed for genetic disorders by methods involving the **polymerase chain reaction** (**PCR**) (*page 628*). The healthy embryos can be placed in the uterus immediately, or frozen for embryo transfer on a future occasion. Any unhealthy embryos may then be discarded.

All these remarkable developments culminated in the birth, in 1990 and 1991, of five babies whose embryos had been screened at the 8-cell stage. The women given this treatment had all had previous terminations of pregnancy.

Research on spare human embryos will continue to be necessary in order to devise new techniques, improve existing ones and ensure their safety. Only embryos which have been subjected to such rigorously tested techniques should be used for transfer to the potential mother.

Henry Leese is Professor in the Department of Biology at the University of York and a member of the Human Fertilisation and Embryology Authority.

30.3 Extra-embryonic membranes

The events described on page 528 apply to all chordates. In fact a transverse section through the trunk region of *any* chordate after neurulation looks more or less like the diagrams in figure 30.9. However, mammals (together with reptiles and birds) have an additional feature, namely a system of membranes which, because they are located *outside* the embryo, are called **extra-embryonic membranes** (*figure 30.10*). They are as follows:

- **Yolk sac** This is situated below the embryo to whose gut it is connected by a stalk. In most mammals the yolk sac is small and does not contain any yolk; it provides no food for the embryo and eventually shrivels up. It is the evolutionary equivalent of the much larger, functional yolk sac of reptiles and birds (*extension box on the next page*).

- **Amnion** and **chorion** These membranes grow up around the embryo and eventually enclose it in a protective, fluid-filled **amniotic cavity** (*figure 30.11*). The amnion is the inner of the two, so it forms the lining of the cavity. As the embryo grows, the amniotic cavity expands and pushes the amnion and chorion outwards until eventually they lie against the inner surface of the uterus.

- **Allantois** This arises as an outgrowth from the embryo's gut. The far end of the outgrowth expands into a balloon-like sac whose lining fuses with the chorion to form the placenta. The chorion develops finger-like **chorionic villi** which become invaded by blood capillaries and project into blood spaces in the wall of the mother's uterus (*page 509*).

The above description of the placenta applies to eutherian mammals (*page 101*). It does not apply to marsupials and monotremes. Marsupials, such as the kangaroo, have a placenta which arises differently from, and is simpler than, the allantoic placenta of eutherian mammals. Monotremes, such as the spiny anteater, lay eggs and have no placenta.

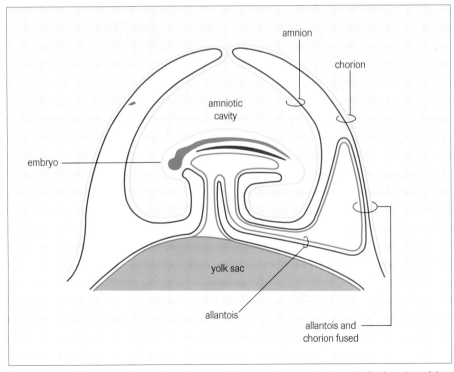

Figure 30.10 The extra-embryonic membranes of a mammal as seen in a longitudinal section of the embryo and associated structures. The functions of the various membranes and cavities are explained in the text.

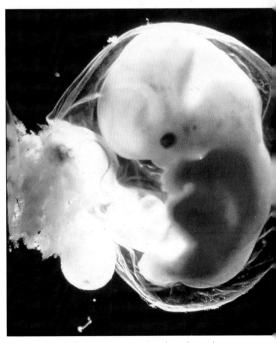

Figure 30.11 In this photograph, taken through a tube introduced into the uterus, the amnion can be seen surrounding the fetus. The fetus is just over 5 weeks old and is just 15 mm in length.

The extra-embryonic membranes of reptiles and birds

The extra-embryonic membranes of reptiles and birds develop differently from those of mammals:

- The yolk sac is particularly well developed in reptiles and birds. It is full of **yolk**, a highly nutritious fluid, and its lining is well supplied with blood vessels which carry the nutrients to the developing embryo.

- The fluid-filled amniotic cavity has the same function as in mammals, namely protecting the embryo.

- The allantois becomes a depository for nitrogenous waste. Since the embryo is surrounded by a shell, there is no way of getting rid of excretory matter, so it has to be stored out of harm's way. As the embryo grows and develops, the allantois becomes full of crystals of **uric acid** which simply stay there until the egg hatches. Uric acid as an excretory product is explained on page 294.

Meanwhile the allantois fuses with the chorion, as it does in mammals, but instead of developing into a placenta it forms a highly vascularised surface just beneath the porous shell. It enables gaseous exchange to take place between the embryo and surrounding atmosphere.

▶ Functions of the amniotic cavity and placenta, page 509

The fetal circulation

The placenta is the means by which the fetus obtains oxygen. Because of this, the fetus' lungs are not functional and the fetal circulation is different from that of the adult.

The basic plan of the fetal circulation is shown in the illustration. The **umbilical artery** carries deoxygenated blood from the dorsal aorta of the fetus to the placenta where the blood is oxygenated. The **umbilical vein** then carries the oxygenated blood from the placenta to the posterior vena cava of the fetus, whence it enters the right atrium of the heart. As the lungs are non-functioning, most of the blood bypasses them by flowing through a hole in the heart, the **foramen ovale**, which connects the right and left atria. Blood which misses it can take an alternative bypass, the **ductus arteriosus**, a short vessel which connects the pulmonary artery with the aorta. The foramen ovale is guarded by a valve which prevents blood flowing back from the left to the right atrium.

Changes at birth

At birth, the placenta is replaced by the lungs as the organ of gaseous exchange. This means that blood must now start flowing to them fully.

Within a few minutes after birth, the ductus arteriosus constricts so that from now on all the blood in the right ventricle is sent to the lungs. This, coupled with the closure of the umbilical vein, results in the blood pressure in the left atrium exceeding that in the right atrium. This has the effect of closing the valve of the foramen ovale, like the slamming of a door.

Within a few days after birth, the foramen ovale becomes sealed up by the fusion of its valve with the atrial wall. With the loss of the placental circulation, and the closure of the ductus arteriosus and foramen ovale, the adult circulation becomes established.

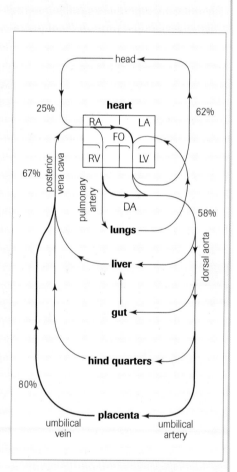

Plan of the fetal circulation. The thick arrows indicate the routes taken by blood in the fetus which are absent in the adult. The figures give the percentage saturation of the blood with oxygen in some of the major vessels. Investigations on the fetal circulation of sheep have shown that about half the blood entering the right atrium of the heart from the venae cavae passes through the foramen ovale into the left atrium. Of the blood which enters the right ventricle, nearly 80 per cent flows via the ductus arteriosus to the aorta. **RA** right atrium, **LA** left atrium, **RV** right ventricle, **LV** left ventricle, **FO** foramen ovale, **DA** ductus arteriosus.

30.4 Larvae

In the type of development described so far, the embryo develops directly into the adult. In some animals, however, the egg develops first into a **larva** which then changes into the adult. The larva is usually very different from the adult in form and habit, and the process by which it is transformed into the adult is called **metamorphosis**.

The way a larva fits into an animal's development is seen particularly clearly in amphibians. The larval stage is the tadpole, and it differs from the adult not only in its structure but also in its habitat, food and behaviour.

Amphibians are virtually the only vertebrates to have larvae. Larvae are more common amongst invertebrates. The best known are those of insects, such as the caterpillars of butterflies and moths, the maggots of flies, and the grubs of ants and beetles. These larvae are all adapted to life on land.

Other invertebrates have aquatic larvae which may be propelled by cilia, a flapping tail or jointed legs (*figure 30.12*).

Though varied in structure, all these larval forms have three basic features in common:

- They are markedly different in structure from the adult.
- They are self-supporting and lead an independent life, fending for themselves in ways that are generally different from those of the adult.
- They cannot reproduce sexually, and only in certain specialised instances can they reproduce asexually.

The fact that larvae and adults are so different means that they can exploit different habitats and never come into direct competition with each other.

The functions of larvae

Looking at animals in general, larvae have four basic functions:

- Motile larvae help to distribute the species. This is particularly important to slow-moving or sessile animals such as sea anemones and corals.
- In the case of parasitic species, the larva may enable the parasite to get from host to host. For example, the ciliated larvae of flukes swim through the water and infect new hosts (*page 712*).
- In some species the larva is primarily responsible for feeding and growth, prior to the formation of the adult whose principal function is to reproduce sexually. Such is the case with certain insects, notably butterflies and moths.
- In certain specialised cases, notably parasitic flukes, the larvae may be capable of asexual reproduction, thereby increasing the number of offspring produced (*page 712*).

Metamorphosis

Metamorphosis, the change from larva to adult, generally involves a profound reorganisation of the body. Nowhere can this be better seen than in insects.

Insect metamorphosis

Insects show two types of metamorphosis:

- **Incomplete metamorphosis**: We see this in locusts, grasshoppers, cockroaches, termites and dragonflies. The egg develops into the adult via a series of **nymphs** which are essentially miniature adults lacking wings. Moulting and growth take place between each nymphal stage (**instar**), giving the intermittent stepwise growth described on page 525. 'Incomplete' is not a very apt adjective for this kind of metamorphosis – 'gradual' might be better, since each moulting brings the animal closer to the adult form (*figure 30.13*).

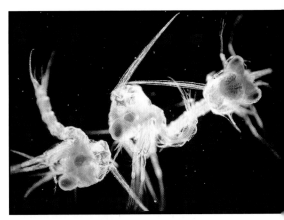

Figure 30.12 Larvae of the shore crab, *Carcinus maenus*, propel themselves through the water by flapping their jointed abdomen and appendages.
Magnification ×100.

Figure 30.13 The final moult of a dragonfly into the adult. From the shape of the old cuticle you can see that the adult is really an enlarged version of the preceding nymphal stage. Apart from size, the only major difference is that the adult has wings. The cuticle of the newly emerged adult is soft enough to allow an immediate increase in size. The abdomen lengthens by the swallowing of air, and the wings expand by blood being pumped into them from the thorax. Once the adult's cuticle hardens, no further growth can take place.

Metamorphosis, a radical transformation

Think of a cabbage-white butterfly and its larva, the caterpillar. They lead completely different lives, the larva crawling around and eating cabbage leaves, the adult flying from flower to flower and sucking up nectar.

It follows that metamorphosis must involve radical changes in the structure and functioning of the body. Not only must a completely different method of locomotion be catered for (wings instead of legs), but the change in diet makes it necessary for the biting and chewing mouthparts of the larva to be replaced by a long, flexible proboscis capable of removing nectar from flowers.

The larva and adult also need different digestive enzymes to cope with their respective diets. The adult also needs a reproductive system and the necessary behaviour to enable it to mate. These are unnecessary in the larva as it does not reproduce.

So the changes that occur at metamorphosis are not only structural, they are physiological too. To control the transition certain genes have to be switched off, and others on.

■ **Complete metamorphosis:** We see this in butterflies, moths, beetles, flies, bees, wasps and ants. The egg develops into a **larva** which is totally different from the adult. After an active life of feeding and growth, typically with several moults, the larva changes into a **pupa** which is usually dormant. Inside the pupa the larval tissues are broken down by phagocytes into a fluid mass. The only structures to escape this dissolution are the central nervous system and small groups of undifferentiated cells called **imaginal discs**. From these the adult organs are formed, nourishment coming from the now dissolved remains of the other larval tissues. Once the new body is complete, and environmental conditions permitting, the insect emerges from the pupa as the adult or **imago**.

Amphibian metamorphosis

The change of a tadpole into a frog does not entail complete destruction of the larval tissues – except for the tail which is digested by lysosome action. Amphibian metamorphosis involves more a modification of existing structures than their total replacement.

These changes are associated with the move from water to dry land: the tail is lost, the gills are replaced by lungs, and the legs (already present in rudimentary form) develop fully. Meanwhile changes take place in the heart and blood vessels, and a double circulation is established.

30.5 Seeds and germination

In flowering plants, development begins with the growth of the zygote into a simple **embryo** inside the **seed**. So to see the earliest stages of development we need to look inside seeds.

Structure of a generalised seed

The internal structure of a generalised seed is illustrated in figure 30.14. The embryo consists of an embryonic shoot (**plumule**), an embryonic root (**radicle**) and one or two 'seed leaves' (**cotyledons**). (Monocots have one cotyledon, dicots two – *page 95*.) The embryo is surrounded by a variable amount of **endosperm tissue**, and the whole is enclosed and protected within a tough **seed coat** (**testa**).

Recall, if you will, that the seed is derived from the ovule (*page 487*). The seed coat is pierced by a small aperture, the **micropyle**, derived from the pore in the wall of the ovule through which the pollen tube gained access to the egg cell. Close to the micropyle a small scar may be seen, a relic of the stalk of the ovule.

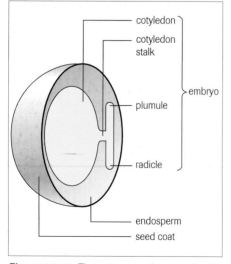

cotyledon
cotyledon stalk
embryo
plumule
radicle
endosperm
seed coat

Figure 30.14 The main parts of a generalised seed. The seeds of different species differ in the number and size of the cotyledons, and the amount of endosperm present.

Different types of seeds

Seeds differ in all sorts of ways but the most fundamental difference is in the size and thickness of the cotyledon(s), and in the amount of endosperm tissue present.

The function of the endosperm is to provide nourishment for the embryo and – if there is enough – for the young plant when it grows out of the seed. The embryo is always surrounded by endosperm tissue during the early stages of seed development, but in some species such as beans and peas it is used up so quickly by the embryo that there is none left by the time the seed matures.

Basically there are two types of seed:

- Seeds with thick, food-filled cotyledons and little or no endosperm. In such seeds, the *cotyledons* provide nourishment for the newly emerging plant. Examples are broad beans and peas.
- Seeds with lots of endosperm and thin, scale-like, cotyledons. In this case the *endosperm* nourishes the newly emerging plant. Examples are wheat and maize seeds.

Extension

Seeds as a source of food

Seeds contain a dehydrated, and therefore concentrated, store of food for nourishing the emerging plant before it can support itself. This makes them a good source of food for humans and other animals. Sometimes the stored food is in the cotyledons, sometimes in the endosperm. The main food stored is usually starch or oil, though other nutrients such as protein, vitamins and minerals may also be present in varying amounts.

Starch seeds

Examples include broad beans, wheat and maize. The starch is in the cotyledons (peas and beans) or endosperm (wheat and maize) – see illustration.

The cotyledons of the broad bean are full of starch while appreciable amounts of sodium, calcium and a variety of vitamins, including vitamin C, are also present in the seed coat.

Wheat seeds ('grain') are, of course, used for making bread. The endosperm is largely starch, with some protein too (about 12 per cent). The bran (seed coat and fruit wall fused together) contains cellulose (fibre), which is one reason why wholemeal bread is particularly recommended. Various vitamins and minerals and a little oil are also present in wheat seeds.

Maize seeds are used for feeding livestock and are a staple part of the human diet in many parts of the world. In Mexico, for example, tortillas are made from maize.

Starch, from whichever types of seeds, can be readily converted into sugars and/or alcohol which are then used for various purposes (*pages 134 and 148*).

Oil seeds

Examples include castor bean, sunflower, rape (the bright yellow-flowered crop which increasingly adorns the British countryside in the spring) and the oil palm (*page 493*). The oil is either in the endosperm (castor bean) or cotyledons (sunflower and rape).

Seed oils are used in cooking and for manufacturing margarine. For health reasons, vegetable oils are generally preferable to animal fats in the diet (*page 24*). The castor bean provides castor oil which is a laxative, linseed oil (obtained from flax seeds) is a constituent of paints and is used for treating wood, and oils from seeds such as sunflower and grapes are used for dressing salads. The residue left after extracting oil from rape and flax seeds makes a useful feed for livestock.

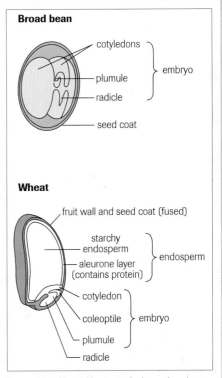

The seeds of broad bean and wheat showing the various parts, some of which are used as sources of food. Strictly speaking the wheat seed is a fruit as it includes the fruit wall, which is fused to the seed coat.

Germination

The process by which a new plant emerges and grows out of the seed is called **germination**. The radicle appears first and grows downwards into the soil to obtain water which is so vital for cell processes. Then the shoot appears and grows upwards out of the soil. Once the shoot is in the light, green leaves develop. Meanwhile lateral roots grow out from the main root, anchoring the plant and absorbing water and nutrients. The young plant is called a **seedling**.

Figure 30.15 shows a young broad bean seedling on which the above description is based. Notice that the shoot emerges in such a way that the plumule is bent back on itself. This prevents the delicate growing points and young leaves from getting damaged as the shoot pushes its way up through the soil. In the seedlings of wheat and other grasses the plumule is covered by a protective sheath, the **coleoptile**, which breaks open when the first leaves appear.

Types of germination

There are two types of germination which differ from each other in what happens to the cotyledons:

- In **hypogeal germination** (*figure 30.16A*) the plumule is thrust upwards out of the soil, leaving the cotyledon(s), still enclosed within the ruptured seed coat, in the soil (*hypogeal* means 'below the ground'). Seeds germinating this way include broad bean and wheat. During its early growth the seedling is nourished by food reserves in the seed – in the cotyledons of the broad bean and the endosperm of the wheat seed.

- In **epigeal germination** (*figure 30.16B*) the plumule *and* cotyledons are thrust upwards out of the soil (*epigeal* means 'above the ground'). Seeds germinating this way have thin cotyledons which, once exposed to light, develop chlorophyll and start to photosynthesise. Before this happens nourishment is provided by the endosperm which is usually extensive in this kind of seed. Most seeds germinate this way, including sunflower and French bean.

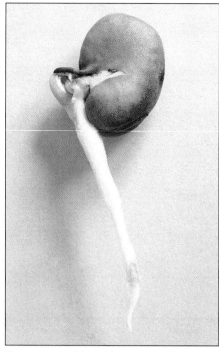

Figure 30.15 A broad bean seed germinating. The radicle has forced its way out of the seed coat and is growing downwards, and the shoot, with the plumule bent back, is just emerging. One of the cotyledons is just visible beneath the ruptured seed coat.

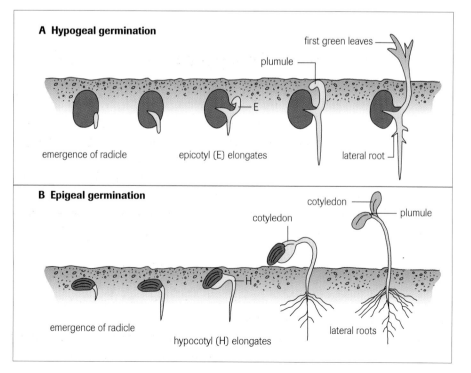

Figure 30.16 Diagrams showing the two types of germination. In hypogeal germination the shoot elongates at the point marked **E**, so the cotyledons remain below the ground. In epigeal germination the shoot elongates at the point marked **H**, so the cotyledons are thrust up above the ground taking the seed coat with them. In these diagrams, hypogeal germination is based on the broad bean, epigeal on the sunflower.

What happens during germination?

Germination starts with a rapid uptake of water by the seed, usually through the micropyle. This results in a dramatic increase in mass – more than 1.5 times the original mass of the seed in the case of the broad bean.

How is the water taken up? You will recall that the final event in the formation of the seed is the drying out of the embryonic tissues inside. This creates a massive water potential gradient acting inwards. When the time comes, water is absorbed by the dried-out cells and cell walls, first in the seed coat and then in the endosperm and embryo itself. This is called **imbibition**. With the hydration of the tissues, the soluble substances in the seed go into solution creating a solute potential which results in water being taken up by osmosis.

The uptake of water by the embryonic tissues causes the embryo to swell. This ruptures the seed coat, allowing the growing root to emerge. The shoot follows shortly after. By this time the enzymes are in solution and have started working, and the rate of respiration may increase a thousand-fold. The stored food materials in the seed (e.g. starch and lipids) are hydrolysed by appropriate enzymes into soluble products which are capable of being translocated to the tip of the root and shoot where growth occurs. One of the most important enzymes is **amylase** which hydrolyses starch into the soluble disaccharide maltose. This rapid mobilisation of food reserves is a requirement for successful germination.

Conditions needed for germination

Controlled experiments can be carried out in which seeds are deprived of the various conditions thought to be necessary for germination, and the effects observed.

Such experiments indicate that seeds require **water** (seeds won't germinate in dry soil), a **suitable temperature** (the requirements vary greatly but relatively few seeds will germinate in severe cold), **oxygen** (needed for respiration of the hitherto dormant embryo) and **appropriate illumination** (light for some species, dark for others).

These and other aspects of how germination is controlled are discussed in the next chapter.

Control of seed dormancy and germination, pages 567 and 568

30.6 Primary growth of the shoot and root

In plants, growth is achieved by cell division in certain localised regions called **growing points** or **meristems** (*figure 30.17*).

The principal meristems are at the tips of the shoot and root (**apical meristems**), and also at their sides (**lateral meristems**). The meristems of the shoot are enclosed in, and protected by, buds – the apical meristem in an **apical bud** and the lateral meristems in **axillary buds**. The term *axillary* derives from the fact that the buds occur in the angle (**axil**) between the stem and a leaf – or what may become a leaf. Leaves and axillary buds occur at regular intervals called **nodes**; the region of the stem between two successive nodes is called an **internode**. Axillary buds are potentially capable of forming **branches** or **flowers**.

The apical meristems of the root are protected by the **root cap** whose surface cells are brushed aside as the root grows through the soil. Root cap cells lost this way are replaced by new ones from the meristem. The lateral meristems of roots are located in the pericycle (*page 539*) and they can give rise to **lateral roots**.

If the apical meristem of a stem or root gets damaged, for example by frost or being cut off, then a lateral meristem can take over and allow continued growth to occur.

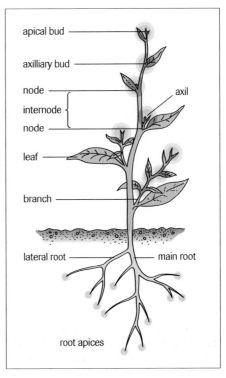

Figure 30.17 Diagram showing the positions of the primary meristems (growing points) of a plant. The meristems are ringed in pink.

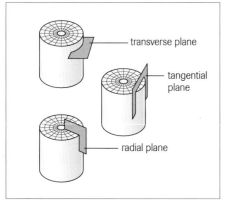

Figure 30.18 The planes in which cell divisions occur in a growing shoot or root.

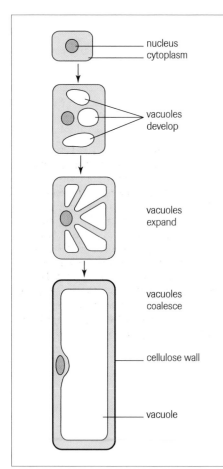

Figure 30.19 Expansion of a cell in the growing region of a flowering plant takes place by the osmotic uptake of water into the developing vacuole. To begin with only the primary cell wall has been formed (*page 42*). This is soft and stretchable, allowing the cell to expand as shown. When the cell reaches its full size the secondary wall is added, making the cell wall tougher and preventing any further expansion.

Cell division, expansion and differentiation

Meristematic cells in the stem or root are potentially capable of dividing in three different planes, and this determines the direction in which growth takes place (*figure 30.18*).

- Divisions in the transverse plane increase the length of the stem or root.
- Divisions in the tangential plane increase the diameter, i.e. the thickness.
- Divisions in the radial plane increase the circumference.

In the apical meristems most of the cell divisions are in the transverse plane, so the emphasis is on increase in length.

As new cells are formed, the older ones further back expand. Figure 30.19 shows how this happens. At first, the cell is full of cytoplasm with the nucleus in the middle. Then several small **vacuoles** appear in the cytoplasm. These soon coalesce to form the large, sap-filled vacuole typical of mature plant cells. Expansion takes place by the osmotic uptake of water into the developing vacuole.

The shape acquired by the cell depends on the elasticity of the cell wall in different directions, which in turn is determined by how the cellulose is laid down. The process is rather like blowing up differently shaped balloons. If cellulose is laid down uniformly all round the cell, expansion occurs equally in all directions and a more or less spherical cell results. This is how parenchyma cells develop. If cellulose is laid down unevenly, expansion occurs more in one direction than another and an elongated cell such as a xylem vessel may be formed. A plant cell may increase in length by as much as 40 times during its development.

Differentiation of the cells into particular types involves further elaboration of the cell wall. For example, deposition of extra cellulose at the corners results in collenchyma cells, and impregnation of the cellulose with lignin results in vessels, tracheids and sclerenchyma fibres.

Stem and root apices

The developmental processes outlined above fit in with what we see if we examine shoot or root apices under the microscope. Basically, three zones can be distinguished from the tip backwards:

- **zone of cell division**, where the cells are dividing;
- **zone of cell expansion**, where the cells are expanding;
- **zone of cell differentiation**, where the cells are developing into specialised types.

> **Support**
>
> ### Differences between animal and plant growth
>
> There are three fundamental differences between the growth of animals and plants:
>
> - Animals stop growing when they reach a certain size whereas plants go on growing throughout their lives – except of course when growth is suspended for environmental reasons.
> - In flowering plants growth is restricted to certain regions (meristems), whereas in animals growth takes place all over the body, though at different rates.
> - If part of a plant is cut off, the detached part will often grow into a new plant (*see page 490 for an example*). Apart from certain 'lower' animals such as *Hydra* and free-living flatworms, such powers of regeneration do not occur in animals.
>
> The versatility of plant growth, in particular the ability to regenerate, makes many plants capable of surviving assaults by even the most destructive gardeners.

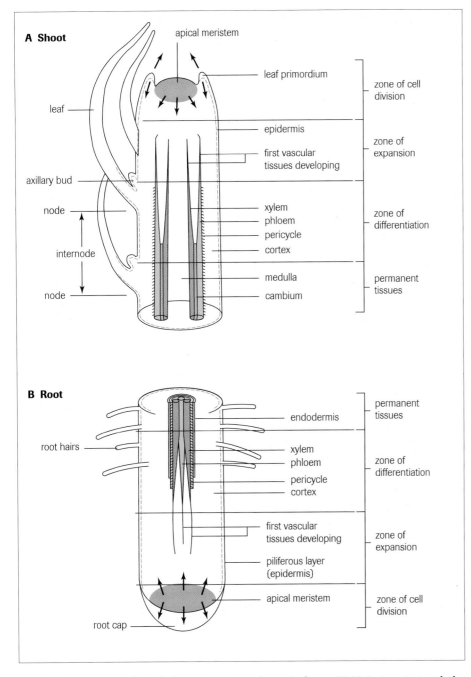

Figure 30.20 The internal structure of a dicotyledonous shoot and root apex to show how they grow and develop. Cell divisions in the apical meristem produce daughter cells which, with continued formation of new cells at the tip, enter the zone of expansion. Further back, the cells differentiate into specific types of tissue: xylem, phloem, parenchyma and so on. There is no sharp distinction between the zones of expansion and differentiation; the cells begin to differentiate while they are still expanding. In the diagram of the shoot, vascular tissues are not shown in the lower leaf although it would have started to develop by this stage.

These three zones in a dicotyledonous plant are shown in figure 30.20. Let us start with the shoot.

One of the first tissues to start differentiating, apart from the epidermis, is the vascular tissue (xylem and phloem). In fact the first vascular tissues make their appearance in the zone of expansion where they form a temporary transport system which develops early so as to nurture the apex. The bulk of the vascular tissues develop further back and form the xylem and phloem in the fully developed stem.

At the tip of the shoot, rudimentary leaves called **leaf primordia** arise just behind the apical meristem. These grow up and envelop the apex, forming the **apical bud**. In this way the delicate meristematic tissues are afforded protection. In the angle (axil) between each leaf (or leaf primordium) and the main stem an **axillary bud** may be found. Meristematic cells at the tips of the axillary buds have the potential to form side branches or flowers.

Now for the root. Though positioned differently, the vascular tissues arise in much the

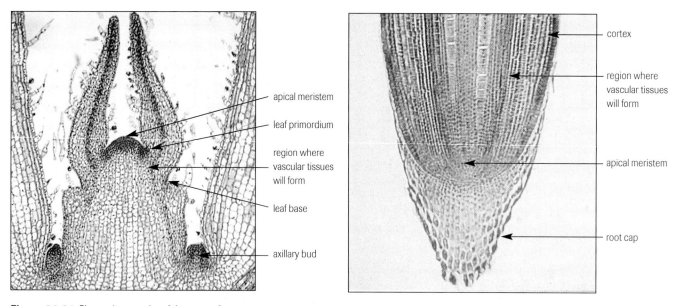

apical meristem

leaf primordium

region where
vascular tissues
will form

leaf base

axillary bud

cortex

region where
vascular tissues
will form

apical meristem

root cap

Figure 30.21 Photomicrographs of the apex of a shoot (*left*) and a root (*right*).

▶ The primary structure of dicotyledonous stem, page 250; and roots, page 248

same way as in the shoot, xylem and phloem developing at an early stage. The meristematic tissue at the tip is protected by the **root cap** which is formed by cells at the extreme tip of the meristem. Further back, the root is covered by delicate **root hairs** which increase the surface area for the absorption of water and mineral nutrients (*page 248*).

Photomicrographs of shoot and root apices are shown in figure 30.21. The tissues formed so far are the result of **primary growth** and constitute the primary structure of the stem or root.

30.7 **Secondary growth**

Primary growth, as just described, increases the length of stems and roots but it does not add appreciably to their width. How, then, is the girth of such plants increased? This is achieved by **secondary growth** which takes place extensively in woody perennials like trees and shrubs, but only slightly in annuals and herbaceous perennials which die back each year.

Secondary growth depends on the presence, within the primary tissues, of meristematic cells which retain the capacity to divide after all the other cells have become fully differentiated. These meristematic cells comprise the **vascular cambium**, so-called because it is destined to give rise to new vascular tissues. It is usually just referred to as the **cambium**.

Initially the vascular cambium is a layer of undifferentiated cells wedged between the primary xylem and phloem – you can see it in the shoot apex in figure 30.20. Notice that the primary xylem is situated on the inside of the cambium tissue, the primary phloem on the outside. Secondary growth takes place by the cambium cells dividing repeatedly to form new xylem inwards and new phloem outwards. In practice more xylem is formed than phloem, so the cambium and phloem gradually get pushed further and further out. As the stem increases in girth the epidermis is replaced with **cork** which becomes the familiar 'bark' of trees and shrubs.

The xylem, when fully developed, is dead and comprises the **wood**. This provides strength and carries water and mineral salts from the soil to the leaves. The phloem, on the other hand, is very much alive. It carries soluble products of photosynthesis from the leaves to the roots and other parts of the plant.

Figure 30.22 shows in more detail how secondary growth occurs in the stem of a dicotyledonous plant during the first year. Comparable events, similar in principle but different in detail, occur in the roots.

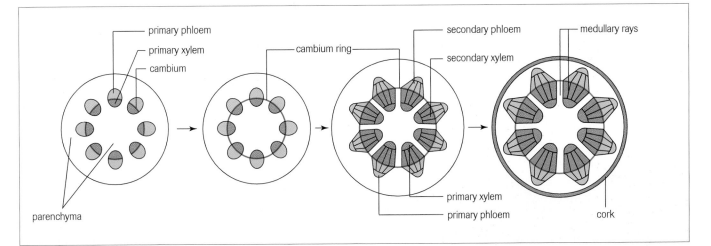

Figure 30.22 Secondary growth in a dicotyledonous stem during the first year. Initially the cambium tissue, shown here in green, is restricted to each vascular bundle, but soon the cambium cells divide radially and join up to form a ring. The cells of the cambium ring then divide tangentially to form secondary phloem on the outside and secondary xylem on the inside. As new cells are cut off, the older ones get pushed further away from the cambium ring, so the youngest cells are closest to the cambium and the oldest ones are furthest away. In places the cambium cells form parenchyma rather than vascular tissue, thus creating a series of radiating medullary rays within the mass of vascular tissue. The medullary rays are composed of living cells which transport nutrients radially across the stem. In practice more tissue is laid down inside the cambium ring than outside it, so the ring gets pushed further and further out. Periodically, the cambium cells divide radially to keep pace with the stem's ever-increasing circumference.

Annual rings and big trees

Secondary growth does not take place all the time. In temperate regions it stops in the winter. The secondary xylem formed the following spring contains a high proportion of vessels with thin walls and large lumens to carry water and mineral salts quickly to the developing leaves. As the summer progresses, the vessels become narrower and thicker-walled, and an increasing number of sclerenchyma fibres are formed. The summer wood is therefore harder and denser than the spring wood (*figure 30.23*).

The result of this seasonal growth is the formation of a series of concentric **annual rings**. These can be counted if a tree trunk is cut across, and they provide an accurate method of measuring the age of the tree. For example, counting the annual rings of some of the giant conifers in California has shown these trees to be over 3000 years old.

For the tree the importance of secondary growth is that, because it increases the strength of the trunk, the trunk can get taller and the canopy can be raised to a much greater height than would otherwise be possible. Figure 30.24 bears this out.

Sapwood and heartwood

If you look at the cut end of the trunk of a felled tree, you will notice a difference between the old wood at the centre and the younger wood further out (*figure 30.25*). The younger wood tends to be lighter in colour and is called the **sapwood**. Its cells are not fully lignified and it contains living parenchyma cells. It is the physiologically active part of the wood, transporting water and mineral salts from the roots to the leaves.

The older wood at the centre is called the **heartwood**. Often dark in colour due to the presence of tannins, resins and dyes, its cells are completely dead and they no longer transport water and mineral salts. Their only function is to support the plant.

The trunk is permeated by radiating **medullary rays**. Their function is to transport soluble food substances from the phloem to the living cells in the sapwood, to store starch, and to carry the soluble precursors of tannins, resins and dyes to the heartwood. The heartwood is much denser and harder than the sapwood, and the tannins and resins make it resistant to decay and to attack by insects. As you can imagine, this is the part of the wood that is favoured by the timber industry.

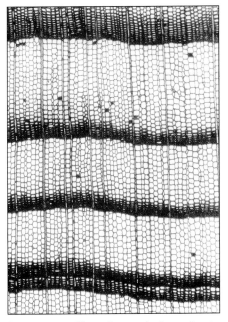

Figure 30.23 Photomicrograph of a small part of the secondary xylem of a redwood tree (*Sequoia sempervirens*) as seen in a transverse section. Each ring represents one year's growth. Notice the marked contrast between the thin-walled, large-celled spring wood and the thick-walled, small-celled summer wood.

Secondary growth occurs in conifers and dicotyledonous angiosperms. However, it does not occur in monocotyledons. There is therefore no secondary wood in monocots and that is why there are virtually no trees in this group of plants. One of the few exceptions are palm trees. Their stems are supported by numerous fibres and scattered vascular bundles formed as a result of primary growth.

Cork and bark

The great increase in girth resulting from secondary growth would rupture the surface tissues were it not for the fact that they, too, undergo a secondary growth process. Between the epidermis and the cortex, there is another layer of meristematic cells called the **cork cambium**. The cells of the cork cambium divide towards the inside and the outside to form new surface tissues (*figure 30.26*).

Cells formed inwards develop into **secondary cortex** which, like the primary cortex, is composed of living parenchyma tissue. Cells formed outwards become **cork**. Their walls are impregnated with **suberin**, a fatty substance which renders these cells impermeable to water and gases. The cells towards the surface of the cork form the hard, dead tissue characteristic of **bark**. (Bark, in the proper botanical sense, includes all the tissue, both living and dead, outside the wood – including the phloem.)

By the continued meristematic activity of the cork cambium, the surface of the ever-thickening tree trunk is kept intact and the living tissues underneath are protected against physical damage, attack by parasites and herbivores, and winter frosts.

Cork is impermeable to oxygen and carbon dioxide, so how do the living tissues underneath exchange gases? The answer is that here and there the suberised cells of the cork, instead of being tightly packed, form a loose mass called a **lenticel**. Here intercellular spaces allow gaseous exchange to take place freely between the inside and outside of the stem. This is particularly important for the phloem, whose transport activities require energy from aerobic respiration.

Figure 30.24 The General Grant tree (*Sequoiadendron gigantea*) in the Sierra Nevada, California. One of the largest trees in the world, it is well over 80 metres tall, and the base of the trunk has a mean diameter of over 11 metres. At 66 metres above the ground the trunk is still over 4 metres wide. The tree is estimated to be over 3000 years old. Fortunately, from the conservation point of view, the wood of these massive trees does not make good timber for building. It is, however, suitable for making toothpicks: there is enough wood in a tree of this size to make 5000 million toothpicks!

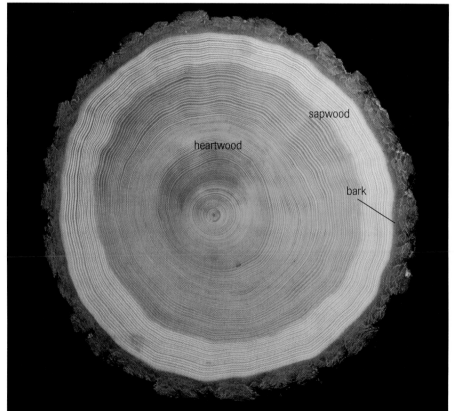

Figure 30.25 The cut surface of the trunk of a felled tree showing the heartwood, sapwood and bark.

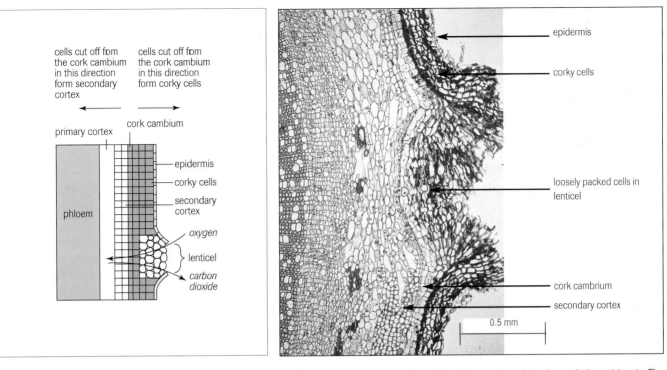

Figure 30.26 The formation of cork at the surface of a stem or root depends on the meristematic activity of the cork cambium beneath the epidermis. The cells on the immediate outside of the cambium layer are the youngest: they have cellulose walls and are alive. The older cells further out have impermeable walls impregnated with suberin and are therefore dead. They form the corky part of the bark. In the lenticel the corky cells are loosely packed, permitting gaseous exchange. The photomicrograph is a section through the bark of a tree and shows the same structures that are visible in the diagram.

Extension

Wood and the timber industry

Guest author Dr Tim King looks at the properties of wood and how they relate to the way we use this ubiquitous material.

The secondary xylem of trees – that is, wood – is light, strong, durable, flammable, easily shaped and relatively resistant to decay. Because of these properties, it is in great demand as timber and is of considerable economic importance. If you are in any doubt about this, think how many well-known objects are made of wood.

Softwood and hardwood

A basic distinction can be made between **softwood** and **hardwood**. Softwood comes from coniferous trees, whereas hardwood comes from angiospermous trees (*page 94*). Softwood is less dense than hardwood, and has a higher proportion of cellulose relative to lignin. Most of the cells in softwoods are relatively thin-walled tracheids whose primary function is to conduct water,

whereas most of the cells in hardwoods are thick-walled, heavily lignified sclerenchyma fibres, providing support.

Rapidly growing conifers are grown on a renewable basis in many parts of the northern hemisphere. One of the most widely grown is the robust Sitka spruce, native to North America but introduced on a large scale into Europe. The softwoods produced by these conifers are suitable for building, making cheap furniture and paper-making.

Angiospermous trees, on the other hand, tend to be slower-growing and longer-lived. Most of those that are used for timber, oaks for example, are extracted from semi-natural communities and are not replaced. The hardwoods they yield are used to make expensive furniture and veneers. Veneers are thin, polished sheets of wood, showing the characteristic hardwood grain, which can be stuck onto the surfaces of cheaper woods to make them

look more attractive.

Wood is also used nowadays as a renewable energy source for power stations. The woods used are mainly poplar and willow which are grown in large plantations and cropped regularly.

Special woods for special jobs

Many trees produce wood which is used for specialised purposes. For example, matchsticks are made from a variety of poplar which is grown in large even-aged plantations in southern Britain. Hazel has strong flexible stems suitable for making hurdles. This has been grown for centuries in coppices: the straight vertical stems are cut near the ground on an approximate 15 year rotation.

What makes particular woods suitable for particular functions? In some cases it is because of their chemical composition. For example, flammable woods such as the American torchwood have a high resin content which makes them ideal for firewood; and the Australian turpentine tree is particularly useful for underwater construction because its high silica content makes it resistant to the shipworm, a marine mollusc which bores into wood and can do untold damage.

In other cases the structure and arrangement of the xylem elements is the important factor. Here are three examples:

- Cricket bats are made from a certain variety of willow. The willow's xylem elements are resilient, having an ability to rebound after deformation – like a pneumatic tyre. If lighter woods were hit by cricket balls, the thinner-walled xylem elements would shatter; and if heavier woods were used, their thicker-walled xylem elements would not be flexible enough to be deformed.

- Pencils are made from the pencil cedar. The wood of this tree has an even texture without marked annual rings, making it easy for narrow grooves to

be made in it for accommodating the lead. It can be sharpened obliquely with a relatively blunt instrument, takes paint and varnish well, presents a smooth surface comfortable to hold, and – last but not least – it does not taste unpleasant to those who chew their pencils!

- Elm wood is cross-grained, some of the xylem fibres being arranged horizontally. This makes it tough, enabling it to resist splitting and shearing. It is therefore ideal for such things as chair seats, mallet heads and butchers' blocks.

Paper-making

This is one of the most important uses of wood. In Britain over 150 kg of paper products are used per person per year. These include writing paper, cardboard boxes, packaging, wallpaper, paper handkerchiefs and tickets. The major

trees used in paper-making are pine, spruce, eucalyptus and birch. The walls of their xylem elements consist of cellulose impregnated with up to 25 per cent lignin by mass.

Paper consists of a meshwork of cellulose fibres bound together. In the production of paper the wood is first ground into pulp. The cellulose is then separated from the lignin by chemical digestion carried out in a giant pressure cooker. Next, the bleached pulp is suspended in water over a fine sieve and, as the water drains away, the cellulose fibres begin to bind. After gradual dehydration in a complex mechanised paper mill, the paper is treated in various ways to make it suitable for its intended purpose.

Dr King researched in plant science and ecology at Oxford and, after teaching at Westminster School and Magdelen College School, is now Senior Master (Studies) at Abingdon School.

Summary

1. Growth results from **cell division**, **assimilation** and **cell expansion**.

2. You can measure growth by determining the increase in a linear dimension (e.g. height), volume, total mass or dry mass. Each has its difficulties, one being that different parts of the organism may grow at different rates (**allometric growth**).

3. Growth may be expressed graphically by a **growth curve** from which the **absolute** or **relative growth rate** may be derived. Growth curves may be obtained by measuring individuals of different ages at the same time, or individuals of the same age at different times.

4. In most organisms growth takes place smoothly, but arthropods show **intermittent growth**. This is caused by the presence of the hard **cuticle** which must be shed (**moulting**, **ecdysis**) before the body can expand.

5. The embryonic changes through which a chordate passes as it develops can be divided into **cleavage**, **gastrulation**, **neurulation** and **organogenesis**.

6. Mammals possess **extra-embryonic membranes** which form the **amnion** and **placenta**.

7. Fundamental changes occur in the circulatory system of a newborn mammal associated with the replacement of the

placenta by the lungs for gaseous exchange.

8. Some animals have a **larva** in the course of their development. The larva develops into the adult by **metamorphosis**.

9. In flowering plants, the embryo develops into a **seedling** when the seed **germinates**.

10. Two types of germination are recognised: **hypogeal** and **epigeal**.

11. Conditions required for germination include water, warmth, oxygen and suitable illumination. Internally a rapid mobilisation of food reserves takes place.

12. **Primary growth** of the stem and root takes place by cell division in **apical meristems** followed by cell expansion and differentiation.

13. **Secondary growth** takes place by means of secondary meristems which produce, amongst other things, **wood** and **bark**.

14. Wood is made use of in the timber industry. **Softwood** comes from coniferous trees and **hardwood** from angiospermous trees. Both have their uses, paper-making being one of them.

For general advice on these questions and advice on answering essay-type questions, see pages vii and viii.

1. (a) Distinguish between *absolute growth rate* and *relative growth rate*. (2)

The graph shows the growth of a human fetus during the later stages of pregnancy.

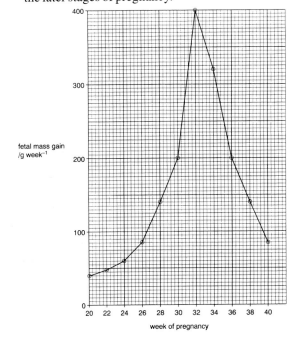

(b) With reference to the graph describe the changes in growth rate of the fetus during the last 20 weeks of pregnancy. (4)

(c) It has been suggested that fetal growth during the later stages of pregnancy is limited by the size of the placenta. Suggest why this may be so. (2)

(d) Describe the roles of the amnion during fetal development. (2)

(Total 10 marks)

UCLES 1997

2. In a survey of muscle growth, the widths of the upper arm and calf muscles in a sample of boys were measured and added together. The graph (top right) shows the mean rate of increase in total muscle width.

(a) Copy the graph and sketch a curve to show the mean rate of increase in total muscle width you would expect for a sample of girls over this age range. (2)

(b) If the total muscle width in an 8-year-old boy were 9.3 cm, predict what it would be at 9 years of age. (1)

(c) A longitudinal study was used to collect the results in this survey.

Explain one advantage of a longitudinal study over a cross-sectional study in conducting surveys of human growth. (2)

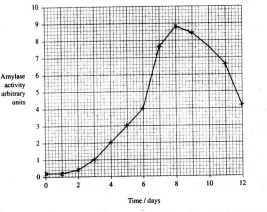

(Total 5 marks)

AEB 1996

3. Some barley grains were soaked in water and allowed to germinate. The graph below shows changes that took place in amylase activity in these germinating barley grains during the following 12 days.

(a) Calculate the rate of increase of amylase activity in the germinating barley grains between day 2 and day 6. Show your working. (2)

(b) Describe and explain the function of amylase in a germinating barley grain. (3)

(c) Suggest reasons for the change in amylase activity between day 0 and day 8. (4)

(d) The rate of amylase activity falls between day 8 and day 12. Suggest why a high rate of amylase activity is not required at this stage of growth. (2)

(Total 11 marks)

London 1998

4. Describe how secondary growth takes place in a plant stem. What advantages does it give to the plant?

(Total 10 marks)

Chapter 31

Control of growth

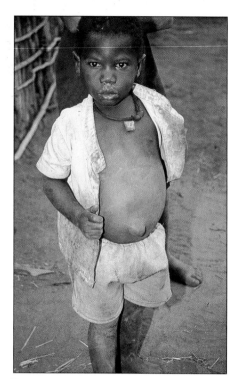

Figure 31.1 This child is suffering from protein deficiency disease (kwashiorkor). The disease is most common in developing countries where children are undernourished. Notice the swollen abdomen which at first sight might give the impression that the children are well fed. It is caused by severe retention of fluid in the tissues (oedema) which is one of the symptoms of protein deficiency.

In Chapter 30 we explained that growth is brought about by cell division, cell expansion and assimilation. Obviously any factor that directly or indirectly affects these processes will influence growth.

In this chapter we shall look at some of the main factors influencing the growth of plants and animals. We shall be concerned with the growth of the whole organism and of specific structures such as flowers.

31.1 Factors affecting growth

For convenience we can make a distinction between external and internal factors affecting growth.

External factors

External factors include a whole host of environmental influences: light, temperature, oxygen, food supply and so on. One of the most important is food supply. An organism has to be supplied with the necessary chemicals from which to make its structures and obtain energy. If any of these are in short supply, poor growth may result.

Protein

Protein forms the structural foundation of the body. For a growing child laying down tissues, at least 20 per cent of the food taken in should be protein. Even in a fully grown person the figure is around 15 per cent, as protein is needed for the maintenance and repair of the tissues. If protein is in short supply because of inadequacies in the diet, the person may suffer from **protein deficiency disease (kwashiorkor)**. A child suffering from this condition is physically weak and shows retarded growth (*figure 31.1*).

Plants of course synthesise their own proteins, but to do so they must be supplied with the necessary inorganic raw materials such as nitrates. Plants growing in nitrogen-deficient soil may not be able to synthesise enough protein, and in consequence may show stunted growth and development. Some species have special adaptations for obtaining the necessary nitrogen compounds for making proteins (*page 259*).

Light

This is one of the most important external factors influencing plant growth. Light is needed for the synthesis and action of chlorophyll without which photosynthesis cannot take place.

If you grow a seedling in the dark it becomes **etiolated** (*figure 31.2*). The plant is yellow, due to lack of chlorophyll, the leaves fail to expand, and the stem is long and spindly, the distance between successive nodes being greater than usual. On the other hand, growth of the *roots* may be exceptionally strong.

Temperature

Unless it can control its body temperature, an organism's metabolic rate is increased by a rise in temperature. It is therefore not surprising to find that growth and development take place more rapidly the higher the temperature. Provided other conditions are favourable, a plant will grow more quickly in warm weather than in cold weather, and a tadpole will develop faster in a warm pond than in a cold pond.

Temperature is one of several factors controlling germination and flowering, as we shall

Figure 31.2 Etiolated bluebells which had been covered by a board that was lying on the soil.

see later. It also affects secondary thickening. Because of its effect on the rate of cell division, more secondary xylem is formed in warm conditions than in cooler conditions. This means that warm summers tend to give thicker annual rings than cool summers. Of course, light and availability of water also influence secondary growth and it is sometimes difficult to decide which have been most significant in a particular summer.

Nevertheless, by analysing the annual rings of felled trees scientists can work out the climatic changes which have occurred in the past, and this provides a useful way of studying long-term weather patterns.

Oxygen

Growth of organisms, or parts of organisms, exposed to the atmosphere is not directly influenced by oxygen because there is always enough of it available. However, the oxygen content of water may vary, and this can have a pronounced effect on the growth of fish and other aquatic organisms.

Soil too can vary in its oxygen content and this can affect the growth of roots as figure 31.3 clearly shows. This in turn may affect the rest of the plant. It follows that well-aerated soil is essential for good plant growth. This is a major concern of farmers in managing their soil. Waterlogged soil has a greatly reduced oxygen content, so efficient drainage is essential in agriculture.

Internal factors

Internal factors affecting growth include the **genetic constitution** of the organism and the concentration of certain chemicals, including **hormones**, in the body *(page 564)*. These two factors are connected, for the genes generally influence growth through the action of such chemicals – and the latter, in turn, may affect the expression of genes.

Internal chemicals may of course be influenced by external factors. For example, lack of iodine in the human diet results in stunted growth because iodine is an essential constituent of the hormone **thyroxine** *(page 15)*.

The general principle here is that growth, like so many other aspects of an organism's functioning, depends on an interaction between external and internal factors. Nowhere can this be seen better than in the way growth is controlled in flowering plants.

31.2 The control of plant growth

Consider the basic problem: after a seed has germinated the shoot grows upwards and the root downwards. What makes the shoot and root behave in this way? Over the years many experiments have been done in an attempt to answer this fundamental question.

We shall take an historical approach as it illustrates how science progresses. Some of the investigations provide 'textbook' examples of the scientific method. Be critical though, as you read about them, and try to think of alternative explanations of the results. Many of the experiments involve using **coleoptiles**. The coleoptile is a sheath that covers the young shoot of members of the grass family. It lends itself readily to experiments of the kind that we shall be describing.

Evidence for the involvement of a growth-promoting substance

If you cut off its tip, a coleoptile stops growing; if you put the tip back, growth starts up again. This and other observations carried out in the early years of the 20th century gave scientists the idea that the tip of the coleoptile exerts an influence over the region further back, causing growth to take place.

What form might this influence take? One possibility is that it is a chemical which passes down the coleoptile from the tip. This hypothesis was tested by the simple experiment summarised in figure 31.4. The tip of a coleoptile was cut off and placed on a

Figure 31.3 The effect of oxygen concentration on the growth of tomato roots. The plants were grown in separate culture solutions. The concentration of oxygen in the air was, from left to right: 1, 3, 5, 10 and 20 per cent. The normal oxygen content of atmospheric air is approximately 20 per cent. Notice the pronounced retardation of growth resulting from the lower oxygen concentrations.

▶ Other soil factors affecting plant growth including pH, pages 655-9

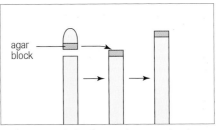

Figure 31.4 A simple experiment testing the hypothesis that a growth-promoting chemical is produced in the tip of a coleoptile. The experiment is explained in the text.

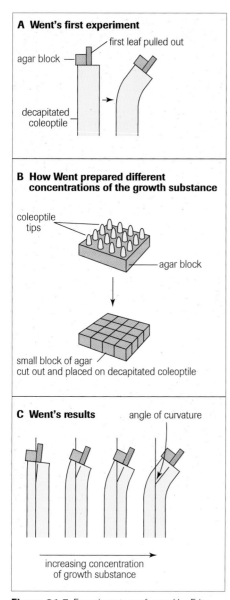

Figure 31.5 Experiments performed by Fritz Went to test the growth regulator hypothesis.
A The effect of placing an agar block containing the growth substance on one side of the cut end of a decapitated coleoptile.
B How Went prepared an agar block containing the growth substance at a particular concentration.
C The effect of increasing concentrations of the growth substance on the curvatures developed by decapitated coleoptiles. Measuring the angle of curvature is the basis of Went's coleoptile curvature test.

small block of agar jelly. Agar jelly does not affect the tissues, and soluble substances can diffuse through it freely. After about two hours the tip was discarded and the agar block placed on the cut end of the coleoptile. The result was that growth, temporarily inhibited by removal of the tip, resumed.

The conclusion was that a growth-stimulating substance, produced in the tip, accumulated in the agar and diffused back into the stump. Of course this experiment had to have a control – what do you think it should be?

Further experiments testing the growth substance hypothesis

In the late 1920s, Fritz Went, a young Dutch botanist, carried out a more detailed investigation to test the growth substance idea. First he collected the supposed substance in an agar block, as in the previous experiment. Then he placed the agar block on top of a decapitated coleoptile so that it covered only half the cut end (*figure 31.5A*). The result was that more growth took place on the side with the block on it than on the other side, so the coleoptile bent.

This experiment is not as easy as it sounds. For one thing, an agar block placed on one side of a decapitated coleoptile has an irritating tendency to fall off. Went got round this in an ingenious way. The first leaf of the shoot is just under the tip of the coleoptile. After decapitating the coleoptile, Went carefully pulled this leaf out slightly and cut the end off. In this way he made a natural partition which could be used to stabilise the agar block.

Went predicted that the more concentrated the growth substance was in the block, the more the coleoptile should bend. He tested this prediction by measuring the degree of curvature produced by different concentrations of the substance. He prepared different concentrations by standing varying numbers of coleoptile tips on identical blocks of agar for a given period of time (*figure 31.5B*). By spreading through the relatively large volume of agar, the substance became diluted. The final concentration depended on how many tips were placed on the agar: the greater the number of tips, the more concentrated the substance. The large blocks of agar were then cut up into smaller blocks, and placed on the cut ends of decapitated coleoptiles as before.

Obviously it is important that conditions should be the same for all the coleoptiles used. The tests were carried out at constant temperature, high relative humidity (to prevent the agar block drying out) and in dim red light of uniform intensity. Curvature was assessed after two hours, the angle being measured from photographs.

Went found, as predicted, that the greater the concentration of the substance, the larger was the degree of curvature (*figure 31.5C*). In fact, provided the concentration was not too great, *the degree of curvature of the coleoptiles was directly proportional to the concentration of the substance.*

The technique described above provides a convenient way of estimating the concentration of a growth-promoting substance which has been collected from a coleoptile or shoot: the biological activity of the substance is expressed in terms of the curvature of the coleoptile. It is known as the **coleoptile curvature test**.

Auxin and its effects on growth

The growth-promoting substance whose actions are described above is known as **auxin** from the Greek word *auxein* meaning 'to grow'. Early attempts to find out what it consists of chemically were fraught with difficulty because it occurs in plants in such minute quantities. Eventually a successful analysis was made and it turned out to be a ring compound called **indoleacetic acid** or **IAA** for short. That was in 1934, but it was many years before this substance became accepted as the auxin of earlier investigations.

IAA has an extremely powerful effect on growth. A solution of 0.01 mg in a litre of water applied to the side of a shoot is sufficient to cause bending (*figure 31.6*).

With a ready source of auxin at hand, quantitative experiments were carried out to show the precise effects of different concentrations on the growth of shoots and roots. The results of one such experiment are shown graphically in figure 31.7. Notice that over a particular range of concentrations auxin *stimulates* growth of the shoot but *inhibits* growth of the root. The suggestion in the graph that auxin at very low concentrations stimulates root growth should be treated with caution because the evidence is slender and depends on the species.

Auxin's principal function is to **stimulate growth**. It is synthesised in actively growing regions of plants such as shoot tips, apical buds and developing leaves and flowers. After being synthesised it is transported to regions further back, becoming more dilute as it moves along. As a result there is a concentration gradient along the main axis of the plant. Opinions differ on whether auxin is produced in root tips or gets there by transport from the shoot.

The reason why the concentration of auxin decreases as it moves along is that it is readily destroyed with time, mainly by being oxidised. The products of this degradation are biologically inactive, so this provides a natural way of removing auxin after it has done its job. The fact that auxin is so readily destroyed limits its use commercially, which is why artificial growth promoters are not auxin itself but synthetic substitutes (*extension box on page 552*).

How do auxins work?

How does auxin promote growth? There are two possibilities: it might increase the rate of cell division or it might facilitate cell expansion.

Evidence suggests that auxin works mainly by facilitating cell expansion. It allows the cell walls to be stretched more easily by the pressures which develop in the vacuoles (*page 538*). It is thought that auxin (indirectly) breaks the links between adjacent cellulose microfibrils, allowing them to slide readily past each other.

Does auxin have *any* effect on cell division? The answer is yes, but the effect is only very slight unless another growth substance is present. We shall meet this substance presently.

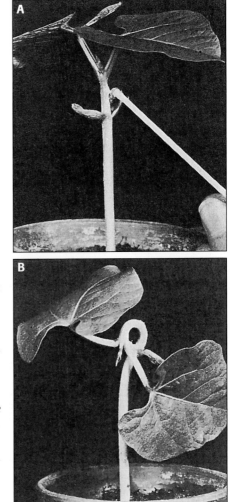

Figure 31.6 Some plants respond particularly quickly to growth regulators and are used for testing the effectiveness of different chemicals. Application of the substance in a suitable carrier such as lanolin to the stems or leaves of the test plant (**A**) may induce a marked growth response within a matter of hours (**B**).

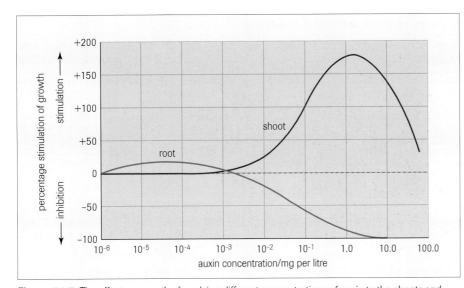

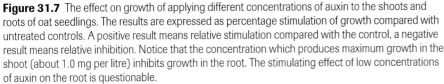

Figure 31.7 The effect on growth of applying different concentrations of auxin to the shoots and roots of oat seedlings. The results are expressed as percentage stimulation of growth compared with untreated controls. A positive result means relative stimulation compared with the control, a negative result means relative inhibition. Notice that the concentration which produces maximum growth in the shoot (about 1.0 mg per litre) inhibits growth in the root. The stimulating effect of low concentrations of auxin on the root is questionable.

Figure 31.8 The effect of removing the shoot apex of *Coleus*. The top photograph shows the plant shortly after the apex had been cut off. The lateral buds lower down are just beginning to develop into side branches. The lower photograph shows the same plant four weeks later. Notice how bushy it has become as a result of the growth of side branches.

Other auxin effects

Auxin is now known to influence many other aspects of plant growth and development. Here are four of its effects.

- **It inhibits the development of side branches**. This can be demonstrated by removing the apical bud from the top of a plant stem. After a short time, one or more lateral buds give rise to side branches. If, however, auxin is applied to the cut end of the main stem immediately after the apical bud has been removed, no such branching occurs.

  Auxin therefore suppresses the lower parts of the plant, a phenomenon known as **apical dominance**. Only if the inhibitory influence of the apex is removed will lateral growth take place. This is the theory behind **pruning**: cutting the top off the main stem removes the source of auxin, encouraging the sprouting of side branches lower down (*figure 31.8*).

- **It stimulates the growth of adventitious roots**. Adventitious roots are roots that grow out of the stem, such as happens when you take **cuttings** of a plant (*figure 31.9*). Cuttings can be encouraged to 'take' by dipping the cut end of the stem or branch in auxin or a synthetic substitute. Of course cuttings will often sprout roots without the assistance of externally applied auxin, but applying auxin speeds up the process.

- **It stimulates the formation of fruit**. Fruits develop from the ovary or receptacle in the flower (*page 487*). Normally this will only happen if fertilisation has taken place: auxin is produced by the embryo and this then causes the fruit to develop. In certain circumstances fruits are formed without prior fertilisation, a process called **parthenocarpy** (*extension box on page 553*).

Auxin also plays an important part in the way shoots, and perhaps roots, respond to external stimuli, a function which we shall return to later. In addition it is involved in secondary thickening and the falling of leaves.

Other plant growth substances

Since auxin was discovered, other substances which influence the growth and development of plants have been found. All these substances, including auxin, used to be called **plant hormones**. However, they are not really hormones in the same sense as in animals, so it is customary nowadays to call them **plant growth regulators** (**PGRs**). Let us look at them briefly.

Figure 31.9 Adventitious roots sprouting from the cut end of a stem of busy Lizzie (*Impatiens* sp.), an auxin-induced response.

Gibberellins

Way back in the 1920s a Japanese farmer noticed that some of his rice seedlings suddenly started growing fantastically tall. He called these plants 'foolish seedlings'. It was discovered subsequently by Japanese research workers that this condition was caused by a fungus, *Gibberella fujikoroi*, which secretes a mixture of related compounds called **gibberellins**. We now know that plants produce their own gibberellins in varying quantities and these have a very powerful effect on growth. The main one is **gibberellic acid** (**GA**).

Gibberellins **stimulate growth of stems**. They achieve this by increasing the length of the internodal regions. If a dwarf variety of a plant is treated with gibberellin it will grow to the height of the tall variety.

A spectacular demonstration of gibberellin's action is seen in a phenomenon called **bolting**, the precocious growth and flowering of certain plants. For example, the cabbage plants in figure 31.10 were each treated with less than one milligram of gibberellin. As a result they developed stems five metres long with flowers at the top!

Like auxins, gibberellins exert their growth-promoting effects mainly by causing cell elongation, though they stimulate cell division too. Some of their effects augment auxin's, others oppose them. For example they *stimulate* the growth of side branches from lateral buds.

Cytokinins

Another group of active growth substances was discovered in 1956. Known as **cytokinins**, they were first extracted from coconut milk but are now known to occur more widely in flowering plants. They are all purines related to adenine, one of the bases in DNA.

Cytokinins occur in very small quantities in plants but are most abundant in tissues where rapid cell division is taking place. Their principal function is to promote **cell division and differentiation** in developing roots, stems, leaves and flowers, but they will do this only in the presence of auxin (*extension box on page 554*).

Abscisic acid

In the mid-1960s two scientists at the University of California found high levels of a substance in cotton plants which appeared to cause the leaves to fall off. The falling of leaves and fruits is called **abscission**, so this newly discovered substance was called **abscisin**. Its chemical structure is now known, and it is called **abscisic acid (ABA)**.

Subsequent research has indicated that abscission is the one thing that this substance is *not* responsible for – at least not in natural circumstances. The most established role of abscisic acid is to bring about the **closure of stomata** in leaves suffering from severe water shortage. It works by stimulating the expulsion of potassium ions from the guard cells, which causes the stomata to close (*page 159*). Since this has nothing to do with leaf and fruit fall, the name abscisic acid now seems inappropriate.

Ethene

All the plant growth substances mentioned so far are complex compounds. However, plants also produce small quantities of the gas **ethene** (C_2H_4) which is involved in a wide range of developmental processes.

One of ethene's most important functions is the **ripening of fruit**. It promotes the conversion of starch to soluble sugar and triggers a sudden and dramatic increase in the respiration rate which leads to ripening.

Another important function of ethene is **wound-healing**. If a plant is damaged, ethene is released at the site of the wound. The gas then stimulates the formation of callus tissue which plugs up the damaged area. Ethene has also been implicated in **leaf and fruit fall**, as we shall see later.

The idea of a growth regulator being a gas may strike you as odd, but in fact it is rather sensible because it can diffuse rapidly from the place where it is formed to its site of action.

Figure 31.10 Bolting in cabbages. The three plants on the right were treated with 0.1 mg of gibberellic acid weekly. The control pair on the left received no such treatment. Normally cabbages do not flower until the second year. However, first year plants treated with gibberellin show enormous elongation and produce flowers, as shown here. With the cabbage plants is S.H. Wittwer of Michigan State University who discovered this particular response.

Commercial aspects of plant growth regulators

Plant growth regulators or their synthetic equivalents have all sorts of uses. Their main uses are summarised here by guest author Dr John Land.

Ever since the chemical structure of auxin (IAA) was discovered in 1934, scientists have explored the possibility of using it, and other growth regulators, in agriculture and horticulture.

The same approach has been adopted as in the search for medical drugs: a naturally occurring substance is discovered, its possible uses are explored, and attempts are then made to synthesise it – or an equivalent substance – in the laboratory.

Over the years numerous artificial growth regulators have been made in the laboratory and are now produced commercially. Although these **analogues**, as they are called, differ chemically from the natural substances, they share enough features in common to function in the same way. Natural IAA is compared with its analogues in illustration 1.

When, in agriculture, we apply a naturally occurring chemical to an organism, we are simply adding a little more of what is already there, so we are enhancing a *natural* effect. Moreover, after the chemical has produced its response it is broken down naturally in the environment. A naturally occurring chemical is therefore the ideal chemical. The same principle applies to substances used in medicine.

In assessing the usefulness of an analogue, various criteria must be taken into account. In particular, the substance should be effective for its chosen purpose but should not harm other organisms. It should be rapidly destroyed after being released into the environment – in other words it must be **non-persistent**. The manufacturer has a responsibility to avoid the use of persistent, broad-spectrum chemicals that may be toxic.

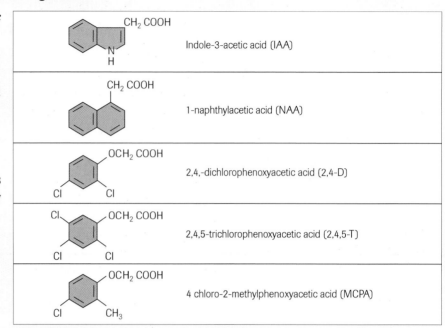

Illustration 1 The molecular structure of natural auxin (IAA) and its analogues. The names given are those currently used in the industry. Notice that the aromatic ring (coloured) is common to all the substances, which is why they all produce the same effects.

What then are the main uses of plant growth regulators? In the following account we shall refer to the analogues listed in illustration 1.

As selective herbicides

This is probably the best-known use of plant growth regulators – **hormone weedkillers**, as they are called. They are taken up by the leaves and translocated to all parts of the plant, so they kill the roots as well as the leaves. They exert their effect by interfering with the plant's growth and metabolism.

The beauty of these herbicides is that, when applied in the right concentration, they kill the broad-leaved (dicotyledonous) weeds but have no adverse effect on the narrow-leaved (monocotyledonous) plants, including grasses. MCPA and 2,4-D are often used to remove broad-leaved weeds from lawns or cereal stands (*illustration 2*).

Woody plants are killed by 2,4,5-T. During the Vietnam war, the United States Air Force applied vast quantities of this substance to the forests in Vietnam to remove the natural cover.

As growth promoters

NAA, as an analogue of IAA, induces root formation in cuttings. It is an ingredient of **rooting powders**. When applied to the cut surface of a stem or branch it supplements the plant's own IAA, increasing its concentration relative to cytokinins. This change of balance encourages the undifferentiated callus tissue which forms at the cut surface to develop into roots.

As growth retardants

Some artificial growth regulators are antagonists to naturally occurring gibberellins, so they have the effect of *reducing* the length of the internodes. When such a substance is applied to a cereal crop such as wheat or barley, it stops the stalks growing too long. This prevents the plants falling over (**lodging**), making them easier and cheaper to harvest.

When sprayed onto houseplants such

as chrysanthemums, these growth retardants restrict growth, making the plant more compact and attractive, and easier to manage.

As flower inducers

Gibberellin antagonists have another use: they induce flowering in woody perennials such as apple and pear trees which do not normally flower until they are several years old. Application of the substance causes the vegetative apex to become floral in the first year, thus ensuring a supply of fruit even when the tree is young.

Biennials such as sugar-beet and cabbage, which do not normally flower until the second year, can be made to flower at the end of the first year by applying gibberellin or one of its analogues.

Ethene is also used to induce flowering. For example, when applied to commercial pineapple plants it causes simultaneous flowering of the whole crop.

As fruit inducers

Normally a signal passes from the developing embryo to the ovary wall or receptacle, encouraging it to develop into a fruit (or 'false fruit' in the case of the receptacle). This signal is IAA, and it can be mimicked by NAA. When applied to unpollinated flowers of, say, a tomato plant or pear tree, fruits are formed without prior fertilisation (parthenocarpy, *page 550*). These fruits look very similar to the ones produced naturally when the plant's own IAA provides the stimulus. However, there is one notable difference – they are pipless!

When pollination of a flower is poor and some of the ovules escape being fertilised, the quantity of IAA released may be insufficient to cause full development of the fruit. Application of NAA can supplement the natural IAA and ensure the production of high-quality fruit (*illustration 3*).

IAA and its analogues are not the only way of influencing commercial fruit development. The gibberellin family of chemicals is used for producing seedless grapes and satsumas – very popular in supermarkets. Bananas that we eat are always seedless because they undergo parthenocarpy naturally.

As fruit ripeners

Ethene is given off naturally by many types of ripening fruit, and it accelerates the ripening process. Certain manufactured chemicals which release ethene can be used for ripening fruit. This is particularly useful for fruits such as bananas, which are picked and shipped green but have to be sold yellow. The fruit is sprayed with ethephon in the ship's hold and ethene is gradually released, encouraging the ripening process.

What about the future? In an ideal world we need crop plants which are highly responsive to growth regulators, but not susceptible to damage by herbicides. Producing such plants necessitates combining normal plant breeding practice with the skills of the genetic engineer (*page 629*).

Dr Land carried out research in plant physiology at Nottingham and Oxford Universities before taking up a teaching post at Marlborough College.

Illustration 2 The effects of a selective weedkiller on a broad-leaved plant. It has grown excessively and become distorted.

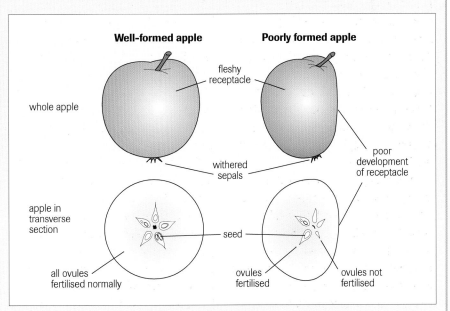

Illustration 3 An apple is a 'false fruit' formed by expansion of the receptacle of the flower (*page 487*). When only some of the ovules are fertilised, a lopsided apple may result. This can be avoided by spraying the flowers with NAA which causes the receptacle to develop into an apple without prior fertilisation (parthenocarpy).

Plant growth regulators working together

Here are two interesting experiments which help us to understand how plant growth regulators influence growth and development.

Experiment 1

This experiment concerns the formation of secondary vascular tissue from cambium tissue in stems. Short pieces of stem were prepared from which the buds (the normal source of growth regulators) had been removed. Auxin and/or gibberellin were then applied to the stems.

It was found that for xylem *and* phloem to be formed, auxin and gibberellin were needed together. Neither substance on its own produced complete secondary tissue. In fact the relative amounts of xylem and phloem formed depended on the *ratio* of auxin to gibberellin.

Experiment 2

In this experiment pieces of undifferentiated callus tissue were immersed in a series of solutions containing different proportions of IAA and a synthetic cytokinin called kinetin.

The callus tissue formed shoots or roots *or* proliferated into more callus tissue *or* stopped growing altogether, depending on the relative quantities of auxin and kinetin in the solution.

From these and other findings, a general principle emerges, namely that in flowering plants the pattern of development is determined to a large extent by the relative amounts of, and interactions between, a limited number of growth substances. Some of these substances oppose each other's actions: they are described as **antagonistic**. Others work together to produce the same effect: they are described as **synergistic**.

Figure 31.11 Positive phototropism in the shoots of cress seedlings. The seedlings were illuminated from the left-hand side. Notice that the plants have bent towards the light.

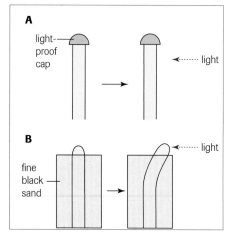

Figure 31.12 An experiment carried out by Charles Darwin and his son Francis on the cause of the phototropic response of coleoptiles. They illuminated a seedling of ornamental canary grass from one side, **A** with the tip of the coleoptiles shielded from light, and **B** with all parts of the coleoptile shielded from light except the tip. In **B** the coleoptile was buried in fine black sand with only the tip protruding.

31.3 Plant growth responses

Plants often respond to an external stimulus acting from a particular direction by a bending movement which involves differential growth – that is, more growth in one region than another. Such growth responses are called **tropisms** from the Greek word *tropos*, meaning 'turn'.

Two types of stimulus are particularly important in evoking tropic responses in plants: light and gravity.

Response to light

Growth responses to light are called **phototropism**. In general, shoots grow towards light, i.e. they are **positively phototropic**. Roots, if they respond at all, grow away from light, i.e. they are **negatively phototropic**.

The response of shoots to directional illumination can be seen in figure 31.11. More growth takes place on the darker side of the shoots than on the lighter side, with the result that they bend towards the light. Quantitative experiments in which coleoptiles are subjected to light of varying intensity and duration suggest that the response is generally proportional to the total amount of light received. Thus strong light of short duration produces the same degree of curvature as weak light of long duration.

The survival value of the phototropic response is obvious: it enables shoots to grow towards places where there is plenty of light for photosynthesis. But what is the mechanism?

The mechanism of phototropism

One of the earliest investigations into this question was carried out by Charles Darwin. Darwin is so famous for his theory of evolution that his many other contributions to biology are often overlooked. In 1880, shortly before his death, he produced a book called *The Power of Movement in Plants* in which he describes an experiment which he did with his son Francis. The experiment is illustrated in figure 31.12.

The Darwins experimented on grass seedlings. They found that a coleoptile failed to bend towards light if its tip was covered with a light-proof cap. If, however, a coleoptile completely covered *except* for the tip, it bent towards light in the usual way. The Darwins concluded that the stimulus of light was detected by the tip of the coleoptile and that some kind of influence was then transmitted to the lower part where it caused the bending to occur.

The idea that this influence might be a chemical is suggested by the two experiments illustrated in figure 31.13. In the first experiment a thin piece of mica was inserted into the side of a coleoptile just behind the tip. The mica created a barrier, preventing any chemicals passing back from the tip, but it did not affect the surrounding tissues. It was found that if the mica barrier was inserted into the coleoptile on the dark side, the coleoptile failed to bend towards the light. However, if the mica was inserted on the illuminated side, bending occurred in the usual way. It was argued that the mica prevented a growth-promoting chemical passing back from the tip on the dark side of the coleoptile.

The second experiment seemed to support this idea. The tip of a coleoptile was cut off. As you would expect, the decapitated coleoptile was completely unresponsive and did not grow at all. However, when an agar block was inserted between the tip and the lower part of the coleoptile, the latter bent towards light in the usual way.

It was concluded that a chemical from the tip had diffused through the agar into the lower part of the coleoptile (the zone of elongation) where it accelerated cell elongation on the darker side, thus bringing about the bending response. The chemical was believed to be auxin.

Is there an unequal distribution of auxin in the coleoptile?

A possible explanation of phototropism is that light causes an unequal distribution of auxin in the tip of the coleoptile, more on the dark side than on the light side. To test this hypothesis the experiment summarised in figure 31.14 was carried out. The tip of a coleoptile was cut off and placed on an agar block divided in two by a thin piece of mica. The excised tip was then illuminated from one side. After a time the tip was discarded and the divided agar block placed on the cut end of a decapitated coleoptile. The latter bent towards the right. It was concluded that the left half of the agar block contained more auxin than the right half.

This experiment was originally carried out in the 1920s by Fritz Went, whom we met earlier in connection with his coleoptile curvature test. He used the test to compare the concentrations of auxin on the dark and light sides of numerous unilaterally illuminated coleoptiles, and he claimed that approximately two-thirds of the auxin accumulated on the dark side.

Is auxin destroyed or does it move?

If directional light causes an unequal distribution of auxin, how is this brought about? Is it caused by destruction of auxin on the illuminated side of the coleoptile, or by the auxin moving across to the darker side?

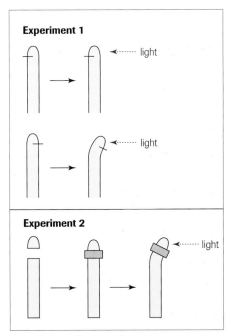

Figure 31.13 Two experiments to test the hypothesis that the phototropic response of coleoptiles is caused by a chemical produced in the tip. In the first experiment the thin piece of mica acts as a barrier to chemicals in the coleoptile but has no adverse effect on the tissues. In the second experiment the agar blocks are brown.

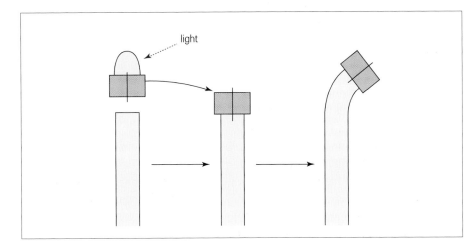

Figure 31.14 An experiment, carried out by Fritz Went in 1928, investigating the effect of directional illumination on the distribution of auxin in the tip of a coleoptile. Explanation in text.

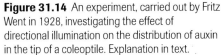

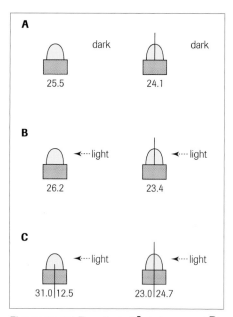

Figure 31.15 The effect of **A** darkness, and **B** and **C** directional illumination on the distribution of auxin in intact and divided maize coleoptiles. Explanation in text. The auxin concentrations were determined by Went's coleoptile curvature test. The figures represent degrees of curvature obtained when the agar blocks were placed on top of decapitated oat coleoptiles.

Information on this question is provided by the experiment illustrated in figure 31.15. Auxin is collected from intact coleoptiles and from coleoptiles which have been partially or completely divided down the middle by mica barriers. Study the diagrams carefully and draw your own conclusions.

The results, taken at their face value, support the idea that light affects the distribution of auxin within the coleoptile but does not destroy it – at least not at the relatively low light intensities used in this experiment. So it would seem that when a shoot is illuminated from one side, auxin is transported laterally to the other side where it causes the bending to occur.

With all these discoveries, the explanation of phototropism in terms of auxin became generally accepted. In recent years, though, it has been the focus of some very careful research which throws it into doubt. You are urged to read the extension box on page 558.

Response to gravity

Suppose you placed a young broad bean seedling horizontally in a dark chamber and left it to continue its development. After a day or so you would probably find that the shoot had bent upwards. This is a plant's normal response to gravity, and it is called **geotropism** (or **gravitropism**). In general, shoots grow away from gravity and are described as **negatively geotropic**. Roots tend to grow towards gravity and are therefore **positively geotropic**. The effect of gravity on broad bean seedlings is shown in figure 31.16.

As with phototropism, the survival value of these geotropic responses is obvious: it means that, however the seed is orientated in the soil, the shoot will grow upwards towards the light, and the roots downwards into the soil.

There are exceptions of course. Trailing plants, tree branches and side roots grow at all sorts of angles relative to gravity, and mangroves, which grow in tropical swamps where there is little or no oxygen, have 'breathing' roots which grow vertically upwards and project from the surface of the water where they can absorb oxygen from the air.

The mechanism of shoot geotropism

One way of explaining the negative geotropism of shoots is to propose that in a horizontally orientated seedling, auxin accumulates on the lower side of the shoot. This will cause growth to occur faster on the lower side than on the upper side, resulting in an upward curvature.

This hypothesis is consistent with the graph in figure 31.7 on page 549, which shows that, except at very low concentrations, auxin accelerates shoot growth.

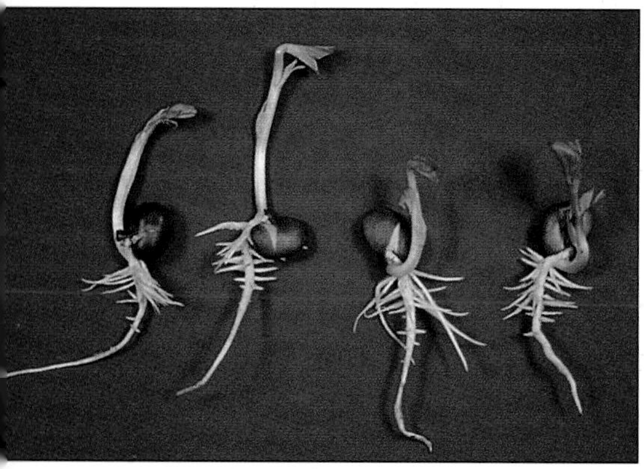

The mechanism of root geotropism

How can we explain the root's positive response to gravity? The most obvious explanation is that auxin accumulates on the lower side of the root where it inhibits growth, causing a downward curvature. This too is consistent with the graph in figure 31.7 which shows that, except at very low concentrations, auxin inhibits root growth.

For many years this was believed to be the explanation. However, an interesting discovery was made in the mid-1970s implicating the **root cap** in the response. Root caps were carefully removed from the roots of maize seedlings, and the seedlings were then orientated so that the roots were horizontal. It was found that the roots continued to grow horizontally instead of bending downwards. In other words, removing the root cap had abolished the geotropic response.

Figure 31.16 Geotropism in broad bean seedlings. Broad bean seeds were pinned in different orientations to a vertical surface and allowed to germinate. Notice that, whatever the orientation, the shoot has grown upwards and the root downwards.

In further experiments half the root cap was removed and the effect on the geotropic response observed. The effect of inserting barriers behind the root cap was also investigated. The results are shown in figure 31.17, and they suggest that a growth inhibitor is produced by the root cap. It was argued that in a horizontally orientated root this inhibitor might accumulate on the lower side, causing downward bending.

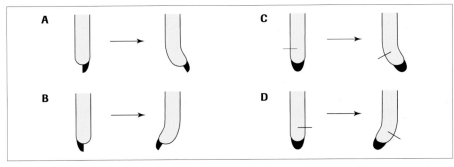

Figure 31.17 Experiments investigating the role of the root cap in geotropism. The root cap is shown in black. Removal of half the root cap encourages growth on that side, as does the insertion of a barrier just behind the root cap.

What might this growth inhibitor be? Research in the 1980s, in which the cut surfaces of decapitated roots were treated with growth regulators, suggested that it might be **abscisic acid** (*figure 31.18*). However, it has since been found that the roots of mutant wheat seedlings, which have no detectable ABA in them, give excellent geotropic responses!

Recently the focus of attention has been on calcium ions. One possibility is that these ions accumulate on the lower side of a horizontally orientated root where they make the cells more sensitive to a growth inhibitor, probably auxin.

Whatever is responsible for root geotropism, this whole story illustrates how science progresses in fits and starts, contradictory data spurring scientists on to put forward alternative hypotheses.

Other plant responses

Plants respond to other directional stimuli besides light and gravity. For example, roots appear to grow towards moisture (**hydrotropism**) and towards certain chemical substances in the soil (**chemotropism**). However, it is very difficult to show that roots really do respond to such stimuli and some plant scientists question the validity of these tropisms. (Why do you think hydrotropism is particularly difficult to demonstrate?) A less disputed example of chemotropism, though, is the growth of the pollen tube towards the ovary in flowering plants (*page 486*).

Some plants show tropic responses to touch (**thigmotropism**). An example is provided by the tendrils of climbing plants such as grape vines and sweet peas, which bend around solid objects with which they come into contact. Growth is slowed down on the side of the tendril experiencing the stimulus of touch (*figure 31.19*). In plants such as honeysuckle the stems and branches respond to touch, and this enables them to grow around objects such as drainpipes.

Nastic responses

Plants respond to a variety of stimuli that do not come from any particular direction, for example temperature, humidity and the general level of illumination. These are called **nastic responses**.

The opening and closing of flowers provides a good example. For instance, crocus flowers open when it is warm and close when it is cold (**thermonasty**), and the flowers of certain daisies open in the light and close in the dark (**photonasty**). In these cases the response involves differential growth or cell expansion in one part of the plant, resulting in a localised bending movement. In crocuses, for example, a rise in temperature causes

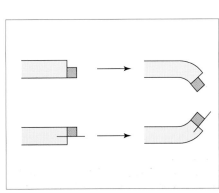

Figure 31.18 Another experiment on geotropism. If an agar block containing abscisic acid is placed in contact with one side of the cut end of a decapitated root, growth is inhibited on that side.

Figure 31.19 Response to touch shown by young grapevine tendrils. The top photograph shows part of a grapevine with young tendrils. Immediately after this photograph was taken a twig was placed in contact with one of the tendrils, and this is shown in the middle photograph. The bottom photograph shows the same tendril one hour later. Notice that the tendril has curved around the twig.

accelerated expansion on the inner side of the petals, so the petals bend outwards and the flower opens.

Much faster nastic responses, comparable to those of animals in their speed, are seen in the spectacular closing of the leaves of the sensitive plant, *Mimosa pudica*, in response to touch, and the rapid reactions of carnivorous plants such as the Venus fly-trap when small animals such as flies alight on them (*page 181*).

What sort of message is transmitted from the site of stimulation to the part of the plant which responds? There is some evidence that it may be electrical, with an ionic basis comparable to that which occurs in the nerves of animals. It has recently been shown that merely touching a tobacco plant causes calcium ions to be released from the plasma membranes into the cytoplasm of the cells. Perhaps this is the first step in the excitation process by which a stimulus generates an impulse.

Extension

Is the auxin story correct?

In recent years, doubt has been cast on the conventional explanation of phototropism. Dr Tim King explains.

The explanation of why coleoptiles bend towards light proposes that auxin moves across the tip of the coleoptile to the darker side where it stimulates elongation, thus bringing about curvature towards the light.

Let us ask some awkward questions about the proposed movement of auxin. For example, it has been estimated that in a single coleoptile, 200 million particles of light (photons) cause the movement of 2 million million molecules of auxin. How can one light photon possibly make 10 000 auxin molecules move? And if auxin does move, how does it do it? The cells in a shoot apex are relatively unspecialised, and there are no obvious transport cells. Presumably the auxin molecules move across the cells via the endoplasmic reticulum and from cell to cell through the plasmodesmata (*page 44*). Within the endoplasmic reticulum, however, what propels the auxin in a particular direction? What happens when auxin reaches a *dividing* cell, in which the normal structure of the endoplasmic reticulum is disrupted?

The answers to these and other questions may become clearer when more research has been done on plant cells. However, important evidence, inconsistent with the usual explanation of phototropism, has come to light which

simply cannot be explained away. This evidence is based on three main findings:

- Time-lapse photography has shown that for the first half hour or so after a coleoptile is illuminated from one side, growth markedly *slows down* on that side. This response, which is too rapid to be accounted for by changes in auxin concentration, can be induced by blue light on its own and it obviously contributes to the curving of the coleoptile.

- Oat coleoptiles and sunflower shoots will bend towards light even when their apices have been cut off, or when their tips have been covered with light-proof caps.

- The distribution of auxin in directionally illuminated coleoptiles has been investigated using Went's coleoptile curvature test and three different modern techniques which measure auxin concentration directly. The results of the coleoptile curvature tests closely resembled those obtained by Went. However, when the auxin concentrations were measured directly, they turned out to be the same on the light and dark sides of the coleoptiles, just as they were in dark-grown controls!

This last experiment has been repeated on sunflower and radish seedlings, with similar results. One possible explanation is that cells exposed to light make an inhibitor which inactivates auxin

molecules. If this happens on the illuminated side of a coleoptile, the latter would be expected to bend towards the light. This suggestion overcomes many of the difficulties, mentioned earlier, of explaining how auxin moves across the tip of the coleoptile or shoot. Perhaps auxin does not move at all! The blue-light growth reaction could be caused by a rapid synthesis of an auxin inhibitor, and the positive phototropism of decapitated coleoptiles could occur in seedlings which are capable of manufacturing the inhibitor well below the apex.

Some progress has been made towards identifying such an inhibitor. In radish seedlings, for example, a compound has been found which binds with IAA and can cause the shoots to bend when applied to the side of the apex in microgram quantities. Compounds like this might have considerable economic importance. For this reason the search is now on to identify this auxin inhibitor.

Dr King researched in plant science and ecology at Oxford and, after teaching at Westminster School and Magdelen College School, is now Senior Master (Studies) at Abingdon School.

31.4 How do plants detect stimuli?

We have seen that shoots and roots respond to light and gravity, but how do they detect these stimuli? We will look at gravity first, then light.

Gravity detection

Certain cells in shoots and roots contain special starch grains (or amyloplasts as they should more properly be called) which are believed to give the plant its gravitational sense. On account of their function, these starch grains are called **starch statoliths**. When a seedling is laid on its side, the statoliths fall under gravity to the lower side of the cells (*figure 31.20*). It is thought that this initiates the geotropic response, possibly as a result of the pressure exerted by the statoliths on the plasma membranes. There is a close parallel here with the otolith organ of animals (*page 398*).

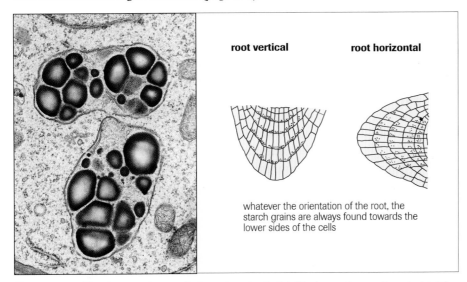

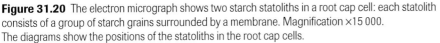

root vertical   root horizontal

whatever the orientation of the root, the starch grains are always found towards the lower sides of the cells

Figure 31.20 The electron micrograph shows two starch statoliths in a root cap cell: each statolith consists of a group of starch grains surrounded by a membrane. Magnification ×15 000. The diagrams show the positions of the statoliths in the root cap cells.

Evidence for this idea comes from the observation that if a vertically growing seedling is placed in a horizontal position and then returned to the vertical, a bending response is given only if the seedling was horizontal for a certain minimum period of time. This is called the **presentation time**. Now it has been found that if you raise the temperature, the time taken for the statoliths to fall and the presentation time both decrease. Indeed there is an almost perfect correlation between the two, as you can see in figure 31.21. Further, if you destroy the statoliths (by keeping the seedling at 35°C for a couple of days), the root will no longer respond to gravity at all.

These ideas fit in with experiments carried out years ago in which a horizontally orientated seedling is suspended in an apparatus called a **klinostat** and slowly rotated on its own axis. The result depends on the speed of rotation. If the rotation speed is very slow, the root becomes twisted like a corkscrew. This is because each side of the root is exposed to the gravitational stimulus for a sufficient length of time for a response to begin. If, however, the rotation is fast enough, the root grows straight. In this case each side of the root is exposed to the gravitational stimulus for such a short period that there is not time for a response to be given.

The starch statolith mechanism may seem plausible but there are some anomalies that need to be explained. For example, some roots respond too quickly for the response to be initiated by the settling of starch grains, and the roots of certain mutant plants which lack starch show perfectly normal geotropic responses.

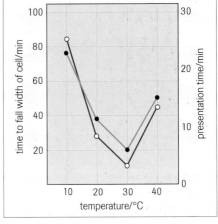

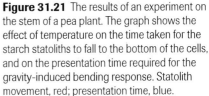

Figure 31.21 The results of an experiment on the stem of a pea plant. The graph shows the effect of temperature on the time taken for the starch statoliths to fall to the bottom of the cells, and on the presentation time required for the gravity-induced bending response. Statolith movement, red; presentation time, blue.

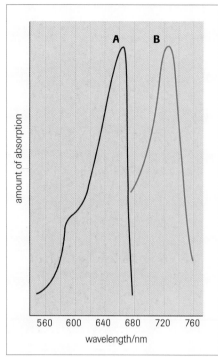

Figure 31.22 Absorption of light by phytochrome.
A Red absorbing form (P$_r$) with maximum absorption at 665 nm wavelength.
B Far-red absorbing form (P$_{fr}$) with maximum absorption at 725 nm wavelength.

Light detection

Animals can only respond to light if the light is first absorbed by a photoreceptor substance (*Chapter 22*). The same applies to plants, though discovering the nature of their photoreceptors has not been easy.

Phytochrome

It has been known for a long time that the seeds of certain plants, Grand Rapids lettuces for example, will germinate only if they are exposed, at least briefly, to light. Sometimes only a quick flash of light is needed.

In the early 1950s research workers in the United States Department of Agriculture carried out systematic tests on Grand Rapids lettuce seeds to find out which particular wavelengths of light were effective in bringing about germination. They discovered that red light in the range 580 to 660 nm was the most effective, whilst far-red light between 700 and 730 nm, inhibited germination. Far-red light is at the end of the visible spectrum, almost at the beginning of the infra-red band. It is barely visible to us, indeed some people cannot see it at all.

The interesting thing is that if a flash of red light is followed immediately by a flash of far-red, the stimulating effect of the red light is cancelled and germination in inhibited. In fact if seeds are exposed to alternating flashes of red and far-red light, the response is determined by the last flash in the series: the seeds germinate if the last flash is red, but fail to do so if the last flash is far-red.

On the basis of these and other experiments it was suggested that light is absorbed by a single photoreceptor substance which can exist in two forms, one capable of absorbing red light and the other capable of absorbing far-red light. This hypothetical substance was given the name **phytochrome** which means 'plant pigment'.

Subsequent research showed that such a substance really does exist. It occurs in extremely small amounts, about 1 part in 10 million, in the tips of growing shoots. Despite the tiny quantities involved, it was successfully extracted and isolated around 1960 and was shown to be a pale blue-green compound consisting of a pigment molecule attached to a protein.

The absorption spectrum of phytochrome corresponds nicely with the results of the germination experiments described above. It does indeed exist in two forms. One absorbs red light and has its absorption peak at 665 nm; the other absorbs far-red light with its peak at 725 nm (*figure 31.22*). These two forms of phytochrome are designated **P$_r$** and **P$_{fr}$** respectively.

The relationship between P$_r$ and P$_{fr}$

The two forms of phytochrome are interconvertible. When P$_r$ absorbs red light it is rapidly converted into P$_{fr}$ and when P$_{fr}$ absorbs far-red light it is rapidly converted into P$_r$. In the dark, P$_{fr}$ is slowly converted into P$_r$:

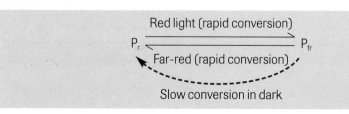

In natural sunlight, P_r is converted into P_{fr}, and P_{fr} into P_r. However, the former reaction predominates because sunlight contains more red than far-red light and in any case less energy is needed to convert P_r into P_{fr} than vice versa. So P_{fr} tends to accumulate during daylight hours, whilst at night it is converted slowly back into P_r:

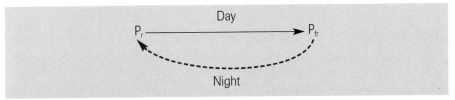

An important point about the phytochrome system is that, almost without exception, P_{fr} is biologically active whereas P_r is inactive. This does not mean that P_{fr} invariably stimulates growth; on the contrary, it sometimes inhibits it, as we shall see later.

Returning now to the lettuce experiment, we can see why far-red light inhibits germination. Treatment with red light causes the conversion of inactive P_r to active P_{fr}. But if red treatment is followed immediately by far-red, the P_{fr} is converted back into P_r before it has time to act.

Responses associated with phytochrome

Phytochrome is now known to be involved in many plant responses and developmental processes including germination, straightening of the plumule, stem elongation, leaf expansion, leaf fall, chlorophyll formation and flowering.

Of its many roles perhaps the most dramatic is the control of flowering. Flowering depends on alternating periods of light and dark, and the way this is synchronised by the phytochrome system demonstrates the delicate interplay between external and internal factors in the behaviour of plants.

Extension

Light perception in phototropism

Although phytochrome is responsible for many light-induced responses in plants, it is not involved in phototropism. Experiments in which seedlings are illuminated from one side with different coloured lights indicate that the phototropic bending of shoots is brought about by (mainly) blue light in the range 450 to 475 nm, so we have to look for a pigment which is sensitive to light in this part of the spectrum.

What is this pigment? The range of wavelengths which induce phototropism (that is, the action spectrum) corresponds to the absorption spectrum of carotenoids, so for some years this was considered a likely candidate. However, experiments carried out in 1995 seem to rule it out.

Mutant seedlings were produced which failed to give a phototropic response. It was found that these mutants contained normal amounts of carotenoids but lacked a certain protein which is present in normal seedlings and rapidly phosphorylated when irradiated with blue light. This protein is believed to be attached to a pigment – possibly a flavin – which perceives the light stimulus in phototropism.

The use of mutants in research on plant responses

The above story illustrates the use that can be made of mutant plants in research on plant responses.

The mutant plant is produced by treating the seeds with a mutagenic chemical (*page 742*). The seedling is then tested to see if it fails to give a particular response. It is then analysed chemically to find out if it lacks a particular substance which is present in the normal (wild type) plant. If it does, we may conclude that this particular substance is involved in the response.

We can go further than this, for the mutant tells us the function of the gene in the normal (wild type) plant. Using techniques of molecular biology described in Chapter 35, this and other comparable genes can be mapped.

A plant much used in this sort of work is *Arabidopsis*, a member of the mustard family. This plant is small, grows quickly and well in the laboratory, and produces thousands of seeds. Moreover, it has a relatively small number of genes (about 28 000) which makes the genetic analysis easier.

31.5 **The control of flowering**

Why do some plants in temperate regions flower in the spring and others in the summer or autumn? The principal factor is the relative duration of day and night. Figure 31.23 shows a striking example. Many other responses shown by both animals and plants are regulated by daylength, i.e. the duration of the photoperiod. The general term for this phenomenon is **photoperiodism**.

Let us consider the basic principle before we get into the details. In order to respond to daylength, the plant must be able to 'measure' the duration of the light period or the dark period – or both. It is now known that the critical factor is the duration of the dark period, in other words the time that elapses between two consecutive light periods.

On the basis of their differing responses to the photoperiod, flowering plants can be divided into three main groups:

- **Long-day plants**, e.g. petunia only flower if the period of uninterrupted darkness is *less* than a certain critical length each day. Long-day plants can be induced to flower by nights that are shorter than the critical length. On the other hand, they can be prevented from flowering by nights that are longer than the critical length.
- **Short-day plants**, e.g. chrysanthemum only flower if the period of uninterrupted darkness is *more* than a certain critical length each day. Short-day plants can be induced to flower by nights that are longer than the critical length. Conversely, they can be prevented from flowering by nights that are shorter than the critical length.
- **Day-neutral plants**, e.g. geranium are indifferent to daylength and will flower irrespective of the relative durations of light and dark which they receive each day.

Long-day plants tend to inhabit temperate regions where, at least in summer, days are long and nights short. Short-day and day-neutral plants, on the other hand, tend to live nearer the equator where days and nights are about the same length all the year round. Within the temperate zone, long-day plants tend to flower in the summer whereas short-day plants flower in the autumn. Spring cereals such as wheat and rye are long-day plants.

The dependence of flowering plants on the photoperiod is important commercially. For example, plants like chrysanthemums can be made to flower early by giving them extra darkness. In this way horticulturists can ensure that there is a good supply of colourful plants for the winter festive season.

More importantly, by careful adjustment of the photoperiod, early- and late-flowering varieties of particular species can be made to flower at the same time, thereby enabling plant breeders to cross them.

The role of phytochrome in flowering

Many experiments, too numerous to describe in detail, indicate that the phytochrome system is involved in the photoperiodic control of flowering. To mention the results of one experiment, it has been found that only red light inhibits the flowering of short-day plants, and this inhibitory effect can be cancelled by following the red treatment with far-red light.

Bearing in mind that far-red light converts P_{fr} back into P_r, it seems that a short-day plant will only flower if a sufficient proportion of its phytochrome is in the P_r form. The trigger to flowering could be either a high enough concentration of P_r or a low enough concentration of P_{fr}. Current opinion favours the latter view, i.e. P_{fr} inhibits flowering and its conversion back to P_r removes the inhibition, thus allowing flowers to develop. In other words, flowering of short-day plants is promoted by the absence of P_{fr} rather than the presence of P_r.

In long-day plants the reverse seems to be true: accumulation of P_{fr} resulting from long exposure to light, stimulates flowering.

For both short-day and long-day plants the critical factor is not just the amount of P_{fr} or P_r which is present, but also the duration of its presence. Rarely is phytochrome all P_{fr} or all

Figure 31.23 The influence of daylength on the flowering of *Kalanchoe*. The plant on the left was given 14 hours of light and 10 hours of darkness per day. The plant on the right was given 10 hours of light and 14 hours of darkness per day. In all other respects the conditions were the same. The two plants were genetically identical, having been grown from cuttings taken from the same parent plant. *Kalanchoe* is a tropical succulent which is grown as a pot plant in temperate countries.

P$_r$; both will be present together and how much there is of each will depend on the quality of the light. In natural conditions there is a dynamic equilibrium between these two forms of phytochrome and their relative proportions will determine whether or not flowering occurs.

Putting it very simply, the phytochrome system provides the plant with a way of telling what time of year it is, so that it knows when to flower.

How does phytochrome exert its effects on flowering?

The photoperiodic stimulus is detected by the leaves. This has been shown by covering the whole of a plant with a light-proof cover except for one leaf which is then subjected to light/dark treatment. Under these conditions the flowering response still takes place.

From the leaves the message is transmitted to the buds, some of which respond by changing into flower buds. These buds, instead of giving rise to side branches and leaves, develop into flowers.

The message itself takes the form of a chemical substance. This has been demonstrated ingeniously by grafting a short-day plant which has been induced to flower by exposure to short days to another short-day plant which has been prevented from flowering by being kept in long-day conditions. The result is that the latter blooms. The substance has been named **florigen**, but it has not been isolated and identified chemically. Functionally it seems to behave like a hormone. A scheme incorporating these ideas is given in figure 31.24.

Temperature and flowering

In view of its importance in influencing growth and development generally, it would be surprising if temperature did not play a part in the flowering process. Flowering is usually favoured by an increase in temperature, the optimum temperature being related to the part of the world that the plant comes from. In general, tropical plants tend to germinate and subsequently flower at higher temperatures than temperate, arctic and alpine plants.

Some plants need to experience a period of cold before they will come into flower. This is called **vernalisation**. Plants of this sort need to go through the winter before they will flower. In other words, the plant will not flower in its first year but will do so in the second year. This is typical of biennials such as foxgloves and cabbages.

We find the same thing in winter varieties of wheat and other cereals. The seeds are sown in the autumn and the seedlings survive the winter before resuming their growth and flowering the following year. Most root vegetables such as carrots, turnips and sugar beet, produce a large store of food in their first year. If this is left instead of being eaten by humans, the plant will use the stored food as a reserve for flowering in the spring or summer of the second year.

Many plants can be induced to flower early by vernalising them artificially. This is done by exposing the germinating seeds to a period of cold. The cold has to be applied just as the radicle starts to emerge, and it should be continued for several weeks. A temperature just above freezing (1–10°C) is required. By chilling seeds like this you can get plants to flower in the same year that the seeds are sown. In other words you trick them into thinking that they have been through the winter! In parts of Russia where wheat seedlings cannot survive the freezing temperatures of winter, the partially germinated seeds are artificially vernalised by keeping them in cold storage. They are then planted in the spring and will flower in the summer a few months later.

How do plants respond to cold treatment in this way? The stimulus is detected by the apical meristem. Grafting experiments suggest that the meristem then produces a substance which, directly or indirectly, initiates flowering. In most cases gibberellic acid will substitute for the cold treatment, suggesting that it might be the substance involved.

In many biennials vernalisation is only effective if it is followed by exposure to long periods of light each day, such as would happen in the spring and early summer. This has

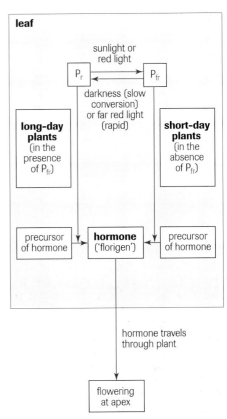

Figure 31.24 Scheme summarising the probable sequence of events that occurs in the photoperiodic control of flowering. Some of the research on which this scheme is based is described in the text.

Figure 31.25 An exceptionally tall woman is seen here with her family and pet poodle. Her tallness was caused by excessive production of pituitary growth hormone during childhood.

led to the suggestion that cold treatment may cause the production of a precursor which is subsequently activated by light.

Some plant species need to be exposed to a very high temperature before they will flower. Such is the case with cotton. This is one reason why such plants can only be grown in parts of the world with a hot climate.

31.6 The control of animal growth

We have seen that plant growth is regulated by chemicals. The same is true of animals. Here growth is controlled by **hormones**.

Human growth hormone

In humans and other mammals the hormone that has the most direct effect on growth is **growth hormone (somatotrophin)** produced by the anterior lobe of the pituitary gland. Having been secreted, it is carried in the bloodstream to the epiphyses of the bones and other sites where growth takes place. It stimulates growth by increasing the metabolic rate, the extra energy being diverted to cell division and protein synthesis.

The secretion of growth hormone by the pituitary gland is normally kept under tight control. Its release is triggered by a **releasing hormone** from the **hypothalamus** in the brain (*releasing hormones are explained on page 376*). Moment to moment control of growth hormone secretion is achieved mainly by varying the amount of releasing hormone produced, through a negative feedback mechanism

Despite this natural control mechanism, a person's pituitary may persistently secrete too much growth hormone. If this happens in a child who is still growing, the rate of growth increases uniformly throughout the body, resulting in a very large but correctly proportioned individual. This condition is called **gigantism** (*figure 31.25*).

Occasionally, over-secretion of growth hormone occurs in adult life, in which case new bone tissue is laid down in the body's extremities, particularly the hands, feet and jaws. These parts become greatly enlarged, a condition called **acromegaly** (from the Greek *akros*: end, *megas*: great).

If the pituitary secretes too little growth hormone in the adult there are few noticeable effects. However, if this happens while the person is still growing, the rate of growth may be severely reduced and the person becomes short and stunted (**dwarfism**). Intelligence and reproductive functions are, however, unimpaired. This condition cannot be rectified once adulthood is reached, but during childhood it can be treated by regular injections of growth hormone obtained from human sources or from genetically engineered bacteria.

Other mammalian hormones controlling growth

Pituitary growth hormone is not the only hormone that promotes growth in humans and other mammals. Insofar as it increases the general metabolic rate, **thyroxine** does so too, and under-secretion of it during childhood can result in stunted growth (*page 373*).

Another hormone that affects growth is the male hormone **testosterone**. Injections of testosterone can enhance the growth of muscles. This fact has been exploited by meat-producers for increasing the mass of their livestock, and by certain over-ambitious athletes for improving their performance. Neither is legal.

Control of breeding in mammals and birds

We saw earlier in this chapter that the flowering of plants is controlled by daylength, in other words the stimulus is a photoperiodic one. The same applies to many animals which have a **breeding season**, including numerous species of mammals and birds. It is obviously important that such animals should produce offspring at a time of the year when

Commercial aspects of mammalian hormones

Mammalian hormones, natural or synthetic, have a number of uses. Briefly they are as follows.

Controlling the time of ovulation

Farmers can influence the time of ovulation by administering carefully controlled doses of artificial hormones to their livestock such as sheep and cows. Take cows, for example (*page 514*). The strategy is to manipulate the duration of the luteal phase of the oestrous cycle so that the time of the next ovulation can be predetermined. Two alternative approaches are used: the luteal phase may be prolonged by administering progesterone and then ended by suddenly withdrawing the treatment, or the luteal phase may be ended early by administering prostaglandin. Either way, a new follicle will start developing in the ovary, leading to ovulation.

To be able to control the time of ovulation in a herd of cows is desirable for a number of reasons. It means that all the cows can be inseminated at the same time and the birth, feeding and rearing of the calves can be synchronised. Much the same applies to other livestock such as sheep.

Hormone treatment is also used for producing large numbers of embryos for cloning.

Promoting the growth of muscle

Muscle is meat, and hormones can be used to promote the growth of muscle. Steroid hormones, for example testosterone (anabolic steroids), and cow growth hormone (**bovine somatotrophin**, **BST**), have been used to increase the efficiency of muscle growth in cattle with obvious commercial benefits to farmers.

Stimulating milk production

It has been known for a long time that injections of BST will increase the milk yield of cows by 10–15 per cent or more without a corresponding increase in food consumption. The hormone causes the udder to increase in size and develop a more efficient blood supply, thereby increasing the rate at which milk is produced.

The side effects of anabolic steroids and BST on cattle, and possible long-term effects on human health, are debatable. Since 1994 the use of these hormones has been permitted in the United States and a number of other countries, but banned in the European Union.

The whole question is highly contentious. Some people feel that to enhance food production by unnatural means is morally wrong, while others feel that it is a practical and justifiable way of feeding the world's ever-increasing population. Between these two extremes are all shades of opinion. The controversy is further complicated by the fact that BST is made by genetic engineering and many people have a natural aversion to genetically engineered products.

---

environmental conditions are favourable and there is plenty of food available. Generally this is the spring or summer.

In animals which mate and produce offspring in the spring or early summer, increased daylength is the stimulus which brings them into the breeding condition. However, some animals mate in the autumn and produce offspring the following year. In these animals decreased daylength is the effective stimulus. Such is the case with red deer.

Numerous investigations have shown that the photoperiodic response is mediated by the hypothalamus and pituitary gland (*page 361*). The sequence of events is outlined in figure 31.26. The stimulus is received by the eyes from which nerve impulses are sent to the hypothalamus. The latter then produces **gonadotrophin releasing hormone** which passes to the anterior lobe of the pituitary gland. The pituitary responds by secreting **gonadotrophic hormones** into the bloodstream. These hormones cause the ovaries and testes to grow to maturity.

What exactly constitutes the stimulus in this photoperiodic response? Is it the duration of the light period each day, or the duration of the dark period? In plants we saw that the critical factor is the duration of the dark period, i.e. the interval between two consecutive light periods. The same applies to animals – at any rate to the Japanese quail which has been much used for studies on this topic. For quails to come into breeding condition, successive light periods must be separated by about 14 hours. In the laboratory you can get quails to breed at any time of the year by giving them light periods separated by this amount of darkness.

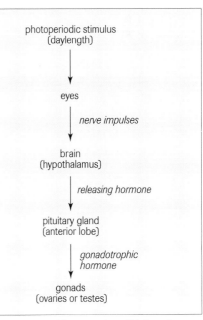

Figure 31.26 Many species of birds and mammals have a breeding season whose timing is controlled by daylength. This scheme summarises the chain of events which brings such animals into breeding condition.

The control of metamorphosis

Metamorphosis is the transformation of a juvenile form (larva) into the adult (*page 533*). This process, which involves extensive changes in the animal's anatomy and physiology, is controlled by hormones. Here we look at a well-known group of animals in which it occurs: amphibians.

Amphibian metamorphosis

Metamorphosis in amphibians such as frogs and toads involves the tadpole (larva) changing into the adult.

Amphibian metamorphosis is controlled by the hormone **thyroxine** secreted by the **thyroid gland**. Injecting thyroxine into a tadpole results in premature metamorphosis. Conversely, removing the thyroid from a tadpole prevents metamorphosis and results in an oversized tadpole.

More precise data have been obtained by treating tadpoles with radioactive iodine. These experiments are based on the premise that thyroxine contains iodine; tracing what happens to radioactive iodine should therefore tell us what the thyroid gland is doing at different times. It turns out that at metamorphosis there is a marked decrease in the radio-iodine content of the gland. This is because the gland has discharged its hormone into the bloodstream. The hormone then causes metamorphosis.

Further research suggests that metamorphosis is brought about partly by an increase in the amount of thyroxine in the bloodstream and partly by an increased ability of the tissues to respond to it. The hormone exerts its effects by influencing the genes responsible for the production of adult structures.

Growth hormones in general produce their effects by influencing the action of genes, and this notion is consistent with what we know about how other hormones work (*page 377*).

It seems that the animal can 'measure' the time between the light periods. In flowering plants we saw that this is achieved by the phytochrome system. In animals like the quail it is achieved by the hypothalamus functioning as a 'clock'. When successive light periods are separated by the correct interval, the activity of the hypothalamus – and hence the pituitary gland – is such that the animal is brought into season.

31.7 Dormancy and suspended growth

In certain conditions an organism may enter a state of **dormancy**, either as an adult or at some stage in its life cycle. Growth and development cease, and the metabolic rate may fall to the point that it is only just sufficient to keep the cells alive. In this way the organism can survive for many months, even years, without exhausting its food reserves.

Dormancy is closely geared to the environment. It enables organisms to withstand unfavourable conditions such as drought, food shortage and winter cold. It also allows time for dispersal by agents such as wind and water, whilst at the same time permitting any necessary internal changes to take place.

Seeds, buds, spores, eggs and plant storage organs can all be dormant. So can insect nymphs, larvae, pupae, and adults. The dormancy of seeds is usually associated with the hard, resistant **seed coat**. The fertilised eggs (zygotes) of many fungi and protoctists secrete a thick wall around themselves, thereby becoming resistant **zygospores** which may remain dormant for long periods of time. Much the same applies to asexually produced spores, including those of bacteria.

Plant storage organs such as tubers and bulbs enable plants to survive the winter from one growing season to the next, for which reason they are known as **perennating organs**. Buds provide a means whereby new leaves and flowers can develop after a period of suspended growth. This is important in deciduous trees and shrubs which shed their leaves before winter sets in, and form new leaves the following spring.

The mechanism of dormancy

The phenomenon of dormancy raises two fundamental questions: what induces it, and what brings it to an end?

The general answer is that dormancy is brought on, and subsequently ended, by environmental factors, particularly temperature and light, acting either directly or via internal chemicals. As a broad statement this would apply equally to animals and plants. One can further predict that there may be two interacting chemicals, one for promoting dormancy and the other for breaking it. With these general ideas in mind let us look at some specific examples of dormancy.

Dormancy in plants

Plants in general produce a number of dormant structures. In flowering plants the main ones are seeds, buds and perennating organs such as bulbs, corms and tubers.

Dormancy of seeds

Seed dormancy may be caused by a variety of environmental factors, including lack of oxygen, lack of moisture (causing the seed to dry out), or the presence of inhibitory substances which prevent germination. Also it may be necessary for the embryo within the seed to undergo further development before it can germinate, or the seed coat may be so hard and impervious to water or oxygen that germination simply cannot occur. In some cases it may be necessary for the seed coat to be scratched or partially digested in an animal's gut before it will germinate.

The seeds of many types of plant, particularly in temperate regions, must be subjected to a period of cold before they can germinate. This is known as **stratification** (not to be confused with *vernalisation* which is the exposure of plants to a period of cold before they will flower (*page 563*). Seed merchants stratify the seeds of some species before packaging them so that they will germinate as soon as they are sown.

Inside the seed, growth regulators have a role to play. For example, it has been discovered that the reluctance of certain seeds to germinate is caused by the presence of high concentrations of abscisic acid which acts as a germination inhibitor. On the other hand, dormancy can often be broken by treatment with gibberellic acid. The idea that the germination inhibitor may be opposed by gibberellic acid is supported by the observation that the concentration of gibberellic acid rises towards the end of dormancy. During germination gibberellic acid, released from the embryo, triggers the conversion of starch into soluble sugars which are then absorbed by the developing embryo.

▶ Structural and physiological aspects of seed germination, page 537

Dormancy of buds

Experimental evidence suggests that the cessation of growth and the formation of dormant buds in deciduous trees and shrubs is induced by the longer nights of autumn, so the stimulus is a photoperiodic one. As with seeds, buds require a period of low temperature, typical of winter, before growth can be resumed the following spring.

The lengthening days (or shortening nights) as spring approaches may be the trigger that breaks dormancy. However, increase in temperature is also important towards the end of the dormant period. Horse-chestnut buds, if brought into a warm house in the spring, will open much earlier than if they are left on the tree.

Internal processes controlling bud dormancy are highly controversial. Some years ago it was claimed that abscisic acid, extracted from buds, would inhibit growth but this is now questioned. Bud dormancy can often be ended by treatment with IAA or gibberellic acid, suggesting that one or both of these substances may be involved.

Extension

Leaf fall

Leaf fall (**abscission**) is associated with the formation of buds and winter dormancy in deciduous trees. The details vary from one species to another. However, the central event, common to most species, is the development of a layer of cells, the **abscission layer**, at the base of the leaf stalk (*illustration*). In the course of time the primary wall of the abscission cells dissolves under the action of enzymes, and the cementing effect of the middle lamella is lost. The result is that the cells separate from one another and the leaf becomes loose. At the same time the cells expand laterally, and this causes the leaf stalk to slough off the stem. Meanwhile, a layer of corky cells forms across the stump of the leaf stalk, protecting it from invasion by microorganisms and reducing water loss. This corky layer becomes the **leaf scar**, clearly visible in winter twigs.

At one time it was thought that abscisic acid was responsible for leaf fall. However, it now seems that ethene is responsible (*page 551*). Ethene becomes highly concentrated towards the base of the leaf stalk at the time of abscission. Moreover, placing a jacket of ethene around the base of the stalk can cause premature abscission. Ethene makes the cells of the abscission layer expand, breaking the leaf stalk. The ethene response is stimulated by long nights, acting via phytochrome.

Auxin is also involved in leaf fall. If the leaf blades are removed from a deciduous tree before autumn, leaving the leaf stalks still attached to the tree, the leaf stalks soon fall off. However, if auxin is applied to the cut ends of such leaf stalks, they stay on the tree. These observations suggest that during the summer auxin passes from the leaf blade down the stalk and inhibits abscission.

It therefore seems that the action of ethene is opposed by auxin. During the life of a leaf, auxin production gradually decreases until eventually leaf fall occurs. So here we have another example of a process which seems to be controlled by two growth regulators that oppose each other's actions.

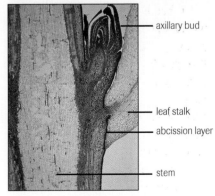

Photomicrograph of a vertical section through the leaf stalk of an old leaf, showing the abscission layer.

Survival during dormancy

There is much variation in the length of time a dormant organism can survive and remain viable. Seeds of lotus plants have been found embedded in peat on the site of an ancient lake in Manchuria. After their coats had been softened by brief immersion in concentrated sulphuric acid, most of them germinated successfully. Radioactive carbon dating showed them to be over 1000 years old. The current record is held by seeds of the Arctic lupin found in frozen silt in the Yukon. The seeds germinated successfully and were estimated to be between 8000 and 13 000 years old!

On the animal side, the record for longevity in the dormant state is probably held by the beetle *Buprestis aurulenta* whose larvae can survive for well over 40 years. Pupae of the gall midge *Sitodiplosis mosellana* are known to remain viable for at least 18 years.

There is also considerable variation in the severity of the conditions which can be endured by dormant tissues. Overwintering buds and perennating organs can of course endure freezing, and spores and seeds can survive long periods of drought. Dry seeds can survive freezing in liquid nitrogen ($-250°C$), and cysts of the unicellular ciliate *Colpoda* can withstand boiling. Dormancy is therefore an efficient way of coping with adverse conditions. Freezing is now used for the long-term storage of seeds.

It is interesting to speculate on how the tissues inside these dormant structures manage to survive. In seeds, the water content declines to a very low level, mitochondria and other organelles shrivel up and respiration can hardly be detected even with the most sensitive apparatus. If the tissues are dry, the formation of ice crystals within the cells, normally damaging, ceases to be a problem.

▶ The way organisms survive extremes of temperature, page 314

Dormancy of perennating organs

Perennating organs are formed by the swelling up of roots, stems or leaves (*page 490*). The formation of a swollen structure from one that is normally long and thin involves a suppression of the normal elongation process and its replacement by lateral expansion. Once formed, the organ becomes dormant and remains so until the following year.

The development of perennating organs such as tubers can be induced by a photoperiodic stimulus similar to that which induces bud formation. There is evidence that the stimulus is detected by the leaves, from which one or more hormone-like substances are translocated to the parts of the plant where the perennating organs are formed.

For subsequent development perennating organs need to experience a period of cold, similar to that which is required by seeds. Bulbs sold in garden shops have usually been 'prepared' by chilling so that they will sprout into new plants in the same year that you plant them.

Dormancy in animals

Amongst animals, a type of dormancy akin to that seen in plants is shown by many species of insects. It is called **diapause**, and can occur at any stage in the life cycle: egg, larva, pupa or adult. In the dormant state, the animal may survive and remain viable for months or even years. Typically it occurs during the winter, which is why you don't see many insects around at that time of the year.

Diapause, like dormancy in plants, is controlled by internal chemicals regulated by the environment. An insect's growth and development is promoted by a hormone secreted by its brain. Diapause seems to be caused by this growth-promoting hormone not being produced, at any rate in adequate quantities.

The hormonal changes which induce diapause are related to daylength. As soon as the hours of daylight fall below a certain critical level, diapause sets in. The critical amount of daily light varies from one species of insect to another. In the cabbage-white butterfly it is about 12 hours. When the light falls below this level, the pupae enter diapause and do not resume their development until the following spring. Surprisingly, insects do not register the photoperiodic stimulus with their eyes: covering their eyes does not abolish the diapause response. The light penetrates the cuticle and acts directly on the brain.

How is diapause ended? In some species the change to longer days may be the effective stimulus, but in many insects a period of cold has been found to be necessary before growth can be resumed – another parallel with plants.

Hibernation and aestivation

Hibernation is superficially similar to diapause (*page 313*). It occurs on a seasonal basis in many animals, including certain mammals such as the dormouse. As in diapause and other forms of dormancy, the metabolic rate falls to a low level with the result that the animal draws on its reserves only very slowly. Some hibernating animals, bats for example, wake up to feed from time to time, but otherwise all activities including growth are suspended.

Hibernation is brought on mainly by the fall in environmental temperature at the beginning of winter, and it is primarily a means of avoiding the need to maintain a high body temperature during the winter cold. To do so would necessitate keeping up a consistently high metabolic rate, a task which would require the consumption of more food than the animal could reasonably obtain during the winter.

Aestivation is like hibernation but it occurs in summer. This type of dormancy is a response to drought or excessive heat and some examples are given on page 295.

The distinction between hibernation and aestivation is not always clear. Many animals go into a state of partial or complete dormancy (**torpor** as it is called) at any time of the year, and for periods of varying duration, depending on environmental conditions.

1. Growth is influenced by a variety of external and internal factors.

2. In flowering plants, growth is regulated by **plant growth regulators** (**PGRs**). One of the main ones is **auxin** (**indoleacetic acid**, **IAA**) which promotes growth of the shoot and performs other functions as well.

3. Other plant growth regulators include **gibberellins**, **cytokinins**, **abscisic acid** and **ethene**. All have specific functions.

4. Plant hormones, or synthetic substitutes, are important commercially as growth regulators and, in the case of auxins, **selective herbicides**.

5. Plants respond to directional stimuli by growth movements (**tropisms**), e.g. **phototropism** and **geotropism**. Evidence suggests that these responses are brought about by an unequal distribution of hormone within the responding structure.

6. Plants also respond to stimuli which do not come from a particular direction (**nastic responses**).

7. Plants detect light by means of the photoreceptor substance **phytochrome**.

8. Phytochrome is involved in many light-induced responses including germination, stem growth, leaf expansion, leaf fall and flowering.

9. Flowering depends on the daylength and is an example of **photoperiodism**. Flowering plants can be divided into **long-day**, **short-day** and **day-neutral plants**.

10. In the photoperiodic control of flowering, it is the length of the dark period (night) rather than the length of the light period (day) that matters. The link between the stimulus and the response appears to be hormonal.

11. Temperature is also important in flowering. In some species flowering will only occur if the plants or germinating seeds are subjected to a period of cold beforehand (**vernalisation**).

12. In animals, growth is controlled by hormones, e.g. **growth hormone** from the pituitary gland and **thyroxine** from the thyroid gland.

13. Evidence suggests that the hormones controlling growth exert their influence by suppressing or activating the relevant genes.

14. Animals with **breeding seasons** are brought into breeding condition by changes in daylength, another example of photoperiodism. As in flowering, it is the length of the dark period (night) that matters.

15. Growth and development may be temporarily interrupted by **dormancy**. Dormancy is initiated and terminated by a combination of external and internal factors.

16. The dormant seeds of some plants require a period of cold before they will germinate (**stratification**).

17. In insects, **diapause** is comparable to dormancy in plants. **Hibernation** and **aestivation** are types of dormancy found in certain animal groups.

Part 5

Practice questions

For general advice on these questions and advice on answering essay-type questions, see pages vii and viii.

1. An experiment was carried out to investigate the effect of an auxin, indole acetic acid (IAA), and gibberellic acid (GA$_3$) on the elongation of segments of pea stem.

   A control group of pea segments received no added IAA or GA$_3$; other groups of pea segments were treated with equivalent quantities of IAA only, GA$_3$ only or both IAA and GA$_3$. The results are shown in the graph.

   (a) Calculate the percentage increase in the mean length of the stem segments between 12 hours and 24 hours in the control. Show your working. (2)

   (b) Comment on the growth of the stem segments over 48 hours:

       (i) when IAA only was added; (2)

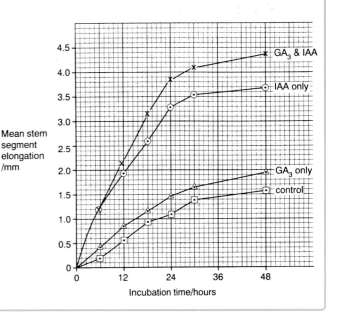

(ii) when GA₃ only was added; (2)

(iii) when IAA and GA₃ were added together. (4)

(c) Explain how IAA causes stem elongation. (3)

(d) Explain the part played by GA₃ in seed germination. (3)

(e) IAA related substances are often used in gardening. State one such use. (1)

(Total 17 marks)

O&C 1997

2. (a) Auxins and cytokinins are both plant growth regulators.

What are the particular functions in plant growth of

(i) auxins (1)

(ii) cytokinins? (1)

(b) In an investigation of the effects of auxin and cytokinin on growth, samples of tissue from tobacco plants were cultured. The medium used for each sample contained the same concentration of auxin, but differing concentrations of cytokinin. The results are shown in the table.

Concentration of auxin/ μmol dm⁻³	Concentration of cytokinin/ μmol dm⁻³	Appearance of tissue after incubation	Summary of effect
10	0		No growth
10	0.1		Roots growing
10	1.0		Disorganised growth
10	2.5		Several shoots
10	10.0		A few shoots; considerable growth
10	50.0		Limited, disorganised growth

From these results

(i) at what ratio of auxin to cytokinin do shoots grow best; (1)

(ii) at what ratio of auxin to cytokinin do roots grow best; (1)

(iii) what results would you expect at an auxin to cytokinin ratio of 2:1? (1)

(c) (i) Name **one** other plant growth regulator that would need to be present for the growth of roots and shoots. (1)

(ii) Briefly describe its role. (1)

(Total 7 marks)

NEAB 1997

3. Give an account of growth regulators in plant stems, in controlling growth and phototrophic responses.

(Total 20 marks)

O&C 1997

4. In order to maximise photosynthesis, plants grow or bend towards light, a process known as phototropism. Outline **two** experiments that could be carried out to support the hypothesis that phototropism is caused by a chemical (auxin) produced by the growing tip.

(Total 8 marks)

CCEA 1998

5. Flowering in the cocklebur plant occurs as a result of exposure to a period of darkness. The development of the flower has been divided into eight stages (0 - no flower, up to 8 - fully developed flower). The graph shows the average stage of flower development for two batches, each of ten plants, one of which was kept in the dark for 16 hours and the other for ten hours.

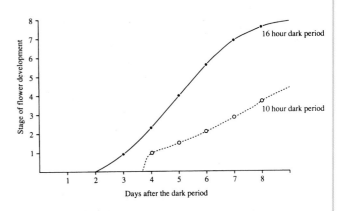

(a) Give **two** differences between flowering in the two batches of plants. (2)

(b) What system of communication in plants links the dark period to the development of flowers ? (1)

(c) Suggest explanations for

(i) the delay between the exposure to darkness and the start of flower development, (1)

(ii) the difference between the two batches after eight days. (1)

(d) Explain fully **one** practical application for this type of research. (2)

(Total 7 marks)

WJEC 1997

Chapter 32

The principles of heredity

W hat do giraffes have that no other organisms have? The answer is not long necks – ostriches have long necks – but baby giraffes (or parent giraffes). No one can help being struck by the often remarkable similarity between parents and their offspring, but it is just as noticeable that parents and offspring differ from each other in many respects. The science of heredity, or genetics, attempts to explain both the similarities and the differences between parents and offspring. Genetics began as 'pure' science, but applied genetics soon developed, and today the subject is of central importance to medicine and agriculture (*figure 32.1*).

We now know that information is contained in the chemicals that make up the **genes** which are located on the **chromosomes**. In recent years spectacular advances have been made in understanding the structure and functioning of genes. But the first major breakthrough in the study of heredity took place over 130 years ago, long before genes or even chromosomes had been recognised. The person responsible for this was a Moravian monk, Gregor Mendel, and the story of heredity starts with him (*figure 32.2*).

Mendel was born in 1822 and entered the monastery in Brunn, Moravia (now Brno, Czech Republic) in 1843. The monastery was unusual in that the young monks were encouraged to continue their academic studies. Mendel went to Vienna University where he became interested in plant breeding.

Starting in about 1856, Mendel carried out a vast number of breeding experiments in the garden of his monastery. He concentrated on the garden pea which has a number of pairs of clearly distinguished characteristics, for example, long versus short stems and smooth versus wrinkled seeds. With great perseverance and diligence he carefully isolated plants, transferred pollen from one to another, collected and sowed the seeds, and laboriously counted and recorded the different types of offspring. The conclusions he drew from his studies form the foundations on which the science of heredity is built.

32.1 Monohybrid inheritance

In the early stages of his work Mendel studied the inheritance of just one pair of contrasting characteristics, which is nowadays called **monohybrid inheritance**. In one such experiment he took a pure-breeding tall pea plant and crossed it with a pure-breeding short pea plant. (Pure-breeding plants are ones which, when crossed among themselves, always give rise to offspring which are like the parents.) The way Mendel crossed plants was to take pollen grains from one plant and dust them onto the stigma of another plant, having first removed the anthers of this second plant to ensure that it could not pollinate itself.

Mendel collected the seeds that resulted from crosses between tall pea plants and short ones, and sowed them. He found that the seeds, once they had germinated and grown into adult plants, always developed into tall offspring (*figure 32.3*). This was the case whether pollen grains from tall plants were placed on the stigmas of short plants, or pollen grains from short plants were placed on the stigmas of tall plants.

In these crosses, the original pure-breeding parent plants are referred to as the **parental generation (P** for short), and the offspring belong to what is called the **first filial generation (F$_1$)**.

Mendel then took these F$_1$ plants and self-pollinated each of them, precautions again being taken to prevent them being pollinated by any other kind of pollen. The resulting seeds were sown and the offspring – belonging to the **second filial (F$_2$) generation** –

Figure 32.1 A Einkorn wheat, an ancient species of wheat known from over 11 000 years ago before the cultivation of wheat began.
B Modern wheat, a result of applied genetics. Today's wheat differs from einkorn wheat in many ways as a result of selective breeding over thousands of years. Modern wheat has a far higher yield of grain. In part, this is because it is much shorter, meaning that more of each plant's photosynthesis can be channelled towards seed production.

Figure 32.2 Gregor Mendel, who first put the study of heredity on a firm scientific basis.

were examined. Mendel found that some of these F_2 plants were tall and some short. Overall he counted 1064 plants. Of these, 787 (74 per cent) were tall and 277 (26 per cent) short. It seemed as though approximately three-quarters (75 per cent) of the F_2 generation were tall and one quarter (25 per cent) short. In other words, the ratio of tall to short plants was approximately 3:1.

The results of these crosses can be summarised as follows:

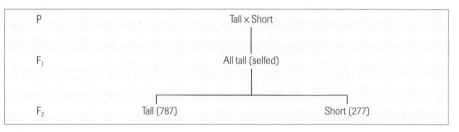

Other monohybrid crosses that Mendel carried out produced very similar results as you can see from table 32.1.

Table 32.1 Summary of Mendel's experiments on the inheritance of single pairs of characters in the garden pea *Pisum sativum*. Notice that for all the characters investigated, a ratio close to 3:1 was obtained.

Character investigated	Cross	F_2 products	Ratio
Form of seed	Smooth × wrinkled	5474 smooth, 1850 wrinkled	2.96:1
Colour of cotyledons	Yellow × green	6022 yellow, 2001 green	3.01:1
Colour of petals	Purple × white	705 purple, 244 white	3.15:1
Form of pods	Inflated × constricted	822 inflated, 299 constricted	2.95:1
Colour of unripe pods	Green × yellow	428 green, 152 yellow	2.82:1
Position of flowers	Axial × terminal	651 axial, 207 terminal	3.14:1
Height of stem	Tall × short	787 long, 277 short	2.84:1

Conclusions from Mendel's monohybrid crosses

What conclusions can be drawn from these results? The first striking fact to notice is that in neither the F_1 nor the F_2 generations are there any medium-sized plants, that is plants intermediate between the tall and the short parents. From this we conclude that inheritance is not a process in which the features of the two parents are blended together to produce an intermediate result, like the mixing of black and white paints to produce grey. Rather, it is a process in which definite structures, or particles, which may or may not show themselves in the outward appearance of the organism, are transmitted from parents to offspring.

That such particles exist is borne out by the observation that they can be combined in one generation but separated in the next, as is witnessed by the recovery of the short form in the F_2 generation despite its absence in the F_1 generation. For these reasons inheritance is described as **particulate**.

Nowadays we call these particles genes, but Mendel simply referred to them as factors. Although he never saw them, nor knew what they were made of, he appreciated their existence and is rightly credited with their discovery.

The second conclusion that can be drawn derives from the observation that there were no short plants in the F_1 generation, despite the fact that one of the parent plants was short. However, short plants did reappear in the F_2 generation. From this we can conclude that although the F_1 plants are tall, they must receive from their short parent a factor for shortness which remains 'hidden' in the F_1 plants and does not reveal its presence in the outward appearance of the plants until the F_2 generation.

A third conclusion is that, as the factor for shortness fails to show itself in the F_1

Figure 32.3 Mendel found that tall garden peas (1.9–2.2 m) crossed with short garden peas (0.3–0.5 m) always gave rise to tall garden peas (1.9–2.2 m).

▶ The chemical structures of genes, page 603

generation, it must in some way he swamped by the factor for tallness. Only in the absence of this factor will the factor for shortness show itself in the outward appearance of the plant. In other words, the factor for tallness is **dominant** to the factor for shortness. Shortness is described as **recessive**.

Although Mendel knew nothing of chromosomes and genes, he suggested that his factors must be transmitted from parents to offspring via the gametes. If we are right in assuming that the F_1 plants contain factors for shortness as well as for tallness, it is reasonable to suppose that each F_1 plant receives via the gametes one factor for tallness from its tall parent and one factor for shortness from its short parent. That is, the gametes contain only one of the two factors for size, while the plants to which these gametes give rise contain a pair of such factors. This is the essence of **Mendel's First Law** (*page 579*).

Genes and their transmission

All these ideas are summarised in the genetic diagram shown in figure 32.4. The gene controlling height in the pea plant exists in two forms. One of them is responsible for producing a tall plant. The other, however, influences development in such a way that, if two are present together, a short plant is produced. These different forms of a gene are known as **alleles**, from the Greek word for 'other'. Alleles, therefore, are alternative forms of a gene. The place on a chromosome where a gene is found is known as its **locus**, from the Latin word for place.

In figure 32.4 the allele for tallness is represented by **T**, and the allele for shortness by **t**. For reasons that will become clear shortly, we shall assume that each parent plant (or, more strictly, each cell of each parent plant) contains a pair of identical alleles: **TT** in the case of the tall parent, **tt** in the case of the short parent. When an organism contains identical alleles like this, it is said to be **homozygous**. In making this statement we are describing the genetic constitution of the parent plants, or at least that part of it which determines their size. The genetic constitution of an organism is known as its **genotype**. The outward appearance of the organism, i.e. the way the genes express themselves in the structure of the organism, is known as its **phenotype**. So in the case of the parent pea plants, the genotype of the tall parent is **TT**, its phenotype being 'tall'; the genotype of the short parent is **tt**, its phenotype being 'short'.

Each of the gametes produced by the tall parent will contain one **T** allele, and each of the gametes produced by the short parent one **t** allele. Fertilisation brings the **T** and **t** alleles together so that all the F_1 offspring have the genotype **Tt**. Phenotypically they are all tall, as the **T** allele is dominant to the **t** allele. When an organism contains two dissimilar alleles, as here, it is said to be **heterozygous** (contrasting with the homozygous condition when the two alleles are identical). In this particular instance the **T** allele is dominant and expresses itself in the phenotype. The **t** allele, however, being swamped by the dominant **T** allele, is described as recessive.

A dominant allele, by definition, can express itself whether it occurs in the homozygous or the heterozygous condition. A recessive allele, however, can only express itself when in the homozygous condition. An individual homozygous for a recessive allele is said to be **homozygous recessive**, and an individual homozygous for a dominant allele is described as **homozygous dominant**.

To return to our example, each of the F_1 plants, being heterozygous, produces two types of gamete: half the gametes will contain the **T** allele, the other half the **t** allele. On self-pollinating the F_1 plants, these two types of gamete will fuse randomly to produce offspring possessing all three possible genotypes: **TT**, **Tt** and **tt**.

There are various ways of showing how this comes about. One was illustrated in figure 32.4. Another, which avoids having lots of lines crossing each other, is called a **Punnett square** because it was first used by the Cambridge geneticist R. C. Punnett (*figure 32.5*). In this device the gametes of one parent are written along the top of a series of boxes, and the

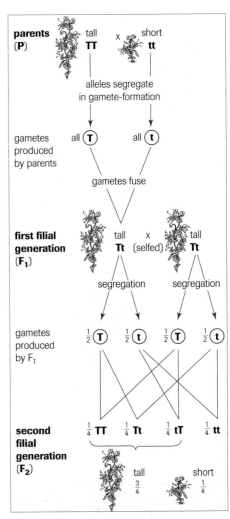

Figure 32.4 Interpretation of what happens when a pure-bred tall pea plant is crossed with a pure-bred short plant. Gametes are circled. This is an example of monohybrid inheritance.

Figure 32.5 R. C. Punnett in his youth. He devised what is now known as the Punnett square for summarising the fusion of gametes in genetic crosses. Punnett was Professor of Genetics at Cambridge. He wrote a large number of papers between 1900 and 1958, most of which helped to confirm and extend Mendel's work.

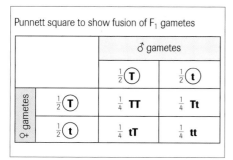

Punnett square to show fusion of F₁ gametes

		♂ gametes	
		$\frac{1}{2}$ T	$\frac{1}{2}$ t
♀ gametes	$\frac{1}{2}$ T	$\frac{1}{4}$ **TT**	$\frac{1}{4}$ **Tt**
	$\frac{1}{2}$ t	$\frac{1}{4}$ **tT**	$\frac{1}{4}$ **tt**

Figure 32.6 A Punnett square can be used to show the fusion of gametes when the F₁ individuals of figure 32.4 are selfed and give rise to the F₂ generation.

gametes of the other parent are written down the side (*figure 32.6*). The products of the various fusions are written in the appropriate boxes and their relative numbers can be estimated.

In our example, the **T** allele is possessed by half the male gametes and half the female gametes. The proportion of zygotes which end up **TT** will therefore be $\frac{1}{2} \times \frac{1}{2} = \frac{1}{4}$. The same reasoning applies to the **t** alleles: half the male gametes and half the female gametes contain the **t** allele so the proportion of zygotes receiving **tt** will be $\frac{1}{4}$.

In the case of the heterozygous (**Tt**) offspring there are two possibilities. Such offspring can either result from the fusion of a male **T** gamete with a female **t** gamete, the probability of which is $\frac{1}{2} \times \frac{1}{2} = \frac{1}{4}$, or they can result from the fusion of a male **t** gamete with a female **T** gamete, the probability of which is again $\frac{1}{2} \times \frac{1}{2} = \frac{1}{4}$. Thus the total proportion of **Tt** zygotes will be $\frac{1}{4} + \frac{1}{4} = \frac{1}{2}$.

So, $\frac{1}{4}$ of the F₂ offspring will have **TT** as their genotype, $\frac{1}{2}$ will be **Tt** and $\frac{1}{4}$ will be **tt**. As **T** is dominant to **t**, the plants whose genotype is **TT** and those whose genotype is **Tt** will all be tall. Thus $\frac{3}{4}$ will be tall and $\frac{1}{4}$ short, which agrees with the 3:1 ratio found by Mendel.

Why did Mendel get a 3:1 ratio?

Why did Mendel get a 3:1 ratio in the F₂ generation of his monohybrid crosses? The answer lies in the behaviour of the chromosomes at meiosis, although Mendel himself knew nothing of this process.

In meiosis, homologous chromosomes separate from each other, as a result of which the haploid gametes receive only one of each type of chromosome instead of the two present in diploid cells. In diploid cells alleles occur in pairs, each of the pair being located on one of two homologous chromosomes.

When homologous chromosomes separate in meiosis they take their alleles with them, and thus each gamete receives only one of a pair of alleles – just as they receive only one of a pair of homologous chromosomes (*figure 32.7*).

Historically, it was the striking similarity between the segregation of Mendel's factors in inheritance and the separation of homologous chromosomes in meiosis as observed under the light microscope that provided evidence that genes are carried on chromosomes.

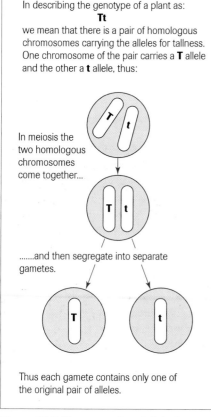

In describing the genotype of a plant as:

Tt

we mean that there is a pair of homologous chromosomes carrying the alleles for tallness. One chromosome of the pair carries a **T** allele and the other a **t** allele, thus:

In meiosis the two homologous chromosomes come together...

.......and then segregate into separate gametes.

Thus each gamete contains only one of the original pair of alleles.

Figure 32.7 The segregation of alleles in inheritance corresponds to the segregation of homologous chromosomes in meiosis.

Support

Probability and the role of chance in genetic ratios

It is important to be clear about what we mean when we say that, for example, $\frac{3}{4}$ of an F₂ generation will be tall and $\frac{1}{4}$ short. For one thing, this only applies when quite a large number of F₂ individuals have their phenotypes described. Another way of putting it is to say that if an F₂ plant is selected at random, there is a 3 in 4 chance of its being tall and a 1 in 4 chance of its being short. In other words, the *probability* of its being tall is $\frac{3}{4}$, and of its being short is $\frac{1}{4}$.

Even if we looked at a large number of F₂ plants, we would not expect the ratio of tall to short individuals to be exactly 3:1. Rather, we would expect *approximately* three-quarters of the plants to be tall. After all, the random fusion of gametes would mean that we *could* end up with all the offspring being heterozygous and so being tall.

For such reasons the actual ratios obtained in genetic crosses only approximate to the expected ratios. However, the more individuals that are counted, the closer the observed ratios tend to be to the expected ones. For this reason Mendel looked at *thousands* of pea plants. Only then was he confident that the ratios he observed were valid.

How genes are arranged on chromosomes

The illustration on the right summarises the relationship between the genes and chromosomes of a diploid organism, and the terms used to describe them.

The letters (**Tt**, **Aa**, etc.) represent a series of hypothetical genes. These can differ in length. Only five genes are shown here. In reality, a chromosome usually carries over a thousand genes.

The loci (singular: locus) are the positions along the length of the chromosomes where the genes occur. Alleles of the same gene occur at the same locus. Only one allele can be present at any particular locus on one chromosome.

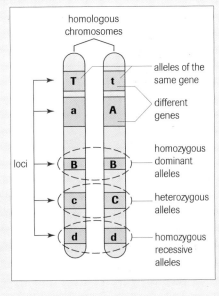

Breeding true

One of the facts to emerge from Mendel's monohybrid crosses is that a particular phenotype may be produced by more than one genotype. For example, a tall pea plant may be **TT** (homozygous) or **Tt** (heterozygous). Either way it will be tall, and there is no way of distinguishing between the two genotypes from their external appearance.

One way of establishing whether a given tall plant is homozygous or heterozygous is to self-pollinate it. If the resulting offspring are all tall, we can conclude that the parent plant has the genotype **TT**. If, however, we get a mixture of tall and short plants, the parent plant must have the genotype **Tt**.

The point is that when an organism which is homozygous for a particular gene is self-fertilised it produces offspring all of which are identical with the parent. Exactly the same result occurs if the organism is crossed with another organism that is homozygous at the same locus. In both cases the organism is said to **breed true**. The organisms are said to belong to a **pure line** for the characteristic in question. Pure lines are of considerable importance in commercial plant breeding (*extension box on page 580*).

Test crosses

So, one way of establishing whether an organism is homozygous dominant or heterozygous for a particular gene is to self-fertilise it, but what do we do if the organism is incapable of self-fertilisation, as most animals are? One technique is to cross the individual whose genotype is unknown with an individual that is homozygous recessive at the locus in question. We can illustrate this with an animal which is much used in genetic experiments, the fruit fly *Drosophila melanogaster*.

Drosophila melanogaster exists in a large number of variants or forms. For instance, most individuals have red eyes, but some have white eyes. Similarly, most individuals have long wings, but some have vestigial wings which are short and functionless (*figure 32.8*). The allele for the long-winged condition (**Vg**) is dominant to the allele for vestigial wing (**vg**).

Figure 32.8
Top Normal-winged *Drosophila*.
Bottom Vestigial-winged *Drosophila*.

If a pure-bred long-winged fly is mated with a vestigial-winged fly, the F₁ individuals are all heterozygous at this locus and have long wings. If two of these F₁ flies mate with each other, a mixture of long-winged and vestigial-winged flies is produced in a ratio of approximately 3:1:

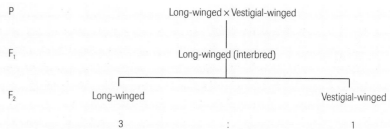

This is what we would expect by analogy with Mendel's experiments. But how can we decide whether a given F₂ long-winged fly is homozygous dominant (**VgVg**) or heterozygous (**Vgvg**)? The simplest way is to cross it with a vestigial-winged fly. We know that a vestigial-winged fly must be **vgvg** (homozygous recessive) – it cannot be anything else. If the long-winged fly whose genotype we wish to determine is **VgVg**, then crossing it with a vestigial-winged fly will give nothing but long-winged flies. If, however, the unknown fly has the genotype **Vgvg**, then the cross will give a mixture of long- and vestigial-winged flies in approximately equal numbers. This is summarised in figure 32.9.

Because this experiment is designed to determine the organism's genotype, it is called a **test cross**. Test crosses with individuals known to be homozygous recessive at the locus in question are a routine method of establishing an organism's genotype.

Figure 32.9 The principle underlying a test cross. Crossing a long-winged fruit fly with a vestigial-winged fly reveals whether the long-winged fly is homozygous dominant (*left*) or heterozygous (*right*).

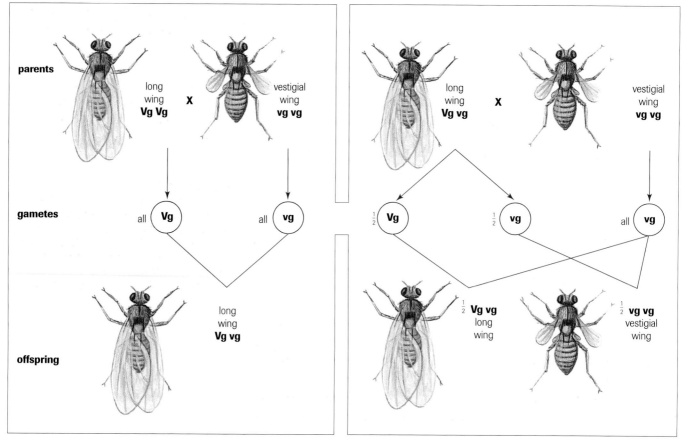

Monohybrid inheritance in humans

A number of human conditions are associated with single pairs of alleles which are inherited in a Mendelian fashion. Here are some examples.

Albinism

Albinism is an affliction in which the skin is pink and fails to tan, the hair white and the iris pink (*figure 32.10*). The reason is that albinos are unable to make the black pigment **melanin** because they lack an enzyme required for its synthesis. They therefore lack the protection from ultraviolet light which this pigment normally confers on the skin.

The allele for albinism is recessive (**a**) so it only exerts its effect in the homozygous state (**aa**). The allele for melanin production (**A**) is dominant. The genotype of a person with normal pigmentation is therefore **AA** or **Aa**.

Suppose a couple each with normal pigmentation have an albino child. For this to happen, the child must have the genotype **aa**. Therefore, aside from the possibility of a rare mutation, each parent must be heterozygous (**Aa**). In other words the parents, though not themselves albino, carry the albino allele, for which reason they may be described as **carriers**.

If this happened in practice, the couple would probably want to know the likelihood (i.e. probability) of their next child also being an albino. The answer to this can be worked out quite easily (*figure 32.11*). Both parents are heterozygous (**Aa**), so each produces **A** and **a** gametes in about equal numbers. These fuse randomly to produce three types of genotype: **AA**, **Aa** and **aa**. The phenotypes are in the ratio 3:1. In practical terms this means that the probability of any of their subsequent children being an albino is $\frac{1}{4}$, one chance in four.

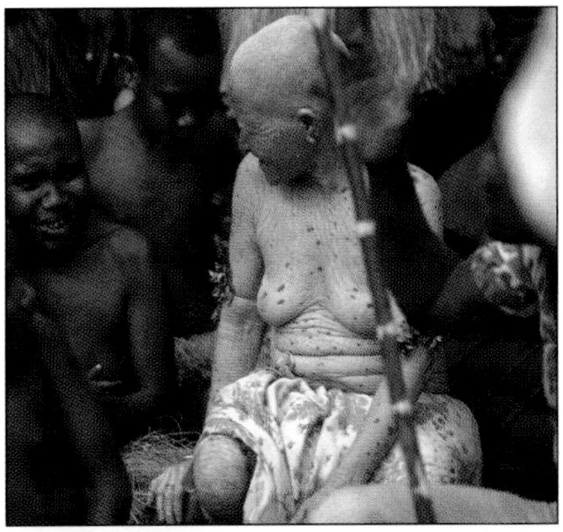

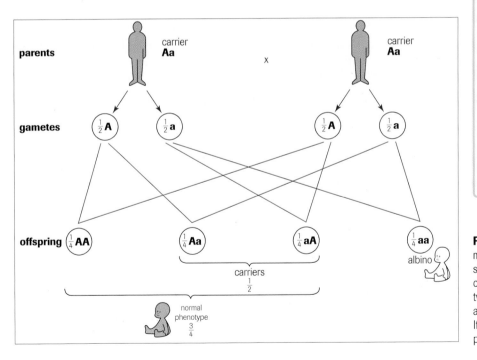

Figure 32.10 An albino woman in the Trobriand Islands, Papua New Guinea.

Albinism and its history

Albinism is probably the earliest recorded rare human condition with a genetic basis. According to the Book of Enoch, which dates from the second century BCE (before the common era), Noah had 'flesh as white as snow and red as a rose; the hair of his head was white like wool, and long; and his eyes were beautiful'.

Today albinism has an incidence of about 1 in 40 000. Fortunately, it is not a life-threatening condition, though albinos are susceptible to sunburn, have difficulty seeing in strong light, and have a higher than average incidence of skin cancer. In some societies they may be ostracised.

Figure 32.11 Albinism, an example of monohybrid inheritance in humans. The diagram shows the genotypes and phenotypes of the children that might result from a union between two carriers of the albino allele. Note that there is a one in four chance of any child being an albino. If a carrier marries an albino what is the probability of a child of theirs being an albino?

Cystic fibrosis

Cystic fibrosis is a distressing condition in which a person produces abnormally large amounts of mucus, particularly in the lungs, pancreas and digestive tract. Vigorous physiotherapy is needed daily to help the person breathe, and enzymes have to be taken with every meal to aid digestion. Cystic fibrosis is therefore an example of a disease where some of its harm is due to changes in the concentration and distribution of enzymes in the body.

Thankfully cystic fibrosis is caused by a recessive allele, like albinism, so that only people who are homozygous recessive are actually affected by the condition. However, one in 24 white Europeans carries the allele which means that one in 2000 children born to white European parents has cystic fibrosis. Many do not live beyond their 20s, though a tremendous amount of medical research is currently underway which is improving the survival rate and quality of life of people with the condition (*page 633*).

Achondroplasia

Not all examples of monohybrid inheritance in humans are caused by recessive alleles. One of the more common sorts of restricted growth in humans is called **achondroplasia** (*figure 32.12*) which is caused by a *dominant* allele. Heterozygotes have a mean height of about 130 cm. Achondroplasics often get bad backaches, but a worse problem is the discrimination they suffer from many taller people.

Eye colour

Eye colour in humans is given in many biology textbooks as an example of monohybrid inheritance. Most books state that brown eye colour is dominant to blue eye colour, blue eye colour being due to the presence of a pair of recessive alleles. In fact the inheritance of human eye colour is more complicated than this. For example, it *is* possible for you to have brown eyes even if both your parents have blue eyes! The reason for this is that eye colour is actually determined not just at one locus but by the actions of genes at several loci (*page 596*).

Figure 32.12 A family in which one of the parents has achondroplasia.

32.2 Dihybrid inheritance

So far we have considered the inheritance of only *one* pair of contrasting characteristics. But Mendel did not stop at this. He went on to study the inheritance of *two* pairs of characteristics, i.e. a **dihybrid cross**.

In one experiment Mendel crossed a pure-bred tall pea plant possessing purple flowers with a short plant possessing white flowers. In the F_1 generation all the plants produced were tall and had purple flowers. These were then self-pollinated. In the F_2 generation four different phenotypes were observed: tall plants with purple flowers; tall plants with white flowers; short plants with purple flowers; and short plants with white flowers. In other words, the offspring showed the two pairs of characteristics (tall versus short, purple versus white) combined in every possible way.

As before, Mendel counted the different types of plant and in one particular case he got 96 tall purple, 31 tall white, 34 short purple and 11 short white, giving a ratio of approximately 9:3:3:1. The experiment can be summarised as follows:

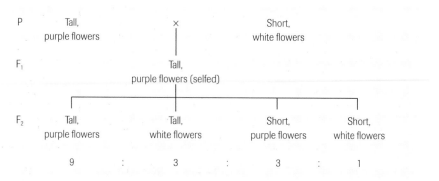

Conclusions from the dihybrid cross

What conclusions can we draw from these results? To begin with, the fact that all the F_1 plants are tall and possess purple flowers confirms that tall is dominant to short and purple flower is dominant to white flower. This is as expected from the results of the monohybrid crosses (*table 32.1 on page 572*).

Figure 32.13 shows how the alleles are transmitted in this dihybrid cross. **T** represents the allele for tallness, **t** for shortness, **P** for purple flower and **p** for white flower. Mendel always started his experiments with pure-bred plants, so the parent plants must be homozygous for both genes. The genotype of the tall plant with purple flowers is therefore **TTPP**, and that of the short plant with white flowers **ttpp**. From Mendel's earlier work we know that the gametes produced by the parent plants are **TP** from the tall purple parent and **tp** from the short white parent. All the F_1 offspring will therefore have the genotype **TtPp**.

Mendel argued that if all four possible combinations of characteristics are to show up in the F_2 generation, the F_1 plants must produce four kinds of gamete: **TP**, **Tp**, **tP** and **tp**. The Punnett square in figure 32.13 shows the different ways these gametes can fuse, together with the genotypes of the F_2 offspring. To be tall, the genotype of the plant must contain at least one **T** allele; to be purple, it must contain at least one **P** allele. From the Punnett square it can be seen that there are 16 possible fusions. Of these, 9 give tall purple plants, 3 tall white, 3 short purple, and 1 short white. The observed 9:3:3:1 ratio can be accounted for if all the possible fusions occur with equal likelihood.

What general conclusion emerges from all this? The main one, surely, is that the alleles of the two genes are transmitted independently of each other from parents to offspring, and therefore assort freely. In other words, each of the alleles of one gene may combine independently with each of the alleles of another gene. **This is Mendel's Second Law.**

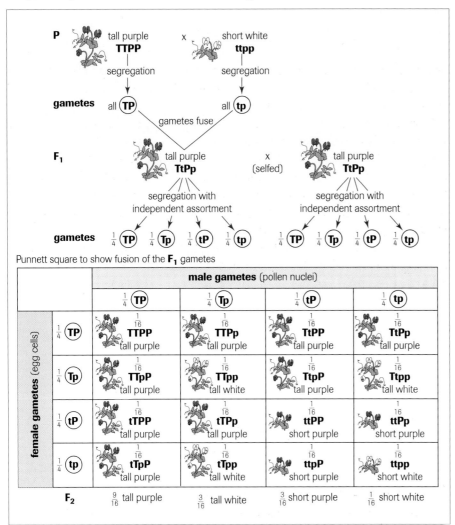

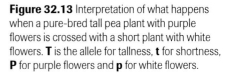

Figure 32.13 Interpretation of what happens when a pure-bred tall pea plant with purple flowers is crossed with a short plant with white flowers. **T** is the allele for tallness, **t** for shortness, **P** for purple flowers and **p** for white flowers.

Part 6

Interpreting dihybrid ratios in terms of probability

Expressed in terms of probability, transmission of the genes determining stem height and flower colour in the garden pea are **independent events**. If we consider the alleles for height on their own, the probability of any one F_1 plant being tall is $\frac{3}{4}$, and of its being short is $\frac{1}{4}$. You can see this in figure 32.13: $\frac{9}{16}$ of the plants are tall and have purple flowers, and $\frac{3}{16}$ are tall and have white flowers. Combining these figures we can see that a total of $\frac{12}{16}$, i.e. $\frac{3}{4}$, of the F_2 plants are tall.

Similarly, if we consider the flower colour alleles alone, there is a probability of $\frac{3}{4}$ that an F_2 plant will be purple, and of $\frac{1}{4}$ that it will be white. What, then, is the probability of an F_2 plant being both tall and purple? Assuming that the alleles are transmitted independently, the answer is $\frac{3}{4} \times \frac{3}{4} = \frac{9}{16}$. This means that the chance of any one F_2 plant, chosen at random, being both tall and purple is 9 out of 16, slightly over 50 per cent. It also means that in a large random sample of F_2 plants, approximately 9 out of 16 of them can be expected to be tall and purple.

We can apply similar reasoning to the other possible combinations of characteristics. The probability of an F_2 plant being tall and white is $\frac{3}{4} \times \frac{1}{4} = \frac{3}{16}$; short and purple $\frac{1}{4} \times \frac{3}{4} = \frac{3}{16}$ and short and white $\frac{1}{4} \times \frac{1}{4} = \frac{1}{16}$. These figures agree with those obtained by the Punnett square method and with the results of Mendel's experiments. They can be explained by postulating that the two pairs of alleles are transmitted independently and assort freely.

Genetics and agriculture

Plant breeding has been important since prehistoric times and in many respects the techniques used then are still valid today.

Suppose a plant breeder has two varieties of wheat, both of which breed true. One variety is tall stemmed and relatively resistant to mildew; the other is short stemmed and relatively susceptible to mildew. Let us imagine that the breeder wants to create a new variety which is short stemmed but relatively resistant to mildew.

The obvious first step is to cross a plant from the tall stemmed, resistant variety with a plant from the short stemmed, susceptible variety. Now let us suppose that all the F_1 offspring are tall stemmed and resistant to mildew. The simplest assumptions to make are that tallness is dominant to shortness, that resistance to mildew is dominant to susceptibility to mildew, and that the two genes are inherited independently.

If this is the case, then calling **T** the allele for tallness, **t** the allele for shortness, **R** the allele for resistance, and **r** the allele for susceptibility, we can say that the tall resistant variety has the genotype **TTRR** and the short susceptible variety the genotype **ttrr**. The F_1 offspring that result when these two varieties are crossed will have the genotype **TtRr**.

Now suppose that the breeder crosses the F_1 offspring among themselves. There are nine possible genotypes which may occur in the F_2 generation (*illustration*).

Our plant breeder wants to end up with a pure line of short resistant plants with the genotype **ttRR**. Just two of the F_2 genotypes have the required phenotype: **ttRR** and **ttRr**. These two genotypes can be distinguished either by selfing the plants, or by test crossing them with short, susceptible plants. Only the **ttRR** genotype will breed true. Thus a new pure breeding line can be established within three generations.

Of course, most plant and animal breeding is much more complicated than this, but this illustrates the general principles.

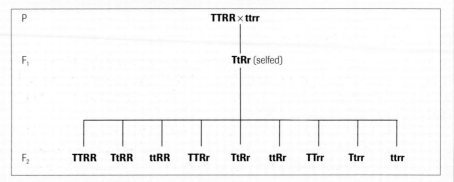

Test crosses and dihybrid ratios

It is clear from the Punnett square in figure 32.13 that the same phenotype may result from several different genotypes. For example, a tall purple plant may have one of four possible genotypes: **TTPP** (homozygous for both genes), **TTPp** (homozygous tall, heterozygous for colour) **TtPP** (heterozygous for height, homozygous purple) or **TtPp** (heterozygous for both genes).

The easiest way of establishing the genotype of a tall purple plant is to cross it with a short white one (**ttpp**). You will appreciate that if the 'unknown' plant is homozygous for both characters, all the offspring from the test cross will be tall and purple (note why).

Now consider the outcome if the unknown plant happens to be heterozygous for both genes. In this case it will produce four types of gametes: **TP**, **Tp**, **tP** and **tp**. The short white plant, however, produces only one type of gamete: **tp**. The fusion of the gametes is shown in figure 32.14, from which it is clear that four types of offspring should be produced in approximately equal numbers: tall purple, tall white, short purple and short white. Mendel carried out this experiment and this is just what he found. In one case, for instance, he obtained 47 tall purple plants, 40 tall white, 38 short purple and 41 short white.

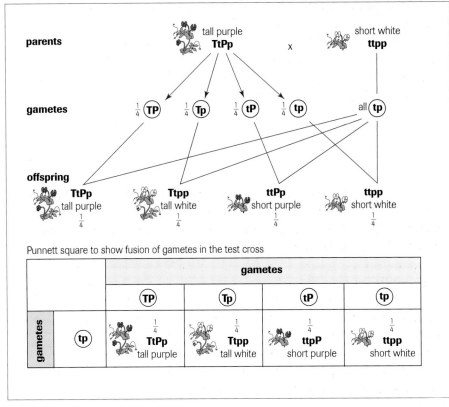

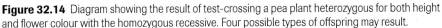

Figure 32.14 Diagram showing the result of test-crossing a pea plant heterozygous for both height and flower colour with the homozygous recessive. Four possible types of offspring may result.

Explanation of dihybrid ratios

The observation that characters like height and flower colour are inherited independently of each other is known as **independent assortment**. The explanation lies in the behaviour of the chromosomes at meiosis, just as was the segregation of alleles that Mendel observed in his monohybrid crosses.

Independent assortment requires that the genes concerned are carried on different chromosomes: for example, the alleles of the gene for flower colour are located on one pair of chromosomes and the alleles of the gene for height on another pair of chromosomes (*top of figure 32.15*).

In describing the genotype of a plant as:

TtPp

we mean that there are two pairs of chromosomes, one pair carrying the alleles of the gene for tallness and the other pair carrying the alleles of the gene for flower colour.

The two chromosomes carrying the 'tallness' alleles are homologous with one another, and the two chromosomes carrying the 'flower-colour' alleles are homologous:

In meiosis the homologous chromosomes come together (**assort**) but they arrange themselves on the spindle **independently** of each other. Thus they may arrange themselves ...

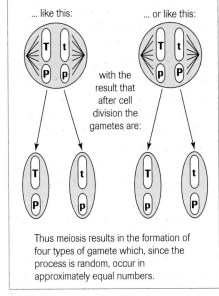

Thus meiosis results in the formation of four types of gamete which, since the process is random, occur in approximately equal numbers.

Figure 32.15 Meiosis provides the explanation for the independent assortment Mendel found in his dihybrid crosses. The free assortment of alleles in inheritance corresponds to the free assortment of chromosomes during meiosis.

Independent assortment in the fruit fly

As with segregation, independent assortment can be demonstrated in other organisms beside peas. Take *Drosophila* for example. As well as flies with long wings and vestigial wings, there are flies with grey-coloured bodies and ebony-coloured bodies.

The allele for the usual grey colour is dominant to the allele for ebony colour. If we cross a fly possessing long wings and a grey body with one possessing vestigial wings and an ebony body, the F_1 offspring are all long-winged and grey-bodied. If two of these are crossed, the F_2 generation yields four types of fly: long-winged and grey-bodied, long-winged and ebony-bodied, vestigial-winged and grey-bodied, and vestigial-winged and ebony-bodied. These occur in a ratio of 9:3:3:1 respectively.

From these results we can conclude that the genes determining wing length and body colour are located on different pairs of chromosomes. The genes segregate and assort freely, just as the genes for height and flower colour did in Mendel's experiments with peas.

In metaphase of the first meiotic division, homologous chromosomes line up side by side on the spindle prior to separating at anaphase. In doing this, different pairs of homologous chromosomes behave independently of each other: the way one pair of homologous chromosomes arrange themselves on the spindle and subsequently separate has no effect whatsoever on the behaviour of any other pair of chromosomes.

The consequence of the independent behaviour of non-homologous chromosomes in meiosis is shown in the lower part of figure 32.15 which illustrates how the four different types of gametes (**TP**, **Tp**, **tP** and **tp**) can be formed from a plant that is heterozygous for height and flower colour (**TtPp**).

We can summarise the situation by saying that the alleles for height and flower colour segregate and assort independently because they are carried on separate chromosomes which themselves segregate and assort independently in meiosis.

32.3 Mendel in retrospect

Mendel's research reveals the mind of a genius. There are three main reasons for this. Firstly, he saw the importance of studying one phenomenon at a time. He did not attempt to follow the inheritance of the many characteristics of pea plants simultaneously, but started by confining himself to one pair of characteristics. Secondly, he was not content merely to *describe* the different types of offspring produced; he *counted* them as well. In other words, he realised the importance of expressing his results quantitatively. Thirdly, and this is where his greatest insight lay, he interpreted his results and drew general conclusions from them. It is all the more impressive that he managed to do this without any knowledge of chromosomes or meiosis.

Mendel worked on inheritance in the garden pea for 10 years. During this time he examined, classified and counted over 28 000 garden peas. In 1866 he published his results in the journal of the local scientific society. However, it received little publicity and made no impact on the scientific world. Until recently, historians of science assumed that this was because hardly anyone read Mendel's work. We now know that this is not the case. Many scientists, including Charles Darwin, read his paper. Why then was Mendel's work ignored? The truth is simply that Mendel was ahead of his time. It is difficult for us to realise how unimportant the mechanism of heredity seemed to 19th century biologists. Mendel's work was not ignored because it was not understood; rather it was thought to be irrelevant.

Before he died in 1884 Mendel told a close friend 'my time will come'. He was right. In 1899 three biologists, Hugo de Vries, Carl Correns and Erich von Tschermak, independently recognised the pioneering importance of Mendel's work. By this time chromosomes had been discovered and meiosis described. Only then, 33 years after its publication, was the full significance of Mendel's work realised.

The limitations of Mendel's work

Although Mendel's work forms the basis of heredity, it does not cover all situations: if it did, genetics would be far easier and less interesting than it is! The fact is that Mendel's work applies to *diploid* organisms, and not all organisms are diploid. Moreover, a gene may have more than two alleles, and it is not always the case that one is dominant to another. Further, some characteristics are determined by several genes, not just one. Finally, genes do not always assort independently. We shall look at these exceptions in the next chapter.

1. The first quantitative experiments on heredity of any significance were carried out in the middle of the 19th century by **Gregor Mendel** on the garden pea.

2. In his first investigations Mendel studied the inheritance of a single pair of contrasting characteristics (**monohybrid inheritance**).

3. From monohybrid crosses it can be concluded that:

■ Inheritance is particulate (nowadays the particles or factors are called **genes**).

■ **Alleles** occur in pairs and may be **dominant** or **recessive** with respect to one another (from which the concepts of **homozygosity** and **heterozygosity** emerge).

■ Only one allele of a gene may be carried in a single gamete.

4. The conclusion that only one allele of a gene may be carried in a single gamete is enshrined in **Mendel's First Law**, the **Law of Segregation**.

5. Examples of monohybrid inheritance in humans include albinism, cystic fibrosis and achondroplasia (a form of growth restriction).

6. In later experiments on the garden pea Mendel studied the inheritance of two pairs of characteristics (**dihybrid inheritance**).

7. From dihybrid crosses it can be concluded that each allele of one gene is equally likely to be inherited with each allele of another gene. This conclusion is enshrined in **Mendel's Second Law**, the **Law of Independent Assortment**.

8. Mendel's Laws and conclusions can be interpreted in terms of the structure of chromosomes and their behaviour during meiosis.

9. Mendel's work was published in 1866 but its significance was not realised until 1899 when it was rediscovered by de Vries and others.

Practice questions

For general advice on these questions and advice on answering essay-type questions, see pages vii and viii.

1. In humans, two genes affect the hands. One gene determines the ability to curve the thumb, the other controls the presence of hair on the middle segments of the fingers. The allele for curved thumb, **T**, is dominant to the allele for straight thumb, **t**. The allele for hair on the middle segment of the fingers, **H**, is dominant to that for an absence of hair, **h**.

   (a) Give all the possible genotypes of individuals who are able to curve their thumbs but have no hair present on the middle segments of their fingers. (1)

   (b) (i) Copy and complete the table to show the possible genotypes resulting from a cross between two individuals heterozygous for both of these genes.

	Genotypes of female gametes			
Genotypes of male gametes				

   (2)

   (ii) What is the probability that one of the offspring of this cross would have hair on the middle segments of the fingers? (1)

   (iii) What is the probability that the first child born to this couple would be a girl with straight thumbs? (1)

   (Total 5 marks)
   AEB 1998

2. Phenylalanine is an amino acid which is essential in the human diet. In normal metabolism excess phenylalanine is converted to tyrosine by an enzyme, phenylalanine hydroxylase. About 1 in 16 000 babies are unable to produce this enzyme because they are homozygous for a recessive allele. Such babies suffer from phenylketonuria and, untreated, phenylalanine builds up in their blood. Excess phenylalanine causes severe brain damage, which usually results in an untreated sufferer requiring lifelong care in an institution.

   A blood test is routinely carried out on babies about ten days after birth to find out whether there is an unusually high level of phenylalanine in the blood. The test uses a nutrient medium without phenylalanine and a strain of bacterium whose rate of growth depends on the amount of phenylalanine present. The blood sample is placed on a small piece of absorbent paper, which is then put on the surface of the nutrient medium in a Petri dish with a culture of the bacteria.

The damaging effects of phenylketonuria can be avoided by feeding affected babies and young children a diet which is very low in phenylalanine. Brain development is most rapid during early childhood. Older children and adults are less sensitive to excess phenylalanine, so the strict diet can usually be relaxed.

(a) Draw a genetic diagram to show how phenylketonuria can be inherited from parents who do not suffer from phenylketonuria. (3)

(b) (i) Explain why phenylalanine builds up in the blood of babies suffering from phenylketonuria. (1)

(ii) Suggest why the blood test is carried out ten days after birth rather than immediately after birth. (1)

(iii) Assuming that about 800 000 babies are born each year in the UK, calculate the number of cases of phenylketonuria that might be expected. (1)

(c) The screening programme for phenylketonuria is generally considered to be effective and worthwhile. Use the information in the passage and your knowledge of screening programmes to explain the features that make this a successful programme. (3)

(d) Cystic fibrosis is another inherited disorder. It may be caused by any one of several different mutant alleles of the cystic fibrosis gene. The most common of these mutant alleles accounts for about 70% of cases of cystic fibrosis. This particular allele can be detected by a specific test. A possible screening programme would involve testing adults of reproductive age to find if they are carriers of the commonest mutant allele. Suggest the possible drawbacks of such a screening programme. (3)

(Total 12 marks)

NEAB 1998

3. Night blindness is a condition in which affected people have difficulty seeing in dim light. The allele for night blindness, **N**, is dominant to the allele for normal vision, **n**. (These alleles are *not* on the sex chromosomes.)

The diagram shows part of a family tree showing the inheritance of night blindness.

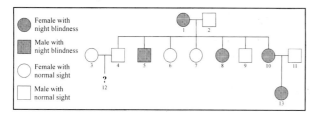

(a) Individual 12 is a boy. What is his phenotype? (1)

(b) What is the genotype of individual 1? Explain the evidence for your answer. (2)

(c) What is the probability that the next child born to individuals 10 and 11 will be a girl with night blindness? Show your working. (2)

(Total 5 marks)

AEB 1998

4. The pedigree shows the inheritance of cystic fibrosis for four generations.

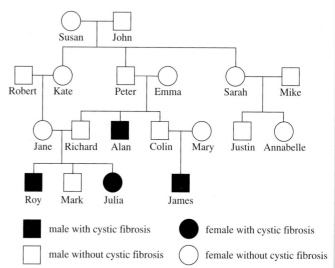

(a) Explain how Roy and Julia could have inherited cystic fibrosis from John or Susan. (4)

(b) People with cystic fibrosis secrete mucus which is very thick and sticky.
Explain how this will affect
(i) gaseous exchange;
(ii) digestion and absorption of food. (8)

(Total 12 marks)

NEAB 1998

I n Chapter 32 we considered examples of monohybrid and dihybrid inheritance where the genetic ratios agree with Mendel's findings. However, this is not always the case. Apart from their intrinsic interest, these exceptions are important because they tell us much about the relationship between chromosomes and genes.

33.1 Linkage

One of the many inherited characteristics in *Drosophila* concerns the width of the abdomen. Most flies have a broad abdomen but some have a narrow one. The allele for broad abdomen is dominant to the allele for narrow abdomen.

If a fly with long wings and a broad abdomen is crossed with one having vestigial wings and a narrow abdomen, the F_1 offspring all have long wings and broad abdomens, as we would predict. But if two of these flies are mated, the F_2 generation fails to yield the 9:3:3:1 ratio we might expect. Instead about $\frac{3}{4}$ of the offspring have long wings and a broad abdomen and nearly all the remaining flies, about $\frac{1}{4}$ of the total, have vestigial wings and a narrow abdomen, thus:

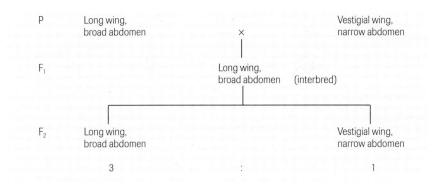

The explanation is that the genes determining the length of the wings and the width of the abdomen are located on the *same* chromosome. This results in their being transmitted together (*figure 33.1*). Such genes are said to be **linked**, and the phenomenon is known as **linkage**. Genes linked together on a chromosome make up a **linkage group**.

It is not the case, though, that the alleles of linked genes can never be separated. If you looked at a very large number of F_2 flies in the example cited above, you would find that a few show independent assortment, i.e. a few long-winged narrow flies and vestigial-winged broad flies turn up in the F_2 generation. The reason for this will be considered later (*page 591*).

Linkage groups and chromosomes

Our knowledge of the relationship between chromosomes and genes is based on experiments started in the early part of the 20th century by T.H. Morgan and his co-workers in the United States. Morgan trained as an embryologist and only started breeding *Drosophila* because he was sceptical about Mendel's results. However, he soon became convinced that Mendel's Laws were essentially correct. In further studies Morgan discovered linkage. He hypothesised that genes which failed to show the ratios characteristic of independent assortment were located on the same chromosome. For this and related work Morgan was awarded a Nobel Prize in 1933.

From a long series of experiments it was shown that *Drosophila melanogaster* has four

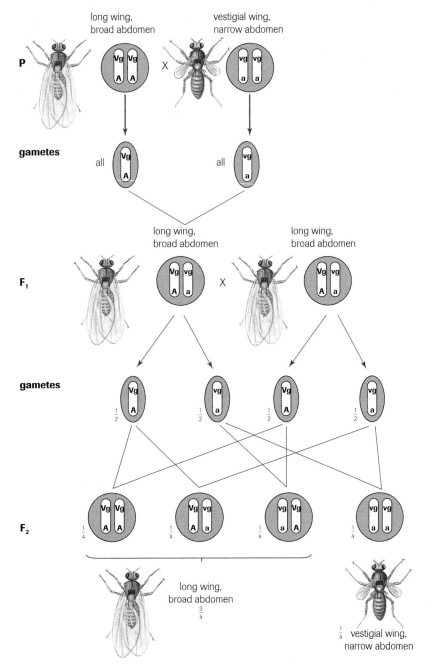

Figure 33.1 Linkage in the fruit fly. The genes for wing length and abdomen width are located on the same chromosome with the result that they are transmitted together and fail to show independent assortment. Allele symbols: vestigial wing (recessive), **vg**; long wing (dominant), **Vg**; narrow abdomen (recessive), **a**; broad abdomen (dominant), **A**.

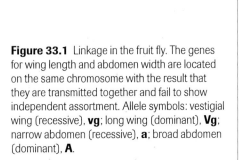

linkage groups. The genes in any one linkage group are transmitted together but independently of the genes in the *other* linkage groups. The interesting thing is that there are also four pairs of chromosomes, early evidence that genes are located on chromosomes.

The same pattern is found in other species. In all cases the number of linkage groups equals the haploid number of chromosomes found in that species. In humans there are 23 linkage groups, corresponding to 23 pairs of chromosomes.

Studies of linkage groups enable us to predict not only the number of chromosomes in a particular species, but their relative sizes as well. If a linkage group contains a large number of genes, we expect the chromosome concerned to be relatively large. This is what we find. In humans, for example, chromosome 1, the longest chromosome, has many more genes than chromosome 22, the shortest.

33.2 Sex determination

In humans, sex is determined by the **sex chromosomes**. Females have two so-called **X chromosomes**; males one X and one much shorter **Y chromosome**. These sex chromosomes are an exception to the rule that homologous chromosomes are identical in appearance. All the *other* pairs of chromosomes, which are identical in appearance, are called **autosomes** (Greek for 'same bodies'). The sex chromosomes, just like the autosomes, are transmitted in a normal Mendelian manner (*figure 33.2*).

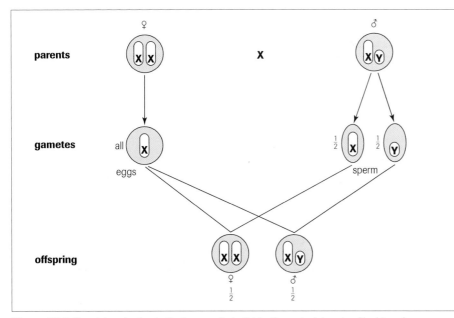

Figure 33.3 A female Morelets crocodile, *Crocodylus moreleti*, on her nest mound. In such species the sex of the offspring is determined by the temperature at which the eggs are incubated during a critical period.

Figure 33.2 Sex determination in the human. An individual's sex is determined by his or her sex chromosomes. Females possess two X chromosomes; males an X and a Y. The sex chromosomes are transmitted in the normal Mendelian fashion as shown here. In determining an individual's sex, the X and Y chromosomes are only important at a relatively early stage of development when the gonads (ovaries and testes) are developing. Once the gonads have been formed, a process completed before birth, sex hormones controlled by autosomal chromosomes take over. The symbols X and Y do not refer to alleles, but to the chromosomes.

There is considerable variation between species as to how sex is determined. For example, in birds, females are XY and males XX. A quite different system of sex determination is found in alligators and crocodiles. Here the sex of the offspring is determined by their environment (*figure 33.3*). Males and females do not differ in their chromosomes. Instead there is a critical period in the early development of the fertilised egg during which the ambient temperature determines the sex of the individual! In some species high temperatures lead to males; in others, high temperatures result in females.

Sex linkage

In organisms with sex chromosomes, such as *Drosophila* and ourselves, all the genes carried on the sex chromosomes are transmitted along with those determining sex – that is they are **sex-linked**.

Consider, for example, the inheritance of eye colour in *Drosophila* where, as with us, females are XX and males XY. The result of crossing a red-eyed *Drosophila* fly with a white-eyed fly depends on which parent is red-eyed and which is white-eyed. If the father is white-eyed, the F₁ gives nothing but red-eyed flies, half being males and half females:

P	White-eyed ♂	×	Red-eyed ♀
F₁	½ Red-eyed ♂		½ Red-eyed ♀

Part 6

There is nothing surprising in this. The allele for red eyes is evidently dominant to the allele for white eyes. If, however, the father has red eyes and the mother white eyes, half the F_1 flies have red eyes and half white, all the red-eyed ones being females, and all the white-eyed ones being males:

At first sight these results seem extraordinary, but they can be explained by assuming that the gene controlling eye colour is carried on the X chromosome, but not on the Y chromosome. Indeed, in *Drosophila* and humans, the Y chromosome carries very few genes, compared to over a thousand carried on the X chromosome. A full explanation of the sex-linked inheritance of eye colour in *Drosophila* is given in figure 33.4.

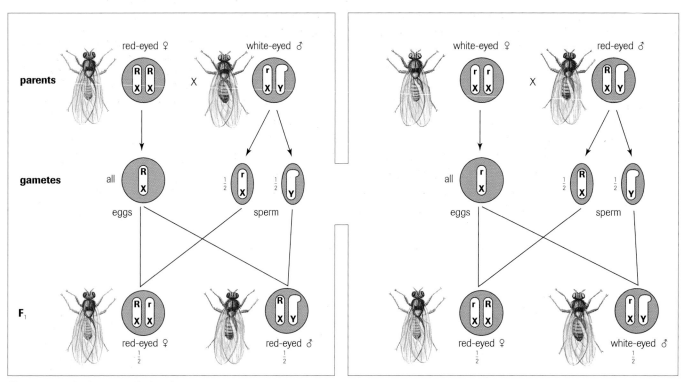

Figure 33.4 Sex linkage in the fruit fly (*Drosophila*). The gene controlling eye colour is located on the X chromosome, and so is sex-linked. The result of crossing red- and white-eyed flies depends on which parent is red-eyed and which white-eyed. This can be seen by comparing the two genetic diagrams above. Allele symbols: red eye (dominant), **R**; white eye (recessive), **r**.

Note that in *Drosophila* and in humans – indeed in all species where females are XX and males XY – males never inherit their father's X chromosome. To all intents and purposes, the Y chromosome carries no genes and all sex-linked genes are therefore carried on the X chromosome. Because fathers never pass their X chromosomes to their sons, a male cannot inherit his father's sex-linked traits. Daughters, however, always receive their father's X chromosome. There is therefore a 50 per cent chance that they will transmit this chromosome to their offspring.

Colour blindness

In humans, **red-green colour blindness** is inherited as a sex-linked characteristic. The allele for this form of colour blindness is carried on the X chromosome and is recessive in females.

Suppose a colour-blind man and a woman with two alleles for normal colour vision have several children. Any daughters will receive a normal functioning allele from their mother, and since this allele is dominant to the allele for colour blindness they will not be colour blind. However, they will *carry* the defective allele. Any sons the couple have will have normal colour vision because they will not receive their father's defective allele (*figure 33.5*).

As you might expect, red-green colour blindness is more common in males than in females. The only way a female can be red-green colour blind is for her to have two copies of the faulty allele. About 8 per cent of males are colour blind, but fewer than 1 per cent of females. Try showing figure 33.6 to large numbers of males and females.

Haemophilia

A much more serious sex-linked trait in humans is **haemophilia**. In this condition the blood takes an abnormally long time to clot, resulting in profuse and prolonged bleeding from even minor wounds.

Haemophilia, like red-green colour blindness, is caused by the recessive allele of a gene which is carried on the X chromosome. As can be seen in figure 33.7, if a man who does not have haemophilia and a woman who happens to carry the allele for haemophilia have children there is a probability of $\frac{1}{2}$ that if they have a son he will be a haemophiliac. If they have a daughter, she will be phenotypically normal, but has a 50 per cent chance of being a carrier.

This is precisely what has happened in the royal families of Europe during the last 150 years. It seems that a haemophilia allele arose by mutation in one of the gametes (it might have been the egg or the sperm) which gave rise to Queen Victoria. Of her nine children, one was a haemophiliac (Leopold) and two were carriers (Beatrice and Alice). As a result of marriages between the various royal families, the defective allele spread to several European countries. Beatrice transmitted the haemophilia allele to the Spanish royal family and Alice to the Russian royal family. Figure 33.9 shows how this happened.

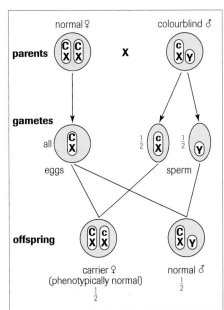

Figure 33.5 Red-green colour blindness, an example of sex linkage in humans. Allele symbols: allele for colour vision (dominant), **C**; allele for colour blindness (recessive), **c**.

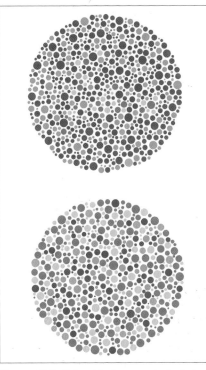

Figure 33.6 Colour blindness can be tested using simple dot patterns like these. People with normal colour vision can read the number embedded in each dot pattern. Those with red-green colour blindness cannot distinguish the number or see a different one.

▶ Physiology of haemophilia, page 228

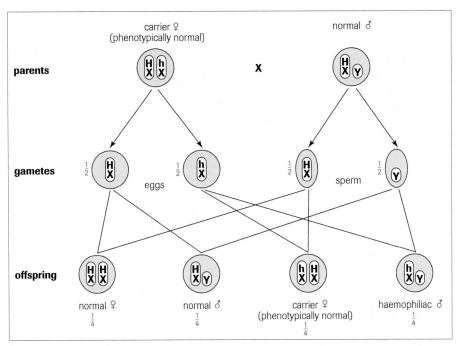

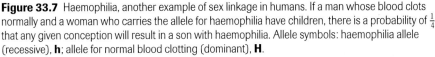

Figure 33.7 Haemophilia, another example of sex linkage in humans. If a man whose blood clots normally and a woman who carries the allele for haemophilia have children, there is a probability of $\frac{1}{4}$ that any given conception will result in a son with haemophilia. Allele symbols: haemophilia allele (recessive), **h**; allele for normal blood clotting (dominant), **H**.

Figure 33.8 Queen Victoria and some of her relatives. Three of the women here were carriers of haemophilia, namely Victoria herself (seated left of centre and wearing a crown), one of her daughters, Beatrice (seated slightly right of centre with a cluster of children, one of whom has his arm on her right shoulder), and one of Queen Victoria's granddaughters, Alice (standing almost at the extreme right of the portrait with the hands of Prince of Schleswig-Holstein on her shoulders).

One of the most famous haemophiliacs on the Russian side was Alexis Nicholaievitch, son of the last Tsar of Russia and heir to the throne. He was badly afflicted with the disease and was often close to death. However, the monk Rasputin was said to have strange powers over the boy and was alleged to be able to cure him of his bleeding attacks. Through this and other means Rasputin gained great influence in the Russian court, to such an extent that for a short period just before the 1917 revolution he was virtually the ruler of Russia.

Do women ever suffer from haemophilia? For a woman to be afflicted, she would need to be homozygous for the malfunctioning allele, as it is recessive. However, the haemophilia allele is so rare that the chances of having two copies of it are extremely remote. It is not known for certain whether there have ever been women with haemophilia. Before the advent of modern medicine, such women would have had little chance of surviving for long beyond puberty, once menstruation had begun.

Support

Genetic counselling

Suppose a couple have had a child with haemophilia and want to know if there is a risk of any other children they may have also having haemophilia. They can go a **genetic counsellor** for advice.

Genetic counsellors need to have a sound understanding of human genetics and must also be able to explain their knowledge clearly and sensitively. People often go for genetic counselling feeling worried or guilty. A good genetic counsellor will help to ease their worries and allay any feelings of guilt.

Sometimes a pregnant woman goes to a genetic counsellor having had a diagnostic test (*page 748*) which showed that, if she has her child, the baby runs a significant risk of having an abnormality. In such circumstances the genetic counsellor needs to explain all the medical and legal options available, which may include termination of the pregnancy. However, this needs to be done in such a way as to allow the woman to make her own decision.

A genetic counsellor needs to able to explain genetic ratios and probabilities so that they can be understood by non-specialists. For example, it is no good telling a couple that their children have a one in four chance of suffering from cystic fibrosis if the couple do not understand what this means. A couple may assume that because their first child has cystic fibrosis, the next three are certain not to.

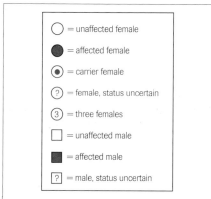

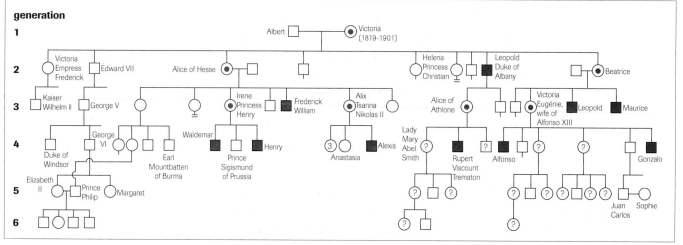

Figure 33.9 A pedigree chart showing the transmission of the allele for haemophilia from Queen Victoria into several of the Royal families of Europe.

Sex linkage and the Y chromosome

We have seen that certain human genes are carried on the X chromosome – those that cause colour blindness and haemophilia, for example. Are genes also carried on the Y chromosome?

If a gene is Y-linked, we would expect its effects to show themselves *only* in men. Can you think of a definite example of such a trait?

The answer is 'maleness'. To be more specific, we now know that the Y chromosome has several copies of a **testicular differentiating gene**. This gene acts on the undifferentiated gonads of the young embryo and causes them to differentiate into testes. In the absence of the product made by these genes, the gonads develop into ovaries.

There are no other conclusive examples of Y-linked inheritance in humans, though some species of fish and mice show several instances of Y-linked inheritance.

33.3 Crossing over

We have seen that linked genes are carried on the same chromosome. This being so, we might expect that their alleles would always stay together and never separate. However, this is not the case. When studying the inheritance of linked genes it is unusual to find complete linkage. More often that not, a small proportion of the offspring show new combinations, as in independent assortment. Let's illustrate this with maize which, like *Drosophila*, has been a favourite in genetic research.

In maize, a single cob is covered with several hundred kernels. Each kernel is the product of a single fertilisation. The kernels show several clear-cut characteristics including colour and shape (*figure 33.10*). If a maize plant from a pure line for kernels which are coloured and smooth is crossed with one from a pure line having colourless, shrunken kernels, the F_1 all have coloured, smooth kernels. Evidently coloured is dominant to colourless, and smooth to shrunken.

Now what would we expect to happen if one of the F_1 plants is test crossed with the double recessive? If the genes for colour and shape are on separate chromosomes, we would expect the test cross to produce all four combinations of characteristics in approximately equal numbers. If the two genes are on the same chromosome we would expect the progeny to show only two types of kernel: coloured, smooth and colourless, shrunken.

In fact, neither of these two possibilities turns out to be the case. What we find is that about 48 per cent of the kernels are coloured, smooth and about 48 per cent are colourless, shrunken, while about 2 per cent are coloured, shrunken and about 2 per cent are colourless, smooth. In other words, all four combinations of characteristics are found, but not in the proportions we would expect if the two genes were located on separate chromosomes.

How can we explain this? The answer is that the genes are situated on the same chromosome and for the most part they are transmitted together through the gametes to the offspring. However, in the formation of a small proportion of the gametes, the alleles of these genes, instead of staying on their own chromosome, change places. This is called **crossing over** and it has the effect of separating alleles that were previously linked, allowing them to recombine with other alleles. The result is that, while the majority of offspring have the same combination of characteristics as the parents, a few show new combinations; they are known as **recombinants**. This is summarised in figure 33.11.

Figure 33.10 Maize cobs have kernels that can differ considerably in colour and shape.

Explanation of crossing over

The explanation of crossing over lies in the behaviour of the chromosomes during meiosis. During prophase of the first meiotic division, when homologous chromosomes become intertwined, the chromatids of homologous chromosomes can be seen to be in contact with each other at certain points along their length (*page 464*). At these points, known as

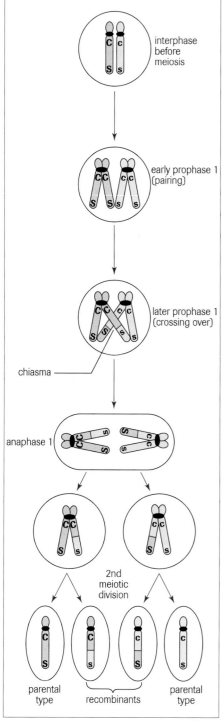

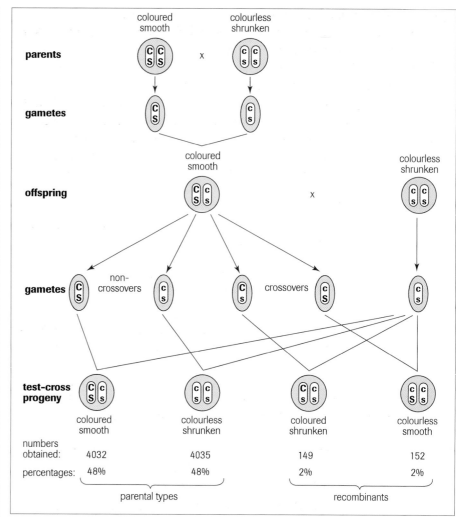

Figure 33.11 Diagram showing the result of crossing maize homozygous for coloured, smooth kernels with maize having colourless, shrunken kernels. The genes controlling colour and shape of the kernels are linked. The small percentage of recombinants in the progeny can be explained by postulating that crossing over takes place between homologous chromosomes during gamete formation. Allele symbols: coloured (dominant), **C**; colourless (recessive), **c**; smooth (dominant), **S**; shrunken (recessive), **s**.

Figure 33.12 Meiosis provides the explanation for crossing over. In prophase I of meiosis, homologous chromosomes become intimately associated with one another and adjacent non-sister chromatids may break and rejoin as shown here. The result is that previously unlinked alleles may become joined and new combinations established.

▶ Variation and evolution, page 740

chiasmata (singular: **chiasma**), the chromatids break and rejoin. The result is that portions of the chromatids belonging to the two homologous chromosomes change places, taking their alleles with them. So the chiasmata result in crossing over. Eventually the chromatids finish up in separate gametes and, after fertilisation, give rise to new combinations of alleles in the offspring – the so-called recombinants (*figure 33.12*).

The number of chiasmata formed in a bivalent during meiosis, and therefore the amount of crossing over, varies from one species to another and, within a species, from one pair of homologous chromosomes to another. Occasionally no chiasmata are formed, sometimes as many as eight. Generally, the longer the chromosomes in a homologous pair, the greater the number of chiasmata.

Because it establishes new combinations of alleles, crossing over is an important source of genetic variation.

Locating genes on chromosomes

A useful consequence of crossing over is that it enables geneticists to work out the relative positions of genes on a chromosome. In 1911, the same T.H. Morgan who discovered linkage (*page 585*) suggested that the extent of recombination that occurs between genes on the same chromosome is a measure of the distance between them.

To see how this works, imagine two linked genes **A** and **B**. The further apart **A** and **B** are on their chromosome, the more likely it is that during meiosis the chromosome will break and rejoin at some point between them. Conversely, the closer they are, the less likely it is that breakage and crossing over will occur between them.

So, if in a breeding experiment we find that a relatively large percentage (say 20 to 40 per cent) of the offspring are recombinants, we can conclude that the genes are relatively far apart on the chromosome. If, though, only a low percentage (say 1 to 5 per cent) of the offspring are recombinants, we can conclude that the genes lie quite close together. The percentage of offspring which show recombination is called the **cross-over value** (**COV**).

Mapping chromosomes

Imagine that in a breeding experiment it is found that the COV of **A** and **B** is 14 per cent. We can represent the distance between the genes thus:

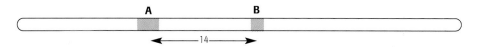

Remember that we only know the *relative* positions of **A** and **B**. We do not know precisely where on the chromosome they lie. For example, they might lie in the middle of the chromosome or at one end of it.

Suppose now that we investigate the transmission of these genes (**A** and **B**) with a third linked gene **C**. If we find that **A** and **C** give a COV of 20 per cent, whereas **B** and **C** give only 6 per cent, we can conclude that **B** is located between **A** and **C**, as follows:

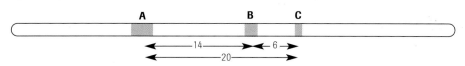

If, on the other hand, **A** and **C** give a COV of 8 per cent, and **B** and **C** 6 per cent, we conclude that **C** lies between **A** and **B**:

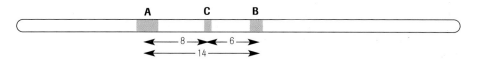

Another possibility is that **A** and **C** might again give a COV of 8 per cent, but the COV between **B** and **C** is 22 per cent. From this we can conclude that **A** lies between **B** and **C**:

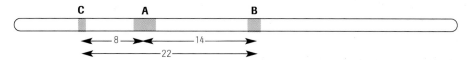

Although this may look like a powerful technique for mapping chromosomes, there are some snags:

- The approach only works if you can look at very large numbers of offspring. It is therefore much easier to determine the positions of, for example, *Drosophila* genes than human genes.

- Even in organisms like *Drosophila* and maize, it may be difficult to determine the relative positions of genes that lie very close to one another.

- If two genes are widely separated on a chromosome, recombinations may take place at two points between them, resulting in a **double cross-over**. This will go undetected and means that the distance between widely separated genes will be underestimated.

Mapping human chromosomes

One way of finding out if two human genes are linked is to follow the inheritance of the characteristics which they determine over two or more generations. This technique is called **pedigree analysis** and we have already come across it in connection with haemophilia (*figure 33.9*).

We can be confident that haemophilia is caused by a gene on the X chromosome for two reasons: firstly, haemophilia is far more common in males than in females; and secondly, males may pass the allele to their daughters but never to their sons. These characteristics are typical of genes carried on the X chromosome, so it is relatively easy to find out which human genes are sex-linked. Among these are genes for haemophilia, red-green colour blindness and Duchenne muscular dystrophy, a distressing condition in which the muscles progressively waste away, leading to an early death.

The cell fusion technique

But how can human geneticists determine on which autosomal chromosomes genes occur? One approach relies on a procedure known as **cell fusion**. To use this technique, you must first establish a colony of human cells which will reproduce themselves in the laboratory. Such **cell lines** are commonly derived from **fibroblasts**, one of the principal cells found in connective tissue (*page 65*).

Once a cell line of fibroblasts is established, one of the cells is placed with a diploid tumour cell from a hamster or other small mammal in the presence of various chemicals and a type of virus, called a Sendai virus. The virus causes the two kinds of cell to fuse, thereby forming a 'hybrid' cell (*illustration 1*). The cytoplasms of the two cells coalesce but at first their nuclei remain separate. The cell then undergoes mitosis. A spindle is formed and chromosomes from

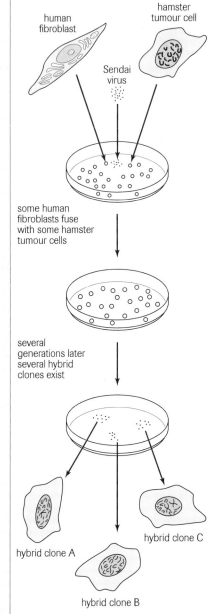

Illustration 1 The technique of cell fusion. Human fibroblasts and hamster tumour cells are placed with Sendai viruses and various chemicals. (Tumour cells are used because they carry on dividing indefinitely, unlike normal cells, which only go through a certain number of cell divisions and then die.) Fused hybrid cells result. These cells give rise to hybrid clones which differ in the chromosomes they contain. The clones can be used to assign genes to particular chromosomes as described in the text.

both cells become attached to it. However, not all the chromosomes succeed in doing this. As a consequence, some of the daughter cells end up with fewer chromosomes than others.

Over successive generations, more and more chromosomes are lost. Eventually classes of cells may result that contain only *one* human chromosome and a number of hamster chromosomes. It may then be possible to detect proteins made by the cell which are known to be produced by *humans* but *not* by hamsters. We may then conclude that this one human chromosome must be producing the protein.

The next step is to examine the cell under the microscope and identify the human chromosome. This is done by comparing it with a prepared set of human chromosomes: a **karyotype**, as it is called. In a human karyotype, the 23 pairs of chromosomes can be distinguished by their size and reaction with certain stains (*illustration 2*). Thus this method allows geneticists to determine the precise chromosome on which the gene is located.

The human genome project

Pedigree analysis, cell fusion and other techniques of cell and molecular biology are making it possible to map the entire human **genome** – genome being a collective word for the genetic material of an organism. This is known as the **human genome project** and it is overseen by the **Human Genome Organisation** (known as **HUGO**), founded in 1988. By August 1998 some 16 000 of the 80 000 to 100 000 human genes had been mapped and had their gene sequences worked out (to an accuracy of at least 99.9 per cent).

HUGO is truly international with many research groups around the world tackling different chromosomes or portions of chromosomes. The largest single centre is the Sanger Centre just outside Cambridge (named after Frederick Sanger, *page 33*). The Sanger Centre is doing 29 per cent of the whole project. If you go there the reception area has a digital read-out, updated every few seconds, of the total number of base pairs mapped to date. Each night the latest information is published on the internet and is available for anyone to use.

Mapping the whole human genome will probably be completed around the year 2003, 50 years after Watson and Crick worked out the structure of DNA (*page 605*). By then the total cost will have been about $2 billion, some 60 cents (40 pence) a base pair.

What is learnt in the Human Genome Project will not only increase our understanding of the nature of inheritance, but also lead to cures being found for some of the distressing human diseases caused by faults in the genetic material. Approximately 60 million people world-wide are affected by these directly, while many more common diseases have an underlying genetic component.

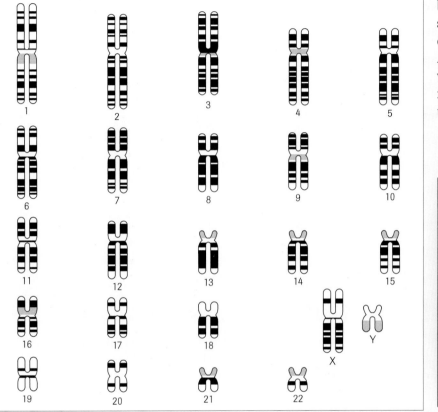

Illustration 2 Human chromosomes can be individually recognised by their size, position of centromere and banding pattern with certain stains. The bands correspond to large groups of genes. The photomicrograph shows a full set of human chromosomes arranged and numbered according to size and centromere position in a male. The diagram shows the banding patterns in detail.

33.4 Degrees of dominance

Mendel's experiments might lead us to conclude that alleles are always either dominant or recessive. However, this is not always so.

Take flower colour in snapdragons, for example. Here, a cross between two pure-bred individuals of differing genotypes results in offspring which are identical with neither parent but are intermediate between the two. A snapdragon with red flowers crossed with a snapdragon with white flowers gives plants with pink flowers in the F_1, a result which contrasts sharply with those obtained by Mendel for the garden pea. The snapdragons with pink flowers are heterozygous for the allele for flower colour, but instead of one allele being dominant to the other, both express themselves equally in the phenotype. Such alleles are said to be **codominant**.

When codominance occurs, the gene should be designated by a capital letter and the alleles by appropriate superscript letters. In the snapdragon example, we might call the gene for colour **C**. The red allele would then be C^R and the white allele C^W. Crossing snapdragons with pink flowers among themselves gives a phenotypic ratio of approximately 1 red: 2 pink: 1 white (*figure 33.13*).

Between the extremes of complete dominance and no dominance (codominance) are various shades of **partial dominance**. In such cases an offspring's phenotype resembles one parent more than the other for a given characteristic.

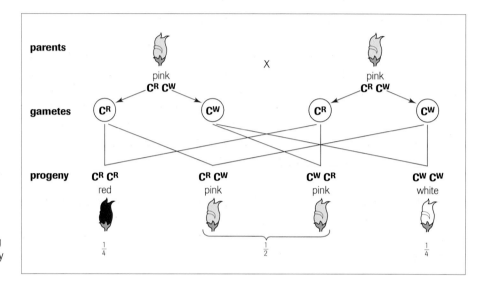

Figure 33.13 Diagram showing the result of crossing snapdragons with pink flowers among themselves. A phenotypic ratio of approximately 1 red: 2 pink: 1 white results.

33.5 **Multiple alleles**

Often genes have more than two alleles at a given locus, though in any one individual only two alleles can be present. An example of such **multiple alleles** is provided by the alleles controlling the **ABO blood group system** in humans.

The ABO system is controlled by three alleles referred to as I^A, I^B and I^O. The physiology of the ABO system is explained in Chapter 19; here we are only concerned with the transmission of the alleles responsible for determining the blood groups.

The I^A allele is responsible for the production of type A antigens in the person's red blood cells, and the I^B allele for the production of type B antigens. The third allele in the series, I^O produces neither antigen. As only two of the three alleles can be present at any one time, an individual may possess any of the following six genotypes $I^A I^A$, $I^A I^O$, $I^B I^B$, $I^B I^O$, $I^A I^B$ or $I^O I^O$.

The I^A and I^B alleles show equal dominance with respect to one another (i.e. they are codominant), but each is dominant to I^O. Thus:

- a person with the genotype $I^A I^A$ or $I^A I^O$ belongs to **blood group A**;
- a person with the genotype $I^B I^B$ or $I^B I^O$ belongs to **blood group B**;
- a person with the genotype $I^A I^B$ belongs to **blood group AB**;
- a person with the genotype $I^O I^O$ belongs to **blood group O**.

The fact that there are more than two alleles responsible for determining the blood groups makes no difference to their transmission, which takes place in a normal Mendelian fashion. Thus a child whose parents are both blood group O must be blood group O (note why). However, offspring may result whose genotypes differ from both of their parents. Work out, for example, the blood groups that can result when a couple with the genotypes $I^A I^O$ and $I^B I^O$ have children (*see figure 33.14*).

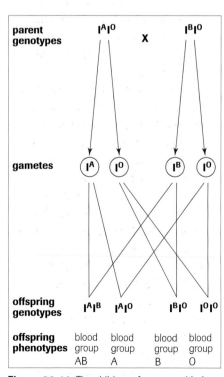

Figure 33.14 The children of parents with the genotypes $I^A I^O$ and $I^B I^O$ may have genotypes and phenotypes that differ from both their parents.

It is probably true that in genetic studies more has been learned about genes from abnormal ratios than from normal ones. Consider, for example, the inheritance of fur colour in mice.

In mice, the allele for yellow fur (**Y** – not to be confused with the Y chromosome with which it is quite unconnected) is dominant to the allele for grey (**y**). If a pair of yellow mice known to be heterozygous for the coat colour gene are mated, the result is always the same: two thirds of the offspring are yellow, and one third grey. Yet from our knowledge of monohybrid ratios, we naturally expect three quarters of the mice to be yellow and only a quarter to be grey. What is going on?

A possible explanation is that individuals homozygous for the yellow allele (i.e. with the genotype **YY**) die before birth. In other words, the genotype **YY** represents a lethal combination of alleles. As can be seen from figure 33.15, the death of such individuals in the embryonic state would have the effect of removing a quarter of the offspring from the litter. The dead embryos would represent a third of the potential yellow offspring, thus reducing the proportion of yellow offspring from what would have been $\frac{3}{4}$ to $\frac{2}{3}$.

Evidence for this hypothesis comes from two observations:

■ Crossing yellow with yellow never produces exclusively yellow offspring; a ratio of two yellow to one grey always results. This can be explained by assuming that viable yellow mice are always heterozygous and that a living homozygous yellow mouse is an impossibility.

■ Examination of the uteri of yellow female mice which have mated with yellow males usually reveals one or more dead embryos. Few if any dead embryos are found either in the uteri of yellow females which have mated with grey males or in the uteri of grey females which have mated with yellow males. This is presumably because in neither case can an offspring arise with the genotype **YY**.

There is therefore good evidence to support the hypothesis that the **YY** combination is lethal. Should the **Y** allele be described as dominant or recessive? The answer is that it depends on how we look at it. As the allele controlling fur colour it is dominant, but as a **lethal allele** it is recessive, exerting its effects only when in the homozygous state.

Dominant and recessive lethals

In most cases, lethal alleles are recessive, for which reason they are called **recessive lethals**. Occasionally, though, the presence of an allele in the heterozygous state is sufficient to cause death. Such alleles are known as **dominant lethals**. An example of a medical condition in humans caused by a dominant lethal is Huntington's disease, characterised by deterioration of the nervous system. Here, individuals with a single copy of the malfunctioning allele die, usually after reaching adulthood. The population genetics of Huntington's disease are discussed further on page 639.

Lethal alleles are known to exist in a wide range of organisms. Each of us, on average, carries four lethal alleles. Fortunately they are all recessive, so problems do not arise provided they are in the heterozygous state. Exactly which four lethal alleles we carry varies from one person to another, so if two people reproduce, the children are unlikely to be homozygous for any of these lethals. However, children produced by matings between close relatives are more likely to be homozygous for these alleles. This is why inbreeding is disadvantageous.

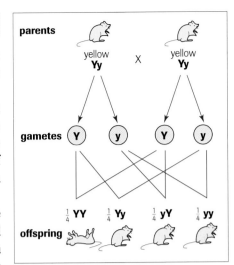

Figure 33.15 Inheritance of fur colour in mice. The allele for yellow coat (**Y**) is dominant to that for grey (**y**), at least as far as coat colour is concerned. Mice that are homozygous **YY** die before birth. As a result, a cross between two mice with the **Yy** genotype fails to produce the 3:1 ratio typical of monohybrid crosses.

Alleles which have more than one effect

Think about those mice in figure 33.15. It seems incredible that simply being homozygous for the colour yellow kills them! Presumably the allele we have called **Y** has two effects, *one* on coat colour, the *other* on viability. An allele which has two or more effects is said to show **pleiotropy**.

Another example of pleiotropy is the allele for cystic fibrosis (*page 577*). A person with cystic fibrosis produces abnormally large amounts of mucus. This has several consequences. The mucus blocks the alveoli and bronchioles in the lungs, leading to severe problems with breathing. It also blocks the exit for digestive enzymes in the pancreas, leading to inadequate digestion. These digestive enzymes, unable to leave the pancreas, may result in autodigestion – that is, they start to eat away the pancreas itself, leading to the development of diabetes.

So, you can see how the cystic fibrosis allele has a whole series of phenotypic effects.

33.7 Interactions between genes

So far we have dealt only with cases where a characteristic is controlled by the alleles of one gene. Sometimes, however, a single characteristic is controlled by the alleles of two or more genes interacting with one another. The transmission of a character controlled by more than one gene is called **polygenic inheritance** and the character itself is called a **polygenic character**.

An example of polygenic inheritance is found in the wheat *Triticum vulgare*. In wheat seeds, colour is determined by three genes, each on a different chromosome. Each of these genes has two alleles. Seeds with dark red coats have the genotype $R^1R^1R^2R^2R^3R^3$ At the other extreme, seeds with white coats have the genotype $r^1r^1r^2r^2r^3r^3$. The colour of a wheat seed is simply determined by how many **R** as opposed to **r** alleles it has. Seeds can have any number of **R** alleles from zero to six. For example, a seed with five **R** alleles is fairly red but not quite as red as one with all six **R** alleles.

If a wheat plant which has all six **R** alleles is crossed with one that has all six **r** alleles, the resulting offspring have seeds that are an intermediate red colour, as you would expect. The interesting thing, though, is what happens when these offspring are crossed among themselves. As you can see from figure 33.16, the full range of seed colours is seen in the F_2 with an expected ratio of 1:6:15:20:15:6:1! Can you work out what ratio would have been expected if only two genes, not three, had been involved?

Many characters are polygenic, and it is a cause of **continuous variation**. A character is said to vary continuously if individuals show a range of phenotypes with a smooth graduation from one extreme to another, rather than falling into a small number of discrete categories. An example in humans is height.

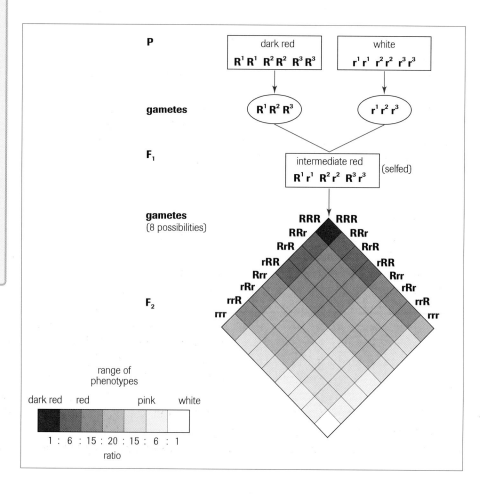

Figure 33.16 In wheat, seed colour is determined polygenically. A total of three genes are involved. This diagram illustrates the complicated phenotype ratios that can result when characters show polygenic inheritance.

Characters that show continuous variation, if they have a genetic basis at all, are usually polygenic. Other characters, such as those that Mendel studied in his garden peas, show **discontinuous variation**. Mendel could unambiguously assign all his pea plants to a small number of phenotypes, such as tall or short. This is because only one gene is involved, and is quite different from the continuous variation in height seen in humans.

Epistasis

Another sort of gene interaction is seen when one gene modifies or masks the action of another gene. This is known as **epistasis**, and it can give rise to unusual ratios in genetic crosses. We are not talking about dominant and recessive *alleles* which, by definition, occur at the same loci on homologous chromosomes. The genes involved in epistasis occur at different loci.

An example of epistasis is provided by the inheritance of certain coat colours in mice. Most mice have a coat colour described as agouti, a greyish pattern formed by alternating bands of pigment on each hair (*figure 33.17*). However, some mice are black and others white.

The allele for agouti coat colour (**A**) is dominant to the allele for black (**a**). White coat colour is due to the presence of a recessive allele (**w**) at a *separate* locus, so that white mice are homozygous recessive (**ww**). A mouse that is homozygous recessive has a white coat *irrespective* of the alleles at the other locus. Thus **AAww**, **Aaww** and **aaww** are all white. The relationship between the genotypes and phenotypes is summarised in table 33.1.

One way to explain these results is to suppose that the following pathway determines coat colour:

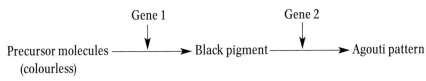

Lack of the product made by gene 1 leads to a white coat colour, irrespective of the actions of gene 2, because the colourless precursor molecules accumulate unless the product made by gene 1 is present.

You might find it instructive to consider the outcome of crossing the various genotypes listed in table 33.1. For example, try crossing two mice with the genotypes **AaWw**. You should get a 9:3:4 ratio. One can't help thinking that if Mendel's crosses had produced such ratios, he would have found them rather difficult to explain.

Figure 33.17 Adult female house mouse with her three-day-old young. Notice her agouti coat colour.

Table 33.1 The relationship between genotype and phenotype in the determination of mouse coat colour.

Phenotype	Genotypes
Agouti	AAWW, AaWW, AAWw, AaWw
Black	aaWW, aaWw
White	AAww, Aaww, aaww

> ### Extension
>
> ### The inheritance of intelligence
>
> Few topics cause as much argument in human heredity as the genetics of intelligence. On the one hand some people argue that intelligence is a polygenic trait which, though influenced by the environment, is essentially inherited. At the other extreme there is the view that, with the exception of people with moderate or severe learning disabilities, a person's upbringing is overwhelmingly the most important determinant of his or her intelligence.
>
> Another view is that it is difficult to agree on precisely what is meant by intelligence and that even if a compromise definition can be agreed, intelligence is very difficult to measure.
>
> Some of the best data supporting a strong genetic component to inheritance come from studies of identical twins reared apart. Not surprisingly, there are not many such twins. However, in several countries careful studies have been made of the **intelligence quotient (IQ)** of identical twins adopted into different families from very early childhood. The twins' IQs can be measured by giving them **IQ tests**. These tests are meant to quantify how intelligent a person is, though there is considerable disagreement about their validity.
>
> If intelligence lacks any genetic component, there should be no relationship between the IQs of separated identical twins. In other words, the **correlation coefficient** between the IQs of the twins should be zero. On the other hand, if intelligence lacks any environmental component, the

correlation coefficient should be 1. In fact it varies from 0.49 to 0.78, which is quite high for a correlation coefficient and shows that there is quite a strong relationship between the IQs of separated identical twins. (These data do not include the results obtained by the English geneticist Cyril Burt, as he seems to have made up some of his data.)

This looks like strong evidence for a genetic *and* an environmental tw component to intelligence. However, it has been pointed out that just because the twins were brought up in different homes, it does not necessarily mean that their environments will have been dissimilar. After all, a child who is adopted is not sent randomly into any family, but goes to carefully selected parents who have to fulfil certain criteria showing that they can care for the child. Indeed, most adoption agencies try to 'match' children and the families in which they are placed.

Adoption studies provide some of the strongest evidence that the environment plays a very important role in the determination of intelligence. If you look at the intelligence of unrelated children adopted into the same family, correlations between the children's IQs vary from 0.12 to as high as 0.65. The extreme view that intelligence is innately determined and uninfluenced by the environment would predict a correlation of 0.

Perhaps the most valid conclusion to draw is that both heredity and environment play a part in determining intelligence and that it is difficult to assess their relative importance.

Summary

1. In dihybrid crosses, genes sometimes fail to assort independently. This can be explained by postulating that such genes are carried on the same chromosome (**linkage**).

2. Genes linked together on the same chromosome constitute a **linkage group**. The number of linkage groups equals the haploid number of chromosomes, and the number of genes in the linkage groups corresponds to the lengths of the chromosomes.

3. Homologous chromosomes are normally identical in appearance (**autosomes**). In many species an exception is provided by the **sex chromosomes**.

4. In mammals and birds, sex is determined by the presence of the **X** and **Y chromosomes**. In mammals, females are **XX** and males **XY**.

5. In humans, genes are carried on all the autosomes and also on the X chromosome. Examples of X-linked inheritance (**sex linkage**) include red-green colour blindness and haemophilia.

6. Crosses involving linked genes usually produce a small proportion of offspring with new combinations (**recombinants**) in addition to the parental combinations. This can be explained by the formation of **chiasmata** and **crossing over** during meiosis.

7. Crossing over enables geneticists to work out the relative positions of genes on a chromosome. In general the distance between two genes is proportional to their **cross over value** (**COV**). In this way chromosome maps can be established.

8. The **Human Genome Project** is an international collaboration to sequence the entire human **genome**.

9. In **codominance**, two alleles both exert a phenotypic effect when present together in the heterozygous state.

10. Some characteristics are controlled by **multiple alleles**. In the case of the **ABO blood group system**, three alleles are involved, although only two can be present in any one individual. These alleles are inherited in a normal Mendelian manner.

11. Sometimes the presence of two particular alleles at a locus results in the death of an organism. Such alleles are **recessive lethals**. Occasionally the presence of just one allele is sufficient to cause death, in which case the allele is a **dominant lethal**.

12. Some alleles affect two or more characteristics of an organism. This is called **pleiotropy**. The allele for yellow fur colour in mice and the cystic fibrosis allele in humans are examples.

13. The transmission of a character, such as height in humans, which is influenced by the presence of several genes is called **polygenic inheritance**.

14. Polygenic characters generally show **continuous variation**. In contrast, characters such as height in Mendel's pea plants, which are caused by single genes, show **discontinuous variation**. The **environment** is also important in producing continuous variation.

15. Sometimes one gene modifies or masks the action of another gene. This is known as **epistasis**.

For general advice on these questions and advice on answering essay-type questions, see pages vii and viii.

1. The way in which sex is determined in birds is different from that in mammals. In birds, the male has two X chromosomes while the female has one X and one Y chromosome. In poultry, the gene for chick colour is sex linked and carried on the X chromosome. The allele for light colour is dominant to that for dark colour.

(a) Copy and complete the genetic diagram below to show the cross in which all the male chicks will be light coloured and all the female chicks will be dark coloured.

	Male (XX)	Female (XY)
Phenotype of parents:		
Genotype of parents:		
Gametes:		
Genotype of chicks:		
Phenotype of chicks:	Light-coloured male : Dark-coloured female; 1:1	

(3)

(b) Poultry farmers who keep hens for egg laying usually buy young chicks from a poultry breeder. Explain why sex linkage may be of practical use in poultry farming. (1)

(Total 4 marks)

AEB 1997

2. (a) Describe two examples of the effect of the environment on the phenotype. (8)

(b) Explain how interaction at one locus, and between loci, affects phenotypic variation. (10)

(Total 18 marks)

UCLES 1997

3. The table above right shows data from studies of twins and their siblings (brothers and sisters).

	Mean differences			
Trait	Identical twins		Non-identical twins reared together (52 pairs)	Siblings of the same sex reared together (52 pairs)
	reared together (50 pairs)	reared apart (19 pairs)		
Height/cm	1.7	1.8	4.4	4.5
Mass/kg	1.9	4.5	4.6	2.1
Head length/mm	2.9	2.2	6.2	not available
Head width/mm	2.8	2.9	4.2	not available
Intelligence	5.9	8.2	9.9	9.8

(a) Identical twins are sometimes called 'monozygotic twins'. Suggest why. (1)

(b) Using the information in the table,

(i) give **one** trait, the difference in which was largely due to genetic factors.
Explain the evidence for your answer. (2)

(ii) give **one** trait, the difference in which was largely due to environmental factors.
Explain the evidence for your answer. (2)

(c) Explain why any conclusions about identical twins drawn from these data should be viewed with caution. (1)

(Total 6 marks)

NEAB 1998

4. The following pedigree shows the inheritance in a family of a type of blindness:

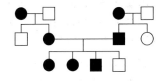

The circles are females and the squares are males; filled in symbols indicate affected (blind) individuals; empty symbols indicate unaffected individuals.

Indicate whether each of the following patterns of inheritance is consistent with the pedigree:

(a) autosomal recessive;

(b) autosomal dominant;

(c) X-linked recessive;

(d) X-linked dominant

(e) Y-linkage.

(Total 5 marks)

Part 6

Chapter 34

The nature of the gene

Figure 34.1 Modoris Ali and his wife, Aygun Bibi, photographed with four of their five children in London. Modoris Ali applied in 1975 for his family to join him in Britain from Bangladesh but the British authorities did not believe that Aygun was his wife or that the children were his. Subsequently, DNA fingerprinting proved that Modoris Ali and Aygun Bibi were the parents of all five children. Aygun and the four younger children were allowed to enter Britain in 1988. However, entry was refused to Boshir, the eldest child, identified by Aygun in the photograph the parents are holding, because he was over 18 by then – even though he was only 13 years of age when they applied for entry. Some of the documentation in the case is shown at lower left.

In this chapter we shall explore the chemical nature of the gene, and we shall see that an understanding of how it works lies in its molecular structure. This is not of purely academic interest. It has practical applications too – see figure 34.1 for example. But before getting down to details let us see what general *predictions* we can make about the nature of the gene.

Genes help to determine an organism's characteristics. This means that genes must contain **information**, a set of instructions if you like, telling the organism how to develop. It also follows that genes must be able to reproduce themselves, or **replicate**, without losing this information, otherwise the instructions they carry will be progressively diluted in successive generations.

In searching for the chemical nature of the gene, scientists therefore looked for molecules that contain information and are capable of replication. Nowadays everyone accepts that **nucleic acids** fulfill this role.

Extension

Early evidence that nucleic acids carry genetic information

For many years proteins were considered the only possible candidates for carrying genetic information because they alone seemed to have the structural diversity necessary to perform this role. But in 1944, Oswald Avery of the Rockefeller Institute in New York produced evidence that nucleic acids rather than proteins are the carriers of genetic information.

First, some background information. The bacteria that cause pneumonia, *Pneumococcus*, exist in two different strains: **capsulated** and **non-capsulated**. The former are characterised by a thick capsule which surrounds the cells. In the non-capsulated strain this capsule is missing. Avery and his colleagues prepared a sample of dead capsulated bacteria. They then extracted the polysaccharides from these cells and added them to a medium in which non-capsulated bacteria were growing.

Nothing remarkable happened. The non-capsulated bacteria simply gave rise to more non-capsulated bacteria. Exactly the same result followed when lipids, proteins or ribonucleic acid (RNA) were tried. However, when deoxyribonucleic acid (DNA) was extracted from the dead capsulated bacteria and added to the medium, capsulated bacteria appeared amongst the non-capsulated ones. This showed that DNA carries the information that determines whether the bacteria are capsulated or non-capsulated.

Avery's was one of a number of early studies into the nature of the genetic material. Twenty years before Avery, an English medical officer, Frederick Griffith, had worked on a non-virulent strain (a strain that does not cause disease) of the bacterium *Pneumococcus*. Griffith showed that this non-virulent strain could be made virulent by taking up something from a virulent strain that had been heat-killed. Avery's subsequent work showed that this something was DNA.

The virulent strain of bacteria in Griffith's experiment is the *capsulated* strain worked on by Avery. They are virulent because their capsules make it difficult for phagocytes to destroy them (*page 321*). These early investigations admirably demonstrate the effectiveness of DNA in determining an organism's characteristics.

The structure of nucleic acids

Nucleic acids occur in all living cells and in viruses. Unravelling their structure has been one of the most exciting adventures in modern science. It has brought us to a better understanding of heredity and development, and has opened the doors to understanding the nature of life itself.

The components of nucleic acids

Two types of nucleic acids are found in cells: **deoxyribonucleic acid (DNA)** and **ribonucleic acid (RNA)**. By means of chemical tests on eukaryotic cells, it can be shown that DNA is found in the nucleus, mitochondria and chloroplasts, whereas RNA is found in the nucleus and cytoplasm, though mainly in the latter. Like proteins, nucleic acids are long chain molecules, but the chains are mostly longer than those of proteins and the sub-units more complicated than amino acids.

The building blocks of a nucleic acid are called **nucleotides**. DNA and RNA are therefore **polynucleotides**, DNA being a particularly stable polynucleotide. A nucleotide consists of three molecules linked together: a **pentose sugar**, **phosphoric acid** and an **organic base**. We shall look at each in turn.

A pentose sugar has basically the same structure as a hexose sugar such as glucose except that there is one less carbon atom in the ring. As a result, the molecule is constructed as follows:

> Hexose and pentose sugars, page 16

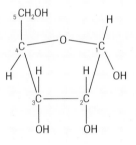

This particular sugar is **ribose** and it is found in ribonucleic acid.

Deoxyribonucleic acid has a different sugar, **deoxyribose**, which differs from ribose only in that the hydroxyl group at position 2 is replaced by a hydrogen atom. Notice how deoxyribose has one less oxygen atom than ribose – hence its name *deoxy*ribose:

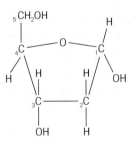

The second constituent of a nucleotide is **phosphoric acid** (H_3PO_4) which has the structural formula:

Part 6

The third component is the **organic base**. DNA contains four different organic bases: **adenine**, **guanine**, **cytosine** and **thymine**, abbreviated respectively to **A**, **G**, **C** and **T**. RNA too contains adenine, cytosine and guanine, but has **uracil** (abbreviated to **U**) rather than thymine. All these five bases are ring compounds composed of carbon and nitrogen atoms which for simplicity we can represent thus:

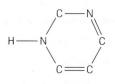

Putting the components together

How do the three components link up to form a nucleotide? As in the construction of so many other organic compounds, the process is one of condensation (*figure 34.2A*). A sugar attaches itself to a phosphoric acid molecule at position 5, and to one of the five bases at position 1. Two molecules of water are removed in the process.

To form a nucleic acid, the nucleotides are then strung together. This also involves condensation. The sugar of one nucleotide joins to the phosphate radical of another nucleotide at position 3 and a molecule of water is released. The addition of further nucleotides produces a long chain of linked nucleotides whose backbone consists of alternating sugar and phosphate groups with the bases projecting sideways from the sugars (*figure 34.2B*).

The sugar and the phosphate groups are identical all the way along the chain; in other words the backbone is absolutely uniform and shows no variation in structure. In RNA the sugars are all ribose; in DNA they are all deoxyribose. The phosphate groups are the same in RNA and DNA.

The bases, however, show no such uniformity. We have already noted that there are five different ones: A, G, C, T and U. DNA contains A, G, C and T; RNA A, G, C and U. The

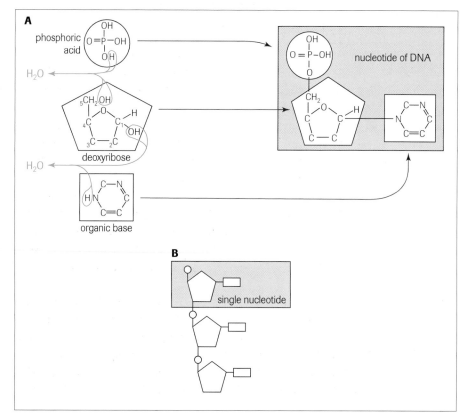

Figure 34.2 How a nucleic acid is built up.
A A pentose sugar, in this case deoxyribose, binds with a phosphoric acid molecule and an organic base to form a nucleotide.
B Nucleotides join through their phosphate groups to form a chain of nucleotides. As well as being the building blocks of nucleic acids, nucleotides are the basis of ATP and enter into the structure of NAD, NADP and FAD, coenzymes involved in respiration and photosynthesis (*pages 144 and 209*).

sequence in which these bases occur along the length of the nucleic acid chain varies from species to species and from individual to individual. It is in this sequence of bases that the nucleic acid carries information controlling the organism's development.

At first sight it may seem incredible that all the instructions required to produce an organism as complicated as, say, a human being, should be conveyed by only four kinds of base. However, it should be borne in mind that a single molecule of DNA may contain five million nucleotides, and the number of possible combinations is almost infinite.

The bases are, in fact, like letters in a four-letter alphabet. From these four letters innumerable words can be constructed. It is worth remembering that computers use only two 'letters' (0 and 1) so perhaps it is not too surprising that four letters are enough to specify a human.

The Watson–Crick hypothesis

In 1953 James Watson and Francis Crick, working together at the Cavendish Laboratory in Cambridge, put forward a possible structure for DNA. How did they arrive at their conclusions?

Some years earlier an American chemist, Erwin Chargaff, had used chromatography to separate the four bases in DNA samples from various organisms. Quantitative techniques were then used to work out the amounts of the four bases. Some of Chargaff's original data are given in table 34.1.

Figure 34.3 James Watson (left) and Francis Crick with their model of DNA. Watson and Crick worked together in the Cavendish Laboratory at Cambridge in the early 1950s when Watson, an American, was on a post-doctoral visit to Europe. Their collaboration led to the discovery of the structure of DNA, for which, together with Maurice Wilkins, they were awarded a Nobel Prize in 1962.

Table 34.1 Chargaff's original data on the base composition of DNA.

Source	Approximate per cent			
	A	C	G	T
Yeast	32	17	18	33
Avian tubercle bacilli	16	34	36	14
Ox thymus	30	18	24	28
Ox spleen	30	18	24	29
Human sperm	30	19	19	32

What do you notice about Chargaff's results? You can see that the ratio of adenine to thymine is close to one, as is the ratio of guanine to cytosine. How can this be explained? Watson and Crick suggested that DNA might consist of two parallel strands held together by pairs of bases; adenine being paired with thymine, and guanine with cytosine.

Meanwhile attempts had been made to work out the structure of DNA by X-ray diffraction analysis (*page 33*). Despite formidable technical difficulties, mainly caused by DNA's reluctance to crystallise, some clear X-ray photographs were obtained by Rosalind Franklin and Maurice Wilkins at King's College, London.

Interpreting X-ray diffraction patterns is no easy matter at the best of times and for a large and complex molecule like DNA it is particularly difficult, especially when the patterns are rather diffuse. However, Watson and Crick set to work on the X-ray patterns, and after months of effort they suddenly realised that both Chargaff's results and the X-ray diffraction data could be explained if DNA consists of two chains twisted around each other to form a **double helix**.

From the relative positions of certain spots in the X-ray photographs, Watson and Crick concluded that the two chains are cross-linked at regular intervals corresponding to the nucleotides, and that there are 10 nucleotides for one complete turn of the helix. Watson and Crick thus envisaged DNA as a kind of twisted ladder, the two uprights consisting of chains of alternating sugar and phosphate groups, the rungs as pairs of bases sticking inwards towards each other and linked together in a specific relationship: A with T, and C with G (*figure 34.5*).

Figure 34.4 Rosalind Franklin worked on the structure of DNA at King's College, London in the early 1950s. An expert X-ray crystallographer, she showed in 1952 that the phosphate groups of DNA must lie on the outside of the molecule. Her work was pivotal in enabling Watson and Crick to propose their hypothesis for the structure of DNA. Her career was cut short in 1958 when she died tragically of cancer at the age of 37, four years before Crick, Watson and Wilkins were awarded the Nobel Prize. Nobel Prizes cannot be awarded posthumously.

What is the evidence that A bonds with T and C with G?

There are two main lines of evidence that A bonds with T and C with G. Firstly, such a relationship would explain Chargaff's discovery that cells contain the same amount of A as T, and the same amount of C as G. Secondly, when Watson and Crick made accurate cut-out models of the four different nucleotides with all their atoms and bonds in the right places, they found that the only way they could make a model of DNA was to have the two strands running in opposite directions (i.e. **antiparallel**) with the bases linked A to T and C to G by hydrogen bonds.

Thymine and cytosine are **pyrimidine** bases consisting of a single hexagonal ring. Adenine and guanine, on the other hand, are **purine** bases consisting of a hexagonal ring joined to a pentagonal ring (*figure 34.6*). The rungs in the DNA ladder can only be formed by linking a purine with a pyrimidine. The sizes of the four bases are such that there would be insufficient room for two purines and too much room for two pyrimidines. The bases in each rung are held together by hydrogen bonds. The positions of the hydrogen atoms in relation to the shape of the molecule ensure that A links with T, and C with G, rather like the fitting together of complementary pieces in a jigsaw puzzle.

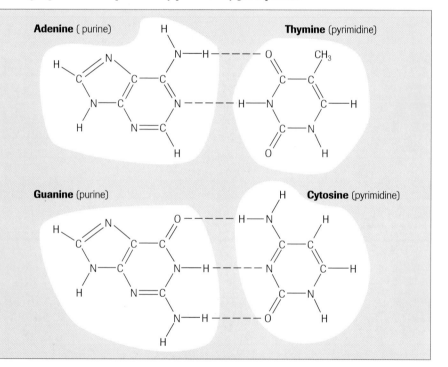

Figure 34.6 Diagram showing the structural formulae of the four organic bases in DNA and how they form hydrogen bonds with one another. The configuration of the molecules is such that two hydrogen bonds are formed between A and T, and three between C and G. In RNA uracil replaces thymine. Uracil's structure is the same as thymine's except that the CH_3 group of the latter is replaced by H. U therefore links with A just as T does.

34.2 **DNA replication**

It was said at the outset of this chapter that an essential property of the genetic material is that it should be able to replicate accurately. Watson and Crick realised that an attractive feature of their model was that it provided a possible method of replication.

Look at figure 34.5. It isn't difficult to imagine the two chains separating from each other rather like a zip unfastening – it should be remembered that hydrogen bonds (which link the bases of one chain with the bases of the other) are not very strong. Any free nucleotides

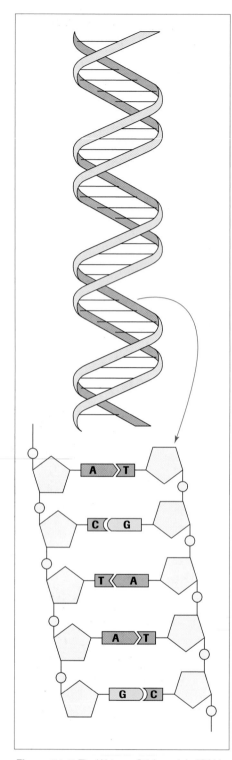

Figure 34.5 The Watson–Crick model of DNA. At the top is shown a short length of the double helix: the two strands are cross-linked at intervals by hydrogen bonds, 10 cross-linkages for every complete turn of the spiral. Below is shown a short length of the DNA helix untwisted to show the positions of the sugars, phosphates and organic bases (A, C, G and T) in the two strands. Note that A pairs with T, and C with G.

would then come along and form hydrogen bonds with each of the two chains. If these nucleotides then joined together through their sugar and phosphate groups, two DNA molecules would result. The complementary relationship between the bases would ensure that each of these DNA molecules was identical to the original one. Because the sequence of bases in the two daughter molecules is exactly the same as in the parent molecule, accurate replication will have occurred, just as required. This process is illustrated in figure 34.7.

What evidence is there that accurate replication of DNA does indeed take place? If the hypothesis is correct then we should be able to demonstrate DNA synthesis *in vitro* outside the cell. All that should be needed for this is a liberal sprinkling of the four types of nucleotide, an energy source (ATP), the enzyme needed to join together neighbouring nucleotides and intact DNA to act as the **template** for the synthesis of new DNA.

The first successful attempt to replicate DNA in a test tube in this way was carried out by Arthur Kornberg, then at the University of Washington. This was a triumph of molecular biology. Kornberg's greatest difficulty was isolating the enzyme that joins the nucleotides together, but after overcoming great technical problems he managed to extract and purify the necessary enzyme from the colon bacillus *Escherichia coli*. He called the enzyme **DNA polymerase**. The stage was now set for the synthesis of DNA.

Kornberg and his colleagues found, as predicted, that if intact DNA was added to a solution containing nucleotides, DNA polymerase and ATP, new DNA molecules were formed. Not only that, but on analysis the new DNA was found to have the same proportions of the four bases in its structure as the original parent DNA, a strong indication that accurate replication had occurred.

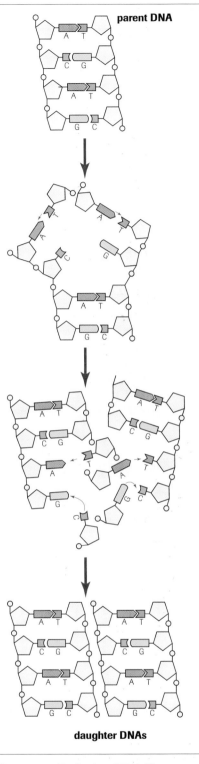

Figure 34.7 Replication of DNA. The two strands of the double helix part company and free nucleotides align themselves in relation to each of the two strands. The specific relationship between A and T and between C and G ensures that the sequence of bases in the daughter DNAs is exactly the same as in the parent DNA.

Conservative versus semi-conservative replication

The zip-fastener idea is a neat and economical way of explaining replication, but it is not the only one. For instance, another possibility is to suppose that the double helix remains intact and in some way stimulates the synthesis of a second double helix identical with the first.

These two alternative hypotheses were put to the test in the late 1950s by Matthew Meselson and Franklin Stahl in a classic investigation which admirably demonstrates the scientific principles of hypothesis-making and testing.

If the zip-fastener hypothesis is correct, neither of the products of DNA replication should be completely new; rather, in both daughter DNA molecules one of the two strands

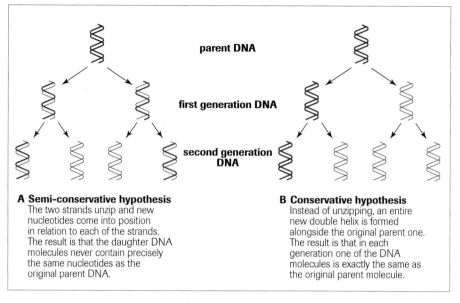

Figure 34.8 Diagram comparing the two ways in which DNA might replicate. The original DNA is shown as thick red lines, the new DNA strands as thin red lines.

A Semi-conservative hypothesis
The two strands unzip and new nucleotides come into position in relation to each of the strands. The result is that the daughter DNA molecules never contain precisely the same nucleotides as the original parent DNA.

B Conservative hypothesis
Instead of unzipping, an entire new double helix is formed alongside the original parent one. The result is that in each generation one of the DNA molecules is exactly the same as the original parent molecule.

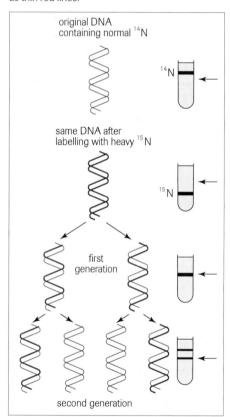

Figure 34.9 The Meselson–Stahl experiment. On the right are shown the results of centrifuging the DNA from bacteria grown for many generations in ^{15}N and then transferred to ^{14}N. A band above the arrow indicates normal 'light' DNA; a band below the arrow indicates 'heavy' DNA, i.e. DNA containing ^{15}N; a band situated on the arrow indicates DNA of intermediate density. On the left is the interpretation in terms of DNA replication: the 'heavy' DNA (containing ^{15}N) is shown by thick red lines, the normal DNA by thin red lines. Notice that the interpretation supports the idea of semi-conservative replication and satisfactorily explains the results of the centrifugation.

should be new, while the other should be one of the two parental strands. On the other hand, if the second hypothesis is correct, one of the two daughter DNAs will be completely new, while the other one will be the original parent molecule.

These two hypotheses are summarised in figure 34.8 and are known as the **semi-conservative hypothesis** and **conservative hypothesis** respectively. To decide between them, Meselson and Stahl designed an elegant experiment involving *E. coli*.

Cells of *E. coli* were grown for many generations on a medium in which normal nitrogen, ^{14}N, was replaced with the heavy isotope, ^{15}N. Once enough time had passed for most of the nitrogen atoms in the DNA molecules of *E. coli* to be of the heavy type, the bacteria were introduced into a new medium containing normal ^{14}N. Samples of bacteria were then withdrawn at time intervals equal to the generation time, and the relative amounts of the two types of nitrogen estimated by a technique which relied on the fact that molecules containing ^{15}N are very slightly heavier than those containing ^{14}N. Ultracentrifugation was used to separate the DNA molecules according to the ratio of ^{14}N to ^{15}N that they contained.

The results, shown in figure 34.9, give unequivocal support to the semi-conservative (zip-fastener) hypothesis. In the first generation after being switched back to normal ^{14}N, the DNA was found to have a density midway between what it would have if it contained only ^{14}N or only ^{15}N; in other words it contained equal amounts of each. In the second generation, two sorts of DNA were detected: one sort contained only ^{14}N; the other sort was the same as that obtained in the first generation, i.e. it contained equal amounts of ^{14}N and ^{15}N. These results fit in perfectly with what we would expect from the semi-conservative hypothesis.

34.3 How does DNA work?

So far in this chapter we have considered the evidence that DNA is the molecule of heredity. But how are the instructions that are embodied in DNA translated into action?

To answer this question we must first appreciate what exactly responds to DNA's instructions. An analogy may be helpful here. An architect's plan contains information for building a house. The complete set of instructions may be contained on a few sheets of paper. However, if the house is to be built, these instructions must be interpreted and put into action by a builder. With nothing more than the necessary materials and the architect's blueprint, the builder must be able to construct the house exactly as the

The double helix

Model-building played an essential part in Watson and Crick's discovery of the structure of DNA. Here Watson reflects on the building of their final model.

The following morning I felt marvellously alive when I awoke. After contentedly poring over *The Times*, I wandered into the lab to see Francis, unquestionably early, flipping the cardboard base pairs about an imaginary line. As far as a compass and ruler could tell him, both sets of base pairs neatly fitted into the backbone configuration. As the morning wore on, Max and John successively came by to see if we still thought we had it. Each got a quick, concise lecture from Francis, during the second of which I wandered down to see if the shop could be speeded up to produce the purines and pyrimidines later that afternoon.

Only a little encouragement was needed to get the final soldering accomplished in the next couple of hours. The brightly shining metal plates were then immediately used to make a model in which for the first time all the DNA components were present. In about an hour I had arranged the atoms in positions which satisfied both the X-ray data and the laws of stereochemistry. The resulting helix was right-handed with two chains running in opposite directions.

Only one person can easily play with a model, and so Francis did not try to check my work until I backed away and said that I thought everything fitted. While one interatomic contact was slightly shorter than optimal, it was not out of line with several published values, and I was not disturbed. Another 15 minutes' fiddling by Francis failed to find anything

wrong, though for brief intervals my stomach felt uneasy when I saw him frowning. In each case he became satisfied and moved on to verify that another interatomic contact was reasonable. Everything thus looked very good when we went back to have supper with Odile.

Abstracted from *The Double Helix* by James D. Watson (Weidenfeld and Nicolson, 1968).

The Francis to whom Watson refers is of course Francis Crick. Max and John are Max Perutz and John Kendrew who discovered the molecular structure of haemoglobin and myoglobin respectively. Odile is Francis Crick's wife and the 'shop' is the workshop in the Cavendish Laboratory.

architect intended. In the same way the coded information in DNA must be interpreted and translated into action in the cell.

DNA as a code for proteins

In earlier chapters we have seen how everything a cell does – what it develops into, what it synthesises and how it operates – is determined by, more than anything, its enzymes and other proteins. It is not surprising therefore that the central role of DNA, apart from replicating itself, is to tell the cell what proteins to make.

How might this be done? A protein may contain up to 500 amino acids of 20 different types. It is the order in which these amino acids are arranged and their relative abundance that gives a particular protein its individuality. Somehow the DNA with its four different bases has got to determine the sequence in which the 20 different types of amino acid are put together in the protein. The question is: how can a code with a four-letter alphabet (for that is what DNA amounts to) specify a protein which at any given point contains one of 20 different amino acids?

Clearly a single base cannot specify a single amino acid, for then only four different amino acids could be coded for, and proteins containing only four kinds of amino acids would be formed. Nor is it feasible for just two bases to specify a single amino acid since only 16 amino acids could be coded for $(4 \times 4 = 16)$. But three bases is sufficient: with these a total of $4 \times 4 \times 4 = 64$ bases can be specified, more than enough to account for the 20 different amino acids commonly found in cells. Of course, four bases would give even more possibilities (how many?), but this is unnecessary.

The idea that a combination of three bases codes for one amino acid – a **triplet code** – was first put forward by Francis Crick on purely theoretical grounds, but since then a firm body of experimental evidence has been established to support it. A triplet of bases is known as a **codon**; codons form the basis of the genetic code.

▶ Evidence that genes control the synthesis of proteins, page 614

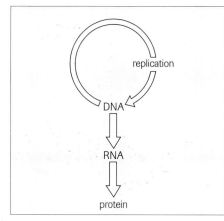

Figure 34.10 The central dogma of molecular genetics is that information flows from DNA to RNA and from RNA to protein. In addition DNA is capable of self-replication.

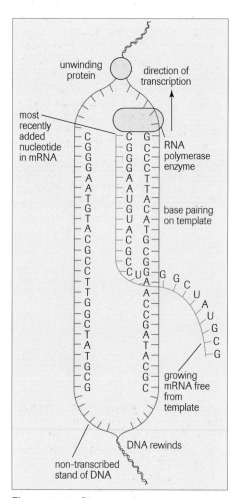

Figure 34.11 Diagrammatic representation of the synthesis of messenger RNA by DNA. When the DNA molecule unwinds, RNA nucleotides pair with one of the exposed strands of DNA which serves as a template. These nucleotides are then joined together by the enzyme RNA polymerase, resulting in messenger RNA.

How does DNA communicate with the cytoplasm?

We are now confronted with the problem of how the instructions embodied in the triplet code are carried out by the cell. DNA is located in the chromosomes in the nucleus, yet proteins are made in the cytoplasm on ribosomes (*page 611*). Somehow the information held by the triplets of bases in the DNA has got to be conveyed from the nucleus to the sites of protein synthesis in the cytoplasm.

How might this happen? Two possibilities suggest themselves. One is that the DNA itself, or part of it, moves out from the nucleus into the cytoplasm. The other is that the DNA stays in the nucleus and another molecule, acting as a go-between or messenger, carries instructions from the DNA to the cytoplasm. The first hypothesis can be discounted on the grounds that chromosomal DNA is never detected in the cytoplasm, which leaves us with the second.

We now know that DNA in the nucleus acts as the basis or **template** for the production of another sort of nucleic acid called **messenger RNA**. Messenger RNA gets its name from its ability to convey the instructions needed for protein synthesis from the nucleus to the cytoplasm. It is similar in structure to DNA in that it is made up of a string of nucleotides. However, it differs from DNA in four ways:

- it contains the sugar ribose instead of deoxyribose;
- it is single-stranded rather than double-stranded;
- it contains the base uracil instead of thymine;
- it is much shorter than DNA, usually containing fewer than a thousand nucleotides.

The idea that DNA makes protein via an intermediate, RNA, is known as the **central dogma of molecular genetics** (*figure 34.10*). Enshrined in this principle is the notion that information can only flow from DNA to proteins, not from proteins to DNA. In other words, changes in DNA may change the resulting proteins, but changes in proteins cannot feed back and change the DNA.

Formation of messenger RNA

How is messenger RNA formed? Before attempting to answer this question let us think about what messenger RNA has to do. A typical polypeptide might contain 200 amino acids. The instructions required for assembling such a molecule will involve 600 bases. However, a typical chromosome contains millions of bases. This means that a given messenger RNA molecule is required to carry instructions from only a very short section of a DNA molecule. The sequence of bases in the messenger RNA must exactly match the sequence of bases in this short section of DNA.

Bearing in mind how DNA replicates (*page 606*) you may be able to suggest how DNA makes RNA. The process is illustrated in figure 34.11. The double-stranded DNA first unwinds and then unzips in the relevant region. Free RNA nucleotides then align themselves opposite one of the two strands. Because of the complementary relationship between the bases in DNA and those in the free nucleotides, cytosine in the DNA attracts a guanine, guanine a cytosine, thymine an adenine, and adenine a uracil. An enzyme called **RNA polymerase** then joins these nucleotides together, resulting in the synthesis of messenger RNA. The whole process is known as **transcription**: DNA has been *transcribed* into RNA.

Once assembled, the messenger RNA molecule peels off its DNA template and moves out of the nucleus into the cytoplasm via the pores in the nuclear envelope. Meanwhile the relevant section of the DNA zips up and winds itself back into a helix again. Note that the sequence of bases in the messenger RNA molecule is the same as that of one of the two strands of the DNA – the one which did not act as the template. The only difference is that RNA has uracil whereas DNA has thymine.

34.4 Protein synthesis

When messenger RNA gets out into the cytoplasm it attaches itself to a ribosome where it causes amino acids to assemble in the right order. This it does with the help of yet another kind of nucleic acid called **transfer RNA**.

Transfer RNA takes its name from its function: its molecules *transfer* (carry) amino acids to ribosomes. They are comparatively small molecules and, unlike messenger RNA which is usually linear in shape, they are folded back on themselves to form a compact three-dimensional structure shaped rather like a clover leaf (*figure 34.12*). Their most important property is that they can bind to amino acids at one end and to messenger RNA at the other.

It has been shown that cells possess over 20 different types of transfer RNA – more than enough for the different amino acids. What happens is shown in figure 34.13. The **amino acid binding site** of the transfer RNA is attached by an enzyme to a specific amino acid. The transfer RNA and accompanying amino acid then move to the messenger RNA on the ribosome. The three bases at the **messenger RNA binding site** then form hydrogen bonds with the appropriate three bases in the messenger RNA molecule. The three bases in the messenger RNA are the codon, and the corresponding bases in the transfer RNA comprise the **anticodon**.

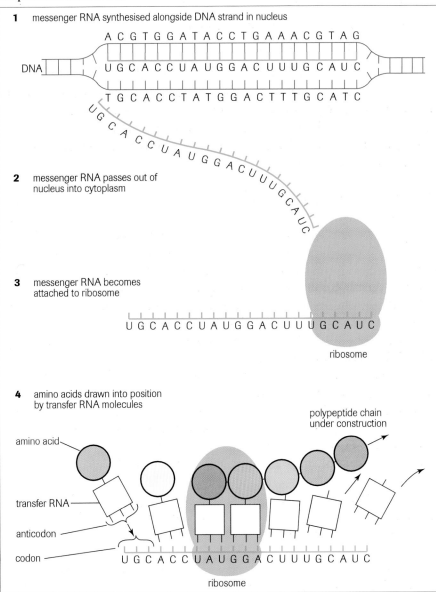

Figure 34.12 The structure of transfer RNA. The molecule has been untwisted, so it appears here as a flat molecule shaped like a clover leaf. There are over 20 different sorts of transfer RNAs in each cell. Some nucleotides occupy the same positions in all transfer RNAs; these are shown in green. The other nucleotides vary according to the particular transfer RNA. The symbols D, γ, ψ and T represent unusual bases characteristic of transfer RNA. Base pairings occur only in certain regions as shown. The three bases at the bottom constitute the messenger RNA binding site, or anticodon. They form hydrogen bonds with the appropriate triplet of bases in messenger RNA. The amino acid binding site is at the top of the molecule.

Figure 34.13 Diagram summarising how DNA in the nucleus controls the assembly of a polypeptide in the cytoplasm. Through the action of transfer RNA, the messenger RNA dictates the order in which amino acids link up to form the polypeptide chain. The anticodons at the ends of the transfer RNA molecules complement the codons (base triplets) in the messenger RNA. Thus the anticodon belonging to the left-hand transfer RNA molecule in this diagram is ACG. In this diagram the transfer RNA molecules are represented as squares; in reality they are shaped like clover leaves as indicated in figure 34.12.

In this way the amino acids are linked up in an order corresponding to the sequence of base triplets in the messenger RNA. As the latter is determined by the sequence of base triplets in the original DNA, it follows that the base sequence in the DNA determines the order in which the amino acids line up on the ribosome.

Once aligned, peptide bonds are formed sequentially between adjacent amino acids and a polypeptide chain is eventually formed. The process of assembly starts at one end of the chain, the end with a free amino group, and proceeds, amino acid by amino acid, to the other end – the end with a free carboxyl group. As the amino acids join up, the completed polypeptide chain peels off from the transfer RNA molecules. The job of the transfer RNAs complete, they detach themselves from the messenger RNA and return to the pool of transfer RNAs in the cytoplasm, from which they can be drawn upon again when required.

As might be expected, the process described above requires energy and this is provided by ATP and related compounds. A large proportion of the fuel our bodies burn up is needed for protein synthesis. Enzymes too are involved at various stages, for instance to attach the amino acids to the transfer RNAs, and to join the adjacent amino acids together.

Earlier, we said that the synthesis of messenger RNA from DNA is known as transcription. The synthesis of proteins from messenger RNA is known as **translation**: messenger RNA has been *translated* into protein.

The role of the ribosomes

The function of the ribosomes is to provide a suitable surface for attachment of messenger RNA and the assembly of protein. But there is more to them than this. Ribosomes may occur in chains called **polyribosomes**. Under the electron microscope a polyribosome is seen to consist of five to 50 individual ribosomes. Special staining techniques show that they lie on a single strand of messenger RNA.

How does a polyribosome function in protein synthesis? What seems to happen is that a ribosome attaches itself near one end of a messenger RNA strand and then progresses towards the other end. As the ribosome passes a triplet of bases the appropriate transfer RNA molecule takes up position, bringing its amino acid with it. The ribosome then moves on to the next section of the messenger RNA strand and another amino acid is drawn into position, and so on. As the ribosome moves along the messenger RNA, more and more amino acids are added to the growing polypeptide chain. Meanwhile the other ribosomes follow suit so that several ribosomes may move along the messenger RNA strand simultaneously, each synthesising a polypeptide chain as it does so. On reaching the end of the messenger RNA strand the ribosome drops off and releases its polypeptide chain. This process is summarised in figure 34.14.

More about ribosomes

Ribosomes consist of protein combined with a type of RNA known as **ribosomal RNA**. The structure responsible for the manufacture of ribosomes is the **nucleolus** (*page 42*). Abnormal cells lacking nucleoli fail to manufacture ribosomal RNA, and are thus unable to make ribosomes.

Eukaryotic ribosomes exist in the cytoplasm in two sub-units, a smaller one called a **40 S sub-unit**, and a larger one called a **60 S sub-unit**. (S is a unit of size.) Both contain numerous protein molecules together with ribosomal RNA.

Some eukaryotic ribosomes are bound to rough endoplasmic reticulum. Others are found unbound throughout the cytoplasm. Generally proteins which are secreted from cells are synthesised on bound ribosomes, whereas those which remain in the cytosol are made on free ribosomes.

Ribosomes are also found in prokaryotes and in mitochondria and chloroplasts. They are smaller than the ribosomes found in the cytoplasm of eukaryotic cells, though they too consist of two sub-units and are involved in protein synthesis.

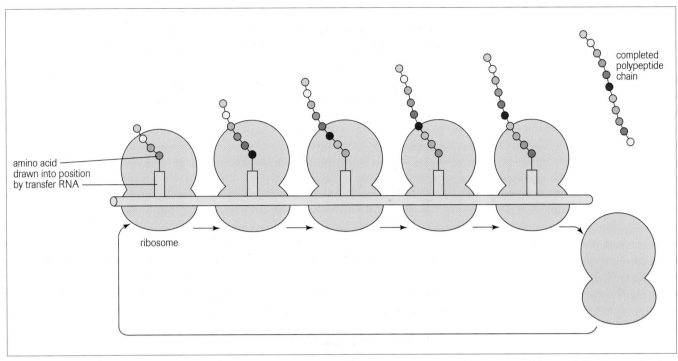

amino acid
drawn into position
by transfer RNA

ribosome

completed
polypeptide
chain

Figure 34.14 How a polyribosome works. A series of ribosomes moves along a messenger RNA molecule (or the messenger RNA moves along a chain of ribosomes depending on how you look at it). Each ribosome synthesises a polypeptide molecule as it moves along the messenger RNA. Transfer RNA molecules draw the appropriate amino acids into position as the ribosome passes each triplet of bases in the messenger RNA. When the ribosome reaches the end of the RNA strand, it releases its polypeptide chain and returns to the beginning.

The advantage of polyribosomes is that they allow a large number of polypeptides to be made from a single messenger RNA strand in a comparatively short time. It has been calculated that in red blood cells, for example, the time required for a single ribosome to travel the full length of a messenger RNA strand and produce a completed polypeptide chain is about one minute. By having 10 or more ribosomes all making proteins from a single messenger RNA strand at the same time, the rate of protein synthesis is greatly increased.

Is the code overlapping or non-overlapping?

Consider the following hypothetical sequence of bases in a short length of messenger RNA:

ACUGAC

If the code is non-overlapping, this sequence would consist of two codons one after the other like this:

ACUGAC

and obviously only two amino acids could be coded for. However, it is possible that the codons might overlap like this:

ACUGAC

in which case four amino acids would be coded for. A less compact sort of overlapping code would be one in which the codons overlap like this:

AGUGAC

The main advantage of an overlapping code is that it would permit a small number of bases to code for a relatively large number of amino acids, and this would enable an entire polypeptide to be programmed by a relatively short length of DNA. On the other hand, an overlapping code would impose a constraint on the sequencing of the amino acids.

The one gene – one enzyme hypothesis

The foregoing account of protein synthesis rests on the basic premise that genes (DNA) code for the synthesis of proteins, including enzymes. Evidence for this was first obtained in the 1940s by George Beadle and Edward Tatum. Beadle and Tatum, then at Stanford University in California, were interested in the genetics of the bread mould *Neurospora crassa*. They found that this mould would thrive on a minimal medium containing nothing but minerals, sucrose and the vitamin biotin. Evidently the mould could synthesise all its other organic compounds from these few precursors.

Beadle and Tatum subjected samples of this mould to radiation treatment and found as a consequence that some of the progeny failed to grow on the minimal medium. By systematically testing the growth of these mutants on different media, Beadle and Tatum discovered that each had acquired, through mutation, an inability to synthesise one specific organic compound. For instance, one mutant could only grow if provided with the amino acid arginine; another mutant could only grow if the medium contained ornithine.

When Beadle and Tatum crossed these mutants with normal moulds able to grow on the minimal medium, they found that the inability to synthesise the extra chemical was transmitted in a normal Mendelian manner.

Beadle and Tatum suggested that the mutants lacked specific enzymes; for example, that the mould which could only grow on the medium supplemented with arginine lacked an enzyme required for the synthesis of arginine. Beadle and Tatum therefore put forward the hypothesis that a single gene controls the production of a single enzyme, the **one gene – one enzyme hypothesis**.

In the case illustrated here, the mutant fails to grow on the first 19 media, but grows on the 20th, indicating that the

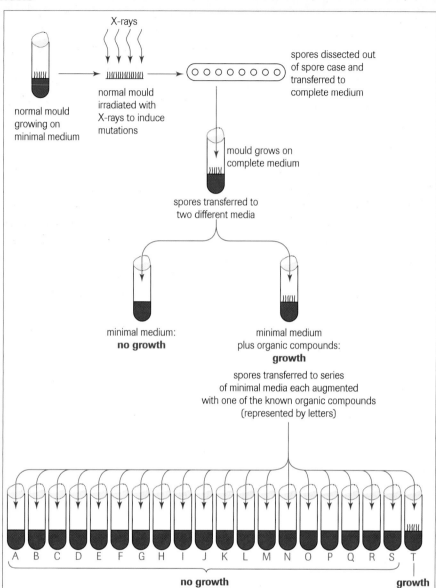

organic compound added to the minimal medium to make up this medium, compound T, is the one which the mutant cannot make for itself. Like many other microorganisms, *Neurospora* is haploid, each individual possessing a single allele rather than a pair as in diploid organisms. Crossing this mutant with a normal mould able to grow on the minimal medium produces spores, half of which are able to grow on the minimal medium while the other half can only grow on a medium to which T has been added. The defect is therefore transmitted in a Mendelian fashion, suggesting that the enzyme

responsible for the synthesis of T is controlled by a single gene.

Numerous experiments in biochemistry and genetics have shown that genes control the production not only of enzymes but of other proteins as well. Moreover, a single protein may contain several different polypeptides, each the result of a different gene. In view of this it would be more accurate to restate Beadle and Tatum's hypothesis as the **one gene – one polypeptide hypothesis**. Even this is an oversimplification as it is now known that not all genes code for polypeptides. Some carry out other functions (*page 623*).

For instance, in the first example of an overlapping code above, as the first amino acid is coded by ACU, the second one will have to be coded by a triplet whose first two bases are CU, and so on. Obviously this would limit the flexibility of the code.

We now know that the code is non-overlapping. This was first shown by making synthetic messenger RNA in the laboratory with the sequence GUAGUAGUAGUA and so on. The resulting protein made consisted only of one type of amino acid (valines). This suggests that the code is a non-overlapping one, being read in this instance as GUA, GUA, GUA, GUA. Had the code been overlapping it would have been read as GUA, UAG, AGU, GUA... or perhaps as GUA, AGU, UAG, GUA... In either case we would have expected the resulting polypeptide to consist of more than one amino acid.

The genetic dictionary

Painstaking work of the sort just described resulted, in 1966, in the complete elucidation of the genetic code – a triumph of modern biology. Table 34.2 summarises the **genetic dictionary**. It shows the relationship between the triplets of bases in messenger RNA (i.e. the codons) and the amino acids that they code for. From this you should be able to work out the relationship between the bases in the original DNA and the amino acids that result.

You can see that most of the amino acids are coded for by more than one codon. So the code contains more potential information than is actually used by the cell: to use the cybernetic term, the code is **degenerate**. Three of the codons do not actually code for an amino acid. Instead they stop the polypeptide chain at that point, acting as termination signals. These **stop codons** play an essential role in the cell, allowing polypeptides of precisely the right length to be produced.

Although the code is non-overlapping, certain viruses have found ways to squeeze additional information out of their relatively small supply of DNA. In some cases, genes overlap. That is, the start of one gene overlaps with the end of another, allowing the overlapping portion to be used both for the end of one protein and the beginning of another.

Breaking the code

In 1993, Manuel Santos and Mick Tuite at the University of Kent proved that the genetic dictionary is not universal. They found that in the yeast *Candida albicans* (which causes thrush), CUG, instead of coding for leucine (*table 34.2*), often (but not always) codes for serine. Five years later they found out why this is the case.

It turns out that the cause is a mutant transfer RNA which binds to the CUG codon but at its other end binds either to leucine or to serine. Fascinatingly, instead of weakening the yeast, the mutation seems to make it stronger! Experiments have shown that it makes the yeast better able to tolerate high temperatures, heavy metals, powerful oxidising agents and cyclohexamide (an antibiotic).

➤ What are mutations? Page 742

Table 34.2 The genetic dictionary. The messenger RNA codons corresponding to the 20 amino acids made in cells are shown in this genetic dictionary. Three triplets act as stop codons, and under certain conditions the codon AUG initiates protein synthesis. The dictionary is known to hold for almost all organisms. Other, rarer, amino acids are made by cells from the amino acids listed here.

Second base

First base		U	C	A	G	Third base
U		UUU ⎫ Phe UUC ⎭ UUA ⎫ Leu UUG ⎭	UCU ⎫ UCC ⎬ Ser UCA UCG ⎭	UAU ⎫ Tyr UAC ⎭ UAA Stop UAG Stop	UGU ⎫ Cys UGC ⎭ UGA Stop UGG Try	U C A G
C		CUU ⎫ CUC ⎬ Leu CUA CUG ⎭	CCU ⎫ CCC ⎬ Pro CCA CCG ⎭	CAU ⎫ His CAC ⎭ CAA ⎫ Gln CAG ⎭	CGU ⎫ CGC ⎬ Arg CGA CGG ⎭	U C A G
A		AUU ⎫ AUC ⎬ Ile AUA ⎭ AUG Met	ACU ⎫ ACC ⎬ Thr ACA ACG ⎭	AAU ⎫ Asn AAC ⎭ AAA ⎫ Lys AAG ⎭	AGU ⎫ Ser AGC ⎭ AGA ⎫ Arg AGG ⎭	U C A G
G		GUU ⎫ GUC ⎬ Val GUA GUG ⎭	GCU ⎫ GCC ⎬ Ala GCA GCG ⎭	GAU ⎫ Asp GAC ⎭ GAA ⎫ Glu GAG ⎭	GGU ⎫ GGC ⎬ Gly GGA GGG ⎭	U C A G

Ala = alanine
Arg = arginine
Asn = asparagine
Asp = aspartic acid
Cys = cysteine
Gln = glutamine
Glu = glutamic acid
Gly = glycine
His = histidine
Ile = isoleucine
Leu = leucine
Lys = lysine
Met = methionine
Phe = phenylalanine
Pro = proline
Ser = serine
Thr = threonine
Try = tryptophan
Tyr = tyrosine
Val = valine

Introns and exons

In 1977 the exact sequence of bases in the gene that codes for the β chain of haemoglobin was determined for the first time. Much to everyone's surprise it turned out that the β-haemoglobin gene contains two regions of DNA whose base sequence does not correspond to the known amino acid sequence of β-haemoglobin. Further study revealed that the entire gene is transcribed into messenger RNA, but some of the RNA is cut out and discarded before translation occurs. Altogether, 670 of the 1660 bases are discarded, as shown in the illustration.

In the illustration, the portions of the DNA that end up coding for amino acids are shown in white. These *expressed* portions of DNA are known as **exons**. The pieces of DNA that code for those sections of messenger RNA that are removed before translation are red. These unused pieces of messenger RNA are, in a sense, *interruptions* and are called **introns**.

What is the function of these introns? One possibility is that they are parasitic bits of DNA, of no benefit to the rest of the cell, but just hanging in there, ensuring that they get reproduced generation after generation. Another interpretation is to suppose that they have some function, even if it is not to code for the amino acids in β-haemoglobin.

What, then, might be their function? We now know that there is a type of blood disease that can result from a mutation in one of the *introns* of the β-haemoglobin gene. The abnormal allele has a thymine instead of the usual guanine, 19 bases away from the junction of the first intron with the second exon.

The presence of the thymine does not affect transcription but causes the messenger RNA to be improperly edited and spliced before it is exported from the nucleus to the cytoplasm for translation. The net result is that although the first 29 amino acids of the polypeptide are correct, there then follow six incorrect amino acids and then the polypeptide stops. A normal β-haemoglobin molecule contains 141 amino acids.

So a single faulty base in one of the introns causes a short defective β-haemoglobin to be released. A person homozygous for this mutation suffers from **thalassaemia major** which results in severe anaemia, growth retardation and a number of other abnormalities.

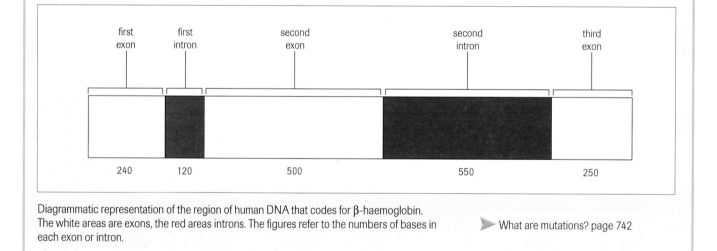

first exon	first intron	second exon	second intron	third exon
240	120	500	550	250

Diagrammatic representation of the region of human DNA that codes for β-haemoglobin. The white areas are exons, the red areas introns. The figures refer to the numbers of bases in each exon or intron.

▶ What are mutations? page 742

In at least one case an even more remarkable adaptation is found. The same piece of DNA is read in one direction to produce one sort of protein and in the other direction to produce another sort of protein.

34.5 Viral reproduction and genetics

Much of the evidence for the role of DNA has come from the study of viruses that attack bacteria. These viruses are known as **bacteriophages** or just **phages**, from the Greek word for 'to eat' – meaning that they 'eat' bacteria. One species of bacteria readily infected by bacteriophages is the colon bacillus *Escherichia coli* which lives in the mammalian large intestine and can be cultured quite easily in the laboratory.

The structure of bacteriophage is shown in figure 34.15. Chemical analysis and electron microscopy show it to consist of DNA surrounded by a protein coat. A long thread of DNA containing about 150 genes is packed into a **head** from which a short **tail** projects. Though larger than most viruses, bacteriophages are nevertheless exceedingly small, the head being only 65 nm wide.

When a phage attacks a bacterium it adheres to the bacterial surface by its tail (*figure 34.16*). By a process analogous to the action of a hypodermic syringe, the DNA thread is injected into the bacterium where it proceeds to replicate prolifically. Experiments in which the viral DNA is labelled with radioactive phosphorus have shown that only the DNA enters the bacterial cell.

Under the influence of the viral DNA, new virus heads and tails are manufactured and then assembled within the bacterial cell. After about 30 minutes the bacterium bursts open, releasing some 300 viruses which then repeat the process in other bacteria.

RNA viruses

We now know that many viruses contain RNA instead of DNA as their genetic material. In some of these viruses the RNA functions as messenger RNA once it gets into the host cell, directing the production of viral protein.

Other RNA viruses, known as **retroviruses**, possess an enzyme called **reverse transcriptase** which transcribes their RNA into DNA. The newly synthesised viral DNA then inserts itself into the host's DNA, remaining there for months or years before it starts to make any proteins.

Retroviruses include **Human Immunodeficiency Virus (HIV)** which can cause AIDS (*page 506*). Note that as their RNA is used to make DNA, they do not conform to the central dogma of molecular genetics illustrated in figure 34.10 on page 610, namely that DNA makes RNA makes protein.

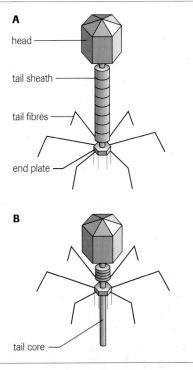

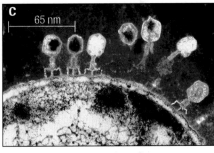

Figure 34.15
A Diagram of a bacteriophage before injecting its genetic material into its host. The head, a bi-pyramidal hexagonal prism, contains a long coiled thread of DNA. The tail consists of a hollow tube (core) surrounded by a sheath. Attached to the distal end of the sheath is a hexagonal end plate from which six tail fibres project.
B Diagram of a bacteriophage after injecting its DNA into its host. The tail sheath has contracted, causing the tail core to be thrust into the body of the bacterium.
C Electron micrograph of bacteriophages injecting their genetic material into the host.

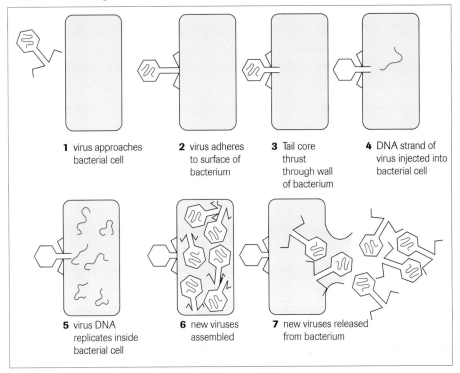

1 virus approaches bacterial cell
2 virus adheres to surface of bacterium
3 Tail core thrust through wall of bacterium
4 DNA strand of virus injected into bacterial cell
5 virus DNA replicates inside bacterial cell
6 new viruses assembled
7 new viruses released from bacterium

Figure 34.16 Life cycle of a bacteriophage. Only the viral DNA enters the bacterial cell, the protein coat remains outside. The viral DNA contains all the necessary instructions for directing the synthesis of new viruses within the bacterium. In reality far more viruses are formed than are shown here. All viruses work by taking over the biosynthetic machinery of their hosts, though the way they do this varies. In the case of certain small viruses which attack animal cells, the whole virus enters the cell and then releases its nucleic acid. Plant viruses may be injected through the cell walls of the host's cells by insect vectors such as aphids.

Proviruses and the role of viruses in cancer

Viruses which actively attack and proliferate in cells are described as **virulent**. Sometimes, however, a virus may infect a cell and then remain in a quiescent state for a long period of time. Instead of replicating, the viral DNA inserts itself into the host's DNA, replicating only when the host's own DNA replicates. In this **temperate** state the virus is known as a **provirus**.

A provirus exerts little influence over the cell, though it may prevent re-infection by another virus. Later on, the virus may lose its benign nature and give rise to a crop of new viruses which burst out of the cell. This is why some virus diseases, such as herpes, tend to recur even in the absence of re-infection.

As described in Chapter 26, some cancers are caused by viruses. A cancer is basically a mass of cells that divide too much and are growing out of control (*page 466*). Viruses seem to cause cancers in two ways.

Firstly, some of the viral genes may make proteins which coincidentally affect the regulation of the host's genes, causing them to produce more of a certain type of messenger RNA. This may result in a protein being produced that causes the cell to grow and divide more.

Secondly, some viruses carry genes that they do not require for the manufacture of their own proteins. Rather, these genes cause the host cell to become cancerous. They do this by producing proteins which closely resemble those produced by the host to increase the rate of cell growth and division. Such genes are known as **oncogenes**.

How can a virus possess genes that are almost identical to the host's genes? It has been suggested that some viral oncogenes are the result of messenger RNA from the host becoming incorporated into the viral genetic material, which in these viruses is RNA not DNA.

Summary

1. Two types of nucleic acid exist in cells: **deoxyribonucleic acid (DNA)** and **ribonucleic acid (RNA)**. Both consist of chains of **nucleotides**. Each nucleotide consists of a **pentose sugar**, a **phosphate group** and one of five **organic bases** (**A, C, G, T** and **U**). DNA contains A, C, G and T; in RNA, T is replaced by U.

2. According to the **Watson–Crick hypothesis**, DNA is a **double helix** consisting of two coiled chains of alternating phosphate and sugar groups, the latter being connected by pairs of bases which form hydrogen bonds with each other in a specific way: A with T, and C with G.

3. During interphase, prior to cell division, DNA undergoes accurate **replication**, the mechanism being **semi-conservative**.

4. A gene is a segment of the DNA chain. In general a single gene is responsible for the synthesis of a single polypeptide chain (originally known as the **one gene – one enzyme hypothesis**).

5. DNA controls protein synthesis by determining the order in which amino acids are linked together on the ribosomes. Each amino acid is coded for by a triplet of bases (**codon**) in the DNA. For this reason the genetic code is called a **triplet code**.

6. In controlling protein synthesis, the relevant portion of DNA in the nucleus is first **transcribed** into **messenger RNA**. This then moves to the cytoplasm where, with the help of **transfer RNAs**, it is **translated** into protein. This is summed up in the **central dogma of molecular genetics** which says that DNA makes RNA makes protein.

7. Ribosomes are made in the **nucleolus** and are often found in chains called **polyribosomes**. Polyribosomes help to speed up the assembly of amino acids into polypeptides by moving in convoy along the messenger RNA strand.

8. Most amino acids are coded for by more than one triplet. The genetic code is therefore **degenerate**. Of the 64 base triplets, 61 code for amino acids; the other three act as **termination codons**.

9. The genetic code is **non-overlapping**, i.e. a given triplet codes for one amino acid, and none of the three constituent bases in the triplet codes for another amino acid.

10. Generally only part of the DNA within a gene is expressed, i.e. used for protein synthesis. The parts that are expressed are called **exons**; the unused parts are called **introns**.

11. The potency of DNA in controlling protein synthesis can be seen in **viruses**, notably bacteriophages, whose nucleic acid can take over the metabolic machinery of the host cell.

12. Some viruses, known as **retroviruses**, can make DNA from RNA, thus causing the central dogma of molecular genetics to be modified.

For general advice on these questions and advice on answering essay-type questions, see pages vii and viii.

1. Write an essay on the structure and function of DNA.

(Total 20 marks)

O & C 1997

2. (a) Name the type of bond that holds together the two strands of nucleotides in a DNA molecule. (1)

Genetic drugs are short sequences of nucleotides. They act by binding to selected sites on DNA or mRNA molecules and preventing the synthesis of disease-related proteins. There are two types.

Triplex drugs are made from DNA nucleotides and bind to the DNA forming a three-stranded helix.

Antisense drugs are made from RNA nucleotides and bind to mRNA.

(b) Name the process in protein synthesis that will be inhibited by:

(i) triplex drugs; (1)

(ii) antisense drugs. (1)

(c) The table shows the sequence of bases on part of a molecule of mRNA.

Base sequence on coding strand of DNA								
Base sequence on mRNA	A	C	G	U	U	A	G	C	U
Base sequence on antisense drug								

Copy and complete the table to show:

(i) the base sequence on the corresponding part of the coding strand of a molecule of DNA; (1)

(ii) the base sequence on the antisense drug that binds to this mRNA. (1)

(Total 5 marks)

AEB 1998

3. The diagram below shows the structure of part of a molecule of deoxyribonucleic acid (DNA).

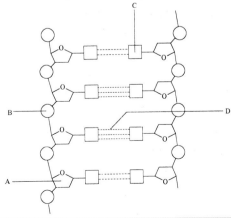

(a) Name the parts labelled A, B, C and D. (4)

(b) (i) On a copy of the diagram, draw a ring around *one* nucleotide. (1)

(ii) What type of chemical reaction is involved in the formation of a molecule of DNA from nucleotides? (1)

(Total 6 marks)

London 1996

4. The polymerase chain reaction is a technique used by biologists to make large amounts of DNA from very small samples. The process is explained in the diagram.

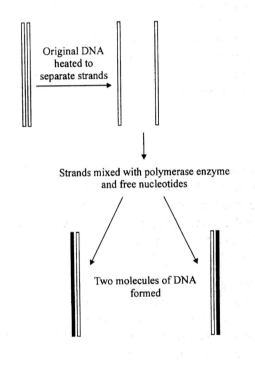

(a) Explain why the DNA produced in this reaction is exactly the same as the original DNA. (2)

(b) At the end of the first cycle of this reaction, there will be 2 molecules of DNA. How many molecules of DNA will there be at the end of 5 cycles? (1)

(c) Give two ways in which this process differs from transcription. (2)

(Total 5 marks)

AEB 1997

Part 6

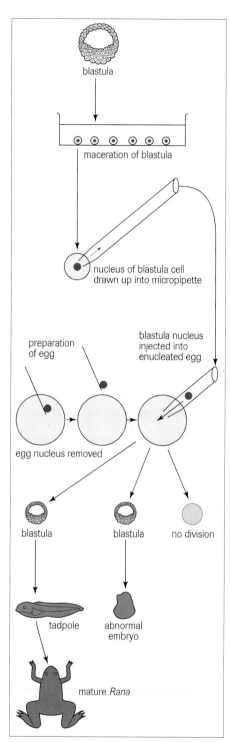

blastula

maceration of blastula

nucleus of blastula cell
drawn up into micropipette

preparation
of egg

blastula nucleus
injected into
enucleated egg

egg nucleus removed

blastula   blastula   no division

tadpole   abnormal
embryo

mature *Rana*

Figure 35.1 Briggs and King's method of
transplanting nuclei in the frog *Rana*. A nucleus is
extracted from a blastula cell and injected into an
enucleated egg. The latter is found to develop
normally in a significant number of cases, though
sometimes it gives rise to an abnormal embryo or
does not develop at all.

T he development of a complex organism from the fertilised egg to the adult involves a
highly ordered sequence of events in which the various cells, interacting with one
another, **differentiate** at just the right time and in precisely the right place within the
embryo.

For development to proceed appropriately, there must therefore be a mechanism by
which it is controlled in both space and time. To elucidate the nature of this mechanism is
one of the central problems of developmental biology. In this chapter we shall look at the
role of genes in this process and at the way the environment can affect their expression. We
shall also look at new technologies such as genetic engineering which can affect
profoundly the way organisms develop and function.

35.1 The role of genes in development

Nowadays we are used to the idea that genes influence the structure and functioning of
individual cells. However, there is a problem when we consider a multicellular organism
such as ourselves.

The problem is this. Our cells are of many different types, each highly specialised in
structure and function (*page 62*). And yet all of them are derived from one original single
cell, the fertilised egg, and thus, except for the occasional mutation, they presumably all
have exactly the same genetic make-up. So we are faced with a paradox. *The cells of an
adult differ from each other, yet their genes are the same.*

There are two ways of getting around this difficulty. One is to suppose that the
replication of DNA is not in fact complete and different genes are passed on to different
cells at cell division. The second way is to suppose that all the cells in an adult *do* contain
identical genetic material, but that different genes are *expressed* in different cells at
different times.

In order to decide between these two hypotheses an experiment can be done which is
attractive in its simplicity and directness. If it is true that the genetic code remains
unaltered during development, then all the nuclei of an embryo, and indeed an adult, must
contain all the necessary genetic information required for producing a complete adult
organism. This being so, it follows that if a nucleus is extracted from an embryo or adult
and implanted into an egg which has had its own nucleus removed, the egg should give
rise to a normal individual. All this assumes, of course, that such a finicky operation can be
done without unduly damaging either the nucleus or the egg into which it is implanted.

This operation was first performed successfully in 1952 by two American biologists,
Robert Briggs of Indiana University and Thomas King of the Institute for Cancer Research
in Philadelphia. They used frogs for their experiments.

Cloning frogs

What Briggs and King did was to take a frog embryo at the late blastula stage
(*page 526*) and immerse it in a fluid which caused the cells to separate from one another
(*figure 35.1*). A nucleus was then extracted from one of the cells by means of a
micropipette. Meanwhile, an egg was prepared for receiving the nucleus. Its nucleus was
removed by means of a fine glass needle. Now it only remained for the donor nucleus to be
implanted into the **enucleated** egg. The egg with its new nucleus was then left to develop.

This experiment has been repeated many times since Briggs and King first did it in 1952. Despite a high mortality rate at first, the results are now reasonably consistent. In general, nuclei obtained from late blastulae are capable of sustaining normal embryos which, on occasions, develop right through to adults. The conclusion is that, at least up to the late blastula stage, no irreversible changes occur in the genetic information contained within the nucleus.

But might it not be possible that genetic changes occur *after* the blastula stage? The most obvious way of testing this possibility is to repeat the experiment with nuclei taken from later stages. The technical difficulties are formidable, due partly to the delicacy and small size of the cells involved. However, in 1962 John Gurdon of Oxford University found that when he took nuclei from the skin of an adult frog and injected them into enucleated eggs, a few of the eggs developed into tadpoles which subsequently metamorphosed into normal adults. In other words, a nucleus taken from a fully differentiated adult cell *can* direct the development of a complete animal.

The individuals produced by this technique are genetically identical to the individual from which the nucleus was taken: that is, they all belong to one **clone**. This technique is therefore known as **cloning**.

Cloning plants

A rather different kind of experiment has shown that, in plants too, adult cells contain the same genetic information as the fertilised egg cell.

In the 1950s, F.C. Steward of Cornell University took mature cells from a carrot root and cultured them on their own. When reared in the right conditions they grew into complete new carrot plants (*figure 35.2*). This technique is now of great commercial importance in plant breeding (*page 491*).

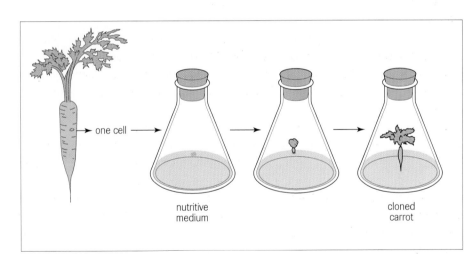

Figure 35.2 A single cell taken from a mature carrot can give rise to a new carrot plant. This suggests that the single adult cell contains the same genetic information as a newly fertilised egg cell.

Cloning mammals

In 1997, Ian Wilmut and his colleagues at the Roslin Institute in Edinburgh succeeded in cloning Dolly the sheep (*figure 35.3*). Prior to Dolly, clones had been made by the **splitting of embryos**, including mammalian embryos (*page 526*). However, it was widely believed that it would not be possible to clone a mammal from a single cell taken from an *adult* individual. Dolly disproved this.

Dolly was produced in much the same way that Briggs and King cloned their frogs. A single donor cell taken from the mammary gland of a sheep was fused with an enucleated recipient egg and the resulting cell, after it had gone through a certain number of cell divisions, placed in a surrogate ewe. After a normal pregnancy, Dolly was born and announced to the full glare of publicity.

Figure 35.3 Dolly, the first mammal to be cloned from a cell taken from an adult.

Within just over a year other researchers had successfully cloned mice, increasing the likelihood that the procedure would work on humans if tried. However, many countries have passed legislation outlawing any attempt to clone humans, believing that this would be ethically unacceptable. Certainly it would be technically difficult. Dolly herself was preceded by 276 unsuccessful attempts by the Roslin team to produce a cloned sheep!

What these cloning experiments indicate is that the genetic make-up of a cell does not change during development. We can therefore conclude that differentiation is brought about by different parts of an organism's genetic material being used in different cells and at different times as development proceeds.

Gene switching

If different parts of an organism's genetic material are used at different times, there must be a mechanism which ensures that the right parts of the DNA operate at the correct time. Such a mechanism must, in effect, *switch* the appropriate genes on or off, as and when they are required.

Before considering the evidence for this, it will help to look at an example to illustrate the basic idea. When adult, we have two sorts of polypeptide chains in the haemoglobin in our red blood cells, **α chains** and **β chains** (*page 218*). In the fetus, however, **γ chains** are produced instead of β chains. The differences between the β and γ chains, though slight, are sufficient to confer the markedly different oxygen-carrying powers discussed in Chapter 14. At birth, the production of fetal haemoglobin (which has two α and two γ chains) ceases and is replaced over the next three months by adult haemoglobin (which has two α and two β chains) (*figure 35.4*).

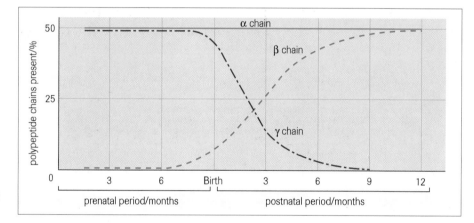

Figure 35.4 Two of the four polypeptide chains, which together with four haem groups make up a single haemoglobin molecule, change during development. Before birth each haemoglobin molecule consists of two α and two γ chains. Around the time of birth, production of the γ chain ceases and is replaced by the β chain.

There is strong evidence from genetic studies that the formation of each of these polypeptide chains is controlled by a single gene. This evidence comes mainly from studying people with abnormal haemoglobin. In every case the abnormalities are associated with a difference in the amino acids in one or other of the polypeptide chains. Pedigree analyses show that these abnormal haemoglobins are inherited in a normal Mendelian manner.

From these studies a hypothesis can be put forward to explain in genetic terms the replacement of fetal with adult haemoglobin at birth:

■ The gene which specifies the α chain works all the time, that is, both before and after birth.

■ The gene which specifies the γ chain works only before birth, and is then switched off.

■ The gene specifying the β chain is inactive during embryonic life, and is then switched on around the time of birth.

We can also postulate the existence of one or more other genes, responsible for switching the γ gene off and the β gene on.

The Jacob–Monod theory of gene action

Over the years, considerable evidence has come to hand to support the idea of genes being switched on and off. During the late 1950s, François Jacob and Jacques Monod of the Institut Pasteur in Paris carried out a series of brilliantly designed experiments on the genetic control of enzyme synthesis in the bacterium *E. coli*.

Briefly, what they found was this. *E. coli* only synthesises certain enzymes if and when it is appropriate to do so. For example, it produces enzymes for breaking down sugar for the release of energy. One such sugar is lactose. If lactose is present in the nutrient medium in which the bacteria are growing, they produce an enzyme, **β galactosidase**, to break it down. However, if lactose is absent from the medium, this enzyme is not produced. If lactose is added to a medium which previously lacked it, then, and only then, will the bacteria start synthesising the enzyme.

From these experiments, together with other investigations into the genetics and biochemistry of *E. coli*, Jacob and Monod put forward a theory to explain how the gene responsible for the production of β galactosidase is regulated. The basic scheme is outlined in figure 35.5.

The section of the DNA strand which codes for the enzyme is called the **structural gene**. Acting via messenger RNA, it brings about synthesis of the enzyme. Situated close to the structural gene is another section of the DNA strand called the **promotor region**. At times when the enzyme is needed, the promotor region activates the structural gene, causing it to produce the messenger RNA which is then translated into β galactosidase.

However, between the promotor region and the structural gene lies an **operator gene**. The operator gene, according to Jacob and Monod's theory, comes under the influence of yet another gene, the **regulator gene**, situated further along the DNA chain. The regulator gene codes for a **repressor substance** which inhibits the operator gene when the enzyme is not required, thereby preventing the structural gene from doing its bit. All this is shown in figure 35.5A.

When the enzyme is required, the repressor substance is inhibited (in this case by lactose), the operator gene becomes unblocked, the promotor region becomes functional, the structural gene is activated and the enzyme is produced (*figure 35.5B*).

If you find all this rather heavy going, don't lose heart. It took Jacob and Monod years to unravel it, and they got a Nobel Prize for it!

The original version of the Jacob–Monod hypothesis postulated that the structural gene is switched off except when needed. More recent evidence suggests that microorganisms also possess other systems in which the structural gene is switched *on* except when it is *not* needed.

Figure 35.5 The Jacob–Monod theory of the control of messenger RNA synthesis.
A Structural gene inactivated as a result of repressor protein made by a regulator gene.
B Structural gene making messenger RNA as a result of inactivation of the repressor protein by a repressor inhibitor molecule such as lactose. Full explanation in text.

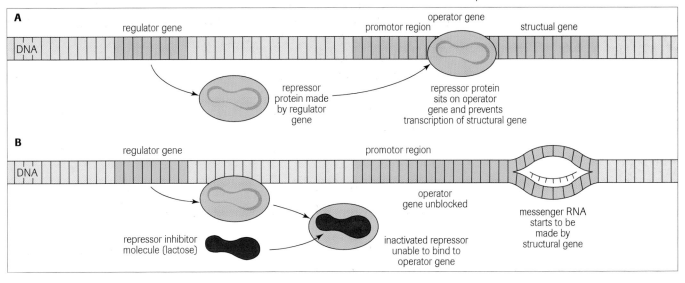

Chromosome puffs

Evidence supporting the idea that differentiation is brought about by different parts of an organism's genetic material being used at different times comes from observations on the **giant chromosomes** of flies.

In 1933, it was found that chromosomes in the salivary glands of *Drosophila* (fruit-fly) larvae are thousands of times broader than those found elsewhere in the body. What happens is that during the larval stage of the insect these cells do not divide. However, the chromosomes continue to replicate, over and over again.

As a result the chromosomes contain thousands of DNA double helices lying side by side. The significance for geneticists of the 1930s and 1940s was

that these giant chromosomes could be seen clearly under the light microscope. This was a great advantage, as the electron microscope had not yet been invented.

How does the existence of giant chromosomes help in our understanding of cell development and differentiation? Well, occasionally the DNA strands which make up these chromosomes become less tightly packed in certain regions, and sections of the chromosomes puff up. The regions where this occurs are called **chromosome puffs**.

Experiments with special stains and radioactive tracers have shown that chromosome puffs are the sites of messenger RNA synthesis. Moreover, puffing occurs in different parts of the

chromosomes at different times as the insect develops, suggesting that different parts of the DNA in the chromosome are being used at different times. For example, puffing has been observed in a particular part of the chromosome just before the larva moults. Moulting is brought about by a hormone called ecdysone). If this hormone is experimentally injected into an immature larva, puffing occurs prematurely in this very part of the chromosome.

All this makes sense, but how can a hormone cause a particular region of the DNA in a chromosome to start producing messenger RNA? One possibility is that the hormone might switch on the relevant part of the DNA. The concept of gene switching is explained on page 626.

Gene regulation in eukaryotes

Precisely how gene regulation occurs in eukaryotes such as ourselves is still far from clear. It is known that transcription is regulated by proteins that bind to specific sites on the DNA molecule, just as in *E. coli*. However, it seems that gene regulation is far more complicated in eukaryotes than in prokaryotes, particularly when multicellular eukaryotes are considered. For instance, the sites at which proteins made by regulator genes bind to the DNA may be thousands of base pairs away from the promotor gene, quite different from the situation in *E. coli* as depicted in figure 35.5.

What is clear is that eukaryotes have a number of types of gene control which are absent from prokaryotes. For instance, about 5 per cent of the cytosine bases in eukaryotic DNA have methyl ($-CH_3$) groups added to them. This is known as **DNA methylation**. When one looks at the same gene in cells from different tissues, it is usually found that the genes are more heavily methylated in those cells where they are *not* expressed. Further, drugs that inhibit methylation often cause genes to start synthesising messenger RNA. So DNA methylation may be a mechanism for gene regulation in eukaryotes.

How DNA is packed into chromosomes

Measured from end to end, the DNA in a human chromosome is about 100 000 times longer than a chromosome at metaphase. This means that when a cell divides in two its DNA is packed incredibly tightly, far more tightly than, say, a ball of string. The reason for this should be clear if you imagine what cell division would otherwise be like. The DNA belonging to the different chromosomes would get in the most hopeless tangle and there would be no chance of cell division resulting in the genetic material being evenly apportioned between the daughter cells.

So how is DNA packed in the chromosome of a dividing cell? The answer is that it is tightly wrapped around special protein molecules called **histones**. Histones are basic proteins that are present in very large numbers in a cell. There are five types of histones, rather unimaginatively called H1, H2A, H2B, H3 and H4. Chromosomes are mainly protein; the DNA makes up less than half the mass of each chromosome.

The histones serve two main functions. Firstly, they protect the DNA from damage; secondly, they allow the long length of DNA to be packaged in such a way that it can be moved around the cell at cell division.

Careful studies using the electron microscope, X-ray diffraction and a battery of biochemical techniques have helped to elucidate the relationship between the histones and the DNA. The complex of DNA and protein in a chromosome is called **chromatin**. The fundamental unit of chromatin is the **nucleosome**. A nucleosome is composed of DNA wrapped around a group of histone molecules (*illustration 1*).

These units occur at regular intervals along the length of the DNA, like a string of beads. Illustration 2 shows how it is thought that the nucleosomes are clustered together in a chromosome.

During interphase the chromosomes uncoil, which allows messenger RNA to be made by the appropriate genes. However, the histones remain associated with the DNA.

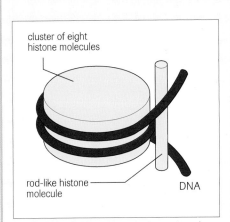

Illustration 1 The structure of a nucleosome, the basic unit of chromatin.

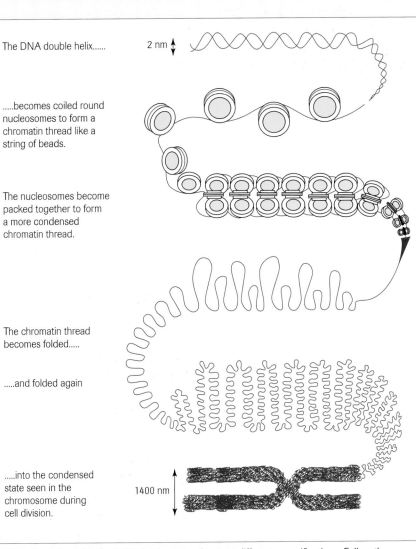

The DNA double helix......

2 nm

.....becomes coiled round nucleosomes to form a chromatin thread like a string of beads.

The nucleosomes become packed together to form a more condensed chromatin thread.

The chromatin thread becomes folded.....

.....and folded again

.....into the condensed state seen in the chromosome during cell division.

1400 nm

Illustration 2 The structure of a chromosome shown at different magnifications. Follow the diagrams from top to bottom and notice the different scales.

Gene switching and the germination of barley seeds

Guest author Tim King discusses a commercially important example of gene switching, in the germination of barley seeds.

In the brewing of beer from barley, the barley seeds (strictly speaking they are fruits) are induced to germinate. During the early stages, the starch stored in the endosperm is hydrolysed to the sugar, maltose, which is an ideal substrate for yeast to ferment to alcohol. Once the barley seeds contain a high enough concentration of maltose, they are killed and the 'malt' is extracted. Because of its economic importance, much time has been spent working out the details of this process.

To understand what happens you need to be familiar with the structure of this kind of seed: on page 535 there is a diagram of a wheat seed which is very similar to barley.

A couple of days after the seed has begun to absorb water, prior to germination, the shoot tip of the embryo releases the plant growth substance gibberellic acid (*page 550*). This travels through the embryo and is released into the endosperm. When it reaches the aleurone layer, a mixture of enzymes is secreted from the aleurone cells into the endosperm. These enzymes break down large insoluble storage molecules in the endosperm into smaller soluble molecules suitable for transporting to the germinating embryo. One of the enzymes is β-amylase which converts starch into maltose.

By isolating various parts of a barley seed, it has been shown that only the cells of the aleurone layer secrete β-amylase, and that gibberellic acid triggers this process. Is the enzyme, which of course is a protein, already present and merely released under the stimulus of gibberellin, or is it synthesised from scratch by the aleurone cells?

This question has been investigated by adding radioactively labelled amino acids to aleurone tissue. The labelled amino acids are rapidly incorporated into new molecules of β-amylase under the influence of gibberellin. This process can be prevented, however, by drugs such as actinomycin D which inhibit messenger RNA synthesis on the DNA template. It seems therefore that molecules of gibberellin, which are lipid-soluble, pass across the plasma membranes of the aleurone cells and then act on the DNA, switching on the genes responsible for synthesis of the enzyme.

This theory has been confirmed by several elegant experiments. For example, when isolated nuclei of aleurone cells are exposed to gibberellic acid, their rate of synthesis of messenger RNA increases by a factor of between six and fourteen. If this messenger RNA is isolated, and added to a cell-free preparation containing ribosomes, transfer RNA and the necessary enzymes and amino acids, β-amylase is produced.

Dr King researched in plant science and ecology at Oxford and, after teaching at Westminster School and Magdalen College School, is now Senior Master (Studies) at Abingdon School.

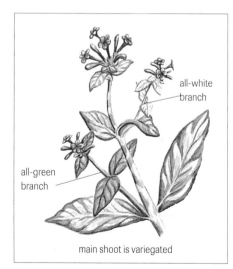

Figure 35.6 Leaf variation in the four-o'clock plant *Mirabilis jalapa*. Flowers may be found on green, white or variegated branches. The results of crossing these flowers cannot be explained by conventional Mendelian genetics. The genes involved are carried in the chloroplasts, not in the nucleus.

35.2 Cytoplasmic control of gene expression

In the type of regulation considered so far, unwanted genes are prevented from being transcribed into messenger RNA. In other words, regulation takes place in the nucleus at the **level of transcription**. However, cells have another avenue of control, namely in the cytoplasm at the **level of translation**. The idea here is that the cytoplasm exerts some control over the rate at which messenger RNA is translated into proteins.

However, there is no evidence that the cytoplasm can control *which* proteins are synthesised. This fundamental element of control seems to reside at the level of transcription in the nucleus. Cytoplasmic control should therefore be seen as a supplement, rather than as an alternative, to nuclear control.

Cytoplasmic inheritance

In 1909 Carl Correns reported some surprising results from breeding experiments he had carried out on four-o'clock plants (*Mirabilis jalapa*). These plants have three sorts of leaves on their branches. Some branches carry only green leaves, others only white leaves and others variegated leaves (*figure 35.6*). Flowers occur on all three types of branches.

When Correns crossed plants, he found that the phenotypes of the progeny depended only on the phenotype of the maternal branch from which the flower came. The phenotype of the paternal branch was irrelevant (table 35.1). This sort of inheritance is known as **maternal inheritance**.

Table 35.1 Results of crosses of four-o'clock plants showing the significance of maternal inheritance.

Phenotype of branch bearing egg parent (♀)	Phenotype of branch bearing pollen parent (♂)	Phenotype of progeny
White	White	White
White	Green	White
White	Variegated	White
Green	White	Green
Green	Green	Green
Green	Variegated	Green
Variegated	White	Variegated, green or white
Variegated	Green	Variegated, green or white
Variegated	Variegated	Variegated, green or white

The white plants produced in Correns' crosses soon died, through their inability to photosynthesise. However, the variegated and green plants grew well and were used in further breeding experiments. Again, maternal inheritance was found.

How can these results be explained? The different leaf colours are due to the presence or absence of chloroplasts. What seems to happen is that leaf colour is determined not by nuclear genes, but by genes carried in the chloroplasts. The egg cell contains chloroplasts, but the pollen grain does not. Accordingly, the phenotype of the offspring, as far as its chloroplasts go, is determined by the mother's chloroplasts.

We now know that both chloroplasts and mitochondria carry their own DNA. This DNA is circular in shape and is involved in the replication of these organelles. However, chloroplasts and mitochondria are not entirely autonomous: nuclear genes also play a part in their synthesis. The inheritance of characteristics through genes in the cytoplasm is known as **cytoplasmic inheritance**.

35.3 The role of the environment

So far we may have given the impression that development is entirely under the control of the genes. However, the environment also plays its part. A well-known case of environmental control is provided by fur colour in the Himalayan rabbit. The Himalayan rabbit has a white body with black ears, nose, feet and tail (*figure 35.7*). It might be thought that this pattern is solely under genetic control, but a simple experiment shows that this is not the case. If a cold pad is fixed to the rabbit's back, left in position for a few weeks and kept cold, black hair starts to develop beneath the pad.

What seems to be happening is that the heat prevents the development of the black pigment. Only in those parts of the body which are cool enough, i.e. the extremities, does black fur grow. The same thing happens in seal-point Siamese cats. Owners of such cats sometimes find that in winter the black areas enlarge, only to regress in warmer weather.

There are many other cases of the environment influencing an organism's development by affecting the expression of genes. For example, in plants, chlorophyll will only develop if light is available, and flowers will only appear if the day-length is right and the temperature suitable, and so on. These and other examples are discussed in Chapter 31.

It is easy to underestimate the importance of the environment on the development of organisms and to assume that everything is under genetic control. In reality, development is the result of a subtle and complex interaction between heredity and the environment. Consider, for instance, communication in humans. Even blind babies smile, which suggests that smiling is genetically determined. Yet the way we use our hands in communication, our facial expressions and above all the language we speak are the result of both genetic and environmental influences.

Figure 35.7 Influence of environment on development. In the Himalayan rabbit, black fur develops at the extremities such as the ears and nose due to the lower temperature of these exposed parts of the body.

The development of behaviour, page 436

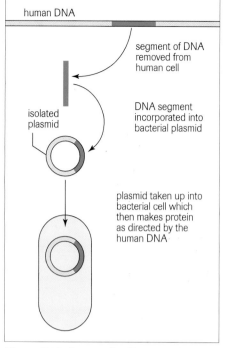

human DNA

segment of DNA removed from human cell

DNA segment incorporated into bacterial plasmid

isolated plasmid

plasmid taken up into bacterial cell which then makes protein as directed by the human DNA

Figure 35.8 An example of how genetic engineering (recombinant DNA technology) is done. In this case a short piece of DNA from a human is transferred to a bacterial cell which then makes the protein coded for by this foreign bit of DNA.

35.4 Genetic engineering

Are there any ways by which we can alter an organism's genetic constitution so that it develops and functions differently? The answer, of course, is yes. Such manipulations have been carried out for centuries in **selective breeding** of crop plants and farm animals. However, a more direct approach has been made within the last decade by **genetic engineering**, also known as **recombinant DNA technology**.

How is genetic engineering carried out?

The first step in genetic engineering usually involves inserting a short piece of foreign DNA into the DNA of a host organism. For example, to insert a piece of DNA from a human into a bacterium, you break open the DNA ring of a bacterial plasmid and insert the human DNA into it (*figure 35.8*). This procedure is called **gene splicing**. The bacterium then acquires the ability to synthesise the protein for which the foreign DNA codes.

Gene splicing relies on an important group of naturally occurring enzymes called **restriction endonucleases**. A given restriction endonuclease cuts a bacterial plasmid open at a specific site which is determined by the sequence of bases in that region. The same enzyme will cut foreign DNA wherever an identical base sequence occurs.

It is characteristic of most restriction endonucleases that they cut the two strands of the DNA at slightly different points. The result is that each end of the foreign DNA segment has a short row of unpaired bases which match the complementary bases at each end of the opened up plasmid. These are referred to as **sticky ends**. In suitable conditions the unpaired bases of the foreign DNA and the plasmid join up, so the foreign DNA gets incorporated into the plasmid (*figure 35.9*). The bonding is made secure by another enzyme, **DNA ligase**. Once in position, the foreign DNA replicates along with the rest of the plasmid every time the bacterial cell divides.

Another enzyme often used in genetic engineering is **reverse transcriptase**. Reverse transcriptase makes DNA using mRNA (messenger RNA) as a substrate (*page 617*). For example, cells of the human pancreas that produce large amounts of the hormone insulin can have their mRNA extracted. Using reverse transcriptase this mRNA can be used to make single strands of DNA, sometimes called **complementary DNA** (**cDNA**). Single-stranded complementary DNA can then be made into the appropriate double-stranded DNA by the enzyme **DNA polymerase** (*page 607*).

The enzymes used in genetic engineering – restriction endonucleases, reverse transcriptase, DNA ligase and DNA polymerase – did not evolve for the benefit of genetic engineers; they occur naturally both in prokaryotes and eukaryotes and have important functions in their own rights. For example, in eukaryotes restriction endonucleases and DNA ligase enable the chromosomal DNA to break and rejoin during chiasma formation. What genetic engineers have done is to exploit these enzymes, extracting them and using them as tools in genetic manipulation.

Once a bacterium has taken up a piece of foreign DNA successfully, it may divide repeatedly and give rise to a large population of bacterial cells, all of which contain replicas of the foreign DNA. The latter has thus been cloned and can be used for the large-scale synthesis of the particular protein for which it codes. The production of large quantities of identical genes by means of genetic engineering is called **gene cloning**. The bacteria which contain the genes are mass-produced in industrial fermenters of the kind described on page 134.

Other ways of moving genes in genetic engineering

Various other techniques are used to move genes from one species to another. One way is simply to fire them in via a tiny gun! The DNA is mixed with tiny metal particles, usually made of tungsten. These are then fired into the organism, or a tissue culture of cells of the

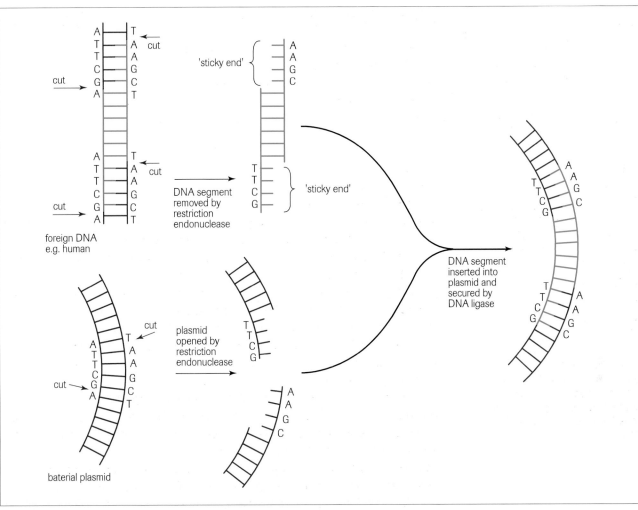

Figure 35.9 Gene splicing. The particular restriction endonuclease depicted here cuts DNA between the bases T and A in the sequence TAAGCT, and between G and A in the sequence ATTCGA. The sequence of unpaired bases in the segment of foreign DNA and the opened up plasmid allow the foreign DNA to become incorporated into the plasmid as shown. Only a small part of the plasmid is shown in these diagrams.

organism. The chief advantage of this method is its simplicity, and it is widely used in the genetic engineering of plants. One problem, not surprisingly, is the damage that may be caused as a result of the firing process. Another is that only a small proportion of the cells tend to take up the foreign DNA.

A further way of getting DNA into a new organism is by injecting it directly into the nucleus of an embryonic cell. This approach is quite widely used in the genetic engineering of animals. This method ensures that at least some of the cells of the organism take up the foreign DNA.

Yet another approach involves using viruses to carry the DNA from one species to another. The chief advantage of this approach is that viruses are rather good at getting DNA into cells! The main disadvantage, though, is that the virus may itself cause problems. For this reason, genetic engineers usually disable the virus in some way.

Applications of genetic engineering

Genetic engineering has opened up all sorts of exciting possibilities in agriculture, medicine and the food industry. However, it has also raised questions about safety and whether it is ethical to change the genetic make-up of species in this way.

Cloning tiny amounts of DNA

Advances in modern biotechnology can enable minute amounts of DNA to be cloned and so multiplied. Suppose, for example, you find a few white blood cells or a tiny sample of sperm at the scene of a crime. You might want to clone the DNA to see if you can match it against possible suspects (*support box below*). The most frequently used technique for this makes use of the **polymerase chain reaction**.

In the polymerase chain reaction you basically start with the DNA you want to clone – even a single molecule is sufficient – and separate its two strands by heating. You then provide all the constituents needed for DNA replication – including DNA polymerase and a mixture of the four different DNA nucleotides. The two DNA strands undergo base pairing and now you have two DNA molecules. The chain of events is then repeated giving 4, 8, 16, 32 DNA molecules and so on.

Once the DNA has been multiplied up you now have enough for various things to be done with it. For example, restriction endonucleases, labelling (e.g. radioactive labelling) and electrophoresis can be used to determine DNA nucleotide sequences. Or it can be used in DNA fingerprinting as explained in the box below, or in genetic engineering.

DNA fingerprinting

It has long been known that no two people have precisely the same pattern of dermal ridges on their fingertips: our fingerprints are unique. This fact is often used by the police in detective work.

It isn't only our fingerprints that are unique to each of us. Thanks to mutations, independent assortment and crossing-over, our DNA is too. In 1984 Alec Jeffreys, a geneticist at Leicester University, discovered a technique that could readily distinguish one person's DNA from another's. This is the basis of **DNA fingerprinting** (also known as **genetic fingerprinting** and **DNA profiling**).

The essence of the method is to take some of a person's DNA and cut it up into lots of bits with restriction endonucleases. These enzymes recognise specific sequences in the DNA (*page 629*). Because each of us has a unique sequence of nucleotides in our DNA, the lengths of these bits will vary from person to person. Electrophoresis is then used to separate out these bits according to their size and charge. The net result is a pattern of bands unique to each of us. The only exceptions are identical twins – they share the same pattern.

So much for the technique. How can it be used? Here's an example that became known as the 'Babes in the Wood' trial. In 1988 a girl came down from Durham to see the pantomime at The London Palladium. She was picked up by a student on the underground, taken back to his flat, plied with drink and then raped. After escaping from his flat she appealed to two men in a red Cortina to drive her to a police station. Instead they drove her to a park where they both raped her.

Eventually she did get to a police station and a vaginal swab produced enough semen for DNA fingerprinting. The analysis confirmed that she had indeed had intercourse with three men that day. The police caught one of them and he was sent to prison for 12 years. The other two have not yet been caught but their DNA fingerprints are on permanent record.

Some DNA fingerprints from another criminal investigation (a murder case) are shown in the illustration. You can see at once which suspects are unlikely to have committed the crime by matching up the bands.

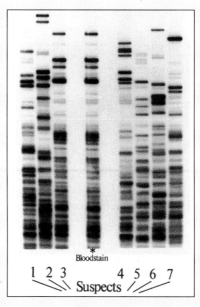

Bloodstain

1 2 3 4 5 6 7
Suspects

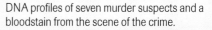

DNA profiles of seven murder suspects and a bloodstain from the scene of the crime.

Human insulin

Our blood sugar level is regulated by the production of insulin and glucagon (*pages 269 – 271*). In **insulin-dependent diabetes**, a person produces insufficient insulin and so suffers from diabetes mellitus. This can be treated by the injection, up to four times a day, of insulin. Until the advent of genetic engineering, the insulin came from cattle (**bovine insulin**) or pigs (**porcine insulin**). Neither bovine nor porcine insulin is identical to human insulin. Although all three hormones are proteins with 51 amino acids, bovine insulin differs from human insulin by three amino acids; porcine insulin by one.

Bovine and porcine insulin are obtained from the pancreases of cattle and pigs slaughtered for food. Although these kinds of insulin have allowed literally millions of people, who would otherwise have died, to lead relatively healthy lives, there are problems with their use. For one thing, the fact that their amino acid sequences differ from human insulin means that some diabetics develop reactions to them. A second problem is that if the animals from which the insulin is obtained are contaminated, for example with certain viruses, the contaminants may be passed onto diabetics. In addition, some people have ethical objections to the use of insulin obtained from cattle or pigs.

Since the 1980s, synthetic **human insulin** has been available through genetic engineering. Sometimes bacteria are used; sometimes yeast. But in both cases the basic idea is the same: the gene that codes for human insulin is spliced into the microorganism which dutifully multiplies and churns out human insulin. This can be collected, purified and injected by diabetics.

However, a word of caution. Some diabetics who switched from bovine or porcine insulin to genetically engineered human insulin have found that its effects are slightly different. In particular, it may be more difficult for the person to realise when his or her blood sugar level is getting dangerously low. In a few cases this may even have led to the death of diabetics.

Support

Other uses of genetically modified microorganisms

It isn't just human hormones such as insulin and human growth hormone that can be made from genetically modified microorganisms. Other products include:

- enzymes for use in the food and cleaning industries;
- antibiotics;
- human factor VIII (involved in blood clotting);
- antigens for the manufacture of vaccines (such as a vaccine to prevent hepatitis B);
- non-human hormones such as BST (*page 565*).

One example of an enzyme that has been made for many years by genetically modified microorganisms is **chymosin**. Chymosin (also known as rennin) is used in cheese-making. It acts on the milk protein casein to make the soft curd known as junket.

Traditionally, chymosin has been obtained from the stomachs of young calves. However, by 1994 about half the world-wide market for chymosin was being supplied by genetically engineered chymosin made by a yeast into which the chymosin gene had been inserted. The production of chymosin by genetic engineering has proved to be extremely successful. One reason for the commercial success of this instance of biotechnology was widespread consumer acceptance. Genetically engineered chymosin does not involve the use of animals and is therefore acceptable to vegetarians, Jews and Muslims.

Extension

Human proteins from sheep's milk

Before the arrival of Dolly (*page 621*), Tracy was the most famous sheep in the world. Tracy had been genetically engineered so that she produced a human protein called α_1-antitrypsin (**AAT**) in her milk.

AAT protects human lungs from damage. People who lack AAT suffer a form of **emphysema** in which their alveoli degenerate (*page 167*). Currently emphysema is incurable. AAT can also be used to help treat cystic fibrosis. Tracy and her daughters hold out the hope of obtaining quite large amounts of AAT fairly easily. By 1999, clinical trials were underway to check that genetically engineered AAT would be safe and effective.

Genetically engineered crops

Genetic engineering of plants is becoming more common. Several companies have developed strains of crop plants that make the plant resistant to the powerful herbicide **glyphosate** (trade name Roundup or Tumbleweed). The idea is that glyphosate could be applied to such crops, killing the weeds but not damaging the crops. The companies concerned argue that this is advantageous for farmers *and* environmentally friendly as glyphosate is non-toxic to most animals and quickly breaks down to harmless components. These two advantages are not shared by many other herbicides that are widely used.

On the other hand, environmentalists argue that genetically engineering plants to be resistant to herbicides makes farmers dependent on herbicides. Perhaps we should be decreasing, not increasing, our reliance on herbicides.

Whatever the arguments for and against using genetic engineering to produce herbicide resistance, many crops are being genetically engineered to be resistant to certain pests and diseases. For example, the European corn borer is an insect which is a major pest of maize, causing global losses of around $1 billion a year. Maize has been genetically engineered to be resistant to the European corn borer and is now being grown commercially (*figure 35.10*). The crop doesn't need to be sprayed with insecticides – which is good for the environment – and it produces higher yields than its conventional, non-genetically engineered counterpart.

Figure 35.10 Corn on the cob and seed from maize genetically engineered to be resistant to the European corn borer. One concern about such genetically modified crops is that pollen from them may 'contaminate' conventional crops. Organic farmers are particularly concerned about this possibility.

At one time, scientists hoped to take the genes responsible for nitrogen-fixation (*page 669*) out of bacterial cells and introduce them into a crop plant such as wheat, thereby conferring on the wheat the ability to fix atmospheric nitrogen. This would save a fortune on nitrogen fertilisers and reduce the problem of high nitrate levels in water due to fertiliser run off. Now, though, it is felt that the large number of genes involved in nitrogen fixation may make this unfeasible.

A more modest piece of genetic engineering has been to move a gene from the Jerusalem artichoke into sugar-beet plants. The introduced gene turns sucrose into fructans. Fructans taste exactly like ordinary sugar but cannot be absorbed by the human digestive system. So the sugar tastes sweet but doesn't lead to the person who eats it putting on weight.

Gene therapy

Gene therapy means using genetic engineering to change a person's genetic make-up for medical benefit. To understand what's involved we need to distinguish between two types of cells in our bodies:

- **germ-line cells** are found in the ovaries of a female and the testes of a male and give rise, respectively, to eggs and to sperm;
- **somatic cells** are all the other cells in the body.

The importance of this distinction is that any genetic changes to somatic cells cannot be passed onto future generations. On the other hand, changes to germ-line cells can be passed on to children and thence to succeeding generations. Currently, the genetic engineering of human somatic cells, known as **somatic gene therapy**, is allowed under certain tightly regulated circumstances, whereas the genetic engineering of germ-line cells, known as **germ-line therapy**, is not permitted in any country.

In the late 1990s, trials to investigate the possibility of treating **cystic fibrosis** by means of somatic gene therapy began in the UK and the USA. Cystic fibrosis is a disease that results from individuals being homozygous recessive for the faulty form of the cystic fibrosis gene (*page 577*). Individuals with cystic fibrosis lack the ability to make a protein known as the CFTR protein. The CFTR protein is responsible for exporting chloride ions across cell membranes. Normally, water follows such exported ions by osmosis. In the absence of this protein, any mucus made by the cell is therefore much less watery, and so more sticky, than usual. It is this sticky mucus that causes all the problems of cystic fibrosis.

Gene therapy opens up the possibility of giving affected individuals nasal sprays which would contain the healthy form of the cystic fibrosis gene packaged in a harmless virus, a hollow sphere of lipid molecules or some other vector. The idea is that the healthy genes would enter some of the lung epithelial cells, become incorporated in their nuclear DNA and start to make the CFTR protein. This should allow the mucus secreted by these cells to have its normal runny consistency.

By 2000, many hundreds of trials for somatic gene therapy had been approved. In addition to trials on people with cystic fibrosis, somatic gene therapy is being trialed for a wide range of conditions including β-**thalassaemia**, **cancers**, **Duchenne muscular dystrophy**, **familial hypercholesterolaemia** and **haemophilia**.

The limitations of gene therapy

Somatic gene therapy has been heralded as a possible cure for a great range of medical problems. However, some human diseases caused by faulty genes can already be treated quite effectively by conventional means. For example, **phenylketonuria** is a condition which, if untreated, leads to the person being severely mentally retarded. Since 1954, though, it has been realised that the condition can be prevented by giving children with the faulty gene a special diet. This illustrates an important truth about human development: both genes *and* the environment play essential parts.

A second reason why we should not see gene therapy as the likely solution to all medical problems is that diseases such as cystic fibrosis, phenylketonuria and sickle-cell disease are the exception, not the rule. These conditions are caused by inborn errors in *single* genes. However, *less than 2 per cent* of our total disease load is due to errors in single genes. Most human diseases have a strong environmental component, and genetic defects at most *predispose* the person to develop the condition. In addition, the genetic component is usually the result of many genes, which makes gene therapy much more difficult.

Genetically modified tomatoes

A form of genetic engineering different from the usual has been carried out on tomatoes. Here, instead of introducing a gene from another species, an artificial gene called an **antisense gene** was introduced. The antisense gene has this name because it makes mRNA that is complementary to the mRNA made by one of the tomato's genes – the PG (polygalacturonase) gene. The first 15 bases in the coding region of the PG gene are ATGGTTATCCAAAGG. The corresponding bases of the antisense gene (as you should be able to work out) are TACCAATAGGTTTCC.

As a result, the mRNAs made by the PG and the antisense genes fit snugly together. *In consequence, the PG mRNA is not translated into protein.* The normal effect of the PG protein is to cause the tomato to ripen quickly. In its absence, the genetically modified tomato ripens far more slowly. This means that it stays firm for longer and is much less likely to go rotten. It also tastes better and develops its red colour naturally without needing to be sprayed with ethene. Just what consumers, farmers and food retailers all want.

During 1997 and 1998, genetically modified tomatoes had excellent sales in the UK. However, in 1999 widespread doubts about **genetically modified food** – dubbed 'Frankenfoods' by some sections of the media – led to them being withdrawn 'on commercial grounds'.

Using genetic engineering on humans for non-medical reasons

Might gene 'therapy' be used to affect traits such as **intelligence**, **beauty**, **criminality**, **sporting prowess** and **sexual preference**? There are frequent reports in the popular press of 'a gene for homosexuality' or 'a gene for criminality' and maybe much human behaviour has a genetic component to it. However, attempts to find genes for such traits are, at best, the first steps to understanding the rich and complex ways in which we develop and behave. At worst, they are misguided attempts to stigmatise certain members of society. We are more, far more, than our genes.

Germ-line therapy

At the moment it is generally felt that human germ-line therapy is too risky. Researchers cannot control precisely where new genes are inserted. This raises the possible danger that the inserted gene might damage an existing gene, which could lead to diseases, including cancers.

However, although human germ-line therapy may currently be too risky, it is unlikely that this will remain the case indefinitely. Probably scientists will develop methods of targeting the insertion of new genes with sufficient precision to avoid the problems that presently attend such procedures. Suppose human germ-line therapy does one day become safe. Should we permit it?

To answer this we should first ask whether germ-line therapy is necessary. It is not easy to demonstrate what is 'necessary'. Value judgements are involved, so that there may be genuine controversy about whether something is needed. Is the motor car necessary? Or tigers? Or confidentiality between doctors and their patients? It is likely that most improvements resulting from germ-line therapy could also be achieved by somatic gene therapy or conventional medicine.

Suppose that one day germ-line therapy becomes relatively safe and allows certain medical conditions to be treated better than by other approaches – would it then be right or wrong?

Some people have expressed the fear that germ-line therapy might be used by dictators to produce only certain types of people – a modern application of eugenics (*page 757*). A major problem with this objection is that it assumes too much of genetic engineering. It is easy to overstate the extent to which we are controlled by our genes. Dictators have had and will continue to have far more effective ways of controlling people.

A more likely problem is that germ-line therapy will be permitted before people have grown sufficiently accustomed to the idea. The speed of technological change is so fast nowadays that it can outpace ethical considerations and people end up feeling bewildered by the sheer number of new possibilities.

35.5 Senescence

So far in this chapter we have considered the processes leading to the formation of a fully efficient adult organism. But in many species a process of **senescence** ensues in which the smooth functioning of the organism declines (*figure 35.11*), culminating in death.

The manifestations of senescence in humans are well known and include:

- greying and loss of hair;
- wrinkling of the skin;
- loss of cardio-vascular efficiency and capacity, resulting in faster, shallower breathing and a decrease in cardiac output;
- a reduction in the basal metabolic rate (BMR);
- reduction in libido (sexual desire);

Figure 35.11 One person, F. S. (1899–1981), at different times in her life. From top to bottom, aged 3, 12, 21, 35 and 79 years.

- a decline in fertility leading, in women, to a cessation of normal ovulation cycles (as a result of changes in the secretion of gonadotrophins and ovarian hormones);

- muscular weakness due to the replacement of muscle fibres by connective tissue;

- sensory impairment including a decrease in visual acuity, a tendency towards long-sightedness, an inability to hear high frequencies or to appreciate some tastes and smells;

- slower reaction times resulting from a decrease in nerve conduction velocity;

- reduction in body size due to progressive atrophy of the bones and other tissues;

- inefficient homeostasis as the body adjusts less effectively to variations in temperature, blood sugar and so on.

There is no precise age at which senescence begins. Many of the changes listed above start in one's 20s, others much later. In addition, old age *may* ultimately be accompanied by mental senility, brittle bones or incontinence.

What causes senescence?

There is no simple answer to this question but research in recent years has suggested that senescence results from the gradual accumulation of genetic and biochemical defects. Some of these are listed below.

- **Mistakes in protein synthesis** Old age appears to be accompanied by changes in the metabolic processes occurring in cells, particularly those involved in protein synthesis. In most species, as individuals get older there is a gradual decline in the accuracy of DNA replication with the result that the genetic make-up of the cells formed in mitosis is abnormal. Since these abnormalities arise as a result of errors in the production of the body (somatic) cells as opposed to the reproductive (germ) cells, they are called **somatic mutations** (*page 742*).

   Many somatic mutations are not too serious, but some lead to cellular misfunction. In some cases this results in the death of a cell. In other cases quite the opposite may happen: a cell may go out of control and divide repeatedly, possibly because it is no longer making the repressor molecules which prevent excessive division. The cell has become cancerous (*page 466*). This is the reason why most types of cancer are more common in older people.

- **Cell loss** In most tissues new cells are formed by mitosis throughout life, with the result that dead cells are constantly replaced by new ones. However, there are certain tissues, notably muscle and nerve, whose cells are not replaced. Once you reach your early 20s, your brain loses about 100 000 neurones a day! Inevitably there comes a time when such continued losses contribute to senescence.

- **Chemical changes in tissues** As one gets older the formation of extra cross-linkages in structural proteins such as collagen and elastin result in the loss of suppleness in one's limbs. Arteries too become harder and less elastic.

- **Auto-immunity** There is evidence that as people get older they may start to produce antibodies against their own antigens. The explanation lies partly in the fact, already mentioned, that ageing is accompanied by mistakes in protein synthesis. Since the protein molecules so formed are new to the body, they may be treated by the immune system as foreign and attacked accordingly.

   Another explanation for auto-immunity is that the suppressor T lymphocytes, which normally prevent the body from attacking its own cells, stop functioning properly. The result is that the person's own cells get destroyed. (T lymphocytes are explained on page 326.)

   Certain diseases associated with old age are due to auto-immunity. These include diabetes, motor neurone disease and rheumatoid arthritis (*figure 35.12*).

Extension

Why don't we live for ever?

Cells taken from a human fetus go through about 50 cycles of cell division before they die. The older you are, the fewer the number of cell divisions your cells have left in them.

In 1990 Dr Calvin Harley, of McMaster University in Canada, and his colleagues reported a study on specialised pieces of DNA, called **telomeres**, that occur at the ends of chromosomes. They found that telomeres shorten in proportion to the number of cell cycles a cell has gone through. This suggests that loss of telomere DNA might be related to senescence.

It is known that an enzyme called **telomerase** can lengthen telomeres. Harley pointed out that this raised the possibility that methods might be found to boost telomerase and so lengthen life span. Indeed, in 1998 a team of North American scientists significantly extended the life span of cultured human cells by adding telomerase.

At first sight this might seem like good news, but is it really desirable for people's life span to be lengthened any more than it is already?

Part 6

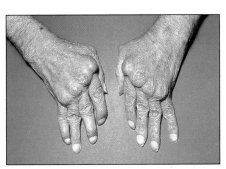

Figure 35.12 A severe case of rheumatoid arthritis, a disease resulting from autoimmunity.

Alzheimer's disease

The general term for disorders which gradually affect the brain as a person gets older is **dementia**. Dementias make it more difficult for a person to think clearly and to cope with everyday life. There may also be changes in personality and behaviour.

In countries where people live a long time, about half the cases of dementia are due to **Alzheimer's disease**, a condition which becomes more common as people get into their 70s and 80s. Another cause of dementia is a series of small **strokes** – a stroke being a sudden interference with the circulation of arterial blood to a part of the brain (*page 360*).

In the early stages of Alzheimer's, sufferers may appear muddled or depressed. As the disease progresses, they eventually lose their memory and fail to recognise even close family members. Often more recent memories are lost first, so 80-year-olds may recall their childhood quite well but not know whether they have been married or had children.

At present little is known about the causes of Alzheimer's. Some forms have a genetic component, and aluminium has been implicated as an environmental trigger for the condition. There is still no cure for Alzheimer's through drugs have been developed which can help in the early stages.

▶ Lack of acetycholine in Alzheimer's disease, pages 364–5

Summary

1. **Development** involves a highly ordered sequence of events, carefully controlled in space and time.

2. **Genes** in the nucleus are primarily responsible for determining how organisms develop, though the **cytoplasm** also plays an important part.

3. **Cloning** experiments in amphibians, plants and mammals show that the DNA in the nuclei of cells remains unaltered during development. **Differentiation** is brought about by different parts of the genetic code being used at different times and in different cells as an organism develops.

4. At a given moment only some of the genes in a cell synthesise messenger RNA; other genes are masked or 'switched off'. This concept is supported by **Jacob and Monod's work** on the synthesis of sugar-splitting enzymes in the colon bacillus *Escherichia coli*.

5. In eukaryotes, the control of gene regulation is far from being understood. Most control probably resides at the level of **transcription** (messenger RNA synthesis), though control at the level of **translation** (protein synthesis from messenger RNA) may also be involved.

6. In eukaryotes, DNA is found in close association with **histone** proteins.

7. The **environment** as well as the genes is important in development.

8. An organism's genetic make-up can be altered by **genetic engineering (recombinant DNA technology)**. A frequent approach involves removing genes from the DNA of one species and inserting them into the DNA of another.

9. Genetic engineering is being used increasingly in medicine, agriculture and the food industry but remains controversial.

10. **Senescence**, a natural process of decline culminating in death, is caused by a combination of factors including **somatic mutations**, **mistakes in protein synthesis**, **cell loss**, **chemical changes in tissues** and **auto-immunity**.

For general advice on these questions and advice on answering essay-type questions, see pages vii and viii.

1. (a) Many older people find it difficult to run to catch a bus. Describe **three** of the physiological changes which occur with ageing that may contribute towards this. (6)

(b) Explain how changes in each of the following may contribute to the ageing process:

(i) genes;

(ii) tissues;

(iii) the immune system. (6)

(Total 12 marks)

NEAB 1997

2. (a) Explain the theoretical basis of genetic fingerprinting and suggest uses for the process. (16)

(b) Outline how genetic fingerprinting is carried out. (6)

(Total 22 marks)

UCLES 1997

3. The diagram below shows how a genetically modified organism may be produced by inserting a gene from a human into a bacterium.

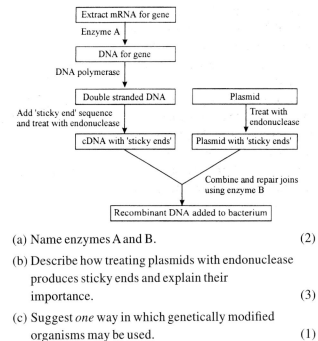

(a) Name enzymes A and B. (2)

(b) Describe how treating plasmids with endonuclease produces sticky ends and explain their importance. (3)

(c) Suggest *one* way in which genetically modified organisms may be used. (1)

(Total 6 marks)

London 1996

Chapter 36

Population genetics

What determines the frequencies of alleles in populations of organisms? In this chapter we shall address this question. We shall also look at the connection between allele frequency and phenotype frequency. If, for example, 20 per cent of the loci for eye colour in a population of humans are occupied by alleles for blue eye colour, what percentage of people will have blue eyes? As we shall see, the answer is not 20 per cent!

36.1 Populations and allele frequencies

A **population** is a collection of individuals that breed with one another and are reproductively isolated from other individuals of the same species (*page 690*). This means that all the individuals must belong to the same species and must live in the same geographical area: rabbits in Yorkshire do not belong to the same population as rabbits in Norfolk. Indeed, there are doubtless many different rabbit populations both in Norfolk and in Yorkshire.

Other examples of populations besides rabbits would be frogs in a pond, beech trees in a copse, *Paramecium* in a ditch or wood mice in a small wood surrounded by agricultural land (*figure 36.1*).

Although there may be considerable movement of individuals to and from it, a population generally perpetuates itself by the interbreeding of the individuals within it. It thus represents a genetic unit, and what happens to it in evolutionary terms depends on the genes it contains. The genetic constitution of a population, i.e. the sum total of all the different genes in the population, is known as the **gene pool**. Just as the future of an individual organism depends to a large extent on its genetic constitution, so the evolutionary future of a population depends on its gene pool.

The frequency of any given allele in a population, relative to other alleles at the same locus, is known as the **allele frequency**. Sometimes, rather confusingly, allele frequencies are called **gene frequencies**, although the former term is better.

Figure 36.1 Aerial photograph showing patches of woodland, many of which are connected by hedges. The more isolated geographically a patch of woodland is, the more likely it is that organisms in it are isolated genetically from organisms of the same species in another patch of woodland. Of course, two small woods may be genetically isolated from each other for some species (e.g. slugs), but not for others (e.g. songbirds).

Calculating allele frequencies

Consider a population of fruit flies. Suppose the population contains 100 flies and we want to know the frequencies of the alleles that determine wing length.

To arrive at an answer, we must bear in mind that fruit flies are diploid and that each cell therefore contains two alleles for wing length. Imagine that 160 of the 200 alleles are alleles for normal wings and that 40 are alleles for vestigial wings. Then the proportion of the alleles that are alleles for normal wings equals 160 divided by 200, i.e. 0.8. The proportion of the alleles that are alleles for vestigial wings equals 40 divided by 200, i.e. 0.2. As we expect, the sum of these two proportions, 0.8 and 0.2, equals 1.0, as all the alleles at this particular locus are either alleles for normal wings or alleles for vestigial wings.

Allele frequencies are sometimes expressed as **proportions**, in which case they lie between 0 and 1, and sometimes as **percentages**, in which case they lie between 0 per cent and 100 per cent. Converting from a proportion to a percentage simply involves multiplying by 100 and adding a percentage symbol (%). In the above case, the allele for normal wings has a frequency of 0.8 or 80%, while the allele for vestigial wings has a frequency of 0.2 or 20%.

Factors that change allele frequencies

Under certain conditions, allele frequencies may remain constant over time. However, a number of factors can lead to changes in allele frequencies. They are as follows.

Allele-specific mortality or emigration

Let us return to the population of fruit flies. Suppose that vestigial-winged flies are more likely to die than normal-winged flies. Vestigial-winged individuals are homozygous for the vestigial-winged allele (*page 575*). Greater **mortality** among vestigial-winged individuals would therefore lead to a *decrease* in the frequency of the allele for vestigial wings and a corresponding *increase* in the frequency of the allele for normal wings.

Similarly, if one of the two phenotypes is more likely to **emigrate** than the other, allele frequencies will change. Note that mortality or emigration by themselves have no effect on allele frequencies. Only if such mortality or emigration is allele-specific – that is, more likely for one allele than another – will mortality or emigration lead to changes in allele frequencies.

Allele-specific reproduction or immigration

In the same way, if one allele is associated with a higher probability of **reproduction** or **immigration**, allele frequencies will change accordingly. For example, normal-winged fruit flies might be more likely to immigrate into other fruit fly populations than vestigial-winged fruit flies, simply because the latter cannot fly. Of course, immigration into one population is always balanced by an emigration from another one. Immigration and emigration may therefore change allele frequencies within individual populations – but for the species as a whole they are of no consequence.

Chance

Suppose, for the sake of argument, that colour blindness is not associated with a decrease or increase in mortality, emigration, reproduction or immigration. Nevertheless, different populations of humans might still differ in the frequencies of their alleles for colour blindness and normal colour vision purely by **chance**.

Suppose that in one population, a woman homozygous for the colour-blind allele had a very large family for reasons quite unconnected with her possession of two alleles for colour blindness. The next generation would see an increase, albeit a small one, in the frequency of the allele for colour blindness. Chance increases or decreases in allele frequencies over time are known as **genetic drift**.

The importance of genetic drift is greatest when population sizes are very small. This is most clearly seen when a group of individuals founds a new population. If the group is large, its gene pool will probably be very similar to that of the parent population. If, however, only a few individuals found a new population, the gene pool of the new population may be quite different from that of the parent population. This phenomenon is known as the **founder effect** (*extension box alongside*).

Mutation

Consider a population in which a particular locus can be occupied by one of two alleles, **A** and **a**. Suppose that the two alleles have no differences in their effects on an individual's survival, reproduction, immigration or emigration. Despite this, it is still possible that, for example, **A** may steadily increase at the expense of **a**, if the frequency with which **A** mutates to **a** is less than the frequency with which **a** mutates to **A**.

36.2 Allele and phenotype frequencies

The factors that can change allele frequencies will obviously change phenotype frequencies too. But what is the precise relationship between allele frequencies and phenotype frequencies? To return to the question posed at the beginning of this chapter, if 20 per cent of the loci for eye colour in a population of humans are occupied by alleles for blue eye colour, what percentage of the population will have blue eyes?

The founder effect in humans

A clear instance of the founder effect in humans is provided by the geographical distribution of a rare neurological condition known as **Huntington's disease** or **Huntington's chorea**, characterised by the degeneration of the nervous system.

Affected people find motor coordination difficult so their hands shake and they have problems with balance. As the condition worsens, they find it more and more difficult to look after themselves. The disease usually manifests itself in people aged between 30 and 50, and death generally follows within five to ten years.

The condition is caused by the possession of a mutant dominant allele on one of the pairs of autosomes (non-sex chromosomes). This means that individuals homozygous or heterozygous for the allele are affected.

Fortunately, Huntington's disease is uncommon. In Britain, for instance, the average incidence of people with the mutant allele is about seven per 100 000. However, in the Moray Firth area in Scotland the figure is 560 per 100 000, while there are villages in Venezuela where the figure is over 1000 per 100 000, i.e. in excess of 1 per cent.

The condition was probably introduced into Venezuela in the 1860s by a sailor aboard a German trade ship. A particularly large number of descendants resulted from a relationship between the sailor and a Venezuelan woman, and many of these descendants inherited the harmful allele.

Figure 36.2 G.H. Hardy. Although his name is nowadays most widely known for his derivation of the Hardy–Weinberg principle, Hardy was a leading pure mathematician during the first half of the 20th century. At the age of 15 he read a novel called *A Fellow of Trinity* and decided that he wanted to be one. He duly arrived at Trinity College, Cambridge as an undergraduate and spent most of the rest of his life there. His daily routine altered little throughout his adult life. Over breakfast he read *The Times*, paying particular attention to the cricket scores. From nine to one, unless he was giving a lecture, he worked at his own mathematics. 'Four hours creative work a day is about the limit for a mathematician' he used to say. After lunch he spent the afternoon watching cricket, unless it was winter in which case he would play a game of real tennis. About two to three weeks before his death he heard from the Royal Society that he was to be given their highest honour, the Copley Medal. He grinned and remarked to a close friend, the novelist C. P. Snow, 'Now I know that I must be pretty near the end. When people hurry up to give you honorific things there is exactly one conclusion to be drawn'.

Note, first of all, that if we were haploid organisms, the answer to this question would be 20 per cent, as individuals with a copy of the allele for blue eye colour would have blue eyes and individuals with alleles for other eye colours would have brown or green or grey eyes, depending on the allele they possessed. However, we are, of course, diploid, not haploid and this makes the relationship more complex.

The Hardy–Weinberg principle

Let us make the simplifying assumption that a particular population of humans has eye colour alleles only for blue or for brown eyes, and that the allele for blue eye colour is recessive to the allele for brown eye colour.

If we let **B** stand for the allele for brown eyes and **b** for the allele for blue eyes, individuals will have the following genotypes and phenotypes:

Genotype	Phenotype
BB	Brown eyes
Bb	Brown eyes
bb	Blue eyes

We can represent the frequency of the allele for brown eyes by the symbol p, and the frequency of the allele for blue eyes by the symbol q. As we have made the assumption that the population in question has eye colour alleles only for brown or for blue eyes, no other alleles can be present at the locus for eye colour. Therefore, p and q are related to one another by the simple equation:

$$p + q = 1$$

What we need is an equation which will relate the allele frequencies p and q to the phenotype frequencies given by the percentage of people who are blue-eyed and brown-eyed.

It was this relationship between allele frequencies and phenotype frequencies that bothered the geneticist R.C. Punnett (the originator of the Punnett square), as he travelled back to Cambridge on a train from a Royal Society of Medicine meeting in London in 1908. Fortunately he was a close friend of the mathematician G.H. Hardy, with whom he used to play cricket (*figure 36.2*). On his return to Cambridge, Punnett sought out Hardy and explained the problem to him. Hardy at once replied 'p^2 to $2pq$ to q^2'.

Punnett assured Hardy that although he might find the solution to the problem trivial, he had made an important contribution to genetics. Hardy was persuaded to publish his result. In the same year the German physician W. Weinberg independently published the same conclusion, for which reason it is now known as the **Hardy–Weinberg principle**.

Put less succinctly, the Hardy–Weinberg principle states that if the frequency of one allele, which we may call **A**, is p, while the frequency of the other allele, **a**, is q, then the frequencies of the three possible genotypes **AA**, **Aa** and **aa** are respectively p^2, $2pq$ and q^2. A population to which it applies is said to be in **Hardy–Weinberg equilibrium**.

Explanation of the Hardy–Weinberg principle

What is the explanation of this relationship? Consider what happens at meiosis and at fertilisation with respect to the two alternative alleles, **A** and **a**.

As a result of meiosis, a proportion p of the gametes will carry the **A** allele, simply because gametes are haploid and a proportion p of the alleles at the locus in question are **A** alleles. Similarly, a proportion q of the gametes will carry the **a** allele.

Now we can construct a Punnett square to see what happens to these gametes on fertilisation:

Gametes	**A**	**a**
Frequency	*p*	*q*
A	**AA**	**Aa**
p	p^2	*pq*
a	**Aa**	**aa**
q	*pq*	q^2

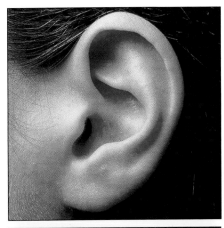

You can see that the frequency of the **AA** genotype is p^2, that of the **Aa** genotype is $pq + pq = 2pq$, and that of the **aa** genotype is q^2.

This gives us the relationship between allele frequencies and *genotype* frequencies. The relationship between allele frequencies and *phenotype* frequencies is now easily worked out. Suppose that **A** is dominant to **a**. In that case, there are only two phenotypes to consider, one displayed by the homozygous recessive genotype, **aa**, and the other by the genotypes **AA** and **Aa**. The frequency of the recessive phenotype is simply q^2, while that of the dominant phenotype is $2pq + p^2$.

Using the Hardy-Weinberg principle

To illustrate how the Hardy-Weinberg principle can be used, consider the inheritance of ear lobes in humans. Human ear lobes may be attached or free (*figure 36.3*). This difference is largely controlled by the actions of a single gene.

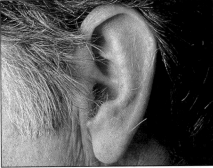

Figure 36.3
Top Attached ear lobe.
Bottom Unattached ear lobe.

The allele for free ear lobes, **F**, is dominant to the allele for attached ear lobes, **f**. As a result, people with free ear lobes are either homozygous dominant for the allele in question (**FF**) or heterozygous (**Ff**); people with attached ear lobes are homozygous recessive (**ff**).

Suppose that in a population 84 per cent of people have free ear lobes whereas the remaining 16 per cent do not. Using the Hardy-Weinberg principle we can calculate the frequencies of the **F** and **f** alleles and also work out the frequencies of the three different genotypes.

The genotypes will be distributed according to the equation:

$$p^2 + 2pq + q^2 = 1$$

where p^2 is the frequency of the homozygous dominant individuals (**FF**), $2pq$ the frequency of heterozygous individuals (**Ff**) and q^2 the frequency of the homozygous recessives (**ff**).

The 16 per cent of the population with attached ear lobes must have the genotype **ff**. 16 per cent is 0.16, so:

$q^2 = 0.16$

Therefore:

$q = \sqrt{0.16}$
$\quad = 0.4$

But:

$p + q = 1$

Therefore:

$p = 1 - 0.4$
$\quad = 0.6$

So, by using the Hardy-Weinberg principle we have determined both *q*, the frequency of the recessive allele, and *p*, the frequency of the dominant allele.

Note that we used proportions when working out q from the information that $q^2 = 0.16$. You are advised always to use proportions, rather than percentages, when using the Hardy-Weinberg principle. This is because most people tend to assume that the square root of 16 per cent is 4 per cent, when in fact it is 40 per cent! (Remember that 'per cent' is the Latin for 'out of a hundred', so that 16 per cent equals 16/100, the square root of which is 4/10, not 4/100.)

When to use the Hardy–Weinberg principle

Phenylketonuria (PKU) is a hereditary disease found in 1 in 10 000 people in Britain who are homozygous recessive at a particular locus. People with the disease lack an enzyme which acts on the amino acid phenylalanine. As a result, phenylalanine in the diet is converted instead into a toxic compound which impairs brain development. Fortunately, mental subnormality can be avoided if a phenylalanine-free diet is taken during early childhood. Because of this, all children born in Britain are routinely tested for PKU and placed on such a diet if the test proves positive.

Question
What percentage of people in Britain are carriers of PKU?

Answer
Carriers are heterozygotes. Assuming Hardy–Weinberg equilibrium, we therefore need to calculate $2pq$. We know that 1 in 10 000 people are homozygous recessive. So:

$$q^2 = \text{1 in 10 000}$$
$$= 0.0001$$

which means that:

$$q = 0.01$$

So:

$$p = 0.99$$

Therefore:

$$2pq = 0.0198$$
$$= 0.02$$
$$= 2\%$$

We conclude that approximately two per cent of people in Britain carry the allele for phenylketonuria.

Having worked out the values of p and q, the proportion of the population who have the genotype **FF** can easily be calculated as it equals p^2. So:

$$p^2 = 0.6 \times 0.6$$
$$= 0.36$$

Similarly, the frequency of the heterozygotes equals $2pq$. So:

$$2pq = 2 \times 0.6 \times 0.4$$
$$= 0.48$$

As a check, the frequencies of these three different genotypes should, of course, add up to 1, as each individual in the population must have one of these three genotypes. So:

$$p^2 + 2pq + q^2 = 0.36 + 0.48 + 0.16$$
$$= 1$$

as expected.

Assumptions made by the Hardy–Weinberg principle

Although the Hardy–Weinberg principle is a powerful tool in the study of population genetics, it does make a number of assumptions, and these need to be appreciated if the principle is not be used inappropriately.

First assumption: the population consists of diploid sexually reproducing organisms

The Hardy–Weinberg principle considers the relationship between allele frequencies and genotype frequencies for a diploid population. It also assumes that reproduction is sexual. Indeed, the whole question of what a population is takes on a new meaning if reproduction is asexual. Species that reproduce only by asexual means consist of large numbers of clones (*page 620*). Each clone contains individuals genetically identical with one another, apart from the occasional mutation. Over time clones gradually diverge from one another through the slow accumulation of distinct mutations.

Second assumption: the allele frequencies do not change over time

Earlier we saw that allele-specific mortality, reproduction, immigration or emigration all lead to changes in allele frequencies over time. Clearly any of these could invalidate the Hardy–Weinberg principle.

To take an extreme example, let us suppose that people with attached ear lobes always die in their early 20s (fortunately this does not happen). Were this to occur, then in the population we were considering just now, the genotype frequencies would be as follows:

	FF	**Ff**	**ff**
People aged under 20	36%	48%	16%
People aged over 30	43%	57%	0%

Although people aged under 20 are in Hardy–Weinberg equilibrium, this is not the case for people aged over 30. In the same way as allele-specific mortality can invalidate the Hardy–Weinberg principle, so can allele-specific emigration, reproduction and immigration.

Third assumption: the population size is large

In very small populations, chance effects may generate ratios that appear not to conform with the Hardy–Weinberg principle. Just as a family of six children might consist of five girls and a single boy, or even of six girls, so small populations may have genotypic and phenotypic ratios that differ from those expected from the allele frequencies. Statistical procedures can be used, however, to see whether such ratios can be accounted for by small population sizes.

Fourth assumption: mating is random with respect to genotype

Suppose that people with free ear lobes tend not to have children with people who have attached ear lobes. In that case the population will show a deficit of heterozygotes.

The easiest way to see this is to make the rather extreme assumption that people always have children with people who have the same genotype for ear lobe attachment as themselves. In that case children can result from one of three sorts of mating:

1 **FF** × **FF**
2 **Ff** × **Ff**
3 **ff** × **ff**

Matings 1 and 3, in the absence of mutations, lead only to homozygotes. In the case of mating 2, one quarter of the children are **FF**, one quarter **ff** and a half **Ff**. So in one generation the frequency of heterozygotes has halved, although there has been no change in allele frequencies. In the next generation the frequency of heterozygotes will again halve if children only result from the union of people with the same genotype.

After all this you might suppose that the assumptions of the Hardy–Weinberg principle are so strict that it can hardly ever be used in real life. In practice, however, it turns out that unless the assumptions of the principle are violated quite substantially, allele frequencies can usually be used to determine genotype and phenotype frequencies with some accuracy, and vice versa.

Is mating random or non-random?

For almost every physical and mental characteristic, people tend to marry individuals more similar to themselves than would be expected by chance. By and large tall people marry tall people, people with blue eyes marry people with blue eyes and people with outgoing happy-go-lucky personalities marry people with outgoing happy-go-lucky personalities. This is how most dating agencies work. Once you have paid your fee, all the computer does is to arrange for you to meet someone of similar age, physical appearance and interests who doesn't live too far away – though most dating agencies do ensure that you and your date are of opposite sex.

The tendency for individuals to mate with individuals of similar phenotypes is called **assortative mating**. One of the very few examples known where people are more likely to marry individuals who *differ* from them in appearance occurs in respect of red hair. For some reason red-heads are less likely to marry red-heads than chance predicts.

Non-random mating with respect to genotype occurs in **inbreeding** when individuals are more likely to mate with relatives. Relatives, of course, are more likely to have the same genotypes, so that assortative mating and inbreeding both disrupt the Hardy–Weinberg equilibrium. The difference is that assortative mating usually disrupts the Hardy–Weinberg equilibrium at only a few loci, whereas inbreeding leads to a loss of heterozygosity at a very large number of loci.

When not to use the Hardy–Weinberg principle

In the MN human blood group system alleles **M** and **N** are codominant. Individuals with the genotype **MM** have the phenotype M, those with the genotype **MN** have the phenotype MN, and those with the genotype **NN** have the phenotype N.

Question
Suppose that 26 per cent of the population are blood group M and 44 per cent are blood group MN. What is the frequency of the **N** allele?

Answer
This is a population genetics question that should be answered *without* the use of the Hardy–Weinberg principle. The reason is that the two alleles, **M** and **N**, are codominant, which means that heterozygotes can be distinguished from both sorts of homozygotes. A good way of answering this question is as follows:

Consider 100 people in this population. Twenty-six of them will have the genotype **MM** and 44 the genotype **MN**. Between them the 100 people have a total of 200 of the alleles in question: each person with blood group M has two **M** alleles, each person with blood group MN has one **M** and one **N** allele, and each person with blood group N has two N alleles. Of these two hundred alleles, the total number of **M** alleles is:

$$(2 \times 26) + 44 = 96$$

The frequency of the **M** allele is therefore:

$$96/200 = 0.48$$

Therefore the frequency of the **N** allele is:

$$1 - 0.48 = 0.52$$
$$= 52\%$$

Having seen how the frequencies of alleles, genotypes and phenotypes are interrelated, we shall now look at two instances where these may change over time or space.

Variation in the peppered moth

One of the best researched examples of population genetics in nature is furnished by the peppered moth (*Biston betularia*) which has been studied by Bernard Kettlewell and others for over 50 years.

The peppered moth is very common in Britain and normally rests in shaded sites on trees, either under horizontal branches or where branches join the main trunk. Here it depends on its cryptic coloration to blend in with the background. The normal or *typica* form of the moth is speckled white, but another form is very much darker. This is called the **melanic** or *carbonaria* form (*figure 36.4*).

The first melanic moths were reported in 1848 near Manchester. After that the number increased prodigiously in various parts of Britain. In the 1950s, Kettlewell conducted an extensive survey on the relative abundance and distribution of the normal and melanic forms in different parts of the country (*figure 36.5*).

Figure 36.4 The light and dark forms of the peppered moth (*Biston betularia*) at rest on a tree in an unpolluted area.

Figure 36.5 Map summarising the relative frequencies of the dark and light forms of the peppered moth (*Biston betularia*) in different parts of Britain in the 1950s. In each disc the white sector represents the light form and the black sector the dark form. The sizes of the discs indicate the number of moths examined at each locality. The dark form predominates in areas blackened by industrialisation.

The interesting fact to emerge was that the melanic form abounded in industrial regions where smoke and soot from factory chimneys had blackened the bark of trees and killed off pale lichens. Around Manchester, for example, the frequency of the melanic form exceeded 95 per cent. In non-polluted areas, however, the light form predominated. In the north of Scotland and the extreme south-west of England it even reached 100 per cent.

Explanation of Kettlewell's results

How can we explain this distribution? The peppered moth is preyed upon by birds, such as great tits, which peck them off the trees. In polluted areas the dark form is almost invisible against the darkened branches, whereas the light form stands out like a beacon. In clean areas the reverse is true: the light form is admirably camouflaged against the background of unsooted lichens, but the dark form is clearly seen.

Kettlewell showed that in polluted woods, such as those near Birmingham, far more light moths were picked off the trees by birds than the better-camouflaged dark forms. As a result the frequency of dark moths was significantly higher. In non-polluted Dorset woods, however, it was mainly the dark moths that fell prey to the birds, so the frequency of the light moths was higher.

In each case differential mortality was achieved by **selective predation**. The darkening of trees with the coming of the industrial revolution meant that the dark body colour was favoured over light. In the last 40 years, however, there has been a significant reduction in industrial pollution in Britain. As a result the frequency of melanic moths has declined in industrial areas.

Genetics of the peppered moth

What about the genetics of the two forms of moth? Breeding experiments have shown that the normal and the melanic forms differ at a single locus. The *carbonaria* allele is dominant to the *typica* allele so that heterozygotes are melanic.

However, the story is more complicated than it first appears. Kettlewell noted that in the 19th century the dominance of *carbonaria* over *typica* was not complete, so that heterozygotes were lighter than moths homozygous for the *carbonaria* allele. What seems to have happened is that as the *carbonaria* allele spread, the darker a heterozygote looked, the more it was favoured. As a result the *carbonaria* allele *evolved* to be dominant to the *typica* allele.

To understand why the *carbonaria* allele evolved to be dominant, consider the position of an unfortunate heterozygous moth that looked intermediate between the melanic and typical forms. Such a moth would be conspicuous both on lichen-covered trees and on dark trees. It would have had the worst of both worlds.

Working out *how* the *carbonaria* allele has evolved to be dominant is more complicated and is still not fully understood. It involves genetic changes at other loci which produce proteins that *modify* the effects of the *carbonaria* allele.

Sickle cell anaemia in humans

Sickle cell anaemia is a blood condition found in some black people, inhabitants of Mediterranean countries, Arabs and Indians. In sickle cell anaemia the normal haemoglobin in the red blood cells is entirely replaced by an abnormal haemoglobin known as **haemoglobin S**. Haemoglobin S is much less soluble than normal haemoglobin and it begins to crystallise when the oxygen concentration falls, as it does in the blood capillaries. This causes the red blood cells, normally biconcave disc-shaped, to assume the shape of a sickle or crescent (*figure 36.6*).

With their abnormal haemoglobin, the sickled red cells are less efficient at carrying oxygen. Not only that, but they may block the capillaries and smaller arterioles. This can lead to acutely painful attacks called **crises**. The pain, rather like the pain of a heart attack, is connected to the lack of oxygen at the affected parts.

In Britain, sickle cell anaemia is found in about 1 in 200 babies of West African origin, and in about 1 in 300 babies of Afro-Caribbean origin. Although some people with the disease live to a ripe old age, many die before reaching adulthood and few have any children.

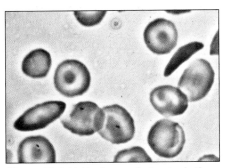

Figure 36.6 Light micrograph showing both disc-shaped (i.e. normal) and sickle-shaped red blood cells.

What causes sickle cell anaemia? Following the discovery that people with sickle cell disease have a different form of haemoglobin, intensive research centred on finding the precise biochemical difference between haemoglobin S and normal haemoglobin. The difference was discovered in 1956 and turned out to be remarkably slight. In haemoglobin S there is one position in each of the two β polypeptide chains in the haemoglobin molecule where the amino acid valine takes the place of glutamic acid. By causing this seemingly trivial change, the defective allele has far-reaching effects on the person's physiology.

Recent studies of haemoglobin S using techniques such as X-ray diffraction and electron microscopy have shown that as haemoglobin S crystallises, the growing crystals distort the shape of the red blood cell. If a way could be found to prevent haemoglobin S from crystallising, then we would have a cure for sickle cell anaemia.

Global distribution of sickle cell anaemia

In some countries sickle cell anaemia is much more frequent than in the United Kingdom. In parts of Africa as many as 1 in 25 children are born with the condition. Given that someone with sickle cell anaemia has two copies of the recessive sickle cell allele, you should be able to use the Hardy–Weinberg principle to show that if 1 in 25 people have the condition, the frequency of the allele responsible must be 1 in 5 (0.2 or 20 per cent).

Why is it that the sickle cell allele is so common when people with sickle cell anaemia usually die young, having left few if any children? A clue can be found by comparing the geographical distribution of the sickle cell allele with the geographical distribution of **malaria** (*figure 36.7*). Places with a high incidence of malaria also have a high frequency of the sickle cell allele.

It turns out that people who are heterozygous for the sickle cell condition are at an advantage in areas where malaria is common. This is because they are less susceptible to malaria than people who lack the sickle cell allele. This may sound surprising unless you know that the parasite responsible for malaria spends part of its life cycle in the human red blood cell (*page 708*). Presumably it is less well adapted to living in red blood cells, half of whose haemoglobin is haemoglobin S. Confusingly, however, people homozygous for the sickle cell allele are very susceptible to malaria.

Heterozygotes have what's called **sickle cell trait** although phenotypically they are the same as people who are homozygous for the normal allele. Only by exposing their blood to

Figure 36.7 A The distribution of the sickle cell allele in Africa, southern Europe, the Middle East and India. Notice how this correlates with **B** the distribution of malaria in this region.

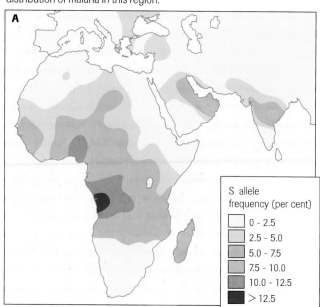

S allele
frequency (per cent)
- 0 - 2.5
- 2.5 - 5.0
- 5.0 - 7.5
- 7.5 - 10.0
- 10.0 - 12.5
- > 12.5

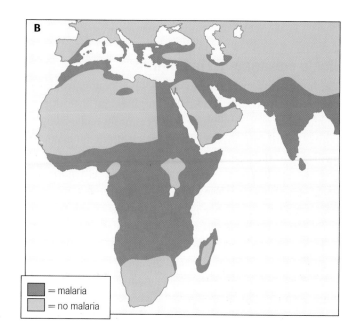

= malaria
= no malaria

unnaturally low oxygen concentrations are their red blood cells made to sickle. Such a state of affairs is known as **heterozygous advantage** because the heterozygote is fitter than either of the homozygotes. It is because of heterozygous advantage that both the sickle cell allele and the normal allele persist. All this is summarised in table 36.1.

Table 36.1 The relationship between genotype and phenotype at the sickle cell locus. **Hb^A**, normal allele; **Hb^S**, sickle cell allele.

Genotype	Name given to genotype	Suffers from sickle cell anaemia?	Susceptible to malaria?
Hb^{A}Hb^A	Normal	No	Yes
Hb^{A}Hb^S	Sickle cell trait	No	Slightly
Hb^{S}Hb^S	Sickle cell anaemia	Yes	Very

36.4 Genetic polymorphism

The peppered moth (*Biston betularia*) and many other animal and plant species exhibit the phenomenon of **polymorphism**. Literally this means 'having many forms' and it may be defined as the existence within a particular species of two or more distinct types of individual. In some cases the different types may result from differences of environment, but in **genetic polymorphism** the different forms, or **morphs** as they are termed, have a genetic basis and their distinctive characteristics are transmitted in a Mendelian manner. Genetic polymorphism occurs when two or more alleles in a population are maintained at levels above those that can be accounted for by mutations alone. An example in humans is the ABO blood group system (*page 596*).

The difference between a genetic polymorphism and one which results from environmental factors is seen in the different sorts of individuals found in a honeybee colony (*page 450*). The colony contains a queen, a number of drones and a very large number of workers. The queen and workers are all females and the differences between them result from the way they are reared as larvae. However, drones are males and differ genetically from the other members of the hive.

Genetic polymorphisms usually result from the possession of alternative alleles by the various morphs. One, or at most a few, loci are involved. In the case of colour variation in the peppered moth, just one locus (i.e. one gene) is involved. This is also true for sickle cell anaemia in humans.

Types of polymorphism

Two types of genetic polymorphism are recognised: **transient** and **balanced**.

- In **transient (unstable) polymorphism** a genetically-controlled morph is in the process of spreading through a population. Eventually the population may become uniform and the polymorphism disappears. In industrial areas the spread of the melanic form of the peppered moth provides us with an example of a transient polymorphism.

- In **balanced (stable) polymorphism** the different morphs – and thus the alleles responsible for them – occur in fairly constant proportions within a given population. A balanced polymorphism is achieved by the existence of relative advantages and disadvantages, each morph being favoured in the particular conditions that occur within a varied environment. The sickle cell condition in humans provides an example of a balanced polymorphism.

Consequences of genetic polymorphism

Often in a balanced polymorphism the various forms possess what appear to be trivial differences which one can hardly imagine would contribute to survival and reproduction.

The concept of race

Within a species there may be sub-divisions of individuals which share common biological characteristics that distinguish them from other such groups. Such sub-divisions are often referred to by biologists as races. For example, the herring gull (*Larus argentatus*) is divided into several races, among which are the Western European race (*L. argentatus argentatus*) and the Eastern Scandinavian race (*L. argentatus omissus*). These two races differ in that the Western European form has a pale silver grey back and pink legs, while the Eastern Scandinavian race has a dark slate grey back and yellow legs (*illustration 1*). However, both races belong to the same species, as they produce viable offspring when interbred.

How great do the differences between the sub-divisions of a species have to be for them to be described as races? It is difficult to answer this categorically. Certainly no one would describe the melanic and pale morphs of the peppered moths as belonging to distinct races as only one locus is involved and the morphs must usually be geographically separated in nature so that interbreeding, though possible, is rare.

To what extent can races be identified in humans? Until the 1960s most biologists classified humans into a number of distinct races. In 1962, for instance, the anthropologist C.S. Coon recognised five racial groupings (*illustration 2*):

■ **Capoids** – cape bushmen of southern Africa;

■ **Negroids** – other black people south of the Sahara;

■ **Caucasoids** – white people indigenous to Europe and West Asia;

■ **Mongoloids** – people indigenous to East Asia and North and South America;

■ **Australoids** – aboriginal people of Australia and New Guinea.

Over the last 30 years, however, many people have increasingly felt it unhelpful to classify people into races. For a start, the genetic diversity *within* each of the above five racial groupings is considerably greater than the genetic distance *between* them. Secondly, over the last few centuries travel has been such that in almost every country of the world, significant numbers of people are to be found belonging to more than one of these racial groupings, thus blurring the distinctions between them. Thirdly, the concept of race in humans has on occasions been abused for political ends, as in apartheid in South Africa, so that the concept is now felt by many to be distasteful.

A A woman of the Bushman people.

B Zulu man from southern Africa.

C Caucasian woman.

D Chinese woman.

Illustration 1   Two races of herring gull.
A Western European race.
B Eastern Scandinavian race.

E Aboriginal man from Australia.
Illustration 2

However, it can sometimes be demonstrated that the various forms do affect important features, such as viability and fecundity.

For example, at first sight there would appear to be no advantage in having a particular blood group within the ABO system. But in fact there is evidence that people belonging to blood groups A and AB were more susceptible to smallpox (now extinct) than people belonging to groups O and B. On the other hand, members of group O are about 40 per cent more likely to develop duodenal ulcers than members of the other three blood groups.

The present global distribution of the three alleles responsible for the ABO blood group syustem (I^A, I^B and I^O) is probably due partly to such factors and partly to migrations of people from one place to another.

Extension

Cyanogenesis in clover

Most populations of white clover (*Trifolium repens*) are polymorphic at two particular loci. Between them these loci are responsible for the production of hydrogen cyanide.

In 1954, the geneticist H. Daday showed that the occurrence of the cyanogenic phenotypes across Europe correlated closely with mean January temperatures. The warmer the winters, the more clover plants contain hydrogen cyanide.

Subsequent studies have shown that slugs, snails and voles prefer to eat clover plants that lack the ability to produce hydrogen cyanide. As cyanide is a poison which inhibits respiration, this is hardly surprising. However, clover plants that can produce hydrogen cyanide are more susceptible to frost damage.

There are thus two opposing environmental pressures. The action of herbivores favours hydrogen cyanide production, but the occurrence of frost favours the absence of hydrogen cyanide production. The result is a more or less uniform change of gene frequencies across Europe. The milder the winters, the greater the proportion of clover plants that produce hydrogen cyanide.

Summary

1. A **population** is a collection of individuals that breed with one another and are reproductively isolated from other individuals of the same species.

2. The frequency of any given allele in a population is known as the **allele frequency**.

3. Over time, allele frequencies can be changed by **allele-specific mortality**, **emigration**, **reproduction**, **immigration**, **genetic drift** and **mutation**.

4. The total of all the different genes in the population is known as its **gene pool**. If only a few individuals start a new population, the gene pool may differ from that of the parent population, a phenomenon known as the **founder effect**.

5. The **Hardy–Weinberg principle** states that, provided certain conditions are met, if the frequency of allele **A** is p, and of the alternative allele **a** is q, then the frequencies of the three genotypes **AA**, **Aa** and **aa** are respectively p^2, $2pq$ and q^2.

6. The Hardy–Weinberg principle assumes that the population consists of diploid sexually reproducing organisms, that there are no changes in allele frequencies over time, that the population size is large and that there is random mating with respect to genotype.

7. Provided its assumptions are met, the Hardy–Weinberg principle can be used to work out allele frequencies from phenotype frequencies, or vice versa.

8. The **peppered moth** provides an example of natural variation in populations which have been extensively studied by population geneticists.

9. **Sickle cell anaemia** is a blood condition in which the normal haemoglobin in the red blood cells is replaced by abnormal **haemoglobin S**. The allele responsible is recessive, though heterozygous individuals are less likely to die from malaria than either of the two homozygotes.

10. A **genetic polymorphism** occurs when two or more alleles in a population are maintained at levels above those that can be accounted for by mutation alone. They may by **transient** (unstable) or **balanced** (stable).

11. Balanced genetic polymorphisms often result from **heterozygous advantage** in which heterozygotes are fitter than either homozygote.

For general advice on these questions and advice on answering essay-type questions, see pages vii and viii.

1. The peppered moth, *Biston betularia*, produces a black variety from time to time. The mutation causing this black variety results in a dominant allele, **B**. The black variety was first observed in 1848 in Manchester, but by 1895 it had increased to 96% of the population in the city.

(a) What was the frequency of the dominant allele, **B**, in the 1895 population of the moth?
Show your calculations. (3)

(b) Explain why there were always some light-coloured forms of the moth present in urban populations after 1895. (2)

(c) Explain why, in rural populations, the black form of the moth remains very rare. (2)

(Total 7 marks)

CCEA 1998

2. (a) In the inheritance of sickle-cell anaemia, the normal allele is represented by **Hb^A** and the sickle-cell allele by **Hb^S**.

(i) Copy and complete the genetic diagram to show the possible phenotypes and genotypes of the offspring of a couple heterozygous for these alleles.
Parental phenotypes
Parental genotypes
Genotypes of gametes
Genotypes of offspring
Phenotypes of offspring

(ii) The first child born to this couple had sickle-cell anaemia. What is the probability that their second child will have sickle-cell anaemia? (4)

(b) Of 12 387 adults examined in Nigeria, 29 were **Hb^S Hb^S**, 2993 were **Hb^{A}Hb^S**, and 9365 were **Hb^{A}Hb^A**. Explain why there were so many heterozygotes in this population compared to the low number of individuals homozygous for sickle-cell anaemia. (3)

(Total 7 marks)

NEAB 1997

3. A single gene with two alleles controls variation in haemoglobin type in sheep. There are three different phenotypes, corresponding to genotypes **S^{A}S^A**, **S^{A}S^B** and **S^{B}S^B** respectively.

In a flock of 175 sheep the frequency of allele **S^A** was found to be 0.6 and the frequency of allele **S^B**, 0.4.

(a) (i) If the animals mated randomly, what frequencies of allele **S^A** and allele **S^B** would be expected in the next generation? (1)

(ii) Using the Hardy-Weinberg equation, calculate the number of sheep with each phenotype in the flock. Show your working. (4)

In humans, the phenotypes and genotypes with respect to the condition of sickle-cell anaemia are as follows:

Phenotype	Genotype
Unaffected	Hb^{A}Hb^A
Sickle-cell trait	Hb^{A}Hb^S
Sickle-cell anaemia	Hb^{S}Hb^S

(b) Explain why:

(i) individuals with sickle-cell anaemia may be at a disadvantage; (1)

(ii) the **Hb^S** allele remains at a relatively high frequency in many populations. (2)

(c) Explain briefly the part played by the following in genetic variation:

(i) mutation; (1)

(ii) the behaviour of chromosomes during meiosis. (3)

(d) The graph shows the frequency distribution of a continuous character.

(i) Draw a line on a copy of the graph to represent changes that would occur under directional selection pressure. (1)

(ii) Explain the shape of the line you have drawn. (1)

(Total 14 marks)

AEB 1996

Chapter 37 Biomes, habitats and environment

A s far as we know, our planet is the only one on which life exists. In this chapter we shall first look at the distribution of organisms around the globe. We shall then look in more detail at what is meant by an organism's environment, paying particular attention to the importance of soil for terrestrial organisms.

37.1 The biosphere

If you look at the Earth from space, you can see the blue of the oceans, the white of the clouds and the green and brown of the land (*figure 37.1*). The part of the Earth and its atmosphere that is inhabited by living things is called the **biosphere**.

We can subdivide the biosphere into large areas which, though separate spatially, are linked by a common type of vegetation. These areas are called **biomes**.

Ecologists argue about how many different biomes there are. To some extent it is a matter of opinion and depends on whether you want to combine the world's plants (**flora**) and animals (**fauna**) into a few very large categories or split them into a large number of smaller categories.

In any event it is convenient to look at **terrestrial biomes** separately from **aquatic biomes**, as different environmental variables are important for each.

Terrestrial biomes

The two most important environmental variables for life on land are **rainfall** and **temperature**. Desert areas such as the Sahara and Central Australia receive little rain, while Central America and Western Central Africa are much wetter. So far as temperature is concerned, as you would expect, it gets hotter towards the tropics and colder towards the poles. Armed with this information, we can now look at the major terrestrial biomes (*figure 37.2*).

Figure 37.1 The Earth from space. Satellite images such as this can reveal changing patterns of land use, for instance loss of forests through burning.

Figure 37.2 The world's major terrestrial biomes. Boreal forest is dominated by evergreen conifers. Sclerophyll vegetation consists of small trees and shrubs with small thick leaves.

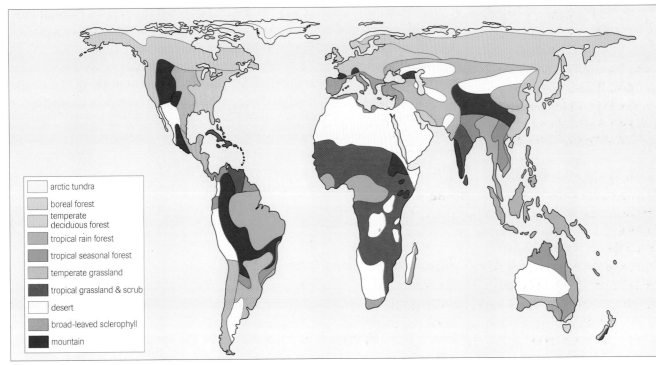

- arctic tundra
- boreal forest
- temperate deciduous forest
- tropical rain forest
- tropical seasonal forest
- temperate grassland
- tropical grassland & scrub
- desert
- broad-leaved sclerophyll
- mountain

PART 7 ORGANISMS AND THEIR ENVIRONMENT

Tropical rain forest

Tropical rain forests are found wherever it is hot and wet throughout the year. Mean monthly temperatures usually lie between 24 and 28°C and frosts are unknown. The annual rainfall is between about 2000 and 3000 mm and rain falls throughout the year; there is no dry season. This climate is found in South-East Asia, Western Central Africa, the Amazon basin, Indonesia and parts of Australia.

The vegetation has a distinctive structure. The most obvious feature is the occasional very large tree, typically 35–45 m tall, whose crown projects above the other trees. Beneath these **emergents** is a second layer of large trees which, together with the emergents, make up a continuous **canopy**. A third tree layer is made up of smaller trees which complete their life cycle without ever reaching the main canopy. Still nearer the ground are young trees, palms, vines and herbs. By the time sunlight reaches the forest floor, most of it has already been intercepted so that it is dark with relatively sparse vegetation.

Many organisms live in the canopy. This is one reason why we know so little of the ecology of tropical rain forests. Only recently have ecologists started to climb the trees or use balloons to investigate the canopy, though early in the 20th century one ingenious botanist used monkeys to collect specimens for him.

Once in the canopy, the contrast with the dark forest floor is striking. Here all is colour and noise. Beautiful epiphytic orchids grow on the branches of the trees. Colourful insects and birds live here without ever descending to the ground. They feed on the copious flowers and fruits available throughout the year. These flowers and fruits are produced by an impressive variety of trees – a single hectare of tropical rain forest may contain over 100 different tree species!

The leaves of the trees tend to be tough and impossible for most animals to digest. The most successful leaf-eaters in Central and tropical South America are sloths (*figure 37.3*). A sloth's entire life is organised around eating large quantities of tough leaves. Because their food is so difficult to digest, sloths have huge stomachs which hold cellulose-digesting bacteria. Food may spend up to a month in the stomach before digestion is complete. It takes a sloth so long to obtain nourishment from its food that it has to conserve as much energy as possible. Although sloths are mammals, their body temperature fluctuates, falling several degrees Celsius at night. They also conserve energy by moving very slowly. Consequently they cannot run away from predators. Instead they rely on **camouflage**. Camouflage is provided by cyanobacteria which live in their fur. These organisms give the fur a greenish tinge which helps the sloths to blend into their background.

Tropical rain forests probably contain more species than any of the world's other biomes. Perhaps surprisingly, their soils are generally **nutrient poor**. This is because decomposition occurs very quickly and any available minerals are rapidly taken up by the many plants.

One result of the soil being nutrient poor is that if the trees are cut down and removed or burnt to provide agricultural land, the resulting soil is only suitable for a few years' farming. After this, the soil becomes so poor that the land has to be abandoned.

In Central America, large areas of tropical rain forest are cut down every year to provide space for cattle ranching, crop-growing and industry. Many of the cattle are subsequently made into beefburgers and sold in fast-food outlets.

Temperate deciduous forest

The north temperate zone lies between the tropic of Cancer and the Arctic Circle. The south temperate zone lies between the tropic of Capricorn and the Antarctic Circle. In these two zones is found **temperate deciduous forest**. This type of forest is dominated by broad-leaved trees that lose their leaves in winter. The biome experiences cold winters, warm summers and intermittent rain throughout the year with a peak in summer.

Figure 37.3 Two-toed sloth in a rain forest. Sloths are adapted for feeding on the leaves of the trees.

Among the major types of temperate deciduous forest found in Europe are those dominated by lime, those by oak and hazel, those by birch and those by beech (*figure 37.4*). The location of each type of forest depends on the climate and, to a lesser extent, the soil.

Until the dawn of agriculture, huge areas of temperate deciduous forest existed. However, over the last few thousand years, these forests have been extensively cleared for cultivation and pasture. Those that remain have almost always, at some time in their past, been managed by people for their wood and other products. Indeed, few undisturbed examples of this biome are found anywhere. We shall look at an example of this biome in more detail later (*pages 633-4*).

Tundra

Tundra occurs at low altitudes and is characterised by the absence of trees and permanently frozen subsoil. It is found in northern Canada, northern Asia and parts of northern Europe. Here it is impossible for trees to grow because the growing season is too short and the soil is too unstable. For much of the year the soil is frozen. Only in summer does the surface thaw. Beneath the surface is soil with water that never melts. This is called **permafrost**.

For much of the year the tundra appears almost lifeless. Then, during the brief growing season, which may last only six weeks, many plants produce spectacular flowers which attract insects for pollination. The Arctic poppy has flowers which rotate during the day, following the Sun. The petals are shaped so as to focus the rays of the Sun on to the stigma and stamens. Here insects gather, attracted by the warmth. In the process, the insects transfer pollen from one plant to another and so bring about cross-pollination.

The most abundant large herbivores of this biome are reindeer, which graze on lichens (*figure 37.5*). Lemmings are also common. Contrary to popular belief, lemmings do not commit mass suicide by flinging themselves into the sea. What happens is that every three to four years their numbers increase to the point at which overcrowding forces large numbers of them to disperse to less populated areas. During this dispersal lemmings will indeed jump into rivers and lakes, but they have exceptionally good long-distance vision and will only jump into water if they can see land at the other side. Once in water they are surprisingly good swimmers and rarely drown.

Desert

Deserts are found throughout the world. Some famous ones are the Sahara of northern Africa, the Kalahari of southern Africa, the Gobi of Central Asia and the Atacama of Peru and Chile. Rain is scarce – usually less than 50 mm a year. Moreover, what little rain there is falls irregularly throughout the year. Some deserts may get no rain for years, only suddenly to receive a downpour of several centimetres within a few hours.

To survive in a desert, organisms have to take advantage of the sudden rains. Many of the smaller desert plants survive as **seeds**. When it rains heavily, they germinate, mature, flower and produce seeds within as little as two weeks (*figure 37.6*). Other plants are **perennials**, surviving the dry periods in the vegetative state. Some of them, such as the cacti of America and the euphorbias of Africa, are **succulents**, storing water and possessing features that minimise water loss. They have thick cuticles, a very low surface–volume ratio and sunken stomata which only open at night (*page 297*). Some desert perennials survive the long periods of drought as underground bulbs or corms. They produce their above-ground parts only when it rains.

Desert animals too have to contend with the problem of water shortage, but they face other difficulties as well. Although it may be very hot during the day, the nights can be surprisingly cold as cloudless skies allow the daytime heat to radiate from the ground. Another difficulty is that sand is hardly an ideal soil. Larger animals need to expend quite a bit of energy in walking over it, while smaller ones find it difficult to maintain burrows.

Figure 37.4 Mature beech wood. Beech trees intercept so much sunlight that very little reaches the ground. As a result, few plants can grow at ground level in a beech wood.

Figure 37.5 Reindeer grazing on lichens beneath the snow.

Figure 37.6 The Judean desert in the spring. Notice the profusion of camelthorn flowers. Soon after this photograph had been taken, the flowers had gone and the plants were producing seeds.

Desertification

Deserts are growing! The spread of deserts into semi-arid lands is known as **desertification**. Desertification results from two causes:

- the actions of people;
- adverse weather conditions.

The main way in which people contribute to desertification is through **overgrazing** by domestic animals such as sheep and goats, or through **deforestation**, i.e. a decrease in the number of trees as they are cut down for firewood. The consequent loss of vegetation leads to a sharp increase in **soil erosion**, whether by winds or the occasional flood, and to a loss in biodiversity (*page 652*).

Desertification can be reversed. For example, the Kenyan Green Belt Movement has shown the value of tree planting and demonstrates the benefits of **sustainable management** in which no more is taken from an area than can regenerate. This project started in the 1970s, and has largely been managed by Professor Wangari Maathai. She has worked with traditional wood-gatherers of Kenya. Over 7 million trees had been planted by the late 1990s. These trees have reduced soil erosion, been a source of foliage for cattle and have provided wood for fuel.

How animals survive dry conditions, page 293; how plants survive dry conditions, page 296

Some of the physiological adaptations shown by animals to the problems of desert life are remarkable. For example, certain frogs can survive for years without water by burying themselves deep into the sand. When the rains eventually come they dig themselves out, mate and lay their eggs in shallow puddles. Here the tadpoles grow very quickly, metamorphosing into adults before the puddles disappear.

Aquatic biomes

The most important variables that operate in aquatic biomes are the salinity, nutrient availability, depth of the water and how permanent it is. Imagine, at one extreme, a puddle in a field. Here the water is not salty. It is shallow and temporary and may be rich in nutrients. At the other extreme, the deep ocean has conditions that are constant throughout the year. The water is salty, dark, cold and nutrient poor. With these extremes in mind, we shall look at two contrasting aquatic biomes.

Lakes and ponds

The crucial factors that determine the ecology of **lakes** and **ponds** are their size and nutrient content. Small ponds may dry up. This has a profound effect on their ecology. Organisms living in such ponds must be able to survive dry periods in some sort of resting stage. Such organisms tend to be small and they complete their life cycle within a few months or even weeks. For this reason fish are not usually found in temporary ponds, but insects and crustaceans are abundant. Indeed, certain crustaceans such as *Chirocephalus*, the fairy shrimp, actually *require* a period of drought in order to complete their life cycles.

An important feature of most lakes is that the water is divided into layers (**strata**) which tend not to mix. Many temperate lakes exhibit **thermal stratification**. In the summer the top few metres of the lake may reach a temperature of 20°C, a pleasant temperature for swimming. However, at a depth of 20 m, the summer temperature may be only 5°C. Most humans would die from hypothermia within an hour of being in water this cold. In winter the reverse happens; the surface of the lake is *colder* than lower down. Stratification can be understood if one remembers that water is densest at 4°C. Consequently, water that is either cooler or warmer than this will rise.

Because the surface and deeper waters of a lake may remain distinct for much of the year, they can differ not only in temperature but also in nutrient concentration and oxygen content. This means that a lake can provide a home for organisms with very different ecological requirements.

Nutrients in lakes and ponds

The most important environmental variable in permanent fresh water is the amount of nutrients available. Paradoxically, lakes which are low in phosphates and nitrates (**oligotrophic lakes**) contain more species than lakes which have high levels of these nutrients (**eutrophic lakes**).

In eutrophic lakes the high levels of nitrates and phosphates promote the growth of large numbers of algae and other small photosynthetic organisms. These in turn support large numbers of aerobic bacteria which decompose the photosynthetic organisms when they die. However, these aerobic bacteria take up so much of the oxygen in the water that the oxygen saturation of the water may fall from nearly 100 per cent to around 60 per cent (*page 682*). Many invertebrates and fish are unable to live unless the oxygen saturation is over 90 per cent.

Marine rocky shore

Marine rocky shores are found on coasts where the waves are too strong to allow the build-up of sand.

One of the most characteristic features of rocky shores is **zonation**. Zonation is the occurrence of organisms in bands – that is, **zones**. On rocky shores zonation occurs because at any one locality the most important environmental variable is the amount of time the organisms are submerged by water (*figure 37.7*). Low down on the shore, organisms may only be exposed at low spring tides. High up on the shore, they may only be submerged at high spring tides. The seashore therefore exhibits a gradation from the terrestrial to the aquatic.

A classic example of rocky shore zonation is provided by four seaweeds in parts of North-West Europe. Lowest on the shore, and submerged for most of the time, is saw wrack (*Fucus serratus*); higher up, saw wrack is replaced by bladder wrack (*F. vesiculosus*); still higher, bladder wrack is replaced by spiral wrack (*F. spiralis*). Finally, at the top of the shore, and only occasionally submerged, is the drought-tolerant channelled wrack (*Pelvetia canaliculata*).

Experiments show that if the species characteristic of the lower shore are transplanted to areas higher up the shore, they die from desiccation. When the species characteristic of the upper shore are transplanted to areas lower down the shore, they become overgrown by the species that normally grow there because they cannot compete with them.

Animals too may show zonation, especially if they are immobile, like barnacles. *Semibalanus balanoides* and *Chthamalus montagui* are two barnacles commonly found on British shores. *Chthamalus* is more drought resistant than *Semibalanus* and so is found higher up the shore. As with the seaweeds, competition is important lower down the shore. Here *Semibalanus* outcompetes *Chthamalus*, probably because it has a looser and more porous shell which is quicker to produce. This allows young *Semibalanus* to grow faster and so cover and crush the young *Chthamalus*. Higher up the shore, though, the loose porous shell of *Semibalanus* renders it susceptible to desiccation. Here the slower growing *Chthamalus* does better.

Figure 37.7 Rocky coastline showing zonation of seaweeds on a moderately sheltered shore.

37.2 Habitats and microhabitats

A **habitat** (Latin for 'it dwells') is the place where an organism lives. Within each biome are numerous habitats, each with a particular set of conditions and associated organisms. Typical habitats include freshwater ponds, slow-flowing streams, rock pools, hedgerows and beech woods.

We can subdivide a habitat into **microhabitats**, small localities each with its own particular conditions. The conditions (or **microclimate**) on the underside of a leaf, in a hedge for instance, will differ from those on the upper side; similarly the lower side of a stone in a stream will be markedly different from the top side. A particular microhabitat will support certain organisms but not others, as you can easily see for yourself by turning over a fallen log in a wood (*figure 37.8*).

The ecological units mentioned so far are essentially *localities* of one size or another. Fundamental to all terrestrial localities is **soil**. Soil forms a link between terrestrial organisms and the rock on which the plants, and therefore the other species in a locality, ultimately depend. For this reason we shall look in some detail at the biology of soil.

Figure 37.8 The organisms that live on the underside of a fallen log differ greatly from those found on its upper surface. This is due to the different microhabitats available to the organisms in those two regions.

37.3 Soil

Soils are derived from rocks by **weathering**. Percolating water is especially important in the formation of soils. Young soils are stabilised when they become colonised by plants and animals. Eventually dead organic matter builds up and a mature soil is formed. Although

Measurements of diversity

Biologists sometimes find it useful to have a quantitative measure of the **diversity** of organisms in an area. For instance, such a measure would allow the following hypotheses (often *assumed* to be ecological truths!) to be tested:

- In extreme environments (e.g. very cold or very dry ones), the diversity of organisms is low.

- A low diversity results in an unstable ecosystem in which populations are usually dominated by abiotic (physical) factors.

- A high diversity results in a stable ecosystem in which populations are usually dominated by biotic factors.

There are a number of different indices of diversity. One widely used one is provided by the following formula:

$$d = \frac{N(N-1)}{\sum n(n-1)}$$

where N is the total number of organisms of all species, n is the total number of organisms of each species and $\sum$ means the sum of.

For example, suppose that a small wood has just 30 individual birds in it, 10 belonging to one species and 20 to another. Its diversity, d, is given by:

$$d = \frac{30 \times 29}{(10 \times 9) + (20 \times 19)}$$
$$= 1.85$$

Fortunately, computers and hand-held calculators can easily be programmed to do the actual calculations, but it is worth stressing one important point. Suppose you are comparing two habitats. Each has 1000 individuals belonging to a total of 10 species. However, one habitat (habitat 1) has 910 individuals of species A and 10 individuals of each of species B, C, D, E, F, G, H, I and J, whereas the other (habitat 2) has 100 individuals of each of species A, B, C, D, E, F, G, H, I and J. Interestingly enough, every index of diversity will conclude that habitat 2 is much more diverse than habitat 1.

At first this may seem surprising. After all, each habitat has 10 species. But now imagine you are walking through the two habitats. Habitat 1 will seem pretty boring – almost every organism you see will belong to species A. Habitat 2 *appears* more species rich because you are equally likely to see any of the 10 species. Appropriately, the various indices of diversity conclude that habitat 2 *is* more diverse than habitat 1.

the underlying **parent rock** influences the type of soil formed, the climate and vegetation are just as important.

Soil content

Soils contain:

- **inorganic particles**
- **water**
- **air**
- **organic matter**
- **dissolved minerals**.

The balance of these components varies considerably in different soils. Sand dune soils, for example, are high in sand, air, sodium ions and chloride ions. Usually they are low in organic matter, most dissolved minerals and water. On the other hand, soils in acid peat bogs are very high in organic matter and water, but low in inorganic particles, dissolved minerals and air.

Inorganic particles in soil

The inorganic particles found in soil are classified by their size (table 37.1). Few soils contain particles all of the same size. Usually a range of particle sizes is found. With experience you can tell the composition of a soil just by rubbing it between your fingers. A soil that contains a mixture of sand, silt and clay is called a **loam** and generally this is the best sort of soil for plant growth.

Clay particles are found in most soils and greatly influence the properties of the soil. The particles have an overall negative electrical charge which means that they attract cations such as H^+, K^+, Na^+, Ca^{2+} and Mg^{2+} to their surfaces. Because of this, clay soils tend to hold on tightly to their cations. Clay soils therefore resist **leaching**, the process in which percolating water washes out dissolved minerals.

Table 37.1 Soil consists of different kinds of particle, classified according to size.

Particle diameter	Particle name
<2 μm	Clay
2 μm – 20 μm	Silt
20 μm – 200 μm	Fine sand
200 μm – 2 mm	Coarse sand
2 mm – 20 mm	Gravel

Table 37.2 The properties of sand and clay.

Property	Sand	Clay
Texture	Coarse	Fine
Structure	'Light'	'Heavy — forms large clods when wet
Aeration	Good	Poor
Drainage	Fast	Slow
Water retention	Poor	Excellent but may lead to waterlogging
Nutrient content	Poor	Good

Sandy soils consist mainly of small particles of silica, SiO_2. Sand and clay are compared in table 37.2. In a loam, individual soil particles become bound together into **soil crumbs** by the binding properties of fungal mycelia and bacterial polysaccharides.

Soil water

Water plays a crucial part in soil. It is necessary for all the soil organisms, holds dissolved minerals in solution and helps to weather the soil.

There are four types of soil water:

- **Hygroscopic water** forms a very thin layer around soil particles. It is so tightly bound to the particles by surface tension that it is unavailable to plants.

- **Osmotic water** forms a thin layer around hygroscopic water. Though less tightly bound, it can be used only by the roots of certain plants.

- **Capillary water** is still less tightly bound. It is the most important regular source of water to plants. Capillary water takes its name from its ability to move upwards against gravity under the influence of capillarity, should the surface of the soil start to dry out.

- **Gravitational water** drains out of soil under the influence of gravity. It is therefore only found in the soil after periods of rain, after which it sinks below the water table to join the ground water.

The relationship between the soil particles and these types of soil water is shown in figure 37.9.

The total amount of water that can be held by a soil against the force of gravity is called the **field capacity**. Farmers value soils with high field capacities as such soils effectively store water that can be used by crops. Clays and loams may have a field capacity equivalent to 15 per cent of their mass.

Soil air

If you look at figure 37.9 you will see a **pore** which is filled with air. **Soil air** differs from air in the atmosphere. It is usually saturated with water vapour and contains less oxygen, but more carbon dioxide. Ammonia and methane, the products of microbial activity, may also be present.

A **waterlogged** soil contains so much water that it has little or no air. Many plants cannot survive such soils for more than a day or so as their roots are unable to obtain the oxygen they need.

Organic matter in soil

Dead **organic matter** is derived both from soil organisms and from organisms that live above the soil surface. Fungi and bacteria in the soil **decompose** this organic material into **humus**.

Humus is a complex mixture of many substances. Most of it consists of partly decomposed, insoluble, dark material. Humus is extremely resistant to further decomposition. It is generally acidic and, like clay, holds on to its cations. Humus, again

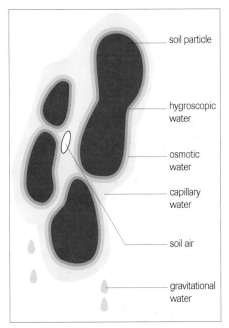

Figure 37.9 The relationship between soil particles, soil air and the four types of soil water.

soil particle

hygroscopic water

osmotic water

capillary water

soil air

gravitational water

Part 7

Figure 37.10 An oblong-leaved sundew, *Drosera intermedia*, that has trapped a white-legged damselfly. Like all carnivorous plants, sundews obtain much of their nitrogen by catching and digesting insects and other small animals. The leaves of the sundew bear numerous sticky hairs which trap and immobilise small prey. Once the victim is caught, the hairs fold over, further securing it. Enzymes are then secreted. These digest the prey, allowing nutrients to be absorbed by the plant.

Digestion, page 182

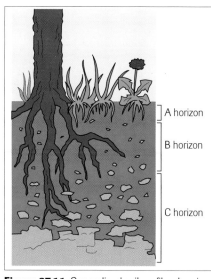

Figure 37.11 Generalised soil profile, showing the A, B and C horizons in relation to surface vegetation and plant roots.

Soil organisms

In addition to *dead* organic material, soil also contains living **soil organisms**. These play a vital role in decomposition. Soil organisms range from bacteria and protoctists to fungi, nematodes, insects, earthworms and a few mammals, such as moles.

When present, earthworms help to aerate and fertilise the soil. Charles Darwin was fascinated by earthworms and wrote a book on them at the end of which he concluded: '*It may be doubted whether there are many other animals which have played so important a part in the history of the world, as have these lowly organised creatures*'.

One thing earthworms cannot do is decompose cellulose and lignin, the main chemicals of which wood is made. Cellulose decomposition is carried out mainly by bacteria and fungi. Lignin decomposition is even more difficult and can only be achieved by a few genera of fungi.

like clay, can act as a **colloid**: the particles are so small that they remain suspended in a fluid and do not settle out under gravity.

For humus to be formed, oxygen must be present as most decomposers are aerobic. Under waterlogged conditions, little oxygen is present and large amounts of undecomposed organic material may accumulate. This is essentially how **peat**, **coal** and **oil** are formed.

Dissolved minerals in soil

The nature of the **dissolved minerals** in soil water depends on the parent rock, the pH, the organisms growing in and above the soil, and whether or not aerobic conditions prevail.

Chalk soils, for example, are high in calcium carbonate but low in phosphate, nitrate and iron. In terms of their vegetation, species diversity is high. More flowering plants are found in a square metre of chalk grassland than in any other European habitat.

When soils are waterlogged and consequently short of oxygen, ions capable of existing in either an oxidised or a reduced state are found in their reduced form. Fe^{2+}, for instance, occurs instead of Fe^{3+}. Some plants are very sensitive to Fe^{2+}, so the vegetation found on waterlogged soils differs from vegetation found on well-drained soils.

Soil pH

Soil pH normally lies between 3.0 (acidic) to 8.0 (alkaline). Bogs often have soils with a pH of less than 4.5. In these acidic conditions, nitrogen and phosphorus become unavailable to plants. On the other hand, the concentration of toxic Al^{3+} ions increases as the pH falls. These factors mean that few plants can grow in acid bogs. Those that do so are often carnivorous and this supplies them with extra nutrients (*figure 37.10*).

Soil profiles

A vertical section through any soil reveals a series of horizontal layers which constitute the **soil profile**. These layers are called **horizons** (*figure 37.11*).

- The **A horizon** is at the top. This gains organic material from above, but loses material through leaching to layers beneath.

- The **B horizon** lies underneath the A horizon. It gains material leached from the A horizon above.

- The **C horizon** is the lowest of the horizons. It consists of the weathered parent material – broken up pieces of rock. Beneath the C horizon is the parent material itself – solid rock.

Soils differ considerably in their profiles. For example, a typical soil under a temperate deciduous woodland is 1–2 m in depth and shows a gradual transition from parent rock through C, B and A horizons to thick leaf litter at the surface. On the other hand, soils under tropical rain forests can be as much as 30 m in depth, have only a thin leaf litter at the surface and lack a B horizon altogether.

37.4 The physical environment

Central to ecology is the concept of the **environment**, that is the surroundings of an organism.

The environment includes all the conditions in which an organism lives. It can be divided into two sorts: the **physical environment** (also known as the **abiotic environment**) and the **biotic environment**. Here we shall restrict ourselves to a consideration of the physical environment, leaving the biotic environment to subsequent chapters.

Traditionally the physical environment is divided into **edaphic**, **climatic** and **topographic** factors.

Edaphic factors

Edaphic factors are those to do with the soil, such as soil water, pH, particle size and so on. We have already discussed them in detail.

It should be remembered that most aquatic ecosystems contain soil too. Lakes, for instance, have soil at their edges and bottoms. Some marine ecosystems also have soils – for example, mangrove swamps and salt marshes.

Climate

Climate should be distinguished from weather.

- **Climate** refers to the predictable long-term patterns of rainfall, temperature and light. For instance, we talk about Ireland having an oceanic climate, meaning that it is warm and wet for its latitude.

- **Weather**, though, is more short term. It may be cold, windy and wet one day and warm, calm and dry the next.

Differences in climate are largely responsible for differences between the world's biomes as we shall now see.

Water

Water is necessary for all life. For terrestrial organisms the **annual rainfall** is the most important variable. However, its **predictability** and **pH** are also important. Organisms living in dry places usually have specialised mechanisms which reduce water loss (*Chapter 17*).

For aquatic organisms, the **temperature**, **salinity**, **oxygen saturation** and **nutrient content** of the water are vital. In addition, **wave action** limits the distribution of many aquatic species. Limpets, barnacles and some seaweeds cling on to the rocks, while many organisms living on beaches burrow out of the way during storms.

In rivers and streams, the rate of **current flow** is important. It is noticeable that free-floating aquatic plants are absent from most streams and rivers, but are widespread in lakes and ponds.

Temperature

Few organisms can grow if the ambient temperature falls outside the range 0–40°C, though, remarkably, some **thermophilous** (heat-loving) bacteria can complete their entire life cycles at temperatures in excess of 100°C. Emperor penguins breed on the

▶ Biotic environment: predators and prey, page 715; symbionts, page 705; ecological communities, page 663

Part 7

Figure 37.12 Emperor penguin incubating its egg on ice in the Antarctic.

Antarctic ice during the long midwinter darkness when the temperature can get as low as −80°C (*figure 37.12*). Many organisms have physiological or behavioural adaptations which enable them to avoid or survive extremes of temperature (*Chapter 18*).

Light

Light is needed for photosynthesis (*Chapter 12*). It is also used by many animals for vision. Light can vary in its **wavelength**, **intensity** and **daily duration**. In temperate regions, changes in day length (hours of light) are used by many organisms as indicators of the season. Many plants, for example, start to flower when the days exceed a critical length (*Chapter 31*). In aquatic environments, the depth to which light can penetrate limits the distribution of photosynthetic organisms.

Atmosphere

One of the most important components of the atmosphere is **oxygen**. Few organisms can live without it. In the atmosphere, oxygen levels remain constant, but in water the concentration of oxygen can vary greatly. Warmth and the presence of aerobic organisms decrease the amount of oxygen carried by water, though plants release oxygen during photosynthesis. When fully saturated, salt water holds less oxygen than fresh water. Turbulence can increase the oxygen content of water by dissolving oxygen from the air.

When conditions are warm and moist, **carbon dioxide** may limit the rate of photosynthesis. The concentration of carbon dioxide in the atmosphere varies little, being present at a concentration of about 0.035 per cent. Only in the soil does the carbon dioxide concentration often get much greater than this on account of all the respiration of soil organisms.

The **relative humidity** of the atmosphere can vary greatly. When it is low, organisms lose more water through evaporation, and therefore face the risk of dehydration. On the other hand, if it is very hot and humid, a low rate of evaporation may be harmful, as evaporation serves to remove heat from an organism and so cool it down.

Winds are the atmospheric equivalents of water currents and waves. Occasional strong winds can flatten trees that are hundreds of years old. Continuous strong winds can prevent trees from becoming established. This is the case, for example, in the Shetland Islands off Scotland. Wind serves a useful function in the pollination and seed dispersal of many plants. Migratory birds may use winds to minimise the energy needed for flight.

Fire

Fire can only burn if organic matter has accumulated. Nowadays fires are often the result of human carelessness. However, in many biomes, fire has always been a natural phenomenon (*figure 37.13*). In nature, fires are caused by lightning strikes or, more rarely, by volcanoes.

Topography

By **topography** is meant the **altitude**, **slope** and **aspect** of a place. As you climb a mountain, many features of the physical environment change. It may become colder, wetter and windier. The air pressure drops (i.e. the air 'gets thinner'), so that oxygen and carbon dioxide become scarcer and more ultraviolet light penetrates.

Slope is important because it reduces the chance of a soil becoming waterlogged. On very steep slopes, soil cannot form, so many plants cannot establish themselves.

Aspect is most important to sessile (immobile) organisms. In the northern hemisphere, south-facing slopes receive more light and heat energy than north-facing slopes (the reverse is the case in the southern hemisphere). This fact is well known to gardeners, who position their plants accordingly. It also influences the distribution of plants in the wild.

Figure 37.13 Trees on fire in Yellowstone National Park, USA. Such fires are a natural phenomenon in the park. Before this was realised, great efforts were made at Yellowstone Park to eliminate fires. The result was a change in the vegetation, with some of the most interesting plant species being replaced by more common ones. Also, when eventually there was a fire, the build-up of dead organic matter over several decades was so large that the fire did far more damage than usual.

The Gaia hypothesis

Guest author, James Lovelock, originated the Gaia hypothesis in 1972. Here he explains his ideas.

The Gaia hypothesis is now almost 30 years old. Those few scientists who have worked closely with it see it as reasonable science and growing ever more plausible as evidence and models map together. Many other scientists disagree and see Gaia as little more than a metaphor – some even denounce it as anti-science.

Gaia was the Greek word for Mother Earth. The Gaia hypothesis supposes that the Earth is a self-regulating planet, able to keep its climate and chemical composition constant and always favourable for life. The hypothesis arose when the Earth's atmosphere was compared with the atmospheres of Mars and Venus. Astronomical observations in the 1960s showed the atmospheres of Mars and Venus to be constant in composition and close to chemical equilibrium. By contrast the Earth's atmosphere, although stable in composition for long periods, profoundly departs from chemical equilibrium.

Gaia theory is not contrary to Darwin's theory of natural selection. The step that distinguishes Gaia from Darwinism lies in the tightness of the coupling between the organisms and their physical environment. Almost everyone now accepts that life profoundly influences the environment. It is equally obvious that life is influenced by and adapts to the environment. The real debate is how important and how tight is the coupling?

Gaia asserts that this close coupling of organisms and their environment is strong enough to have greatly influenced the way in which the life-environment system on Earth, and on other planets with life, has evolved.

Gaia is a theory that can be tested experimentally. It makes predictions such as that oxygen has been held at its current level of 21 per cent for at least the last 200 million years. It predicts that the atmosphere in the archean period over 2.5 billion years ago was chemically dominated by methane, with oxygen as a trace gas at the parts per million level. It successfully predicted that the gases iodomethane and dimethyl sulphide would be found to be the dominant carriers of the elements iodine and sulphur from the oceans to the land surfaces.

Among other insights from Gaia is the recognition that pollution with greenhouse gases, and the widespread destruction of natural habitats, are insults to a weakened system. Forced too far, a sudden transition could occur to a new homeostasis, possibly at a much higher global temperature.

In Gaia we are part and partners of a democratic entity. The rules insist, through natural selection, that species which harm the environment are voted out. If we are truly concerned for mankind then we must respect other organisms. If we think of nothing but people and ignore the natural life of the Earth, the scene is set for our own destruction and that of the comfortable Earth we know. Just now we seem like the Gadarene swine, driving our polluting cars down to a sea rising to meet us.

Dr Lovelock, originator of the Gaia hypothesis, is currently Vice-President of the Marine Biological Association of the United Kingdom.

Summary

1. **Ecology** is the study of organisms in relation to their environment.

2. The part of the Earth and its atmosphere inhabited by life is called the **biosphere**. The biosphere can be divided into **biomes**.

3. The most important variables for terrestrial biomes are the **amount of rain** and the **temperature**.

4. The most important variables for aquatic biomes are the **salinity** of the water, its **depth**, **permanence** and **nutrient availability**.

5. A **habitat** is a specific locality where an organism lives.

6. A habitat is divided into numerous **microhabitats**, each with its own particular conditions (**microclimate**).

7. For terrestrial organisms, **soil** is particularly important. All soils contain **inorganic particles**, **air**, **organic matter** and **dissolved minerals**. However, soils may differ greatly from one to another.

8. The **environment**, namely the conditions in which organisms live, can be divided into the **physical** (or **abiotic**) **environment** and the **biotic environment**.

9. The abiotic (physical) environment includes **edaphic factors** (to do with the soil), **climatic factors** (water, temperature, light, atmosphere and fire) and **topographical factors** (altitude, slope and aspect).

10. The **Gaia hypothesis** proposes that the Earth is a self-regulating system.

For general advice on these questions and advice ing essay type questions, see pages vii and viii.

1. Read the following extract.

Dumb waiters that square the ocean's food circle

Almost all the inhabitants of the ocean from the haddock to the carnivorous great white shark, depend ultimately upon sea-dwelling algae - the floating vegetation of the oceans. But how do the algae obtain the nutrients they need while still getting the sunlight necessary for photosynthesis? It is a tricky problem, because the nutrients, derived from dead organic matter, tend to be deep in the sea out of the reach of the sunlight. According to the science journal *Nature*, the algae form tiny submersible 'mats'.

These mats seem to play an astonishing role in the transport of nutrients. Researchers found that tangled *Rhizosolenia* mats only a few square centimetres in size appear able to travel vertically for hundreds of metres to carry nutrients to the surface waters.

Divers collected samples of algal mats close to the surface of the Pacific Ocean. They then left the mats standing in jars of sea water for several minutes. To their surprise, the investigators found that some of the mats rose to the top of the jar while others fell to the bottom. Even more surprisingly, the mats travelling upwards turned out to be transporting much larger amounts of nitrate than those travelling downwards.

Further investigation showed that the tiny mats can penetrate right down to the rich pools of nitrate at the bottom of the ocean and transport nitrate back to the surface. They appear to rise with their load, bask in the sunlight while using up the nutrients then fall back to the deep water to replenish their stocks.

(Adapted from an article in the *Independent* Newspaper)

(a) Explain briefly why the great white shark depends on sea-dwelling algae. (2)

(b) (i) Explain how nitrates are usually made available to plankton near the surface in aquatic ecosystems. (2)

(ii) Suggest **one** explanation for the lack of nitrates in the surface layers of the Pacific Ocean. (2)

(c) The algal mats descend to the bottom of the ocean to 'rich pools of nitrate'.

Using your knowledge of the nitrogen cycle, describe in detail how the floor of the ocean becomes rich in nitrates. (6)

(Total 12 marks)
NEAB 1996

2. Write an essay on the physical factors affecting the distribution of organisms in a named habitat.

(Total 15 marks)
London 1998

3. Diatoms are microscopic photosynthetic organisms that live in water. They have a protective outer covering made from the mineral silica. The graph shows the number of diatoms and the concentration of dissolved silica in the water of a lake over several months.

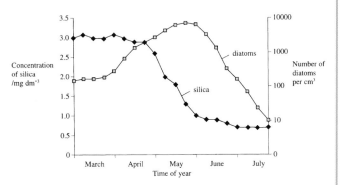

(a) Explain how the concentration of silica may affect the size of the diatom population. (2)

(b) Suggest **two** other abiotic factors which could account for the increase in the number of diatoms in this lake. Explain how each would have its effect. (4)

(Total 6 marks)
NEAB 1997

J ohn Donne, the 17th century English poet, once wrote 'No man is an Island, entire of itself; every man is a piece of the Continent, a part of the main'.

Donne meant that none of us can lead a life totally independent of others. Humans depend on one another. In the same way, no other organism can exist on its own. Without plants, animals would starve through lack of food and in the long term would run short of oxygen. Without bacteria and fungi, decomposition and nutrient cycling would stop. In the absence of animals, many plants would be unable to reproduce. This chapter is about the ways in which organisms depend on each other. Each provides an important aspect of the other's **biotic environment**.

38.1 Communities

A **community** is the sum of the organisms found in a habitat. Some communities are named after an obvious feature of the environment – rock pool and sand dune communities for example. Other communities are named after the dominant plants – heathland and pine forest communities for example (*figure 38.1*).

If you examine any community carefully, you find that the species in it interact with each other. Sometimes these interactions are mutually beneficial. For example, many trees produce fruits which are eaten by birds. Clearly the birds benefit; they obtain food from the tree. But the tree benefits too. Its seeds are dispersed by the birds into new areas. There, they may grow into trees.

Sometimes the interactions between two species are such that one species benefits at the *expense* of the other. This is the case when one species eats or parasitises another. With these basic ideas in mind, let's look at the interactions in an oak-wood community.

Oak woodland

Most of Europe has been so influenced by agriculture and human settlements that little virgin forest remains. Only in Poland and some other parts of Eastern Europe is truly undisturbed woodland left. A number of European countries, though, have **ancient woodland**. This is woodland which is known to have existed for at least several hundred years. Often it has been used by humans, for instance as a source of **timber**. Nevertheless, these ancient managed woods are similar in structure to the few remaining undisturbed ones. Such managed woods show how resources can be obtained in a sustainable fashion.

Much of Europe was once dominated by the pedunculate oak (*Quercus robur*). Oak is usually found with other tall trees such as lime, elm and ash. Beneath the tall trees in an oak wood is an **understorey** of shrubs such as hazel and small trees such as hawthorn. Lower still is the **herb layer**. This is at its most spectacular early in the year before the leaves of the trees have opened in the late spring. Here we find bluebells, wood anemones and violets among others (*figure 38.2*). In the traditional woodland management practice of **coppicing**, the understorey shrubs are cut down every 10 years or so. The resulting timber is used for many purposes and the spring flowers bloom even more profusely than usual.

The plants in an oak wood provide food for a rich variety of animals. Many insects and molluscs are found. Oak in particular supports numerous insect species. These insects in turn are eaten by a number of birds including great tits and great spotted woodpeckers. Many insects are also eaten by spiders. Other birds take a greater variety of food. The blackbird and song thrush eat berries and earthworms as well as insects. The smaller of

Figure 38.1 A pine forest community in Scotland.

Figure 38.2 A British oak woodland in spring, with bluebells in flower.

Figure 38.3 The fruiting bodies of bracket fungus on a felled tree, in the New Forest, Hampshire, in autumn.

Figure 38.4 A pond in the forest of Dean, Gloucestershire, England. Notice the way the pond is being colonised by plants. Reeds are particularly evident.

▶ Soil, page 655

these birds may be hunted by sparrowhawks.

Mammals too are common in oak woods. Shrews make runways through the thick **leaf litter** resulting from the fall of dead leaves, and tunnel through the soil. They feed on earthworms, beetles, spiders, centipedes, woodlice, snails and slugs. The bank vole is found in areas with thick cover and feeds mainly on fleshy fruits and seeds. In winter, though, it will eat dead leaves. The wood mouse has a more varied diet, feeding on seedlings, buds, fruits, nuts, snails and arthropods. Another mammal found in oak woods is the stoat. Stoats are carnivorous. They eat rabbits, birds and small rodents such as bank voles and wood mice.

Many other species are found in oak woods. Fungi and bacteria are abundant but easily overlooked. Some break down dead animals and plants; others attack living species. Fungi are at their most obvious in the autumn when their fruiting bodies appear (*figure 38.3*).

This description of the organisms in an oak wood should convince you of the complexity of their interactions. We shall consider the feeding relationships found in communities in more detail later (*page 670*). However, the organisms in a community interact not just with each other but also with their physical environment. This brings us to the concept of the ecosystem.

38.2 Ecosystems

An **ecosystem** consists of all the interacting organisms in an area together with the non-living constituents of their environment. For example, an oak wood ecosystem includes not only the organisms that make up the oak wood community but also the relevant aspects of the physical environment, such as rain, the inorganic components of the soil, sunlight and atmospheric oxygen and carbon dioxide.

Ecosystems are relatively self-contained. Any ecosystem tends to perpetuate itself by the cycling of minerals within that ecosystem. In a wood, for instance, leaves fall and decompose and their nutrients are returned to the soil. In turn, the plants remove these nutrients from the soil and use them in growth. It was the English ecologist Sir Arthur Tansley who first used the term ecosystem in 1935. He realised that organisms and their immediate environment need to be considered together as a functional unit.

Examples of individual ecosystems include salt marshes, coral reefs and ponds (*figure 38.4*). Several different ecosystems may be present in one area, and sometimes it is not possible to decide where one ecosystem stops and another one begins. The Amazon rain forest, for instance, is too large to be described as a single ecosystem. Despite this limitation, the concept of the ecosystem has proved very useful to ecologists.

To give a full account of an ecosystem it is necessary both to list the organisms there and to describe the relevant aspects of their environment. For instance, an adequate description of a lake requires a detailed account of the water as well as of the species found in it. We would need to look at the temperature of the water at different depths throughout the year. The pH, oxygen and nutrient content are also important, as is the depth to which light penetrates. In terrestrial ecosystems soil forms an important link between organisms and their physical environment.

Analysing an ecosystem involves studying how different species interact in a community. Typically the first step is to identify the organisms living in the ecosystem, though occasionally this is left until later. Identification can be done with the aid of **systematic keys** (*Chapter 5*). It is then necessary to find out exactly where in the ecosystem the different species occur.

Ecologists usually want to know why species occur in some places but not others. Answering this question is rarely easy. It involves trying to see how a species interacts with other species and with the physical environment. Often experiments are needed to test the various hypotheses generated.

38.3 Succession

If a lawn is left unmown, the grass soon grows long. If the lawn is left unmown for several years, it will no longer be a lawn. New plants will have invaded it and become established. This is an example of **colonisation**. These plants will probably be taller than the grasses. Because of this, the grasses may become shaded, so they don't get enough light. In most parts of the world, a lawn that is left uncut will eventually turn into a wood.

The lawn example illustrates a widespread observation: *communities do not remain in the same state indefinitely*. They change. This change in a community over time is called **succession**. Each step in a particular plant succession is known as a **sere**. Two of the easiest examples of succession to interpret are those that occur on bare rock and in a pond.

Succession on bare rock

Think of a bare area of rock, for example at the base of a retreating glacier. At first there are no organisms on the rock, except for the occasional insect blown on to it by the wind. Soon, however, organisms begin to establish themselves.

The first organisms to become established are often **lichens**, one of the few types of organism that can subsist on bare rock. These lichens trap windblown dust particles. They also promote the break-up of the rock surface, so allowing a very shallow and simple soil to accumulate. This soil allows **mosses** to colonise the area and, later, **grasses** and **ferns**.

Over the years, enough soil builds up for various **herbaceous perennials** to take root. Often these early invaders can fix atmospheric nitrogen, thus compensating for the poor nutrient status of the shallow soil. In time small **shrubs** colonise the area. Eventually the soil is deep enough to allow the establishment of tall **trees** (*figure 38.5*).

Throughout the course of the succession, changes in the animal species accompany changes in the plants. Even mosses have a characteristic fauna. You can show this by pipetting a few drops of water on to a moss tuft, waiting for half an hour and then squeezing the water from the moss. If the water is examined under a microscope, tiny animals can often be seen.

The progressive colonisation of a previously unoccupied area is called a **primary succession**. The earliest communities in a succession are typically the simplest. They have the fewest species and the interrelationships between them are relatively straightforward. Later communities have more species and show more complex interactions. For instance, insect pollination is generally more frequent in the later stages of a succession. It may take hundreds or even thousands of years for succession to result in a forest growing on what was once bare ground.

Succession in a pond

Most ponds and lakes have plants growing at their edges. Some of these plants take root in the mud at the bottom and hold their leaves beneath the surface of the water. Other plants, such as bulrushes and reeds, grow at the edge and raise their leaves above the water level.

The effect of these plants is to cause a steady accumulation of organic matter at the edge of the pond. This organic matter comes mainly from the dead remains of the plants. In time, the pond becomes shallower due to the accumulation of organic matter, and the rooted plants extend towards the centre. You can see this in figure 38.4 the previous page. Gradually, the pond becomes filled up. Eventually the succession may result in forest, just as is the case for succession on bare ground.

Why does succession occur?

There are two reasons why communities change with time.

■ The organisms themselves cause a change in their environment which in turn makes the environment more suitable for other species. This is what happens, for instance, in

Figure 38.5 Succession on a cleared area of oak-hornbeam forest in southern Poland. From *top* to *bottom* the succession has occurred for 7, 30 and 150 years.

the succession from bare ground to forest. The lichens are responsible for the accumulation of a rudimentary soil suitable for mosses. In turn the mosses help to generate a soil suitable for vascular plants. This type of change is called **autogenic succession**.

■ The physical environment changes for some reason not directly related to the organisms in the community. For instance, at the start of an ice age it gets colder and both the vegetation and the fauna change. This sort of change is called **allogenic succession**.

The result of succession

What happens at the end of a succession? Eventually a single **climax community** may establish itself. Across much of the Earth's land surface, forest is the climax community. However, this is not always the case. In the tundra the climate and soil do not allow trees to grow. Instead, the climax vegetation is a mixture of short grasses, herbs and lichens.

While primary succession starts with an area previously unoccupied by organisms, **secondary succession** begins in an area where at least some organisms are already present. For instance, the successions that occur in a cleared area of forest, on a burnt moorland or in a meadow flooded with river silt, are examples of secondary succession. Secondary succession usually takes place more rapidly than primary succession.

Sometimes succession may not proceed to a climax community. For example, many grasslands are maintained as grasslands by a combination of grazing and fire. In the absence of these factors, grassland usually develops into shrubland and then into forest. Instances where natural successions are halted in this way are known as **deflected successions** or **plagioclimaxes**. Permanent grassland is frequently the result of a deflected succession.

If the cause of a deflected succession is removed – for example if grazers are taken away from a grassland – then the succession may proceed towards the climax in the normal way (*extension box alongside*).

▶ Tundra and other biomes, page 653

Extension

Turning rabbits into forests

A classic example of how succession from grassland to forest can proceed if grazers are removed is provided by the introduction of the myxomatosis virus into Britain in 1953.

This was done in an attempt to reduce the number of rabbits, which are generally considered to be agricultural pests. Within two years over 99 per cent of the British rabbit population died from the disease. The grass on chalk downs, until then kept short by rabbit grazing, grew rampant, displacing many low-growing wild flowers. The rabbits had also included hawthorn seedlings in their diet. With the demise of the rabbits, these seedlings soon grew into young trees.

As well as causing large areas of grassland to change into shrubland, myxomatosis had a number of other effects. With the collapse in the rabbit population, foxes, stoats, weasels and buzzards failed to breed in the years immediately after 1953 and declined in numbers. As a result, vole numbers reached an unusually high level in 1956–7, allowing the carnivores to recover in numbers.

38.4 Cycling of matter and flow of energy in ecosystems

In almost all ecosystems, the organisms fall into three nutritional groups.

■ **Producers:** autotrophic organisms, so called because they can make organic compounds, such as starch and proteins, from inorganic precursors. Producers include plants, some protoctists and certain prokaryotes (*pages 84-5*).

■ **Consumers:** heterotrophic organisms, so called because they need to feed on the organic compounds made by autotrophs. Consumers include animals, parasitic fungi, some protoctists and certain bacteria.

■ **Decomposers:** heterotrophic organisms, responsible for breaking down the organic waste products and dead remains of organisms into the inorganic substances needed by the producers. Decomposers mainly comprise bacteria and fungi. Such organisms are known as **saprobionts**.

Producers, consumers and decomposers interrelate as shown in figure 38.6. Organic materials synthesised by the producers are eaten and assimilated by the consumers. Thanks to the activities of the decomposers, all the organic materials incorporated into the bodies of the consumers are eventually broken down into inorganic materials. These are then rebuilt into organic compounds by the synthetic activities of the producers.

So matter circulates in nature. An individual atom may find itself at one time in a producer, at another time in a decomposer and at another time in water, air or soil. However, there is little overall loss of matter from the system.

Although matter circulates repeatedly around an ecosystem, this is not the case with energy. Instead, energy is continually lost from ecosystems as heat energy. The photosynthetic producers transfer some of the radiant energy of sunlight to chemical energy in plant carbohydrates. By their respiratory activities, the producers, consumers and decomposers transfer this energy to ATP, whose subsequent hydrolysis provides energy for the cells' vital activities. Both in the formation of ATP, and in its subsequent usage, a proportion of the energy is lost from an ecosystem as heat energy.

Ultimately *all* the energy in an ecosystem is transferred to heat energy. However, the continual trapping of the energy of sunlight by green plants makes good this loss and maintains the flow of energy.

Nutrient cycles

For organisms to maintain themselves, grow and reproduce, they need a supply of the elements of which they are made. These they receive from the cycling of matter, or **nutrient cycles** as they are called.

Nutrient cycles have two components: a biological component showing how the element cycles through organisms, and a geochemical component showing how the element cycles through rocks, water and the atmosphere. For this reason, nutrient cycles are also called **biogeochemical cycles**.

The carbon cycle

The **carbon cycle** is unique among nutrient cycles because it need not involve decomposers. This is because autotrophs take in their carbon as carbon dioxide, and carbon dioxide is given out by all organisms as a result of respiration. Figure 38.7 shows the carbon cycle on a global scale, but even in the absence of any decomposers, carbon would still be able to circulate for some time within an ecosystem.

▶ Respiration and energy, page 138

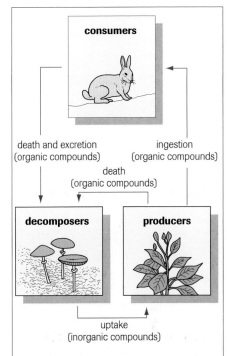

Figure 38.6 Cycle illustrating the interdependence of producers and consumers in an ecosystem. The autotrophic activities of the producers (green plants, etc.) produce organic materials which are fed on by the consumers. The saprotrophic activities of the decomposers (mainly certain bacteria and fungi) free inorganic materials from the dead bodies and waste products of the producers and consumers, thereby ensuring a continual supply of raw materials for the producers. The carbon and nitrogen cycles are detailed instances of this general principle.

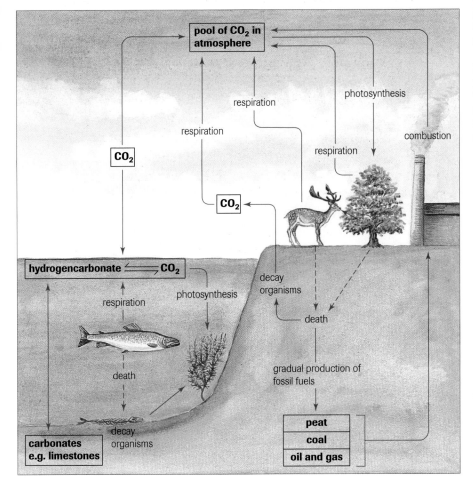

Figure 38.7 The carbon cycle. The amount of carbon dioxide in the atmosphere is maintained by a balance between photosynthesis (which withdraws carbon dioxide from the atmosphere) and respiration and combustion (which add carbon dioxide to the atmosphere). In fact, the level of carbon dioxide in the atmosphere has risen this century for reasons discussed on page 677.

Not all dead material decays. In anaerobic or highly acidic conditions decomposers may be unable to break down all the remains or waste products of organisms. In such situations these may accumulate to form **fossil fuels** such as peat, coal, oil and their gaseous derivatives. In natural circumstances these deposits represent a **sink**.

Sinks are diversions from cycles. However, in practice humans burn fossil fuels as a source of energy (**combustion**). But, even without human activity, some of the carbon in fossil fuels would eventually return to the carbon cycle when natural geological processes return these substances to the Earth's surface. Oxidation might then return the carbon to the air as carbon dioxide.

Human activity is currently reducing the amount of carbon trapped in the sinks of the carbon cycle at a speed vastly in excess of that at which fossil fuels are made. As a result, atmospheric levels of carbon dioxide have been, and still are, rising at a worrying rate (*page 677*). If we carry on burning fossil fuels at the current rate, the world will have exhausted its accessible fossil fuel deposits within one to two hundred years.

Figure 38.8 The nitrogen cycle. The amount of nitrogen available to plants is determined by the relative activities of the various bacteria involved in the nitrogen cycle. Meanwhile the amount of nitrogen in the atmosphere is maintained by a balance between the processes which withdraw nitrogen from it (nitrogen fixation) and those which add nitrogen to it (denitrification and volcanic emissions).

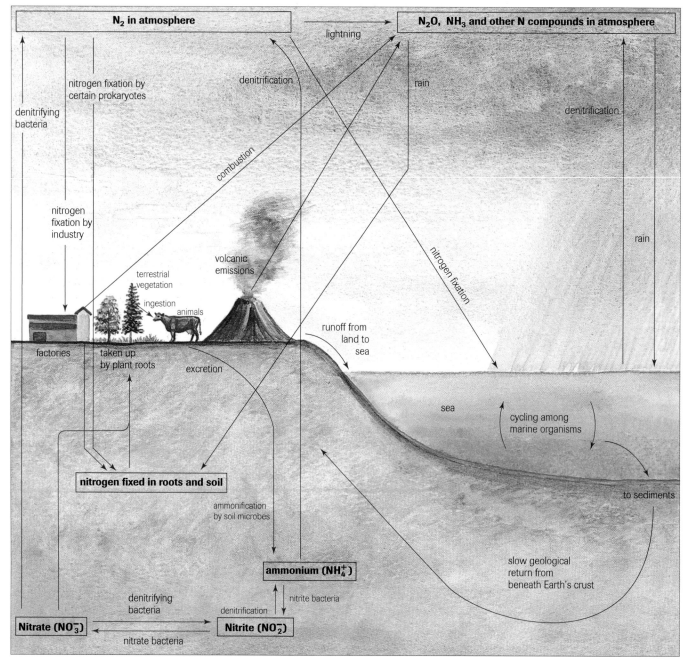

Nitrogen fixation

The best known nitrogen-fixing organisms are bacteria that live in the roots of **leguminous plants** (family Papilionaceae) such as peas, beans and clover. It has long been known that such plants are able to thrive in soils deficient in nitrates, and we now know that they owe this ability to the nitrogen-fixing bacteria such as saprobiontic *Rhizobium* in their roots.

The bacteria enter the young plant through its root hairs, and they cause the cortical cells of the root to proliferate, forming a swelling called a **root nodule**. A vascular strand connects the nodule with the vascular tissues in the main root. In the cells of the nodule the bacteria multiply rapidly, fixing atmospheric nitrogen which is then built up into amino acids and proteins.

The association between the bacteria and their plant host is mutually beneficial, both partners gaining from the relationship. Some of the products of the bacteria's nitrogen fixation pass into the host plant and are utilised by it. This has been confirmed by supplying an infected plant with the heavy isotope of nitrogen, ^{15}N. Eventually the ^{15}N gets into the whole of the plant, not just the part containing the bacteria. Legumes that lack nitrogen-fixing bacteria grow far less well than control plants provided with their usual nitrogen-fixing partners.

What do the bacteria gain from the host apart from protection? From the host's photosynthesis they obtain carbohydrates. These provide a source of

Nodules of *Rhizobium*, the nitrogen-fixing bacterium, on the roots of the bean, *Phaseolus vulgaris*, a legume. Magnification ×1.5.

carbon for the synthesis of protein, and also serve as an energy source. However, not all nitrogen-fixers live inside the tissues of other organisms. Many free-living examples (e.g. *Azotobacter*) are also known.

There are only two ways for us to postpone or avoid this **energy crisis** (strictly a **fuel crisis** since energy is conserved). One is to use far less fuel. The other is to obtain energy from other sources, such as the Sun (**solar power**), wind (**wind power**) or **nuclear power**.

The nitrogen cycle

The nitrogen cycle is more complex than the carbon cycle. The way it relates to the biosphere as a whole is illustrated in figure 38.8.

Gaseous nitrogen makes up about 80 per cent of the atmosphere where it is in the form N_2. N_2 is a very stable molecule. It can be removed from the atmosphere in only two ways: by **lightning** and by **nitrogen fixation**. Nitrogen fixation can be carried out naturally by certain prokaryotes, and in industry by the **Haber process** which is used to make nitrogen-rich fertilisers.

Plants are unable to take in nitrogen directly from the atmosphere. Most plants can absorb only **nitrate** (and sometimes ammonium) from the soil. Some plants, though, have **nitrogen-fixing bacteria** in their roots and can thus grow in soils which have very little nitrate. Either way, nitrogen finishes up in proteins inside the plants.

Animals in turn rely on plants for their source of nitrogen. The nitrogen bound up in animal or plant protein can be converted to nitrate via ammonium and nitrite by the sequential activities of various **nitrifying bacteria**. *Nitrosomonas* and *Nitrococcus* obtain energy by oxidising ammonium to nitrite while *Nitrobacter* oxidises nitrites to nitrates.

At the same time reactions carried out by various **denitrifying bacteria** work in the opposite direction and so *reduce* the amount of nitrate in the soil.

In the oceans, some of the available nitrogen (as nitrate and ammonium) brought in by rain and the activities of nitrogen-fixing organisms circulates through the plants and animals found there. Some of the available nitrogen, however, sinks beneath the upper 100 metres or so to which photosynthetic organisms are confined because it is too dark below. It may then sink to the sediments at the bottom of the ocean. Here it is unavailable to most

Why do denitrifying bacteria remove nitrates from soils?

Denitrifying bacteria (such as *Pseudomonas* and *Thiobacillus*) reduce nitrates to nitrites and nitrites to ammonium even though they have to expend energy in the process. The reason why they do this is that they tend to live in conditions of oxygen shortage, and they use oxygen from nitrate in respiration as the final acceptor in the hydrogen carrier system (*page 144*). This yields ATP, whose subsequent hydrolysis releases energy for the synthesis of organic compounds.

Part 7

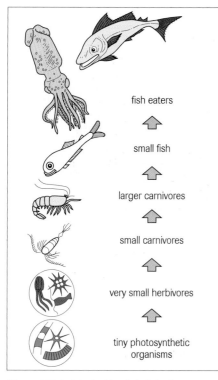

fish eaters

⬆

small fish

⬆

larger carnivores

⬆

small carnivores

⬆

very small herbivores

⬆

tiny photosynthetic organisms

Figure 38.9 A typical food chain in the ocean. Notice the number of trophic levels. The smaller organisms in this food chain make up plankton, the millions of organisms which float or drift in surface water.

organisms unless it is eventually returned to the atmosphere by volcanic emissions and other processes.

This loss of nitrate and other nutrients makes the ocean a relatively impoverished environment. Close to the shore and in estuaries, powerful upcurrents bring nutrients to the surface. In these situations plant and animal life is more abundant. This is why fishing is so successful in such regions.

The carbon and nitrogen cycles are of particular ecological significance, but other elements, such as oxygen, phosphorus and sulphur, also circulate. Water circulates too, though this of course is not an element but a compound made up of two elements.

Food chains

In figure 38.6 on page 667 the consumers are shown feeding directly on the producers. In reality the situation is usually more complicated, the producers being eaten by herbivores (**primary consumers**) which are then eaten by carnivores (**secondary consumers**). Moreover, there may be several carnivores in the series, with first level carnivores (secondary consumers) being fed on by second level carnivores (tertiary consumers). Sometimes these second level carnivores are eaten by third level carnivores. Eventually, **top carnivores** are reached. These are not preyed upon. Instead they die of old age, disease or injury.

The nutritional sequence that leads from producers to top carnivores is known as a **food chain** (*figure 38.9*). *A food chain is a series of organisms through which the organic compounds initially produced by plants, or other autotrophs, are transferred.* Each organism in the series feeds on, and therefore derives energy and nutrients from, the preceding one. In turn it is consumed by, and provides nutrients and energy for, the next organism. The levels in a food chain are called **trophic levels**, *trophic* meaning feeding.

38.5 Food webs

If you study communities in detail, you find that simple linear food chains are rare. Many herbivores feed not on just one species of plant, but on several. In the same way, herbivores are generally eaten by a number of different predators. A diagram showing such feeding relations in a community is referred to as a **food web**.

In general, a food web consists of a number of interconnected food chains. In most ecosystems, food webs are extremely complicated. A typical oak wood, for instance, contains thousands of species of plants, fungi and animals, as well as many different

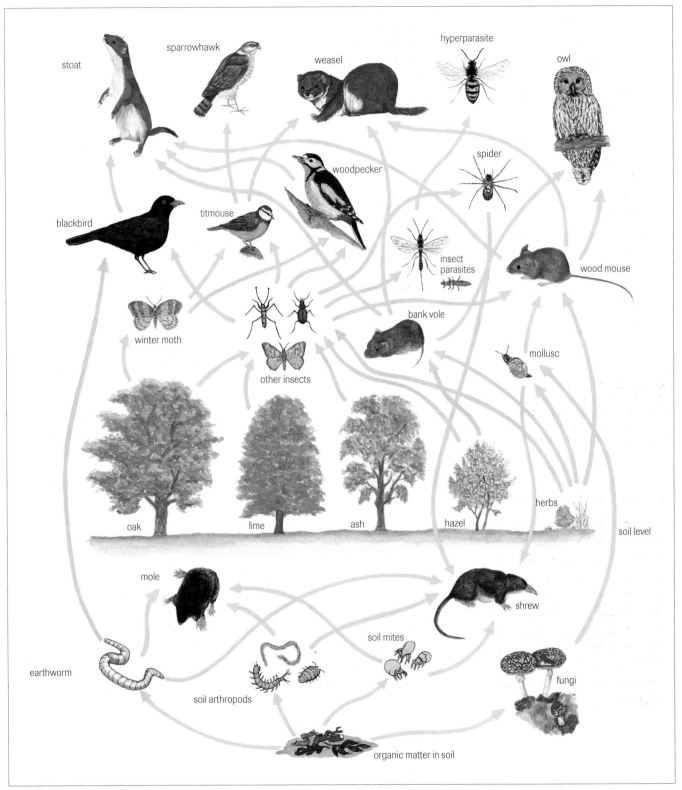

species of bacteria and protoctists. A simplified food web in an oak wood is shown in figure 38.10.

Figure 38.10 Simplified diagram of a food web in an oak wood (Sun not shown). Notice how some species cannot be allocated to a single trophic level. Hyperparasites are parasites that attack parasites.

If you study a food web, such as the one in figure 38.10, you will realise that it is difficult to assign organisms to specific trophic levels. To what level, for example, does the wood mouse belong? It eats both herbs and insects. As such it is classified as an **omnivore**. The same applies to the blackbird. It eats plant berries, insects and earthworms, which are respectively producers, primary consumers and decomposers.

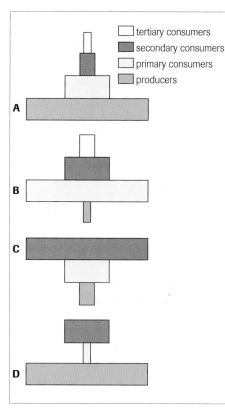

Figure 38.11 Four different pyramids of numbers.
A Typical pyramid of numbers showing how the number of individuals found at each trophic level decreases as you go up a food chain. The width of each rectangle is indicative of the number of organisms in each trophic level.
B The producer is a single plant such as a tree.
C The producer is a single plant which is infected with parasites (primary consumers) and the latter are parasitised by further parasites (hyperparasites).
D A large number of producers are eaten by a single primary consumer which is infected with parasites (secondary consumers).

Legend:
- tertiary consumers
- secondary consumers
- primary consumers
- producers

38.6 Ecological pyramids

Food webs give a useful description of the feeding relationships in a community. However, they are non-quantitative. The first attempt to provide a quantitative account of the feeding relationships in a community was made by the English ecologist Charles Elton.

Pyramids of numbers

In 1927, Elton pointed out that if you study the animals in an oak wood in summer, you find vast numbers of small herbivorous insects like aphids, a large number of spiders and carnivorous ground beetles, a fair number of small birds and only a few hawks. In other words, *as you go up a food chain there is a progressive drop in the numbers of the organisms found at each trophic level.* This progressive drop in numbers is shown in figure 38.11A and is known as a **pyramid of numbers**.

Pyramids of numbers, despite their name, need not always be pyramidal in shape. Consider the situation where a single very large producer, such as a tree, supports a large number of primary consumers. In this case, an **inverted pyramid of numbers** results (*figure 38.11B*).

Inverted pyramids of numbers can also result when communities contain parasites. Imagine, for instance, a mammal infected with ticks or fleas. These parasites are in the trophic level above the mammal, yet their numbers will be much greater. Inverted pyramids of numbers involving parasites are shown in figure 38.11 C and D.

Pyramids of biomass

Another type of ecological pyramid which can be constructed for a community is the **pyramid of biomass**. Here, instead of counting the number of individuals at each trophic level, you measure their total mass at each level. This is called the **biomass**.

Pyramids of biomass are time-consuming to construct and only a few have ever been determined with any precision. As you might expect, those that have been constructed are almost always pyramidal in shape. The greatest mass of organisms is found in the producers. These support a smaller mass of herbivores, which in turn support a smaller mass of carnivores. Although top carnivores, such as eagles, leopards and wolves, may be large (*figure 38.12*), they are few in number with the result that top carnivores always have a relatively low biomass in a given area.

Figure 38.12 Wolves at the edge of a forest in eastern Canada.

In certain circumstances, however, measurements of the biomass at the various trophic levels in a community may also give an inverted pyramid. For instance, at certain times of year the biomass of the tiny herbivorous organisms that float in lakes and oceans (**zooplankton**) may exceed the biomass of the tiny photosynthetic organisms (**phytoplankton**) on which they feed (*figure 38.13*). This is because biomass refers to the mass of organisms present at a particular moment, the so-called **standing crop**. However, the organisms which constitute the phytoplankton are smaller than the zooplankton that depend on them. Because of this, the phytoplankton have shorter life cycles. As a result, at any one time the biomass of the phytoplankton may be less than that of the zooplankton, the latter being supported by a tremendously rapid turnover of phytoplankton.

Pyramids of numbers and biomass provide ecologists with useful information. However, to get a fuller understanding of what happens in communities, pyramids of energy are often constructed.

Pyramids of energy

A **pyramid of energy** shows the transfer – or *flow* – of energy through a community. As a result, pyramids of energy are expressed in units of energy per area per time, e.g. kilojoules m^{-2} yr^{-1}. They show the rate at which energy is transferred from one trophic level to another. This dynamic view of a community contrasts with the static picture provided by pyramids of numbers or biomass which are taken at an instant in time rather than over a measured period of time.

Figure 38.14 shows a generalised pyramid of energy and a specific example. These pyramids can never be inverted, as pyramids of numbers or biomass sometimes are. To understand why, look at figure 38.15. Consider the energy of sunlight which the producers have transferred to photosynthetic products. Three things can happen to this energy: it can be respired by the producers, it can pass to the herbivores or it can pass to the decomposers. In the same way, some of the energy stored in the herbivores will be respired, some will pass to the carnivores and some to the decomposers.

We can see therefore that the energy transferred from the producers to the herbivores must be greater than the energy transferred from the herbivores to the carnivores. This is an application of the **Law of Conservation of Energy**, the first law of thermodynamics (*page 122*).

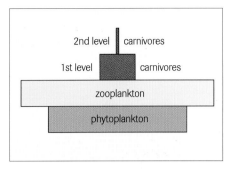

Figure 38.13 An inverted pyramid of biomass, showing how a small mass of phytoplankton can, at some times of the year, support a larger mass of zooplankton.

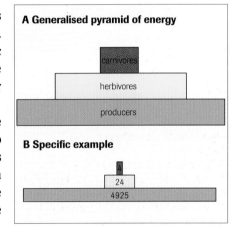

Figure 38.14
A Generalised pyramid of energy, showing how the energy flowing through a trophic level decreases as you go up a food chain.
B Pyramid of energy from the Arctic tundra, Devon Island, Canada. Units are kJ m^{-2} yr^{-1}.

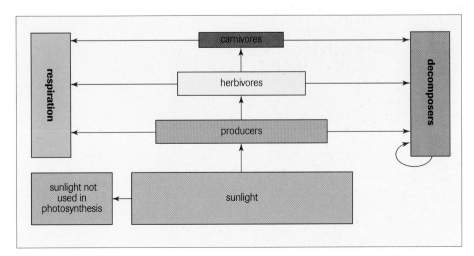

Figure 38.15 Generalised diagram showing the flow of energy through a community. Only some of the energy stored in a trophic level goes to the trophic level above. The rest is respired or passes to the decomposers. This is why pyramids of energy can never be inverted.

38.7 Energy budgets

An **energy budget** for a species shows what percentage of the energy ingested by an individual is assimilated. It then looks at the fate of the assimilated energy. Some of this energy is respired, some is used for growth and building up tissues, and some is used for the production of gametes (reproduction). How much energy is allocated to each of these three functions depends on a number of factors. A juvenile individual, for example, will allocate quite a bit to growth, but nothing to reproduction.

Energy budgets can be constructed either for individual species or for whole communities. It takes a lot of careful experimental work to determine the energy budget for a species. It takes even longer to determine the energy budget for a whole community. Yet such studies can tell us a lot about the dynamics of ecosystems.

The first study to investigate the energy budget of a community was carried out by the American ecologist E.P. Odum at Silver Springs, a pool plus its associated five mile river, in Florida (*figure 38.16*). Odum spent four years painstakingly measuring the energy flow at Silver Springs and his results are summarised in figure 38.17.

Notice from figure 38.17 how little of the sunlight that struck the producers was actually trapped by the chloroplasts and used to fix carbon dioxide. The total amount of light striking the producers (the insolation) was about $7\,100\,000$ kJ m^{-2} yr^{-1}, whereas the energy fixed in photosynthesis was only $87\,402$ kJ m^{-2} yr^{-1}.

From these figures we can calculate the **efficiency of photosynthesis**:

$$\text{Efficiency of photosynthesis} = 87\,402 \text{ kJ m}^{-2}\text{ yr}^{-1} \div 7\,100\,000 \text{ kJ m}^{-2}\text{ yr}^{-1}$$
$$= 1.2\%$$

This figure seems very low, but is similar to that found in many other communities. The highest photosynthetic efficiencies are found in tropical rain forests and in crops growing under intensive agriculture. Even here, the efficiency of photosynthesis is only 3–4 per cent.

Productivity of ecosystems

The total organic material made in photosynthesis is known as the **gross primary production**. However, only some of this is available to herbivores. The remainder is respired.

Figure 38.16 Silver Springs, Florida.

Figure 38.17 The energy flow in the Silver Springs community, Florida. The units are kJ m^{-2} yr^{-1}. Notice how little of the sunlight that strikes the plants (insolation) ends up trapped in glucose. Some of this trapped energy is respired, some goes to the decomposers, some is carried downstream and some is consumed by the herbivores. In turn, some of the energy transferred to the herbivores goes to the first level carnivores, and some of the energy transferred to these goes to the second level carnivores.

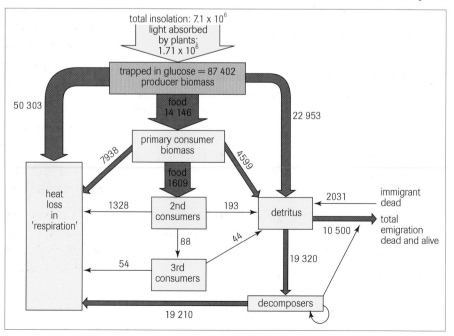

The amount of organic material actually available to the herbivores is called the **net primary production**.

The percentage of the energy at one trophic level which ends up in the next trophic level is called the **trophic efficiency**. The trophic efficiency of herbivores, for instance, is the percentage of the net primary production that is converted to the growth and reproduction of herbivores.

Ecologists have now calculated trophic efficiencies for a number of ecosystems. The values range from less than 1 per cent to over 40 per cent. Some of the highest are found in the oceans. The trophic efficiencies of zooplankton feeding on phytoplankton, for example, can be over 40 per cent.

Applied aspects of energy budgets

Farmers rely on energy budgets to stay in business and provide the rest of us with food. Although plants only convert about 1–3 per cent of incident sunlight into vegetation, sunlight doesn't cost anything and there's a lot of it around.

Over the centuries, selective plant breeding has increased the proportion of photosynthetic product that is channelled into the part of the plant we eat. Wheat, for instance, used to stand almost 2 m tall, as can be seen from paintings of medieval harvests. Nowadays, it is less than a third of that height. This means that more of the plant matter ends up in the grain.

Animal farmers want a high proportion of the energy ingested by their flock or herd to go towards production (i.e. growth and reproduction) rather than respiration. They therefore use a variety of techniques to maximise the economic value of their animals. Strategies include:

- ensuring that food fed to the animals is highly digestible so that as much of it as possible will be absorbed and assimilated;

- using young animals (older animals put less of their energy intake into growth);

- minimising energy expenditure by the animals – for example, by keeping the animals warm and in the dark.

Pigs have the highest growth efficiency of any domestic mammal, transforming up to 15 per cent of the energy they ingest into meat. This is why pork is a relatively inexpensive meat, despite the fact that pigs require more looking after than many other farm animals.

Summary

1. A **community** consists of the organisms found in an area. These organisms interact with one another in many ways.

2. An **ecosystem** consists of the interacting organisms and their **physical (abiotic) environment** within an area.

3. The change in the species found in a community over time is known as **succession**.

4. **Primary succession** is the progressive colonisation of a previously unoccupied area, such as bare rock or open water. **Secondary succession** begins in an area which has been previously colonised.

5. The end point of a succession is known as a **climax community**. Over much of Europe, mixed deciduous forest is the climax community.

6. Species can be classified into **producers** (autotrophic organisms), **consumers** (heterotrophic organisms) and **decomposers (saprobionts)**.

7. **Nutrient cycles** show how matter circulates around an ecosystem. They have two components: a biological component and a geochemical component.

8. The nutritional sequence that leads from producers to **top carnivores** is known as a **food chain**. Food chains rarely have more than six **trophic levels**.

9. A **food web** shows the feeding relationships of a community more fully than do food chains. A food web consists of interconnected food chains.

10. A **pyramid of numbers** shows the number of organisms at each trophic level in a community. A **pyramid of biomass** shows the mass of organisms at each trophic level.

11. A **pyramid of energy** shows the rate at which energy flows through the trophic levels of a community.

12. Pyramids of numbers are quite often **inverted**, pyramids of biomass occasionally and pyramids of energy never.

13. The highest **photosynthetic efficiencies** are found in tropical rain forests and in crops growing under intensive agriculture. Even here, only some 3–4 per cent of the incoming sunlight is fixed in photosynthesis.

For general advice on these questions and advice on answering essay-type questions, see pages vii and viii.

1. Bacteria of the nitrogen fixing *Rhizobium* species that live in a mutualistic association with legumes are important to agriculture. A good crop of clover with active nitrogen fixation can yield up to 400 kg of nitrogen per hectare per year.

   (a) Outline the ways in which *Rhizobium* benefits from this mutualistic relationship. (3)

   (b) Explain the significance to agriculture of this high yield of fixed nitrogen. (4)

   Industrial waste tips are often very difficult to reclaim. One reason for this is the low levels of nutrients in the covering soil. Legumes with associated nitrogen fixing bacteria have been used early in reclamation because they improve the nitrogen content of the soil.

   (c) Suggest how this improved nitrogen content of the covering soil might affect the succession of plants on such a spoil tip. (2)

   Host plants are infected when *Rhizobium* penetrates root hair cells. The bacteria migrate to the root cortex and nodule formation begins. For successful nitrogen fixation to occur conditions inside the nodule must be anaerobic.

   (d) Suggest

   (i) why conditions must be anaerobic; (2)

   (ii) how anaerobic conditions develop inside the nodule. (1)

   (Total 12 marks)
   UCLES 1997

2. Give an account of the roles of bacteria in the nitrogen cycle.

   (Total 10 marks)
   London 1997

3. The table shows the ratios of biomass between successive trophic levels in a number of grassland ecosystems.

Ecosystem	Biomass ratio	
	Producer / Primary consumer	Primary consumer / Secondary consumer
Bunchgrass	1984	2
Tallgrass	1376	18
Southern shortgrass	2071	7
Northern shortgrass	1657	4

From this table it can be seen, for example, that in the bunchgrass system, 1984 units of producer biomass are required to yield 1 unit of primary consumer biomass.

   (a) How many units of producer biomass are required to yield 1 unit of secondary consumer biomass in the northern shortgrass ecosystem?
   Show your working. (2)

   (b) Which of the ratios shown in the table represents the most efficient conversion of biomass? (1)

   (c) (i) Explain why it is not possible to have a ratio of 1 in this table. (1)

   (ii) Suggest **one** explanation for the fact that the figures in the second column of the table are much larger than those in the third column. (1)

   (Total 5 marks)
   AEB 1996

4. (a) Explain why, in most ecosystems, less than 5% of sunlight is converted into chemical energy by green plants. (8)

   (b) With reference to pyramids of energy, discuss the transfer of energy between trophic levels. (10)

   (Total 18 marks)
   UCLES 1997

U ntil a few thousand years ago humans were just one species among countless others and our impact on the world as a whole was minor. But today there are few areas in the world that have not been influenced by our activities. As we shall see in this chapter, even the ice of the Arctic and Antarctic and the waters of the largest oceans have been significantly affected by our species (*figure 39.1*).

Let us look at what we have done and what we can do about it.

39.1 Pollution

Pollution is the damaging release by humans of materials or energy into the environment. The things released are referred to as **pollutants**.

Of course, whether an action is 'damaging' can be a matter of opinion. Is the addition of insecticides to the environment damaging? On the one hand, the pesticide may accumulate in food chains to the point at which it prevents some species from breeding and may be poisonous to humans. In this respect the pesticide is damaging. On the other hand, it may kill organisms that transmit diseases or eat crops, and so be used to our benefit. To understand pollution you need to understand biology, chemistry, economics, sociology and psychology!

Carbon dioxide

It may seem strange to describe this odourless, invisible gas as a pollutant, especially as it is needed for photosynthesis and occurs in the atmosphere at a concentration of less than one part in a thousand. However, on a global scale carbon dioxide may prove to be the most serious pollutant over the next hundred years. This is because it contributes to the **greenhouse effect**.

The greenhouse effect takes its name from the fact that the so-called **greenhouse gases** (carbon dioxide, along with water vapour, methane and some other atmospheric components) help to warm the Earth in much the same way that glass helps to warm a greenhouse.

Light rays (*short* wavelength electromagnetic radiation) from the Sun pass through the glass into a greenhouse. They strike objects in a greenhouse, warming them. These objects give out heat rays (*long* wavelength electromagnetic radiation) which cannot get through the glass. So heat energy is held within the greenhouse.

The same process happens in the Earth's atmosphere. Light rays from the Sun heat up the Earth's surface. Some of the Earth's reflected heat is trapped by the greenhouse gases.

Measurements of the carbon dioxide concentration of air bubbles trapped in the ice of Antarctica show that from about 500 BC to AD 1880 the carbon dioxide concentration remained fairly steady at roughly 270 ppm (parts per million). Since then, however, the global carbon dioxide concentration has been rising at a gradually increasing rate and has now reached over 360 ppm, an increase of 33 per cent (*figure 39.2*).

What has caused this increase in the level of atmospheric carbon dioxide? The main answer is that we are burning more and more fossil fuels. This releases carbon dioxide into the atmosphere from coal, oil, gas and peat formed over several hundred million years. A second cause is that the world's forests are being cut down at an ever-increasing rate, thus removing plants that would otherwise take up the carbon dioxide. To some extent, negative feedback comes to the rescue. As the amount of carbon dioxide in the atmosphere increases, plants automatically photosynthesise more rapidly. Unfortunately, this only uses up about a third of the extra carbon dioxide being released into the atmosphere.

Figure 39.1 Tropical island off Malaysia. Even in this idyllic setting the water contains detectable levels of pollutants. More worrying still is that a rise in sea level, possibly resulting from increased atmospheric levels of carbon dioxide, could destroy such islands.

▶ Photosynthesis, page 196

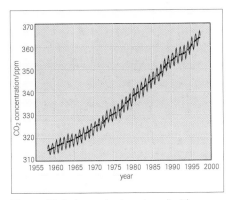

Figure 39.2 Atmospheric carbon dioxide concentrations measured at Mauna Loa Observatory, Hawaii between 1958 and 1997. Fluctuations, caused by seasonal differences in the amount of photosynthesis, are superimposed on a steady upward trend.

Biodegradable and non-biodegradable pollutants

A useful distinction can be made between biodegradable and non-biodegradable pollutants.

- **Biodegradable pollutants** such as sewage and waste paper are broken down by microorganisms to harmless substances fairly quickly.

- **Non-biodegradable pollutants** such as certain insecticides cannot so readily be broken down. They tend to accumulate and are therefore potentially more dangerous.

Possible consequences of the greenhouse effect

Scientists know that during the last 100 years, average world temperatures have risen by between 0.5 and 1.0°C. This may not sound very much, but it is greatest at the poles and, given time, warming by only a few degrees centigrade could lead to much of the polar ice melting. We now know that this has begun to happen.

Scientists still cannot predict with confidence what the long-term outcome of the greenhouse effect is likely to be. However, it is thought that over the next few decades, world temperatures may increase by a further 1 to 3°C. Possible consequences include the flooding of much of the world's coastal land and more droughts in sub-tropical latitudes (5–35°N).

Possible remedies

The greenhouse effect is an example of **global pollution**. No one government on its own can hope to overcome it. International cooperation is needed.

There are several possible ways in which the rise in carbon dioxide concentrations could be halted or at least slowed:

- The use of alternative energy sources such as solar power and wind power could be expanded.

- More energy-saving measures could be introduced.

- A switch could be made from burning fossil fuels to using nuclear power.

- We could stop expecting our standard of living (and therefore energy consumption) to go on rising.

- Massive tree-planting programmes could be started, allowing carbon dioxide to be 'locked up' in wood.

- Nutrient enrichment of the oceans might increase the number of photosynthetic organisms there, which would again trap carbon dioxide in organic matter.

Oil pollution

Oil is an important fuel, but is found only in certain parts of the world. Because of this, vast amounts of oil are carried every day by supertankers around the globe. Inevitably accidents happen and **oil spills** result.

Oil pollution may also occur when ballast water taken into empty tankers to provide stability on the return voyage is discharged, and in times of war when oil refineries are bombed or when a country deliberately spills oil into the sea for military purposes.

Oil is lighter than water and, being non-polar, does not dissolve in it. As a result, large **oil slicks** form on the surface of the water. These may persist for weeks or months, before being washed up on coastlines or eventually dispersing.

The most obvious victims of oil pollution are oceanic birds and other large animals, thousands of which may die as a result of oil spills. However, such damage is only the tip of the iceberg. Many other species are killed by the oil which carpets the water, preventing photosynthesis and smothering organisms.

Early attempts to treat oil pollution involved using **detergents** to disperse the oil, much as washing-up liquid helps grease to dissolve in water. However, such treatment often caused more pollution than it prevented, as detergents are themselves pollutants, generally being non-biodegradable.

More recent methods at treating oil pollution involve:

- using floating booms to prevent slicks reaching the shore;

- setting fire to the oil;

- pumping the oil back into special collection ships;

- adding naturally occurring bacteria that can digest oil;

- adding special oil spill cleansers that are relatively non-toxic and more biodegradable than previously used detergents.

A common guillemot whose feathers are oiled from a spill. Even modest amounts of oil can lead to death of sea birds. This is partly because of damage to the insulating properties of the feathers.

Damage to the ozone layer

Ozone, O_3, occurs at low concentrations in the Earth's stratosphere, 15 to 50 km up. Here it serves the useful function of intercepting much of the dangerous ultraviolet radiation that would otherwise strike the Earth from the Sun and damage the genetic material in cells. During the late 1980s, measurements above Antarctica showed a seasonal collapse in the amount of ozone there. A hole in the ozone layer was appearing and getting bigger each year.

The chemicals found to be damaging the ozone layer were identified as **chlorofluorocarbons** (**CFCs**). Until recently CFCs were widely used in refrigerators, aerosol sprays and fast-food packaging. Thanks to intensive lobbying by scientists and environmentalists, a number of international measures have now been agreed which hopefully will cut back the use of CFCs.

In 1987, the **Montreal Protocol** signed by over 30 countries laid down targets to ensure that fewer CFCs were released into the atmosphere. It was followed by increasingly stringent amendments in London in 1990 and in Copenhagen in 1992. The decade after the signing of the Montreal Protocol saw a reduction in CFC use in many countries. However, alternatives to CFCs are expensive and some countries are *increasing* their use of CFCs. In addition, other long-lived ozone-depleting substances are still being produced.

If measures to repair the ozone layer are not successful, a rise in the number of cases of skin cancer in humans is likely, particularly in countries close to Antarctica, as more ultraviolet radiation gets through to ground level. The effects on other species are less clear though there is some evidence that amphibian populations are already being damaged by increased surface levels of ultraviolet radiation.

How CFCs damage the ozone layer

In the atmosphere CFCs break down, releasing atoms of chlorine. The chlorine atoms then react with ozone as follows:

$$Cl + O_3 \rightarrow ClO + O_2$$

The ClO so formed then reacts with an oxygen atom thus:

$$ClO + O \rightarrow Cl + O_2$$

As a result of these two reactions, a molecule of ozone is destroyed without any chlorine being used up. Chlorine atoms can therefore be said to *catalyse* the destruction of ozone. The English scientist Joe Farman, who discovered the hole in the ozone layer, calculates that a single CFC molecule can remove hundreds of thousands of ozone molecules.

Pesticides

Pests are organisms which people consider a nuisance or harmful. Pesticides are substances deliberately introduced into the environment to kill pests. This is called **chemical control**. The main classes of pesticides are:

- **herbicides**, which kill weeds;
- **fungicides**, which kill fungi;
- **insecticides**, which kill insects.

Pesticides are most likely to cause environmental problems when they are **persistent** or **non-specific**. Herbicides rarely cause serious problems even though they are widely used. Most of them can, within months, be broken down by microorganisms to harmless chemicals: in other words, they are biodegradable. Fungicides, however, can be important pollutants. Many of them contain either copper or mercury, as fungi are very sensitive to these two elements. Mercury is toxic to humans. Cases have arisen, for instance in Japan, where people have died as a result of eating fish and molluscs which had accumulated high concentrations of mercury.

Many substances, from cyanide and nicotine to synthetic organochlorines, have been used as insecticides. A general problem with many insecticides is that they don't just kill the intended insects. Often the insecticide also kills useful insects which may parasitise, eat or compete with the harmful species. This means that when the time comes for the insecticide to be used a second or third time, the natural checks to the population growth of the pest will have been removed (*figure 39.3*). A farmer may then become locked into an expensive dependency on the insecticide, being forced to spray more often and in greater amounts than was originally required.

A further problem with pesticides is that pests may evolve resistance to them, requiring ever-increasing doses to be applied (*page 752*).

Use of biological control, page 697

The case of the peregrine falcon

In Britain, the peregrine falcon (*Falco peregrinus*) began to decline in numbers in the 1950s. By the 1960s its numbers were less than half of what they had been 25 years earlier. Careful research by the ecologist Derek Ratcliffe established that the decline of the peregrine was due to the accumulation of organochlorine residues. These caused the birds to lay eggs with thinner shells. These thin shells resulted in the eggs being more likely to get broken.

Fortunately, the story has a happy ending. As a result of this research, the British government introduced strict restrictions on the use of organochlorine pesticides and by the late 1980s peregrine numbers had completely recovered – an example of how the harmful effects of a pollutant can be reversed, provided the political will is there.

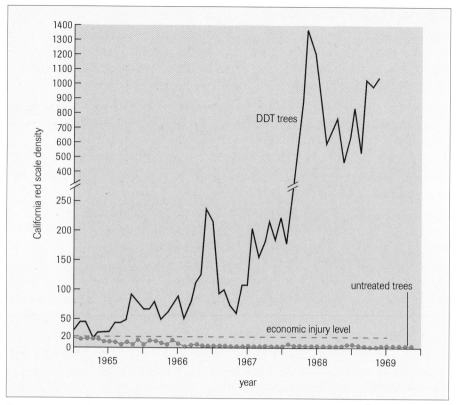

Figure 39.3 Increases in California red scale (*Aonidiella aurantii*) infestation on lemon trees caused by monthly applications of DDT spray. Nearby untreated lemon trees suffered no economic damage because various insect parasites and predators kept the red scale under control.

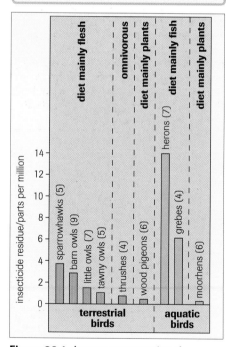

Figure 39.4 Average concentration of organochlorine insecticide residues in the breast muscle of different types of bird. Notice how the insecticide residue levels are higher in those birds that eat flesh or fish. The number of specimens analysed is given in brackets after the name of each type.

The organochlorines

Some of the most widely used insecticides have been the **organochlorines**. These are relatively non-biodegradable. One such compound, 1,1-bis(*p*-chlorophenyl)-2,2,2-trichloroethane, better known as **DDT**, was widely used during and after the Second World War against mosquitoes and other insects. Thanks to its use, millions of people survived who would otherwise have died of malaria or starvation.

However, there is a problem. DDT and other organochlorine insecticides become amplified in food chains. This is because they are not very soluble in water, and so tend not to be excreted. Instead, they are stored in tissue fat where they accumulate. Because an animal generally eats lots of animals belonging to the preceding trophic level – a single heron eats hundreds of fish for example – the concentration of the insecticide increases as it goes along the food chain.

Because of this effect, carnivores are more at risk than herbivores from organochlorines and a number of other insecticides (*figure 39.4*). A 1998 study found that Inuits, who live in the Arctic and eat large amounts of seal meat and fat, have especially high levels of various synthetic organic compounds, such as PCBs, which are known to be harmful.

Acid rain

Acid rain results from a variety of processes which together lead to acidic gases from the atmosphere being deposited on land and in water (*figure 39.5*). The main sources of these acidic gases are power stations that burn coal or oil, and motor vehicles. The gases involved are sulphur dioxide (SO_2) and various oxides of nitrogen (collectively labelled NO_x). When these gases dissolve in rainwater, the rain that falls typically has a pH of between 4.0 and 4.5. Unpolluted rainwater has a pH of about 5.6.

Ecological impact of farming

In every country, farming has a significant impact on the ecology of an area. In industrialised countries this impact is especially severe for a variety of reasons:

- Crops are generally grown in **monocultures** so that only one species (e.g. wheat, oil seed rape) is found in large fields.

- Trees and hedgerows may be removed and wetlands drained.

- The widespread use of fertilisers can lead easily to eutrophication caused by nitrates and phosphates in organic effluents (*page 682*).

- Extensive use of pesticides not only kills unwanted pests such as aphids, but deprives insectivorous birds and other animals of food.

Such practices constitute **intensive food production**. Some farmers are striving to halt or even reverse these developments. For example, **organic farmers** use only natural pesticides and organic fertilisers.

Organic farming is an example of **extensive food production**. In Western countries, a possible advantage of organic farming is that it may prove to be more **sustainable** in the long run. Disadvantages include the fact that yields are lower while organic food generally costs more. Some of this extra cost is because governments subsidise intensive food production.

In developing countries various types of extensive food production are practised. For example, legumes are still widely used in **crop rotation** while two different crops may be grown in alternate rows in a field – a practice known as **intercropping**. One advantage of intercropping is that the two crops may make slightly different, complementary, demands on the soil and on pollinators.

Lichens are among the organisms most sensitive to atmospheric sulphur dioxide. Different species of lichen vary in their tolerance to this gas, but most are so susceptible that they cannot grow in industrial areas. That is why tree trunks and tombstones in cities often have fewer lichens than in rural areas. Lichens can therefore be used as **pollution indicators** and are known as **indicator species**.

The distribution of lichens around major industrial centres shows that sulphur dioxide pollution drifts downwind. Nowadays coal- and oil-fired power stations are equipped with very tall chimneys. These enable the pollutants to be carried hundreds of miles away. Much of Britain's industrial pollutants falls as acid rain on Germany and Scandinavia, although great progress has been made by the major UK electricity generating businesses in reducing sulphur dioxide emissions.

Figure 39.5 Acid rain is caused by the emissions of various gases resulting from the burning of fossil fuels. The principal gases involved are sulphur dioxide (SO_2) and several oxides of nitrogen (NO_x). Dry deposition happens in the absence of rain. The action of sunlight on NO_x and hydrocarbons in the atmosphere can give rise to photochemical smog in which ozone (O_3) and organic nitrates are important secondary pollutants. Wet deposition is particularly severe in upland areas covered with mists for long periods of time.

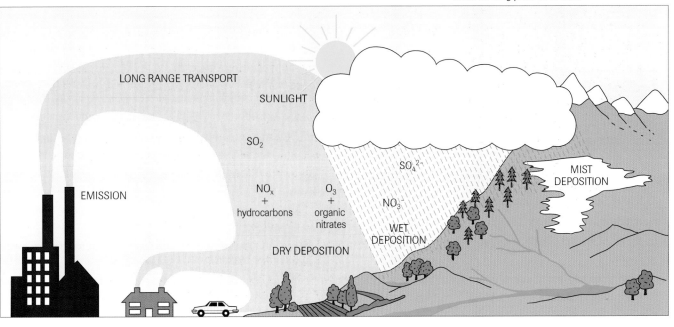

LONG RANGE TRANSPORT

SUNLIGHT

SO_2

EMISSION

NO_x + hydrocarbons

O_3 + organic nitrates

DRY DEPOSITION

SO_4^{2-}

NO_3^-

WET DEPOSITION

MIST DEPOSITION

Part 7

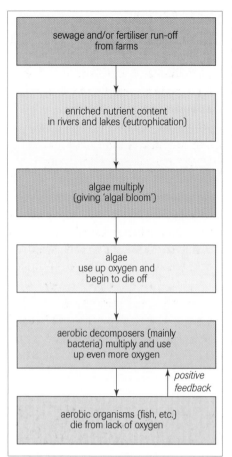

Figure 39.6 Flow chart showing the sequence of events which may result from eutrophication.

The flow chart shows:
- sewage and/or fertiliser run-off from farms
- enriched nutrient content in rivers and lakes (eutrophication)
- algae multiply (giving 'algal bloom')
- algae use up oxygen and begin to die off
- aerobic decomposers (mainly bacteria) multiply and use up even more oxygen
- *positive feedback*
- aerobic organisms (fish, etc.) die from lack of oxygen

Acid rain has led to fish, molluscs and other invertebrates being lost from many lakes in Europe and North America. It may be damaging European and North American forests too, though that is less certain. The passing in 1970 of the Clean Air Act in the USA led to major falls in SO_2 emissions. However, it can take a long time to undo the effects of acid rain. In the Hubbard Brook Experimental Forest, USA, average stream-water pH only rose from 4.85 in 1963 to 5.01 in 1993, although the Clean Air Act had been in force for over 20 years.

Sewage

Sewage is society's water-borne waste.

- **Domestic sewage** contains human faeces and urine, the water used to wash these away and the dirty water that flows from our baths and sinks.
- **Industrial sewage** includes the dirty water from industry, hospitals and abattoirs.
- **Agricultural sewage**, derived from farms, is not allowed to mix with domestic and industrial waste, and is treated separately.

Eutrophication

If untreated sewage or agricultural fertilisers are allowed to enter lakes or rivers, **eutrophication** may occur. Eutrophication is the enrichment of water with nutrients when large amounts of organic matter, or nitrogen and phosphorus, enter the water. A chain reaction then occurs, as a result of which the oxygen level of the water falls and many organisms die (*figure 39.6*).

The degree of eutrophication in a body of water can be determined by measuring the rate at which a sample of the water takes up oxygen in the dark. This is known as the **biological oxygen demand** (**BOD**). The higher the BOD, the greater the number of aerobic microorganisms in the water and the greater the degree of eutrophication.

At a sewage treatment works, the BOD of the sewage can be reduced by a factor of over 20. This means that the water discharged into lakes or rivers after treatment is far less likely to cause pollution.

Treatment of sewage

The principles of sewage treatment are outlined in figure 39.7. First, the solid matter such as gravel and condoms are removed by screening or by being allowed to settle under gravity. The sewage then passes to the **primary treatment tanks**. Two main techniques are available for treating the effluent from these tanks.

- In a **biological filter system**, the soluble supernatant from the primary sedimentation tanks is allowed to trickle down through a **filter bed** under the influence of gravity. This filter bed is usually composed of rock chippings and provides a large surface area for the growth of aerobic bacteria and fungi. These microbes support a complex community of protoctists, annelids, nematodes, flies and other small animals. Between them, these organisms remove most of the organic matter from the effluent.

- In an **activated sludge system**, the supernatant fluid from the primary sedimentation tanks is fed into large tanks and mechanically aerated. Again, aerobic bacteria and fungi feed off the sewage, but the mechanical agitation prevents the growth of larger organisms.

With either system the end result is much the same, with the great majority of the organic matter being removed from the sewage by aerobic decomposition. Anaerobic decomposition, though, also plays a part. Indeed, some sewage works are built to encourage it. Such works produce large amounts of **methane** and this can be burnt to generate energy.

Despite all the decomposition that takes place in a sewage works, the water finally discharged still has lots of nutrients and a biological oxygen demand about six times that of clean river water. Figure 39.8 shows what happens when such sewage enters an otherwise unpolluted and well-oxygenated river.

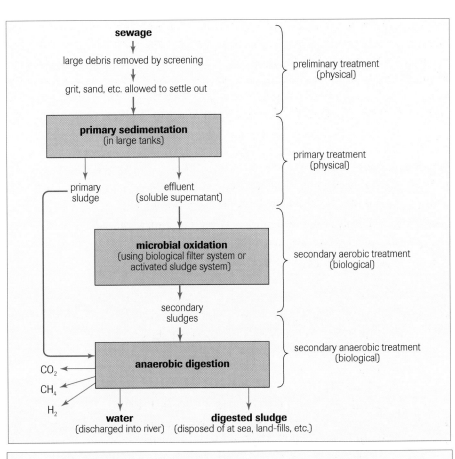

China clay waste tips

In Cornwall and Devon, china clay has been mined for over 200 years to make chinaware and high-quality paper. The resulting tips are nutritionally deficient in nitrogen, phosphorus, potassium, magnesium and calcium.

Natural colonisation is extremely slow. However, covering the tips with topsoil which is then seeded soon allows a dense vegetation to develop.

This illustrates the general point that, if we have the will and resources, most types of pollution can be remedied. There is more about this in the extension box on the next page.

Figure 39.7 Major stages in the treatment of sewage.

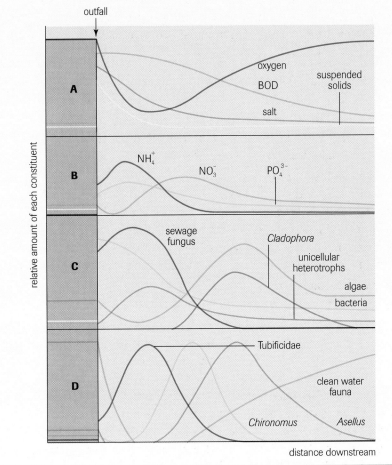

Figure 39.8 Diagrammatic representation of the effects of sewage discharge into a river. Typical levels upstream of the discharge are indicated by horizontal lines at the left of the outfall.
A and **B** Physical and chemical changes.
C Changes in microorganisms. *Cladophora* is a filamentous alga known as blanket weed because its thick growth can cover large areas.
D Changes in aquatic invertebrates. The Tubificidae are annelids that can tolerate water with almost no dissolved oxygen. *Chironomus* are midge larvae. *Asellus* is an aquatic woodlouse.

Reclaiming colliery spoil

When coal is mined, huge mounds of unwanted colliery spoil accumulate near the mine. Plants are often very slow to colonise these spoil tips, with the result that for many years ugly naked heaps scar the landscape.

Restoring land which has been scarred in this kind of way so that it is covered with vegetation is called **reclamation**. Soil analyses show that colliery spoil often has a pH of less than 3.5 and is frequently very low in essential plant nutrients. Reclaiming such spoil usually first involves adding lime to the area. This helps to neutralise the soil, though as much as 60 tonnes of lime per hectare may be needed. Fertilisers can then be added to provide essential nitrogen and phosphorus.

Seeding is then carried out. The type of seed used depends on whether or not it is intended to graze the land. If it is to be grazed, a plant like rye grass (*Lolium perenne*) is often used as this is palatable to grazing animals. If, however, grazing is not envisaged, a plant such as wavy hair grass (*Deschampsia flexuosa*) may be more suitable. Wavy hair grass can grow well on quite acid soil and therefore less lime has to be added.

Legumes are nearly always sown along with the grasses. This is because most legumes can fix atmospheric nitrogen (*page 669*). Once established, they reduce the need for further applications of fertiliser, thus making the reclamation operation cheaper.

Although colliery spoils are unsightly, limestone quarries often make attractive nature reserves if they are left alone once quarrying has finished. The nutrient-poor soil allows a wealth of beautiful chalk-loving plants to colonise the site over the years.

Radioactivity

The average person living in the United Kingdom receives a total radiation dose of about 2 millisieverts per year. About 87 per cent of this is natural radiation which comes either from outer space (e.g. cosmic rays) or from rocks in the Earth's crust that contain radioactive materials.

The other 13 per cent of the radiation we receive is the result of human activity. The great majority of this 13 per cent comes from radioactivity used for medical purposes. This includes radioactivity from X-rays, used for diagnostic purposes, and from radiotherapy used in the treatment of many cancers. Only about 1 per cent of the radioactivity to which we are exposed is due to radiation from nuclear power stations or nuclear weapons.

Advocates of nuclear power use these figures to emphasise how safe nuclear power is. However, most of the worries about nuclear power centre on what would happen if there was a major accident at a nuclear power station.

The Chernobyl disaster

So far the world's worst nuclear accident was the explosion at Chernobyl in the then Soviet Union on 26 April 1986. This released approximately 80 kg of **radionuclides** (radioactive substances) into the atmosphere and led to the authorities having to evacuate 115 000 people from within a 30 km radius of the plant. The radionuclides produced were eventually deposited throughout the northern hemisphere. In Britain, the worst affected regions were upland areas in North Wales, Cumbria and Scotland. These areas were severely affected because they receive a lot of rain. The rain washed the radionuclides down and deposited them on the ground.

The radioactive substances in the Chernobyl fallout that proved most significant in the long term were caesium-134 (half-life = 2 years) and caesium-137 (half-life = 32 years). Considerable quantities of iodine-131 were also released but as this has a half-life of only eight days, most of the radioactivity from this source soon disappeared.

As a direct result of Chernobyl, rates of cancer and birth malformations nearby approximately doubled. Children born in the aftermath of the disaster have twice as many mutations. All in all, an estimated 10 000 people will be killed by the radioactivity; countless more will suffer either medically or economically. The economic losses of neighbouring Belarus, the most affected country, are comparable to those of the Second World War.

Work has also been carried out on the wider ecological implications of Chernobyl. Conifers are some 10 times more sensitive to radioactivity than are deciduous trees. Over an area of some 4400 ha around the reactor, all the mature *Pinus* (pine) trees died. These are expected to be replaced by *Betula* (birch) and other deciduous trees. Vertebrates are more affected by radioactivity than invertebrates though it is unclear what the precise consequences of Chernobyl will be for the animals of the area.

Almost every country in the northern hemisphere has been affected by Chernobyl. For example, restrictions were placed on the sale of sheep in certain parts of Britain because the grass they were eating became infected by radioactive caesium-137. At first it was thought that these restrictions would be required for approximately three weeks but in 1998 restrictions still remained in place on over 47 000 sheep on 23 farms in Scotland.

39.2 Conservation

Conservation involves managing the Earth's resources so as to restore and maintain a balance between the requirements of humans and those of other species.

There are two main reasons why we should conserve.

- The **ethical reason** is that we have a moral duty to look after the environment: we have no right to destroy ecosystems or allow species to become extinct.

- The **pragmatic reason** is that it is to our advantage to ensure the integrity of our environment: if we preserve the tropical rain forests, the greenhouse effect will be lessened; if we conserve fish stocks, we can get more food from the seas; and if we reduce water pollution, people will be able to swim on unpolluted beaches and fish in clean rivers.

We shall look at the issue of conservation at four levels: the **international level**, the **national level**, the **local level** and the **individual level**.

Conservation at the international level

Conservation at the international (global) level requires the concerted action of many nations. We have already discussed the damage to the ozone layer and the problems of the greenhouse effect. Resolving both these problems will require cooperation between the major industrial nations of the world, just as measures to reduce the risk of nuclear war require international negotiation.

There are other ecological issues which require international agreement. Within Europe, for example, there is a mass of legislation on air and water quality as well as the **EU habitats directive** which relates to the conservation of natural habitats and wild fauna and flora. Here, we shall focus on the preservation of tropical rain forests and the hunting of elephants.

Saving the tropical rain forests

Why should we get so fussed about the world's tropical rain forests? Well, one ethical argument for conserving them is that they are the most diverse biome in the world. They contain millions of species, most of which haven't even been named yet. These species have worth in themselves, whether they are of use to us or not. Another ethical reason is that tropical rain forests are the home of many native people.

The pragmatic argument is that the tropical rain forests play a vital part in the health of our world. Quite apart from their possible role in averting excessive global warming, many pharmaceutical drugs of immense value are probably obtainable from plants found only in the rain forests.

A second pragmatic reason for preserving the tropical rain forests is that in countries where forests have been extensively cut down (**deforestation**), whether for wood or to provide land for agriculture, severe **erosion** has often followed. Normally the vegetation prevents heavy rains from washing away the soil. The plants in a rain forest hold on to rainwater, rather like a sponge, and only slowly release it into rivers. Once this protective blanket is removed, several interrelated changes occur:

- **sheet erosion** of surface soils leads to loss of fertility;

- **gully erosion** increases the rate at which water runs off, leading to flooding;

- there is disturbance to carbon and nitrogen cycling;

- changes in the amount of light reflected back by the forest into the atmosphere alter patterns of precipitation. The result is heavier and less frequent rain which exacerbates the flooding.

A study in 1989 of an Amazon rain forest in Peru showed that each hectare of the forest produced fruit and latex (rubber) with an annual market value of $700. If, however, the trees are cut down, the total value of their wood is $1000. Trees can only be felled once, but fruit and latex can be harvested every year. This study of the sustainable provision of resources provides a ray of hope for the Amazonian rain forest. If governments can be persuaded that more money can be made from rain forests by exploiting them on a

Extension

Thermal pollution

Thermal pollution occurs when excessive heat energy is produced with damaging consequences. It is most noticeable in rivers downstream from industries that use river water for cooling purposes. Once the water has done its job, it is returned – warmer – to the river. In the River Trent, temperature rises of over 20°C have been recorded more than 1.5 km downstream of a certain electricity generating power station.

You might suppose that such warming would have no ill effects. However, as the temperature of water rises, the water holds less dissolved oxygen. At 5°C a litre of water can hold up to 9 cm³ of dissolved oxygen. At 20°C, the same volume of water can hold only 6 cm³ of oxygen.

Changes in the temperature of a river can therefore lead to fish and other organisms dying through asphyxiation. The problem is compounded by the fact that the warmer the water, the greater the metabolic rate of the organisms and therefore the greater their oxygen requirements.

Figure 39.9 Landslide resulting from deforestation, Cascade mountains, Washington.

Figure 39.10 There is a real possibility that the African elephant may become extinct in the wild.

Figure 39.11 Elephant tusks from the Kruger National Park, South Africa.

sustainable basis than by destroying them, it may be worth their while to protect them.

During the 1990s, an area the size of Belgium was burnt each year in the Amazon rain forest. The destruction of the rain forests is an international issue because much of the pressure to cut them down comes from countries such as Japan and the USA which import large amounts of tropical hardwoods. We should remember, though, that when countries like Brazil and the Philippines cut down their forests they are only doing what many other countries, such as the USA and those in Europe, have already done over many centuries.

Saving the African elephant

In the 1960s there were around two million African elephants (*figure 39.10*). During the 1970s the price of ivory soared and more and more elephants were killed for their **tusks** – outgrowths of two of the teeth found in both males and females.

By the 1980s, poachers were using guerrilla tactics and sophisticated automatic weaponry. With limited money to fund anti-poaching operations, exclusion of determined poachers became virtually impossible. In an attempt to stem the demand for ivory, **CITES**, the Convention on International Trade in Endangered Species of Wild Fauna and Flora, agreed in 1989 to a total ban on the ivory trade (*Figure 39.11*). Ivory prices fell sharply and poaching declined.

In 1995 there were probably around 600 000 African elephants. In some countries their numbers were still declining; in others they were increasing. With the partial recovery in elephant numbers, Botswana, Namibia and Zimbabwe argued for a restoration of culling and/or trade in ivory. At their 1997 meeting, the 138 nations that belong to CITES agreed to allow these countries to start a limited ivory trade again.

African elephants are worth conserving in themselves. In addition, they are a **keystone species**: they play a pivotal role in the maintenance of their ecosystem and many other species depend on them. They create and enlarge watering holes by trampling the mud and carrying it away after wallowing. In addition, their paths to the water holes help funnel the rainwater to them. Elephant dung – which is produced in large quantities – provides a habitat for dung beetles and other species, replenishes the fertility of the soil and distributes tree seeds. Elephants also open up scrubland, providing grassland for grazers such as gazelles and impala. The loss of elephants would have far-reaching consequences for other species.

Conservation at the national level

Although some conservation requires international cooperation, there is a tremendous amount that individual countries can do. We shall look at an example in Australia.

The problem of introduced species in Australia

Australia has been an island separated from other continents for approximately 55 million years. This has allowed its flora and fauna to evolve in their own unique way. Unfortunately, during the last 200 years a great many animals and plants have been introduced into Australia and these have done untold harm. For instance, the sensitive mimosa bush (*Mimosa pigra*) has been introduced from South America. In Kakadu National Park it is spreading at such a rate that four men employed full time cannot control it. As a result it is turning the wetlands into shrubby heath.

Another example is the bitou bush (*Chrysanthemoides monilifera*). This was introduced from South Africa between 1950 and 1970 to help stabilise sand dunes. However, it is forming vast impenetrable thickets over much of the New South Wales coast, where it is now choking out native vegetation.

Introduced animals also cause great problems in Australia. Rabbits and house mice eat enormous amounts of food, and rats eat the eggs of many native birds.

There are cases where species introduced into Australia have been brought under control (*page 697*). However, many more species continue to cause great ecological damage. Whether the Australian government is prepared to put in the necessary finance to preserve what is left of Australia's unique fauna and flora remains to be seen.

Sites of Special Scientific Interest

In many countries, national conservation has been greatly helped by the setting aside for conservation of areas of land, specially protected in various ways. In the UK there are:

- **National Parks** (some 13 in all);
- **Environmentally Sensitive Areas** (some 22 in all);
- **National Nature Reserves** (some 275 in all);
- **Sites of Special Scientific Interest** (some 6000 in all).

A Site of Special Scientific Interest (SSSI) is 'an area of land which is of special interest by reason of its flora, fauna, geological or physiographic features'. However, approximately 5 per cent of SSSIs are damaged each year due to roads, housing, leisure amenities or other causes. Many National Parks and National Nature Reserves face these problems too. In some cases, such as the Lake District, the sheer number of visitors is a major problem.

Figure 39.12 Black-footed ferret. One of the few examples where captive breeding has saved a species from extinction.

Conservation at the local level

It is encouraging just how much can be achieved by local action. We shall look at two examples which differ in scale. At one extreme is the rescue from extinction, at a cost of several million dollars, of the black-footed ferret. At the other is churchyard conservation which costs almost nothing.

Saving the black-footed ferret

The black-footed ferret is a large weasel that was once widespread throughout the western prairies of the USA (*figure 39.12*). It is a specialist carnivore, feeding only on large squirrel-like rodents called prairie dogs. Prairie dogs have been hunted as pests throughout the 20th century on account of the damage they can do to crops. As a result, the number of black-footed ferrets has crashed.

By 1986 the total known population of the black-footed ferret was less than 30 individuals. The Wyoming Game and Fish Department made the controversial decision to capture as many of these as possible to try and establish a programme of **captive breeding**. In September 1986 eleven females and six males were trapped; a further male was trapped in February 1987. Fortunately, the ferrets proved easier to breed in captivity than many had feared, and by 1999, more than 2500 of them had been born in captivity.

The aim of the recovery plan is to establish, by the year 2010, ten or more separate populations in the wild, each numbering around 150 ferrets.

Churchyard conservation

In many places, urban or rural, churchyards are an oasis of wildlife (*figure 39.13*). Every churchyard is unique and has to be managed as such, but some broad guidelines can be given.

Most churchyards are essentially 'old pasture'. In Britain they were often used for grazing the priest's sheep. With a bit of care, many churchyards can support over 50 species of native flowering plants, together with a rich fauna of butterflies, moths, other invertebrates, birds and mammals.

Figure 39.13 A churchyard in Yorkshire showing a variety of habitats. The ecological value of this particular churchyard would be increased if some of the grass was kept short. Why do you think this would be beneficial from the conservation point of view? It would certainly be appreciated by people visiting graves and having wedding photographs taken.

The churchyard should provide a variety of habitats. Some of the grass should be cut regularly, say by mowing once a week during the growing season. Other areas should be cut less frequently, including some areas that are cut only once a year in the autumn. Where possible, grass cuttings should be removed to a compost heap.

A corner of the churchyard should be left almost untended. Here, brambles, nettles and native shrubs can grow up. These will provide nesting sites for birds, breeding grounds for butterflies and winter food for many animals. Where possible, one should ensure that the trees and shrubs in the churchyard are native. The use of pesticides should be avoided as far as possible.

In Britain, churchyards are the responsibility of individual Parochial Church Councils. Usually they are only too pleased for an offer of help, provided that access to the church and graves is kept clear. By looking after a churchyard, a small group of people can make a major impact on local conservation within just a few years.

NGOs and conservation

Non-government organisations (**NGOs**) play an important role in conservation. These voluntary, independent organisations are supported by millions of people. In the UK, for example, the **Royal Society for the Protection of Birds** (**RSPB**) has over a million members who do much to promote conservation nationally and locally.

The RSPB owns and manages nature reserves. It also campaigns with considerable success, on nature conservation issues.

Conservation at the individual level

Ultimately, conservation is the responsibility of each of us individually. Even at the international level conservation relies on the pressure exerted by individuals.

Ten things you can do to help conservation are listed in the box on the left.

Summary

1. Pollution is the damaging release by humans of materials or energy into the environment. The materials or energy released are called **pollutants**.

2. Biodegradable pollutants, such as waste paper, are fairly quickly broken down to harmless substances by microorganisms. However, **non-biodegradable** pollutants cannot be so readily broken down.

3. The **greenhouse effect** takes its name from the fact that carbon dioxide and certain other atmospheric gases help to warm the Earth in much the same way that glass helps to warm a greenhouse.

4. Atmospheric carbon dioxide levels have risen at a steadily increasing rate over the last 100 years. This is due to the accelerating combustion of fossil fuels and destruction of the world's forests, and has resulted in an increase in the average temperature of the Earth (**global warming**).

5. Chlorofluorocarbons (**CFCs**) are damaging the **ozone layer** high in the Earth's atmosphere, thereby increasing the amount of ultraviolet radiation that reaches the Earth's surface.

6. Substances deliberately introduced into the environment to kill pests are called **pesticides**. They include **herbicides**, **insecticides** and **fungicides**.

7. The burning of coal, petrol and oil leads to the release into the atmosphere of sulphur dioxide and various oxides of nitrogen. When these gases dissolve in rainwater, the rain acquires an unnaturally low pH and is known as **acid rain**. Acid rain has contributed to the acidification of many lakes and rivers.

8. The release of untreated sewage or agricultural fertilisers into rivers or lakes may lead to **eutrophication** as the levels of nutrients and organic matter rise. This generally results in a fall in oxygen levels and the loss of oxygen-demanding species.

9. Conservation involves managing the Earth's resources so as to restore and maintain a balance between the requirements of humans and of other species. There are ethical and pragmatic arguments in favour of conservation.

10. Captive breeding programmes may help to save some endangered animals.

11. Effective conservation often requires careful legislation, but ultimately it relies on individual efforts.

*For general advice on these questions and advice on
answering essay-type questions, see pages vii and viii.*

1. The graph below shows changes in the atmospheric carbon
dioxide concentrations at Mauna Loa, a site on an island in
the middle of the Pacific Ocean, between 1958 and 1988.

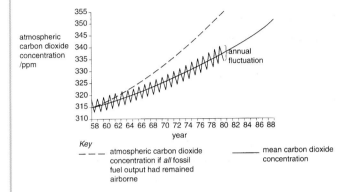

Key
- – – – atmospheric carbon dioxide
       concentration if *all* fossil
       fuel output had remained
       airborne
——— mean carbon dioxide
       concentration

(a) Suggest why Mauna Loa is regarded as a particularly
    suitable place to measure concentrations of carbon
    dioxide. (2)

(b) With reference to the graph,

   (i) explain why there is an annual fluctuation in the
    concentration of carbon dioxide; (2)

  (ii) showing your working, calculate the percentage
    increase in carbon dioxide concentration over the
    30 years between 1958 and 1988; (2)

 (iii) state the year in which the 1988 mean carbon
    dioxide concentration would have been reached if
    all the carbon dioxide from the burning of fossil
    fuels had remained in the atmosphere. (1)

(c) Explain why all the carbon dioxide from the burning of
    fossil fuels does not remain in the atmosphere. (2)

Although chlorofluorocarbons (CFCs) are more
powerful greenhouse gases than carbon dioxide, it is the
increasing concentrations of carbon dioxide which are
blamed for enhancing the greenhouse effect.

(d) (i) Explain what is meant by the *greenhouse
    effect*. (4)

  (ii) Explain why carbon dioxide is of more concern
    than CFCs. (1)

 (iii) Suggest **one** other factor in the atmosphere which
    contributes to the increased concentrations of
    carbon dioxide. (1)

(Total 15 marks)
UCLES 1997

2. The table shows the results of measuring three factors in a
lake. The first set of measurements was made before the
widespread use of fertilisers near the lake; the second set
was made after the surrounding land had been improved
with fertilisers.

Factor	Before use of fertilisers	After use of fertilisers
Mean mass of chlorophyll/ µgdm^{-3}	2.5	9.2
Mean depth to which light penetrates/m	4.8	1.6
Mean rate of oxygen use in lower layers of water/µg m^{-3} day^{-1}	37	56

Explain how the use of fertilisers would have resulted in
the changes in each of the factors measured.

(Total 6 marks)
NEAB 1997

3. The Norfolk Broads (large areas of fresh water) have
become heavily contaminated with phosphate over the last
100 years. The drawings show the effect this has had on the
community of plants and animals which live there.

Nineteenth century.

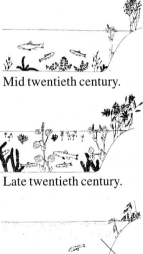

Phosphate concentration
20 µgdm^{-3}

Sedimentation rate
1 mm per year

Mid twentieth century.

Phosphate concentration
100 mgdm^{-3}

Sedimentation rate
2 mm per year

Late twentieth century.

Phosphate concentration
1000 mgdm^{-3}

Sedimentation rate
10 mm per year

Vast numbers of phytoplankton

(a) Give one function of phosphates in plants. (1)

(b) Suggest one reason for the large increase in the
    phosphate concentration in the Norfolk Broads over
    the last hundred years. (1)

(c) Explain the reasons for the changes in the community
    that had occurred

   (i) by the middle of the 20th century. (3)

  (ii) between the middle and late 20th century. (3)

(Total 8 marks)
NEAB 1996

Chapter 40

Populations and the niche concept

Figure 40.1 A male Brewer's blackbird. Just by looking at it, you can't tell the population to which it belongs. However, different populations of songbirds are reproductively separated from each other and have subtle differences in their songs.

▶ Speciation, page 751

In this chapter we shall look at the ecology of individuals within species. We need to do this to fully understand the ecology of an area. After all, natural selection operates on individuals rather than on whole species.

40.1 Populations

In everyday speech the word 'population' is used to mean the number of individuals of an organism. For ecologists, however, the word has a more precise definition. A **population** is a collection of individuals that breed with one another and are reproductively isolated from other individuals of the same species (*figure 40.1*). The *number* of individuals in a population is called the **population size**.

You might think that this definition of population is rather fussy. However, the question of whether or not the individuals in an area have the potential to breed with one another has important consequences for evolution. Suppose that on an island a species of insect is divided into two separate populations. This means that over time these two populations might give rise to two distinct species. However, this is much less likely to be the case if the insects on the island all belong to one population.

We shall consider how new species arrive later. Now we shall look at the way populations increase in size.

Support

Estimating population size

How you estimate the size of a population depends on the species concerned. The most direct way is simply to count all the individuals in the population. However, this only works for large, sessile individuals that are reasonably spread out. Other species require **samples** to be taken from the population using **quadrats** or some other method.

A useful technique for motile species is the **capture–recapture** method. The procedure is as follows. First a sample of individuals is caught, counted and marked in some way. Then these individuals are released. After being allowed to mix with the rest of the unmarked population, a second sample is caught and counted and the number of marked individuals noted. An estimate of the population size can then be made.

Suppose you catch 50 wood mice, mark and release them. Then a couple of days later you come back and catch 40 wood mice, four of which bear the mark you put on the 50 wood mice. In that case one in 10 of the mice you caught the second time (four out of 40) had already been caught. The chances are, therefore, that when you caught and marked your original 50 wood mice, you only managed to mark one in 10 of the population. In that case the best estimate you can make of the total population size is 500.

The formula for working out the population size by this method is as follows:

$$\text{Population size} = \frac{n_1 \times n_2}{n_m}$$

where n_1 is the number of individuals marked and released; n_2 is the number of individuals subsequently caught; and n_m is the number of *marked* individuals caught.

This formula, called the **Lincoln index**, can be used to estimate population sizes in different localities or to study changes in the population in a given locality over a period of time.

Different methods of capture and marking are needed for different species. For instance, small mammals can be trapped in **Longworth traps** (metal or plastic boxes with a trapdoor that closes, trapping the live animal inside) and marked by clipping off a small piece of their fur. Ground beetles can be caught in **pitfall traps** (plastic or glass jars, sunk into the ground, into which certain invertebrates stumble) and marked by placing a minute drop of waterproof paint on one of their hardened front wings (elytra).

The capture–recapture method is quite easy to apply, and can be the basis of some fascinating investigations. However, if quantitative conclusions are to be drawn you should realise that the method makes a number of major assumptions. For example, it only works if marking the animals doesn't affect the chances of their being caught a second time. Can you think of any other assumptions the method makes?

40.2 Population growth

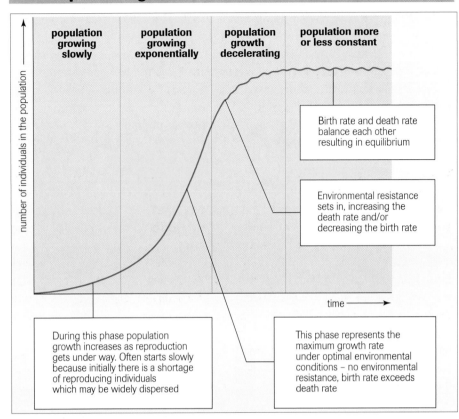

Figure 40.2 Generalised graph of population growth.

In the figure:

population growing slowly | **population growing exponentially** | **population growth decelerating** | **population more or less constant**

number of individuals in the population

time →

Birth rate and death rate balance each other resulting in equilibrium

Environmental resistance sets in, increasing the death rate and/or decreasing the birth rate

During this phase population growth increases as reproduction gets under way. Often starts slowly because initially there is a shortage of reproducing individuals which may be widely dispersed

This phase represents the maximum growth rate under optimal environmental conditions – no environmental resistance, birth rate exceeds death rate

Consider what happens if a few individuals enter an unoccupied area. Assuming there is enough food and that predation and disease are not too severe, reproduction will occur and the number of individuals will increase as shown in figure 40.2.

At first, there may be a **lag phase** as the individuals settle into their new environment. As reproduction gets under way, the population shows **exponential growth**. Suppose that over a unit of time the population doubles from 20 to 40 individuals. Then over the next unit of time, the population will increase from 40 to 80 individuals; over the next unit of time from 80 to 160 individuals, and so on. In other words, the population size *doubles* at regular intervals. During this exponential phase the population is said to grow **geometrically**. This is because the population sizes at successive time intervals form a geometric series (20, 40, 80, 160 in our example).

The exponential part of the growth curve takes place in environmental conditions that permit maximum population growth. During this phase there is little competition for food and space and the effects of predation and disease are slight. We can sum this up by saying that there is little **environmental resistance**. Under these circumstances the struggle for existence is not too severe, survival is high and the species realises its full reproductive potential.

Figure 40.3 shows exponential growth in a species of tree from over 9000 years ago. The abundance of the pine *Pinus sylvestris* is plotted as the density of pollen grains in peat samples of different ages. You can see that over the 500 years from 9500 BP (years before the present) to 9000 BP, the pollen density of the pine increased exponentially.

Exponential growth cannot go on forever, otherwise we would be knee-deep in aphids and the sea would be full of jellyfish! The great Swedish botanist Carl von Linné (Linnaeus) calculated what would happen if a plant produced only two seeds a year and then died, and these two seeds in turn matured and each produced two seeds, and so on. (Incidentally, no plant is as *un*productive as this.) Linnaeus found that in 20 years there would be over a million plants. You can check his calculation.

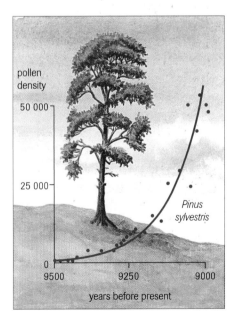

Figure 40.3 Exponential increase of pine trees in Norfolk, England over 9000 years ago. The density of pollen grains in peat samples taken from the bottom of Hockham Mere (a lake in Norfolk) gives a measure of the population size of the tree.

Even organisms that take a long time to reach maturity would eventually overpopulate the Earth if their numbers continued to grow exponentially. Charles Darwin calculated that a single pair of elephants would give rise to a total of 15 million descendants after five centuries.

In reality, exponential growth ceases as environmental resistance builds up. Eventually, as you can see in figure 40.2, the population reaches its maximum size. This is known as the **carrying capacity** for the particular environment in which the population occurs.

The curve in figure 40.2 is idealised. Populations rarely increase in such a regular manner. However, the pattern shown by this curve is important to our understanding of how populations change over time. It is called a **sigmoid curve** because its shape looks rather like an 's', the Greek letter *sigma*.

Extension

The mathematics of population increase

The sigmoid growth curve can be represented mathematically by the logistic equation:

$$\frac{dN}{dt} = rN\left(1 - \frac{N}{K}\right)$$

In this equation:

N is the population size;

t is time;

dN/dt is the rate at which the population is increasing;

K is the carrying capacity;

r is the intrinsic rate of increase.

The **intrinsic rate of increase** (r) equals the number of offspring born to each individual over a unit period of time when the population is growing exponentially. Suppose a pair of organisms can produce four offspring per year; then $r = 2 \text{ yr}^{-1}$ and the population will double in size each year if individuals die after reproducing.

To get to grips with this logistic equation, consider what happens when the population size is very small, relative to the carrying capacity of the environment. This means that $\frac{N}{K}$ is very small. Consequently $1 - \frac{N}{K}$ almost equals 1 and the equation for population growth reduces to:

$$\frac{dN}{dt} \approx rN$$

This is an equation for exponential growth, as we expect. Now, as the population builds up, $\frac{N}{K}$ gets bigger. Eventually N almost equals K, so that $\frac{N}{K}$ almost equals 1. Consequently $1 - \frac{N}{K}$ is very close to zero and the equation

for population growth reduces to:

$$\frac{dN}{dt} \approx 0$$

In other words, the population no longer increases in size but simply maintains itself. As we expect, the population levels off.

If time is plotted linearly along the horizontal axis, but population size is plotted logarithmically up the vertical axis, the exponential phase of population growth now falls on a straight line (*illustration 1*). This is called a **semi-logarithmic plot**, and is a useful way of identifying the period over which population growth is exponential (*illustration 2*).

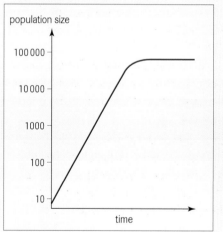

Illustration 1 A semi-logarithmic plot of the logistic equation. Time is plotted linearly (normally) along the horizontal axis, but population size is plotted logarithmically up the vertical axis. The result is that during the exponential phase of population increase the data fall on a straight line. As the population size approaches the carrying capacity of the environment, it begins to level off. A semi-logarithmic plot is therefore a useful way of seeing whether a population is increasing exponentially or not.

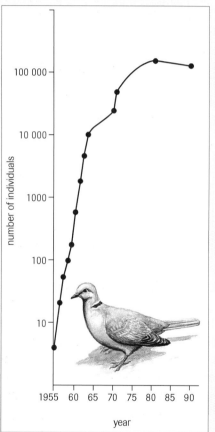

Illustration 2 A semi-logarithmic plot showing the population size of the collared dove in Great Britain since 1955. You can see how from 1955 till about 1965 the increase was exponential. Nobody knows why the collared dove has increased in numbers so tremendously. Until about 1930, the birds were restricted in Europe to Turkey and parts of Albania, Bulgaria and Yugoslavia. Then they reached Hungary in 1932, Czechoslovakia in 1936, Austria in 1938, Germany in 1943, the Netherlands in 1947, Denmark in 1948, Sweden and Switzerland in 1949, France in 1950 and Belgium and Norway in 1952. By the mid 1970s the birds had even reached the Faeroe Islands and Iceland.

Births, deaths, immigration and emigration

So far we have only considered births as a factor affecting population size. But the number of individuals in a population is affected by four factors: **births**, **deaths**, **immigration** and **emigration**. The change in the size of any population over a period of time can be summed by the equation:

Change in population size $= B + I - D - E$

where $B =$ births, $I =$ immigrations, $D =$ deaths and $E =$ emigrations.

Births and deaths are obviously important. However, immigrations and emigrations can be important too. During the Irish potato famine from 1845 to 1849 the potato harvest was devastated by potato blight. As a result, the population fell from almost 9 000 000 to about 6 500 000. About a million people died in the famine and about one and a half million emigrated, mostly to the USA.

Throughout this period, Irish farmers continued successfully to produce cereals, cattle, pigs, eggs and butter. All in all, enough food was produced to ensure that no one need have starved. However, farmers had to export these crops to England to get the money they needed to pay the rents they owed their English landowners. Farmers who failed to export their produce were evicted from their farms and had their cottages razed to the ground.

Environmental resistance

The pattern of population growth is much the same, irrespective of the species. The sigmoid growth curve in figure 40.2 is shown equally by bacteria on an agar plate, yeast cells in a flask of cider and rabbits when they were first introduced to Australia. However, the form that environmental resistance takes depends on the species in question.

Here are the main factors that make up environmental resistance and therefore limit the sizes of populations:

- **Lack of food or water** Probably all species have populations whose size is limited by insufficient food or water. Possible exceptions include some species of insects whose numbers may never build up to the point where food becomes limiting.

- **Lack of light** This is particularly important for the growth of plant populations both on land and in water. Even in the calmest and cleanest waters, enough light for photosynthesis cannot penetrate more than about 50 metres.

- **Lack of oxygen** Insufficient oxygen may limit the population size of some aquatic species. This is because oxygen diffuses much more slowly through water than through air. In most home aquaria the level of oxygen saturation of the water is well below 100 per cent even with an aerator pumping continuously.

- **Predators and parasites** The presence of organisms that prey on or parasitise a particular species may play a crucial role in keeping down the population of that species. Parasites are often more important than predators in this respect because, being small, they have high rates of natural increase and can respond quickly to changes in the numbers of their host. On the other hand, many parasites do not kill their host, whereas predators do.

- **Disease** This can be one of the most potent forces in checking the uncontrolled growth of populations. Diseases can spread more rapidly where large numbers of individuals are crowded together. This is why so much pesticide is used in intensive agriculture. A field of wheat is a paradise for mildews and rusts.

- **Lack of shelter** This may be shelter from predators or shelter from physical factors of the environment such as excessive heat.

- **Accumulation of toxic waste** The build-up of a high concentration of, for example, carbon dioxide and nitrogenous waste can limit the population growth of certain organisms, for example insect pests of stored grain.

Measuring the growth of microorganisms

Various techniques can be used to quantify the growth in population size of a microorganism.

For bacteria, **serial dilution** can be used. Here, samples are taken and successively (i.e. serially) diluted 10 times, 100 times, 1000 times and so on. Each of these samples is plated out onto an agar Petri dish. After incubation, the number of colonies is counted. It is assumed that each colony develops from a single bacterium.

Yeast cells are bigger than bacterial cells and can be counted directly under a light microscope using a special microscope slide called a **haemocytometer**. The slide is called a haemocytometer because it is normally used for carrying out blood cell counts. A sample of yeast cells whose population size one wishes to determine is mounted in the centre of the slide under a coverslip. This part of the slide has a known volume and is etched with a grid which enables the number of cells in the sample to be estimated.

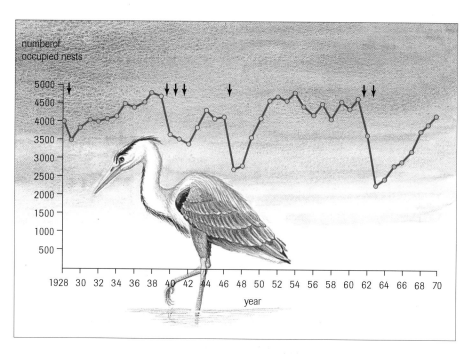

Figure 40.4 Bad winters significantly reduce the numbers of herons. The severest winters are arrowed.

■ **Stress** In some cases overcrowding causes excessive stress leading to abnormal behaviour. In some mice and voles stress leads to very high levels of certain hormones, notably adrenaline and adrenocorticotrophic hormone (ACTH), which may cause the animals to collapse and die.

■ **Weather and other catastrophes** Weather conditions, and climate generally, may drastically reduce populations. The effects are generally most severe for small organisms, but in a particularly bad winter the population sizes of even large species may decline significantly. The European heron relies on open water so that it can catch fish. In bad winters, when lakes are frozen over for long periods, herons may starve to death. Figure 40.4 shows the effects of bad winters on the numbers of herons breeding the following year in England and Wales. Other catastrophic effects include fire in dry scrub and grasslands, and landslides in mountainous rain forests.

Some of the factors listed above are **density independent**: their effectiveness is unrelated to the density of the population, i.e. to the number of individuals per unit of space. Others are **density dependent**: their effectiveness depends on the number of individuals in the population.

Density dependence means that the more individuals there are in the population, the greater the proportion of the population that dies or fails to reproduce.

Population regulation

Populations do not remain constant in size; they fluctuate. Figure 40.4 shows how heron numbers fall after bad winters but then recover. You can see, however, that although heron numbers vary, they do so between limits: from 1928 to 1970 there were always about 2500 to 5000 breeding pairs of herons in England and Wales.

Careful fieldwork has shown that the numbers of most species do not fluctuate widely and erratically. Instead they seem to lie near an equilibrium point which we can call the **norm** or **set point**. For a given species in a particular environment there is a certain equilibrium population which the environment can support. If the population rises above the set point, environmental resistance in the form of competition, predation or some other density-dependent factor reduces breeding or increases mortality to such an extent that the population falls. If the population falls below the set point, environmental resistance is temporarily relieved so that the population rises again (*figure 40.5*).

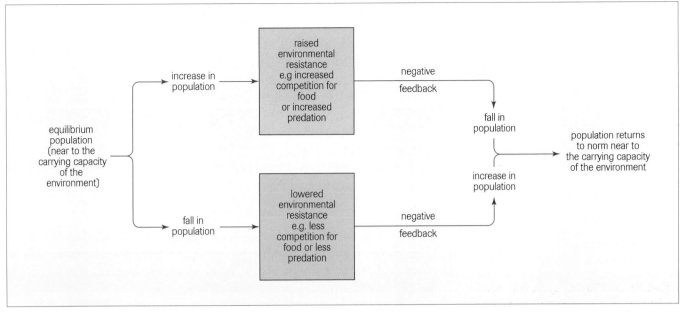

In the normal course of events, populations fluctuate on either side of the set point, but the regulatory processes described above prevent the fluctuations being excessively large. We have here an example of **homeostasis**, the principles of which are explained in Chapter 16. *An increase or decrease in population sets in motion processes which keep the population on an even keel.* This is an example of **negative feedback**, so called because an increase in the population above the norm leads to a decrease, while a decrease in the population leads to an increase. An apparent exception to this control process, though, is the human population.

Figure 40.5 Scheme summarising the homeostatic control of populations. The equilibrium population (norm) is the set point in a negative feedback process by which the population is kept more or less constant. Can you predict what effect a permanent change in the environmental resistance would have?

Growth of the human population

Figures for early human populations are difficult to come by, but archaeological and historical evidence suggest that there have been three major population explosions, each corresponding to a 'cultural revolution' which allowed more people to survive:

- The first human population explosion took place over 20 000 years ago and was probably associated with the use of tools which allowed improvements in hunting and food-gathering techniques (**tool-making revolution**).

- The second, some 10 000 to 6000 years ago, was brought about by improvements in farming and the widespread domestication of animals and plants (**agricultural revolution**).

- The third, which got underway about 300 years ago and is still in progress, has been caused by improvements in food production, industry and medicine (**scientific–industrial revolution**).

Each of these bursts was associated with a substantial rise in the population set point; the birth rate rose, the death rate fell and the population surged upwards towards a new level.

The current situation

Nowadays the world's population increases by some 250 000 people every day. Figure 40.6 shows how the world's population has increased over the last 2000 years. The increase is huge! The data have been plotted on a semi-logarithmic plot, so an exponential growth in population would be shown by a straight line (*page 692*). In fact, the curve bends upwards. That means that during the last 2000 years the human population has been increasing *faster* than exponentially.

Another way of putting this is to say that the time taken for the world's population to

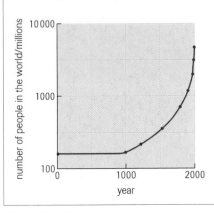

Figure 40.6 The world's human population size has increased hugely over the last 2000 years.

Part 7

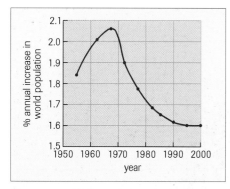

Figure 40.7 The annual percentage increase in the world's population. Since the late 1960s the rate at which the world's population is increasing has been slowing down. However, an annual increase of 1.6 per cent still means that the world's population doubles every 40 years.

Figure 40.8 World population distribution. Each dot stands for 100 000 people. The 10 most densely populated countries of the world (figures are people per km²) are Hong Kong (4174), Singapore (3825), Malta (950), Bangladesh (533), Mauritius (448), Taiwan (431), Puerto Rico (361), South Korea (345), Netherlands (339) and Belgium (319).

double has been decreasing. It took until the start of the 17th century for the world's population to double from what it was in New Testament times, approximately 250 million, to 500 million. However, it then doubled to 1000 million in under 250 years. It then doubled to 2000 million in about 100 years, and then to 4000 million in about 50 years.

A good way of seeing whether the population is growing exponentially over a relatively short period like this is to look at the **annual percentage increase in population**. These data are shown in figure 40.7. You can see that until the late 1960s the annual percentage increase was increasing. This means that the world's population was increasing more rapidly than exponentially.

However, since the 1970s the annual percentage increase has begun to fall, so that the population growth is now slower than exponential.

The future

It is too soon to be sure at what level the world's population is likely to stabilise. United Nations' projections suggest that by the year 2020 the world's population will be approximately 8000 million (eight billion), almost 35 per cent more than what it currently is (year 2000). By 2050 it should peak at around 9500 million.

At the moment, those countries in which the population is still growing most rapidly tend to be those in which the average income per person is low. Countries such as Britain, Japan and the USA have populations which are increasing less rapidly. These countries also have a high standard of living. Some people argue that the way to stabilise the world's population is to ensure that contraceptive methods are more widely available. Others maintain that a country does not stabilise its population until its economy has improved. Only then will its sanitation and medical services reduce child mortality sufficiently for people to be willing to have small families, i.e. for human fertility rates to fall significantly.

It is all too easy for developed countries to blame less developed countries for the world's population problem. In fact, developed countries often have more people per unit area of land than less developed countries (*figure 40.8*). The United Kingdom, for instance, has a population density of 230 people per square kilometre while Uganda has 68, Kenya 37 and Brazil 16. It can be argued that the less developed countries are now going through the population growth which countries in the West have already experienced.

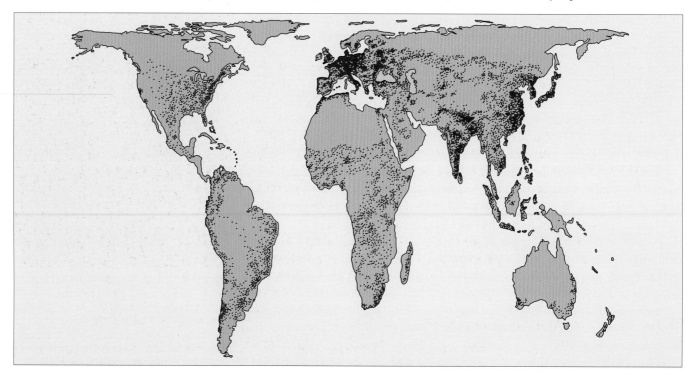

Two views about the human population

In 1948 an international congress was held at Cheltenham on world resources in relation to the family. Here are two views about the human population which were expressed at the meeting.

Sir John Boyd Orr

When Darwin came forward with the theory of the survival of the fittest, that seemed to prove that the best thing to do was to let these people die out. That argument has been used to me – 'Why reduce mortality? You only further overcrowd an already overcrowded planet'. I think you can take it, however, that if modern science is applied and Governments are willing to do it, we can feed and clothe and house as large a population as is likely to come in the next 50 or 100 years, and that is as far as we can see.

P. K. Whelpton

It seems to me that even in countries like the USA, the population is above the economic optimum; that is, we have more people even there than is most desirable from the standpoint of the natural resources which we possess. That does not mean that a rapid decrease in population would be desirable, but I think it does mean that if we would choose between a stationary population of say, 100 million and 150 million or 200 million we should without question be better off with the former.

Consider these two views in the light of events which have happened since 1948. (The population of the USA in 1998 was 275 million.)

Figure 40.9 Caterpillars of the cactus moth (*Cactoblastis cactorum*) eating the prickly pear cactus.

40.3 Biological control

Control of pest numbers with chemicals often has unfortunate consequences (*page 679*). An alternative is to use one species to control the numbers of another species. This is called **biological control**. The earliest recorded instance of this was around 2000 BC when the Chinese used ants to kill leaf-eating insects, thus protecting valuable crops. Here are two recent examples.

Control of the prickly pear cactus in Australia

The prickly pear cactus (*Opuntia*) is not native to Australia. As with so many of Australia's animals and plants, it was introduced into the country after the arrival of Europeans.

In 1840 a certain Dr Carlyle brought some specimens from America and planted them in his garden. They quickly ran wild and by the turn of the century had spread over more than four million hectares of land, rendering it unsuitable for agricultural use. By 1910 the cactus was spreading at a rate of nearly 400 000 hectares per year.

The Australian government responded by setting up a research programme to find an animal that would eat the prickly pear cactus. Studies were made of the species that attacked the plant in its native America, and in 1925 eggs of the moth *Cactoblastis cactorum* were introduced to Australia from Argentina (*figure 40.9*).

Fortunately this was a great success. The caterpillars ate the cacti and within a few years almost all of them had been destroyed (*figure 40.10*). Today the cactus and the moth coexist at low densities. Every now and again the population of the prickly pear flares up, only to crash again as the moth's numbers increase in response.

Myxomatosis and the control of rabbits

The rabbit is not native to Britain. It was introduced by the Romans, who liked eating it, but it then died out. It was reintroduced by the Normans, and this time it stayed.

Figure 40.10 The introduction of the cactus moth (*Cactoblastis cactorum*) devastated the prickly pear cactus in Australia.
Top Dense prickly pear in the Chinchilla area, Queensland, in 1926.
Bottom The same area three years later after biological control of the cactus by the moth.

Figure 40.11 Rabbits keep grassland vegetation short and prevent colonisation by shrubs and trees.

➤ Succession, page 665

Figure 40.12 A Large Blue butterfly. This butterfly went extinct in Britain as a consequence of myxomatosis.

For centuries the rabbit was thought beneficial: it provided valuable meat and its fur was widely used. However, by the 1950s its numbers had increased to between 60 and 100 million – more than one for every person in Britain. By then it was considered a pest, as it ate large quantities of wheat and other crops.

Myxomatosis is a disease caused by a virus that attacks a certain species of South American rabbit. The European rabbit belongs to a different genus from the South American rabbit but the myxomatosis virus can attack it with devastating results. The disease was first recorded in Britain in Kent on 13 October 1953. It is not known for certain how it got to Britain, but there is more than a suspicion that it was deliberately introduced by a farmer to reduce his crop losses. The consequences were remarkable. The disease spread like wild-fire. Within a couple of years 99 per cent of all British rabbits were dead.

Effect of the myxomatosis epidemic

To an ecologist, what is particularly interesting is the effect that myxomatosis had on the rest of the flora and fauna. It soon became clear that rabbits were responsible for maintaining much of the beautiful chalk grassland in lowland Britain. In the absence of rabbits, the grass, hitherto kept short by grazing, grew rampant, ousting many of the wild flowers. Shrubs and trees began to invade these areas as there were no rabbits to eat the young seedlings (*figure 40.11*).

The myxomatosis epidemic also affected many other species of animals. Hares increased in numbers, presumably because rabbits had previously competed with them for food. One might have expected predators such as foxes and buzzards to have crashed in numbers. However, for a few years after the introduction of the virus the numbers of such predators actually increased. This may have been because they fed on the large numbers of dead and dying rabbits. Studies have shown that later on foxes changed their diet to smaller animals such as voles, whose numbers had increased. Voles may have increased because of the growth of grass caused by the disappearance of the rabbit. Buzzards, however, were adversely affected in the long term: their numbers decreased by around 30 to 40 per cent.

The crash in rabbit numbers in 1953 also led to the extinction in Britain of the Large Blue butterfly some 30 years later (*figure 40.12*). The habitat for the Large Blue is south-facing slopes with short turf. The butterfly relies on wild thyme and the larvae of certain ants to complete its life cycle. Both the wild thyme and the ants are restricted to short grassland, and the reduction in the number of rabbits thus led eventually to the extinction of the butterfly. Attempts are now being made to restore the habitat and reintroduce the butterfly.

One thing we learn from the myxomatosis story is how difficult it is to predict the effects of introducing a biological control agent into a new area. Indeed, there have been many disastrous instances when attempts at biological control have gone wrong and an introduced species has wiped out a harmless native species. The approach of **integrated pest management** combines the best of both biological and non-biological methods.

40.4 **Fluctuating populations**

Rabbit and prickly pear numbers crashed because in each case an organism was introduced to control their populations. However, some species regularly decline in numbers without the introduction of a new predator or parasite.

Such a species is the Canadian lynx. This beautiful animal has long been trapped for its fur which is then turned into coats. Annual records of the numbers trapped were kept by the Hudson Bay Company from 1821 to 1934 and these numbers are shown graphically in figure 40.13.

Much to the surprise of the trappers they found that however hard they worked there were some years when lynx were hardly ever trapped. In other years, though, huge

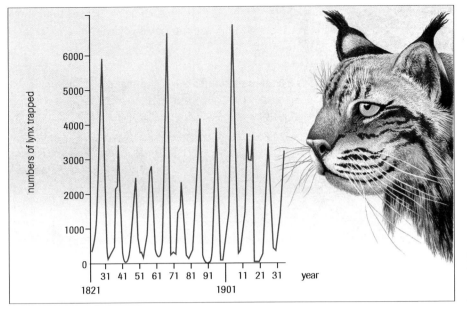

Figure 40.13 The number of lynx trapped for the Hudson Bay Company from 1821 to 1931. Notice how the numbers cycle, showing peaks every 10 years or so.

numbers were trapped. You can see from figure 40.13 that the numbers of lynx peak every 10 years or so. What could cause these large fluctuations?

In northern Canada, lynx feed mainly on snowshoe hares. When you look at the numbers of hares as well as the numbers of lynx, you find that the hares also go through a 10-year cycle (*figure 40.14*).

For many years it was thought that the cycles might be caused by the following sequence of events:

- When lynx numbers are low, few hares are eaten and so the number of hares increases greatly.

- The large number of hares allows lots of lynx to survive and reproduce, leading to a great increase in the number of lynx.

- There are now so many lynx that they eat most of the hares, causing the hare population to crash.

- The shortage of hares leads to many lynx starving and being unable to reproduce, leading to a crash in the number of lynx.

- Finally, the very low number of lynx allows the hare population to recover, causing the cycle to start again.

Unfortunately there is one thing wrong with this explanation. Certain islands off the east coast of Canada have hares but no lynx. On these islands the hares go through exactly the

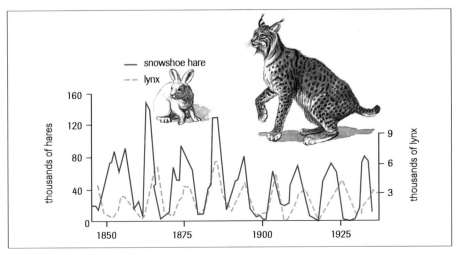

Figure 40.14 The numbers of snowshoe hares and lynx from 1845 to 1935 as shown by the number of pelts taken by the Hudson Bay Company. Notice the close correspondence between the two sets of numbers.

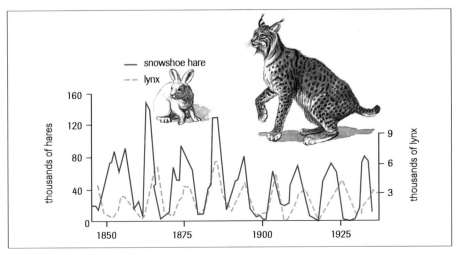

same sort of cycles that they do on the mainland of Canada, again with a periodicity of about 10 years! So the hare cycle is clearly not dependent on the number of lynx, at least not on the islands.

Scientists are still not certain why snowshoe hare numbers fluctuate in the way they do. It is known that when there are large numbers of hares, the plants they normally eat respond by producing shoots with high levels of toxins. These toxins make the shoots unpalatable to the hares. Maybe it is the plants that cause the hares to cycle. It certainly seems that changes in the numbers of hares cause the lynx cycles, even if the lynx are not responsible for the hare cycles.

40.5 Population pyramids and life expectancy

Any population consists of individuals that differ in age and sex. A **population pyramid** is a convenient way of showing this. Its shape can be used to make predictions about how a country's population size is likely to change in the future.

Figure 40.15 shows population pyramids for India and the USA in 1978. The broad base to the Indian population pyramid suggests that the population size will increase rapidly with more and more babies born each year. In fact the population size of India has increased substantially since 1978. However, another possible explanation for broad-based pyramids is that infant and child mortality is high.

The population pyramid for the USA in figure 40.15 is typical of a country with a fairly constant number of people. In fact the population size of the USA has increased since 1978. This is the result of a high birth rate, a low death rate and a high immigration rate.

You can see in figure 40.15 that the two halves of each pyramid are not quite symmetrical. In most developed countries women tend to live longer than men.

A person's **life expectancy** is the further number of years he or she can expect to live. Obviously this depends on the person's age and gender. Average life expectancies are used by insurance companies to calculate the premiums they charge on life insurance policies so that they can be confident of making a profit. Some insurance companies take into account their clients' life styles. You may have to pay more than the average if you smoke or have a history of heart disease, for instance.

Figure 40.15 Population pyramids for India and the USA in 1978. Notice that in India a far greater proportion of the population are children than in the USA.

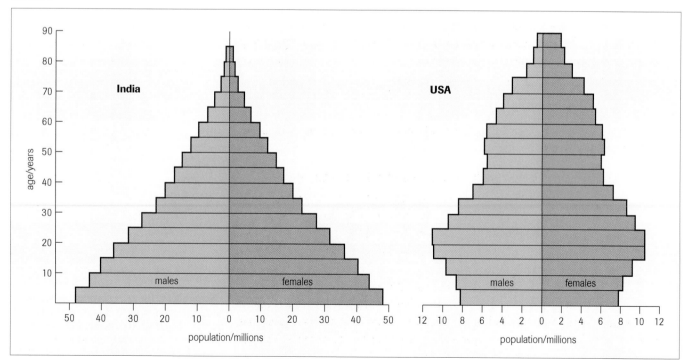

Survivorship curves

The chance an individual has of surviving to a given age can be shown by means of a **survivorship curve**. Imagine a population of 100 individuals born at the same time. A survivorship curve shows how many of them are likely to be alive at any particular age.

There are three main types of survivorship curves and these are shown in the illustration:

■ The upper curve is typical of organisms, such as ourselves, that have few young. After an initial period of relatively low juvenile mortality, mortality is very low until late in life.

■ The middle curve is found in many small birds. Notice that as the vertical axis is logarithmic, the curve actually shows an exponential decline in the number of individuals surviving over time.

■ The lower curve is typical of many plants and fish. Thousands or millions of young are produced, few of which mature into adults. The vast majority die as juveniles.

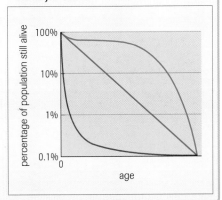

40.6 The niche concept

In 1934, the Russian biologist G.F. Gause published a book called *The Struggle for Existence*. In it he included the results of careful experiments he had carried out on two species of the unicellular ciliate *Paramecium* (*page 91*).

Gause found that he could easily keep *Paramecium caudatum* and *P. aurelia* in separate containers in his laboratory. However, when he tried to keep the two species in the same container, *P. caudatum* always died out after a few days.

The importance of Gause's experiments was not realised at the time. However, some 10 years later his results were seen in a new light by ecologists looking at the question of what allows different species to coexist in a habitat. Gause's results were put into a general statement called the **competitive exclusion principle**. This states that *two species cannot coexist in the same habitat unless there are significant differences in their ecologies*. In the case of Gause's two species of *Paramecium*, their ecologies were too similar. This meant that only one species could survive when they were kept together.

Another way of looking at Gause's competitive exclusion principle is to say that *each species has its own unique niche*. An organism's **niche** is what it *does* in its community. Niches are sometimes distinguished from habitats by saying that the habitat of an organism is its address, while its niche is its role in the community.

Describing the role of an organism is no easy task. For an animal, the most important aspect of its niche is usually its food. Describing the niche of a leopard, for instance, involves discovering, amongst other things, the sorts of prey on which leopards feed. This is called its **feeding niche**.

How can the competitive exclusion principle be tested?

To test the competitive exclusion principle, ecologists have looked at similar species that coexist to see whether differences can be found between their niches. For instance, many woods contain birds that seem to have very similar ecologies. However, if you study them carefully, you nearly always find that they feed on slightly different foods or build slightly different sorts of nests or have different parasites.

Some ecologists argue that these differences support Gause's competitive exclusion principle. Others are more suspicious. After all, if you look hard enough you are bound to find *some* differences between the ecologies of any two species. The important question is just how different do the niches of two species have to be to allow coexistence? There is considerable uncertainty about the answer to this question.

We can explore the significance of niches by considering red and grey squirrels in Britain.

The niches of red and grey squirrels

The red squirrel is native to Britain. Until the end of the 19th century it was found throughout the British Isles in both deciduous and coniferous woods. Nowadays it is largely confined to coniferous woods (*figure 40.16A*).

The reason for the red squirrel's decline is the introduction of the larger grey squirrel (*figure 40.16B*). During the 19th century, many attempts were made to introduce the grey squirrel to Britain from North America where it is native to deciduous forests. Exactly why people were keen to establish it in Britain is not entirely clear. One introduction was made by an American who released over 100 individuals in Richmond Park, Surrey. Perhaps he was homesick for them.

By the beginning of the 20th century, grey squirrels were firmly established in Britain. As they increased their range, the red squirrel became rarer. Today red squirrels are only found in coniferous woods, mixed woods dominated by conifers and on some islands which have never been colonised by the grey squirrel.

Exactly why the red squirrel has declined is still uncertain. However, it is not because the grey squirrels attack their red relatives. Rather, it may be an instance of Gause's competitive exclusion principle in action. It seems that the niches of the two squirrels are so similar that only one of them can survive in any one habitat. In most habitats the grey squirrel **out-competes** the red.

Figure 40.16
A Red squirrel feeding in a pine forest.
B Grey squirrel feeding in an oak wood.

Extension

How much food can we take from the wild?

Farmers cannot allow all their produce to be eaten. If they did, they would not be able to produce any food the next year. Some of the produce has to be kept back to 'seed' the next generation. This is true whether we are talking of arable farming such as wheat and rice or pastoral farming such as sheep and cows.

The same principle should hold when we obtain food from the wild. Too often humans have overhunted or overfished species to extinction or near extinction. So what, then, is the optimal harvest or catch? How can we decide how many fish or oysters or deer to catch so as to maximise the harvest without jeopardising the continuity of the population? Obviously this is an important number to know. It is called the **maximum sustainable yield**. Knowing it should make it possible for us to manage ecosystems to provide resources in a sustainable fashion.

Look at the left-hand graph in the illustration. It shows that the numbers of births and deaths in a population depends on the population size. When the population size is very small, the numbers of births and deaths will also be very small, though obviously there will be more births than deaths as the population grows. As the population increases, the difference between the number of births and the number of deaths also increases. However, as the population size approaches the carrying capacity (K) the number of deaths starts to catch up with the number of births.

The right-hand graph shows the *same* information in a different form. The difference between the number of births and the number of deaths is called the **net recruitment** to the population. This is plotted as a function of the population size. You can see that at a population size somewhere between 0 and K, the net recruitment reaches a maximum. This population size is the optimum if you wish to maximise the sustainable yield of the population.

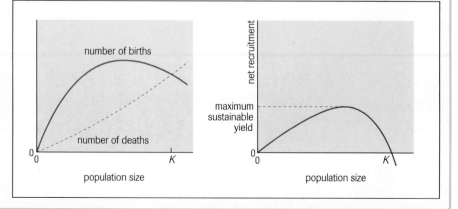

So much for the theory. Unfortunately, the political difficulties in setting quotas in line with scientific predictions are immense. For example, each year scientists advise the European Union on the fishing quotas that should be set for the following year. Almost invariably the actual quotas set exceed the levels recommended by scientists for a sustainable harvest.

Why do you think the governments of the European Union rarely accept the scientific advice on fishing quotas?

Extension

Fisheries and fish farming

Fishing is an example of harvesting from a natural ecosystem. With improvements to fishing vessels has come the need for regulation to try to prevent **over-fishing**. Over-fishing occurs when the number of fish caught from a population exceeds the maximum sustainable yield of that population (*extension box on previous page*).

Ways to regulate fishing include having:

■ **mesh size restrictions**, to prevent young fish from being caught;

■ **quotas**, to control the total number of fish caught each year;

■ **close seasons**, i.e. times of each year during which fishing is illegal;

■ **exclusion zones**, i.e. areas from where no fish are permitted to be taken.

Despite such regulations, more and more of the world's natural fisheries have been over-fished. Partly in response to this, **fish farming** is growing in importance. Such farming can take place in either open or closed systems, depending on the extent to which the water in which the farmed fish live circulates freely with 'natural' water, whether fresh water or marine.

The main advantages of fish farming are that the fish are easy to catch (!) and that productivity can be greatly enhanced by providing the fish with added food. However, there are disadvantages:

■ The fish live at unnaturally high densities so diseases spread easily.

■ The combination of added food and pesticides (to treat the diseases) can have a profound effect on the local ecology.

■ There are fears that if genetically engineered fish start to be kept, they may escape and breed with their wild relatives.

Summary

1. A **population** is a collection of individuals that breed with one another and are reproductively isolated from other individuals of the same species.

2. After a **lag phase** a population may grow **exponentially** before reaching a **norm** or **set point** about which it then fluctuates.

3. Populations may change in size as a result of **births**, **deaths**, **immigrations** and **emigrations**.

4. Populations are prevented from growing indefinitely by **environmental resistance** which may take many forms.

5. The **carrying capacity** of a habitat is the maximum number of individuals of a species that it can sustain over a long period of time.

6. There are approximately 6000 million people alive today – more than at any previous time in our history. Each day the world's population increases by about 250 000 people.

7. Until recently the world's human population was growing faster than exponentially. However, since the late 1960s the rate of increase has declined, giving some hope that the world's population may eventually level off.

8. **Biological control** is achieved when humans use one species to keep down the numbers of another species. Attempts at biological control sometimes have unforeseen and undesirable consequences.

9. Two successful instances of biological control are the use of the moth *Cactoblastis cactorum* to control the numbers of prickly pear cactus in Australia, and the use of the myxomatosis virus to control the numbers of rabbits both in Australia and in Britain.

10. Some populations fluctuate in size on a cyclical basis. Ecologists still do not fully understand why.

11. **Population pyramids** show the age composition of a population. They can help to indicate whether the population has been increasing or decreasing in size and what is likely to happen in the future.

12. Gause's **competitive exclusion principle** states that two species cannot coexist in the same habitat unless they differ sufficiently in their ecologies.

13. The **niche** of a species describes the role of that species in its community.

For general advice on these questions and advice on answering essay-type questions, see pages vii and viii.

1. The diagram represents four ways in which changes can take place in the number of organisms in a population.

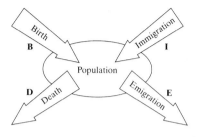

(a) Explain what is meant by a population. (1)

(b) Use the letters **B**, **I**, **D** and **E** to write a formula to show

   (i)   a stable population which is in equilibrium;

   (ii)   a population which is increasing in size. (2)

(c) The size of a population may be limited by density-dependent factors or density-independent factors. Explain how these two types of factor operate to limit population size. (2)

(Total 5 marks)

NEAB 1998

2. (a) Describe how biological control of one named pest is achieved. (3)

(b) Give two advantages of using biological control rather than pesticides to control insect pests. (2)

(Total 5 marks)

NEAB 1996

3. The wren is a small, insect-eating bird. The percentage change in size of the wren population from one year to the next was estimated over a number of years. The number of days with snow lying in the previous winter was also recorded. This information is shown on the graph.

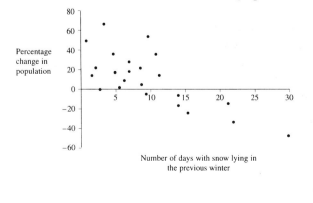

(a) (i) Describe the relationship between the number of days with snow lying and the change in population size. (2)

   (ii)   Suggest and explain a reason for this relationship. (2)

(b) A comparison was made between the number of breeding pairs of wrens each year and their breeding success.

Number of breeding pairs of wrens/millions	Percentage increase in population size
1.2	55
2.5	435
23.9	25

Suggest an explanation for the relationship between the size of the breeding population and breeding success. (2)

(Total 6 marks)

NEAB 1997

4. The diagram shows population pyramids as percentage distribution by age for Algeria and Sweden in 1955.

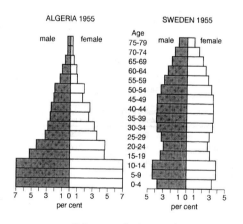

The percentage of the population under 15 years of age in Sweden was 23%.

(a) With reference to the diagram,

   (i)   calculate the percentage of the total population in Algeria that was also under 15 years of age; (1)

   (ii)   outline the consequences of a large percentage of under 15 year olds in a country such as Algeria. (3)

(b) Suggest what the future consequences could be for a country with an age population pyramid similar to that for Sweden in 1955. (3)

(Total 7 marks)

UCLES 1997

There are many situations in which individual organisms form close associations with one another. Such associations may occur within the same species (**intraspecific associations**) or between different species (**interspecific associations**). Either way, the environment of each individual is profoundly influenced by the presence of the other.

Intraspecific associations, involving communication, mating behaviour, aggression and parent–offspring behaviour, form the basis of **social organisation**. They are dealt with in the chapter on behaviour. In this chapter we shall look mainly at interspecific associations, concentrating on how the ecology of one species shapes the ecology of the other.

▶ Behaviour, page 436

First, though, we must define what is meant by the biotic environment because an organism's interspecific associations form part of its biotic environment.

41.1 Biotic environment

In Chapter 37 the physical environment of an organism was defined as the sum of the non-living factors that influence that organism – factors such as climate, soil and topography. The **biotic environment**, on the other hand, is the sum of the living factors that influence the organism.

Consider a female red deer (*figure 41.1*). Her biotic environment includes other red deer with which she interacts, such as her offspring, any males with which she mates, and other red deer with which she spends her time. These individuals are all members of her species. However, her biotic environment also includes the plants on which she feeds, the mites, ticks, flies and other parasites that bother her, the golden eagles that may carry off her young, and the soil organisms that will decompose her body when she dies.

Figure 41.1 Red deer hind with calf. How many features of the hind's biotic environment can you see in this picture?

Intimate associations

Intimate associations are found when the body of one organism (called the **host**) serves as the habitat for another organism. The host may be the only habitat in or on which the organism can survive or reproduce, in which case the association is described as **obligatory**. If the host is not essential, the association is described as **facultative**.

In these intimate associations we can see with particular clarity the workings of natural selection. No one looking at how a tapeworm is adapted to living in the intestine of its host can fail both to be horrified yet intrigued by the way in which all aspects of its anatomy, physiology and ecology are geared to its way of life.

The general term used to describe intimate associations between pairs of species is **symbiosis** which, loosely translated from the Greek, means 'living together'. Some older books restrict the term symbiosis to cases where the association benefits both species. However, most ecologists nowadays use symbiosis in its wider sense and divide the term into three categories distinguished by the consequences of the association to each party.

- **Parasitism** Here one organism, the **parasite**, lives in or on the other organism, the host, for at least part of its life cycle. The parasite, which is smaller than its host, benefits from the relationship at the expense of the host.

- **Commensalism** In this case, one of the two organisms, usually the smaller, benefits from the association, while the other organism neither loses nor gains.

- **Mutualism** Here the association benefits both participants, i.e. the gain is mutual.

Part 7

Intimate associations between species

How do we decide if a particular association is a case of mutualism, parasitism, predation or herbivory? Guest author Geoffrey Harper reflects on these four terms.

Assuming that in an intimate association one species always benefits, we can see that the four terms tell us something about the other species. They tell us whether it also benefits (mutualism) or is harmed (parasitism) or given the chop (predation).

You might think that these terms are easy to use, but consider a horse grazing on grass (herbivory): the grass plant has its leaves eaten, presumably making it worse off than if they were not, yet the horse may at the same time be killing off the grass plant's competitors, by grazing or trampling, so benefiting the grass. A tree may have mycorrhizal fungi associated with its roots which can benefit the tree in poor soil, while the same fungi may be parasitic where the soil is more fertile. Individual microorganisms in a cow may be killed and digested, but the microorganism population continues to thrive.

Even if we were clear what 'harm' and 'benefit' mean in biological terms, it is often difficult to measure them. In the case of many lichens, for example, it is not obvious whether the relationship is mutualistic or whether the fungus is parasitic on the alga.

The four terms we have been discussing are arranged along the horizontal harm/benefit axis of the illustration. Vertically, the examples are distributed according to the intimacy of the relationship, ranging from permanent intracellular contact at the top to no physical contact at all at the bottom. In the illustration, just a few examples have been plotted, and in each pair of species the larger organism always benefits.

Which of the two axes is more 'important' to the organisms themselves? The question is vague, but can be improved by adding 'as seen in the organisms' adaptations to the association'. Grass leaves are adapted to grazing by growing continuously at the base, and the plants are strongly rooted. Bees' mouth parts are adapted for obtaining nectar from flowers, and there are pollen baskets on their legs. Fig wasps can recognise fig trees.

All these adaptations are directly related to the kind of contact between the associated species, and probably would be little different if the grass, flowers and figs did not benefit. If this seems to be a general rule – and you can check it by thinking about other adaptations in intimate associations – it would suggest that whether an association is mutualistic, parasitic or whatever is less important than the intimacy.

Dr Harper, formerly research zoologist and Head of Biology at Watford Grammar School, is now a freelance scientific writer and translator.

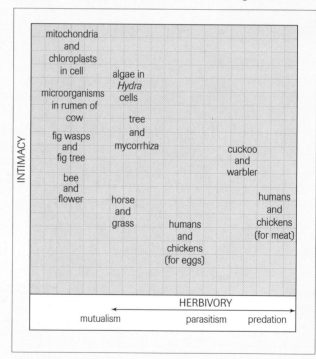

41.2 Parasitism

The association between a parasite and its host can be of two types:

- **Ectoparasites** live on the surface of the host. An example is provided by the ticks in figure 41.2.

- **Endoparasites** live inside the host. An example is the parasite that causes sleeping sickness (*figure 41.3*).

Parasitism is tremendously important. Most species, including humans, harbour parasites. Parasites may have a major impact on their hosts, reducing their health and in some cases causing their death.

We shall look at several parasites and then draw some general conclusions about how parasites are adapted to their way of life and how their hosts respond to their presence.

Figure 41.2 Parasitic ticks on a mammal. Ticks have specially adapted mouth parts which enable them to feed on the host's blood.

Potato blight

Potato blight is caused by a fungus-like organism called *Phytophthora infestans* whose life cycle is shown in figure 41.4.

The parasite overwinters in infected potato tubers as a system of slender, branched threads called a **mycelium**. The individual threads are called **hyphae**. In the spring, the hyphae grow through the tubers and, on reaching the air, they branch into tree-like **aerial hyphae** which bear asexual reproductive structures called **sporangia** at their tips. The sporangia are small, pear-shaped bodies which – being light – are readily dispersed by wind or rain. When a sporangium lands on a wet potato leaf it may burst open, releasing about six motile **zoospores**. Equipped with a pair of flagella, the zoospores swim through the water on the surface of the leaf. They then settle down and send out hyphae which may penetrate the leaf cuticle or enter through a stoma.

Once inside the potato plant, the hyphae spread rapidly through the plant. They grow between the cells of the host, obtaining nourishment by sending out short side branches which penetrate the cellulose walls of the host cells (*figure 41.5*). They gain entrance by secreting the enzyme **cellulase** at their tips. Once the cell wall has been breached, finger-like **haustoria** are produced. These secrete enzymes which cause the plasma membrane to leak. Substances leaked from the host cell are absorbed by the haustoria and passed back to the rest of the mycelium, allowing further growth to take place.

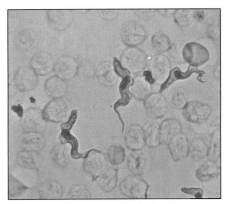

Figure 41.3 Light micrograph of a trypanosome in a human blood smear. This particular form is *Trypanosoma gambiense* which causes acute sleeping sickness in humans. Trypanosomes are flagellated protoctists that live in the bloodstream. Precisely why they are so dangerous is still not known for certain. It is possible that the immune system over-reacts to the infection. At any rate, sleeping sickness is frequently fatal if untreated, though it may take several years for the victim to die.

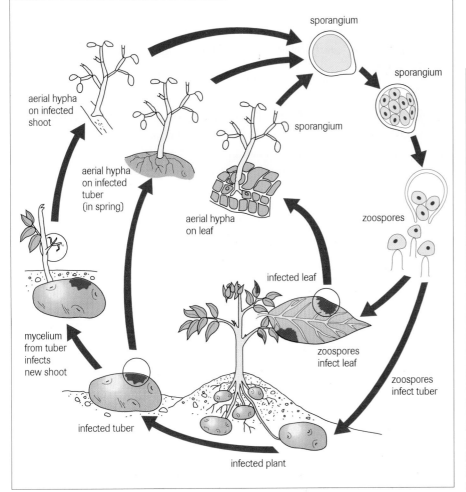

Figure 41.4 Life cycle of the organism that causes potato blight, *Phytophthora infestans*. The disease is transmitted by sporangia which produce motile zoospores. These can infect either the leaves or the tubers of potato plants, sending out hyphae which grow through the host's tissues. Sporangia are formed at the tips of hyphae which grow out of the tubers, seedlings and adult potato plants.

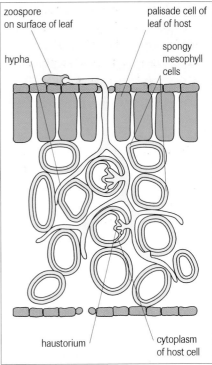

Figure 41.5 *Phytophthora infestans* is partly intercellular and partly intracellular. Specialised haustoria allow the organism to obtain its nutrients from the cells of its host, the potato plant. Haustoria are here seen attacking the spongy mesophyll cells in the leaf. They penetrate the cell walls (yellow) and then absorb nutrients from the cytoplasm (blue).

The success of this parasite is due to its combination of rapid intercellular growth coupled with intracellular feeding and mass production of sporangia. Infection can rapidly turn a healthy potato plant into a black, putrid mass. Eventually sporangia are produced and new plants become infected. In most countries reproduction is almost always asexual. In some countries, however, separate plus and minus strains are found and sexual reproduction can take place between these strains.

Potato blight is found in most parts of the world where potatoes are grown. When the weather is warm (16–22°C) and moist (80–100 per cent relative humidity) the disease can cause the total destruction of an entire potato crop within a week. The disease swept through Ireland in the late 1840s and was responsible for the death of about a sixth of the people living there (*page 693*). Thankfully it is now relatively easy to control.

How potato blight is controlled

Infected potato tubers should be burnt and only disease-free potatoes should be used for 'seed'. Chemical sprays can also play an important role. Traditionally these were based on copper, as fungal and related parasites are especially sensitive to copper. Copper, however, is toxic to a wide range of other organisms and nowadays a variety of non-copper chemicals is available. In many countries farmers receive advice from meteorological stations so that they can spray in advance of warm, moist weather.

Plant-breeding programmes have produced resistant varieties of potato plant which are less susceptible to the parasite than older traditional varieties. However, no variety is completely immune to potato blight. *Phytophthora* has a short generation time and produces enormous numbers of offspring. As a result, despite the frequent absence of sexual reproduction, natural selection is working to produce new strains better able to infect their hosts.

Malaria

Malaria is probably the world's most important disease with approximately 250 million people suffering from it, of whom about two million die each year. Most deaths occur in children under the age of six. Usually adults survive, though they often continue to suffer periodic attacks for a number of years.

Describing the disease is complicated by the fact that no fewer than four different species can cause it. All are members of the genus *Plasmodium*, sporozoans in the kingdom Protoctista. The most common is *P. vivax* which thankfully is less dangerous than the next most widespread species, *P. falciparum*. The other two species are *P. malariae* and *P. ovale*.

Although the four different species have fundamentally the same life cycle, the diseases they produce differ significantly. For example, the fever produced by *P. falciparum* is worse than that produced by *P. vivax*.

For the parasite to complete its life cycle, two hosts are required: a human and a mosquito in the genus *Anopheles*. Only female mosquitoes bite humans, and so spread malaria. Females use protein from human blood for manufacturing their eggs. When an infected female mosquito pierces the skin with her proboscis, she is searching for a capillary. At the same time saliva from her salivary glands is injected into the bloodstream. The saliva contains an **anticoagulant** which stops the blood clotting until the mosquito has finished her meal. Unfortunately, from our perspective, when the mosquito injects her saliva she will, if infected, also inject a large number of malarial parasites which at this stage are slender cells called **sporozoites**.

Within about 30 minutes these cells make their way via the bloodstream to the liver (*figure 41.6*). Here, each sporozoite gives rise asexually to up to 1000 or more cells called **merozoites** (*figure 41.7*). This remarkable process, called **schizogony**, is described on page 470. The merozoites are released from the liver cell and may then attack red blood

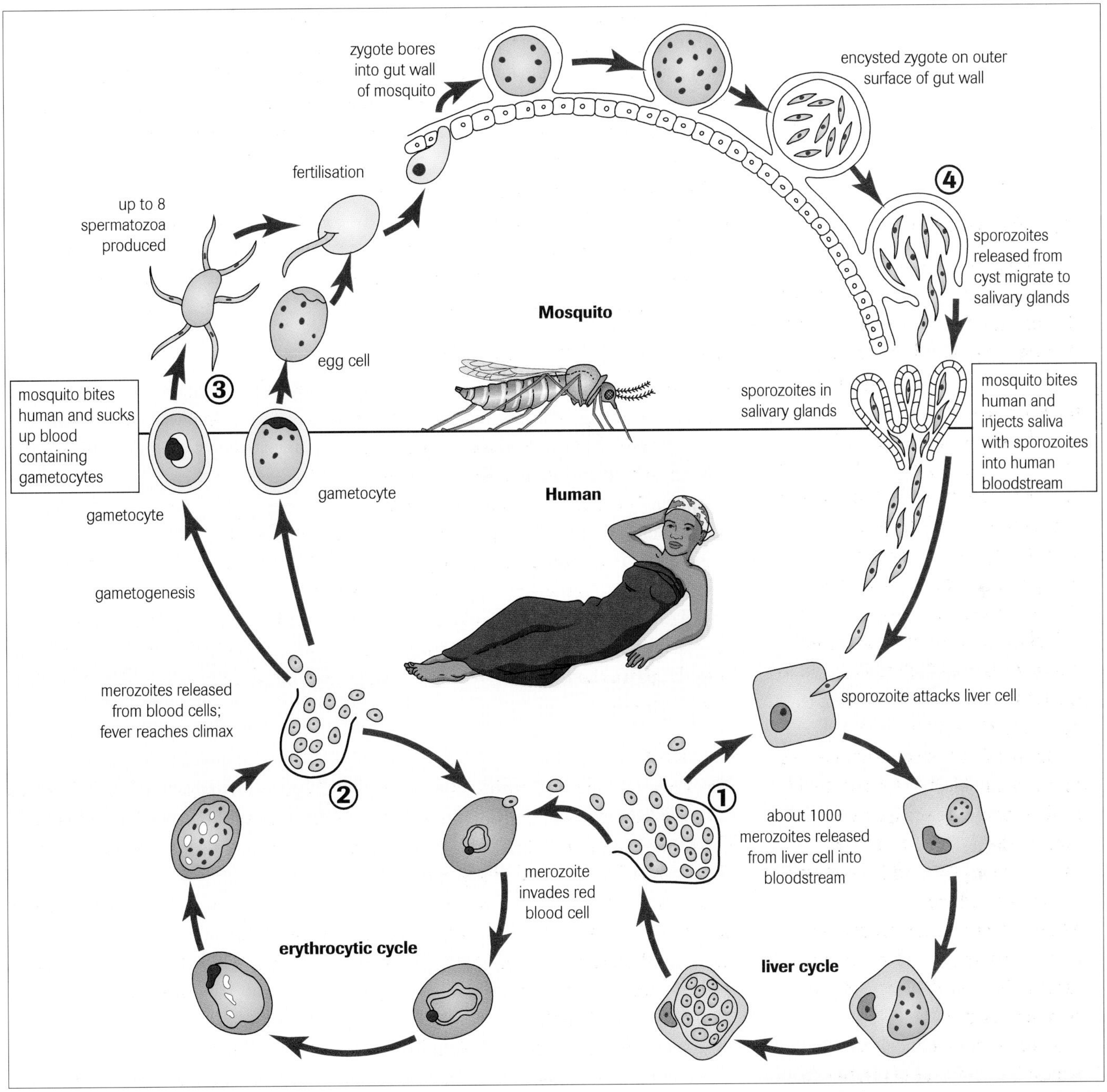
zygote bores
into gut wall
of mosquito
encysted zygote on outer
surface of gut wall
fertilisation
4
up to 8
spermatozoa
produced
sporozoites
released from
cyst migrate to
salivary glands
Mosquito
egg cell
sporozoites in
salivary glands
mosquito bites
human and sucks
up blood
containing
gametocytes
3
mosquito bites
human and
injects saliva
with sporozoites
into human
bloodstream
gametocyte
gametocyte
Human
gametogenesis
merozoites released
from blood cells;
fever reaches climax
sporozoite attacks liver cell
2
1
about 1000
merozoites released
from liver cell into
bloodstream
merozoite
invades red
blood cell
erythrocytic cycle
liver cycle

Figure 41.6 Life cycle of the malarial parasite showing the four stages where reproduction occurs (numbered 1 to 4).

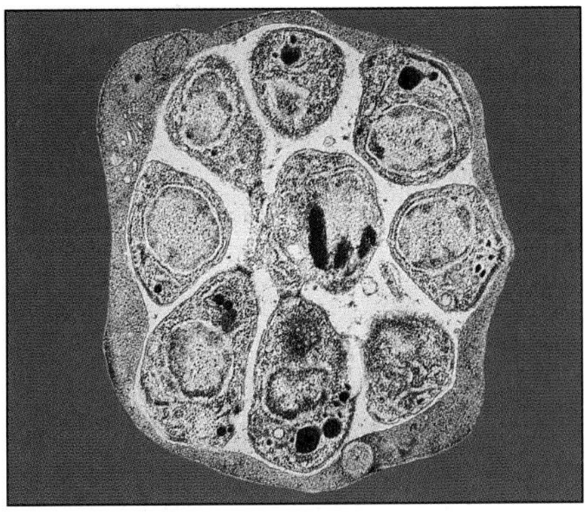

Figure 41.7 Electron micrograph showing merozoites of the malarial parasite *Plasmodium falciparum* in a human liver cell. Magnification × 1200.

cells. (In certain *Plasmodium* species, but not *P. vivax*, some of these merozoites may also attack other liver cells.)

Once inside a red blood cell, further asexual reproduction takes place and the products are released and then attack further red blood cells. As the infection progresses, the asexual stages in the red blood cells become synchronised so that a blood sample taken at any one time shows most of the parasites at the same stage of development. Because of the synchronous release of merozoites from countless red blood cells, the person suffering from malaria goes through a characteristic cycle of symptoms which correspond to different stages in this so-called **erythrocytic cycle**.

After several generations, some of the merozoites develop into sexual forms (**gametocytes**). These develop no further until taken up by an *Anopheles* mosquito. In the mosquito's gut, the male gametocyte produces up to eight **sperm** while the female gametocyte develops into a single **egg**. Fertilisation then takes place and diploid **zygotes** are formed. These burrow into the wall of the mosquito's gut where they form wart-like **cysts**. Within these cysts, meiosis takes place, followed by asexual reproduction. The result is that typically 10 000 haploid sporozoites are released from each cyst. Many of these sporozoites then migrate to the mosquito's salivary glands ready to be injected into the next human she bites.

Extension

Combating malaria

To control any parasite, the life cycle must be broken. Malaria has traditionally been combated in three ways:

- by attacking the parasite itself;
- by eliminating its vector, the mosquito;
- by preventing the vector from biting humans.

The third of these options, protection from the vector, is the most straightforward. **Mosquito nets** can be used or, more simply, the risks of infection may be reduced by keeping away from places with standing water and by staying indoors at dawn and dusk, when most species of anopheline mosquito are most active. For tourists, **insect-repellents** are valuable.

The mosquito may be attacked in a number of ways. Traditionally, **draining potential breeding grounds** has been used. This technique was extensively employed in historical times throughout much of Europe. The expense and difficulties involved are an indication of the seriousness of the disease.

More recently, a variety of **insecticides** has been used, notably DDT. Two problems have been found with the widespread use of insecticides. One is that the mosquitoes evolve resistance, requiring ever higher doses or the application of new pesticides to kill them. The second is that many insecticides do more harm than good, either killing insects beneficial to humans or becoming concentrated in

food chains and harming carnivores (*page 679*).

Another technique is to **spray the breeding grounds with oil**. The oil is taken into the breathing tubes of the larvae and kills them. There have also been attempts at **biological control**, for instance by introducing guppies which eat the mosquito larvae. However, biological control has not proved as effective as was hoped.

Drugs against malaria

For over 300 years it has been widely known that the drug **quinine**, obtained from the bark of the cinchona tree (*Cinchona ledgeriana*) can cure malaria. The tree gets its name from the Countess of Chinchon. The story is told of how the Countess caught malaria while in Peru in about 1640. She was given the bark of a local tree by her physician and experienced a miraculous cure. As a result some of the tree bark was carried back to Spain and used to cure others of malaria. Unfortunately for the story, recent historical research has shown that while the Countess was in Peru she was in remarkably good health and never suffered from malaria.

Whatever the origins behind its discovery, quinine remained the only drug against malaria until the interruption of transatlantic shipping by the Germans during the First World War prompted North American research into alternatives. By now a number of other drugs have been developed, though

quinine is still widely used. Such drugs form the basis of 'malaria tablets' which can be taken by tourists when visiting malaria-infested regions.

A vaccine against malaria?

It is hoped that an effective **vaccine** against malaria can be developed. So far this has proved extremely difficult. Among the problems are the fact that, as we have seen, four different species of *Plasmodium* can cause the disease, and the sporozoites take only 30 minutes to infect a liver cell once they have entered their host. Further, it seems that the parasite has a high rate of mutation and new strains are always evolving.

However, in 1999 successful trials of a malaria vaccine were reported using rabbits as an experimental system. The new vaccine targets the most dangerous *Plasmodium* species, *P. falciparum*.

By examining blood from children who develop natural immunity to malaria caused by this species of *Plasmodium*, the research team found that several specific regions of the parasite's proteins were most likely to be recognised and attacked by the children's antibodies. These proteins come from the various stages of the parasite's life cycle in a human. The researchers then created an artificial gene to make a protein with all these specific regions. Injecting the protein made by this gene into the rabbits resulted in an excellent immune response, exactly what is wanted for a successful vaccine.

Parasitic adaptations

The parasitic way of life is a precarious one. For example, a parasite needs to have a way of locating its host, must be able to prevent rejection by its host, and must be able to spread to new hosts. Parasites show many different ways of overcoming these problems, depending on whether they are ectoparasites or endoparasites.

▨ Many endoparasites show **degeneration or loss of certain organs**. They may lack sense organs, particularly eyes, and frequently have a reduced nervous system. Gut parasites like the tapeworm lack an alimentary canal, though their free-living relatives have one. Endoparasites that wallow in their host's body fluids often lack osmoregulatory devices.

▨ Some parasites have **penetrative devices** for gaining entrance into the host and its cells. The miracidium larva of the liver fluke, for example, has a slender tip on to which opens a group of glands which secrete tissue-digesting enzymes (*figure 41.8*). By softening the tissues, these enzymes enable the larva to bore into the foot of a freshwater snail, the intermediate host.

We have already seen how *Phytophthora*, the organism that causes potato blight, secretes **cellulase** at the tips of its hyphae thereby enabling it to penetrate the cell walls of its host. Many parasitic fungi also produce cellulase, while related enzymes are produced by a number of parasitic bacteria.

▨ Many parasites, especially ectoparasites, have **attachment devices** for clinging to the host. For instance, many species of trematode inhabit the gill passages of fish. The constant flow of water over the gills would sweep them away were it not for **suckers**, **hooks** or **anchors** which enable them to cling to the epithelium. Hooks and suckers are also used for attachment of the scolex of the tapeworm *Taenia taeniformis* to the wall of the cat gut (*figure 41.9*).

▨ Gut parasites live in a particularly hazardous environment. They have various **protective devices** which prevent them being harmed by the host's digestive processes. These devices include the possession of a thick, protective **cuticle**, the secretion of large quantities of **mucus** and the production of **inhibitory substances** which locally inactivate the host's digestive enzymes.

▨ It is not only gut parasites that must protect themselves against the host's defence mechanisms. The blood fluke *Schistosoma*, responsible for the human disease bilharzia, synthesises chemicals which **switch off the host's immune system**: the parasite coats itself with molecules which the host recognises as 'self'.

▨ One of the greatest problems facing any parasite is getting from one host to another. As parasites are often specific to only one species of host, a possible strategy for an animal parasite is to **wait until the host mates**. The various organisms responsible for sexually transmitted diseases in humans spread in this manner.

▨ A related strategy is to **pass from mother to offspring**. Again, the organisms responsible for a number of sexually transmitted diseases in humans can spread this way, including those that cause gonorrhoea and AIDS. In gonorrhoea, the bacterium can pass from mother to offspring during birth. In AIDS, the causative agent, HIV, can cross the placenta and may be found in breast milk.

▨ Many parasites employ a **secondary** or **intermediate host** which conveys the parasite from one **primary host** to another. Thus the *Anopheles* mosquito transfers the malarial parasite *Plasmodium* from one human to another. (Of course, from the mosquito's point of view, it might be argued that we are the secondary hosts and they the primary ones!) An organism, such as the mosquito, which carries a parasite from one primary host to another is called a **vector**.

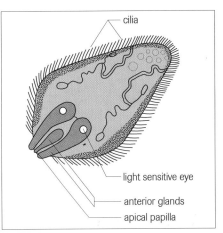

Figure 41.8 Miracidium larva of the liver fluke *Fasciola hepatica*. The cilia enable the larva to swim through water to the intermediate host, a snail. The protrusible apical papilla adheres to the snail's foot and a secretion from the anterior glands dissolves the flesh, thereby permitting the larva to penetrate. The larva then wriggles through the snail's tissues by contraction of circular and longitudinal muscles in its body wall.

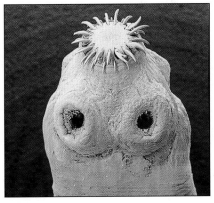

Figure 41.9 Attachment devices of *Taenia taeniformis*, a parasitic tapeworm found in cats. The head (scolex) is buried in the gut wall which it grips by means of its hooks and suckers. Magnification ×25.

▶ Sexually transmitted infections, pages 505–6

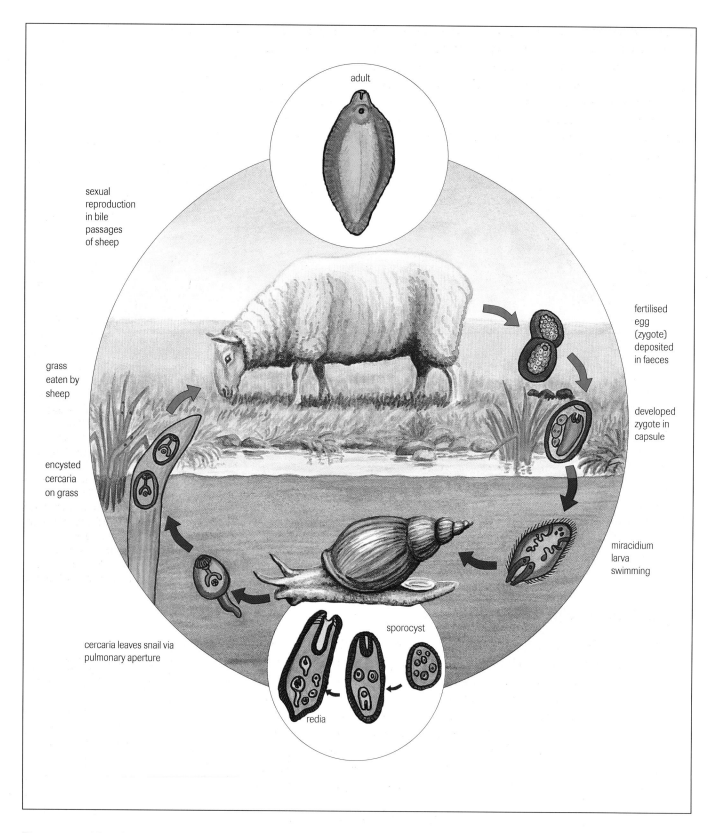

Figure 41.10 Life cycle of the liver fluke *Fasciola hepatica*. The adult fluke lives in the bile passages of sheep where it reproduces sexually, producing numerous encapsulated zygotes. The ciliated miracidium larva emerges from the capsule and, swimming through water on the ground, penetrates the fleshy foot of the snail *Limnaea truncatula* where it turns into a sporocyst. Inside the sporocyst special propagatory cells divide to form rediae larvae which burrow into the liver of the snail, feeding on the tissues. Inside each redia, propagatory cells give rise to either more rediae or numerous cercariae larvae. The latter usually work their way to the mantle cavity and leave the snail via its pulmonary aperture, encysting on blades of grass. If and when it is eaten by a sheep, the cyst bursts open, releasing a small immature fluke which migrates from the host's gut to its liver. Here it feeds and grows to maturity, thus completing the cycle.

Infection of new hosts is a hazardous business for a parasite. To raise the probability of success **vast numbers of offspring** are produced. The reproductive powers of many parasites are phenomenal. Countless millions of wind-dispersed spores may be produced by a single parasitic fungus, and figure 41.6 on page 709 gives some idea of the reproductive powers of the malarial parasite. You can see that reproduction occurs at no less than four stages in the life cycle, two of them in the human host and two in the mosquito. In the type of malaria caused by *Plasmodium vivax*, the number of parasites in the blood may exceed 30 000 per mm³.

Endoparasites with a primary and secondary host may have a succession of structurally distinct **larval stages**, each allowing rapid asexual multiplication in a different environment. This is illustrated by the liver fluke *Fasciola hepatica* whose life cycle is summarised in figure 41.10.

The liver fluke illustrates another important principle, namely the advantage of having a **dormant resistant stage** in the life cycle. Provided they are immersed in water, the encysted cercariae of the liver fluke remain viable for up to a year, though they can only survive for a few weeks if exposed to air. Many other parasites have stages that remain in a dormant, yet viable, state until a suitable host is found.

Some parasites are so closely linked with their host that their **tissues are interconnected**. For example, certain plant parasites plug into other plants and tap off nutrients from the host's vascular tissues. One such plant is dodder (*Cuscuta*), shown in figure 41.11.

Minimising the harm

Interestingly, many parasites seem to cause surprisingly little harm to their hosts. In part this may be because, over time, hosts have evolved defences against the worst effects of their parasites. However, there may be another reason. When you think about it, it may not be the interests of a parasite to cause too much damage to its host. Suppose that a parasite killed its host within a short time. In that case the parasite would either perish with the host or be forced to begin again the hazardous business of finding a new host. This is an instance of the parasite and host evolving together – a point to which we shall return later.

Figure 41.11 Dodder (*Cuscuta*) on a host plant. The genus *Cuscuta* contains about 100 species, all of which parasitise other plants. All dodders have thin stems which wind around the shoot of the host. At intervals short side branches, known as suckers, are given off and these penetrate the host's stem. The suckers contain vascular tissues which link up with those of the host. As a result the parasite can obtain all its water, minerals and soluble organic substances from the host. In consequence dodder has leaves that are small and scale-like and once the plant is established the roots wither away.

41.3 Commensalism

For a relationship to be commensal it must be shown that one partner gains, while the other neither gains nor loses. In practice, it is doubtful if any relationship can be shown to be truly commensal, for it is almost impossible to demonstrate that a host fails either to benefit a little or to incur a minute penalty from the association. Nevertheless, there are associations where one partner benefits substantially, while the other *appears* to be unaffected.

One such instance is the association between the colonial hydroid *Hydractinia echinata* and the hermit crab *Pagurus bernhardus* (*figure 41.12*). The hermit crab is a distinctive creature whose asymmetrical abdomen fits snugly into the coils of an empty whelk shell. *Hydractinia* is one of several organisms commonly found attached to shells occupied by hermit crabs.

In this particular association the hydroid obtains food particles from the crab and, more importantly, is taken into regions which otherwise would be unsuitable for it because of the softness of the substratum – the hydroid can stand on rocks or empty shells, but not on soft mud.

Although the hydroid clearly gains from the association, as far as is known the crab neither benefits nor loses. Indeed, when selecting an empty shell, the crab's choice seems unaffected by the presence or absence of hydroids on it.

Figure 41.12 Hermit crab with colonial hydroids. This relationship seems to benefit the hydroids and neither benefits nor harms the crab.

41.4 Mutualism

For an association to qualify as mutualistic it must be demonstrated that both partners benefit. There are all possible grades of mutualism, ranging from rather loose associations in which the two organisms gain relatively little from each other, to associations so intimate that the two partners may be regarded as a single organism.

Mutualism includes cases when one partner lives inside the other. One instance is the complex community of microorganisms that occur in the rumen of cows, sheep and other ruminants. The host benefits from the enzymes of the microorganisms which, unlike those of the host, include **cellulase** which can break down cellulose. In return the microorganisms are guaranteed a safe and constant environment. However, we should hesitate before assuming that the relationship is harmoniously balanced. The microorganisms eventually pass out of the rumen and are digested by the host (*page 706*).

▶ Ruminant digestion, page 191

Green hydra and zoochlorella

The ultimate in intimacy is achieved when one of the partners lives inside the cells of the other. An example is provided by the green hydra *Chlorohydra viridissima* which harbours large numbers of the green protoctist *Chlorella* (in this case referred to as zoochlorella) in its endodermal cells.

Various lines of evidence indicate that this association is mutually beneficial. For instance, even when *Chlorohydra* is kept in the dark, the zoochlorellae survive. This suggests that, although unable to photosynthesise, they derive essential nutrients from their host. Conversely, specimens of *Chlorohydra* kept in the light but prevented from feeding heterotrophically, survive for longer than closely related species of hydra that lack zoochlorellae.

What, then, do these two organisms obtain from each other? The protoctist is afforded shelter, protection, nitrogenous compounds from its host's excretory waste and possibly a significant supply of carbon dioxide from its host's respiration. In return the hydra obtains carbohydrates made by the protoctist's photosynthesis and possibly a significant supply of oxygen, again from photosynthesis.

Lichens

▶ Blue-green bacteria, page 89; fungi, page 92; lichens, page 93

A similar metabolic relationship is found in those extraordinary organisms, **lichens**. A lichen is the result of a union between a fungus and a unicellular photosynthetic organism. The fungus partner is usually an ascomycete or a basidiomycete. The unicellular organism is either a green alga or a blue-green bacterium.

The fungus forms most of the lichen (*figure 41.13*). However, it can apparently only survive when in partnership with its algal or bacterial companion. On the other hand, most lichen algae can survive on their own. The complications of this relationship make it difficult to know where to classify lichens. Usually they are put in the Fungi, but they could equally well be in the Prokaryotae, the Protoctista or in a group of their own.

Lichens are astonishingly hardy organisms and can thrive in the most unlikely places, for example on exposed rocks at high altitudes and in the Arctic and Antarctic. Often they flourish in places where no other organisms can survive through lack of water. Frequently they are the first species to colonise exposed rock.

Both partners gain from being able to live in a greater range of habitats. The green algae or blue-green bacteria are protected from desiccation and in turn they give the fungus carbohydrates from their photosynthesis. Lichens containing blue-green bacteria have the added bonus of receiving organic nitrogen compounds from the bacteria as they can fix atmospheric nitrogen.

▶ Nitrogen fixation, page 669

Figure 41.13 Section through a lichen showing fungal hyphae and algal cells. Soredia are units by which lichens reproduce. They contain both algal cells and fungal hyphae.

Figure 41.14 Greater horseshoe bat. Bats are nocturnal and can locate objects in their flight path by sensing the delay between the emission of an ultrasonic squeak and the return of its echo. The sound is produced by the larynx and emitted through the mouth or nose – in the case of the horseshoe bat through the nose. The echo is detected by the ears with their large pinnae.

41.5 Predation

Predators differ from parasites in that they are usually larger than their 'hosts'. More importantly, they kill their prey before eating it. There are so many examples of predators being adapted for catching their prey, and of prey being adapted to avoid their predators, that it is difficult to know where to begin. We shall concentrate on just one example: that of bats catching moths.

There are almost a thousand species of bats and they occur throughout the world except in the Arctic, the Antarctic and on the highest mountains. **Echolocation** is probably the key to their evolutionary success, for this allows them to forage for insects at night when many other predators are disqualified by darkness. Sounds are emitted by the bat through its open mouth or nostrils, depending on the species. Bats with elaborate noses, such as horseshoes and false vampires, emit sounds through their noses (*figure 41.14*).

Whether a bat emits sounds through its mouth or its nose, the pattern with which the sounds are produced depends on precisely what the bat is doing. For example, the rate and frequency with which sounds are produced by the North American big brown bat depend on whether the bat is searching, approaching or attempting to capture prey (*figure 41.15*).

The contest between a bat and its prey is not as one-sided as you might imagine. True, the bat can measure the delay between sending out a pulse of sound and hearing it return, thus pinpointing the position and movement of its prey. However, certain insects have evolved counter-adaptations. Some moths have listening membranes that detect the bat's sonar pulses, giving the moth the chance of escape. Other moths can even produce their own ultrasound, thus confusing the bats.

Echolocation in bats

Nowadays we are so used to the idea that bats use echolocation that it is hard to imagine the incredulity with which the idea was first received. When the zoologist Robert Galambos first reported his evidence for bat echolocation to a conference in 1940, one distinguished scientist was so indignant that he seized Galambos by the shoulders and shook him, complaining that he could not possibly make such an outrageous suggestion!

Today we know that not only bats, but whales and their relatives and even some cave-dwelling birds can echolocate.

Figure 41.15 Sonogram showing the search, approach and capture phases of the hunt of the North American big brown bat. When searching, the bat emits five to six pulses per second, each lasting about 10 ms and descending in frequency from about 70 to 30 kHz. Once a potential prey is located, the pulse rate increases dramatically. At the point of capture (or near miss) the bat is producing about 100 pulses per second and receives the same number of pieces of information on its prey's whereabouts.

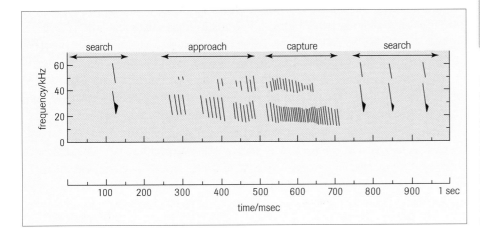

The presence of large herbivores leads to the coevolution of large carnivores. Much of the evolution of large mammalian herbivores and carnivores over the last 60 million years has centred on both getting faster. Evidence for this comes from fossils over this period which show elongation of limb bones, a sure sign that the animals were running faster.

Not only did the limbs of the herbivores and carnivores evolve for greater speed, but their brains became larger too. Looking today at the way large carnivores such as wolves, lions and jaguars hunt their prey, it is clear that intelligence favours both the hunter and the hunted. Survival is a battle of wits. It could be that coevolution has forced both herbivores and carnivores to become more intelligent.

If coevolution has led to greater speed *and* intelligence in large carnivores and their prey, we would expect the hunting success of a modern cheetah or lion to be no better than that of its ancestors 60 million years ago. The American evolutionary biologist Leigh Van Valen calls this the **Red Queen effect**. The Red Queen, you may recall from Lewis Caroll's *Through the Looking Glass*, described how her country was one where you had to run ever so fast just to remain in the same place.

It is easy to imagine that an organism which has been living commensally (or even mutualistically) might start to exploit its host in some way, thus becoming a parasite. Equally, a parasitic association might gradually become so well-balanced that no harm at all is inflicted on the host, thus turning it into a commensal relationship. It is likely that many different sequences have occurred in evolution but in all cases symbiotic organisms seem to have evolved in response to each other, a process called **coevolution**.

The English biologists John Krebs and Richard Dawkins have argued that coevolution is essentially an **arms race** between two organisms in selfish competition. Even when the relationship is mutualistic, natural selection still favours traits that benefit whichever partner possesses them. Only if this is the case can natural selection allow mutually beneficial traits to evolve.

Pollination is considered in more detail in Chapter 28, but it is clear that in insect pollination the insect and the plant have evolved together. From the plant's point of view the insect serves only to pollinate it. Gaudy petals, quantities of nectar and seductive scents are simply necessary advertisement and bribery. From the insect's perspective, getting covered in sticky pollen is a hazard. The benefit comes from eating nectar or pollen.

Grasses and large herbivores

Everyone likes to chew on a piece of grass on a nice summer's day while contemplating the meaning of life, but few of us would choose to live on it. Indeed, we can't. Grass simply doesn't contain enough protein for us. Not only that, but it contains a surprisingly large amount of silica (SiO_2), an abrasive mineral which would soon damage our teeth.

It is thought that grasses have evolved the ability to deposit silica in their leaves and stems to reduce their risks of being grazed. In turn, large herbivores have evolved complex molars with enamel ridges for grinding up grass (*page 179*). In other words, grasses and large herbivores have coevolved. Even so, elderly red deer sometimes die of starvation through having had their teeth worn down by the silica in their food.

Colour, patterns and mimicry

If an organism is to avoid being eaten, an obvious strategy is to blend into the background and be inconspicuous. This is known as **crypsis** and is common throughout the animal kingdom.

If you have ever seen certain stick insects and crickets you will know how effective crypsis can be, for these animals can look remarkably like the plants on which they feed in both colour and shape. Many ground-nesting birds provide examples of crypsis for they make nests that are exceptionally difficult to find (*figure 41.16*).

A quite different strategy is to be distasteful and to advertise the fact by looking especially conspicuous! This is known as **warning coloration**, and an example is provided by the monarch butterfly (*Danaus plexippus*) illustrated in figure 41.17.

This colourful North and Central American butterfly lays its eggs on milkweeds in the genus *Asclepias*. The milkweeds produce a number of poisonous chemicals (cardiac glycosides) which deter most herbivores. However, the larvae of the monarch butterfly feed on milkweeds and store the poisons in their body. When the caterpillars metamorphose into adults, they fly away still with the stores of poisonous cardiac glycosides.

Monarch butterflies are sometimes caught by birds called blue jays. Within half an hour of eating a monarch butterfly the bird is violently sick. When the bird next sees a monarch butterfly, it refuses to eat it. It seems that the blue jay learns to associate the butterfly's distinctive coloration with the traumatic consequences of eating it. In this way the bright colouring may reduce the chance of the butterfly's relatives being eaten (*page 448*).

Mimicry

There are a number of other butterfly species that look very similar to the monarch butterfly yet are completely palatable. This is an example of **Batesian mimicry**, named after the Victorian explorer, Henry Bates, who first suggested it.

In all cases of Batesian mimicry there is a distasteful species, the **model**, and one or more palatable species, called **mimics**, which resemble the model. The mimics obviously benefit because the risks of their being eaten are reduced. For example, hoverflies, with their yellow and black striped abdomens, are Batesian mimics of bees and wasps (*figure 41.18*).

What are the costs and benefits of the relationship from the model's point of view? If the mimic becomes too abundant, the model will suffer. This is because once the mimic is more common than the model, the chances are that a predator will eat a mimic before it first takes a model. If this is the case, it will learn to associate the distinctive patterning of the model and the mimic with a safe and tasty meal! This will be to the disadvantage of both the model and the mimic.

There is another sort of mimicry, known as **Müllerian mimicry** after the German zoologist Fritz Müller. In this case both the model and the mimic are unpalatable or dangerous. Here both partners benefit so the relationship is mutualistic.

Figure 41.16 Ringed plover nest with cryptic eggs on shingle.

Figure 41.17 Monarch butterflies resting during their migration in Mexico.

Figure 41.18 A A media wasp which can sting painfully. **B** A harmless hoverfly which mimics bees and wasps.

Summary

1. The **biotic environment** of an organism is the sum of the living factors that influence that organism.

2. The general term used to describe intimate associations between pairs of species is **symbiosis**.

3. **Parasitism** is an association between two organisms in which the smaller, the **parasite**, lives either temporarily or permanently in or on the larger, the **host**. The host is harmed by the parasite, but is usually not killed by it.

4. **Commensalism** is an association in which one of the two organisms benefits, while the other neither loses nor gains.

5. **Mutualism** is an association which benefits both participants.

6. **Potato blight** is a disease of potato plants caused by a parasitic fungus-like organism.

7. **Malaria** is a disease of humans caused by parasitic microorganisms belonging to the genus *Plasmodium*. The parasites require a **vector**, a mosquito in the genus *Anopheles*, to complete their life cycles.

8. Parasites show many adaptations to their way of life, depending on whether they are **endoparasites** or **ectoparasites**.

9. **Predators** differ from parasites in that they kill their prey before eating it.

10. Over time each organism in an association may evolve in response to how the other organism has evolved. This is called **coevolution**.

11. Many organisms reduce the risk of predation by blending into the background, that is, by being **cryptic**. However, if poisonous or dangerous, it may pay an organism to advertise the fact by, for example, **warning coloration**.

12. **Mimicry** occurs when a palatable (or distasteful) **mimic** resembles a distasteful **model**.

For general advice on these questions and advice on answering essay-type questions, see pages vii and viii.

1. (a) Describe a named predator–prey relationship and a named parasite–host relationship. Outline the main differences between them. (12)

(b) Explain how population sizes of predators and prey, and of parasites and hosts, may be influenced by their relationships. (6)

(Total 18 marks)
UCLES 1997

2. Read the passage.

Return to the Wild

Conservationists want to reintroduce the wolf to the Highlands of Scotland and the Rocky Mountains of North America. But talk of a pilot project on the Scottish island of Rhum is already causing a stir.

Rhum, a soggy, deer-infested island off the coast of Scotland, was first suggested as a site for introducing wolves some twenty years ago. Overgrazing by the island's huge population of red deer is one of the reasons why the native pine woods cannot regenerate. So why not introduce wolves to prey on the deer and ease the pressure?

Red deer, which humans hunted to extinction during the second half of the eighteenth century, were re-introduced to the island in 1845. Since then, their numbers have been controlled by culling (selectively killing some individuals). The Scottish Natural Heritage is using the island to study the dynamics of the deer population. By culling, the wardens can alter the proportion of males to females of a particular group and monitor the effect. To these ends the Scottish Natural Heritage has traditionally set itself the target of culling about 16 per cent of the deer population. But the culling is both labour intensive and time-consuming.

"Wolf predation would be a far more efficient way of controlling the red deer," says Derek Yalden, a zoologist at the University of Manchester, "and it would be more in keeping with the objectives of a National Nature Reserve." He estimates that the annual cull on Rhum produces over 25 000 kg of meat - enough, he says, to sustain a population of 19 wolves. Separate research led by Martyn Gorman at the University of Aberdeen says likewise.

But there is more to survival than an adequate food supply. Other evidence suggests that deer and wolf populations can only coexist if there is enough space. When two pairs of wolves were introduced to Coronation Island in Alaska in 1960 the experiment ended in spectacular failure. The wolf population grew to 13 in four years and deer numbers declined drastically. By 1968 only one wolf survived. The island had supported a large population of deer but the area of the island was only 73 square kilometres. The Alaska Department of Fish and Game concluded that Coronation Island was too small to support both deer and wolves. Yet at about 100 square kilometres, Rhum is not significantly larger.

(Adapted from an article in New Scientist)

(a) (i) Suggest and explain why the Scottish Natural Heritage finds it necessary to cull the deer population on Rhum. (2)

(ii) Suggest and explain why the wardens find it an advantage to alter the proportion of males and females in a group of deer. (2)

(b) Should wolves be introduced to Rhum? Give scientific arguments either for or against the introduction of wolves. (4)

(c) Describe the processes which might lead to regeneration of native pine forests in Scotland if deer populations were reduced. (4)

(Total 12 marks)
NEAB 1997

3. European carp feed on plants. They were introduced into Australia in the last century. One strain of carp, the Boolarra strain, was used to stock fish farms on the Murray River. From there it spread rapidly through the neighbouring river systems. In some sections of the Murray River, the carp is now almost the only type of fish left. The Boolarra strain can grow to a length of 80 cm and a mass of 10 kg.

(a) Suggest and explain why the carp is now almost the only type of fish left in the Murray River. (2)

(b) To solve the carp problem, river authorities are considering releasing a European virus called spring viraemia which is known to kill carp.

(i) Suggest **one** test the authorities should carry out before releasing spring viraemia into Australian rivers.

(ii) Explain why it would be necessary to carry out this test. (2)

(Total 4 marks)
NEAB 1997

Chapter 42

Evolution in evidence

A s far as we know, our planet is unique in possessing living organisms. Of course, life may yet be discovered elsewhere in the Universe, but it is possible that life exists only on the planet Earth. Here it is certainly found in abundance, often in inhospitable places. There are an estimated 20 to 30 million species in existence today, while from the air most land looks green, witnessing to the presence of countless photosynthetic autotrophs. The question is: how did such tremendous diversity of life come to exist on this planet?

42.1 Darwin and the theory of evolution

The person whose name is most closely associated with this question is Charles Darwin (1809–1882), shown in figure 42.1. Ever since his days as a student at Cambridge, Darwin had been a keen naturalist, devoting much of his time to collecting animals and plants, especially beetles. But his real opportunity came in 1831 when he was offered a berth on *HMS Beagle*, a small ship which was to sail around the world on a map-making survey. The journey took nearly five years and the many stops, some of them several months long, gave Darwin an unparalleled opportunity to explore the flora and fauna of many different parts of the world.

During his long voyage, Darwin was gradually forced towards the conclusion that organisms have **evolved** by a slow and gradual change over successive generations, this being brought about by **natural selection**.

For 20 years after returning from his voyage Darwin consolidated his data and filled in the details of his theory, seeking support for his ideas from geology, embryology and other branches of biology. On 24 November 1859 his book *The Origin of Species by means of Natural Selection or The Preservation of Favoured Races in the Struggle for Life* was published. The entire first print run sold out on its day of publication and a second one was quickly produced. The book has been in print ever since and is without doubt the most important biology book ever written.

The reason why Darwin's book was so important was that it was the first theory of evolution to be fully supported by evidence and backed up by a credible theory to explain the mechanism by which evolution occurs.

This was not in fact the first announcement of the theory, as the previous year Darwin had published a short paper with Alfred Russel Wallace who had independently thought of the same mechanism for evolution as Darwin. However, despite the fact that they published their theory jointly, Darwin is the one better remembered for the theory, partly because of the huge mass of evidence he collected in its defence, but also because he published his ideas in a book.

What did Darwin do?

Darwin did two things. First, he marshalled powerful evidence supporting the proposition that species have not remained unaltered through time, but have gradually changed from one form into another. This was not an entirely new idea – it is found in the writings of some earlier naturalists and philosophers – but Darwin was the first person to put it on a sound scientific basis. Some of Darwin's evidence was based on the geographical distribution of the animals and plants he had observed during his five-year voyage.

Darwin then went on to argue that if species have arisen by gradual change it should be possible to learn something about their ancestry from the similarities and differences between them, and from their embryology and fossil record. This he set out to do with

Figure 42.1 Charles Darwin at the age of 40.

Darwin and society

Nowadays most people take evolution for granted, but the climate of opinion in the middle of the 19th century far from favoured the notion. Although the idea had been in the air for some time, most people preferred to believe that animals and plants had arisen by a supernatural act of special creation – each kind of organism being formed separately.

It had even been calculated by the ingenious Dr Lightfoot, vicar of the University Church at Cambridge, that the world had been created at 9 a.m. on 23 October 4004 BC. Although many people felt that the exact date could not be determined as precisely as this, it was generally thought that the Earth was no more than 10 000 years old. Darwin's theory required the Earth to be many millions of years old and this was widely held to be ridiculous, particularly as the chronologies of the Jewish scriptures (The Old Testament), if interpreted literally, required Adam and Eve to have been created by God only about 6000 years ago.

Darwin therefore found himself immediately at the centre of controversy. He was opposed not so much by the Church, for many leading theologians had little difficulty in accepting his ideas, but by Victorian society in general. The idea that humans were descended from other animals was felt to be insulting, even blasphemous. On hearing of Darwin's theory, the wife of the Bishop of Worcester is said to have exclaimed 'Descended from apes! My dear, let us hope it is not so; but if it is, that it does not become generally known'.

Darwin was a shy man. However, the biologist Thomas Henry Huxley, a close friend, soon became known as 'Darwin's bulldog' as he tirelessly defended Darwin's theories both in print and in public debate. The most famous confrontation Huxley experienced was with the Bishop of Oxford, Dr Samuel Wilberforce, whose fluency as a speaker had earned him the nickname of Soapy Sam. In a public debate the bishop asked Huxley if he traced his descent from an ape through his grandfather or his grandmother; whereupon Huxley replied that he would rather be descended from an ape than from an intelligent being 'who uses his gifts to discredit and crush humble seekers after truth'.

The newspapers of the day were divided as to whether Huxley or Wilberforce had won the argument, but despite these stormy beginnings Darwin's theory has stood the test of time and, with certain modifications, is accepted today by practically all biologists. Those who accept the theory of evolution are known as **evolutionists**.

painstaking care and thoroughness. The result was that he gave a new purpose and direction to biological enquiry. The old disciplines of comparative anatomy and palaeontology took on a new form. No longer purely descriptive, they increasingly became concerned with tracing the ancestral history of organisms and this helped to underpin Darwin's theory.

The next thing Darwin did was to put forward a plausible theory explaining the mechanism by which species have changed. As a naturalist, Darwin was enormously impressed with the remarkable way organisms are adapted to their surroundings. Darwin explained this by proposing that individuals of a species differ from each other in the degree to which they are suited to their environment. The poorly adapted ones, he argued, perish while the well-adapted ones survive and hand on their beneficial characteristics to their offspring. This is what is meant by natural selection, nature as it were selecting the 'fit' and rejecting the 'unfit'.

To Darwin, natural selection provided an explanation of the extinct forms seen so clearly in the fossil record. We shall return to natural selection in Chapter 43. In the present chapter we shall be concerned with the way evolution reveals itself – or appears to reveal itself – in different areas of biology. The areas we shall discuss are:

- geographical distribution
- comparative anatomy
- molecular biology
- embryology
- taxonomy
- palaeontology.

Why did Darwin take so long to publish his theory?

When Darwin set out on his Beagle voyage in 1831 he believed that species were created separately in much the form as they exist today. By 1838 he was convinced that all species, including humans, had evolved by natural selection.

Darwin realised that his ideas were important and in 1842, and again in 1844, he wrote them out in detail leaving strict instructions with his wife to publish them should he die. Yet he didn't publish his ideas until 1858 when Wallace's independent discovery forced his hand.

So why did Darwin take so long to publish his theory? One suggestion is that he spent the time gathering evidence. No doubt there is some truth in this, but 20 years!

Another explanation is that he was afraid of public reaction. It is difficult for us nowadays to recognise the impact of his ideas on Victorian England. When an entire society, tens of millions of people, believe that they are recently descended from Adam, a perfect, sinless immortal being created by God in his own image out of the dust of the Earth, it takes

courage to publish a theory which implies that we are descended from a seemingly endless series of animal forms that date back countless millions of years to the beginnings of life itself.

By all accounts Darwin was a quiet man. Though not a recluse, he seems to have cared little for the cut and thrust of academic debate and public life, preferring instead the company of his family. It is an intriguing question whether he would ever have published his theory had it not been for Wallace.

42.2 Geographical distribution studies

Consider Africa and South America. Both contain approximately the same range of latitude, and both have much the same variety of habitats – humid jungles, dry plains, high mountain ranges and so forth – and yet each supports a very different fauna. Africa has short-tailed (Old World) monkeys, anthropoid apes, the African elephant, the dromedary (one-humped) camel, antelopes, the giraffe and the lion, to mention but a few of the mammals. South America, however, has none of these. Instead we find such mammals as long-tailed (New World) monkeys, llamas, tapirs, the puma ('mountain lion') and the jaguar.

If we take Australia into consideration as well, we find even greater differences despite the fact that it, too, lies on the same latitude as much of South America and Africa. In Australia we find pouched mammals (**marsupials**), such as kangaroos, which are totally absent from Africa and are represented in South America only by opossums. It is in Australia that we find the duck-billed platypus and spiny anteater, the only living representatives of a group of egg-laying mammals (the **monotremes**) found nowhere else in the world. So distinctive are these animals that when the first stuffed duck-billed platypus was brought back to Europe in 1798, it was widely believed by reputable zoologists to be a fake, made by stitching together parts of a duck with parts of a mammal.

Australia is also distinctive in the mammals it lacks. It has very few placental (**eutherian**) mammals, except those that have been introduced by humans, their place being taken by the many different types of marsupials (*figure 42.2*). The marsupials occupy the ecological niches filled on other continents by eutherian mammals.

Africa, South America and Australia are all in the Southern Hemisphere. If, however, we examine the mammals of the Northern Hemisphere, we find that the differences are far less pronounced. In both North America and Eurasia we find reindeer, red deer (called wapiti or elk in North America), bison, beavers, hares, wild goats, mountain sheep, bears and the lynx. In some cases the same species is found in North America and Eurasia, e.g. the lynx. In other cases, one species occurs in North America and another very similar species in the same genus is found in Eurasia. This is the case with beavers: the North American beaver is *Castor canadensis*; the European beaver *C. fiber*.

Figure 42.2 Australasian marsupials.
A Red kangaroo.
B Marsupial wolf (now almost certainly extinct).
C Sugar glider possum.

Explanation of continental distributions

We are left, then, with the general picture of the two great continents of the Northern Hemisphere having quite similar mammals, whereas the three southern continents have sharply contrasting mammals. How can we explain this? A glance at a map of the world will remind you that whereas South America, Africa and Australia are separated from one another by great bodies of water, North America and Asia are separated only by a shallow strait (the Bering Strait), less than 100 km wide. Moreover, there is evidence that in the geological past a continuous land bridge linked these two northern continents across what is now the strait.

A possible hypothesis to explain the geographical distribution of mammals is that evolution gave rise to new species and genera, some of which moved from North America to Eurasia, or vice versa. In other words, different mammals evolved in these two continents, but the geographical closeness of the two regions kept their faunas together and prevented them from diverging very greatly.

On the other hand, the wide separation of the three continents of the Southern Hemisphere meant that only very rarely was there any exchange of mammals between them, so the mammals of each evolved independently along their own lines. Marsupials in Australia evolved to fill niches occupied in the Northern Hemisphere by placental mammals.

A fuller understanding of continental distributions is provided by the theory of continental drift.

Continental drift

Consider the fossil reptile, *Mesosaurus* (*figure 42.3*). *Mesosaurus* lived about 270 million years ago. Measuring about a metre in length, it had webbed feet, a long tail and numerous sharp teeth. It appears to have been well adapted to living in freshwater, where it probably fed on small fish.

In itself, *Mesosaurus* is of no tremendous importance, unless you have a particular interest in fossil reptiles. However, its geographical distribution is striking. It is found in fossil deposits in only two places: the eastern side of South America and the western side of southern Africa (*figure 42.4*). How can we explain this?

It is unlikely that this reptile could have migrated from one of these two continents to the other via a northern land route without leaving any fossil remains in between; and it seems unlikely that it could have swum over 3000 miles across the Atlantic. There is, however, another possible explanation which would help to explain the distribution not only of Mesosaurus, but of many other animals and plants as well.

If you look at a map of the *modern* world (such as that in figure 42.4), the complementary shapes of South America and Africa are striking. If you bring them into close proximity, they fit together quite snugly like pieces of a jigsaw puzzle. This has led to the suggestion that at one time South America and Africa were joined together. But if this was indeed the case, how come they are now so far apart?

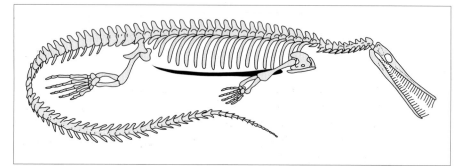

Figure 42.3 The skeleton of *Mesosaurus*, a fossil reptile about a metre in length that lived around 270 million years ago. This animal is found in fossil deposits in the eastern side of South America and the western side of southern Africa.

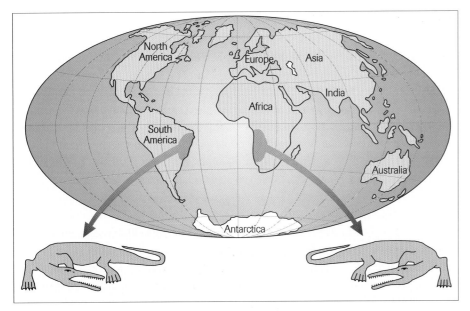

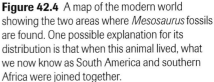

Figure 42.4 A map of the modern world showing the two areas where *Mesosaurus* fossils are found. One possible explanation for its distribution is that when this animal lived, what we now know as South America and southern Africa were joined together.

One theory is that America and Africa have gradually moved away from each other. This theory of **continental drift** was proposed by the geologist Alfred Wegener in 1912. At the time very few scientists took his ideas seriously, mainly because they could not envisage a mechanism for continental drift. However, since the 1960s more and more geophysical and oceanographic evidence has come to light suggesting that the continents, far from being fixed in their present positions, have indeed moved about the surface of the globe and are still doing so. Further, the theory of **plate tectonics**, as it is called, provides an understanding of how continents move and allows geologists to reconstruct what the surface of our planet may have looked like in previous eras (*figure 42.5*).

You can see from figure 42.5 that at about the time when *Mesosaurus* existed, what we now know as South America and Africa may have been united, along with the other land masses, into a single supercontinent called **Pangea** ('all the earth'). There is considerable argument over the timing, but it is generally agreed that South America, Antarctica and Australia had separated from the other continents, but were still joined to each other, when the first marsupials were evolving. Fossil marsupials have recently been found in Antarctica, exactly as this would predict.

The Galapagos Islands

On his voyage aboard the Beagle, Darwin visited the **Galapagos Islands** which are situated on the equator some 900 km west of Ecuador in South America. It is thought that these islands were formed by volcanic action and so were at first devoid of life. Later, they became colonised by organisms from the mainland. These then evolved along their own lines into species which, though fundamentally similar to the mainland forms, differ from them in certain respects.

Despite the harmful effects of animals that have been introduced there by humans within the last few hundred years, the Galapagos Islands are a biologist's paradise. This is not because of their climate, for it is generally exceptionally hot on the islands, and some of them lack fresh water. Rather it is because they demonstrate the effect that isolation can have on subsequent evolution.

What Darwin saw on the Galapagos Islands during the month that the Beagle anchored there shaped his ideas about evolution more forcibly than any other single experience during his five-year voyage. As he himself wrote: 'Here, both in space and time, we seem to be brought somewhat near to that great fact – that mystery of mysteries – the first appearance of new beings on this Earth'.

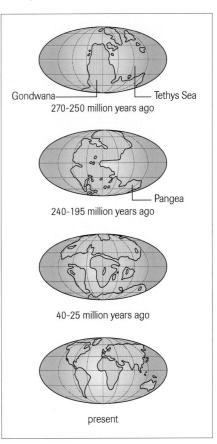

Figure 42.5 The theory of plate tectonics predicts that the continents have slowly moved and changed shape over time. This series of diagrams shows what the distribution of land and sea is thought to have been at various times over the last 270 million years.

Figure 42.6 Giant iguana lizards on the Galapagos Islands.
Top The terrestrial iguana.
Bottom The marine iguana.

Among the more distinctive inhabitants of the Galapagos Islands are the **giant land tortoises**. These unique animals give their name to the islands, as galapagos is the Spanish for tortoise. The first fact about them to strike Darwin was their size. They may reach a metre in height and weigh up to 225 kg.

However, there's more to them than simply their size. At dinner one evening, Mr Lawson, an Englishman who was acting as vice-governor of the Galapagos archipelago, remarked to Darwin that he could tell by looking at a tortoise which island it had come from. Thus the tortoises on Albemarle Island have a different sort of shell from those on Chatham, and both differ again from those on James. What was Darwin to conclude from this? Had a different form of tortoise been created on each island, or had a single ancestral form evolved into different forms? The islands are separated by deep water, so the tortoises would have been isolated from each other.

Also prominent on the islands are the **giant iguana lizards** (*figure 42.6*). About 1.25 m long, there are two species, one terrestrial and the other marine. The marine species is the only known aquatic lizard, and is adapted for living in water by having webbed feet and a laterally flattened tail which it uses for propelling itself rather like a newt. The terrestrial species was extremely abundant at the time that Darwin visited the islands, and it is thought that the marine form evolved from it as a result of overcrowding and competition for food on land. Both species are herbivorous; the land species feeding on leaves and other types of vegetation, the marine species on seaweed.

Darwin's finches

While on the Galapagos Islands Darwin also collected a number of small birds – all **finches** of one kind or another. At the time these did not interest him as much as some of the other organisms, but later he saw in these finches the key to understanding the evolutionary process.

Darwin was familiar with similar finches on the mainland of South America. There, they all possess short, straight beaks which they use to crush seeds. On the Galapagos islands, however, there are 13 species of finch which fall into six main types, each having a beak specially adapted for dealing with a particular kind of food (*figure 42.7*).

Between them, the Galapagos finches exploit a wide range of ecological niches which on the mainland are mainly occupied by other types of bird. The **ground finches**, the closest to the mainland finches in form and habit, have typical finch-like beaks for crushing seeds. In contrast, the **cactus finches** have long, straight beaks and split tongues with which they obtain nectar from the flowers of the tree-sized prickly pear cactus which grows in abundance on the islands. The **vegetarian tree finch**, on the other hand, has a curved parrot-like beak with which it feeds on buds and fruits. The **insectivorous tree finches** have similar beaks which they use for feeding on beetles and other small insects. Then there is the **warbler finch** which is so like a true warbler that at first it was thought to be one. It uses its slender beak for feeding on small insects which it catches on the wing just as true warblers do.

Perhaps the most remarkable of all the Galapagos finches is the **woodpecker finch**. This resembles a true woodpecker in its ability to climb up tree trunks and bore holes in wood in search of insects. But whereas true woodpeckers use their long tongues to seek out insects, the woodpecker finch, which lacks a long tongue, picks up a cactus spine in its beak and pokes this into holes (*figure 42.8*). When the insect emerges, the bird drops the spine and devours the insect. Although the operation is time-consuming compared to the way a true woodpecker feeds, the technique allows the woodpecker finch to exploit a niche that would otherwise be vacant, as there are no true woodpeckers on the Galapagos islands. Quite apart from its evolutionary implications, the woodpecker finch is remarkable for being one of the few species other than ourselves to use a tool.

Figure 42.7 The heads of the 13 species of finches found on the Galapagos Islands arranged according to their possible evolutionary relationships.

The Galapagos finches afford an excellent example of **adaptive radiation**. It is assumed by evolutionists that a stock of ancestral finches reached the islands from the mainland and then, in the absence of much competition, evolved to fill many of the empty ecological niches occupied on the mainland by species absent from the islands.

Isolating barriers

It is clear from this brief review that the distribution of organisms, and the form they take in different localities, depend to a considerable extent on migration and isolation. These in turn depend on the existence of **natural barriers** which restrict movement in one direction or another. Barriers limiting the movement of terrestrial organisms include water, mountain ranges, deserts, temperature differences and other environmental factors. Aquatic organisms are limited by such factors as salinity, oxygen concentration, currents and tides.

Isolating barriers do not remain static throughout geological time but change from one period to another. Routes that have served as a pathway for the migration of animals during one period may become closed in a subsequent period, thus isolating groups of organisms from each other and allowing them to evolve independently.

42.3 **Comparative anatomy**

If it is true that widely separated groups of organisms share a common ancestor, as their geographical distribution suggests, we would expect them to have certain basic structural features in common. In fact the degree of resemblance between them should indicate how

Figure 42.8 A woodpecker finch on the Galapagos islands using part of a twig to obtain insects from beneath bark.

closely related they are in evolution: groups with little in common are assumed to have diverged from a common ancestor much earlier in geological history than groups which have a lot in common. Establishing evolutionary relationships on the basis of structural similarities and differences is the business of **comparative anatomy**.

In deciding how closely related two organisms are, a comparative anatomist looks for structures which, though they may serve different functions, are fundamentally similar in structure, suggesting a common origin. Such structures are described as **homologous**.

In deciding whether or not two structures are homologous, many considerations must be taken into account: their relative positions, morphology, histological appearance and so on. In cases where the structures serve different functions in the adult, it may be necessary to trace their origin and development in the embryo if fundamental similarities are to be discerned.

The pentadactyl limb

A clear example of homology is provided by the **pentadactyl limb**, so called because typically it has five digits (*figure 42.9*). It is found in all four classes of terrestrial vertebrates (amphibians, reptiles, birds and mammals) and some of the limb bones can even be traced back to the fins of certain fossil fishes from which the first amphibians are thought to have evolved.

Throughout the terrestrial vertebrates, the structure of the pentadactyl limb is fundamentally the same, conforming to a greater or lesser extent to the generalised pattern shown in figure 42.9. However, if we look at individual animals we find that their limbs have become adapted for different functions, in some cases involving major structural modifications. This can be seen in figure 42.10 which shows how the forelimb is modified for grasping, walking, swimming and flying in a selection of vertebrates.

In some cases evolution has resulted in extreme reduction, even total loss, of a structure. In a bird's wing, for instance, the third digit is very much reduced and the fourth and fifth are missing altogether. Structures which are greatly reduced are described as **vestigial**, and their existence has been used as evidence for evolution: it is thought that vestigial structures performed a function in the ancestor but have since been reduced to such an extent that they have lost or greatly changed their original function. Well-known examples are the wings of the kiwi and other flightless birds, the muscles of our ear lobes, and the reduced pelvic girdles and hind limbs of whales and pythons.

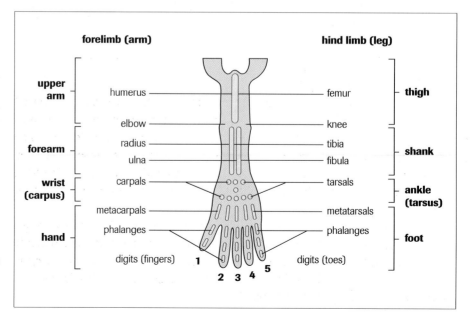

Figure 42.9 A generalised pentadactyl limb. This kind of limb is possessed by most terrestrial vertebrates. The edge of the limb that generally points towards the main axis of the body is to the left. The forelimbs and hind limbs both conform to the pattern illustrated: the nomenclature used for each is shown to the left and right of the diagram respectively.

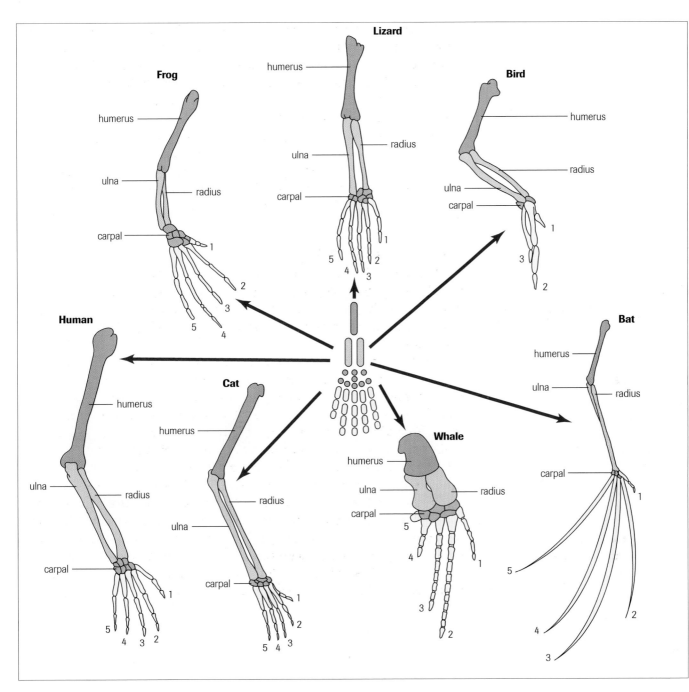

Figure 42.10 The principle of homology illustrated by the adaptive radiation of the forelimb of a selection of vertebrates. All conform to the basic pentadactyl pattern shown in the centre of the diagram but are modified for different uses.

Divergent evolution

We can explain variations in the pentadactyl limb by suggesting that from an ancestral stock numerous lines of evolution resulted in the basic pattern being modified to serve different functions, thus enabling the descendants to fill a wide variety of ecological niches. This is described as **divergent evolution**, and clearly it results in adaptive radiation. The end products have certain structural features in common with each other and with the ancestral stock from which they arose. These structural similarities are the basis of homology.

Comparative anatomy permits evolutionists to do more than relate a handful of diverse organisms to a common ancestor. In certain situations it allows **evolutionary trees** to be constructed. The principle is straightforward. The more similar two organisms are, the more recently they are assumed to have diverged. However, there is a possible danger here, namely the occurrence of convergent evolution.

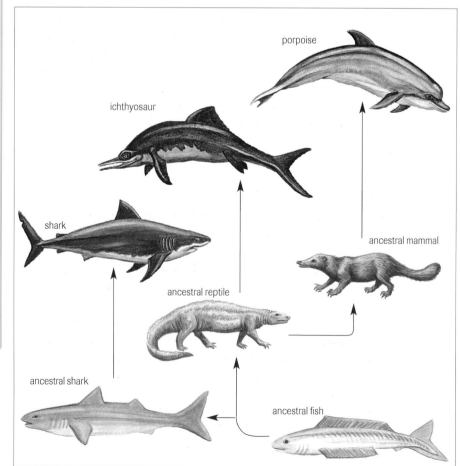

Taxonomy

Taxonomy is the study of the principles, rules and methods of classification (*page 79*). Modern classification dates from the time of the Swedish biologist Carl Linnaeus (1707–1778). Along with virtually all his contemporaries, Linnaeus believed in the fixity of species. Yet his classification system, worked out 100 years before Darwin's *Origin of Species* was published, is in many places very close to the evolutionary relationships thought to hold by most modern biologists. How could this be?

The answer is that Linnaeus classified organisms into common groups (**taxa**) if they shared certain essential characteristics. Mammals, for instance, were classified together because they possess hair, have adult females that produce milk, and are warm-blooded. Exactly the same principles are used today by biologists attempting to discern evolutionary relationships. Viewed this way, taxonomy is not so much evidence for evolution as the inevitable result of it.

Taxonomy only reflects evolutionary affinities when a **natural system of classification** is used. Other classification systems exist. Indeed, even Linnaeus had some groupings that failed to reflect evolution. If a classification is to reflect evolutionary relationships it must be based on homologous and not on analogous structures. Determining whether similar structures are analogous or homologous is sometimes difficult, though molecular biology and embryology can help, as can fossils.

Figure 42.11 Convergent evolution in three marine carnivores brought about by adaptations for sustained rapid swimming in the same environment: the sea. Ichthyosaurs were reptiles that lived at the same time as the dinosaurs. Like sharks and porpoises, they had a streamlined shape and 'fins' and were probably excellent swimmers.

Convergent evolution

Consider a shark and a porpoise. They look similar, and one might suppose that they are closely related. Yet one is a cartilaginous fish and the other a mammal. The similarity in their shapes is thought to be the result of **convergent evolution**. In this process complete organisms (or their parts) come to resemble each other as a result of their sharing similar environments and performing the same function (*figure 42.11*).

Structures arising from convergent evolution are described as **analogous**. Examples include the legs of spiders and mammals, and the wings of butterflies and birds. It can easily be seen that the legs of spiders and mammals, although performing the same task, have quite different structural organisations. Similarly, the wings of butterflies and birds, although both used for flight, are constructed on different principles.

In these two cases of analogy, a cursory glance is enough to tell us that the structures bear no fundamental resemblance to each other. But this is not always the case. The eyes of octopuses and vertebrates, for instance, are remarkably similar in a number of respects and an observer might well conclude that they are homologous. However, there is one telling difference between them: in the vertebrate eye the nerve fibres lie *in front of* the sensory cells of the retina, whereas in the octopus eye they lie *behind* them. Because of this, the vertebrate eye has a 'blind spot' where the optic nerve emerges from it (*page 384*). The octopus eye, though, lacks one.

The reason for this difference presumably lies far back in the mists of time. However, it suggests to an evolutionist at once that vertebrate and octopus eyes are the products of two distinct lines of evolution, resembling each other as a result of convergent evolution.

Careful study can uncover cases of convergent evolution and prevent us from attributing evolutionary relationships when they do not exist. Even so, there is a limit to how much conventional comparative anatomy can tell us about evolutionary relationships. Major advances had to wait until the 1960s when techniques of cell and molecular biology were brought to bear on the problem.

42.4 Molecular biology

Research on the structure and function of cells leads to the conclusion that the cells of different organisms are remarkably alike in many details of their biochemistry and fine structure. Chemicals such as nucleic acids, ATP and cytochrome, and certain organelles including ribosomes, appear to be of almost universal occurrence. This supports the view that all living things have had a common ancestry. Even viruses, which at first sight appear very different from living organisms, possess nucleic acid and proteins.

However, certain structures and chemical substances are not ubiquitous but are confined to specific groups of organisms. For example, most plants contain chlorophyll, cellulose and starch, all of which are absent from animals; vertebrates possess adrenaline and thyroxine, neither of which is found in other groups, and the brown algae are the exclusive possessors of the orange pigment fucoxanthin.

Organisms sharing the same chemical characteristics are considered to be more closely related than those lacking such affinities. This principle, known as **biochemical homology**, has been used in recent years to identify and confirm evolutionary relationships. The analysis of proteins and DNA has been particularly revealing.

Protein and DNA structure

Since Sanger developed a technique for working out the sequence of amino acids in proteins (*page 32*), **amino acid sequence analysis** has become an important tool in establishing possible evolutionary affinities. For example, the sequence of amino acids has been analysed in part of the fibrinogen molecule of various mammals. It turns out that the sequence differs in varying degrees from one species to another, and this has enabled scientists to draw up a possible evolutionary tree for mammals (*figure 42.12*).

Another way of determining possible evolutionary relationships is to compare the sequence of bases in the DNA of different organisms. The more alike the sequences, the closer the organisms are presumed to be in evolution. The comparison is normally carried out by the technique of **DNA hybridisation** (*extension box below*).

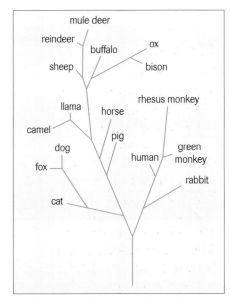

Figure 42.12 An evolutionary tree for a selection of mammals based on a comparison of the sequence of amino acids in part of their fibrinogen molecules. Mammals with similar fibrinogen molecules are assumed to be more closely related than mammals with dissimilar fibrinogen molecules.

Part 8

Extension

How DNA hybridisation is carried out

To carry out DNA hybridisation you first extract the DNA from one species and separate the two strands by heat treatment. You then do the same thing with the DNA of another species. The single strands of the two species are then mixed together, whereupon they join up, sometimes with the complementary strand from their own species, but sometimes with the complementary strand from the other species.

On heating the mixture, the DNA separates into two strands. However, the double-stranded DNA that contains one DNA strand from one species and its other strand from the other species separates into two strands at a lower temperature. This is because the hydrogen bonding holding the two strands together is weaker, as some of the bases fail to pair up.

The closer the temperature at which such hybrid DNA separates compared to the temperature at which the double-stranded DNA of each individual species separates, the more closely related the two species are thought to be.

Figure 42.13 A group of adult sea squirts from the Great Barrier Reef, Australia. Despite their modest appearance, these creatures belong to the phylum Chordata, just as we do.

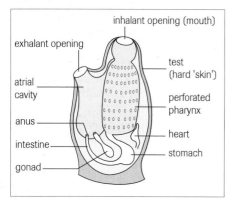

Figure 42.14 The adult sea squirt bears little resemblance to a chordate. There is no trace of a notochord and, except for the perforated pharynx, none of the other chordate characteristics are seen. The inhalant and exhalant openings, perforated pharynx and atrial cavity are associated with this animal's filter-feeding habits.

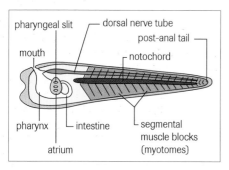

Figure 42.15 The evolutionary affinity of sea squirts with the chordates is revealed by its free-swimming larva which shows the characteristic features of a chordate.

42.5 Embryology

There are times when it is necessary to study an organism's embryological development in order to establish evolutionary relationships. Sometimes the embryonic stages give us an insight into what the ancestors may have been like. Used in this way, embryology becomes a special type of comparative anatomy.

However, there is a problem. Although embryology can be indispensable in establishing evolutionary relationships, there has been a tendency in the past to take it too far. Thus Ernst Haeckl (1843–1919) suggested that during its embryological development an organism repeats its ancestral history, or, to use Haeckl's own way of putting it, 'ontogeny recapitulates phylogeny'.

There is a grain of truth in this: the presence of branchial grooves (relics of gill slits) and segmental muscle blocks in the human embryo, for example, are suggestive of a fish ancestry. But it is wrong to assume that an animal literally 'climbs up its family tree' during its development. After all, many of the steps in its ancestral history will have no usefulness in embryological development and will have long since dropped out of the developmental sequence, if indeed they were ever there.

Moreover, there is every reason to suppose that embryological stages, particularly later ones, have themselves evolved and may be markedly different now from what they were in the past. This is well illustrated by insects, whose larvae show almost as much diversity of form as the adults. Indeed, research by Michael Richards published in 1997 showed that the larval stages of the species studied by Haeckl actually vary far more from one another than his drawings show! There may have been some wishful thinking on Haeckl's part.

Bearing in mind these provisos, let us see how embryology helps us to place an organism in a particular group. As an example we shall consider the evidence that sea squirts (tunicates) belong to the phylum Chordata.

The tadpole larvae of sea squirts

Chordates are characterised by the presence of a notochord, a hollow dorsal nerve cord, visceral clefts, segmental muscle blocks and a post-anal tail (*page 100*). Included in the phylum are sea squirts, fish, amphibians, reptiles, birds and mammals.

At first it seems extraordinary that sea squirts are included in the chordates. After all, the adult sea squirt looks nothing like the other members of this phylum (*figure 42.13*). It is a sessile filter-feeder and lacks any trace of a notochord and other chordate characteristics (*figure 42.14*).

However, a detailed examination of its motile larvae makes its affinity with the other chordates abundantly clear (*figure 42.15*). Not only is there a notochord but there are pharyngeal clefts, a dorsal tubular nerve chord, segmental muscle blocks and a post-anal tail.

Eventually the larva attaches itself to a rock or piece of weed by its head and undergoes metamorphosis into the sessile adult, thereby obscuring its evolutionary relationships.

42.6 Palaeontology

The evidences for evolution presented so far are based on studying organisms living today. Further evidence comes from studying the organisms of the past as seen in the **fossil record**, a branch of biology known as **palaeontology**.

How fossils are formed

Fossils are generally preserved in **sedimentary** rock, which is formed by the deposition of silt, sand or calcium carbonate over millions of years. Silt deposits give **shales**, sand gives **sandstone**, and calcium carbonate (derived from the shells of organisms or precipitated from solution) gives **limestone**.

The most common method of fossilisation involves the ultimate conversion of the hard parts of the body (such as shells, bones or teeth) into rock. What happens is that when an animal such as a bivalve mollusc dies, the organic material in its shell gradually decays away, resulting in the shell becoming porous. If the animal subsequently becomes buried in mud, mineral particles may infiltrate the shell and slowly fill up the pores. If and when the mud turns into rock, the shell hardens and may be preserved for hundreds of millions of years.

On occasions, dead animals become covered by wind-blown, mineral-enriched sand or volcanic ash, and if this is followed by flooding or heavy rain, the same process of mineral infiltration may occur. Fortunately, sedimentary rock is comparatively soft, so that it may not be too difficult for a palaeontologist, armed with hammer and chisel, to separate the fossil from the softer rock or **matrix** surrounding it.

Fossilisation is not confined to animals. For example, there are instances of entire tree trunks being preserved in fossilised forests in Antarctica and elsewhere (*figure 42.16*). In the case of the famous 'Petrified Forest' of Arizona, the original organic matter of the wood became replaced, particle by particle, by silica, which was carried into the logs by water from the sediment in which the trees were buried. The result was that the wood was literally turned into rock, a process called **petrifaction**. So detailed is the transformation that the individual xylem elements and annual rings can clearly be seen. It is even possible to measure the widths of the individual rings and determine what the climate was like at the time.

Sometimes an organism, particularly when buried in rapidly hardening mud, decays completely and the space it occupied – the **mould** – becomes filled with another kind of material. This process results in the formation of a **cast**. For instance, in the case of many shells the cast is composed of silica while the surrounding rock is made of limestone. Recovery of the fossil can then be carried out by chemical means, the limestone being removed by hydrochloric acid.

Occasionally, footprints or other marks made by animals on mud become covered over by a layer of deposit which subsequently hardens. If a line of weakness between the two layers splits, it may reveal the marks as **trace fossils**. Although the information they provide may be fragmentary, such impressions can tell us quite a lot about the organisms that made them (*figure 42.17*).

In certain circumstances, an organism may be preserved by being immersed in some kind of natural preservative. Spectacular examples are provided by insects trapped in **amber**. Such creatures were caught in resin exuding from coniferous trees. On hardening, the resin turned to amber, preserving the animals intact. Subsequent serial sectioning of the embedded specimens can enable their internal anatomy to be described in detail.

Other natural preservatives are found in **tar pits** and **asphalt lakes** in various parts of the world. Complete skeletons of the sabre-toothed tiger and other extinct mammals have been obtained from tar pits in southern California.

Yet another means of preservation is **freezing**. Complete specimens of mammoths and woolly rhinoceroses have been found preserved in the frozen soil of northern Siberia. The mammoth's flesh is said to have been in such a good state of preservation that it was eaten by wolves.

In 1984, the preserved body of a man, now known as **Lindow Man**, was found in a peat bog in Cheshire (*figure 42.18*). His skin, hair and main internal organs were all intact, thanks to the preservative effects of the acid peat which contained very little oxygen, so greatly slowing the process of decay. Radiocarbon dating showed the body to be about 1900 years old.

Figure 42.16 View of the 'Petrified Forest' in north-eastern Arizona, USA. These great logs are the remains of trees that flourished about 160 million years ago. The trees were washed downstream in flood waters and rapidly buried, their wood becoming replaced by silica.

Figure 42.17 An example of a trace fossil. Footprints of an upright primate made in soft, damp, volcanic ash some 3.6 million years ago at Laetoli, Tanzania, as found by Mary Leakey in 1978. The footprints belong to two adults and a child.

Figure 42.18 (*right*) Lindow Man died approximately 1900 years ago. His remains were well preserved in the peat of a Cheshire bog and found in 1984. The body was sufficiently well preserved for a forensic pathologist to determine that death was caused by strangulation with a rope, while his last meal consisted of a flat, unleavened griddle cake made from emmer wheat, spelt wheat and barley cooked over a heather fire at a maximum temperature above 300°C.

What are the chances of an organism ending up as a fossil?

The impression may have been given that fossilisation is a common process. On the contrary, it is a very rare occurrence, requiring precisely the right circumstances. Only a very small percentage of organisms become preserved after they have died and this, coupled with the fact that many fossils get destroyed by erosion or are inaccessible, means that the geological record is for the most part scanty and incomplete.

Further, the fossils we have provide us with a very biased account of life long ago. Organisms with shells, bones or teeth are much more likely to be preserved than those whose bodies lack hard parts. This means that our knowledge of, for instance, fossil fungi or flatworms is extremely patchy.

Despite the small chances of fossils being preserved and subsequently uncovered, there are certain places where large numbers of fossils have been found concentrated together in a comparatively small area (*illustration 1*). In some cases it is thought that such concentrations of fossils are the result of a cataclysmic change in the environment, killing many

Illustration 1 Dinosaur bones exposed in the famous quarry in north-eastern Utah, USA. Parts of over 300 individual dinosaurs, belonging to 10 different species, have been excavated from the quarry which dates from approximately 140 million years ago.

Illustration 2 An artist's reconstruction of some of the different animals and plants to be found at various times in the fossil record. The left-hand half is the older, dating from about 240 to 200 million years ago; the right-hand half dates from about 170 to 100 million years ago.

organisms all at once. Excavation of these fossils and careful reconstructions have enabled palaeontologists to build up a partial picture of the flora and fauna that appear to have existed on this planet during past ages (*illustration 2*).

Figure 42.19 The Grand Canyon in Arizona. At its greatest width the canyon measures 28 km from rim to rim. Its depth is over 1700 m. Horizontal strata can be seen clearly and these consist of sedimentary rocks which span some 500 million years of geological history.

Reconstructing evolutionary pathways from the fossil record

By arranging extinct animals and plants into some kind of geological sequence, it is possible to suggest how one group may have evolved into another. The fact that fossils are formed in sedimentary rocks helps palaeontologists to do this. In the formation of sedimentary rock, a layer of silt, sand or calcium carbonate hardens and another layer is subsequently formed on top of it, and so on. The resulting rock consists of a series of horizontal layers or **strata** (singular **stratum**), each containing fossils typical of the time when it was laid down. The oldest rocks, and therefore the earliest fossils, are contained in the lowest strata; the youngest rocks, and most recent fossils, are in the highest strata.

But how do we get at the lowest layers? Fortunately nature has come to our aid by eroding sedimentary rock in such a way that the different strata are exposed. This can be seen spectacularly in the Grand Canyon in Arizona (*figure 42.19*). Almost two kilometres deep, the canyon has been cut by the eroding action of the Colorado River, which has exposed a series of strata spanning some 500 million years of geological history.

Studying the fossil inhabitants of different strata in places such as these has made it possible to trace the evolution of successive groups of animals and plants during geological time. In order, though, for scientists to obtain the maximum information from any fossil, it is necessary for that fossil to be dated. How this is done is explained in the extension box on the next page.

The evolution of horses

What kind of evolutionary sequences have been established from the fossil record? There are far too many for us to look at all of them, so we shall choose one for detailed discussion: the evolution of horses.

The evolution of horses can be followed through a series of fossils obtained from successively younger rock strata. The series starts with a small animal called *Hyracotherium* (old name *Eohippus*), which lived in North America in the Eocene epoch about 50 million years ago and then spread across to Europe and Asia. It finishes up with the modern horse *Equus*. In between, there are many intermediate forms, with numerous offshoots from the main line.

Compared with most fossil sequences, the record for horses is pretty complete, although it is pieced together from a number of different sites: there is no one place where the whole sequence can be seen in its entirety. Further, palaeontologists believe that there were numerous complications. For one thing, the rate at which evolution took place was probably not uniform, but sporadic and irregular. For another, there are thought to have been times when certain of the trends were reversed when, for instance, horses became smaller for a while.

With these cautions in mind, we can now turn to the overall changes in this particular evolutionary story. Fossil remains of *Hyracotherium* obtained from Eocene rocks in North America show it to have differed from modern horses in three important respects:

- it was very much smaller;
- it had well-developed digits (four on the forefoot, three on the hind foot);
- it possessed low-crowned molar teeth lacking the serrated surface typical of modern horses.

We believe that *Hyracotherium* lived in rather marshy, well-wooded country in which its spreading toes would have afforded it much better support than a hoof. It probably fed on soft vegetation and fruit, for which its non-grinding molars would have been perfectly adequate.

In the subsequent evolution of horses three major changes took place:

- The animals increased in size. *Hyracotherium* was barely 0.4 m tall. The later fossils show a progressive increase in size, finishing up with the modern horse which typically stands approximately 1.6 m off the ground.
- The third digit got stouter and longer. At the same time the other digits were reduced or lost so that by the Pliocene, some five million years ago, they no longer touched the ground. The lengthening of the third digit was brought about by great elongation of the metacarpal and metatarsal, this being accompanied by the conversion of the distal phalange (strictly speaking, its nail) into a hoof. Thus the modern horse stands on the tip of its third digit.
- The molar teeth, from being low-crowned in *Hyracotherium*, acquired higher crowns with a complete covering of cement. Subsequent wearing of the surface resulted in the serrated structure typical of the modern horse. These changes were accompanied by a transformation of the premolars into molar-type teeth.

These three changes can be related to changes in the environment. The fossil plants found in the different strata tell us that the marshy, wooded country in which *Hyracotherium* lived was gradually replaced by a drier type, and the Miocene descendants of *Hyracotherium* found themselves living in open prairie offering little concealment from predators.

Survival now depended on the head being in an elevated position for gaining a good view of the surrounding countryside, and on a high turn of speed for escape from predators – hence the increase in size and replacement of the splayed-out foot by the hoofed foot. The

Dating fossil remains

How can fossils be dated? Very rough estimates can be made from knowing how long it takes for sedimentary rocks to be laid down, but such estimates may be very wide of the mark.

More accurate methods are based on the fact that the older a rock is, the less radioactive it will be. Strata can often be dated by analysis of radioactive isotopes contained in crystals of igneous rock. Such rock is formed from the molten material beneath the Earth's surface. The radioactive clock starts once the crystalline rock is formed, so the older the rock, the less of the original radioactive material remains.

By estimating the rate at which uranium decays to lead, or potassium to argon, it is possible to make reasonably accurate datings of rocks and fossils. The **potassium–argon** method is particularly useful because potassium is a common element found in all sorts of rocks, and it decays into argon extremely slowly. In this way it is even possible to date rocks that are over three billion years old.

For younger fossils which still contain some organic material, radioactive **carbon dating** can be used. This method is based on the fact that after an organism dies the radioactive carbon (^{14}C) it contains gradually disintegrates into nitrogen (^{14}N). As disintegration is rapid, this method can only be used for dating fossils not more than about 50 000 years old. However, it is an accurate method and has been used to make precise datings, not only of fossils but also of archaeological remains. Carbon dating was used to age Lindow Man (*page 731*).

drier, harder ground made the original splayed-out foot unnecessary for support.

The changes in the teeth can be explained by a change in diet from soft vegetation to grass. Grass has a high silica content which wears down teeth. This is why evolution from *Hyracotherium* to *Equus* was accompanied by enlargement of the grinding area and deepening of the teeth.

The sequence of changes in the evolution of the modern horse from *Hyracotherium* is summarised in figure 42.20.

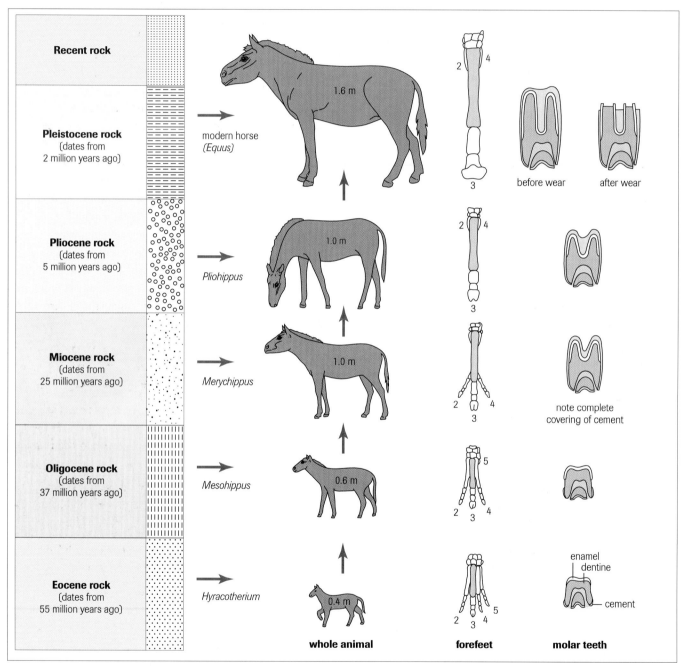

Figure 42.20 The main steps in the evolution of the horse, showing reconstructions of the fossil species obtained from successive rock strata. The foot diagrams are all front views of the left forefoot. The 3rd metacarpal is brown throughout. The teeth are shown in vertical section.

Scientific arguments against evolution

The theory that all life today is descended through evolution from original inorganic precursors differs from many other scientific theories in the extent to which it is directly testable.

However, the theory of evolution is a scientific theory. It makes predictions which can be *indirectly* tested. For instance, if a single fossilised human was ever found in the same sedimentary rocks as dinosaurs, this would disprove the hypothesis, currently accepted by most biologists, that humans evolved long after the dinosaurs had become extinct. In this sense evolution is a science rather as astronomy is. Scientists cannot directly experiment on the history of the universe, but they can make predictions about what we should see today if certain astronomical theories hold.

Granted, then, that the theory of evolution is indirectly testable, what can we say about the evidence for and against it? Perhaps the best evidence in favour of evolution is the fossil record. Yet fewer than 300 000 fossil species have been described. This is almost certainly fewer than one in a thousand of the species that have existed. In other words, the fossil record is very incomplete and there are those who argue that it can be explained without assuming that evolution has occurred.

Indeed, there are some quite major difficulties with the theory of evolution. How did DNA replication and protein synthesis get going, for example? Without these processes it is difficult to imagine any form of life, however simple, and yet even in the smallest prokaryotes the biochemical sophistication required for these metabolic processes is immense. Are they really the blind product of chance? Can evolution account for the existence of humans? Has the human brain really evolved from the inorganic precursors of life?

Although the great majority of scientists alive today would answer 'yes' to these questions, it must be admitted that such an answer cannot be proved. The evidence for evolution is less good than, say, the evidence that the Earth goes round the Sun rather than vice versa.

Summary

1. Charles **Darwin** and Alfred Russel **Wallace** proposed a plausible theory of evolution in 1858.

2. Evolution reveals itself in the **geographical distribution of organisms**, **comparative anatomy**, **molecular biology**, **embryology**, **taxonomy** and **palaeontology**.

3. The present-day Australian fauna can be understood by suggesting that marsupials evolved there to occupy the ecological niches filled elsewhere by eutherian mammals.

4. The theory of **plate tectonics** explains **continental drift** which in turn allows the distribution of organisms on the various continents to provide evidence for evolution.

5. Darwin visited the Galapagos islands during his voyage on the Beagle. The finches, tortoises and other species there provided him with some of his clearest evidence of evolution.

6. From comparative anatomy the principle of **homology** emerges. This can be explained in terms of **divergent evolution** and **adaptive radiation** and provides evidence for evolution. A clear example is the vertebrate pentadactyl limb.

7. Groups with separate evolutionary origins may appear to be similar as a result of **convergent evolution**.

Superficially similar structures shared by such groups are called **analogous structures**.

8. The fundamental similarities in the structure and functioning of all cells and the ubiquitous occurrence of many biochemicals suggests a common ancestry for all organisms.

9. **Biochemical homology**, established by techniques such as amino acid sequence analysis and DNA hybridisation studies, provides further evidence for evolutionary affinities within certain groups.

10. Sometimes **comparative embryology** can provide evidence for evolutionary affinities which are not evident from studying the adult forms.

11. **Taxonomy**, the classification of organisms, is not so much evidence for evolution as a consequence of it.

12. The most direct evidence for evolution derives from **palaeontology**, the study of **fossils**. The fossil record can be used to trace evolutionary pathways in detail as in the case of the evolution of horses.

13. The theory that all life today is descended through evolution from original inorganic precursors is testable, albeit only indirectly, and is therefore a scientific theory. However, the evidence in favour of it, although held by many to be convincing, is not absolutely conclusive.

For general advice on these questions and advice on answering essay-type questions, see pages vii and viii.

1. Haemoglobin in mammals is made up of four polypeptide chains, two identical α chains and two identical β chains. The sequence of amino acids in these chains has been determined for a number of different mammals.

Table 1 below shows a sequence of fifteen amino acids in an α chain from four different primates: a chimpanzee, a human, a gorilla and an orang-utan.

Table 1

Primate	Amino acid sequence
Chimpanzee	K A A W G K V G A H A G E Y G
Gorilla	K A A W G K V G A H A G D Y G
Human	K A A W G K V G A H A G E Y G
Orang-utan	K T A W G K V G A H A G D Y G

Key: A = alanine   D = asparagine   E = glutamic acid
       G = glycine   H = histidine   K = lysine
       T = threonine   V = valine   W = tryptophan
       Y = tyrosine

(a) (i)   What differences are there between the amino acid sequence for the orang-utan and for the chimpanzee? (1)

    (ii) Name *one* other pair of primates in the table in which there is a difference in the amino acid sequence. (1)

(b) Comparisons of amino acid sequences have been used to determine evolutionary (phylogenetic) relationships in the primates.

    (i) Using evidence given in Table 1, copy and complete the evolutionary tree diagram below to show the possible evolutionary relationship between chimpanzees, gorillas, humans and orang-utans. (3)

Common ancestor ——————— Chimpanzee

    (ii) Give *two* ways in which the data in Table 1 support your suggested evolutionary relationship. (2)

(c) When human blood serum is injected into a rabbit, the rabbit produces antibodies against human serum proteins. When blood serum from humans and other mammals is mixed with rabbit serum containing these antibodies, precipitation occurs.

Table 2 below shows the percentage precipitation when this rabbit serum was mixed with serum from a human, a gibbon, a spider monkey and a hedgehog.

Table 2

Mammal	Percentage precipitation
Human	100
Gibbon	79
Spider monkey	58
Hedgehog	17

What do these data suggest about the phylogenetic relationship of the four mammals in Table 2? (2)

(d) (i)   Describe how fossils can be used to provide evidence for human evolution. (3)

    (ii) Give *one* disadvantage of the use of fossils in providing evidence for human evolution.

(1)

(Total 13 marks)

London 1998

2. (a) What do you understand by the term 'adaptive radiation'? Illustrate your answer by reference to either the Australian fauna or to that of the Galapagos Islands. (2)

(b) Construct a fully labelled diagram of the foot of the following hypothetical animals:

    (i)   a large swamp-dwelling reptile, (2)

    (ii) a tree-dwelling primate, (2)

    (iii) a large desert animal, (2)

    (iv) an aquatic amphibian. (2)

(Total 10 marks)

3. Make a list of the principal lines of evidence which support the theory of evolution. Which ones do you find the least convincing and the most convincing? Go on to discuss in detail one piece of evidence which you personally find most convincing.

(Total 10 marks)

The mechanism of evolution

Natural selection, as proposed by Darwin and Wallace, is still thought to be the driving force for evolution. In this chapter we shall look at the theory of natural selection and see that although Darwin and Wallace's ideas are still considered correct in their essentials, a great deal more is now known about how evolution takes place.

43.1 The theory of natural selection

Darwin and Wallace's theory of natural selection is so simple that when Darwin's close friend, T. H. Huxley, read of it, he said 'how stupid of me not to have thought of it first'. The theory can be summarised by means of four hypotheses which result in two conclusions:

- **Hypothesis 1** Individuals differ from one another, the differences arising as a result of chance variation (*figure 43.1*).
- **Hypothesis 2** Offspring generally resemble their parents (*figure 43.2*).
- **Hypothesis 3** More offspring are born than can survive to maturity and reproduce (*figure 43.3*).
- **Hypothesis 4** There is a **struggle for existence**; some individuals being better **adapted** to their environment and therefore more successful than others (*figure 43.4*).
- **Conclusion 1** The better adapted individuals that survive and reproduce pass on their beneficial characteristics to their offspring.
- **Conclusion 2** In time, the individuals in a species may give rise to a new collection of individuals that are sufficiently distinct to be classified as a separate species.

Lamarck's theory

A central feature of the theory of natural selection is that the variations which form the 'raw material' for natural selection arise spontaneously. They are in no way dictated by the environment or purposefully geared towards making the organism better adapted. This idea is in direct contrast to an alternative theory put forward in 1809 (coincidentally, the year of Darwin's birth) by the French naturalist Jean-Baptiste Pierre Antoine de Monet, Chevalier de Lamarck, generally referred to as Lamarck.

Lamarck's idea was based on the observation that structures which are subjected to

Figure 43.1 Individual variation within a species of snail (*Cepaea hortensis*).

Figure 43.2 In all species, offspring usually resemble their parents.

Figure 43.3 The chance of all these young blue tits surviving to adulthood is very small.

Figure 43.4 A group of elm trees, some of which have succumbed to Dutch Elm disease. The healthy trees have proved better able to withstand the effects of the fungus.

Alfred Russel Wallace

Alfred Russel Wallace was born on 7 January 1823. He was one of eight children and left school at the age of 14 because of his family's financial difficulties. In 1843 he became a teacher at a Leicester boarding school. There he had a stroke of good fortune: he met the naturalist Henry Bates (remembered today for Batesian mimicry – *page 717*).

As a result of this meeting, Wallace found himself at the age of 25, despite his lack of biological education, deep in the Amazon basin with Bates on a four-year expedition. Short of food, and suffering periodically from malaria, tropical ulcers and other infections, Wallace nevertheless collected nearly 15 000 animal species, some 8000 of which were new to science.

Then disaster struck. On the return journey in 1852 the ship caught fire and Wallace lost all his specimens and most of his notes. Undeterred, he set off in 1854 for what was to prove to be an eight-year expedition to the Malay Archipelago. It was here in 1858 that, as he lay ill with

fever, he wrote 'Why do some die and some live?... from the effects of disease, the most healthy escape; from enemies, the strongest, the swiftest, or the most cunning; from famine, the best hunters or those with the best digestion'. On his recovery, Wallace wrote a 12-page paper on his ideas and sent it to Darwin.

Darwin received Wallace's letter on 18 June 1858 and was stunned. Its basic argument was identical to his own. Sixteen years before, in 1842, Darwin had sketched out his theory of natural selection and two years later had expanded it into a 160-page manuscript. However, he had published neither his sketch nor the essay. Wallace's letter came out of the blue. Darwin wrote in confusion to the geologist Charles Lyell, the botanist Joseph Hooker and others. The result was that a meeting of the Linnean Society in London was presented with Wallace's letter together with a five-page summary of Darwin's theory. For these reasons we should think of the theory of natural selection not just as

Darwin's theory, but as the **Darwin–Wallace theory**.

Wallace returned from his eight-year expedition in 1862, having collected an incredible 125 660 specimens. For the rest of his long life he remained in England, writing and lecturing. He seems to have been a very modest man, calling, for instance, his own book on natural selection *Darwinism*.

He had a great belief in social reform, exposing, for example, the greed of absentee English landlords in Ireland and Scotland. His passion for social justice brought him into conflict with the establishment and he wasn't elected a Fellow of the Royal Society until he was 69 years old.

He lived for another 21 years, dying in 1913. By that time the Darwin–Wallace theory of natural selection had become almost universally accepted as the cornerstone of modern biology.

Figure 43.5 Giraffe browsing a tall tree in East Africa. Alternative explanations as to how the long neck evolved were offered by Lamarck and by Darwin.

constant use become well developed, whereas those that are not tend to degenerate. Lamarck proposed that when an organism develops a need for a particular structure, this causes the appearance of the structure.

This in itself is not an unreasonable proposition; after all, everyone knows the effect that exercise and training can have on the development of muscles in an athlete or swimmer. But Lamarck suggested that these beneficial characteristics, acquired during an individual's lifetime, could be handed on to the offspring. In other words, evolutionary change could be achieved by the **transmission of acquired characteristics**. This implies that a swimmer who has developed large powerful arm muscles would produce children born with especially large powerful arm muscles.

Darwin and Lamarck compared

To illustrate the difference between Darwin's and Lamarck's theories, consider the case of the giraffe (*figure 43.5*). Palaeontologists are confident, from fossil evidence, that the ancestors of the modern giraffe had short necks, and that in the course of geological history the neck gradually got longer. How do we explain this?

A Lamarckian explanation would go something like this. The ancestors of the giraffe fed on the leaves of bushes and trees and, competing with each other for a limited food supply, stretched their necks in order to reach the higher branches. This condition was transmitted to the offspring who therefore started with somewhat longer necks and repeated the process. Hence the descendants of the original stock acquired progressively longer necks.

The Darwinian explanation is based on a quite different premise, namely that the occasional occurrence of a giraffe with a longer than average neck was a chance event and not the result of environmental need. In past generations some individuals *happened* to have longer necks than others. Since they could reach the leaves on higher branches than their shorter-necked contemporaries, such individuals were more successful in the struggle for existence and passed on this characteristic to their offspring.

Darwin and Lamarck today

How do the Darwinian and Lamarckian theories stand today? In the course of the last 100 years a mass of evidence has been marshalled in support of the Darwin–Wallace theory of natural selection. On the other hand, with possibly one or two exceptions, no decisive evidence has been found in favour of Lamarck's theory.

Just because Lamarck's theory is now thought to be incorrect, it does not mean that the theory is worthless or that Lamarck was somehow to blame for this! It is the way of science that most theories, however successful they are for a while, eventually become superseded. Lamarck's theory is perfectly reasonable. It just doesn't happen to be supported by the evidence. In its time it was a valuable theory, not least because it helped Darwin to propose an alternative one.

When Lamarck and Darwin put forward their ideas, practically nothing was known

Extension

Evolution: a gene's eye view

Are we just vehicles for our genes? Guest author Richard Dawkins suggests that we are, and briefly explains his reasoning.

Why are we living things so good at doing what we do? It is because we are descended from an unbroken line of successful ancestors. Almost all individuals die young, but not a single, solitary one of your ancestors did. From an unbroken line of successful ancestors, all living things inherit what it takes to be successful. This tells us what adaptation really is. An adaptation is a device for becoming an ancestor.

We inherit what it takes to be successful and this means, of course, successful genes. Adaptations are devices created by successful, as opposed to unsuccessful, genes. Udders exist, and are well-adapted for suckling, for one reason only: genes that give mothers good udders save copies of those very same genes in the bodies of the young suckled. Penises are well-adapted for inserting sperm into females because genes that make good penises have shot their way down the generations through a long succession of ancestral good penises, and that is why those genes are still around. Genes that made ineffective penises are no longer present in the world. Of course many adaptations work by fostering individual survival – strong teeth, sharp claws, swift limbs, keen eyes – but this is not the end; it is a means to the end of preserving copies of the genes inside the individual.

An adaptation – it might be an organ or an entire body – is best seen as a device for preserving and propagating the genes that made it. You can usually get away with saying that an adaptation is a device for enhancing the 'fitness', in the sense of reproductive success, of an individual. But even this is incorrect for worker ants, termites and bees which, being sterile, have no offspring but only brothers and sisters, nephews and nieces. This difficulty disappears the moment we take a gene's eye view of evolution. Genes that make sterile bees work and sacrifice themselves for their hive are preserved, not in the workers' own bodies nor, obviously, in their offspring, but in the young queens and drones emerging from the hive. Those new queens and drones will begin new hives, and produce new sterile workers driven to similar action by copies of those very same genes.

Natural selection, if it is to have a long-term effect on evolution, must choose between alternative entities that aspire to being long term. These entities must have at least the potential to survive indefinitely through generation after generation in the form of copies. Genes have this potential immortality. Bodies, even the best of them, are mortal. The most natural view of adaptive evolution is the gene's eye view. A body is the genes' way of making more genes. A body is a 'throwaway survival machine' for its genes.

Richard Dawkins, author of The Selfish Gene *and other books on evolution, is Professor of the Public Understanding of Science and a Fellow of New College, Oxford.*

about heredity. Subsequent research by geneticists, including the pioneering work of Mendel reviewed in Chapter 32, has provided a clearer understanding of inheritance and firm support for the Darwinian theory. This reappraisal of the theory of natural selection in terms of modern genetics is sometimes called **neo-Darwinism**.

We shall look at the key points in neo-Darwinism one at a time.

43.2 **Variation**

Both environmental and genetic differences contribute to variation (*page 571*). From the evolutionary point of view, genetic variation (i.e. the kind that can be transmitted from parents to offspring) is what is important, not environmental variation (*figure 43.6*). With this in mind, let us look into the causes of genetic variation and assess their role in evolution.

The causes of genetic variation

There are several causes of genetic variation. In the first place, as explained on page 462, during metaphase of the first meiotic division homologous chromosomes come together in pairs and subsequently segregate into the daughter cells independently of each other. The result of this **independent assortment** is the production of a wide variety of gametes which differ from each other according to which particular chromosomes end up with one another in each daughter cell. This in turn depends on the way the various chromosomes line up on the spindle prior to separating.

The number of possible different combinations depends on how many pairs of chromosomes there are in the parent cell. To illustrate this, consider three pairs of chromosomes. From figure 43.7 you can see that the various ways in which they can segregate give a total of eight possible combinations in the gametes. In general terms, the number of different combinations that can occur is 2^n, where n is the haploid number of chromosomes, in this case three. In humans, with a haploid number of 23, the number of combinations is 2^{23}, almost 10 million.

The mechanism described above, though important in promoting genetic variety, can only mix up alleles of genes carried on different chromosomes. It can play no part in separating and recombining alleles carried on the same chromosomes. This second source

Figure 43.6 Some of the differences in the appearance of these birch trees in Siberia will be genetic in origin, others environmental. For instance, trees at the edge of a wood experience greater differences in light intensity and wind strength than those trees inside the wood. Even if all the trees in a wood are genetically identical, as can happen with large clones of elm trees, we expect to see differences in their growth form.

▶ Meiosis, page 461

Figure 43.7 These diagrams show how different kinds of gametes can be formed even in the absence of crossing over, depending on how homologous chromosomes segregate during meiosis. The parent cells show the different ways chromosomes can arrange themselves on the spindle prior to separating. The gametes show the different combinations of chromosomes resulting from meiosis. Note that up to eight different gametes may be produced (2 to the power of 3), three being the haploid number in this example. The two members of each pair of homologous chromosomes are here given different colours (red and yellow). Although homologous chromosomes are identical in size and shape, they may differ in the complement of dominant and recessive alleles that they carry.

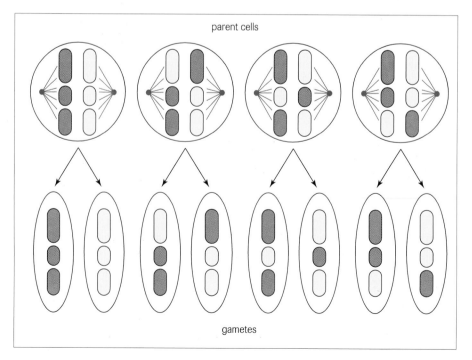

parent cells

gametes

of genetic variation is provided by **crossing over**.

In prophase of the first meiotic division, when homologous chromosomes are in intimate contact with one another, the chromatids of homologous chromosomes may break and rejoin at any point along their length. The places where this happens are called **chiasmata** (*see page 462*). The number and positions of the chiasmata relative to the sequence of genes determines the different combinations possible in the gametes (*figure 43.8*).

As each chromatid typically carries hundreds or thousands of alleles, and as the number of chiasmata per chromatid may vary from zero to as many as eight, you can see that the amount of variation that may result from crossing over is enormous.

A third source of variety is achieved on **fertilisation**. Union of gametes results in the alleles present in one gamete being united with the alleles in another gamete. If a population consists of large numbers of breeding individuals, the amount of variation that may result from this is again enormous.

Despite the tremendous amount of variation that these three processes may generate, they play only a limited role in evolution. The reason is that although they may establish a new combination of alleles in one generation, they do not *generate* long-lasting variation of a novel kind. This kind of genetic variation is the result of mutations, to which we now turn.

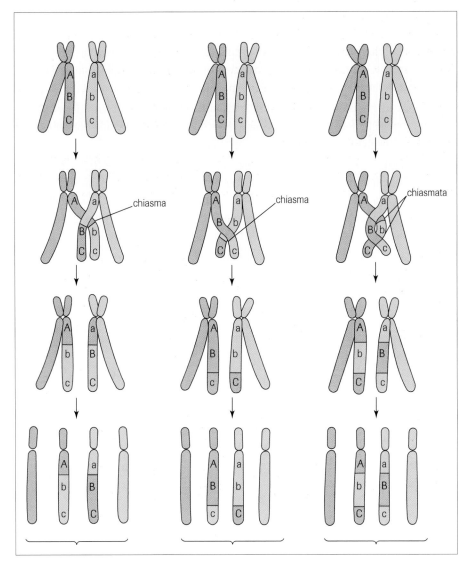

Figure 43.8 These diagrams show how crossing over between the chromatids of homologous chromosomes can lead to new combinations of alleles. The exact genotypes produced depend on the number of chiasmata and the positions of the genes relative to the sites of crossing over (chiasmata). The letters represent alleles on the chromosomes.

Figure 43.9 Bluebells, as their name suggests, normally have blue flowers. Occasionally, though, a mutant white-flowered individual occurs.

Table 43.1 Some mutagens and their effects. Colchicine is a drug extracted from the autumn crocus *Colchicum autumnale*. Its effects are described in more detail on page 747. The mutagenic effects of mustard gas (bis–2-–chloroethyl sulphide) were discovered in the 1940s when it was being investigated as a possible chemical warfare agent. Cyclamate is an artificial sweetener, now banned. Acridine orange is a dye used as a biological stain and in the dyeing industry.

Mutagen	Effect
X-rays	Gene and chromosome aberrations
UV light	Structural distortion of DNA
Colchicine	Prevents spindle-formation in mitosis and so doubles chromosome number
Cyclamate	Chromosome aberrations
Mustard gas	Guanine in DNA replaced by other bases
Nitrous acid	Adenine in DNA deaminated so it behaves like guanine
Acridine orange	Addition and/or removal of bases in DNA

What are mutations?

Every now and again a natural population of organisms throws up an individual with some characteristic that is strikingly different from the rest of the population (*figure 43.9*). Examples include haemophilia and cystic fibrosis in humans, white eyes and vestigial wings in *Drosophila*, resistance to penicillin in bacteria and to DDT in flies – the list is unending. It can be shown from studies of inheritance that these conditions are nearly always transmitted in a Mendelian fashion. Such novel genetic conditions are known as **mutations** and individuals showing them are referred to as **mutants**, though it would be insulting to refer to humans in this way.

It is characteristic of mutations that they are comparatively rare, at least from the perspective of a particular gene. In most organisms the mutation rate at any given locus varies between 1 and 30 mutations per million gametes. The exact number is variable since genes at different loci have different **mutation rates**. Low mutation rates bear witness to the tremendous accuracy with which DNA replicates.

Because mutation rates are low, geneticists found it difficult to investigate mutations until the American biologist H.J. Muller discovered in 1927 that the mutation rate in *Drosophila* can be greatly accelerated by irradiation with X-rays. Since then it has been found that other factors also speed up the mutation rate. These **mutagens** include gamma rays, ultraviolet light and a number of chemicals (*table 43.1*).

The discovery of mutagens made it easier to study the cause and transmission of mutations. Most experiments are carried out on bacteria and plants, though animal cells in tissue-culture may also be used. From these studies three main facts emerge:

- Mutations arise spontaneously and are in no sense 'directed' by the environment. Environmental influences can greatly affect the mutation *rate* but they cannot cause a particular mutation to occur.

- Mutations are persistent. They tend to be transmitted through many generations without further change, though there is always the possibility that they may mutate again, either producing another novel characteristic or reverting to the original condition.

- The vast majority of mutations confer disadvantages on the organisms that inherit them. Often mutations cause enzymes to function less efficiently or not at all. The occurrence of a useful mutation is an extremely rare event but does occasionally happen (*page 752*). Natural selection prevents harmful mutations surviving but ensures that beneficial mutations persist and spread through the population.

We can distinguish between two types of mutation: **chromosome mutations** and **gene mutations**. The former involve changes in the gross structure of chromosomes. The latter are chemical changes in individual genes.

Chromosome mutations

During meiosis when chromosomes become intertwined, there is plenty of opportunity for various kinds of structural aberration to take place.

For example, a chromosome may break in two places and the section in between may drop out, taking all its genes with it. If the two ends then join up, a shorter chromosome results with a chunk missing in its middle (*figure 43.10A*). This is called a **deletion** and, as it leads to an absence of certain genes, it can have a profound effect on the development of an organism. In fact all but the shortest deletions are usually fatal.

Another kind of chromosome abnormality occurs if a chromosome breaks in two places and the middle piece then turns round and joins up again, so that the normal sequence of genes is reversed. This is called an **inversion** (*figure 43.10B*).

Sometimes a section of one chromosome breaks off and becomes attached to another chromosome. This is known as a **translocation** (*figure 43.10C*). Inversions and translocations result in neither the loss nor the gain of genetic material, but change the

Why do people with HIV take so long to develop AIDS?

The significance of mutations is illustrated by HIV (human immunodeficiency virus). One of the unusual things about infection with HIV is that it typically takes years before any symptoms are seen. Indeed, some people infected with HIV never seem to progress to AIDS. (*The symptoms of AIDS are described on page 506.*)

Why is this? Recent research suggests that the answer may be related to the extraordinarily high mutation rate of HIV. HIV mutates up to a million times faster than some other viruses. In a person infected with HIV, the virus replicates and, because the mutation rate is so high, sooner or later the host's antibodies fail to recognise the viral antigens. Eventually enough of these mutant viruses accumulate to start attacking the person's immune system. That is approximately when the first symptoms of AIDS appear.

Support for this theory comes from observations on a group of Scottish haemophiliacs thought to have been infected with the same strain of HIV via contaminated blood products. Several years later all were infected with different strains of HIV.

If this theory turns out to be correct, then finding a cure for AIDS is going to be even harder than previously thought, and finding a vaccine exceptionally difficult. From the biological point of view, it is an impressive example of just how rapidly evolution can take place.

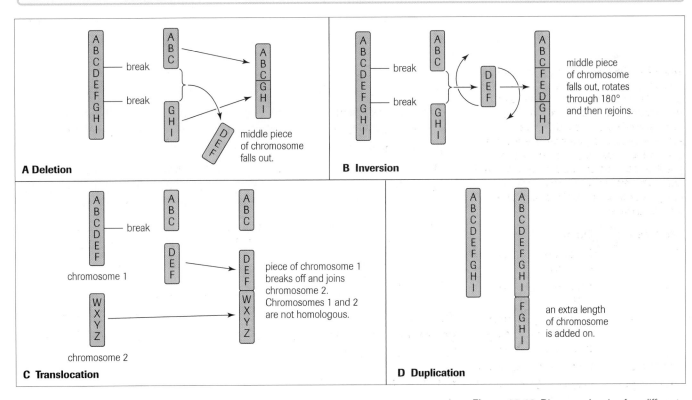

A Deletion — break, break, middle piece of chromosome falls out.

B Inversion — break, break, middle piece of chromosome falls out, rotates through 180° and then rejoins.

C Translocation — chromosome 1, chromosome 2, break. piece of chromosome 1 breaks off and joins chromosome 2. Chromosomes 1 and 2 are not homologous.

D Duplication — an extra length of chromosome is added on.

order in which genes occur on chromosomes. Often this disrupts gene regulation and very occasionally the resulting change in gene expression may benefit the organism.

Yet another abnormality occurs when a section of a chromosome replicates so that a set of genes is repeated: this is called **duplication** (*figure 43.10D*). Again, duplication is frequently harmful. However, on occasions it may be beneficial and selected for. The various genes that control the different haemoglobins produced in human red blood cells are thought to have arisen by duplications.

Another kind of chromosome abnormality is caused by the addition or loss of one or more whole chromosomes. Normally in meiosis homologous chromosomes come together and then segregate into separate cells, so that the gametes finish up with only one of each type of chromosome. However, on some occasions the two homologous chromosomes, instead of separating, go off into the same cell.

Figure 43.10 Diagrams showing four different types of chromosome mutation. Each type of mutation results in an alteration in the number and/or sequence of genes (represented by letters) on the chromosome.

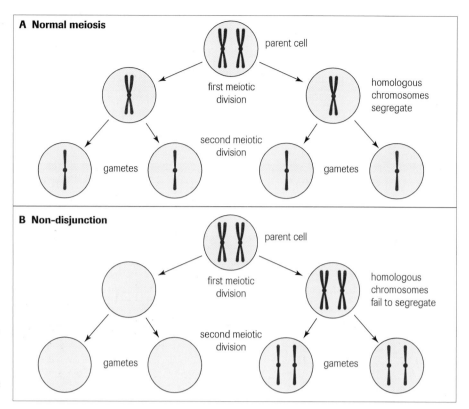

Figure 43.11 Diagram comparing normal meiosis with non-disjunction for one pair of chromosomes. In normal meiosis the homologous chromosomes segregate, so the gametes each contain one chromosome. In non-disjunction the chromosomes fail to segregate, so half the gametes contain two chromosomes each and the other half contain no chromosomes. Generally non-disjunction takes place with respect to just one pair of homologous chromosomes, the rest behaving normally. It can occur during either the first or the second meiotic division.

This phenomenon is known as **non-disjunction** and it results in the formation of two types of gametes in equal proportions: one type has two of the chromosomes whilst the other type has none (*figure 43.11*). The fusion of the first kind of gamete with a normal gamete gives a zygote with three such chromosomes, i.e. the normal pair plus an extra one. This condition is called **trisomy**. Fusion of the second kind of gamete with a normal gamete gives an individual with only one of this particular type of chromosome in each cell.

Chromosome mutations in humans

Quite how important non-disjunction has been in generating useful genetic novelty is uncertain, but there is no doubt that it can have a profound effect on an organism's development, as we can see by looking at two human examples.

Down's syndrome

Down's syndrome in humans is caused by the presence of an extra chromosome in each cell, chromosome number 21 to be precise (*figure 43.12*). This is one of the smallest of the human chromosomes, yet presence of an extra one plays havoc with the individual's normal development.

Children with Down's syndrome have a characteristic appearance with almond-shaped eyes and a roundish face (*figure 43.13*). They are mentally retarded and can rarely read or write more than a limited number of words. They often die before they are 30-years old as they are susceptible to infections and frequently have congenital heart disease. On the other hand, they are usually delightful children, happy and affectionate, enjoying both home life and school.

Since Down's syndrome affects one of the autosomes, i.e. the non-sex chromosomes, it is known as an **autosomal trisomy**. It is by far the commonest autosomal trisomy in humans. Its incidence increases, the older the mother is (*table 43.2*). However, as most women have their children in their 20s or early 30s, the majority of babies with Down's syndrome are born to women under the age of 40. Approximately a quarter of Down's syndrome cases are the result of non-disjunction in the father, and here, too, age has a significant effect: older men are more likely to father a Down's syndrome child.

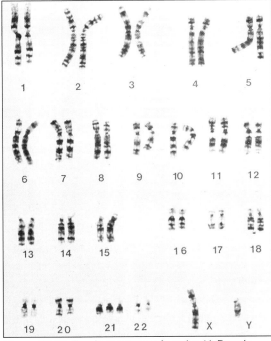

Figure 43.12 The chromosomes of a male with Down's syndrome. Notice that there are three copies of chromosome 21, giving a total of 47 chromosomes instead of the usual 46.

Figure 43.13 A young girl with Down's syndrome. In recent years considerable advances have been made in caring for people with Down's syndrome. The education of children with Down's syndrome is now much more appropriate, and many children with this syndrome have surprised their parents and teachers by showing how much they can learn. Better medical care also means that the outlook for adults with Down's syndrome has improved significantly.

Sex chromosome abnormalities

Various sex chromosome abnormalities in humans are also caused by non-disjunction. For example, approximately two in a thousand men have the genetic constitution XXY – **Klinefelter's syndrome**. This may result either from the fusion of a Y sperm with an XX egg, or from the fusion of an XY sperm with an X egg. Although XXY individuals are phenotypically men, they have very small genitals and are infertile; in addition, they may develop breasts. However, the condition is not usually associated with below-average intelligence, and testosterone therapy at puberty can often help alleviate the symptoms.

Another abnormality is due to the absence of one of the sex chromosomes. Fetuses with 22 normal pairs of autosomes and a single Y chromosome never survive to birth. However, children may be born with 22 normal pairs of autosomes and a single X chromosome. Such individuals are said to have the genetic constitution XO. They are females and occur with an incidence of approximately 0.4 per 1000 liveborn girls. The condition is known as **Turner's syndrome**. Individuals are usually shorter than normal with a characteristic webbed neck. Intelligence is not usually affected, but the person is infertile. Treatment with oestrogen can allow normal pubertal development, and growth can be stimulated by injections of growth hormone.

Polyploidy

Sometimes cell division fails altogether, resulting in half the gametes having two of each type of chromosome (i.e. being diploid), the rest having none. If a diploid gamete fuses with a normal haploid gamete the resulting individual is **triploid**, i.e. it has three of each type of chromosome. If two diploid gametes fuse, a **tetraploid** individual results. It is thus possible for an organism to acquire one or more complete extra sets of chromosomes, a phenomenon called **polyploidy**.

Polyploidy also occurs if the whole chromosome set doubles after fertilisation. In this case the chromosomes replicate as they would prior to mitosis. Sometimes, however, the

Table 43.2 The risk of a child being born with Down's syndrome increases the older the mother becomes.

Maternal age at birth of child	Risk of child having Down's syndrome
20 years	1 in 1925
25 years	1 in 1205
30 years	1 in 885
35 years	1 in 365
40 years	1 in 110
45 years	1 in 32
50 years	1 in 12

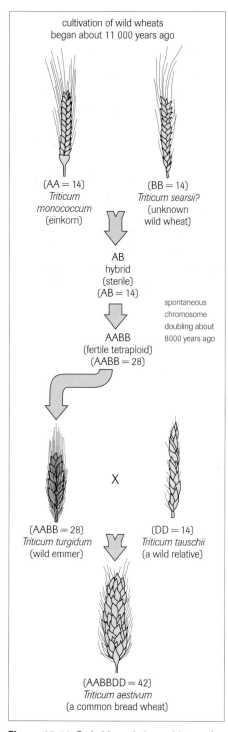

cultivation of wild wheats
began about 11 000 years ago

(AA = 14)
Triticum monococcum
(einkorn)

(BB = 14)
Triticum searsii?
(unknown wild wheat)

AB
hybrid
(sterile)
(AB = 14)

spontaneous
chromosome
doubling about
8000 years ago

AABB
(fertile tetraploid)
(AABB = 28)

(AABB = 28)
Triticum turgidum
(wild emmer)

X

(DD = 14)
Triticum tauschii
(a wild relative)

(AABBDD = 42)
Triticum aestivum
(a common bread wheat)

Figure 43.14 Probable evolutionary history of modern wheat over the last 10 000 years or so as revealed by a combination of archaeology and genetics. The letters A, B and D each refer to a different set of seven chromosomes. For example, *Triticum aestivum* has two sets of A chromosomes, two sets of B chromosomes and two sets of D chromosomes.

spindle fails to form and the cell does not divide, finishing up with twice the normal number of chromosomes. If this happens to a diploid cell, a tetraploid results; if it happens to a triploid cell, a hexaploid results.

Such post-fertilisation polyploidy can be particularly important in cases where two different, but closely related species, are crossed. The diploid offspring will be incapable of producing gametes, and are therefore sterile, because the chromosomes, being non-homologous, will be unable to pair during meiosis. (If you find it difficult to follow this explanation, try drawing what happens at anaphase I of meiosis in a cell with, say, four chromosomes, two from one species and two from another, remembering that none of the chromosomes will be homologous.) However, if the diploid number is doubled, giving the tetraploid condition, each chromosome will have a homologous one with which it can pair. As a result, successful meiosis will be possible.

Examples of polyploidy

Polyploidy is thought to have been important in the evolution of wheat. Modern wheat – the type we use for bread-making – is believed to have evolved from a sterile hybrid whose chromosome number doubled about 8000 years ago (*figure 43.14*). In 1998, evidence from DNA analysis suggested that there have been at least two distinct domestications of wheat. It seems as though wheat began to be farmed at about the same time across a wide area of the Middle East, rather than starting in only one place and spreading from there.

A more recent example of polyploidy is provided by the evolution of the cord grass *Spartina anglica* whose remarkable success is discussed in the extension box below.

Extension

Polyploidy in *Spartina*

In 1829, a plant with the name of *Spartina alterniflora* (2n = 62) was first recorded in the British Isles after being introduced to Southampton Water in shipping ballast. This species hybridised with *S. maritima* (2n = 60), a plant which, on the south coast of England, is at the northern limit of its natural distribution. The result was a sterile hybrid called *S. x townsendii* (2n = 61) which first appeared in Southampton Water around 1870.

About 1890, *S. x townsendii* doubled its chromosome number and gave rise to *S. anglica*, a fertile tetraploid with 122 chromosomes. *S. anglica* is a tough, vigorous halophyte which uses the C_4 pathway in photosynthesis (*page 213*). It spread rapidly both vegetatively and by seed, outcompeting the other species. It is now widely distributed around the coast of the British Isles. Indeed, certain areas are choked with it. There is some

evidence that the number of over-wintering birds, dunlin for example, have declined as a result. This is because such birds find it difficult to penetrate the dense sward to reach their invertebrate food supply in the nutrient-rich intertidal sediment. This illustrates the far-reaching ecological consequences of an organism doubling its chromosome number.

Cord grass (*Spartina anglica*), a vigorous halophyte which has evolved as a result of polyploidy, is here seen flourishing in the salt marshes around Poole Harbour, Dorset.

Polyploidy is rare in animals, but common in plants. In fact, approximately half of all plant species are polyploid. Polyploidy is often associated with advantageous characteristics such as increased size and greater hardiness, though such advantages are sometimes offset by reduced fertility.

Reduced fertility is particularly common when individuals are triploid (3n), or when tetraploidy (4n) results not from the crossing of individuals from two different species, but simply from a doubling of the chromosome number in one species. Infertile triploids and tetraploids are commercially significant precisely because they are infertile. Many of the seedless bananas, grapes and other fruit we eat are the result of such polyploidy.

Gene mutations

Gene mutations are thought to have been very important instigators of evolutionary change. A gene mutation arises as a result of a chemical change in an individual gene. An alteration in the sequence of nucleotides in the part of a DNA molecule that corresponds to a particular gene may change the order of amino acids making up a protein. This may have far-reaching consequences on the fitness of an organism, as in the case of sickle cell anaemia (*page 645*).

The kind of gene mutation that causes sickle cell anaemia is called a **substitution**. This is because the mutation results from the substitution of one base for another in the DNA. In sickle cell anaemia, instead of the triplet coding for the sixth amino acid of haemoglobin being CTT, it is CAT – in other words thymine is replaced by adenine at this particular point in the DNA molecule. As a result, the sixth amino acid is valine rather than the usual glutamic acid.

When a gene mutation involves a change in only a single base, as in the case just mentioned, it is called a **point mutation**. However, some gene mutations involve a change in two or more bases.

If we look upon DNA as a conveyor of coded information, we can see at once that even a very slight change may be enough to alter completely its information content. As an analogy, consider the faulty information which might be conveyed by a sentence in which a single incorrect letter is substituted for the intended one:

Intended message:	SUSAN IS NOW ARRIVING BY AIR FROM NEW YORK.
Actual message:	SUSAN IS NOT ARRIVING BY AIR FROM NEW YORK.

Let us consider some other misprints. Here is an example of an extra letter creeping into a message. A geneticist would call it an **insertion**:

Intended message:	PLEASE SAY WHERE YOU ARE.
Actual message:	PLEASE STAY WHERE YOU ARE.

On the other hand a letter might be left out (**deletion**):

Intended message:	RE YOUR ENQUIRY ABOUT ROOMS NONE AVAILABLE.
Actual message:	RE YOUR ENQUIRY ABOUT ROOMS ONE AVAILABLE.

Another possibility is that two or more letters might be printed the wrong way round, resulting in an **inversion**:

Intended message:	WOULD YOU LIKE TO PLAY A LEADING PART IN OUR PRODUCTION?
Actual message:	WOULD YOU LIKE TO PLAY A LEADING PRAT IN OUR PRODUCTION?

Actual examples of all these types of gene mutation are known.

Extension

Inducing polyploidy

Polyploidy can be induced experimentally by heat or cold shock or by various chemical agents, notably **colchicine**, an alkaloid substance extracted from the crocus *Colchicum*. Applied in the correct amounts, colchicine prevents spindle-formation during mitosis. The chromosomes replicate in the usual way but the absence of a spindle means that anaphase fails and when the nuclear envelope reforms, cells often result with twice the normal number of chromosomes.

Prenatal diagnosis

A number of techniques are now available to test for chromosomal and gene mutations in human fetuses. At the moment these techniques are mostly used to detect abnormalities, on the basis of which the parents may be offered the option of a termination of pregnancy. However, in the future some of the techniques may be developed to allow certain genetic disorders to be treated.

The best known technique for prenatal (before birth) diagnosis is **amniocentesis** (*illustration 1A*). A long, hollow needle with a fine point is inserted through the mother's abdominal wall into the amniotic cavity in the uterus, and a sample of amniotic fluid is drawn off. This fluid contains fetal cells, some of which are alive and can be cultured. The cultured cells are then stained to show up the chromosomes and reveal any chromosome abnormalities, such as that responsible for Down's syndrome.

The procedure is usually carried out around 14–16 weeks into gestation and it takes about three to four weeks for the cells to be cultured and chromosome mutations revealed (*page 742*). The risk that the procedure will give rise to a miscarriage is about 0.5 per cent. It is also possible to test the amniotic fluid by DNA analysis for a number of gene mutations.

Another, more recent, approach to prenatal diagnosis is **chorionic villi sampling** (*illustration 1B*). Here, a narrow tube is inserted through the cervix and a tiny sample is taken of the chorionic villi from the placenta. This is embryonic, rather than maternal, in origin, so that chromosome staining and examination can be carried out to test for chromosome mutations in the fetus.

More fetal cells are obtained in chorionic villi sampling than in amniocentesis, which means that this technique can be carried out earlier (from around 8–10 weeks into gestation) and the results obtained more quickly (within

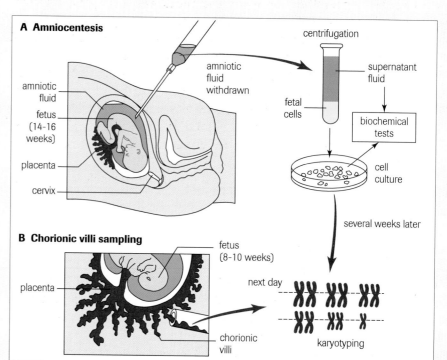

Illustration 1 The techniques of amniocentesis and chorionic villi sampling compared.

a couple of days). However, the risk that the procedure will give rise to a miscarriage is higher than for amniocentesis, being about 2 per cent.

A quite different approach is provided by **α fetoprotein screening**. In this procedure the concentration in the *mother's* blood of a particular protein called α fetoprotein is determined. About 80 per cent of cases of open neural tube defects (spina bifida) and over 90 per cent of cases of anencephaly (in which a part of the skull and brain fail to develop) can be detected by an increased maternal serum concentration of α fetoprotein. On the other hand, an unusually low α fetoprotein concentration in the mother's blood is associated with an increased risk of Down's syndrome. This technique carries no risk to the fetus.

Other approaches used in diagnosis and screening programmes include the use of **X-rays**, various imaging techniques (including **CAT scans**) and **endoscopy**. In endoscopy, a tube with a light source transmitting illumination via

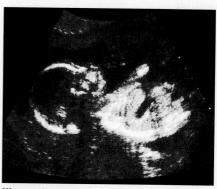

Illustration 2 Ultrascan showing a healthy human fetus around 21 weeks gestation.

bundles of glass fibres is used to visualise interior parts of the body. Cameras can be attached to such endoscopes.

A final approach involves **ultrasound** (*illustration 2*). This technique very probably carries no risk to the fetus and can be used to test for a wide range of structural abnormalities including hydrocephaly ('water on the brain'), various types of congenital heart disease, clefts of the lip and palate, and bone abnormalities. Ultrasonography also tells the mother whether or not she is carrying twins.

Somatic mutation

Sometimes a mutation occurs in a non-reproductive (i.e. somatic) cell of an organism. This is called a **somatic mutation**. The resulting genetic change will be present in all the cells descended from the original mutant cell and, as such, may profoundly affect the individual. However, as the genetic change is only in non-reproductive cells, it will not appear in the gametes and so cannot be transmitted to future generations.

Somatic mutations cause such phenomena as birthmarks in humans. Whatever their manifestations, somatic mutations result in some cells of the organism having a different genetic constitution from the rest. Such an individual is described as a **genetic mosaic**.

The proportion of cells affected depends on how early in development the mutation occurs: obviously, more cells will show the genetic change if the mutation occurs in the early embryo rather than in the adult. Somatic mutations can occur at any stage in life and an accumulation of them in older individuals is thought to contribute to senescence (*page 634*).

43.3 The struggle for existence

If you turn back to the four hypotheses of the Darwin–Wallace theory of natural selection (*page 737*), you will see that they include the idea that more offspring are born than can survive to maturity and reproduce, and that there is a struggle for existence, some individuals being better adapted for this struggle than others.

Let us consider these propositions in more detail. First, see if you can answer the following question. In a species consisting of equal numbers of males and females, how many offspring would each sexually reproducing female need to produce during her lifetime for the population to remain constant in numbers, assuming no infant mortality?

The answer is two. Now there is no species in the world in which adult females only produce two offspring during their lifetime. Even in elephants, a female typically produces about eight young during her lifetime. This means that in every species more offspring are born than can possibly survive to reproduce.

Malthus and the limit to exponential growth

The first person to realise the importance of the fact that more individuals are born than can survive was Thomas Malthus, an English clergyman, who in 1798 argued that while the human population increases geometrically (i.e. exponentially), the food supply only grows arithmetically, as shown in figure 43.15. This means that in time the number of people alive will always tend to outstrip the available food supply, leading to 'famine, pestilence and war'.

It was a grim doctrine which challenged the optimism of the time. Many of Malthus' contemporaries disagreed with his argument, partly because England was then enjoying a period of prosperity and sustained population growth. Indeed, with hindsight it is difficult to see why food supply should only increase arithmetically. However, despite any logical imperfections in the argument, both Darwin and Wallace were much impressed with it. They each saw that it applied to all organisms, not just humans. In the Malthusian argument they could see the seeds of a mechanism for evolution.

While Malthus appreciated that exponential growth cannot continue forever, it was Darwin and Wallace who, separately, realised that the mortality that keeps population sizes from increasing for ever is not random, i.e. it does not affect all individuals equally. It strikes more fiercely at those individuals that are least well adapted for survival. In other words the population is kept in check by a process of *differential* mortality.

As well as keeping the population on an even keel, differential mortality favours the perpetuation of beneficial characteristics. However, it does not necessarily follow that the

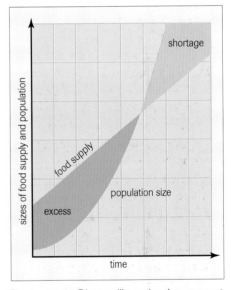

Figure 43.15 Diagram illustrating the argument of Thomas Malthus that in time human population growth will always outstrip the food supply. Although the reasoning behind Malthus' argument is open to question, his ideas played a crucial role in helping both Darwin and Wallace to come up with the theory of natural selection.

individuals which are the fittest physically are also the fittest genetically. Only if there is a genetic basis to differential survival and reproduction can evolution by natural selection occur, as we shall now see.

43.4 **Natural selection**

From the evolutionary point of view, differential mortality is important because, if it occurs before the individual has had a chance to reproduce, it eliminates unfavourable alleles from the population.

However, death is not the only way of achieving this. Any process that encourages the transmission of favourable alleles and hinders the transmission of unfavourable ones contributes towards evolution. Given enough time, an allele which is associated with only a very slight reduction in viability, fertility or fecundity will usually be eliminated from the population.

Natural selection as an agent of constancy as well as change

A central conclusion from Darwin's theory is that species change over time. In proposing his theory, a major difficulty Darwin had to contend with was that species appear to remain remarkably constant. This was seized upon by some of his critics as a weakness in the argument.

But in fact, natural selection is responsible both for maintaining the constancy of species and for changing them. To see how this works, imagine that we construct a frequency distribution curve for mass in a population of organisms and obtain the result shown in figure 43.16A. Now suppose that we identify those individuals that reproduce and leave viable offspring. These individuals are shown in figure 43.16B. You can see how only those individuals whose mass is close to the average reproduce. None of the very light nor any of the very heavy individuals contribute to the next generation. This kind of selection is known as **stabilising selection** because it maintains the constancy of species over generations.

Stabilising selection normally occurs when the environment remains constant over time. If, however, the environment changes, for instance by becoming colder in winter, then it may be an advantage to be larger than before. A new mass becomes the 'ideal' or 'optimum' and the result is that the frequency curve of the breeding individuals becomes shifted to the right. The net effect is to achieve an overall increase in the mean size of individuals in the population – provided, of course, that mass is at least partly heritable. This kind of selection favours the emergence of new forms and is called **directional selection**.

Figure 43.16

A Hypothetical diagram showing a frequency distribution curve for the mass of individuals in a population.
B Hypothetical diagram for the same individuals illustrated in **A**, but showing (by colour) which individuals breed.

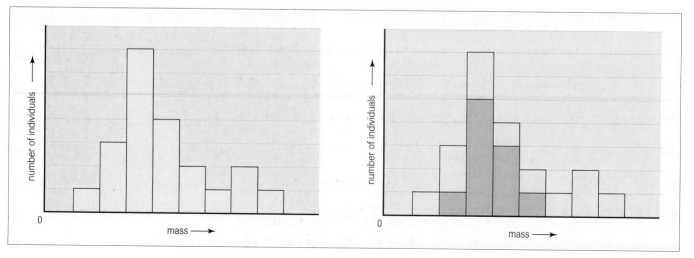

A hypothetical example of a population subjected to alternate periods of stabilising and directional selection is shown in figure 43.17. However, in reality such evolution would usually take hundreds or thousands of generations, rather than the very few shown here. A third kind of selection is **disruptive selection**. Here, natural selection results in the formation of two new forms from a single existing form.

Natural selection in action

Another weakness in Darwin's original theory was that he was unable to demonstrate natural selection actually taking place. This is understandable, for palaeontologists calculate that it often takes over a million years for one species to evolve into another!

Today, though, we do have examples of natural selection in action. Remember, for example, the evolution of the cord grass *Spartina anglica* which we discussed earlier in this chapter. Here, within 150 years, a new species evolved and spread hundreds of miles, outcompeting other species as it did so.

Another instance of natural selection was discussed in detail on page 644, namely the evolution of melanism in the peppered moth (*Biston betularia*). Other, more recent examples are given in the extension box on the next page.

43.5 The origins of species

A species can be defined as a group of organisms which are potentially able to breed amongst themselves but not with any other species. Often, though, we cannot employ this definition directly. Palaeontologists, for instance, never have the opportunity to see whether their fossils can breed with one another or not. In such situations a different criterion is used, one of **morphological similarity**.

Morphological similarity makes use of the common observation that species can be distinguished by their appearance – a song thrush looks recognisably different from a blackbird, for instance. However, there are dangers in using morphological similarities as the sole criterion for what constitutes a species. For example, in many species of animals, males and females look very different from each other.

The importance of isolation

Over time, one species may evolve into another. This process is called **speciation**. If, however, one species is to evolve into two, it is necessary for the species to become split up into at least two separate populations, each with its own gene pool. These populations must be almost totally isolated from each other because if more than a tiny amount of gene exchange occurs between them they will effectively behave as one population and any genetic differences which might arise between them will not be perpetuated. If they are isolated, mutation and selection can take place independently in the two populations and each may develop into a distinct species.

Isolation is often geographic in origin. Such isolation provides the opportunity for each population to evolve along its own lines. If the two populations subsequently come together, each may have changed to such an extent that for physiological or genetic reasons interbreeding is impossible. If this is the case, the two populations have become separate species. In time it is likely that they will diverge even further, unless one of them becomes extinct.

Isolating mechanisms

Two main kinds of isolating mechanisms can lead to the emergence of new species:

   Geographical isolation When a population becomes geographically split into separate populations, the evolution of new species is very probable, given the passage of enough time. This sort of speciation is known as **allopatric speciation** (literally

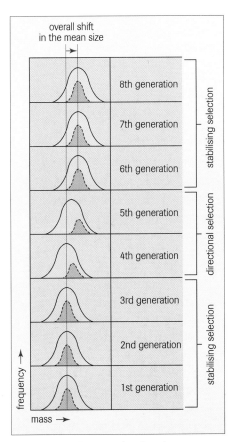

Figure 43.17 Diagram showing alternate periods of stabilising and directional selection. Stabilising selection is responsible for maintaining the constancy of species. Directional selection causes, in this case, a shift in the mean mass by favouring heavier individuals. In each generation the frequency curve for all individuals born is shown as a continuous line. The curve for breeding individuals is shown as a broken line.

'speciation in different countries'). Clear examples are provided on oceanic islands, such as the Galapagos Islands (*page 723*).

- **Reproductive isolation**. This occurs when ecological, behavioural or genetic barriers arise *within* a population and prevent certain individuals from breeding with each other. Suppose, for instance, that within a species of insect which is active during the day a mutation occurs that causes a few individuals to be active at night. There is a

Recent examples of natural selection

Natural selection is not just a process of the past. It still happens and is responsible for a continuous process of evolution. Some recent examples are given here.

Heavy metal tolerance in plants

One of the most convincing examples of natural selection is provided by the evolution in certain grasses of tolerance to heavy metals, such as copper, zinc and lead, enabling them to flourish on the spoil from mines. Work in the 1950s and 1960s by A.D. Bradshaw of the University of Liverpool showed that this tolerance could evolve in less than 30 years.

Various physiological mechanisms have evolved which allow these plants to grow and reproduce in soils where heavy metals are present at concentrations that kill normal plants. In some species the toxic metals bind to organic molecules in the cell walls where they remain trapped, unable to harm the cell's contents. In other species the metals are stored in the vacuole, again out of harm's way. Other species trap the metals at special membrane sites. Some plants simply expel the metals from their cells to the external environment.

Whatever the mechanism, the net result is the same: these plants are able to flourish in an environment which would otherwise remain unexploited. Indeed, the plants have become so well adapted to living in such conditions that on unpolluted soil they do not fare so well and are outcompeted by normal plants.

Antibiotic resistance in bacteria

A more sinister example of the power of natural selection is provided by the evolution of antibiotic resistance by

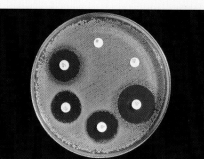

Bacteria growing on an agar plate on which have been placed six different antibiotics (white disks). Notice that the bacteria fail to grow in the presence of four of the antibiotics but can grow in the presence of two of them.

certain bacteria. Antibiotics are widely used in medicine and veterinary practice to kill pathogenic bacteria. On many farms they are routinely fed to even apparently healthy animals because this can increase the growth rate by up to 5 per cent. They act as growth promoters by removing gut bacteria that interfere with digestion.

However, bacteria have very short generation times, are haploid and can reproduce sexually in a variety of ways (*page 473*). These features enable bacteria to evolve rapidly in response to changes in their environment.

With the widespread use of antibiotics over the last 50 years, many bacteria have evolved mechanisms enabling them to grow in the presence of a great many antibiotics (*illustration 1*). For example, the production of penicillinase allows a bacterium to nullify the effects of the antibiotic penicillin. A few bacteria have even evolved the ability to feed off certain antibiotics! Nowadays doctors tend to be more restrained than they were about how many different antibiotics they prescribe. That way, a few really effective

ones can be kept in reserve to be used only if a bacterium arises which is resistant to all the more common antibiotics. The problem is especially serious as resistance genes can even move from one species of bacterium to another.

Antibiotic resistance is continuing to spread and threatens to become an even more serious problem. In 1999, in response to this, European Union agriculture ministers banned the use of four antibiotics from animal feed.

DDT resistance in insects

The widespread use of DDT to control insect pests has lead to the evolution of resistance to this chemical by many species. One Nigerian survey of mosquitoes in the species *Anopheles gambiae* found that in unsprayed villages almost no flies were resistant to DDT. However, in villages which had been subject to regular spraying, approximately 90 per cent of the flies were homozygous for resistant alleles.

In houseflies, several mechanisms are known which permit resistance. Four genes are involved and each has a distinct function. Two of the DDT-resistant genes enable the poison to be detoxified, each by a different route. Another gene reduces the rate at which DDT penetrates the cuticle. The fourth gene acts by an unknown route.

Many more examples of natural selection in action could be given, though the clearest instances, such as those given above, generally result from the activities of humans. It is widely believed that over time natural selection has been the prime mechanism driving evolution and still operates today.

chance that such a mutation might lead to a new niche being exploited. If individuals carrying the nocturnal mutation never meet the diurnal individuals to mate with them, this could result in the evolution of a new species. This sort of speciation is known as **sympatric speciation** ('speciation in the same country').

In plants, both sympatric and allopatric speciation are important, while in animals allopatric speciation is probably the more important. One of the most frequent causes of sympatric speciation is polyploidy (*page 745*).

How is interbreeding prevented?

Whatever the type of speciation, two species will only remain as separate entities if interbreeding is impossible or very rare, or if the resulting hybrids are at a significant disadvantage.

Often interbreeding is prevented by geographical isolation. In this case the two species may interbreed if brought together. For example, the wild cat (*Felis silvestris*) found in Scotland will interbreed with the domestic cat (*Felis catus*). Indeed, the gene pool of the wild cat is being infiltrated by genes from domestic cats (*figure 43.18*). Given time, geographically separated populations may eventually become so different that interbreeding is impossible.

Apart from geographical isolation, interbreeding between separate species may be prevented by a lack of attraction between males and females of the two species or by physical non-correspondence of the genitalia. In the case of flowering plants it may be due to the fact that pollination is impossible between the two species. In animals with elaborate behaviour patterns, such as ducks, it may be because the courtship behaviour of one fails to stimulate the other.

Even if mating is possible, fundamental differences in genetic constitution may prevent reproduction being successful. Thus, the gametes may be prevented from fusing, as, for example, when the pollen grains of one species of plant fail to germinate on the stigmas of another (*figure 43.19*). Even if fertilisation does occur, the zygotes may be inferior in some way and fail to develop properly. Sometimes offspring are produced but the hybrids may die before reaching adulthood. Or they may be sterile, as in the case of the mule, formed by crossing a donkey with a horse.

Figure 43.19 Where many species of flowering plant co-exist, it is vital that they do not interbreed. Usually interbreeding is prevented because pollen grains can only germinate on the stigmas of the same species.

Figure 43.18 Scottish wild cat, *Felis silvestris*. This species can interbreed with the closely related domestic cat, *Felis catus*.

Naming organisms, page 81

Figure 43.20 The coelacanth. In 1938, a trawler fishing off the coast of South Africa caught one of these fish. Until then the species had been thought to be extinct for 70 million years. Because it has changed so little over so long a period, it is called a 'living fossil'.

Figure 43.21 Leafy branch of a ginkgo tree. This tree is native to China but is grown as an ornamental tree in mild climates all over the world. Plants that look virtually identical to this tree are found in the fossil record over 150 million years ago.

Altruism and kin selection, page 448

Figure 43.22 A peacock with dazzling plumage attempts to attract the attention of a peahen.

Sub-species and speciation

It is clear that, far from being fixed and immutable, species change and may evolve into new species. This raises a practical difficulty, for if a species shows signs of evolving into a new species, what do we call the intermediate forms? Normally, recognisably distinct forms within a species are called **sub-species**. Only when such sub-species fail to interbreed can they be said to have evolved into separate species.

The rate of evolution

The rate at which evolution occurs varies enormously. At one extreme are so-called living fossils such as the coelacanth (*figure 43.20*) and ginkgo tree (*figure 43.21*). These organisms have remained almost unchanged for tens of millions of years or longer.

At the other extreme are organisms such as the banana-feeding moths in the genus *Hedylepta* found only in Hawaii. There are five species of this moth. Bananas were only introduced to Hawaii approximately 1000 years ago, so it seems likely that these five species have evolved from a common ancestor within the last 1000 years.

Another example of rapid evolution is provided by a lake which was cut off from Lake Victoria in Uganda approximately 4000 years ago. This lake contains five species of cichlid fish, each similar to, but distinct from, one of the cichlid species in Lake Victoria.

43.6 Extensions of natural selection

Darwin extended the Darwin–Wallace theory of natural selection in two ways:

Kin selection This happens when a characteristic is favoured in evolution, not for the benefit it confers on the individual that possesses it, but for the benefit it confers on its relatives. For example, the stinging behaviour of worker bees does not benefit the individual workers, for they die after using their sting, but it does benefit the offspring of the queen.

Sexual selection One way in which this happens is when characteristics have evolved to allow individuals to compete amongst themselves for access to mates. For example, in most mammals males are larger than females. Why is this? The reason is that adult males often compete amongst themselves for access to females. The result is that some adult males never get to breed. Instead, other males monopolise the breeding. This leads to selection for large, strong males.

There is a second way in which sexual selection can occur and this is by **female choice**. In a number of birds, males are more brightly coloured than females and may display bizarre courtship behaviour or possess exotic plumage (*figure 43.22*).

In 1930, the English geneticist R.A. Fisher suggested that if such males are more likely to breed, a runaway form of sexual selection will occur. Suppose, for instance, that females are more likely to notice a male with a long tail. This might make a particular male marginally more likely to attract the female into mating with him. Then this male will breed more successfully than other males and pass on his long tail to his sons, who will in turn be more attractive to females.

Sexual selection for increased tail length will continue until the advantage of having an exceptionally long tail is cancelled out by a disadvantage: for example, a very long tail might make the male poorer at flying, or the bright plumage might make him more vulnerable to predation.

43.7 Artificial selection

For thousands of years, humans have altered certain species by imposing on them a process of **artificial selection**. This forms the basis of **animal** and **plant breeding**.

Gradual change or sudden jumps?

Darwin assumed that species gradually change over long periods of time from one form to another (a process called **phyletic gradualism**).

If this idea is correct, one would expect to find intermediate forms between one fossil species and the next in successive rock strata. However, intermediate forms in the fossil record are surprisingly rare.

The rarity of intermediate forms is seen by **creationists**, who believe in **special creation** rather than in the evolution of species, as evidence that evolution has not occurred. However, two American palaeontologists, Niles Eldredge and Stephen Gould, have put forward a different interpretation. They suggest that new species may often arise rapidly, perhaps within a few thousand years, and then remain almost unchanged for millions of years before changing again. Moreover, the sudden evolution of a new species may occur in a marginal part of the population, containing only a small number of individuals.

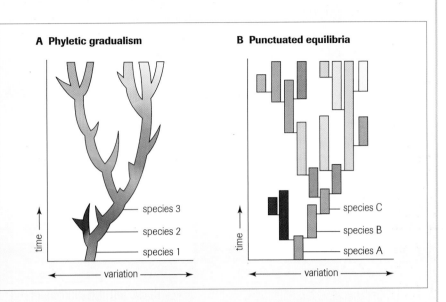

In these circumstances we would not expect to find a gradation between successive species in the fossil record. This idea is embodied in the term **punctuated equilibria** – 'punctuated' referring to the short periods of rapid evolution, 'equilibria' to the long periods of almost no change.

Phyletic gradualism and punctuated equilibria are compared diagrammatically in the illustration. Some people have felt that the idea of punctuated equilibria is contrary to Darwinism. However, it can be explained in terms of natural selection, and Darwin himself recognised that it could happen. It is quite possible that both processes have occurred in the course of geological history.

Breeders select individuals with the characteristics that are wanted, and allow them to interbreed. Individuals lacking the desired qualities are prevented from breeding. By rigorous selection over many generations special **breeds** or **varieties** may be developed for particular purposes. Identifying suitable individuals from which to breed by looking at their offspring (progeny) is known as **progeny testing**.

Animals that have been subjected to artificial selection include:

- cattle for milk and beef;
- sheep for wool and meat;
- horses for racing and hauling;
- pigs for lean meat;
- pigeons for flight capacity and plumage type;
- poultry for egg and meat production;
- dogs for hunting, retrieving, racing and appearance.

Amongst plants, crops such as wheat, barley, rice and potatoes have been bred for higher yield, greater resistance to disease and so on, while many plants have been bred for ornamental purposes.

In all these cases the different varieties, each with its distinctive characteristics, have arisen by a process of artificial selection in which humans play a role analogous to that normally performed by nature.

The green revolution

Since the 1960s, agriculturists have produced many new varieties of the world's major food crops, such as rice, wheat, maize and barley. This process has been called the **green revolution**. In general, these new varieties display some or all of the following advantages over the older ones:

- Their stems are shorter, resulting in dwarf varieties which are less likely to be flattened by wind and rain and can more easily be harvested.

- They give a higher yield per unit area.
- They show a greater response to water and fertilisers.
- They are relatively insensitive to day length and/or temperature, with the result that two or even three crops may be grown per year.
- They are more resistant to pests and diseases.

In developing countries, the green revolution has had a pronounced effect on food production, with great increases in crop yields. However, one problem is that these new varieties require high levels of fertiliser which are expensive and not always available in developing countries. This has led some economists to question the benefits of the green revolution. It has been argued that the introduction of these varieties concentrates wealth in the hands of a minority of farmers who can afford artificial fertilisers.

Practicalities of plant and animal breeding

Because artificial selection, like natural selection, relies on genetic variation, an important part of being an animal or plant breeder is recognising and selecting individuals with advantageous characteristics. A plant breeder, for example, who wants to develop a variety of wheat tolerant to salty soils might grow large numbers of young wheat plants in salty soils and then select those plants that survive and grow best.

The next stage of any artificial breeding programme is to multiply the numbers of the new variety and check that it does not have any disadvantageous characteristics. The temptation here may be to use only a few individuals to give rise to a new variety. The problem with this approach is the danger associated with the crossing of closely related individuals, namely **inbreeding**.

Inbreeding leads to a loss in fitness known as **inbreeding depression**. This is because an individual produced as a result of crossing two close relatives is more likely to have two copies of a harmful or even lethal recessive allele. So damaging is inbreeding depression that animal and plant breeders may try to produce **hybrids**.

A hybrid is the result of a cross between individuals belonging to two different varieties (**outbreeding**). Such individuals show **hybrid vigour**. This is because hybrids tend to be heterozygous at many of their loci. Any harmful alleles therefore have their effects masked by healthy ones.

Gardeners often grow F_1 hybrid plants (*figure 43.23*). These are the result of crossing two different parent lines, each parent line being pure bred. On the animal side, many of the lambs produced in Britain are hybrids.

In farm animals, **artificial insemination** is frequently used as a rapid means of spreading the beneficial characteristics of a particular male throughout the stock. For example, the semen from a single bull can be used to sire as many as 90 000 cattle a year. With so large a number it becomes extremely important for farmers to maintain accurate breeding records if they are to avoid the problems of inbreeding.

Sperm banks are kept and **embryo transfer** may be used as a way of increasing the reproductive rate of genetically superior females. Sperm banks, and the equivalent **seed banks** in plants, serve as **gene banks** or **gene pools**, which provide ways of maintaining genetic diversity.

Artificial selection in humans

Could the kind of artificial selection we have been discussing be imposed on humans? To most people this idea seems repugnant, conjuring up visions of selective breeding and

Figure 43.23 An F_1 hybrid Brussels sprout plant (*left*) with one of its pure bred parents (*right*).

▶ Embryo transfer, page 526

compulsory birth control. But in fact it already happens to a slight degree as when, for example, a couple with a history of abnormality in their children or close relatives decide, perhaps on the basis of information given them by a genetic counsellor, not to have any more children.

There is nothing intrinsically evil about wanting to improve the quality of the human race, especially when it involves minimising the frequency of harmful alleles, such as those that cause haemophilia and certain mental defects. The theory and practice of improving the human species by means of selective breeding is known as **eugenics**, and despite its sinister undertones many people feel it is acceptable provided that it is carried out for the right reasons and on a voluntary basis.

During the late 1990s, advances in molecular genetics and human reproductive physiology made it possible not only to carry out *in vitro* fertilisation (*page 508*) – which gives rise to so-called 'test-tube babies – but also to check certain genes of very young embryos. It is possible, at a considerable number of loci, to detect whether or not a single cell is homozygous for a recessive disease-causing allele or heterozygous for a dominant disease-causing allele. These checks can be carried out on a single cell removed from the 8–16 cell stage of an embryo (*figure 43.24*).

Removing a single cell from the embryo causes it no harm. If it is found that the embryo will *not* develop into a child suffering from the disease, it is implanted into the mother's womb as in 'normal' *in vitro* fertilisation. If though, it turns out that the embryo *would* develop into a child suffering from the disease, the mother-to-be is given the option of having the embryo destroyed. In the future, it may be possible to put such defects right through genetic engineering (*page 629*).

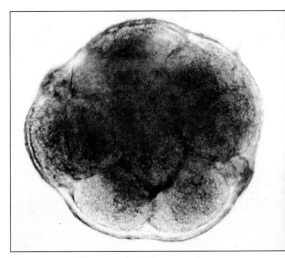

Figure 43.24 Photograph of a human embryo at the 8–10 cell stage. It is now becoming possible to carry out genetic tests on such embryos to see whether or not they carry genes for certain genetic diseases. Magnification ×4500.

Summary

1. According to the Darwin–Wallace theory, evolution occurs by **natural selection** of chance variations.

2. The variation on which natural selection depends arises by **mutations**, but is aided by the reshuffling of genes in meiosis through **independent assortment** and **crossing over**, and by **fertilisation**.

3. Mutations may be caused by changes in the gross structure of chromosomes (**chromosome mutations**) and by changes in the structure of genes (**gene mutations**).

4. Mutation frequencies are generally very low. However, the mutation rate can be increased by various **mutagenic agents**.

5. Mutations occur spontaneously and are long-lasting. Usually they are harmful but occasionally they may confer beneficial characteristics on an individual.

6. Types of chromosome mutation include **deletion**, **inversion**, **translocation** and **duplication**. Also one or more entire chromosomes may be gained or lost as a result of **non-disjunction** during meiosis.

7. Sometimes an organism may gain a complete set of extra chromosomes. This is known as **polyploidy**. In certain situations polyploidy is associated with beneficial characteristics.

8. Gene mutations involve changes in the sequence of the nucleotide bases in DNA. These may be brought about by **substitution**, **insertion**, **deletion** or **inversion**.

9. Mutations sometimes occur in an organism's non-reproductive cells. These are called **somatic mutations**.

10. The conflict between organisms and their environment, physical or biotic, has been described as the **struggle for existence**.

11. The fact that more offspring are born than can survive is the basis of **differential mortality**, an essential part of natural selection.

12. Natural selection can maintain species constancy by **stabilising selection**, but if the environment changes it favours the emergence of new forms by **directional selection**.

13. For new species to arise (**speciation**) **genetic isolation** is necessary. This may result from geographical isolation between populations (**allopatry**) or from reproductive isolation within a population (**sympatry**).

14. The principles of genetics and evolution are employed by humans in **animal** and **plant breeding**, in which natural selection is replaced by **artificial selection**.

For general advice on these questions and advice on answering essay-type questions, see pages vii and viii.

1. (a) Give two symptoms of Down's syndrome. (2)

(b) The diagram shows the chromosomes of a male with Down's syndrome.

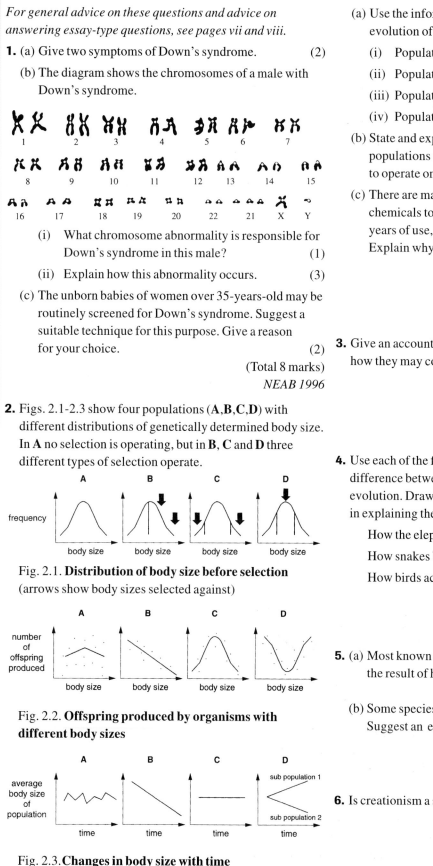

(i) What chromosome abnormality is responsible for Down's syndrome in this male? (1)

(ii) Explain how this abnormality occurs. (3)

(c) The unborn babies of women over 35-years-old may be routinely screened for Down's syndrome. Suggest a suitable technique for this purpose. Give a reason for your choice. (2)

(Total 8 marks)

NEAB 1996

2. Figs. 2.1-2.3 show four populations (**A,B,C,D**) with different distributions of genetically determined body size. In **A** no selection is operating, but in **B, C** and **D** three different types of selection operate.

Fig. 2.1. **Distribution of body size before selection** (arrows show body sizes selected against)

Fig. 2.2. **Offspring produced by organisms with different body sizes**

Fig. 2.3. **Changes in body size with time**

(a) Use the information in Figs. 2.1-2.3 to outline the evolution of body size in populations **A, B, C** and **D**.

(i) Population **A** (no selection) (3)

(ii) Population **B** (3)

(iii) Population **C** (3)

(iv) Population **D** (3)

(b) State and explain one example from natural populations where a selection process has been shown to operate on a character other than body size. (2)

(c) There are many examples where humans have used chemicals to control pests, only to find that after a few years of use, these chemicals are no longer effective. Explain why this is so. (2)

(Total 16 marks)

O&C 1998

3. Give an account of chromosome mutations and describe how they may contribute to genetic variation.

(Total 10 marks)

London 1998

4. Use each of the following phenomena to illustrate the difference between Lamarckian and Darwinian theories of evolution. Draw attention to any difficulties you encounter in explaining the phenomena by each theory.

How the elephant got its trunk

How snakes became legless

How birds acquired wings.

(Total 9 marks)

5. (a) Most known examples of natural selection in action are the result of human activity. Why do you think this is? (3)

(b) Some species evolve more rapidly than others. Suggest an explanation. (3)

(Total 6 marks)

6. Is creationism a scientific theory? Explain your answer.

(Total 5 marks)

Chapter 44

Major steps in evolution

I t is remarkable to think that you, the person sitting reading this chapter, and we, the authors of it, are – if current scientific opinion is to be believed – the products of an evolutionary process that began some 13 billion years ago with the birth of the Universe itself. In this chapter we shall survey some of the major events in the history of life. We shall start by going back some three and a half to four billion years, when it is thought that life first arose on this planet.

44.1 The origins of life

In 1953, Stanley Miller, then a 23-year-old graduate student at the University of Chicago, succeeded in synthesising amino acids, the building blocks of proteins, by putting a spark across a mixture of simple gases in a closed system. This was a momentous achievement, not because he synthesised amino acids as such, but because he managed to produce them under the primitive conditions that are thought to have existed on this planet some 4×10^9 years ago.

What were the first organisms like?

Before discussing how life might have arisen, it is worth asking what form the first organisms might have taken. In particular, what would they have used as a source of energy?

There are really only two possibilities: they must have been either **autotrophs** or **heterotrophs**. At first sight autotrophism might seem more likely as we are used to food webs with autotrophs at the base supporting a mass of heterotrophs. However, the metabolic equipment required to synthesise organic substances from inorganic raw materials, which is what an autotroph does, is generally more complicated than that needed by a heterotroph which feeds on ready-made organic matter. On these grounds it is generally believed that the first organisms were heterotrophs.

This immediately raises a whole host of questions. If the first organisms were heterotrophs, how did the organic substances, on which they were dependent for food, come into being? How did these first organisms originate? How did they metabolise these organic substances to release energy? And so on!

The hypothesis that the first organisms were heterotrophic was first put forward by the Russian scientist Alexander Oparin in the 1930s and, subject to various additions and refinements, it is still largely adhered to today. Let us examine its various propositions, step by step.

Synthesis of organic molecules

The age of the Earth has been calculated to be about 4.6×10^9 years, and the first indications of primitive life, as revealed in the fossil record, occurred about 3.5×10^9 years ago. In the early stages of its existence, the Earth would have been too hot for life to exist, and we can therefore narrow down the origin of life to around 3.5×10^9 years ago, give or take a couple of hundred million years!

Geochemical evidence suggests that at this time the Earth's atmosphere was dominated by four simple gases: **methane** (CH_4), **ammonia** (NH_3), **hydrogen** (H_2) and **water vapour** (H_2O). It is thought that oxygen was probably not present as a gas (O_2) since the atmosphere was too hot: it would have combined with other substances, such as iron and silicon, whose oxides form much of the Earth's crust. Water vapour is thought to have been

The beginnings of life

Ever since the beginning of recorded history, people have speculated on the beginnings of life. Of course, people have always known that ducklings only come from ducks, lambs from sheep and babies from women, but common experience seemed to suggest that worms came from the soil and maggots from rotting meat (*illustration 1*). It was even widely supposed that rats came from garbage and mice from stored grain.

Until the 17th century it was almost universally believed that some organisms arose spontaneously from non-living matter – **the theory of spontaneous generation**. However, in 1668 Francesco Redi, an Italian physician, argued that the maggots which appeared on decaying meat were introduced from the outside in some way, not spontaneously generated within the meat itself. By covering meat with a very fine gauze, which prevented female flies from laying their eggs on the meat, he showed that maggots did not arise from meat. Surprisingly though, Redi did believe that grubs could appear spontaneously in decaying vegetable matter.

For the next 200 years the question as to whether or not life could arise spontaneously was one of the great intellectual debates of the time. Evidence in favour of spontaneous generation was obtained in the middle of the 18th century by John Needham, an English scientist who became the first director of the Royal Academy of Belgium. It was known that boiling killed organisms, so Needham boiled some mutton gravy and sealed it in a glass flask. After some days the gravy was swarming with life. Surely here was proof that life could arise spontaneously.

It was not until 1862 that the theory of spontaneous generation was finally disproved in a series of experiments performed by the French chemist and microbiologist Louis Pasteur. Pasteur performed much the same experiment as Needham had 100 years earlier, except that he boiled the nutrient broth *after* it had been placed in its glass container, not before. Can you see why this made all the difference?

Pasteur found that it was not even necessary to seal the flask. If the neck of a flask containing broth was drawn out into a long S-shaped tube, and the broth then boiled, microorganisms often failed to develop. If, later, the tube was broken off close to the flask, microorganisms quickly appeared and multiplied. Pasteur reasoned that microorganisms entered the flask from the atmosphere. In the first case they became trapped on the walls of the tube and so failed to reach the broth (*illustration 2*).

From Pasteur's work grew the idea that all life comes from pre-existing life, and all notions of spontaneous generation died a quiet death. In fact this theory became so unfashionable that some people could not even accept that the first organisms on this planet arose from non-

Illustration 1 Maggots on a drowned kestrel carcass. Until the 17th century almost everyone thought that maggots were spontaneously generated by meat itself.

Illustration 2 Louis Pasteur in his laboratory in Paris. One of his 'swan-necked flasks' with nutrient broth can be seen in the centre of his laboratory bench. Pasteur found that if the broth was boiled inside the flask, it would remain fresh. At the Pasteur Institute in Paris there is a swan-necked flask containing broth which has remained fresh ever since it was set up over 100 years ago!

living matter, preferring to believe that they were brought here by meteorites from other planets. Most scientists think this theory unlikely, and in any case it merely begs the question as to how life began in the first place.

formed mainly from volcanic activity: about 10 per cent of the material in a modern volcanic eruption is water.

The first step towards the origin of life must presumably have been the synthesis of simple organic molecules. Many suggestions have been put forward to explain how this might have happened, but the most generally accepted theory is that they were formed by the action of lightning and ultraviolet radiation, or possibly gamma radiation, on the four simple gases mentioned above. Partial evidence for this rests on the fact that scientists have been able to repeat such syntheses in the laboratory. A photograph of the apparatus used by Stanley Miller in his experiment, with which we started this chapter, is given in figure 44.1. Figure 44.2 shows a diagram of the apparatus, emphasising its main features.

Since Miller's original work, several other steps in the synthesis of organic molecules have been carried out under primitive earth conditions. Miller himself synthesised amino acids from the four gases using an electric spark. From the same raw materials, Melvin Calvin, using gamma radiation, managed to produce a mixture of amino acids, simple 6-carbon sugars, and purine and pyrimidine bases – i.e. constituents of nucleic acids.

Since then, more complex organic molecules have been made: polypeptides have been synthesised from amino acids simply by heating them to melting point and then cooling; nucleic acids have been formed from nucleotides merely by heating under pressure. These laboratory syntheses do not, of course, prove that similar events happened millions of years ago, but they do suggest that such events *could* have taken place.

Assuming that the synthesis of organic molecules took place in the atmosphere, it is supposed that they were subsequently brought down to the Earth's surface in heavy rain and that, in the course of time, they accumulated in oceans and lakes. One can imagine that these great bodies of water may have been teaming with organic molecules, a kind of 'organic soup'.

Figure 44.1 Stanley Miller in his laboratory in 1990 with a replica of the apparatus with which he had shown, 37 years earlier, how the first organic chemicals might have evolved.

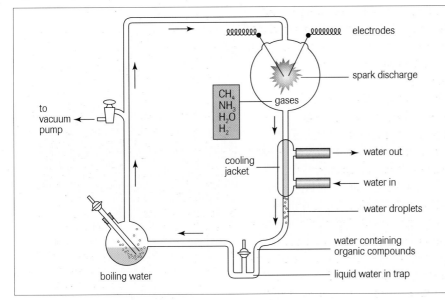

Figure 44.2 Diagram of the apparatus which Stanley Miller used to synthesise organic compounds under primitive earth conditions. Some 15 amino acids were synthesised including glycine, alanine, glutamic acid and aspartic acid.

Life from clay?

Since Miller's work, some earth scientists have questioned whether the Earth ever had a reducing atmosphere lacking oxygen, and whether it really was as hot as had previously been supposed. The existence of an 'organic soup' has also been questioned, as has the idea that life arose from it.

These doubts have led to the formulation of alternative hypotheses. One of the most fascinating is the notion that the first organisms arose on land from clay crystals. At first this idea sounds far-fetched, but it has been championed over the years by its original proponent, A.G. Cairns-Smith, a chemist from Glasgow.

Cairns-Smith begins by pointing out that the ordinary clays found in soils are astonishingly diverse in structure. Scanning electron micrographs and X-ray studies reveal a tremendous number of different sorts of clay crystals. They are mostly built up from silicic acid, $Si(OH)_4$, a compound of silicon whose tetrahedral shape is much the same as that of methane, CH_4. Silicic acid readily polymerises, again in much the same way that methane polymerises to give a carbon chain.

Clays are by no means simple homogeneous crystals. Rather they contain many irregularities. These irregularities may be in the pattern of polymerisation – whether, for instance, the silicic acids join in a straight line or in a branching arrangement. Irregularities also arise depending on the occasional presence of ions such as Mg^{2+}, Al^{3+} or Fe^{2+}. These

The origin of carbon

All organisms rely on carbon for their organic compounds. Carbon is made inside stars by fusion reactions which can only take place at tremendous temperatures and pressures. The essence of the reaction is that three helium nuclei, each with two protons and two neutrons, fuse to form a single carbon nucleus with six protons and six neutrons.

It is thought that when a star gets to the end of its life it either collapses inwards under gravitational pressure or explodes, scattering its contents to an enormous distance. Planets form from the scatterings of exploded stars.

As John Polkinghorne, a former Cambridge Professor of Mathematical Physics who is also an Anglican priest, puts it: 'We are made from the ashes of dead stars'.

irregularities are akin to mutations in a genetic code. Further, clays, being crystalline, can be said to replicate, in the sense that they grow and then break into smaller units. Not only that, but the precise pattern they display depends on the elements they contain and on the way these elements are arranged.

Finally, clays can behave as catalysts much as some other inorganic substances such as iron and platinum can. Indeed, the variety of clay structures allows them to be quite specific as to which chemical reactions they catalyse. For example, Aharon Katchalsky of the Weizman Institute of Science in Israel has found that certain clays will faithfully catalyse the formation of polypeptides from amino acids.

By now a significant minority of scientists think that there may be something in Cairns-Smith's ideas. However, it is difficult to see precisely how life based on carbon could have evolved from life based on silicon. Perhaps we will one day find that life elsewhere is based on silicon.

The first organisms

Whether life began in an 'organic soup' or as inorganic clays, somehow certain compounds must have come together to form the first living organisms, i.e. they must have combined in such a way as to produce a stable and integrated chemical system capable of transferring energy and replicating itself. However, this is an enormous step and one about which very little is known.

A possible clue as to what may have happened comes from the study of certain macromolecules such as proteins and carbohydrates. When mixed together in the right conditions, they form what look like little droplets. When surrounded by water, these droplets are remarkably stable and show a number of properties similar to living matter. For example, in the presence of certain oils they can become coated with lipid membranes through which various substances are selectively absorbed.

However they were put together, there are certain things that the earliest organisms must have been able to do if they were to qualify as living beings. First and foremost they must have been able to obtain energy, presumably by the breakdown of organic molecules. If there was little or no oxygen present at this time, their respiration would have been anaerobic. Secondly, they must have been able to reproduce. Presumably at this early stage of evolution reproduction was a simple asexual process involving nothing more than the synthesis of new macromolecules and the splitting of the organism in two.

It seems likely that replication of whatever chemical made up the genetic material in these early days of life would not be absolutely accurate. Any inaccuracies would allow natural selection to proceed. The likely result would be the rapid evolution of more complex and better-adapted forms. Any early form of sexual reproduction would hasten this evolution.

Today, all organisms use DNA (or RNA in the case of some viruses) as their genetic material. So how did the first DNA arise, and how did the familiar pattern 'DNA makes RNA makes protein' (*page 610*) become established? The problem is that, on its own, DNA is a rather delicate molecule, susceptible to mechanical damage and to chemical alteration by ultraviolet radiation. One possibility is that DNA only evolved *after* RNA, which is a more robust molecule.

Cairns-Smith argues that the presence of crystal genes, based on silicic acid, paved the way for organic genes, such as those based on RNA or DNA. Other biologists, such as James Watson, the discoverer with Francis Crick of the structure of DNA, agree that RNA preceded DNA.

One reason for believing that RNA came first is that ribose, the sugar in RNA, is much more readily synthesised than deoxyribose, the sugar in DNA, under simulated pre-life conditions. Another reason is that RNA can act as a catalyst.

It is now known that relatively short stretches of just 52 RNA nucleotides can catalyse the synthesis of a complementary RNA chain. Other RNA molecules can synthesise a variety of other reactions. In other words, it is possible that early organisms relied on RNA both for their genetic material and for their enzymes. A genetic material made of DNA and enzymes made of protein may have evolved later.

Evolution of autotrophs

So we envisage that the first organisms were heterotrophs which evolved either from clays or from 'organic soup'. What happened next? It is likely that the supply of organic molecules, originally present in vast quantities in the primitive oceans, was gradually exhausted by the ever-growing population of heterotrophs. The competition must have been increasingly fierce, and this would have placed a premium on any organisms capable of an alternative method of feeding. In other words the evolution of autotrophs would be strongly favoured.

Of course we have no certain idea what kind of autotrophism the first autotrophs indulged in. It may have been a form of **chemosynthesis** akin to that used by certain present-day bacteria. Or it may have been **photosynthesis**, perhaps similar to that performed by present-day green and purple sulphur bacteria which, living in anaerobic conditions, use hydrogen sulphide as the source of hydrogen for reducing carbon dioxide.

Aerobic respiration and the further evolution of heterotrophs

The arrival of photosynthesising autotrophs would have led to the production of oxygen (O_2). At first this probably combined with other elements such as iron. But eventually photosynthesis would have resulted in oxygen gas accumulating in the atmosphere.

The build-up of oxygen gas was important for three reasons:

- It resulted in the formation of a layer of ozone (O_3) high in the Earth's atmosphere. This forms a barrier to the Sun's radiation and would have reduced the chances of further organic compounds being synthesised in the atmosphere.

- In subsequent stages of evolution, ozone would have protected organisms from exposure to harmful radiation.

- The presence of oxygen allowed some organisms to evolve so as to utilise this free oxygen for aerobic respiration, thereby achieving a more thorough breakdown of organic substances with the release of additional energy (*page 138*).

The presence of autotrophs and heterotrophs would have led to natural selection for predation. Predatory heterotrophs would have attacked other organisms rather than relying on the presence of free organic molecules in their environment.

So we end up with autotrophs and a range of heterotrophs coexisting side by side. These provide the basic components of a balanced ecosystem. Both were presumably unicellular at this early stage of evolution. It is supposed that bacteria (both autotrophic and heterotrophic) and early eukaryotes arose from this stock.

44.2 From prokaryotes to eukaryotes

The earliest fossils that have ever been found – estimated by the potassium–argon method to be over 3000 million years old – are very similar in structure to some modern prokaryotes. Most biologists believe that at some point eukaryotes evolved from prokaryotes. How might this have happened?

One possibility is that a heterotrophic prokaryote may have ingested an autotrophic prokaryote which, instead of being digested, became a symbiont inside the heterotroph, enabling it to carry out photosynthesis. Equipped with its own DNA, the symbiont may have divided inside the host cell every time the host cell itself divided, and in this way the

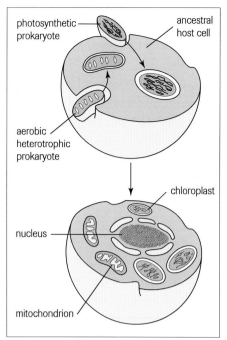

Figure 44.3 Diagrammatic representation of the endosymbiotic theory in which the eukaryotic cell is envisaged as a consortium of prokaryotes that established a particularly intimate symbiotic relationship. A photosynthetic prokaryote is here depicted becoming a chloroplast, and an aerobic heterotrophic prokaryote is depicted becoming a mitochondrion.

Figure 44.4 Lynn Margulis, the leading advocate of the endosymbiotic theory for the origin of eukaryotes. Marginalised by the established scientific community for much of her life, her views are now widely accepted. Now professor of Geosciences at the University of Massachusetts in the USA, she is also responsible, with Karlene Schwartz, for the five kingdom classification system outlined on page 85.

Figure 44.5 Diagrammatic representation of the theory that some cell structures, notably the endoplasmic reticulum and nuclear envelope, may have originated as infoldings of the plasma membrane.

symbiont may have become a chloroplast inside the host cell.

This **endosymbiotic theory**, as it is called, may also explain the origin of mitochondria. The ancestors of mitochondria may have been bacteria that were aerobic heterotrophs. Perhaps they first gained entry into a larger prokaryote as undigested prey or internal parasites. One can imagine how the 'capture' of appropriate prokaryotes might lead to a large prokaryote having protochloroplasts and protomitochondria (*figure 44.3*).

The endosymbiotic theory has been passionately advocated over the last 30 years by the biologist Lynn Margulis (*figure 44.4*). There are several lines of evidence for it:

- It explains why mitochondria and chloroplasts, unlike other organelles, have a double membrane. The inner membrane in each case presumably belonged to the original free-living organism. The outer membrane is assumed to be comparable to the membrane that surrounds a food particle in phagocytosis.

- Mitochondria and chloroplasts have their own DNA and this is in the form of a ring, just as in present-day prokaryotes.

- The inner membranes of mitochondria and chloroplasts have several enzymes and transport systems that closely resemble those found in the cell membranes of modern prokaryotes.

- Mitochondria and chloroplasts divide by a splitting method reminiscent of binary fission in bacteria.

- The ribosomes in mitochondria and chloroplasts are the same size as those found in modern prokaryotes, and significantly smaller than those found in the cytosol of a eukaryote.

Other cell structures, such as the endoplasmic reticulum and nuclear envelope, may have originated as infoldings of the plasma membrane. Simple infoldings are found in some present-day bacteria (*page 43*) and it is not difficult to imagine them eventually pinching off from the plasma membrane to become separate structures (*figure 44.5*).

44.3 **Origin of multicellular organisms**

Like so many other aspects of early evolution, this is a controversial matter and we can do no more than touch on the possibilities.

One possibility is that the first multicellular organisms may have arisen as a result of a unicellular organism dividing and the daughter cells then failing to separate. We see this today in the green protoctist *Pleurococcus* which lives on damp tree trunks and in other moist places. When the cell divides a cross-wall is formed, but frequently the daughter cells, instead of separating, remain attached to one another in small groups as shown in figure 44.6. It is possible that simple multicellular organisms may have originated in this way.

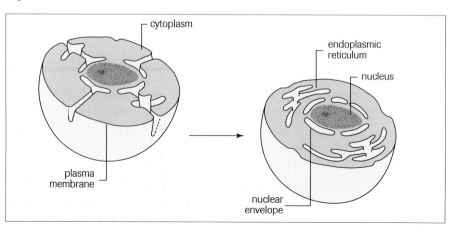

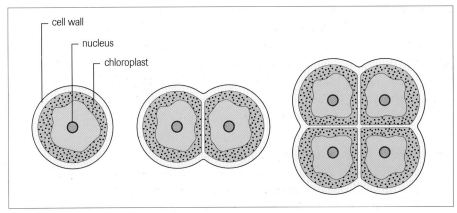

Figure 44.6 The green protoctist *Pleurococcus* occurs singly or, if the daughter cells fail to separate after cell division, in small groups. Might some multicellular plants have arisen in this way?

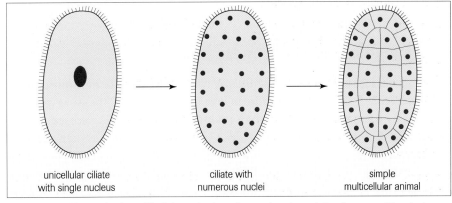

unicellular ciliate with single nucleus   ciliate with numerous nuclei   simple multicellular animal

Figure 44.7 How a simple multicellular animal may have arisen in evolution from a multinucleate protoctist.

An alternative possibility is that the nucleus of an ancestral unicellular organism may have divided repeatedly to give a **multinucleate cell**. If plasma membranes were to form between the nuclei, a simple multicellular organism would result (*figure 44.7*).

One piece of evidence in favour of this theory is that multinucleate protoctists do exist, and indeed this condition is quite common among ciliates. Furthermore, there are certain flatworms in which the plasma membranes between adjacent cells are incomplete. Like other free-living flatworms, these animals are ciliated, and it is just possible that they may have arisen from a multinucleate ciliate which developed membranes between its nuclei.

The divergence of animals and plants

The theory just propounded assumes that animals and plants had a common ancestry, a belief that is substantiated by their many biochemical similarities. If this is so, might we not expect to see, even today, unicellular organisms capable of existing both autotrophically and heterotrophically?

In fact such organisms do exist in the protoctist phylum which includes euglenoid flagellates (*page 91*). Euglenoid flagellates are generally green (because they contain chlorophyll) and have one or two flagella. Most of them feed exclusively by photosynthesis and will die if kept in the dark. However, some of them can thrive in darkness. This is because they can feed heterotrophically by absorbing soluble organic matter through their cell wall. Certain species can even feed on solid matter by phagocytosis (*figure 44.8*).

However multicellular organisms arose (and they may well have arisen in more than one way), once they existed there seems to have been an explosion of evolution, as witnessed by the fossil record. Although the first multicellular organisms appeared only about 600 million years ago, they quickly diversified into a tremendous variety of forms.

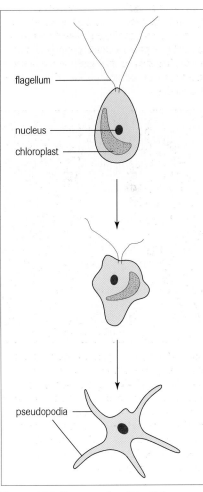

Figure 44.8 The green flagellate *Ochromonas* can change from a photosynthetic flagellated form into a heterotrophic amoeboid form. The latter takes in solid particles of food by phagocytosis.

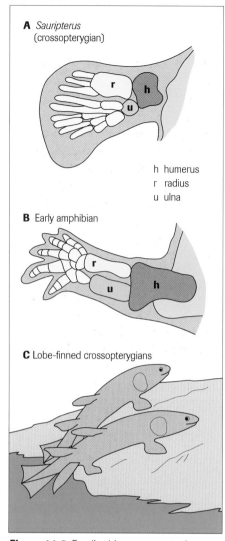

A *Sauripterus* (crossopterygian)

h humerus
r radius
u ulna

B Early amphibian

C Lobe-finned crossopterygians

Figure 44.9 Fossil evidence suggests that animal migration from water to land took place in the Devonian period about 380 million years ago when a group of freshwater fish, the crossopterygians, gave rise to the first amphibians. The crossopterygians had lobed fins, constricted at the base, which in some cases showed a marked tendency towards the pentadactyl limb. It is thought that these were used for locomotion on land. The Devonian included long periods of seasonal droughts and any fish capable of struggling overland from one body of water to another would have been at an advantage.
A Pectoral fin of a crossopterygian showing its likeness to the pentadactyl limb.
B Forelimb of an early amphibian for comparison.
C Artist's reconstruction of a pair of lobe-finned crossopterygians clambering out of water.

44.4 The colonisation of land by animals

Life probably began in the oceans. Even if the very first organisms were crystal clays, there is little doubt that the early carbon-based organisms were restricted to water. Many millions of years later, armed with the appropriate adaptations, organisms began to leave their aquatic home and move onto land.

This migration from water to land seems to have happened on several occasions in evolutionary history, in both plants and animals. The best known instance, well documented by fossils, is the movement onto land by a group of fish in Devonian times some 380 million years ago. Known as crossopterygians, they, and the early amphibians to which they gave rise, show a gradual transformation of paired fins into the pentadactyl limbs typical of modern tetrapods (*figure 44.9*). Adaptations necessary for animals to move onto land are outlined in the extension box on the next page.

44.5 Evolutionary trends in animals

Some animals, such as *Hydra*, are constructed of two layers of cells: the **ectoderm** covers the outside of the body, and the **endoderm** lines the 'gut' (enteron). These two layers are separated by a jelly-like mesogloea which is virtually devoid of cells. Such animals are described as **diploblastic**.

In more complex animals there are three layers of cells: ectoderm (covering the outside), endoderm (lining the gut) and, between these two, a third layer of cells, the **mesoderm**. Such animals are described as **triploblastic**. The development of the mesoderm has been a most important step in evolution because in the embryology of triploblastic animals it is the mesoderm that gives rise to most of the individual's organs (*page 527*).

In flatworms, the mesoderm forms a solid mass of tissue between the ectoderm and endoderm. In all other animals a **body cavity** develops in this region, though the way it is formed varies in different phyla. In annelids and chordates the body cavity is enclosed by mesoderm and is known as the **coelom**; in arthropods it lies between the ectoderm and endoderm and becomes a blood-filled **haemocoel**.

The development of a body cavity, be it a coelom or haemocoel, is yet another important advance because it provides a space in which the organs can be suspended and it permits the body wall and gut to move independently. Moreover, in certain soft-bodied animals such as the earthworm it serves as a **hydrostatic skeleton** which is important in locomotion (*page 41*).

In chordates, the dorsal part of the mesoderm splits up into a series of identical units called **somites**. This results in certain structures and organs being repeated along the length of the body – a phenomenon known as **metameric segmentation**. Metameric segmentation is fundamental to the organisation of most animals including chordates (*page 528*). It is seen particularly clearly in the chaetae and fluid-filled coelomic compartments of the earthworm and the muscle blocks (**myotomes**) of fish, where its main advantage is to provide an effective means of locomotion. In birds and mammals, metameric segmentation has become obscured, but traces of it can still be seen in, for example, the repeated pattern of the spinal nerves.

By and large evolution has led to an increase in complexity. When we look at the animal kingdom we see a trend towards more sophisticated organs and systems.

To say that evolution tends to produce more complex forms is not to imply that it is never regressive. There are many instances of what are thought to have been quite active animals taking up a sedentary or parasitic existence. Resorting to such passive modes of life generally involves the degeneration or even total loss of many organs, though parasites frequently show complex biochemical adaptations to their hosts.

How animals have been able to colonise dry land

For an animal to move from water onto land requires a number of anatomical and physiological changes:

- Air is a much less dense medium than water, so there would have to be **new means of movement and support**. This particularly applies to large, land-dwelling vertebrates, in which the skeleton holds the head and abdomen clear of the ground (*Chapter 24*).

- Aquatic animals like fish breathe by means of gills, but these need to be suspended in water and collapse when on land. Terrestrial animals have evolved **air-breathing organs** such as lungs (*Chapter 10*).

- Terrestrial animals are liable to lose water by evaporation. As explained in Chapter 17, both active and passive mechanisms of **water conservation** have evolved for coping with this. The passive technique of developing an impermeable cuticle is common to animals and plants.

- Water, particularly in the oceans, is a comparatively stable medium, not liable to the wide fluctuations in temperature which characterise the terrestrial environment. Land animals, whether endothermic or ectothermic, must have structural, physiological or behavioural means of **controlling their body temperature** (*Chapter 18*).

- Air's low resistance to movement means that **higher speeds can be achieved**. Almost all birds can fly faster than the swiftest of fish can swim. It does not, of course, follow that all terrestrial animals are fast movers; some, such as worms and snails, withdraw instead to protected environments.

- In many aquatic animals fertilisation is external, eggs and sperm being shed into the surrounding water. As this is impossible on land, terrestrial animals have other means by which females can obtain sperm. In many cases this involves the use of an intromittent organ such as the penis, by which sperm are deposited inside the female and **internal fertilisation** takes place. However, some terrestrial animals, such as amphibians, still have external fertilisation and return to water for breeding.

- With internal fertilisation comes the possibility of **internal development and viviparity**. This is an enormous advantage to a terrestrial animal, for the environmental hazards that plague an adult can have an even more devastating effect on its helpless eggs and young. Of course, birds still produce eggs, but these have a hard protective shell and are looked after carefully by one or both parents.

44.6 Evolutionary trends in plants

Because of the scantiness of the fossil record, it is not easy to reconstruct the evolutionary history of the plant kingdom. However, analysis of what fossils there are and examination of modern algae and plants enable us to detect certain trends.

For example, in some multicellular green algae, such as certain members of the colonial Volvocales and the filamentous *Spirogyra*, all the cells are alike and all have the capacity to reproduce sexually. But in other green algae the cells have become differentiated into those that reproduce (**gonadic cells**) and those that carry out non-reproductive functions such as photosynthesis (**somatic cells**). The rudiments of such differentiation are seen even in *Volvox*, but the process is carried much further in plants. The separation of 'sex and soma' is one of the earliest and most fundamental evolutionary trends in the plant kingdom.

In the life cycles of most plants there is a distinction between **sporophyte** and **gametophyte generations**. The diploid sporophyte undergoes meiosis to produce haploid spores; and the haploid gametophyte produces haploid gametes. In vascular plants such as ferns, conifers and flowering plants there has been a trend towards suppression of the gametophyte. Eventually, in flowering plants (angiosperms), the gametophyte becomes incorporated into the body of the sporophyte itself (*page 478*). This is associated with the development of pollination, enclosed egg cells and production of seeds. As such it may be seen as an adaptation to life on land.

Alternation of generations, page 475

Many of the fundamental trends in the evolution of plants relate to the colonisation of land, just as was the case for animals. These trends are discussed in the extension box on the next page.

Early land plants

The colonisation of the land by plants was one of the most important events in the Earth's history. Here guest author Dianne Edwards takes a look at some fossil plants.

The colonisation of the land by plants was probably a gradual process with origins in the early Palaeozoic or even in the Precambrian, but there is no direct fossil evidence for these early stages. It seems likely that most terrestrial surfaces were initially coated by mats of cyanobacteria and algae, followed by 'turfs' of bryophyte-like plants.

However, it was the advent of vascular plants in the Silurian which was of major importance in changing the face of our planet, both in modifying geological processes and in creating a diversity of ecological niches and habitats on land.

Vascular plants exhibit a number of biochemical and anatomical adaptations that allow them to grow in a wide range of environments from moist to arid. This is because they maintain their own internally hydrated environment. The **cuticle** is a waterproofing layer that greatly reduces evaporation from these hydrated tissues. **Stomata** permit exchange of gases for photosynthesis and respiration and connect to an extensive system of **air spaces** for their diffusion. Specialised absorption regions (rhizoids) developed on extensive **rooting systems**, enabling large volumes of soil to be exploited for water and mineral nutrients.

Once plants had colonised the land, taller individuals were probably at an advantage for the dispersal of spores by air currents. However, an increase in height necessitates the presence of water-conducting systems. The best developed is the **xylem** of vascular plants composed of tracheids or vessels. These utilise the complex polymer, **lignin**, to resist collapse under tension, and to provide structural support.

The early vascular plants are exemplified by *Rhynia gwynne-vaughanii* from the Rhynie Chert which shows all the anatomical 'inventions' associated with the invasion of the land. The Rhynie Chert deposit offers a unique window into the plant life of a wetland in Lower Devonian times (*illustration 1*). Earlier representatives, such as *Cooksonia*, in the lowermost Devonian and late Silurian, are smaller and even simpler, but – being preserved as thin films of coal – they usually lack anatomical detail (*illustration 2*). Exceptionally preserved tiny fossils show that *Cooksonia* possessed a cuticle and stomata plus a central strand of tracheids in its upright forking axes.

Questions about the ancestry of vascular plants cannot be answered just by reference to the fossil record. Nucleic acid sequencing shows that the bryophytes and vascular plants had a common ancestor, probably in the charophyte algae.

Dianne Edwards, a palaeobotanist, is Professor in the Department of Geology at the University of Wales, Cardiff.

Illustration 1 Reconstruction of early land plants growing in the vicinity of hot springs in Lower Devonian times in what is now Scotland.

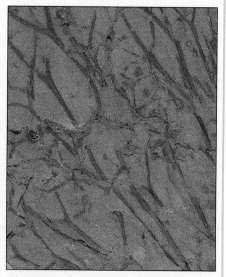

Illustration 2 A fossil *Cooksonia* from Wales, one of the first land plants (×5). With simple branched stems ending in sporangia the shape and size of small pinheads, it would have looked like a mossy green carpet – very unassuming compared with the land vegetation we know today.

44.7 Large size and its implications

In both plants and animals there have been trends towards larger size over the course of evolutionary history. Some of the problems attendant on this are discussed on page 217. On a more positive note, increase in size generally goes hand in hand with the development of ever more complex tissues and organs.

A tendency towards increased size has evolved in many groups. One of the classic examples is provided by the **dinosaurs**, a group of reptiles, some of whose members carried size to perhaps its ultimate conclusion. These great animals were the dominant fauna during the Cretaceous from 150 to 65 million years ago. Some, like *Tyrannosaurus rex*, were

Extension

Evolution of flight

Many animals, including even one species of snake, have evolved the ability to glide downwards from tree to tree or from tree to ground. However, true powered flight is found in only four groups: insects, birds, bats and the extinct pterosaurs. Rather little is known from the fossil record about how flight evolved in insects or bats: fossil bats are extremely scarce, and even the earliest fossil insect wings seem superbly adapted for flight.

More is known about the evolution of flight in birds. In 1861, just two years after Darwin's *Origin of Species* was published, a remarkable fossil was found at Solnhofen in present-day Germany. This fossil appeared to be a 'missing link' between reptiles and birds. Given the name *Archaeopteryx* (literally 'ancient wing'), it was found in rocks from the Upper Jurassic, some 150 million years old.

By now a total of six relatively complete specimens have been found, all belonging to the same species. *Archaeopteryx* was about the size of a small chicken. It combined features found in reptiles of the time and in present-day birds. Its jaws bore teeth, as in a reptile, and it lacked the keeled extension of the sternum to which, in modern birds, the flight muscles are attached. Other reptilian features include the retention of abdominal ribs, the presence of a long vertebral column in the tail and three fingers on each forelimb which were not incorporated into the wings but were freely movable as claws.

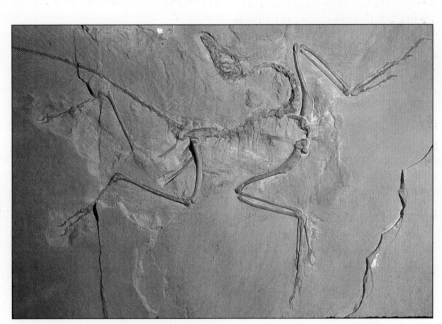

Archaeopteryx, a fossil bird, showing a combination of reptilian and avian characteristics.

Despite its many reptilian characteristics, *Archaeopteryx* had one vital feature which immediately distinguished it from all other reptiles: it had **feathers**. Indeed, the feathers were so well developed that they are indistinguishable in their structure and distribution from the flight feathers of modern birds. It is generally supposed that feathers evolved from reptilian scales, but no living or fossil reptile has any trace of feathers to show how this may have happened.

Archaeopteryx existed at the same time as a group of flying reptiles, the **pterosaurs**. Close relatives of the dinosaurs, these were the first backboned animals to fly. They had light, hollow bones and their wings were made of skin that stretched from the tail to an immensely elongated fourth finger. The presence of an enlarged cerebellum, as revealed by the shape of their skulls, presumably helped them to maintain their balance. The smaller pterosaurs were the size of sparrows and probably flew actively by flapping their wings; the largest ones glided over prehistoric lakes and oceans and may have fed on surface fish.

Some of these pterosaurs were huge. The record is held by *Quetzalcoatlus*, a pterodactyl that stood over 3 metres tall and had a wing span of 15 metres.

Figure 44.10 *Brachiosaurus*, one of the largest herbivorous dinosaurs. Whether it supported its huge mass by spending most of its time half submerged in water (as the picture suggests) is still controversial, though the consensus is that they *could* walk on dry land.

savage carnivores; others, like *Apatosaurus* (which used to be known as *Brontosaurus*) were vegetarian. Although some dinosaurs were only the size of a domestic cat, others reached fantastic sizes: *Brachiosaurus*, for instance, was about 22 m long, stood 13 m tall and had a mass of some 75 000 kg, i.e. 75 tonnes.

The main problem facing enormous terrestrial animals is how to support the body. The largest male elephants, for instance, only lie down (to go to sleep) on ground that slopes; otherwise they find it extremely difficult to get up again.

The mass of an animal varies with the cube of its linear dimensions. In other words, if the animal's size doubles in all directions (length, height and breadth), its mass increases by about eight times. But the strength of its legs varies with their cross-sectional area. If a large animal had legs that were proportionately the same size as a smaller animal of similar shape, the strength of its legs might be unable to support the mass of the animal. This is because an eight-fold ($2 \times 2 \times 2$) increase in mass would be accompanied by only a four-fold (2×2) increase in the cross-sectional area of the legs.

The result of this argument, which was appreciated by the 17th century Italian scientist Galileo Galilei, is that for a large animal to support itself, the width of its legs must increase at a greater rate than the rest of the body. Judging by their fossils, the legs of the larger dinosaurs were indeed extremely thick, rather like elephants' legs are today.

Even so, some zoologists are doubtful if the legs could have supported such heavy bodies. For this reason, it has been suggested that the largest dinosaurs spent much of their time wallowing in shallow lakes where the water would buoy up their massive bodies (*figure 44.10*). This idea seems to be supported by evidence from fossil footprints which sometimes appear to show the animals on tip toe. However, others have argued that if they were aquatic creatures the water pressure at such depths would have collapsed their lungs.

Extinction of the dinosaurs

By the end of the Cretaceous, some 65 million years ago, none of these dinosaurs remained: they had all died. What led to their extinction? We do not know for certain, but at the last count there were over 100 separate theories!

Figure 44.11 Why did the dinosaurs become extinct? Chris Nichols of the Department of Earth Sciences at Cambridge puts forward four ideas.

There is good evidence that the end of the Cretaceous saw marked changes in climate: land levels changed and there may have been a pronounced drop in temperature over much of the world. Large animals, such as dinosaurs, may have been particularly sensitive to such climatic changes, partly because of the large amounts of food they required and partly because their huge size may have made thermoregulation more difficult.

However, this latter explanation assumes that dinosaurs were ectothermic. A number of dinosaur experts now believe that dinosaurs were in fact **endothermic**. The evidence for this comes from a variety of sources. Anatomical details of bone structure suggest that dinosaurs were fast moving and agile, while there are indications from fossil dinosaur nests that juvenile dinosaurs had growth rates typical of mammals and birds and far in excess of present-day reptiles (*figure 44.12*). This suggests that they were able to maintain a body temperature higher than that of their surroundings.

Another theory was proposed by Luis Alvarez, a Nobel laureate, and his son, Walter, a geologist, in 1980. They argued that an **asteroid** 10 km in diameter crashed into the Earth 65 million years ago close to what is today the Gulf of Mexico. The impact could have triggered volcanic eruptions leading to the release of copious amounts of dust that blocked out the Sun for a few years, leading to massive starvation, particularly among larger animals. Evidence in favour of this theory comes from the unusually high abundance of the element **iridium** in rocks that date from precisely this period. It is known that asteroids contain considerably more iridium than the Earth's crust.

Whatever the cause of the extinction of the dinosaurs, their disappearance allowed another group of animals to blossom forth. This group had been around for upwards of 100 million years, remaining small and insignificant, probably living in caves and trees and feeding on insects and buds. But as soon as the great age of dinosaurs came to an end, they underwent an explosion of adaptive radiation and in a short period of time gave rise to the many species that we know as **mammals**. Humans, of course, are members of this group.

Figure 44.12 In 1987 Wendy Sloboda, a farm hand who is also an amateur palaeontologist, found some hadrosaur nests in southern Alberta, Canada, with adults on top of the eggs. This discovery suggests that these dinosaurs incubated their eggs in carefully constructed nests, as shown in this artist's reconstruction. (A more mundane explanation is that the adults died while laying.) The adults weighed from four to six tonnes. The eggs are about 20 cm in length. There is some evidence from the remains of young hadrosaurs that they grew by as much as 280 cm in their first year after birth. Such dramatic growth suggests that the animals were endothermic.

Two brains are better than one

Being one of the larger dinosaurs presents problems. For instance, how do you overcome the length of time taken for nervous impulses initiated by the brain to reach your tail? One solution was suggested by Bert Taylor, an American rather fond of dinosaurs:

> Behold the mighty dinosaur,
> Famous in pre-historic lore,
> Not only for his power and strength
> But for his intellectual length.
> You will observe by these remains
> The creature had two sets of brains.
> One in his head (the usual place),
> The other at his spinal base.
> Thus he could reason *a priori*
> As well as *a posteriori*.
> No problem bothered him a bit
> He made both head and tail of it.

> So wise was he, so wise and solemn,
> Each thought filled a spinal column.
> If one brain found the pressure strong
> It passed a few ideas along.
> If something slipped his forward mind
> 'Twas rescued by the one behind.
> And if in error he was caught
> He had a saving afterthought.
> As he thought twice before he spoke
> He had no judgement to revoke.
> Thus he could think without congestion
> Upon both sides of every question.
> Oh, gaze upon this model beast,
> Defunct ten million years at least.

Some of the larger dinosaurs did indeed have an enlargement of the spinal cord at the base of the spine, as revealed by their fossil remains. In *Stegosaurus*, this bundle of nerve tissue was some 20 times

Stegosaurus, one of a number of dinosaurs with a second 'brain'.

the size of the brain in the head. It was presumably used to control the massive hind legs and spiked tail (*illustration*).

44.8 The emergence of humans

By any account, humans are a remarkable species. In 1945 the American anthropologist George P. Murdock listed the following characteristics that have been recorded in every human society:

> Athletic sports, Belief in the afterlife, Bodily adornment, Calendars, Cleanliness training, Community organisation, Cooking, Cooperative labour, Cosmology, Courtship, Dancing, Decorative art, Division of labour, Dream interpretation, Education, Etiquette, Faith healing, Family feasting, Fire making, Folklore, Food taboos, Funeral rites, Games, Gestures, Gift giving, Government, Greetings, Hair styles, Hospitality, Housing, Hygiene, Incest taboos, Inheritance rules, Joking, Kin groups, Language, Law, Magic, Marriage, Mealtimes, Medicine, Obstetrics, Penal sanctions, Personal names, Population policy, Property rights, Puberty customs, Religion, Sexual restrictions, Superstitions, Surgery, Tool making, Trade, Visiting, Weaving and Worship.

From time to time people have tried to single out just one or two characteristics that make humans unique – such as tool use or worship. One problem with this approach is that the characteristic may be shared by other species. For example, chimpanzees and the Galapagos woodpecker finch both use tools. Another problem is that some individual humans may not display a particular characteristic, such as worship.

A more fruitful approach is to look at some of the ways in which we differ from our close evolutionary relatives, gorillas and chimpanzees:

- We walk on two legs, that is we are **bipedal**.
- Our hands have **opposable thumbs** which make it easier to perform very fine manipulations.
- Our brains are exceptionally large (1350 cm³ on average).
- Our **gestation period** is unusually long (40 weeks).
- We remain highly dependent on our parents for a very long time (10–20 years).
- We have a long life span (often 70 years or more).
- We have a highly developed **communication system** (most people have a vocabulary of at least 5000 different words).
- We are almost hairless (Desmond Morris' 'naked ape').
- Females have no oestrous period and breeding may occur at any time of year.
- We sometimes live in very large **societies** (over 20 million people live in Mexico City).
- We can control our environment to an unparalleled degree.
- We are found throughout the world.

How did all this come about? A combination of the fossil record and evolutionary trees derived from DNA hybridisation studies and analysis of the amino acids in certain proteins suggests that we shared a common ancestor with chimpanzees from which we split about five to eight million years ago. Unfortunately the fossil record is not at all clear about exactly what happened subsequently. Conclusions have to be drawn from a limited number of fossil remains, none of which is complete. As one scientist has put it: 'deciphering the course of evolution from those fragments is like trying to follow the story of *War and Peace* from 12 pages torn randomly from the book'.

Fossil remains of early humans

In 1924, the British anthropologist Raymond Dart announced the discovery of a fossil skull from a South African quarry. The fossil was named *Australopithecus africanus* (Southern

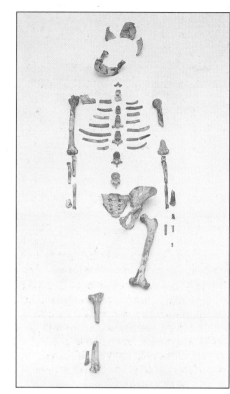

Figure 44.13 Fossil remains of Lucy, a member of the species *Australopithecus afarensis*, which dates from some three million years ago. This species may have been a direct ancestor of our own species. When she died she was about 20 years old and between 107 and 122 cm in height.

Figure 44.14 Fossil skull of *Homo habilis* found in 1972 and dating from 1.8 million years ago.

ape). Subsequent discoveries indicated that *Australopithecus* walked fully erect and had human-like hands and teeth. However, the brain of *Australopithecus* was only about one-third the size of a modern human's.

The genus has by now been split into several species. One of these is called *A. afarensis* because the first fossil of this species was found in the Afar region of Ethiopia (*figure 44.13*). This fossil was discovered in 1974 by a team led by the American palaeoanthropologist Don Johansen. Its significance lies partly in the fact that it is 40 per cent intact, making it one of the most complete fossil hominids known. The fossil is known as 'Lucy' after the Beatles' track 'Lucy in the sky with diamonds' which was playing in camp on the night of her discovery.

Lucy lived some three million years ago. She stood only 110 cm tall and weighed about 30 kg. The shape of her pelvis identifies her as an adult female. Her cranial capacity was only about 400 cm³ and, although she was bipedal, her walk was probably more rolling than ours. There are differences between modern-day humans and *Australopithecus* in foot anatomy and leg musculature.

Between *Australopithecus* and ourselves – *Homo sapiens* (literally 'wise man') – lie a number of other species including *Homo habilis* and *Homo erectus*. Of these two, *H. habilis* is the older, existing about two million years ago (*figure 44.14*). *H. erectus* evolved about 1.5 million years ago, probably in Africa, from where it migrated to Asia, where the first fossils were found (Java Man and Peking Man). Judging by the artefacts found in the vicinity of the fossils by Mary Leakey and others, both species used tools. *H. erectus* individuals seem to have lived in huts and caves, built fires and clothed themselves in animal skins.

The oldest fossils classified as *H. sapiens* date from about 130 000 years ago. *H. sapiens* is distinguished from *H. erectus* by a number of precise anatomical differences, including the possession of a significantly larger brain. In addition, archaeological remains suggest that the early members of *H. sapiens* buried their dead (*figure 44.15*).

How did humans evolve?

The details of human evolution are unclear, particularly the early stages (*figure 44.16*). Indeed, although most anthropologists think we evolved on the savannahs of Africa, Alister Hardy and Elaine Morgan have championed the idea that we are 'aquatic apes'. This theory argues that we passed through a semi-aquatic phase during which we lost most of our body hair, acquired large amounts of subcutaneous fat, became bipedal, began to copulate face to face, learned to cry and began to talk. Elaine Morgan writes most convincingly and her books *The Descent of Woman* and *The Aquatic Ape* are well worth reading.

Whether we evolved on land or at the sea's edge, the evolution of the delicate muscles that control our fingers and thumbs must have been of paramount importance. **Hands** probably originated in primates long ago as prehensile grasping devices for climbing

Figure 44.15 Evidence suggests that we have been burying our dead for a very long time. The picture shows Silbury Hill in Wiltshire. It is the largest man-made mound in Europe, having a height of 39 metres and a base area of 2 hectares. Dated at around 2745 BC, it was probably a burial chamber though there is no certain evidence for this.

Figure 44.16 Exactly how humans evolved is still shrouded in doubt. Here are two theories as to how *Homo sapiens* may have descended from species in the genus *Australopithecus*.

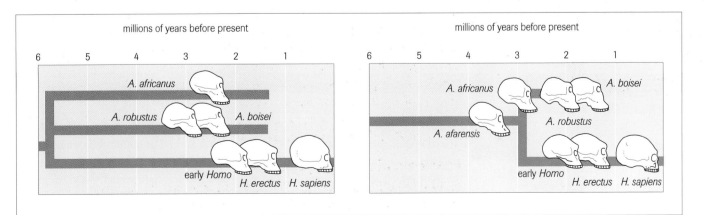

Figure 44.17 Bushmen cave art from at least 15 000 years ago, Nswatugi Cave, Matopos, Zimbabwe.

trees. In early humans they became efficient manipulative devices with opposable thumbs for making tools and hurling weapons. Today they provide the means by which we show our creativity and transmit our achievements down the generations (*figure 44.17*).

Full use of the hands would not have been possible had it not been for our ancestors becoming **bipedal**. This necessitated major changes in the musculo-skeletal system, particularly the vertebral column and pelvis. These changes are part of the reason why many people get backache and why childbirth is painful for mothers. However, the evolution of bipedalism freed our hands from their former function of locomotion and allowed them to be used for other purposes. Precisely why bipedalism evolved is debatable. It may have helped our ancestors to see predators at a distance. Or perhaps it prevented overheating, by exposing a smaller surface area to the tropical Sun.

In the emergence of *Homo sapiens* as a dominant species, the development of **speech** has been extremely important. Of course, many organisms can make a variety of sounds and communicate thereby. What is unique to our species is the ability to produce such an extensive repertoire of sounds by subtle movements of the lips and tongue.

Human speech depends on the production of sound by the larynx. In the sound-producing process two elastic strands of tissue, the **vocal cords**, are vibrated by blasts of air emitted from the lungs. Pitch is determined by the tension on the vocal cords, together with the size of the glottal aperture; loudness by the strength of the blast of air.

Our hands and voice are coordinated by complex neural mechanisms initiated by the brain. In fact, while all these developments were taking place there was a dramatic increase in **brain size** (*figure 44.18*). The increased **mental ability** which this would have allowed must have helped our ancestors to think rationally, predict the behaviour of others, foresee the outcome of their actions, solve problems and appreciate the difference between right and wrong. Such abilities have been helped by our **prolonged parenting**, which gives many years for us to learn from our parents.

Figure 44.18 Brain volumes of various hominids showing the mean and 95 per cent population limits in each group.

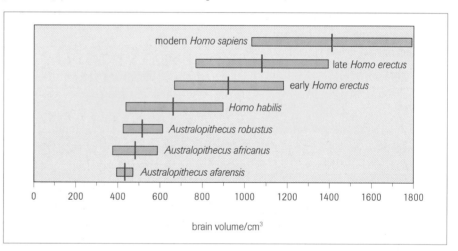

brain volume/cm³

44.9 The future course of evolution

Today, in many human societies, natural selection is not the potent force that it is in other species, or indeed used to be in human communities. Modern science and medicine have seen to that.

Does this mean that the human species is no longer evolving? The answer is no. Natural selection still operates, though on a more limited scale and in more subtle ways than in past ages. But, more importantly, humans have entered a new phase in their evolution, a phase in which advances depend not so much on structural changes in the body as on the transmission of accumulated experience from one generation to the next (*figure 44.19*). This can be termed **cultural evolution**.

Figure 44.19 Learning from previous generations has enabled *Homo sapiens* to undergo a process of cultural evolution which hopefully will continue in the future.

Extinction

The evolution of species has been accompanied by extinction. Guest author Tim Halliday explains why animals become extinct and how this relates to conservation.

The extinction of animal and plant species is of considerable concern at the present time, because of the very high rate at which species are being exterminated by the direct and indirect effects of human activities, such as habitat destruction and pollution.

It is important to remember, however, that extinction is also a natural process and that it is the ultimate fate of all species to become extinct or evolve into new species. The 30 million species that inhabit the Earth today represent only a minute fraction of all the species that have existed; the history of life on Earth has involved a process of continuous turnover, in which new species replace previous ones. From time to time, however, the rate of turnover has shown dramatic increases, leading to mass extinctions, the best known being the demise of the dinosaurs. At the present time there is a comparable mass extinction caused, not by natural events, but by the harmful activities of humans.

A species will inevitably become extinct if mortality among existing individuals persistently exceeds the addition of young individuals to the population. While this is self-evident, it provides the essential basis for effective conservation of endangered species, since it is necessary to decide whether efforts should be directed towards reducing mortality or enhancing reproduction. The great auk, for example, was exterminated by the uncontrolled slaughter of adult birds, whereas the decline of many large birds of prey, such as the peregrine falcon, has been caused by pesticides like DDT that caused them to lay eggs with very thin shells.

Active conservation of several birds of prey has involved efforts to enhance their reproductive rate, whereas protection of other species, such as the once endangered elephant seal and polar bear, has been achieved through restrictions on hunting.

Naturally occurring extinctions are primarily the result of two interacting processes: competition between species and environmental change. As environments change, they impose pressures on species to adapt to such changes. Species that cannot adapt are replaced by species that can. For example, the ice ages in Britain caused widespread changes in the fauna and flora. What were once semi-tropical forests were replaced by coniferous and deciduous woodlands which were better able to survive in the changed environment.

A distinction can be made between **real extinctions** and **pseudo-extinctions**. All the species existing at a particular time are direct descendants of ancestral species, and it will often be the case that an ancestral species is no longer present. In a sense it did not become extinct but became transformed into a different species over a long period of time. For example, the direct ancestors of *Homo sapiens* did not suffer real extinction but pseudo-extinction. In other instances, however, species and entire groups of organisms have gone extinct without leaving any descendants. Contemporary extinctions, caused by human activities, are real extinctions because they do not involve the transformation of existing species into new ones.

Clearly, certain kinds of species are more prone to extinction than others. One such category are large, predatory species, such as eagles and other birds of prey. Because they are at the top of a food chain, they tend to exist in small numbers and to be adversely affected by any disturbance lower down the chain.

Another group susceptible to

A snail kite with its prey.

extinction are species with very specialised habits. For example, the snail kite (*illustration*) is adapted to feed exclusively on a particular species of snail, and it is endangered because its prey species has declined. The corollary of this is that species with very generalised habits, such as starlings and sparrows, prosper and spread as a result of habitat changes brought about by humans.

The highest rates of extinction in recent times have occurred among species endemic to small oceanic islands. Because of their isolation, such islands commonly contain species that are uniquely adapted to the local conditions and are found nowhere else. Because islands are often small, they are quickly devastated by human activities and the resident species have no escape. The classic example of a recent extinction, the dodo, provides an example of a common pattern among birds. In adapting to life on the island of Mauritius, where there were no ground-living predators, it lost the ability to fly. As a result it was helpless when hunted by humans and the predators that humans brought with them, such as rats and cats.

Tim Halliday, ethologist and artist, is Professor of Biology at the Open University.

Figure 44.20 We may yet be able to plan ahead and avoid catastrophe. Members of the European Parliament Green Group address a press conference at the 1998 Buenos Aires Conference. This conference discussed ways of cutting emissions of greenhouse gases.

We are such a dominant species on this planet that the Earth's entire future may depend on what we do within the next generation or two. At one extreme, we have the potential to destroy the majority of the world's population through the use of nuclear weapons. A nuclear war could herald a nuclear winter in which enormous amounts of dust generated by the explosions might block out the Sun's rays for years.

In much the same way that the dust thrown up by an asteroid impact may have caused the extinction of the dinosaurs (*page 771*), the dust from nuclear explosions might lead to a collapse in agricultural production with accompanying mass starvation. Of course, we don't know whether the human species would become extinct, or whether sufficient individuals would survive to repopulate the Earth.

Even in the absence of a nuclear winter, there are other ways in which our activities may threaten ourselves and other species. As we saw in Chapter 39, global warming and the destruction of the ozone layer are recent phenomena, the outcome of which is still unclear. However, where there is great potential for harm, there is also great potential for good. We are unique as a species. The next 50 years are likely to show whether we are heading towards heaven or hell.

Summary

1. Pasteur, in his famous swan-necked flask experiment, disproved **the theory of spontaneous generation**.

2. The first step in the formation of living organisms may have been the synthesis of organic molecules from simple gases. This has been repeated in the laboratory under conditions thought to resemble those found on Earth four billion years ago.

3. Another possibility is that the first organisms arose from clay crystals.

4. Whether life began in an '**organic soup**' or as inorganic clays, somehow certain compounds must have come together to form the first living organisms.

5. The first organisms were probably anaerobic **heterotrophs**. **Autotrophs** evolved later, eventually releasing oxygen into the atmosphere and paving the way for **aerobic respiration**.

6. The transition from a **prokaryotic** to a **eukaryotic** cell structure may have occurred as a result of **endosymbiosis**.

7. **Multicellular organisms** probably arose either as a result of a failure of cells to separate after cell division, or from a multinucleate ancestor.

8. A major development in the evolution of both animals and plants has been the exploitation of dry land. For this to take place various anatomical and physiological changes were necessary to cope with the shortage of water, loss of buoyancy and other environmental problems.

9. Evolutionary trends in animals include the evolution of **triploblastic organisation**, body cavities (**coelom** and **haemocoel**) and **metameric segmentation**.

10. On the plant side, an early trend led to the separation of **reproductive** and **somatic** cells, and a later trend to the distinction between **sporophyte** and **gametophyte**.

11. In both animals and plants there have been trends towards larger size. The largest ever terrestrial organisms were certain **dinosaurs**. The reason the dinosaurs became extinct some 65 million years ago is still hotly debated.

12. Although **extinction** of species is a natural process, the rate of extinction has greatly increased recently as a result of human activities.

13. Humans probably shared a common ancestor with chimpanzees from which we diverged five to eight million years ago.

14. The evolution of the human species (*Homo sapiens*) has been marked by **bipedalism, increased intelligence, manipulative hands, speech, prolonged parenting, loss of body hair** and a sense of **right and wrong**.

15. Over the last few thousand years we have become increasingly dependent on the transmission of accumulated experience, termed **cultural evolution**.

16. The future of the planet is largely in our hands.

For general advice on these questions and advice on answering essay-type questions, see pages vii and viii.

1. The diagrams below show the reconstructed hands of a modern chimpanzee and Neanderthal man.

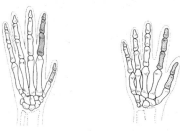

   Chimpanzee   Neanderthal man

   (a) The ratio of the length of the first finger to that of the thumb (shown shaded on the diagram) in the chimpanzee is 2.3:1.

   (i) From the diagram of the hand of Neanderthal man, determine the ratio of the length of the first finger to that of the thumb. Show your working. (3)

   (ii) Comment on these ratios in relation to the mode of locomotion of chimpanzees compared with that of Neanderthal man. (2)

   (b) Explain the significance of one other feature of the hand of Neanderthal man in relation to the evolution of the genus *Homo*. (2)

   (Total 7 marks)

   London 1998

2. Early humans are thought to have had highly pigmented dark skins and to have evolved in tropical Africa. These populations then spread out into the rest of the world, where natural selection produced a range of skin pigmentation in the various populations.

   (a) Explain the advantage of dark skins to humans living in tropical Africa. (2)

   (b) Explain how natural selection might have produced populations with lighter coloured skins in Europe. (4)

   (Total 6 marks)

   NEAB 1996

3. Archaeologists have found a 50 000 year old skeleton of a human male in the Shanidar cave. It shows a congenital (present from birth) withered right arm. This arm had been amputated below the elbow some years before the man died. The skeleton indicated that the man had died at the relatively advanced age of about 40 years old. The teeth showed a high degree of wear.

   (a) Explain the evidence that the archaeologists could have used to determine

   (i) that this human had an upright posture. (4)

   (ii) that the skeleton was approximately 50 000 years old. (1)

   (iii) that this human belonged to a group which had a reasonable degree of cooperative social behaviour. (2)

   (b) The development of speech and control of fire were two very important stages in early human cultural evolution.
   Explain why **each** of these was important. (5)

   (Total 12 marks)

   NEAB 1998

4. One of the many changes that are believed to have taken place in the evolution of humans from a pre-human ancestor is the loss of the tail.

   (a) Suggest **two** functions of the tail in primates. (2)

   (b) What possible selection pressures may have led to the loss of the tail in the evolution of humans? (2)

   (c) Discuss the possible consequences, advantageous and disadvantageous, if a tail had been *retained* in the human. (4)

   (Total 8 marks)

5. (a) Why do you think there was strong selection in favour of increased mental capacity in *Australopithecus* and *Homo*? (2)

   (b) Suppose that humans still exist in 50 million years. What course may evolution have taken by then, and by what kind of mechanism? (4)

   (Total 6 marks)

Appendix: Statistics

It is often the case in biology that more can be learnt from quantitative data if they are analysed statistically. This brief statistics appendix concentrates on two important statistical tests:

- the t-test;
- the chi-squared (or χ^2) test.

The t-test

The **t-test** allows you to see whether the means of two samples differ significantly. Here is a hypothetical example to illustrate how it works. Suppose you measure the height of six trees of a particular species in a wood, and the height of five trees of the same species growing nearby as separate, solitary specimens. All in all you get 11 bits of data, as follows:

Height of trees in wood: 8 m, 9.5 m, 7.5 m, 10 m, 8.5 m, 11 m.
Height of solitary trees: 7 m, 8 m, 7.5 m, 8 m, 7.5 m.

It looks as though woodland trees are taller than solitary ones but can we be sure of this? The first thing to do is to calculate the **mean**.

Calculating means

You have almost certainly calculated means before. All you have to do is to add up the individual values and divide by the total number of measurements. So, in this case, the mean height of the woodland trees is:

$$(8 + 9.5 + 7.5 + 10 + 8.5 + 11) \text{ m} \div 5 = 9.08 \text{ m}$$

The general formula is:

$$\bar{x} = \frac{\Sigma x}{n}$$

where:
  $\bar{x}$ is the mean
  Σ stands for 'sum of'
  x refers to the individual values of the sample
  n is the total number of individual values in the sample.

Repeating this exercise with the solitary trees, we find that their mean height is 7.6 m. Now 7.6 m is less than 9.08 m but this doesn't prove that woodland trees are taller than solitary ones. Indeed, the two tallest solitary trees (each 8 m in height) are taller than the shortest woodland tree (which is 7.5 m in height). *What we are interested in seeing is whether the mean height of the trees in the wood differs significantly from the mean height of the solitary trees.*

The first thing we need to do is to calculate **standard deviations**. The standard deviation is a measure of the extent to which individual measurements *vary* around the mean. The greater the variation among the individual measurements, the bigger the standard deviation; the less the variation among the individual measurements, the smaller the standard deviation.

It helps to have a calculator that works out standard deviations. If you *don't* have such a calculator, read the next section entitled *'Calculating standard deviations'*. If you *do* have a calculator that works out standard deviations, you may want to skip this section and go to the section entitled *'Using a calculator to obtain standard deviations'*.

Calculating standard deviations

The standard deviation, s_x, is given by the following formula:

$$s_x = \sqrt{\frac{\Sigma x^2 - \frac{(\Sigma x)^2}{n}}{n - 1}}$$

where:
  Σ stands for 'sum of'
  x refers to the individual values of the sample
  n is the total number of individual values in the sample.

In the case of our six trees in the wood, the six individual values, i.e. values of x, were: 8 m, 9.5 m, 7.5 m, 10 m, 8.5 m and 11 m. The sum of these five values, i.e. Σx, equals 54.5 m. (You can forget about the units while actually doing the calculations provided you put them in at the end – the mean and standard deviation have the same units as the individual values of x.) Using these values of x and Σx in the above formula, we have:

$$s_x = \sqrt{\frac{8^2 + 9.5^2 + 7.5^2 + 10^2 + 8.5^2 + 11^2 - \frac{54.5^2}{6}}{s}}$$

$$= 1.32 \text{ m}$$

Using a calculator to obtain standard deviations

You may need to have your calculator in standard deviation mode, and type the data into a memory. Then there will be a key, often labelled $\bar{x}$. This key gives you the mean of the data. Another key, often labelled s or σ, gives you the standard deviation. If you have the key σ_{n-1} or s_{n-1} use it in preference to σ_n or s_n for working out the standard deviation.

Using standard deviations to calculate the significance of the difference between two means

If you have a decidedly superior calculator (or access to a statistical package) you may have a key labelled t. This stands for 't-test' because that is the name of the test we are going to carry out. If you do have such a key, use it as instructed by the calculator or statistical package and go to step 8 below. If you don't have a key labelled t, proceed as follows:

1. Work out the means of the two sets of data.

2. Subtract the smaller mean from the larger one.

3. Work out the standard deviation of one set of data. Multiply this number by itself (i.e. square it) and divide it by the number of pieces of data in that set of data.

4. Work out the standard deviation of the other set of data. Multiply this number by itself (i.e. square it) and divide it by the number of pieces of data in that set of data.

5. Add together the figures you calculated in steps 3 and 4.

6. Take the square root of the figure calculated in step 5.

7. Divide the difference between the two means (step 2) by the figure calculated in step 6. This is your **t value**.

8. Now use Table A.1 to see whether your value of t could be expected by chance. Note that you need to know something called the **degrees of freedom**. For a t-test, the degrees of freedom are simply two less than the total number of individual measurements in the two samples.

- If your value of t is *bigger* than the critical value shaded in Table A.1 you can be at least 95% confident that the difference between the means is significant. Your result is said to be **statistically significant** and you can reject the **null hypothesis** that there is no difference between the means. It's called a 'null' hypothesis because you start off by making the hypothesis that there is no significant difference between the two means. You then test this hypothesis. You only reject this hypothesis if you are at least 95% confident that the hypothesis is falsified by the data. Statistics is never about certainties, only about probabilities. By convention, statisticians like to be at least 95% sure of their findings before drawing any conclusions.

- If your value of t is *smaller* than the critical value shaded in Table A.1 you are less than 95% confident that the difference between the means is significant. Your result is not statistically significant and you cannot reject the null hypothesis that there is no difference between the means.

Carrying out a t-test: an example

As an illustration we shall use the data listed earlier on the heights of trees. Our null hypothesis is that there is no difference between the heights of the woodland and solitary trees. The value of t has no units so we can leave out units in the calculation, but note that you must use the same units throughout. You can't, for example, use m for the heights of the woodland trees and cm for the heights of the solitary ones!

1. Mean height of the woodland trees = 9.08; mean height of the solitary trees = 7.6.

2. Difference between the means = 1.48.

3. Standard deviation of the height of the woodland trees multiplied by itself, divided by the number of pieces of data in that set of data = $1.32 \times 1.32 \div 6 = 0.29$.

Table A.1 Table of t values (based on Zar).

Degrees of freedom	t values					
1	1.00	3.08	6.31	12.71	63.66	636.62
2	0.82	1.89	2.92	4.30	9.93	31.60
3	0.77	1.64	2.35	3.18	5.84	12.92
4	0.74	1.53	2.13	2.78	4.60	8.61
5	0.73	1.48	2.02	2.57	4.03	6.87
6	0.72	1.44	1.94	2.45	3.71	5.96
7	0.71	1.42	1.90	2.37	3.50	5.41
8	0.71	1.40	1.86	2.31	3.36	5.04
9	0.70	1.38	1.83	2.26	3.25	4.78
10	0.70	1.37	1.81	2.23	3.17	4.59
11	0.70	1.36	1.80	2.20	3.11	4.44
12	0.70	1.36	1.78	2.18	3.06	4.32
13	0.69	1.35	1.77	2.16	3.01	4.22
14	0.69	1.35	1.76	2.15	2.98	4.14
15	0.69	1.34	1.75	2.13	2.95	4.07
16	0.69	1.34	1.75	2.12	2.92	4.02
17	0.69	1.33	1.74	2.11	2.90	3.97
18	0.69	1.33	1.73	2.10	2.88	3.92
19	0.69	1.33	1.73	2.09	2.86	3.88
20	0.69	1.33	1.73	2.09	2.85	3.85
21	0.69	1.32	1.72	2.08	2.83	3.82
22	0.69	1.32	1.72	2.07	2.82	3.79
24	0.69	1.32	1.71	2.06	2.80	3.75
26	0.68	1.32	1.71	2.06	2.78	3.71
28	0.68	1.31	1.70	2.05	2.76	3.67
30	0.68	1.31	1.70	2.04	2.75	3.65
35	0.68	1.31	1.69	2.03	2.72	3.59
40	0.68	1.30	1.68	2.02	2.70	3.55
45	0.68	1.30	1.68	2.01	2.70	3.52
50	0.68	1.30	1.68	2.01	2.68	3.50
60	0.68	1.30	1.67	2.00	2.66	3.46
70	0.68	1.29	1.67	1.99	2.65	3.44
80	0.68	1.29	1.66	1.99	2.64	3.42
90	0.68	1.29	1.66	1.99	2.63	3.40
100	0.68	1.29	1.66	1.99	2.63	3.39
Probability (p) that chance alone could produce the difference	0.50 (50%)	0.20 (20%)	0.10 (10%)	0.05 (5%)	0.01 (1%)	0.001 (0.1%)

4. Standard deviation of the height of the solitary trees multiplied by itself, divided by the number of pieces of data in that set of data = $0.42 \times 0.42 \div 5 = 0.035$.

5. The sum of the figures calculated in steps 3 and 4 = $0.29 + 0.035 = 0.325$.

6. The square root of the figure calculated in step 5 = 0.57.

7. The difference between the two means (step 2) divided by the figure calculated in step 6 = $1.48 \div 0.57 = 2.60$.

8. It is clear from table A.1 that 2.60 is greater than the critical value of t, which for a total of 11 pieces of data, i.e. for 9 degrees of freedom, equals 2.26. This means that we are at least 95%

confident that the mean heights of the woodland and solitary trees differ. Note that our value of t would have had to equal at least 3.25 for us to have been 99% confident that the mean heights of the woodland and solitary trees differ.

We can sum up the way to calculate the value of t by these steps as follows:

$$t = \frac{\bar{x} - \bar{y}}{\sqrt{\dfrac{(s_x)^2}{n_x} + \dfrac{(s_y)^2}{n_y}}}$$

where:
$\bar{x}$ equals the mean of sample X
$\bar{y}$ equals the mean of sample Y
s_x is the standard deviation of X
s_y is the standard deviation of Y
n_x is the number of individual measurements in sample X
n_y is the number of individual measurements in sample Y.

The degrees of freedom are equal to $n_x + n_y - 2$.

One final point. The larger your sample sizes, the more likely you are to detect a significant difference – if it exists. You normally need a *minimum* of half a dozen individual measurements in each sample.

The chi-squared (χ^2) test

The **chi-squared (χ^2) test** allows you to see whether the ratio of your results is what you expect, i.e. if your *observed* numbers differ significantly from your *expected* numbers. For example, does a genetics ratio differ significantly from the 3 to 1 ratio you expected? Note that while the t-test can be carried out on any quantitative data, the χ^2 test can only be carried out on whole numbers that vary discontinuously. This means that the χ^2 test is normally only used if you have counted distinct individuals or quadrats or something. It cannot be used if the units of what you have measured are those of time (e.g. seconds or hours), nor can it be used on percentages.

To see if observed numbers differ from expected numbers you need to work out exactly what your expected numbers are. An example will help. Suppose, in an ambitious project, a group of biology students cross pairs of rabbits, each of which is heterozygous at the same locus for coat colour. We can represent this as **Aa × Aa**. Now if **A** is dominant to **a**, we might expect to get a 3:1 ratio of phenotypes among the offspring, e.g. black coat : white coat. Let us suppose the students actually end up with 47 baby rabbits, 38 of which are black and 9 of which are white – a ratio of 4.22:1. The question is, does this ratio of 4.22:1 differ *significantly* from the expected one of 3:1?

The first thing to do is to work out the expected numbers. In this case we expect one-quarter of the 47 offspring (i.e. $47 \times 0.25 = 11.75$) to have one set of characteristics (white coat), and three-quarters (i.e. $47 \times 0.75 = 35.25$) to have the other set of characteristics (black coat). It may look odd expecting non-whole numbers, but this is the only way to get a ratio of *exactly* 3:1 (i.e. 35.25 black : 11.75 white).

Now we complete the following table:

	black	white
Observed (O)	38	9
Expected (E)	35.25	11.75
O – E	2.75	–2.75
(O – E)^2	7.56	7.56
(O – E)^2 ÷ E	0.21	0.64
Sum of {(O – E)^2 ÷ E} $= 0.21 + 0.64 =$		0.85

Here, 0.85 is called the **chi-squared value (χ^2 value)**. The bigger it is, the greater the chance that the observed results differ significantly from the expected ones. To see if the difference is significant, use Table A.2. Note that you need to know the number of classes of data to work out the degrees of freedom. For a chi-squared test, the degrees of freedom are simply one less than the number of classes of data. In our example the number of classes of data equals two, because each offspring fell into one of two classes, black or white. If the expected ratio had been 1:2:1 (e.g. black : grey : white), the number of classes of data would have been three and the expected numbers would not have been 35.25 and 11.75, but 11.75, 23.5 and 11.75.

Table A.2 Table of χ^2 values (based on Fisher).

Degrees of freedom	Number of classes	χ^2 values					
1	2	0.46	1.64	2.71	3.84	6.64	10.83
2	3	1.39	3.22	4.61	5.99	9.21	13.82
3	4	2.37	4.64	6.25	7.82	11.34	16.27
4	5	3.36	5.99	7.78	9.49	13.28	18.47
Probability (p) that chance alone could produce the deviation		0.50 (50%)	0.20 (20%)	0.10 (10%)	0.05 (5%)	0.01 (1%)	0.001 (0.1%)

If the value of chi-squared is bigger than the critical value shaded in Table A.2, we can be at least 95% confident that the difference between the observed and expected results is significant. The result is said to be statistically significant. You can see that in our example the value of chi-squared we calculated (0.85) is much smaller than the critical value (3.84). This means that the ratio of 4.22:1 (i.e. 38:9) is not significantly different from a 3:1 ratio for our sample size of 47.

The general formula you need to carry out a chi-squared (χ^2) test is given by:

$$\chi^2 = \Sigma \left\{ \frac{(O - E)^2}{E} \right\}$$

The degrees of freedom are equal to one less than the number of classes. As always in statistics, the more data the better. For technical reasons a chi-squared test needs each expected value to equal at least 4.

Index

There isn't enough space to include everything in this index. If you cannot find the word or phrase you want, look for one similar in meaning, or for one which is more inclusive (e.g. instead of 'mushroom' look for 'fungus').

In the case of a phrase, try looking up more than one word in the phrase, e.g. 'plasma protein' might be under 'plasma', 'protein' or 'plasma protein'.

If several page references are given for a word, you are recommended to start from one printed bold, which will take you to a definition, a general introduction to the concept, or to the main description.

Some important topics are mentioned so often in the book that not all page references can be given. We have tried to include the most useful ones.

carboxyl group **23**, 26, 183
  and decarboxylase 124
  and hydrogen bond 28
carboxylase 212
carboxypeptidase 183, 189
carcinogen(ic) 174, 466
cardiac arrest 240
cardiac cycle **232**-3
cardiac frequency **232**, 242, 244
  maximum 425
cardiac infarction 229, **240**
cardiac muscle 233-5, **401**-8
cardiac output 232, 634
cardiovascular centre 238-44, 361
cardiovascular disease 240-42, 275, 517
cardiovascular system: *see* circulatory system
carnassial 180
carnivore, carnivory 178, **180**, 670-74, 680
  and Red Queen effect 716
carnivorous plant 110, 180, 259, 658
carotene 202-3
carotenoid 202, 561
carotid body 172, 244-5
carotid sinus 238-**239**, 242
carrier, genetic **577**, 589-90, 642
  of infection 505
carrier protein **105**-7, 114
carrying capacity 692
cartilage 30, **67**, 100
  articular 419
  and bone 414, 417
  hyaline 425
cascade **59**, 228-9
Casparian strip 26, **249**-50
CAT scan 748
catabolism 118-19
catalase 15, **125**, 127, 132
  in liver 273, 277
catalyst 123
cataract 386
cavitation 255
CD4 328
cell **41**-59
  animal 41-2, 45, 54, 119
  germ-line 633
  plant 42, 44-5, 119
  somatic 633
cell cycle 59, **455**-68
cell division **455**-65, 523
cell fusion 594
cell line 594
cell migration **525**, 527
cell plate 460
cell recognition 58
cell sap 42, 109-10
cell wall 22, **42**, 47, 55
  of bacterium 43
  in cell division 460
  and osmosis 109-10
  primary, secondary 55-6, 460
cell-to-cell pathway 249-50, 256
cellulase, in food industry 134
  of *Phytophthora* 707
  in gut microorganisms 191, 714
cellulose 19, **21**-2, 42, 91, 94
  digestion 191
  in diet 154
centipede 99
central dogma **610**, 617, 762
central nervous system (CNS) **345**, 527
centrifugation 51, 135, 144, 607
centriole 42, 45, **54**-5
  and cell cycle 456

centromere 457
cephalisation 366
Cephalopoda 99
cereal crop 93, 95, 148
cerebellum 359, **361**, 422
cerebral cortex 172-3, 362
cerebrospinal fluid **359**-60
cerebrum, cerebral hemisphere 359-**362**-4
cervix **497**, 505, 748
Cestoda 97
chaeta **97**-8, 431, 437
channel protein 104-5
cheese 90, 148
chemical messenger 370
chemiosmotic theory 145, 210
chemoautotroph 196, 214
chemoreceptor 172-173, **380**
chemosynthesis 87-88, **196**, 214, 763
chemotaxis 59, **321**, 503
chemotherapy **331**-3, 468
chemotropism 557
Chernobyl 684
chiasma 462-**464**-5, 592, 629
  and genetic variation 741
Chilopoda 99
chi-squared test 781
chitin 23, 92
chlamydia 506
chloramphenicol 332
chlorenchyma tissue 70
chloride, chlorine 13-15, 633
  and ozone 679
chloride secretory cells **292**-3
chloride shift 221
chlorocruorin 221
chlorofluorocarbon (CFC) 679
chloromycetin 90
chlorophyll 122, 196, 201, **202**-9
  a and *b* 91-2, 94, **202**-3
  a 89, 208-9
  c 92
  and magnesium 14
Chlorophyta 92
chloroplast **44**-5, 70, 94
  in guard cells 158-9
  origin of 763-4
  structure and function 207
chlorosis 15
cholecalciferol (vitamin D₃) 35
cholecystokinin-pancreozymin (CCK-PZ) 190
cholera 58, **318**, 326, 341
cholesterol **26**, 241
  and bile salts 275
  in diet 24-5, 155
  formation of 275
  and plasma membrane 57-8
cholinergic synapse 357
cholinesterase 130, **356**-8
Chondrichthyes 100, 164
chondrin 67
chondroblast 67, 417
chordate, Chordata **100**, 472, 730
  coelom 766
chorion 531
  see also villus
chorionic villus sampling (CVS) 530, **748**
choroid plexus 360
chromatid **457**-65, 591-2, 608, 741
chromatin 42, 456, 625
chromatophore 43
chromosome 42, **455**-65, 571-648
  giant 624
  homologous **462**-5, 740-41

and linkage 585-7
  maternal, paternal 504
  sex **587**-91, 745
  structure of 625
chromosome puff 624
chyle 191
chyme **187**, 190
chymosin 290, 631
chymotrypsin 189
Ciliophora, ciliate 91
ciliated epithelium 63
cilium **54**-5
  in disease prevention 319
  on epithelium 63
  and locomotion 74, 91, 97, 433
  in mollusc 162
  in reproductive system 507
circadian rhythm 362, 371, **440**
  see also diurnal rhythm
circulation 104, 106
  fetal 532
  in mammal **230**-45
  open, closed 222
circulatory system 217, **222**-4
circumcision 498
cirrhosis, of liver 274, 317
CITES 686
citric acid cycle 144
CJD 76
cladistics 82
clam (foot) 432
class 79-80
classification **79**-85
  five kingdoms **84**-5, 764
  natural system 728
clay, and origin of life 761-2
cleavage 459, **526**
climate 659
  see also global warming
clitoris 497-**498**, 505
cloaca 295
clonal selection 325, 336
clone, cloning **470**, 493, 620-22
  of DNA 629, 630
  of embryos 526, 565
  of genes 628
  of lymphocytes 323
clotting, of blood 15, 35-6, **228**-9, 275
  and disease prevention 320
Cnidaria 73, 97, 402
  germ layers 527
  life cycle 471-2, 476
coagulation, of blood 509
coal 658, 667-8, 677, 680
cobalamin (vitamin B₁₂) 35
cocaine 366, 511
coccus 88
cochlea 393-**394**-5
codominance 595
codon **609**-11, 615
coelenterate: *see* Cnidaria
coelom **97**, 431, 527-8, 766
coenzyme 132
  A 35
coevolution **716**-17
cofactor 132
cohesion-tension theory 254-5
coitus interruptus 520
colchicine 742, **747**
cold, common 319
cold injury 306
cold stress 306
coleoptile 536, 547-56
  curvature test 548
colitis 191
collagen 30, 55, 62, 65-7

collagen fibre **65**, 237, 418
collagen tissue 65
collar cell 96
collenchyma **70**, 538
  in leaf 206-7
  in stem 250-51
colloid 30, 658
colon 193
colonisation, ecological 665
  of land 766-8
colony 73
colostrum 512
colour blindness **391**, 588-9, 594
columnar epithelium 63
combustion 667-8
commensalism 705, **713**
communication **444**-7
community, climax 666
  ecological **663**-4
companion cell 258-64
compensation period, point 201
competitive exclusion principle 701
competitive inhibition 130-31
concentration gradient **103**-5, 113-14
conception **507**, 512, 519
condensation **17**-18, 24, 27, 124, 604
conditioning 367, **440**-41
  operant 440
condom 506, **520**
cone (eye) **386**-91
conifer, Coniferophyta 94, 543-4
  sensitivity to radioactivity 684
conjugation, in reproduction 91-3, 472-**473**
conjunctiva 384
connective tissue 22, 29-30, **65**-6
conservation 2, **684**-8
  of endangered species 775
  global 685
consumer **666**-73
continental drift **722**-33
continuous culture 134
contraception **517**, 519-20, 530
  and population growth 696
contractile vacuole 74, 292
control (in experiment) 4, 548, 669
control centre, in homeostasis, in homeostasis 272
convoluted tubule 53, 63, **281**-5, 288
coordination 348, 360
copper 13-15, 132, 221
  as toxin 708, 752
coppicing 663
coprophagy 191
copulation: *see* mating
coral 73, 97
cork 42, **70**, 540-43
corm 73, **490**, 566, 653
cornea 30, **384**-5
coronary artery 233
coronary heart disease 24, 154, **240**, 317, 340
corpus callosum **362**, 364
corpus luteum 501, **512**, 515, 517
corrective mechanism, in homeostasis 272
correlation 599-600
cortisol 271, **334**, 371
cortex, of adrenal gland 290, 334, **370**-71
  in kidney 280
  in plant 248-**249**-50, 539-42
  secondary 542
cot death 175
cotyledon 95, **487**, 534-6
coughing 320

countercurrent **285**, 312
counterflow 165
courtship 443, 753
covalent bond **16**–17, 27, 29, 59, 66
cowpox 324
cranial nerve **345**, 367
cramp, muscular 15
crassulacean acid metabolism (CAM) 213, 298
phosphate **141**
creationism 755
crenation 109
cretinism 373
Creutzfeldt-Jacob disease: *see* CJD
Crick: *see* Watson–Crick theory
crista 50, 398
critical temperature **310**–11
crop rotation 681
cross, dihybrid **578**–81
　monohybrid 572
　test 575–6
crossing over 465, **591**–2
　double 593
　and genetic variation 740–41
Crustacea 99
crypsis 716
crypt of Lieberkühn 188–90
cryptosporidiosis 329
cuboidal epithelium 63
cupula 397–9
curare 358
cuticle, arthropod 62, 99
　insect 47, 294, 525
　in fossil plants 768
　of parasite 711
　plant **157**, 205–6, 251
　and temperature control 314
　in xerophytes 297
　see also cutin, wax
cutin 26
cutting **491**, 493, 550
cyanide 113, 130, 648
　as insecticide 679
cyanobacteria 83–5, **89**, 652
　in lichen 714
cyanogenesis 648
cycle, biogeochemical 667
　nutrient **667**–70
cyclic AMP 59, 377
cyclosis 264
cyst 710
cysteine 26–7
cystic fibrosis **577**–8
　and genetic counselling 590
　as genetic disorder 32, 317, 530
　and pleiotropy 597
　treatment 631, 633
cytochrome 14–15, 33, **144**
cytochrome oxidase 130, 132, **144**
cytokinin **551**–2, 554
cytology 1
cytomegalovirus 329
cytoplasm **41**–3, 74, 90
cytoplasmic division 455, **459**–60
cytoplasmic filament 259
cytoplasmic streaming 52, 181, 264
cytosine **604**–15
cytoskeleton 46, 52
cytosol 44, **45**–6, 50, 59, 144
　in muscle 411

D

dark adaptation 388
data 2
Darwin, and earthworms 658
　and evolution 9, **719**–28, 737–8,

749, 754–5
　and Mendel 582
　and phototropism 554
　and population growth 692
Darwin–Wallace theory **738**, 754
dating, carbon 731, **733**
　potassium-argon **733**, 763
DDT **680**, 710, 752, 775
dead space 169
deafness 395–7, 436, 635
deamination 151, 274
death 361
　and population growth 693, 700
decarboxylase 124
decarboxylation 142, 147
decomposer **666**–73
defaecation 192–3
deficiency disease 11, 35, **317**
deforestation 654, 685
degenerative disease 317
dehydration 292, 296, **307**, 310
dehydrogenase 124
　in respiration 141–4
dehydrogenation 141–2, **147**
deletion, in chromosome mutation 742–4
　in gene mutation 747
dementia 636
denaturation 126–**127**, 133, 301
dendrite 348–9
density dependence 694
dental formula 181
deoxyribonucleic acid: *see* DNA
depolarisation **350**–57, 383, 411
depression 317–18, 366
　winter 362
dermatitis 35
dermis 303, 381
desert(ification) 653–4
detergent 127
detoxification, in liver 273, 277
development **523**
　in animals 525–34
　in plants 534–43
diabetes 135, 154, **269**–71, 284, 336
　and auto-immunity 635
　and cystic fibrosis 598
　and heart disease 242
　insulin-dependent 631
diagnosis, prenatal 748
dialysing membrane **282**–3, 286
dialysis **286**–7, 336
　peritoneal 528
diapause 568
diaphragm 101, 166
diarrhoea 35, 317–20, 340
diastema 179
diastole **231**–7
diastolic pressure **238**, 241
dicotyledon, Dicotyledoneae **95**, 250, 534, 552
diet 24
　balanced 11
dietary reference value (DRV) 31
dieting 154
differentiation 620
　of plant cell 538–9
diffraction pattern: *see* X-ray
diffusion **103**–7, 157–9, 222
　in insect 163
　in mammal 238
　in small organisms 217
diffusion distance 104
diffusion gradient 157, 165
diffusion shell 257
digestion 178, 180, **182**–92

digestive enzyme **183**–91
dinosaur 732, 769–71
dioecious 483
dipeptide 27
diphtheria 318–19
diploblast(ic) **97**, 766
diploid 92, 450, **455**, 461–4
　in life cycles 471–8
Diplopoda 99
disaccharide 17–18
Discomitochondria 91
disease **317**–41
　and environmental resistance 693
　genetic 530
　in plants 338
　see also sexually transmitted
dislocation 420
dispersal 94, **492**–4
　of larvae 533
　of seed 660, 686
　of spores 471, 477
displacement activity 443
distal 75–6
diurnal rhythm 440
　in body temperature 302
diuresis 288
diversity, of cells 58
　of organisms 656
diving 244
division of labour 74
DNA 6, 42, **603**–18
　breakage 59
　complementary (cDNA) 628
　foreign 628–9
　of mitochondrion and chloroplast 764
　ubiquity of 762–3
　in virus 617
DNA fingerprinting 630
DNA hybridisation **729**, 772
DNA ligase 124, 628
DNA profiling 630
dominance, behavioural 448, 451
　apical 550
　genetic **573**, 595–6
　incomplete/partial 596, 645
dopamine **364**, 366
dormancy **566**–8, 713
dorsal 75
dorsal root 346
double circulation 223–4
douche, vaginal 520
dough 148
Down's syndrome **744**–5, 748
downstream processing 134
drainpipe cell **64**–5
Drosophila **575**–6, 582, 585–8
drug **331**, 511
　anti-inflammatory 375
　fertility 517
　immunosuppressive 334, 336
　psychoactive 366
　from rain forest 685
duct 64
duodenum 127, **184**, 189–90
duplication, in chromosome mutation 743–4
dwarfism 564
dysentery 319, 90

E

ear **393**–9
ear ossicle 393–6
earthworm 69, 431, 658
　behaviour 437–8
ecdysis 525

ecdysone 624
Echinodermata 100
echolocation 715
ecology 2, 273, 651–717
ecosystem **664**, 763
'ecstasy' 366
ectoderm 97, **526**, 766
ectoparasite 707
ectoplasm 433
ectotherm(y) **301**–2, 312–14
edaphic factor 659
effector 401–2
　in nervous system 345–6
　in homeostasis 272
efficiency, of human body 153
egg, as laid **474**, 531–2, 767
　of peregrine falcon 680, 775
egg (cell) 372, 499, **503**–5, 510, 512
　in cloning 620
egg-laying mammal 101
ejaculation **504**–5, 513
elastase 189
elastic cartilage 67
elastic fibre **65**, 418
elastic tissue **66**, 236–7
elastin 31, **66**
electric organ 402, **405**
electrocardiogram (ECG) 233, 240–41
electrochemical gradient 145, 211
electroencephalogram (EEG) 365
electron acceptor 209
electron carrier
　in chloroplast 205
　in mitochondrion 144–5
electron transport/chain 144–5
　in photosynthesis 208–11
electro-osmosis 264
electrophoresis 32, 83, 628
elephant 686, 749
　sleeping on slopes 770
　see also tooth
elephantiasis 97
Eloclea: see Canadian pondweed
embolus 240
embryo 68, 508–10, **525**–32
　in flowering plant 487, 534–7
　splitting of 621
embryo sac 485
embryo transfer **526**, 529–30
　see also transplant
embryology 1
　and evolution 730
emigration 639
emphysema 175, **317**, 506, 631
emulsification, emulsifier 37, **189**
end plate potential 356
endemic disease 341
endergonic 118–19
endocrine: *see* gland
endocytosis **115**, 373
endoderm 97, **527**, 766
endodermis **248**–50, 254, 258
endoparasite 707
endometrium **507**, 508, 511–12, 515
endonuclease, restriction **628**–30
endopeptidase 183
endoplasm 433
endoplasmic reticulum **44**–46, 55, 59
　and endosymbiotic theory 764
　rough, smooth 46–7
endorphin 366
endoskeleton 431
endosperm 460, 487, **534**–7
endosymbiotic theory 764
endothelium **62**, 237–8
　in kidney 282–4

gene switching **622**, 626
generalisation 5
generator potential **382**-3, 388
genetic counselling 590
genetic drift 639
genetic dictionary 615
genetic engineering 9, **628**-34,
  in crops 338, 553
  and genetic defects 757
  and hormones 565
  of microorganisms 90, 133
  and vaccines 710
genetically modified food 633
genetics, principles of 1, 571-82
  population **638**-48
genitalia, genitals **497**-8, 513
  abnormal 745
  mismatch 753
genome 594
genotype **573**-81
genus 79-80
geographical distribution 639, **721**-3
geometrical: *see* exponential
geotropism **556**-9
germ layer **527**-8
germination **536**-7, 561
  and temperature 546
gestation period **512**, 748, 772
giberellic acid, giberellin **550**, 553-4,
  563, 567, 626
  as terpene 26
gigantism 564
gill 98-9, 106, **160**-65
gland 63-4
  as effector 402
  endocrine 64, **370**
  exocrine **64**-5, 370
  see also pituitary, salivary
glandular epithelium 63
glandular fever 317
glia **349**, 360
global warming 547, **678**, 685, 776
  and disease 708
globin **217**
globular protein 28, **30**, 57, 124, 128
globulin 30, 275
glomerular filtrate 282-3
glomerular filtration rate **292**-5
glomerulus 281
glottis 184-6
glucagon **270**-72, 284, 370-71
  and second messenger 377
gluconeogenesis 269
glucosamine 23
glucose **16**-20, 104
  in blood 289-91
  in respiration 138-41
glucose oxidase 135
glucose 6-phosphate 104, **142**
glutamic acid **27**, 646, 747, 761
  see also monosodium
glutamine 27
glyceraldehyde 3-phosphate (GALP)
  142, 212
glycerate 3-phosphate (GP) 212-14
glycerol **23**, 56, 183
  and freezing tolerance 314
glycine 26-**27**, 761
glycocholate 26
glycogen 19-**21**, 35, 41
  in exercise 244, 403
  in liver 277
  in respiration 141
glycogen loading 141
glycolipid 57-**58**
glycolysis 141-7

glycoprotein **29**, 47
  blood groups 337
  in cell wall 22
  in fertilisation 504-5
  as hormone 371
  outside plasma membrane 53, 57-8
  as prion 76
glycoside 716
glycosidic bond, link **17**, 21, 128, 183
glycosuria 269
goblet cell 63
Golgi apparatus 42, 45, **47**, 115
  in cell division 460
  in liver 277
goitre 15, 374
gonad 497
gonadotrophin 371, **376**, 510, 513-17
  and releasing hormone 516, 565
gonorrhoea 331, 505-**506**, 711
Goodall, Jane 447
gp120 328
Graafian follicle **501**, 510, 512-13
  and sexual cycle 515-17
graft(ing) 492
Gram staining, negative, positive 88
granum 204-5
gravity, and plants 556-7, 559
grazer, grazing 260, 654, 666
  in Africa 686
greenhouse effect, gases **677**-8, 685,
  776
grey matter 346-**347**
ground substance: *see* matrix
growing point 537
growth 7, 59, **523**
  allometric 524
  in animals **523**-5, 538, 564-6
  control of **546**-68
  intermittent 525
  and mitosis 461
  in plants **537**-43, 547-64
  primary **537**-40
  secondary 95, **540**-42, 547
  suspended 566-8
growth hormone 371, **564**
  and blood glucose 271
  and genetic engineering 133, 631
  in plants 547
  as treatment 745
growth rate **524**-5
growth regulator 59
guanine **604**-15
guard cell 110, **157**-8, 206-7
guttation 298

H
habitat 655
habituation 440
haem 29, **33**, 132, 217-18
haemocytometer, haemocytometry 7,
  693
haemocoel **98**-9, 222, 766
haemocyanin 221
haemoerythrin 221
haemoglobin 33
  and bile pigments 275
  fetal 511
  gene(s) of 616, 743
  and gene switching 622
  in insects and worms 162
  containing iron 14-15
  carrying oxygen 106, 217-**218**-21,
  228
  in Quechuas 243
  S 645-6
haemoglobinic acid (HHb) 221

haemolysis 109
haemolytic disease 338
haemophilia 228-**229**, 317, 530,
  589-90, 594, 633
hair 101, 293-4, 304-5
hair follicle 101, **303**-4
hair-pin countercurrent multiplier 285
halophile 87
halophyte 298
hand, importance in evolution 772-4
haploid 92, 450, **455**, 461-5
  in life cycles 471-8
haplodiploid 450
Hardy-Weinberg principle **640**-43
Harvey, William 234
haustorium 707
Haversian canal **67**, 417
hay fever **333**, 484
head 76, 97-8
health 339-40
hearing aid 396-7
heart 222, 230-**231**-6, 528
  and autonomic system 367-8
  transplant 336
heart attack: *see* cardiac infarction
heart disease 58, 175
heart rate: *see* cardiac frequency
heart surgery 306
heat cramps, stress 307
heat exchange system 312
heat stroke 273, 307, 310
heat tolerance 315
heavy metal tolerance 752
helix, alpha (protein) **28**, 33
  double (DNA) **605**-9
  triple (collagen) **30**, 66
hemicellulose **22**, 42, 460
heparin 229
hepatic artery **276**-7
hepatic portal vein 183, 193, **276**-7
Hepaticae 94
hepatitis 229, 506, 631
hepatocyte 276-7
heptose 16
herbaceous plant **110**, 113, 200
herbicide 552, 632, **679**
herbivore, herbivory **178**-80, 191
  and Red Queen effect 716
heredity: *see* genetics
Hering-Breuer reflex 172
heritability 598
hermaphrodite 97-8, **487**-8
heroin 366, 511
herpes 506, 618
heterotroph(ic) 84, 92, **178**-93
  as first organisms 759
heterozygote, heterozygous **573**-82,
  645
heterozygous advantage 647
hexaploid(y) 745-6
hexose **16**-19, 22, 141
hibernation 312-**313**, 315, 568
hierarchy, social 450
high blood pressure: *see* hypertension
Hill reaction 210
Hirudinea 98
histamine 321, 333
histidine 27
histology 1, 62
histone 625
HIV 76, 229, 327-**328**-30
  and central dogma 617
  see also AIDS
Hodgkin, Dorothy 36
Hodgkin-Huxley theory of nerve
  impulse 350-52

holistic approach 2
homeostasis 8, 267-**268**-73
  examples 29, 132, 159, 173-4, 289,
  308-9, 319, 334, 374, 422, 515-16,
  564, 677, 694-5
homogenate 51
homoiothermy: *see* endothermy
homologous, homology
  biochemical 729
  chromosomal **462**-5, 574, 740-41
  of organs, structures **726**, 728
homozygote, homozygous **573**-81, 645
Hooke, Robert 41
Hopkins, F.G. 35
horizon, of soil 658
hormone 59, 64, **370**-77
  ovarian 514-16
  plant: *see* plant growth regulator
  releasing **376**, 510, 516, 565
  sex 500, **513**
  see also growth hormone
hormone replacement therapy (HRT)
  418, 513
horse evolution 733-4
horticulture 552, 562
  see also plant breeding
host **705**, 711, 715
hot spring 87, 315
human chorionic gonadotrophin (HCG)
  517
human genome project 594-5
human immunodeficiency virus:
  see HIV
human species, origin of **772**-4
humidity 257, 305, 660
humus 657-8
Huntingdon's disease/chorea 317, 530,
  639
hyaline cartilage 67
hybrid 753
hybrid vigour 756
hybridoma 325
hydathode 263, **298**
hydrocarbon chain **23**, 56, 58
hydrocephaly 748
hydrochloric acid 185, 187
hydrogen 16
  in early atmosphere 759
  in respiration 144-5
hydrogen acceptor 144
hydrogen bacteria 214
hydrogen bond **12**, 21, 28-9, 128
  in nucleic acid 606-7
hydrogen carrier **141**-2, 669
hydrogen ion 211, 221
hydrogen peroxide 125, 132
hydrogen sulphide 88
  bacterial oxidation of 196, 214, 763
hydrogen transport system 145-7
hydrolase 124
hydrolysis **17**-18, 24, 54, 124
hydrophilic 58, **105**
hydrophyte 296
hydroponics 200
hydrotropism 557
hypercholesterolaemia 633
hyperglycaemia 269
hyperparasite 671
hypersensitivity 333
hypertension 154, **241**-2, 509
hyperthermophile 87
hyperthyroidism 374
hypertonic solution 109
hyperventilation 243
hypha, fungal 23, **92**-3, 259,
  in potato blight 707

oomycete 91
hypodermis 303-4
hypoglycaemia 270
hypothalamus 271, **361**-2
    and growth 564
    and pituitary 374-6
    and sexual cycle 514-19
    as osmoreceptor 288
    and photoperiodism 565
    in thermoregulation 307-9
hypothermia **306**, 310, 654
hypothesis **2**-5
    examples 128, 263, 407-10, 445, 547,
        557, 735, 737
hypothyroidism 373
hypotonic solution 108
hypoxia 171, 174

I
imago 534
imbibition 537
immigration 639
    and population growth 693, 700
immobilisation, of enymes 133
immune response, system **320**-30
    and parasitism 711
immunisation **330**-31
immunity, acquired 322
    active 330
    artificial 330-31
    cell-mediated **327**, 329
    humoral (antibody-mediated) **326**-7
    innate, natural 322
    passive 330, 509
immunodeficiency **328**, 333
immunoglobulin **323**, 333
immunological tolerance **336**-7
implantation **507**-8, 512, 515-16
    delayed 514
    prevention of 520
    and research on embryos 529
imprinting 442-3
in vitro fertilisation (IVF) **510**, 530
inbreeding 487, 643, 756
inbreeding depression 756
incisor 179-81
independent assortment **579**, 581-2,
    740
indicator species 93
indoleacetic acid (IAA) **548**, 554
induced fit hypothesis **128**-9
infanticide 449
infectious diseases 317-**318**-41
infertility 517
inflammation **321**-3, 334
    of pericardium 506
inflammatory response 375
inflorescence 488
influenza 58, **317**, 319, 341
ingestion 178
inheritance, cytoplasmic 626-7
    dihybrid 578-82
    maternal 626-7
    monohybrid **571**-8
    polygenic 598
inhibin 518
inhibition, inhibitor, of active transport
    254
    of auxin 558
    in clotting 229
    and dormancy 566
    and drugs 366
    of enzymes **129**-32, 143
    of gene 623
    of growth 560-61
    in hormones 270

lateral 388
    in muscles 347, 422
inorganic ions 13
insect, Insecta **100**, 294, 366
    gaseous exchange 162-3
    flight 432
    growth 525
    haemocoel 222
    and metamorphosis 533-4
    as pollinator 488-9
    reproduction 472, 475-6
insecticide 130, 358, 678-**679**-80
    against mosquitoes 710
insemination 756
insertion, in gene mutation 747
inspiration 166-7
instar **525**, 533
instinct **437**-9
insulation **25**, 66, 304, 306
    of neurone 349
insulin 370-**371**
    and genes 59
    and genetic engineering 133
    as globular protein 30
    in homeostasis 269-71, 284
    and membrane receptor 377
    structure 33, 36
    used in treatment 631
integrated pest management 698
integration 360
intelligence 436, **441**, 599-600, 745
interbreeding 753
intercostal muscle 166, 173
intercourse: *see* mating
intercropping 681
interferon 327
internal environment 267-8
interoceptor 380
interphase 463-**464**, 625
interstitial cell **500**, 519
intracellular digestion 115, 181
intracellular enzyme 124, 127
intracytoplasmic sperm injection (ICSI)
    530
intrinsic muscle 423
intrinsic rhythmicity 173
intron 616
inversion, in chromosome mutation
    742-4
    in gene mutation 747
invertebrate 100
involuntary: *see* autonomic
iodine, iodide 13-15, 92, 113, 372-4
    from Chernobyl 684
iodopsin **388**-91
ion channel 382-3
ionic bond **16**, 29
ions, control of **289**-290
iris, of eye **384**-5
iron 13-15
    bacterial oxidation of 196, 214
    as cofactor 132
    in cytochrome oxidase 130
    in haemoglobin 217-18
    in waterlogged soil 658
islet of Langerhans **270**-71, 598
isogamy 472
isolation **751**-3
    geographical 751, 753
    reproductive 752
isoleucine 27
isomer **17**, 124, 388
isomerase 124
isometric contraction 421
isotonic contraction 421
isotonic solution 109

isotope **120**, 210
see also label (isotope), radioactive
    label, tracer

J
Jacob-Monod theory 623
jaundice 275
Jenner, Edward 331
jet lag 362
joint 414, **419**-20
    synovial **419**-20
joulometer 139

K
karyotype 594, 745, 748
keratin **28**, 30, 65, 293, 304
keto group 31
keystone species 686
kidney 53, **280**-95
    transplant 335
kidney machine 286
kin selection 448-9
kinesis 437
kinetic energy 121
kingdom **79**-80, 83-5, 87
Kleinfelter's syndrome 745
Koch's postulates 319
Krebs cycle 141-**142**-51, 244-5
kwashiorkor 15, 317, **546**

L
label (isotope) **120**, 210, 258, 607, 669
    see also tracer
lactase **189**-90
lactation **474**, 511, 518
lacteal: *see* capillary, lymph
lactic acid **147**-9, 163
    in exercise 244-5, 403-4
    in vagina 320
lactose **17**, 19, 623
Lamarck 737-9
lamella, in bone 67
    of gill 164
language **446**-7
    evolution of 774
    how acquired 436, 513, 627
    ubiquity of 772
larva 100, **533**-4
    and cilia 54
    in life cycle **475**-6
    and metamorphosis 566
    moulting of 624
    of parasites 713
    of sea squirt 730
    of sponge 96
latent period 402
lateral 75
law, scientific 6
leaching 656
lead 130, 752
leaf 73, 157-9, **205**-8, 253, 256
leaf area 314
leaf fall 59, 297-**298**, 550-51, 561, 567
leaf litter 664
leaf mosaic 201
learning, insight, latent 441
    trial and error **440**-41
leg 99-100
    see also limb
legume, leguminous plant **669**, 684
lens 384-5
lenticel 157, **542**-3
leprosy 319
leucine 27
leucocyte: *see* white blood cell
leucotomy 364

leukaemia 467
libido 634
lichen 93, **714**-15
    as coloniser 665-6
    and pollution 681
life cycle 470, **475**-9
    of flowering plant 478-9, **481**-94,
        767
life expectancy 700
ligament 30, 66, **418**-20, 425
ligase 124
    DNA 628
light, in environment 660
    and growth 546
    and plant response 560
light harvesting 208-209
light-producing organ 402
lignin **70**-71
    in cell wall 22, 42, 252, 538
    and collapse of xylem 768
    in wood 22, 543-4
lignification 22, 249, 251, 541
limb 76, 99
limiting factor **199**-200, 693
Lincoln index 690
link reaction 141
linkage, linkage group **585**-6
Linnaeus, Carolus 81
lipase **124**, 127, 129, 134-5
    in digestion 183, 189-90
lipid **236**, 56
    in liver 273
lipid bilayer 104
lipoprotein **29**, 273
liquid feeder 178, **181**
liver 20, 46, 125, **273**-7
    in digestion 183, 188-9
    and fat 273
    functions of **273**-5
    and malaria 708-10
    transplant 336
liverwort **94**, 475-7
lock-and-key mechanism 128
locomotion 54, **414**-33
    in air 429-30, 432
    in water 427-8
locus **573**, 575-6
lodging, of cereal crops 552
longevity 568, 635
loop of Henlé **281**-5, 295
LSD (lysergic acid diethylamide) 366
luciferase, luciferin 149
lumen 185, 252
luminescence 122, 140
lung 106, 160-61, **167**-76, 528
    transplant 336
luteal phase **512**, 514-15, 565
luteinising hormone (LH) 371, 508
    and sexual cycle **514**-19
lyase 124
lymph **268**, 322
lymph node 239, 321-**322**, 326-9
lymphatic capillary 239
lymphatic system 69, 97, 192, **239**, 321
lymphocyte 322-37
    B 322-**323**-9
    T 322, **326**-8, 371, 635
lymphokine 327
lysine 27
lysis 332
lysosome 47, **52**, 115-16, 321
    in tadpole 534
lysozyme 28, **128**, 190
    and bacteria 320

ultrasound, ultrasonography 748
ultraviolet radiation 467, 679
    as mutagen 742, 762
umbilicus, umbilical cord **508**, 532
unicellular organism 73, 90
unsaturated fatty acid 24
uracil **604**, 610
urea 11, 127, 151, **274**
    excreted 280-86, 293-4
    in cattle feed 191
urea cycle 274
ureter 280
urethra 280, 498
uric acid 284, **294**-5, 532
urinary system **280**-95
urination 280, **287**-8, 437
    inhibition during ejaculation 505
    and gonorrhoea 506
urine 153, **280**-95
uterus **497**, 505-7, 512
utricle 397-8

V

vaccination, vaccine 317, **330**
    against AIDS 743
    and genetic engineering 631
    against malaria 710
    against smallpox 342
vacuole 52-**53**
    contractile, food 74
    gas 89
    in plant cell **42**, 45, 109-11, 158, 538
vacuole membrane: *see* tonoplast
vagina 65, 320, **497**, 504-5, 511-12
vagus nerve 345, **367**-8
    and heart 235-8, 242, 357
valine 27, 646, 747
valve 217
    in blood vessel **231**-3, 237
    in insect 294
    in plant 253
variation, causes of **740**-41
    continuous **598**
    and crossing-over 465
    discontinuous **599**
    and selection 737, 756
    and sexual reproduction 472, 474
variety 80, 755
vas deferens 498
vascular bundle **250**-51, 541
vascular cylinder 248-51
vascular plant 94, 768
vascular tissue (plant) 71-2, 94, **206**-7,
    539-40
    secondary 554
vasoconstriction **304**, 367
vasodilation 245
vector 711
vegetarian 32
vegetative reproduction 73
vein 230, 234, **236**-7
vena cava 231, **280**
ventilation 101, 163-70
ventilation centre 172, 242, 361
ventilation rate 244
ventral root 346
ventricle, of brain **359**-60
    of heart 224, **230**-35
venule 192, 230
vernalisation **563**, 567
vertebral column 100, 360, **415**, 425,
    528
vertebrate 100
vesicle **115**
    in egg cell 503-4
    pinocytic 53, 284

secretory 47
synaptic 355
vessel 217
    in plants 71, 206-7, **252**-8, 538
    see also circulation
vestibular apparatus 393, **397**-9
vestigial structure 726
Viagra 517
villus **187**, 192
    chorionic 508, 531
    placental 508-10
    trophoblastic 508, 526
virology 1
virus **76**, 317-23, 326-8
    living or non-living 84
    and cancer 466-7
    in genetic engineering 630
    genetics 616-17
    herpes 329
    myxomatosis 698
    reproduction of 616-17
    retro- 617
    RNA 617
    temperate 618
    tobacco mosaic 76
    virulent 618
visceral cleft 100
vision: *see* eye
visual acuity **390**-92
visual purple: *see* rhodopsin
vital capacity **169**, 174
vitamin **34**-6
    B₁₂ 191, 275
    K 26, 228-9
    storage 275
viviparity, viviparous 101, **767**
voluntary nervous system 288, 356-7
von Frisch, Karl 446

W

Wallace 719, 721, 739, 749, 737-**738**
warning coloration 716
warts 506
washing powder 134
    biological 135
water 11-13, 107
    in early atmosphere 759
    density 654
    in environment 659
    as greenhouse gas 677
    metabolic 25, 296
    in photosynthesis 197-8
    in plants 248-58
    in respiration 138, 144
    in soil 657
water balance: *see* osmoregulation
water potential 14, **108**-13, 158, 267-8
    gradient 224, 249-50, 253-6, 537
water stress **113**, 159, 256
Watson–Crick hypothesis **605**-7, 609
wax 26, 70, 94, 205
    impermeability 294
weather 659, 694
weathering 655
weedkiller **552**-3
wheat, evolution of 746
    and genetic engineering 632
    and green revolution 756
white (blood) cell **227**, 320-21
white fibrous cartilage 67
white fibrous tissue 65
white matter 346-**348**
whooping cough 330
wilting **113**, 256, 314
wind 660
    chill factor 306

wing, of bird 101, **429**-32, 726
    of insect 100, 728
wood 22, 42, 72, **540**-44
wound-healing 551

X

xanthophyll 202-3
xerophyte **296**-298
X-ray, and cancer 467
    diffraction, crystallography 33, 66,
    128, 323, 410, 605, 646
    as mutagen 742
    for screening 748
xylem 71-2, 224, 248-**252**-61
    fossil 731, 768
    in leaf 206-7
    and growth regulators 554
xylose 22

Y

yeast **93**, 123, 133, 148
    in disease 318, 320, 615
    reproduction 471
yellow elastic cartilage 67
yellow elastic tissue 66
yoga 367
yoghurt 90, 148
yolk, yolk sac 531-2

Z

zinc 13-15, 132, 752
zonation 655
zoology 1
Zoomastigina 91
zoospore 707
zwitterion 29
zygomorphic flower 483
zygomycete, Zygomycota 93
zygospore 93, 566
zygote 461, **475**-8, 504, 507, 574
    in *Plasmodium* life cycle 710

Acknowledgements

Photographs

The authors and publisher are grateful to the following for permission to reproduce copyright material. Every effort has been made to trace all relevant copyright holders, but if any have been inadvertently overlooked, the publishers will be pleased to make necessary arrangements at the first opportunity.

Photo research by Zooid Pictures Ltd.

Chapter 1

p1 Cambridge University Library
p2 top Geoff Tompkinson/Science Photo Library
p2 bottom Corbis UK Ltd.
p7 top David A. Northcott/Corbis UK Ltd.
p7 centre Ann Purcell/Corbis UK Ltd.
p7 bottom Bruce Coleman
p8 top Lee Snider/ Corbis UK Ltd.
p8 bottom Walter Singer, New York

Chapter 2

p13 top Heather Angel/Biofotos
p13 bottom Jeffrey L. Rotman/Corbis UK Ltd.
p14 Harry Smith
p18 left Paul Hutley/Corbis UK Ltd.
p18 right Jose F. Poblete/Corbis UK Ltd.
p20 left Bruce Iverson/Science Photo Library
p20 right Biophoto Associates
p22 Biophoto Associates
p25 Dan Guravich/Corbis UK Ltd.
p31 left W. Wayne Lockwood/Corbis UK Ltd.
p31 right Sir John Randall
p33 Fred Sanger
p35 Jeffrey L. Rotman/Corbis UK Ltd.
p36 top Lester V. Bergman/Corbis UK Ltd.
p36 bottom Clements/Corbis UK Ltd.

Chapter 3

p41 Wellcome Centre for Medical Science
p43 Biophoto Associates
p44 Biophoto Associates
p46 left Michael Roberts
p46 right Michael Roberts
p47 Biophoto Associates
p48 left Biophoto Associates
p48 right Biophoto Associates
p49 top left Biophoto Associates
p49 top centre Biophoto Associates
p49 top right Biophoto Associates
p49 bottom David Sharf/Science Photo Library
p50 Prof Ruth Bellairs

p51 Dr Don Fawcett/Science Photo Library
p52 Dr Brij Gupta/Michael Roberts
p53 left Gene Cox
p53 right Biophoto Associates
p54 Dr A Boyde/Michael Roberts
p55 left Drs Vi Barber, Patricia Holborow and MS Laverack/The Editor, Zeitschrift fur Zellforshng und Mikroskopicae Anatomie/Michael Roberts
p55 right Drs Vi Barber, Patricia Holborow and MS Laverack/The Editor, Zeitschrift fur Zellforshng und Mikroskopicae Anatomie/ Dr V Grimstone
p56 left BE Juniper/Michael Roberts
p56 right Bawie Juniper

Chapter 4

p62 Gene Cox
p66 top Gene Cox
p66 bottom Lester V. Bergman/Corbis UK Ltd.
p68 Gene Cox
p70 top Gene Cox
p70 bottom Gene Cox
p72 Bruce Coleman
p73 Biofoto
p75 top Robert Maier/Bruce Coleman
p75 bottom D.P. Wilson/Corbis UK Ltd.
p76 NIBSC/Science Photo Library
p77 Omikron/Science Photo Library

Chapter 5

p81 left Lynda Richardson/Corbis UK Ltd.
p81 bottom right Woodfall Wild Images
p81 top Klaus Honal/Corbis UK Ltd.
p81 centre B.J.W. Heath
p83 top Biophoto Associates
p83 bottom Biophoto Associates

Chapter 6

p88 centre left AB Dowsett/Science Photo Library
p88 left CNRI/Science Photo Library
p88 centre right CNRI/Science Photo Library
p88 right RB Dowsett/Science Photo Library
p89 top Dr Jeremy Burgess/Science Photo Library
p89 bottom Prof David Hall/Science Photo Library
p90 top Francis Leroy/Science Photo Library
p90 centre CAMR, Barry Dowsett/Science Photo Library
p90 bottom Michael Abbey/Science Photo Library
p91 top centre Andrew Syred/Science Photo Library

p91 bottom centre Sinclair Stammers/ Science Photo Library
p91 top Eric Grave/Science Photo Library
p91 bottom Woodfall Wild Images
p92 top Biofotos
p92 bottom Biofotos
p93 top centre European Journal of Cell Biology/Namboori J. Raju
p93 bottom centre Biofotos
p93 top Gene Cox
p93 bottom Ian Harwood/Corbis UK Ltd.
p94 top centre Tony Wharton/Corbis UK Ltd.
p94 bottom centre Heather Angel/Biofotos
p94 top Biophoto Associates
p94 bottom Martin B. Withers/Corbis UK Ltd.
p95 top left David Woodfall/Woodfall Wild Images
p95 bottom left Grace Monger
p95 top right Biofotos
p95 bottom right Heather Angel/Biofotos
p97 top centre John Heath/Biofotos
p97 top Brandon D. Cole/Corbis UK Ltd.
p97 centre M.I. Walker/Science Photo Library
p97 bottom Lester V. Bergman/Corbis UK Ltd.
p98 top centre Heather Angel/Biofotos
p98 bottom centre Biofotos
p98 top Rodger Jackman/Oxford Scientific Films
p98 centre Robert Pickett/Corbis UK Ltd.
p98 bottom George Lepp/Corbis UK Ltd.
p99 top centre Biofotos
p99 bottom centre Biofotos
p99 top Biofotos
p99 bottom John Robinson/Woodfall Wild Images
p100 top centre Andy Harper/ Windrush Photos
p100 bottom centre Joel W. Rogers/Corbis UK Ltd.
p100 top Anthony Bannister/Corbis UK Ltd.
p100 bottom Biofotos
p101 centre left Mike Lane/Woodfall Wild Images
p101 bottom left Animals Animals/Oxford Scientific Films
p101 top centre Mark Hamblin/Woodfall Wild Images
p101 bottom centre David Woodfall/Woodfall Wild Images
p101 top right Michael Fogden; Patricia Fogden/Corbis UK Ltd.
p101 bottom right Adam Woolfitt/Corbis UK Ltd.
p101 centre David Hosking/Corbis UK Ltd.

Chapter 7

p109 top Gene Cox
p109 bottom Gene Cox
p113 top Heather Angel/Biofoto
p113 bottom Heather Angel/Biofoto
p115 Biophoto Associates
p116 SECCHI-LECAQUE/Roussel-UCLAF/
CNRI/Biophoto Associates

Chapter 8

p121 Babraham Institute
p122 top Paul A. Souders/Corbis UK Ltd.
p122 bottom Jeffrey L. Rotman/Corbis
UK Ltd.
p125 top B.J.W. Heath
p125 bottom B.J.W. Heath
p134 Roger Ressmeyer/Corbis UK Ltd.

Chapter 9

p139 St. Batholemew's Hospital/Science
Photo Library
p140 Wellcome Centre for Medical Science
p143 Michael Roberts
p148 Adam Woolfitt/Corbis UK Ltd.
p152 Bob and Clara Calhoun/Bruce Coleman

Chapter 10

p157 top Gene Cox
p157 bottom Barry Juniper
p158 top Dr. Colin Willmer
p158 bottom Dr. Colin Willmer
p164 top Geoff Tompkinson/Biofotos
p164 bottom John Davenport/Biological
Sciences Review
p168 Gene Cox
p170 B.J.W. Heath
p172 Dr J. Clarke, St Bartholomew's Hospital
p174 John A. Clarke
p175 left James Stevenson/Science
Photo Library
p175 right James Stevenson/Science
Photo Library

Chapter 11

p178 top left Michael S. Yamashita/Corbis
UK Ltd.
p178 bottom left Staffan Widstrand/
Corbis UK Ltd.
p178 bottom centre Anthony
Bannister/Corbis UK Ltd.
p178 bottom right Bruce Coleman
p179 top Grace Monger/Michael Roberts
p179 centre Paolo Ragazzini/Corbis UK Ltd.
p179 bottom David Thompson/Oxford
Scientific Films
p180 top centre Biofotos
p180 bottom centre Michael Roberts
p180 top Gunter Ziesler/Bruce Coleman
p180 bottom Claude Nuridsany and Marie
Perennou Biofotos
p181 top centre B.J.W. Heath

p181 bottom centre BBC Natural History/
Premaphotos Wildlife
p181 top Biophoto Associates
p181 centre Richard T. Nowitz/Corbis UK Ltd.
p181 bottom Claude Nuridsany and Marie
Perenou/Science Photo Library
p182 top Biofotos
p182 centre Peter Parks/Oxford
Scientific Films
p182 bottom Peter Parks/Oxford
Scientific Films
p187 Biophoto Associates
p188 BBC Natural History/
Professor Henry Leese
p189 Gene Cox
p193 Fawcett/Hirokawa/Heuser/Science
Photo Library

Chapter 12

p200 left Roger Tidman/Corbis UK Ltd.
p200 centre Chinch Gryniewicz/Corbis
UK Ltd.
p200 right Pat Jerrold/Corbis UK Ltd.
p201 Biofotos
p205 Michael Roberts
p207 top Gene Cox
p207 bottom Gene Cox
p208 CR Photography
p213 left Lawrence Berkley National
Laboratory
p213 right Lawrence Berkeley Laboratory/
University of California

Chapter 14

p228 top Dr Dennis Kunkel/Phototake
NYC/Robert Harding Picture Library
p228 bottom NIBSC//Science Photo Library
p232 Sally Morgan/Corbis UK Ltd.
p234 top centre Corbis UK Ltd.
p234 bottom centre Corbis UK Ltd.
p234 top Corbis UK Ltd.
p234 bottom Corbis UK Ltd.
p234
p235 left Michael Roberts
p235 right Michael Roberts
p237 Gene Cox
p240 top Science Photo Library
p240 bottom Science Photo Library
p241 Mehau Kulyk/Science Photo Library
p243 Corbis UK Ltd.
p244 Rick Price/Oxford Scientific Films

Chapter 15

p248 Biophoto Associates
p249 JC Rew/Biophoto Associates
p249 Biophoto Associates
p251 Biophoto Associates
p251 Biophoto Associates
p251 Gene Cox
p251 Biophoto Associates
p252 Biophoto Associates
p253 top left Biophoto Associates

p253 bottom left Biophoto Associates
p253 top right Springer/Biophoto Associates
p253 bottom right Biophoto Associates
p259 bottom left Biophoto Associates
p259 bottom right Michael Roberts
p259 top Bryan Knox/Corbis UK Ltd.
p261 top George McCarthy/Corbis UK Ltd.
p261 bottom Biophoto Associates

Chapter 16

p267 Michael Roberts
p268 Science Photo Library
p270 Astrid and Hang-Frieder Michler/Science
Photo Library
p275 Martin/Custom Stock Photo/Science
Photo Library
p276 Gene Cox
p277 WHO/Michael Roberts

Chapter 17

p281 Lester V. Bergman/Corbis UK Ltd.
p283 Biophoto Associates
p287 Simon Fraser, Royal Victoria Infirmary,
Newcastle upon Tyne/Science Photo Library
p291 Pat O'Hara/Corbis UK Ltd.
p295 Ford Kristo/Planet Earth Pictures
p295 David Liittschwager; Susan Middleton/
Corbis UK Ltd.
p296 top Christine Osborne/Corbis UK Ltd.
p296 bottom Hal Beral/Corbis UK Ltd.
p297 bottom left Gene Cox
p297 bottom right Gene Cox
p297 top Christine Osborne/Corbis UK Ltd.
p298 Heather Angel/Biofotos

Chapter 18

p309 Naval Medical Research Institute
National Naval Medical Center,Bethseda,
Maryland,USA/Michael Roberts
p311 left Galen Rowell/Corbis UK Ltd.
p311 right Francesc Muntada/Corbis UK Ltd.
p312 top Norbert Rosing/Oxford Scientific
Films
p312 bottom Steve Kaufman/Corbis UK Ltd.
p313 Heather Angel/Biofotos
p314 top Andrew Brown/Corbis UK Ltd.
p314 bottom Heather Angel/Biofotos
p315 Biofoto

Chapter 19

p320 Lester V. Bergman/Corbis UK Ltd.
p321 Biophoto Associates
p325 Secchi, Lecaque, Roussel, UCLAF,
CNRI/Science Photo Library
p330 S Nagendra/Science Photo Library
p331 WHO/Michael Roberts
p332 top St Mary's Hospital Medical
School/Science Photo Library
p332 bottom St Mary's Hospital Medical
School/Science Photo Library
p333 NASA/Science Photo Library
p335 top Sir Roy Calne/Michael Roberts

p335 bottom Norbert Rosing/British Heart Foundation
p337 Sir Peter Medawar, National Institute for Medical Research/Michael Roberts
p339 IACR-Long Ashton
p342 left Paul Almasy/Corbis UK Ltd.
p342 top right WHO
p342 bottom right WHO

Chapter 20

p348 Dee Conway
p355 Professor EG Gray/Michael Roberts
p362 CNRI/Science Photo Library

Chapter 21

p373 Gene Cox
p374 Du Vivier Biophoto Associates

Chapter 22

p380 Professors P Motta and T Naguro/Science Photo Library
p388 Biophoto Associates
p392 David Scharf/Science Photo Library
p394 Dr. G. Oran/Science Photo Library
p397 top Starkey Laboratories
p397 bottom Starkey Laboratories

Chapter 23

p405 Biofotos
p406 Professor Hugh Huxley/Michael Roberts
p407 Professor Hugh Huxley/Michael Roberts
p408 top Biophoto Associates
p408 bottom Biophoto Associates
p409 Professor Hugh Huxley

Chapter 24

p414 THOMAS NELSON & SONS LTD.
p417 Topham Picturepoint
p418 Gene Cox
p419 Chris Bjornberg/Science Photo Library
p423 top left Professor Hugh Huxley/Michael Roberts
p423 centre left Professor Hugh Huxley/Michael Roberts
p423 bottom left Professor Hugh Huxley/Michael Roberts
p423 top right Professor Hugh Huxley/Michael Roberts
p423 centre right Professor Hugh Huxley/Michael Roberts
p423 bottom right Professor Hugh Huxley/Michael Roberts
p424 top Karl Weatherly/Corbis UK Ltd.
p424 bottom James L. Amos/Corbis UK Ltd.
p427 Charles Philip/Corbis UK Ltd.
p430 top Peter Johnson/Corbis UK Ltd.
p430 bottom BJW Heath/Michael Roberts
p433 Biophoto Associates

Chapter 25

p436 Kevin Schafer/Corbis UK Ltd.
p438 Windrush Photos

p443 Michael Roberts
p445 David Cumming/Corbis UK Ltd.
p447 Kennan Ward/Corbis UK Ltd.
p448 top Chase Swift/Corbis UK Ltd.
p448 bottom Craig Lovell/Corbis UK Ltd.
p450 Clive Bromhall/Oxford Scientific Films
p451 top JM Pearson/Biofotos
p451 bottom Richard Bickel/Corbis UK Ltd.
p452 Brenda Prince/Format Photographers

Chapter 26

p459 bottom left Dr Brij Gupta/University of Cambridge
p459 top centre CNRI/Science Photo Library
p459 bottom centre CNRI/Science Photo Library
p459 bottom right CNRI/Science Photo Library
p459 top CNRI/Science Photo Library
p459 centre CNRI/Science Photo Library
p460 left Dr A Bajer/Michael Roberts
p460 right Michael Roberts
p461 left Dr. Jeremy Burgess/Science Photo Library
p461 right Dr. Jeremy Burgess/Science Photo Library
p464 Gene Cox
p464 Biophoto Associates
p465 centre left Biophoto Associates
p465 left Biophoto Associates
p465 centre right Biophoto Associates
p465 right Biophoto Associates
p465 Biophoto Associates
p465 Biophoto Associates
p467 Novosti/Science Photo Library

Chapter 27

p470 top Audrey Glauert
p470 centre Audrey Glauert
p470 bottom Audrey Glauert
p471 top Michael Fogden; Patricia Fogden/Corbis UK Ltd.
p471 centre Gene Cox
p471 bottom Corbis UK Ltd.
p472 top George McCarthy/Corbis UK Ltd.
p472 bottom Biofotos
p473 Dr L Caro/Science Photo Library
p474 Kennan Ward/Corbis UK Ltd.
p476 Biofotos
p477 London Scientific Films/Oxford Scientific Films
p478 left Tony Wharton/Corbis UK Ltd.
p478 right Heather Angel/Biofotos

Chapter 28

p482 top Patrick Johns/Corbis UK Ltd.
p482 centre Biofotos
p482 bottom Deni Brown/Oxford Scientific Films
p483 left Biofotos
p483 right David Hosking; Eric Hosking/Corbis UK Ltd.

p484 top Deni Brown/Biophoto Associates
p484 centre Deni Brown/Biophoto Associates
p484 bottom Deni Brown/Biophoto Associates
p484 Gene Cox
p485 top Biophoto Associates
p485 bottom Andrew Syred/Science Photo Library
p486 Dr Jeremy Burgess/Science Photo Library
p487 Dr Jeremy Burgess/Science Photo Library
p488 top Dr Jeremy Burgess/Science Photo Library
p488 centre Dr Jeremy Burgess/Science Photo Library
p488 bottom Biofotos
p489 bottom left Biofotos
p489 bottom right Biofotos
p489 top Biofotos
p490 Biophoto Associates
p492 KG Preston-Mafham/Premaphotos Wildlife
p493 bottom left UNILEVER
p493 bottom right Edward Parker/Oxford Scientific Films
p493 top UNILEVER
p494 top left Biofotos
p494 bottom left Tony Wharton/Corbis UK Ltd.
p494 top right Steve Austin/Woodfall Wild Images
p494 bottom right Sally Morgan/Corbis UK Ltd.

Chapter 29

p500 Secchi-Lecaque/CNRI/Science Photo Library
p501 Gene Cox
p502 Dr A Bajer/Michael Roberts

Chapter 30

p523 George Lee White/Corbis UK Ltd.
p526 top centre G.I. Bernard/Oxford Scientific Films
p526 bottom centre G.I. Bernard/Oxford Scientific Films
p526 top G.I. Bernard/Oxford Scientific Films
p526 centre G.I. Bernard/Oxford Scientific Films
p526 bottom G.I. Bernard/Oxford Scientific Films
p531 Petit Format/Nestle/Science Photo Library
p533 top Andrew Syred/Science Photo Library
p533 bottom Manfred Pfefferle/Oxford Scientific Films
p536 Gene Cox
p540 left Biophoto Associates
p540 right Biophoto Associates
p541 Gene Cox
p542 top Galen Rowell/Corbis UK Ltd.

p542 bottom Doug Wilson/Corbis UK Ltd.
p543 Biophoto Associates

Chapter 31

p546 top Andy Crump, TDR,WHO/Science Photo Library
p546 bottom Biofotos
p547 Dr LC Erickson/Botanical Society of America/Michael Roberts
p549 top United States Department of Agriculture
p549 bottom United States Department of Agriculture
p550 top Michael Roberts
p550 centre Michael Roberts
p550 bottom Biofotos
p551 Dr SH Wittwer/Michael Roberts
p553 John Land
p554 B.J.W. Heath
p556 B.J.W. Heath
p557 top Michael Roberts
p557 centre Michael Roberts
p557 bottom Michael Roberts
p559 Biophoto Associates
p562 Dr. J.W. Hannay
p564 Science Photo Library
p567 Biophoto Associates

Chapter 32

p571 top Biofotos
p571 centre Judyth Platt/Corbis UK Ltd.
p571 bottom Science Photo Library
p573 Wellcome Centre for Medical Science
p575 top Darwin Dale/Science Photo Library
p575 bottom Owen Newman/Oxford Scientific Films
p577 Charles Lenars/Corbis UK Ltd.
p578 Rex Features

Chapter 33

p587 Carol Farnei/Planet Earth Pictures
p590 Mary Evans Picture Library
p591 Scott Camazine/Oxford Scientific Films
p595 CNRI/Science Photo Library
p599 Liz & Tony Bomford Oxford Scientific Films

Chapter 34

p602 David Parker/Science Photo Library
p605 A Barrinton Brown/Science Photo Library
p605 Science Photo Library
p617 Eye of Science//Science Photo Library

Chapter 35

p621 Ph Plailly/Eurelios/Science Photo Library
p627 Hans Reinhard/Bruce Coleman
p630 Michael Roberts
p632 Bruce Coleman
p635 James Stevenson/Science Photo Library

Chapter 36

p638 Biofotos
p640
p641 top Martin Dohrn/Science Photo Library
p641 bottom Tony Craddock/Science Photo Library
p644 Biofotos
p645 Eric Grave/Science Photo Library
p648 top centre Guy Stubbs/Corbis UK Ltd.
p648 bottom centre Karen Su/Corbis UK Ltd.
p648 top David Reid/Corbis UK Ltd.
p648 centre Bob Krist/Corbis UK Ltd.
p648 bottom Michael S Yamashita/Corbis UK Ltd.

Chapter 37

p651 Corbis UK Ltd.
p652 Kevin Schafer/Corbis UK Ltd.
p653 top Andrew Brown/Corbis UK Ltd.
p653 centre Biofotos
p653 bottom Richard T. Nowitz/Corbis UK Ltd.
p655 top Biofotos
p655 bottom Pat Jerrold/Corbis UK Ltd.
p658 Fritz Polking/Corbis UK Ltd.
p660 top Doug Allan/Oxford Scientific Films
p660 bottom Jeff Vanuga/Corbis UK Ltd.

Chapter 38

p663 top Dr Rod Preston-Mafham/Premaphotos Wildlife
p663 bottom Biofotos
p664 top Biofotos
p664 bottom John Heseltine/Science Photo Library
p665 top Dr Z. Glowacinski
p665 centre Dr Z. Glowacinski
p665 bottom Dr Z. Glowacinski
p669 Dr Jeremy Burgess/Science Photo Library
p672 Tom Brakefield/Corbis UK Ltd.
p674 Silver Springs Wild Waters Waterpark

Chapter 39

p677 Ted Streshinsky/Corbis UK Ltd.
p678 George Lepp/Corbis UK Ltd.
p685 Natalie Fobes/Corbis UK Ltd.
p686 top W. Perry Conway/Corbis UK Ltd.
p686 bottom Anthony Bannister/Corbis UK Ltd.
p687 top D. Robert Franz/Corbis UK Ltd.
p687 bottom Biofotos

Chapter 40

p690 Tim Zurowski/Corbis UK Ltd.
p697 top Australian News and Information Bureau/Michael Roberts
p697 centre Australian News and Information Bureau/Michael Roberts
p697 bottom Australian News and Information Bureau/Michael Roberts
p698 top Biofotos
p698 bottom Jeremy Thomas/Biofotos
p702 top Roger Tidman/Corbis UK Ltd.
p702 bottom George McCarthy/Corbis UK Ltd.

Chapter 41

p705 Biofotos
p706 David Spears/Corbis UK Ltd.
p707 Gene Cox
p709 Masanichi Aikawa, MD/Phototake NYC/Robert Harding Picture Library
p711 Eye of Science//Science Photo Library
p713 top Hal Horwitz/Corbis UK Ltd.
p713 bottom Jeffrey L. Rotman/Corbis UK Ltd.
p715 JLG Grande/Bruce Coleman
p717 bottom left David Fox/Oxford Scientific Films
p717 bottom centre KG Vock/Okapia/Oxford Scientific Films
p717 bottom right W. Perry Conway/Corbis UK Ltd.
p717 top Biofotos

Chapter 42

p719 National Library of Medicine/Science Photo Library
p721 top Charles Philip/Corbis UK Ltd.
p721 centre Seth-Smith/Zoological Society of London
p721 bottom Francisco Futil/Bruce Coleman
p724 top Buddy Mays/Corbis UK Ltd.
p724 bottom Galen Rowell/Corbis UK Ltd.
p725 Mary Plage/Bruce Coleman
p730 Bill Wood/Bruce Coleman
p731 top David Muench/Corbis UK Ltd.
p731 centre John Reader/Science Photo Library
p731 bottom British Museum/Munoz-Yague/Science Photo Library
p732 top James L. Amos/Corbis UK Ltd.
p732 bottom Liz Hymans/Corbis UK Ltd.

Chapter 43

p737 bottom left Kim Taylor/Bruce Coleman
p737 bottom right Roger Tidman/Corbis UK Ltd.
p737 top Jane Burton/Bruce Coleman
p737 centre Laura Dwight/Corbis UK Ltd.
p738 David Hosking/Corbis UK Ltd.
p740 Wolfgang Kaehler/Corbis UK Ltd.
p742 John Urling Clark
p745 left East Anglian Regional Genetics Service/Science Photo Library
p745 right Hattie Young/Science Photo Library
p746 Heather Angel/Biofotos
p748 Mehau Kulyk/Science Photo Library
p752 John Durham/Science Photo Library
p753 left Steve Austin/Corbis UK Ltd.
p753 right Steve Austin/Corbis UK Ltd.

p754 top Peter Scoones/Planet Earth Pictures
p754 centre Kevin R. Morris/Corbis UK Ltd.
p754 bottom K.G. Preston-Mafham/
Premaphotos Wildlife
p756 Dr Chris Wood/Horticultural Research
International, Wellesbourne
p757 Omikron/Science Photo Library

Chapter 44

p760 top Biofotos
p760 bottom Corbis UK Ltd.
p761 Roger Ressmeyer/Corbis UK Ltd.
p764 Lynn Margulis
p768 Biophoto Associates
p769 Sinclair Stammers/Science Photo Library
p772 top John Reader/Science Photo Library
p772 bottom John Reader/Science
Photo Library
p773 Yann Arthus-Bertrand/Corbis UK Ltd.
p774 top Charles Lenars/Corbis UK Ltd.
p774 bottom Sally & Richard Greenhill
p775 Fritz Polking/Corbis UK Ltd.
p776 EPA/Press Association

Illustrations

Certain material in this book is taken from
already published sources as follows:

Chapter 2

Page 12 E.J. Wood and W.R. Pickering,
Introducing Biochemistry (John Murray);
2.12 C. Starr and R. Taggart, *Biology: The
Unity and Diversity of life* (Wadsworth);
2.17 A.L. Lehninger, *Principles of
Biochemistry* (Worth Publishing);
2.18, 2.21 and **2.22** F.B. Armstrong,
Biochemistry (Oxford University Press);
2.20 P. Sheeler and D.E. Bianchi, *Cell and
Molecular Biology* (John Wiley & Sons).

Chapter 3

3.5 Modified after Brechet;
3.21 J.A. Ramsey,
The Experimental Basis of Modern Biology
(Cambridge University Press);
3.22 and **3.23** J. Singer and G.L. Nicholson,
Science, **175**, 1972.

Chapter 4

4.3 Modified from A.W. Ham, *Histology* (Pitman);
page 66 B. Alberts *et al.*, *Molecular Biology of
the Cell, 3rd edn* (Garland Publishing);
page 74 K. Vickerman and F.E.G. Cox,
The Protozoa (John Murray);
4.19B P. Freeland, *Microbes, Medicine and
Commerce* (Hodder and Stoughton).

Chapter 5

5.6 G. Monger and M. Sangster, *Systematics
and Classification* (Longman).

Chapter 6

Page 96 G. Monger and M. Sangster.

Chapter 7

7.3 and **7.11** B. Alberts *et al.*, *The Molecular
Biology of the Cell* (Garland Publishing);
7.5 Based on J.F. Sutcliffe.

Chapter 8

Page 120 G.H. Harper, *Tools and Techniques*
(Nelson);
8.2 G.G. Simpson and W.S. Beck, *Life, an
Introduction to Biology* (Harcourt Brace
Jovanovich);
8.12 M. Boxer and Z. Towalski, *New Scientist*,
19 January 1984.

Chapter 9

Page 138 D.G. Mackean, *Experimental Work
in Biology No 7: Respiration and Gaseous
Exchange* (John Murray);
9.10 S. Davidson and R. Passmore,
Human Nutrition and Dietetics
(Churchill-Livingstone).

Chapter 10

Page 159 illustration 1 After Noel, 'Some
new techniques in plant physiology', *School
Science Review*, **142**, 1959;
page 159 illustration 2 S. Boussiba and
A. Richmond, 'Abscisic acid and the after-effect
of stress in tobacco plants', *Planta*, **129**, 1976;
page 162 illustrations 1 to **5** Based on
Alison Leadley Brown;
10.7 and **10.8** V.B. Wigglesworth, *The
Principles of Insect Physiology* (Methuen);
10.11A and **page 165** G.M. Hughes,
*Comparative Physiology of Vertebrate
Respiration* (Heinemann);
10.13 C. Starr and R. Taggart;
10.15 D.G. Mackean, *Introduction to Biology*
(John Murray);
10.16 Teresa Tetley, 'Holy smoke: smoke
damage in the lungs', *Biological Sciences
Review* Vol. 2, No. 5, May 1990;
page 170 T. Turvey, *Revised Nuffield
Advanced Science Biology*, Practical Guide 1
(Longman);
10.19 G. Monger (ed.), *Revised Nuffield
Advanced Science Biology* (Longman);
page 175 Graphs reproduced by courtesy of
the Health Education Authority.

Chapter 11

A.W. Ham; **11.18** G.L. McCulloch, *Man Alive*
(Aldus Books).

Chapter 12

12.3 Data by Gaastra;
12.7 After Haxo and Blinks;
12.9 Mainly after Clayton;
12.10 Professor Rachel Leech, University
of York.

Chapter 13

13.2 Professor M.F. Perutz;
13.4, 13.5, 13.6, 13.9 and **13.10** G. Monger
(ed.), *Revised Nuffield Advanced Science
Biology* (Longman).

Chapter 14

14.5 G.J. Tortora, *Principles of Human
Anatomy* (Canfield Press);
14.6 Based on C.R.W. Edwards *et al.* (eds) in
Davidson's *Principles and Practice of Medicine*
7th edn (Churchill-Livingstone);
14.8, 14.10 and **14.16** C. Starr and R. Taggart;
14.9 Winton and Bayliss, *Human Physiology*
(Churchill-Livingstone);
page 241 Courtesy of Dr Geilan Ismail.

Chapter 15

15.4 G. Monger (ed.), *Revised Nuffield
Advanced Science Biology* (Longman);
15.12 K. Esau, *Plant Anatomy* (John Wiley
& Sons);
15.14 Data after Professor J.F. Sutcliffe;
15.16 After Zimmerman;
15.18 Data by Hoagland;
15.19 Data provided by Dr Richard Gliddon;
15.22 F.A.L. Clowes and B.E. Juniper, *Plant
Cells* (Blackwell);
15.26 M. Wilkins, *Plant Watching* (Macmillan).

Chapter 16

16.2 Data after T.E. Isles and Hazel Barker.

Chapter 17

17.1 C.H. Best and N.B. Taylor, *The Living Body*
(Chapman and Hall);
17.5 G. Monger (ed.), *Revised Nuffield
Advanced Science Biology* (Longman);
page 286 illustration 1 A.C. Guyton, *Basic
Human Physiology* (Saunders);
page 286 illustration 2 G. Monger (ed.),
Revised Nuffield Advanced Science Biology
(Longman);
page 287 R. Gabriel, *A Patient's Guide to
Dialysis and Transplantation* (MTP Press
Limited);
17.13 Data after Sir James Beament;

17.14 H.G.Q. Rowett, *Dissection Guides V Invertebrates* (John Murray).

Chapter 18

18.1 Data after C.J. Martin;
page 302 Data after Samson Wright;
18.2 A.C. Guyton, *Physiology of the Human Body* (Saunders);
page 309 Data after T.H. Benzinger;
18.6 M.S. Gordon, *Animal Physiology* (Macmillan);
18.7 P.F. Scholander *et al., Biological Bulletin* Vol. 99.

Chapter 19

19.2 and **19.10** L. Gamlin, 'The human immune system', Part 1, *New Scientist*, **1605**, 24 March 1988;
19.6 Courtesy of Dr Basiro Davey;
19.13 G. Monger (ed.), *Revised Nuffield Advanced Science Biology* (Longman);
19.15 Data from the World Health Organisation.

Chapter 20

20.4 G.L. McCulloch, *Man Alive* (Aldus Books);
20.6C and **20.14** Alberts *et al.;*
20.17 P.R. Wheater *et al., Functional Histology* (Churchill-Livingstone);
page 365 C. Blakemore, *The Mind Machine* (BBC Books).

Chapter 21

21.1 G.J. Tortora, *Principles of Human Anatomy* (Canfield Press);
21.7 and **21.8** R. Guillemin and R. Burgus in D. Emslie-Smith *et al.* (eds), *Textbook of Physiology* (Churchill-Livingstone).

Chapter 22

Page 381 Based on A. Vander, J. Sherman and D. Luciano, *Human Physiology: the Mechanisms of Body Function 7th edn* (McGraw-Hill);
22.3 W.R. Lowenstein;
page 389 illustration 1 E.G. Boring;
page 389 illustration 2 Barbara Gillam, 'Geometrical illusions', *Scientific American*, January 1980;
22.11 George Wald and others;
page 392 V.B. Wigglesworth, *The Life of Insects* (Weidenfield and Nicholson);
22.14 W. Bloom and D.W. Fawcett, *A Textbook of Histology* (Saunders);
22.15 D. Emslie-Smith *et al., Textbook of Physiology* (Churchill-Livingstone);
22.16 R.F. Schmidt (ed.), *Fundamentals of Sensory Physiology* (Springer-Verlag);
22.17A and **22.18A** G.L. McCulloch, *Man Alive* (Aldus Books).

Chapter 23

23.8 C. Starr and R. Taggart;
page 410 Based on Peter Kohn.

Chapter 24

24.1 G.J. Tortora, *Principles of Human Anatomy* (Canfield Press);
24.4 C. Starr and R. Taggart;
24.6A Henry Gray, *Anatomy, Descriptive and Surgical* (Running Press, Philadelphia);
24.14A J.Z. Young, *The Life of Vertebrates* (Oxford University Press);
24.20 Sir James Gray.

Chapter 25

25.2 A.J. Premack and D. Premack, *Teaching Language to an Ape* (Scientific American);
25.3 J. Alcock, *Animal Behaviour: an Evolutionary Approach* (Sinauer Associates, Inc.);
25.6 N. Tinbergen, *The Study of Instinct* (Oxford University Press);
25.7A N. Tinbergen;
25.8 A.P. Brookfield, *Animal Behaviour* (Nelson);
25.9 Drickamer and Vessey, and A.P. Brookfield;
25.11 Data taken from I.C.T. Nisbet, 'Courtship feeding, egg size and breeding success in common terns', *Nature*, **241**, pp141–2;
25.12 F. Huntingford, *The Study of Animal Behaviour* (Chapman and Hall);
25.14, 25.15 and **25.16** M.J. Reiss and Harriet Sants, *Behaviour and Social Organisation* (Cambridge University Press).

Chapter 26

26.6 B. Alberts *et al.;*
26.12 V. Rich, 'An ill wind from Chernobyl', *New Scientist*, 20 April 1991, pp 26–8.

Chapter 27

27.10 C. Starr and R. Taggart, and N.A. Campbell, *Biology* (Benjamin/Cummings);
27.11 C. Starr and R. Taggart.

Chapter 28

28.1, 28.2 and **28.13** C. Starr and R. Taggart;
28.5 G. Beckett, *The Secret Life of Plants* (Octopus) based on an original text by J. Pazourek;
28.22 R.B. Whellock, *General Biology* (Harrap);
28.23 A. Gemmell and P. Swindells, *Your Gardening Questions Answered* (Reader's Digest).

Chapter 29

29.1, 29.2A, 29.12 and **29.13** R.J. Demarest and J.J. Sciarra, *Conception, Birth and Contraception* (McGraw-Hill/Hodder and Stoughton);
29.2B M. Dym in L. Weiss and R.O. Greep (eds), *Histology* (McGraw-Hill);
29.4C B.I. Balinsky, *An Introduction to Embryology* (Holt Saunders);
29.6 D.W. Fawcett, *The Cell* (Saunders);
29.10 Based on A.W. Ham;
29.11 H. Tuchmann-Duplesses, G. David and P. Haegel, *Illustrated Human Embryology Vol. 1 Embryogenesis* (Springer Verlag/Chapman and Hall);
29.14 Courtesy of Professor Henry Leese;
page 513 J.M. Tanner, *Fetus into Man* (Open Books).

Chapter 30

30.2 J.M. Tanner, *Growth and Adolescence* (Blackwell);
30.3 G.G. Simpson and W.S. Beck, *Life: An Introduction to Biology* (Harcourt Brace Jovanovich);
30.4 Data after G. Teissier;
30.8 B.I. Balinsky, *An Introduction to Embryology* (Holt Saunders);
30.17 A.S. Foster and E.M. Gifford, *Comparative Morphology of Vascular Plants* (W.H. Freeman);
30.20 K. Esau, *Anatomy of Seed Plants* (John Wiley & Sons).

Chapter 31

31.7 Data after L.J. Audus;
page 553 J.B. Land and R.B. Land, *Food Chains to Biotechnology* (Nelson);
31.15 Data after Briggs *et al.;*
31.17 M.B. Wilkins;
31.20 K. Esau, *Anatomy of Seed Plants* (John Wiley & Sons);
31.21 Data after L. Hawker;
31.22 After Hendricks.

Chapter 33

33.9 and **page 594** S. Singer, *Human Genetics: An Introduction to the Principles of Heredity* (W.H. Freeman).

Chapter 34

34.11 S. Singer;
34.12 and **34.15** H. Curtis and N.S. Barnes, *Biology* (Worth);
34.14 After Rich.

Chapter 35

35.1, 35.6 and **table 35.1** D.T. Suzuki, A.J.F. Griffiths, J.H. Miller and R.C. Lewontin, *An Introduction to Genetic Analysis* (W.H. Freeman);
35.4 and **35.5** H. Curtis and N.H. Barnes.

Chapter 36

36.7 S. Singer.

Chapter 37

37.2 P. Colinvaux, *Ecology* (John Wiley & Sons);
37.11 T.R.G. Gray and S.T. Williams, *Soil Micro-organisms* (Longman).

Chapter 38

38.7 P.R. and A.H. Ehrlich, *Population, Resource, Environment* (W.H. Freeman);
38.9 J. Krebs, *The Message of Ecology* (Harper and Row);
38.10 J.P. Kimmins, *Forest Ecology* (Macmillan/Collier Macmillan);
38.17 T.J. King, *Ecology, 2nd edn* (Nelson) taken from E.P. Odum, 'Trophic structure and productivity of Silver Springs, Florida', *Ecological Monographs*, **27**, 1957.

Chapter 39

39.3 J. Krebs;
39.4 Data by Moore and Walker;
39.5 J. Lee, 'Acid rain', *Biological Sciences Review*, **1**(**4**), pp 15–18, 1988;
39.7 H. Pearson, 'Muck an' brass: the sewage story', *Biological Sciences Review*, **1**(**4**), 1989;
39.8 K. Mellanby, *The Biology of Pollution* (Edward Arnold).

Chapter 40

40.3 J.W. Silvertown, *Introduction to Plant Population Ecology* (Longman);
page 692 illustration 2 G.E. Hutchinson, *An Introduction to Population Ecology* (Yale University Press);
40.4, **40.13** and **40.14** M. Begon, J.L. Harper and C.R. Townsend, *Ecology: Individuals, Populations and Communities* (Blackwell Scientific Publications);
40.8 B. Knapp, *Systematic Geography* (Collins);
40.15 P. Gadd, *Individuals and Populations* (Cambridge University Press).

Chapter 41

Page 706, G.H. Harper;
41.4 G.N. Agrios, *Plant Pathology* (Academic Press); **41.6** W.C. Marquardt and R.S. Demaree, *Parasitology* (Macmillan/Collier Macmillan);
41.13 P.H. Raven, R.F. Evert and H. Curtis, *Biology of Plants* (Worth);
41.15 D. Macdonald (ed.), *The Encyclopedia of Mammals: 2* (BookClub Associates by arrangement with George Allen and Unwin).

Chapter 42

42.3 A.S. Romer, *Vertebrate Paleontology* (University of Chicago Press);
42.4 Based on Hallam;
42.5 C. Starr and R. Taggart;
42.9 Grove and Newell, *Animal Biology* (University Tutorial Press);
42.10 and **42.11** M.W. Strickberger, *Evolution* (Jones and Bartlett);
42.12 After Eck and Dayhoff;
42.15 R. Buchsbaum;
42.34 Sir Gavin de Beer.

Chapter 43

43.14 C. Starr and R. Taggart;
page 748 N.A. Campbell, *Biology* (Benjamin/Cummings);
page 755 G.H. Harper and A. Cruickshank.

Chapter 44

44.2 C. Starr and R. Taggart after Stanley Miller;
44.3 and **44.5** N.A. Campbell;
44.8 After Pascher;
44.9A and **B** Mainly after A.S. Romer;
44.9C The American Museum of Natural History;
44.16 C. Starr and R. Taggart;
44.18 S. Tomkins.

Design, illustration and page layout by Ian Foulis & Associates, Plymouth, PL7 1RQ